The Cambridge Handbook of Historical Orthography

The study of orthography (spelling and writing systems), and its development over the history of language, is central to many areas of linguistic inquiry, offering insight into syntactic and morphological structures, phonology, typology, historical linguistics, literacy and reading, and the social and cultural context of language use. With contributions from a global team of scholars, this *Handbook* provides the first comprehensive overview of this rapidly developing field, tracing the development of historical orthography, with special emphasis on the last and present centuries. Chapters are split into five key thematic areas, with a focus throughout on the interplay between theory and practice. The *Handbook* also explores the methods used in studying historical orthography, and the principles involved in the development of a spelling system. Providing a critical assessment of the state of the art in the field, it is essential reading for anyone with an interest in writing systems and historical linguistics.

MARCO CONDORELLI has a PhD in English language and has worked as a researcher and lecturer at various academic institutions. His previous publications include *Introducing Historical Orthography* (2022), *Standardising English Spelling* (2022) and *Advances in Historical Orthography, c. 1500–1800* (editor, 2020).

HANNA RUTKOWSKA is Associate Professor at the Faculty of English, Adam Mickiewicz University in Poznań, Poland. Her previous publications include *Orthographic Systems in Thirteen Editions of the* Kalender of Shepherdes *(1506–1656)* and *Graphemics and Morphosyntax in the (1472–88)* Cely Letters.

CAMBRIDGE HANDBOOKS IN LANGUAGE AND LINGUISTICS

Genuinely broad in scope, each handbook in this series provides a complete state-of-the-field overview of a major subdiscipline within language study and research. Grouped into broad thematic areas, the chapters in each volume encompass the most important issues and topics within each subject, offering a coherent picture of the latest theories and findings. Together, the volumes will build into an integrated overview of the discipline in its entirety.

Published titles

The Cambridge Handbook of Phonology, edited by Paul de Lacy
The Cambridge Handbook of Linguistic Code-switching, edited by Barbara E. Bullock and Almeida Jacqueline Toribio
The Cambridge Handbook of Child Language, Second Edition, edited by Edith L. Bavin and Letitia Naigles
The Cambridge Handbook of Endangered Languages, edited by Peter K. Austin and Julia Sallabank
The Cambridge Handbook of Sociolinguistics, edited by Rajend Mesthrie
The Cambridge Handbook of Pragmatics, edited by Keith Allan and Kasia M. Jaszczolt
The Cambridge Handbook of Language Policy, edited by Bernard Spolsky
The Cambridge Handbook of Second Language Acquisition, edited by Julia Herschensohn and Martha Young-Scholten
The Cambridge Handbook of Biolinguistics, edited by Cedric Boeckx and Kleanthes K. Grohmann
The Cambridge Handbook of Generative Syntax, edited by Marcel den Dikken
The Cambridge Handbook of Communication Disorders, edited by Louise Cummings
The Cambridge Handbook of Stylistics, edited by Peter Stockwell and Sara Whiteley
The Cambridge Handbook of Linguistic Anthropology, edited by N. J. Enfield, Paul Kockelman and Jack Sidnell
The Cambridge Handbook of English Corpus Linguistics, edited by Douglas Biber and Randi Reppen
The Cambridge Handbook of Bilingual Processing, edited by John W. Schwieter
The Cambridge Handbook of Learner Corpus Research, edited by Sylviane Granger, Gaëtanelle Gilquin and Fanny Meunier
The Cambridge Handbook of Linguistic Multicompetence, edited by Li Wei and Vivian Cook
The Cambridge Handbook of English Historical Linguistics, edited by Merja Kytö and Päivi Pahta
The Cambridge Handbook of Formal Semantics, edited by Maria Aloni and Paul Dekker
The Cambridge Handbook of Morphology, edited by Andrew Hippisley and Greg Stump
The Cambridge Handbook of Historical Syntax, edited by Adam Ledgeway and Ian Roberts
The Cambridge Handbook of Linguistic Typology, edited by Alexandra Y. Aikhenvald and R. M. W. Dixon
The Cambridge Handbook of Areal Linguistics, edited by Raymond Hickey
The Cambridge Handbook of Cognitive Linguistics, edited by Barbara Dancygier
The Cambridge Handbook of Japanese Linguistics, edited by Yoko Hasegawa
The Cambridge Handbook of Spanish Linguistics, edited by Kimberly L. Geeslin

The Cambridge Handbook of Bilingualism, edited by Annick De Houwer and Lourdes Ortega
The Cambridge Handbook of Systemic Functional Linguistics, edited by Geoff Thompson, Wendy L. Bowcher, Lise Fontaine and David Schönthal
The Cambridge Handbook of African Linguistics, edited by H. Ekkehard Wolff
The Cambridge Handbook of Language Learning, edited by John W. Schwieter and Alessandro Benati
The Cambridge Handbook of World Englishes, edited by Daniel Schreier, Marianne Hundt and Edgar W. Schneider
The Cambridge Handbook of Intercultural Communication, edited by Guido Rings and Sebastian Rasinger
The Cambridge Handbook of Germanic Linguistics, edited by Michael T. Putnam and B. Richard Page
The Cambridge Handbook of Discourse Studies, edited by Anna De Fina and Alexandra Georgakopoulou
The Cambridge Handbook of Language Standardization, edited by Wendy Ayres-Bennett and John Bellamy
The Cambridge Handbook of Korean Linguistics, edited by Sungdai Cho and John Whitman
The Cambridge Handbook of Phonetics, edited by Rachael-Anne Knight and Jane Setter
The Cambridge Handbook of Corrective Feedback in Second Language Learning and Teaching, edited by Hossein Nassaji and Eva Kartchava
The Cambridge Handbook of Experimental Syntax, edited by Grant Goodall
The Cambridge Handbook of Heritage Languages and Linguistics, edited by Silvina Montrul and Maria Polinsky
The Cambridge Handbook of Arabic Linguistics, edited by Karin Ryding and David Wilmsen
The Cambridge Handbook of the Philosophy of Language, edited by Piotr Stalmaszczyk
The Cambridge Handbook of Sociopragmatics, edited by Michael Haugh, Dániel Z. Kádár and Marina Terkourafi
The Cambridge Handbook of Task-Based Language Teaching, edited by Mohammed Ahmadian and Michael Long
The Cambridge Handbook of Language Contact: Population Movement and Language Change, Volume 1, edited by Salikoko Mufwene and Anna Maria Escobar
The Cambridge Handbook of Language Contact: Multilingualism in Population Structure, Volume 2, edited by Salikoko Mufwene and Anna Maria Escobar
The Cambridge Handbook of Romance Linguistics, edited by Adam Ledgeway and Martin Maiden
The Cambridge Handbook of Translation, edited by Kirsten Malmkjær
The Cambridge Handbook of Chinese Linguistics, edited by Chu-Ren Huang, Yen-Hwei Lin, I- Hsuan Chen and Yu-Yin Hsu
The Cambridge Handbook of Intercultural Pragmatics, edited by Istvan Kecskes
The Cambridge Handbook of Role and Reference Grammar, edited by Delia Bentley, Ricardo Mairal-Usón, Wataru Nakamura and Robert D. Van Valin Jr.

The Cambridge Handbook of Historical Orthography

Edited by
Marco Condorelli
University of Central Lancashire, Preston
Hanna Rutkowska
Adam Mickiewicz University, Poznań

Shaftesbury Road, Cambridge CB2 8EA, United Kingdom

One Liberty Plaza, 20th Floor, New York, NY 10006, USA

477 Williamstown Road, Port Melbourne, VIC 3207, Australia

314–321, 3rd Floor, Plot 3, Splendor Forum, Jasola District Centre, New Delhi – 110025, India

103 Penang Road, #05–06/07, Visioncrest Commercial, Singapore 238467

Cambridge University Press is part of Cambridge University Press & Assessment, a department of the University of Cambridge.

We share the University's mission to contribute to society through the pursuit of education, learning and research at the highest international levels of excellence.

www.cambridge.org
Information on this title: www.cambridge.org/9781108487313

DOI: 10.1017/9781108766463

First published 2023

A catalogue record for this publication is available from the British Library.

Library of Congress Cataloging-in-Publication Data
Names: Condorelli, Marco, 1990- editor. | Rutkowska, Hanna, editor.
Title: The Cambridge handbook of historical orthography / edited by Marco Condorelli, Hanna Rutkowska.
Description: Cambridge, United Kingdom ; New York, NY : Cambridge University Press, 2023. | Series: Cambridge handbooks in language and linguistics | Includes bibliographical references and index.
Identifiers: LCCN 2023026046 | ISBN 9781108487313 (hardback) | ISBN 9781108720052 (paperback) | ISBN 9781108766463 (ebook)
Subjects: LCSH: Language and languages--Orthography and spelling. | Historical linguistics. | LCGFT: Essays.
Classification: LCC P240.2 .C36 2023 | DDC 417/.7--dc23/eng/20230721
LC record available at https://lccn.loc.gov/2023026046

ISBN 978-1-108-48731-3 Hardback

Contents

List of Figures *page* ix
List of Tables xi
List of Contributors xiii
List of Abbreviations xxiii

Part I Introduction

1 Historical Orthography: Purposes, Ambitions and Boundaries *Marco Condorelli and Hanna Rutkowska* 3

Part II Structures and Theories

2 Classifying and Comparing Early Writing Systems *Amalia E. Gnanadesikan* 29

3 Elements of Writing Systems *Stefan Hartmann and Renata Szczepaniak* 50

4 Orthographic Conventionality *Aurelija Tamošiūnaitė* 74

5 Theoretical Approaches to Understanding Writing Systems *Hanna Rutkowska* 95

6 Grapholinguistics *Vuk-Tadija Barbarić* 118

7 Typologies of Writing Systems *Terry Joyce* 138

Part III Organization and Development

8 Comparative Historical Perspectives *Per Ambrosiani and Elena Llamas-Pombo* 163

9 Systems and Idiosyncrasies *Benjamin W. Fortson IV* 183

10 Multilayeredness and Multiaspectuality *Justyna Rogos-Hebda* 204

11 Adapting Alphabetic Writing Systems *Anetta Luto-Kamińska* 224

12 Variation and Change *Michelle Waldispühl* 245

13 What Is Spelling Standardization? *Marco Condorelli* 265

Part IV Empirical Approaches

14 Studying Epigraphic Writing *Katherine McDonald and Emmanuel Dupraz* 285

15 Materiality of Writing *Giedrius Subačius* 305

16 Data Collection and Interpretation *Anja Voeste* 324

17 Philological Approaches *Annina Seiler and Christine Wallis* 338

18 Exploring Orthographic Distribution *Javier Calle-Martín and Juan Lorente-Sánchez* 360

19 Comparative and Sociopragmatic Methods *Marija Lazar* 381

20 Reconstructing a Prehistoric Writing System *Ester Salgarella* 395

Part V Explanatory Discussions

21 Scribes and Scribal Practices *Peter J. Grund* 419

22 Orthographic Norms and Authorities *Carol Percy* 436

23 Networks of Practice across English and Dutch Corpora *Marco Condorelli and Chris De Wulf* 457

24 Literacy and the Singular History of Norwegian *Agnete Nesse* 477

25 Authorship and Gender *Mel Evans* 498

26 Sociolinguistic Variables in English Orthography *Juan Manuel Hernández-Campoy* 520

27 Sociolinguistic Implications of Orthographic Variation in French *Sandrine Tailleur* 537

28 Orthography and Language Contact *Israel Sanz-Sánchez* 555

29 Discourse and Sociopolitical Issues *Laura Villa Galán* 578

30 Transmission and Diffusion *Gijsbert Rutten, Iris Van de Voorde and Rik Vosters* 596

31 Analogy and Extension *Yishai Neuman* 617

Bibliography 644

Name Index 789

Subject Index 801

Figures

2.1 The extension of initial logograms along the phonological and semantic dimensions into further logograms and beyond to phonograms and semantic determinatives *page* 38
3.1 Graphemes as the smallest suprasegmental units 55
3.2 The minuscule p 60
3.3 The length hierarchy of letter heads 61
3.4 Stroke order for 你 'you' (pīnyīn *nǐ*) 62
3.5 Combining marks as character type in typography 65
3.6 Relation between characters and glyphs 65
3.7 Variant glyphs of the characters 'A' and 'a' 66
3.8 The features [+/− empty] and [+/− vertical] according to Bredel (2008) 68
10.1 Syllabic suspension 213
10.2 Abbreviation of final m 213
10.3 The macron symbol used for contraction 213
10.4 Some variants of the macron 214
10.5 "Abbreviation marks significant in themselves" 216
11.1 Alphabet according to Jan Kochanowski 232
11.2 Alphabet according to Łukasz Górnicki 232
11.3 Alphabet according to Jan Januszowski 233
12.1 The elder futhark consisting of 24 signs (c. AD 100–700) 261
12.2 Swedish variant of the younger futhorc consisting of 16 signs (c. AD 700–1200) 262
13.1 Percentage of orthographic forms per year coming into widespread use 273
13.2 Percentage of orthographic forms per year undergoing a rapid decline in usage 274
14.1 Dedication to Augustus, Herculaneum, first century AD 288

14.2	Table 5 of the Iguvine Tables, showing the end of the older text (in the Umbrian alphabet) followed by the beginning of the newer text (in the Latin alphabet)	297
16.1	*Die sieben Herzensleiden Unserer Lieben Frau*, with highlighted uppercase and lowercase letters of *nomina sacra*	330
16.2	Maria in lower case (vocative after full stop)	331
16.3	Percentages of final e in singular and plural	333
16.4	Undesired combination of i-dot and ascender	335
16.5	Percentages of <y> and <i> in relation to following ascenders/nonascenders (Σ 92)	335
18.1	Margins and writing space in MS Hunter 497	362
18.2	Nominal and adjectival compounds in handwritten texts	368
18.3	Nominal and adjectival compounds in printed texts	369
18.4	Reflexive forms in handwritten texts	370
18.5	Reflexive forms in printed texts	370
18.6	Other adverbs and prepositions in handwritten texts	371
18.7	Other adverbs and prepositions in printed texts	371
18.8	Development of *shalbe* and *asmuch* in handwritten texts	372
18.9	Development of *shalbe* and *asmuch* in printed texts	373
20.1	LB tablet from Knossos (KN Da 1156)	415
22.1	A page from *Simplified Spelling. For the Use of Government Departments*	452
24.1	Runic stick from Bergen, the Middle Ages	485
26.1	Germanic alphabet of runes	523
28.1	Distribution of sibilant spellings in the loanwords in Nahuatl manuscripts	572
29.1	Reformed alphabet implemented by Madrid teachers in the 1840s	590
30.1	The incremental change of <ae> to <aa> across centuries	612
30.2	The change from <ae> to <aa> across regions and centuries	613
31.1	The English vowel system	631

Tables

3.1	The grapheme as a minimal contrastive unit in different types of writing systems	*page* 54
3.2	Heads and codas of letters	60
6.1	Phoneme/phone vs. grapheme/graph	126
14.1	Lejeune's analysis of vowel orthography in Oscan in the Greek alphabet	293
14.2	Zair's analysis of vowel orthography in Oscan in the Greek alphabet	294
14.3	Front vowels in Umbrian (simplified presentation)	297
17.1	Spelling variation in T2 and T4	352
18.1	Type of division in OE	373
18.2	Phonological boundaries in OE	374
18.3	Morphological boundaries in OE	374
18.4	Type of division in ME	375
18.5	Phonological boundaries in ME	375
18.6	Morphological boundaries in ME	376
18.7	Type of division in EModE	376
18.8	Phonological boundaries in EModE handwritten texts	376
18.9	Phonological boundaries in EModE printed texts	377
18.10	Morphological boundaries in EModE handwritten texts	377
18.11	Morphological boundaries in EModE printed texts	377
19.1	Clusters of features in Novgorodian writings with different authors' referential perspectives	390
20.1	The LB 'basic' syllabary	397
20.2	The LB 'additional syllabary'	409
20.3	The LB 'undeciphered' syllabograms	414
27.1	Conservative vs. innovative use of orthographic variables according to writer and generation	547

27.2 Conservative vs. innovative use of orthographic variables according to writer and place of birth 548
27.3 Frequency of vernacular features/spelling errors in Wallace Landry's letters 550
28.1 Medieval central Castilian system of sibilant fricatives 567

Contributors

Per Ambrosiani is Professor Emeritus of Russian at Umeå University (Sweden) and Affiliate Professor of Russian at Stockholm University (Sweden). His research interests include Slavic historical linguistics, Slavic book history, Russian historical onomastics and translation studies. He has recently published 'Slavic alphabets and languages in publications by the Propaganda Fide during the 17th and 18th centuries' (in S. Kempgen and V. S. Tomelleri, eds., *Slavic Alphabets and Identities*, 2019), 'Graphematic features in Glagolitic and Cyrillic orthographies' (in M. Condorelli, ed., *Advances in Historical Orthography, c. 1500–1800*, 2020) and the online database *The Smolensk Archives, 1604–1611* (with E. Löfstrand and A. Selin, 2020–).

Vuk-Tadija Barbarić is Research Associate at the Institute of Croatian Language and Linguistics, Zagreb (Croatia). His main interests are textual criticism, historical sociolinguistics and the history of Croatian language. During the last decade, his research has focused on the oldest Croatian lectionaries. This particular research interest peaked in 2017 when his book *Nastajanje i jezično oblikovanje hrvatskih lekcionara* [Genesis and Linguistic Formation of Croatian Lectionaries] was published. In recent years, his attention has drawn him closer to historical orthography, as he embarked on a project at the Institute of Croatian Language that deals with Croatian historical orthography in Roman script.

Javier Calle-Martín is Professor of English Linguistics at the University of Málaga (Spain), where he teaches History of English and Quantitative Linguistics. He is the editor of *The Middle English Version of De viribus herbarum* in MS Hunter 497 (2012), *A Late Middle English Remedybook* in MS Wellcome 542 (2013) and a synoptic edition of John Arderon's *De judiciis urinarum* housed in MS Hunter 328 and MS Rylands 1310 (2020). He is also lead researcher of the early and late modern English components of *The Málaga Corpus of Early English Scientific Prose*. His research interests are the history of the English language and manuscript studies, and late Middle English and early Modern English scientific manuscripts in particular. In the last few years, he has also developed some interest in the standardization of English and the connection between usage and prescription in late Modern English.

Marco Condorelli completed his PhD at the University of Central Lancashire and has held research and teaching positions at the University of Manchester (UK), the University of Giessen (Germany), Leiden University (the Netherlands) and the Herzog August Bibliothek (Germany). His previous publications include *Introducing Historical Orthography* (2022), *Standardising English Spelling* (2022), *Advances in Historical Orthography, c. 1500–1800* (editor, 2020), and a number of articles which have appeared in, for example, *English Language and Linguistics*, *English Studies* and *Neuphilologische Mitteilungen*.

Chris De Wulf is Senior Lecturer for Dutch Studies at the University of Zurich (Switzerland) and has held teaching and research positions at various universities in Belgium, the Netherlands, Switzerland and Germany. His fields of expertise include phonology and graphematics, both from a topological and a diachronic perspective. He has authored a reference work on fourteenth-century Dutch phonology and spelling, the *Klankatlas van het veertiende-eeuwse Middelnederlands. Het dialectvocalisme in de spelling van lokale oorkonden* [Sound Atlas of Fourteenth-Century Middle Dutch. Dialect Vocalism in the Spelling of Local Charters] (2019). His current project, *Development of Dutch Orthography*, focuses on the history of Dutch spelling from Middle Dutch to the present time.

Emmanuel Dupraz is Professeur chargé de cours of Classics at the Université libre de Bruxelles (ULB, Belgium). He defended his *Habilitation à diriger des recherches* at the Ecole Pratique des Hautes Etudes (Paris, France) in 2010 and his doctoral thesis at the Université Paris-IV (France) in 2003. His research deals with ancient inscriptions and languages of Gaul and Italy. He has been working both from a linguistic (syntax, semantics) and a sociolinguistic perspective (uses of writing, pragmatics of inscriptions). His most recent monograph is entitled *Aufbau und Inhalt der umbrischen Gebetstexte. Untersuchungen zu den Fachbegriffen uestisia, uesticatu und uest(e)is* [Structure and Content of the Umbrian Prayer Texts: Studies on the Technical Terms *vestisia*, *vesticatu* and *vest(e)is*] (2020).

Mel Evans is Lecturer in English Language (with Digital) at the University of Leeds (UK). Her research explores the relationship between language, identity and technology, particularly in Early Modern English. She draws on sociolinguistic and pragmatic frameworks for interpretation, and experiments with interdisciplinary methods from linguistic, digital humanities and literary fields. Her most recent book is *Royal Voices: Language and Power in Tudor England* (2020).

Benjamin W. Fortson IV specializes in Indo-European historical linguistics. He received his BA from Yale (USA) and his PhD from Harvard (USA), both in Linguistics. He is the author of *Indo-European Language and Culture*, a textbook on Indo-European linguistics. Most of his research concerns the prehistory of Latin and the Italic branch of the family, but he has also published on various topics in Hittite, Indo-Iranian, Greek, Old Irish and Armenian. Since 2003, he has taught in the Classical Studies and Linguistics departments at the University of Michigan (USA); previously he was on the faculty at Harvard, Northeastern, and universities in Germany, and was an editor and lexicographer for *The American Heritage Dictionary of English*.

Amalia E. Gnanadesikan has recently retired from a post as Research Scientist and Technical Director for Language Analysis at the Center for Advanced Study at the University of Maryland (USA). She received her doctorate from the University of Massachusetts Amherst (USA) and served as Assistant Professor at Holy Family University (USA) and Assessment Specialist at the Educational Testing Service. Her three areas of specialty are writing systems, phonology and South Asian languages. She is the author of *The Writing Revolution: Cuneiform to the Internet* (2009) and *Dhivehi: The Language of the Maldives* (2017).

Peter J. Grund is Senior Lecturer and Research Scholar in the Divinity School and the English Department at Yale University (USA). He is the author of *The Sociopragmatics of Stance: Community, Language, and the Witness Depositions from the Salem Witch Trials* (2021), co-author of *Testifying to Language and Life in Early Modern England: Including a CD Containing an Electronic Text Edition of Depositions 1560–1760 (ETED)* (with M. Kytö and T. Walker, 2011) and co-editor of *Records of the Salem Witch-Hunt* (with B. Rosenthal et al., 2009), *Speech Representation in the History of English* (with T. Walker, 2020) and *Boundaries and Boundary-Crossings in the History of English* (with M. Hartman, 2020). He serves as co-editor of *Journal of English Linguistics*.

Stefan Hartmann is Associate Professor of Germanic Linguistics at the University of Düsseldorf (Germany). He obtained his PhD at the University of Mainz (Germany) and has worked at the Universities of Hamburg and Bamberg (Germany). His research interests include language acquisition, language evolution and change. In particular, his recent work has focused on corpus linguistic approaches to language acquisition and language change. In the domain of historical orthography, he has worked on the history of sentence-internal capitalization in German and other languages.

Juan Manuel Hernández-Campoy is Professor in Sociolinguistics at the University of Murcia (Spain), where he teaches English sociolinguistics, varieties of English and history of English for undergraduate students, as well as sociolinguistic research methods for postgraduates. His research areas include sociolinguistics, dialectology, the history of English and socio-stylistics, with special interest in language variation and change. His publications include *Sociolinguistic Styles* (2016), *Style-Shifting in Public: New Perspectives on Stylistic Variation* (with J. A. Cutillas-Espinosa, 2012), *The Handbook of Historical Sociolinguistics* (with J. C. Conde-Silvestre, 2012) and *Sociolinguistics and the History of English: Perspectives and Problems* (edited with J. C. Conde-Silvestre, 2012), as well as numerous articles in leading journals.

Terry Joyce is Professor of Psychology at the School of Global Studies, Tama University (Japan). He is the president of the Association for Written Language and Literacy, which convenes regular international conferences on writing systems and literacy. He is also associate editor of the *Written Language and Literacy* journal and has co-guest-edited four of its special issues, the latest including an article about graphematic variation in the Japanese writing system (co-authored with H. Matsuda, 2019). His research interests include writing systems typology, the visual word recognition of Japanese compound words and the Japanese mental lexicon.

Marija Lazar wrote her PhD on genre development of the East Slavic business letter from the eleventh to the eighteenth century. She specializes in a variety of areas within historical linguistics, ranging from digital humanities, historical lexicology, orthography of the East and West Slavic languages, and the eastern European cultural space. In 2014–2020, she contributed to a project on the German Law in East Central Europe at Saxon Academy of Sciences and Humanities in Leipzig (Germany), exploring the transfer of this cultural heritage in legal orders and their languages applied to Slovakia, Czechia, Poland, Belorussia, Ukraine and Russia. Currently she is employed in the translation industry and leads a software localization team.

Elena Llamas-Pombo is Reader in French Historical Linguistics and Researcher at the Institute of Medieval and Renaissance Studies and of Digital Humanities (IEMYRhd) at the University of Salamanca (Spain). She has recently published a section on punctuation in the *Grande Grammaire Historique du Français* [Great Historical Grammar of French] (2020) and she is co-author of *Enregistrer la parole et écrire la langue dans la diachronie du français* [Recording Speech and Writing Language in the Diachrony of French] (with G. Parussa and M. Colombo Timelli, 2017).

Juan Lorente-Sánchez is a member of the Department of English, French and German Philology at the University of Málaga (Spain), where he has taught English for International Tourism, and currently teaches English Language as well as English Phonetics and Phonology. He has recently completed his PhD dissertation, which deals with the edition, corpus compilation and philological study of Glasgow University Library, MS Ferguson 7. He has collaborated in the compilation and tagging of the Late Modern English component of *The Málaga Corpus of Early English Scientific Prose*. His research interests include text palaeography and codicology, historical linguistics and corpus linguistics.

Anetta Luto-Kamińska currently works at the Nicolaus Copernicus University in Toruń (Poland), where she conducts research in the field of language history and teaches practical Polish language at the university's Study of Polish Culture and Language for Foreigners. She also cooperates with the Institute of Polish Language of the Polish Academy of Sciences, where she received her habilitation in 2019. For over twenty years she was associated with the Institute of Literary Research of the Polish Academy of Sciences, where she contributed approximately 1,000 entries to *The Dictionary of the 16th-Century Polish Language* and worked as scientific editor of selected volumes from this dictionary. Her most recent research topic is Polish feminatives in their historical, linguistic, comparative and cultural aspect. She is the author of *Polska wersja przekładowa "Ex P. Terentii comediis latinissimae colloquiorum formulae ..." Mateusza z Kęt. Studium języka autora na tle polszczyzny XVI wieku* [The Polish Translation of "Ex P. Terentii comediis latinissimae colloquiorum formulae ..." by Matthaeus of Kęty. A Study Comparing the Language of the Author of the Translation with the Polish Language of the Sixteenth Century] (2010).

Katherine McDonald is Assistant Professor in Roman History at the University of Durham (UK). After completing her PhD on Oscan/Greek bilingualism in Cambridge in 2013, she became a Research Fellow at Gonville and Caius College, Cambridge (UK), and then a Lecturer at the University of Exeter (UK). Her other major works include *Oscan in Southern Italy and Sicily* (2015), *Italy before Rome: A Sourcebook* (2021) and, as co-editor, *Migration, Mobility and Language Contact in and around the Ancient Mediterranean* (with J. Clackson et al., 2020). Her research has previously been funded by the AHRC and the British School at Rome.

Agnete Nesse is Professor of Scandinavian Linguistics at the University of Bergen (Norway). Both her teaching and research fall across the fields of sociolinguistics, dialectology and historical linguistics. Some of her projects have focused on language contact between Norwegian and Low German in the Hanse era, radio language in Norway from 1936 until 1996, and language and text in autograph albums in the years 1819–1978. She was co-editor of *Norsk språkhistorie I–IV* (2016–2018). Her latest publications include 'En analyse av språket i Anna Hansdatter Tormods brev fra perioden 1714–1722' [An analysis of the language in Anna Hansdatter's letters from the period 1714–1722] (*Maal Og Minne* 113/1, 2021) and 'Poetic resistance: girls' autograph albums during WWII in Norway' (*Scandinavian Studies* 94/4, 2022).

Yishai Neuman is Senior Lecturer of Hebrew and Semitic linguistics at David Yellin Academic College in Jerusalem (Israel) and at Al-Qasemi Academic College in Baqa al-Gharbiyye (Israel). His particular fields of research are Hebrew and Semitic linguistics, historical linguistics, lexical semantics in cognate languages, language shift and substrate, Arabized Hebrew, and language–writing relations. Current research projects include two main pillars of Hebrew and Arabic ancient and recent relations: Lexical Semantics of Hebrew and Arabic, studied as cognate languages using anthropology and cognitive semantics; and Native Arabized Hebrew, mapping the linguistic features of the recently nativized interlanguage which results from the Arabic-to-Hebrew language shift ensuing from the immigration of Arabic-speaking Jews to a Hebrew-speaking society.

Carol Percy is Professor of English at the University of Toronto (Canada). Her work on eighteenth-century English normative texts includes 'The orthography of opposition' (*Age of Johnson: A Scholarly Annual* 15, 2004) and studies of grammatical prescriptivism in book reviews as well as in grammars by Robert Lowth and by women authors. More recently she has surveyed 'British women's roles in the standardization and study of English' for *Women in the History of Linguistics* (edited by W. Ayres-Bennett and H. Sanson, 2020). Her co-edited essay collections include *Prescription and Tradition in Language: Establishing Standards across Time and Space* (with I. Tieken-Boon van Ostade, 2016) and *The Languages of Nation: Attitudes and Norms* (with M. C. Davidson, 2012).

Justyna Rogos-Hebda is Assistant Professor in the Department of the History of English at the Faculty of English, Adam Mickiewicz University in Poznań (Poland). Her research interests concern the Early English book trade, paleography of medieval English manuscripts, visual textuality and medieval multimodalities. She has published on scribal spelling systems and on visual pragmatics of the manuscript page, and she was principal investigator in a postdoctoral project entitled *Latin-based Abbreviations in Middle English Literary Manuscripts: Evolution of Forms and Functions*, funded by the National Science Center.

Hanna Rutkowska is Associate Professor at the Faculty of English, Adam Mickiewicz University in Poznań (Poland). Her publications include *Orthographic Systems in Thirteen Editions of the* Kalender of Shepherdes *(1506–1656)* (2013) and *Graphemics and Morphosyntax in the* Cely Letters *(1472–88)* (2003), and she has co-edited *Scribes, Printers, and the*

Accidentals of Their Texts (with J. Thaisen, 2011). She is also the author of several articles and chapters on various aspects of historical orthography and historical sociolinguistics, visual pragmatics, and late medieval and Early Modern English morphosyntax.

Gijsbert Rutten is Professor of Historical Sociolinguistics of Dutch at Leiden University Centre for Linguistics (Netherlands). His research focuses on topics such as historical multilingualism and language contact, norm–usage interaction, language history 'from below' and historical language ideologies. His recent publications include the monograph *Language Planning as Nation Building. Ideology, Policy and Implementation in the Netherlands (1750–1850)* (2019) and a special issue of *Language Policy* on 'Revisiting Haugen: historical-sociolinguistic perspectives on standardization' (co-edited with R. Vosters, 2020).

Ester Salgarella's research focuses on Bronze Age Aegean scripts (Linear A, Linear B and Cretan Hieroglyphic). She completed her PhD in Classics (Peterhouse, Cambridge) in 2018, which was later published as a monograph entitled *Aegean Linear Script(s): Rethinking the Relationship between Linear A and Linear B* (2020). Her current research aims to investigate paleographical relations between Cretan scripts, ultimately leading to a refinement of their sign repertories and a more nuanced appreciation of Cretan writing traditions as a whole.

Israel Sanz-Sánchez is Professor of Spanish and Linguistics at West Chester University (USA). His research focuses on the history of dialect and language contact in the Americas, the Spanish colonial documentary record in Southwest USA and the history of Spanish in the USA. His recent work focuses on the results of various forms of acquisition in the phonology and morphology of early colonial varieties of Spanish. His contributions have appeared in journals such as *Diachronica, Hispania, Spanish in Context, Studies in Hispanic and Lusophone Linguistics, Transactions of the Philological Society* and *Journal of Historical Linguistics*. He is one of the editors of the *Journal of Historical Sociolinguistics*.

Annina Seiler is Academic Associate at the English Department of the University of Zurich (Switzerland). She holds a PhD in English Linguistics from the University of Zurich. She is the author of *The Scripting of the Germanic Languages: A Comparative Study of 'Spelling Difficulties' in Old English, Old High German, and Old Saxon* (2014). Her research interests include the history of the English language, the West Germanic languages, the functions of writing and the connections between Roman and runic script, literacy and orality in the Middle Ages, the history of lexicography and the history of linguistic thought.

Giedrius Subačius is Professor and Director of the Endowed Chair in Lithuanian Studies at the University of Illinois at Chicago (USA) and Research Fellow at the Institute of Lithuanian History in Vilnius (Lithuania). His primary scholarly interests are historical sociolinguistics, development of standard languages, history of linguistic thought, history of orthography, and history of the Lithuanian language and Lithuanian immigration to the USA. His publications include *Žemaičių bendrinės kalbos idėjos: XIX amžiaus pradžia* [Ideas about Standard Lowland Lithuanian: Beginning of the Nineteenth Century] (1998), *Kalikstas Kasakauskis: Lietuvių bendrinės kalbos konjunktūra* [Kalikstas Kasakauskis: Juncture of Standard Lithuanian] (2001), *Upton Sinclair: The Lithuanian Jungle* (2006), *Lietuvių kalbos ekspertai Rusijos imperijos tarnyboje* [The Experts of Lithuanian in Service of the Russian Empire] (2011), *Simono Daukanto Rygos ortografija (1827–1834)* [Simonas Daukantas's Rīga Orthography (1827–1834)] (2018) and *Simono Daukanto Sankt Peterburgo ortografija (1834–1846)* [Simonas Daukantas's St Petersburg Orthography (1827–1834)] (2021).

Renata Szczepaniak is Professor and Chair of Historical German Linguistics at the University of Leipzig (Germany). Her most recent book publications include *Walking on the Grammaticalization Path of the Definite Article* (co-edited with J. Flick, 2020), *Historische Korpuslinguistik* [Historical Corpus Linguistics] (co-edited with L. Dücker and S. Hartmann, 2019) and *Sichtbare und hörbare Morphologie* [Visible and Audible Morphology] (co-edited with N. Fuhrhop and K. Schmidt, 2017). One of her current research projects addresses the usage of sentence-internal capitalization in Early New High German (c. 1350–1650) using a multifactorial, corpus-based account. Her research interests include, in addition to historical orthography, historical phonology, historical sociolinguistics and German language didactics.

Sandrine Tailleur is Associate Professor of Linguistics at the Université du Québec à Chicoutimi (Canada). She specializes in French historical sociolinguistics, with a special focus on morphosyntactic variation in various types of written historical documents. Her research aims at studying intraspeaker variation in personal correspondence from newly created dialectal regions and unveiling Aboriginal voices in French Canadian newspapers (in the nineteenth and twentieth centuries). In addition to publishing a number of book chapters and journal articles, Sandrine has co-edited *Voix autochtones dans les écrits de la Nouvelle-France* [Indigenous Voices in the Writings of New France] (with L. Vaillancourt and E. Urbain, 2019) and *L'individu et sa langue: Hommages à France Martineau* [The Individual and Their Language: In Honor of France Martineau] (with W. Remysen, 2020).

Aurelija Tamošiūnaitė is Lecturer in the Department of Nordic and Baltic Languages and Cultures at Johannes Gutenberg University in Mainz (Germany). Her research focuses on the sociolinguistic history of written

Lithuanian during the long nineteenth century, with an emphasis on orthographic variation and change in Lithuanian ego-documents, in particular texts written by 'ordinary' writers. In her forthcoming book, she explores the use and application of Cyrillic to Lithuanian at the turn of the twentieth century. Her research has been published in *Archivum Lithuanicum*, *Poznań Studies in Contemporary Linguistics*, *Written Language and Literacy* and *Multilingua*.

Iris Van de Voorde holds a PhD in Linguistics from the Vrije Universiteit Brussel (Belgium) and Leiden University (Netherlands). Her PhD is rooted in historical sociolinguistics, examining historical pluricentricity in the Dutch language area. Her research interests include language variation and change, language history and sociolinguistics.

Laura Villa Galán is Tomás y Valiente Fellow at Universidad Autónoma de Madrid and Madrid Institute of Advanced Studies (Spain). She received her PhD in 2010 from The Graduate Center, CUNY (USA). Her research interests fall at the intersection of language and politics. She has studied the development of standard norms amid the economic and political changes brought about by nineteenth-century liberalism in Spain and Latin America, the contemporary international promotion of Spanish led by Spain's geopolitical and economic interests, the linguistic exploitation of USA Latinxs in the neoliberal labor market and the implementation of critical pedagogy in courses for Spanish-English bilingual speakers. Laura Villa is co-editor of *Anuario de Glotopolítica*.

Anja Voeste is Professor of Historical Linguistics/German Language History at Justus Liebig University Giessen (Germany). She graduated with a PhD on the variation of adjective declension of eighteenth-century German, *Varianz und Vertikalisierung* [Variance and Verticalization] (2000), and explored sixteenth-century spelling in *Orthographie und Innovation* [Orthography and Innovation] (2008), outlining the trendsetting role of typesetters. Her research focuses on the synthesis of empirical data and theoretical approaches like historical sociolinguistics and functionalism, sound change and evolutionary theory, spelling history and systems theory. She is co-editor of *Orthographies in Early Modern Europe* (with S. Baddeley, 2012) and *Typographie* (with U. Rautenberg, 2022).

Rik Vosters is Associate Professor of Dutch Linguistics and Historical Sociolinguistics at the Vrije Universiteit Brussel (Belgium), where he is currently also serving as Head of the Department of Linguistics and Literary Studies. He has several ongoing research projects in Dutch historical sociolinguistics, with a focus on language variation and change, language norms, language planning and language contact. He is also one of the editors of the *Journal of Historical Sociolinguistics* and an active member of the *Historical Sociolinguistics Network* (HiSoN).

Michelle Waldispühl is Associate Professor in German Linguistics and Language Acquisition at the Department of Languages and Literatures, University of Gothenburg (Sweden). She specializes in philology, Germanic language history, and language acquisition and teaching in higher education. She has worked on historical spelling variation, especially in runic and onomastic sources, on language contact and on cryptography, and is interested in sociolinguistic, interdisciplinary and digital approaches to historical linguistic data. Her current research projects include the investigation of variation and contact in historical personal names and the documentation and automatic decryption of historical cryptographic manuscripts.

Christine Wallis is Research Associate on the Unlocking the Mary Hamilton Papers project at the University of Manchester (UK). Her PhD (obtained at the University of Sheffield, UK) investigated scribal behavior in shaping the text of the Old English translation of Bede's *Historia ecclesiastica*. Her current work focuses on language variation and change in historical English, examining how wider notions of linguistic norms or language standards impact on individual writers' training and output. Her research and teaching interests lie in the areas of historical sociolinguistics, philology, manuscript studies, textual editing and digital humanities.

Abbreviations

AE	*L'Année Épigraphique*
ARCHER	*A Representative Corpus of Historical English Registers*
CEEC	*Corpus of Early English Correspondence*
CIL	*Corpus Inscriptionum Latinarum*
CNC	*Czech National Corpus*
CoMIK	*Corpus of Mycenaean Inscriptions from Knossos*
CoP	community of practice
CTVA	cross-textual analysis
EEBO	*Early English Books Online*
EEBO-TCP	*Early English Books Online: Text Creation Partnership*
eLALME	*An Electronic Version of A Linguistic Atlas of Late Mediaeval English*
GDL	Grand Duchy of Lithuania
Gmc	Germanic
GVS	Great Vowel Shift
HiSoN	*Historical Sociolinguistics Network*
IPA	International Phonetic Alphabet
ISTC	*The International Short Title Catalogue*
IURA	*Sources from Laws of the Past*
LA	Linear A (syllabary)
LAEME	*A Linguistic Atlas of Early Middle English 1150 to 1325*
LALME	*A Linguistic Atlas of Late Mediaeval English*
LB	Linear B (syllabary)
LION	*Literature Online*
LRL	*Lexicon der Romanistischen Linguistik*
ME	Middle English
MHG	Middle High German
ModE	Modern English

OCS	Old Church Slavonic
OE	Old English
OHG	Old High German
PCEEC	*Parsed Corpus of Early English Correspondence*
RAE	Real Academia Española
s.d.	*sine dato*
s.v.	*sub verbo*
s.vv.	*sub verbis*
SL	Standard Lithuanian
TERVA	intertextual analysis
TRAVA	intratextual analysis
VSR	Vowel Shift Rule

Part I

Introduction

1

Historical Orthography: Purposes, Ambitions and Boundaries

Marco Condorelli and Hanna Rutkowska

1.1 Overview

Before introducing historical orthography as a core field of study for the contributions in this volume, some preliminary assumptions must be established concerning the term *orthography*. Already at this point it should be made clear that this term can be and has been interpreted in various ways. According to the *Oxford English Dictionary Online* (Simpson and Proffitt 2000–), the word *orthography* started to be used in English in the mid-fifteenth century, as a borrowing from Anglo-Norman and Middle French (ultimately derived from Greek), meaning "correct or proper spelling," which has since remained one of the main senses of this word. In the sixteenth century, it also acquired more general senses of "a system of spelling or notation" and "[s]pelling as an art or practice; the branch of knowledge which deals with letters and their combination to represent sounds and words; the study of spelling." Although, as the definitions above indicate, *orthography* can be considered a synonym of *spelling* in popular knowledge, and especially a conventionalized spelling system of a given language, the term has also been used with reference to "[t]he standardized writing system of a language" (Crystal 2003: 257) or "a spelling norm which consists of all the standardized and codified graphic representations of a language" (Rutkowska and Rössler 2012: 214), thus comprising also the capitalization, punctuation and word division agreements followed in a given language. Spelling, from yet another point of view, can be understood as "the graphic realizations of all words" (Rutkowska 2013a: 29) of a given language, and, in that case, orthography, intended as a binding norm in that language, would encompass spelling. Ultimately, the term *orthography* can also refer to a branch of knowledge which studies various aspects of the structure and functions of writing systems, considering not only fully developed normative usages but also writing practices at different stages of standardization, including very early ones, which still involve high levels of variation.

Much like orthography, other essential concepts, such as, for instance, *writing system*, *grapheme* and *allograph*, have been interpreted in different ways, depending on the theoretical approaches adopted by the authors. These include, for example, the relational (or referential) and autonomistic approaches (see Chapter 5). In view of the diversity of definitions of orthography and related terms, as well as the complexity of orthography as a field of study, and its intricate relationships with various levels of linguistic description, including, most conspicuously, phonology and morphology, but also syntax, semantics and pragmatics, we have decided not to attempt to fully uniformize the terminological usage in this volume, considering it to be an unfeasible task. Instead of erasing contrasts, we chose to promote future dialogue among researchers, letting contributors specify their theoretical approaches and provide their own definitions of the relevant terms. Our approach has resulted in a number of partly overlapping definitions of expressions related to orthography across this book.

At first sight, this terminological inclusiveness may seem inconsistent or even overwhelming to an inexperienced user, for example, to an undergraduate student. However, we prefer our volume to reflect the actual state of the art, that is to say, the richness of perspectives taken by the scholars conducting their research in orthography, rather than pretentiously seeking some unconvincing artificial unity. This approach also seems the best solution if we consider that chapters are likely to be frequently consulted individually, for example, as materials for discussion during university courses, or as reading material for researchers or students interested in finding out more about a given topic and/or a specific language. Since terminological considerations are entertained and alternative explanations are offered in various chapters below, and the authors follow a variety of approaches, some of which may show little overlap (such as, for example, the grapholinguistic and sociolinguistic approaches), we limit ourselves here to clarifying the most basic assumptions and distinctions, as well as the conventions followed in this volume.

It also needs to be clarified at this point that although, as editors, we have striven to ensure clarity of the terms and definitions employed by the authors, especially with regard to aspects strictly or loosely related to orthography, we assume that our readers will be familiar with the rudimentary linguistic terminology, particularly within the areas of phonology and phonetics, as well as morphosyntax. Basic information like the symbols inherent to the International Phonetic Alphabet (IPA), for instance, is not explained here, as it is supposed that readers should know the sound values of a given IPA character, or at least that they should be able to look it up independently if needed. This choice has been dictated purely by the sheer length of the volume, which has been, as one might imagine, a rather challenging feature – but also a welcome patience and endurance challenge – of the present project.

So far, we have talked about the boundaries and limitations of the book. But what does it actually do and what information does it provide? Again, this is not an easy question to answer, given the scope of the project, but we attempt to provide here a summary of the most important points. This volume does not merely present current views and terms within the area of synchronic orthography, but it should rather be placed within the area of *historical orthography*, which can be defined as a subdiscipline of linguistics focusing on the study, understanding and comparison of orthographies, including various interpretations of this concept, and their development over time (see Condorelli 2022a: 3). This subdiscipline explores the underlying forces and processes which shaped and directed modifications in historical orthographic systems and features, from the creation of the first writing systems to our contemporary era. As will become evident to the readers of this volume, research within this discipline has followed different strands, according to various geographical areas and periods of time, covering a breadth of interests and goals which include but are not limited to theoretical issues, different types of orthographic change and regularization, empirical methods and models for the study of historical orthography, as well as the linguistic and extralinguistic contexts which shaped orthographies diachronically (Condorelli 2020a: 2–6).

The diversified range of interests in historical orthography is not surprising, if one considers the outstanding differences in terms of the research into the field, the pedagogy of the subject across languages, as well as the number of linguists with divergent fundamental assumptions and methodologies who share an interest in the possibilities, tendencies and causes of orthographic change from a purely national-philology perspective (Condorelli and Voeste 2020: 239–41). Other factors that have affected the way in which historical orthography is formally studied and explored today are the different political decisions made in the administration of higher-education curricula related to profound historical, cultural and political differences across nations and continents. For example, the phenomenon of biscriptality (see, e.g., Bunčić et al. 2016 for more discussion; see also Chapter 8, this volume) is pertinent to the histories of the orthographies of several Slavic languages (e.g. Belarusian and Croatian), but is of less relevance to the writing systems of many other languages. In contrast, the philological approaches and traditions (see, e.g., Fulk 2016; see also Chapter 17, this volume), based on specific languages, seem to have been maintained in various regions, cultures and political circumstances. Among the most popular approaches to studying orthography and historical orthography in recent research, especially among the young scholars' generation, are the theoretical and comparative ones (see, e.g., Meletis 2020a).

While some of the factors mentioned above have caused a relative state of isolation among members of the same scholarly community (see Amirova 1977: 6–7, Baddeley and Voeste 2012b: 1), the existing differences in historical orthography undoubtedly represent an element of richness and diversity which should be valued and looked after in the future in order to ensure that there is some progress in the field. Nevertheless, this divergence also makes it difficult to apply a full-fledged comparative approach when discussing theoretical and methodological developments in historical orthography across various languages, research strands and personal research interests. Also, as a result of the great variety of interests, the relevance of historical orthography as a branch of scholarly inquiry is not defined only in the boundaries of a group of those who are interested in the discipline per se, but rather it is applicable to a much larger audience of researchers, not least those working in historical orthography from the perspective of phonology, etymology, lexicography, sociolinguistics, corpus linguistics, philology, literature, history, art history, bibliology and history of the book.

Aside from some of the most obvious cross-disciplinary links that exist in historical orthography, there is also a much deeper, fundamental reason for the importance of historical orthography as the subject matter for a handbook in linguistics: orthography constitutes the primary witness of the earliest linguistic past and, as such, historical orthography is of vital importance to anyone with an interest in many aspects of historical languages (Condorelli and Voeste 2020: 238, Condorelli 2022a: 1). For example, it is orthography, particularly spelling, that constitutes the basis for any speculation concerning the pronunciation of a given language in the periods preceding the invention of audio recording. Also etymologists, lexicologists and lexicographers draw upon spelling evidence when attempting to trace the histories of individual words and word families. Likewise, variation in orthographic features recorded in historical documents helps sociolinguists discover pertinent information about individual users of a language and the relations among them in terms of, for instance, social networks and other types of communities. Philologists interested in textual history can often find connections between specific texts mainly thanks to their shared orthographic characteristics. In turn, researchers specializing in corpus linguistics may find the preservation of orthographic features in corpora a challenging task, especially when this involves replacing and tagging the symbols which are no longer in use in modern languages. Thus, historical orthography indeed functions as a meeting point for various disciplines, bridging numerous fields which are seemingly not related.

The interest in the study of orthographic variation in our modern understanding started in the late nineteenth century, together with the appearance of dialectology. Traditional dialectologists paid attention to diatopically determined variation (Schneider 2002: 69), with spelling variation being the most readily available and noticeable type. However, despite the importance and relevance of writing, orthography and historical orthography in linguistics, this area of investigation used to be most often considered as subsidiary to other components of linguistics or explicitly excluded from objects of linguistic study (Saussure 1993 [1916]: 41, Sapir 1921: 19–20, Bloomfield 1933: 21; see Stenroos 2006: 9, Rutkowska 2012: 225, 2013a: 37–38, Rutkowska and Rössler 2012: 229). The last thirty years, however, have witnessed profound changes in attitudes and research on writing systems. On the one hand, in the mainly German-centered theoretical tradition, the area of grapholinguistics has developed, raising the description of orthographic features to a full-right level of linguistic investigation, focusing primarily on synchronic aspects of orthographic systems, with much emphasis on the comparative perspective (for details, see Chapter 6, this volume). On the other hand, scholars have shown an increasing awareness of the importance of historical orthography as a discipline in its own right. Recent approaches to investigating historical orthography have been subject to technological advances, the use of new analytical methods, and theoretical experimentation (Condorelli 2020a: 2).

These innovations are especially owed to recent advances afforded by insights derived from historical sociolinguistics, which have given rise to a revolution in historical orthography. While attention has been paid to the importance of intrinsic (i.e. linguistic) determinants for the development of orthographies, the focus has recently moved to the correlation between orthographic practices and social variables, and with focus on the empirical basis for the studies (Condorelli 2020a: 1). The first signs of interest in orthographic variation within a strict diachronic sociolinguistic framework are from the end of the 1990s and the early 2000s (see especially Hernández-Campoy and Conde-Silvestre 1999, 2005, Conde-Silvestre and Hernández-Campoy 2004). Some of the areas that were investigated and discussed in the earliest relevant publications include the diffusion of standard spelling practices, and the influence of authors' age, gender, style, social status and social networks on orthographic developments. Some other areas of interest in the field include patterns about authorial profiles and their relationship with sociocultural and historical influences shaping historical orthography.

Further recent endeavors have explored connections between orthographic elements and various combinations of extralinguistic background features (for overviews, see Rutkowska and Rössler 2012, Condorelli 2020a, as well as Chapter 5 and Chapter 26 in this volume), including gender and text type (see, e.g., Sönmez 2000, Oldireva Gustafsson 2002, Sairio 2009), gender and authorship (see, e.g., Evans 2012, Hernández-Campoy 2016b), genre, text type, register and level of formality (Taavitsainen 2001, Markus 2006, Tieken-Boon van Ostade 2006b, Moreno Olalla 2020, Stenroos 2020b), typographical conjectures (see, e.g., Howard-Hill 2006, Agata 2011, Rutkowska 2013a, 2013b, 2020b, Shute 2017, Voeste 2021, Condorelli 2022b), paleographical factors (see, e.g., Calle-Martín 2009, 2011a, 2011b, Grund 2011, Peikola 2011, Thaisen 2011, Llamas-Pombo 2012, Rogos 2013, Rogos-Hebda 2020) and transhistorical pragmatic aspects (Tagg and Evans 2020). Orthographic changes have also been investigated from the point of view of discourse communities (see, e.g., Taavitsainen 2004), community norms (see, e.g., Voeste 2010, Zheltukhin 2012), ideology (see, e.g., Villa 2012, 2015), code-switching (see, e.g., Zheltukhin 1996, McConchie 2011) and communities of practice (see, e.g., Rogos 2013, Rutkowska 2013b, Sairio 2013, Tyrkkö 2013, Conde-Silvestre 2019, 2020), together with attempts to compare writing features of scribes and printers across editions of the same text (see, e.g., Blake 1965, Aronoff 1989, Horobin 2001, Kopaczyk 2011, Peikola 2011, Rutkowska 2005, 2013a, 2015a, 2016, 2020a). Likewise, the long-established topic of diatopic orthographic variation has not ceased to spark researchers' interest in recent decades (see, e.g., Kopaczyk et al. 2018, Laing and Lass 2019, Stenroos 2020a, 2020b).

Research in historical orthography has also addressed the difficult topic of the relationship between graphemes and phonemes (see, e.g., Laing and Lass 2003, Lass and Laing 2010, Berger 2012, Bunčić 2012, Kopaczyk et al. 2018, Condorelli 2019, Lisowski 2020), as well as different spellings of lexical items and morphological categories (see, e.g., Laing and Lass 2014, Rutkowska 2013a, 2020a). Other apposite areas of discussion include differences in the amount of phonography and morphography in specific orthographies due to the competing influences of phonology and etymology (see, e.g., Baddeley 2012, Cerquiglini 2004, Michel 2012, Voeste 2012). More recent topics of investigation cover interrelations between regional and sociolinguistic variation and standardization (see, e.g., Sönmez 2000, Bunčić 2012, Llamas-Pombo 2012, Nevalainen 2012a, Voeste 2012, Vosters et al. 2014, Vosters and Rutten 2015), short forms of various types (see, e.g., Markus 2006, Kopaczyk 2011, Rutkowska 2013b, Honkapohja and Liira 2020, Rogos-Hebda 2020, Tieken-Boon van Ostade 2006b) and patterns related to punctuation and capitalization (see, e.g., Llamas-Pombo 2007, 2020, Voeste 2018b, Smith 2020b).

Overall, the attempts made toward reaching a bolder, more comprehensive outlook on historical orthography by exploring the areas mentioned above have been positive and encouraging. Today, work in historical orthography is published widely in international world-leading journals like *Diachronica*, *Folia Linguistica Historica*, *Language Variation and Change* and *Historische Sprachforschung/Historical Linguistics.* Research work related to diachronic orthography has also been published in major generalist journals like the *Journal of Linguistics* and *Language.* Some contributions have also been published in platforms closely related to historical sociolinguistics and especially *Written Language and Literacy*, the *Journal of Historical Sociolinguistics* and the *Journal of Historical Pragmatics* (Condorelli 2020a: 7). A growing number of language-specific books and long research articles are being dedicated to topics included in this *Handbook*, some of which focus on the connection between spelling and paleography, typography and transmission from manuscript to print (see, e.g., Thaisen and Rutkowska 2011, Rutkowska 2013a, Hellinga 2014, Shute 2017, Subačius 2018, 2021, Condorelli 2020c, 2022a, 2022b).

The enthusiasm from the academic community for topics related to historical orthography, the extraordinary breadth and diversity of topics in the area, as well as the increased awareness of the importance of orthography for most areas in historical linguistics, are all convincing signs of the subject's maturity and the need for a large-focus, interdisciplinary handbook. The present volume is thus the first attempt to provide the international audience, including both researchers and students, interested in this subject with a handbook devoted specifically to historical orthography, and to make the first step toward research-oriented communication among those members of the academic community whose research involves, or at least touches upon, historical orthography.

The fact that historical orthography has become a mainstream subdiscipline of linguistics only relatively recently has been an additional motivating factor for the production of a handbook entirely devoted to the subject. The present *Handbook* has given scholars an opportunity to reflect about and formalize aspects of the discipline that have so far remained expressed only in the context of specific languages and case studies. The volume leans on the extensive formal knowledge already existing in the field of contemporary orthography and reflects on the application of some of the existing principles to historical questions and dimensions. It attempts to fulfill this task by bringing together in one place a compendium of key topics and issues in historical orthography. The *Handbook* presents an up-to-date, in-depth and comprehensive exploration of historical orthography, combining contributions by scholars of different generations, including both some of the foremost scholars and young researchers in the field, and concentrating on its scientific aspects. The volume touches on areas of inquiry that are applicable to a wide range of linguistic domains, thanks to the complex interrelation of orthographic systems with the phonology, morphology, syntax and lexicon, as well as the semantics and pragmatics of a language (see Rutkowska and Rössler 2012: 213).

The *Handbook* is focused on historical orthographic elements and issues that are largely independent from niche case studies and small language groups. However, whenever contextualization in specific languages is useful and constructive for the development of a given topic, an effort has been made to allow for a broad coverage of language families by inviting authors who specialize in a wide variety of languages to contribute to the volume. Whenever possible, authors also represent a diversity of expertise and cultural backgrounds so as to avoid purely Eurocentric views. Thus, the contributors to the *Handbook* support their discussions with references to and examples from not only Indo-European languages, such as Germanic, Romance and Balto-Slavic ones, but also from non–Indo-European languages. The chapters have been commissioned with the goal of becoming essential reading on both introductory and advanced courses in historical linguistics as well as on general linguistics modules that cover issues related to orthography, integrating existing volumes on the subject (e.g. Condorelli 2020a). Drafts were distributed for peer review among external reviewers and authors of individual chapters, thus enabling comparative insights to be reflected in the volume and also mitigating any glaring contradictions and disagreements among the authors. The chapters collected in the *Handbook* are ordered in a way that enables a unified narrative throughout, and is firmly grounded in the published literature on historical orthography and diachronic linguistics. The aim of the volume is that of tracing the development of historical orthography with special emphasis on the last century as a time that shaped our modern understanding of the subdiscipline, discussing the components of historical orthography as we understand it today and, ultimately, pondering the future of the field. The book also sets out to make productive links between cognate lines of research across different scholarly areas, and while its primary focus is in linguistics, it also lies at the intersection between literary studies, paleography, social history, sociopolitical research, and the history of writing and of the written text, including issues pertaining to, for example, book and script aesthetics, incunabula, typography and bookbinding.

While the *Handbook* definitely fulfills the purposes established above, there are other ambitions that we hope our volume will be associated with. The chapters of this *Handbook* have been developed to seek originality and completeness in two respects. Firstly, they aim to integrate the discussions and findings of different theoretical paradigms, methodological frameworks and contextual parameters to changes in historical orthography, thus addressing the tendency in diachronic linguistics for models and approaches to develop separate agendas. The unitary endeavor afforded by the rise of historical orthography as a self-standing scientific branch of linguistics aims to mitigate the scarcity of interdisciplinary dialogue existing among scholars with different backgrounds and training skills. Secondly, the chapters are written in such a way that they can be used as either pedagogical or scholarly resources, that is as textbook chapters to be discussed with both graduate and undergraduate students but also as research-oriented contributions, with a robust empirical basis, that scholars can consult and cite. The mixed format of the volume contributes to embracing the extent of knowledge in the field, as well as solidifying some of the existing theoretical and methodological foundations and exploring new territories. Some of the ambitions of the volume also include attempting to enhance terminological precision and to overcome the relative incompatibility of existing theoretical approaches to orthography and writing, both from a universal point of view and from a language-specific perspective. We hope that the volume will further the understanding of the interrelation between linguistic and extralinguistic factors in the shaping of orthographic systems, and of the patterns of convergence and regularization of writing practices as a complex process of change on multiple linguistic and nonlinguistic levels.

Let us now focus on the overall structure of the present *Handbook*. The volume is divided into five different, complementary sections: Part I: Introduction, Part II: Structures and Theories, Part III: Organization and Development, Part IV: Empirical Approaches and Part V: Explanatory Discussions. Part I, which is where this introduction is situated, explains the key assumptions, purposes, ambitions and purposes of the book, as well as presenting an overview of the main research interests of historical orthography over the recent decades. Part II introduces the fundamental structures and theories of historical orthography, moving from the classification of early writing systems, the elements of writing systems, orthographic conventionality, early and contemporary theoretical approaches to understanding writing systems, including the most recent developments in grapholinguistics, through the typologies of existing writing systems. In Part III, the volume goes on to discuss aspects of the organization and development of writing systems, which comprise comparative historical perspectives, systems and idiosyncrasies, multilayeredness and multiaspectuality, adaptation of alphabetic writing systems, variation and change, as well as spelling standardization. After all the preliminary and theoretical aspects of historical orthography have been explored and explained, Part IV presents a range of empirical approaches, with the aim of illustrating the application of various theoretical approaches, analytical methods and models for studying orthography in specific languages and contexts, and so case studies constitute the main parts of the discussions in this section. The chapters tackle issues connected with studying epigraphic writing, the materiality of writing, data collection and interpretation, philological approaches, orthographic distribution, comparative and sociopragmatic methods, and issues inherent to reconstructing a prehistoric writing system.

Part V, the largest section in the *Handbook*, discusses factors that lie at the core of and explain the processes of change in historical orthography, with the intention of reassessing the traditional view of historical orthography and pointing to the most promising approaches in the field. This section comprises exploratory discussions on scribes and scribal practices, orthographic norms and authorities, networks of practice, literacy, sociolinguistic variables and implications of orthographic variation, orthography and language contact, discourse and sociopolitical issues, transmission and diffusion, as well as analogy and extension. Most contributions in this final part show the relevance of sociolinguistic and sociopragmatic frameworks to explaining the significance and various functions of orthographic variation, reflecting, as mentioned earlier on, some of the main trends in investigating historical orthography in recent decades. Although some necessary selection of topics to include in the *Handbook* has had to be made, the volume contains material of crucial importance to all with an interest in synchronic and diachronic study of writing systems, historical (socio)linguistics, theoretical linguistics and other subdisciplines of linguistics.

Given the diversity of topics and languages treated in the chapters outlined above, the volume was subject to some inevitable technical decisions, which we explain here in order to facilitate its use. As regards the notations and other conventions adopted throughout the volume, graphemes (irrespective of some differences concerning the definition of the term among the authors) are enclosed within angle brackets, whereas allographs, understood as different realizations of graphemes, are enclosed within vertical lines. However, in the cases where use of vertical lines would cause confusion (e.g. with the runic symbols in Chapter 12), these are omitted, for simplicity. In turn, sets of allographs and variant spellings (sometimes called "allographic spellings"; see Chapter 9) are indicated with a tilde (e.g. |ć| ~ |ci|, *color* ~ *colour*). For graphs and letters, as well as examples of words and short phrases, italics are generally employed, with the exception of the characters and examples in scripts other than Latin (e.g. Devanāgarī and Chinese ones). A hyphen is normally used for indicating word division (e.g. *replic-able*). Italics are also employed to highlight new terms when first mentioned in a given chapter. Moreover, phonemic transcription is used in nearly all the cases where pronunciation is discussed, with phonemes enclosed within slash brackets. However, in some cases, where the authors deem it necessary (e.g. where allophones are discussed), broad phonetic transcription is also used, with allophones rendered in square brackets. A colon between spaces is used for correspondence between letters (or graphemes) and sounds, for example *a* : [ə]. Single inverted commas are used for meanings of words and phrases as well as selected terms, and double inverted commas are employed for quotations. The latter are always accompanied with references to specific pages (if available) in the relevant publications. Any abbreviations are explained, with the full version provided, when used for the first time within a given chapter.

Needless to say, we have tried to make the principles established above as consistent as possible, and we hope that any minor oversight, which may be a natural byproduct of the complexity of the present project in terms of size, number of authors and topics treated, may be forgiven. In any case, we are confident that any remaining issues in the convention system explained above, or indeed any other conventional or structural oversight, will not hinder the reader from grasping the main messages of each chapter, as we, as editors, have read carefully and fully each individual chapter at least twice. This is definitely not one of those projects where one can indulge in the so common scholarly tendency to linger in the smallest details, as the risk of doing so would be that of never getting the book published, or, perhaps even worse, making it available to the public when most of the research efforts made in the volume have become outdated and of little use.

There is now one last word of caution that needs to be given with regard to the material available at the end of this *Handbook*. In order to facilitate the use of the bibliography to those readers who are not familiar with alphabets other than the Latin one, the bibliographical details of the publications originally issued in such (mainly Cyrillic-based) alphabets have been transliterated, using the American Library Association and the Library of Congress romanization tables. Furthermore, because of various possible classifications of specific documents, and because the same publications have occasionally been used as primary sources by some authors and as secondary ones by others, we have decided not to divide the bibliography into sections differentiating between them, but instead offer a continuous list of all the sources, be they printed and electronic publications or manuscripts. We hope that this will allow readers to make a better judgment of the extent of material available in historical orthography beyond the boundaries of a given topic and a specific language. We also trust that some of this comparative perspective will be enhanced by the two indexes available at the end of this book, namely the subject index and the name index. We have aimed to make the subject index as comprehensive as possible, but there were some inevitable limits that we had to take into account here, too. Because some important terms, such as *orthography, writing system* and *orthographic variation*, are discussed in virtually every chapter in this *Handbook*, yielding several hundred instances each, these were not included in the index as separate entries. However, all the personal names mentioned in the chapters, both in the references and in any other context, are recorded in the name index. The following section provides a more detailed summary of each chapter in the *Handbook*, and we hope that it will be useful to readers who approach the volume with the intention of reading about a specific topic.

1.2 Contents of the *Handbook*

1.2.1 Structures and Theories

Amalia E. Gnanadesikan's chapter, the first in Part II, focuses on the terminology and typology relevant to the study of early writing systems from a linguistic perspective. It begins by introducing writing as a linguistic notation system that arose in the context of numerical and iconographic notation systems, and the study of writing systems as a growing subdiscipline of linguistics. Next, it presents the typology of written signs, including the basic divide between logograms and phonograms. It also describes how writing arose independently in three or four places in the world, resulting in writing systems that were heavily logographic, encoding morphemes, which have both phonological and semantic values. Abstraction along the phonological and semantic dimensions led to phonography and semantic determinatives. The author briefly characterizes each of the pristine systems and considers the typology of phonographic writing more closely, following the traditional division into syllabaries and alphabets. This chapter defends the established definition of syllabary and offers some criticism of Daniels's abjad–abugida–alphabet typology of segmental scripts. The chapter presents some early historical examples of phonographic scripts and considers implications of script typology on sign inventory size as well as the evolution of script types, and whether there is directionality in script evolution.

In the next chapter, **Stefan Hartmann and Renata Szczepaniak** define the basic elements of writing and writing systems: graphemic units (graphemes and allographs), graphetic units (letters and graphs) and typographical units (glyphs and characters). Starting with graphemes, they introduce and discuss different definitions of graphemes proposed in the pertinent literature and then tackle the question of the distribution of graphemes in a given writing system and elaborate on the concept of allography. Regarding graphetic units, the authors focus on the internal structure of letters and other graphs and introduce the concept of the 'length hierarchy' of letters, which leads to a discussion of larger graphemic categories, especially the graphemic syllable. Looking more deeply at the functional distribution of letters, they address the question of graphemic inventories and their development. In their discussion, they also include the typographical key concepts of glyphs and characters. The chapter then focuses on the graphemic subinventory of punctuation, the form of punctuation marks, as well as their decoding and encoding functions. The final issue discussed is capitalization as the functional differentiation between uppercase and lowercase, including the development of different functions of uppercase letters in the history of the European writing systems.

Chapter 4, by **Aurelija Tamošiūnaitė**, discusses the notion of orthographic principles, the associated theoretical issues and the relevance of these principles in the (diachronic) study of spelling. More specifically, it provides an overview of aspects of writing that should be taken into consideration when identifying general patterns or rules governing spelling practices within a specific historic orthographic system, such as the typological makeup of the writing system, levels and regularity of linguistic representation, and graphotactic constraints. The discussion focuses on alphabet-based spelling systems and delineates several general pathways for the conventionalization of spelling across various European vernacular spellings systems at different historical periods, making particular illustrative use of Cyrillic Lithuanian. In addition to foregrounding the importance of sound- and meaning-oriented graphic mappings in shaping alphabet-based spelling systems, this chapter emphasizes the role of graphotactic constraints, which have been central in contributing to morphographization of some European spelling systems in the early modern and late modern periods.

Hanna Rutkowska's chapter offers an overview of selected linguistic approaches to writing and writing systems, mainly to alphabetic orthographies, with special emphasis on the English language. The survey starts with the ancient views on the relationship between speech and writing, as they constitute the foundation of premodern and modern perspectives. Since the debate between the relational and autonomistic approaches lasted for several decades of the twentieth century, an important part of the chapter covers their main tenets and representatives. The author argues that, over time, one can observe growing convergence between the previously opposite perspectives, which testifies to the increase in the awareness of the complexity of interrelations between alphabetic writing systems and the other language subsystems. Eventually, scholars, especially those focusing on English in their research, have widened their interest in writing systems to a variety of extralinguistic aspects interrelated with the patterns of orthographic variation. These interrelations are presented and illustrated in the last part of the chapter, devoted to the historical sociolinguistic approach.

In Chapter 6, **Vuk-Tadija Barbarić** provides a brief introduction to grapholinguistics, focusing mainly on its core subdisciplines: graphetics and graphematics (or graphemics). Historically, grapholinguistics can be perceived as a neglected subdiscipline of linguistics, though it also explores the topic of written language in its totality, which is not entirely linguistically oriented. The author specifies that its beginnings, as an organized movement, date back to Germany in the 1970s, but various instances of grapholinguistics emerged at different places (and in different languages). The field now has an established textbook, a special section in the online *Dictionaries of Linguistics and Communication Science*, and, as of quite recently, a proposal for a unifying general theory. This chapter is centered on graphetics and graphematics in order to expose the crucial linguistic dichotomy – that between form and function. Whereas the primary concern of graphetics is the materiality of writing, graphematics deals mainly with the functions of abstract units. The interplay between these two interrelated grapholinguistic subdisciplines is especially evident in the analysis of allography, which focuses on the variation of both concrete and abstract units (graphs and graphemes, respectively).

Terry Joyce's chapter, closing Part II of the *Handbook*, discusses the ongoing enterprise of developing typologies of writing systems, which strives to propose a coherent framework, or tool, for classifying the world's diverse writing systems. The author explains that because different theoretical assumptions about the core entities under analysis can yield divergent proposals, it is valuable to continually assess the conceptual and terminology contrasts that both shape and communicate typology proposals. Therefore, his chapter examines the underlying conceptualizations, the diverse, and often inconsistent, terminology, and the main limitations of existing typologies of writing systems, in seeking to further elucidate the materialization of written language both diachronically and synchronically. More specifically, the chapter's substantial third section illustrates how the majority of typology proposals to date classify writing systems primarily in terms of a core set of representational principles, or mapping relationships, assumed to exist between the linguistic units and graphemes of a language. After commenting on the elusive trinity of key terms (writing system, script and orthography), this section both outlines some of the most influential, controversial and promising typology proposals and reflects on the various conceptual and terminological distinctions propounded to capture the principles of representational mapping. Given the complexities of natural writing systems, such that the mapping principles are at best idealizations, the last section of the chapter briefly considers the merits of exploring complementary or alternative approaches to writing system typologies.

1.2.2 Organization and Development

Per Ambrosiani and Elena Llamas-Pombo's chapter starts Part III of this volume, devoted to aspects of the organization and development of writing systems. This chapter is intended to offer assistance for the linguistic description of writing systems throughout the history of one or, especially, several languages and provide a comparative description of the different units of writing systems. The first section establishes definitions of the concepts of grapheme, graph, allograph and suprasegmental grapheme. The application of these concepts to English and Romance languages is exemplified by three models and methods of diachronic and comparative description of writing systems: Romance scriptology, cultural history of European orthographies and comparative graphematics of punctuation. The second section discusses biscriptality, the phenomenon of employing two or more writing systems for the same language, not rare in the history of languages from different families, and related to different aspects of society and language users. With examples mainly from Russian and other Slavic languages, biscriptality is shown to be present on several levels of written language, and various applications of biscriptality are characterized with the help of dichotomies such as synchronic vs. diachronic biscriptality, mono- vs. pluricentric biscriptality, and societal vs. individual biscriptality.

Chapter 9, by **Benjamin W. Fortson IV**, focuses on the relationship between writing systems and language, which is never perfect, with the result that irregularities and idiosyncrasies arise even in writing systems that ostensibly have a one-to-one correspondence between grapheme and speech sound (or other unit of language). On the basis of a diverse assortment of examples drawn from around the world, this chapter outlines the ways in which writing systems are and are not systematic and discusses various avenues by which idiosyncrasies arise. The survey begins with a consideration of systematicity at the level of individual graphemes, where both aesthetic and functional aspects are discussed, and follows this with an exploration of the various degrees to which phonetic writing systems cover a language's phonemic and subphonemic distinctions and where irregularities can arise. Issues of spelling and orthography, already interspersed in the first two parts, are the dedicated topic of the last section. At various points the chapter showcases the tension between desire for economy and efficiency and desire for regularity.

Justyna Rogos-Hebda's chapter focuses on one of the most conspicuous, yet elusive elements of pre-print textuality, which has both informed and frustrated the efforts of paleographers, textual scholars and historical linguists, trying to date and/or authenticate, or just make sense of historical handwritten documents. Abbreviations, the subject of concern here, were, in a sense, almost a byword for a written document from Antiquity through the Middle Ages right until the early modern period: notwithstanding the language, text type and genre, script type, purpose and audience, these ideographic elements were nearly always to be found in a written document. For the medieval *litteratus*, abbreviations embodied the inextricable link between *logos* and *imago*; for the contemporary reader, they may well have a familiar feel of the multimodality that informs digital textuality we have grown accustomed to. The author outlines the origins, typology and visuality of Latin abbreviations used in medieval and early modern Europe, adding a postscript on the transition from script to print, which ultimately spelled the end of such ideograms in the modern era. This chapter, however, should not be read as a note on 'the days of yore' in the history of orthography in the Latin West: abbreviations do have a *longue durée* in Latin-based textuality and remain a feature of modern writing, if sometimes in a different guise.

In Chapter 11, **Anetta Luto-Kamińska** tackles the subject of contacts between alphabetic systems, defines the role of various types of interferences, and considers the reasons behind them and their consequences. The main area of interest includes the stages of the hybridity of writing systems in the period of the formation of various alphabets as well as their adaptations to the requirements of specific languages. These issues are discussed in three perspectives. Firstly, the chapter draws attention to the role of borrowings and intersystemic influences at the early stage of the formation of alphabets which are herein referred to as the 'grand' ones, including the Greek, Latin, Cyrillic and Arabic alphabets. These are forms of writing of a long tradition, which later became the basis for numerous national alphabets. Adaptations of the latter kind, consisting in adjusting a certain alphabetic system (the base alphabet) to the needs of writing the phones of a different language, constitute the second – narrower – perspective of approaching contacts between alphabets and the transformations within them. The reflections in this part are exemplified by references to the Latin alphabet in its Polish edition. In the subsequent part, the chapter focuses on the narrowest perspective regarding issues under discussion, drawing readers' attention to such alphabet adaptations that, for various reasons, did not achieve the status of national writing. This is exemplified by two – entirely different – models of adaptation, comprising the Polish *graždanka* (Polish Cyrillic alphabet) and the Polish and Belarusian Arabic-graphic writing (*aljamiado*). Additionally, the author briefly discusses Polish texts written in the Armenian alphabet.

Michelle Waldispühl's chapter presents current research demonstrating that orthographic variation does not only occur naturally in historical texts but also shows systematic patterns and functional uses. Premodern orthographic systems are flexible and offer room for innovation. This is a decisive characteristic and an important precondition for orthographic variation and change. This chapter includes an overview of types and functions of historical orthographic variation and different processes of orthographic change on the basis of examples from the history of German and from runic writing. It aims, on the one hand, to give a general introduction to the topic, and, on the other hand, to discuss theoretical and methodological issues in the study of variation and change in historical orthography. These provide a background against which a research question and design for the study of variation and change in historical orthographies can be defined.

In the last chapter of Part III, **Marco Condorelli** introduces readers to the concept of spelling standardization, offering an overview of the *ways* in which spelling standardization occurred, the *agents* behind the modern-like developments in historical spelling, and the *chronology* of the process of development in historical English. The chapter starts from the idea that historical spelling represents one of the most complex facets of linguistic standardization, and one where disagreements exist about its overall process of development. It moves on to discuss the idea that standardization in English spelling was, for some scholars, an intralinguistic, spontaneous process of self-organization, and for others a 'multiparty affair' that involved authors, readers, the printing press and linguistic commentators of the time. The final section of the chapter summarizes findings from recent work that focuses on large-scale developments over the sixteenth and the seventeenth century, and overviews the role and relevance of theoreticians, schoolmasters, authors and readers in Early Modern English spelling.

1.2.3 Empirical Approaches

In Chapter 14, opening Part IV of the present volume, **Katherine McDonald and Emmanuel Dupraz** outline some of the difficulties of studying orthography in fragmentary languages from ancient Italy in the first millennium BC. While these texts are challenging, the authors advocate for a multilevel approach to get the most information from short and (sometimes) poorly understood texts. The chapter includes a number of case studies from Republican Latin, Oscan, Umbrian and Venetic, highlighting the problems posed by different kinds of texts. For Latin, some grammarians provide relevant information about the perceived 'standard' language, but their points of view may not always reflect the usage of their contemporaries. Oscan is written using three main alphabets, which allows a comparison of orthographies and of the execution of spelling rules across different regions. The Iguvine tables, written in Umbrian, are a long and detailed religious document, written by different individuals from a small group of priests, in two main phases, and show a number of orthographic practices specific to these documents. Finally, Venetic furnishes an example of how punctuation can be as important as spelling to a community's orthographic practices.

Giedrius Subačius's chapter explores connections of orthography to *paleography* and *codicology*, and the dependence of historical orthography on the *materiality* of writing and printing environments. He explains that orthography is one of the tools of paleographers, and a key to understanding (deciphering) the written language of ancient and medieval texts, whereas codicologists investigate nonlinguistic (and nonorthographic) peculiarities of early manuscript books (codices). Orthographic research, however, in some cases helps estimate more precisely the origins of codices (time and location). Moreover, this chapter presents some of the ways in which the materiality of writing and printing historically has directed the development of orthographic features (e.g. symmetricity of upper and lower cases, dependence on the limitations of printers' type sets). The author also introduces the dichotomy between the perceived *durability* and *perishability* of a text at its creation phase, and reveals its impact on the differentiation of orthographic approaches such as the historical simultaneous double orthographies of various European languages (i.e. printed versus handwritten manuscripts, books versus newspapers).

Anja Voeste, in her chapter, gives an overview of different approaches to data collection. Three methods of comparative variable studies are presented in detail and illustrated with examples from the early history of printing: intratextual, intertextual and cross-textual variable analyses. The intratextual variable analysis investigates the frequency and range of spelling variants in a single text copy and is particularly useful for the detection of possible internal factors that trigger the choice of a variant. The intertextual analytical method compares the results of two or more intratextual investigations, for example with respect to different external determinants such as time and place. The third method, cross-textual variable analysis, compares the spelling variants of different versions of the same text, and is concerned with alterations from one version to the other in order to detect a pattern of deliberate changes. Both the advantages and disadvantages of the three methods are considered in the chapter, and their inherent theoretical premises are discussed. The author shows that data collection and interpretation are closely intertwined, and also that the chosen approach prestructures the data and leads to preferences for specific interpretations.

Chapter 17, by **Annina Seiler and Christine Wallis**, sketches the history of philology and charts its use as a method for analyzing and understanding orthographic variation. Its chronological arrangement spans the discipline's development, from the roots of philology in the Classical period to present-day incarnations of the approach. Such incarnations have seen philology move from its use as a tool which sought to make sense of orthographic variation in order to facilitate textual editing, to one which, combined with newer theoretical linguistic approaches, gave rise to disciplines such as historical sociolinguistics or pragmaphilology, where extralinguistic contexts are brought to bear on linguistic data. The authors present two case studies exemplifying contemporary philological approaches to historical orthography. The first one uses a manuscript-centered methodology to illustrate the contrasting copying practices of two scribes working on the Tanner version of the Old English translation of Bede's *Historia ecclesiastica*. The second one focuses on the scripting of /w/ in Old English and Old High German and demonstrates how an etymological sound reference system can be employed for graphemic analysis.

Javier Calle-Martín and Juan Lorente-Sánchez's chapter discusses the concept of *distribution* in historical handwritten and printed compositions understood in its widest sense, considering the text not only as a mere arrangement of the sentences and paragraphs on the pages but also as the contribution of other elements associated with spacing in Late Middle English and Early Modern English. For this purpose, the chapter is divided into three parts. First, it describes the rationale behind the composition of early English handwritten documents, reconsidering aspects such as the formatting and the layout of the folios in the preparation of the writing surface, and assessing the use of columns, margins, ruling, number of lines and line justification. Second, the main notions of the concept of spacing are discussed, describing the different types of word division. Finally, two case studies are offered reconsidering the emerging of spacing in the Middle Ages and its development throughout Early Modern English, both in the middle and at the end of lines. The data used as source of evidence come from the Late Middle English and the Early Modern English components of *The Málaga Corpus of Early English Scientific Prose*, the scientific material of the *Early English Books Online* corpus together with other sixteenth- and seventeenth-century scientific compositions.

In the following chapter, **Marija Lazar** draws upon the comparative and sociopragmatic methods in historical orthography research. After first introducing writing systems and describing orthography as a supportive discipline on the fringes of other disciplines, the chapter explains the growing interest in this discipline. It presents the adoption of the comparative method in Slavic studies and principal directions therein. Then, it summarizes theoretical preliminaries in historical sociopragmatics, primarily based upon research on English historical orthography. The author offers an overview of the most important approaches in Slavic studies, pragmaphilology and diachronic pragmatics, illustrating the differences and synergies between them mostly with Russian, Czech and Polish material. Finally, the methods proposed are critically appraised and their applicability for prospective research is demonstrated.

Closing Part IV, **Ester Salgarella**'s chapter investigates the topic of orthographic reconstruction of a historical writing system by taking as case study the Linear B syllabary of Bronze Age Greece. The Linear B syllabary was used to render the oldest Greek dialect attested in written form, so-called 'Mycenaean' Greek (c. 1400–1190 BC). The reader is guided step by step through the stages involved in the reconstruction of the orthography of the Linear B syllabary, so as to understand how to bridge the gap between actual attestations and their phonetic rendering (e.g. Linear B *a-to-ro-qo* representing alphabetic Greek ἄνθρωπος /antʰrōpos/ 'man'). The discussion covers some of the methodological issues scholars had to reckon with when first faced with the task of reconstructing a historical orthographic system in the Bronze Age Aegean context. This complex process eventually allowed for drawing up the 'rules' that govern the system and, by assessing deviations, for evaluating the extent to which these were adhered to. This chapter also illustrates the role played in such reconstruction by the historical and linguistic backdrop, within which the adaptation of an already existing writing system ('Minoan' Linear A) took place to render a linguistically different language (Greek).

1.2.4 Explanatory Discussions

In the final part of the *Handbook*, devoted to explanatory discussions, **Peter J. Grund**'s chapter reviews what we know about scribal practices of orthography (focusing on spelling), how their orthographies have been studied and interpreted, and where avenues of future research lie. The chapter covers fundamental aspects of studying scribes, showing the multidisciplinary interest in scribes and providing a broad background for thinking about scribal variation in orthography. It discusses issues such as the term and concept of a *scribe*, the contexts in which scribes worked, and how the role of the scribe has changed over time. The chapter focuses on research concerning scribal orthographies within three broad contexts: studies focusing on phonology and phonetics, but using scribal orthography as the source of information; research that concentrates on the intersection of phonology/phonetics and orthography; and studies that are interested in orthography as an exclusively or primarily written phenomenon. It also addresses the issue of orthographic standardization specifically, as scribes have been seen as central in this process, and touches on the various frameworks and approaches adopted for the study and interpretation of spelling regularization and standardization. Finally, the chapter points to some of the avenues open for new discoveries in the future.

Carol Percy, on the other hand, explains that linguistic uniformity is rarely characteristic of nation-states. In Europe, she argues, official national languages brought powerful and ongoing consequences for 'minority' languages and their speakers. Nineteenth-century nation- and empire-building also affected regional speakers of national languages, such as Flemish or Austrian German, or Afrikaans among other postcolonial varieties of European languages. Moreover, the author suggests, imposing European languages in settler nations has irrevocably endangered or eliminated Indigenous languages and cultures. The debates about European orthographic authorities surveyed in this chapter expose conflicting cultural allegiances and pedagogical needs. Vernaculars inherited diverse writing practices from different scholarly discourse communities, whether government chanceries or literary scriptoria or national language academies. Representative conflicts include tensions between scholarly traditions and simplified spellings for mass state education. Existing traditions, the author indicates, can be difficult to displace, especially in democracies. Educators' engagement with the state reminds us that pedagogy is often a matter of politics. Journalists can support or undermine proposed norms, whether using or reporting them. Successful reforms sometimes reflect intersections of low literacy and/or authoritarian states, though not always. The chapter goes on to explain that many debates that raged in the nineteenth century have continued into modern times, and with the rise of social media, individuals can not only internalize but also influence and drive discourses of group identity.

Marco Condorelli and Chris De Wulf's chapter formulates some relatively new lines of inquiry for research in historical orthography, which stem from the concept of a community of practice. The authors propose the idea that communities of practice represent a key bridge across material which inevitably stimulates divergent research interests in the field. In order to make their point, they suggest that communities of book producers in England and the Low Countries were not self-standing entities, but engaged in more or less loose, professional and social interactions, forming networks of practice. The respective histories of English and Dutch had some fundamental similarities with reference to early book production and local organization, and there were links existing even between those working on manuscripts and printed material. This chapter provides useful background information on early book production and large-scale professional networks, with a view to inspiring future researchers to explore the intricate correlation between professional organization, culture and society in the complex framework of early modern Europe.

In Chapter 24, **Agnete Nesse** gives a presentation of writing and literacy in Norway from the first runic inscriptions until the present day. Instead of trying to cover all periods in the same depth, certain phenomena and certain texts are used to exemplify the development. Where possible, the author takes the viewpoint of the writers. The aspects discussed include the relationship between orthography and alphabets, the understanding of orthographic use in the light of reading preferences, and the importance of political ideas of nationality and democracy for the codification of the two written standards that are used today. Language-external factors had a major impact on changes concerning writing in Norway. For example, the introduction of the Latin alphabet led to great changes in the runic literacy, and the Black Death caused a general decline in literacy. Later, the political union between Denmark and Norway led to a common, Dano-Norwegian written language. Between 1750 and 1850 this common language was standardized, and variation is less noticeable. After 1850 a Norwegian Ausbau process started, and variation, with two standards and several dialects, became a trade mark of Norwegian writing, which it still is.

Mel Evans, in her chapter, discusses the relationship between spelling and the social background of writers, identifying how access to literacy and literacy practices in the history of English contribute to the spelling forms and conventions used in historical texts. The topic is explored from three perspectives. Firstly, the chapter provides an overview of spelling and literacy in Old and Middle Englishes. Gender and social status inflect the spelling evidence from these periods, with the historical manuscripts largely representing the orthographic preferences of elite men, typically linked to religious houses or royal administration. More recent periods in English provide a broadening picture of societal spelling, as access to literacy increases; even so, it is important to recognize the potential skewing of any dataset when analyzing and interpreting historical spelling practices. The second part of the chapter considers a more applied dimension of spelling and authorship, surveying studies that have made attempts to identify authorship on the basis of orthographic evidence. Citing examples from Shakespeare studies, as well as other works, the discussion identifies the potential of this approach, but also the need for caution when making pronouncements without an empirical baseline of spelling norms for a given historical period. Finally, the chapter homes in on the relationship between gender and spelling in the history of English, particularly in the early and late modern periods, highlighting how negative social attitudes toward women's spelling can be found in a range of historical and more recent publications, and that claims made about women's practices are not always borne out by empirical analysis. The contribution concludes with suggestions for directions for future research relating to spelling and authorship.

Juan Manuel Hernández-Campoy's chapter clarifies that the treatment and reliability of orthographic variables as linguistic variables has already been tested with the application of both macroscopic and microscopic approaches to digitalized historical materials. In this way, patterns of variation and change in past periods of a given language have been evidenced through the observation of its users' sociolinguistic behavior in social interaction. In turn, the recent prolific research output in historical sociolinguistics is reflecting the growth of interest in style and register within the field. The role of new genres and text types (e.g. travel accounts, court records, recipes, diaries and letters) is thus also being highlighted as materials worth studying for both interspeaker and intraspeaker variation. The aim of this chapter is to explore the indexical potential of orthographic variation in style, register, genre and text types. The extralinguistic factors conditioning the use of different spelling forms in cases of variability are usually based on production, geographical location, sociodemographics (sex, age, rank), social networks, text type (and genre), style, register and medium (handwritten vs. printed). In earlier periods, when correspondence and other ego-documents were probably the most frequent means of written communication and without the existence of a well-established and fixed standard variety, orthographic variation constituted a source of social meaning.

In the following chapter, **Sandrine Tailleur** discusses selected studies of orthography that focus on the spelling practices of mere users of the language (in crucial opposition to actors from the literate elite – norm makers), concentrating on what they reveal about processes of language change as exemplified by spelling variation. Her contribution supports the idea that, within the field of historical sociolinguistics, orthographic variables are now considered a type of linguistic variables. The author shows, on the basis of specific historical sociolinguistic studies, that writers' variable choices of orthography can inform us about broader mechanisms of language change, but always alongside other types of variation or linguistic information. This chapter examines almost exclusively material from the French language, with the studies under consideration all addressing either regional French in France or different varieties of French in Canada. The author situates the French orthographic variables within the broader language evolution context, explicating what information spelling variation discloses about the writer's attitudes toward the (written or spoken) norm, toward the written form, and toward the writer's linguistic community as a whole. She also considers how spelling variation compares to other types of language variation in order to contribute to a greater understanding of language change.

According to **Israel Sanz-Sánchez**, language contact settings have historically operated as prime sites for the negotiation of orthographic norms, one of the processes involved in the emergence of orthographic standards. Starting from this basic premise, the goal of his chapter is twofold: firstly, to provide a general review of the literature on language contact and orthography, with a special focus on how situations of language contact can bring about alternation or conflict among various spelling traditions, and spearhead the emergence of new orthographic standards; and secondly, to explore how a historical sociolinguistic approach can contribute to the study of historical orthographies in language contact situations. Specifically, the chapter tests the possibilities of an ecological framework to the study of historical orthographies in contact settings, by considering spelling norms as a reflection of multiple, simultaneous linguistic and cultural environmental forces. This framework is illustrated in the second half of the chapter by means of a case study of the emergence of orthographic norms in a high-contact environment, namely the development of spelling protocols in colonial Nahuatl and the application of these protocols to Spanish loanwords containing sibilants. This case study exemplifies the interface between linguistic, social and cultural effects typical of language contact environments, and illustrates the affordances of an ecological approach to the study of historical orthographies and orthographic normativization in other contact settings.

Laura Villa Galán's chapter addresses the study of orthography from a sociopolitical historical perspective, including a literature review and a case study focused on the politics of spelling in mid-nineteenth-century Spain. She indicates that scholars working with a sociopolitical historical approach to orthography realize that language and power are intertwined. Thus, orthographic processes (such as the selection of a script, the codification of a writing system, and the establishment or reform of specific spelling norms) are no longer understood as ideologically neutral scientific endeavors but rather seen as historically situated political activities. Examples offered in the first sections of the chapter show that orthographies are powerful instruments of inclusion and exclusion, gatekeeping devices that exacerbate and naturalize social inequalities, and ideological mechanisms that reinforce (or challenge) a given political entity. The case study, discussed further on, exemplifies the political nature of orthography by examining the spelling system that was made official in Spain in 1844 (and that, with minor changes, remains as today's standard) as the result of a historical struggle between social actors with different political agendas and different amounts of power to influence the outcomes of the debate. In short, this chapter explains that orthographies are practical and symbolic tools strategically used to impose, maintain or resist particular social identities or politico-economic orders.

In Chapter 30, **Gijsbert Rutten**, **Iris Van de Voorde** and **Rik Vosters** refine the Labovian distinction based primarily on the type of language learning involved by bringing in the contact-based insights of Milroy (2007) on this issue. Exploring the extent to which the transmission–diffusion distinction can also apply to orthographic, rather than phonological or morphosyntactic, changes, the authors discuss a range of different examples of both transmission and – various subtypes of – diffusion, mostly from Dutch, German and English. Their central argument is that diffusion must be seen as the dominant driver of orthographic change, but transmission-type changes are also possible in specific historical contexts, for instance in relation to explicit instruction in schools or in closely knit social networks. Building on different examples and cases, the chapter also explains the link between diffusion and supralocalization, as local and regional spelling practices in medieval times give way to more supraregional writing traditions in postmedieval times. As such, these processes of geographical diffusion of innovations across communities often lay the groundwork for later standardization efforts. However, by discussing a slightly more elaborate case study on spelling change and pluricentricity in Dutch language history, the authors show how the development of such supraregional writing traditions often not only leads to linguistic standardization, but also results in a linguistic landscape which can best be described as pluricentric, consisting of different national and regional normative centers from which innovations spread.

The following chapter closes Part V as well as the whole volume. It is important to indicate at this point that the author of this contribution adheres to the traditional view on graphemics, treating it as external to language (in contrast to, for example, the perspective taken in Chapter 6). In this chapter, **Yishai Neuman** explores various aspects and examples of analogy and extension, with particular attention paid to the interrelations between both phenomena. As the author clarifies, *analogy* can be understood as an automatic cognitive process by which what is known is extrapolated to what is considered as similar, which leads to a similar outcome, that is *extension*. This can be illustrated by an infant confusing cats and dogs, treating them as the same kind of animal, due to this child's short-term past experience. Later cognitive development usually prevents incorrect analogy, as when children start understanding that cats and dogs are different animals. Extension following perceptual analogy in conventional semiotic systems produces changes in the system, so instead of being interpreted as erroneous, it should be considered as a reflection of evolving human perception. Thus, semiotic systems generally evolve via extension generated by analogy, which, according to the author, can be illustrated by language and graphemics. The author specifies that analogy between graphemic systems in contact may induce intergraphemic extension, and analogy between different categories of a given graphemic system may lead to intragraphemic extension. Because graphemic systems are related to language in many ways (e.g. to elements of phonemic and morphemic systems), analogy concerning graphemics may often produce intersemiotic extension, either from language to graphemics or in the opposite direction. Eventually, the seemingly ideal synchronic correlation between graphemics and linguistic elements may have been caused by historical analogy and extension between them, and this evolution can be studied by diachronic analysis of language–writing relations.

Part II

Structures and Theories

2

Classifying and Comparing Early Writing Systems

Amalia E. Gnanadesikan

2.1 Introduction

The task of describing and classifying writing systems begins with defining and classifying writing as a whole. Writing constitutes one of many forms of symbolic notation. Specifically, it is a *linguistic* symbolic notation. While some scholars have embraced a wide definition of writing that includes nonlinguistic notational systems such as mathematical notation (notably Harris 1995), most scholars of writing use a narrower definition under which writing conveys information in linguistic form.[1] Put simply, this means that the messages that writing conveys are conveyed in words – specific words, and not just any kind of words. Writing is dependent on – and therefore historically subsequent to – the human cognitive faculty of language, which is usually expressed in speech but which may also take signed, that is, gestural forms. Historically and conceptually, writing was also dependent on two other forms of interrelated information technology: *notation* and *iconography* (Whittaker 2009: 51). Nonlinguistic notational systems are abstract ways of conveying information that is nonlinguistic or not essentially linguistic. Modern examples are mathematical notation, musical notation, and circuit diagrams. A historical example from pre-Columbian Mesoamerica is the numerical notational system used in the regional calendar system (Marcus 2006: 18). Iconography, on the other hand, is a method of using conventionalized images to convey information: the information may be 'read' in words, but the specific linguistic

[1] Another exception – the more notable for coming from a linguist – is that from Sampson (2015: 21–22), who classifies Blissymbolics (invented in 1949 by Charles Bliss to be a universal writing system independent of spoken language) as a *semasiographic* writing system, that is, a writing system that does not represent a spoken language. Rogers (2005: 265–67) agrees that Blissymbolics (or Bliss symbols) constitute a semantic writing system rather than one that is based on the morphemes or phonology of any specific language, but suggests that in practical use it is not independent of the primary language of its users.

form of the reading is not determined by the symbols used. Stylized symbols on bathroom doors conventionally used to represent 'men' and 'women', 🚻, or baby-changing facilities, 🚼, are modern forms of iconography. A bathroom sign, for example, may be read as *bathroom*, *washroom*, *toilet*, *loo* or many another word in another language. A historical Mesoamerican example of iconography is the system that identified, for example, place names and lordly titles (Houston 2004: 286). These two elements – notation and iconography – were at the root of the development of writing in that region.

A writing system is the conventionalized means of writing a given language, using a script (or signary, a set of written symbols known as signs or graphs) and a set of rules for relating the written signs to units of the language (called the orthography, e.g. Daniels 2018: 155, and/or the graphematics, Neef 2015: 713).[2] A wider definition of *script* includes the signs and their basic linguistic interpretations but not the specific orthographic rules of a particular written language. By this definition a script includes the common elements of a group of signaries that largely share the same signs and are used by related writing systems in similar linguistic functions (Weingarten 2011: 16–17). So, for example, the Roman script is used with a slightly different set of letters and with slightly different orthographic conventions in English, Swedish and Turkish, but is generally referred to as a single script. In this larger sense, two languages sharing a script is quite common. It is, however, rare (though not technically impossible) for two languages to share exactly the same writing system, given the linguistic differences between languages and the historical contrasts between the cultures that use them. Because the specifics of orthographic rules and the differences between the writing systems of individual languages that share a script are not particularly relevant to this chapter, I use both *writing system* and *script* here, depending somewhat on whether the focus is on the systematic nature of a given form of writing or on the history, appearance or name of the set of signs.

The scientific study of writing systems has sometimes been called *grammatology* (Gelb 1963, Daniels 1990, Daniels 1996a), but the term has failed to become fully established, probably at least in part through its association with Jacques Derrida's (2016 [1967]) deconstructionist work *Of Grammatology*. Hockett (1951: 445), while declaring the study of writing systems to fall outside the discipline of linguistics (though being based on linguistics), proposed the term *graphonomy* by analogy to *astronomy*, since *graphology* was already in use for the study of handwriting. This term has achieved some recent traction, being adopted by Daniels (2018). In a bid to establish the study of writing

[2] Sometimes the writing system of a language, including its script, is called its *orthography*. Thus the term *orthography* can have three meanings: (1) the means by which a language is conveyed in writing, here termed its *writing system* (e.g. Cahill and Rice 2014), (2) the rules by which the signs of a writing system are assigned their values in a given language (the sense used here) and (3) the specific rules of standard spelling in a given language (e.g. Neef 2015).

systems as a subfield of linguistics, the field has more recently also come to be called *grapholinguistics* (e.g. in Neef 2015; see also Chapter 6 in this volume). The terms *graphematics* (Weingarten 2011) and *graphemics* (Hall 1960) are also sometimes used in this meaning, though they may be used with a narrower meaning, such as when *graphematics* is used to mean specifically the correspondence between written sounds and phonological units in Neef (2015: 713). I would myself propose the term *philography*, on analogy with *philosophy* and *philology*, if there were not already so many contenders for a name.

The modern scientific study of writing systems is often (e.g. Daniels 1996a: 7, Woods 2010a: 16) traced back to I. J. Gelb's seminal work *A Study of Writing*, with which he considered himself to be laying "a foundation for a new science of writing" (1963 [1952]: v). Although it is true that Gelb attempted to find predictive patterns in the evolution of writing systems, the earlier works of Taylor (1883) and Diringer (1949) stand out for their descriptive thoroughness while employing much the same taxonomy and similar teleological assumptions.

Despite these foundations, the twentieth century saw considerable resistance to the inclusion of writing systems within linguistics. This stance was memorably expressed by Bloomfield (1933: 21) when he dismissed writing as "not language, but merely a way of recording language by means of visible marks." Householder states it even more strongly when he characterizes Bloomfieldian linguistics as including among "the propositions intuitively felt to be basic by friend and enemy alike" the view that "[l]anguage is basically speech, and writing is of no theoretical interest" (Householder 1969: 886). In recent years, however, writing systems have come to be seen as a legitimate object of scientific and linguistic study, and a number of book-length works devoted to the subject have been published by linguists, including Sampson (2015 [1985]), Coulmas (1989, 2003), DeFrancis (1989), Daniels and Bright (1996), Sproat (2000), Rogers (2005), Gnanadesikan (2009) and Daniels (2018). In the following sections, I describe some fundamentals of writing systems: their typology, the birth and development of writing, the historical distribution of writing system types, and some of the hypotheses that have been formulated regarding the evolution of writing system types.

2.2 Linguistic Typology of Sign Types

All writing systems represent an analysis of language (O'Connor 1983, Reiner 2000: 1, Daniels 2013). None of them, despite Bloomfield's memorable dismissal quoted in the preceding paragraph, is a mere recording of spoken utterances. Writing systems present linguistic messages as a series of discrete signs, while a spoken utterance is characterized by stretches of connected sound (Liberman et al. 1967), far more so than literate people tend to assume, habituated as we are to seeing discrete symbols on a page. Writing systems present a sampling of such linguistic analyses made over the course of history, and insofar as the writing systems have been successful, they represent analyses that their users have found effective. While there are many ways in which writing systems could be classified, the conventional way of classifying them (going back at least as far as Taylor, Diringer and Gelb) is by what kinds of linguistic units their signs mainly correspond to. Thus, classifying a writing system is a matter of classifying its signs. However, it is important to keep in mind that a writing system rarely refers to only one type of linguistic unit (Gelb 1963: 199, Justeson 1976: 59). As a trivial example, a mixing of sign type would occur if an otherwise perfectly phonemic writing system also used the numerals <0> through <9> as logograms. In practice, a great deal of mixing of sign types has occurred in the history of writing.

A fundamental distinction can be drawn between *logograms* on the one hand, and *phonograms* on the other. A *logogram* (or *logograph*) is a sign that stands for a word or morpheme of a language.[3] Morphemes are the meaningful building blocks of words: depending a bit on the particular language, a word may contain one morpheme (as in *word*) or more than one (as in *words*, made of *word* + *s*). Morphemes (and the words they compose) have both a meaning and a pronunciation; thus, logograms are also associated with both a meaning and a pronunciation. While a logogram does not directly encode a pronunciation, it encodes a morpheme, which does have a pronunciation.[4] An example of a logogram from modern English is <&>, which means 'and' and is pronounced /ænd/. Since written signs may stand for morphemes (which may or may not be complete words), but not for words independent of their morphemic makeup, the term *morphogram* is sometimes preferred to *logogram* (e.g. Rogers 2005: 14, Daniels 2018: 85). A writing system that was strictly logographic instead of morphographic would use four different signs for the four morphologically related words *walk*, *walks*, *walked* and *walking*. This, however, does not occur. Instead, such a writing system would use a single sign to write the common element *walk*. In this respect, the term *morphogram* is more accurate. However, *logogram* is more traditional, and not without some rationale. It is generally the root morpheme of a word that is written with a logogram, and other (inflectional) morphemes, if the language has inflection, are often (but not always) written with phonograms. The term *logogram* helps to point out that in writing, not all morphemes are treated equally, and the core or root of a word may receive special treatment. In early Sumerian cuneiform, for example, only the lexical roots were written, and

[3] In this chapter I use terms ending in *-gram* for noun forms and terms ending in *-graphic* for adjectival forms.

[4] Thus, I disagree with Daniels's (2018: 155) definition of a logogram as "denoting the meaning but not the pronunciation of a word or morpheme." Rather, a logogram denotes a morpheme, and a morpheme is associated with *both* a meaning and a pronunciation. The pronunciation may vary between dialects of a language, however, or even between two languages using the same logogram.

inflectional morphemes were left unwritten, a practice known as *nuclear writing*. The world's first writing systems and various other early writing systems were all heavily logographic. However, no fully developed writing system is completely logographic, a point which I return to below.

A *phonogram* is a sign that corresponds to an element (or occasionally more than one element) in the phonology of the language. A phonogram has no inherent semantic meaning. It may be pictorial (as in the Egyptian hieroglyph 𓅓) or linear, consisting only of arbitrary lines (as in <M>), but the 'meaning' of such a sign is not a word or morpheme but a phonological unit devoid of semantic content – in both of these cases, the phoneme /m/. There are three main types of phonograms.[5] A *syllabogram* is a sign that stands for a syllable. Most syllabograms stand for V or CV syllables (so-called 'light syllables'), but VC and CVC syllabograms ('heavy syllables') have occasionally occurred historically, particularly in Mesopotamian cuneiform. Scripts mainly composed of syllabograms are known as *syllabaries* (but see Section 2.5 for discussion of controversies surrounding the definition of syllabaries). The Linear B script, used on Bronze Age Crete and in parts of mainland Greece to record Mycenaean Greek centuries before the development of the Greek alphabet, was a syllabary (Hooker 1980, Chadwick 1990; see Chapter 20, this volume). When the phonological unit being represented is a phoneme (sometimes also called a phonological *segment*), the signs are called *letters*. The typology and terminology of segmental writing systems are somewhat controversial, as I explain in Section 2.5. A third type of phonogram represents phonemes in semi-decomposable groups. This type of sign, found in the native scripts of South Asia,[6] is known as an *akshara* (also rendered in Roman script as *akshar* or *akṣara*). A simple akshara stands either for a vowel that is not preceded by a consonant (V) or for a consonant followed by a default (unwritten) vowel, which is /a/ in most but not all of the relevant languages. Examples from the Devanāgarī script (used for Hindi, Marathi and Nepali) are उ *u* and त *ta*. Depending on the language and script, a special diacritic may or may not be required to indicate that no vowel follows the consonant, as in त् *t*. Complex aksharas add a dependent sign to the simple akshara to replace the default vowel with a different vowel, as in Devanāgarī ते *te*, or to combine sequential consonants into a single consonant group, as in स्त *sta*, or both, as in स्ते *ste*.

[5] A few other types exist as well. The units of the Pahawh Hmong script, invented in 1959 by Shong Lue Yang (Smalley et al. 1990), are syllable onsets and rhymes. The *hiragana* and *katakana* syllabaries, used for Japanese, each contain a sign whose function is to lengthen the following consonant, while *katakana* has one whose function is to lengthen the preceding vowel (Taylor and Taylor 2014: 288). The Egyptian hieroglyphic script contained signs whose values were two or three sometimes discontinuous consonantal phonemes. Akkadian cuneiform (Foxvog 2014: 11) and Nahuatl writing (Whittaker 2009: 66) both used occasional disyllabograms: CVCV. The Greek alphabet contains some letters (such as Ψ *psi*) that stand for a sequence of two phonemes, as does the Latin <X>.

[6] The Ethiopic script is formed on similar principles (Haile 1996), but sequences of consonants are not combined, unlike in many of the South Asian scripts.

Generally speaking, a new akshara begins after every vowel, so that a vowel and a following consonant are in different aksharas even if they are in the same syllable. However, there are some exceptions if the following consonant is a nasal.[7]

A writing system may also contain signs that are not pronounced, or not pronounced independently of other signs. These include phonetic complements, semantic determinatives, and of course punctuation, which is dealt with elsewhere in this volume (especially Chapter 8). A *phonetic complement* (or *phonetic indicator* – see Whittaker 2009: 56–57 for the difference between these two terms, for those who make one) is a sign that is used in addition to another sign to disambiguate or to re-enforce the pronunciation of that sign. While phonetic complements are phonograms, they are not pronounced separately from the primary sign with which they appear. A *semantic determinative* (or just *determinative*) is a sign that is used in addition to another sign (or group of signs) to identify the semantic category of the referent of the sign(s). This also helps to disambiguate the sign(s). Phonetic complements and semantic determinatives were both commonly used in the Egyptian hieroglyphic writing system. So, for example, in the word 𓉐𓂋𓂻 *pr* 'go', the 𓉐 is used as a phonogram representing the consonants /p/ and /r/, the 𓂋 is used as a phonetic complement repeating the /r/ of the previous sign, and 𓂻 is a determinative indicating that the word has to do with motion (example from Davies 1990: 103).

Two terms for classifying signs have tended to be misunderstood and misapplied. These terms are *ideogram* and *pictogram*. Ideogram means 'a sign that represents an idea'. An example of an ideogram in modern usage is the circle with a slash through it, ⊘, used to express the idea of something being forbidden. A pictogram is a sign that is a conventionalized picture of something. The iconic symbols for men and women on bathroom doors, 🚻, are pictograms. Emoji are pictograms that may also be used as ideograms, depending on the context and the particular sign. For example, ☺ is both a pictogram (a stylized picture of a smiling face) and an ideogram (used to convey the idea of happiness). Ideograms and pictograms are important to the origin of writing systems, given that they contributed iconographic elements from which writing emerged. For example, a stylized picture of a sun could mean 'sun' and perhaps by extension 'day' or 'time'. However, in order for true writing to develop, ideograms and pictograms had to become logograms, phonograms or determinatives. The terms *ideogram* and *pictogram* therefore do not serve to identify a sign as either writing or not writing, nor do they identify what kind of function a given sign is filling in a writing system or what kind of

[7] Specifically, if the following consonant is a nasal consonant that is in the syllable coda, and its place of articulation is dependent on the first consonant of the following syllable, the nasal consonant may be represented with a diacritic, known as *anusvāra*, on the preceding akshara. Thus तंत writes *tanta* in Devanāgarī, the dot being the *anusvāra*.

writing system a particular system is. As a result, these terms should arguably be avoided by scholars of writing systems (Sampson 2015: 26).

Chinese characters, Egyptian hieroglyphs and Maya hieroglyphs have all been misunderstood as being fundamentally ideographic or merely pictographic. Egyptian hieroglyphs were long thought by European scholars to be ideograms, that is, to represent concepts directly rather than through the mediation of language (Pope 1999). Not surprisingly, this assumption was not helpful to the decipherment of Egyptian. Maya hieroglyphs were thought to be largely a system of mathematical and astronomical notation rather than full-fledged writing (a view espoused by Gelb 1963: 61, and described in detail by Coe 1992). Chinese characters have also often been considered by Westerners to be independent of spoken language and to therefore be a good candidate for a universal writing system (a view discussed and soundly refuted by DeFrancis 1984a, 1989). As a heritage of this belief, the characters are sometimes still inaccurately referred to as ideograms or ideographs, even in the Unicode Standard (Unicode Consortium 2019). A sign that remains pictorial in its quality, particularly if it was used in monumental inscriptions, is often termed a *hieroglyph*. However, the term *hieroglyph* is merely a description of the visual quality of a sign and is not a grapholinguistic classification. A hieroglyph may fill any or all of several functions in a writing system. For example, the Egyptian hieroglyph 𓉐, which pictorially represented the ground plan of a house, could be a logogram (meaning 'house'), a phonogram (representing the consonants /pr/) or a determinative (indicating that the preceding word referred to a building).

2.3 The Emergence of Writing

Writing has only developed from scratch a few times in history – though the exact number of times is not entirely clear. These initial systems are often called "pristine" writing systems (e.g. Cooper 2004: 89, Woods 2010a: 15), on the grounds that their emergence was not influenced by the writing of other peoples. The earliest writing in the world is thought to have arisen in Mesopotamia in the late fourth millennium BC (Cooper 2004: 72, Woods 2010b: 33). Known in its earliest phases as proto-cuneiform, it developed into the script known as Mesopotamian cuneiform, used for the Sumerian and Akkadian languages, and inspired a number of other scripts of cuneiform – that is, wedge-shaped – design. Nearly or perhaps equally as old as proto-cuneiform are Egyptian hieroglyphs, also dating to the end of the fourth millennium BC (Baines 2004, Stauder 2010: 118). While there were trade links between Mesopotamia and Egypt at the time, these two systems are so very different from their very beginnings that they are usually both considered independent inventions. Nevertheless, Daniels's (2006, 2018: 141) claim that all pristine inventions of writing were used for languages with largely monosyllabic root morphemes (a point returned to in Section 2.5) leads him to the conclusion that Egyptian writing was inspired by Mesopotamian cuneiform rather than an independent development. Other writing systems that are numbered among the original inventions are the Chinese writing system and the first of the several Mesoamerican systems. The Chinese script dates from the late thirteenth century BC (Bagley 2004: 190, Bottéro 2004: 250, Shaughnessy 2010: 216) and is the only one of the original scripts still in use. The earliest surviving inscription in Mesoamerica that can unambiguously be classified as writing may be the Olmec La Venta Monument 13, dating to 500 BC or earlier (Houston 2004: 276)[8] or to 450–300 BC (Justeson 2012: 830). This early Mesoamerican writing was not Mayan, contrary to popular belief. Its cultural context is that of the Olmec civilization, but what language it represented is actually unknown. The Maya script, first attested between 300 and 200 BC (Saturno et al. 2006: 1282), is the best understood of several successor scripts that developed in the area prior to European contact and the Spanish Conquest.

Other potential independent inventions include Anatolian hieroglyphs, Cretan hieroglyphs, the Indus Valley script and Easter Island rongorongo (for which see Yakubovich 2010, Olivier 1986, Parpola 1994 and Horley 2009, respectively). Of these, Cretan hieroglyphs, the Indus Valley script and rongorongo have not been deciphered. It has been argued that the Indus Valley script (Farmer et al. 2004) and rongorongo (Sproat 2010: 124–27) are not in fact writing but some other kind of notational system. While firm conclusions in this regard may be unwise in the absence of decipherment or interpretation, the argument against rongorongo being true writing has been more widely accepted than that against the Indus Valley script (e.g. Daniels 2018: 126). Anatolian hieroglyphs are usually considered to have been created by people familiar with Mesopotamian cuneiform, but the argument has been made (Waal 2012) that the system is older than generally thought and was in fact an independent invention. Since Chinese writing postdates cuneiform, and Egyptian writing is often thought to as well, Gelb (1963: 212–20) could credibly argue that writing was only invented once and that all writing was inspired, one way or another, no matter how indirectly, by Mesopotamian cuneiform. Thus, in his view, known as the monogenetic theory, there was only one pristine writing system. Gelb's monogenetic theory was in keeping with the rather ethnocentric view, common at the time, of Mesopotamia as

[8] The dating of the earliest Mesoamerican writing is not uncontroversial, given uncertainties of dating and the fact that the common use of iconography in early Mesoamerica makes it difficult to judge whether a given sign or group of signs is an example of writing or not. Houston (2004: 292) uses the criteria that writing is "(1) a graphic representation of language, (2) detached from the body of its referent, and (3) disposed into linear sequences that can theoretically expand into greater degrees of syntactic complexity." Of course, in the absence of a decipherment, the fulfillment of criterion (1) can only be guessed at.

the single cradle of civilization for the world. Gelb dismissed the Maya glyphs as not being true writing, not having "even approximately reached the phonetic stage of writing which we find so well developed already in the oldest Sumerian inscriptions" (Gelb 1963: 51). This view of Maya glyphs turned out to be flat-out wrong. The decipherment of the Maya glyphs and an increasing understanding of pre-Columbian writing in Mesoamerica in general left the monogenetic theory no longer tenable, and other independent inventions (in China and perhaps Egypt) became plausible again. Although the emergence of writing took somewhat different paths in the different contexts in which it arose, in the remainder of this section I sketch out a somewhat abstract picture of the development of writing that is applicable across instances.[9]

As briefly mentioned in the introduction to this chapter, writing arose in contexts with pre-existing or coexisting systems of notation and iconography. Notation and iconography may each constitute independent systems that are complete within a given communicative sphere. It is in the combination of the two that writing, with its reference to linguistic units, seems to have arisen. Specifically, Justeson (1986) suggests that writing first arose through the combination of previously existing *numerical* notation and iconography. Thus, when a sign for a numeral (e.g. *6*) is combined with an iconographic sign for an entity or object (e.g. *goats*), it is read as 'six goats', with each sign corresponding to a word in a grammatical phrase. In this way, Justeson suggests, the link between sign and word, and thus writing, was born. By contrast, a purely iconographic rendering of six goats (with six distinct goat signs) would not suggest a link between an individual sign and an individual word, and neither would a purely numerical notation. In Mesoamerica, Justeson argues, the linkage of numerical notation and iconography came about in the recording of calendrical dates, while in Mesopotamia numerical notation and iconographic signs were joined in the creation of economic administrative documents. Chrisomalis (2009) further shows that a link between numerical notation and early writing can be found in all four of the writing systems most commonly classified as pristine (independently arising) systems. Whether the numerical notation pre-dated writing or developed in tandem with it, numerical notation is present in the earliest preserved examples of writing, supporting the hypothesis that writing arose in the context of combining systems of numerical notation and iconography. What makes writing, instead of simply the

[9] Histories of writing systems often spend time describing and/or debunking the token theory of the development of writing in Mesopotamia, propounded by Schmandt-Besserat (1986). This chapter does not engage in this debate, for three reasons: (1) the token theory applies only to Mesopotamia, only one of several loci of writing system invention, (2) I find the arguments against the theory convincing (for a summary see Woods 2010b and Sampson 2015), and (3) the theory is more about the origin of using signs impressed on clay tablets as an accounting system (which later developed into writing) than about the crucial intellectual leap by which graphic signs came to convey linguistic messages and thus specifically became writing.

concurrent use of (nonlinguistic) notation and iconography, is that the symbols come to convey information in a given linguistic form, that is, in words.

The pristine writing systems all depended heavily on pictography – though, as mentioned above, for them to become writing systems, signs which were pictographic in *form* had to take on the *function* of logograms. In order for the writing systems to develop fully into systems that could write sentences on any topic, however, further signs were needed. Not all the words of a language contain morphemes that are easily pictured or whose meaning would have been previously encoded in either the culture's numerical notation or its iconography. A morpheme combines a particular lexical meaning with a particular phonological form (i.e. a pronunciation). As a representation of a morpheme, a logogram is associated with both a meaning and a pronunciation. In order to extend the repertory of written signs and the words and morphemes that could be written, the link between meaning and pronunciation (between semantics and phonology) was broken and one dimension of a logogram's interpretation – either the phonology or the semantics – was pursued (see Figure 2.1). A sign originally standing for a word with a particular meaning–pronunciation combination could be used to stand for another word that had either the same or similar pronunciation or a related meaning. The use of a pictorial sign to stand for a homophonous or nearly homophonous morpheme is known as *rebus* writing. At first this was used to derive other logograms, such as when Sumerian cuneiform used the sign for *ti* 'arrow' to mean 'rib', which was also pronounced /ti/, and also for '(to) live', which was pronounced /til/ (Foxvog 2014: 11). The rebus principle was also eventually used, by a greater step of abstraction, to derive syllabograms – signs used only for their pronunciation and no longer associated in any way with an inherent meaning. Another form of greater abstraction on the phonographic side was *acrophony*. Acrophony is the use of a sign to stand for just the first part (the first phoneme or the first CV syllable) of the word corresponding to what the sign is a picture of. Acrophony was used in the Maya script, for example when the sign depicting the head of a gourd, *tzimah*, was used for the syllable /tzi/ (Mora-Marín 2003: 209).

Along the semantic branch, the principle of semantic extension meant that a sign for something easily pictured could be used for something that was

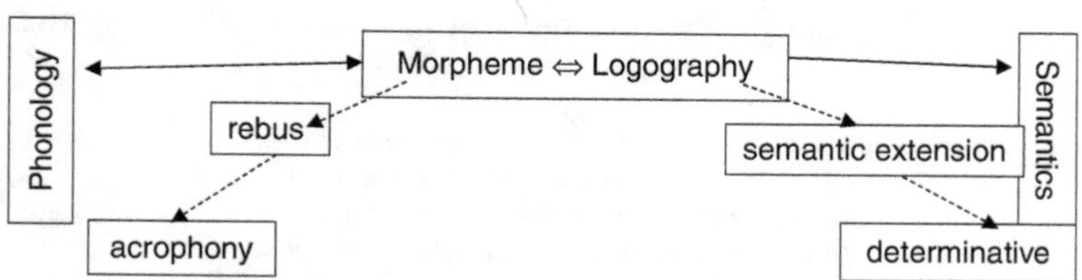

Figure 2.1 The extension of initial logograms along the phonological and semantic dimensions into further logograms and beyond to phonograms and semantic determinatives

semantically related but less easily pictured. This occurred when, for example, the Sumerian cuneiform sign for 'plow', pronounced *apin*, was also used to mean 'farmer', with the totally unrelated pronunciation of *engar*. An additional layer of semantic abstraction was added when signs came to be used as determinatives, associated only with a semantic category and no longer with specific morphemes. All fully developed writing systems have used phonological abstraction to some degree or another and have thus become at least somewhat phonographic, but the principle of semantic extension was also extensively used in early writing systems. The following section gives very short descriptions of the pristine, heavily logographic writing systems. For more details, see Gnanadesikan (2009) and references therein and elsewhere in this chapter.

2.4 Examples of Heavily Logographic Systems

Mesopotamian cuneiform originated in the late fourth millennium BC in southern Mesopotamia. The earliest version of the system (known as proto-cuneiform) was heavily logographic and the texts were highly telegraphic, with inflections and even grammatical word order to be supplied by the reader from context. As time went on, and proto-cuneiform became cuneiform, the phonographic aspect of the script grew (in the form of syllabograms), and the writing of inflectional morphemes increased. The resulting system is classified as *logosyllabic*. The first recognizable language for which cuneiform was used is Sumerian, but it also came, with extension and modification, to be used for Akkadian. It also served as the inspiration for numerous other scripts of cuneiform (wedge-shaped) design. The signs of Mesopotamian cuneiform included logograms, syllabograms (including V, CV, VC and CVC types, with occasional disyllabic CVCV) and determinatives. Cuneiform is last attested in the first century AD.

Egyptian hieroglyphs also originated in the late fourth millennium BC. Sign types included logograms, determinatives and phonograms. The phonograms included signs standing for one, two or three consonants, with no specification of the intervening vowels. Uniconsonantal signs often served as phonetic complements. Because of the use of consonantal signs, the system is classified as *logoconsonantal*. The hieroglyphs never lost their original pictorial quality. About 500 signs were used at any one time over most of the life of the script.[10] The last known hieroglyphic text dates from the end of the fourth century AD. Hieratic, a related but more cursive (and less pictorial) Egyptian script,

[10] Considerably more signs (over 6,000) are attested from near the end of the script's use as religious scribes wrote elaborate, cryptic texts for a very restricted readership.

operating on the same principles as hieroglyphic, is essentially as old as the hieroglyphs (Baines 2004: 169–70).[11]

Chinese characters are first attested from the late thirteenth century BC. Known at first from oracle bone inscriptions used for divination, this system developed into the Chinese system still in use today, although with considerable changes along the way. Its classification has been the cause of considerable controversy (DeFrancis 1989: 89–121, Sproat 2000: 144–54). While it has often been considered logographic (i.e. writing morphemes), this view is complicated by two factors.[12] One is that morphemes in Chinese are almost invariably one syllable in length, confounding the distinction between logography and syllabography: the few morphemes that are longer than one syllable are written with more than one character. In other words, the one-to-one correspondence between characters and syllables is stronger than the nearly one-to-one correspondence between characters and morphemes. The other factor is that although its simplest signs each represent a (monosyllabic) morpheme, most signs are compounds of simpler signs. The most common form of compound includes one part that is a clue to the meaning of the morpheme (functioning as a semantic determinative) and one part that is a clue – though often far from exact in the modern language – to the pronunciation of the morpheme. Thus, using modern Mandarin pronunciations, the compound character 妈 *mā* 'mother' can be seen to be made up of the characters for 女 *nǚ* 'woman', a clue to the meaning, and 马 *mǎ* 'horse', a near-homophone. In this way the system encodes a great deal of phonography. It is therefore often classified as a *morphosyllabic* system.

Mayan hieroglyphs are the best understood of the pre-Columbian Mesoamerican writing systems, so the Mayan system is commonly used as a stand-in for the earlier pristine system of Mesoamerica. Known for elaborately carved signs, often depicting faces, the script is a logosyllabary of about 700 signs. The syllabograms are mostly CV, but occasionally CVC (Justeson 2012: 836). The phonograms can be used as phonetic complements (as in Mesopotamian cuneiform and Egyptian hieroglyphs), but unlike cuneiform and Egyptian hieroglyphs, the system makes little use of semantic determinatives. A single large sign, sometimes with smaller signs appended, constitutes a 'glyph block', and monumental texts are read from left to right and top to bottom, often in double columns of glyph blocks. This system was last used in the seventeenth century AD.

[11] A third Egyptian script, demotic, is considerably younger, dating from about 650 BC (Johnson 2010: 165).

[12] A third complication is introduced if we accept Baxter and Sagart's (2014) reconstruction of Old Chinese as containing derivational prefixes and suffixes (and one infix), which were usually monoconsonantal. If these affixes were still synchronically productive when the Chinese writing system was developed, then the writing system did not write each morpheme with its own sign, but nor did it write each syllable with its own character, as some of the prefixes constituted their own syllables, albeit weak ones.

2.5 Typology of Phonographic Writing

Traditionally, writing systems whose basic units are syllabograms are known as *syllabaries*, while those whose basic units are phonemic letters are known as *alphabets*.[13] Those whose basic units are aksharas have tended to occupy an uncomfortable typological space, sometimes being considered alphabets but sometimes being given terms such as *alphasyllabary* (Bright 1999), *abugida* (Daniels 1996a: 4), or *semi-alphabet* and *semi-syllabary* (Diringer 1949: 329, 360). Syllables and the syllabaries that represent them have played an important but somewhat controversial role in the study of writing systems. Syllabograms are pervasive in the history of writing: while the pristine writing systems were all heavily logographic, three out of four of them (all except Egyptian) were also heavily syllabic once they were fully developed. According to Daniels (1992, 2018: 136–39), the fact that Sumerian, Chinese and Mayan all had a large number of monosyllabic root morphemes enabled the leap from logogram to syllabogram. In his view this was crucial to allowing full writing to develop. However, it is important to realize that the Mayan writing system was not in fact the first writing in Mesoamerica; thus, the nature of Mayan word roots may be irrelevant to his hypothesis, depending on how fully developed the Mesoamerican predecessors of the Mayan system actually were. Daniels's theory also crucially depends on Egyptian writing not being one of the pristine systems.

Various secondary inventions were also logosyllabic or syllabic. As Daniels has pointed out (1992, 1996c), writing systems known to have been invented in modern times by individuals who had heard of writing but who were not themselves literate are generally syllabaries.[14] (Perhaps the most famous of such people was Sequoyah, inventor of the Cherokee script, Scancarelli 1996.)[15] It is entirely reasonable to conclude, as Daniels does, that the

[13] In popular terminology, *alphabet* is sometimes used (especially by users of alphabets) to refer to any script. This is inaccurate in any modern philographic typology.

[14] Pahawh Hmong is an exception, as its units correspond to syllable onsets and rhymes. If Egyptian hieroglyphs are not an independent invention, they would constitute another exception, as the system bears no evidence of design influence from Sumerian cuneiform. Thus they are either an original invention (a pristine system) or they are a secondary invention made by someone(s) who did not actually understand how Sumerian cuneiform worked.

[15] Sequoyah is unanimously described as illiterate and as speaking little or no English in traditional descriptions of his invention, but see Cushman (2012: 23–25) for a discussion of two handwritten letters from the 1830s that may possibly have been written by Sequoyah in English (though dating to after his invention of the Cherokee syllabary). I consider Sequoyah's prior literacy in English to be unlikely, since (1) it is historically common for literate individuals to serve as scribes for illiterate individuals, so letters from Sequoyah may have been translated and transcribed by someone else, (2) contemporaries and close connections of Sequoyah described him as speaking very little English, and (3) the type of writing system that an individual first learns has a profound effect on that person's concept of literacy. A person with prior literacy in English (but in none of the other writing systems of the world) would surely have invented something more like the English writing system, despite the conscious effort to set aside English influence that Cushman ascribes to Sequoyah.

historically widespread preference for syllabaries is due to the relative accessibility to speakers' consciousness of syllables as opposed to phonemes. In other words, the ability of non-alphabet-users to perceive and count syllables is much greater than that for phonemes, which is very poor (Liberman et al. 1974, Read et al. 1986). It has even been suggested that the concept of the phoneme was actually inspired by alphabetic writing and not vice versa, and that the phoneme has no independent (i.e. nonorthographic) reality (Faber 1992). This view is rather more extreme than the evidence warrants, in part because a writing system based on linguistically illegitimate units would certainly fail to become established (Gnanadesikan 2011: 397). Successful writing systems imply successful linguistic analyses, as mentioned above. However, as Aronoff (1992) points out, phonological theory may be more influenced by orthography than we tend to suspect.

The definition of a syllabary has at times been reconsidered. For theory-internal reasons, Gelb (1963: 75–79) classified the Egyptian writing system as logosyllabic and the Phoenician consonantal writing system as syllabic. In these systems, which lack vowel notation, he analyzed signs that stood for consonants as in fact standing for a consonant plus any vowel, rendering them syllabograms with unspecified vowel components. This view has been criticized by various subsequent scholars (e.g. Daniels 1996a: 8, Baines 2004: 178–79, Sampson 2015: 80–81).

Another reconsideration of the definition of the syllabary comes from a series of unpublished talks in which William Poser (1992) claimed that most writing systems that have been called syllabaries in fact use the mora as the linguistic unit to which signs correspond, the mora being the unit of syllable length, whereby so-called light syllables – schematically V or CV – have one mora, and so-called heavy syllables – (C)VV or (C)VC – have two moras. This claim, taken up by Rogers (2005: 276–77), was based on the preponderance of signs that are (C)V – that is, a single mora – in such systems. Gnanadesikan (2011) takes partial issue with Poser's claim, arguing that syllabaries in fact make a considerable amount of reference to syllables, even if they usually (but not always) consist of only (C)V signs. Only a few scripts traditionally known as syllabaries (notably Japanese *kana* and the Vai script) actually represent all the language's moras. By contrast, such systems reliably write all their syllables. Buckley (2018) takes the argument in defense of syllabaries a step further, stating that the reliance on (C)V signs in such systems stems simply from the signs representing the unmarked (i.e. simplest) form of syllables in order to keep the size of the sign inventory low. In the Japanese and Vai cases, additional signs are used to indicate syllable-final moraic consonants, but these constitute a small exception to the overall sign type which does not affect the classification of the system as a whole.

Writing systems whose signs correspond to segmental phonemes are traditionally known as *alphabets*, and the first of the Semitic consonantal writing systems is traditionally taken to be the first alphabet (Naveh 1982, Healey 1990, Lam 2010). However, Daniels (1996a: 4, 2017: 77–81, 2018: 156) divides segmental writing into three types: *abjad*, *abugida* and *alphabet*. This typology has become very popular. An *abjad* is a writing system that writes only consonantal segments (which Gelb classified with the syllabaries). An *abugida* is one in which "each character denotes a consonant accompanied by a specific vowel, and the other vowels are denoted by a consistent modification of the consonant symbols" (Daniels 1996a: 4). The akshara-based scripts are considered abugidas. The term *alphabet* in this typology is reserved for a writing system that writes all vowels as well as consonants. Gnanadesikan (2017) takes partial issue with the Daniels classification, pointing out that this typology divides segmental scripts into types that appear to be no more related to each other than they are to syllabaries, ignoring the fact that in representing segments they have something in common which they do not share with syllabaries or logographies. Additionally, there is virtually no writing system that actually fits the definition of an abjad. The Phoenician script, attested from around 1050 BC (and its lesser-known predecessors, Proto-Canaanite and Proto-Sinaitic), was a pure abjad, but the so-called abjads in modern use, descended from Phoenician's daughter script Aramaic, all write some of their vowels. For example, Aramaic's daughter script Arabic writes all the long vowels of the Arabic language. Its application to languages other than Arabic has resulted in a range of vowel notations, such as in Sorani Kurdish, in which all vowels except one are written (Gnanadesikan 2017: 24). This kind of use suggests that (consonantal) abjads and (fully voweled) alphabets may in fact be two ends of a spectrum of vowel notation rather than two separate types.

The type called by Daniels an abugida, I would argue, is better termed an *akshara* system (or *āksharik*, Rimzhim et al. 2014: 50). The term *akshara* is native to the akshara-writing tradition of South Asia, while the term *abugida* is taken from Ethiopia, a secondary locus of akshara-based writing. Daniels applies the term to the Indic writing systems as though they were in search of terminology, which they are not. The native writing systems of India are also often termed *alphasyllabaries*. Although *abugida* and *alphasyllabary* are often taken to be synonymous, they are not (Bright 1999, Gnanadesikan 2017: 22), as an alphasyllabary does not require the use of an unwritten/default vowel. As described in Gnanadesikan (2017), *akshara* systems are essentially segmental, falling near the 'fully voweled' end of the vowel notation spectrum, but they also include the organization of segments into syllable peaks and margins.

As a further type of phonographic writing system, Sampson (2015: 162–63) assigns Korean Han'gŭl to a type of its own, that of featural system, as the letters of the script carry some information at the subphonemic level – that is, at the level of distinctive phonological features. Others (DeFrancis 1989: 196–97, Sproat 2000: 135–38, Gnanadesikan 2017: 25, Daniels 2018: 156–57), while recognizing the presence of some subphonemic information in the letter shapes, consider the fundamental units of Han'gŭl to actually be segmental, though they are also syllabically clustered. The following paragraphs give very short descriptions of early phonographic writing systems. For more details, see Gnanadesikan (2009) and references therein and elsewhere in this chapter.

2.6 Examples of Phonographic Writing Systems

Linear B was a syllabary used on Crete and part of mainland Greece for Mycenaean Greek between about 1500 and 1200 BC. It used about 87 signs, which stood for simple (C)V syllables. Also used in the accounting tablets that form the Linear B corpus were additional signs comprising numerals and a set of signs categorizing the goods that were being counted (usually called ideograms, as they were not read as words in the texts). Since the Greek language had more complex syllables than CV, numerous rules were used to fit Greek words into Linear B signs. Generally speaking, an sCV syllable would be written as just CV, with the /s/ lost; a $C_1C_2V_3$ syllable (where the first C was not /s/) would be written as C_1V_3-C_2V_3 and a CVC syllable was written as just CV, with the final C lost. Thus, for example, the place name Knossos was written as 𐀒𐀜𐀰, *ko-no-so*. Linear B's predecessors on Crete, Linear A and Cretan hieroglyphic, were used for an unknown language and remain undeciphered.

Phoenician was a consonantal phonemic script, one of the few purely consonantal scripts in history. Dating from 1050 BC (though this date is not uncontroversial and is placed later by some scholars, e.g. Sass 2005), it is a descendant of the first Semitic consonantal script, which was inspired by the use of uniconsonantal signs in the Egyptian writing system. In this script, the name Ahiram, phonemically /ʔaħiram/, with an initial glottal stop, was spelled (reading from right to left) 𐤀𐤇𐤓𐤌, *ʔħrm*. This 22-letter script was in turn the direct ancestor of the Aramaic script. Egyptian, Phoenician and Aramaic are all Afro-Asiatic languages, which build their words based on usually three-letter consonantal roots. Thus a consonantal writing system was appropriate for these languages. The consonantal values of the letters were derived via the acrophonic principle from the first phoneme of the names of the letters.

Archaic Greek was the first phonemic system to write all of its phonemes, consonants and vowels. It seems to have been inspired by a partial misunderstanding of the Phoenician writing system, probably in the eighth century BC. For example, the first letter of the Phoenician script, 𐤀, named *'ālef*, stood for its first sound, which was a consonant, the glottal stop /ʔ/. Since Greek did not have a phonemic glottal stop, the letter was interpreted as standing for the next phoneme, the vowel /a/, becoming A, *alpha*. This reinterpretation of a consonant letter as a vowel letter opened the way for other Phoenician letters that were not needed to write consonants in Greek to also be used as vowel letters. The resulting alphabet wrote all of its vowels. Although all phonemes were written in Greek (except in some cases /h/), letters and phonemes were not in a one-to-one relation: long and short vowels were not always distinguished from each other, and some letters, such as Ψ *psi*, stood for a sequence of two consonants.

Brāhmī was the akshara-based ancestral script of India as well as of parts of Southeast Asia. Originally used for Prakrit and later Sanskrit, it is attested from about the third century BC to the fourth century AD, by which time it had developed northern and southern varieties. The regional varieties became further differentiated and evolved into the modern akshara-based scripts of India and Southeast Asia. It seems to have been inspired by Aramaic, though with significant modifications in design that replaced the consonantal writing with akshara-based writing. The related but extinct Kharoṣṭhī script probably served as something of an intermediate stage between Aramaic and Brāhmī.

2.7 Implications of Typology for Sign Inventory Size

Because a language has many more morphemes than syllables and many more syllables than phonemes, systems that include a large number of logograms have larger sign inventories than pure syllabaries, which in turn are larger than pure alphabets. However, given that a language may have as many as 122 consonants (in the case of !Xóõ or Taa, Maddieson 2013), this is not logically necessary across languages. A pure alphabet for !Xóõ with a one-to-one relationship between letters and phonemes would have over 120 letters, while a syllabary with only CV signs, employed for a language such as Rotokas, with only 6 phonemic consonants (Maddieson 2013) and a similar number of vowels, would need fewer than 40. In practice, however, syllabaries tend to have between 50 and 90 signs, while alphabets tend to have 20 to 50 signs. Logographic systems are in theory unbounded (with any new morpheme calling for a new logogram), but since no mature writing system is purely logographic, unboundedness is not logically necessary. Nevertheless, the total number of signs used in the heavily logographic scripts has tended to vary over time. For example, in the early third millennium BC the Mesopotamian cuneiform script peaked at about 1,200 signs, while by the mid-third millennium it contained about 800 signs, and by the end of the third millennium it was down to about 600, where it stayed for the following millennium (Cooper 1996: 40). In Chinese, the most logographic modern script, common literacy requires 3,500 characters, a scholar may know 6,000, and a large dictionary lists about 50,000 (Taylor and Taylor 2014: 50). Most characters are compounds of simpler characters, however. Akshara systems may contain many hundreds of aksharas, but most of them are decomposable into sequences of simpler phonemic or C+a signs. Because of the large phonemic inventory of Sanskrit, however, even the simple aksharas of South Asian writings systems tend to number in the 40s.

2.8 Evolutionary Theories Regarding Script Type

Theories regarding the evolution of writing systems have been plagued by misunderstandings and outright ethnocentrism. Gelb (1963: 201) claimed that writing "must pass through the stages of logography, syllabography, and alphabetography in this, and no other, order." This concept is known as the principle of unidirectional development. Crucial to making this principle work was Gelb's analysis of the consonantal scripts as syllabic, which allowed him to claim that the Greek alphabet was descended from a syllabary. In fact, as Justeson and Stephens (1993) point out, no true syllabary has ever evolved into an alphabet. Gelb was not the first to chart such a line of evolution, however. Taylor (1883: 5–6) describes five stages in the development of writing: pictures of things, pictorial symbols representing abstract ideas, word signs, syllabic signs and alphabetic letters. Diringer (1949: 35–37) also implies an evolutionary order of logography, syllabography, and alphabetography. Gelb saw alphabetic writing, first adopted by the Greeks, as superior to other forms of writing, a view which has been strongly criticized (Harris 1995: 1–5, Daniels 1996b: 26–28, Trigger 2004: 40–43, Share 2014). In this opinion too he followed Taylor and Diringer, although both Taylor and Diringer included the Semitic consonantal scripts in their category of alphabet. Diringer (1949: 37) states that "[t]he alphabet is the last, the most highly developed, the most convenient and the most easily adaptable system of writing. Alphabetic writing is now universally employed by civilized peoples; its use is acquired in childhood with ease."[16]

The relative ease of acquisition of different types of writing systems is beyond the scope of this chapter; suffice it to say that alphabetic writing is not in fact clearly easier for children to learn than other types of writing.[17] While the views of Diringer with respect to what makes a people "civilized" are so

[16] It is not clear whether the Brāhmī-descended scripts of South and Southeast Asia are included in his definition of "alphabetic writing," as he terms Brāhmī a "semi-alphabet" (Diringer 1949: 329) and its descendant Devanāgarī a "semi-syllabary" which is nonetheless "one of the most perfect systems of writing" (Diringer 1949: 360).

[17] The awareness of syllables precedes the awareness of phonemes in children's cognitive development cross-linguistically and occurs spontaneously in children, whereas the awareness of phonemes develops only in those learning to read a phonemic script (Goswami 2006: 466). Thus, children who are learning a syllabary are learning a system that refers to phonological units of which they are already aware, while those learning an alphabet must grasp the concept of the phoneme in order to learn to read. As a result, Japanese children can often read the *hiragana* syllabary before receiving any formal education (Taylor and Taylor 2014: 333).

blatantly ethnocentric as to appear to require no comment in the twenty-first century, his elevated view of the alphabet is not obsolete. The classicist Eric Havelock has declared that "[t]he introduction of the Greek letters into inscription somewhere about 700 BC was to alter the character of human culture, placing a gulf between all alphabetic societies and their precursors. The Greeks did not just invent an alphabet, they invented literacy and the literate basis for modern thought" (1999: 54).

Havelock's view of the primacy of the Greek alphabet has been so roundly criticized by scholars of writing systems (Houston 1994, Daniels 1996b: 26–28, Taylor and Taylor 2014: 416–20) that it too is almost not worth mentioning here except as an object lesson: it is easier to fall under the spell of one's own writing system than one imagines. It is extremely difficult for literate people to view language separately from their own writing system, even if they are linguists. It is seldom noticed, for example, that the International Phonetic Alphabet, meant to be a system of transcribing the sounds of speech, is actually an alphabet, and it imposes a segmental analysis on the speech signal (Coulmas 2013: 8).

Alphabetic writing codifies the phonology of one dialect of a language at one time in history, while logographic writing is friendlier to dialectal variation and historical change. It is also worth noting that alphabetic writing has tended to move away from purely segmental writing over time: the introduction of word spacing, which is not based on phonemes, has been claimed as an important step in making text easily readable (Saenger 1997); logograms and, in texting, even syllabograms have crept back in (as in *I ♥ my cat* or *YRUL8?*); and emoji, whatever their precise nature in the theory of writing systems, are not segmental phonograms. Yet not all questions about the relative effectiveness of writing systems are illegitimate. Unlike languages, writing systems are deliberate human inventions, and as such they can be more or less effective – a more or less good fit for the language for which they are used, or easier or harder for learners to learn, for writers to write or for readers to read. These are among the many issues that designers of writing systems must wrestle with (for which see Cahill and Rice 2014). Yet it is dangerous to evaluate the effectiveness of historical scripts by modern standards and against modern uses of writing. In a volume with a historical focus, it is perhaps best to leave such questions aside, concluding only that any script that survives in the historical record was considered by its users to be an effective way of conveying their messages.

One of the most ubiquitous traits of writing is its conservatism (Gnanadesikan 2009). Accordingly, changes in writing system type are very rare. They occur where there is a disruption of normal script transmission, when the technology of writing is adapted to a new language in a new cultural context (see Daniels 2000 and de Voogt 2012). In other contexts, the established literate elites are deeply invested in maintaining the status quo. Mesopotamian cuneiform inspired consonantal Ugaritic cuneiform and syllabic Hurrian cuneiform but never lost its own logosyllabic character. Egyptian logoconsonantal writing inspired the direct ancestor of Phoenician consonantal writing but did not itself evolve into a purely phonographic script. The Phoenician consonantal script inspired the Greek fully voweled alphabet, but neither it nor its daughter system Aramaic ever wrote all its vowels. Chinese writing inspired the purely syllabic Japanese *kana* but has never lost its morphemic quality, and nor did the Japanese abandon Chinese characters when they added syllabic writing.

It is an open question to what extent there is directionality in script evolution. Certainly it is the case that all of the pristine and various other very early writing systems, such as Anatolian hieroglyphs, had a high degree of logography, while more purely phonographic scripts came later. It is also true that fully voweled alphabets are relative latecomers to the history of writing (the first, the Greek alphabet, dating from about the eighth century BC). However, the use of phonemic uniconsonantal signs (albeit as part of a larger script) dates back to the first dynasty of Egypt, around 3000 BC (Stauder 2010: 145), nearly at the very beginning of human writing. So phonemic writing is neither new nor 'advanced'. It may be, however, that there are tendencies in what types of scripts are easily learned at the edges of civilization, in the absence of established educational institutions, where writing has historically been adapted to new languages. A reduction in sign inventory may be natural at such a transference point. This would lead to a predominance of phonographic scripts over time, with their smaller inventories. The current predominance of the Roman and Cyrillic alphabets, however, owes so much to global geopolitics that it is well beyond the scope of this chapter to evaluate how much of modern alphabetic popularity may be owed to the philographic design of the scripts and how much to those other factors.

2.9 Conclusion

Writing arose independently in Mesopotamia, China, Mesoamerica and probably Egypt, in each case in the context of systems of notation and iconography. Early writing systems were heavily logographic and (at first) pictographic, representing words or root morphemes by means of stylized pictures. By processes of semantic and phonological abstraction, early pictographic logograms came to also be used for morphemes with similar sounds or meanings, and by further abstraction for syllables or phonemes or for semantic categories. One result of this abstraction is that the systems took on a partly phonographic character. Phonographic writing systems represent syllables or segments (phonemes). Early fully phonographic systems include the Linear

B syllabary, the Phoenician consonantal script (or abjad), the fully voweled archaic Greek alphabet and the Brāhmī akshara-based script.

Writing systems are traditionally classified into logographic systems, syllabaries and alphabets. This classification has been challenged on all points, but not always successfully. The term *logographic* has been challenged by *morphographic*; it has also been shown that no fully developed writing system is purely logographic (or morphographic). Syllabaries have been given a starring role in the development of writing, being considered the most natural form of phonography, yet the very existence of syllabaries has been challenged by the claim that such systems are actually moraic. The definition of the term *alphabet* has also been hotly contested. The tripartite *abjad–alphabet–abugida* classification of segmental scripts, intended to replace the traditional *alphabet*, has gained ground, but not without some disagreement. Other areas of debate concern whether some types of writing systems are better than others, and whether there is a directionality to the development and evolution of writing systems. Specifically, fully voweled alphabets have been held up as the best kind of writing system and the end point of writing system evolution. However, while there are common patterns among the earliest writing systems, it is not clear that the development of writing systems since then has proceeded in any consistent direction, and in fact writing systems tend to be typologically very stable. Nor is it clear that one particular type of writing system can be said to be better than others, especially when taking into account the differences in the languages for which they are used and in the values and needs of their user communities.

3

Elements of Writing Systems

Stefan Hartmann and Renata Szczepaniak

3.1 Introduction

This chapter introduces readers to the basic elements of writing systems. While we largely focus on Western writing systems, which have been the focus of much previous research, we also discuss to what extent the relevant concepts can be applied to non-Western writing systems. Writing systems can be analyzed at different levels of description, according to the branch of scientific inquiry that one wants to use as a lens for analysis. While *graphematics* (or *graphemics*) analyzes writing systems from a functional point of view, *graphetics* studies the material aspects of writing, the physical properties of written signs, and their visual and mechanical aspects (see, e.g., Coulmas 1996: 177, Fuhrhop and Peters 2013: 218–19).[1] Furthermore, graphetics and typography constitute different but related subdomains of the study of written language. Following, for example, Meletis (2015a), typography can be seen as taking a prescriptivist perspective on formal features of written language. Typography focuses on issues like font design and font technologies as well as aesthetic aspects of font perception. Hence, the relationship between typography and graphetics can be compared to the distinction that is sometimes made between graphemics and orthography, where graphemics refers to writing-in-use, while orthography is understood as referring to the system-external codification of graphemic rules (Meletis 2020b: 257; note, however, that *orthography* is often used in a broader sense, as attested by the very title of the present *Handbook*). The units introduced in this chapter belong to all

We are grateful to the editors, two anonymous reviewers, and to Eric Engel and Michael Pleyer for their helpful comments and suggestions on previous drafts of this chapter. Of course, we are solely responsible for any remaining errors or shortcomings.

[1] More about graphematics and graphetics is discussed in Chapter 6, this volume.

three domains. The concept of *grapheme* and the related concept of *allograph* pertain to functional aspects and can therefore be considered graphemic concepts. While graphemes are the smallest units of analysis in graphematics, *graphs* are the smallest elements of graphetics. *Letters* constitute a subgroup of graphs. In typography, abstract *characters* and concrete *glyphs* are distinguished.

In this chapter, we discuss these concepts in turn. Section 3.2 introduces the concepts of grapheme and allograph, and Section 3.3 is dedicated to letters and graphs. In Section 3.4, we address the question of how the graphemic inventory of a language can be defined. Section 3.5 introduces the typographical concepts of characters and glyphs. Sections 3.6 and 3.7 address punctuation and capitalization. Compared to the more abstract concepts introduced in the preceding sections, punctuation and capitalization are comparatively easy to define. However, describing their functions accurately can be challenging and arguably requires taking their historical development into account. Sections 3.6 and 3.7 therefore include a brief overview over the historical evolution of punctuation and capitalization, respectively.

Although the concepts discussed in this chapter are very basic, many of them present major definitional as well as analytic challenges that can be addressed from multiple perspectives. Our own point of view is strongly influenced by concepts that are rooted in recent German-speaking linguistic research, since "German grapholinguistics flourished in the 1980s" (Meletis 2019a: 27).[2] In this research tradition, a grapholinguistic framework was developed that assumes a hierarchically organized graphemic system, rather than conceiving of written words as linear sequences of letters (Evertz and Primus 2013: 1). According to this nonlinear approach to graphemic structure, each graphemic word can be divided into smaller units, graphemic syllables and graphemic feet. This is the reason why Berg and Evertz (2018: 191) call this approach "suprasegmental graphematics." In addition, this approach also conceives of letters as units that can be broken down into smaller units, and consequently assumes a strong correlation between the shapes of letters and their function (see Section 3.3 for discussion). Some of these concepts – as well as ancillary issues such as the length hierarchy, discussed in Section 3.3 below – are not yet well established in the international research landscape of orthography but have been applied quite fruitfully not only in the synchronic description of writing systems but also in studies of diachronic graphemic change (e.g. Elmentaler 2003). They provide a promising framework to analyze the basic elements of writing systems both from a synchronic and from a historical perspective.

[2] See also Fuhrhop et al. (2011: 276), who mention Eisenberg (1983) and Naumann (1989) as pioneers of German grapholinguistics.

3.2 Grapheme

The term *grapheme* has given rise to different interpretations, which we discuss in Subsection 3.2.1. Subsection 3.2.2 is devoted to the term *allograph*, the understanding of which strongly depends on whatever definition of the grapheme is adopted.

3.2.1 The Term *Grapheme* and Its Concepts

The term *grapheme* was first introduced by Baudouin de Courtenay in 1901 (Ruszkiewicz 1972: 10, 1978: 112), shortly after the term and the concept of *phoneme* had been established (Kohrt 1985: 163–67, Kohrt 1986). There are multiple competing definitions of the term, which can partly be attributed to different conceptualizations of the relationship between speech and writing (see, e.g., Dürscheid 2016: 35–41; see also Chapter 6 and Chapter 8, this volume). The *dependency or derivational approach* sees written language as derived from spoken language. On this view, written language represents a secondary system of representation. According to the *autonomy hypothesis*, by contrast, writing is seen as an independent form in which language is manifested (see also Chapter 5, this volume). Interim positions between these views are of course possible and arguably quite common. For instance, one could defend the position that writing should be analyzed on its own terms without denying a close connection between spoken and written language (see, e.g., Neef and Primus 2001). These different basic assumptions strongly influence the definition of the term *grapheme*, which, in modern usage, comprises at least four different concepts (see Henderson 1985, Rutkowska 2012, Berg et al. 2016, Evertz 2018, Klinkenberg and Polis 2018, Meletis 2019a):

(i) a written unit that corresponds to exactly one phoneme;
(ii) a minimal contrastive unit in a writing system;
(iii) the smallest suprasegmental unit within a graphemic hierarchy; and
(iv) a letter.

These concepts are discussed in turn below.

(i) Firstly, the term *grapheme* can be understood as a written representation of a phoneme. Following Klinkenberg and Polis (2018: 70), its relationship to the concept of phoneme can thus be seen as referential. This definition is in line with the dependency/derivational approach mentioned above. From this perspective, graphemes can only be determined in writing systems that follow a strong phonographic principle (i.e. in alphabetic systems). Obviously, the inventory of graphemes in a language determined according to this approach differs from that identified under the assumption that writing systems are autonomous (see Section 3.4 on grapheme inventories). For instance, in English, the letter *x*, which is a grapheme according to the autonomistic approach (presented below in more detail), corresponds to a sequence of two phonemes /k/+/s/, and thus poses a theoretical problem for an account that expects every phoneme to be represented separately in writing. However, the sequence of letters <qu> (e.g. in *question*) corresponds to two phonemes. As the two letters always co-occur in native English words, <qu> is treated as one grapheme by the autonomistic approach. According to the dependency approach, by contrast, it represents a sequence of two graphemes where <q> → /k/ and <u> → /w/ (see Henderson 1985: 137, 144).

(ii) The definition of the grapheme as a minimal contrastive unit in a writing system is based on the methodological assumption that the analysis of written language should be performed independently (i.e. without reference to spoken language; Coulmas 1996: 27–28, 176–77, 202, Neef and Primus 2001: 353, Dürscheid 2016: 35–42). According to this definition, the notion of the grapheme is defined by analogy to the phoneme (see Klinkenberg and Polis 2018: 70). From this point of view, graphemes can be determined in the same way as phonemes by means of minimal pairs. For instance, the graphemic minimal pair <house> ~ <mouse> indicates that <h> and <m> are graphemes. Identifying graphemes based on minimal pairs entails the possibility of complex graphemes. For instance, the sequence of letters <qu> would be considered a complex grapheme in English as it is the smallest inseparable unit that can form minimal pairs, as in <**qu**ote> ~ <vote> or <**qu**ite> ~ <**b**ite>. Note that a graphemic minimal pair does not need to be a phonological one, as the example <quite> ~ <bite> illustrates. Following this distributional criterion, sequences of vowel letters like <ea>, <oa> or <ee> in English should be considered two separate graphemes since – in contrast to <qu> – they are separable and can be combined with each other, for example <mean> ~ <moan> and <beat> ~ <beet>. As we discuss in (iii) below, sequences of letters such as <ea> in <mean> or <oa> in <moan> could alternatively be analyzed as complex graphemes if the higher-order graphemic category – the graphemic syllable – is taken into account. In addition, graphemes with diacritics can be analyzed as complex graphemes, for example <ä>, <ą> or <á> (see however Rogers 2005: 11, for a different view).

The fact that this definition of the grapheme is based solely on the written system, without any reference to the spoken language, does not rule out the possibility of a correspondence between graphemes and phonemes, which is a powerful principle of alphabetic writing systems (see Chapter 4, this volume). However, in contrast to definition (i), the autonomistic approach can better account for the fact that even in alphabetic systems, the phonographic principle can be overridden by other principles (e.g. morphological or syntactic). For instance, the use of <ä> in German is, in most cases, governed by the morphological principle where <ä> (which corresponds to /ɛ:/) marks a given word form as morphologically related to another one written with <a>, as in <Mann> 'man' and <Männer> 'men' (Eisenberg 1996: 620–25). Both word forms contain the stem morpheme {mann}. Because of its autonomous nature, this definition of the grapheme can easily be applied to both alphabetic and nonalphabetic writing systems (see Chapter 2, this volume). Furthermore, this definition allows for what Rogers (2005: 10) calls "nonsegmental graphemes," those units that do not necessarily have a counterpart in pronunciation (e.g. punctuation or whitespace). Table 3.1 lists examples of both segmental and nonsegmental graphemes according to definition (ii).

(iii) The third concept of the *grapheme* is firmly rooted in the nonlinear approach to graphemic structure briefly explained above, that is, the idea that the graphemic system is organized hierarchically, like the phonological system (Primus 2010, Berg et al. 2016). In addition, the concept is based on Primus's (2003: 4) "correspondence theory," which hypothesizes that spoken language, sign language and written language constitute three different modalities that are connected via correspondences as well as modality-independent factors. Consequently, the hierarchical levels that characterize spoken as well as sign language have correspondences in written modality – but importantly, they have to be defined on their own terms, without recourse to phonology (Primus 2003: 4). On this view, graphemes are defined as the smallest suprasegmental units (Berg and Evertz 2018: 191). The individual segments are the letters, as shown in Figure 3.1. Graphemes are in turn organized in syllables, and syllables are organized in higher-level constituents: the *graphemic foot* and the *graphemic word*. The graphemic foot is a sequence of graphemic syllables, with exactly one of them being a head of the foot (Evertz and Primus 2013, Evertz 2016, 2018). The graphemic word is simply defined as a chain of graphemes between two spaces. It can comprise one or more feet (Fuhrhop 2008, 2018). In this framework, the concept of graphemic syllables plays a key role in determining which units count as graphemes – which is why we briefly outline the main idea of the concept here (see Subsection 3.3.1 below for more details). In essence, the notion of graphemic syllable refers to the alternation between consonant and vowel graphemes (see Berg 2019: 70). Like the phonological

Table 3.1 *The grapheme as a minimal contrastive unit in different types of writing systems*

Types of graphemes	Examples
Alphabetic letters or a set of letters	<a>, <qu>
Syllabograms	< カ > (syllabogram corresponding to /ka/ in Japanese *katakana*)
Morphographs (also logograms)	<马> (the Mandarin Chinese for 'horse')
Punctuation marks	<,>, <!>
Numerical digits	<8>, <八>

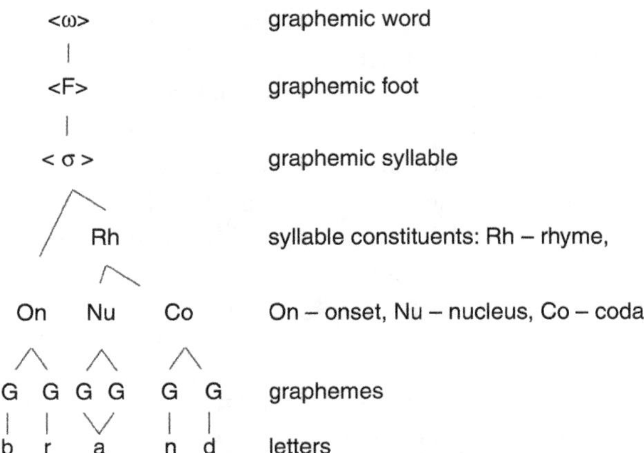

Figure 3.1 Graphemes as the smallest suprasegmental units (Berg et al. 2016: 351)

syllable, the graphemic syllable is conceived of as a skeletal tier with an obligatory V-position (the so-called syllable peak), prototypically represented by a vowel letter (hence 'V'), and optional C(onsonant)-positions. For instance, the word *brand* contains one graphemic syllable <brand>, in which the vowel letter <a> constitutes the syllable peak, as shown in Figure 3.1.

Fuhrhop and Buchmann (2009) suggest that the graphemic syllable is governed by a length-sequencing principle which, roughly speaking, is responsible for the visual integrity of a graphemic syllable. We return to the concept of the so-called length hierarchy when discussing letters in Subsection 3.3.1. The length hierarchy serves as the basis for a number of principles which can be linked to regularities that have been observed across languages – for example, the nucleus of a graphematic syllable tends to be occupied by 'compact' letters (like *a* in *brand*), while the 'longest' segments (here, *b* and *d*) appear at the edges. In the hierarchical model illustrated in Figure 3.1, the nucleus of the 'strong' graphemic syllable is assumed to be binary branching: it dominates two so-called structural G-positions. The 'strong' graphemic syllable is the only syllable in monosyllabic words, and usually the first in bisyllabic ones. As the example in Figure 3.1 demonstrates, the structural G-positions assumed by the model are not necessarily equivalent to graphemes (see Schmidt 2018: 136–45). In Figure 3.1, the letter *a* occupies two G-positions but is still considered one grapheme.[3] In such an approach, letter sequences like <oa> or <ea> in *mean-ing* or *moan-er* are seen as complex graphemes, as they are inseparable in the process of word division and, hence, considered to be part of one graphemic syllable. Note that this approach is not

[3] Newer versions of the model have therefore changed the designation of the skeletal positions from 'G' to 'X' (see Meletis 2019a: 19).

entirely uncontroversial, and especially the notion of the graphemic syllable has been criticized on both theoretical and methodological grounds (see, e.g., Primus 2003: 4). Nevertheless, it has proven quite influential in explanations of graphemic conventions and graphemic change, as also becomes clear in subsequent sections of this chapter. Importantly, the definitions (ii) and (iii) do not exclude each other. They are, rather, complementary: the idea of identifying graphemes with the help of minimal pairs is shared by the proponents of the correspondence theory. However, the units that distinguish minimal pairs from each other are partly established on the basis of their position in a word's graphemic syllable structure.

(iv) In some studies, the word *grapheme* is used synonymously with *letter* (Henderson 1985, Kohrt 1985). Despite the differences between the concepts of the grapheme discussed above, they arguably all show that it makes sense to keep these concepts apart (see also Neef 2005), which is why we do not pursue this concept further here. In Subsection 3.3.1, the letter is discussed in greater detail.

In sum, then, there are different definitions of the grapheme, and as for many of the concepts that are discussed in the subsequent sections, there is neither a universally agreed-upon definition nor a consensus regarding the question of whether or not the term is actually needed for an adequate analysis. For example, Daniels (2001: 67) strongly rejects the concept and especially the parallelism to phonology that is inherent – to varying extents – to all the definitions discussed above: He argues that "writing systems do not work like linguistic systems" (Daniels 2001: 66). However, this does of course not mean that the concept, if properly defined, cannot be fruitfully applied to the investigation of graphemic systems and phenomena. In fact, historical orthography can also serve as a working ground for verifying the validity of some of the approaches outlined above. Different definitions of graphemes make different predictions regarding the diachronic development of graphemic systems, as we see in more detail in Subsection 3.3.1, where we discuss concepts that are closely connected to the third definition of the grapheme mentioned above.

3.2.2 Allograph

Generally speaking, allographs are variants of graphemes. The definition of an allograph depends on the definition of the grapheme (see Subsection 3.2.1). If we follow definition (i) mentioned above, according to which the grapheme is a written unit which corresponds to exactly one phoneme, different written representations of the same phoneme can be seen as allographs, for example |o| and |oo| in English *lose* and *booze* (see, e.g., Coulmas 1996: 9). If, however, graphemes are understood as the smallest functional units of a writing system (see definition (ii) in Subsection 3.2.1), an allograph is a non-contrastive variant of a grapheme (Rogers 2005: 10–11). For example, |ß| and |ss| are allographs in the German writing system, see *beißen* 'bite' (German orthography) vs. *beissen* (Swiss orthography) or *daß* (old German orthography until 1996) vs. *dass* (current German orthography). Meletis (2020b) proposes a basic differentiation between graphetic and graphemic allographs. *Graphetic allography* depends on visual similarities. Hence, graphetic allographs are concrete realizations which can be assigned to graph classes or to "basic shapes" (see Meletis 2020b: 254–57, Meletis and Dürscheid 2022: 153–55). For example, different typefaces lead to graphetic allography of the basic grapheme <a> (e.g. |a|, |a|, |**a**|, |ɑ|). *Graphemic allography*, by contrast, does not depend on visual similarity but on shared functions. Meletis (2020b: 257) proposes various subtypes of graphemic allographs based on three criteria:

(i) *intra- vs. inter-inventory*: allographs occur within one graphemic inventory (interinventory allographs) or between different inventories (intrainventory allographs). The notion of graphemic inventory denotes the set of all graphemes used in a given language and is discussed in more detail in Section 3.4 below;
(ii) *free vs. positional*: positional allographs are complementarily distributed, while free allographs are not. They are often subject to stylistic variation;
(iii) *externally independent vs. externally determined*: allographs are externally independent or determined by linguistic levels other than graphematics (e.g. syntax or pragmatics).

In a similar vein, but independently from Meletis, Fuhrhop and Peters (2013: 207) propose a typology of allographic variation:

- Allographic variation due to different fonts or handwritings – for example, in Roman handwriting, <r> can be written as |ɿ| or |r|, while in printed variants, it can occur in different typefaces, such as |**r**| or |r|. Allography can also be caused by the use of serifs, small lines attached to the end of a letter stem, especially at its top or bottom (compare sans-serif |a| with |a| in a serif font). Such free allographs occur in every type of writing system. For instance, in the Chinese script, regional and/or historical variants of one character co-occur. The word for 'horse', for example, has the traditional form 馬 and the simplified form 马. Stylistic or calligraphic variants of the same character constitute allographs, too. Note, however, that the notion of 'free' allography should not be taken to imply that writers actually switch freely between these variants – just like the concept of 'free allophony', it simply means that the variants are not distributed complementarily. However, writers do not usually switch freely between two graphetic inventories, for example two fonts ('inter-inventory allography' in the terminology of Meletis 2020b). However, a person might use different variants of the same character in their handwriting ('intrainventory allography').

- Distributionally conditioned allography in particular scripts, for example Greek sigma <σ>, which occurs as |ς| at the final position of a word (see Klinkenberg and Polis 2018: 70). In the Arabic script, most of the (consonantal) graphemes, for example the grapheme with the name *tā'*, display word-initial تـ, word-medial ـتـ and word-final ـت variants and an isolated form ت, while for some like the grapheme *dāl* only a bound ـد and an isolated variant د exist. The variation between uppercase and lowercase letters can also be seen as allography in this sense, at least in those cases in which it depends on the syntactic position of the word. For instance, in English and many other languages, words are written with uppercase letters at the beginning of a sentence. An extension to this rule is the sentence-internal capitalization of every noun and nominalization in German (see Section 3.7 for more details). In some cases, however, uppercase and lowercase letters behave like graphemes because they distinguish between two meanings, for instance English *china* and *China* (see Henderson 1985: 144, Rezec 2013: 234).
- There are also instances of distributionally conditioned allography that do not depend on a particular script, such as English <y> and <ie>, or rather |y| and |ie|, for example in *die, dying,* which alternate in a nonidiosyncratic, predictable way (see also Berg 2019: 291).

As the examples above show, the distinction between allographs and graphemes in their own right is not always clear-cut (see, e.g., Meletis 2019a: 40), and the analogy between the concepts of phoneme and grapheme is of course not perfect (see, e.g., Lockwood 2009 [2001] for an extended discussion). One important difference between the concept of phonemes/allophones, on the one hand, and graphemes/allographs in the sense outlined above, on the other, is that letters can be graphemes in some contexts but not in others. For example, Fuhrhop et al. (2011: 284) argue that <c> and <k> can be considered graphemes before <e> and <i> and allographs in all other contexts. While the concept of allographs as outlined above has been broadly applied, especially in approaches that are more or less closely affiliated with the correspondence theory (e.g. Fuhrhop et al. 2011, Berg 2019, among many others), there is no clear consensus yet on how allography should be understood. Both the notion of graphemes and the accompanying concept of allographs have been subject to renewed discussion in recent research (e.g. Klinkenberg and Polis 2018, Meletis 2019a), and as for example Meletis (2019a: 42) points out, the concept of allography needs to be defined in more detail in future case studies.

3.3 Letters and Graphs

This section discusses the concepts of letters and graphs as well as their relation to graphemes. In Subsection 3.3.1, we introduce a decompositional approach to the letters of the Roman alphabet that has proven quite influential, especially in the German literature on graphematics (see, e.g., Primus 2004, 2006, Berg 2014, Berg 2019; for discussion, see Rezec 2010, 2011, Fuhrhop and Buchmann 2011, Primus 2011). Subsection 3.3.2 then takes a broader perspective looking at graphs and the relation between letters, graphs and graphemes.

3.3.1 Letter

The term *letter* "refers to the basic symbols of Semitic-derived writing systems" (Coulmas 2002: 35). In alphabetic scripts, letters represent the smallest units (see, e.g., Coulmas 1996: 291), in the same way as syllabograms, that is signs representing syllables, are the smallest units in syllabic systems and morphographs (or logograms), that is signs representing morphemes, in morphographic (or logographic) systems (see Joyce 2011 for terminological discussion). Coulmas (2002: 35) uses *sign* as a cover term for the smallest units of different kinds of writing systems. In writing systems whose units are not well understood, the term *glyph* is sometimes used as a cover term for morphographs (or logograms), phonetic signs and compound signs (see Coulmas 1996: 168). In this section, however, as mentioned earlier, we focus exclusively on the Roman alphabet. The set of letters in an alphabet is language-specific: for example, the English and the German alphabets share the letters of the Roman alphabet, but the German alphabet contains seven additional letters, as follows (on the distinction between majuscules, i.e. uppercase letters, and minuscules, i.e. lowercase letters, see Section 3.7 below):

Characters of the Roman alphabet
Majuscules: A, B, C, D, E, F, G, H, I, J, K, L, M, N, O, P, R, S, T, U, V, W, X, Y, Z
Minuscules: a, b, c, d, e, f, g, h, i, j, k, l, m, n, o, p, r, s, t, u, v, w, x, y, z
Additional characters in the German alphabet
Majuscules: Ä, Ö, Ü, ẞ[4]
Minuscules: ä, ö, ü, ß

As already mentioned in Section 3.2, the concrete realization of letters can vary. Rezec (e.g. in Rezec 2013) assumes that each letter has one (or in some

[4] The majuscule counterpart to *ß* is a fairly recent development: it was added to Unicode in 2008 and to the official orthographic rules of German in 2017 (Walder 2020: 212–13). In practice, *ß* is often replaced by *SS* in fully capitalized words. Thus, it can be debated whether or not |ẞ| is already a fully fledged member of the German inventory of letters or just a (typographical/prescriptive) addition. However, Walder (2020: 212) also points out that it was already used long before its adoption in Unicode, so there is a descriptive basis to its addition to the German alphabet.

cases more) prototypical shape, for which he adopts the term 'basic shape' from Herrick (1975). Primus (2004, 2006) has argued that letters have an internal structure and can be decomposed into smaller distinctive segments which can be classified as their heads. Extending the notion of head as discussed in other areas of linguistics such as morphology, Primus argues that each letter has an obligatory component: a head (see, e.g., Primus 2011: 65).[5] Heads are the longer ('governing') parts of a letter, while codas are the shorter ('dependent') elements.

The basic idea that underlies this decompositional analysis is that the graphemic space can be divided in three parts, as shown in Figure 3.2: a central space, an upper outer space and a lower outer space defined by four horizontal lines. For the minuscule *p*, for instance, this means that it consists of a straight long head and the curved coda. In Table 3.2, examples of heads and coda are given (see Fuhrhop et al. 2011, for the complete analysis of all letters in the Roman alphabet).

While majuscules always occupy the upper outer space and the central space, minuscules differ strongly in the amount of space they cover. Their spatial structure depends on the type of their heads, which can be systematized according to their length (Fuhrhop and Buchmann 2009, Fuhrhop et al. 2011, Fuhrhop and Buchmann 2016), as follows:

Types of letter heads
Long heads: f, t, j, h, p, b, k, g, d
Slant heads: z, v, w, s, x
Short straight heads: m, n, r, l, i, u
Short bent heads: e, o, a

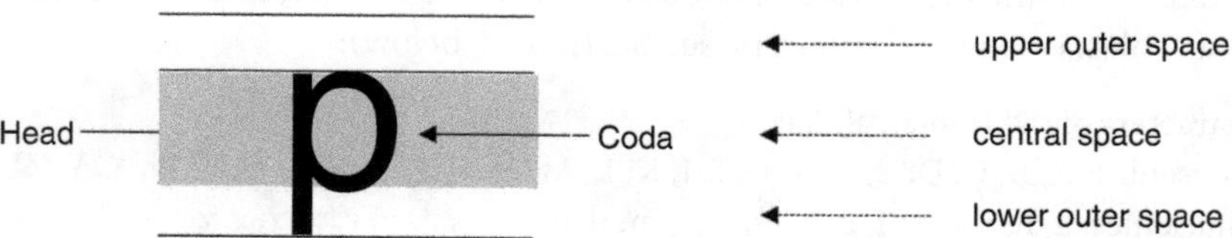

Figure 3.2 The minuscule p

Table 3.2 *Heads and codas of letters*

Letter	Head	Coda
p	|	ͻ
z	/	=
m	|	ɿn
e	C	—

[5] For a related approach that does not use the notion of head, see Brekle (1995).

long head	slant head	short straight head			short bent head	
		connected at the top	not connected at the top			
		bent coda	non-bent coda		bent coda	
b, p, q, d, g, k/c, h, t, j, f, y, β	v, w, x, z, s	m, n	r, l	i	u	a, e, o

← increasing length of letter heads

Figure 3.3 The length hierarchy of letter heads

Based on the length of their heads, letters can be ranked along a 'length hierarchy' (see Fuhrhop and Buchmann 2009), as shown in Figure 3.3.

The length hierarchy principle briefly introduced above allows us to extend the analogy between phonological and graphemic syllables: length hierarchy can be compared to the sonority hierarchy, which governs the structure of the phonological syllable. In length hierarchy, letters with long heads, *f, t, j, h, p, b, k, g, d* can be placed on one end of the continuum. The parameter of length is gradually decreasing from letters with slant heads, through those with short straight heads, to the letters with short bent heads, *e, o, a*, which are the most compact ones. Fuhrhop and Buchmann (2009) use length hierarchy to derive principles for the shape of graphemic syllables. In a canonically structured graphemic syllable, graphemes are structured according to what they call the length-sequencing principle: the syllable core is occupied by the most compact grapheme. The length of the segments that constitute graphemes increases monotonously from the core toward both syllable edges; *brand*, discussed in Figure 3.1, would be a prototypical example, with the most compact letter *a* in the nucleus position and the long-head letters *b* and *d* in the onset and coda, respectively.

Length hierarchy has been used to explain present-day graphemic conventions as well as diachronic developments. For instance, Fuhrhop et al. (2011: 285–86) discuss diachronic developments related to <c> and <k> across different languages in light of the length-sequencing principle. They also argue that the allographic variation between |y| or |ie| in English as in *lady ~ ladies* can be explained by a syllabic principle. The allograph |y| occurs in an open syllable at the end of the graphemic word. If the graphemic syllable closes with an <s>, a more compact allograph |ie| replaces the |y| (Fuhrhop et al. 2011: 285–86). The relevance of the graphemic syllable for graphemic rules and their change has been discussed in the relevant literature exclusively with reference to the Roman alphabet. Similar studies on other alphabetic systems are still needed. For example, length hierarchy and the category of the graphemic syllable may play a minor role in the Cyrillic alphabet, where many of the consonantal letters are compact and occupy only the central space both in hand- and machine-based writing (e.g. п, т, к, г, ж, ч, ш). Hence, contrastive studies could shed some light on the question of whether the graphemic hierarchy can be deemed universal.

3.3.2 Graph and Digraph

A graph is the smallest formal entity of the written language (see, e.g., Coulmas 1996: 173). Letters, syllabograms, punctuation marks, numerals, spaces and special symbols such as *&* or *$* are graphs. As mentioned in Section 3.1, graphs belong to the domain of graphetics. The compositional analysis of letters, as introduced in Subsection 3.3.1, is also a part of graphetics, since the decomposition into specific features shows what, for instance, all graphic realizations of the letter *p* have in common. The mechanical aspects concern the question of how written signs are produced: The letters of the Roman alphabet contain two parts, a head and a coda, which have to be composed in the process of writing from the left to the right. Chinese characters, on the other hand, are made of smaller parts, distributed in a fourpartite square-shaped space, which have to be written from the upper left to the lower right field. This leads to a specific stroke order (Rogers 2005: 40–41) as follows:

Stroke order for Chinese characters

1. top to bottom
2. horizontal before vertical
3. outer before inner finished
4. left to right
5. middle before sides
6. close bottom last

For instance, as shown in Figure 3.4,[6] the character 你 for the word 'you' (Chinese pīnyīn[7] *nǐ*) has to be written in the order of strokes given in Figure 3.4 (see Berkenbusch 1997: 6).

Graphs constitute graphemes when they are functionally used (see Subsection 3.2.1). For example, a graph *h* is a grapheme <h> in *house* because of its function to distinguish this meaningful unit from others, for example *mouse*. In *rhythm, shot, change* or *which*, the graph *h* does not constitute a

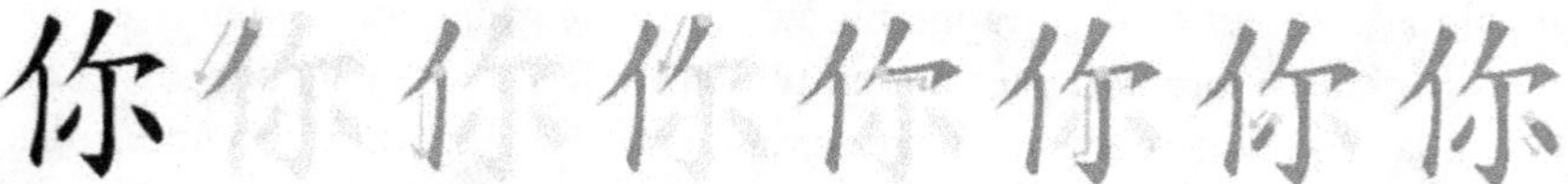

Figure 3.4 Stroke order for 你 'you' (pīnyīn *nǐ*)

[6] Source: https://commons.wikimedia.org/w/index.php?curid=195461, user: M4RC0, CC-BY-3.0. A very similar figure can be found in Berkenbusch (1997).

[7] The term *pīnyīn* refers to the official romanization of Chinese (see Taylor and Taylor 2014: 23). Throughout the remainder of this chapter, Chinese characters are accompanied by their *pīnyīn* transcription.

grapheme of its own, but it is part of complex graphemes, in which two graphs are combined to digraphs <rh>, <sh>, <ch>, <wh> (Fuhrhop et al. 2011: 286–87). The same holds for written Chinese: not every graph is a grapheme. For instance, the Chinese word 垃圾 (*lājī*) 'rubbish, garbage' consists of two signs 垃 and 圾 which cannot be used separately.[8] Both signs together constitute one grapheme (Mair 1996: 202).

3.4 Graphemic Inventories

The graphemic inventory of a written language is a comprehensive set of all graphemes used in this language. Graphemic inventories are not only language-specific, but their exact setup depends on the definition of graphemes that is adopted. Following the view of the dependency model, however, graphemic inventories can, in principle, be independent from individual languages. For instance, the alphabet could be seen as a graphemic inventory. According to the autonomistic model, by contrast, grapheme inventories are language-specific, depending on the distributional rules in a given writing system. As an example, consider the letter *q*. If the grapheme is simply defined as a letter, as in definition (iv) established in Subsection 3.2.1, then the letter *q* would of course qualify as a grapheme in English. If, by contrast, we see graphemes as the smallest distinctive units that are an autonomous part of graphemic syllables (see definition (iii) in Subsection 3.2.1), then *q* does not count as a grapheme as it only occurs in combination with *u* in native words.[9] This is why Berg (2019: 32) proposes the following graphemic inventory of English:

simple: <a>, <b>, <c>, <d>, <e>, <f>, <g>, <h>, <i>, <j>, <k>, <l>, <m>, <n>, <o>, <p>, <r>, <s>, <t>, <u>, <v>, <w>, <x>, <y>, <z>
complex: <qu>

Berg (2019: 32) argues that *q* is not a grapheme, since it cannot by itself be part of a syllable, but only in combination with *u*. Other letter sequences that can be regarded as graphemes in some contexts, for example *rh* (*rhyme*), *sh* (*short*), *ch* (*church*) or *wh* (*who*), are not counted as parts of the graphemic inventory, as every single letter can be an autonomous part of a syllable, for

8 Thanks to Yadi Wu and Andreas Hölzl for pointing out this example to us. Mair (1996: 202) mentions a number of other examples, but many of them are problematic – for instance, as an anonymous reviewer of this chapter has correctly pointed out, the last segment of the Chinese word for 'spider', *zhīzhū* 蜘蛛, can actually be used for 'spider' in other expressions as well.

9 Many approaches only take graphemes into account that are attested in the present-day spelling of native words (see, e.g., Eisenberg 2013: 290, for German), while others, which include nonnative words in their analysis, arrive at a larger graphemic inventory (e.g. Zifonun et al. 1997: 257, for German). In German, for instance, the digraph <ph> for /f/ only occurs in nonnative words and is often replaced by <f> in the process of loanword integration, for example *Telephon* (early twentieth century) → *Telefon* (present-day spelling).

example *rite*, *cite*, *hay*, *way* and so on. Note, however, that this approach differs from the procedure of determining phonemic inventories in phonology, where the parts of a diphthong are seen as one phoneme, for example /oʊ/ in *show*, irrespective of whether they do or do not occur on their own – both vowels, /o/ and /ʊ/, as single units can occupy a syllable peak in English. In contrast, Fuhrhop et al. (2011) analyze the same letter sequences as complex graphemes, rather than combinations of graphemes.

The narrow definition of graphemes as constituents of a graphemic syllable excludes punctuation marks, numerical digits and so on from the graphemic inventory. As discussed in Subsection 3.2.2, uppercase letters can be considered as graphemes in their own right in some contexts if the existence of written minimal pairs is used as a criterion for identifying graphemes (see, e.g., Meletis 2019a for such an approach). Thus, Rutkowska (2012: 232) points out that we could, in principle, distinguish 52 rather than 26 graphemes in English. She also mentions that, from a diachronic perspective, the inventory would have to be extended, taking now-obsolete graphemes like <Þ> into account. This is closely related to the more general question of whether graphemic inventories should be determined from a synchronic or from a panchronic perspective. Most of the concepts introduced so far are defined, for obvious reasons, with a relatively stable graphemic system in mind, which can present a challenge for historical orthography. As for graphemic inventories, they change over time in various ways. For instance, new graphemes can evolve. In German, the graphemes <ä>, <ö> and <ü> developed from the combination of the basic vowel letters <a>, <o> and <u> with a small *e*-letter written mostly above, <å>, <ů>, <o̊> (Elmentaler 2018: 289–97). Additionally, graphemic distribution can change due to phonological developments or due to an internal restructuring of the writing system. One example is the use of the grapheme <h> in German, which has lost its original phonographic value (<h> ↔ /h/) word-internally, see German *drehen* /dʀeːən/ 'to turn over' or *dehnen* /deːnən/ 'to stretch'. The new function of <h> is to mark the syllable onset <dre.hen> and the length of the preceding vowel (here, long /eː/). The historical development of graphemic inventories still requires further research.

3.5 Typography: Characters vs. Glyphs

Before we turn from the core elements of graphemic systems to punctuation and capitalization, we briefly discuss two key notions of typography: characters and glyphs (see, e.g., Moran and Cysouw 2018: 15). This distinction can roughly be connected to the linguistic distinction between grapheme and allograph, but there are some important differences. In the Unicode Standard, a character encoding system that allows for the computational processing of characters from many different writing systems (see Moran and

Cysouw 2018: 14–15), characters are defined as "the abstract representations of smallest components of written language that have semantic value" (Allen et al. 2012: 11). The semantic values of the character include the property of being an alphabetic, numeric, ideographic or punctuation symbol, and the character's case and its directionality, that is the direction of character arrangement (e.g. horizontal from left to right as in Latin scripts or from right to left as in Semitic scripts, see Allen et al. 2012: 40–41). In contrast to graphemes, characters represent not only letters, punctuation, and "other signs that constitute natural language text and technical notation." They also contain diacritics, referred to as 'combining marks', as well as different types of separators. For example, the diacritic U+0301 COMBINING ACUTE ACCENT (shown in Figure 3.5) is a character in its own right. As a combining mark it is thus syntactically related to the preceding character (e.g. U+0061 LATIN SMALL LETTER A), which is its base.

Additionally, one graph can correspond to multiple characters. This is due to the fact that letters used in different languages are grouped into individual scripts. Even if they are graphemically equal and have the same semantic values (in the sense discussed above), they represent distinct characters in Unicode. For example, there are three characters corresponding to the letter form *Đ*, as shown in Figure 3.6.

While characters are abstract, glyphs "represent the shape that characters can have when they are rendered or displayed. In contrast to characters, glyphs appear on the screen or paper as particular representations of one or more characters. A repertoire of glyphs makes up a font" (Allen et al. 2012: 12). Since glyphs are used to represent the abstract entity of the character, they are necessary to determine the so-called character identity as it is presented in the code charts. The character identity includes the character name (e.g. LATIN SMALL LETTER A), the code point (U+0061) and a representative

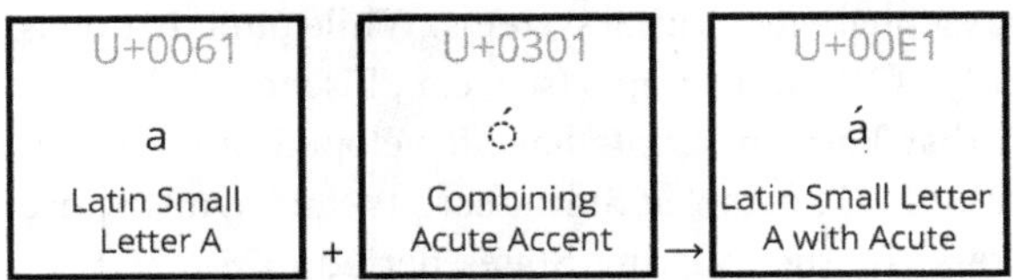

Figure 3.5 Combining marks as character type in typography

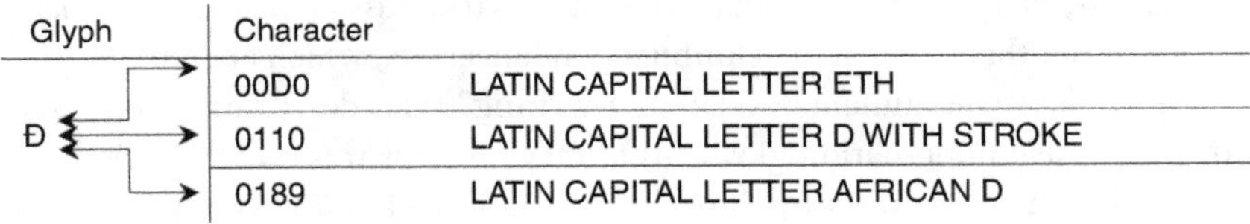

Figure 3.6 Relation between characters and glyphs
(from the code charts Latin-1 Supplement, Latin Extended-A and Latin Extended-B, Haugen 2013: 101)

Figure 3.7 Variant glyphs of the characters 'A' and 'a' (adapted from Haugen 2013: 100)

glyph. One character can be represented by various glyphs which are connected by a certain degree of similarity in shape. However, the degree of similarity can vary considerably. Consider, for example, the distinction between the regular a and the italic *a* or between the serif a and the sans-serif a (Haugen 2013: 100). They are recognized as instances of the same character not only because of their shape but also because of the contexts in which they appear (Haugen 2013: 100, see Figure 3.7).

Note that the terms *character* and *glyph* are used in a more technical sense here than in the graphemic literature, where the former serves as a cover term for "the elementary signs of a written language" (Coulmas 1996: 72), while the latter – as pointed out in Subsection 3.3.1 – is sometimes used as "a collective designation to indicate a logogram, a phonetic sign or a compound sign" (Coulmas 1996: 168), especially for writing systems where the status of the units in question is doubtful.

3.6 Punctuation

Punctuation marks are seen as graphemes in some frameworks but not in others, depending on the grapheme definition. Regardless of whether or not they are seen as graphemes, punctuation marks play a key role in present-day alphabetic writing systems. This section first compares different definitions of punctuation and then discusses formal and functional characteristics of punctuation marks in present-day alphabetic writing systems. While punctuation is often seen as a feature mainly of Western scripts (see, e.g., Fischer 2001: 261), it should be kept in mind that Eastern scripts have developed punctuation marks as well: Kornicki (2018: 157) notes that Sinitic scripts started to acquire additional "attention markers" by the Warring States period (475–221 BC). Already in early China, scribes used signs as well as blanks and indentation to mark the beginnings and ends of texts, and to distinguish between different levels of text, such as main text vs. commentaries (see Kornicki 2018). Kornicki also points out that some of the Dunhuang manuscripts, which are among "the earliest available monuments of Tibetan writing" (van der Kuijp 1996: 431), "carry extensive punctuation glosses that may perhaps represent contemporary practice in other parts of China" (Kornicki 2018: 158). Today's uses of punctuation in Japanese, Korean and Chinese writing systems are partly influenced by the Western practice (see, e.g., Taylor and Taylor 2014: 375).

3.6.1 Defining Punctuation

Coulmas (1996: 421) defines punctuation as "[t]he rules for graphically structuring written language by means of a set of conventional marks such as dots and horizontal, vertical or oblique strokes." Punctuation is sometimes defined even more broadly: Nunberg et al. (2002: 1724) subsume typographical features such as boldface and italics as well as capitalization under "punctuation indicators." Similarly, Müller (1964: 11) argues that the use of spaces between words as well as line breaks between smaller sense units should be considered instances of punctuation. Bredel (2005: 22, 2009: 119) defines punctuation in formal and, more importantly, reception-oriented terms (see also Subsection 3.6.2 below). According to her, punctuation marks are (i) one-element paradigms, that is they have exactly one form (as opposed to letters, which have a majuscule and a minuscule variant); (ii) they do not combine with each other; (iii) they occur independently (unlike diacritics, which are additive); (iv) they cannot be verbalized; and (v) they can be represented without graphic context. The last criterion distinguishes punctuation marks from spaces. From this definition, she also derives the inventory of punctuation marks: < . ?, ( ) ... : ! ' – " " >. While she focuses on the German punctuation system, this inventory is applicable more broadly (although it would have to be extended by, for example, the inverted question and exclamation mark for Spanish < ¿ > and < ¡ >). In addition, there are typographical variants of quotation marks with strong language-specific tendencies to prefer one variant over others, for example „ and " in German or « and » in French. The slash / is not a punctuation mark according to Bredel's (2005, 2009) definition, as she argues that it can be verbalized (e.g. *s/he* 'he or she', *his/her* 'his or her'). Following broader definitions such as those by Coulmas or Nunberg cited above, however, it would also clearly belong to the inventory of punctuation marks.

Apart from the aforementioned marks that have their origin in Western scripts and partly have come to be used in Japanese, Korean and Chinese writing systems as well, there are a number of East Asian marks, some of which differ from the Western ones only in form but not in function (see Taylor and Taylor 2014: 376). Examples include

- the Chinese enumeration comma or *dun comma* 、 used when listing items (Yip and Rimmington 2016: 105);
- the middle dot · indicating juxtaposed items in written Korean (*Marx·Engels*, 'Marx and Engels'), but also used in Chinese, Japanese and Korean to separate individual components of foreign names (e.g. Chinese 亚伯拉罕。林肯, pīnyīn *yàbólāhǎn·línkěn* for 'Abraham Lincoln');
- the iteration mark 々 indicating repeated *kanji* in Japanese.

Other writing systems have script-specific punctuation marks as well – Allen et al. (2012: 261) mention the Armenian hyphen ֊ and the Arabic semicolon ؛ as examples.

3.6.2 Form and Function of Punctuation Marks

The most thorough description of the formal properties of punctuation marks has been offered by Bredel (2005, 2008, 2009). Although she focuses on the German punctuation system, her analysis can also be applied to other languages that share the same inventory of punctuation marks (see Kirchhoff and Primus 2016 for English). Bredel (2008) adopts the idea that the graphemic space can be divided into three parts, as established in Subsection 3.3.1 above: a central space, an upper outer space and a lower outer space, defined by four horizontal lines. Depending on their position in the graphemic space, she posits two features along which punctuation marks differ. The first feature [+/– empty] captures whether or not the sign touches the baseline that separates the central space from the lower outer space. A punctuation mark is [– empty] when it touches the baseline. Otherwise it is [+ empty]. The second, [+/– vertical], concerns the upper space: some punctuation marks have vertical elements in the upper space, others do not (see Figure 3.8).

In addition, the feature [+/– reduplication] is related to the question of whether the sign can be divided into two identical elements. For instance, : and ... can be analyzed as multiple instances of a period . and brackets as well as scare quotes consist of reduplicated elements by definition, so (and), “ and ”. Bredel (2005, 2008) observes a correlation between these formal features on the one hand and functional and even physiological aspects on the other: Assuming that the reading process involves oculomotoric and (possibly optional) subvocalizatoric processes (“inner speech,” see, e.g., Rayner and Pollatsek 1989), she posits that [+empty] signs guide the former and [–empty] signs the latter. Punctuation marks with the feature combination [–reduplicated, +empty], that is the en-dash and the apostrophe, help to decode information at word level, where they mark interrupted or incomplete structures. The punctuation marks < . , : ; ? ! >, with the features [–reduplicated, –empty], on the other hand, operate above the word level. Signs with the feature combination [–reduplicated, –empty, +vertical], that is < ? > and < ! >, fulfill epistemic functions, while, for instance, the round brackets and

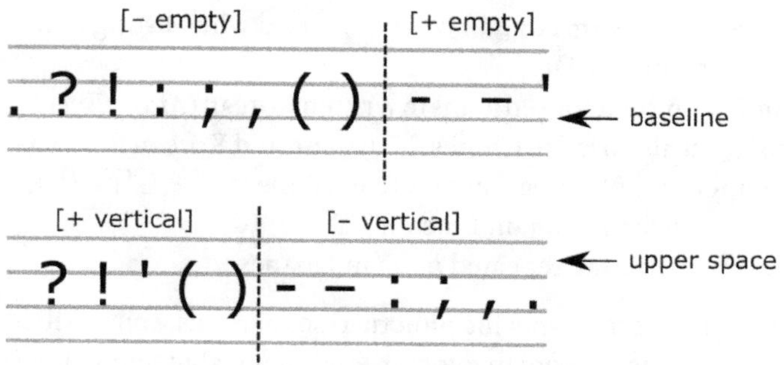

Figure 3.8 The features [+/– empty] and [+/– vertical] according to Bredel (2008)

the double quotation marks, which are [+reduplicated, −empty, −vertical], support the decoding of interactional meaning, for example by signaling a deictic change of role via scare quotes or a communicative change of role from "covert writer" to "overt writer" by means of parentheses (Bredel 2008: 216).

Note that Bredel's analysis focuses on the role of punctuation in the reading process (i.e. in the process of decoding). Traditionally, research on punctuation systems has focused more on the question of how punctuation encodes linguistic properties, distinguishing between prosodic and grammatical punctuation (i.e. from the perspective of the writer). Prosodic, or rhetorical, punctuation is closely connected to the prosodic and intonational properties of oral speech, while grammatical punctuation reflects syntactic and semantic distinctions and is usually assumed to be more strongly conventionalized (see Primus 2007: 104). According to this view, the Romance languages were claimed to be characterized by prosodic punctuation, while the punctuation systems of languages like German, Hungarian and Finnish were seen as grammatical. However, this clear-cut distinction has largely been abandoned in favor of a more pluralistic approach. In particular, punctuation systems that had previously been seen as purely prosodic have increasingly come to be described in grammatical terms (see Primus 2007: 105). Kirchhoff and Primus (2016), for example, discuss the use of comma in English in some detail and argue that its use is better described by syntactic rules than by intonation.

Also for English, Nunberg criticizes the "transcriptional" view, according to which punctuation signals intonational features, and argues in favor of "approaching punctuation (and more) as an autonomous system that admits of study in its own terms" (Nunberg 1990: 15). His analysis of punctuation is guided by the idea that we can distinguish two 'grammars' for written language, a 'lexical grammar' that also pertains to spoken language on the one hand and a dedicated 'text grammar' on the other. The latter pertains to language users' knowledge about how a text is structured via devices such as paragraphs and punctuation. He treats structuring devices such as punctuation marks, spaces, paragraphs, but also font-, face-, case- or size-alternations as 'text category markers', which he groups into three categories:

- delimiters, which mark one or both ends of a category type;
- distinguishers, which set off a piece of text from its surroundings; and
- separators, which are inserted between elements of the same category type (Nunberg 1990: 52–53).

For example, < . ? ! > are right sentence delimiters, while capitalization (see Section 3.7 below) is used as a left sentence delimiter in English. The comma can serve as a delimiter in some contexts (*The key, obviously, has been lost*) and as a separator in others (*The woods are lovely, dark and deep*). The distribution of text category indicators is governed by context-sensitive functional rules and constraints that interact both with each other and, in some cases, with lexical grammar. Despite Bredel's and Nunberg's attempts to provide a systematic account, the linguistics of punctuation can still be considered an understudied area (but see, e.g., Scherer 2013, and Caro Reina and Akar 2021 on apostrophes, Gillmann 2018 on semicolons, and Caro Reina and Engel 2020 on hyphenation; for broader studies of the diachrony of punctuation focusing on German, see Kirchhoff 2017 and Rinas 2017). This holds even more for the diachronic study of punctuation. Note that both Bredel and Nunberg take a largely synchronic perspective. However, a full understanding of the functional potential of punctuation arguably requires taking its historical evolution into account, where a number of factors have influenced the gradual development of punctuation conventions. For instance, the use of the printing press necessitated decisions about standards pertaining, among other things, to punctuation (Eisenstein 1979: 87). The individual factors that are usually assumed to be involved in the conventionalization and standardization of graphemic practices – such as the context of production and the social context as well as prescriptivist influences – are explored further in Chapters 22 to 30, this volume.

3.7 Capitalization

Capitalization shares many linguistic functions with punctuation. In fact, Nunberg et al. (2002) even treat capitalization – along with other nonsegmental features like whitespace, italics, or boldface – as 'punctuation indicators', which they use as an umbrella term for punctuation marks, spaces and modifications (see Subsection 3.6.2). As mentioned above, Nunberg (1990) uses 'text category indicators' as a cover term. Like punctuation, capitalization can be used as a text-structuring device in alphabetic scripts. For instance, it is used for highlighting the beginning of a sentence. In addition, capitalization can be used to highlight specific words sentence-internally. This function is used to a different extent across different languages, as is shown below. Capitalization obviously requires a distinction between uppercase and lowercase letters which – today part of the Roman alphabet – originate from different script types (see Labs-Ehlert 1993: 17–38). Driven not least by technological progress like the development of material on which texts where written, the older scripts consisting only of uppercase letters (majuscules) used in ancient times were gradually replaced by younger minuscule scripts in the Middle Ages.

In the course of this process, majuscule letters did not fall out of use but developed a new function, namely highlighting the beginning of texts first, later of sentences (see Weber 1958: 56). For present-day English, Nunberg et al. (2002: 1757) see two main functions of capitalization: "to mark a left boundary and to assign special status to a unit." They observe that the units that are typically assigned special status are prototypically proper names (*the*

Empire State Building) or functionally equivalent expressions. Additionally, some languages made much wider use of sentence-internal capitalization in the past, to the extent that all nouns and nominalizations tended to be spelled uppercase. This tendency was conventionalized as sentence-internal capitalization in German and Luxembourgish (see, e.g., Bergmann and Nerius 1998, Barteld et al. 2016, Nowak 2019). Gallmann (1986: 63) interprets sentence-internal capitalization as a graphemic classifier, that is graphic devices that "convey additional information, supporting the interpretation of the basic textual content, by marking and thereby classifying certain textual structures." More specifically, he argues for the existence of three subclasses, namely grammatico-lexical classifier (capitalization of nouns), semantico-lexical classifier (capitalization of proper nouns), and pragmatico-lexical classifiers (capitalization of some forms of address, e.g. polite *Sie* or sometimes its informal equivalent *Du* 'you').

The diachronic development of sentence-internal capitalization in German has been investigated quite extensively (e.g. Kämpfert 1980, Risse 1980, Moulin 1990, Labs-Ehlert 1993, Bergmann and Nerius 1998, Bergmann 1999, Barteld et al. 2016, Dücker et al. 2020), and it has been shown that it is driven by an interplay of pragmatic, semantic and syntactic principles. Bergmann and Nerius's corpus study (1998), based on printed texts, shows that proper names and *nomina sacra* (nouns referring to deities and saints) are capitalized first, followed by nouns referring to persons and objects. Sentence-internal capitalization has also been used and conventionalized to various degrees in other Germanic languages. For Danish, Ruus (2005: 1286) points out that by the end of the eighteenth century, "capitalization of nouns was the rule." Osselton (1984, 1985) shows a strong trend toward sentence-internal capitalization in English printed prose texts (but see Grüter 2007, 2009, who does not detect a clear chronological development in her corpus, and Nowak 2019, who shows that this tendency is much less pronounced in English Bible prints).

The emergence of capitalization has of course also been documented in languages other than Germanic. For French, Meisenburg (1990) shows a gradual rise in the use of sentence-internal capitals in seventeenth-century French. According to Meisenburg, the use of sentence-internal capital letters is largely determined by pragmatic and semantic factors. On the one hand, majuscules are used to signal reverence, for example when referring to 'sacred' concepts like *l'Ecriture sainte* 'the Holy Scripture', *l'Eglise catholique* 'the Catholic Church'. On the other hand, collective nouns or abstract concepts like *Droit* 'right' and *Justice* 'justice' – which are often allegorically personified – are sometimes capitalized. For Polish, Bunčić (2012: 242) observes a strong trend toward capitalization in the sixteenth century, while it is restricted to the use of sentence-initial majuscules and the capitalization of certain names and proper nouns in present-day usage. Taken together, these observations indicate that the rise of sentence-internal capitalization has been a fairly widespread phenomenon in early modern writing, especially in printed texts. It remains to be investigated how the use of sentence-internal capitalization developed in the individual languages and to what extent these developments were interrelated: for instance, Maas (2007: 387) assumes that German Protestant Bible prints pioneered the use of sentence-internal majuscules that was then adopted in Dutch and other European languages. However, there is not yet enough empirical evidence to back up this hypothesis, and Nowak's (2019) study, comparing English, German and Dutch Bible prints, indicates that the development of sentence-internal capitalization in Dutch may have been more independent from German than previously assumed.

3.8 Conclusion

In this chapter, we have discussed the basic units of writing at three different levels – graphem(at)ics, graphetics and typography. Distinguishing between these levels of description is essential for understanding the different concepts that have been proposed in the literature to describe the basic elements of writing systems. Especially at the graphemic level, the individual elements of writing systems have been subject to quite different definitions, which in turn are contingent upon the relationship that researchers assume between speech and writing. While some approaches see spoken language and writing as inextricably connected, others argue that writing systems have to be described on their own terms, independently from other modalities. Partly as a consequence of these two opposing views, the key concepts of grapholinguistics have been defined differently by different researchers. Particularly the grapheme concept has seen different interpretations. Understanding graphemes as minimal contrastive units in a writing system enables us to apply this concept across different writing systems. If we adopt the concept of a hierarchically organized writing system, as proposed by correspondence theory, graphemes can also be defined as smallest suprasegmental units. As such, graphemes are parts of higher-level units, graphemic syllables and graphemic feet. This approach makes it possible to describe the inventory and the distribution of graphemes and allographs in a given writing system more precisely.

A closer look at punctuation reveals that the internal structure of punctuation marks – which has been studied in detail in the present-day German punctuation system – correlates with their functions in the process of decoding. This approach opens up future research avenues for similar studies in other writing systems. Another major area of future research is the question of what kinds of linguistic properties are encoded by punctuation marks in a given writing system. Finally, our discussion on capitalization has shown that the use of majuscule letters can lead to the emergence of new functions over time. It has also shown that a full understanding of writing systems as well as their individual elements requires a historical perspective, which is also true for punctuation and many other graphemic phenomena. Thus, our understanding of the individual 'elements' of writing systems, introduced in this chapter, can benefit substantially from historical orthography, and it is hoped that more researchers will continue contributing to this subject area.

4

Orthographic Conventionality

Aurelija Tamošiūnaitė

4.1 Introduction

Among the defining features of orthography is its conventional nature. How something is written down and what meanings are attached to different graphic segments, their arrangements and shapes are usually subject to a shared agreement among those involved in the writing and reading process. One of the fundamental tasks of both present-day and historical orthographic research concerns precisely this issue of conventionality, identifying how specific spellings and graphic segments obtain their conventional meanings and what specific aspects underlie and shape the establishment of these conventions, otherwise known as *orthographic principles*. For a researcher investigating orthographic practices of the past, the identification or establishment of orthographic principles is by no means an unproblematic task. The diachronic study of orthography always involves a degree of uncertainty, prompted by the complex, arbitrary and, most importantly, time-contingent relationships between writing and speech. Nevertheless, the investigation of orthographic principles is crucial to unveil the general patterns (or rules) that may govern orthographic practices within a specific writing system at a historical point in time. More specifically, it allows for an understanding of how different graphic signs relate to each other and to units of speech and how these signs operate systematically or idiosyncratically at different structural levels of language. This chapter seeks to illuminate some of the linguistic constraints that more directly inform principles or conventions in orthography. Given the diversity and often language-specific nature of the world's orthographic systems, this chapter focuses on and provides a selective overview of only those general principles of orthography that historically evolved and operated in alphabetically written languages. The discussion is further restricted to linguistic constraints that underlie *spelling* practices, that is "how graphemes of a writing system are used to write a language" (Coulmas 1996a: 477). The mechanisms underlying conventions that determine capitalization, punctuation or word division patterns fall outside the scope of this chapter. Such a restriction in scope, as well as the focus on predominantly European orthographic traditions, presents a rather limited and one-sided view of orthographies; this reflects, however, the *alphabetocentric* or *ethnocentric* focus that has prevailed so far in orthographic research (Meletis 2018: 53; see Harris 1986: 46, Ehlich 2007: 724).

I begin the overview by first outlining how the term *orthographic principle* is employed in the linguistic study of writing systems. After addressing some of the issues with the term itself, I discuss the importance of some of the aspects that underlie or shape the principles of orthography, such as the typological makeup of a writing system, levels and regularity of linguistic representation, and graphotactic constraints. For illustrative purposes I draw on research in Cyrillic Lithuanian (Subačius 2004a, 2005a, 2005b, 2011a, Tamošiūnaitė 2010, 2011, 2013, 2015), the writing system that was introduced to Lithuanian in the 1860s and was officially withdrawn in 1904, as this is my main working language and area of expertise. Although Cyrillic Lithuanian never developed an orthography in the strict sense of the term, its use in a handful of surviving ego-documents and printed texts nevertheless showcases many of the aspects and issues relevant to a discussion on orthographic principles. The final section of this chapter outlines how some general orthographic principles changed, informed and shaped the orthographies of some European languages at different points in time.

Finally, a note on terminology. In its strict modern sense, the term *orthography* is used to refer to a codified or standardized spelling system and its rules (Greek *ὀρθο* 'ortho' + *γραφία* 'graphia' > 'correct spelling') (see Coulmas 1996a: 379–80, 477–78). In this chapter, I employ the term *orthography* in a broader nonprescriptive sense, following the practice that seems to prevail in diachronic empirical treatments of writing (see a collection of studies in Baddeley and Voeste 2012b, Bunčić et al. 2016; see also Emiliano 2011, Rutkowska 2013c, 2016, Subačius 2018: 24–25). That is, I use the term *orthography* to refer to both constant and idiosyncratic *spelling practices* and the conventions that govern their use and interpretation, which may be (but are not necessarily) officially codified, and thus may or may not be perceived as normative or correct at different points in time. Opting for such a broad understanding of orthography[1] results from the diachronically contingent notions of *standard, norm* and *correctness*, which challenge the application of the term *orthography* in its narrow sense to diachronic studies of spelling (see Tieken-Boon van Ostade 1998, Martineau 2013, Martineau and Tailleur 2014, Nevalainen 2014, Rutten and van der Wal 2014, Vosters et al. 2014, Rutten 2016a).

[1] For similar (inclusive) synchronic treatments of *orthography*, see, for instance, Sebba (2007), Jaffe et al. (2012), among others.

4.2 Orthographic Principle as a (Pre)theoretical Concept

The treatment and definition of *orthographic principles* varies across the literature. As Neef (2013: 12) has observed, the very notion of 'principle' is a somewhat fuzzy concept. Some researchers reserve the term to refer *implicitly* to rules, conventions, regularities, patterns or preferences that govern spelling practices, that is how something is written down, and/or their interpretation, that is how what is written is pronounced (see, for instance, Venezky 1970, Scragg 1974, Luelsdorff 1990, Carney 1994, Voeste 2008, Rutkowska and Rössler 2012); some assign principles to higher-order categories,[2] such as the writing system; some interpret the term rather metaphorically as imperatives or guidelines of a spelling system (see Venezky's 1999: 6–10 or Ryan's 2016: 53–56 principles of English spelling); while yet others use the term in a much narrower sense, to refer for instance to graphotactic rules (see Neef 2013: 11–12).

There is generally a divide, especially among German scholars (see Neef 2013), regarding whether the term *orthographic principles* itself is valid as a theoretical concept. For instance, Nerius's (2007) theoretical modeling and structural description of the Standard German orthographic system, on the one hand, relies on the concept of orthographic principles, defined as "general or basic relationships from the graphic level to other levels of the language system" (2007: 87) that form the basis for orthographic rules. Accounting for these functional relationships, Nerius (2007: 89) discerns two major principles that operate in present-day Standard German orthography – the *phonological* and the *semantic* – which are further subdivided into a subset of structural principles according to linguistic levels, that is, *phonemic, syllabic, intonational* (under *phonological*) and *morphemic, lexical, syntactic* and *textual* (under *semantic*). Eisenberg (1983: 66), on the other hand, argues that theoretically one should not speak of writing principles, but rather "linguistic levels." This view is echoed by Glück (2016: 598), who suggests replacing the term *orthographic principles* with "networks of structural relationships" between the graphic and other linguistic levels. Kohrt (1987: 518) rejects the term due to its metaphorical implications, and suggests that it can only be used to refer to hypothetical internal norms.

The major criticism against the employment of term *orthographic principles*, however, concerns the lack of a coherent model that would enable mapping of relationships between different principles in a systematic way. Most of the existing descriptions of orthographic principles employ heterogeneous criteria to discern different types of principles. Neef's (2013: 34–37) list of 102 orthography-related terms (mostly in German) that are expressed as

[2] Coulmas (2003: 33), for example, lists three *analytic principles* of *writing*: "the principle of the autonomy of the graphic system, the principle of interpretation, and the principle of historicity."

principles illustrates a large diversity and heterogeneity in terms of how they are labeled and approached. Heterogeneous approaches to orthographic principles are also characteristic in other language-specific research traditions. For instance, when describing spelling patterns of sixteenth and seventeenth-century Lithuanian texts, Palionis (1995: 28–32) refers to *phonetic, morphological, traditional* and *differential principles*. While the first two refer to the linguistic level of representation, and thus are descriptive and synchronic, the *traditional principle* refers to historical spellings and thus is diachronic and overlaps partly with the first two, while the *differential principle* accounts for the graphic differentiation of homophonous words or morphemes and hence partly overlaps with the morphological principle.

Rutkowska and Rössler (2012: 215–16) provide a rather extensive list of various principles that may operate in different language-specific writing systems, namely, *phonetic, phonological, etymological, historical, heterographic, graphostylistic* or *graphotactic, pragmatic, grammatical, semantic* ones, as well as the *principle of economy*. Many of these principles are by no means consistent, however, and most are "partly conflicting and overlapping" (Rutkowska and Rössler 2012: 215). The list incorporates not only principles that determine spelling regularities, but also graphotactic constraints and rules determining capitalization patterns. Moreover, the listed principles are also unequal in terms of their weight in orthographic systems, as principles that map structural relationships between graphemic, phonological and morphological levels seem to play a more fundamental role in determining spelling regularities across alphabet-based European writing systems, while other principles are more peripheral. What is more, language-specific orthographic systems differ in terms of how these principles have been and are balanced.

More recent attempts to theorize orthographic principles may be found in Wiese (2004), Venezky (2004) and Neef (2013). Wiese (2004) approaches orthographic principles from the point of view of the *optimality theory*, namely, as constraint interaction between different orthographic preferences. He notes that an important advantage of the optimality theory is that it illuminates the ranking order of the constraints, which in turn helps to explain the differences (preferences for one or another way of spelling) across orthographies (Wiese 2004: 326). Venezky (2004) shares a similar approach by treating the mechanisms that operate in modern orthographies as constraints. Neef (2013: 29), on the other hand, proposes treating phonological and morphological orthographic principles as pretheoretical concepts which, according to him, touch upon the essential aspects of writing systems, but are insufficient to serve as robust theoretical categories. While the theoretical validity of orthographic principles as such is evidently contested, all empirically oriented treatments of orthography account for the different types of spelling regularities in one way or another, that is, how different graphic signs relate to each other and to units of speech and how these graphic signs operate on different structural levels in the language. It is in this sense that orthographic principles are approached in this chapter.

4.3 Orthographic Principles: Types and Constraints

The interplay of several factors seems to be important when establishing underlying principles of orthography: language-internal factors (i.e. the typological makeup of a writing system; levels and regularity of linguistic representation; graphotactic constraints); and language-external factors (i.e. origin, tradition and aesthetic value). In the following, I discuss the relevance of these factors in more detail. First, I consider how orthographic principles are affected by the type of script which determines the basic functional unit of linguistic representation (Subsection 4.3.1). In Subsection 4.3.2, I focus on alphabetic orthographies and consider the level and regularity of linguistic representation that determine how graphic signs may operate on different structural levels of language, resulting in phonological, morphological and/or lexical spellings. Subsection 4.3.3 looks at the importance of medium-specific features, namely combinatorial or graphotactic constraints that determine how different graphic signs relate to and combine with each other. Finally, Subsection 4.3.4 considers diachronic and cross-linguistic influences that shape the interpretation of specific orthographic principles over time.

4.3.1 Orthographic Principles and Typological Features of Writing Systems

Orthographies and the principles that guide them are inextricably linked to the typological properties of *writing systems* (see also Chapter 7, this volume). Any language-specific writing system encompasses a *script*, that is, a set of actual graphic signs "with prototypical forms and prototypical linguistic functions" (Weingarten 2011: 16), and language-specific rules (codified and noncodified) that govern the linguistic encoding of the graphic signs (see Gnanadesikan 2017: 15). Although writing systems are language-specific, the selection and implementation of a certain *type* of script (i.e. an *alphabet, abjad* or *syllabary*) determines to a certain degree what kind of mappings between graphic signs and other structural levels of language are expected to operate in its orthographic system. The scripts (and, hence, writing systems)[3] differ in terms of what kind of linguistic units their graphic signs encode,

[3] There is a slight disagreement on what exactly typologies refer to, namely whether typological properties should be assigned to *writing systems* or to *scripts*. Some, such as Weingarten, propose assigning typological qualities (such as alphabetic, abugida and so on) to *writing systems*, which he defines as "an ordered pair of a single language and a single script" (Weingarten 2011: 17), while others argue that it is precisely the *script*, that is the basic set of graphic signs with "prototypical linguistic functions" (Gnanadesikan 2017: 15), that carries typological characteristics.

that is, what serves as their minimal graphic unit of linguistic representation (Coulmas 1996b: 1381, Rutkowska 2017: 204). The most general distinction is often made between *morphograms* (or *logograms*),[4] that is graphic signs that refer to *morphemes* or *words*, and *phonograms*, that is graphic signs that refer to *syllables* or *phonemes* (Rogers 2005: 272). Based on this general distinction, scripts and, more generally, writing systems are classified broadly into *morphographic* (or *logographic*) and *phonographic*. The latter, depending on the segment size of the phonological unit encoded (see Gnanadesikan 2017: 16), may be further subdivided into *syllabaries* (i.e. scripts that denote syllables, such as Japanese *kana*), *alphabets* (i.e. scripts that denote vowels and consonants, such as Latin or Cyrillic), *abjads* (i.e. scripts that denote only consonants, such as Arabic or Hebrew) and *abugidas* (i.e. scripts where a character denotes a consonant accompanied by a particular vowel and other vowels are indicated by additions to consonantal shape, such as Devanāgarī or Ethiopic) (Daniels 1990, 1996a, 2018; also see Joyce and Borgwaldt 2011: 4).[5]

Although a script and orthography are independent from each other, by adopting a *phonographic script* that uses distinct graphic signs to denote vowels and consonants (i.e. an alphabet), one expects the *phonological* principle to operate on that particular orthography to a certain degree. On the other hand, the adoption of a *morphographic script*, where graphic signs principally represent morphemes, such as Japanese *kanji* (as argued by Joyce 2011), implies the operation of the *morphological* principle. In most orthographies, however, the relationships between graphic signs and units of speech operate in a much more complex way than simply following one of these two principles, which are otherwise foregrounded by typological classifications. Moreover, the heterogeneous nature of an orthography may be present from the very inception of a vernacular writing tradition, as, for instance, is the case in written French, which "from the very beginning, was a mixed system, in which the phonogrammic, etymological, morphogrammic and ideographical principles coexisted" (Baddeley 2012: 98).

4.3.2 Levels and Regularity of Linguistic Representation

In alphabetic orthographies, considering the functional relationships between graphemic and other linguistic levels, a more general differentiation can be made between *phonological* and *morphological* or *lexical* spellings. The discernment of these two very broad types of spellings presents an

[4] Joyce (2011) provides a terminological overview and arguments for the use of *morphographic* instead of *logographic* writing; others, for example Tranter (2013), argued for the use of the terms *logogram* and *logographic* writing. For the sake of consistency and for practical purposes I follow Rogers (2005) in using the term *morphographic*.

[5] See also Chapter 2, this volume, for a similar discussion of terminology and categories to the one provided in the present subsection.

oversimplified picture of how graphic signs map onto linguistic levels, but they serve here to showcase that it is precisely an interplay of *sound-oriented* and *meaning-oriented* graphic mappings that shapes alphabetic orthographies. Each of the two categories is further discussed below.

4.3.2.1 Phonological Spellings

The phonological (also *phonemic*; see Ryan 2016: 41, or *phonographic*, *phonetic-phonological*; see Dürscheid 2006: 142) principle assumes a one-to-one mapping between a graphic sign, for example a letter, and a unit of speech. Strictly speaking, one may differentiate between a *phonetic* and a *phonemic spelling*. The former assumes that each graphic sign denotes a distinct sound and for each distinct sound there is a distinct graphic expression (see phonetic transcription using the International Phonetic Alphabet), while the latter assumes that such one-to-one mapping operates on the level of phonemic representation. For the purpose of this chapter, however, I subsume sound and phonemic mappings under the phonological principle. The following Cyrillic Lithuanian examples, taken from a letter written by Stanislovas Prakulevičius, a Lithuanian soldier, in 1879 (see Tamošiūnaitė 2013), largely follow the phonological principle, as each grapheme maps onto a distinct phoneme, and vice versa: *варкстам* /ˈʋɐrkstɐm/[6] 'we are taking pains' (compare with Standard Lithuanian (SL) *vargstam*), *дованом* /do:ʋɐˈno:m/ '(with) gifts' (SL *dovanom*), *ранкелес* /rɐnkɛˈlɛs/ 'hands' (SL *rankeles*). While examples such as *ижгелбету* /ɪʒˈgælbe:tu:/ 'would save' (SL *išgelbėtų*),[7] *ужмекту* /ʊʒmiɛkˈtʊ/ 'I fall asleep' (SL *užmiegtu*) or *ужмерште* /ʊʒˈmęrʃtę/ 'to forget' (SL *užmiršti*) also suggest the application of a 'one-to-one principle', a more accurate analysis of the linguistic values of the grapheme <e> (denoting /æ/, /e:/, /iɛ/ or /ę/) in these examples reveals a more complex picture. More specifically, it points to a *divergence* (Carney 1994: 15) from one-to-one correspondences also known as *polyvalence*, a rather typical phenomenon in alphabetic writing systems and beyond, where a graphic sign has "more than one phonetic value" (Coulmas 1996a: 413).

Polyvalence contributes to the graphic variability of the spelling system in terms of its phonological mappings. The multiplicity of graphic marking can go in both directions: from grapheme to sound (one grapheme to many sounds, aka 'polyphony'; see Haas 1970: 52), and from sound to grapheme (one sound to many graphemes, aka 'polygraphy'; see Haas 1970: 52, and also Coulmas 1996a: 176). Thus, one grapheme can denote several sounds,

[6] The broad transcription employed here does not indicate suprasegmental features of stressed diphthongs, as well as positional palatalization of consonants. Nevertheless, some positional neutralizations of consonants (e.g. fricative retraction, voicing and devoicing) are marked as they are relevant for the discussion.

[7] Here and everywhere else throughout the chapter, boldface in the empirical examples is used to emphasize specific spelling feature(s) under discussion. Empirical examples are provided in their original form, retaining, among other features, capitalization patterns.

as in the previous examples, where the grapheme <e> denotes /ɛ/, /æ/, /eː/, /iɛ/ and /ę/, and the same sound can be denoted by several graphemes. For instance, in the abovementioned Cyrillic Lithuanian letter, the author marked /iɛ/ not only with <e>, as in the examples above, but also with <ѣ> (see *дѣна* /ˈdiɛnɑː/ 'day', compare SL *dieną*) (Tamošiūnaitė 2013: 433–34). Haas (1970: 52) has observed that different orthographies may favor different types of divergencies: some, as in French, may lean more toward polygraphy, while others, for example English, toward both polygraphy and polyphony. Different types of phonemes (i.e. vowels as opposed to consonants) may exhibit different degrees of polyvalence. Vowel spellings in many alphabetic, especially Latin-based orthographies tend to be more variant (i.e. polyvalent), although in many cases this polyvalence may be quite regular or predictable. This observation is also valid for the abovementioned Cyrillic Lithuanian letter, as well as for many other Cyrillic Lithuanian models (see Subačius 2004a, 2011a, Tamošiūnaitė 2010, 2011). While vowel spellings exhibit high variation, with the grapheme <e> corresponding to five different pronunciations, <ѣ> to three, and <o> to two (see Tamošiūnaitė 2013: 433–35), consonant spellings, with a few exceptions, remain mostly invariant.

In addition, different individual phonemes and graphemes may also be prone to different degrees of divergence (Carney 1994: 15–16). For instance, in most Cyrillic Lithuanian models, the spellings of plosive /k/ or nasals /m/ and /n/ are much more regular and invariant in contrast to the spellings of affricates /ʧ/ and /ʤ/ or fricative /ʒ/. Carney (1994: 16) differentiates between real and apparent divergence, drawing a distinction between *conditioned* and *competing* spelling variants. The distribution of conditioned variants (such as, for instance, the use of <pp> spellings for /p/ in English, Carney 1994: 16) is largely predicted by the context of their occurrence, while competing variants lack such an explanation. For instance, the spellings of affricate /ʤʲ/ with <дж> (*джяугтисъ* /ˈʤʲɛʊktɪs/ 'to be happy', compare SL *džiaugtis*) or <дз> (*дзяугесъ* /ˈʤʲɛʊgʲɛs/ 'one is happy', SL *džiaugias*) in one of Jonas Krečinskis's Cyrillic Lithuanian texts (see Subačius 2004a: 160) function primarily as competing variants. If one disregards external influences (e.g. transliteration patterns from Latin Lithuanian texts), the distribution of these particular digraphs is by no means constrained by the context of occurrence (i.e. they interchangeably occur in the same lexemes) or any other system-driven rules.

A number of factors may lead to the polyvalence of the graphic denoting of sounds, such as diachronic changes in the phonological system, differences in phonemic and nonphonemic contrasts within and across languages, orthographic treatment of foreign loanwords, language-specific orthographic developments, and functional 'reinterpretations' of specific graphic signs (Coulmas 2003: 96–101). For example, the loss of nasal vowels in Lithuanian during the eighteenth century remained largely unreflected in the Latin Lithuanian writing system. Moreover, the use of nasal graphemes (i.e. <ą>, <ę>, <į>, <ų>) was retained in modern SL orthography and even ‘transplanted’ by some authors into Cyrillic Lithuanian orthographic models (Venckienė 2006: 332, Subačius 2012: 233) at the end of the nineteenth century. As a result of asymmetrical developments of writing and speech, the originally phonological spelling of nasal vowels thus lost its initial meaning and was ‘reinterpreted’ with new linguistic functions. The Cyrillic Lithuanian models that adapted nasal graphemes primarily adopted them to mark specific inflectional morphemes, for example the accusative singular of nominals as seen in the following examples: *вѣнą* /ˈʋiɛnɑː/ ‘one’ (SL *vieną*), *картą* /ˈkɐrtɑː/ ‘time’ (SL *kartą*) (Mikšas, letter from November 6, 1885; see Venckienė 2006: 332) or *балсą* /ˈbɐlsɑː/ ‘voice’ (SL *balsą*), *гірэлą* /gɪˈræːlɑː/ ‘forest’ (SL *girelę*), *жалę* /ˈʒɑːlʲæː/ ‘green’ (SL *žalią*) (ЛНП 1867: 37;[8] see Subačius 2012: 233). Such a functional reassignment, where a graphic sign becomes a marker of morphological information, points to the morphologization of spelling. More precisely, it highlights the importance of higher-order mappings, that is graphic encoding of morphological and lexical information or *meaning-oriented* spellings, in alphabet-based orthographies. More about this topic is discussed in the following section.

4.3.2.2 Morphological and/or Lexical Spellings

Morphological (also *morphemic* or *lexical*; see Carney 1994: 18, Ryan 2016: 45) spellings refer to constant graphic marking of morphemes in morphologically (i.e. etymologically and semantically) related words. Morphological spellings are meaning-based and as such they visually foreground the connections between related lexical items, irrespective of their pronunciation. Consider the following sixteenth-century morphological words in Early New High German: *blatt* ‘leaf’ corresponding to *blaͤtter* ‘leaves’, *kaͤlte* ‘coldness’ as in *kalt* ‘cold’, and *kind* ‘child’ as in *kinder* ‘children’ (Voeste 2007a: 92, 2008: 15). Constant graphic spellings may be applied to stem or root morphemes (compare German term *Stammprinzip*) and to affixes (compare German term *Morphemkonstanzprinzip*; see Neef 2013: 21). Constant stem spellings, for instance, are retained in the following Cyrillic Lithuanian examples: *вѣшпатисчю* /ʋiɛʃpɐˈtiːʃʧʲuː/ ‘kingdoms’ (УК[9] 1902: 38, *вѣшпатистéсе* /ʋiɛʃpɐˈtiːsteːsɛ/ ‘in kingdoms’, УК 1902: 39); *Ругп’ютис* /rʊkˈpjuːtɪs/ ‘August’ (УК 1902: 19, *ругей* /rʊˈgʲɛɪ/ ‘rye’, АЛР[10] 1865: 40); *ужмокесчіо* /ˈʊʒmoːkɛʃʧʲoː/ ‘of payment’ (ПаЖЖ[11] 1902: 5, *Ужмокести* /ˈʊʒmoːkɛstiː/

[8] ЛНП 1867 = Литовскія народныя пѣсни [...] (= *Litovskīia narodnyia piesni* [...]), 1867.

[9] УК 1902 = Укишкасис календорюс 1902 метамс [...] (= *Ukiškasis kalendorius 1902 metams* [...]), 1902.

[10] АЛР 1865 = Абецеле лѣтувишкай-русишка [...] (= *Abecele lėtuviškaj-rusiška,* [...]), 1865.

[11] Пажж 1902 = Сказка о рыбакѣ и рыбкѣ [...] (= *Skazka o rybakie i rybkie* [...]), 1902.

'payment', ПаЖЖ 1902: 5). Constant graphic marking of the prefix *iš-*, irrespective of its phonetic mapping, has been retained in: ***ишдави*** /ˈɪʒdɐʋɛ̹/ 'issued' (Sartininkai parishioners c. 1901), ***ишгис*** /ɪʒˈgɪs/ 'will heal' (Juška, letter of September 8, 1901) and ***ишгирдом*** /ɪʒˈgɪrdoːm/ 'we heard' (Juška, letter of September 15, 1901). Most of these Lithuanian examples deal with automatic or positional morphonological alternations that involve consonant assimilation (fricative retraction from /s/ to /ʃ/ or voicing of /ʃ/ to /ʒ/) and affrication (/tʲ/ to /ʧʲ/). However, as the spellings in *вѣшпатисз-ю* vs. *вѣшпатист-ѐсе* suggest, while some morphonological alterations of the stem (here the positional assimilation of /s/ to /ʃ/) become subject to morphemic spelling, others (such as the stem final alternation between /tʲ/ to /ʧʲ/ in the same example) are spelled phonetically. This illustrates how the same spelling principle may be subject to different degrees of generalization, which in turn may lead to spelling idiosyncrasies.

The occurrence of morphological spellings in Cyrillic Lithuanian (as well as in its Latin-based orthographic models) is not as high compared to other languages like English (see Carney 1994: 15, 24), French (see Baddeley 2012: 99) or Russian (see Grigor′eva 2004: 34, Bunčić et al. 2016: 121), where the morphological principle has played and still plays a much more significant role. Moreover, the choice between morphology-based vs. phonology-based spellings in Cyrillic Lithuanian is largely constrained by external factors, such as the author's literacy level, education, familiarity with Latin Lithuanian orthographic models and even ideological stance (see Tamošiūnaitė 2015). Most Cyrillic Lithuanian handwritten ego-documents, written by less educated authors with lower exposure to writing and reading, tend to rely primarily on phonetic spellings (even if exhibiting graphemic polyvalence) in contrast to printed texts prepared by hired Lithuanian language 'experts' (see Subačius 2011a). Printed texts tend to show a comparatively higher amount of morphological spellings. In other words, vernacular Cyrillic Lithuanian orthography appears more 'phonetic' (or *transparent*) than the orthography employed in (at least some) printed texts.[12] A correlation between literacy and morphological spellings has also been observed in other vernacular writing traditions (see Section 4.4).

In alphabetic writing systems, the amount of morphological spellings is often employed as one of the measures to determine *orthographic depth* (see Rogers 2005: 274–75).[13] Orthographic depth refers to a scalar dimension that intends to capture the regularity and consistency of mappings between graphic signs and related linguistic levels. The concept originates from psycholinguistic research on reading and writing (Katz and Feldman 1983, Frost et al. 1987) and is based on the (nowadays theoretically challenged)

[12] See Bunčić et al. (2016, 132–34) for an opposite trend in thirteenth-century Novgorod orthographies.

[13] On its problematic applicability beyond alphabetic scripts, see, for instance, Share and Daniels (2016).

assumption that morphological representation is more 'abstract' and thus 'deeper' in comparison to phonological representation, which is perceived as more 'concrete' (Katz and Frost 1992: 71, Neef et al. 2002: 2, Roberts 2011: 93). Therefore, orthographies that map letter and sound relationships in a more transparent or isomorphic way (i.e. adhere to the phonological principle) are characterized as *shallow*, *transparent* and *surface*, while orthographies that deviate from this principle are described as *deep* or *opaque*.[14] The most commonly cited example of a shallow orthography is modern Serbo-Croatian (see Katz and Feldman 1983: 158, Frost et al. 1987: 104–5), which has almost isomorphic mapping between sounds and letters, while English or French are typically seen as examples of deep orthographies, since they exhibit high graphemic polyvalence and prioritize morphological spellings at the expense of the phonemic ones (Coulmas 1996a: 380, Ryan 2016: 42). It should be noted, however, that most orthographic systems often exhibit different degrees of transparency; the descriptors *shallow* or *deep* should not be perceived as bounded or strict categories but rather as opposing ends of a continuum. In addition, the degree of transparency of a specific orthographic system is historically contingent: it may exhibit different degrees of transparency or depth at different periods of time. Such fluctuation is observable among many European vernaculars, as exemplified by an overview of some case studies in Section 4.4.

A further layer of complexity in an orthographic system regards distinguishing visually between otherwise homophonous words or morphemes (Rutkowska 2017: 205). Consider the following English spellings as examples: *hole* vs. *whole* or *hoop* vs. *whoop* (Scragg 1974: 59) and *wright* vs. *write* vs. *right* vs. *rite* (Carney 1994: 403). Ryan (2016: 55) associates such spellings with the *distinctiveness* principle, while Rutkowska and Rössler (2012: 216) associate it with the *heterographic* principle. Distinct spellings can be applied not only to homophonous lexemes, as exemplified above, but also to homophonous morphemes. For instance, in seventeenth-century Lithuanian texts by Danielius Kleinas, the spelling of morpheme *iš(-)* was graphically differentiated: fricative /ʃ/ was spelled with ligature of <ſ> and <ʒ>, that is <ß> as a preposition, but with <ś> as a prefix, as in ***iß** tamſybju **iś**wėde* 'led from the darkness' (KING[15] 1666: 131_{20}; see Šinkūnas 2014: 28). In addition, diacritics were employed to graphically distinguish homophonous inflectional morphemes, for example a circumflex ^ differentiated singular genitive endings (as in

[14] On the use of the terms *deep* vs. *opaque* and *shallow* vs. *transparent* in English and French research traditions, see, for instance, Roberts (2011). For an overview of how orthographic depth and graphematic transparency can be measured, see Neef and Balestra (2011).

[15] KING 1666 = [Kleinas, Danielius] Σὺν τῷ Θεῷ. Neu Littauſches / verbeſſert=und mit vielen neuen Liedern vermehretes Geſangbuch <...>. NAUJOS GIESMJU KNYGOS. <...> KARALAUCZUJE Iśſpaude ſawo iſſirádimais PRIDRIKIS REUSNERIS Metůſe M. DC. LXVI. [1666].

gieſmês 'psalm', KlGr 1653: 48 v(48)$_{29}$)[16] from the homophonous nominative plural inflection (as in *gieſmes*, KlGr 1653: 49$_{1}$). To a certain extent, such heterographic marking of homophonous lexemes and morphological forms is on a par with the morphological principle of spelling as it foregrounds the importance of meaning-oriented encodings of graphic signs. The spellings that distinguish homophonous morphemes or lexemes contribute to the *amount of morphography* (Rogers 2005: 275) within the phonographic writing system. A higher degree of morphography may additionally result from spellings that map directly onto words or other meaningful units rather than sounds. Such traits of morphographic writing, as found in alphabetic writing systems, can be illustrated, for instance, by the use of ampersand *&* for Latin *et* and English *and* (Carney 1994: 5), the employment of Latin or Greek abbreviations *xp͡s* and *x͡p* for *Christus* (Šinkūnas 2016: 185–89; see also Baddeley 2012: 98) and the use of short form *vñ* for *und* in sixteenth-century German printed texts (Voeste 2012: 173). The existence of such morphographic elements in phonographic writing systems point to their mixed and multifaceted nature, suggesting that purely phonemic alphabet-based orthographic systems may likely exist only in theory, and rarely in practice (see Coulmas 2003: 93).

4.3.3 Graphotactic Constraints and Aesthetically Conditioned Spellings

Many alphabetic writing systems, both present-day and historical, tend to contain graphic elements (*markers* in Venezky's terminology; see 1970: 50) that do not stand for any sounds, such as <ъ> in Russian writing system or the lengthening (*Dehnungs*) <h> in German. The opposite is also true: certain speech units may not be marked graphically in writing, for example the consonant /j/ in some word-initial or -internal positions before <ie> in SL (e.g. *ietis* 'a spear' and *paieškoti* 'to look for'). Some of these markers, which otherwise have no sound correspondences, may be employed in so-called *syllabic spellings* to mark specific structural properties of the syllable, for example openness, closedness, length of the nucleus vowel, phonological contrasts, and so on. In Early New High German, syllabic spellings apply to the use of lengthening <h> (e.g. *nehmen* 'to take'), doubling of vowel graphemes (e.g. *eere* 'honor') or gemination of consonants (e.g. *kommen* 'to come') (Voeste 2007a: 91, 2012: 180–81). What these instances suggest is that some graphic signs tend to function independently "from the spoken forms" (Neef et al. 2002: 4), which in turn implies the existence of some at least partial autonomy

[16] KlGr 1653 = [Kleinas, Danielius] GRAMMATICA Litvanica Mandato & Autoritate SERENISSIMI ELECTORIS BRANDENBURGICI adornata, & præviâ Cenſurâ primùm in lucem edita à M. DANIELE Klein <...> REGIOMONTI, Typis & ſumptibus JOHANNIS REUSNERI, ANNO χριστογονίας clɔ. Iɔc. LIII. [1653]. There are two pages paginated as 48 in this particular copy of Danielius Kleinas's *Grammar*. The quoted example appears on the second page (here marked as 48v) in line 29 (here marked in subscript). The number in parenthesis refers to original pagination.

of writing in relation to speech. Furthermore, it highlights the importance of the contextual graphic environment, also known as *graphotactics*, that affects the use and functions of different graphic signs (Coulmas 1996a: 175) and which further challenges the straightforward or bidirectional relationship between graphemes and sounds.

Graphotactics encompasses, among other aspects, the "combinability of letter segments within the graphic word and the interaction of these segments and their combinations" (Voeste 2008: 11). Some of the combinations of graphic segments may be constrained by their position (initial, internal-medial or final) in a graphic word or morpheme, preceding or proceeding segments, as well as their visual shapes, graphetic weight and even aesthetic qualities (symmetry or balancing) (Voeste 2008: 11–12). In most medieval and early modern European vernacular manuscript traditions, for instance, the use of the graphemes <i> vs. <j> vs. <y>, <u> vs. <v>, and <s> vs. <ſ> was graphotactically restricted to different positions within the graphic word, as well as surrounding graphic segments (see Scragg 1974: 10–11, Baddeley 2012: 99, Šinkūnas 2014: 10–11, Scholfield 2016: 148, 153). Similarly, during the second quarter of the seventeenth century, Lithuanian texts of the so-called Western variety interchangeably employed two digraphs to mark the affricate /ʧ/, that is <cʒ> and <tʒ>, whose use, according to Šinkūnas (2014: 34), was graphotactically constrained: <cʒ> was used only word-initially, while <tʒ> was employed in the remaining positions of the graphic word. Both digraphs thus functioned as conditioned variants in complementary distribution (see Subsection 4.3.2.1).

Intertextual analysis of the employment of the grapheme <ъ> in Cyrillic Lithuanian ego-documents (14 hands, 17 ego-documents, 3,482 word tokens) also points to graphotactically determined use.[17] If <ъ> is used, it overwhelmingly tends to appear in word-final positions following consonantal graphemes (in parallel with Russian orthographic practice at the time), with some authors even showing a tendency to generalize the use of <ъ> for all word-final positions irrespective of the preceding grapheme. The following examples found in a book ownership inscription written in 1901 illustrate this generalization: *Таъ* /'tɐ/ 'that', *касъ* /'kɐs/ 'who', *Кнйнгаъ* /knin'gɐ/ 'book', and *монъ* / 'mǫn/ 'to me' (Smilga 1901). In all of these cases the use of <ъ> marks the end boundary of the graphic word, functioning thus as a visual segmentation tool. A number of factors may influence the emergence of different combinatorial restrictions in language-specific writing systems, such as cross-linguistic and cross-cultural influences, as in the case of <ъ> marking in word-final positions for Cyrillic Lithuanian or in the distribution of <u>

17 In the Russian writing system at the time, the use of <ъ> was also graphotactically constrained. It was employed both in word-final positions, following a nonpalatalized consonant, and word-internally, most often after the prefix preceding the vowel to indicate syllable boundary (Grot 1885: 49–52).

vs. <v> or <s> vs. <ſ> across European vernaculars. Other factors include the type of medium (i.e. manuscript vs. print), typographical developments (see Voeste 2008: chapter 3), and even individual preferences of the scribe, which may be based purely on aesthetic grounds (see Voeste 2007b).

Subačius's (2018) analysis of orthographic variation in Simonas Daukantas's manuscript *History of Lithuanian Lowlands* has showcased how the marking of the dialectal diphthong /ẹi/ (which had at least seven competing graphic renderings) was subject to graphotactic variation, which in turn was motivated by visual and aesthetic combinability of specific graphic elements. In word-medial positions, the four most frequently employed graphic renderings, |ei|, |ęi|, |yj| and |ij|, functioned primarily as aesthetic variants[18]: |ei| and |ęi| often followed those root-initial positions that contained a cluster of two or more consonantal graphemes (e.g. after <br->, <gr->, <skr-> and so on, Subačius 2018: 224), while |yj| and |ij| were mostly preceded by only one consonantal grapheme (Subačius 2018: 224–25). In addition to the importance of such segmental density, the graphetic aspects of spelling variants also influenced the choice of the variant: the spellings with long descenders, |yj| and |ij|, were preferred after graphemes with long ascenders and descenders (such as, <l>, <p> and <t>), while |ei| and |ęi| were typically employed after 'short' graphemes or digraphs (such as <s> and <sz>) (Subačius 2018: 224–25). The aesthetic balancing of graphic elements served thus as one of the key motivational factors (Subačius 2018: 226) behind variational spelling of /ẹi/ in Daukantas's manuscript. The exceptions that did not follow these graphotactic spelling patterns were mostly lexically motivated; Daukantas preferred to spell certain lexemes such as *diena* 'day', *Dievas* 'God' or *tiesa* 'truth', and their derivative forms, with the 'short' variants <ei> or <ęi> despite the low graphic density and long ascender at the graphic onset of the root (Subačius 2018: 223–26). All these examples point to the complex simultaneous interaction between different spelling preferences at work and the different degrees of generalization of these principles. They additionally highlight that aesthetically shaped graphotactic spellings contribute to the 'morphographization' of an alphabetic writing system.

4.3.4 Diachronic Changes and Cross-linguistic Influences

Orthographies and writing systems are historical constructs. As a result, different guiding principles for orthographies may be prioritized at different points of time for the same writing system, and the meaning assigned to the relationship between the graphic and the linguistic units is inherently time-contingent.

[18] The relationship between these four orthographic variables was in fact much more complex: in addition to serving as aesthetic variants, they were also diachronic, diaphasic, diatopic and diaprecise variants (Subačius 2018: 226).

The history of sixteenth-century German writing practices may illustrate both points. Voeste (2008, 2012) has shown how Early New High German spelling practices started shifting from predominantly phonological to syllabic and morphemic spellings during the sixteenth century; furthermore, over time, some initially phonemic spellings, such as the gemination of consonants, were reanalyzed as syllabic ones. Voeste (2008: 213–14, 2012: 176–77) attributes these changes to the increasing importance of morphological segmentation of written words, which is evident for example in the changing spelling patterns of <v> and <u>, whose use, following Latin tradition, was graphotactically constrained to specific word positions. The more frequent use of <v> word-internally during the sixteenth century, as in *hervnter* 'down' or *großvater* 'grandfather', shows both a change of spelling habits and increasing graphic segmentation of words, which eventually "set the foundations for etymological spelling regulations" (Voeste 2012: 176) in present-day German.

Orthographic changes and changes to a writing system more generally may be conditioned not only by asymmetric development of writing and speech, but also constrained by external factors, including social, political and cultural (Scragg 1974: chapter 3, Sampson 1985: 198, Rutkowska 2017: 210–11). As Weingarten (2011: 17) points out, the prototypical functions associated with certain graphic signs, for example the linguistic function of the letter <r> in Latin-based or <p> in Cyrillic-based writing systems for a rhotic phoneme of some kind, are transmitted to language-specific writing systems both historically and cross-linguistically. Since the emergence of vernacular writing traditions in Europe was closely linked to the adoption of either Latin Christianity or Byzantine Christianity, it was Latin, Greek and Old Church Slavonic orthographic traditions that served as models for the "scriptualization" (Voeste 2012: 168) of vernaculars. In other words, the linguistic functions of Latin and Greek graphic signs were transferred to European vernacular writing systems (Lass 1997: 46), and subsequently modified to accommodate the graphic rendering "of each vernacular's respective linguistic peculiarities" (Baddeley and Voeste 2012a: 2). Moreover, these very same vernacular writing traditions also exercised influence on newly emerging neighboring written varieties. The Lithuanian graphic inventory of the sixteenth and seventeenth centuries, for instance, was largely modeled on German and Polish (and even Czech, via Polish) writing systems of the time, as evident in the adoption of such spellings as <sch>, <sz> and <ś> for fricatives /ʃ/, /ʃʲ/, <cz> and <ć> for affricates /ʧ/, /ʧʲ/ and <ů> for the diphthong /uɔ/, in addition to the use of geminates in order to mark the quantity of the preceding vowel, following the German orthographic tradition. During the second half of the nineteenth century, when a script reform was introduced in Lithuanian, the adaptation models of Cyrillic for Lithuanian were largely shaped by Russian orthographic conventions and principles (Subačius 2004a, 2005a, 2011a, Tamošiūnaitė 2015).

4.4 A Glimpse at Some European Vernaculars

The diachronic development of certain types of spelling conventions among European orthographies are frequently language-specific. Baddeley and Voeste (2012b), however, in one of the very few comparative and cross-linguistic overviews of diachronic orthography,[19] have pointed to some common developmental trends across written vernaculars in early modern Europe, especially among those writing traditions that emerged with the adoption of Latin Christianity. A comparative look into the vernacular orthographic systems from the early modern period has pointed to two diverging directions: some vernacular orthographies aimed at maintaining and incorporating 'Latinate elements' and thus diverged from phonemic spelling patterns, while others, since the inception of their writing systems, exhibited "greater independence from Latin" by employing "phonographic systems of spelling" (Baddeley and Voeste 2012a: 2). The former direction is observable among the Romance languages, namely vernacular French, Italian and Spanish writing systems. These organically emerged out of Latin writing tradition, so that "there was initially no real break between the emergence of the vernaculars and the development of corresponding written systems" (Baddeley and Voeste 2012a: 2; see also Llamas-Pombo 2012: 18). What is specific to the initial stages of the writing systems of Romance languages is their morphographic rather than phonographic nature, that is, their orientation to meaning rather than only to form.

Baddeley (2012) has provided an illustrative example of how spelling patterns in fifteenth-century French manuscripts became more morphographic. Due to the speed of writing, many of the handwritten graphemes ended up looking alike. This process led scribes to begin inserting mute consonant letters, which not only played a graphotactic role but were also supposed to emphasize the visual connection to cognate words in Latin (e.g. spelling of <l> in French *moult* 'a lot' and Latin *multum*, Baddeley 2012: 116). A number of abbreviations that could stand for either Latin or French words were also employed, for instance the tilde to mark a nasal consonant or <q;> for enclitic *-que* (Baddeley 2012: 99). According to Baddeley (2012: 99), all these morphography-oriented features indicate that the texts were written without an intention to pronounce them, but rather solely for them to be read. Preference for morphological spellings, despite the numerous debates and initiatives over time to reform French orthography in order to make it more sound-based, prevailed since the sixteenth century. This particular orientation set French orthographic development apart from Spanish or Italian vernacular writing traditions, which eventually leaned toward sound-based orthographies (see

19 For the most recent cross-linguistic stance on the development of European orthographies, see the volume edited by Condorelli (2020c).

Llamas-Pombo 2012, Michel 2012). Thus, in terms of the orthographic principles employed and the weight given to them, French, as claimed by Baddeley, was always a mixed system, but it was never a fully "phonetic orthography" (2012: 99).

The latter phonographic path of spelling, that is to say the sound-based system, was adopted by most Germanic, and other Central, Nordic and Eastern European vernaculars. While the starting point for these vernacular writing systems was primarily phonological, the degree of their phonography fluctuated over time (Baddeley and Voeste 2012a: 8): some, like German, English or Dutch, shifted toward morphography, albeit in different ways, while others, such as Croatian (Marti 2012), Swedish (Zheltukhin 2012), Finnish (Nordlund 2012) and Czech (Berger 2012), "remained more or less phonographic" (Baddeley and Voeste 2012a: 11). With regard to German, Elmentaler (2003) has explored graphematic variation in the Early New High German texts of ten Duisburg town clerks from the fourteenth to the seventeenth century. His analysis of spellings used for syllable differentiation, vowel class differentiation, and umlaut marking has highlighted a discontinuous or nonlinear diachronic development in the sense that the orthographic choices and spellings adopted by individual scribes differed from those of their predecessors. Moreover, in terms of spelling regularities, Elmentaler (2003: 291, 307) has argued that, at least in his dataset, there were no systematic attempts to employ either strictly phonological (evident through the high degree of grapheme polyvalence) or morphological (stem constancy) principles of spelling until the middle of the seventeenth century.

Voeste (2007a, 2008, 2012, 2015), however, has provided evidence that processes of spelling 'morphologization' in Early New High German started emerging already during the sixteenth century. Two fundamental changes led to the shift from 'segmental phonography' to morphography. The first concerns the changed perception of the written unit, which eventually resulted in the separation of "word-units with blanks" (Voeste 2012: 168), and the second relates to the invention of Gothic cursive, which made the written word visibly distinct. As a result, written segments, according to Voeste (2012: 169), "began to be visualizations of semantic units, since written word forms refer to the semantic level." During the sixteenth century, in German two types of orthographic principles thus seem to have played a role: phonological, that is "segmental phonography," and morphological, that is "word-bound logography" (Voeste 2012: 169). The evidence for morphography, for instance, comes from the graphotactic changes of <v> and <u>, as in *landuogt* vs. *landvogt* 'baillif' (compare *vogt*), and <ſ> and <s>, as in *biſher* vs. *bisher* 'until now' (compare *bis* 'until'), in compound words (Voeste 2008: 108, 109). In this category of words, the new word-internal positions of the otherwise restricted graphemes <v> and <s> indicates, according to Voeste (2008: 109), the preference to maintain morpheme constancy. Morphologization tendencies are also evident from the spread of umlaut spellings and geminate consonants, which were gradually generalized to other cognate forms (Voeste 2012: 179). These changes did not affect all graphemes, however, with some ("giacomettic"; Voeste 2012: 180) letters, such as <t>, <l> or <f>, more susceptible to participate in the 'etymologization' process, while others, such as <m>, were less so, most likely due to the different graphetic weight (Voeste 2012: 180, compare Voeste 2015: 251).[20] In addition to the emergence of morphological spellings, another development that appears during the sixteenth century is syllabic spelling, most characteristically evident in the use of *mute* <h>, which marked, and still marks, the long vowel in a syllable nucleus, for example *jhar* or *jahr* 'year' (Voeste 2012: 181).

The transition from phonological to syllabic spellings has also been observed by Rutten and van der Wal (2011, 2014) in seventeenth- to eighteenth-century Dutch orthographic practices. One type of evidence for this shift comes from the spelling patterns of the so-called "etymologically distinct long *e*'s" (Rutten and van der Wal 2014: 35). These long *e*'s were graphically distinguished in the Zeeland Dutch orthographic system and initially maintained in the North, but as a result of the sound merger, the Northern orthographic practices eventually started shifting toward morphology-based or syllabic spellings (see also Chapter 30, this volume). Sound-based spelling maintained the distinction between two *e*'s in open syllables: the so-called *softlong ē* was spelled as <e>, as in *leven* 'to live', while the *sharplong ê* was rendered with <ee>, as in *steenen* 'stones' (Rutten and van der Wal 2014: 35). Morphology-based systems also generalized the use of <ee> to those morphologically related word forms that otherwise had softlong *ē*, while syllabic spellings generalized either the use of <e> or <ee> (Rutten and van der Wal 2014: 35). Rutten and van der Wal's analysis of Dutch private letters showed a clear trend over time to generalize the spellings with <ee> to all open syllables regardless of phonological differences, pointing to a diachronic shift across Holland from sound-based spellings, which prevailed in the seventeenth century, to the "syllabification of the writing system" (2014: 69). The researchers have labeled the shift as *graphemization* of the written language, explained as follows:

> the importance of phonology for orthographical practice was reduced, while choices directly linked to the written code became more important. This implies morphologisation and/or syllabification of the spelling, where morphological and/or syllabic aspects decide on the grapheme used, for instance uniformity of inflected forms and root forms, or uniformity of open and closed syllables.
>
> (Rutten and van der Wal 2014: 67)

[20] Graphetic weight refers to visual properties of a letter in terms of its shape (e.g. tall, thin, round, curved), length (e.g. long, short) or width (e.g. narrow, wide). For instance, due to its thinness and tallness <l> would be considered graphetically *lighter* than wider and rounder <m> (see Voeste 2012: 172, 2015: 251).

Graphemization also went hand in hand with supralocalization, a process where local dialect features were replaced with nonlocalizable, supraregional forms (Rutten and van der Wal 2014: 73–74; see also Chapter 13, Chapter 21, Chapter 25 and Chapter 30, this volume). Considering the fact that literacy rates in the Northern Netherlands were comparatively higher than in other parts of Europe (Rutten and van der Wal 2014: 13), the shift toward graphemization of the Dutch writing system seems to support the hypothesis raised by Baddeley and Voeste (2012a: 9) that the emergence of morphological spellings is to a certain extent related to "an increasing degree of literacy." Adopting foreign writing conventions presents another way in which an initially sound-based orthography can move toward 'morphographization'. The history of English orthography is perhaps the best-known example of this, where naturalization (see Scholfield 2016: 145) vs. preservation of the original spelling of loanwords throughout history contributed to the graphemic and phonemic polyvalence within the English writing system and eventually foregrounded the importance and prioritization of morphological spellings (on etymological inputs to the English writing system, see Horobin 2016, Ryan 2016: 49–51, Scholfield 2016: 145–48).

To further illustrate the process of 'morphographization', consider again the example of Cyrillic Lithuanian. The Lithuanian writing system has used the Latin script since the beginning of the sixteenth century, akin to many written traditions that emerged from the adoption of Latin Christianity. After the Polish-Lithuanian social and political uprising in 1863, however, the officials of the Russian Empire initiated script reform in 1865, banning the use of the Latin alphabet for Lithuanian and implementing the use of Cyrillic (for more comprehensive accounts on Cyrillic Lithuanian, see Subačius 2004a, 2005a, 2011a, Tamošiūnaitė 2015). The ban, which lasted for forty years, was eventually lifted in 1904. While the script reform ultimately failed, several orthographic models (initiated by government officials) were proposed during this period for the adaptation of Cyrillic to the Lithuanian writing system. As both Latin and Cyrillic scripts are alphabetic, the initial proposals, and some later individual ones, followed the phonological principle, attempting to account for letter–sound correspondences when adjusting Cyrillic letters to Lithuanian. However, the models that were promoted by the imperial administrators, such as those designed by Jonas Krečinskis, Dmitrii Kashirin and Zakharii Lyatskii (see Subačius 2004a, 2005a, 2011a), followed the morphographic path. These models relied on Russian orthographic conventions of the time, with several orthographic features characteristic of these models, in particular the use of the back *yer* <ъ> and the *yat* <ѣ>. The employment of these graphemes in Russian orthography of the time was based on historical tradition: the back *yer* was a 'silent' letter that indicated the hardness of the preceding consonant and was used in all word-final positions, after a consonant; the *yat*, which had lost its distinctive phonetic encoding in Muscovite Russian by the end of the fifteenth century (Vlasto 1986: 49), was restricted to certain lexemes or morphological positions, such as the marking of the prepositional case. These two graphemes were borrowed with their linguistic functions into Cyrillic Lithuanian. The back *yer* <ъ>, as in Russian orthography of the time, was used in word-final positions ending in consonants (e.g. Krečinskis's *антъ* /ˈɐnt/ 'on', Subačius 2005a: 36), while <ѣ> was mostly used in those lexemes that were cognates with respective Russian words (e.g. Krečinskis's *рѣтай* /rɛˈtɐi/ 'rarely', compare Russian *рѣдко* 'rarely', Subačius 2005a: 38) or was employed to mark locative singular endings (e.g. Kashirin's *савеѣ* /sɐʋeːˈjɛ/ 'in one's own', Subačius 2011a: 71) analogously to the Russian prepositional case. In Krečinskis's, Kashirin's and Lyatskii's orthographic models for Cyrillic Lithuanian, the use of at least these two graphemes was thus motivated by either graphemic shape of a cognate word in Russian or graphotactic features of the Russian writing system. Such 'borrowing' and orientation to Russian orthographic practices in turn largely contributed to the morphographic nature of these Cyrillic Lithuanian models. Leaving the ideological implications aside (see Tamošiūnaitė 2015 or Subačius 2011a for a discussion), one may claim that what guided the development of these particular Cyrillic Lithuanian orthographic models was the principle of morphographic "visualization" (see Voeste 2012: 179).

4.5 Conclusion

Orthographies emerge and develop as both planned and "self-organized" (Voeste 2007a) historical and social constructs. This dual and even conflicting pattern of development implies that orthographies are largely shaped by the tensions between *centripetal forces*, which aim at uniformity, regularization, consistency and stability, and *centrifugal forces*, which embrace heterogeneity, variation, individuality and creativity (see Bakhtin 1975: 83). Heterogeneity, manifesting itself on a number of levels, is inherent in the orthographic system, and this in turn explains why different orthographic principles or spelling regularities may develop, function and operate in complex and even conflicting ways within the same writing system at different points of time. An interplay of several language-internal factors shapes orthographic principles in alphabetic writing systems. Namely, graphotactic constraints, which determine how different units of writing relate to and combine with each other, the type of script, which establishes what serves as the basic functional unit of linguistic representation, and level and regularity in linguistic representation, which determine how graphic signs operate on different structural levels of language. Most alphabetic orthographies, to varying degrees, account for sound-oriented and meaning-oriented mappings, but the balancing of phonological vs. morphological/lexical spellings, as well as their prioritization and interpretation, are contingent upon time, space, language and social agency. The lattermost aspect in particular highlights the ideological and socially constructed nature of orthographies (see Sebba 2007, Jaffe et al. 2012, Spitzmüller 2015, Villa and Vosters 2015a), and reminds us that orthography is by no means a "value-neutral technology" (Vosters et al. 2012: 136). The aesthetic, symbolic or ideological meanings attached to specific graphic signs or spelling variables are largely constrained, negotiated and shaped by individual social actors and discursive communities involved in the writing process. It is these social meanings and social contexts, in addition to the time-contingent relationship between a graphic sign and its linguistic meaning, that need to be accounted for when looking to explain the multi-layered heterogeneity of orthographic practices found in historical texts.

5

Theoretical Approaches to Understanding Writing Systems

Hanna Rutkowska

5.1 Introduction

"The fact is that writing and speech in Western civilization have for centuries been locked in a relationship which is essentially symbiotic." This quotation from Harris (1986: 46) encapsulates the difficulty experienced by both ancient and later scholars with defining precisely the nature of the relationship between speech and writing. Nonetheless, despite the difficulties, various views have been offered over time on this challenging issue. The present chapter offers a diachronic and synchronic overview of theoretical linguistic approaches to defining and understanding writing systems, with reference mainly to alphabetic orthographies and with emphasis on the English language, though a number of observations and principles included here also apply to the orthographies of other languages. The approaches to writing and writing systems through most of the twentieth century could be divided into two main trends, *relational*[1] and *autonomistic*, as first proposed by Ruszkiewicz (1976: 37–46) and summarized by Sgall (1987: 2–3). The basic difference between these approaches is that, in the former, language is equaled with speech and the purpose of writing is merely to represent spoken sounds, whereas, in the latter, the writing system of a language does not only show correspondences with the spoken system, but also contains features and oppositions not related to speech in any way.

The previously heated debate between these two attitudes had virtually disappeared by the eighties of the twentieth century and the distinction seems to have become blurred. Also, as regards linguistic research on historical documents, the earlier approaches have given way to, on the one

[1] Also known as *referential* (see, e.g., Haas 1970: 9–16, Kohrt 1986: 80) or *phonocentric* (Berg 2016, the term ultimately going back to Derrida 1967).

hand, mixed approaches combining some features of the relational and autonomistic perspectives, and, on the other hand, the sociolinguistic (and sociopragmatic) perspectives, where the earlier opposition is mostly irrelevant. Instead, the focus moves to the correlation between patterns of orthographic variation and social identities and practices. This discussion offers an overview of the theoretical approaches to writing systems, and their relation to speech and language. Because the adherents to modern approaches draw upon the opinions expressed by earlier thinkers, I begin my discussion with an overview of the selected, most characteristic comments recorded before the twentieth century.

5.2 Early Views on Speech, Writing and Language

Already in the Classical Antiquity (fifth century BC–fifth century AD), approaches to understanding speech and writing varied to some extent, but all pointed to the close relationship between both notions. However, ancient statements are also interpreted in different ways, depending on particular authors and their points of view. Presumably, the earliest known ancient statement on this subject is the one by Aristotle (fourth century BC), in his work *Peri hermeneias* (better known as *De interpretatione*, in the Latin translation), expounding that spoken sounds are signs of ideas coming from the soul, whereas written marks merely symbolize spoken sounds (Aristotle 1963 [fourth century BC]: 43). This assertion was quoted and discussed in numerous later writings in support of the relational approach to writing, but it may be considered as resulting from incorrect translation. According to Maas (1985, as discussed in Augst 1986: 25–26), Aristotle's opinion on the relationship between speech and writing was actually more complicated than generally assumed, with written marks correlating not with the spoken sounds themselves, but with what is contained in them, that is, the linguistic-grammatical design of the world (*die sprachlich-grammatische Gestaltung der Welt*, Schlieben-Lange 1994: 105).[2]

Quintilian is another frequently cited early authority (first century AD). To him is ascribed the view that "spelling should follow pronunciation because the text is a repository for the *vox*" (Liuzza 1996: 35). However, also in this case, the slightly broader context of his statement shows that his views were not as clear-cut as often presented. The relevant passage from *Institutio oratoria* reads as follows: "Ego (nisi quod consuetude obtinuerit) sic scribendum quidque iudico, quomodo sonat. Hic enim est usus litterarum, ut custodiant voces et velut depositum reddant legentibus, itaque id exprimere debent quod dicturi sumus" (Quintilian 1920: 144), which is translated by Butler (1920: 145)

[2] See also Haas (1970: 10) for other reservations concerning the common translation of Aristotle's words.

as "I think that, within the limits prescribed by usage, words should be spelt as they are pronounced. For the use of letters is to preserve the sound of words and to deliver them to readers as a sacred trust: consequently they ought to represent the pronunciation which we are to use." Thus, in the original passage, Quintilian goes beyond the straightforward dependence of spelling on pronunciation, adding the reservation concerning the usage or custom.

In medieval times, the concept of *littera*, going back to the Stoics, gained appreciation and popularity among scholars. This complex and potentially ambiguous concept was explained in a late-Antiquity Latin grammar by Donatus in the fourth century AD (Keil and Mommsen 2009 [1864]). *Littera*[3] was one entity with three inherent features, including *figura* (the shape of the letter), *potestas* (the way the letter is pronounced) and the *nomen* (the letter's name), so it was "a structural element of language, with two aspects or realizations, one visible and one audible" (Abercrombie 1949: 59). Given the fact that Donatus's grammar was part of the canon of education in the Middle Ages (Haugen 1950: 41), it may be assumed that it had a profound impact on medieval and later grammarians. Indeed, Donatus's claim that "a letter is the smallest part of articulate utterance" (Irvine 2006: 98) as well as the detailed explanation of the concept appear, and are further developed, by Diomedes and Priscian (as discussed in Irvine 2006: 98–99). A few centuries later, it also forms the basis of the theoretical approach to orthography in *The First Grammatical Treatise*, written by an anonymous Icelandic author in the middle of the twelfth century, where he distinguishes among three elements of *stafr* 'letter': *nafn* 'name', *líkneski* 'appearance' and *jartein* 'significance' (Haugen 1950: 40–48).

Continuing the ancient and medieval tradition of *littera*, sixteenth- and seventeenth-century orthoepists, as a rule, used the term *letter* to refer to sounds and letters simultaneously, treating each *littera* as an entity with three attributes. For example, Gil (1619: 11–13) provides a table presenting the *figura*, *nomen* and *potestas* of each letter in English. Smith (1568: 5, my translation) evokes Donatus's statement in "the letter is the smallest part of the articulated voice." The discussions of orthography in contemporary grammars also often contain similar conventional statements asserting that "[l]etters are either vowels, or consonants" (Clement 1587: 11), "letters are vowels, semivowels, and mute consonants" (Smith 1568: 5, my translation), "letters are either vowels or consonants" (Gil 1619: 7, my translation). The lack of clear differentiation between the spoken and the written forms of language, however, often led to unclear and imprecise descriptions and, from the modern point of view, implies confusion on the part of the early phoneticians, for example, in the case of digraphs treated as equivalents of diphthongs, which was evidently problematic for such elements as <ea>.

[3] Spelt *litera* in Abercrombie (1949) and Liuzza (1996).

In general, the main preoccupation of those sixteenth- and seventeenth-century scholars who showed interest in orthography was to advocate bringing spelling as close to pronunciation as possible, with emphasis on the practical rather than theoretical side of the issue. However, a few spelling reformers accompanied their proposals with some theoretical grounding, comprising mainly references to statements made by the ancient and medieval thinkers, especially Quintilian, Priscian and Donatus. They include, apart from Hart (1569), also Smith (1568), Mulcaster (1582), Hume (1617) and Gil (1619), among others. For example, Smith (1568: 5 v) asserts that "[e]st autem scriptura, imitatio sermonis, ut pictura corporis" and Hart (1569: 9 v) comments that "Quintilian would haue the writing to be framed to the speaking." Remarkably, Hart attempts to combine different traditions into one consistent approach, on the one hand drawing on Aristotle's and Quintilian's division between speech and writing, but on the other emphasizing the link between the sound and the letter characteristic of the doctrine of *littera*. The issue can be better understood from the following passage: "[t]he simple voyce is the least part or member of a speech, and the letter wee may wel call a maner of painting of that member for which it is written [...] so the diuers members of the speech ought therfore to haue eche his seuerall [=particular][4] marke" (Hart 1569: 9 r). Also, presumably to justify his own views, he modifies the beginning of Quintilian's statement (discussed above), to "[e]go (non quod consuetudo obtinuerit) sic scribendum quicque iudico quomodo sonat," replacing the conjunction *nisi* ('unless, but') with the adverb *non* ('not, by no means'), and in this way changing the original meaning to (virtually) its opposite, translating the sentence "I doe not allowe that which custome may haue obtained." Interestingly, Mulcaster (1582) engages in a discussion with Hart (not mentioning his name though), taking a firm position against him, explaining that "*Quintilian* speaking of *sound*, saieth expresslie, and in plaine terms, that euerie thing is to be writen, not as the *sound* giues, but as *custom* hath won (which *custom* directeth not *sound*, but the expressing of *sounds*)." And alluding to Hart's trickery: "[t]o win *Quintilian*, naie to wring *Quintilian* to stand for sound against *custom*, by falsifying of euidence & corruption of print [...] argeweth som infirmitie in the alledger" (Mulcaster 1582: 95). In fact, throughout his treatise, Mulcaster recommends a balanced combination of *sound*, *custom* and *reason* when prescribing individual spellings. Similar remarks, postulating that orthography should be based on more than merely sounds, can also be found in Bullokar (1580a) and Gil (1619). For example, Bullokar (1580a: B2 v) argues, if somewhat vaguely, for "such concord of the eye, voyce, and eare, that it will yeelde to the mind a most pleasant harmonie" (see also Chapter 13, this volume).

[4] My interpretation.

Presumably due to the influence of the doctrine of *littera*, sounds and letters were not consistently distinguished throughout the sixteenth and seventeenth centuries. Even though in the eighteenth century *letter* was more often used to refer to writing, confusion continued.[5] Nevertheless, as indicated by McIntosh (1956: 40), the attitude to speech and writing started to change in the seventeenth century, together with the rise of interest in universal language, as the attempts to construct it started with the written form. He points to the innovative views expressed by Wallis, who argues that there is "nothing, in the nature of the Thing it self, why Letters and Characters might not as properly be applied to represent Immediately, as by intervention of Sounds, what our Conceptions are" (Wallis 1670: 1091). To illustrate his opinion, Wallis refers, among others, to numbers and symbols for weights and metals, which denote the same conceptions, though they are pronounced differently in various languages.

In the eighteenth century, new ideas appear also in Douglas (c. 1740) and Sheridan (1762). Douglas, apart from listing a number of rules governing the spelling-to-sound correspondences, also provides some rules linking spelling (although imperfectly) with the morphemic level of language description (Venezky 1970: 22, citing Holmberg 1956). Sheridan (1762: 7), in turn, distinguishes between writing and speech, claiming that "we have in use different kinds of language, which have no sort of affinity between them, but what custom has established; and which are communicated thro' different organs: the one, thro' the eye, by means of written characters; the other, thro' the ear, by means of articulate sounds and tones." Thus, he revives the notion of 'custom' (valued so much by Mulcaster), which can be considered a synonym of 'convention'. He also explains that "to represent ideas [...] might be done without any reference to sound at all" (Sheridan 1762: 250), illustrating his claim with "the language of hieroglyphics" which "was the first kind of written language, or method of communicating ideas by visible marks," whereas later on "the industry of man was set to work to find out a more easy, expeditious, and comprehensive method of communication in writing; and this ended in the invention of letters; which by being made the symbols of articulate sounds, became capable of conveying knowledge" (Sheridan 1762: 251). Thus, according to Sheridan, nonalphabetic writing systems can communicate ideas directly, whereas alphabetic ones express them by the intermediary of sounds.

As discussed in Ruszkiewicz (1976: 12), in the first half of the nineteenth century there was still no clear distinction between letters and sounds. Grimm (1822) divides letters (*Buchstaben*) into vowels (*vocale*) and consonants (*consonanten*), and further describes them as sounds. Later, Rudolf von Raumer (2019 [1870]) points to the necessity of differentiating

[5] See Abercrombie (1949) for an overview, including some earlier examples of modern-like usage, such as Daines (1640).

between sounds and letters, which motivates Grimm's replacement of *letters* with *sounds* in the third edition of his *Deutsche Grammatik*. Among the nineteenth-century scholars preoccupied (not exclusively) with orthography, Venezky (1970: 23–25) singles out Goold Brown and his *Grammar of English Grammars*, pointing to his insightful comments. Brown (1850) goes beyond the assertion that letters represent sounds, arguing that since it is possible to teach those who can neither hear nor speak to write and read, "the powers of the letters are not, of necessity, identified with their sounds" (Brown 1859 [1850]: 15, quoted after Venezky 1970: 23). He also appreciates the links between orthography and other levels of language description, explaining that "words are not mere sounds, and in their *orthography* more is implied than in *phonetics*, or *phonography*. Ideographic forms have, in general, the advantage of preserving the identity, history, and lineage of words" (Brown 1859 [1850]: 203, quoted after Venezky 1970: 24).

5.3 Contemporary Approaches

Because even current views concerning speech and writing, their mutual relationship and their connection with the notion of language are deeply indebted intellectually to the work of numerous earlier authors, the identification of the starting point of what can be considered 'contemporary' is virtually impossible. There is, however, one convenient event which can justify setting that moment at the beginning of the twentieth century. It is the introduction of the term *grapheme* (originally *grafema*) by Baudouin de Courtenay in 1901 (Ruszkiewicz 1976: 25, 31), which, a few decades later, became established as the standard appellation of the unit of writing. As indicated in the chapter introduction, the main division assumed here comprises *relational*, *autonomistic* and *sociolinguistic* perspectives. The first two of these belong to the domain of theoretical linguistics and are often considered as opposite approaches, whereas the last one transcends the boundaries of linguistics to include some pertinent social factors. In each of these approaches, key concepts and terms are defined in different ways.

5.3.1 The Relational Approach

The main characteristic of the relational approach is the conviction that the only purpose of writing is to represent the spoken language. This belief, ascribed already to Aristotle and to Quintilian (but see some controversy discussed in the previous section), reappears in the writings of numerous thinkers and researchers over the centuries. Possibly, the notion of *littera* also contributed to the perceived primacy of speech over writing, as it promotes sound "having 'power'" (Smith 2008: 212). At the beginning of the twentieth (and late nineteenth) century, it can be found in the publications authored by the neogrammarians. For example, Paul (1909: 274, 373, quoted after Ruszkiewicz 1976: 13), claimed that "writing is not language" and that once language has been translated into writing, one must retranslate it in order to study it, but such retranslation can never be perfect, because writing does not preserve the continuity of speech. Also Behaghel (1911: 82, cited in Ruszkiewicz 1976: 13) emphasized that writing records only selective aspects of speech. Similar views did not prevent the comparative philologists Bopp, Rask and Grimm from classifying sounds based on orthographic, not phonetic features (Venezky 1970: 25).

Saussure, himself originally a neogrammarian (Haładewicz-Grzelak 2014) and Indo-European comparative philologist, is likewise of the opinion that writing is not part of language: "[l]anguage and writing are two distinct systems of signs; the second exists for the sole purpose of representing the first. The linguistic object is not both the written and the spoken forms of words; the spoken forms alone constitute the object" (Saussure 2011 [1916]: 23–24). He also complains about the "written image" of "the spoken word" managing "to usurp the main role" even though it "it obscures language" (Saussure 2011 [1916]: 24, 30). The attitudes to writing of the other early structuralists are no different. Sapir (1921: 19) argues that "[t]he written forms are secondary symbols of the spoken ones – symbols of symbols" and, according to Bloomfield (1933: 21), "[w]riting is not language, but merely a way of recording language by means of visible marks." A quarter of a century later, Francis (1958: 36) continues the same discourse: "[w]riting is not language and language is not writing. We have defined language as an arbitrary system of articulated sounds" and "an arbitrary system of written symbols which more or less accurately represents the arbitrary system of sounds."[6]

Even though the structuralists' views on writing are actually not always consistent,[7] the ones just reported have had important consequences on numerous linguists, resulting in the relatively widespread neglect of writing systems as a potential object of study (in its own right) lasting for several decades. Nonetheless, since speech is not always readily available for investigation, orthographic data have been used as one of the main sources of phonological evidence, especially regarding the past, by historical phonologists, even those with a structural penchant. Apart from drawing conclusions from the detailed analyses of whole orthographic systems of individual texts and authors or scribes, also occasional (or naïve) spellings as well as rhymes and puns may prove useful for such purposes. Theoretical discussions on different

[6] It should, however, be admitted that Francis also states that "the English writing system has a structure of its own, which can be studied independently of what the writing stands for" (1958: 437).

[7] See de Beaugrande (2006: 32–35) for examples.

aspects of orthographic data used as phonological evidence are provided in, for example, Penzl (1957), Wrenn (1967) and Liuzza (1996).

The investigations of writing systems from the "symbols of the symbols" perspective have required suitable definitions of the *grapheme*. According to Kohrt (1986: 81–82), "the term 'grapheme' has always been dependent upon the notion of the 'phoneme,'" where the latter "served as a model." Examples such as "any letter or letter cluster which corresponds to a single phoneme" (Coltheart 1984: 69) or "the class of graphs which denote the same phoneme" (Hammarström 1981 [1964]: 97) are rather typical of this approach, with the phoneme, a unit of the phonological system, as the point of reference for the grapheme. Interestingly, also the *Oxford English Dictionary Online* (Simpson and Proffitt 2000–) provides only a typically relational definition: "[t]he class of letters and other visual symbols that represent a phoneme or a cluster of phonemes" ("grapheme, n.").[8] However, as indicated by Henderson (1985), a purely relational approach cannot be easily found among the available publications, as most authors allow for some autonomy in the investigated writing system. She found the only clear case of such an approach in Stockwell and Barritt (1951), who went "so far as to define different spellings as allographic where they represent the same phoneme" (Henderson 1985: 140). In fact, the terms *to represent, to realize* and *to stand for* are often used by linguists with reference to the relation between a grapheme and a phoneme, even if their author is not a determined adherent to a relational approach to speech and writing. Also Bazell's (1956) treatment of the grapheme can be classified as relational, as he sees an analogy between a grapheme and an allomorph on the grounds that allomorphs are identified through a semantic, not distributional procedure, and phonemics should be considered the 'semantics' of graphemics. The relational approach has inspired numerous spelling reformers, since the sixteenth century until the present day, who mostly "viewed writing as a mirror of speech" (Venezky 1970: 31) and advanced proposals for phonemic spelling with each letter corresponding to one sound.[9] This way of thinking has also been sufficiently influential to leave some mark in general use, as echoed in such idioms as "in Wort und Schrift" and "par la parole et la plume" (Augst 1986: 26).

5.3.2 The Autonomistic Approach

The term *autonomistic approach* refers to a set of relatively recent views, not really to one homogeneous and consistent perspective. What they have in common is the awareness that the functions of writing systems go beyond simply representing pronunciation, though the relation to the phonological

[8] This entry has not yet been fully updated (first published 1972).

[9] See Carney (1994: 467–88) for an overview of the efforts aiming at a spelling reform in English.

level of language is not denied. The roots of this perspective are not as old as those of the relational one, but it goes back at least to the sixteenth century, as discussed above, and fully develops in the twentieth century. In this section, the most influential views are discussed, giving due prominence to a few authors, in a roughly chronological order. Such a frame of reference shows the development of, as well as the interrelations between, the concepts important for the investigation and description of writing systems.

As briefly mentioned above (Section 5.3), the linguist who first laid firm theoretical foundations under the autonomistic approach to writing systems was Baudouin de Courtenay. While other contemporary linguists still found the differentiation between sounds and letters somewhat problematic (see Subsection 5.3.1), he had been persistently engaged in investigating the properties of the written language and its association with spoken language for decades, since the 1860s.[10] In contrast to the advocates of the purely relational perspective, to de Courtenay, language does not equal speech. Instead, he treats language as an entirely mental phenomenon which exists in individual minds. He views a national language as a generalizing construct comprising a series of "individual languages" (Ruszkiewicz 1976: 30). This understanding of the concept of language seems quite close to recent definitions such as "a complex system residing in our brain which allows us to produce and interpret utterances" (Rogers 2005: 2), though it does not include the idea of a system (this one seems to have been introduced by Saussure). Baudouin's various research interests include attempts at outlining the principles of orthography, finally arriving at three main ones: etymological (corresponding to what we would rather understand as morphemic today), phonetic and historical (Ruszkiewicz 1976: 27). The several definitions of *grapheme* in his writings can be reduced to two main ones: (1) "a grapheme is the mental representation of a letter" and (2) "graphemes are the simplest elements of written-visual language" (Ruszkiewicz 1976: 32). Nonetheless, this partly psychological, partly linguistic-autonomistic treatment of the unit of the writing system does not mean that de Courtenay was not aware of the correspondences between phonemes and graphemes, as he devoted a substantial part of his research to investigating and describing such relations.

In the first half of the twentieth century, several scholars offer their insightful comments concerning various aspects of the autonomy of written language, likely to have inspired later authors. To begin with, Bradley remarks that "graphic differentiation of homophones does, so far as it goes, render written English a better instrument of expression than spoken English" and that the common practice of silent reading has largely made of written language

[10] See Ruszkiewicz (1976: 24–49) for a concise overview of Baudouin's contribution to the theory of graphemics, as well as Adamska-Sałaciak (1996: 61–129) and Mugdan (1984) for more comprehensive treatments of his theoretical and empiricist linguistic output.

"an instrument for the direct expression of meaning, co-ordinate with audible language," which has resulted in the development of written language "independent of the development of oral speech" (1919 [1913]: 13–15). Stetson (1937: 353) affirms that "[m]uch is written that is not pronounced" and that "[t]he unit of writing may be called the grapheme." According to Edgerton (1941: 149), "the received view, which restricts the function of writing to the recording and transmission of language, is erroneous";[11] he adds that "[w]riting consists in the conventional use of visible symbols for the recording or transmission of ideas, or of ideas and sounds (as in most poetry and much prose), or of sounds unaccompanied by ideas (as in phonetic recording of uncomprehended speech, and perhaps in some nonsense writing)."

Uldall argues that neither speech nor writing is language as such, but each is the substance through which language is manifested, whereas "the something, that which is common to sounds and letters alike [i.e. language], is a form [...] independent of the particular substance in which it is manifested" (1944: 11, quoted after McLaughlin 1963: 21); both manifestations, speech and writing, without primacy of one over the other, coexist as "mutually incongruent" systems "which can express the same language," which "is possible because the orthographic units and the units of pronunciation are functions of the same units of context" (McLaughlin 1963: 21–22). Wrenn (1967 [1943]: 147) points to the fact that "our [English] orthography is symbolic and ideographic rather than phonetic." Bolinger (1946: 333), from the perspective of behaviorist psychology and on the basis of empirical experiments (e.g. concerning homonyms), asserts the existence of "visual morphemes" whose recognition has been impeded by the treatment of writing and "the visual side of language" as secondary to spoken language, emphasizing that "[a]ll that behaviorism requires is that language be viewed as having an anatomical basis," which is not limited to "laryngeal processes" connected with speech.

Among the linguists who have contributed the most to the development of the theory of writing over several decades is Vachek (within his activity in the Prague School of Linguistics). In 1939, he proposes the concept of a universal language norm (equivalent to Saussure's *langue*), comprising a *spoken norm* and a *written norm*[12] (Vachek 1976 [1939]: 115). He admits that the written norm "developed historically from a kind of quasi-transcription" which originally could be treated as a sign of the second order (a sign of a sign), representing speech, but soon "became a primary one, i.e. written signs began to be bound directly to the content" and is now "a more or less autonomous system" and "a system in its own right" (Vachek 1976 [1945–49]: 130–32). In Vachek's theory, the concept of *orthography* is distinguished from the *written*

[11] In the context of Edgerton's paper as well as the currency of the early structural views, one may assume that "language" in this quotation refers to "speech."

[12] Vachek uses these terms interchangeably with *spoken language* and *written language*, respectively.

norm (presumably a more general notion) and is defined as "a kind of bridge leading from spoken sentences to their written counterparts," whereas pronunciation would lead in the opposite direction (1976 [1945–49]: 128). As regards the *grapheme*, Vachek points to the analogy between this unit of the written system and the *phoneme*, where the latter is "a member of a complex phonemic opposition [...] indivisible into smaller successive phonemic units" and the former "a member of a complex "graphemic" opposition [...] indivisible into smaller successive graphemic units" (1976 [1945–49]: 128).

The definition of the *grapheme* as well as the analogy between the *grapheme* and the *phoneme* are the topics undertaken in the 1950s and 1960s by several authors. Stockwell and Barritt (1951) define allographs in purely relational terms (see Subsection 5.3.1), but, surprisingly, provide a definition of the grapheme which could be acceptable for autonomists, arguing that "[t]wo symbols may be stated to be members of one grapheme if they are in complementary distribution or in free variation with each other [...], or both" (Stockwell and Barritt 1951: 8). They also point to the analogy between graph, grapheme and allograph on the one hand, and phone, phoneme and allophone on the other. Pulgram (1951) takes the issue further, pointing to the parallelism between graphemics and phonemics, comprising nine analogies between phonemes and graphemes. For example, he calls graphemes "[t]he smallest distinctive visual units of an alphabet," by analogy to phonemes, which are "[t]he smallest distinctive audible units of a dialect," a graph is "[t]he hic et nunc written realization of a grapheme," whereas a phone is "[t]he hic et nunc written realization of a phoneme," and "all graphs identifiable as members of one grapheme are its allographs" like "all phones identifiable as members of one phoneme are its allophones" (Pulgram 1951: 15). The complementary distribution of allographs and the "significant contrast" between graphemes are, likewise, foregrounded by McLaughlin (1963: 29).

McIntosh (1956) emphasizes the need to recognize the written language as a valid object of linguistic study in its own right, independent of the spoken language. Throughout his paper, McIntosh refers to the *systemic correlation* between them, but admits that both mediums are not fully overlapping and this correlation is not a one-to-one relationship: "written texts [...] manifest [...] distinctions which are in no sense a reflection of, or correlated with, anything in the spoken language" (McIntosh 1956: 33). Simultaneously he stresses that both the written and spoken systems "may be regarded as standing in some sort of filial relation to 'the language system'" (McIntosh 1956: 45), and as such are equivalent and equal at the level of importance and expected rigor of their respective linguistic analyses. However, special techniques and terminology are needed for the analysis and description of written language, that is what he calls "graphematic analysis," with due attention paid to the particular characteristics of this medium (McIntosh 1956: 52). Such analysis involves the examination of features which used to be considered irrelevant (e.g. punctuation, abbreviations, capitals, spaces between words) for determining the characteristics of the system (McIntosh 1956: 53). To facilitate this, closer co-operation is postulated between paleographers and historical linguists at the theoretical and methodological level (McIntosh 1956: 49). At the same time as McIntosh, Crossland, inspired by the suggestions about the need for the terminology to be used in the analysis of written language, expresses very similar ideas, claiming that "'[l]inguistics' should include the study of written languages as well as spoken; the former study can and should be as scientific as the latter, and needs its own terminology which would be basically independent of that of the study of spoken languages" (Crossland 1956: 8). He himself proposes such an analysis, referred to as 'graphic linguistics', to be conducted at the level of graphs, 'graph-classes' or 'sign-classes', and graphemes.

5.3.3 Further Debate and the Emergence of Combined Perspectives

The debate between the relational and autonomistic approaches continues in the second half of the twentieth century. The purely relational approach of early structuralists, stressing the overwhelming dependence of writing on spoken language and treating it virtually as imperfect phonemic transcription, does not find numerous adherents at that time. In fact, most (though not all) authors discussing writing systems are ready to accord them a certain degree of autonomy, but some influences exerted by the followers of the relational perspective can also be noticed in the available publications. Thus, a trend toward synergy between different approaches can be noticed over time.

The calls for specific terminology for studying written language made, apart from McIntosh (1956), also by Uldall (1944), Vachek (1945–49), Abercrombie (1949), Pulgram (1951) and Crossland (1956) evoke a number of responses. For instance, Hall recommends introducing "a comprehensive, unified theory of graphemics," which would "prove instructive in its resemblances to phonemic theory and also in its difference therefrom [...] clarifying the relationships between speech and writing" (Hall 1960: 13). His approach should definitely be regarded as relational, as he considers "[p]honemic representation" to be the main function of alphabetic writing, and his division of the main unit of the writing system into two types, single and compound graphemes (an example of the latter would be <ai>, pronounced /ɛ/, as in French *faire*), is closely dependent on their 'representation' of phonemes. Nonetheless, he departs somewhat from the typical phonocentric views, recognizing the existence of the relations between the writing system and the other levels of language, explaining that "[g]raphemes normally symbolize phonemes, morphophonemic alternations, or morphemes" (Hall 1960: 15). Hall acknowledges other uses, including the etymological, arbitrary (e.g. pseudo-etymological, as in *author*) and semantic (e.g. the graphic difference between the psychological term *phantasy* and the literary term *fantasy*) (Hall 1960: 16–17). He also notices the similarity of hierarchical relation between allographs and the grapheme to the one between allophones and the phoneme, and suggests that allographs occur in complementary distribution (Hall 1960: 14).

Inspired by Bazell (1956), McIntosh (1961: 108) explains that "written language and spoken language *both* symbolize mental experience but [...] written language, by virtue of its graphological system, *also* symbolizes spoken language." He calls the latter "phonic meaning" and argues that it is needed for interpreting "visual graphic material" when reading aloud (McIntosh 1961: 111). McLaughlin (1963) takes the autonomistic side, rejecting Hall's (1960) term "compound graphemes" as useless in the graphemic analysis. However, he admits that Hall's idea can be applied to a different, graphonemic level of analysis, and replaces the term with 'complex graphonemes'. In his approach, 'allographones' of the same 'graphoneme' correspond to a phoneme. He also proposes a set of other terms including, for example, a 'morphograph', an 'allomorphograph', a 'morphographeme' and an 'archigrapheme'. McLaughlin applies them to the analysis of a selected medieval manuscript (London, British Library, Cotton MS Nero A X), so his discussion is not only theoretical, but also related to empirical research. Apparently, his recognition of the autonomous nature of the writing system does not preclude using written data as evidence for a specific phonemic system. However, presumably on the basis of the latter, he warns that the description of the written system "must be particular rather than universal" (McLaughlin 1963: 37) and that "[n]o general theory of relationships between written and spoken expressions of a language is possible" (McLaughlin 1963: 28). Moreover, he argues that "[t]he relationships which exist between the spoken and written systems of various languages appear to demonstrate no observable uniformity from language to language" (McLaughlin 1963: 31).

In the 1960s, orthography attracts the interest of generativists.[13] On the basis of their analysis of the vowel alternations recorded in pairs of etymologically related words such as *divine* vs. *divinity*, *compare* vs. *comparative*, *serene* vs. *serenity*, Chomsky and Halle (1968: 184) state that "conventional orthography is [...] a near optimal system for the lexical representation of English words," because it tends to represent the *underlying form* (corresponding to historical pronunciation) of a particular morpheme or lexical item. Adopting the same perspective, Carol Chomsky (1970) later argues that "[l]exical spellings represent the meaning-bearing items directly, without introducing phonetic detail irrelevant to their identification" (1970: 294), as specific phonetic

[13] The generative approach to English orthography is still live. Among recent works inspired by generative theories (mainly the Optimality Theory, developed in the 1990s) are, for example, Rollings (2004), Ryan (2017) and Evertz (2018).

realizations are predictable by general rule and thus not indicated by spelling (Carol Chomsky 1970: 291, 293). A major contribution to the theory of writing and its relation to speech (recognized as such already by Vachek 1976 [1972]: 138) is Haas (1970). The main import of this publication is the claim that the relation between writing and speech is a symmetrical one and consists in *correspondence*, not *reference*. He explains in detail the operation regularly performed whenever one writes down what is spoken or reads what is written, which he calls *translation*, claiming that it bears close resemblance to translation between different languages (Haas 1970: 12, 15–16). In this theoretical model, writing *translates* into speech (and vice versa), whereas each *refers* directly to *things*, that is, extralingual reality (Haas 1970: 16–17). Opposing Hall (1961) and, to some extent, McIntosh (1961), he considers writing and speech to be two independent mediums (see also Hjelmslev 1961 and Uldall 1944; compare Vachek's norms). A written text conveys meaning directly and does not need mediation by speech to be understood, each serving a different purpose; also, "[t]he biological and historical precedence of speech is no *logical* priority" (Haas 1970: 12). Haas argues that *phonographic divergence* (i.e. the deviation of orthography from the one-to-one correspondence between graphemes and phonemes) is not a flaw in view of the overall efficiency of the writing system, which signals also, among others, lexical and grammatical information (Haas 1970: 3–4).

In the seventies and eighties, Vachek continues explaining and elaborating his earlier ideas, referring to the spoken norm as unmarked and the written norm as marked (Vachek 1976 [1972]: 136). The written norm emerges "when social relations of the members of the community have become so complex and the cultural level of that community has risen so high that functional need for its emergence becomes urgently felt" (Vachek 1976 [1972]: 139). That norm "caters for higher, that is more specialized, cultural and civilizational needs of the language community than its spoken counterpart [...] resorted to both by literature and by research work, as well as by state administration" (Vachek 1976 [1972]: 135). He still treats the written norm as "a relatively autonomous language system" and "a system in its own right" (Vachek 1976 [1972]: 137, see also 1976 [1945–49]: 130–32), but stresses the mutual (functional) complementarity of the spoken and written language (1976 [1972]: 134–35, 138), offering a psychological explanation: "the written utterances enable the language user to react to a given piece of extralingual reality in a documentary and easily surveyable manner, whereas the spoken utterances serve the purpose of reacting to the same piece of extralingual reality in a manner that can be characterized as ready and immediate" (Vachek 1976 [1972]: 135). Vachek ([1976 [1972]: 134, 139–43) emphasizes that the functional differentiation has been overlooked by some scholars who refuse to recognize the status of the written language, like Jakobson (1962) and Hockett (1958).

In the eighties, there appear new voices in the debate on the relation between speech and writing, as well as on the criteria according to which orthographic systems can or should be analyzed. According to Augst (1986: 26), both the spoken and written modes "are in a state of relative dependence and autonomy" and his aim is to determine the exact nature of this relation. He suggests a comprehensive approach via the application of "a trilateral sign" where "[b]oth grapheme schema and phoneme schema access meaning directly, but they activate each other holistically without intervening phoneme-grapheme correspondences" (Augst 1986: 37). The proposed sign takes the form of a triangle with 'meaning', 'the phoneme schema' and the 'grapheme schema' as its vertices. However, the system can only work properly following "morphemic parsing," that is "a segmentation into morphemes allowing the search for grapheme schemata and/or morphographemic rules and the working of phonemic-graphemic correspondences" (Augst 1986: 32). He also proposes a potential explanation for "why later generations so tenaciously conserve traditional spelling patterns," connecting this situation with the way the brain works, with larger areas of the neocortex processing visual information than those processing acoustic information (Augst 1986: 33–34). In the same volume, Catach (1986: 1–2) argues that a writing system is a kind of semiological system, with close links to the spoken language, but also with its own functions and attributes to be studied as such. The key characteristic of this system is "its extreme plasticity, due to the profusion of graphic means compared with the relative limitation of the phonic capacities of man. It stands between the language of phonemes and the language of images, and draws advantage from both" (Catach 1986: 1).

Another relevant voice in the debate is that of Sgall (1987), who offers several insightful comments concerning the description of graphemic systems. For example, he refers to the parallelism between graphemes and phonemes as prototypical for alphabetic systems, the links with the other levels of description remaining closer to the periphery (Sgall 1987: 2–5). The reason is that "when the written form does not correspond to phonemics" it corresponds to other levels of structure, including morphophonemics (e.g. {-s}, {-ed}), morphemics (e.g. in "lexical morphemes" *right* ~ *write*), syntax and semantics (e.g. in punctuation) (Sgall 1987: 5). In his contribution, Sgall (1987: 8–9) also offers a set of complex terminology, including, for instance, "protographemes," "subgraphemes" and "epigraphemes," which has not been generally accepted in later research. This may be considered one of the (admittedly numerous) cases of unnecessarily "blowing up the terminological vocabulary" deplored by Kohrt (1986: 91) as one of the problems contributing to "further irritations in the field of the investigation of written language."

By the end of the eighties, the dispute between the adherents to the relational and autonomistic perspectives had practically died out. Apparently, enough evidence had been gathered and discussed by various researchers by then to prove that orthographies are complex systems endowed with various functions, not solely with signaling pronunciation. In fact, mentions of the previous heated debate become rare in the English-centered research tradition.[14] This does not mean that the interest in the structure and functions of writing systems has ceased. On the contrary, new approaches have appeared over time. Moreover, whereas the earlier discussions on the relationship between writing and speech overviewed above are almost exclusively theoretical and use largely anecdotal evidence, in the seventies there starts a new trend of combining theory with methodological innovation. The combination has resulted in comprehensive synchronic descriptions of the spelling system enabled by technological advancement thanks to the availability of sophisticated statistical methods and of corpora that can serve as the basis for comprehensive studies. Such publications start with Venezky (1970). Other important studies include, for example, Carney (1994) and Rollings (2004). The eighties also saw the rise of interest in the sociolinguistic aspects of writing and of orthographic systems. Intriguingly, since the eighties, one can also observe a division of interests in orthographic research following the German-centered and the English-centered paths. The two routes have few, if any, mutual influences, the former developing the theoretical approaches and the latter moving in the direction of empirical research inspired by sociolinguistics.[15] The sociolinguistic, English-centered path is discussed further below.

5.3.4 The Sociolinguistic Approach

Among the current approaches to orthography, the sociolinguistic perspective has enjoyed ever-growing interest among researchers over the last two decades. As reported by Stubbs (1980: 16), in the seventies (and earlier), sociolinguists were not attracted to studying writing, written language and literacy within the frameworks of their scientific discipline (presumably due to the enduring structuralist influence).[16] However, individual scholars do recognize the correlation of social and cultural factors with both the functions and the development of orthographic systems. It is evident, for instance, in Vachek's discussions of two norms, spoken and written, and their respective functions (see Section 5.3.3). Another example is Haas (1970: 4), who states that "the capacity of orthography for signalling lexical and grammatical values" can extend "its social and cultural use." So far, individual orthographic systems and usages have been approached by sociolinguists from two main

[14] Such references can nevertheless be found in, for example, Berg (2016), Berg and Aronoff (2017).

[15] See Chapter 6, this volume, for a detailed discussion of the recent theoretical proposals in the German-centered publications.

[16] Stubbs mentions Labov (1972b) as an exception.

perspectives, synchronic and diachronic, and within these, both macrosociolinguistic and microsociolinguistic studies can be identified (these perspectives can also be combined).[17] In this section, I focus primarily on the theoretical aspects of the sociolinguistic approach to (alphabetic) writing systems, mainly the English one (as it was the first to be studied within the sociolinguistic framework and studies published on it so far are relatively numerous),[18] referring to several studies as examples, with emphasis on the diachronic approach.

The beginnings of what we can call a sociolinguistic approach to writing and to orthography in particular are not clear-cut. On the one hand, it could be argued that Scragg's (1974) long essay on the history of English spelling marks such a start, as the author considers a number of social factors influencing the development of spelling practices in English, for example, historical and political events (most conspicuously the Norman Conquest of AD 1066), cultural phenomena (like the Renaissance, especially 1500–1700), and technological advances (emphasizing the introduction of the printing press in England in 1476). Scragg's work, on the other hand, was published before the recognized birth of historical sociolinguistics,[19] which is placed in the 1980s, starting from Romaine's (1982) study. Another candidate for a pioneer could be Stubbs (1980: 17), who discusses a variety of social aspects concerning writing and connected with its social priority over spoken language, as well as different functions of writing systems (e.g. administrative, intellectual), depending on a particular community and time, referring to a number of languages and societies. He provides, among others, a list of criteria which must be met by writing systems, including linguistic, psycholinguistic, educational, sociolinguistic, cultural and technological criteria. He announces his contribution to be a development of Vachek's (1973) *functional* approach (using his concept of *functional complementariness* of written and spoken language), combined with Basso's (1974) ethnographic view. Nevertheless, the approach taken by Stubbs could be referred to as predominantly synchronic and macrosociolinguistic.

Investigating the social aspects of written language, rather than individual and group variation, is also characteristic of other (largely) synchronic studies regarding writing systems, for example, Halliday (1985),[20] Coulmas

[17] *Macrosociolinguistics*, also referred to as *sociology of language*, denotes the study of language within society; phenomena typically investigated from this perspective include language shift and language death, diglossia and diaglossia, and language policies. In contrast, *microsociolinguistics* (especially *variationist sociolinguistics*) is concerned with individual and group variation (Millar 2012: 1).

[18] See Chapter 26, Chapter 27, Chapter 28, Chapter 29 and Chapter 30 for discussions of further sociolinguistic studies concerning the writing systems of English and other languages.

[19] See, for example, Nevalainen and Raumolin-Brunberg 2012, Nevalainen 2015, Auer et al. 2015: 1–12 and Russi 2016: 1–8, for an introduction to historical sociolinguistics.

[20] In this book, Halliday discusses both spoken and written language; he also devotes much attention to the general typology and development of writing systems, not only alphabetic ones.

(1989), Harris (1995) and Rogers (2005). Apart from Scragg (1974), none of these monographs focuses specifically on orthography and its diachronic aspects, but they are concerned more generally with types and functions of writing systems, literacy, the relationship between speech and writing, as well as spoken and written norms. Nevertheless, several society-related synchronic aspects of orthography have attracted the attention of scholars, for example, Jaffe (2000b), Sebba (2007), Jaffe et al. (2012) and Tagg et al. (2012). These aspects include, most importantly, language ideologies (e.g. nation-building) and indexicality, that is the potential of standard and nonstandard spelling as well as of orthographic variation to carry meanings and take on individual and group identities.

The authors of diachronic studies concerned specifically with orthographic systems rarely use the term *macrosociolinguistic* when discussing the approach that they adopt, but the influence of social and generally extralinguistic factors on the development of orthographies is discussed in dedicated chapters of language histories, for example Salmon (1999) and Venezky (2001) in the *Cambridge History of the English Language*. However, over the last decade, there have appeared publications concerned primarily with macrosociolinguistic aspects of orthography, such as the pioneering volume edited by Baddeley and Voeste (2012b), which enables a comparison of the impact of such important extralinguistic phenomena as the Renaissance, the Reformation and the introduction of printing technology on the standardization of national orthographic systems of several European languages (Spanish, Italian, French, English, German, Swedish, Polish, Czech, Croatian, Hungarian and Finnish). Another important volume in the area is the special issue of *Written Language and Literacy*, edited by Villa and Vosters (2015b), covering the sociopolitical and ideological aspects of orthographic debates in a number of languages (Dutch, German, Lithuanian, Macedonian, Portuguese and Spanish) from early modern until the present times. A mostly macrosociolinguistic and cross-linguistic approach is also taken in Rutten et al. (2014), a volume not concerned solely with orthography, but devoting much attention to the emergence of orthographic norms, compared to everyday usage, in Dutch, English, French and German.

Both the synchronic and diachronic dimensions of the macrosociolinguistic perspective are combined in the seminal book by Milroy and Milroy (2012 [1985a]). Their main focus is not orthography as such, but since they are mostly preoccupied with attitudes toward language, particularly prescription and consciousness of norms (language ideology), their focus naturally falls on the emergence of the linguistic norm, best visible in the standardization of the writing system,[21] and especially the spelling system, as – in contrast to

[21] Milroy and Milroy (2012: 51) perceive "the writing system" as a more general term than "the spelling system," as the former comprises "conventions of spelling, grammar and word-choice."

pronunciation – it tolerates virtually no variation (Milroy and Milroy 2012: 18, 25, 56). Among their most widely recognized theoretical contributions is the elaboration of Haugen's (1966c) model of standardization, which comprises *selection* of norm, *codification* of form, *elaboration* of function and *acceptance* by the community. Milroy and Milroy (2012: 22–23) add three more stages to what they prefer to call the *implementation* of the standard, that is, firstly, the geographic and social *diffusion* of the variety accepted by influential members of the speech community (e.g. by means of the circulation of official documents); secondly, the *maintenance* of the standard variety once it has become well established; and thirdly, *prescription* of the already codified standard (e.g. in dictionaries and grammars). Both Haugen's and Milroy and Milroy's models form the theoretical basis of numerous studies on various aspects of standardization, most conspicuously the standardization of orthography (see Rutkowska and Rössler 2012 for an overview of studies exploring various aspects of orthographic standardization in English, and Chapter 13, this volume, for further discussion on standardization).

Most diachronic sociolinguistic studies on orthography are *microsociolinguistic* corpus-based studies, focusing on individual and group variation in specific languages. In contrast to Saussure and other early structuralists, who believed that only the system of the language (corresponding to *langue*) carried meaning, whereas the omnipresent variation (*parole*) was meaningless, microsociolinguists argue (and have provided ample evidence for it) that a plethora of meanings can be associated with individual variants. In their interest in variation and departure from structuralism, microsociolinguists, despite many other differences, agree with dialectologists (Chambers and Trudgill 1998: 127, Millar 2012: 3–4). As discussed in detail in Rutkowska and Rössler (2012: 216–19), *orthographic variants* can be divided into several types, including diachronic, diatopic, diaphasic, diastratic, diasituative and aesthetic ones. *Diachronic* variants cover coexisting older and more recent forms (most characteristically spellings), for example *mediaeval* and *medieval*. *Diatopic* ones refer to forms used in different places (dialects, varieties), for example *colour* in British English and *color* in American English. Variants can also be *diaphasic*, different in earlier phases in life (such as childhood, during the process of writing acquisition) and in adult life, for example *hunny* and *honey*. In turn, *diastratic* variants are those used by people of varying social and educational backgrounds; there are no set examples to point to here, but the spellings of well-educated people would be generally expected to conform more closely to the standard orthography (accepted norm) in a given language. *Diasituative* variants appear in different situations or contexts, for example, in British English, *program* is used only with reference to information technology, and *programme* elsewhere. Finally, *aesthetic* variants are forms deliberately diverging from the standard for various purposes, often commercial or literary. Nonstandard spellings are used, among others, to draw attention, provide entertainment or imitate the pronunciation of a group of people (e.g. one associated with a region). An example of an aesthetic variant can be *Bar-B-Quesday*, advertising barbeque sandwiches served at a university bar on Tuesdays (Jaffe 2000b: 497); like numerous other such creative spellings, it has a compound nature (i.e. it does not have a one-element equivalent in standard orthography).

An important abstract notion in variationist sociolinguistics, to some extent shared with dialectology, and helpful in identifying, discussing and explaining variation, is that of a *variable*, which can be either linguistic or extralinguistic. A linguistic variable can be defined as "a linguistic unit with two or more variants involved in covariation with other social and/or linguistic variables" (Chambers and Trudgill 1998: 50). Apart from phonological, grammatical, lexical-semantic and pragmatic variables (see Hebda 2012, Auer and Voeste 2012, Grzega 2012, Jucker and Taavitsainen 2012), one can distinguish also orthographic variables. An orthographic variable can be defined as "a feature of an orthographic system of a given language, related to the phonological, morphological, or lexical levels of that language system, and realized by different variants under specific extra-linguistic circumstances" (Rutkowska and Rössler 2012: 219–20). The extralinguistic variables that can be correlated with the orthographic variables include, most characteristically, the region and time of production, demographics (sex/gender, age, rank), text type and genre (and the audience targeted), register and medium (handwritten or printed).

The remaining part of the present section is devoted to illustrating the main trends followed in the studies on historical orthographic variation over the last decade.[22] The authors of recent studies are usually explicit about their approach, and specify the theoretical framework within which their studies can be placed. The most popular analytical constructs employed include *social networks* (see Milroy 2002 and Conde-Silvestre 2012 for theoretical introduction) and *communities of practice* (see Meyerhoff 2002, Jucker and Kopaczyk 2013). The data for microsociolinguistic studies usually comprise corpora of various sizes, typically collections of either private, handwritten correspondence or printed documents. Occasionally, both kinds of documents are compared. The micro perspective is at times combined with the macro perspective, which usually involves standardization as the most conspicuous macro phenomenon.

Over the last decade, some authors have continued the trend established by the Milroys in the 1980s, studying orthographic variation through the lens of the *social network* concept introduced during the 'second wave' of microsociolinguistics (Millar 2012: 7–8). Examples include the studies investigating diaphasic variation during the individuals' lifespans (communal change),

[22] See Rutkowska and Rössler (2012) for an overview of earlier publications.

based on personal correspondence, for instance, Sairio (2010) and Conde-Silvestre and Hernández-Campoy (2013). In other studies, a generational change is revealed, with the proportions of the innovative variant increasing by generation (e.g. Hernández-Campoy et al. 2019). A rather atypical use of the concept of the term *social network* is made by Berg and Aronoff (2017: 37–38), who claim that the English spelling system "gradually became more consistent over a period of several hundred years, starting before the advent of printers, orthoepists or dictionary makers, presumably through the simple interaction of the members of the community of spellers, a sort of self-organizing social network."[23] The authors also argue that the English spelling system signals morphological information and avoids homography of suffixes and final parts of words homophonous with them. As Berg and Aronoff emphasize, this morphology-related information is encoded specifically in spelling, with no equivalent in phonology. Such conclusions are in line with the views of the autonomists, sketched out in Subsection 5.3.2.

Researching individual (idiolectal) diaphasic spelling variation in correlation with social variables (education and age) is another, well-established trend in sociohistorical studies, with special interest in women's writing. It is represented by Evans (2013),[24] who combines micro- and macro-level approaches, as the idiolectal features are explored against the macro background of general contemporary usage. Gender is also in focus in Hernández-Campoy's (2016b) study on orthographic (and grammatical) variation in personal letters, together with authorship, literacy, representativeness and empirical validity.[25] The analysis reveals that whereas the usage of particular variants of grammatical variables does not seem affected by the scribe's intervention, the orthographic variants reflect the scribe's spelling system, rather than the author's, and thus letters written by different scribes display divergent proportions of the orthographic variants. In turn, Grund et al. (2021) show that research into individual spelling variation does not have to study only personal letters, basing their research on court documents from the witch trials in Salem, MA, in 1692–93 (Rosenthal et al. 2009), in the emerging variety of American English.

The contributions in the pioneering volume edited by Kopaczyk and Jucker (2013) are the first to employ the analytical construct of the *community of practice* (often abbreviated CoP) to the study of the past. The concept itself, borrowed by Eckert (2000) from Wenger (1998) to explain specific patterns of group-centered linguistic variation among youngsters in Detroit, is associated

[23] Berg and Aronoff's proposal has been received as rather controversial; see the ensuing discussion in Sampson (2018a) and Berg and Aronoff (2018).

[24] This discussion focuses only on orthography, but note that Evans (2013) investigates also grammatical (morphological and syntactic) variables.

[25] Most of these aspects are listed among the key theoretical and methodological problems with which historical sociolinguistics has to contend (Hernández-Campoy and Schilling 2012).

with the "third wave" of microsociolinguistics (Millar 2012: 8–9). Four papers in Kopaczyk and Jucker are concerned predominantly with orthographic practices of CoPs involving texts of medieval scribes (Rogos 2013), authors of eighteenth-century private correspondence (Sairio 2013), and early modern printers (Tyrkkö 2013, Rutkowska 2013b).[26]

A recent publication referring to the practices of printers' community is Condorelli (2021a), a large-scale quantitative study (with an extensive qualitative commentary) investigating orthographic regularization and standardization[27] (see also Chapter 13, this volume) on the basis of the huge *Early English Books Online* (EEBO) database, in which the author's discussion combines variationist, pragmatic and macrosociolinguistic approaches. Kaislaniemi et al. (2017) is likewise a macro-level quantitative study, with elements of the micro-level approach. The authors manage to discover long-term tendencies in English epistolary spelling from the fifteenth to the eighteenth century, on the basis of the *Corpus of Early English Correspondence* (CEEC, Nevalainen et al. 1993–98) as well as four smaller collections of handwritten documents, revealing important changes over time: whereas idiolectal variation dominates in the fifteenth and sixteenth century, the seventeenth century witnesses generational change, and in the eighteenth century, clear standardization trends can be identified, with nonstandard spellings decreasing considerably.

Sociolinguistic investigation of historical orthographic variation spanning over a century is also possible with a close-up of various versions of a single text, as offered in Rutkowska (2013a), a longitudinal corpus-based analysis of over 30 orthographic variables in 13 editions of an almanac entitled *The Kalender of Shepherdes*, published between 1506 and 1656. The variables belong to six criteria, namely grapheme distribution, the graphemic realization of lexemes in the full and abbreviated forms, vowel length indication, the level of homography, morphological spelling, and etymological spelling, the last four listed by Salmon (1999: 21) as essential in describing the process of spelling regularization. The detailed comparative analysis of the trends of orthographic variation in this study indicates that, contrary to the generally accepted assumptions (e.g. Blake 1965, Brengelman 1980), early sixteenth-century printers (before relevant normative writings were available) were already regularizing their spelling practice.

Among the most recent innovations in the research on orthographic variation is the attempt at a transhistorical approach taken in Evans and Tagg (2020),[28] who employ the theoretical approach usually taken for analyzing orthographic variation in digital media, to investigate intra- and inter-speaker

[26] See also Chapter 23, this volume.

[27] See also Condorelli (2020b), for detailed considerations of the innovative aspects of his methodology.

[28] See also Tagg and Evans (2020), for a transhistorical pragmatic approach, comparing the sixteenth-century writers' spelling with present-day SMS spelling.

variation and identify points of continuity and difference in the usage of selected sixteenth-century high-rank female writers. A quantitative comparison of individual variation with the macro-level norms in contemporary correspondence (PCEEC, Nevalainen et al. 2006) and in printed documents (EEBO N-gram Browser) reveals a high level of idiosyncrasy among the writers, with some elements of influence from local network practices. Evans and Tagg propose a reformulation of Sebba's (2007) concept of the *zone of social meaning*, used to interpret the socially significant differences from a binding orthographic norm in modern languages, to the notion of flexible "localised zones of social meaning" (Evans and Tagg 2020: 217) as better suited to the analyzed situation where local-level influences are the norm and idiosyncratic variants can be considered "epistolary identity markers."

5.4 Conclusion

The present chapter has overviewed some of the main theoretical approaches to researching orthographic variation. It has started from the ancient views on the role of writing in order to explain the roots of contemporary perspectives on orthographic systems and on orthographic variation. Subsequently, a substantial part of the discussion has been devoted to the debate between the relational and the autonomistic approaches that spanned several decades of the twentieth century, transforming over time into general awareness of the complexity of the relationships between orthography and the other language levels, and eventually leaving room for the approaches taking into account a variety of extralinguistic factors, of which the sociolinguistic approach has been so far the most popular. The aim of this survey, nonetheless, has not been to provide an exhaustive list of available approaches and studies (which would be impossible owing to their abundance), but rather to point to some key directions taken so far by the scholars interested in the field. Considering the main topic of this *Handbook*, special emphasis has been placed on the studies concerned with the diachronic dimension of orthographic variation (with due attention paid to the micro- and macrosociolinguistic perspectives), and so current research in applied and cognitive linguistics has not been covered here. Also, it should be made clear that new, transdisciplinary approaches to historical orthography are currently emerging, for example, sociopragmatic and visual pragmatic ones, which, in due time, will presumably merit their own overview and description.

6

Grapholinguistics

Vuk-Tadija Barbarić

6.1 Introduction

This chapter provides a brief introduction to grapholinguistics.[1] It is impossible, or perhaps unnecessary, to explore grapholinguistics in its entirety without a more comprehensive introduction, a true perspective of the pertinent facts, and convincing clarifications. First and foremost, grapholinguistics could be defined as a "linguistic subdiscipline dealing with the scientific study of all aspects of written language" (Neef 2015: 711). Dürscheid and Meletis (2019: 170) claim that the term *grapholinguistics* is needed to refer "not exclusively to one research domain of written language but to all writing-related aspects." However, they also admit that the use of grapholinguistics is of "programmatic character," which is critical for a proper grasp of the (sub)field in general. This programmatic character stems from linguistics on the whole as a field. Initially, linguistics developed on the assumption that spoken language was its primary concern, while writing was of lesser importance (see Žagar 2007: 11–25). As a consequence, those scholars who were interested in 'grapholinguistic topics' were relegated to the margins of linguistics. The study of written language evolved in isolation from linguistics, on its own, within many disparate and diverging areas, as suggested by the very name given to the discipline. *Grapholinguistics* is an English equivalent of the German term *Schriftlinguistik* (sometimes also known as *Grapholinguistik* in German). Today, its status is recognized primarily due to the dictionary edited by

[1] For the sake of clarity, I somewhat depart from the *Handbook's* convention in visually differentiating between graphetic and graphem(at)ic units (by use of these brackets | |, < >, respectively). This is only relevant as of Section 6.4, where it is explained in more detail.

Neef et al. (2012).[2] To date, this online dictionary comprises roughly 1,500 terms related to grapholinguistics.[3] The terms are described in separate articles of variable length. Throughout this chapter, Neef et al.'s online dictionary is used as a reference to define the basic terms of grapholinguistics with the presumption that its definitions were selected and governed by a strong preliminary consensus.

The term's explicit affiliation to linguistics (grapho-*linguistics*) is undeniable, even though, at least in my opinion, grapholinguistics cannot be compared and contrasted at all with subfields such as psycholinguistics or sociolinguistics. Meletis (2018: 61) draws a parallel between these two linguistic subdisciplines. Notwithstanding, this comparison serves only for terminological purposes, to underscore their similar naming pattern.[4] Grapholinguistics can be viewed as more fundamental than Meletis's comparison might suggest. In reality, it is probably comparable to phonetics or phonology (i.e. to the study of linguistic structures). Hence, it is not surprising that grapholinguistics bears a resemblance to the schools of thought related to structuralism and functionalism. Nonetheless, grapholinguistics stayed out of the due theoretical limelight in linguistics, allowing a more befitting name – *graphology* – to be appropriated by a pseudoscientific discipline. This course of events inevitably led to a number of terminological issues, more evidently pronounced than otherwise in linguistics (e.g. the use of the terms grammatology, graphonomy,[5] or writing system research). Meletis (2019a: 63) considers "*writing system research* as roughly synonymous with *grapholinguistics* – the latter being probably a bit broader."[6]

Unquestionably, 'phonolinguistics' is not usually – or ever, for that matter – contrasted with grapholinguistics, but it is possible that the reader of these lines is encountering the term grapholinguistics for the very first time. Haralambous (2020: 12) concludes that the following questions should be

[2] See Meletis (2020a: 9–11) for more details on the current status of grapholinguistics. Actually, Meletis (2020a: 10) argues that "[t]o this day, Germany remains the heart of the international grapholinguistic community." Interestingly, Neef et al.'s online dictionary contains multiple entries for seemingly identical terms because their definitions are derived from various disciplines. For example, certain terms are assigned somewhat different meanings by grapholinguists than by historical linguists.

[3] Note that my last opportunity to access the dictionary database was in January 2020.

[4] In support of his claim that it is not just a matter of terminology, Meletis (2020a: 3) reveals yet another side of the term, which "reflects the German-language research area's decades-old practice of acknowledging and investigating writing and written language in their own right." From my perspective, Meletis's observation is yet another confirmation in support of the programmatic character, although the term might largely be confined to the German tradition of grapholinguistics, especially because there is only sparse evidence of its recognition or acceptance elsewhere.

[5] The term *graphonomy* was proposed by Hockett (1951: 445), who thought that "[g]raphonomy can only progress on the basis of sound linguistics."

[6] The closest alternative to grapholinguistics is graphic linguistics (see Crossland 1956, Amirova 1977, 1985 – *graficheskaı͡a lingvistika*, originally *графическая лингвистика*, in Russian). For more alternatives, see Amirova 1977: 42–46.

raised: "'Why have I never heard of grapholinguistics?' 'If this is a subfield of linguistics, like psycholinguistics or sociolinguistics, why isn't it taught in Universities?' 'And why libraries do not abound of books about it?'" Haralambous believes it should be ascribed to Saussure's influence,[7] which gave rise to *phonocentrism* in linguistics (i.e. privileging speech over writing, otherwise known as *logocentrism* – see Dürscheid 2016: 13–19). The continuing presence of phonocentrism in linguistics is indisputable, but the inevitability of the advent of phonocentrism is debatable. The example given below shows the spirit of the time that might have fostered Saussure's influence on this topic.

Not so many years before Saussure gave his famous lectures (1907–11), Maretić (1889) published his work on the history of Croatian orthography in Roman script. Maretić's work was monumental, and some of its aspects remain unrivaled to date, but it also comprised a short introduction by the author. In his introduction, Maretić explained his "scientific" principles (obviously under considerable influence of Vuk Karadžić, whose ideas stemmed from Johann Christoph Adelung, see Bunčić forthcoming). Nowadays, Maretić's principles cannot be classified as scientific in any of the usual meanings of the word, but they can be considered as phonocentric. These principles are as follows:

> The script is nothing more than the live word captured and put in written form [...] 1. One sound is to be written by a single letter [...]. 2. One sign is to correspond to a single sound [...]. 3. What is one in speech, should be one in writing [...]. 4. What is separated in speech, should be separated in writing [...]. 5. Whatever is spoken should be written [...]. 6. What is not spoken should not be written [...]. 7. The signs should be written in the particular order in which they are pronounced.
>
> (Maretić 1889: v–vi, my translation)

In keeping with Maretić, any orthography that fulfills the aforementioned requirements would be regarded as a perfect orthography.

Clearly, Maretić's principles adhere to pretheoretical thought, denoting that a written word is a merely secondary instance of the spoken word. Having this in mind, the existence and prevalence of phonocentrism is hardly surprising, particularly in the formative stages of linguistics. Linguistics simply captured what at first seemed more apparent. Something similar could be seen in the writings by Bloomfield (see Žagar 2007: 17, who also highlights the fact that even Edward Sapir, "Bloomfield's senior colleague and countryman" [my translation], had phonocentric ideas), albeit with the awareness of all the difficulties that might accompany a change (simplification) of English

[7] For Saussure's legacy in the context of written language, see Chiss and Puech (1983). See also Chapter 5 and Chapter 17, this volume.

spelling, the spelling that "greatly delays elementary education, and wastes even much time of adults" (Bloomfield 1935 [1933]: 501). See also Anis (1983: 31–32) for several phonocentric quotes by grapholinguists (used as arguments against his idea of autonomous graphematics; see at the end of Section 6.3 for more details on his autonomistic approach).

Grapholinguists have diverging opinions about the relationship between written language and spoken language. As Meletis (2019a: 28) wonders,

> [s]hould the fact that writing operates at another level than language [...] preclude us from analysing it with the same or similar tools and concepts that are used to analyse subsystems of language such as phonology and morphology? [...] Once acquired successfully, are the processes of reading and writing not often dominated by automatisms?

Grapholinguistics clearly lacks a unifying general theory (see Watt 1998: 99–100).[8] At any rate, no such theory is as visible here as it is in linguistics in general, a situation which is facilitated by the vastness of the field. The term *scripturology* has recently been proposed by Klinkenberg and Polis (2018: 58), who suggest that this discipline is "understood as a general theory targeting the establishment of a semiotic typology of writing systems" (see also Chapter 8, this volume). Meletis (2020a: 3) considers the discipline a French (*scripturologie*) equivalent to grapholinguistics. In any case, their proposal considers only one of the areas confined to grapholinguistics – the area comparable to linguistic typology – and relocates it to the realm of semiotics. If this chapter is first time the reader has encountered the term grapholinguistics, they may eventually realize that they are already familiar with some areas of grapholinguistics, but under different names.

The only textbook on grapholinguistics (Dürscheid 2016 [2002]) was written in German. Normally, the textbook's language would be of little importance, but Section 6.2 below, which outlines the history of grapholinguistics, raises a pertinent question about the international reception of grapholinguistic ideas. The textbook defines a few main areas of interest in grapholinguistics: the relationship between spoken language and written language,[9] writing systems,[10]

[8] An attempt to provide a unifying general theory (see Meletis 2020a) is of such a recent date that its publication coincided with the peer review of this chapter. Most importantly, it is written in English and distributed in the open access format. Therefore, it might easily become one of the relevant references for the issues concerning grapholinguistics, and hopefully might precipitate popularization of the entire field.

[9] The section on graphetics (Section 6.3) addresses two important terms – the dependency hypothesis and the autonomy hypothesis – with regard to this area of grapholinguistic research. This area pays much attention to the notions of orality and literacy as well, which lie outside the scope of linguistics.

[10] This area mainly deals with the typology of writing systems. There are many available classification criteria (see Chapter 7, this volume, for details). However, in this case, the distinction between phonographic systems (in which a unit of a writing system is related to a meaning-distinguishing unit of a language, typically a phoneme) and logographic systems (in which a unit of a writing system is related to a meaning-bearing unit of a language, typically a word) is probably best known.

the history of writing,[11] graphematics, orthography, typography,[12] and the acquisition of written language.[13] As indicated previously, not all facets of grapholinguistics can be addressed here in their own right. Fortunately, there is no need to delve into all of them extensively in order to grasp the idea of what grapholinguistics is all about and what its main concerns are. This chapter mainly focuses on *graphetics* and *graphem(at)ics*,[14] legitimately considered as the 'core' grapholinguistic disciplines, by analogy to phonetics and phonology, respectively.

6.2 A Note on the History of Grapholinguistics

The evolution of grapholinguistics is marked by many important dates associated with the German-language area. Dürscheid (2016: 12–13) lists the following events from roughly the last quarter of the twentieth century as crucial: in 1974, the Rostock Orthography Research Group (*Forschungsgruppe Orthographie*) was established; in 1981, the Written Language Study Group (*Studiengruppe Geschriebene Sprache*) in Bad Homburg was founded; in 1985, research on oral and written communication was initiated at the University of Freiburg; in 1994, the annual conference of the German Society for Linguistics was dedicated to the topic of language and script; and in the same year, the first volume of *Schrift und Schriftlichkeit/Writing and Its Use* was published, and the second volume followed in 1996 – see Günther and Ludwig (1994–96). Once again, the events were molded by the programmatic character of grapholinguistics. An outline of the history of grapholinguistics could also include a list of the reflections of prominent historical persons on, for example, the relationship between speech and script (see also Chapter 5, this volume), reminiscent of textbooks on the history of linguistics. All such reflections, however, could only be considered as pre-grapholinguistic. Following this approach, we would have to acknowledge Gelb's (1952) influential work as grapholinguistic.[15] Nevertheless, he used the term *grammatology*, which would be used

[11] This area studies the historical development of scripts and describes historical scripts.

[12] Typography focuses on the writing medium, writing materials and design. It studies the arrangement of visual/graphic units and their organization on the writing surface.

[13] This area is essentially concerned with the acquisition of basic writing and reading skills, but it extends to adulthood to include issues regarding the development of reading and writing competence. In any of these areas of interest, researchers often radically deviate from linguistic interests.

[14] The first part of Meletis's book (2020a) on descriptive structural grapholinguistics is structured similarly, with the exception of orthography, which is explored in a separate chapter of this book. In this chapter, orthography is considered only briefly in Section 6.4, on graphematics, because, although it is undeniably incredibly interesting, I adopt here a view that it is optional (Neef 2015, Meletis 2020a: 15, 28); see the end of the section for more details regarding the theoretical framework that allows such a view. Section 6.5 briefly touches upon the explanatory side of grapholinguistics, to which Meletis dedicates the second part of his book.

[15] It would by no means be wrong to acknowledge it as grapholinguistic. However, for practical reasons which are stated in more detail below, grapholinguistics is restricted to the grapholinguistics proper.

later in a different, more philosophical sense by Derrida (1967) – see Meletis (2018: 61), Klinkenberg and Polis (2018: 58). As it happens, Gelb investigated only a portion of what is recognized today as grapholinguistics.

One of the focal terms of grapholinguistics, the *grapheme* ("the smallest meaning-distinguishing unit in a writing system,"[16] as defined by Birk (2013) in the aforementioned online dictionary of grapholinguistics), was invented much earlier than the 1970s. Reportedly, it was used by several individuals independently, including Baudouin de Courtenay (Meletis 2019a: 27; see also Boduėn de Kurtenė 1912, as well as Chapter 3 and Chapter 5, this volume). Above all, it should not be forgotten that some researchers, Daniels (2017) in particular, consider this term to be redundant. He suggests that a grapheme is "nothing more than a pre-theoretic, fancy, scientific-sounding word for 'letter' or 'character' and ought not to be part of technical discourse" (Daniels 2017: 88). Moreover, the same author argues that "perhaps writing is outside the scope of linguistics" (Daniels 2017: 90),[17] which is in line with his rebuttal of *grapheme* altogether as a valid scientific term. In all probability, the term *grapholinguistics* ("Schriftlinguistik oder Grapholinguistik") was first introduced by Nerius in 1988 (see Nerius and Augst 1988: 1) to designate the birth of a new linguistic discipline (Dürscheid 2016: 12). It is no wonder that the new field depended upon the knowledge accumulated in the study of writing, although it had not been considered a part of linguistics at all times.

At this point, it should be pointed out that this note on the history of grapholinguistics probably conceals more than it discloses. There are some practical reasons for this, the least important of which is possibly the limited space allocated to any one chapter. Above all, the chapter is significantly determined by the choice of the term in its title. While the German term *Schriftlinguistik* has been around for quite a while, the English term *grapholinguistics* is of relatively new provenance, and definitely derives from the writings of German researchers. The choice of a different term in the title would have generated quite a different overview. In other words, grapholinguistics is not viewed here as an umbrella term for all of its possible substitutions, as otherwise this would only exacerbate the incoherence of a field that is already incoherent in and of itself. The overt adherence to the German tradition (or to authors influenced by that tradition) at least reinforces the impression of coherence.[18] Meletis (2020a: 3–8) explains in detail why "the German-language community has been more instrumental in the

[16] Or in written language, as defined by Fuhrhop and Peters (2013: 202).

[17] This opinion is neither trivial nor isolated. For example, Anis (1983: 44) essentially expresses the same concern with the vivid image of "drowning in an interdisciplinary swamp" (my translation), even though he does call for brave modern linguistics, open to semiotics and other disciplines concerned with writing.

[18] This impression should be particularly helpful to readers encountering the term *grapholinguistics* for the first time.

development of grapholinguistics"[19] in comparison to the English-language community.[20] While acknowledging that "drafting a historical reconstruction" of the field is "challenging" (Meletis 2020a: 4), he nevertheless ventures to make such an attempt in spite of serious limitations. He recognizes the problem of the lack of reception of grapholinguistic thought from other countries (also Meletis 2020a: 403) and reveals (Meletis 2020a: 7) that Catach also founded a research group named *Histoire et structure des orthographes et systèmes d'écritures* in France in 1962.[21] And indeed, the French literature on written language is much more developed than this information imparts. Furthermore, for example, Amirova practically established grapholinguistics (or rather, graphic linguistics) in Russia in the 1970s and 1980s (see Amirova 1977, 1985). More recently, grapholinguistics has been studied and practiced by researchers in South Slavic countries as well; for instance, there is a German-edited collection on Serbian and Croatian grapholinguistics (see Brehmer and Golubović 2010). However, the abovementioned data are insufficient; although interesting, they are also very random. A comprehensive history of grapholinguistics has yet to be written.

6.3 Graphetics

Taking the aforementioned into consideration, the first question that comes to mind is the following: Why provide a section on graphetics when this discipline is not even recognized as one of the main grapholinguistic areas of interest in Dürscheid (2016)? In her textbook, graphetics is described relatively briefly within the chapter on typography (Dürscheid 2016: 218–22). There are many reasons for this, but the definitions given below might first explain the main reason why graphetics is believed to have such importance for grapholinguistics. Meletis (2015b) defines graphetics as an "interdisciplinary field concerned with the analysis and description of the materiality of scripts as well as its role in the production and perception of written language." In contrast, Ruge (2013) defines graphematics (otherwise also known as graphemics, even though, in this chapter, the 'German' model is

[19] Ironically, and to complicate things even further, brief overviews of the history of the field published recently have little or no reference to the German-language community (see Bilets'ka 2015, Makaruk 2013).

[20] For instance, one important difference is that the German tradition is generally more theoretically oriented, whereas the English tradition is mainly descriptive. This explains why so many monumental (in terms of their importance and size) books on writing and writing systems were written in English (e.g. Coulmas 2000, Daniels and Bright 1996, Roger 2005). Here, it is important to expand Meletis's observation to include the French tradition, which also has a strong theoretical orientation (see Anis 1983, 2017 [1988], Gruaz 1990, Sébastianoff 1991, Klinkenberg and Polis 2018).

[21] Incidentally, to date, Catach is the only one among the French authors referred to in this overview to have received some citations in Neef et al. (2012), probably because some of her works were published in German editions.

applied – that of *Graphematik*)[22] as a "linguistic subsystem comprising the writing system's basic units and the rules of their combination, as well as its study and analysis."[23] It is worth noting that one linguistic dictionary (Brown and Miller 2013: 200) defines graphetics as "[t]he study of graphic *substance*" and graphemics as "[t]he study of graphemes," while defining graphemes as "[t]he smallest *unit[s]* in a writing *system*" (my emphasis).

The answer to the question raised is relatively simple. By choosing to investigate graphetics and graphematics at the expense of other potential topics, we establish the grounds for introducing and interrogating a crucial linguistic dichotomy (according to structuralism) – that between form and function. It is hardly a coincidence that Meletis, one of the promising grapholinguists of today, first mastered graphetics (see Meletis 2015a), and only then embarked on the quest of building a general theory of grapholinguistics (see Meletis 2018, 2020a). For the conference *Grapholinguistics in the 21st Century*, Haralambous (2020: 14) announced, among others, the topics *Foundations of grapholinguistics, graphemics and graphetics*; *History and typology of writing systems, comparative graphemics/graphetics*; *Computational/formal graphemics/graphetics*; *Typographemics, typographetics*; and *Graphemics/graphetics in experimental psychology and cognitive sciences*, all of which demonstrate the relevance of the abovementioned dichotomy for grapholinguistics. Any area of grapholinguistics that might be under consideration will provoke the discussion about form and function eventually, if not immediately. Regardless of my terminological decision to use the term graphematics instead of graphemics, the concrete *etic* (graph**etic**) and the abstract *emic* (graph**emic**) units (see Meletis 2015: 13, 45) can still be differentiated. Daniels (2017: 88) denies the existence of the *emic* level for writing systems altogether, as "writing systems do not work like linguistic systems." Marković (2015: 80), however, claims convincingly that this is not a valid argument, since even language itself does not have an *emic* level per se. The *emic* level is essentially a construct of the human mind.

Table 6.1, taken and translated from Žagar (2007: 32), applies a structuralist approach to defining terms in keeping with the established and abovementioned parallelism (or analogy) between the units belonging to phonematics

[22] Actually, the model is not German. I simply want to underline that this choice of terminology is determined by what has been explained at the end of Section 6.2. Reference can be made to the terminological legacy of structuralism, or more precisely of glossematics (see Amirova 1977: 66–67, Žagar 2007: 31). French authors also use *graphémathique*, but no evidence has been found for its attribution to the German influence or vice versa (see Anis 2017 [1988], Catach 1990 [1988], Gruaz 1990). The absence of mutual influences is also evident in general. Apparently, structuralism was a good common ground that might have induced similar ideas to develop independently in distant or even relatively close areas. It remains to be seen (upon more detailed examination) whether this is really what happened to grapholinguistics.

[23] As a consequence, graphematics explicitly studies the system of a single language, whereas graphetics is not confined to a single language but studies many facets of the materiality of writing (see Fuhrhop and Peters 2013: 181–82).

(i.e. phonology) and phonetics on one side, and the units belonging to graphematics and graphetics on the other, and with the graph as the central unit of graphetics.[24] Adam (2013) defines the graph as a "concrete realization of a grapheme," which is far more cautious than "[a] symbol representing a phoneme or letter of the alphabet," as defined by Brown and Miller (2013: 200), whose definition is too exclusive.

In accordance with the scheme outlined in Table 6.1, Žagar (2007: 32) claims that *grapholinguistics* is a term best suited to designate a discipline solely concerned with the linguistic aspects of a script, while the term *grammatology* is better for the study of all aspects of writing, which is definitely a legitimate view. Nonetheless, it could be argued that it is impossible to establish full correspondence between the means of written language and the means of spoken language. This is because the two are not entirely dependent on each other, and as a result, written language cannot be regarded as secondary to spoken language (Žagar 2007: 34). Although more relevant to graphematics, specifically to the graphematics of alphabetical writing systems, two important grapholinguistic terms should be introduced at this point – the *dependency hypothesis* (German *Dependenzhypothese*) and the *autonomy hypothesis* (German *Autonomiehypothese*).[25] According to the dependency hypothesis, writing only represents spoken language, while the autonomy hypothesis maintains that graphematics and phonology are two independent subsystems of a language system (see Bunčić forthcoming).

Dürscheid (2016: 36, 38) provides arguments for both hypotheses. In conformity with the dependency hypothesis, script is only a visualization of language (a linguistic argument); it is acquired both phylogenetically and ontogenetically later than language (a developmental psychological

Table 6.1 *Phoneme/phone vs. grapheme/graph*

	Orality	Literacy
Language	**Phonematics**	**Graphematics**
	Phoneme	*Grapheme*
Speech	**Phonetics**	**Graphetics**
	Phone	*Graph*

(taken and translated from Žagar 2007: 32)

[24] Žagar's approach is applied in this overview because of its clarity and simplicity. For theoretically more complex approaches, see Gruaz (1990), who applies frameworks (systemic, semiotic, pragmatic), strata (phonematic, graphematic, morphematic, lexematic) and domains (graphemological, morphemological, lexemological), undeniably under the strong influence of glossematics and stratificational grammar (see Lamb 1966). Gruaz's graphematic stratum (or layer) is based on the notion of supralanguage, combining the oral and graphic sides of language into a single entity (Gruaz 1990: 47–49).

[25] Compare the relational and autonomistic approaches in the English-centered and non-German traditions, as discussed in Chapter 5, this volume.

argument);[26] it exists independently of writing (a logical argument); and spoken language is used on far more occasions than written language (a functional argument). According to the autonomy hypothesis, script consists of discrete units, while spoken language is a continuum (a structural argument); reading and writing do not necessarily refer to spoken language (a logical argument); script enables us to distance ourselves from the object of investigation since it makes linguistic structures accessible to precise observation (a linguistic argument); script prevents us from forgetting (a cultural studies argument); and script has optical-visual characteristics that affect spoken language (a medium-related argument).

Little has been formally expressed about the aims and methods of graphetics (Meletis 2015a: 11). The most common view is that graphetics is an auxiliary field to graphematics, and for this reason, Meletis (2015a: 13) is not inclined to consider it as an established discipline. Klinkenberg and Polis (2018: 62, 81) have no use for the term graphetics in their theoretical framework, but their closest counterpart – the study of 'grammemic signifiers' – also remains "largely to be explored in a scripturological perspective." Moreover, there are few works published on graphetics, which is another reason why the establishment of graphetics as an independent discipline is still a long way off (Meletis 2015a: 19). As a consequence, paleography was used as a substitute for graphetics for a long time. For example, in his work, Žagar (2007) applies a grapholinguistic framework, focusing on graphetics, to revive an area of research that was dominated by paleography for decades, namely research on Croatian Glagolitic texts. Accordingly, he refers to "grapholinguistically based paleography" (see Žagar 2007: 60–65), in which graphetic means are involved in the organization and optimal visual presentation of all linguistic levels. Žagar makes a distinction between four levels: (1) the basic level (mostly graphematic, as this level deals with graphemes, but graphetic when it concerns ligatures or letters borrowed from other writing systems); (2) the morphological level (e.g. assimilation is not recorded on morphemic boundaries); (3) the syntactic level (e.g. punctuation, sentence contraction in rubrics);[27] (4) the textual level (e.g. colors, white spaces, initials, special signs – anything signaling the structural organization of text).

Despite there being a lack of works published on graphetics, Althaus (1973) made an attempt to establish graphetics within linguistics. His attempt provoked a lot of criticism and citations (see Meletis 2015a: 24). Althaus did not invent the term, nor did he refer to the non-German tradition that had taken it into consideration. However, he did draw the attention of German

[26] The oldest evidence of writing is much younger than the advent of *Homo sapiens*, who presumably were able to speak from the beginning. Correspondingly, children produce their first words much earlier than they learn to read and write (see also Bunčić forthcoming).

[27] *Rubric* is a paleographic term used to denote a heading which is typically written in red color.

grapholinguists to the framework in which graphetics is considered auxiliary to graphematics. According to Althaus (1973: 138), graphetics deals with the concrete (material) manifestation of written communication, from which abstract regularities can be derived. Günther (1990) later proposed the model of graphetics as an independent subdiscipline of grapholinguistics. In his view, this subdiscipline observes all the phenomena used in the communication process (see Dürscheid 2016: 219). His perspective is similar to the perception of phonetics today (only in a different medium, and in the areas of research carried out within both the humanities and the sciences). Therefore, graphetics can be established as an independent discipline, especially because its object of investigation cannot be denied.

Nevertheless, the establishment of graphetics seems to be a challenging task. Works that focus on the materiality of writing are dispersed across numerous (mainly nonlinguistic) disciplines (typography, sociology and psychology, to name but a few) and have different objectives and methods. The dual nature of methodological approaches to graphetics can be explained by the following terms used by Günther (1990: 99–100): symbol-graphetics and signal-graphetics. Symbol-graphetics analyzes the graphetic means of the world's writing systems descriptively with recourse to other systems, such as languages and cultures, while signal-graphetics examines writing detached from the language it depicts by using experimental methods. Meletis uses the same distinction to raise what are, in his opinion, the key issues concerning graphetics while avoiding claiming comprehensiveness (see Meletis 2015a: 184–86).

Gallmann (1985), on the other hand, is credited with the systematic classification of typographic elements. His model distinguishes individual segments from suprasegments ('supragraphemes') and incorporates a variety of graphetic variations from the German writing system. However, it should be mentioned that Anis (1983) used the terms *segmental graphemes* and *suprasegmental graphemes* two years earlier. Admittedly, Gallmann's notion of grapheme does not correspond to the abovementioned definition (which identifies graphemes with letters), but is nevertheless included in this account for argument's sake. Gallmann divides graphemes into the following categories: basic graphemes (German *Grundgrapheme*), which correspond to graphemes in the conventional sense; meaningful graphemes (ideograms); classifiers, graphic elements which provide additional syntactic, semantic or pragmatic information (e.g. noun capitalization to help identify the part of speech); boundary signals, graphic elements that mark syntactic, semantic or pragmatic levels or units (e.g. spaces, punctuation and quotation marks, capitalization at the beginning of a sentence); signals of sentence intention (e.g. question marks and exclamation marks); and signals of omission (e.g. apostrophes, ellipsis dots). All of the foregoing graphemes can be contrasted with supragraphemes. Günther (1988) improved Gallmann's terminology by contrasting segments and suprasegments and was able to demonstrate that

Gallmann had mixed the *etic* and *emic* levels. Suprasegments are such typographic properties as italics, underlining, bold, small caps, superscript and the like. Segments with such properties can be considered marked, contrary to those considered as unmarked. It is safe to say that, according to the source literature, typographic elements can be observed within a linguistic framework, but the functions of typographic elements still greatly depend on the situation and context (see Dürscheid 2016: 221–22, Meletis 2015a).

Here it is also worth noting that in his autonomistic approach (in which the graphic is detached from the phonic), Anis (1988: 87–144) distinguishes between three classes of graphemes: alphabetic – *alphagrams*, punctuo-typographic – *topograms*, and logogrammatic – *logograms*. Alphagrams are distinctive units, which belong to the second articulation (like phonemes). More simply put, in writing systems such as French, alphagrams are the letters of an alphabet (with diacritics treated as components of graphemes, and not as a separate class, which is justified by minimal pairs). Topograms are such signs as punctuation (independent of alphagrams/logograms) or italics (modifying alphagrams/logograms). Logograms are the most heterogeneous class, but clearly distinct from alphagrams and topograms, as they indisputably function synthetically and not analytically. Logograms cannot be decomposed, and for this reason, some logograms have their place on the keyboard. These are signs such as *&*, *$*, *5*, *23*, which correspond to words (*at*, *dollar*, *five*, *twenty-three* – regarding possible decomposition, note that the latter cannot be interpreted as *two three*). See also Haralambous and Dürst (2020: 129, 145–46).

Meletis defined three key types of issues (linguistic, typographic semiotic and philosophical) in graphetics. Linguistic issues, inter alia, address the relationship between a graph and a grapheme including the idea of allography, which is crucial to graphematics, besides the segmentation of characters and the detection of distinctive features. Typographic semiotic issues refer to questions of aesthetics vs. legibility (optimization of scripts for the process of reading), and the functions of typography (defining typography more precisely to be able to categorize typographic phenomena). Philosophical issues are mainly concerned with the question of the materiality of writing (see Meletis 2015a: 44–106). At the end of this section, it is important to understand that, nowadays (in the 'digital age'), graphetics extensively deals with issues related to Unicode, emojis and texting (see Coulmas 2013: 126–51, Dürscheid and Meletis 2019, Haralambous and Dürst 2019, Küster 2019).

6.4 Graphematics

Eisenberg (2009: 66) considers graphematics as a branch of grammar. Another definition implies that graphem(at)ics is a "science of graphic constitutive elements of written language, their functions and properties, and also their systemic organization" (Amirova 1985: 53, my translation). However, right at the outset it is essential to make a distinction between *graphematics* and *orthography*, as they are both seemingly similarly focused on written language. Graphematics is concerned with the description of a writing system, while orthography is generally concerned with the standardization of a writing system (Dürscheid 2016: 128). Consequently, Meletis (2020b: 257) does not consider orthographic variation as allographic (see below) in a narrow sense, despite acknowledging the conceivable consideration of systematic variation vs. normative variation. Graphematic regularities are implicit, while orthographic rules are explicit. Communication is the most important graphematical function, whereas conventionalization and standardization are most important for orthography (Meletis 2020a: 155–59; see also Fuhrhop and Peters 2013: 186–88). In one particular case in historical linguistics – in a preorthographic period in the history of a writing system – graphematics and orthography share a common area of interest. A preorthographic (or graphematic) period is characterized by flourishing spelling variation as opposed to an orthographic period, in which this variation tends to be diminished (see Neef 2012: 217–18). Neef's position is that graphematics cannot be conceived as a natural basis for orthography. Since graphematics is not normative, it can easily be recognized as natural. This position is criticized by Neef (2012: 218–19), especially because he does not see how its naturalness could be empirically verified.

There is much evidence that the grapheme is the central concept of grapholinguistics,[28] and for that reason, the grapheme should also be considered as a central concept of graphematics. In this context, Meletis (2019a: 27–34) suggests four strategies: rejecting the grapheme altogether, avoiding defining the grapheme, preferring *letter* over *grapheme*, and, finally, defining the grapheme. In this chapter, pressed for limited space, I am not concerned with the rejection or avoidance strategies, as the very name of graphematics suggests that the notion of grapheme is essential. I therefore only touch upon the preference of *letter* (or *character*) to *grapheme*, since this could be a useful strategy for individual descriptions (i.e. for descriptions of a particular writing system). Rather than defining German <sch> as a grapheme, Neef (2005) prefers the term *fixed letter combination*. Meletis agrees that this is possible in the case of German, which uses the alphabetic writing system. To that effect, for the sake of comparison across different writing systems, including many non-alphabetic writing systems, this will not suffice. Therefore, Meletis (2019a: 30) calls for a definition of the grapheme that "captures the minimal linguistically

[28] "Graphemes and phonemes are each determined in relation to an individual language" (Fuhrhop and Peters 2013: 202, my translation). As with the phoneme in phonology, it is possible to go below the level of the grapheme and analyze its graphematic features. See Primus (2004) for a featural analysis of the modern Roman alphabet, showing, within the Optimality Theory framework, that the internal structure of its letters is highly systematic (e.g. the paper answers exactly how letters are distinguished from digits and punctuation).

functional unit of any given writing system." This definition would reflect that "at the core, they all share a crucial function: visually representing language (and this is not restricted to speech)." Primus (2004: 242–43) also contends that "letter sequences that correspond to one sound or behave graphematically as a single unit" cannot be simply treated as graphemes. It must be said that approaches found in Neef (2005) consider graphematics as a counterpart of segmental phonology. According to such a line of thought, many terms were produced modeled on phonology (e.g. the graphematic syllable, with the onset, nucleus, rhyme and coda; the graphematic foot; and the graphematic word) (see Meletis 2019a: 31, Fuhrhop and Peters 2013: 216–38, 251–68, and especially Berg 2019, for a suprasegmental model of writing).

To attain such a definition, the universal properties of the grapheme had to be identified. First, however, I would like to take a step back to expound briefly on the two strategies noteworthy for the definition of grapheme governed by the *referential* view and the *analogical* view. Kohrt (1986) is credited for coining these important terms (see Lockwood 2001: 307). The two views reflect the position of their respective proponents on the relationship between writing and speech, which was discussed in greater detail in Section 6.3. According to the referential view, writing represents speech (graphemes are signs of phonemes – the dependency hypothesis). In contrast, the analogical view considers writing to be autonomous from speech (graphemes are the smallest functional units – the autonomy hypothesis). Neither of the suggested views is flawless. The referential view can be reduced to absurdity, since it implies equality between graphemes and phonemes, leading to a logical conclusion that there is no need for the notion of grapheme (see Günther 1988: 76). Methodologically, the analogical view strongly depends on phonology and, consequently, graphemes do not necessarily stand for phonemes (they are only parallel to phonemes). The direction of analysis is important here. The referential view supports the direction from phoneme to grapheme, contrary to the analogical view. Therefore, it is not surprising that the advocates of the referential view produced such terms as *phono-grapheme* and *phonological-fit grapheme*, whereas the promoters of the analogical view endorsed the terms *grapho-grapheme* and *graphemic grapheme* (see Kohrt 1986: 81, 92, Lockwood 2001: 314, Meletis 2019a: 34). Since both views disclose essential information on the relationship between graphemes and phonemes, obviously useful but seemingly mutually exclusive, the researchers undertook a challenging task and sought to reconcile them within more complex models (see Meletis 2019a: 32–34).

The notion of allography is another important issue of graphematics. The *allograph* is defined as a "variant form of a grapheme" (Adam 2014), once again by analogy to other linguistic levels (allophone – allograph). In the framework of graphetics discussed in Section 6.3, graphetics could rightfully lay claim on allography. Either way, however, allography has a real impact on graphematics because it sometimes makes the determination of a writing system's inventory of units rather difficult. Meletis (2020b: 253–62), therefore, proposed two major types of allography, assigning allography to both graphetics and graphematics. The former type is called *graphetic allography*, while the latter is called *graphematic allography.* Graphetic allography relies on the visual side of concrete units, while graphematic allography relies on the function. In other words, graphetic allography takes as its task to explain how an occurrence of the four graphs in the following sequence <**m**y> <**m**other> <**m**isses> <**m**e> relates to the basic shape |m|. Taking suprasegmental graphetic units into consideration, this example might as well look like this <***m**y*> <**m**<u>other</u>> <**m**isses> <^{me}>. Nevertheless, it would still relate to variations of the basic shape |m|. It is the task of graphetic allography to explain how this is possible.

The use of angle brackets < > for graphematic units, and vertical strokes | | for graphetic units is a well-known convention, which is used in this chapter. I depart from the *Handbook*'s convention for the sake of clarity as much of my examples make use of specific text formattings. Meletis (2020b: 252) introduces even more conventions into his notation, while Marković (2015) differentiates between angle brackets for graphs and double angle brackets for graphemes. Different conventions could be applied to allographs, for instance, but the notation depends on practical questions as well as on the underlying theoretical background (see, e.g., Primus 2004: 243–44). In this chapter, no such distinction is made.

If the abovementioned example is yet again transformed into <***m**y*> <**M**<u>other</u>> <**M**isses> <^{me}>, the graphetic framework would include two distinct basic shapes |m| and |M|, which are related. In other words, the basic shape is an abstraction within graphetics: <***m***> and <m> are concrete realizations of the basic shape |m|, while <<u>**M**</u>> and <**M**> are concrete realizations of the basic shape |M|. More accurately, <***m***> and <m>, as well as <<u>**M**</u>> and <**M**>, are graphs, and the basic shape is defined by its visual properties. All these graphs (sometimes referred to as glyphs) are considered related by virtue of their functional correspondence at the level of graphemes (see Meletis 2020b: 251–53). This matter becomes quite complex when discussed in the context of handwriting and print. Meletis (2020b: 254–56) goes on to differentiate three types of variation: intrainventory graphetic allography (largely a syntagmatic phenomenon – <<u>m</u>a<u>mm</u>al>), interinventory graphetic allography (exclusively paradigmatic phenomenon – <m>, <m>, <m>, <m>), and suprasegmental graphetic variation (contrastive function – <Give *me* the book!>, i.e. not him), leaving the term allography reserved for segmental alternations exclusively. Since this chapter does not allow for looking at this in more detail, and to avoid any further confusion, Meletis's notation was not adopted here (which, *nota bene*, differentiates graphs, graph classes, basic shapes and graphemes).

As explained below, the discussion of graphetic allography is necessary at this point to understand the types of graphematic allography, which concerns the assignment of basic shapes to graphemes. Meletis (2020b: 257) suggests three relevant criteria supporting a distinction between subtypes of graphematic allography: intrainventory vs. interinventory (establishing whether allographs occur within a given inventory), free vs. positional (free variation vs. complementary distribution) and externally independent vs. externally determined (determination possible according to other linguistic levels). The interinventory free graphematic allography type is exemplified by the pairs of basic shapes that are related at the level of graphemes but lack visual similarity (e.g. |a| and |ɑ|).[29] In this example, the criterion of visual similarity evidently does not play a role, and the association of these basic shapes with the same grapheme is only possible due to their functional equivalence. However, one should notice that |a| and |ɑ| cannot be regarded as graphemes in their own right due to their inability to differentiate meaning through minimal pairs (<area>, <ɑrea>, <areɑ> and <ɑreɑ> are all functionally the same).[30] This is essentially a structuralist concept that has stood the test of time in grapholinguistics.

The intrainventory positional graphematic allography type is the best-known type. This type allows the alternation of visually dissimilar basic shapes. Nevertheless, they never alternate in the same positions, as their distribution is positional. The most common case of this kind is the Greek case of |σ| and |ς|, for which no minimal pair can be found because the latter is reserved for final position (for more examples, see also Klinkenberg and Polis 2018: 70, Bunčić forthcoming). Uppercase and lowercase basic shapes, a special and controversial case, are often treated as an instance of allography (see Fuhrhop and Peters 2013: 207–8). On the one hand, Meletis (2020b: 260–61) shows that uppercase and lowercase basic shapes are in complementary distribution, and on the other hand that their use is determined by external factors (which represents externally determined intrainventory positional allography). Accordingly, they are allographs of the same grapheme rather than distinct graphemes. Klinkenberg and Polis (2018: 78) point out that "allography can indicate a categorisation and thus function as a classifier," which is exemplified by uppercase.

The referential view (the dependency hypothesis) offers an "automatic solution" to the problem of assigning different written shapes to the same grapheme (Lockwood 2001: 308). Consequently, such variations as <f>, <v> and <ph> in German are considered as an instance of allography by virtue of

[29] In other words, they are distinguished at the graphetic level, but not at the graphematic level (see Fuhrhop and Peters 2013: 197, 202).

[30] It goes without saying that this is language-specific. In some languages, the basic shapes |a| and |ɑ| can form minimal pairs.

their correspondence with the phoneme /f/,[31] and the same applies for <f> and <ph> in French (see Klinkenberg and Polis 2018: 70). Meletis (2020b: 261–62) is strongly against such a view, but acknowledges that this is a kind of graphematic variation and subsumes these and similar cases under nonallographic graphematic variation.

It is now time to revisit the attempts at providing a universal definition of grapheme. According to Meletis (2019a: 35–38), a candidate for a grapheme has to fulfill the following three criteria: lexical distinctiveness, linguistic value and minimality.[32] Lexical distinctiveness is tested through minimal pairs found among the existing words of a language. The German <sch> (such as in the word *Schaum*) evidently consists of the following basic shapes: |s|, |c|, |h|. A grapheme candidate <sch> fulfills the criterion of lexical distinctiveness because the minimal pair with *Baum* can be established. The simple fact that <sch> stands for /ʃ/ confirms its linguistic value. The only imperative is the existence of a linguistic value. It is straightforward that a grapheme candidate refers to more than one linguistic unit or that its linguistic reference is unstable. The minimality criterion is decisive to indicate that <sch> is not a grapheme. At the level of graphetics, a basic shape must occupy exactly one segmental space of the writing surface. Having this in mind, the test can be repeated to confirm whether <sch> constitutes a grapheme according to the first two criteria. This time, minimal pairs are found for <s> and <ch> – *Masche* vs. *manche*, and *Masche* vs. *Maske*, and clearly, <sch> cannot be considered as a grapheme, since this sequence of basic shapes is not so exclusive in the writing system as it may seem at first.[33] On the other hand, in German, <ch> meets all the criteria for a grapheme, corroborated by the fact that <c> is not used independently in native words. For the German language, Fuhrhop and Peters (2013: 204–5) recognize only <ch> and <qu> as 'complex graphemes'.[34] The grapheme <ch> is only graphetically polysegmental,

[31] The graphematic solution space for /f/ in German has been worked out in detail by Balestra, Appelt and Neef (2014).

[32] Gruaz (1990: 55–57) considers a graph to be a generic unit which takes two values, that of a graphon (a systemic unit) and of a grapheme (a semiotic unit). For French graphemes, Gruaz recognizes three functions: (1) the phonographic function; (2) the morphological lexical/grammatical function; and (3), the lexical distinctive function between homophones. The phonographic function is comparable to Meletis's linguistic value, and the other two both share some resemblance to the lexical distinctiveness criterion. Even so, the minimality criterion (in Meletis's sense) is not explicitly stated.

[33] The acceptance of such letter sequences as graphemes raises the following issues: it "enlarges the basic inventory of a writing system" and "disregards the fact that the individual letters in such sequences are distinctive" (Primus 2004: 243). This is exemplified by *misch* vs. *milch*, similarly to what was shown above, and *Ship* vs. **SHip*, where it would be expected that something considered as a unit behaves as a unit in all contexts. In this context, this is obviously not the case.

[34] Nonetheless, for practical reasons, Eisenberg (2009: 67–68) considers <sch> to be one of the "consonant graphemes," while acknowledging the theoretical importance of analyzing graphemes without reference to "phonological words."

but conceptually still treated as a unit (basic shape) that occupies one space. This was a fairly simple example, but Meletis (2019a: 38–42) proceeds to show that the same principle can be applied to the writing systems used for Chinese, Thai, Korean, Japanese, Arabic, Tamil and Hindi. However, he acknowledges that more testing is required in other writing systems.

I would now like to briefly consider an attempt by Neef (2015) at developing what he called a 'modular theory of writing systems'. Within this theory, "[a] writing system is a notational system for a natural language," and graphematics is regarded as a module of a writing system that "relates units of a language system to units of a script" (Neef 2015: 708). In other words, graphematics "refers to the linguistic subsystem and not the branch in which it is studied" (Meletis 2019a: 62). Neef's attempt is particularly interesting because it very promisingly casts light on the relationship between graphematics and orthography. Systematic orthography is another module of a written language in this approach, which is optional. All the modules, including the language system module, belong to a writing system. Graphematics deals with the relationships between letters and phonological units which are expressed by rules (or constraints), taking into account the graphematic context or phonological regularities when the relationship is complex in such a way that, for example, a single letter stands for multiple phonological elements (Neef 2015: 714). Here again the direction of analysis is important, as this theory takes a rarely used direction 'from letter to sound' and considers it as basic without dismissing the other perspective. The ultimate aim is to show that a graphematics module contains sets of all the possible spellings of words in a particular language. Neef (2015: 716) calls these sets 'graphematic solution space' and gives an example of it for the phonological representation /raɪt/ that belongs to the English writing system: *right, rite, write, wright, wrightt, ryte, rrryte*. However, the actual spelling of words depends on orthography – a module that prescribes the correct spelling of a word within a given solution space. It is, in fact, "a system of constraints applying to the graphematic solution space" (Neef 2015: 718), which should be differentiated from conventional orthography. The most obvious difference is that a conventional orthography can prescribe a spelling outside a given graphematic solution space. Systematic orthography depends on graphematics to provide graphematic solution space. The only remaining question is that of vocabulary. A graphematics module is not concerned with the spelling of foreign words and can provide the most accurate graphematic solution space for native words only, with native words at the center of the vocabulary and foreign words on the periphery. Even the spelling of proper names is disputable in this respect, as not so many spelling constraints are imposed on them. This corresponds to linguistics in general – one initially describes only the language system of the central vocabulary (see Bunčić forthcoming).

6.5 Toward the General Theory of Grapholinguistics

This short section has a somewhat ambitious title considering the lack of a unifying general theory within the vast area of grapholinguistics as previously established. Nevertheless, due attention should be given to a recently announced attempt to construct such a theory, which has enjoyed substantial progress. Meletis (2018, 2020a) proposes *natural grapholinguistics*, which draws on naturalness theory. This theory considers the processing of linguistic phenomena with little sensomotoric and cognitive effort to be more natural in comparison to more complex phenomena. A trivial but illustrative example is a logical assumption that footnotes are more natural than endnotes because there is less effort involved in finding footnotes (see Meletis 2020a: 244). A more complex example is a finding that native Arabic readers process unvowelized Arabic easier than vowelized Arabic, from which it is concluded that vowelization "produces a situation of visual load and thus does not necessarily facilitate word recognition" (Taha 2016: 140).

Meletis adheres to the comparative graphematics of Weingarten (2011), which studies how given linguistic phenomena manifest themselves through different writing systems, focused on the identification of linguistic parameters underpinning cross-linguistic differences among writing systems. This approach is extended to create comparative grapholinguistics, along with its subdiscipline comparative graphetics, which in turn once again outlines the importance of graphetics within grapholinguistics. The establishment of the aforementioned (sub)disciplines should assist in the evaluation of naturalness in writing and the determination of the extent of naturalness (something can be deemed as either more or less natural in respect to something else). Again, the entire endeavor was preceded by similar attempts to establish natural phonology in the 1960s and natural morphology in the 1970s (see Meletis 2018: 52–58).

It cannot be contested that naturalness at the universal level is determined by human physical and cognitive configuration. Graphetic naturalness can be considered at the micro level, where it is concerned with basic shapes in isolation. At the macro level, the entire inventory is analyzed through relationships between units of a script. For example, the tendency of writing systems to evolve from phonetically based to lexically distinctive was proposed (see Sampson 2018b). This tendency complies with the naturalness theory, since it assumes that, over the course of time, more natural features (i.e. the features more natural to readers/writers) will prevail. On the other hand, symmetry (or asymmetry) can be seriously considered as a candidate for a universal graphetic naturalness parameter. If we look at the Roman script, such pairs of basic shapes as |b| and |d| or |p| and |q| are extrinsically symmetrical at the vertical axis. This area of research is well documented, and begins with the analyses of errors made by children on account of symmetry. Interestingly enough, there is a lack of symmetry in widely used scripts invented a long time ago (see Meletis 2018: 70–71, 80–81). It has already been pointed out in Section 6.1 that Meletis differentiates between description and explanation. Both approaches are ambitious, and they consist of the following: "description deals with the question of how writing systems are built and how they are used, whereas explanation strives to answer why they are built the way they are and why they are used as they are" (Meletis 2020a: 177). It is now up to the scientific community to evaluate the answers provided.

6.6 Conclusion

This chapter has provided some information about grapholinguistics, which, compared to linguistics, is still in its infancy. Grapholinguistics desperately aspires to establish itself as a linguistic subdiscipline, somewhat contrary to its programmatic character propelling it to embrace the topic of writing in its totality. In its extreme, grapholinguistics would surely be concerned with the entire content of this book, and in its nucleus, it would concern nothing more than those aspects parallel to and comparable to the study of linguistic structures. The history of grapholinguistics can be viewed in two ways. In a narrow sense, it can be traced back to the organized research conducted by German universities since the 1970s, and in a broad sense, its history began with the first instances of writing system research. Both of these histories are difficult to sketch owing undoubtedly to various instances of grapholinguistics emerging at different places (and in different languages). Should they be called traditions or schools? This remains to be seen. In my opinion, the solution to this issue requires a joint effort to be invested. Of all the topics that deserve due consideration, this chapter has addressed two of its focal subdisciplines, underpinning grapholinguistic research on the whole – graphetics and graphematics. It has been demonstrated that these subdisciplines are considerably leveraged on the traditions of structuralism and functionalism. Naturally, this might be attributed to the immaturity of grapholinguistics: the discipline will most likely have to endure most of what linguistics has already sustained in its history. The topics addressed in this chapter, together with the list of references, will hopefully suffice to generate more interest and their further pursuit within grapholinguistics. This pursuit could also naturally extend to the study of historical orthography (see, e.g., Žagar 2020 for a recent attempt).

7

Typologies of Writing Systems

Terry Joyce

7.1 Introduction

Writing is arguably the most consequential technology of human history, as testified by both its widespread dissemination around the world and its immense significance within our contemporary societies (Coulmas 1989: 3, 2003: 1, 2013: xi, Robinson 1995: 7, 2009: 1, Rogers 2005: 1, Gnanadesikan 2009: 2, Powell 2009: 1, Sproat 2010: 8, Joyce 2016: 288). And, yet, intriguingly, all writing systems, whether long extinct or still extant, can ultimately be traced back to just a couple of truly independent inventions: Sumerian cuneiform and Chinese characters.[1] The historical diffusion of writing systems has unfolded through myriads of transmissions between neighboring peoples. In some cases, the transition process was plenary adoption, albeit with some form changes over time; in many cases, it was adaptation, where divergences between neighboring languages necessitated modifications of sign inventories; in other cases, simple misunderstandings yielded deeper structural alterations (Haarmann 2006: 2405, Daniels 2018: 139–41). These dissemination mechanisms largely account for the sheer diversity within the world's writing systems.

However, faced with the immense profusion of both historical and modern writing systems, a major challenge for scholars is to appropriately differentiate between the more significant properties, such as mapping principles, and the more marginal ones, such as sign-form variations (Joyce and Meletis 2021). In that context, the enterprise of developing typologies of writing

[1] There is general consensus that writing emerged separately in Sumer, China and Mesoamerica, but less certainty about whether the emergence in Egypt was also independent (Coulmas 2013: 192, Daniels 2018: 136, Gnanadesikan 2009: 2, Rogers 2005: 4, Sproat and Gutkin 2021: 478). Moreover, no modern writing systems are descendent from Mesoamerica.

systems is striving to realize, as its ultimate goal, a coherent framework, or tool, for categorizing the diversity of writing systems; a touchstone for comprehending the multifarious ways of materializing written language. As sampled in Subsection 7.3.2, a number of typologies have been proposed, but, as they incorporate different theoretical assumptions about the deeply interconnected entities involved (i.e. language, speech, writing, writing systems, scripts, orthography, alphabet, grapheme), it is expedient to simultaneously analyze the enmeshed conceptual and terminology contrasts employed within typologies, in order to hone their transparency and validity.[2]

Very much in that spirit, this chapter seeks to highlight the dialectic interaction between such theoretical assumptions and the terminology employed, to potentially contribute to the emergence of more perspicuous typologies of writing systems, which, in turn, can further illuminate our understandings of written language, both diachronically and synchronically. Accordingly, Section 7.3 outlines how the majority of typology proposals have approached the classification of writing systems primarily in terms of a core set of representational principles, while Section 7.4 briefly considers the potential merits of exploring complementary or alternative approaches.

7.2 Writing Systems Research

In light of the initial claims about the significance of writing, it might strike many as rather surprising that, as also argued in Chapter 6, this volume, writing systems have not been a focus of formal linguistic research until comparatively recently. Echoing Weingarten's (2011) observation, there remains a distinct ring of truth to Gnanadesikan's (2017: 14) recent claim that the study of writing systems "is still in its infancy."[3] Naturally, there are a few closely interconnected consequences. These include the relative scarcity of fully developed proposals of writing system typologies and a marked lack of consistency in the application of their basic terminology, such that misconceptions and inappropriate terms continue to muddle matters, with writing systems remaining, in general, poorly understood (Powell 2009: 1–9, Joyce 2016: 288).

Although it is something of a moot point whether the situation primarily reflects the relative neglect of writing as an area of linguistics or is just a quirky

[2] As Coulmas (1996b: 1387) astutely observes, since "writing represents language, typologies of writing systems that are based on the units and processes by means of which this is accomplished can deepen our understanding of language, while a sharpening of the notions for analyzing the units of language can help to improve such typologies."

[3] Although Gelb's (1963) seminal work, *A Study of Writing*, undoubtedly provided the initial groundwork, arguably, the discipline's foundations were not established in earnest until after the mid-1980s, with Sampson (1985), Coulmas (1989), DeFrancis (1989) and Daniels (1990). Moreover, Daniels (2001) was the first chapter on writing systems to feature in a handbook of linguistics, with the journals of *Written Language and Literacy* and *Writing Systems Research* first appearing in 1998 and 2009, respectively.

example of historical inconvenience, it warrants mention that alternative designations for the discipline of writing systems research continue to vie for general acceptance. Without question, the ideal term would be *graphology*, for, in being completely analogous with *phonology* and *morphology*, it could clearly signify the relations between visual form, sound, and meaning that are core to linguistics (Joyce 2002: 269, McIntosh 1961: 107; see again Chapter 6, this volume). The term, however, was earlier misappropriated to refer to the "pseudoscience of divining someone's personality from their handwriting" (Daniels 2018: 5), which has effectively forced scholars of writing and writing systems to propose alternative designations.

Gelb (1952: v) coined one of the first: *grammatology*. Despite Gelb's immense significance for the discipline and the fact that Daniels (1996a, 2000, 2009) has used it in the past, as Coulmas (1996a: 173) points out, the term has not gained wide currency. Indeed, Daniels's (2018: 4–5) preference is now for Hockett's (1951) proposal of *graphonomy*, where the relationship between graphology and graphonomy is taken to be analogous to that between astrology and astronomy. Another, more recent designation is *grapholinguistics*, which Neef (2015: 711) uses to refer to the linguistic subdiscipline concerned "with the scientific study of all aspects of written language." In addition to noting that this is a translation equivalent of the German *Schriftlinguistik*, Meletis (2018: 61), who also adopts the term, suggests, as discussed in Chapter 6, this volume, that this designation has parallels with other subdisciplines of linguistics, such as sociolinguistics and psycholinguistics. While there is some merit in that observation, in contrast to the more interdisciplinary natures of both sociolinguistics and psycholinguistics, debatably, the term grapholinguistics fails to fully accord the study of writing with the central status that it deserves alongside the study of speech. Moreover, while it is difficult to discern all the ramifications that may have arisen from this nomenclature issue and the lack of more suitable designations, there have plausibly been direct consequences in the diverse range of senses that have become associated with the term *orthography*. As Subsection 7.3.1 comments, these senses range from the literal meaning of the prescriptive rules for correct writing, to denoting written representations within research on visual word recognition, and, most inclusively, to the full set of written conventions of a language.

7.3 Writing System Typologies

Constituting this chapter's core, this section consists of three related subsections: the first discusses the three close-related terms of *writing system*, *script* and *orthography*; the second presents a selection of typology proposals; and the third focuses on their conceptual distinctions and terminology.

7.3.1 The Elusive Trinity of Terms

No serious student of writing systems research can deny the truth of Gnanadesikan's (2017: 15) observation that there "is, in general, significant variation in the basic terminology used in the study of writing systems." In fact, given that differences of interpretation are associated with many of the discipline's terms, not just the basic ones, Gnanadesikan's comment is, possibly, at some risk of erring toward understatement. However, setting aside concerns for the ubiquity of interpretive variations, Gnanadesikan laudably highlights the thorny problems concerning the elusive trinity of terms at the heart of writing systems research, namely *writing system*, *script* and *orthography* (Joyce and Masuda 2019).[4] Treatments run the basic gamut of possibilities, with some scholars regarding all three terms as essentially synonymous, while others only treat two as synonymous and, thus, either ignore or seek to differentiate the third. Falling firmly within the first camp is Sampson (2015: 8), who uses all three terms "to refer to *a given set of written marks together with a particular set of conventions for their use*." In contrast, in treating *script* as "a general term for a writing system without regard for its structural nature," Rogers (2005: 261) effectively ignores *orthography*. In also commenting on the terminology issue, Meletis (2018: 73) remarks that *writing systems* and *orthography* "are often shockingly misused as synonyms, or *writing system* is not used at all and *orthography* is employed instead." Certainly, there are considerable degrees of overlap in the historical and conventional usages of these terms, as evidenced, for example, by the following definitions recently provided by Daniels (2018: 155). Starting with *orthography* as the "conventional spellings of texts, and the principles therefore," Daniels defines *script* as "a particular collection of characters (or signs), used to avoid specifying abjad, alphabet, etc." and *writing system* as "a script together with an associated orthography." However, resonating deeply with the concerns expressed by both Gnanadesikan (2017: 14–16) and Meletis (2018: 73–74), Joyce and Masuda (2019: 248–51) recently examine this trinity of terms with specific reference to the contemporary Japanese writing system. As pertinent to this chapter's focus on the conceptualizations and terminology of writing systems typologies, Subsection 7.3.1 briefly recapitulates the most relevant aspects of their discussions.

[4] Most of the examples of terminological variation that Gnanadesikan (2017: 14–15) singles out involve these core terms, but it bears immediate acknowledgment that Gnanadesikan's Figure 1 (2017: 15), entitled "Terminology of writing systems," consists of five terms; *writing system, script, orthography, signary* and *typology.* It also bears stressing that there are significant differences between Gnanadesikan's interpretations of these terms and the approach to writing systems typology presented here. Within Gnanadesikan's Figure 1, the five terms are organized at three levels: "Writing Systems (e.g. Italian writing system)" appears at the top, which is divided into "Script (e.g. Roman Alphabet)" and "Orthography (e.g. <gn> → /ɲ/ ...)" at the middle level, with script further divided into "Signary (e.g. A B C D ...)" and "Typology (e.g. Alphabet") at the lowest level. Thus, while writing system clearly refers to a specific instance (in the secondary sense described below), typology denotes a specific aspect or property of a writing system. More specifically, Gnanadesikan (2017: 15) appears to be using typology to indicate a "type of correspondence to linguistic structures," which, despite her claim that it is not "usually given a name," essentially matches to what is referred to here as a representational mapping relationship.

In contrast to Daniels's (2018) ordering of these core terms, Joyce and Masuda (2019) start by appropriately acknowledging that the term *writing system* has two distinctive meanings within the literature (Coulmas 2013: 17–18, Joyce 2016: 288). While more technical in nature, its primary meaning refers to the narrow range of abstract representational mapping relationships that exist between linguistic units and the graphemes of a language. As highlighted in both Subsections 7.3.2 and 7.3.3, the dominant approach to classifying writing systems has been to focus on the linguistic level – whether it is *morphographic* (*morpheme* + *writing*), *syllabographic* (*syllable* + *writing*) or *phonemic* (segmental) – that is predominately represented by a writing system's unitary symbols (Joyce 2011, 2016: 288–89, Joyce and Borgwaldt 2011). However, as alluded to in Daniels's (2018) definitions, a secondary, yet nonetheless frequently employed, sense of writing system is to refer to the "specific rules according to which the units of the system are interpreted in a given language" (Coulmas 2013: 17–18). Turning to the second term, *script*, as Weingarten (2011) observes, it is often confused with writing system. Yet, its meaning and both sense distinctions of writing system can be clearly differentiated, if script is suitably restricted to refer only to the set of material signs (the signary) of a specific language (Weingarten 2011, Coulmas 2013, Joyce 2016, Joyce and Meletis 2021).[5] These sense distinctions can be illustrated with reference to the notoriously complex Japanese writing system (Joyce 2011, Joyce and Masuda 2018: 182–89, 2019: 251–55). According to the second sense of writing systems, the Japanese writing system refers to all the graphemes that are used to represent the written Japanese language. Moreover, according to the primary sense, it employs all three levels of representational mapping, which are graphematically realized by its four component scripts, namely morphographic *kanji*, the two sets of syllabographic *hiragana* and *katakana*, and the phonemic segmentary of *rōmaji*, which are supplemented with the set of Arabic numerals.

As already touched on at the close of Section 7.2, *orthography* is potentially the most problematic of these terms to pin down because it has acquired a wide range of connotations. From the perspective of writing systems research, however, there are two factors that are particularly germane. The first is that an orthography is always language-specific in nature.[6] The second key

[5] It is worth noting that, consistent with his definition of script as "a set of graphic signs with prototypical forms and prototypical linguistic functions," Weingarten (2011: 16) conceives of writing systems as referring to the pairing of a particular script with a particular language. Thus, for Weingarten, Amharic-Latin and Amharic-Ethiopic are two different writing systems, where the Amharic language is being graphematically represented by a variant of the Latin script and by the Ethiopic script, respectively.

[6] Sebba (2007: 170) stresses this factor within his glossary entry for orthography: "a writing system, as adapted and designed in order to write a particular language. An orthography makes use of a particular script to write a specific language – for example, Russian orthography makes use of the Cyrillic script (alphabet)." An anonymous reviewer has perceptively pointed out that Sebba's reference to "a particular script" is not consistent with the Japanese writing system's complementary employment of multiple scripts. However, Sebba's somewhat lax use of

aspect is that, as substantiated in the term's Greek etymology (ὀρθός /orthos/ 'straight; correct' + γράφειν /graphein/ 'to write'), orthography explicitly pertains to the prescriptive rules for 'correctly writing' a particular language (Coulmas 1996a: 379, Desbordes 1997: 117–18, Sebba 2007: 10, Weingarten 2011: 13, Neef 2012: 217–19, 2015: 709–16). Indeed, as Sebba (2007: 10) aptly observes, "'writing correctly' is exactly what is implied by the term used for spelling in many languages, – for example, German (*Rechtschreibung*, 'correct writing'), Greek (*orthographia*, 'correct writing'), and the French, German and Spanish terms which derive from the Greek."[7]

With these two factors duly noted, it is possible to further elucidate the close interconnections among the three basic terms. Reflecting its focus on correct norms, in its core sense, orthography is concerned with the mediation between the principles of representational mapping (writing system in the abstract sense), on the one hand, and the material script, on the other. That is, for *phonographic* (*sound* + *writing*) writing systems, at least, this sense of orthography closely parallels the abstract sense of writing system in the shared focus on the mapping of graphemes to phonological units. In the contexts of phonemic (segmental) writing systems, the mapping relationships are often referred to either as phoneme to grapheme or grapheme to phoneme correspondences, depending on the direction (Henderson 1982, Katz and Frost 1992b: 67, Rogers 2005, Sebba 2007, van den Bosch et al. 1994: 178).

However, the major problem with this notion of orthography is that it largely fails to adequately account for how most natural writing systems evolve. As Sampson (2018b) argues, given that both spoken languages and scripts (i.e. symbol sets) change over time, the representational consistency of mapping relationships tends gradually to erode. While some irregularities may merely reflect representational deficiencies (mapping inadequacies common to most, if not all, alphabets) that are present from the outset (Desbordes 1997: 119), most emerge due to what Sampson (2018b: 10) refers to as a tendency for orthographies to become less *phonetically based* and more *lexically distinctive* over time.[8]

"a particular script" is clearly evoking the 'conventional' allusion to an entire set of material signs (i.e. a signary); an interpretation that is consistent with Sebba's (2007: 10) earlier remark that "*Script* is usually taken to be a synonym of 'writing system,'" which stands as further testimony to the pervasive mixing of these basic terms.

[7] Consistently, although オーソグラフィー /ōsogarafī/ has also entered Japanese as a phonetic borrowing, the Greek etymology is closely paralleled in the standard Japanese translation of 正書法 /sei-sho-hō/ 'orthography' (literally, 'correct + [write + method]'). Moreover, for clarity, it should be noted that Sebba (2007: 10–11) does make a finely nuanced distinction between orthography and spelling, with orthography being "the set of conventions for writing words of the language" and spelling "the application of those conventions to write actual words."

[8] Sampson (2018b) proposes this generalization based on two separate properties. The first is orthographic constancy, which refers to assigning "a constant written shape to each lexical element – each morpheme, or at least each root (as opposed to grammatical affix morphemes) – even if that element varies its phonetic shape in different environments" (Sampson 2018b: 10), as in *divine* and *divinity*. The second property, acknowledged as potentially more controversial, is sparse orthographic neighborhoods: having fewer "other words which differ by only one letter, or by few letters in a long sequence" (Sampson 2018b: 16).

One solution to this issue could be to simply expand the scope of the term orthography, in order to embrace all the linguistically and sociohistorically derived conventions that contribute to the complexities of determining what to regard as 'correctly written' from among alternative written representations. To the extent that many scholars generally adopt such an inclusive interpretation, that is essentially what has come to pass. However, there is undoubtedly considerable merit in seeking to distinguish assiduously between the distinct linguistic (i.e. applications of representational mapping principles) and the diverse sociohistorical factors (i.e. spelling irregulates, homophone distinctions, loanwords, identity, reform) that underlie both regular and irregular written representations.

While not underestimating the difficulties of formulating meaningful distinctions, the more recent emergence of graphematics may be helpful in this respect, at least, in providing some additional terminology demarcations. Weingarten (2011) and Neef (2012, 2015) both use the term *graphematics* to refer to the interface between abstract representational mappings and graphemes. The close parallels to both the abstract sense of writing system and the core sense of orthography are unmistakable. However, Neef (2015: 713) also defines graphematics as the module or "component of the writing system that captures the relation between letters and phonological units of the language system," where the reference to writing system is clearly on its secondary meaning of the set of material signs. More specifically, within his modular theory of writing systems (2012, 2015), Neef postulates both an obligatory graphematics module, which can potentially generate a set of multiple candidate spellings of a word, referred to as the *graphematic solution space*, and an optional module of *systematic orthography*, as a system of regulating constraints on the solution space. Undeniably, the systematic orthography module requires further elaboration, particularly in regard to Neef's (2015: 716) fleeting mention of 'conventional orthography', but the theory seems to offer a tenable framework for delineating more coherently between linguistic (i.e. representational mappings) and other sociohistorical influences (i.e. deviations and irregularities) on written representations.

Another tangible corollary derives from the notion of the graphematic solution space: the potential for multiple alternative representations to exist free from any prescriptive presumptions of 'orthographic' correctness. As already noted, Joyce and Masuda (2019) deliberate over the trinity of key terms primarily from the perspective of the contemporary Japanese writing system. More specifically, they contend that, although it is reasonable to refer to the conventions that govern its component scripts as orthography, the term's regulatory connotations of 'correct writing' are simply not reconcilable with the fungible nature of the Japanese writing system as a whole, where alternative written representations are the norm (Backhouse 1984: 219, Joyce et al.

2012: 255–60, Joyce and Masuda 2018: 182–89).[9] Although Joyce and Masuda espouse the notion of graphematic representation with specific reference to Japanese, in being unencumbered by any *a priori* concerns for orthodoxy, the concept appears to have more universal relevance, when referring to the presence of multiple alternative written representations within any writing system.[10]

7.3.2 A Sample of Typologies

This section samples some of the most influential, controversial and promising typology proposals to date (see also both Joyce and Borgwaldt 2011 and Coulmas 1996b). It is essentially descriptive in nature, with fuller discussions of the various conceptual and terminology issues deferred to Subsection 7.3.3.

However, before embarking on that in earnest, it is beneficial at this point to make a basic statement, which, on one level, seems quite straightforward and uncontroversial and, yet, on another level, remains as a truism that has still to be fully explicated within writing systems research. Simply put, writing systems represent language. Superficially, the observation might seem rather trivial, and, thus, not worth articulating, but it most definitely justifies periodic repetition. The refrain can be traced from Hill (1967: 92), who claimed that his typology placed "every system of writing in relation to that which all systems represent, language," to Sproat (2010: 9) emphasizing how "all writing systems represent elements of *language* – not ideas or something else," and to Daniels (2018: 157) more recently proclaiming simply that "writing represents language." Read (1983: 143) also frames the insight deftly, when perceptively observing that, because "writing is the representation of specific linguistic forms,"[11] it "requires a writing system, a shared way of pairing representations with linguistic forms." The direct ramification of that realization

[9] The coexistence of multiple graphematic representations is an intrinsic characteristic of the Japanese writing system (secondary sense of all signs), where the multiple material scripts can render alternative graphematic representations according to their different mapping principles (writing system in the primary sense). Thus, 山 (*kanji*), やま (*hiragana*), ヤマ (*katakana*), and YAMA (*rōmaji*) are all equally valid graphematic variants of the Japanese word /yama/ 'mountain' (Joyce and Masuda 2018, Masuda and Joyce 2018). As an approach to identifying the various motivational factors that underlie both conventional orthographic and nonconventional, or variant, written representations, Joyce and Masuda (2019) supplement the notion of conventionality with an inclusive notion of intentionality espoused on the assumption that written representations are always motivated to some degree.

[10] A potential quandary here hinges on whether *orthographic variation* might be construed as an oxymoron. Under an inclusive interpretation of *orthography*, where the term is essentially synonymous with *written representation*, the issue is largely immaterial. On the other hand, if *orthography* is about presiding over what is 'correctly written', given that only one representation can be *orthographically* acceptable, in a narrower, prescriptive sense, the issue has immense significance.

[11] As Read (1983: 143) also points out, "specific linguistic forms" means that, although photographs and paintings may communicate a message, they are not writing, as echoed in Sproat's (2010) caveat about ideas. Presumably, if they had existed at the time, Read would have also classified emoji as images that are not writing.

is that writing systems must essentially function at one of three linguistic levels – either at the levels of *morphemes*, *syllables*[12] or *phonemes* – and the primary goal of the typology of writing systems should be to clearly communicate these core possibilities (see also Chapter 4, this volume). However, the relatively small, but expanding, collection of typologies proposed so far have generally failed to do that adequately, as the following outlines illustrate.

Even though seriously flawed on a pivotal issue, unquestionably Gelb (1952) stands as a seminal work on writing systems, as it attempted to lay the foundations for the scientific study of writing. Gelb's classification recognized five categories in total, but it should be noted that (1) pictorial representation and (2) mnemonic devices were both seen as being the forerunners of writing and so were distinguished from the main grouping of full writing, which included the final three categories of (3) word-syllabic (mixture of *logography* (word + writing) and syllabic), (4) syllabic and (5) alphabetic. Notwithstanding the insightful emphasis on the notion of full writing, Gelb's classification was fundamentally blemished by his zeal to present the evolution of writing as a teleology, which inevitably transitions via logography and syllabary to a final stage of an alphabet. A number of writing systems scholars have discussed the problems with Gelb's classification at length, including Coulmas (1996a), Daniels (1990, 2001), Rogers (2005), Sproat (2000) and Trigger (2004).

Although the 1960s were not completely fallow of proposals, such as those from Diringer (1962) and Hill (1967), the next typology that merits mention is that proposed by Haas (1976, 1983). It stands as an early attempt to move away from the historically oriented approach that Gelb (1952) represents, because it was more conceptual in nature. More specifically, Haas's (1976) classification involved a set of three binary choices or contrasts. They are *derived–original*, where *pictographs* (*picture* + *writing*) are regarded as original because they do not correspond in a regular way to speech; *empty–informed*, depending on whether or not a grapheme directly determines a meaning; and *motivated–arbitrary*, depending on whether or not the relation between a grapheme and its referent is pictorial in nature. These choices are logically independent, but not all of the combinatory possibilities are real, because, for example, an *empty* writing system cannot also be *motivated*. Accordingly, the scheme effectively only recognizes five kinds of writing systems, and although the contrasts are useful for differentiating between types of pictorial representation, only the empty–informed contrast has relevance for other writing systems. On the basis of the Greek words for empty and full, respectively, Haas (1976, 1983) also referred to that contrast as *cenemic–pleremic*, such that cenemic writing

[12] Notwithstanding the debate over the status of the mora, a phonological unit of syllable weight, for writing systems (Rogers 2005, Gnanadesikan 2011, 2012, 2017, Buckley 2018), within the scope of this chapter, it is sufficient to acknowledge Gnanadesikan's (2011: 395) claim that "looking at writing systems for evidence of syllabic structures yields strong evidence for the linguistic reality of syllables."

systems only represent sounds (i.e. phonographic writing systems) but the graphemes of pleremic writing systems are semantically informed in denoting both sounds and meanings (morphography).

The next typology to note is that by Sampson (1985, 2015), which is particularly noteworthy for a couple of reasons. Firstly, it ushered in a flurry of works from the mid-1980s onwards, which started to attract wider interest to the study of writing systems, and, secondly, it has inspired considerable, albeit often misguided, debate about its categories, as evidenced for example by DeFrancis (1989, 2002), DeFrancis and Unger (1994), Sampson (1994, 2016a, 2016b) and Unger and DeFrancis (1995). Within Sampson's typology, the first division is between *semasiographic (meaning, signification + writing)*, a category that Sampson intended to be conjectural in nature, and *glottographic (speech + writing)* writing systems. At the next level, glottographic is divided into logographic and phonographic. Moreover, on the basis of what Sampson also deemed to be a logical possibility, the category of logographic is subdivided into polymorphemic units and morphemic, even though Sampson acknowledges that no systems based on polymorphemic units actually exist. The phonographic category was also further divided into three subcategories of syllabic, segmental and featural (where grapheme components correlate with phonetic features), with the latter included solely to include Korean Han'gŭl, another aspect of Sampson's classification that has prompted much debate.

Also significant for greatly contributing to the growing interest in writing systems from the late 1980s is DeFrancis's (1989) book, which presented his writing classification scheme. At the heart of DeFrancis's classification is the important dichotomy between what he refers to as 'partial' and 'full' writing systems, and, directly linked to that, DeFrancis's conviction in the phonetic basis of all full writing systems. In line with his belief that writing is simply the visual representation of speech, DeFrancis's (1989) scheme distinguishes between six types of writing systems. Although all six types fall under the umbrella of syllabic systems, two types, (1) 'pure' syllabic systems (including Linear B, *kana* and Cherokee) and (2) morpho-syllabic systems (including Sumerian, Chinese and Mayan), are distinguished from the other four types that are referred to as consonantal systems. In turn, these consonantal systems are further differentiated into (3) morpho-consonantal systems (including Egyptian) and (4) 'pure' consonantal systems (including Phoenician, Hebrew and Arabic), with the final two types, (5) 'pure' phonemic systems (including Greek, Latin and Finnish) and (6) morpho-phonemic systems (including English, French and Korean), being classified as alphabetic systems.

Despite the hugely significant contributions that the typological proposals by Gelb (1952), Sampson (1985, 2015) and DeFrancis (1989) have made to the discipline of writing systems research, the classification proposed and developed by Daniels (1990, 2001, 2009, 2018) has undoubtedly been one of the most influential of the last three decades. One of Daniels's primary motivations has been to address the inadequacies that he perceived in the traditional tripartite classification, such as in Gelb's (1952) typology, of writing systems as either word-syllabic, syllabaries or alphabets. More specifically, Daniels has argued for the recognition of two other script types, namely, *abjads*, where each character stands for a consonant, and *abugidas*, where each character stands for a consonant accompanied by a particular vowel, with other vowels indicated by additions to the character (see especially Chapter 2, this volume). Daniels (1990) coined both terms, which have also been the focus of much discussion. Modeled on the exemplar term *alphabet*, as the combination of alpha and beta, abjad is formed from the first letters of the Arabic script, the most widespread example of the kind, while abugida is an Ethiopic word formed from the initial letters according to their traditional ordering. For much of its history, the classification has consisted of six categories: (1) logosyllabary (morphosyllabary), (2) syllabary, (3) abjad (Semitic-type script), (4) alphabet (Greek-type script), (5) abugida (Sanskrit-type script) and (6) featural. However, Daniels's (2018) version no longer recognizes the featural category, for Korean Han'gŭl, which is classified as an alphabet. Deeply connected to the limitations of Gelb's tripartite classification, Daniels challenges Gelb's teleology, for, as Daniels (2001: 68) comments, "once abugidas are distinguished from syllabaries, a different historical sequence can be identified, which no longer privileges the alphabet teleologically."

In addition to the considerable influence of Daniels's (1990, 2001, 2009, 2018) classification, three other typology proposals also merit explicit mention within the present selective sampling. Of those, Sproat (2000) and, subsequently, Rogers (2005) are closely related. In their more radical departures from the traditional inverted-tree typology, both adopt a similar strategy of locating writing systems within a theoretical space defined by two dimensions: the type of phonography (five categories arranged horizontally) and the amount of logography/morphography (represented vertically) involved within a writing system. Although Rogers's (2005) version essentially follows Sproat's (2000) basic tactic, their typologies differ in two key respects. The first is with regard to the category terms used to refer to types of phonography. Sproat distinguishes five categories as consonantal, polyconsonantal, alphabetic, core syllabic and syllabic, whereas Rogers elects to label them as abjad, alphabetic, abugida, moraic and syllabic, respectively.[13] The second key difference relates to the label assigned to the vertical axis. Sproat's original proposal was for *amount of logography*, adopting a rather inclusive interpretation of logography as "any component of a writing system as having a logographic function if it formally encodes a portion of nonphonological linguistic

[13] It should be noted that even though a number of the writing systems common to both typologies are accorded similar treatments, not all of the examples noted are the same.

structure, whether it be a whole morpheme or merely some semantic portion of that morpheme" (Sproat 2000: 134). In contrast, Rogers (2005: 275) refers to this dimension as *amount of morphography*.

Last but not least, Gnanadesikan (2017) tenders another typological proposal. While it is incomplete, in that it currently falls short of explicitly addressing the issues of morphographic writing systems, it is a promising approach to more finely delineating the differences between phonemic writing systems, even though it incorporates a somewhat different notion of writing systems typology. Still, there can be no dispute that, no matter how best conceived of, "writing systems have many components," from their graphemes, their spatial arrangements, their representational mappings, and their orthographic, or graphematic representational, principles, such that "typologies may (and probably should) be constructed which consider any of these components" (Gnanadesikan 2017: 14). Central to Gnanadesikan's (2017: 21) typology proposal is the term *segmentary*, which she defines as "a script all or most of whose signs are used in such a way as to encode individual phonological segments, or phonemes (which may include archiphonemes and morphophonemes)." Moreover, it is worth stressing that Gnanadesikan's typology eschews the inverted-tree structure common to a number of earlier typologies. Indeed, the tabular presentation (Gnanadesikan 2017: 28) of the typology and its terminology rather resembles a decision-tree diagram in key aspects. Arranged under three columns of category, values and term, the highest category distinction depends on whether characters basically represent segments (yes/no), while the lowest divisions are according to the degree to which vowels are included (ranging from all, most, some and none). Illustrative of the detailed classification descriptions that Gnanadesikan's typology yields (2017: 29), for example, Han'gŭl is classified as being "fully vowelled syllabically arranged featural segmentary," Devanāgarī as a "mostly vowelled āksharik segmentary," Greek as a "fully vowelled linear segmentary" and unvocalized Arabic as a "partial vowelled linear segmentary."

7.3.3 Conceptual and Terminology Distinctions

Having outlined a selection of important typologies, this section seeks to highlight some of the key conceptual and terminology contrasts that have shaped the various proposals and underlie the diverse range of category labels. Extending on Joyce's (2016) similar deliberations, the endeavor draws inspiration from both Coulmas's (1996b) observation (see note 2) and Powell's (2009: xv) assertion that writing "can be defined and understood, but only with the help of a careful organization of categories and terms." As even scholarly typologies embody different notions about the inventions and historical diffusion of writing systems (see Henderson 1982, Joyce 2011, 2016, Powell 2009), as well as divergent beliefs about language, it is pertinent to briefly note the problematic tendency, still frequency encountered, to perceive of language primarily in terms of speech. Largely influenced by Bloomfield (1933) and his much-cited comments about writing being merely a means of transcribing speech, many scholars still ascribe to the *language is speech* position (Joyce 2002, 2011), or what Rastle (2019) refers to as the concept of *primacy* (see also Chapter 5, this volume). Essentially, the position confuses *language* with *speech* within the standard refrains that speech, but not writing, exists in all human communities and speech is naturally acquired, whereas writing requires instruction. Yet, only a passing familiarity with sign languages is sufficient to realize that sound is not a defining characteristic of language. In contrast, the *abstract entity* position (Joyce 2002, 2011) merely regards speech, writing and signing as alternative media of expressing language, which are interconnected through conventions that allow for the approximate transformations of linguistic content. Although the *language is speech* view undoubtedly gained wider circulation due to DeFrancis (1989), as Harris (2009: 46) notes, the naïve assumption can be traced back to Graeco-Roman Antiquity. Even though they sometimes function in a complementary manner, speech and writing are "completely independent, having quite different semiological foundations." The specter of the *language is speech* position is discernible in some definitions of writing. For example, Daniels (1996a: 3, 2009: 36, 2018: 156) continues to define writing as "a system of more or less permanent marks used to represent an utterance in such a way that it can be recovered more or less exactly without the intervention of the utterer."

As expressed in the introduction, the ongoing linguistic enterprise of developing typologies is endeavoring to realize a coherent framework, or conceptual tool, that can be utilized to enrich our understanding of writing systems. However, given the elusive, closely interconnected nature of the three core terms and the wider range of terminology labels that the undertaking is generating, it must also be appreciated that, in reflecting certain opinions about what to emphasize, such classifications are, to some degree, always arbitrary in nature. Still, for writing systems typologies to fully contribute to our understandings of written language both diachronically and synchronically, typology proposals should strive to meaningfully reflect the dominant principles of representational mapping that writing systems incorporate and to employ consistent and transparent terminology in signaling those mapping principles (Joyce 2011, 2016: 288–89). Although some typology proposals have explored alternative formats, as noted earlier, many prominent classifications are visually depicted as inverted-tree diagrams. Such diagrams start from the most inclusive categories at the top, with lower category distinctions typically represented as diverging branches, usually terminating with writing systems at the very bottom. In broadly keeping with that directional metaphor, the present discussion progresses from the upper, broader classification categories down toward the lower, more specific ones.

The first concept and term that warrants comment is *semasiography*, a term coined by Gelb (1952) to serve as an inclusive term for various symbolic devices for conveying general meanings. The category has featured within a number of classifications over the years, from Gelb (1952), Diringer (1962), Haas (1983) and Sampson (1985, 2015) to Rogers (2005) and Powell (2009).[14] Arguably, the category has some merit within a broader classification of symbols or pictorial representations, but, as DeFrancis (1989) forcefully argues, it is vital to recognize that forms of semasiography are always extremely limited in what they can express. Consistent with DeFrancis's (1989) classification, a natural outcome of treating forms of semasiography as *nonwriting*, or, at best, as only *partial writing*, is the realization that the semasiography category falls just outside the scope of a typology of writing systems.[15] This key insight seems to bear periodic reiterating, given that, within the more generalist literature on writing, there seems to be something of a re-emergence of the myths that semasiography, ideography and pictography all have the potential to function as full writing systems, particularly in reference to the expressive potentials of emoji (Danesi 2017, Joyce 2019). Although indicative of the tenacity of some misconceptions, that is most assuredly not the case and, in that context, the distinction between partial and full writing also warrants renewed emphasis (DeFrancis 1989, Joyce 2019). Typologies that include semasiography essentially need to generate a new category; this is labeled as *glottography* by Sampson (1985, 2015) and as *lexigraphy* (*word* + *writing*) by Powell (2009). Although Powell (2009: 37) appears, at one point, to endorse the literal interpretation of lexigraphy in glossing it as "writing with words," from his subsequent definition, "writing in which the signs are attached to necessary forms of speech" (2009: 51), it would seem that the superficial difference from glottography is immaterial.

Before turning to the three linguistic levels at which writing systems generally function, it is appropriate to comment on the other terms that have historically overlapped to considerable degrees with semasiography; namely, *pictography* and *ideography* (*idea* + *writing*). As already suggested, the term pictography is regaining wider circulation since the emergence of 絵文字 /emoji/ 'emoji' (literally, 'picture' + 'character'), a regrettable trend that potentially perpetuates certain oversimplifications concerning the origins

[14] Sampson (1994: 119–20) has subsequently stressed that, rather than arguing for the existence of such systems, his intention was conjectural in nature (as the dotted line in his figures sought to indicate, see Sampson 1985, 2015) and he was merely speculating on "whether there might ever be a semasiographic system comparable in expressive power to a spoken language." Within a glossary entry, Rogers (2005: 297) defines "semasiographic writing" as an "alternative name for semantic writing system," the term he uses. Although Rogers (2005) argues for the existence of one semantic writing system in Bliss symbols (Bliss 1965), Sproat (2010) astutely stresses the limitations of Bliss symbolics as a writing system.

[15] In this respect, it is worth recalling Read's (1983) remarks about writing requiring consensus about the mapping relationships between linguistic forms and symbols.

of writing systems. Of course, there is a grain of truth in claiming that the core signs in all three independent inventions of writing in Sumer, China and Mesoamerica originally involved some degree of pictographic resemblance to the objects that they signified (such as 口 /kuchi/ 'mouth', 火 /hi/ 'fire' and 魚 /sakana/ 'fish'). However, the serious limitations on pictorial representation, from both the production and perception perspectives, underscore the fact that pictographs alone simply cannot function as a full writing system. In many ways, the issues associated with semasiography, pictography and ideography relate to what has been the most evasive typological distinction to conceptualize, namely that between nonphonographic and phonographic writing systems, which remains one of the major sources of confusions about writing (Joyce and Borgwaldt 2011: 2, Joyce 2016: 293, Sampson 2016a: 561, 2018b: 4).[16] At times, the division has been cast as being between ideography, the most problematic of these terms, and phonography. However, now that the myth of ideography (i.e. that it is possible to have a full system of writing based solely on *graphs* which directly express *ideas* independently from language) has largely been dispelled, the contrast is usually framed as being between phonography and logography. The deeper significance of this typological division becomes clearer once one realizes that it is essentially the same as the *pleremic* and *cenemic* contrast within the writing system typology proposed by Haas (1976, 1983). As noted in Subsection 7.3.2, the graphemes of cenemic writing systems only represent sounds (i.e. phonography), but the graphemes of pleremic writing systems denote both sounds and meanings – the modern exemplar being Chinese characters. As Joyce (2011: 67) points out, the enduring dilemma for advocators of the *language is speech* perspective is to provide an adequate account of the existence and function of the nonphonological, or semantic elements, of Chinese characters, if writing is merely representing speech.

As already noted, it turns out that there are basically three levels of linguistic structure at which writing can function in (generally) systematic ways of representing language – the morpheme, syllable and phoneme levels. Moreover, the implications for a typology of writing systems should be immediately obvious: it should consist of three basic typological categories that correspond to these levels, and these should be clearly distinguished with terminology that is both informative and consistent. Unfortunately, misconceptions and confusions are present at these levels too. Taking the morpheme level first, the main problem appears to be that of conservatism. As Joyce (2011: 70) argues, given the consensus among scholars of writing systems

[16] As Sampson (2016a: 561) insightfully comments, although researchers generally differentiate between alphabetic and syllabic scripts, that "is a relatively minor distinction, set against the contrast between logographic scripts, which assign distinct marks to meaningful units of a language, i.e. words or morphemes, and phonographic scripts which represent phonological units of one size or another."

(Hill 1967: 93, Sampson 1985: 32, Taylor 1988: 203, Daniels 1996: 4, 2001: 43, Fischer 2001: 170, Rogers 2005: 14, Gnanadesikan 2009: 8) that morphography is a more precise typological label than logography, typologies should cease to perpetuate this particular confusion. Indeed, as Daniels (2018: 156) explicitly acknowledges, "'morphography' would actually be preferable to 'logography.'"[17] The sheer number of symbols necessary for a purely word-based writing system means that the only level above the syllable level that a writing system can function at is the morpheme level, taken to be inclusive of both free (i.e. words) and bound morphemes. As Hill (1967) astutely pointed out some time ago, in contrast to the phonological analysis of words within cenemic writing systems, the analysis of word meaning for pleremic writing systems naturally settles on the morpheme, the smallest element of linguistic meaning.

Turning next to the syllable level, or the syllabography category, although failures to consistently apply coherent criteria are highly endemic among typologies, the ramifications are especially conspicuous at this level. The primary criteria for typologies should be the linguistic level that is predominately represented by the unitary symbols of a writing system. If it is the syllable, then it should be classified as being syllabographic, irrespective of whether or not the symbols only provide approximate indications of a target syllable and regardless of whether or not they possess internal structure or share visual similarities. As testimony to Daniels's (2001: 68) observation that the "key to the history of writing is the primacy of the syllable," it is hardly surprising that syllabographic writing has actually been realized in different ways. However, for a principled typology, it is vital to preserve the integrity of the linguistic level and to locate further method demarcations at a new level within a typology. Notwithstanding his keen insight about the significance of the syllable, Daniels's (1990, 1996a, 2001, 2009, 2018) classification is perhaps the most influential example of a typology that is greatly undermined by this basic confounding problem. As outlined earlier, his classification now distinguishes five categories, but from a typological perspective, it is clearly mixing heterogeneous typological criteria in its confusion of linguistic levels (categories 1 and 2) with exemplar names (categories 3, 4 and 5).

[17] Although the following comments from Daniels (2018: 99) are being noted here primarily in relation to the problems with the term *logographic*, they are also of relevance to the evasive division, noted earlier, between cenemic and pleremic writing systems in terms of full writing systems. "The solutions ultimately hit upon around the world were surprisingly similar: develop characters for their sounds, but also use characters for their meanings. In the latter use, the characters are called 'word-signs,' or logograms. The term *heterogram* appears sometimes in Iranian studies. [...] Since it's noncommittal as to the level of grammatical analysis involved – it doesn't specify 'word' or 'morpheme,' just 'otherness' – it might be convenient to adopt it for general use." However, as Joyce (2019) remarks, it is quite difficult to see how being noncommittal in nature on a key issue for writing systems research can be considered an appropriate justification for proposing a new term, when, rather than elucidating, it would merely serve to obscure matters further.

The serious consequence is that these typological categories essentially obscure the key point that syllabography is the common underlining principle for *syllabaries* (basically separate symbols), *abjads* (underspecification of the target syllable's vowel), *abugidas* (extensions to graphemes for core syllables) and *featural* (elements combined as a block; a grapheme gestalt). A similar underappreciation for the importance of maintaining coherent typological conventions also appears to underlie a number of muddled compound labels, such as *consonantal alphabet* for abjad (Gnanadesikan 2009: 10) and *alphasyllabic* for abugida (Bright 1999: 45). These are defective as informative typological labels on two counts: they fail to specify the more salient linguistic level and convey little about grapheme structures.

The firm hand of conservatism is also the major source of distortion at the final linguistic level of phonemic writing. Despite Diringer's (1962: 24) claim that "alphabetic writing has within the past three thousand years assumed such importance as to deserve a category of its own," the practice of labeling the category after its sole exemplar is absolutely antithetical to the objectives of a typology to be informative and consistent (Hill 1967: 92, Coulmas 1996b: 1381). From the perspective of illustrating the possible relationships between language and writing, it is vital to appreciate two related points about phonemic writing systems that consist of symbols for both consonants and vowels. The first is that all extant alphabets trace back to the Greek alphabet, "a single invention that took place at a single time" (Powell 2009: 231). The second point, which also underscores its uniqueness, is the unnaturalness of phoneme segmentation, which Faber (1992: 112) argues to be a consequence of alphabetic writing rather than being a necessary precursor (for related experimental findings, see also Read et al. 1986). One of the crucial challenges for typologies of writing systems is to discern the core set of principles of representational mapping that operate within the apparent diversity of the world's writing systems (Joyce and Borgwaldt 2011: 5, Joyce 2016: 291). As Coulmas (1996b: 1380) rightly notes, the typology of writing systems must find the right balance between too many categories that overlook key commonalities and too few categories that obscure important distinctions. Accordingly, the present discussions have been shaped largely by two typological tenets. The first is that the primary categories of the typology should match to the relevant linguistic units – either the morpheme, syllable or phoneme. The second is that, because further demarcations (whether attempting to capture different methods of realization or principle mixtures, see Subsection 7.4.1) are typologically different in nature, they require additional levels of categories. While it remains to be seen whether Gnanadesikan's (2017) typology of phonemic writing systems can be extended to encompass all writing systems, it certainly has considerable merit in highlighting the limitations of single-term classification labels, such as abjads and abugidas.

7.4 Complexities of Writing Systems

This section consists of two related subsections, which seek to highlight the limitations of representational principles as a typology criterion and briefly consider the possibilities of exploring some complementary or alternative criteria, respectively.

7.4.1 Representational Mapping Principles as Idealizations

As Subsection 7.3.2 sought to exemplify, on the whole, existing proposals of writing system typologies have invariably attempted to classify writing systems based on the dominant principle of representational mapping, or graphematic representation, that underlies different systems (i.e. at either the morpheme, syllable or phoneme levels). However, as those levels and their mapping principles combine in complex ways, in reality, most writing systems are, to varying degrees, mixed in nature (Gelb 1952: 199, DeFrancis and Unger 1994, Trigger 2004: 46, Joyce and Meletis 2021: 2). Thus, it is vital to keep in mind that the principles of graphematic representation are to, a considerable extent, essentially idealizations. To underscore that point, this subsection discusses a relevant commentary and two related typological proposals, where the issues of typological purity are particularly salient.

Reflecting its somewhat complicated theoretical motivations, on the one hand, and that it falls short of constituting a systematic typology proposal, on the other hand, DeFrancis and Unger (1994, see also Unger and DeFrancis 1995) can be viewed more as a commentary on the evasive cenemic–pleremic contrast (and, hence, not covered in Subsection 7.3.2). Envisaging *pure* phonography and *pure* logography as representing opposing extremes of a theoretical continuum, DeFrancis and Unger (1994) advocate for what they consider to be a *realistic* view of writing system typology. Juxtaposing their realistic view with what they take to be *naïve* typologies in assuming two distinctive groupings of writing systems falling toward the two opposing extremes with an empty middle space, DeFrancis and Unger (1994) claim that the actual range of writing systems occupies only the middle area of the continuum. More specifically, DeFrancis and Unger (1994) posit six writing systems within the middle section, with three on the phonographic side of the continuum and three on the logographic side. Thus, Finnish is positioned closest toward the extreme of pure phonography, with French and then English placed progressively closer to the center, while Chinese is set closest toward the extreme of pure logography, with Japanese more central than Chinese and Korean situated more centrally still. Clearly, the typology proposals of most relevance in this context are those proposed by Sproat (2000) and by Rogers (2005). As already outlined, they are highly similar in terms of applying the same basic strategy of locating writing systems within a theoretical space. In contrast, however, to the one-dimensional phonography–logography continuum hypothesized by DeFrancis and Unger (1994), the theoretical spaces in both Sproat's (2000) and Rogers's (2005) typology proposals are two-dimensional in nature. Within both, five categories of phonography are organized along the respective horizontal axes, but the vertical axes represent the amount of logography within Sproat's (2000) typology and the amount of morphography within Rogers's (2005) typology.

However, regardless of the number of dimensions actually theorized, there are a couple of fundamental issues that are common to DeFrancis and Unger (1994), Sproat (2000) and Rogers (2005). The first is that, in all cases, the locating of writing systems is highly arbitrary in nature, whether along the single continuum in DeFrancis and Unger (1994), or at various degrees, or depths, of logography or morphology in Sproat (2000) and Rogers (2005), respectively (although Sproat and Gutkin (2021) subsequently propose a measurement approach). The second issue, albeit less conspicuously highlighted in DeFrancis and Unger (1994), is how the phonographic dimension entails different categories that are assumed to be mutually exclusive. However, advocating mutually exclusive categories would appear to entirely miss the deeper insight that any representational inconsistencies that exist are the direct consequences of a particular writing system simultaneously employing a mixture of graphematic principles, of which morphography is one, rather than constituting a separate dimension completely. This is particularly telling, because Rogers (2005: 275) explicitly sought to differentiate the amount of morphography from what he claimed to be a related, but separate, notion of orthographic depth (see Katz and Frost 1992b). In reality, although the concept of orthographic depth was formulated primarily to account for varying degrees of consistency in grapheme–phoneme correspondences within the context of investigating the psychological processes of reading, it is, of course, intimately related to the insight that representational mapping principles are idealizations and, thus, all writing systems are to some extent mixed in nature.

Moreover, although the basic dichotomy has been around for some time, the distinction between partial versus full writing is of immense significance for writing systems typologies (Joyce 2019). The contrast was certainly acknowledged in Gelb (1952: 194), but, arguably, it is first accorded its appropriate prominence in DeFrancis (1989: 3), even though his formulation is not entirely without flaws. For DeFrancis, partial writing is "a system of graphic symbols that can be used to convey only some thought," while full writing "can be used to convey any and all thought." Two crucial caveats to note immediately, however, are that the contrast is actually about the potential to represent language, as the medium of thought, and that the dichotomy is also an idealization. The significance of this dichotomy for writing systems typologies hinges on the simple, yet key, observation that only cenemic writing systems can become full writing, but partial pleremic writing systems still warrant special attention within writing systems research. More specifically, the discipline still needs to develop coherent accounts of just how the graphemes of a pleremic writing system represent the morphemes of the specific language. Such expositions are critical not only to account for historical examples but to also adequately elucidate the contemporary examples of the Chinese and Japanese writing systems, as well as comprehensively expounding the full complexities of mixed writing systems, such as the notoriously complicated English writing system. In developing such accounts, it is also vital to stress a couple of key points. Firstly, pleremic writing systems are always partial writing systems, because it is simply not possible to represent all the words of a language by the morphographic principle alone, as there are simply too many words in all languages (and, thus, other graphematic principles must also be employed simultaneously). Secondly, morphography is the only feasible level for pleremic writing systems, as it is essential to have consensus-based associations between graphemes and linguistic units for a writing system to be fully functional. The point about the importance of consensus regarding sign–language associations also underscores why emoji are unlikely to ever become a partial pleremic writing system, despite rising popular misunderstandings to the contrary. In seeking to establish more realistic accounts of how the semantic elements of Japanese *kanji* function, for instance, one might do well to consider Robertson's (2004: 19) insightful observation on the possibility of writing emerging from the intersection between "highly developed avenues of human perception – visual (iconic) and auditory (symbolic) perception."

7.4.2 Exploring Alternative Criteria

Undoubtedly, there is considerable merit in classifying writing systems based on their dominant principles of representational mapping, as it endows typologies with sound linguistic foundations. It is, however, also worth exploring a far wider range of the characteristics and properties associated with writing systems, in terms of their potentials to serve as either complementary or alternative criteria for investigating and differentiating writing systems.

That noted, however, given the complexities of writing systems and their various component elements (Gnanadesikan 2017: 14), it is also extremely important to assess the many candidate characteristics and properties that have already been singled out for consideration, in order to determine which of the three core notions is of most relevance. That is especially so in light of the considerable confusions that continue to surround them, as Subsection 7.3.1 outlined. For example, Altmann (2008: 150) enumerates ten properties of scripts that can be beneficially investigated. However, although a number of them do indeed relate specifically to the material shapes of signs (graphemes) and their shared attributes as a set, some of the proposed properties are clearly more germane to the principles of graphematic representation.

Thus, although (1) *inventory size*, (2) *complexity*, (3) *frequency*, (4) *ornamentality*, (5) *distinctivity* and (6) *variability* are unquestionably characteristics of the material script, the rest are not, including (7) *phonemic load*, (8) *grapheme size*, (9) *graphemic load* and (10) *graphemic utility* or letter usefulness. Moreover, even if the properties or dimensions under investigation are sufficiently restricted to just one of the basic terms, such as script, that does not necessarily make them suitable for valid comparisons across multiple writing systems. For example, a recent study by Chang et al. (2018) focuses on four dimensions that undeniably relate primarily to script forms, namely, (1) perimetric complexity (ratio of form to white space), (2) number of disconnected components, (3) number of connected points and (4) number of simple features (strokes). Chang et al.'s (2018: 427) claim that the graphic complexity across the world's writing systems "is associated with variable mappings that graphic units can have to linguistic units (abjad, alphabetic, syllabary, alphasyllabary, and morphosyllabary)" is reasonable *prima facie*. However, the striking dissociation within their data plots between the morphosyllabary writing system example of Chinese and all the other writing systems examined blatantly indicates that these dimensions are reflecting more than a simple notion of graphic complexity; once again the evasive contrast between the variable mappings of pleremic and cenemic writing systems has been entirely confounded.

Similar to Altmann's (2008) script properties, the problems of not sufficiently specifying the aspect of most relevance are also highly apparent in the related studies by Share and Daniels (2016) and Daniels and Share (2018), even though their intention to highlight a wider range of ten dimensions that potentially underlie writing system variation is certainly laudable.[18] Clearly, Daniels and Share's (2018) dimensions of *inventory size* and *visual uniformity and complexity* are concerned primarily with properties of the material script, which could also be potentially extended to *ligaturing*. However, the other dimensions, including *linguistic distance, spatial arrangement and nonlinearity, historical change, spelling constancy despite morphophonemic alternation, omission of phonological elements* and *allography*, as well as *dual purpose letters*, quickly merge into the overlapping domains of representational mapping (writing system in its primary sense) and an inclusive interpretation of orthography. As consistently alluded to, writing systems research needs to accord greater attention to carefully and consistently differentiating between writing system, script and orthography and to tracing out their complicated interactions. Adopting a different approach to thinking about the potential

[18] To provide some brief context to their dimension proposals, Daniels and Share (2018) specifically claim that the two dominant approaches to studying cross-script diversity, namely, orthographic depth (Katz and Frost 1992b) and psycholinguistic grain size theory (Ziegler and Goswami 2005) are both "deeply entrenched in Anglophone and Eurocentric/alphabetist perspectives."

merits of evaluating alternative criteria, Meletis (2018, 2019b) suggests that candidate criteria can be beneficially organized under three categories that embody the notion of fit. The categories are (1) *linguistic fit* (the match between a language and its writing system), (2) *processing fit* (encompassing both physiological and cognitive aspects) and (3) *sociocultural fit* (embracing a range of communicative and social functions). Naturally, with such diverse factors, there are bound to be dynamic interactions between them, even to the extent of often being in conflict, which also necessitates meticulous consideration. Crucially, however, they are also likely to afford further valuable insights into the complexities of writing systems and how they both evolve diachronically and function synchronically (Joyce and Meletis 2021).

7.5 Conclusion

As noted at the outset, as a technology of immense significance, understandably, the widespread dissemination of writing around the world has generated a plethora of diverse writing systems, both historical and contemporary. Thus, for research that targets many aspects of written language, a major challenge is to identify the key properties of writing systems – such as their mapping principles, rather than more superficial aspects, such as variations in sign shapes – that can serve as an effective classification criteria for coherent writing system typologies.

However, as also acknowledged from the start, to the extent that different theoretical assumptions yield divergent typology proposals, it is also valuable to continually assess the conceptual contrasts that shape typology proposals and the terminology employed in communicating them. In that vein, by outlining a selective sample of the most significant typology proposals to date, this chapter has sought to underscore the dialectic interaction between the conceptualizations and the diverse, and often inconsistent, terminology embodied within typologies. Moreover, although the basic typological strategy of classifying writing systems according to their dominant principle of representational mapping is unquestionably well motivated, this chapter has also argued that, because such principles are essentially idealizations, that strategy alone fails to fully capture the complexities of natural writing systems that are often mixed in nature. Accordingly, while also not without inherent challenges, future contributions to the ongoing enterprise of developing typologies might benefit from exploring alternative, or complementary criteria in seeking to further elucidate the materialization of written language both diachronically and synchronically.

Part III

Organization and Development

8

Comparative Historical Perspectives

Per Ambrosiani and Elena Llamas-Pombo

8.1 Introduction

Since its birth as a science for the objective observation of languages, linguistics has emerged as a comparative study of different tongues. For example, Indo-European linguistics has been dealing with, since the late eighteenth century, the common origin of some of the languages in Europe and Asia before they had access to writing (for a synthesis on Indo-European linguistics, see Klein et al. 2017), and Romance linguistics has been engaging with, largely by means of written content, the coincidences and dissimilarities of languages descended from Latin. The cultural globalization of the twenty-first century is promoting the comparative approach over the study of isolated systems. This cultural rationale is shown in the current interest in a general and typological theory of writing that describes units in all languages or compares them over time. Thus, comparative and historical graphematics is an emerging field of research, as a discipline within the umbrella of historical orthography that compares the graphic units of languages. Comparison is the first methodological imperative of the following new disciplines that study writing.

(a) *Comparative graphematics*, as it has been proposed by Weingarten (2011: 13–14, 35), "deals with the writing systems of the world. It aims to identify the linguistic parameters that underlie cross-linguistic differences between writing systems [...] The analysis of at least two languages can provide greater insight into the relevant linguistic structures than can be derived from the analysis of a single language alone." Comparative

Research for Section 8.2 was supported by the research project PID2020-113017GB-I00 on 'Enunciation and French historical pragmatics' from the Ministerio de Ciencia e Innovación, Spain.

graphematics "does not compare writing systems as a whole" because only "detailed linguistic analyses are possible." Comparisons of writing systems are important tools for the decipherment of yet unknown writing systems, as the typological studies that determine the universal parameters along with writing systems vary and so do various fields of applied linguistics (see also Meletis 2022, Meletis and Dürscheid 2022: 119).

(b) The status of the comparative concept is also central in linguistic typology (see *Linguistic Typology* 2016).

(c) *Grapholinguistics* is an emerging interdisciplinary and general area of research that studies all types of writing, not only alphabetic writing systems, and reflects on the role that writing and writing systems play in neighboring disciplines, such as computer science and information technology, communication, typography, psychology and pedagogy (Neef et al. 2012, Neef 2015, Haralambous 2019, 2021, Meletis 2019a: 27, 2020a: 78, 173, 2020b: 250, 2021: 133–34, Meletis and Dürscheid 2022). See also Chapter 6, on grapholinguistic approaches.

(d) *Scripturology* is a new discipline established by Klinkenberg and Polis (2018: 57–59) which concerns the study of different facets of writing but whose scope is wider than in *graphematics* or *graphemics*. Scripturology is understood as "a general theory aiming at the establishment of a semiotic typology of writing systems"; "[...] as a search for the universals of writing, as with the language universals." That said, for Klinkenberg and Polis describing, classifying and ordering the diversity of systems remains an urgent task and it assumes the possibility of comparison (see also Chapter 6, this volume).

This chapter is intended to offer assistance for the linguistic description of writing systems throughout the history of one or several languages. The first decision of the researcher for a comparative analysis of writing systems is to adopt a valid definition of the *grapheme*, the core unit of written language. This is an essential methodological step, since different schools of linguistics consider different elements to be graphemes. In the first section, we consequently establish a working definition of the grapheme, paying special attention to English and Romance languages. The application of this concept is subsequently exemplified by three different methods of diachronic and comparative description of writing systems: Romance *scriptologie*, cultural history of European orthographies and comparative graphematics of punctuation. In the second section of this chapter, we discuss *biscriptality*, which studies the use of two or more writing systems for representing the same language – a phenomenon that is not rare in the history of languages from different families, and that is related to different aspects of society and language users. With examples mainly from Slavic languages, biscriptality is shown to be present on several levels of written language. Biscriptality situations are characterized by dichotomies such as synchronic vs. diachronic biscriptality, monocentric vs. pluricentric biscriptality, and societal vs. individual biscriptality.

8.2 Comparative Graphematics and the Units of Writing Systems

8.2.1 The Concept of Grapheme

The grapheme is the minimal graphic unit with a linguistic (i.e. distinctive) function that is used compositionally in closed systems to build larger units in written language. Graphemes are discrete and combinable units with a spatial manifestation. However, the understandings of the term grapheme diverge considerably as different authors consider it from the following four distinct points of view (see Catach 1990, Pellat 1988, Weingarten et al. 2004: 15–18, Klinkenberg and Polis 2018: 70, Meletis 2019a: 26, 32, 2020a: 77–99, Meletis and Dürscheid 2022: 119–25; see also Chapter 3, Chapter 5 and Chapter 6, this volume).

(a) Following the referential view, the grapheme is the written unit which refers to a phoneme. For example: following the 138 phoneme–grapheme correspondences in British English established by Brooks (2015: 253–65), the phoneme /f/ corresponds to a main system of graphemes: <f> (*full*), <ph> (*physical*) and <ff> (*staff*). These last two units are named *digraphs* or *two-letter graphemes*. The phoneme /f/ also corresponds to other less common two-letter graphemes: <fe> (*carafe*), <ffe> (*giraffe*), <ft> (*often*) and <gh> (*enough*) (Brooks 2015: 260). In this system, English presents *single-letter graphemes* such as <f>, *digraphs* such as <ph>, *trigraphs* such as <ffe> for the phoneme /f/ in *giraffe*, or <cch> for the phoneme /k/ in the word *saccharine*, and even *four-letter graphemes* such as <ngue> for the phoneme /ŋ/ in the word *harangue* /hə'ræŋ/. Brooks (2015: 5) proposes a wide concept of graphemes as "single letters or letter-combinations that represent phonemes."

(b) Following the analogical view, the grapheme is the smallest functional unit of writing, that is, the written unit that is lexically distinctive and identified by commutation, which is tested via written minimal pairs such as <house> and <mouse>, analogously to phonological minimal pairs which can be used to identify phonemes (Klinkenberg and Polis 2018: 70, Meletis 2019a). This is, for example, the concept of grapheme (Spanish *grafema*) used by the Real Academia Española (RAE) in its Spanish *Ortografía*, a work that is both theoretical and normative, aimed at all Spanish language users: "just as phonemes are the minimal distinctive units in the phonic sphere, graphemes are the minimal distinctive units in writing. They are minimal because they cannot be divided into smaller units. They are distinctive because they can differentiate one linguistic sign from another" (RAE 2010: 60–61, our translation). For example, the difference between the words *basta*, *vasta*, *hasta*, *casta* and *pasta* is established in Spanish by opposition of the graphemes <b>, <v>, <h>, <c> and <p>. According to the theory supported by the RAE, the linguistic term grapheme is a synonym for the common word letter, intended as a simple distinctive graphic unit that cannot be divided into smaller units. Therefore, when a phoneme is represented by several graphemes or letters, the RAE refers to these as *digraphs*, *trigraphs* or *tetragraphs*, depending on the number of graphemes they contain. In Spanish, there are only digraphs: *ch* is a digraph representing the phoneme /tʃ/ as in the word *chocolate*, composed of two different graphemes <c> and <h>; *rr* is a digraph representing the voiced apical-alveolar trill /r/, as in *carro* ('car', 'cart'), as opposed to a single *r*, representing /ɾ/, as in *caro* ('expensive'); *ll*, *qu* or *gu* are also digraphs in words such as *llama*, *queso* or *guitarra*. This system includes a grapheme, <h>, which does not correspond to any phoneme in the standard phonological system: for example, the grapheme <h> that appears in the word *hasta* ('until'), which is pronounced /asta/, makes it possible to differentiate between this and the word *asta* ('pole for a flag', 'horn'), also pronounced /asta/ (for the whole phoneme–grapheme correspondences in Spanish, see RAE 2010: 72–188).

Therefore, we can see that there can be two different meanings for the term grapheme in didactic or normative works applied to the description of a single language: (1) according to the referential perspective, a grapheme may be made up of several letters; (2) according to the analogical or functional perspective, grapheme is a synonym for letter, which means that, from this perspective, a grapheme may only contain one letter. Nevertheless, the linguistic graphematic theory does not include letter as a term because of its lack of precision, as we shall see below.

(c) The third definition of the grapheme is far broader than that of the two perspectives mentioned in (a) and (b). In particular, Catach (1995 [1980]) has established three categories of graphemes required for the description of the *plurisystem of French spelling* and has defined *graphème* as "the minimal distinctive unit in a written sequence, consisting of a letter, a group of letters (*digramme*, *trigramme*, and so on) or a letter with an accent or with an auxiliary sign that refers to a phonic or a semic unit of the speech sequence" (Catach 1995 [1980]: 16, our translation). It means that a grapheme can represent a phoneme, as well as a whole unit provided of a meaning, that is, a semic unit. In the first case, French linguists refer to the *phonographic principle of writing*. In the second case, they refer to the *semiographic principle of writing*. Let us consider some examples of the different classes of graphemes distinguished by Catach.

Thus, graphemes named *phonograms* (French *phonogrammes*) represent phonemes. For example, the verb *pourchasser* is formed by 11 letters and 8 graphemes (<p>, <ou>, <r>, <ch>, <a>, <ss>, <e>, <r>), which correspond to 7 phonemes /p/, /u/, /ʁ/, /ʃ/, /a/, /s/ /e/. Following Catach, the word *faim*

/fɛ̃/ is formed by 4 letters (*f, a, i, m*) and 2 graphemes: <f> and <aim>. Catach (1995 [1980]: 9–15) states three levels of phoneme–grapheme correspondence in French, from the lowest to the highest number of graphemes, depending on their frequency:

Level 1: 45 basic and frequent graphemes (as <eu> in *peur*, <ou> in *fou* or <ss> in *basse*).
Level 2: 70 graphemes (the basic ones and some infrequent graphemes, as <eau> pronounced /o/ in *eau*).
Level 3: 130 graphemes (the basic, the infrequent and the exceptional graphemes, as <aim> in *faim*, representing /ɛ̃/).

The graphemes named *morphograms* (French *morphogrammes*) represent morphemes, independently of whether they are pronounced or not; for example, in the word *rat* pronounced /ʁa/, <t> is a *nonphonogramic grapheme* that represents a *lexical morphogram* related with other words of the same family, as *dératiser* /deʁatize/. In the word *petit* /pəti/, the final <t> is also a nonphonogramic grapheme that represents a lexical morphogram related with the feminine *petite* /pətit/ and the noun *petitesse*.

The graphemes named *logograms* (French *logogrammes*) represent complete lexemes and their function is to give a specific visual image of the homophonic words; for example, *ver, vers, verre, vert* and *vair* are different logograms all pronounced /vɛʁ/. Jaffré has adapted Catach's model, used to analyze the French writing system, in order to establish a more general distinction between the phonographic and the semiographic principles in writing systems that could more readily accommodate nonalphabetic systems (see Fayol and Jaffré 2016).

Just as in Catach's theoretical framework, the more recent model of Meletis (2019a, 2020a: 92–99, Meletis and Dürscheid 2022: 126–33) puts forward a definition of the grapheme that can encompass the properties common to the units in a large variety of writing systems such as those of Arabic, Chinese, Japanese, Korean, Thai, Tamil and so on, because referential and analogical views are restricted to alphabetic writing systems. For Meletis, a grapheme is a basic unit of writing that (1) must distinguish meaning (i.e. it is lexically distinctive); (2) must relate to a linguistic unit or linguistic information of some kind (mostly by referring to phonemes, syllables, morphemes and so on); and (3) must be a minimal unit, not composed of smaller units which are themselves graphemes. Thus, in this framework, the linguistic value of the grapheme can be that of a phoneme, an entire morpheme as in Chinese writing (where complex graphemes have one component signaling meaning and another component pronunciation), or one syllable as in Japanese writing. Meletis (2020a: 105–15, 2020b: 249–53, Meletis and Dürscheid 2022: 155–58) has also established a model for the description of structural graphic variation (named *allography*), based on the comparison of different types of writing systems, and has redefined the hierarchy of units of writing systems including, among others, the concepts of *graph* and *allograph*. Meletis's model is not only valid to compare all sorts of current languages but could also be useful to present a diachronic description of one or more languages, to account for their variation over time with a comprehensive and terminologically coherent approach.

(d) We can also find a fourth extension of meaning for the term grapheme in authors who include punctuation marks as part of it, as in the case of French graphematics. Anis developed a model of autonomistic graphematics, that is, a description of graphemes independently from phonetics and orality (Anis 1983, Anis et al. 1988). If the grapheme is the "minimal unit of the graphic form of expression," Anis (1983: 33) distinguishes two types of graphemes: *segmental graphemes* (e.g. alphabetic graphemes) and *suprasegmental graphemes* (including punctuation marks).

8.2.2 Graphemes and Punctuation Marks

According to Anis (1983: 33), a suprasegmental grapheme is "a grapheme located in the graphic chain that modifies the structure or the enunciative status of an utterance or part of an utterance." It can be said that a punctuation mark is suprasegmental if we consider its *scope* (*portée* in French), that is, the extension of the graphic sequence that is affected by the mark. This extension ends whenever there is an intervention by another mark of the same level or of a higher level within the hierarchy of graphic segments (Anis et al. 1988: 121, Dahlet 2003: 27–28, 32). For example, opening and closing punctuation marks such as parentheses or em dashes are hierarchical discourse markers that show their scope to the right and the left of the segment they demarcate. Another example: when a colon introduces an element or series of elements that amplifies the information that preceded this punctuation mark, its scope spreads to either side of its location, until it reaches the full stops that are found before and after it.

The inventory of suprasegmental graphemes includes three formal types (Anis 1983: 41–42, Dahlet 2003: 19–32):

(a) Graphemes formed by the *regulation of the blank spaces*. The main difference between oral language and written language lies in the fact that, in the oral medium, speech is developed through time, whereas in the visual medium, speech is developed linearly through space. The space is the visible support of the writing system insofar as it contributes to demarcate the units of the written language; for example, different blank spaces separate words, utterances, paragraphs and chapters. The French term *ponctuation blanche*, 'white punctuation', refers to this regulation of space and has been widely used in French studies on the history of the page, the book and reading (see Laufer 1972, Catach 1980, Berrendonner and Reichler-Béguelin 1989, Védénina 1989, Arabyan 1994, 2018, Favriaud 2004). The duality of the French terms *ponctuation blanche/ponctuation noire*, 'white punctuation'/'black punctuation' is formed by a synecdoche based on the most widespread form of printed books: black ink on white paper. Additionally, it refers to the opposition between blank spaces and punctuational graphemes.

(b) *Punctuational graphemes* or 'black punctuation' are inscribed manually or mechanically on the writing space: < . : ; , ? ! ( ) [ ] « » - – — >, and so on.

(c) *Coalescent graphemes* or *linked graphemes* are shown through a formal but significant variation of *segmental graphemes* (alphabetic graphemes or other types of graphemes). The duality roman/italic, light/bold, underlined/nonunderlined, or lower case/upper case (or lower case/*littera notabilior* in medieval texts) represents linguistic and enunciative values. For example, an uppercase initial graphically underscores the status of the proper noun (e.g. proper noun *Rose* vs. common noun *rose*); and in literature and the press, italics usually distinguish reported speech from reporting speech or a narration.

8.2.3 Comparative and Diachronic Methods for the Study of Orthographies

The comparative study of graphic systems over time has been approached through different linguistic models and methods which, in turn, reflect the different meanings (a, b, c, d) behind the term grapheme that have been defined above (Subsections 8.2.1 and 8.2.2). We present here three important methods for European languages:

Historical Graphematics: The Comparative Model of Romance *Scriptologie*

The *scriptologie* is a methodology applied to the description of the diachronic, diatopic and diastratic variation of medieval handwritten spelling of Romance languages.[1]

Romance-speaking Europe, which was the group of territories where Latin-derived languages were born, showed significant dialectal fragmentation in the Middle Ages: each of the linguistic domains of Gallo-Romance, Ibero-Romance, Italo-Romance and Balkan-Romance included a group of dialects

[1] *Scriptologie*, a French term coined by Gossen in 1967 as a calque of the German word *Skriptaforschung*, is equivalent to the Italian *scrittologia* and the Spanish *escriptología*. It refers to a methodology of historical graphematics of Romance languages. It must not be mistaken for the English term *scriptology*, which refers to a much larger area of study, as a 'general discipline that studies all writing systems'. In this wider sense, the English term *scriptology* corresponds to the general description of writing that contemporary linguistics finds in the disciplines named *grapholinguistics* and *scripturology-scripturologie* (according to the term recently proposed by Klinkenberg and Polis 2018).

that were intercomprehensible, but with their own linguistic peculiarities. The institutions in some of these regions developed standardized written varieties which are not an exact transcription of the spoken dialects and have therefore been called *scriptae*. A *scripta*, a term coined by Louis Remacle in 1948, shows a combination of graphic features: on the one hand, it includes diatopic features (regional and dialectal); on the other hand, it presents atopic features (common for the entire linguistic domain), and finally, it has diastratic or sociolinguistic features (insofar as a graphic feature reflected the social status of the scriptors). For example, within the Gallo-Romance domain, in the twelfth century, the *langue d'oïl* (i.e. Old French language) existed in the form of several oral dialectal variants that were characteristic for each region (Wallonia, Picardy, Normandy, England, Burgundy, Champagne, etc.). Some of these regions developed a *scripta*, which was a hybrid continuum of common and particular spellings. As a methodology for the study of graphematic variation, *scriptologie* is applied on specific original manuscripts, and it focuses the evolution and the structure of medieval spelling during the period prior to its unification into a hegemonic orthography. The *scriptologie* has been comprehensively applied to the Gallo-Romance (see Glessgen 2012 and Glessgen et al. 2010) and Italo-Romance (see Videsott 2009) domains and, to a lesser extent, to the Ibero-Romance area (see Sánchez-Prieto Borja 2012), but not to the Germanic and English domains, because they did not contain the same diversity of writing centers in their regions in the Middle Ages (see Goebl 1975: 3–9, Gossen 1979 and Glessgen 2012: 8, following Seiler 2011: 167–83).

The objective of *scriptologie* is to carry out a global and comparative typological analysis of the different medieval *scriptae*; this typology would be equivalent, according to Goebl's metaphor to the view of the whole house, whereas the analysis of the writing features of each *scripta* would correspond to the bricks of that house (see Goebl, *Lexicon der Romanistischen Linguistik*, henceforth abbreviated LRL, Holtus et al. 1995: 315). The major current treatises of Romance linguistics present a global overview of all written varieties that is adequate for a comparative analysis. For example, the LRL (1995: 290–405) provides a synthesis of all the *scriptae* of medieval French. Nonliterary documents that have been studied by *scriptologie* have a more ephemeral character than literature, which means that their spelling closely reflects the features of their era and the phonetic peculiarities of the geographical area in which they were written. Thus, the diatopic research model of *scriptologie* employs the first (a) concept of grapheme that was described above: phonology and graphematics are complementary descriptions in the LRL, so that the graphemes of a *scripta* are studied with regard to their phonological equivalences.

A Comparative Cultural History of Orthographies in Early Modern Europe

As stated by Condorelli (2020b: 1), "for approximately two decades now, and in connection with the development of historical sociolinguistics as a separate subdiscipline, the focus of several studies in historical orthography has shifted to exploring the sociolinguistic aspects of writing systems." The history of orthography studies the norms that restrict and regulate the graphematic resources of a language, as well as the relationship between those norms and society over time. From this sociological perspective, an emerging field of research is the systematic comparison of orthographies of several languages and societies. Methodologically, comparability across languages requires in the first place that the field of comparison be defined precisely and be focused on relevant parameters of comparison. "First of all, we need to agree on a historical period of focus" and on a "geographical limit" (Condorelli and Voeste 2020: 241).

This emerging field has uncovered surprising parallels in the histories of quite distinct orthographic systems used in regions which are geographically remote. Baddeley and Voeste (2012b) have put forward a new approach toward this comparative history in a work focused on the Romance, Germanic, Slavonic and Finno-Ugrian language groups, languages that currently all use the Latin alphabet at the key moment of the early modern era. These authors have demonstrated how the evolution of the orthographic systems of European languages shows a large number of convergences, due to the mobility of scholars, ideas and the technological innovations in printing throughout the period. They have thus established some parameters useful for comparative studies about the history of orthographies. For example:

(a) A typology of writing systems, oscillating between, on the one hand, traditional semiographic systems of spelling, often incorporating etymological spellings (such as the French language), and others indicating greater independence from Latin (i.e. phonographic systems of spelling, such as the Italian or Spanish languages).
(b) A comparative view of the experimentation in the graphic expression of each vernacular's phonetic peculiarities, particularly when representing the 'new' phonemes that were unknown to the Latin phonological system, such as palatals and fricatives. This line has also been developed in German studies, for example, in the works by Seiler (2011, 2014) on spelling difficulties in Old English, Old High German and Old Saxon.
(c) A consideration of language contact and the orthographic influence of some languages upon others, for example, the influence of written French as a prestige language in England or the introduction of the medieval Spanish letter *ç* into the French language in the sixteenth century.

In order to develop the methodology of comparative graphematics as a new and future international research area, Condorelli (2020c) has collected a number of chapters which discuss innovative empirical models and methods in historical orthography. While the chapters focus on individual languages, the volume as a whole could enlighten the comparison of several languages in the early modern period (c. 1500–1800):

(a) If spelling variation is the core object of historical orthography, one who wants to explore variation should first decide on a method of data collection, depending on the focus on the variants of a single text copy or on a comparative analysis of different copies: *intratextual variable analysis* involves an investigation of variants in a single text copy, *intertexual variable analysis* aims to compare results of two or more intratextual investigations and *cross-textual variable analysis* examines the variants of different versions of the same text (Voeste 2020: 142).
(b) Future comparative research can follow methods and pertinent parameters such as:
   - The understanding of material and aesthetic influence in the standardization of orthographies in early modern Europe, as in the case of Lithuanian spelling (see Subačius 2020);
   - A multifactorial model for the development of capitalization in handwritten texts, including not only grammatical but also semantic, syntactic and pragmatic domains (as exemplified in Early New High German by Dücker et al. 2020);
   - The graphetic/graphemic distinction in order to provide a more systematic framework for an analysis of orthography, as applied by Žagar (2020) for Early Modern Croatian.

Graphematics of Punctuation: The Emergence of Comparative Models

Let us now consider some recent works that have started to develop methodologies of comparative history of punctuation, not only as a paleographic or codicological subject, but as a linguistic system that contributes to different syntactic, semantic, enunciative and pragmatic aspects in written texts.

(a) On the level of 'white punctuation', the history of the separation between words by means of a blank space is a common feature in all Romance languages and other written European languages that employ the Latin alphabet between the ninth and the sixteenth century. It has been analyzed from the paleographic and the linguistic perspectives that different languages as Latin, Irish, Spanish or French presented the same two trends of graphic variation in the Middle Ages (see for Irish, Parkes 1987: 18, 26; for Latin, Parkes 1992: 264 and Saenger 1997: 31; for French, Baddeley and Biedermann-Pasques 2004; for Spanish, Llamas-Pombo 2009). On the one hand, there is the union or agglutination of two or several grammatical words in a whole graphic segment (in Latin, *deparadiso* instead of *de paradiso*; in Old Irish, *isaireasber* instead of *is aire as-ber*, 'it is therefore he says'; in French, *laueintre* instead of *la ueintre*, 'defeat her'; in Spanish, *conderecho* instead of *con derecho* 'with rights'). On the other hand, there is the disjunction of a word into two or more graphic segments (in Latin, *reli quit* instead of *reliquit*; in French, *ar gent* instead of *argent*; in Spanish *di sputar* instead of *disputar*).

(b) One emerging field in comparative graphematics is linguistic and comparative history of punctuation in European languages, as proposed by Hungarian linguist Keszler (2003, 2004), who has highlighted the unitary nature of European punctuation as a significant factor in the cultural history of the continent. The publication in 2008 of a history of punctuation marks in Europe directed by Mortara Garavelli has provided an innovative overview that includes 23 languages or linguistic areas. In the introductory chapter of the *History*, Lepschy and Lepschy (2008: 3) observe that punctuation in European languages has both a unitary and a multiple character at the same time: the considerable unity of the sign system, together with the intrinsic variability in the diachronic evolution of each language and the typological variability of the different language families. These authors set the foundations for a future methodology of contrastive linguistics of punctuation, whose history is yet to be written and has already been researched in some studies.

The hypothesis on the European unity of medieval punctuation that came from Latin still has to be developed by comparative studies that prove this is a manifestation of the cultural unity of medieval literacy in Europe. The separation of words, the signs for quotes, and the structure of the page as a reading support are aspects that allow us to envisage medieval punctuation, to some extent, as a 'program for text processing' which would have been the same, regardless of the language that was being edited on the page (see Llamas-Pombo 2007, 2009, 2019, 2020).

The unity of European thought during the period in which the norms and the grammar of vernacular languages were emerging (sixteenth and seventeenth centuries) is a field that still needs to be studied, and which has recently been discussed in a comparison between the analogous ideas about punctuation of French and Spanish standardizers at that time, following a methodology of diachronic and comparative graphematics based on parameters of variational linguistics: punctuation varies diachronically following social or diastratic parameters, diaphasic or stylistic purposes, and different degrees of correspondence between the phonic and the graphic codes (Llamas-Pombo 2020). Similarly, following these same parameters, it would be interesting to compare the punctuation of Romance languages such as Italian, French and Spanish with that of Germanic languages such as English and German in the sixteenth and seventeenth centuries, in order to contrast the linguistic ideas of standardizers and typographers on how to standardize written languages.

The recent book entitled *Vergleichende Interpunktion – Comparative Punctuation* (Rössler et al. 2021) offers some models for a contrastive analysis of different current norms of punctuation, whose conclusions are useful for translation, language teaching and foreign language acquisition. The authors have focused, for example, on the cases of the dash in Italian and English; the comma and the semicolon in Italian and German; quotation marks in Russian and Polish; the colon in German, English and Swedish; the exclamation mark in German and Danish; punctuation marks in English, Swedish and Norwegian fiction texts; punctuation in the bilingual acquisition of German and Italian; punctuation in the acquisition of German by Hungarian speakers; and also, from a diachronic and contrastive approach, functions of punctuation in Italian and in Polish.

8.2.4 New Perspectives on the Comparative Orthotypography of Languages

If orthotypography can be defined as the set of rules that make it possible to write correctly and according to a norm by means of types or characters, that is, the set of orthographic and typographical rules (spaces, italics, upper case and so on), the field of comparative orthotypography presents a gap in its applied research that requires the inclusion of punctuation into the definition of a grapheme, according to concept (d) which was described in Subsection 8.2.1. See also 8.2.2.

Students, editors, translators and teachers who work with two or more languages often find an extensive range of orthotypographical differences (as well as frequent errors and interferences) between languages (see Sassoon 2004 [1995]). Let us mention four short examples:

(a) French requires a nonbreaking space before the punctuation marks < :>, < ;>, < ?>, < !>, < »>, and so on, which is not the case in Spanish or in English. One writes « *en français* » with blank spaces, but "*en español*" or " in Spanish" with no space between the letters and the quotation marks.

(b) With regard to the rules for splitting words at the end of a line, English allows for both morphological and syllabic word division (the latter in cases where multisyllabic words cannot be broken down according to morphological criteria), whereas French and Spanish only allow for syllabic. For example, English norm requires the division *account-able*, whereas in Spanish only the division *con-table* is correct and this word may not be divided as **cont-able*.

(c) In Spanish, all the letters are separated (e.g. in the word *oeste* 'the West'), whereas in French the correct typography requires in a certain number of words that the *e* is joined together with the *o* (*l'e dans l'o*); for example, the correct writing is *œuvre* instead of **oeuvre*.

(d) For a quote within a quote, Spanish and French use three types of quotation marks alternatively [«quotation 1 ... "quotation 2 ... 'quotation 3' ... " ... »], whereas in Hungarian, texts are edited with a different sequence of signs [„quotation1 »quotation 2» quotation 1″].

Autocorrection systems include these normative differences, but are neither explicit nor systematic, and standardizers must have to have established them previously for computer programmers. In the age of written electronic communication and fast circulation, translation and copying of texts, there is an urgent need for a systematic comparative orthotypography of languages, with equivalences and usage contrasts. If there is a linguistics applied to language acquisition, then an applied orthotypography is needed to compare the different typographical criteria of languages, an inheritance from centuries of norms in the art and techniques of handwriting and printing. New empirical perspectives based on computerized corpora should be developed for comparing different orthotypographies across objective quantitative and qualitative data.

8.3 Biscriptality

Comparative historical perspectives are always related to different aspects of society and language users. In Section 8.2, we have described different methodologies for diachronic comparison of writing systems of different languages. In the present section, we also deal with the analysis of different graphic sets of signs used for one and the same language.

8.3.1 Theoretical Remarks

In the following, under the term biscriptality, we discuss the phenomenon of using two or more writing systems for the same language (for the opposite perspective, using a writing system for a language other than the one for which the writing system was originally devised, the term *allography* has sometimes been used, see den Heijer et al. 2014). This phenomenon has been named differently: the most established term, at least prior to the publication of Bunčić et al. 2016, seems to be *digraphia* (see, for example, Dale 1980, Berlanda 2006, Bunčić et al. 2016: 26–50). After a discussion of different definitions, Bunčić et al. (2016: 54) arrive at a definition of the term biscriptality, adopting a "slight modification" of the definition of *digraphia* by Dale (1980: 6): "Biscriptality is the simultaneous use of two (or more) writing systems (including different orthographies) for (varieties of) the same language" (for a critical discussion of the terminology, see also Mechkovskai͡a 2017, Ambrosiani 2020). In the present discussion, we use the term biscriptality in a somewhat wider sense than Bunčić et al. (2016), including also situations where two or more writing systems are used for the same language not only simultaneously, but also within a diachronic perspective (see below). Following mainly Bunčić et al. (2016), biscriptality normally uses the term *script* for a "set of graphic signs for writing languages" (Bunčić et al. 2016: 20), *writing system* for the use of graphic features to write a particular language, and *orthography* for a particular standardization of the use of graphic features within a particular writing system (see also Cook and Bassetti 2005, Zima 1974, DeFrancis 1984b, Cheung 1992). Within biscriptality, a distinction needs to be made between different levels of *manifestation*. Biscriptality can be identified on at least three levels.

(a) The *script* level, that is, the use of two or more scripts for the same language, as in, for example, contemporary Serbian, which is written with either Latin or Cyrillic letters, and Tatar, since the beginning of the twentieth century written with either Arabic, Cyrillic or Latin letters (see Wertheim 2012), Classical Egyptian (see von Lieven and Lippert 2016: 276, "the complex linguistic situation of Egyptian is best categorized as *intrasystemic bi-* or rather *trigraphism* throughout its biscriptal history, i.e. from the emergence of hieratic in addition to hieroglyphs around 2600 BCE until hieroglyphs and hieratic fell out of use around 400 CE"), and so on. For biscriptality on this manifestation level we use the term *bigraphism*.
(b) The *orthography* level, that is, within a certain writing system, the use of two or more inventories and/or organizations of the written signs. Examples include the use of Russian 'pre-reform' orthography vs. contemporary Russian orthography, or the use of the *taraškevica* vs. *narkomovka* orthography for Belarusian, or the use of traditional vs. simplified *hanzi* for Standard Chinese. For biscriptality on this manifestation level we use the term *biorthographism*.
(c) The *glyph* level, that is, within a certain writing system, the use of two or more glyphic variants. Examples include the use of blackletter glyphs vs. 'Roman' glyphs (Antiqua) for German and several other languages (see, for example, Spitzmüller 2012: 262–69). For Cyrillic, Franklin (2019: 103–4) refers to four main traditional types of Cyrillic lettering in Muscovite and Russian manuscripts: *ustav*, *poluustav*, *skoropis'* and *viaz'* (see, however, Cleminson 2015 and Lomagistro 2008, who problematize the *ustav/poluustav/skoropis'* distinction). For biscriptality on this manifestation level we use the term *biglyphism*.

The terms bigraphism, biorthographism and biglyphism, adapted from Bunčić et al. (2016), are here used as blanket terms for all types of biscriptality on the respective manifestation levels. As should be clear already from the above definitions, the three manifestation levels cannot be seen as completely independent. For example, within a particular script, such as, for example, the Latin script, it can be possible to identify both the orthography and glyph levels of biscriptality, whereas it is seldom meaningful to discuss orthography or glyph distinctions between different scripts, even if they appear in situations of bigraphism. From a different perspective, there are cases of biscriptality where more than one manifestation level is included, as, for example, in Russian Cyrillic biscriptality during the early eighteenth century. This example concerns both the orthography and glyph manifestation levels, juxtaposing the 'new', Westernized letter shapes and orthography and the traditional 'Church Slavonic' letter shapes and concomitant orthography. In addition to the manifestation level distinctions, biscriptality situations can be further characterized by several different perspectives.

(a) Within certain scholarly traditions, a distinction has been made between the use of two or more writing systems for the same language *at the same time* (synchronic biscriptality) and the use of two or more writing systems for the same language *at different times* (diachronic biscriptality, see Dale 1980, Berlanda 2006, but compare Bunčić et al. 2016: 53–54, who explicitly exclude diachronic biscriptality from their definition of biscriptality). From a sociolinguistic point of view, cases of synchronic biscriptality seem to be of more relevance, as these situations concern complex linguistic relationships within existing language communities during defined time periods. However, from a historical perspective, the analysis of the use of two or more writing systems for the same language at *different* times is undoubtedly of considerable interest. Diachronic biscriptality is not seldom accompanied by a period of synchronic biscriptality, when both the 'older' and the 'newer' writing systems are used at the same time in a language community. Thus, for research in historical biscriptality, it is often rewarding to make a complex analysis of both synchronic and diachronic aspects of biscriptality situations. Examples of diachronic biscriptality include, for example, the gradual replacement of the Glagolitic script with the Cyrillic script for Old Church Slavonic, the replacement of Scandinavian runes with Latin script, the replacement of the Arabic script with the Latin script for Turkish during the twentieth century, and so on.[2]

(b) A distinction has often been made between situations where the use of two or more writing systems for the same language is attested within a certain geographical or political entity (*monocentric biscriptality*), and situations where the same language, or close varieties of the same language, are written with different writing systems in different geographic, social or political communities (*pluricentric biscriptality*). Examples of pluricentric biscriptality include both cases of bigraphism, such as, for example, the relationship

[2] Compare the discussion on the hybridity of writing systems and orthographies in Chapter 11, this volume. In that chapter, the author takes a slightly different view of biscriptality, in the sense that it is seen mainly as a synchronic phenomenon.

between Hindi, written with the Devanāgarī writing system and Urdu, written with Arabic letters – at least when it comes to their spoken forms, Hindi and Urdu are often considered to be the same language (see Brandt 2016); Romanian, written with Latin letters, and Moldovan, written with Cyrillic; Bosnian, written with Arabic letters (arebica) and with Latin and/or Cyrillic letters; and cases of biorthographism, such as, for example, the relationship between Post-reform Russian orthography in the Soviet Union during the 1920s and the 1930s and Pre-reform orthography in Russian émigré publications at the same time; Catholic and Protestant Upper Sorbian; Warsaw- and Kraków-centered Polish during the late nineteenth and early twentieth century (see Bunčić et al. 2016: 204–9, 219–27).

(c) In some studies, a distinction is made between situations where more than one writing system is officially recognized as standard for a particular language (*official biscriptality*; for example, modern Serbian, where both a Cyrillic script and a Latin script-based writing system are formally recognized, see Ivković 2013: 337), and situations where the standard language is, in principle, monoscriptal, but more than one writing system can be used on a less formal level, as in advertising, personal communication, graffiti and so on (*informal biscriptality*; see, for example, Dickinson 2015: 509, who criticizes an earlier dominant "monographic norm" and instead emphasizes the "wide range of competencies, uses, and meanings attached to the use of more than one writing system"). Studies on informal biscriptality are often conducted within a linguistic landscape paradigm (see, for example, Ivković 2015a, 2015b). Examples of informal bigraphism in the Slavic-speaking countries include, for example, the presence of Glagolitic graffiti in medieval Russia (see Franklin 2002: 95), and the relationship between Latin and Cyrillic standard and nonstandard orthographies in Serbian online forums (see Ivković 2013).

(d) In biscriptal situations, a distinction can also be made between cases where the same text includes two or more writing systems, that is, hybrid-script texts, and monoscriptal texts, which interact in different ways with other monoscriptal texts in a biscriptality context. This distinction can be connected with the question of the intended receiver of the text: a *hybrid-script* text is, arguably, intended for a biliterate reader, whereas *monoscriptal* texts, even within biscriptal contexts, can be intended for monoliterate readers (see further below). Examples of hybrid-script texts may include, for example, personal ads (see Angermeyer 2005, 2011).

(e) So far, the focus has primarily been on biscriptal situations at a society or group level. However, a distinction can also be made between biscriptality within a particular society or group (*societal biscriptality*), and the use of two or more writing systems for the same language by an individual person (*individual biscriptality*). Most of the extant scholarly literature discusses biscriptality situations on the society level, within different theoretical and methodological paradigms. When it comes to individual practices, the focus has often been on situations where different writing systems are connected to different languages (see, for example, Bassetti 2012, Cook and Bassetti 2005, who discuss 'bilingual biliterates') – that is, for situations where two or more monoscriptal languages are used by the same individual – but individual biscriptality, although perhaps less common on a global scale, can certainly be attested for many individuals literate in modern Serbian or earlier Serbo-Croatian (see, for example, Feldman and Barac-Cikoja 1996).

When studying biscriptality from a historical perspective, particularly within a sociolinguistic context, analyses usually concentrate on societal biscriptality, but there are cases where conclusions can be drawn also on the individual level (see, for example, von Lieven and Lippert 2016: 270, on the presumed reading skills of different groups of people in ancient Egypt, or Miltenov 2009–10, on medieval Slavic scribes producing texts with both Glagolitic and Cyrillic letters).

(f) Sometimes, particularly when the focus is on individual biscriptality, a relevant distinction can be made between what can be called a 'producer' perspective, when the same producer produces texts in more than one writing system, and a 'receiver' perspective, which focuses on the reception of biscriptality situations: in a biscriptal society, some readers can be monoliterate, other readers biliterate or multiliterate (see Sebba 2011: 8, who discusses mixed-language texts from a literacy perspective).

As we have tried to outline above, biscriptality can be studied on different manifestation levels and from several different perspectives. However, the dichotomies suggested here – synchronic vs. diachronic, monocentric vs. pluricentric, societal vs. individual biscriptality, and so on – should be seen not as clear-cut tools offering unequivocal answers to simple questions, but rather as tentative labels for diverse analytical approaches to the complex realities of written languages and writing in general. In the next section, we take a closer look at some attested situations of historical biscriptality, which illustrate some of these complexities.

8.3.2 Biscriptality on the Script Level (Bigraphism)

Glagolitic and Cyrillic Old Church Slavonic

It is generally accepted that the first alphabet used to write Old Church Slavonic was the Glagolitic alphabet, and that the Cyrillic alphabet was invented somewhat later: the earliest extant Glagolitic manuscripts are thought to date from the tenth to eleventh centuries (see Žagar 2013, Marti 2014). The change from Glagolitic to Cyrillic can be seen as an example of diachronic biscriptality, but it is clear that there was a substantial period during which both writing systems were used at the same time, sometimes even by the same individual scribes. For example, Glagolitic letters and phrases occur in otherwise predominantly Cyrillic manuscripts in several different situations: they can be included in the main Cyrillic text, used for paratexts relating to the Cyrillic main text, either by the same scribe or by a later scribe, or inserted into Cyrillic paratexts (see Franklin 2002: 96, Lomagistro 2004, Musakova 2004, Miltenov 2009–10, 2013; for a detailed analysis of three Glagolitic texts in the thirteenth-century Middle Bulgarian Cyrillic *Šafařík-Triodion*, see Trunte 2004). Also the opposite, the use of Cyrillic in a predominantly Glagolitic Old Church Slavonic manuscript, was possible (see, for example, the discussion by Miklas et al. (2016) of the eleventh-century *Psalterium Demetrii Sinaitici*).

Thus, for Old Church Slavonic (and at least also for the later Middle Bulgarian Church Slavonic) we can identify situations both of diachronic and synchronic bigraphism both on the society and the individual levels. An interesting case of 'informal' bigraphism can be deduced from the presence of Glagolitic graffiti on the walls of Saint Sophia's cathedral in Novgorod (see Franklin 2002: 95), which can be contrasted with the predominantly Cyrillic writing for both formal and informal writing during the same time (see below, on the birchbark documents from Novgorod).

Glagolitic, Cyrillic, and Latin-script Sixteenth-century Croatian/South Slavic

In Croatia, the Glagolitic alphabet continued to be used until at least the nineteenth century, and here we can consequently talk about a prolonged bigraphic relationship between the Glagolitic and primarily the Latin alphabet, but also the Cyrillic alphabet. Thus, in Tübingen in the 1560s, translations of the New Testament and other books were printed in Croatian using the Glagolitic, Cyrillic and Latin writing systems (see Ambrosiani 2020, with further references). These monoscriptal publications were probably intended for monoliterate (in either Glagolitic, Cyrillic or Latin) readers of Croatian. Later, the *Propaganda Fide* in Rome used the same metal type pieces to print books in all three writing systems (see Ambrosiani 2019).

Arabic- and Cyrillic-script Medieval Bosnian

In medieval Bosnia, particularly in manuscripts intended for Muslim speakers, a revised version of the Arabic writing system, the so-called *arebica*, was used. It was based on the Ottoman adaptation of the Arabic script for Turkish (see Lehfeldt 2001: 269–75, Gažáková 2014, Selvelli 2015). The Slavic language used in Bosnia was also written with a particular variety of the Cyrillic script, the so-called *bosančica* or 'Western Cyrillic'. This arebica/bosančica bigraphism can be characterized as pluricentric: Muslims tended to use arebica whereas non-Muslims used bosančica, at least during certain periods. Arebica also appeared in newspapers from the end of the nineteenth to the beginning of the twentieth century (Gažáková 2014: 463).

8.3.3 Biscriptality on the Orthography Level (Biorthographism)

Russian 'Everyday' Orthography in Novgorod Birchbark Documents from the Eleventh to Fourteenth Centuries

In many Russian birchbark documents, which have been found mainly in Novgorod since the 1950s, a particular 'everyday' Cyrillic orthography has been identified and described in detail (see Zalizn͡iak 2000, 2004: 21–36, Franklin 2002: 35–45, 183–84, Schaeken 2019). The coexistence of a standard Cyrillic orthography with this particular type of orthography, in which the function of certain letters characteristically diverges from that standard, can be seen as an instance of biorthographism, where the two varieties function as two orthographic registers, 'formal' and 'informal'.

Russian Cyrillic Pre- and Post-1918 Orthography

After the Russian orthographic reforms of 1917–18 (see Comrie et al. 1996: 284–95), which were officially adopted by the new Bolshevik government, most printed texts produced in Soviet Russia (and, later, in the Soviet Union) were printed in the 'new' orthography, whereas the 'old' orthography continued to be used for many publications printed outside Russia, at least up until the 1930s (see Grigor′eva 2004: 139–46), thus forming a situation of pluricentric biorthographism.

8.3.4 Biscriptality on the Glyph Level (Biglyphism)

Russian Cyrillic Biglyphism during the Eighteenth Century

At the beginning of the eighteenth century, Tsar Peter I introduced a new 'civil' typeface, which led to a situation of biglyphism between the new typeface and the traditional Cyrillic typefaces used mainly in Church-related publications and, less and less often, in secular publications (see Nemirovskiĭ 2008, Franklin 2019: 105–9).

8.4 Conclusion

Comparison is the first methodological imperative of the new disciplines that study writing: comparisons of writing systems are important tools for the decipherment of yet unknown writing systems, for typological studies that propose to determine universal parameters for the variation between and within diverse writing systems, and for various studies within applied linguistics. Thus, the comparability of orthographies of different languages and societies across time constitutes an emerging field of investigation within international linguistics. An essential methodological step in this field is the definition of the grapheme as the core unit of written language. The grapheme definition determines different methodologies and approaches of comparison, such as, for example, Romance *scriptologie*, the common cultural history of European orthographies in the period of early modern Europe, or the comparative graphematics of punctuation and orthotypography. If we include punctuation signs in the definition of the grapheme, then comparative graphematics and the comparative cultural history of orthographies may fill in some gaps in the multidisciplinary research on writing systems. Similarly, the renewed scholarly interest in the use of two or more writing systems for one and the same language underscores the fact that biscriptality – with differing definitions and in a multitude of perspectives – constitutes an important feature of many language situations throughout the history of writing.

9

Systems and Idiosyncrasies

Benjamin W. Fortson IV

9.1 Introduction

We may begin with the following quotations, which are useful springboards for the issues discussed in this chapter:

> Ego, nisi quod consuetudo optinuerit, sic scribendum quidque iudico quomodo sonat. Hic enim est usus litterarum ut custodiant voces et velut depositum reddant legentibus. Itaque id exprimere debent quod dicturi sumus.
>
> For my own part, I hold that (except where usage prevails) we should write everything just as it sounds. The use of letters is to keep safe sounds entrusted to them, as it were, and to restore them faithfully to readers. They ought therefore to represent what we are going to say.
>
> (Quintilian, *The Orator's Education* 1.7.30–31, trans. by Donald A. Russell, Loeb Classical Library)

> My son William has hit upon a new method of spelling Fish. As thus: —G.h.o.t.i. *Ghoti*, fish. Nonsense! say you. By no means, say I. [...] *Gh* is *f*, as in *tough*, *rough*, *enough*; *o* is *i* as in *women*; and *ti* is *sh*, as in *mention*, *attention*, &c. So that *ghoti* is *fish*.
>
> (Charles Ollier, letter to Leigh Hunt, December 11, 1855, quoted in Zimmer 2008)

The passage quoted from the first century AD Roman author Quintilian's treatise on public speaking argues for what many surely regard as a self-evident truth about the relationship between spelling and pronunciation: the former should accurately reflect the latter. He is not dogmatic about it, however, as his parenthetical insert *nisi quod consuetudo optinuerit* 'except where usage prevails' makes clear: he allows custom to override this principle even if causing deviations from it.[1] If the pseudo-spelling *ghoti* for *fish* in the second quote above (later made famous by George Bernard Shaw, see also Chapter 31) in fact had the weight of customary usage behind it, it might occasion some consternation on the part of those learning how to spell, but once it became fixed in the memory and used countless times, few if any people in the English-speaking world would probably bat an eye over it. The question of when customary usage should be given the green light to buck otherwise systematically applied orthographic principles is old and vexed, and will likely never find true resolution because of an essential fact about writing systems (by which is meant not just the written symbols *per se* but also the principles of their use and combination): contrary to Quintilian's stated goal, systems of spelling have never in practice behaved like mathematical functions or computer algorithms where a single output is mechanically, unconditionally and exceptionlessly generated from a particular input – or, to put it less abstractly, where a particular unit of language is exceptionlessly and uniquely signaled by a particular written symbol. This chapter is a brief exploration of some of the ways in which writing 'systems' are and are not, in fact, systematic, and some of the ways in which idiosyncrasies, irregularities, inconsistencies and ambiguities can crop up, especially in the mapping of speech onto writing.

By way of outlining what is to come, after some further preliminaries, the first subject treated is graphemes in a given writing system as entities separate from issues of their orthographic use, with focus on those that form an internally coherent set of symbols as regards their construction, visual appearance or organization. After this, the relationships between graphemes or orthographic systems and speech sounds (both phonemes and allophones) are treated, with abundant exemplification of various degrees and levels of systematicity and idiosyncrasy. The discussion then advances to the level of whole words and their spelling, before a brief conclusion. The topics naturally overlap to some extent and should not be taken as too strictly imagined; some of the material under one heading is relevant to other headings as well. The examples, collected from a wide variety of languages and scripts, are selective and specific and, even when going into detail, are not intended to provide comprehensive descriptions of any of the relevant orthographic systems, which are treated elsewhere in this volume and in other works.[2] The reader is assumed to have some knowledge of basic terms pertaining to writing systems (such as grapheme, pictogram, logogram and syllabary, as discussed in Chapter 2 and Chapter 3, this volume).

[1] See also Chapter 5, this volume, for more discussion of Quintilian's views.

[2] Global reference is made to Daniels and Bright (1996) for fuller discussions of the various non-Latin scripts discussed below for which no other specific reference is given.

9.2 Sources of Inconsistency and Idiosyncrasy

At the most basic physical level, audible speech is an acoustic signal consisting of a continuous series of pressure waves, while writing consists of static and discrete visible symbols: no writing system has any direct physical connection to speech. The discovery that the acoustic signal – and/or the articulatory gestures that produce it – is composed of recurring units (be they words, morphemes, syllables or individual speech sounds) and that these units can be indexed in a completely different medium by a set of arbitrarily devised visual symbols was a brilliant act of analytic genius, no less so for having been achieved multiple times in human history.[3] One might indeed think that the creation of such symbols to represent linguistic units would result in a neat, one-to-one system, where each visual symbol always corresponded to one and the same linguistic unit. For various reasons, though, this has been rarely accomplished. For example, many writing systems started out as pictographic, but one cannot draw a picture of everything; to represent abstract concepts, metaphoric and metonymic usage of pictograms had to be introduced, resulting in some symbols becoming polysemous. Thus, in Sumerian cuneiform, for example, the symbol for the word for 'heaven' (*an*), in origin a picture of a star, came to be used logographically also for the word for 'god' (*diĝir*) by metonymic extension (✱), whereas 'star' or 'constellation' (*mul*) was represented by a different pictogram consisting of three stars (i.e. ⁂). This strategy, too, only takes one so far, and it is in any event not possible to devise a logogram for every word in a given language; the set is unbounded, since humans have an unlimited ability to create novel words.

For this reason, all systems that started out as pictographic or logographic evolved to include a phonetic component so that words could be represented not only according to what they meant but also according to what they sounded like. This means that many signs came to be used both as pictograms/logograms and as phonograms, further departing from any one-symbol, one-meaning principle. This was the course of development seen in, for example, Mesopotamian cuneiform, Egyptian hieroglyphics, Chinese writing and Mayan hieroglyphics. In the case of purely phonetically based writing systems – syllabaries and alphabets – we might expect that it would be easier to achieve thoroughgoing one-to-one correspondence between written symbol and speech sound or sound sequence. In practice, though, this is not the case here, either. Although total regularity can in theory be achieved for a given variety of speech at a particular moment, pronunciation naturally varies at any given time within a speech community, meaning the spelling system

[3] The earlier notion that this act happened only once, in the region cherished in the West as the 'cradle of civilization' (see, e.g., Maisels 1993), is baldly ethnocentric and has in any event been long since discredited empirically.

might be slightly 'off' for some speakers right from the time of the introduction of the writing system. Furthermore, the ineluctable effects of sound change slowly increase the distance between the static written norm and the spoken form in any case. Modern English spelling is an immediate and familiar example of this: many words, such as *knight, make* and *listen*, contain so-called 'silent letters' that were actually pronounced at the time their spelling became fixed hundreds of years ago, but have since disappeared from speech. Even if spelling at the level of the word could be perfectly regular and systematic, difficulties of implementation arise at higher levels: if, for example, the writing system signals word divisions, should a particular short idiomatic phrase or compound be written as a single word or not (as with *smart phone* vs. *smartphone*)?[4]

The ever-widening gap between speech and writing over time has of course resulted in reform efforts to bring orthographies in line with pronunciation after the latter has changed, but these are not always consistently implemented. In theory, the gap could be repaired every few generations, but the problem never really goes away; the histories of countless spelling systems, including notably English, are littered with the bones of successive layers of reformation and attempts thereat.[5] But conservative cultural forces – not to mention (especially in modern times) economics and practical realities – can prevent reform from being implemented in whole or in part. Noah Webster's long-term campaign to regularize American English spelling, which had a strongly moralistic underpinning relating to views of language and national character (see Bynack 1984: 104–6), succeeded in a few straightforward cases where he advocated simpler variants already in existence (*-or* for *-our* as in *color*, *-er* for *-re* as in *center*, etc.) but otherwise failed, as people balked at changes that appeared too drastic, such as *masheen* for *machine*.[6] The set of orthographic reforms instituted in Germany in 1996 – nearly a century after the previous set of reforms in 1901 – to make spelling more 'logical' evoked a hue and cry from educators and prominent intellectuals; implementation wound up proceeding differently in different places and not to the same extent everywhere, and now, nearly a quarter-century later, unresolved issues with it continue to linger.[7]

It should be recalled that the purpose of writing systems is first and foremost communicative: they are a means for transmitting information. This can be readily effected without representing all the potentially relevant linguistic units of a language and/or representing them consistently. Native speakers

[4] The issue of how to quantify orthographic regularity is outside my scope in this chapter; for a survey of approaches see Borleffs et al. (2017).

[5] For more information, see, for example, Jespersen (1909) and Crystal (2012).

[6] In his remarks on orthographic reform in the preface to his first dictionary (Webster 1806: vii–viii), he actually advocated a middle ground between complete overhaul and hidebound conservatism.

[7] Based on personal experience during periods of residence in Germany. See also Martin (1997–).

can recover much from context that is not directly expressed in written form. This, plus the factors outlined above that can lead to irregularities, leave little room for surprise that writing tends to be imperfectly systematic in the mapping of spoken language.

9.3 Systematicity at the Level of the Grapheme

When all the written symbols of a given writing system are considered together, there are a couple of levels at which they can exhibit systematicity. The first and most visually obvious one is the *stylistic* or *aesthetic* level. Many writing systems have undergone the imposition of aesthetic principles that lend most or all of the written symbols a unified look. This has generally involved either the establishment of a small set of constitutive graphic elements out of which most or all of the symbols were built (or were retrofitted to be built out of), or the introduction of a unified styling in the absence of separate elements. The proto-cuneiform used at the end of the fourth millennium BC in Sumer that marked the beginnings of a writing system for Sumerian is a hodgepodge of incised images of varying sizes composed of curved and straight strokes. As a result of changes in writing technology in the third millennium BC, whereby reed styluses cut at an angle came to be used for impressing the signs, the wedge-shaped strokes that give cuneiform its 'classic' look became (by default) the norm, and cuneiform symbols came largely to be made out of only three elements: horizontal wedges, vertical wedges and wedges set at roughly a 45-degree angle. Symbols also came to take up more or less the same amount of vertical space in a line of text (though their width varied considerably).

Similarly, the earliest preserved Chinese characters, most of them incised on flat bones or shells such as scapulae and tortoise plastra in the second millennium BC, had some general aesthetic commonalities but differed widely in size; these too evolved into a system comprising a fixed number of standardized constitutive elements (eight distinct basic stroke-types plus numerous additional combining and compound strokes) with every character in a line of text filling the same amount of space (an imaginary square box) regardless of the number of strokes it contained. The shapes of the strokes themselves also underwent stylistic unification under the influence of brush writing, which occasioned variations in stroke thickness depending on the direction of the stroke (horizontal strokes are normally thinner than vertical and certain angled strokes) as well as, for example, the leftward 'hook' at the bottom end of vertical strokes.[8] The evolution of the look of the Latin alphabet is comparable: the earliest inscriptions in Latin, such as the seventh century BC Forum Inscription from Rome,

[8] For more detail see Fazzioli (1986), especially pages 9–20.

look crude and jumbled by comparison with the aesthetic that was to develop over a half-millennium later, where letters on official and monumental inscriptions were evenly spaced and of a uniform height, and the strokes of each letter varied in thickness according to their orientation and ended flared out in serifs. This look, which survives intact today in traditional typography, was also due to influence from brush writing.

Less frequently, the graphemes of a writing system can explicitly and systematically encode information about specific features of the represented linguistic unit, in being constructed out of a common set of parts with linguistic meaning. More than nine-tenths of Chinese characters are combinations of two simpler characters where one is used as an indicator of the semantic domain and the other provides phonetic information, and there is a standardized fixed set of the semantic indicators (so-called 'radicals'). A few signs in Mesopotamian cuneiform were similarly compounded out of simpler signs as a way of combining semantic with phonetic information. The vast majority of the world's writing systems, however, do not evince graphemes whose component parts – if distinct component parts they even have – convey information on their own and/or form a group with parallel parts of other graphemes.[9] Not infrequently, characters in a writing system are formed by modifying other characters that have a related phonetic value. In Cyrillic, which is fundamentally a modified and expanded version of the Greek alphabet, the letter Б : /b/ is a modification of В : /v/, which was an adoption of the Greek letter *beta* after the latter's ancient pronunciation as /b/ had evolved to /v/. In Brāhmī, several of the characters for aspirated stops (or, more precisely, aspirated stops plus the inherent vowel *a*) appear to be related to those representing the corresponding unaspirated stops, in that the former were derived from the latter by the addition of a stroke or the latter were derived from the former by the subtraction of a stroke (or a mixture of both). This can still be seen today in some such pairs in Nāgarī, the most widely used descendant of original Brāhmī, such as unaspirated *ṭa* ट beside aspirated *ṭha* ठ and unaspirated *pa* प beside aspirated *pha* फ. But only in one writing system are the shapes of the characters explicitly designed to pictorialize oral gestures involved in the articulation of the respective sounds; that system is Korean Han'gŭl. There is some dispute about which models were used by its promulgator, King Sejong (and/or his scholars), traditionally credited with inventing it in the fifteenth century, but the resulting product is clear: in the case of the velars and dentals, for example, the letters depict the position of the tongue viewed laterally as in a modern cut-away depiction of the vocal tract with the lips to the left, so that the velar *g* ㄱ shows the back part of the tongue raised toward the roof of the mouth, while symbols for the dentals *n* ㄴ and *d* ㄷ show the tip of the tongue raised toward the alveolar ridge. Adding a horizontal stroke inside of *g* and *d* produces symbols for the aspirated stops *k* ㅋ and *t* ㅌ.

[9] Excepted from this, of course, are diacritics.

Systematicity at the level of the grapheme can also sometimes be seen in the ordering of the symbols constituting a writing system, ordering which is sometimes language-specific. There is no recoverable rationale to either of the two attested orders of letters in the Semitic alphabet,[10] but the ordering of at least one major family of scripts, Brāhmī, has been systematically informed by linguistic principles. The character order here is reflective of the highly developed Indian grammatical tradition described in Section 9.5, and proceeds according to phonetic principles, both in general terms – vowel graphemes and other syllabics are grouped together as a series preceding the nonsyllabic sounds – and at numerous levels of detail. The vowel graphemes/syllabics are grouped into short–long pairs, themselves ordered relative to one another according to natural classes. Thus the three characters corresponding to vowels at the corners of the vowel triangle start things off, beginning with mid or low (*a* : [ə] *ā*) followed by high front and high back (*i ī u ū*); next come the symbols for the two pairs of syllabic sonorants (*r̥ r̥̄ l̥ l̥̄*), rounded off by the graphemes corresponding to the mid vowels and diphthongs again going from front to back (transliterated nowadays as *e ai o au* but in earlier literature *ē āi ō āu*, which is actually a better reflection of the phonetic reality). With this last set, matters are additionally interesting because of two other facts. First is a further feature of all these letters: each long member of a short–long pair is the same character as the short member plus an added stroke (thus, e.g., अ *a*, आ *ā*). For *e/ai* and *o/au*, this may seem puzzling, but *e* and *o* are historically monophthongizations of the (short) diphthongs **ai* and **au*, and in historical times still alternate with them (or their equivalents *ay* and *av* with off-glides) in certain contexts; additionally, *e o ai au* are all metrically long.[11] Similar systematicity is evinced by the arrangement of the obstruents, which are grouped overall according to manner of articulation (stops, glides, liquids, fricatives); the stops furthermore are divided into groups ordered according to place of articulation from the back of the mouth forward (velar, palatal, retroflex, dental, labial), and within each of these groups they are further arranged according to manner of articulation (plain voiceless first, followed by voiceless aspirated, voiced, voiced aspirated and nasal).

As Buddhism and, with it, the Brāhmī writing system spread eastward, the system's linguistically informed ordering proved influential on the arrangement of characters in some unrelated writing systems, particularly the two Japanese *kana* syllabaries and Han'gŭl. The ordering of the Han'gŭl consonant graphemes is similar to that of Brāhmī (in the original 1446 version of

[10] Alongside the more familiar Semitic alphabet that begins *ʾ b g d h* is the South Semitic alphabet beginning *h l ḥ m q*, still used in Ethiopia, where it has evolved into an abugida. Both alphabetic orders are attested in the cuneiform alphabets of ancient Ugarit. See Haring (2015) for the earliest known evidence for the South Semitic alphabetic order.

[11] There is no evidence that *e* and *o* were still pronounced as diphthongs at the time the writing system was developed, however.

the former, *k/g kh ng t/d th n p/b ph m j ch s h ʔ l/r z*),[12] though the vowel symbols come after the consonant ones. The *kana* syllabaries of Japanese follow the Brāhmī order more faithfully, especially when one takes sound changes into account. These syllabaries begin with the vowel symbols in the Brāhmī order (*a i u e o*) followed by the *k-*, *s-*, *t-*, *n-*, *h-*, *m-*, *y-*, *r-* and *w-*series;[13] representation of voiced *g*, *z*, etc. is achieved by the addition of two small strokes (thus, for example, く *ku* and ぐ *gu*, と *to* and ど *do*). The position of the *s*-series, curious at first glance, is due to the fact that it corresponds to the Brāhmī palatal series: the phonemes corresponding to *s* and *z* are allophonically palatalized to the sound reflected by *sh* and *j* before *i*, and *j* in Brāhmī belongs to the palatal series. As for *h*, it is historically the weakened descendant of earlier *p*, which is why adding the diacritic for voicing to members of the *h*-series produces a *b*-series; thus, for example, は *ha* (< *pa*) and ば *ba*. Since *p* remained in some positions, a special diacritic was devised to represent it that looks like a degree sign; thus, for example, ぱ *pa*.

An unusual case of alphabetical order (going hand in glove with a perhaps unique alphabetic genesis) is represented by the Thaana alphabet used since the seventeenth century to write Dhivehi (Maldivian), which consists of letters that are historically the Arabic numerals from one to nine, followed by the corresponding Indian numerals that had been used in the predecessor Brāhmī-derived script, with vowels indicated by letters derived from the vowel diacritics of Arabic (Gippert 2013: 96–98). Previously, Dhivehi had been written in a Brāhmī-derived script that ran left to right, which made it cumbersome to mix in Arabic words (written right to left); Thaana solved that problem since it is written just right to left. However, no rationale has yet been uncovered for the assignation of the specific phonetic values to the numerical symbols, or why numbers were chosen in the first place.

9.4 Phonemic Indication

It is often assumed that phonetically based writing systems typically cover all the sounds of a language at the phonemic level.[14] This assumption is largely true of the more prominent Western systems, but, as also briefly discussed in Chapter 3, cases where some phonemic distinctions are not represented are far from rare. In writing systems where each written symbol represents

[12] *ʔ* represents a glottal stop.

[13] Since kana is a syllabary and not an abugida like Brāhmī and vowels are not indicated with diacritics, the syllables *ka*, *ki*, *ku*, *ke* and *ko* are each represented by a separate syllabogram (か き く け こ, in hiragana), and similarly for the other consonant–vowel combinations.

[14] Phonemes are, informally, the basic sounds of a language, and can alter meaning when interchanged, as the /t/ and /d/ in English *cat* and *cad*. Other features of a language's pronunciation, such as stress and tone, can be phonemic as well, but are less frequently indicated in writing.

a phoneme (i.e. in alphabets) or a syllable (i.e. in syllabaries), decisions have to be made as to how many phonemes or phonemic sequences are to be represented. Pure abjads represent only consonantal, not vocalic, phonemes, and do not, for example, graphically encode differences between single and geminate (double) consonants. Such, historically at least, are the Semitic alphabets like Phoenician, Old Hebrew and Nabataean. Over time, of course, such systems can expand to encode further information: certain consonantal letters can take on the additional role of indicating long vowels (such as the use of aleph, normally representing a glottal stop, to represent *ā* also; these are the so-called *matres lectionis*). Syllabaries, although they represent vowels by default, do not necessarily indicate differences in vowel length or the doubling of consonants, such as Linear B, described directly below. Semitic alphabets historically have not had dedicated letters for the short vowel phonemes; diacritics exist for representing short vowels but these are typically not employed outside of sacred texts and some children's literature.

An extreme case of phonemic underrepresentation is the Linear B syllabary used for writing Mycenaean Greek in the second millennium BC (see, e.g., Hooker 1980; see also Chapter 20, this volume). Linear B contained only symbols for V and CV syllables, and the consonant inventory encoded in the script fell considerably short of the number of phonemic distinctions in the language.[15] Greek had a three-way distinction between voiceless, voiced and voiceless aspirated stops (e.g. /p/, /b/, /pʰ/), but the script only reflected the first two of those and only in the case of the dentals (/t/ and /d/); for labials, palatals and labiovelars, a single set of CV symbols had to be used for all three manners of articulation.[16] Furthermore, the script did not distinguish between /r/ and /l/. Although theoretically long vowels could have been indicated with spellings of the CV-V type, the Linear B scribes appear to have had no interest in representing vowel length, and only devised workarounds for syllable-initial consonant clusters, which were indicated with a dummy copy vowel (e.g. *ko-no-so* for *Knossos*). As this example shows, gemination of consonants was not indicated either, nor were consonants in syllable codas.

A not dissimilar case, at least in its end result if not in its origins, is provided by the limitations of the Pahlavi alphabet (Mackenzie 1971), a modified form of the Aramaic alphabet used to write Middle Persian and some other Iranian languages. Over time, numerous letters merged in form, resulting in only a dozen distinct letters representing twice as many phonemes. The multiple ambiguities that arise from this can hamper scholarly interpretations of Pahlavi texts, but appear not to have caused Pahlavi speakers themselves any difficulty. Indeed, it can almost be stated as a rule that orthographies try to

[15] The script appears to have been originally used for an unrelated language, which, one can reasonably speculate, lacked a number of those distinctions, though it may be a mistake to imagine that it was perfectly designed for that language either.

[16] One sign, pu_2, seems to have been in use secondarily to represent aspirated /pʰu/.

maximize economy; if a particular phonemic distinction does not have to be indicated, it often will not be. For example, Spanish and Italian indicate the position of the word stress (with an accent mark) only if the accent does not fall on the syllable that the productive stress-positioning rules would lead one to predict; thus in Spanish *Alcázar* (which violates the rule that words ending in *-r* are normally end-stressed) and Italian *àncora, città* (which violate the rule that words are normally stressed on the penult) the stress is written in, but not in, for example, Spanish *doctor* (stressed on the final syllable) or Italian *fiore* (stressed on the penultimate syllable). This already provides more information than some other orthographies, such as Russian, where stress is very unpredictable but not represented in writing at all. For example, the word *мука* means 'flour' if stressed on the first syllable but 'torture' if stressed on the second, with no distinction in writing. English is not so different; compare *project* (noun, first syllable stressed) versus *project* (verb, second syllable stressed) and many other such pairs where the stress difference is not indicated in spelling.

Sometimes the desire to maximize economy can lead to ambiguities and an actual increase in complexity through the rise of so-called 'positional rules'. Italian has two phonemes, /k/ and /tʃ/, that can each be represented in two partially overlapping ways depending on context: *c* before a back vowel is always /k/ and before a front vowel, /tʃ/; /k/ before a front vowel is represented by *ch*, while /tʃ/ before a back vowel is represented by *ci*, a sequence of letters that in other contexts represents the syllable /tʃi/. Thus *cosa* 'thing' /kɔsa/ ~ *cento* 'hundred' /tʃɛnto/ ~ *che* 'that' /ke/ ~ *ciao* 'bye' /tʃao/ (not *[tʃiao]) but *cinque* 'five' /tʃiŋkwe/. This system arose for a couple of reasons. First, historically the phoneme represented by *c* had two different pronunciations depending on the context: it sounded like /k/ before the back vowels /ɑ/, /o/ and /u/, but more like /tʃ/ before front vowels (/e/ and /i/), and subsequent changes resulted in these originally predictable variants becoming separate phonemes. Second, this change in the phonemic inventory was not matched by the introduction of any new written symbols (or resuscitation/recycling of ones in disuse, like *k*), probably because of a desire to preserve *c* in all its historically justified contexts. This resulted in the letters *h* and *i* being marshaled into service with new roles as indicators of the quality of a preceding *c*. The desire to maximize economy, which would have been most easily satisfied by adopting a one-grapheme-equals-one-phoneme approach, has in this case conflicted with the desire to keep things looking basically as they always did. This desire itself was not consistent; for example, *z* was introduced as a replacement of Latinate *ti* after the latter's pronunciation had changed to [ts] (for more see Demartini 2011). Spanish has a similar situation with respect to the voiced counterpart of /k/, namely /g/. This is represented orthographically by *g*, but *g* is pronounced /x/ before *e* or *i*. To indicate the sequence /ge/ or /gi/, Spanish orthography uses *gu* instead, with *u* acting as a 'buffer letter' like the *h* in Italian *ch*. However, unlike *h* in Italian, which is always silent, *u* in Spanish is not, and *gu* in other contexts represents /gu/ or /gw/ (often weakened to just /w/). Thus to indicate the sequence /gui/ or /gue/ in pronunciation, Spanish orthography makes use of an additional feature, namely, it adds a diaeresis over the *u*, as in *averigüé* 'I found out' [-gu'e] from the verb *averiguar* 'to find out' [-gu'aɾ].

An especially interesting case of the ambiguities and idiosyncrasies that can arise through the use of positional rules – however systematic the rules themselves are – comes from Classical Old Irish orthography (Thurneysen 1946). Here, letters were pronounced differently depending on their position in a word, resulting in some sounds being unambiguously represented and others not. A *c*, for example, represented /k/ word-initially but /g/ after a vowel; thus *cath* /kaθ/ 'battle', *éc* /eːg/ 'death'. To represent a voiceless stop after a vowel, the letter was written double: *macc* /mak/ 'son', accusative plural *maccu* /maku/. Certain proclitics (unstressed particles that form a phonological unit with a following stressed word) induced a morphophonological set of mutations to word-initial consonants, but because they were written together with their hosts without a break, this sometimes resulted in changes to the spelling of those initial consonants and sometimes not. One of the mutations resulted in the voicing of a word-initial /k/ to /g/. The genitive plural of the definite article, *inna* or *na*, is an example of a proclitic that induced this mutation; 'of the battles' was pronounced /(ɪ)nə gaθə/ but written *(in)nacathae*. The internal *-c-* unambiguously represents /g/. However, ambiguity sets in when the mutation was induced by a full lexeme, since full lexemes were written separately. Such a word was *secht* /ʃɛχt/ 'seven'; 'seven battles' was pronounced /ʃɛχt gaθə/ but written *secht cathae*.[17] In certain other cases, however, the change in pronunciation *was* indicated. If the initial consonant was a voiced stop, such as /g/, a word like *secht* caused the addition of a homorganic nasal, which was represented orthographically: *glais* 'locks' but *secht nglais* 'six locks'. Thus in the same context, words beginning with voiceless stops were written morphematically and the reader had to mentally supply the sound changes, while words beginning with voiced stops were written phonetically. In other contexts, though, the situation could be reversed. The numeral *cóic* 'five' caused a following word-initial stop to become a fricative; thus /k/ became /χ/ and /g/ became /ɣ/. While /χ/ was unambiguously represented as *ch*, /ɣ/ was written *g*, just like /g/. Thus 'five battles' was written *cóic chathae* while 'five locks' was written *cóic glais* /ɣlaʃʹ/. Here it is the words beginning with voiced stops, not voiceless stops, where the reader has to mentally supply the changes.

[17] To make matters worse, normalized modern editions of Irish works also write proclitics separate from their hosts (e.g. *(in)na cathae*); without knowing the effects on pronunciation of the article, there would be no way to tell from the spelling that the *c-* was pronounced /g/.

Many alphabetic and syllabic writing systems use single and double letters or characters in order to signal contrastive (phonemic) length of vowels and/or consonants. In the cuneiform syllabary described above that was used for Hittite, not all possible consonant-vowel-consonant sequences had a dedicated sign in the script. Those that did not thus had to be represented with a CV sign followed by a VC sign, each encoding the same vowel sound, for example, *pa-ak* for the syllable /pak/. Since the doubling of the vowel is orthographic only, necessitated by the limitations of the script (*p-ak* and *pa-k* were not possible because there were no true consonant letters), in order to indicate a phonetically long vowel, an extra V-sign had to be inserted: *pa-a-ak*. But a double consonant was always significant (*ap-pa*) and represented gemination,[18] since the orthography easily allowed a contrast between that and *a-pa* with a single intervocalic consonant (see further Melchert 1994).[19]

In contrast with modern orthographic systems like those of Italian and Finnish, where geminate consonants are regularly indicated as such, the Hittites were inconsistent, but even Italian and Finnish are not perfect in this regard. In certain syntagms in both these languages where word-initial gemination occurs, the gemination is not signaled orthographically. The case of *raddoppiamento sintattico* in Italian is one example: certain vowel-final monosyllables trigger gemination of the initial consonant of the following word, but without this being reflected in the spelling; for example, *va bene* 'okay' is pronounced /va bːɛne/ as though *va bbene*. However, such phrases are spelled with doubling if they have been univerbated, such as *frattanto* 'meanwhile' < *fra* 'between' + *tanto* 'as much, still'. A similar situation arises in Finnish, though with a bit less regularity as regards univerbations. Nouns and adjectives in *-e* like *terve* 'well, healthy' ended historically in a consonant that assimilated to following consonants in a variety of contexts, resulting in a geminate consonant in speech. As in Italian, the initial geminate is not indicated when the words are separate; but, somewhat more complicated than the Italian situation, within single words, gemination is not always indicated either. Case-endings undergoing the change regularly reflect the gemination, as in the partitive singular (*terve-ttä* < *terve* + *-tä*). However, in a compound like *tervetuloa* 'welcome' (*terve* + *tuloa* 'coming'), pronounced as though *tervettuloa*, gemination of the initial *t* of *tuloa* is not indicated, and whether a word induces gemination is not always predictable—in many cases it is lexically determined. Here Finnish evinces a genuine irregularity in its otherwise very regular spelling system.[20]

[18] At least in Assyrian, whence the Hittites borrowed the script. Whether doubling represents (or always represents) gemination in Hittite itself is an unsettled question.

[19] The sequence *a-pa* was strongly preferred over *ap-a*, presumably reflecting the syllabification of single intervocalic consonants as onsets.

[20] For more examples of gemination not indicated in the orthography see Karlsson (1983: 17).

Doubling of a letter is not the only way to indicate gemination or length of the sound indicated by that letter. In Dutch, vowel length can be indicated by whether the *following consonant* is written single or double: single indicates the preceding vowel is long (e.g. *maken* with /aː/); double, short (e.g. *Bakker* with short /a/). This system, however, is only used if the consonant is intervocalic; otherwise, the vowel letter is written single or double depending on the length (e.g. short vowel in *van, best, word*; long vowel in *aan, twee, woorden*). The practice of using the following consonant letter to signal length of a preceding vowel is found in the orthographies of other West Germanic languages, including English (whence the contrast between *hoping* and *hopping*, for example).[21] Long vowels can also be indicated by the addition of an extra 'silent' letter, such as an *h* (German *Ahl* 'awl') or an *e* (Low German placename *Coesfeld* /koːsfɛlt/). The 'silent *e*' in English that is synchronically interpreted as an orthographic indicator of vowel 'length' (as in *made* vs. *mad*) is not isolated either; a comparable usage is found in the Mayan hieroglyphic script (see Coe 1992). In this logosyllabic script, only syllables of the structure V or CV are represented by dedicated signs. There being no unambiguous way to represent word-final consonants, a dummy vowel was used that copied the vowel of the preceding syllable: thus a syllable like *pan* was written *pa-na*. To indicate that the vowel in the preceding syllable was long, the dummy vowel *i* was used instead, so *pa-ni* indicated /paːn/. It may seem peculiar that these systems and others like them do not make use of unambiguous symbols like diacritics for indicating length, but rather use workarounds based on the number of graphemes or a particular combination of graphemes or the equivalent. Again, it is often not important for the writing cultures in question that all these details be represented at all; and diacritics in general are something of a latecomer historically, though there are a few examples from the ancient world. Oscan, a relative of Latin in ancient Italy, added a modified *I* and *U* to its alphabetic inventory around 300 BC that consisted of the old *I* and *U* with an added stroke at the top, used to indicate different vowel qualities. Latin inscriptions and manuscripts sometimes made use of the so-called apex to indicate vowel length, a mark that looks similar to a modern acute accent. In both of these traditions, use of these diacritics was optional.[22]

Besides not always representing the full phonemic inventory or all phonemic distinctions of a language, written cultures have sometimes seen fit to

[21] Technically the salient distinction here is not one of length or duration (in spite of the traditional grammar-school terminology) but one of tenseness (tense vs. lax), often combined with presence or absence of diphthongization. *Hoping* has the diphthong /oʊ/ beginning with the tense vowel /o/, while *hopping* has the undiphthongized lax vowel /ɑ/. Similarly (see further below in the main text), the 'long' vowel in *made* is the tense diphthong /ej/ while the 'short' vowel in *mad* is lax /æ/. Tense vowels in English can be secondarily longer than lax vowels, but whether a following consonant is voiced or voiceless has a much greater effect on English vowel length: the vowels in *made* and *mad*, coming before a voiced consonant, have more than two times the duration of the same vowels in *mate* and *mat*, coming before a voiceless one.

[22] See Buck (1928) for an overview of Oscan, and Fortson (2020) for an overview of scholarship on the apex.

ignore entire morphemes. An extreme example comes from ancient Sumer, where the earliest layer of true writing contained logograms for a variety of full lexical concepts (the root meanings of nouns, verbs and adjectives) but had not yet developed syllabograms to represent inflectional morphology.[23] A less extreme example, from the modern world, comes from Farsi (Thackston 1993). In this language's so-called *ezâfe* construction, a clitic particle *-e* or (after vowels) *-ye* is inserted between the elements of certain phrases, such as noun phrases (e.g. *mard-e xub* 'a good man', *hanâ-ye xub* 'good weather'). Because the language is written in the Perso-Arabic script, which is an abjad and does not indicate short vowels, this grammatical element is completely absent from writing in phrases like the first one above (written مرد خب *mrd xb*), but it is reflected in phrases like the second one since *-ye* begins with a consonant (حناط خب *hn'y xb*, with aleph ا ' used for *â*).

But is phonetic regularity even a desired feature of writing systems? Specialists in language, who are steeped in the International Phonetic Alphabet, might put a premium on writing systems that have a one-to-one relationship between written symbol and sound, but particular writing cultures often put their priorities elsewhere. Sebba (2007: 81–82) notes the interesting cases of Romanian and Moldovan, the name for Romanian as spoken in the Republic of Moldova and, historically, in much of Moldavia (which stretched over what is now part of eastern Romania, Moldova, and parts of Ukraine and Russia). Until relatively recently, the Cyrillic alphabet was used to write Romanian/Moldovan. In early nineteenth-century Romania, the Latin alphabet was introduced on the grounds that this was appropriate given the language's descent from Latin; Cyrillic was banned in 1863. In Moldavia, Cyrillic continued to be used until the 1920s, when the switch to the Latin alphabet also occurred; but after the eastern part of Moldavia was annexed as Moldova by the Soviet Union in 1941, Cyrillic was reintroduced. In 1989, though, the country reverted to the Latin alphabet, two years before it declared its independence. The interesting fact for the purposes of the present discussion is that the Cyrillic alphabet is better suited for representing Romanian and Moldovan than the Latin alphabet because of its larger number of letters, allowing it to represent all the sounds of the language individually. However, ideological desire (in the nineteenth century) to showcase descent from Latin and (in the late twentieth) to assert independence from the Soviet Union, together with the Moldovans' wish to reunite the writing system with that of their Romanian kin, rendered any relevant linguistic or functional concerns utterly inconsequential.

It is, moreover, far from clear in any case that a precise phonetic script is always the 'ideal' writing system. Mandarin Chinese illustrates this issue very

[23] The syllabograms developed as a specialization of certain logograms, to a large extent under Akkadian influence.

clearly. On the one hand, the traditional logographic writing system is highly complex, requiring the mastery of several thousand characters for competent literacy. On the other hand, the language has an extremely high rate of homophony due to a combination of two factors: first, most morphemes are monosyllabic, and second, the number of distinct syllables is small, due to historical loss of most final consonants and reduction or simplification of initial complex onsets and various consonantal contrasts.[24] Thus an alphabetic rendering of a syllable such as *yì*, while simple to learn in the abstract, would be horrendously ambiguous (especially outside of context) since this syllable corresponds to over thirty homophonous morphemes,[25] but when each homophone is represented by a different character, the ambiguity is erased. A similar case can be made for preserving the heterography of English homophones like *air*, *heir*, *ere* and *e'er*. On these grounds alone it is not mysterious why the various ways of writing Chinese phonetically that have been invented over the centuries (whether based on traditional characters, like *bopomofo* or *zhùyīn*, or using the Latin alphabet, like *pīnyīn*) have never been adopted for general employment. Probably the most widespread use to which such phonetic systems have been put is as so-called 'ruby characters' written above or to the right of a character to indicate pronunciation in children's books; Japanese children's books use *kana* for the same purpose to indicate the pronunciation of *kanji*. Chinese characters also have an important unifying role at the cultural and political level, as they are used throughout the country as the standard written medium across regions with mutually unintelligible local varieties of Chinese.[26]

9.5 Subphonemic Indication

Phonemes are pronounced differently in different contexts; these variants are called allophones and comprise the subphonemic level of speech. In relaxed speech in most varieties of English, the /t/ of *top* is pronounced quite differently from the /t/ of *butter*, and also (if a bit more subtly) differently from the *t* of *stop* and *tray*. The occurrence of a given allophone is always predictable based on the surrounding context. Subphonemic distinctions such as these are generally ignored in writing systems (native speakers may not even be

[24] To be sure, in principle almost every morpheme is a monosyllabic word, but in practice there is a high rate of compounding, which reduces the meaning load borne by each syllable significantly. For example, although the morpheme 茄 *qié* means 'eggplant' all on its own, in practice when talking about eggplants one adds the nominalizer 子 *zǐ*, literally 'child', forming the compound 茄子 *qiézi* 'eggplant'.

[25] A sampling: 易 'to change', 邑 'country, capital', 乂 'to manage', 挹 'to ladle', 劓 'punishment in which the nose is cut off', 毅 'decisive'.

[26] Actually, the written standard, based on Mandarin, does not map directly onto regional Chinese languages even at a logographic level because of sometimes large differences in vocabulary.

aware of them). A notable exception is Sanskrit (Whitney 1889). The intellectual life of ancient India was focused on grammar, whose analysis was developed with a sophistication unique in the ancient and medieval worlds. This left an indelible stamp on the orthography of Sanskrit, which encodes an unusual amount of subphonemic detail. In particular, the phonetic changes that happen at word junctures (external sandhi rules) are clearly indicated, in contrast to the orthographies of other languages, where such aspects of pronunciation are routinely ignored. Thus the English verb *hit* is so written regardless of whether, in relaxed speech, one pronounces it as /hɪʔ/ with a glottal stop (as in *he hit me*), /hɪɾ/ with a flap (as in *I hit him*), or /hɪtʃ/ (as in *he hit you*) where the /t/ coalesces with the following /j/ to form a /tʃ/-sound. Notably, Sanskrit reflects such variants in its spelling. Hence, for example, the ablative singular form *nagarāt* 'from (the) city' undergoes changes in spelling in combinations such as the following (due to the nature of the script, which is an abugida or alphasyllabary, words ending in a consonant are written together with the following word): नगरात् *nagarāt* + अगन् *agan* '(s)he went' > नगरादगन् *nagarādagan*, नगरात् *nagarāt* + शुक्रात् *śukrāt* 'shining' > नगराच्छुक्रात् *nagarācchukrāt*, नगरात् *nagarāt* + जगाम *jagāma* 'I went' > नगराज्जगाम *nagarājjagāma*, नगरात् *nagarāt* + नव्यात् *navyāt* 'new' > नगरान्नव्यात् *nagarānnavyāt*.

Though this system is carefully followed in all word-combinations in modern editions of Sanskrit texts and is described in detail by the Sanskrit grammarians, fidelity to it varies widely in manuscripts and inscriptions. In the prenormative language of the oldest Sanskrit text, the Rigveda,[27] the external sandhi rules are not always the same as in the Classical language and are not applied in a number of circumstances. In Middle Indic, sandhi is only indicated in word-groups that are closely connected syntactically. All this suggests that the rigid, across-the-board orthographic representation of external sandhi is artificial and not reflective of the reality obtaining in speech.[28] More normal in the ancient world is sporadic indication of external sandhi, typically in close syntactic contexts like short prepositional phrases. This is found frequently, for example, in Greek and Latin inscriptions.

[27] Technically, the language of the Rigveda is not Sanskrit, since specialists often limit that term to the later normative language (Classical Sanskrit) that was prescriptively codified in the second half of the first millennium BC; but in practical terms the differences are not especially large, somewhat comparable to the differences between Homeric and Classical Attic Greek.

[28] Typologically analogous is word-final elision in Greek and Latin. In the scansion of Greco-Latin poetry, it occurs across the board regardless of the syntactic connection between the elided word and the word that follows, and even across change of speaker in a dramatic piece. Thus in Plautus's comedy *The Menaechmi*, line 547, where one character says *Non habeo* 'I don't have (it)' before another character says a sentence beginning *At tu* ... 'But you ...', the final *-o* of *habeo* is elided before the initial *a-* of *At* spoken by the other character. In natural speech, however, there is good evidence that elision was more limited. On this and similar phenomena in other poetic traditions, see Devine and Stephens (1994: 263).

Elsewhere, indication of subphonemic detail is sporadic at best. Probably the sandhi phenomena that are most consistently observed in spelling systems are elision and contraction, the former of which in particular can be mandatory even at the slowest talking speeds. Thus French *l'ami* 'the friend' is never written *le ami* because it is never so pronounced (versus, e.g., in the placename *Le Havre*). One of the earliest Greek alphabetic inscriptions, on the so-called Nestor's Cup from around the late eighth century BC (see Watkins 1976), indicates elision in the sequence (with restorations) ΗΟΣΔΑΝΤΟΔΕΠΙΕΣΙΠΟΤΕΡΙΟ *hosdantōdepiēsipotēriō* = *hos d' an tōde piēsi potēriō* 'but he who drinks from this cup ...', where the adversative conjunction *de* is elided to *d'* before the vowel-initial modal particle *an*. Elision in French is regularly indicated as well; this is true also of the opposite phenomenon, liaison, an external sandhi phenomenon whereby etymological word-final consonants that are not ordinarily pronounced come out of hiding (as it were) before a vowel in certain syntactic contexts. Liaison is normally indicated by default since the majority of such consonants are already present in the spelling for historical reasons but are otherwise silent (due to their having been lost through sound change over the centuries); in certain cases, however, the consonants do not normally occur in spelling but are restored in liaison contexts, for example, *elle parle* 'she speaks' but *Parle-t-elle?* 'Does she speak?', *donne-le-moi* 'Give it to me!' but *donnes-en* 'Give some of it!', with restoration of the historical verb personal endings *-t* and *-s* that dropped out of pronunciation in all other contexts.

A common subphonemic rule of many languages is the devoicing of word-final voiced consonants. In some written traditions, such as those of the Slavic languages, this devoicing is not reflected in spelling: thus Czech *hradu* /ɦradu/ 'of castle' (genitive singular) but nominative singular *hrad* even though pronounced /ɦrat/. Others, nonetheless, do spell out the alternation, such as Middle High German, for example, dative singular *lobe* 'fame' but nominative *lop*. This practice, however, died out; in present-day German, spelling is morphophonemic, whence nominative singular *Lob* even though the final *b* is devoiced.[29] In all the examples given so far where a spelling system represents a subphonemic distinction, the allophones in question nevertheless are the same as other phonemes that are already represented by graphemes. Thus in the Middle High German example, *lop* is written with a *p* because a *b* in that position sounded like a *p*, which is itself a phoneme (a different phoneme from *b*, of course). Many allophones, however, do not sound like phonemes elsewhere in the system, as is the case with several of the English examples: the *t* of *matter* (in the variety of English described here) is a flap, which is not

[29] Perhaps relevant to this is the fact that the degree of final devoicing varies considerably and the resultant sound is not always identical to that of *p*; in some analyses, the process is not actually best labeled as devoicing at all. See Iverson and Salmons (2007).

a phonemic sound, and likewise the *t* of *hit* (a glottal stop). It is very rare for writing systems to create dedicated symbols for allophones of this type. Once again, Sanskrit provides a couple of examples, though usage is not consistent at all historical periods and in all varieties of the Brāhmī abugida; one such example is the symbol ळ *ḷ*, which stands for an allophone of *ḍ* between vowels.

9.6 Beyond the Level of the Grapheme and Phoneme

To those used to the fixity of spelling in our contemporary orthographic world, where usually only one way of spelling a word is prescriptively 'correct', the looser practices that obtained throughout most of the rest of human history can seem puzzling and disorienting. One of many examples that could be cited comes from Hittite. Though the cuneiform writing system was perfectly capable of indicating contrasts in vowel length (*pa* versus *pa-a*) and single versus geminate consonantism (*a-pa* versus *ap-pa*), it was not part of the scribal culture to indicate such distinctions consistently except in certain words. There is consequently much fluctuation in spelling. The variety only increases when another factor is added, namely, that the distinction between voiced and voiceless stops that the syllabary actually encodes was not in fact implemented by the Hittites when they adopted the script, and they used the corresponding symbols interchangeably. Thus the stem of the noun for 'body, self', which was phonetically [twe:k-], shows up in no less than five different spellings, as witnessed by fluctuations in spelling like *tu-eg-ga-az, tu-e-eg-ga-az, du-eg-ga-az, tu-e-ek-ki* and *tu-ek-ku-uš* (the different endings reflect different grammatical forms of the word).[30]

Of course contemporary orthographic systems have their inconsistencies as well, but these tend to be standardized for individual lexemes rather than the result of free variation/choice. The same symbol or orthographic sequence can have several different pronunciations (as the sequence *ough* in English *though, through, rough, cough, thought, bough*, plus the British *hiccough*) and the same phonetic entity can have several different ways of being represented in spelling (as with long /a:/ in the German words *Tal, Wahl, Aal*, versus only one way to indicate short *a* in the same environment: *Fall*); but the spelling of each word is fixed in these traditions. Sometimes having more than one spelling for the same phonetic sequence can serve to disambiguate. Thus in German, the diphthong /aj/ is normally spelled <ei>, but <ai> is also used,

30 That the different spellings of this word represented different phonetic realities is unlikely. On the other hand, it is very difficult to know in all cases when to take differences in Hittite spelling at face value, and consequently this is a long-standing area of scholarly debate. One could, for example, argue that *ga* is a simpler sign to write than *ka* and may have influenced the choice in the ablative; but this does not explain why *ka* is on the whole much more commonly used than *ga* across the Hittite corpus. *gi* and *ki* have about the same number of strokes, while *ku* is simpler than *gu*.

especially for the less frequent of two homonyms (e.g. *Weise* 'way, manner' vs. *Waise* 'orphan', *Seite* 'page' vs. *Saite* 'string of an instrument'). A present-day language where spelling still has a bit of freedom is Japanese, though the freedom operates within a fairly limited set of choices. As briefly discussed in Chapter 7, three separate writing systems are used, *kanji* (logographic Chinese characters representing lexical sememes) and the two syllabaries (*hiragana* and *katakana*) collectively called *kana* that have already been mentioned and that are purely phonetic. While one could theoretically use *kana* to write an entire text phonetically, this is rarely done: *kanji* and *kana* are used side by side, with the root meaning of full lexical words typically expressed with *kanji* and stem and inflectional endings added using *kana*. The latter, nevertheless, can always be used instead of *kanji* depending on authorial choice and stylistic factors; broadly speaking, the more *kanji* that are used, the more formal the style. The fixity of orthographies over much of the present-day world is a product only of the last very few centuries, often the result of the workings of a centralized normative institution or academy, but sometimes (as in English) the combined result of efforts by individual eminent literary figures who took it upon themselves to promulgate orthoepic norms. In parts of the ancient world where alphabets were used and where there was close to a one-to-one correspondence between letter and sound, one sometimes sees a high degree of regularity in spelling (e.g. in Classical Attic Greek inscriptions); but it is not clear if the regularity resulted by default from the general accuracy of the script, or whether it was purposefully imposed.

Many times in the history of writing, cultural movements arose resulting in broad spelling reforms through imitation of the orthography of a prestige language. Throughout the last two millennia of Western European history, Latin and Greek have enjoyed such prestige status and have influenced the spelling (and vocabulary) of most Western European languages to a sometimes remarkable degree. A particular wave of such respellings gripped these literary cultures during the Enlightenment in the seventeenth century. Brengelman (1980) regards the central impact of this intellectual movement on spelling to have been rationalization or regularization, with the result that, for English at least, by the 1660s the plethora of earlier spelling variants had largely disappeared and a widely agreed-upon system was in place that has remained mostly unaltered to the present day. Words of Latinate origin underwent consistent respelling according to their etymologies, many of which resulted in changes to pronunciation on the basis of the new spellings (e.g. *adventure*, earlier *aventure*), others of which did not (e.g. *debt*, earlier *dette*, compare Lat. *debitum*).[31] In French, there were parallel efforts. The

[31] Brengelman (1980: 350) notes, "[i]t is this development which makes possible a curious fact about English spelling: the longer and more bookish a word is, the easier it is to spell."

French descendant of Latin *grandis* 'large' was spelled *grant* (masculine) and *grande* (feminine) in Old French, which was phonologically accurate (the dental had undergone final devoicing in the masculine); but the masculine was later respelled as *grand*, even though the historically correct pronunciation with /t/ persists to this day in liaison contexts (e.g. *grand homme* 'great man' /gʁɑ̃t‿ɔm/). As these examples show, such reforms do not result in greater regularity or systematicity across the board, and can actually increase the divide between spoken and written language.

9.7 Conclusion

In spite of being perforce cursory, the above overview has attempted to showcase the great variety of factors – many of them linguistic but just as many of them not – that can either advance or impede the achievement of systematicity in writing and orthographic systems. Given the number of different modes of pronunciation that obtain even within a single speech community and given humans' great ability to make do with and make the best of imperfect conditions and tools, it is not surprising that so few (if any) systems of writing or orthography are fully consistent at any level of abstraction.

It may have been noticed that the words 'systematicity' and 'idiosyncrasy' have not been given strict definitions in this chapter beyond anything that their ordinary usages denote. This was done on purpose since, at least to an extent, whether something can be called systematic or idiosyncratic is in the eye of the beholder and depends on factors like the level of resolution and the context: what might seem systematic at one level or in one context can appear an idiosyncrasy in another. Not only do writing systems exist on many planes, they are also not merely the products of individual intellects, nor merely visual symbolizations of structures of spoken language, but expressions of culture at various aesthetic and functional levels. Exactly how the connections between writing and culture are to be theoretically modeled is a very complex one and is far beyond our scope; other scholars may find it useful to explore this area against the backdrop of more general anthropological investigations of specific cultures or the human species more broadly. Of course it need not be the case that each and every discrete aspect of a writing system is culturally underpinned, and the same goes for any specific instance of systematicity in writing or its absence.

Regardless of the resolution of this question, its very existence creates challenges for another issue that has not been considered in this chapter, namely, whether any useful comparative typology of idiosyncrasies can be catalogued. It would appear to emerge (at least preliminarily) from the foregoing that such a typology, however descriptively or conceptually useful, would nonetheless be of limited intellectual or explanatory value, focusing as it would on epiphenomena. Systematicity is an imposed structure or framework that is deployed to varying degrees by the creator(s) of a given writing system; idiosyncrasy arises (or can arise) wherever this framework is not applied. The *motivations* for its application or nonapplication are really of greater interest, assuming they are recoverable from the historical record or indirectly through other historical and cultural investigations.

10

Multilayeredness and Multiaspectuality

Justyna Rogos-Hebda

10.1 Introduction

When exasperated language purists post online indignant comments on 'the current state of the language' they frequently pin the imminent demise of 'proper language' on abbreviations. Young people in particular, they claim, obsessively and compulsively truncate every other word when they engage in written interactions, manifesting their 'sloppiness' and 'laziness' in utter disregard for the sanctity of the dictionary form. Yet those very same people who lament the abbreviative nature of modern communication will roam the streets of Rome or take a trip around Cyprus with nothing but admiration for the monumental architecture, adorned with inscriptions, of which abbreviation is a common element. Still, despite their ubiquity, signs of truncation and curtailment would prove problematic even for the students of diachronic orthographies (with the notable exception of paleographers) who did not quite know how to incorporate scribal abbreviations into linguistic analyses of historical texts (see, e.g., *A Linguistic Atlas of Late Mediaeval English*, McIntosh et al. 1986a). Indeed, truncating frequently recurring, familiar items has always been part of the written culture. Limitations of space, workability of the writing surface or the time necessary to do the job all required the development of 'coping strategies' from the writers, whether they worked with stone or parchment. Rather than marking any 'impoverishment' of the language, abbreviations were a direct appeal to readers' literacy competence, which entailed a knowledge of sometimes intricate but mostly stable mappings between these visual symbols and their orthographic interpretation. Indeed, to abbreviate (and to understand what abbreviation stood for) meant to be a *litteratus* and, in a way, this still holds true in the modern digitally oriented written communication.

This chapter, while limited in its scope, is thus a reminder of the *longue durée* of abbreviation in scribal practices of the early-to-late Middle Ages in parts of Western Christendom, specifically England and Ireland. The Anglo-Irish context is both typical and idiosyncratic in the ways in which abbreviations were integrated into literacy practices of textual communities in the medieval and early modern periods. On the one hand, Irish and English scribes would access the same pool of symbols with the same range of meanings that were available for all writers and readers in the Latin West. Barring regional modifications to a handful of symbol shapes, the Latin system of abbreviations transgressed geographic and political boundaries in times when vernacular languages were not the default option for all written works, and when, regardless of their mother tongue, scribes from all over medieval Europe were practitioners of a form of Latin-based literacy. On the other hand, both geographic and, in a sense, cultural distance from continental influences (including a very distinct path of Christianization of the British Isles) facilitated a distinct 'vernacularization' of insular abbreviations.

By tracing the origins of abbreviations in late Antiquity and recounting their spectacular success in the Middle Ages, followed by their gradual (yet never complete) fall from grace in the early modern period, this chapter points to the lasting impact of abbreviation on contemporary abbreviating habits in written communication. Not unlike their contemporary manifestations, the abbreviations which are the focus of this chapter were always 'shape-shifters': not only would they change their form depending on the type of script, position on the page, or the language of the text but also they were ever negotiating between *logos* and *imago*, text and image, shape (*figura*) and its phonetic interpretation (*potestas*). In that sense, they serve as links between the different modalities which informed premodern textuality, entreating the reader always to shift between the linguistic, visual and spatial elements of the manuscript (or early printed) page to make sense of the text before their eyes. Medieval abbreviations can therefore help us to better understand the multimodality which informs modern, digitally based communication. Abbreviations are not and never have been foretellers of some kind of linguistic apocalypse; if anything, they reflect the multilayeredness and multiaspectuality of visually based transmission of ideas.

Arguably, one of the factors contributing to the 'problematic' reputation of abbreviations is the fact that these symbols span the boundary between the linguistic, visual and spatial components of the manuscript page. As such, they are neither the focus of linguistics *sensu stricto*, nor do they belong with visual studies. Moreover, the near-identicality of forms for Latin and vernacular languages suggests the commonality of functions in both linguistic contexts, even though they demonstrate patterns of distribution more complex that what could be explained away by the different structures of Latin and vernacular orthographies. The "half-graphic" structures – as Traube

(1907) once referred to them – sit inconveniently between image and text, the visual and the linguistic, the *figura* and the *potestas* (i.e. shape and sound value), Latin and the vernacular. Historically, abbreviations were applied to frequently recurring grammatical items (including prepositions, particles or inflectional endings) and for words which either could not be spelled in full out of reverence for the deity (*nomina sacra*) or needed not be spelled out because they belonged to a specialist jargon (*notae iuris*). However, in translation from Latin to vernacular languages those contexts and connotations were largely lost and what remained was their orthographic similarity (or identicality) with particular vernacular forms. Thus, from the linguistic point of view, the function of abbreviations shifted from that of grammatical or lexical markers to shortcuts for a specific orthographic sequence, which might signal a specific morpho-lexical category.

At the same time, what is becoming increasingly clear is that, far from being just a scribal shorthand, symbols of abbreviation are a crucial element of medieval multimodality (see Amsler 2012, 2016, Maxwell 2016). That is to say, they often participate in the creation of meaning of the text alongside other semiotic resources: it is not just the linguistic layer but also the visual makeup of the manuscript page (and the interactions between such visual elements as ink colors, script sizes, letter shapes), the spatial arrangement of its components or the tactile experience of the page itself all add to the pragmatic reading of the text. It is also through multimodality that one can access the multilayered functions of abbreviations, more about which is said in the subsequent parts of the chapter.

10.2 Polyvalent Functions of Abbreviations

"Take a foreign language, write it in an unfamiliar script, abbreviating every third word, and you have the compound puzzle that is the medieval Latin manuscript" – with these words Heimann and Kay (1982: i) begin their translation of Adriano Cappelli's *Dizionario di abbreviature latine ed italiane* (1899), which is to date one of the key references for those who work with medieval manuscripts. Indeed, so critical are abbreviations to pre-print textuality and so common are they in scribal output that the disciplines of paleography and diplomatic(s) (invested in the study of old handwriting and critical analysis of historical documents, respectively) trace their late seventeenth-century/early eighteenth-century origins to the very practical need to decipher symbols with which medieval scribes interspersed their writing. In the most basic definition, abbreviation is the shortening of a word either by disposing of some letters from the end (or from the body *and* the end) or by curtailing the letters from the middle but leaving the initial and final letters intact (Thompson 1893: 75). While individual abbreviation shapes would undergo mild-to-serious modifications and the number of types belonging to active scribal repertoires would fluctuate from one period and one geographical region to another, their primary purpose has always been to facilitate the efficacy of writing; either by truncating the familiar and recurrent orthographic strings and thus speeding up the copying process or by pointing to the nontextual reality (e.g. through legal shorthand[1] or *nomina sacra*).

Abbreviations are peculiar to pre-printed texts also because they are a link between text and image: in the highly visual literacy of the Middle Ages they are the forms combining *littera* with *imago*. Now based on individual letter shapes, sometimes modified by additional strokes, now entirely 'un-letter like' and arbitrary, symbols of abbreviation sit somewhat uncomfortably between the visual and the textual. Hence, no wonder that they should have been approached from either of the two perspectives (visual, i.e. paleographic, or textual, i.e. linguistic) rather than a combination of the two. The typical manner in which medieval abbreviations have been presented to the modern reader is in the form of abbreviation dictionaries, the most influential of which were composed in the eighteenth and nineteenth centuries. Apart from Cappelli, mentioned above, one should also mention Chassant (1846) and Trice Martin (1892), both of whose dictionaries problematize Latin abbreviations in the context of vernacular medieval sources (French and English, respectively).

While extremely useful for the modern reader of medieval sources, these dictionaries, with their impressive lists of Latin abbreviations, give an appearance of stasis, which belies the actual reality of the early-to-late Middle Ages. One would be arguably hard-pressed to gather from the lists collated by Chassant, Cappelli or Trice Martin that these scribal (and, to a certain degree, typographical) symbols were actually a context-bound, dynamic and open category, reflecting the linguistic, cultural and very pragmatic needs of the people who applied them to parchment or paper. Just as the Latin of the Roman republic (with which period the increasingly widespread use of abbreviations is typically associated) bears little semblance to the Latin of the medieval Church, so the system of abbreviations used in the legal documents of late Antiquity is different from that of religious texts of the high-to-late Middle Ages. Apart from historical depth, there is also diatopic differentiation in the abbreviation systems applied throughout our period of interest: even before the vernacularization of writing scriptoria in different parts of medieval Europe (and often, too, different scriptoria within the same political unit) there were specific in-house practices for abbreviations. Of course, in the era of Latin as a written *lingua franca*, there needed to be limits to the

[1] The practice of abbreviating elements of legal formulae and business transactions goes back to the Roman era. Legal scribes would resort to *litterae singulares* or *notae iuris* for commonly recurring words and terms (Bischoff 1990 [1979]: 150).

inventiveness of the scribes and an adherence to a general set of rules was necessary, lest written communication collapse. There are peaks and troughs in the history of abbreviations: the 'need for speed' ultimately had to be reconciled with practicality, and the scribes needed to know how to strike the balance between efficient copying and readability of their texts. Up until the twelfth century AD, the number of abbreviations was on the rise, with the Carolingian Renaissance of the ninth and tenth centuries contributing significantly to the expansion of the system and creation of new forms (Derolez 2003: 72). When Latin lost the hegemony of being *the* written medium of the educated *litterati*, abbreviation systems started to be regulated by vernacular orthographies. A number of forms (like ꝝ for *-rum*, *bꝫ* for *-bus*, *qꝫ* for *-quae* abbreviations) had to go, simply because vernacular languages did not have appropriate referents for them.

At the same time, scribes operating in vernacular systems devised new abbreviations for items not encountered in Latin (Irish scribes are said to have been particularly fond of that practice; see Bischoff 1990: 91). For late medieval and early modern scribes, abbreviation was as much a matter of the economy of copying as it was a marker of the formulaicity of written language: some types of texts and some formats of manuscripts are just more likely to contain more abbreviations in general or to contain abbreviations of specific type(s). For instance, the most densely abbreviated manuscripts in the Middle Ages are those which were intended for study, whereas those meant to be recited from – like liturgical manuscripts – contain relatively few abbreviations (Clemens and Graham 2007: 89). As such (and as has been argued elsewhere; see Rogos-Hebda 2016, 2020) they too, along with elements of the visual makeup of the manuscript page, indicate the pragmatic functions of the text, rather than simply encode specific orthographic strings to save the scribe's time. This richness of forms and functions stems from centuries-long processes of adaptations and modifications, which still resonate in the post-print world of today. This chapter traces the origins of symbols of abbreviation in the Latin West and outlines linguistic and cultural contexts for their changing graphic forms from late Antiquity to late Middle Ages (first century BC to fifteenth century AD). Section 10.3 focuses on sources for abbreviations in the written culture of the Latin West. Section 10.4 discusses typologies of abbreviation systems, circulating in manuscript studies, paleography and codicology and characterizes each of the types. Section 10.5 looks into modifications (or, better perhaps, adaptations) of the system inherited from late Roman practices and introduced by scribes translating that system into vernacular forms. Moreover, a link between the types of script and the type of abbreviation forms is made explicit. Finally, Section 10.6 hints at the transition period between the gradual decline of handwritten book production and the burgeoning print market, signaling some of the printers' responses to the abbreviations.

10.3 Sources for Abbreviations: *Sigla*, *Notae Iuris* and *Nomina Sacra*

All writing is abbreviative, to a degree. Limitations of the writing surface, pressure of time and the scribe's own predilections have always featured in the decisions to implement abbreviation. Some textual contexts would entail abbreviation as a matter of course, as students of numismatics and epigraphy will testify. Words encarved in metal and stone would be abbreviated for practical reasons (the availability of space), but they would also serve as visually encoded markers of power structures (coin issuance and architectural commissions were the prerogatives of the powerful). Yet it was inscriptions that, despite their abbreviative character, were able to communicate longer portions of text, thus becoming a template for the practices of scribes engaged with more 'workable' materials. In paleographic literature, the origins of what became the Latin-based system of abbreviations, used in the Latin West between late Antiquity and the early modern period (approximately seventh to sixteenth century), are traced to the *sigla* system and the Tironian notes of the Roman Republic on the one hand (Cappelli 1899: 1) and, on the other, to the *nomina sacra* of the early Greek manuscripts of the Scriptures (Traube 1907: 45).

A *siglum* was form of abbreviation in which a word was truncated to its initial letter (as in *A.D.*, *S.P.Q.R.*). Common in inscriptions, they gradually made their way to shorthand, which was becoming more widespread in the late Republic (approximately first century BC). These so-called *litterae singulares* were commonly applied to first names, calendar signs or common formulae in legal and business writings of the Classical Latin period (i.e. first century BC to third century AD) (Bischoff 1990: 150). Cappelli (1899: 3) refers to *sigla* as the most important but also the most notorious type of abbreviation by means of truncation (where the only unabbreviated part of a word is its initial part), which could only be efficient so long as it was limited to the most frequent lexemes. *Sigla* usually took the form of a majuscule initial followed by a period, although in written documents it is also possible to find *sigla* written as minuscules, often not followed by a period but marked by a horizontal stroke above the *siglum* (Cappelli 1899: 4). Moreover, in medieval written documents, one can find *sigla* made by the *middle* rather than initial letter of a word (e.g. *h* for *nihil*). Doubling the majuscule, in turn, would indicate plurality or the superlative degree (e.g. *FF.* would stand for *fratres*). For female first names and titles, *sigla* would have been tilted or written upside down (e.g. *W.* for *Mulier*). Cappelli (1899: 6) links the gradual decline of the *sigla* system to its inherent inefficacy: there are only so many words which can be unambiguously assigned to this category, and the eighth and ninth centuries witnessed the appearance of abbreviations which truncated fewer elements than *sigla* did and thus improved the legibility of such abbreviations.

From truncating words to just the initial letters developed the practice of leaving either the first letter of every syllable in a word unabbreviated, or else of leaving the first and final letter. This principle of contraction was applied in *notae iuris* – a system of legal abbreviations which, albeit more systematic than *sigla* ever were, were often ambiguous (Di Renzo 2000: 7). Lack of punctuation and adequate spacing in writing, combined with the propensity for abbreviating legal formulaic language, which was of little use and even less practicality beyond the legal context, made *notae iuris* hardly amenable for use in more general contexts.[2] That much was apparently noticed by Marcus Tullius Tiro, the secretary of Cicero, who needed a system for recording his master's dictations, public speeches and business transactions efficiently. His system, which came to be known as *notae Tironianae*, relied on three pillars: Latin letters, elements of Greek shorthand, and abstract symbols devised by Tiro himself (Di Renzo 2000: 8). A distinguishing feature of Tiro's system, and one of the causes of its success and subsequent expansion, was that, apart from developing abbreviations for individual words, it also took care of broader grammatical categories. Thus, Tironian notes included symbols for recurring inflectional endings, prefixes or function words (viz. abbreviations for *et*, *enim*, *esse*, *sunt*). Combinations of abbreviated letters, syllables and entire words then were used as shorthand for recording whole sentences and thus became the most varied and accurate shorthand system in the Antiquity (Di Renzo 2000: 8).

The system of 'slashes, curves and hooks' (Teeuwen 2014) would survive until the Middle Ages, when it was used predominantly in the context of legal and administrative writing. The system of Tironian notes would be further expanded and, from the early medieval period onward, combined with other abbreviations (Russon 2016). The original system swelled to more than a dozen thousand symbols by the beginning of the Carolingian period (mid-eighth to ninth century), after which the numbers still in use were significantly smaller. Teeuwen (2014) highlights the fact that the presence of Tironian notes in a medieval manuscript is indicative of the scribe's high level of education; an education most likely received in a monastic institution invested in scholarly activity. While one can tease out individual symbols for particular abbreviated items (lexical and/or functional) from the extant sources, it can be frustratingly difficult to interpret actual Tironian notes in a medieval text. The basic elements (i.e. strokes and curves which make up the *notae*) can be connected with following *figurae* (i.e. letter shapes) in highly idiosyncratic manners. Simply put, it is a challenging task to decipher the Tironian shorthand of a writer whose hand one is not familiar with (see Teeuwen 2014). With time, the number of Tironian notes used by the scribes was significantly limited, as limited was the audience able to read this shorthand. It is with a scholarly

[2] Saenger (2000: 40–42) argues that, while abbreviations facilitated reading in *scripto continua*, they became superfluous when word division became standard scribal practice.

setting that one should associate this system of abbreviations and, apart from a brief period of rekindled interest in the system during the twelfth century, it mostly went out of use, save for a few remnant symbols, which survived up until modern times (e.g. the Tironian *et*: ⁊ in Irish and Scottish signs).

The third source for medieval abbreviations are the early Greek translations of the Septuagint or, more specifically, the small set of abbreviations for terms referring to the names and attributes of God. Thompson (1893: 76) connects the emergence of the *nomina sacra*, as these abbreviations came to be known, with the practice of Hellenistic Jews, working on the translation of the Septuagint from Hebrew into Greek. To illustrate, rather than spell out the name *Yahveh*, these scribes tended to either copy the Hebrew Tetragram *YHVH* (the vowel-less version of the name of God) into the Greek text or, similarly, omit vowels in the Greek *ΘΕΟC* to *ΘC*, out of reverence to the deity. Along the same lines, *KYPIOC* for 'Lord' would become *KC* and both abbreviations would receive a horizontal stroke above. In the Hebrew tradition of copying, using such strokes would typically single out specific words as foreign or emphatic, but since a horizontal line was applied to abbreviated forms of 'God' and 'the Lord', it came to be used as a general symbol of abbreviation and would extend over the entire abbreviated word (Thompson 1893: 77). Initially, the group of sacred names (the *nomina sacra*) was limited only to five *nomina divina*, 'godly names', namely *God, the Lord, Jesus, Christ* and *Son*. It later expanded to 15 items, including words for *Spirit, father, savior, heaven, man, Israel, Jerusalem, David, cross* and *mother* (the latter only appearing as *nomen sacrum* in the fourth century AD).

Unlike *notae iuris* or *notae communae, nomina sacra* were not motivated by considerations of space or the speed of copying. The scribes' decision to resort to contracted forms of the 15 terms listed above was one guided by reverence rather than economy. The abbreviating principle with this category of lexemes was one of contraction, that is, abbreviating the middle of a word, leaving the first and final letters unabbreviated (and thus allowing an easy identification of case ending). While in principle biblical manuscripts precluded abbreviation (so as not to lead to interpretative ambiguity), by the Roman period "abbreviations of terms central to Christian worship" (Bischoff 1990: 152) were common enough. In Latin copying tradition, Greek *nomina sacra* were transliterated, with one notable exception, namely *XPC*, which often retains its Greek lettering in Latin texts, albeit receiving Latin inflections (Horsley and Waterhouse 1984: 211). Thus, *Deus, Iesus, Christus, spiritus, dominus (noster), sanctus* (and later also *David, Israel, Ierusalem*) become, respectively, *DS, IHS, XPS, SPS, DMS (N)* and *SCS*. Toward the early Middle Ages (sixth to tenth century) a number of abbreviations which originated as *nomina sacra* came to be used with nonreverent meanings, for example, forms like *DMS* or *SPS* for *dominus* and *spiritus*, respectively, were largely restricted to their everyday connotations (Bischoff 1990: 152). With the expansion of the institutional Catholic Church in the high Middle Ages, the same principle of contraction resulted in the coinage of new abbreviations, denoting names of Church officials (*episcopus* and *presbyter* abbreviated as *EPS* and *PRB* are cases in point) (Bischoff 1990: 153).

10.4 Typologies of Abbreviations

Reading historical handwriting is largely an act of decoding: the unfamiliar scripts, the idiosyncrasies of letter shapes, the nonalphabetic symbols, some of which are ornamental flourishes while others abbreviate specific orthographic sequences; all these elements require a well-trained eye. The study, description and interpretation of historical handwritten material are the tasks of paleography, a discipline which, from its inception in late seventeenth century, would try to embrace the vast and inherently variable documentary corpus of late antiquarian and medieval texts under a comprehensive nomenclature. However, paleographic terminology has always been somewhat fluid: descriptive terms used for characterizing letter shapes and symbols encountered in a medieval manuscript can vary in detail among paleographers, although a common core of typology is generally accepted. Specifically, terms like *lobe, shaft, bowl, arm, ascender, descender*, etc. to describe elements of letter *figurae* recur in publications on the topic, although authors differ in the manner in which they describe the scribal hands or the ways in which they characterize pen lifts. Similarly, typologies of abbreviation symbols have differed slightly from one author to another, depending on the criterion adopted for organizing the system. Brown (1990: 1), in fact, insists that terminology is one of the most controversial (although also the most basic) issues in paleography. One cause for this is that a number of such categorizations are based on mixed criteria, for example: context/text type appears next to shape (viz. *nomina sacra* vs. *special symbols*); mode of abbreviation next to 'whatever does not fit' (suspensions vs. contractions vs. brevigraphs); position within the line next to orthographic context (superior letters vs. signs significant in context). Even though abbreviation symbols feature in the works of both 'founding fathers' of paleography and diplomatics (the study of documents, as opposed to, e.g., literary texts), namely Mabillon (1681a) and Montfaucon (1708), it was not until the nineteenth century that some sort of taxonomy for abbreviations as a distinct category of scribal output began emerging (a historical outline of these taxonomies can be found in Honkapohja 2013). The most comprehensive and most general categorization, followed by many contemporary handbooks, is the one comprising suspensions, contractions and special signs (also termed 'special symbols' or brevigraphs). This type of classification combines the categories of 'mode of abbreviation' with the 'physical appearance of the symbol' as classificatory criteria. The most straightforward typology, reiterated in many publications, introduces the categories of suspensions, contractions and some sort of 'special symbols' type. While specific authors differ in their descriptions of details, general similarities in this tripartite division of abbreviation symbols can be observed.

Suspensions are those abbreviations which truncate the end of a word; they appear under this name in Chassant (1846), whereas Cappelli (1899: 1) refers to this category as "abbreviation by truncation." An example of this abbreviation type are Roman *sigla* (e.g. *D.* for *dux/dominus*, *J.C.* for *iuris consultus*, Cappelli 1899: 4), but usually more than just the initial letter is left unabbreviated in this category (e.g. *BO.ME.* for *Bonae Memoriae*, Cappelli 1899: 5). Often, suspension is indicated by means of a *punctus*, following the letter which was left unabbreviated (Cappelli's example is *.n.* for *enim*; (Cappelli 1899: 4)). Cappelli (1899: 1) further differentiates between general and specific signs used for suspension: the former only indicate that the word has been truncated, the latter that abbreviation concerns the ending of a word. An example of general signs is the horizontal stroke, which, positioned above the abbreviated word, may indicate syllabic suspension (Clemens and Graham 2007: 89) or, when positioned above a word-final vowel letter, indicates the truncation of a following *n* or *m* (in fact, Cappelli (1899) treats abbreviation of final *m* and *n* as a distinct class). For example, the abbreviated form of *amen* in Figure 10.1 (Cappelli 1899: 6) is a case of syllabic suspension, whereas Figure 10.2 (Cappelli 1899: 14) abbreviates word-final *m* in *aliam*.

Abbreviation by *contraction*, in turn, depends on shortening the middle part of a word – it may be only one letter or more. Here, too, the symbol indicating this form of abbreviation is one of general abbreviation, that is, a horizontal (straight or curved) stroke placed above the letter(s) that precede(s) the abbreviated sequence. This abbreviation symbol, also known as 'macron', was by far the most versatile and the most common graphic symbol of abbreviation used in medieval manuscripts (see Figure 10.3).

am̄ = amen

Figure 10.1 Syllabic suspension (Cappelli 1899: 6)

aliā = aliam,

Figure 10.2 Abbreviation of final m (Cappelli 1899: 14)

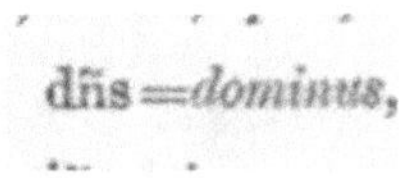

dn̄s = *dominus*,

Figure 10.3 The macron symbol used for contraction (Trice Martin 1892: v)

That same symbol also happens to be the most common form of a word-final flourish, which can be easily mistaken for abbreviation. This 'otiose' pen stroke would be added to the final letter of a word for purely decorative purposes, a practice quite common among Middle English scribes (Derolez 2003: 187) but potentially confusing for the readers. Otiose spellings in English vernacular manuscripts include forms like *meñ* for *men*, *sonñ* for *son*, *foundeñ* for *found* or *torñe* for *turn* (all examples found in late fifteenth-century manuscript: London, British Library, Royal MS 18 D II, of John Lydgate's *Siege of Thebes*). In fact, English vernacular manuscripts of the later Middle Ages are notorious for this potential for confusion.

In principle, no abbreviation symbol was invariable: its particular shape was always adjusted to the type of script selected by the scribe, the amount of interlinear space, the position of the abbreviated word on the page (within the ruled column vs. the margins) or the shape of the neighboring letter. The macron, however, was possibly the most variable symbol of abbreviation, both in terms of its forms and specific functions (linguistic and pragmatic). For one thing, the *figura*, or shape representing this particular abbreviation type, has the largest number of allographs available to scribes. Interestingly enough, one can see that variety within the confines of a single copying stint performed by a single scribe. Depending as much on scribal idiosyncratic preferences as on the type of script and the amount of space between the x-height (i.e. the body of the letter, minus ascenders and descenders, which extend toward the headline and baseline, respectively) and the headline, that horizontal stroke would appear as a short thick line (typical but not exclusive to more formal scripts, like *littera textualis*), a wavy line (both in *textura*-type and cursive scripts), a crescent-shaped symbol, with occasional *punctus* underneath (especially popular with cursive hands, see Petti 1977: 22) or a long hairline stroke (see Figure 10.4).

With cursive scripts the macron abbreviation is often physically attached to the letter it precedes by means of a counter-clockwise stroke, exercised without lifting the pen. This is especially true of letters *m* and *n* (the latter often indistinguishable from the *u littera*), occasionally word-final *a*. A variant of that same type is a counter-clockwise stroke with a change in the direction of writing, likewise attached to word-final *m*'s and *n*'s. There does not seem to be much compelling evidence that these graphic variants had different functions, other than highlighting a scribe's reactions to the dynamics of script and the word/line context. The complicating factor, rather, lies in their orthographic interpretation in vernacular manuscripts (especially English, but also

Figure 10.4 Some variants of the macron (Cappelli 1899: 2)

French), when word-final stroke can be interpreted both as abbreviation for *n* and as an otiose flourish, that is, a penstroke devoid of any linguistic meaning (forms like *governaũce* for *governaunce* are clear enough, but that same word might well be spelled *governauce* in an English manuscript of the later Middle Ages).

Further complicating the distinctions between the categories of suspensions and contractions is the fact that both types can be operated by the same sets of symbols, the most common of which is the general abbreviation sign, mentioned above. Traube (1907: 47) suggested that the difference between the two types lies in their distribution: while contractions typically occur with Christian Latin items, suspensions are more typical of Greco-Roman vocabulary, but this distinction is by no means categorical. The third category, superscript (or, superior) letters, is sometimes treated as a subtype of contractions (e.g. Petti 1977: 22), as it depends on abbreviating some elements from the middle of a word. As the name suggests, superscript letters are vowels or consonants raised above the x-height of the preceding letter. They typically truncate orthographic sequences comprising the raised letter and the letter *r* (thus abbreviating *ar, ra, er, re, or, ro, ir, ri, ru, ur*)[3] and with this function they are easily transferable from Latin to the vernacular (e.g. g^{a}*ce* is a frequent spelling for *grace* in English literary manuscripts between the thirteenth and sixteenth centuries). In Latin manuscripts, superscript vowels have a fixed meaning (Cappelli 1899: 32) and operate more like contractions proper (e.g. a^{a} stands for *anima* or *alia*, o^{i} for *omni*, u^{o} for *uno* or *vero*). In English manuscripts, in turn, superscript *e* and sometimes *u* become near-abbreviations (Brown 1990: 11) in $þ^{e}$, $þ^{u}$ for *the(e)* and *thou* respectively.

In less frequent cases, when the raised letter is a consonant, its interpretation depends on that particular consonant: it can abbreviate just two letters or entire syllables, so superscript consonants are much more context-dependent than vowels. For instance, a raised *c*, superscripted to another consonant, usually meant *ec* or *iec* (e.g. ob^{c}*to* for *obiecto*; Cappelli 1899: 33). Superscript *n*, in turn, when preceded by a *q*, abbreviated *quando*, and superior letter *t* next to a consonant would represent *it* (e.g. $m^{t}t^{t}$ for *mittit*; Cappelli 1899: 33–34). Another recurring superscript consonant is *r*, which, when preceded by *t*, abbreviates *ur* (here the 2-shaped *figura* for *r* alternates with superscript *u*, in its 'regular' and 'serrated line' version), for example *cēt*^{r}*io* for *centurio* (Cappelli 1899: 33). In English, a raised *t* is a common abbreviation for two recurrent function words, *with* and *that*, which are often spelled w^{t} and $þ^{t}$, respectively. Occasionally, a superscript *s* appears line-finally, both in Latin and vernacular manuscripts.[4] Finally, special symbols, or *brevigraphs*, can

[3] In fact, the *ur* sequence is more typically represented by the raised *2* symbol or by a serrated line in the upper index. Superscript *u*, in turn, nearly always stands for *ru* or just *u*, as in the Middle English $þ^{u}$.

[4] Cappelli (1899: 33) dates this usage to the twelfth century but it recurs in later copies as well.

either resemble one of the letters omitted or be arbitrary in shape (Petti 1977: 23). More recently referred to as simply "symbols" (Brown 1990: 5, Clemens and Graham 2007: 89), they are a cover term for what most nineteenth- and early twentieth-century paleography handbooks saw as distinct categories: "signs significant in themselves," also termed "signs significant in context" (Cappelli 1899: 18), "conventional symbols" (Cappelli 1899: 39), "abbreviative signs" or "special signs" (*signes abréviatifs* in Chassant 1846: 26). What binds all these symbols together are their arbitrary shapes: although some of them do resemble actual letters of the Latin alphabet, they are nearly always modified by some additional *figura* (e.g. the '*p*-bar' or '*p*-loop' abbreviations for *per, par, por* and for *pro*, respectively, which feature in medieval manuscripts as variants of *p* and *ꝓ*). Still others are ideograms with no relation to actual letters of the alphabet (e.g. the ⁹ abbreviation, standing in for *con/com*, the ₉ for *us* or the *ƒ* for *is/es/is*).

Since a number of those special symbols represented orthographic sequences recurring not only in Latin but also in vernacular languages, many survived beyond the Classical period well into the late Middle Ages (fourteenth to fifteenth century), and some of them still feature in early printed books. Among them were the 9-like character for *con/com*, the supralinear hook-symbol indicating *re/er*, the loop for final *is/ys/es*, the *p*-bar, the *p*-loop, the serrated line/*oc*-version of *a* supralinear symbol for *ra*, the 2-like or *a*-like supralinear symbol for *ur*, or the 9-like symbol in the supralinear position for *us* (Petti 1977: 23–24; see Figure 10.5).

Somewhat limited distribution became the fate of the *ser*-abbreviation *ƒ*, which can be encountered until well into the sixteenth-century in English manuscripts. The so-called 'hook' abbreviation, representing the *er* or *re*

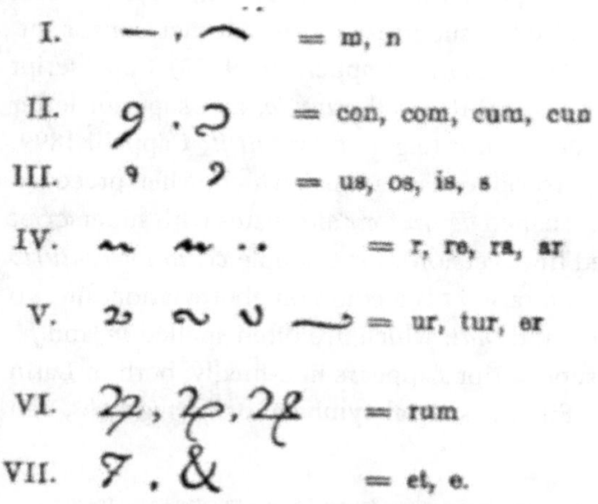

I. = m, n
II. = con, com, cum, cun
III. = us, os, is, s
IV. = r, re, ra, ar
V. = ur, tur, er
VI. = rum
VII. = et, e.

Figure 10.5 "Abbreviation marks significant in themselves" (Cappelli 1899: 13)

sequences (or, *e*, when attached to word-final *r*), was nearly as multifaceted as the macron. Most typically, it would take the form of a counter-clockwise curl, either physically attached to the preceding letter or separate from it. In some variants it would be similar to *punctus interrogativus*, the 'question mark' (minus the dot); in others it would look not unlike the hairstroke variant of the macron (this form can occur in cursive scripts). Most typically the curl would have been small, although some scribes would elongate the stroke to reach a few letters to the left. Other abbreviations, such as ꝝ for *rum*, *b*ʒ for *bus*, *q*ʒ or ꝙ for *quod*, truncating Latin grammatical categories, were lost in transition to vernacular book production. Otherwise, although the grammatical referents of some of the abbreviations were gradually lost (like ꝰ and ꝭ, which in Latin represented inflectional endings), their orthographic interpretation remained available for vernacular languages too. Thus, in English the ꝰ and ꝭ brevigraphs remained in use to indicate plural ending or the possessive inflection. From the eleventh century onward, abbreviations became increasingly more common in manuscripts and new forms were introduced to cater to the needs of an expanding book market (an example of such innovation was the Tironian ⁊ for *et*; Derolez 2003: 66).

The peak of abbreviating practices, however, occurred in the thirteenth and fourteenth centuries, when the concurrently progressing vernacularization of book production and the emergence of new (i.e. lay, nonscholarly) readers marked the beginning of a gradual reduction of the numbers. Scholastic and scientific works, designed for limited audiences of professional *litterati* tended to retain their highly abbreviated nature, but works of literature and those produced for display (whose purposes would often overlap and coincide with public reading practices) were characterized by a significantly lower number of abbreviations, only limited to truncating the most common grammatical words and some conventionally abbreviated items. It is in those vernacular manuscripts that abbreviations acquire new, pragmatic functions, for example, when they signal code-switching along with other visual elements on the manuscript page (Rogos-Hebda 2023) or when they aid the scribes in organizing the discourse on the page by combining with other visual discourse markers (see Carroll et al. 2013, Rogos-Hebda 2020).

10.5 Abbreviations and Medieval Scripts

Textbooks of paleography typically provide lists of Latin abbreviation symbols with their canonical orthographic interpretation(s), offering limited commentary on their diachronic and diatopic developments. While on the whole, the 'meaning' (in the sense of orthographic interpretation) of abbreviation symbols, which originated in Latin, remained unchanged throughout the Middle Ages and beyond, the morpho-lexical and visual contexts for those symbols did not remain unchallenged. Since every act of translating from one medium to another is inherently interpretative, whatever paleography textbooks, translating from manuscript to print, represent as 'medieval abbreviation symbols' is at once an approximation and a simplification of the visual-orthographic contents of the manuscript. Whether traced by hand from the actual manuscript (see Cappelli 1899) or printed in the so-called Record Type (a special type of font used up until mid-twentieth century to represent the *minutiae* of medieval manuscripts in near-facsimile editions, e.g. Trice Martin, 1892), the symbol presented on the page to the contemporary reader is both an idealization and a 'catch-all' shape for the variety of forms available for one abbreviation. One source of that variety is the variation of post-Roman scripts themselves. Often referred to as 'national hands' (a term as anachronistic as it is misleading), scripts pre-dating the pan-European Carolingian minuscule were "fluid, interactive variants, in an unstable political climate" (Marcos 2017: 22), each with their idiosyncratic approach to abbreviations. For example, the most successful (and longest-living) of these scripts, Insular minuscule (in its Anglo-Saxon minuscule variant), developed a series of contractions for the most frequently recurring elements of lexicon: *and/ond ~ 7* (and its crossed variant 7̵), *æfter ~ æft̄*, *for ~ f̄*, *ge ~ ḡ*, *þæt/þat/þet ~ ꝥ*, *sancte ~ sc̄e*, *þonne ~ þon̄*, *-um/-un ~ ū* (Rumble 1994: 14). Also, an Anglo-Saxon innovation was the *tur* abbreviation in the form of a "<t> with a downstroke through the bar" (Bischoff 1990: 91).

Even beyond the Carolingian period (ninth century), well into the reign of Gothic scripts, which leveled the differences between regional hands, one can notice geographically determined differences in abbreviating practices. Examples of such differences are distinct *figurae* of the *bus*-abbreviation in German-speaking and Scandinavian countries (*b* with a vertical zig-zag line instead of the more usual *b* followed by a semicolon-like character); idiosyncratic forms of *con*/*cum* abbreviations in Central Europe and Germany (inverted *c* formed with two strokes, rather than a *2*-shaped, a *9*-shaped or an inverted-*c figura*); and the Insular forms of *enim*- (*n* between two dots) and *est*-abbreviations (horizontal stroke with a dot or flourish above and below) (Derolez 2003: 67). Individual scribes too had at their disposal more than one graphic variant of a given abbreviation and would sometimes apply different forms of the same abbreviation on the same page. Earlier textbooks would often attribute this variety to the "caprice or carelessness of the scribe" (Trice Martin 1892: v), a judgment clearly colored by the standardizing effects of print, but inadequate to the context-driven motivations of scribes. The type of script as a geographical criterion has already been mentioned, but it needs to be emphasized that, beyond the 'local flavor' in abbreviating practices, scripts, whether transnational (however inadequate the 'national' attribute is when discussing premodern phenomena), like Roman or Carolingian scripts, or more 'regional', like the Insular or Merovingian, also came with elaborate visual-semiotic and linguistic systems. Simply put, abbreviations depended as much on scribal preferences as on the way the script *looked* (i.e. on the so-called *aspect* of the page) and the way it would have *sounded* (i.e. on the language of the page). Ter Horst and Stam (2018) point to the ways in which Latin abbreviations were incorporated into eleventh- to fourteenth-century Irish manuscripts as visual diamorphs, that is, items whose graphic form prevents one from assigning them to a specific language (Laura Wright 2011: 203). For instance, the form *aps.* was devised to abbreviate Latin *apostolus*, but when applied to Gaelic, it would have rendered *apstal* (Ter Horst and Stam 2018: 234).

Scribes copying in European vernaculars indeed adopted and adapted Latin bases for abbreviation to suit language-specific purposes. While on the whole, the orthographic 'meaning' of abbreviation symbols originating in Latin remained relatively unchanged throughout the Middle Ages, the morpho-lexical and visual contexts for those symbols provided a dynamic background for scribal abbreviating practices. The shift from Latin to vernacular languages necessitated the loss of some abbreviations, while others were successfully carried over, even if to encode purely orthographic, rather than grammatical categories, like they used to. As an example mentioned above, the *-rum* abbreviation for genitive plural of Latin third and fourth declensions in the form of *figura ꝝ* would no longer feature in vernacular scripts because it lacked a non-Latin equivalent in vernacular languages. On the other hand, an abbreviation like *ꝭ* – *is*, which marked the genitive plural of the same third declension in Latin, worked equally well as an indicator of plurality in English. Conversely, because some recurrent orthographic sequences in 'national' [*sic*] scripts did not have their equivalents in Latin, scribes would devise new abbreviation symbols. Mixed-language manuscripts demonstrate how differently scribes were thinking about abbreviations in Latin and in vernacular languages – not only are the symbols distributed differently in linguistic terms (with Latin portions of the text typically containing more abbreviations than the vernacular fragments) but they are also *visually* different. Simply put: if the sheer number of abbreviations in the Latin text does not separate it from the vernacular fragments, then manipulating the type, size and/or color of the script surely does. In other words, it is through a combination of visual means (like the color of the ink, the size of the script, the type of the script, position on the page) *and* an increased incidence of abbreviations that switches between two (or more) linguistic codes are signaled (in the late fourteenth and fifteenth centuries, copies of works by John Gower or Geoffrey Chaucer are illustrative of these practices). The distribution of abbreviations on the page was also determined by their immediate word and line context. First of all, the position relative to other letters in the abbreviated word was significant, as that determined both the size and shape of the abbreviated symbol (whether or not it was attached to the preceding letter; if so, what letter that was, how much space there was between the *x*-height and the headline). Equally important was its position within the line: line-final and column-final contexts tend to attract abbreviations, whereas proximity to the right-hand margin or to the gutter of the page affects the dimensions of the abbreviation symbol. Marginal abbreviations (both in Latin and vernacular manuscripts) tend to occur with much more density and variety of types than those occurring within the ruled column, at the center of the page.

A more elaborate, formal type of script, like the *textura*, would encourage fewer abbreviations, as it would be typically applied to more costly manuscripts, often Latin ones, where saving time and space was not a concern.[5] In such scripts, abbreviations tend to be more formulaic in nature: they appear on items commonly abbreviated (like function words: prepositions, pronouns, conjunctions) or abbreviate words at the very ends of the ruled column so as to ensure visual coherence to the text on the page.[6] Vertical orientation of the script required the scribes to maintain larger distances between the lines (Derolez 2003: 125). As a result, there was more interlinear space to fit abbreviation symbols, but because the script would be compressed, it was easier to fit words into the ruled column(s). Cursive scripts, in turn, are characterized by a more 'open' character and a horizontal orientation, which contributes to a more 'sprawled' aspect, giving scribes more trouble with keeping the text within the ruled grid and thus facilitating a more widespread use of abbreviations. Initially the development of the cursive did, indeed, contribute to a rapid expansion of abbreviation symbols, but when *cursiva* was adopted as a bookhand (rather than as a documentary script) in the fourteenth and fifteenth centuries, the number of abbreviations used in cursive manuscripts decreased significantly to facilitate the readability of the text and to enable access to the nonscholarly reader (Derolez 2003: 154).

10.6 Abbreviations in Transition: From Manuscript to Print

Although abbreviations are commonly associated with manuscript books, their popularity and use continued well into the late fifteenth and sixteenth centuries, when the printing press was gradually becoming central to the book market. As pointed out by Honkapohja and Liira (2020: 269), "[a]s parchment began to be replaced by a cheaper material, paper, and the printing press made it possible to produce multiple copies with ease, the two main needs for

[5] There are, of course, exceptions to this rule, when a *textura* script, or one modeled on *littera textualis*, is applied in a manuscript with considerable abbreviation, for example, Oxford, Balliol College, MS 224a – a copy of works by Richard Rolle. Cambridge, University Library, MS Mm. 5.37 of Rolle's *Incendium amoris* is at the other end of the extreme in that it contains virtually no abbreviation symbols.

[6] Abbreviations were just one of the tools used by scribes concerned with adjusting the text on the manuscript page to the *ordinatio* (i.e. the layout of the page); see Bergeron and Ornato (1990).

using an abbreviation and suspension system lost their importance." Even so, abbreviations did not prove to be among the first casualties of "the printing revolution in early modern Europe" (see Eisenstein 1983). Initially, printers attempted to present their codices in a format as visually similar to the handwritten book as possible: the *mise-en-page* (or, page layout), the illuminated initials, the illustrations, the incipits and explicits and the blackletter typeface, modeled on *textura* scripts, were all meant to look like typical elements of a manuscript. Matters were no different with abbreviations: such a familiar component of the codex would not go away with the arrival of new technology, and printers would sometimes go to extraordinary lengths to reproduce abbreviation symbols familiar from scribal practices (Edwards 2000: 65).

Before long, however, this labor-intensive process of book production proved untenable, as any advantage the printing press had over the man-hours devoted to handwriting was dwarfed by the costs (financial and otherwise) of printers' efforts to replicate in metal casts the ligatures, variant graph forms and abbreviations (Hellinga 1999: 70). Hellinga also points to the short-lived nature of founts of types which comprised a number of graphic variants for individual letter forms. These were gradually replaced by "long-lived type, carefully designed but with a smaller number of sorts," which meant that in due course "a simplification in the presentation of graphic forms had to be accepted" (Hellinga 1999: 71). In the end, abbreviations remained in use as one of three methods for right-justifying the text (the other two being breaking words over lines and altering spaces between words; see Shute 2017: 15), and several studies of the English material (e.g. Shute 2017, Honkapohja and Liira 2020) have indeed pointed to a higher incidence of abbreviation in line-final contexts.[7] Similar motivation was noted in French texts (Cottereau 2005, Camps 2016, as quoted by Honkapohja and Liira 2020: 298). Honkapohja and Liira (2020: 301) link this development to a change in the layout of printed works from one to two columns of text, which exerted even more pressure on compositors to ensure right-margin justification (this change was also related to genre, as it was the *de luxe* books which were more typically printed in a two-column layout).

While mass publication increasingly became the norm for book production, various types of ephemera and legal or administrative documents continued to be handwritten (see Kytö et al. 2011). For instance, in English, letters, personal notes, accounts, legal depositions and local documents (Stenroos 2020a: 39 incorporates into this category "records of cities, churches, manors, local courts and private transactions") remained the *loci* for abbreviation, oftentimes more elaborate than what was typical of handwritten manuscript

[7] A similar propensity for increasing the ratio of abbreviations in the line final position has also been discerned in manuscript material; see, for example, Petti (1977), Thaisen (2011), Smith (2018), Rogos-Hebda (2020); see Wakelin (2011: 49), ascribing the same function to otiose strokes on word-final letters in a line-final position.

copies (especially literary ones) toward the close of the fifteenth century. It is not without significance that documentary texts ("formulaic texts, and texts intended for internal use by administrators," Stenroos 2020a: 67) continued to be written in Latin well into the sixteenth century.

Accounts and inventories, on the other hand, often used abbreviations to obscure linguistic boundaries: this is what Laura Wright (2011: 203) referred to as the "visual diamorph" effect, by which abbreviation symbols applied in word-final (i.e. inflectional) contexts would often make it impossible to tell the difference between an English or a French or a Latin item. This visual overlap between Latin and the two vernacular languages used in medieval written accounts (Wright 2002: 472) was one of the staples of code-intermediate phenomena, featuring in mixed-language texts prior to the emergence of a vernacular standard in the early modern period (Wright 2002: 471). Yet another type of document characterized by a similarly prolonged use of abbreviations are the custom rolls. Like other types of handwritten accounts in late medieval England, these were heavily mixed-language texts with a system of abbreviations, which Needham (1999: 152) referred to as "makeshift."[8]

Ultimately, "sometime in the sixteenth century" (Honkapohja 2013) abbreviations went out of use altogether. Honkapohja and Liira (2020: 269) connect this development in England with the vernacularization of written documents. During the short-lived Commonwealth period of 1649–60, Latin abbreviations were abolished; they returned to use with the Restoration, only to be abolished again, along with Latin, in 1731 (Hector 1966 [1958]: 29). Indeed, with the transition from monolingual Latin or Anglo-French through mixed-language to monolingual English in handwritten, and later, printed documents, only a handful of abbreviation symbols remained in active use and some of those are still used today (like *e.g.*, *i.e.*, *etc.*) as conventionalized markers of (often specialist) discourse.

10.7 Conclusion

Despite the fact that the modern reader would find it hard to infer this much from contemporary editions of historical texts (which tend to expand suspensions and contractions), abbreviations are intrinsically linked to pre-print literacy. Spanning late Antiquity through the early-to-late Middle Ages only to be laid to rest in the latter part of the early modern period, they belong to the commonplace community practices of premodern *literati*. Developed for the very pragmatic purpose of signaling oft-repeated words in legal and

[8] Judging from Needham's comments on the nature of this 'makeshiftness', it seems that abbreviations used in custom rolls displayed a similar extent of visual diamorphy to what Wright (2002, 2020a) found characteristic of other types of written accounts.

administrative records and of avoiding spelling out the *nomina sacra*, abbreviations became recognizable elements of scribal shorthand, which not only helped the scribes economize on their time and writing surface but were also employed in structuring the visual discourse (e.g. abbreviations were often used in running titles or in *incipit/explicit sections* to signal elements of text structure), signaling code-switching in multilingual texts (along with accompanying changes in ink color, type of script or position on the page) or, very generally, underscoring the *Latinitas* of the text (e.g. by reference to external authorities in the margins of the manuscripts). In a way, abbreviations are a truly protean element, not only changing in function but also in form: scribes adjust their shapes according to the amount of space available in the interlinear context and to the type of script selected for the copying process. In many ways they are a shorthand for medieval literacy: marrying the linguistic and the pragmatic, the visual and the textual, Latin and the vernacular through their multilayeredness and multiaspectuality.

11

Adapting Alphabetic Writing Systems

Anetta Luto-Kamińska

11.1 Introduction

This chapter focuses on adapting different alphabetic writing systems to the requirements of a given language.[1] For the needs of the present chapter, my main linguistic basis for analyzing writing systems are Slavic languages, with particular consideration given to the Polish language, which is used for detailed exemplification of the adaptation of writing systems under discussion. This chapter provides an analysis of examples of the way a variety of alphabetic systems were adapted to the Polish language, in order to showcase the complications behind the process of 'recording' (in the sense of rendering) a given language by means of a particular system of signs. The classical alphabet established for the Polish language consists in the appropriately modified Latin alphabet; however, one needs to realize the length of time involved in adaptation processes before a fully functional national alphabet takes shape. While users of a given language are typically unaware of this, any attempt at using an alphabet other than the classical alphabet makes clear the complexities of the mechanisms accompanying the alphabetization of a language. This process is presented here on the basis of several examples displaying the use of a different alphabet than the Latin alphabet for recording Polish: *graždanka*, the Arabic alphabet and the Armenian alphabet.

Adapting Lotman's terminology, Ong (2005 [1982]: 8) deemed writing a "secondary modeling system" which is always dependent on the "prior primary system," that is, the spoken language. Analogically, regarding the

[1] I am using the notion of *writing system* or *system of writing* in what is perhaps the most traditional sense, whose basic differentiator connects the smallest graphic elements with a specific type of linguistic unit, for example, a phoneme, a syllable, a word (see, e.g., Daniels 1996a: 8–10, Coulmas 1991: 55–201, Coulmas 2003: 1–17, Joyce and Borgwaldt 2011). Since only alphabet-based writing systems are analyzed in detail here, I also, alternatively, use a more precise term: *alphabetic system*.

development of writing systems and indicating the ways in which particular alphabets have formed, one may introduce the term 'prior modeling system' referring to the alphabetic system on the basis of which the Ongian 'secondary modeling system' was formed – understood here as writing adapted to the needs of a given community. One may thus note two aspects of the way writing systems form within a certain language for a specific group of users: on the one hand, there is a transition from the oral system to the graphic system (prior primary system → secondary modeling system). On the other hand, the emergence of writing in a particular language concerns the very system of forming a set of signs, which never happens in isolation, as it draws on other, existing graphic systems, used by a different community, which usually communicates in a different language. As such, I consider the 'prior modeling system' a broad notion which, rather than a single system of signs, might contain several such systems; these systems, due to the influence of interferences, have given rise to a different alphabetic system. This aspect, in contrast to Ong's cultural and social, or even philosophical reflections, emphasizes the technical issues pertaining to the graphic shape of linear alphabets.

The initial stages of the formation of almost every alphabet are characterized by a certain level of *hybridity*, resulting from adopting a borrowed graphic base and attempting to adapt it to one's own needs. This stage tends to be marked by a diversity of technical solutions used to adapt the adopted graphic system that are imposed by features of the recipient language. As a result of further transformations and unifying actions, some solutions are forgotten, while, in time, others become established methods of alphabetic writing in a given language (national alphabet).[2] In this chapter, the broadly understood hybrid nature of writing systems pertains to every situation wherein an alphabet originally serving to record statements in a different language was adopted at an early stage of its adaptation connected with introducing new and individual graphic solutions. Conversely, writing systems that were genetically connected with a specific language, or a language family, and then entered a stage of relative stabilization are considered base systems; however, at an initial stage of their formation they might also have developed on a different base graphic system.[3] Fully formed systems are most frequently characterized by centuries-long traditions of using a specific system of signs for a given language, and its gradual evolution. The most desirable result of such outlined changes is the best possible regulation of the phone–sign relationship.[4]

[2] For a general overview of the formation of alphabetic systems see, for example, Coulmas (1991: 159–78); about the hybridity of scripts, see Daniels (2017a: 109–17).

[3] Compare the discussion on synchronic and diachronic biscriptality in Chapter 8, this volume.

[4] This constitutes a simplification of the problem I have signaled. However close the rules of writing would be to its ideal realization, in which one phone corresponds to one sign, these systems tend to change. This may be due to clear changes in the language itself, including changes in its phonological subsystem.

Below, in Section 11.2, I present the process of the crystallization of alphabetic systems, and the significance of contacts and interferences between them. In Section 11.3, the hybridity of both writing systems and orthographies is considered on the level of the formation of a national writing system, while in Section 11.4, it is analyzed from an even narrower perspective. I discuss here particular cases of transposition and utilization of a different alphabet from that used as a standard in a given language.

11.2 Alphabet Formation: Adaptations and Interferences

Without fully investigating the genesis and the stages of the formation of an alphabetic system of recording speech, it may be assumed that they began to appear during the second millennium BC in Western Semitic writing (see, e.g., Diringer 1943, Strelcyn 1952, Cohen 1956: 45–46, Gelb 1969: 190–205, Gieysztor 2009: 40), although it is very likely that graphic elements of earlier pictographic origin were used and transposed (Cohen 1956: 44, Gieysztor 2009: 41). Indisputably, one of the most significant achievements in the development of writing is the creation of Phoenician writing, with its abjad alphabet[5] and its considerable influence on the development of other graphic systems.[6] This section discusses two examples that document the adaptation and changes in the base systems of signs.

The assumptions outlined in Section 11.1 may be exemplified by the development and evolution of the Greek alphabet, which was based on the Phoenician alphabet. In order to record their language, the Greeks modified the system previously used by the Phoenicians (Cohen 1956: 50). Although particular city-states used local varieties of the adapted letters, a common feature was that the Phoenician consonantal alphabet took on the form of a full consonant-and-vowel alphabet in its Greek variety. To mark vowels, Phoenician letters denoting phonemes absent from the Greek language tended to be used, and several signs unknown to the Semitic prototype also appeared. Neither the Phoenician nor the early Greek writing separated words; it was only with time that Greek writing abandoned this continuous style of writing (Cohen 1956: 45, 52–53). In contrast to the Phoenician script, which had a fixed direction from right to left, only some of the oldest records retain this direction, while others are written *boustrophedonically* (Cohen 1956: 45, 51), a manner, discarded in approximately the sixth century BC, for a single-direction

[5] The term abjad describes alphabets which use letter signs only for consonants. This word is formed by the first letters of the alphabet used in Semitic languages (compare Arabic ابجد with the letters read from right to left: *alif, bā', ǧīm, dāl*). See Subsection 11.4.2 and overviews of typologies of writing systems, for example Daniels (1996a: 8–10) as well as Chapter 2, Chapter 4, Chapter 7 and Chapter 8, this volume.

[6] A brief overview of geographic, chronological and linguistic aspects of the transfer of Phoenician writing to the West are to be found, for example, in Swiggers (1996).

arrangement from left to right. The present-day Greek alphabet is a bicameral script with a clear differentiation between uppercase and lowercase letters.[7]

An even more interesting example may be the emergence of the alphabet known as the Glagolitic alphabet (from *glagolъ* 'word, letter' in Old Church Slavonic, OCS for short; see Brajerski 1990: 58) and of its subsequent transformations. The creation of this alphabet is usually attributed to the missionary brothers Cyril and Methodius, who arrived in the vicinity of Great Moravia with a mission to Christianize the region in the second half of ninth century (see also Chapter 8, this volume). They recorded the translated liturgical texts in an alphabet created to reflect the phones of the OCS, the contemporary Slavic dialect of Solun (a Bulgarian-Macedonian dialect from the region of Thessaloniki). The prototype of the letters of the Glagolitic alphabet is thought to be found, above all, in the Greek minuscule of the eighth and ninth centuries, although features of Southern Semitic alphabets and Latin cursive are also frequently pointed out.[8] The letters were written, as in contemporary Greek, horizontally from left to right. This graphically uniformly stylized alphabet should, however, certainly be considered an original creation, individually tailored to the phonetic and phonological needs of the language it was intended to record.[9] The original Glagolitic alphabet underwent certain modifications concerning the shape of its letters; for example, in Bulgaria the so-called *round* Glagolitic alphabet persisted, while in the Croatian Primorje region and Istria the so-called *angular* Glagolitic alphabet developed, most likely under the influence of the Gothic script. In the tenth century, a new alphabet began to spread in the place of the Glagolitic alphabet, the Cyrillic alphabet (so called to honor Cyril), whose basis is believed to be found in the majuscule of the Greek alphabet (in its uncial version)[10] together with simplified Glagolitic letters denoting phones without equivalents in the Greek alphabet (Diringer 1948: 478–83, Lehr-Spławiński and Bartula 1976: 7). Although genetically both scripts under discussion show specific dependencies, the Glagolitic alphabet with the minuscule and the Cyrillic alphabet with

[7] For a discussion of Greek writing and Greek palaeography, see also Schubart (1925), Gelb (1969: 176–83), Cavallo and Maehler (1987) and Harrauer (2010).

[8] Deciding who created the Glagolitic alphabet and when, and what alphabetic system had the greatest influence on the graphic shape of Glagolitic letters remains a moot point, and it frequently has almost ideological connotations. Greek minuscule is usually recognized as the basis for the alphabet, while Constantine-Cyril is thought to be its author (Jagić 1913, Lehr-Spławiński and Bartula 1976: 7). Diringer (1948: 485–87) presents this along with other theories, according to which the prototype of the Glagolitic alphabet may be sought among such alphabets as the Hebrew, Phoenician, Samaritan, Ethiopic, Armenian, Georgian and Albanian. Approaches suggesting a much earlier emergence of the Glagolitic alphabet, and one that denies Cyril's authorship, have also been debated. The prototype is sought in, among others, the Latin alphabet and the Gothic runes. About theories concerning the genesis of the Glagolitic alphabet, see Dąbrowska-Partyka (2000), Oczkowa (2004) and Stęplewski (2018: 128–45).

[9] See Diringer (1948: 484) and his understandable associations with the shape of Ethiopian letters.

[10] The uncial script derives from the Roman capitals; it is a handwriting consisting of rounded, large-sized, separately written capital letters.

the majuscule, both are bicameral scripts, with the uppercase and lowercase letters differing not in shape, but in size.

11.3 National Scripts and Alphabets in a Variety of Linguistic Editions

The contacts and interferences between alphabets take place on two planes. The basic plane, as discussed in Section 11.2, showcases the stages of the formation of alphabets such as the Greek, Latin, Cyrillic and Arabic ones, taking place with the use, adaptation or transformation of basic systems of writing. These may be described as the 'grand' alphabets: not only the ones most commonly used but also constituting the basis for a number of variants (i.e. national scripts). On this plane, we are dealing with already specific adaptations of an established alphabet for the needs of a given language, with the use of conventionalized methods of modification. The formation of national scripts, that is, individualized systems of alphabetic writing adjusted to the needs of given peoples, usually consists in variations of adaptations of the most frequently used alphabets. One such basic European alphabet is, above all, the Latin alphabet, in its original form used to record the Latin language. The modifications of this alphabet for the needs of other languages, such as Romance, Germanic, Finno-Ugric and Slavic, may be schematically presented as follows:

AL—L → ALX—X

where the Latin alphabet (AL) used in the Latin language (L) is adapted for recording another language (X) with the use of the adapted Latin alphabet (ALX).

The appropriate adaptation of the adopted basic alphabet (AL → ALX), suitable for recording language L, to the particular needs of language X would take place in several ways. To graphically represent a phone from language X that is absent from the phonetic system of language L and, thus, has no graphic equivalent therein, required several resolutions. The basic elements of new graphemes were, above all, graphically or functionally modified letters from the original alphabet: (a) letters with diacritics (usually representing a phonic value close to the original letters), for example with signs used originally to mark different accents: dots, curves, strokes, curls or double marks; (b) letter combinations (digraphs, trigraphs, etc.) or ligatures corresponding to a single phone of language X; (c) letters whose shape has been modified; (d) letters that have no phonic equivalents in language X in a different function from that of language L. A less common way of acquiring graphemes reflecting the specificity of the recipient language (X) consists in borrowing letters from alphabets different from AL, whereas entirely new letters were created only sporadically (see also Diringer 1948: 553–54). The methods by which the basic script would be adapted to the needs of the national scripts presented here pertained not only to the Latin alphabet, or even to national scripts as such, but also other ones (see the adaptations of the Latin, Cyrillic, Arabic and Armenian alphabets discussed in Subsections 11.3.1, 11.4.1, 11.4.2 and 11.4.3).

In our discussion of national scripts we may use the analogy to OCS, which became the language of the liturgical writing system for Slavs from the Byzantine culture. At the same time, it absorbed elements of a number of local dialects. We are therefore dealing with the same language, but in different permutations, in academic literature known as editions, for example OCS in the Ruthenian, Croatian and Bulgarian editions. A similar situation pertains to alphabets. In a given culture's sphere of influence, the adapted alphabet would function to record other national languages, and would later be modified to the needs of their own writing system. Analogically to languages, we may thus refer to alphabets in a given national edition, such as the Latin alphabet in a German, Czech, French or English edition, or the Cyrillic alphabet in a Belarusian, Macedonian or Bulgarian edition. The Cyrillic alphabet, presented in Section 11.2, underwent subsequent stages of evolution. Peter the Great's reform at the beginning of the eighteenth century introduced a modified and graphically modernized version of the Cyrillic alphabet to Russia, the so-called *graždanka*, or civil script (from a Russian adjective in the term *гражданский шрифт* 'civil, secular script'). Over the following two centuries the inventory of the letters in the script changed. Some letters that had no equivalent in Russian were omitted (e.g. letters used to denote nasal vowels in OCS) and new letters were added to better differentiate between phones (e.g. to denote iota).

With certain modifications modeled on the Russian alphabet, the Cyrillic alphabet became the basis for the alphabet that is used today in, among other countries, Bulgaria, Serbia, Montenegro, Macedonia, Bosnia, Herzegovina, Moldavia, Belarus and Ukraine. After 1991, some former republics of the USSR (e.g. Turkmenistan, Azerbaijan, Uzbekistan)[11] ceased to use the general Cyrillic alphabet and adapted the Latin alphabet to the phonic needs of their languages. In Bosnia and Herzegovina, as well as in Uzbekistan, both the Cyrillic alphabet and a modified Latin alphabet are used, while in Tajikistan the Persian alphabet is also used. The oldest alphabet in Croatia, the Glagolitic

[11] It should be noted that the Turkmen, Azeri and Uzbek languages use multiple alphabets. These languages belong to the group of Turkic languages, and in order to record them, the Arabic alphabet was used, over time superseded by the Latin alphabet. At the time of the existence of the Union of Soviet Socialist Republics, the Cyrillic alphabet was enforced on them by the authorities, and after the fall of the USSR they returned to the Latin alphabet. Voices advocating using the Latin alphabet to represent the Kazakh and Kyrgyz languages have begun to appear. The history of changes in the alphabets used in the countries of the former Soviet Union has been the subject of many press articles and TV programs. Basic information on this subject can also be found on websites such as *Ethnologue* (ethnologue.com) or *OLAC: Open Language Archives Community* (olac.ldc.upenn.edu).

alphabet, was long used, but for a considerable period of time Croatian writing was characterized by its tri-alphabeticity, as simultaneous use was made of the Glagolitic, Cyrillic and Latin alphabets. In Czechia, the Glagolitic alphabet was superseded by the Latin alphabet as early as at the end of the eleventh century (Oczkowa 2004: 57). This brief overview of the evolution of alphabets, mainly those used to write Slavic languages, simultaneously showcases fluid changes from the original graphic systems to systems of a hybrid nature, which, subsequently, having gone through a number of stages of adjustment, begin to constitute a system congruent with the phonetic layer of the given language. Against the background of these examples, the Glagolitic alphabet stands out as the alphabet whose functional perfection is already confirmed in the oldest inscriptions.

11.3.1 The Polish Edition of the Latin Alphabet

To record the Polish language, the Latin alphabet began to be used in the thirteenth and fourteenth centuries. The letters available, however, were insufficient to represent all the phones in the Polish language, and thus only when the Latin alphabet was considerably expanded and a set of orthographic rules added was it possible to record Polish phonically adequately and unambiguously. The development and expansion of printing in the sixteenth century played a significant role in the standardization of the rules of Polish writing, although the creation of a unified and consistent system was still a long way off.[12] An analysis of the way vowels were written at the time adequately demonstrates the methods of adjusting the Latin alphabet by dint of the adaptative techniques discussed above (see Section 11.3).

A more extensive vocal system required the introduction of new graphemes. Most frequently, this consisted in using a suitable letter with a diacritic. For nasal vowels denoting a nasal version of the /ɔ/ and /ɛ/ vowels, the letters *a* and *e* were written with a diagonal stroke at the bottom of the stem, or, less frequently, with an *ogonek* (*littera caudata*);[13] indeed, the latter method persists in the modern Polish alphabet: <ą>, <ę>. Earlier and for a long time, the Polish language had only one nasal vowel of a quality approximate to that of the /a/ vowel. In order to denote this, Parkosz (c. 1470: 44, Kraków, Jagiellonian Library, MS 1961, pp. 3–16),[14] author of a medieval orthographic

[12] In Europe, the beginnings of the development of modern standard languages date precisely to the Renaissance era (Coulmas 2013: 106). At the same time, it may be assumed that the processes of standardizing particular vernacular writing systems also began during this era.

[13] The so-called *e caudatum* was found in the standard set of fonts in printing houses, as this font was used in typesetting Latin texts as a replacement for the *ae* diphthong (Luto-Kamińska 2015: 37).

[14] It is assumed that the manuscript of the orthographic treatise preserved in the Jagiellonian Library (Poland) is a copy dated to c. 1470. Parkosz's original text was probably created approximately thirty years earlier (Parkosz c. 1470: 6–7, Łoś 1907: 3–4).

treatise, recommended the use of <ø>, which was already available in this function at the end of thirteenth century. In the sixteenth century, former quantitative differences (duration) between vowels were replaced with a differentiation in sound. Former long vowels, usually denoted by double letters (e.g. *long a* as <aa>; see Parkosz c. 1470: 44) in medieval texts, underwent raising in the Renaissance (the sixteenth century), becoming what are now called leaning or narrow vowels. The quality of short vowels (so-called bright vowels) did not change in pronunciation.[15] Two such vowels, /ɛ/ and /ɔ/, continued to be written with unchanged graphemes, while the /a/ vowel was usually written with an acute accent <á>. New vowels with raised articulation were written, respectively, as <é>, <ó> and <a>[16] (see Januszowski 1594: E). This notational system may be considered the most typical, but other methods were also utilized. In a Renaissance description of the Polish alphabet in three different lessons proposed by three humanities scholars of the time, Jan Kochanowski, Łukasz Górnicki and Jan Januszowski (Januszowski 1594),[17] we also find different suggestions for diacritic signs with letters denoting vowels, for example in Kochanowski's version /a/ : <á>, /ä/ : <à>;[18] /ɛ/ : <é>, /ɛ̇/ : <è>; /ɔ/ : <o>, /ɔ̇/ : <ò> or <ó> (Januszowski 1594: G3). In the earlier texts of this period there were sometimes instances of a notation parallel to that discussed above, denoting a narrow vowel by means of doubling the letter, and sometimes additionally with a diacritic sign, for example /ä/ : <aa>, /ɛ̇/ : <eé>, /ɔ̇/ : <uó>. Another sporadically utilized method of adapting the Latin alphabet to denote vowels of the Renaissance Polish language was borrowing from another alphabet. The grapheme <α> (derived from a Greek letter), for instance, could be used as an equivalent of the Polish nasal front vowel, while the grapheme corresponding to the same letter with a stroke across the stem, <α̸>, represented the nasal back vowel. In present-day Polish, there remain two nasal vowels /ɔ̃/, /ɛ̃/, written by means of a letter with an *ogonek* <ą>, <ę>, and oral vowels in a single articulative variant, so there is no further need to differentiate <a>, <e>, <o> (or <i>, <y>, <u>) graphically. The two formerly narrow vowels are currently pronounced in the same way as their bright equivalents /a/, /ɛ/, while the previous *narrow o* /ɔ̇/ is pronounced as /u/. Historical spelling has, however, been retained and the /u/ vowel derived from the old leaning /ɔ̇/ vowel is denoted by the grapheme <ó>.

15 The terminology used here reflects that established by Lisowski (2020) for Renaissance Polish and represents what I believe are the most correct nuances for describing vowels in the Polish phonetic system.

16 The /i/, /ɨ/ and /u/ vowels, as high vowels, appeared only in one tone and thus were denoted with single letters, mainly <i>, <y>, <u>.

17 Full sets of letters of the Polish alphabet according to the three authors (Januszowski 1594) are presented later in this chapter (Figures 11.1, 11.2, 11.3).

18 This is Kochanowski's early approach to denoting both *a* vowels (Januszowski 1594: D4v). The poet's subsequent ideas are discussed later in the chapter.

Sixteenth-century texts also make use of other methods of adapting the Latin alphabet with respect to consonants: ligatures, modifications of the letter shape, changes in the function of a letter, and the creation of new letters (together with the creation of new ligatures). The most common ligature consisted in the grapheme borrowed from German script (with a change in function), resembling the Greek letter *β*, the so-called *Eszett* or *scharfes S* (sharp *s*). In the Polish writing system, it denoted a particular front-tongue postalveolar consonant /ʃ/,[19] written in two variants depending on the typeface: one close to the German original <ß> (e.g. Januszowski 1594: G3, H3 v) and, more frequently, one consisting in a ligature combination between a long *s* and a *z* with a *cauda* <ſʒ>. Górnicki (Januszowski 1594: G3 v) proposed his own ligature for the consonant /ʧ/, consisting of two connected *c* letters. Like Kochanowski, he also advocated the use of a ligature for the voiced equivalent of this consonant, modeled stylistically on German ligatures (Januszowski 1594: G3–G3 v). Kochanowski denoted the soft /ɕ/ consonant either with the letter *s* with an acute <ś> or with a considerably modified letter *s* with a closed lower bowl, approximating in its shape the Arabic digit *6* written in cursive (Januszowski 1594: G3). In Czernecki's (1902: 12) opinion this was a new grapheme created by Kochanowski. As suggested by Parkosz (c. 1470: 45–47)[20] as early as during the Middle Ages, differentiating between hard and soft consonants on the basis of differentiating the shape of the letters generally failed to catch on. It found its continuation, however, in the sixteenth-century *Ortografia Polska* by Murzynowski (1551). Like Parkosz, this author also suggested the use of the letter *b* with a top bow to denote the palatal consonant, but only in word-final position, while he denoted the palatal /ʑ/ phoneme by means of <ʐ> (*z* with a 'swash tail') (Murzynowski 1551: Bv, B3).

Figures 11.1, 11.2 and 11.3 show three Renaissance suggestions for a Polish national alphabet (including allographs in Januszowski's version):

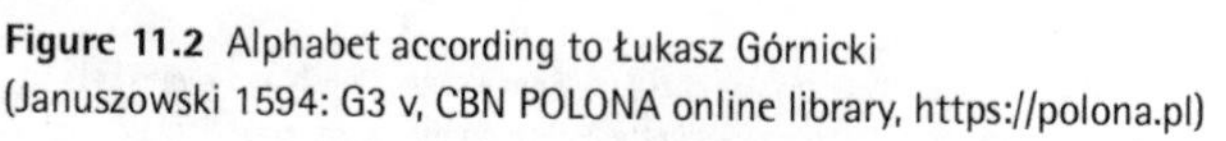

Figure 11.1 Alphabet according to Jan Kochanowski
(Januszowski 1594: G3, CBN POLONA online library, https://polona.pl)

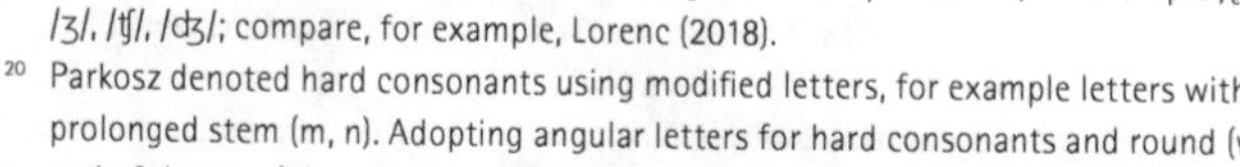

Figure 11.2 Alphabet according to Łukasz Górnicki
(Januszowski 1594: G3 v, CBN POLONA online library, https://polona.pl)

19 For Polish phonemes, I use IPA symbols as established by Wolańska (2019). However, it should be borne in mind that some researchers use different markings for some phonemes, for example /ʂ/, /ʐ/, /t͡ʂ/, /d͡ʐ/ instead of /ʃ/, /ʒ/, /ʧ/, /ʤ/; compare, for example, Lorenc (2018).

20 Parkosz denoted hard consonants using modified letters, for example letters with a square bowl (p, b) or with a prolonged stem (m, n). Adopting angular letters for hard consonants and round (with an additional bow at the end of the stem) for soft consonants, he used musical notation as a model.

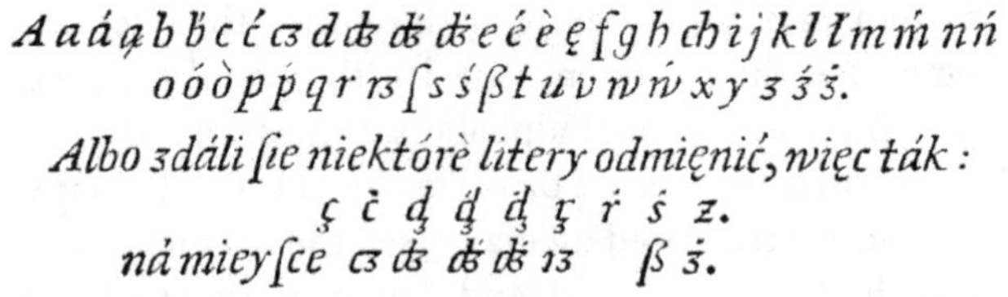

A aá ą b b̓ c ć cz d dz dź dż e é è ę f g h ch i j k l ł m ḿ n ń
o ó ò p p̓ q r rz ſ s ś ß t u v w ẃ x y z ź ż.
Albo zdáli ſie niektóre litery odmięnić, więc ták :
ç č ḑ ḑ́ ḑ̇ ŗ ŕ ś ż.
námieyſce cz dz dź dż rz ß ż.

Figure 11.3 Alphabet according to Jan Januszowski
(Januszowski 1594: H3 v, CBN POLONA online library, https://polona.pl)

The current Polish alphabet consists of 32 letters:[21] *Aa, Ąą, Bb, Cc, Ćć, Dd, Ee, Ęę, Ff, Gg, Hh, Ii, Jj, Kk, Ll, Łł, Mm, Nn, Ńń, Oo, Óó, Pp, Rr,* Ss, *Śś, Tt, Uu, Ww, Yy, Zz, Źź, Żż,* of which nine have diacritic signs.[22] Every letter corresponds to a specific phone with distinctive features. The graphemes <u> and <ó>, however, represent the same phoneme, /u/, and their usage is motivated by morphological and historical reasons. Digraphs <ch>, <cz>, <dz>, <dź>, <dż>, <rz>, <sz> which, with the exception of particular cases, denote the following seven phones: /x/, /ʧ/, /ʣ/, /ʥ/, /ʤ/, /ʒ/, /ʃ/, are not included in the Polish alphabet.[23] Soft consonants, denoted by a letter with an acute accent, are written without a diacritic if they occur before a vowel, and their palatal character is denoted by a following, additional letter *i*,[24] with which they create two- or three-piece signs: |ć| ~ |ci|, |ń| ~ |ni|, |ś| ~ |si|, |ź| ~ |zi|; |dź| ~ |dzi|. In contrast to the aforementioned digraphs, they correspond not to separate sounds, but constitute only orthographic (positional) allographs of appropriate diacriticized letters.

11.4 Alphabet Adaptations with a Narrow Scope of Usage

The above-discussed adaptations of alphabets aimed at rendering a particular language may be considered to represent an adaptation of a general range. They are, firstly, connected with a top-down regulation regarding the usage

[21] For a detailed and multifaceted analysis of the graphemic system of the present-day Polish language with references to other writing systems, see the recent work by Wolańska (2019).

[22] The codification of Polish orthography is the responsibility of the Polish Language Council at the Presidium of the Polish Academy of Sciences. The order of the letters of the Polish alphabet is presented by a brochure published by the Council (Rada Języka Polskiego 2007: 4). In addition to the aforementioned letters belonging to the alphabet, it is permissible, albeit only in borrowings, to use the letters *Qq, Vv* and *Xx*.

[23] It should be noted that comparing national alphabets based on the Latin alphabet, one may notice differences not only of a quantitative (a different number of letters) or a qualitative (various phonic equivalents of some letters) nature, but also sequential (different sequences of letters, especially with regard to the position of new graphemes) or technical differences, including poligraphemes. In the Renaissance era, the Polish alphabet tended to contain digraphs and trigraphs, which thus had the value of individual graphemes. Today, they are treated as two (or three) separate letters rather than individual graphemes. Examples of present-day alphabets in which multigraphs are considered individual graphemes and find a place in the alphabetic order include the Czech <ch> and the Hungarian units <cs>, <dz>, <gy>, <ly>, <ny>, <sz>, <ty>, <zs>, <dzs>.

[24] An exception is to be found in the use of an appropriate soft consonant before the vowel /i/. In this case, the vowel letter also constitutes a grapheme corresponding to an individual phone, and not only a graphic sign of softness (e.g. in the word *ciszo*).

of a specific alphabetic system, and subsequently, with refining the relationship between the phonemes and the graphemes, and with formulating the orthographic rules. This is the way national alphabets and scripts may be born. Due to their national nature, they have a broad group of users. In many countries, the rules of writing are regulated officially (see the example from note 22); they are relatively highly normalized, and they may frequently be characterized by gradual evolution, resulting from long tradition. Writing "as a public good" (Coulmas 2013: 104) is a source in the public sphere in many aspects, including the institutional. There also exist examples of adaptations of alphabets whose range of usage is considerably narrower than those described in Section 11.3 above. In such cases, we are dealing with a different kind of hybridity of the writing systems than that connected with the early stages of adjusting an alphabet to the general needs of a community that speaks a particular language. This pertains to scripts that only partly fulfill the same criteria as do national scripts. In some republics of the former Union of Soviet Socialist Republics, the lack of a longer writing tradition stems, above all, from political conditions. Due to the relatively frequent changes in the general alphabetic system of the languages that prevail there, as well as the ordinances governing the official language, many of the alphabets imposed have failed to proceed from the stage of early adaptation to the level of solid stabilization, as had been the case in the aforementioned systems of writing for the Turkmen, Azeri and Uzbek languages (see references in note 11).

There may be a variety of reasons behind adaptations of a narrow scope of usage, that is, adaptations of a provisional rather than general nature, for example, political, ideological, religious adaptations. There may also be different dependencies between alphabets used in a general scope and in a narrow scope. On the one hand, an alphabet utilized provisionally in order to record a given language may already be broadly used to record other languages in the same language group, as in the case of the traditional use of the Cyrillic or the Latin alphabet to record Slavic languages. On the other hand, it is also possible to transpose an alphabet that generally serves to record languages from an entirely different language group (see Subsection 11.4.2 about *aljamiado*). The difficulties connected with transposition of this kind should be considered on two levels. The first pertains to the differences of an interlanguage nature, among which the most significant are differences in the phonological subsystems of languages from distantly related language groups: a different stock of phones, different realizations of phones, their distinctive functions, positional variants, etc. The very systems of writing are frequently different (e.g. full alphabet or abjad). There are other significant differences of an external nature, such as the prevalent writing practices, orthographic rules and the direction of writing, but these do not receive any further attention here due to space limits.

11.4.1 The Polish Graždanka

Although the above process by which alphabets would be changed frequently or where multialphabeticity with regard to a given language did not serve to stabilize national scripts, the latter were still characterized by a relative degree of normalization. The so-called Polish Cyrillic alphabet was an example of an unstable alphabetic system.[25] Different variants of this alphabet have appeared in the history of Polish writing, and their episodic nature connected with the limited number of users resulted in the Polish Cyrillic alphabet never graduating from the stage of graphic hybrids, not even approaching the initial adaptations of a general nature as described in Subsection 11.3.1. Only a small community in the Siberian village Vershina (the Bokhan Region, near Irkutsk) currently uses *graždanka* in order to record the Polish language. *Graždanka* is used there for the handwritten texts of songs performed by the local choir and printed religious texts, as well as in grave inscriptions, alongside the Latin alphabet (Głuszkowski 2012, Ananiewa 2013). The system used in Vershina is not fully standardized. Its usage is partly connected with assimilation processes within the local community, although they involve only using a 'foreign' alphabet, and not a foreign language as such.

The first serious example of the use of *graždanka* to record the Polish language may be referred to as a provisional adaptation. It occurred in a dictionary published in St. Petersburg in 1787 (vol. 1) and 1789 (vol. 2), entitled *Linguarum totius orbis vocabularia comparativa; augustissimae cura collecta* [...] *Linguas Europae et Asiae complexae* (Pallas 1789). The dictionary is frequently referred to as 'The Dictionary of Empress Catherine the Great', as it was her interest in Antoine Court de Gébelin's theory of the genetic unity of all languages of the world that gave the impulse to the creation of the work. It was a large lexicographic undertaking, involving the translation of 273 Russian words into 200 languages, with the addition of numerals translated into 222 languages (Pallas 1789: 472–91). All the lexical equivalents, including the Polish, were written in *graždanka*.[26] A brief overview of the transliteration rules was provided after the Latin foreword by Peter S. Pallas, the main author of the project. It is a list of the letters of *graždanka* with their equivalents, the letters of the Greek and Latin alphabets, sometimes together with remarks on spelling in different languages, Italian, German, French and English (Pallas 1787: *s.n.* 6–7). The list included two Cyrillic signs that denoted the particular sound values of phones in different languages. Jakubczyk (2014b, 2014a)

[25] Although the expression Polish Cyrillic alphabet is frequently used for the alphabet described here, it should be borne in mind that formally it was already the modernized Russian version: *graždanka*. In this part, I use the terms interchangeably.

[26] Examples include: *Мальчикъ*: 10. *Польски* – Хлопѣцъ, 32. *Аглински – Бой*; *Человѣкъ*: 10. *Польски – Чловѣкъ*, 32. *Аглински – Мянъ* (Pallas 1787: 36, 42–43); *Дубъ*: 10. *Польски – Донбь*, 32. *Аглински – Оокъ*; *Воинъ*: 10. *Польски – Жо́лнѣръ*, 32. *Аглински – Соджїэръ, Варїоръ* (Pallas 1789: 1, 187).

describes in detail the history of the creation of this dictionary together with an analysis of the graphemes of Polish *graždanka*.

Nineteenth-century attempts at adapting the Cyrillic alphabet to render the Polish language were of a more systematic nature. They were connected, above all, with politics, aiming at the denationalization of Poles living in the Russian partition, but it also resulted from the current of Slavophilia in Russian Romanticism. Although the first projects of a Polish Cyrillic alphabet were created as early as the 1840s,[27] only a subsequent project, prepared by the Russian bibliophile Pëtr P. Dubrovskiĭ, was used in practice. In 1852, Dubrovskiĭ published fragments of Polish works of literature (including translations), written in the Cyrillic alphabet in an anthology entitled *Образцы польскаго языка въ прозѣ и стихахъ для Русскихъ*, which was reprinted in 1866. The selections were divided into three parts, including proverbs and short fragments of prosaic and poetic texts. The anthology was preceded by an introduction, in which the editor presented the rules of transposing the Latin alphabet into the Cyrillic alphabet, first in Russian, then in Polish (Dubrovskiĭ 1866: 1–11). The transliteration of the majority of the letters was facilitated by the identical sound of the phones in both languages, and only the rules of writing phones characteristic solely for Polish were discussed in greater detail. The Polish Cyrillic alphabet of Dubrovskiĭ's design was, however, no mechanical transliteration, but rather a well-considered system of writing which could be seen as more phonetically successful than the use of the Latin alphabet. For instance, the vowel denoted by means of <ó> or <u> Dubrovskiĭ (1866: 4, 10) marks according to phonetic writing with <y> (Latin <u>). He also writes the consonant /ʒ/ derived from soft *r* /rʲ/ as <рж> (Dubrovskiĭ 1866: 4, 10).

Dubrovskiĭ was familiar with 'The Dictionary of Empress Catherine the Great' and the transliteration methods it suggested (Dubrovskiĭ 1866: 10). He also referred to a very similar publication from the year before, which focused on Jaroslav Puchmír's effort involving a project of adapting *graždanka* bearing in mind the needs of the Czech language (Dubrovskiĭ 1866: 9). Dubrovskiĭ apparently knew only the improved edition of Jaroslav Puchmír's *Pravopis rusko-český* (1851), first published in 1805. A number of similarities may nevertheless be found between the Polish and the Czech publications. The subsequent project of transposing the Polish Latin alphabet to the Cyrillic alphabet was prepared by Pan-Slavists: Aleksander F. Gilferding and Stanisław J. K. Mikucki, with co-operation from Jan Papłoński. A new manual for reading and writing was introduced in schools: *Элемэнтаръ для дзеци вейскихъ* (= *Elementarz dla dzieci wiejskich*, henceforth *Elementarz*), published first

[27] An early project of adapting the Cyrillic alphabet to the needs of recording Polish was created in 1844–45 under the direction of the Minister for Education of the Russian Empire, Sergey S. Uvarov, and was of a purely theoretical character (see Uspenskiĭ 2004, Strycharska-Brzezina 2006: 11–14).

in 1865 in St. Petersburg, then in Warsaw in 1866, where it was reprinted in 1869. The introduction to this book presents the new Polish alphabet, *graždanka*, with traditional equivalents of Latin letters (in both majuscule and minuscule) written beneath it in the order of the sequence of letters in *graždanka*. The following pages contain the alphabet written in cursive, as is particularly important with regard to *graždanka*, due to the fact that straight script sometimes differed significantly from the cursive, as well as sample syllables and words (Elementarz 1866: 2–14). At the end of the next section there are some texts. The transposition tended to be based on the simple transliteration of phones of similar sound in the Polish and Russian languages. Due to the fact that the Russian language and its phonological system lack nasal and narrow vowels, diacriticized graphemes, as in Polish, were used in the following cases: for the vowel /ɔ̃/: <ą>; for /ɛ̃/ the *graždanka* equivalent of the Latin grapheme <e> with an *ogonek*: <э̨>; and for the vowel derived from the narrow vowel /u/ (←/ɔ̇/), a grapheme with a circumflex: <ô>. In the Polish version of the Latin alphabet, as in *graždanka*, vowels had their diphthong equivalents appearing in the form of individual graphemes (<e> ~ <ie>, <ë> ~ <io>, <ю> ~ <iu>, <я> ~ <ia>), and analogical signs were also created for the vowels peculiar to Polish by adding an *ogonek* or a circumflex to particular letters: <ę> ~ <ię> /ɪɛ̃/, <я̨> ~ <ią> /ɪɔ̃/, <ю̂> ~ <ió> /ɪɔ̇/.

As mentioned in Subsection 11.3.1, in the traditional Polish alphabet there are no separate letters equivalent to the laminal postalveolar phones /ʃ/, /ʒ/,[28] /ʧ/, /ʤ/, and they are written using appropriate digraphs: <sz>, <rz>, <cz>, <dż>. In *graždanka*, there exist graphemes for two phones that are close in quality in both languages: /ʃ/ <ш> and /ʧ/ <ч>, for example *koszt* ~ *кошть*, *czas* ~ *часъ* (Elementarz 1866: 11, 10),[29] while for the consonant /ʒ/ derived from /ṛ/ the *graždanka* equivalent of the Latin grapheme <r> with a *caron* was used: <р̌>, for example *brzeg* ~ *бр̌егъ* (Elementarz 1866: 10). Digraphs analogical to the Latin alphabet were only used for Polish hardened consonants /ʤ/ and /ʥ/: <dż> ~ <дж>, <dz> ~ <дз>, for example *drożdże* ~ *дрожджe*, *dzban* ~ *дзбанъ* (Elementarz 1866: 12, 10). The grapheme <щ> was retained, as equivalent to the Russian palatal consonant cluster /ʃʧ/, and to the two Polish hardened laminal 'rustling' phones, traditionally written by means of digraphs: <sz>, <cz>, for example *szczur* ~ *щуръ* (Elementarz 1866: 10).

Palatal consonants in Polish, traditionally denoted either with an acute accent or with an added <i> (in the past also <y>), were also written in two ways in the Polish Cyrillic alphabet. The *graždanka* equivalent of a letter

[28] The fricative consonant derived from soft *r* /rʲ/, written in Polish with the use of the digraph <rz>, and not the original vowel whose Latin diacriticized grapheme is <ż> (in *graždanka*: <ж>).

[29] All Polish equivalents of words written in an alphabet other than Latin are always given in modern orthography (Latin alphabet in the Polish edition).

with a diacritic sign was a digraph consisting of the appropriate letter and a soft sign, for example *wieś* ~ *весь*, *nać* ~ *наць*, *broń* ~ *бронь*, *bliźniemu* ~ *близьнему* (Elementarz 1866: 9, 10, 48). An analogical rule pertained to writing the phone /ʥ/, whose corresponding digraph in the Latin alphabet was <dź>, but, in *graždanka*, the trigraph <дзь>, for example *miedź* ~ *медзь*, was used (Elementarz 1866: 10). Conversely, the soft sign would not be used when the given palatal consonant appeared before a front vowel or a diphthong: *zięć* ~ *зęць*, *sieć* ~ *сець*, *cios* ~ *цёсь*, *dziś* ~ *дзись*, *dziad* ~ *дзядь* (Elementarz 1866: 9, 10). The method of denoting Polish soft vowels may be considered surprisingly consistent. This also pertains to rendering in writing the consonants which remain hard due to the morphological boundary, although it is followed by a softening phone. In such cases, the lack of softening is signaled by a hard sign, for example *zjazd* ~ *зъяздь*, *zjadać* ~ *зъядаць* (Elementarz 1866: 10). The historical differentiation between /x/ ~ <ch> and /ɣ/ ~ <h>, was retained. The Latin digraph <ch>, corresponding to /x/, found its individual equivalent in the grapheme <x>, while the Polish grapheme <h>[30] was rendered by the same grapheme with a vertical tilde <x̍>, for example *duch* ~ *духъ*, *mchy* ~ *мхы*; *hak* ~ *x̍акъ*, *hej* ~ *x̍эй* (Elementarz 1866: 9–11). In contrast to Dubrovskiĭ's project, which was close to a phonetic transcription, here we clearly see transliteration from the Latin alphabet to *graždanka* with the use of new graphemes (diacriticized letters and poligraphs) to denote phones specific to Polish, in order to retain characteristic phonic features of the Polish language. The differences between the two alphabetic systems, the Latin alphabet and *graždanka*, sometimes result in significant differences in the number of letters used to write the same Polish words, for example *pszczoły* 'bees' (8 letters, including 2 digraphs) ~ *пщолы* (5 letters), *chrząszcze* 'cockchafers' (10 letters, including 4 digraphs) ~ *хр̆ąщэ* (5 letters), *odwilż* 'thaw' (6 letters) ~ *одвильжь* (8 letters, including 2 digraphs). This brief overview of Polish *graždanka* is based on several texts. In addition to the aforementioned publications, other classroom aids, such as textbooks for studying literature, grammar, arithmetic and religion, were also printed in *graždanka* as a part of the nineteenth-century Russification policy.

11.4.2 Polish and Belarusian *Aljamiado*

The Polish language is part of the Slavic group of languages, and thus it may seem relatively unproblematic to use *graždanka*, an alphabet at the base of many Slavic national scripts, to render it. The situation is entirely different when a given alphabet is used to write a language from a different

[30] The pronunciation differentiation between the voiceless /x/ and the voiced /ɣ/ (written as <ch> and <h>, respectively) has disappeared in the present-day standard Polish language, and both consonants are pronounced voicelessly.

language group, for example when the Arabic alphabet is used to write Polish. Structural differences between Polish and Arabic are reflected in two different traditions of writing (recording traditions): vowel-containing roots in Indo-European languages and consonantal roots in Semitic languages. The list of differences between these two kinds of writing, the Latin and the Arabic, is clearly broader and pertains also to other aspects in the alphabetic system itself. On the one hand, we have the bicameral full Latin alphabet in its Polish edition; on the other, the unicameral Arabic abjad, in which the only phones written are consonants, long vowels (/aː/, /iː/, /uː/) and diphthongs (represented as digraphs: <ay>, <aw>), with the possibility of vowel marks for short vowels. The Latin alphabet has two separate classes of letters, the lowercase and uppercase, and thus every letter occurs in two variants where usage is dictated by grammatical and lexical-semantic convention. In the Arabic alphabet, the appearance of the letters depends only on their location in a given word, and thus graphemes usually occur in four variants: in an isolated position, at the beginning, at the end, or in the middle of a word. In both cases, Latin and Arabic, the writing has a linear horizontal direction. The Polish Latin alphabet runs from left to right with spaces between words, while the Arabic system of writing is continuous with a different technique used to signal the borders of the words and it runs from right to left. Latin is characterized by a clear demarcation of phrases and sentences due to punctuation marks, which is generally absent when writing Polish in the Arabic alphabet. Considerable differences between the Polish and Arabic phonetic systems, pertaining both to the number and the quality of phones (see, e.g., Danecki 1994: 55–67), require the use of well thought-out and legible techniques of transposition. When used to write the Polish language, the Arabic script generally retains all the characteristic features discussed above. With few exceptions, such texts commonly use Arabic vocal marks to denote vowels. The basic difference, however, lies in the scope in which either alphabet is used for the Polish language. The Polish Latin alphabet constitutes an adaptation of a general nature; texts in the Arabic script constitute only a small fraction of the entire literary legacy of the Polish language. They include relics of Muslim religious literature composed in Polish (and Belarusian) by the Tatars living in the historical terrain of the Grand Duchy of Lithuania (GDL).[31]

The writings of the Muslim Tatars from the GDL consist of texts in Polish and Belarusian, or, more precisely, as Shirin Akiner (2017: 403) succinctly refers to this language, "a mixture of Polonised Belarusian and Belarusianised Polish," written in an appropriately adapted Arabic alphabet. Although the oldest preserved manuscripts date back to the seventeenth century, their prototypes had certainly already existed in the previous century. As the faithful grew increasingly unfamiliar with the Arabic language, they found the

[31] The expression Slavic languages used henceforth refers to Polish and Belarusian.

Quran, which constituted not only the basis of the prayers, but also a precise collection of rules according to which an orthodox Muslim should live, practically incomprehensible. As a result, there began to appear translations of fragments of the Quran, and, in time, it appeared translated in its entirety. Other religious texts of different form, content and length were also translated and compiled, drawing inspiration not only from Oriental sources, but also from Old Polish literature and the Bible (see Wexler 1988, Drozd 1997, Konopacki 2015).[32]

Detailed descriptions of selected relics of writing, together with an analysis of their writing system, not infrequently connected with the transliteration of the entire text or its fragments, were presented by Stankevich (1933), Meredith-Owens and Nadson (1970), Łapicz (1986), Dziekan (1997), Miškinienė (2001), Tarėlka and Synkova (2006, 2008), Akiner (2009) and Miškinienė et al. (2009) among others. The philological dissertation, the first of such length and degree of detail, of Antonovich (1968), a Vilnius scholar, is today considered a classic text. In this pioneering work, Antonovich discussed the writing system and language of 24 handwritten texts. In the so-called kitabistics literature (from the Arabic *kitāb'* – 'book'), whose area of research is the texts by the GDL Tatars in the Arabic writing system,[33] a number of scholars use a variety of ways of reproducing Arabic graphemes with the letters of the Latin alphabet or *graždanka*.[34] In this section, I focus only on the manner of writing the Polish (and Belarusian) language by means of an appropriately adapted Arabic alphabet. Polish *aljamiado* was not a normalized or codified system.[35] There happen to be more or less common graphic solutions for particular phones.

In order to render Slavic vowels, the vocal marks, alone or connected to appropriate letters, of the Arabic abjad were used. Only three vowels were thus denoted, namely /a, i, u/, in two variants: long and short. Even omitting the Polish narrow vowels and Ruthenian diphthongs, a way to render the vowels /ɛ/, /ɨ/ and /ɔ/ needed to be established, together with, in the case of Polish, a way of denoting the back and the front nasal vowel. The vowel /a/ was usually denoted as /ā/ in the Arabic script, that is, with the letter *alif*.[36] A

[32] On the genres of literature of the GDL Tatars, see, for example, Drozd (2000), Konopacki (2010: 125–60), Danecki (2011), Dziekan (2011), Lewicka (2016).

[33] On the history and the subject of research of kitabistic studies, see, for example, Lewicka (2015), Miškinienė (2015), Tarėlka (2015) and Łapicz (2017).

[34] A detailed overview of nine authorial systems of transliteration and transcription of Tatar texts was presented in the form of a table by Radziszewska (2015: 180–94). She additionally juxtaposed them with the International Organization for Standardization standards (standard ISO 233: 1984 for Arabic language), and, in the case of Turkish and Persian graphemes, with the standard DIN 31635 (Das Deutsche Institut für Normung) from 1982.

[35] I am using the term *aljamiado* (from Arabic *al-'ağamiyyai* 'foreign' < *al-luğa al-'ağamiyya* 'foreign language'), initially used in Oriental studies in order to denote Romani dialects written in the Arabic alphabet, in its broadest scope, referring in general to non-Arabic writing, see Dziekan (2015: 201–2).

[36] It should be noted that in Belarusian dialects in which *akanye* occurred, the unaccented vowel /o/ was usually pronounced as /a/. Examples of mixing these two vowels could thus appear in texts.

combination of *alif* and *fatḥa* <اَ>, however, was most commonly used for this. In a specific position, especially in word-initial position, an *alif* would appear with a *madda* <آ>, or a ligature of the letters *'ayn* and *alif* with *fatḥa* <عَا>, for example *nad* ~ نَاْدْ[37] (TL: 3 v); the conjunction *a* ~ عَا, *amin* ~ آمِـنْ (*Ivan Łuckievič's kitab*, henceforth KL: 140). A ligature consisting of the letters *lām* and *alif* with *fatḥa* <لَا>, for example *chwała* ~ خْوَالَا (KL: 140), was also commonly used. An independent *fatḥa* <◌َ>, which served, in a nonobligatory way, to denote *short a* in the Arabic script, was typically used to denote the vowel /ɛ/ in Polish *aljamiado*, for example *nie* – نَ (TL: 3 v).

Initially, a method of differentiating between the /u/ and /ɔ/ vowels was not developed, but from the beginning of the nineteenth century, two ways of rendering these phonemes in writing were employed most frequently: (1) a traditional one for /u/, with the use of *ḍamma*, either on its own <◌ُ> or with a *wāw* <وُ>, and (2) for /ɔ/, with the use of a *wāw* together with a *fatḥa* <وَ>, for example *bogu* ~ بوَغُ (*Milkamanowič's kitab*, henceforth KM: 379).[38] No graphic differentiation between the vowels /i/ and /ɨ/ was, however, introduced, and words using a *kasra* <◌ِ> had to be deciphered intuitively on the basis of context. For example, the words مِ or بِـلْ could be interpreted as two different Polish lexemes: the former as *my* 'we' or *mi* 'me', and the latter as *był* 'he was' or *bił* 'he was beating'. Another feature adapted from the Arabic script was the *sukūn* <◌ْ>, denoting the lack of a vowel, which was also used in the consonant word-final position, and thus played a delimitating role (see the examples above). The rules pertaining to writing Polish nasal vowels tended not to differ from those proposed by Dubrovskiĭ (1866: 3–4, 9) for Polish *graždanka*. The nasal vowels were thus denoted by the corresponding oral vowels, individual or connected with a nasal consonant: <n> or <m>.

In order to denote particular Slavic consonants, several of the methods of graphic adaptations of letters discussed in Section 11.3 were utilized. One of these methods consisted of using new diacritic marks with the traditional Arabic letters. In this way, the graphemes for the hardened consonants /ʣ/ and /ʦ/ were created by means of adding to the letters *dāl* <د> and *ṣād* <ص> diacritic marks unused for them, in the form of three dots under the letter: <ࢮ> and <ڝ>, for example *ochłodzeniu* ~ وَخْلوُࢮَنيـُو (KM: 386), *pomocy* ~ پُومُوڝ (TL: 3 v). Such a modification of the letter *sīn* <ڛ>, used mainly to denote the soft or softened consonant *s*, for example *świata* ~ ڛْـوَاطَا (TL: 3 v), also made sporadic appearances. Borrowed signs that had enriched the Arabic alphabet in its Turkish and Persian editions were also used. In the Arabic script, there existed graphemes for the voiced consonants /b/ and /ʤ/: *bā'* ~ <ب> and *ğīm* ~ <ج>, whereas the letters for /p/ ~ <پ> and /ʧ/ ~ <چ>

[37] In Arabic writing, I do not include various, basically allographic, variants of the signs used in manuscripts; for example, *ḍamma* frequently resembled an apostrophe, and *sukūn* an inverted apostrophe.

[38] In word-initial position, both characters could be preceded by an alif.

were introduced for their nonexistent voiceless counterparts. In accordance with the same rule, a letter was added for the voiced phone /ʒ/ ~ <ژ>, as in the classic Arabic alphabet there only existed a sign for the voiceless phone /ʃ/: *šīn* ~ <ش>. Additionally, as has been discussed above, the Persian-Turkish letter *kāf*, diacriticized with three dots, was also adopted; in exceptional cases it could have only one dot (Drozd 1994).

The third method of adapting the Arabic alphabet for the needs of Slavic languages consisted of changing the functions of particular letters. The most systemic way was to 'utilize' the letters corresponding to the pairs of clear (nonpharygealized) and pharyngealized consonants (distinctive phonemically)[39] to reflect the Slavic opposition between hard and soft (or softened) consonant phonemes. As may be seen from the examples above, the softness of a given consonant was usually indicated by the following vowel /i/ or /ɛ/. Following the rule of similarity of sound, it was also possible to use several Arabic letters to denote certain Slavic phones.

11.4.3 Ephemeras of Armenian Script

As a final example of the use of an alphabet other than the Latin alphabet to record the Polish language, let us look at records made with the Armenian alphabet. The scope of its usage was a great deal narrower than the previously discussed alphabets, *graždanka* and the Arabic alphabet. Moreover, there remain only a very small number of such records available, emphasizing their ephemeral character (see Tryjarski 1976, Urbańczyk 1986, Reczek 1987: 6–7). The Armenians, who began to come to Poland in the middle of fourteenth century, used the Kipchak language as their mother tongue and they acquired Polish. In time, they grew to use Polish commonly. This was the result not only of their assimilation, but also of the arrival of Armenians escaping Armenia and the wars that ravaged the country in the sixteenth and seventeenth centuries. Rather than the Kipchak language, they spoke a variety of dialects of Armenian, and so Polish began to function as the common language for old and new settlers alike. They were additionally connected by the traditional alphabet,[40] because they wrote their documents in Polish by means of their own Armenian alphabet, which they had brought to Poland, for example *twoja* ~ Դւվօյա, *chwała* ~ խւվալա, *wieczny* ~ վէչնի (Grigoryan and Pisovich' 1964: 229).[41]

[39] The pharyngealized phones are frequently referred to with their actual hypernym: emphatic phones.

[40] For more on the subject of Polish Armenians, their origins, language and writing (especially in the sixteenth and seventeenth centuries) see Tryjarski (1960), Grigoryan and Pisovich' (1964), Grigori͡an (1980: 117–56), Stopka (2000), Stachowski (2010) and Pisowicz (2000, 2014 [2001]: 24–25).

[41] All examples of Armenian script referred to in this part of the chapter are derived from the article by Grigoryan and Pisovich' (1964), which contained two texts: one from 1573, found in court reports from Kamieniec Podolski, and the other a religious hymn dating back to the eighteenth century.

The Armenian alphabet is considered a mystical work, the creation of Mesrop Mashtots (Մեսրոպ Մաշտոց) from the fifth century. Before that, the Armenian language had been written for some time in the Greek script, then the Syrian and Pahlavi scripts (Cohen 1956: 65). In the alphabet created by St. Mesrop, attuned to denote the phones of the Old Armenian language (*grabar*), graphic methods may be found partly based on the abovementioned alphabetic patterns (Pisowicz 2014 [2001]: 24). The Armenian script is bicameral with horizontal orientation written from left to right. Polish Armenians used the Western Armenian dialect, as evidenced by the use of letters to denote selected voiced and voiceless consonants; for example, in the word *Tobie* ~ Դօպիէ (Grigoryan and Pisovich‘ 1964: 229), the written letters *da* <դ> and *peh* <պ> correspond, respectively, to the voiceless /t/ and the voiced /b/ phones in this dialect (see also the word *twoja* above). In the classic Eastern Armenian writing, these graphemes denote different consonants: <դ> ~ /d/, <պ> ~ /p/. Similarly, in the notations of *panie* ~ բանիէ the word-initial letter *ben* <բ> denotes the voiceless consonant /p/, while in the verb form *padamy* ~ բատամի one also encounters the word-initial letter <բ> ~ /p/, and in the word-middle position the letter *tiwn* <տ> – /d/ (Grigoryan and Pisovich‘ 1964: 229).

Similarly, as in the case of the methods of recording the Polish language by means of *graždanka* and the Arabic alphabet (above), writing in the Armenian alphabet also had a mostly phonetic character that took into account the similarity of phonemes in both languages. In order to represent individual Polish phones, a variety of provisional methods were used. For example, the writing instances frequently do not distinguish between the Polish narrow vowel /ȯ/ and the vowel /u/, and use the classic method of denoting the /u/ vowel in both cases, a combination of the letters <ո> and <ւ>,[42] for example *który* ~ քդուրիլ, *panów* ~ բանուվ, *mówił* ~ մուվիլ, *fantów* ~ փանդուվ, a variation of *długu* ~ տլուկու (Grigoryan and Pisovich‘ 1964: 228). The narrow vowel /ȯ/ may also, however, be written by means of the letters *vo* <ո> or *oh* <օ>, which correspond to the vowel /o/ in the Armenian language – their usage being determined by their position in the word, not reflected in Polish texts, for example *kupców* ~ քուպցով, *grzeszników* ~ կրժէշնիկքով, *którą* ~ քդօրօ (Grigoryan and Pisovich‘ 1964: 228, 230).

The nasal vowels /ɔ̃/ and /ɛ̃/ were most frequently rendered by means of a combination of two letters denoting a sonically correlated oral vowel and a nasal consonant, or, slightly less frequently, using the oral vowel letter itself. The /ɔ̃/ vowel was usually written by means of combining the letters <օն> ~ Latin <on>, for example *sądem* ~ սօնտէմ, *takową* ~ դաքօվօն, *wszystką* ~

[42] This medieval method of denoting the /u/ vowel by means of two graphemes shows a connection with Greek writing (/u/ : <ou>). In present-day writing, the sign combination <ու> is treated as a single letter (Pisowicz 2014 [2001]: 43).

վըիադօն, *twą* – դվօմ, or a single grapheme <o> ~ Latin <o>: *twą* ~ դվօ, and less frequently the <ու> ~ Latin grapheme: *stanąwszy* – ստանուվըի (Grigoryan and Pisovich‘ 1964: 228, 230). The same rule pertained to rendering the vowel /ɛ̃/, using a combination of letters reflecting its positional pronunciation <են> ~ Latin <en>, <էմ> ~ Latin <em>, for example *święcie* ~ սվենցէ, *piniędzmi* ~ բինենձմի, *Wstępując* ~ Վստէմբույօնց (Grigoryan and Pisovich‘ 1964: 228, 230). The /ɛ̃/ vowel could also be represented by one or two letters denoting the oral vowel /ɛ/ ~ <է>, <եէ>, for example *imię* ~ իմէ, *ugodę* ~ ուկօտէ, *się* ~ սէ; *się* ~ սեէ, *sumę* ~ սումեէ (Grigoryan and Pisovich‘ 1964: 228).

Even a cursory overview of the ways of recording only the vowels specific for the Polish language showcases the way the spelling in this script was far from normalized.

11.5 Conclusion

This chapter has focused, above all, on the stages of the hybridity of writing systems during the formation of various ways of writing, that is, the adaptation of a certain alphabetic system (the base alphabet) for the needs of the phones of a different language. I have pointed out various paths of adaptation, different scopes and diverse reasons for adopting one and not another base system. In Section 11.2, attention was drawn to the crystallization of 'grand' alphabets (Latin, Greek, etc.). The discussion then moved to the modifications of established base systems, which sought to create a well thought-out, uniform system of rendering of another language. I focused on two levels of adapting base alphabets for the needs of other languages. Broadly, the adaptation of writing is of a universal nature, common to the languages discussed in Section 11.3, as was seen from the example of the Latin alphabet in its Polish edition (11.3.1). The adaptation of an alphabet of narrow usage scope (Section 11.4) for various reasons would not achieve the status of a national script. I analyzed the following examples: the Polish Cyrillic alphabet (11.4.1), the Polish and Belarusian *aljamiado* (11.4.2) and the use of the Armenian alphabet to write Polish texts (11.4.3). While the examples of national alphabets (Section 11.3) and alphabets of narrow scope of usage (Section 11.4) concern the recording of the Polish language, the universal nature of certain methods related to adaptation techniques of alphabetic systems also needed to be addressed. The aforementioned ways of recording the Polish language illustrate an entire spectrum of dependencies connected with choosing which alphabetic system should be used: cultural, religious, political, social or utilitarian.

12

Variation and Change

Michelle Waldispühl

12.1 Introduction

This chapter provides insights into crucial findings on variation and change in orthography and into current theoretical and methodological issues.[1] It gives an overview of types and functions of historical orthographic variation in Section 12.2 and different patterns of orthographic change in Section 12.3. Its aim is to introduce the subject and to highlight important preliminaries, methodological considerations, relevant research questions and *desiderata*. This chapter shall, on the one hand, contribute to a broader general understanding of orthographic variation and change in historical texts and, on the other hand, provide a background against which a research question and design for the study of variation and change in historical orthographies can be defined and created.

The topics covered in this chapter are limited in three important respects. First, it includes only alphabet writing, that is, writing systems with distinctive segments that systematically map to phonic units.[2] Second, the chapter concerns mainly the history of German and runic writing.[3] Lastly, within the

This work was partly supported by the Swedish Research Council, grants 2018-01556 and 2018-06074.

[1] 'Orthography' is understood here as a general term to capture regularities in spelling and includes nonnormalized spelling. The term furthermore implies a focus on linguistically functional units, that is, the focus here is on the linguistic code underlying the system of a certain written language. Thus, paleographic, typographic or graphetic (e.g. letter shapes) components are touched upon only if they involve functional differences in the spelling system, when, for example, a letter component is graphically modified or a diacritic mark is added to denote linguistic or indexical difference.

[2] A phonic unit is a sound unit and it can refer to a phoneme or an allophone of a phoneme.

[3] Runic writing is a phonographic writing system and was used by Germanic people from the second century AD. Most runic inscriptions are from the Viking Age and medieval Scandinavia where runes were popular also after the introduction of the Roman alphabet around AD 1000. The runic alphabet is called *futhark* or *futhorc* derived from the first six letters in the runic row (ᚠ 'f', ᚢ 'u', ᚦ 'þ (th)', ᚨ 'a', ᚱ 'r', ᚲ 'k'). Runes were mainly used epigraphically (i.e. for inscriptions on solid materials, such as stone or wood).

history of German, the main focus rests on the Middle Ages (AD 750–1350) and the beginning of the early modern period, before convergence processes toward a supraregional variant began. These restrictions reflect the focus of my own research. However, the examples from two writing systems and different time periods provide insight into various processes and contexts for orthographic practice and I hope that the conclusions on historical orthographic variation and change presented here are transferable to other historical written languages. Moreover, insights into variation patterns and developments in premodern writing are not only relevant for linguistic sister fields, particularly historical phonology (see the chapters by Lass 2015, Minkova 2015a and Unger 2015 in the *Oxford Handbook of Historical Phonology*), but can also be of interest from an interdisciplinary perspective, given that historical texts are investigated in other disciplines, including paleography, history, literary studies and cryptography.

In my description of written language, I use the following technical terms: *sign* and *letter* to refer to the basic, visually distinct, individual units in an alphabetic writing system, such as the Roman alphabet letters *a, b, c, d* and the runic signs ᚠ, ᚢ, ᚦ, ᚼ; *graph* (German: *Graphie*) or *graph type* for signs or a combination of signs that map to a phonic unit of a reference variety;[4] and *grapheme* for the combination of a graph and the phonic unit of the historical reference system it represents in a particular spelling system.[5]

12.2 Variation in Orthography

Spelling variation is one of the key characteristics of premodern writing. Various spellings of the same word are common not only in a language of a certain period, for example the spellings *kind, chind, chint, khind, kint, kynt, kindt, kinth* for the lemma *Kind* 'child' in Early New High German,[6] but can also occur in the same text written by the same scribe. While modern written language users are familiar with linguistic variation on the grammatical and the lexical levels, spelling variation is in sharp contrast with most present-day, standardized orthographies. Here, invariability in word spelling and a predefined set of letters and graphs are crucial principles.

In traditional linguistic research, spelling variation in historical texts was perceived and empirically approached through the lens of present-day orthography. It was often classified as chaotic and random and the scribes

[4] The term 'graph' (*Graph* in German; *graf* in Swedish/Norwegian/Danish) is in some studies also used to refer to a concrete realization of letters in real-life documents. Since this level of analysis is not relevant in the discussion of orthography in this chapter, the ambiguity of the term is neglectable here. The term 'graph type' is common in runological and Nordic studies and is used to refer to the runic writing system in this chapter.

[5] These terms are discussed more extensively in Chapter 3, this volume.

[6] *Das Bonner Frühneuhochdeutschkorpus* (2020).

were judged as inconsistent and careless.[7] More recent research has shown, however, that historical orthographic variation is not only an integral part of historical languages, but also follows systematic patterns and has functional uses. Premodern orthographic systems are not standardized and, therefore, there is room for innovation. This is a definitive characteristic and an important precondition for orthographic variation and change. Hence, premodern systems and uses of written communication were very different from present-day orthography. This "otherness" (Mihm 2016) has to be taken into consideration in approaching historical orthographies, and "our job is to develop a hermeneutic that non-anachronistically provides techniques for anything we are likely to come across in past writing" (Lass 2015: 107).

While linguistic variability as an inherent characteristic of all languages is widely investigated on the levels of phonology, morphology, syntax and lexicon, the study of orthographic variability has attracted somewhat less attention. Interest in the structural description and functional explanation of orthographic variation patterns has grown only in the last decades. Consequently, theoretical and methodological aspects of the study of orthographic variation are still subject to ongoing development and refinement. In this section, theoretical and methodological challenges for the study of orthographic variation in historical documents as discussed in recent studies are presented. This discussion is followed by an overview of approaches to different types and functions of orthographic variation using examples from the history of alphabetic German and runic writing.

12.2.1 The Study of Orthographic Variation

Languages vary between different places, social groups, situations, text types and time periods. With regard to orthographic variation, this means that spelling practices can vary from one place to another or from one social group to another. However, *variability* is a relative term. What varies and to what degree is always dependent on the measurement parameters and on the criteria to delimit the investigated material. A first aspect to consider is that orthographic variation patterns may present a completely different picture if they are analyzed in a single text, in various texts written by the same scribe, in texts from a specific region, or in various varieties of a language. For instance, while 15 different graphs for /iː/ were used during the period of Early New High German (Ebert et al. 1993: 53), the scribe Egbertus working

[7] See, for example, von Polenz (2020 [1978]: 100) on Martin Luther's use of double consonants: *Er stand noch auf dem Höhepunkt der Verwilderung im willkürlichen Setzen von überflüssigen Buchstaben* 'He was still at the height of carelessness in the arbitrary use of superfluous letters'. For an overview of statements on spelling variation in older research, see Mihm (2000: 368), Elmentaler (2003: 23).

at the Duisburg chancellery at the beginning of the fifteenth century primarily used only two graphs in a distinct distribution (<ij> for /iː/ in closed syllables, <y> for /iː/ in open syllables; Elmentaler 2003: 249–50, 358). Hence, what seems an extremely wide, perhaps even chaotic range in consideration of a language period can be explained with reference to structural phonological patterns in a particular subsystem. Consequently, research questions and designs within orthography have to consider the range within which variation shall be measured.

Second, measurement parameters have to be clear with respect to what units of the written language are to be analyzed and to what linguistic unit they are mapped. For the analysis of variation and change in the mapping of graphic units to phonic units in alphabet writing, a method that analyzes spelling systems in relation to a reconstructed (etymological) sound reference system has been proven to be most adequate.[8] In practice, this means that for every occurring word in a corpus of investigation, the reconstructed form is elicited from etymological dictionaries (e.g. West Germanic **deupa-* for the token *dyep* 'deep' in a Middle Low German text).[9] Thereafter, the graph inventory of a spelling system is determined with respect to what graphs are used in order to represent the phonic units of the historical reference system. For **deupa – dyep*, these are <d>, <ye> and <p>. Here, <d> for the etymological phonic unit {d}[10] and <p> for {p} can be matched one-for-one between the etymological reconstructed form and the word token, and the Germanic diphthong {eu} is represented by a digraph <ye>. The result of this analysis is a list of graphs and their quantitative occurrences for the respective etymological vowels and consonants. On the basis of this list, the preferences of individual historical scribes, chancelleries or schools can be shown and compared. Following on, the mapping of graphs to the respective etymological phonic units (or sound positions)[11] is analyzed in order to establish graphemes. As a result, structural distributions in the use of graphs come to the fore. With this procedure, it can be determined which sound distinctions a scribe selected to render in their spelling system (e.g. long vowels in open vs. closed syllables). The fact is, however, that even a historical spelling system that shows a fairly consistent mapping of segments to phonic units may nevertheless display

8 Mihm and Elmentaler refined the sound relational method as part of the Duisburg research project on the history of the Low Rhenish language (see Elmentaler 2003: 49–63) on the basis of earlier sound relational studies (Fleischer 1966, 1969, 1970, Glaser 1985). The brief description presented here is based on their research. For a more detailed account of the approach and further examples, see most recently Elmentaler (2018: 234–59) and Palumbo (2020: 99–109) for the transfer of the method to epigraphic runic sources.

9 In cases where the underlying etymological sound cannot be established unequivocally, the spellings are generally excluded from the investigated corpus (Seiler 2014: 95).

10 The etymological phonic units are given in curly brackets.

11 A sound position is a phonic unit of the reference variety in one particular phonological (or graphetic; Seiler 2014: 89) context.

variation in the spelling of morphemes (see Subsection 12.2.6). This is why an approach which takes account only of phonographic patterns might fail to explain some variation and overlooks other potentially relevant variation patterns which rely on bigger linguistic units.

Third, possible factors that may explain the variation patterns have to be evaluated. Variation in spelling is usually explained either by language-external factors that rely on diatopic, diastratic/social, disituative (genre-based), diaphasic, diachronic and aesthetic differences (for brief definitions of these terms, see Chapter 5, this volume; see also Chapter 26 and Chapter 27), or by (internal) linguistic factors such as phonology and ongoing sound changes, graphotactics, morphology and semantic-lexical categories. Generally, it can be said that when a spelling system shows a certain systematic distribution (i.e. correlations with sound patterns or lexemes/morphemes), the variation is likely to be functional. A diffuse distribution of spelling variation, on the other hand, may reveal mistakes that indicate the insecurity or negligence of a scribe. Analysis of possible external factors (e.g. the level of education or mobility of a scribe) depends on the availability of data about the scripting situation and the scribes, which – and this is a general problem in historical sociolinguistics – is not always retrievable.

In addition to these methodological preliminaries, two other principles have proven to be highly relevant for the study of historical orthography. The first is a strict separation of scribes (and typesetters) and a main focus on original written material (see Mihm 2016: 276). This first principle takes account of the significant position in premodern times of individual scribes, whose key role in the choice of orthographic variants has been highlighted (see Subsection 12.2.7). The second principle, instead, tries to limit linguistic influences that stem from copying exemplars and to keep control of possible language-external variables, such as the type of genre or the addressee (see Mihm 2016: 276). However, the second principle excludes a large proportion of early premodern sources, as original, spontaneously written text types were clearly underrepresented in comparison to copies. Furthermore, the copying process and the scribes' agency in this process is an interesting field of study in its own right at the intersection between philology and linguistics (see, e.g., Laing 2004; see also Chapter 21, this volume).

Lastly, absolutely crucial for the investigation of historical orthography is, of course, the work either with original texts (or facsimile editions) or with reliable diplomatic editions that keep original spelling. When working with editions, it is therefore important to check the editing principles that had been applied to a historical text. Especially in older editions, but also in more modern ones with a focus on the text work in a manuscript, spelling variation is sometimes normalized. Such editions are of course not reliable for the investigation of historical orthography.

12.2.2 Phonographic Writing by Means of a Foreign System: Old High German in the Latin Alphabet

Old High German (OHG) serves as an excellent example with which to illustrate the importance of scribal separation in the analysis of orthographic variation. In the scriptualization process of German, as with other vernaculars in Western Europe, the Latin alphabet was adapted as a writing system. This process posed challenges to the OHG scribes who had been schooled in Latin, since various vernacular sounds lacked graphic representation in the Latin alphabet, such as the dental fricatives /θ/ and /ð/ or the results of the High German Consonant Shift, a sound change that took place before AD 700 (e.g. the affricates /pf/, /ts/, /kχ/ or the fricatives /s(s)/, /χ/). OHG scribes had to find creative solutions for the spelling of these sounds. They based their vernacular writing mainly on the sound analysis of their own spoken variety, which is why there is a wide range of regional spelling variation within OHG. Their spelling solutions mainly consist of di- and trigraphs (e.g. <ch> for /χ/, <phf> for /pf/) and the use of so-called 'superfluous' letters (<z> and <k>), that is, letters that were passed down as part of the Latin alphabet although unnecessary for its spelling. Even though the scribes could find inspiration in spellings for Germanic names present in Merovingian Gaul texts (e.g. in the use of *h* in <th>, <dh>, <ch> to indicate fricatives; see Seiler 2014: 211), interwriter spelling variation within the regions shows that the spelling solutions for the aforementioned phonological peculiarities were not straightforward. Vernacular writing by means of the Latin alphabet required a major effort and posed challenges to the scribes. This is illustrated nicely in the metalinguistic reflections on certain spelling problems for German expressed by the scribe Otfrid von Weissenburg, for example the use of letters <k> and <z> for the results of the High German Consonant Shift (see Mattheier 1990) and <uu> for /w/.

However, as Seiler (2014: 211, 218–28) showed, the spelling systems of individual scribes were systematic and highly consistent with respect to their representation of sound positions by distinct graphs. Furthermore, OHG scribes made independent choices regarding which graphemic differences their systems would distinguish and by how many and which graphs this would be performed. As a consequence, OHG is characterized by idiosyncratic orthography and no tendencies toward straightforward borrowing between scribes or larger spelling traditions can be seen in the OHG sources. These two facts corroborate the high literate proficiency and independence of the scribes. In contrast to the practice in OHG, a much stronger tradition of vernacular writing evolved in early Old English (675–850) where three diachronic phases with their respective graphemic 'trends' can be distinguished irrespective of the individual scribe (Seiler 2014: 204–10, 216). In later Old English, from the second half of the ninth century onward, a 'standardized' literary dialect (late West Saxon or Winchester standard) developed and was used also by scribes in other dialect regions.

12.2.3 Over- and Underdetermined Systems: Orthographic 'Design Styles'

Premodern orthography is characterized by idiosyncratic solutions. Not only was this the case in OHG, but studies in the orthography of different German dialects in the early modern period have also shown that both the number and form of the graphs and the number of distinct graphemes varied from scribe to scribe (Moser 1977, Elmentaler 2003, Ravida 2012, Mihm 2016). This indicates on the one hand that there were various options for structuring the phonological units of a certain dialect and mapping them to written units within the same time period (see Ravida 2012: 361, Mihm 2016: 293), and on the other hand that scribes had considerable freedom in their orthographic practice. In Elmentaler's (2003) investigation of the grapheme inventories for vowels used by ten Low German scribes working at the Duisburg city chancellery between 1360 and 1660, for instance, three scribes only differentiate between 7 and 9 vowels, while the other seven make 11–12 distinctions. Hence, the latter group applies a spelling system with a finer degree of sound distinction, whereas the systems of the former group are more abstract with respect to the representation of sounds in writing. The scribes are also responsible for specific structural preferences. For instance, some of the scribes distinguished between long vowels in open and closed syllables (*koep* 'purchase' with digraphic <oe> for /oː/ in a closed syllable and *kopen* 'to buy' with <o> in an open syllable) while others considered qualitative differences between umlaut and nonumlaut vowels (<o> for /o(ː)/ vs. <oe> for /ø(ː)/) more relevant to mark (see also Elmentaler 2018: 261). Most recently, in a more comprehensive study of the spelling systems of 50 Alemannic scribes (1300–1450), Mihm (2016) demonstrated that systems with different levels of graphemic distinctions are dependent of their respective scribes and also existed side by side in one scriptorium at the same time.

Regarding the functions of such a strong tendency toward interindividual orthographic variation, Mihm (2016: 282–83, 287–88, 293) suggests that scribes and schools developed their distinct orthographic styles. In his classification of these styles, Mihm (2016: 288, 293) defines two extreme poles: underdetermined, more abstract systems with fewer graphemic distinctions, which he terms *strenger Orthographiestil* 'strict orthographic style', and overdetermined, more differentiated systems that form a *reicher [Orthographie] stil* 'rich orthographic style'. The definition of these two poles ties in with Lass's (2015: 110) ideas on the function of interwriter variation. The terms he uses are "economical" vs. "prodigal" orthographic "design styles." Both the scribes and the literate community as a whole obviously considered all of these various orthographic practices as being adequate for the expression of communicative meaning (see Elmentaler 2011: 24–25). The coexistence of different orthographic systems was an integral feature of premodern writing culture. Consequently, we can assume that premodern readers were more tolerant of spelling variation and flexible in their reading perception than present-day readers today.

12.2.4 Subphonemic Distinctions in Phonographic Spelling Systems

In premodern German and in runic writing in general, segmental phonological spelling was the main orthographic principle and the scribes' spoken reality was one of the main guiding factors. This could result in the reflection of ongoing sound changes on the subphonemic level. Such tendencies can be studied in a distributional analysis of the use of different graphs for a particular sound position. One of the spelling systems from the Straßburg scriptorium (1330) presented in Mihm's (2016: 295–96) study, for instance, makes use of seven different graphemes (<e>, <eͮ>, <ev̀>, <eͥ>, <y>, <ei>, <ıͨ>) for the etymological sound position {ë} (< Gmc **e*). A distributional analysis in consideration of the phonological context reveals a complementary distribution of the graphs <e> (predominant graph), <ev̀, eͮ> (in open syllables before {b, d}) and <eͥ> (before {g}). Mihm (2016: 295–96) interprets this distribution as a marking of ongoing conditioned sound changes. These results make it clear that historical orthographies can map written units to allophonic (subphonemic) units, a conclusion drawn also in other studies (e.g. Elmentaler 2003: 152–57; see also the runic examples in Subsection 12.3.4 of this chapter).

12.2.5 Innovative Spellings as Orthographic Trends

Innovative spellings do not necessarily need to represent structural patterns based on the spoken variety but may also rely on independent developments in the written language. The complicated entanglement of written and spoken language can create problems for the phonological interpretation of innovative spellings. This has been demonstrated in a recent sound-relational analysis of the medieval Swedish material recorded in runic inscriptions. Palumbo (2020: 228–32) showed that there are regional differences in the representation of front vowels in Western and Eastern Sweden. In inscriptions from Western Sweden, the Old Swedish monophthongized *e* (< Gmc. **ai*, e.g. **stainaz* > *sten* 'stone') and *e* (< ancient Nordic /e/, /eː/) were distinguished by two graphemes, <e> (represented by the graph type ᛂ 'e') and the new grapheme <æ> (with its graph type ᛅ 'æ'), respectively. In Eastern Sweden, on the other hand, only one grapheme, <e> (ᛂ 'e'), was used for both phonic units. Interestingly, in the region of Western Sweden also other spelling innovations concentrate, such as the use of diacritic dots (ᛑ 'd', ᛔ 'p', ᚵ 'g') to distinguish voiced from unvoiced plosives. These innovations spread to Eastern regions but only at a later stage. There are possible cultural explanations for the Western innovations, such as the contact with Danish or Norwegian writing traditions or the rise of Latin literacy in Western clerical hubs. In Eastern

Sweden, by contrast, the earlier Viking writing tradition had been stronger than in the West, and medieval runic spelling remained more conservative. Thus, the finer distinction of the front vowels in Western Sweden could as well have been a consequence of general innovative tendencies toward a more phonemic spelling system, whereas the lack of distinction in Eastern inscriptions relies on traditional spelling. Hence, the divergent orthographic traditions do not necessarily represent regional phonological differences.

Furthermore, phonographic orthographic systems do not map all the sound contrasts that must have been perceivable, and the principle behind a scribe's selection of what phonological entities to represent in writing is often unclear. In his analysis of overdetermined orthographic systems in Early Modern Alemannic, Mihm (2016: 293–94) detects regional patterns that apparently do not originate in the spoken dialect but are characteristic of the written language only. The Alemannic written dialects west of Bodensee (Lake Constance), for instance, lack distinction within the group of palatal vowels {ẹ, ë, ē, ä, ā̈} even though these sounds most probably were pronounced differently, as rimes in West Alemannic texts suggest. East of Bodensee, a distinction of the classes {ẹ, ë, ē} and {ä, ā̈} is common. Against this backdrop, Mihm (2016: 293–94) argues that overdetermined systems are not designed to reflect semantically relevant distinct phonological units, but rather that the written units map phonic entities that must have been salient to a respective scribe. Which characteristics of a phonological entity exactly lead to its being perceived as salient is, however, still an open question. Possible factors might be particularly innovative developments in pronunciation, or important sociolinguistic or regional features (see Mihm 2016: 297–98).

12.2.6 Word-bound Spelling Variation

Orthographic variation not only occurs on the level of graphs but also at word level, such as in the variants *chimt, chůmpt, chůmt, cumpt, kumpt, kumt, kūpt* for third person singular present of 'come' in a copy of the Augsburg 'Stadtbuch' from 1373 written by a single scribe (Glaser 1985: 379). This type of spelling variation in German has been noticed previously in older graphemic studies and classified as lexically bound, free variation (e.g. Glaser 1985: 67). In more recent studies, this kind of variation was linked to the marking of a sophisticated writing style according to the aesthetic principle *variatio delectat* 'variation delights', which is still valid for the lexical level today insofar as variation in vocabulary is stylistically valued, that is, repetition of the same word in a paragraph or even text is avoided (Voeste 2008: 31–38, 2012: 171–72). Hence, word spelling variation can be seen as an intentionally applied stylistic device. According to Voeste (2012: 171), this "striving for diversification functioned as a license or even a pressure to coin and try out new variants."

Two more aspects have been identified with regard to word spelling variation. First, this type of variation might serve to emphasize certain words in a text, indicating that the allographic marking had semantic function. In a text written by the secretary of the city of Duisburg in 1660, for instance, the word *Rat* 'counselor', which often occurs as part of the honorific formula *Ein Ehrsamer Rat*, is spelled in 11 different ways. In this case, it seems likely that the variation is indicative of an intentional choice to emphasize this specific word in order to 'honor' the addressee (Mihm 2000: 383–84). The fact that this kind of variation has been observed particularly in relation to names corroborates this hypothesis. However, further studies are needed to investigate possible patterns in connection with certain word types. Second, even for this type of variation, interwriter distributions can be found. In the Alemannic corpus presented by Mihm (2016: 299–300), for instance, the lexeme *meier* 'trustee' is written in 11 different ways by a scribe of St. Georgen in 1400, whereas another scribe in St. Blasien in 1360 uses only one variant, despite the token occurrence of the lexeme being comparable in the texts of both scribes.

12.2.7 The Crucial Role of the Scribe: Aspects of Inter- and Intra-individual Variation

The scribes, and later the typesetters, were crucial decision-makers in the choice of orthographic variants, and their choices were guided by both linguistic and external factors. From an interindividual perspective, the scribes' orientation toward the spoken reality in segmental phonological spelling (see Subsection 12.2.4) could result in a wide range of regional variation. However, the scribes did not just follow the principle of 'write as you speak'. The orthographic practice was more complicated than that and also other factors influenced the scribes' choices. If the spoken reality had been the single factor, contemporaneous scribes from the same origin presumably would have exploited the same or at least a similar system. Instead, scribes and typesetters developed and employed their own orthographic systems (see Subsections 12.2.2 and 12.2.3) and used that system consistently. Hence, premodern orthography was characterized by a very strong tendency toward idiosyncratic practices from an interindividual perspective, but also by a high systematic consistency on the intraindividual level. This theoretical 'constellation' is exemplified clearly in the spelling variation seen in Nordic personal names that were written down by Upper German scribes in a memorial book of the Reichenau monastery in South West Germany around AD 1000–1200. The name Old Norse *Þorkel/Þorketill*, for instance, occurs 18 times (= tokens) in 10 different spelling variants. These variants appear in separate lists written by 11 different scribes. Only two scribes use the same variant, and the respective scribes consistently employ their variant when the name occurs more than once in the same list (Waldispühl 2018: 141–45). Moreover, the sound-relational analysis of one particular list shows high consistency in the mapping of graphic and phonic units (Waldispühl 2020a: 24–25, 34).

Other factors involved in interindividual spelling variation can be determined from studies where data on single scribes are available and the respective biographies traceable. One such factor studied in earlier research on orthographic variation is mobility. Meissburger's (1965) study on externally educated scribes working in chancelleries in Freiburg, Konstanz, St. Gallen and Basel between the thirteenth and early sixteenth centuries showed that mobile scribes generally adapt their orthography only to particularly salient, regional features at their new place of work and retain their own spelling system wherever possible (Meissburger 1965: 81). Features characteristic for specific chancelleries can be classified as spelling regularities (see, e.g., Müller 1953, Boesch 1946, 1968). They should, however, not be understood as an invariable norm that was passed on within the chancellery, but rather as a local framework of spelling possibilities within which scribes, both local and migrant, could make individual choices (see Moser 1977).

Another factor contributing to interindividual variation is the level of education and experience. Moser's (1977: 229–300) study of seven scribes working at the Maximilian court chancellery between the end of the fifteenth and beginning of the sixteenth century showed that despite every individual having their own spelling system, some scribes had more in common than others. The two scribes whose work shows the greatest deviations are a novice and a scribe who held fast to older spelling traditions. Glaser (1998: 489–90) notes differences in dialect features in her comparison of the spelling systems of the professional scribe Clara Hätzlerin and her less experienced contemporary Sebastian Ilsung, both working in Augsburg in the fifteenth century. While Hätzlerin used a specific, highly consistent orthographic system in her text copies, Ilsung's spellings exhibit more fluctuation in the graphic mapping of phonic units and many features of the local spoken dialect. Hätzlerin, on the other hand, seemed intentionally to avoid local dialect features and was oriented toward specifically written conventions.

Although single scribes tend to use consistent orthographic systems, their spelling could vary intraindividually over time, with respect to communicative situations or functions. The processes by which novice or mobile scribes adapted to a new spelling practice, for instance, is evidence for intraindividual variation over time. Such a process required effort and did not occur suddenly. Consequently, scribes can be seen to use different variants in earlier and later stages of their written production (Kettmann 1967: 305, Moser 1977: 218–22). Moreover, premodern scribes, especially when well educated, were not only multilingual, but also multilectal and disposed over various diasituational written varieties. Moser (1977: 229), for example, found a genre-based spelling variance in the writing of seven scribes at the Maximilian chancellery who employed a graphemically more differentiated spelling system and used a wider variety of abbreviations in letters than in administrative genres. Mihm (2017) discovered similar features in his analysis of the private writing of four sixteenth-century men from Cologne. He showed that the men chose to use local dialectal spellings to express a language of proximity in the informal genre despite their knowledge of the more formal written language. Scribes could furthermore be multiscriptal and use different writing or coding systems, for example cryptographic writing (see, e.g., Nievergelt 2009) or the combination of Roman and runic writing among Anglo-Saxons (see, e.g., Waldispühl 2020b).

12.3 Orthographic Change

This section begins by providing an overview of general tendencies in orthographic change. Two case studies are then presented, the first from the history of alphabetic German and the second from runic writing, that illustrate different structural paths of orthographic development and their triggering factors.

12.3.1 Discontinuous Changes 'from Below' rather than Planned Innovations

Regarding the nature of orthographic change in premodern writing systems, recent studies on medieval and early modern writing have shown three important tendencies. First, developments of German orthographic systems before standardization tendencies emerged proved to be discontinuous and inconsistent rather than linear. Neither the number of different graphs used by single scribes working at the same chancellery nor the range of graphemes in their orthographic systems develop into one particular direction (see Elmentaler 2003, Ravida 2012, Mihm 2016). This fact corroborates the strong and independent position of premodern scribes, who typically did not follow the model of more senior scribes in their chancellery but defined their own orthographic style. Moreover, there are divergent variation patterns and developments in different regions which, on the one hand, reflects the fact that phonographic spelling was the main orthographic principle and hence, scribes generally were oriented toward their pronunciation; on the other hand, it demonstrates the central importance of regional traditions.

Secondly, a certain similarity to the dynamics and complexity of 'natural' language variation and change has been pointed out. Such developments emerge slowly over a long period of time, including a period of overlap between older and innovative variants, and involve processes such as reanalysis (see Subsection 12.3.3) or iconism, in which 'more' in terms of phonological substance relates to 'more' in terms of graphic form, for example marking long vowels by double signs <aa>. Hence, unlike changes in modern, standardized orthographies, premodern orthographic changes usually were not planned innovations brought forth as reforms ‘from above’.

Lastly, and in connection with the aforementioned point, contemporary grammarians had a low impact on the effective practice of the scribes or typesetters. A famous medieval example is the so-called Icelandic *First Grammatical Treatise*, composed around or shortly after 1150 (Benediktsson 1972), which gives a thorough account of how the Latin alphabet can be adapted most accurately to unambiguously map Old Icelandic phonemes, that is, to achieve a 1:1 fit between phonemic segments and graphic symbols (see Raschellà 1994, Huth 2003). However, these guidelines were only partially followed, and this orthographic system cannot be found in other Icelandic medieval manuscripts (see Karlsson 2002). In the history of German, the influence of the grammarians on orthographic practices is also limited. During the emergence of morphological spellings in the sixteenth century (see Subsection 12.3.3) and also later in the development of sentence-internal capitalization, grammarians described the principles, but they did not ‘invent’ them. Rather, they based their rules on the common conventions and spelling practices already in use at the time. In describing these practices, however, they contributed to the shaping and transparency of the underlying principles (Bergmann and Nerius 1998: 963–73, Bergmann 1999: 73–74, Ewald 2004, Moulin 2004).

12.3.2 Strategies in Graph Inventory Change

Regarding the changing graphemic inventories of written languages, eight different strategies can be observed:

(1) *Graphetic modification of sign elements* involves a change in the basic graphic components of written signs and is common in runic writing but not in the history of German written in the Roman alphabet. An example of this strategy is the modification of the older runic character ᚨ ‘a’ (/a(:)/) to ᚩ (/ɔ̃(:)/) and to ᚪ (/a(:)/) in the Old English futhorc as a consequence of phonological changes that altered the original sound value of ᚨ (see Subsection 12.3.4).

(2) The *use of diacritics* for the creation of new graphs occurs frequently in the history of alphabetic German. Graphs with diacritic marks such as <aͤ>, <oͤ>, <uͤ>, etc. became particularly plentiful in the course of the development of the German umlauts in Middle High German and Early New High German. In runic, diacritic dots were introduced during the late Viking Age (shortly before AD 1000) to disambiguate polyfunctional signs, for example to render the distinction between voiced and unvoiced consonants (e.g. ᚴ /k/, ᚵ /g/), or the vowels ᛁ /i(:)/, ᛂ /e(:)/ (see Subsection 12.3.4).

(3) The *invention of completely new signs* is generally rare and does not occur in alphabetic German. An example of an invented sign in the history of runic writing is ᛤ for a velar allophone of Old English /k/ occurring in the seventh century Ruthwell Cross inscription in the Old English futhorc (Waxenberger 2017: 221–22). However, this innovation most probably constitutes a unique creation of a single, creative writer/carver rather than a change with a wider geographical distribution (see Subsection 12.3.4).

(4) In the history of German, the *import of letters from other writing systems* can only rarely be observed, for example in the Old Saxon *Heliand* where the Old English letter *ð* is used for a dental fricative. More famous for this strategy is the import of runic <ƿ> *wynn* and <þ> *thorn* for the typical Germanic sound values /w/ and /θ/ into Old English manuscript writing. In runic writing proper, no such tendencies occurred, but we find inscriptions mixing the runic and the Roman alphabet (see, e.g., Okasha 2018, Källström 2018: 70–74).

(5) In German, the *combination of signs* can be found much more frequently as a strategy to compose new graphs than the previously mentioned strategies of modification, innovation and import of signs. Two, or more rarely three, four or five letters are combined to map single phonic units. In German, especially in the Early New High German period, this strategy is extensively used, as demonstrated by the 139 digraphs (e.g. <aa>, <ch>, <mm>), 53 trigraphs (e.g. <sch>, <cck>), 11 tetragraphs (e.g. <ppfh>, <tsch>) and two pentagraphs (<czsch>, <tzsch>) listed for New High German (Ebert et al. 1993: 49–63, 84–151, see Elmentaler 2018: 71). In contrast, this strategy is not popular in runic writing. To the best of my knowledge, there are no such examples at all.

(6) *Loss.* Letters that lose their function can disappear completely, as for example in the case of the aforementioned imported letter *ð* in Old Saxon. Since the dental fricative developed into a /d/, the previously rendered distinction was superfluous and the letter *d* sufficient. In the history of runic writing, the reduction of the graph inventory from 24 to 16 signs during the early Viking Age was a more complicated, typological change that led from a phonemically determined graphemic system to a more abstract one (see Subsection 12.3.4).

(7) *Reinterpretation of allographs.* Graphic variants of the same grapheme appeared as two distinct graphemes in the history of runic writing. For instance, the so-called long twig ᛅ and short twig ᛆ variants of the grapheme <a> split into two graphemes <æ> (ᛅ) and <a> (ᛆ). Spurkland (2017: 151) refers to this phenomenon as "graphemic split."

(8) Lastly, *recycling of 'superfluous' or previously lost signs* that were transmitted with the alphabet can be observed in the use for new sounds, for example <z> and <k> in German (see Subsection 12.2.2) or the Old English *yew*-rune ᛇ for /ç/, /χ/ (see Subsection 12.3.4).

12.3.3 Development of Orthographic Depth in Historical German

Present-day German orthography is characterized by orthographic depth, that is, spellings with an orientation toward higher linguistic levels (syllable, morpheme, word). Especially important in present-day standardized German is the morphological spelling principle, which entails that cognates and corresponding morphemes in word paradigms are spelled consistently, neglecting possible phonological differences. In *Hand/Hände* 'hand/hands', for example, the final devoicing of /t/ in /hant/ is not expressed in the written form and the umlaut spelling <ä> for /hɛndə/ instead of <e>, which phonographically also would be an option for /ɛ/, makes a morphological connection graphically more transparent. Tendencies toward morphological spelling principles in German develop over the course of the sixteenth century. According to Voeste (2008, see also 2012: 176–77), the change of the distribution of <v> and <u>-spellings for /u/ shows a first step toward a morpheme-based segmentation of words. While before the sixteenth century, <v> was used in the beginning of words (e.g. *vnter* 'under') and <u> within words and in final position (e.g. *herunter* 'downward'), <v> was used even in initial morpheme position in compounds thereafter (i.e. *her+vnter*). Furthermore, the spread of <aͤ> (later <ä>) and <aͤu>- (<äu>)-umlaut spellings for /ɛ/ and /ɔʏ/ in words that had flectional or derivational cognates containing <a> or <au> (e.g. *garten/gaͤrten* 'garden/gardens') marks the rise of morphological spelling in sixteenth-century German. Originally, the spelling <aͤ> had been used in medieval Upper German (i.e. Southern German dialects) to render a secondary umlaut vowel /æ/ (e.g. in <naͤht> 'nights') that was pronounced more openly than the primary umlaut vowel /e/ (see Moser 1929: 27–29, Paul and Klein 2007: 89–90). Thus, the <aͤ>-spelling marked a phonological distinction in these dialects. By the end of the fifteenth century, however, <aͤ>-spellings began to emerge in other geographical areas where such a phonic variant did not exist in the spoken dialects and, at the same time, they declined in Upper German in words without <a>-cognates. Hence, the <aͤ>- as well as the <aͤu>-spellings were reanalyzed as morphological spellings and their occurrence rose significantly during the sixteenth and seventeenth centuries (Ruge 2004: 79, diagram 1). However, this spelling convention emerged slowly as a variant, and both Ruge's (2004) and Voeste's (2007b) studies of printed texts have shown that <e> and <aͤ> coexisted side by side, even in a single text for which a single typesetter was responsible. Hence, this orthographic change was discontinuous and neither planned nor applied generally in premodern texts.

The presence of the morphological umlaut spellings alone does not, however, imply that sixteenth- and seventeenth-century scribes and typesetters were oriented toward a morphological orthographic principle. In fact, other morphological spellings occur more frequently only in the eighteenth century (e.g. *soll, sollt* instead of the earlier *sol, solt* in accordance with the infinitive *sollen*; see Ruge 2004: 181–205), and as long as texts employed word-bound spelling variation (see Subsection 12.2.5), there was no room for the advent of the idea of a fixed-word spelling (Ruge 2004: 33–34). The development of fixed-word spelling, the crucial principle in modern standardized orthographies, is still an unexplored field in the history of German, and empirical studies that could outline the pathway of development and its triggering factors are lacking (see Elmentaler 2018: 285–88). Regarding the linguistic factors involved in the development of morphological spellings, Ruge (2004: 96–99) points out that the morphological principle tended to involve flectional pairs earlier and more intensely than derivational pairs. Furthermore, it affected nouns first, followed by adjectives and verbs. Within the verb paradigm, subjunctive forms were marked with an umlaut spelling (*wåre* 'would be', cognate of *war* 'was') before this was the case for inflected forms of person and number (e.g. *fährst* second person indicative present, *fährt* third person indicative present). Nübling et al. (2017: 255) point out that this process of change reflects the following hierarchies in cognitive processing principles: "nominality" before "verbality," statics before dynamics, and concreteness before abstractness. From a cultural historical perspective, Voeste (2012: 186) emphasizes that the professionalization of writing production with regard to technical, economical and individual aspects, and the rise of literacy in general, had an effect on orthographic development in the sixteenth century. The graphic transparency of the morphological connection between words facilitates the reading process and is interpreted as a consequence of the rise in literacy at that time (see also Baddeley and Voeste 2012a: 8–9). However, morphological spellings also serve the (grammatically educated) writer, as it is easier to produce words when they correspond in form.

12.3.4 Graphemic Change in Runic Writing

In the history of runic writing, two opposite trends can be observed: developments toward more phonological determination on the one hand and toward a more abstract, reductive system on the other hand. While the former developments have been linked to the external factor of a multilingual and multiscriptal, Latin-learned milieu, explanations for the latter trend are based on internal, structural conditions. A case for the shift to a phonologically more determined runic orthography is the development from the common-Germanic elder futhark to new versions in Anglo-Saxon England. On the basis of a sound-relational analysis of the Old English runic corpus, Waxenberger (2017) divides the process of change into three phases. The triggers in the first phase (c. AD 400–600) were phonological changes in the vowel system (e.g. the phonemic split of West Germanic */aː/ into pre-OE /aː/ and /ɔ̃ː/) that led to changes in the graphemic system. New symbols were created by graphic modification (e.g. ᚩ for /ɔ̃(:)/ and ᚪ for /a(:)/), and former signs changed their sound values (e.g. ᚫ from */a(:)/ > /æ(:)/ and ᛟ */o(:)/ > /ø(:)/).

While these changes are evident throughout the Old English runic corpus, the innovations of the second phase (c. AD 650–750) clearly originate in one inscription, the Ruthwell Cross in Northumbria, a wooden cross featuring a devotional Christian poem in Old English. The innovations include a new sign ᛠ for the diphthong /e(:)a/, three completely new creations and a recycled use of an older sign ᛇ to render products of velarization and palatalization. Only the use of ᛠ for /e(:)a/ spread to southern regions, whereas the other innovations were either restricted to the Ruthwell Cross or only influenced a few neighboring inscriptions in the North-West of Northumbria (see also Waxenberger forthcoming). The third and final phase is characterized by the recycling of older runic signs that had become superfluous to distinguish sub-phonemic palatal and velar consonant allophones in different sound positions. Waxenberger (2017: 244) points out that the later innovations clearly "were carried out by learned scholars."

The social embedding of the later Old English innovations in a Latin-based, learned, Christian context is emphasized by Schulte (2015: 97) as a crucial external factor which is absent in the runic developments in the Scandinavian context around AD 600–700. In the North, the runic sign inventory was significantly shortened from 24 to 16 signs (see Figures 12.1 and 12.2) and, as a consequence, a number of graphs mapped to more than one sound value, that is, became polyfunctional (e.g. ᚢ 'u' – /u(:)/, /y(:)/, /o(:)/, /ø(:)/, /w/; ᛏ 't' – /t(:)/, /d(:)/). The outcome clearly is an economical writing system. Additionally, in contrast to the Old English changes in the sign inventory, the innovation strategies in Scandinavia did not include either the creation of completely new or the recycling of superfluous signs, but rather loss of signs and graphic simplification. Schulte (2011, 2015: 101–2) argues that the developments that led to the younger futhark in the North are part of an invisible, structural change based on the writing principle of polyfunctional runes and resulting in "the abandonment of phonemic distinctions and the creation of maximum contrast" (Schulte 2015: 101). Schulte (2011: 57–60) sketches the development as originally being triggered by a phonological change, the umlaut, which led to the polyfunctional use of the rune ᚢ 'u' to render both

ᚠ **f**	ᚢ **u**	ᚦ **þ**	ᚨ **a**	ᚱ **r**	ᚲ **k**	ᚷ **g**	ᚹ **w**
ᚺ **h**	ᚾ **n**	ᛁ **i**	ᛃ **j**	ᛇ **?**	ᛈ **p**	ᛉ **z**	ᛊ **s**
ᛏ **t**	ᛒ **b**	ᛖ **e**	ᛗ **m**	ᛚ **l**	ᛜ **ng**	ᛞ **d**	ᛟ **o**

Figure 12.1 The elder futhark consisting of 24 signs (c. AD 100–700)

ᚠ **f**	ᚢ **u**	ᚦ **þ**	ᚭ **ą**	ᚱ **r**	ᚴ **k**
ᚽ **h**	ᚿ **n**	ᛁ **i**	ᛆ **a**	ᛌ **s**	
ᛐ **t**	ᛓ **b**	ᛙ **m**	ᛚ **l**	ᛧ **R**	

Figure 12.2 Swedish variant of the younger futhorc consisting of 16 signs (c. AD 700–1200)

/u(:)/ and /y(:)/. This polyfunctionality of a single sign would have developed into a writing principle and was analogically transferred to the consonant system, diminishing the distinction between voiced and unvoiced plosives (ᛒ 'b' for both /p/ and /b/, ᛏ 't' for /t/ and /d/, ᚴ 'k' for /k/ and /g/). The exact course of the change and plausible explanations for single developments involved are still lacking within runology. It is, for instance, unclear why certain signs were abandoned while others changed their sound value (Barnes 2012: 54–59). Furthermore, there are no explanations for the diffusion of the changes throughout Scandinavia. A concise, sound-relational analysis of the 'transitional' inscriptions as well as the consideration of geographical and, as far as possible, chronological and other external factors might shed new light on variation patterns and the diffusion of innovative spellings. Such an analysis might also add to the discussion on whether the change occurred gradually as a natural language change or rather constitutes a planned reform 'from above', or a combination of both.

In the 1000s AD, structural changes aiming at differentiating polyfunctional signs emerged in Scandinavian runic writing. This was mainly achieved by adding diacritic dots to render distinctions between, for example, ᚢ 'u' /u/ and ᚤ 'y' /y ~ ø/, ᛁ 'i' /i/ and ᛂ 'e' /e/, ᚴ 'k' /k/ and ᚵ 'g' /g/. The origins of this practice are still obscure even though an emergence in the multiscriptal (runes, Roman alphabet, ogham)[12] and multilingual (Latin, Celtic, English, Scandinavian) context of the British Isles, where at that time there was lively exchange with Denmark and Norway, seems most appealing (Hagland and Page 1998, Schulte 2020). The practice spread to the whole of Scandinavia, but it is worth mentioning that it was not employed consistently; ᚴ could still denote /g/, for instance. Moreover, the dotted characters were integrated only very seldom in so-called 'futhark inscriptions', inscriptions where the runic signs were listed as an inventory in their traditional sequence. This fact suggests that the additional characters were considered to be spelling variants by the carvers (see Spurkland 2017). At the same time, further changes occurred that contributed to a more accurate rendering of phonological distinctions. The use of these spelling innovations is usually linked to the rise of

[12] Ogham is an ancient Celtic writing system used in Ireland and Britain roughly between AD 300 and 900.

Latin literacy and the introduction of the Roman alphabet in the North in the later Viking Age. However, a recent study of Swedish runic inscriptions in Latin (Palumbo 2022) has shown that the "encounter between the Latin and the runic written culture [...] is a multifaceted phenomenon where processes are at work that are more intricate than a simple one-way influence from one tradition to another." Among other sociolinguistic factors, spelling practices rely on different levels of competences among carvers.

12.4 Future Prospects

Two recent systematically executed sound-relational graphemic studies on runes, both of which follow a corpus-oriented approach and take a macro perspective (Waxenberger 2017, Palumbo 2020, see Subsections 12.2.5 and 12.3.4), showed chronological and geographical patterns in spelling variation and identified crucial phonological and cultural factors behind spelling variation and change. Systematic research on orthographic variation and change is, however, still rather sparse. For German, research is moreover confined to micro-studies covering single scribes or smaller groups of scribes and typesetters in certain regions and in certain time periods. On this basis, it is not yet possible to give a more detailed and general picture of spelling variation patterns and diachronic developments of historical orthography, and the explanation for some patterns occurring in micro-studies must remain open due to the lack of comparable data. There is a need for both more micro-level studies for regions and contexts not yet covered in previous research and comparative studies covering larger datasets. The methodological approach in the *Atlas of Late Medieval Written Languages of the Low German 'Altland' and Neighboring Areas* (Peters 2017) might serve as a model for projects covering other regions, or even larger areas. It is based on dated and geographically located original sources, and both synchronic variation and diachronic developments are visualized and thoroughly documented. Furthermore, such systematically collected and presented data on tendencies in orthographic variation and change can serve to date and locate manuscripts (see, e.g., Rutkowska 2016: 186, Seelbach 2016).

Challenges for future research certainly lie in the complexity of the interplay between different factors for spelling variation and the various functions single spellings may perform. This applies especially to large-scale projects that become laborious and time-consuming when factors such as origin, provenance, dating, the scribe or typesetter and their educational and professional background, the possible presence of an exemplar, and other philological factors must be collected and evaluated for every text witness. Moreover, metadata are often not available, especially in epigraphic data such as runic inscriptions, where a scribal separation only can be carried out in rare cases. However, future studies benefit significantly from the availability of a growing number of reliable editions that are also accessible digitally (see, e.g., the collection of historical corpora in the CLARIN ERIC infrastructure and the HistCorp collection presented in Pettersson and Megyesi 2018). Such digital corpora might, in the future, even be applied to reduce the number of mistakes in optical character recognition (OCR) and in handwritten text recognition (HTR)[13] of historical texts where spelling variation still poses problems.

Another way forward in the analysis of orthographic variation and change are digital methods. An example where digital methods are exploited to good effect is Korkiakangas's (2018) study on spelling variation in administrative Latin writing from seventh- to eighth-century Tuscany. Korkiakangas applies the Levenshtein distance (see Levenshtein 1966) whereby the deviation of an actual word spelling from a normalized type is measured automatically (for a thorough discussion of the approach, including its limitations for historical material, see Korkiakangas 2018: 577–81). The computer-assisted correlation analysis is visualized in a series of different diagrams (see also Korkiakangas and Lassila 2018) and has shown both significant interwriter variation throughout the material and a reduction in variation over time. Lastly, the field of historical orthography would profit from more comparative studies on variation and change not only in different vernacular languages (see Baddeley and Voeste 2012b, Seiler 2014, Nowak 2019, Dücker et al. 2020: 86–89) but also taking practices employed for contemporary Latin writing into consideration.

12.5 Conclusion

This chapter has given an overview of current tendencies in the research of variation and change in historical orthography and has outlined relevant methodological considerations for its study. Examples from historical varieties of alphabetic German and runic writing have served to illustrate different types and functions of spelling variation and tendencies in graphemic change. In current research, micro-studies prevail and, to date, only little can be said about larger processes and about similarities and differences of orthographic variation and change in different languages. More research is needed in order to shed light on larger tendencies in variation patterns, on their functions and on the historical development of orthographic practices. Moreover, comparative perspectives including the comparison of orthographies in different vernacular languages and in Latin will likely push forward the understanding of what impact the cultural context had on premodern writing. Future studies in this field will certainly profit from further development of digital historical corpora and digital methods for language analysis.

[13] Optical character recognition (OCR) is the automatic conversion of text in an image into machine-readable text. In handwritten text recognition (HTR), image processing methods converse handwritten text into machine-readable text.

13

What Is Spelling Standardization?

Marco Condorelli

13.1 Introduction

Any piece of writing that seeks to deal with issues related to spelling standardization in a serious way cannot do so without first providing an overview of the meanings behind the term *standardization*. This chapter aims to do just that – to provide an overview of previous thoughts and frameworks for understanding 'standardization', both from a theoretical point of view, and with specific reference to recent preliminary, large-scale work in English spelling. Standardization is normally described as a process that involves several stages and follows some objectively identifiable steps, namely the selection of a norm, characterized by the minimization of variation in form, the extension of the standard to a wide range of functions, also known as elaboration of function, the codification of the forms which emerge as minimally variant, the maintenance of the standard, and the prescription of the standard to the community (Haugen 1966a: 933, 1987: 59, Agha 2003: 231, 2006: 190, Nevalainen and Tieken-Boon van Ostade 2006: 274–86, Milroy and Milroy 2012 [1985a]: 23). The foundational model of description above has been modified a few times, so that the stages of standard development most commonly identified are not necessarily understood as successive, but rather they may overlap with each other or can even be cyclical (Leith 1983: 32, Deumert and Vandenbussche 2003: 4–7). Most recently, the understanding of standardization outlined above was updated by Agha, who sees the set of linguistic norms that come about from the process of standardization as a linguistic repertoire, which can be differentiated within the language as a socially recognized norm and linked with a framework of cultural and societal values (Agha 2003: 231, 2006: 190).

All of the versions of the foundational model above have a shared, relatively straightforward and fundamental understanding of standardization. For

Haugen, a standard combines the two requirements of "minimal variation in form" and "maximal variation in function" (Haugen 1966a: 931). According to Milroy (1992a: 129, 2001: 531), "the process of standardization works by promoting invariance or uniformity in language structure [and] consists of the imposition of uniformity upon a class of objects." For Nevalainen and Tieken-Boon van Ostade, standardization follows two fundamental processes, maximum application, that is *generality*, and minimum variation (i.e. *focusing*; Nevalainen and Tieken-Boon van Ostade 2006: 310). These two conditions are best fulfilled in the spelling system, but they are never likely to be met in full in any given standard or norm. Having mentioned the term *norm* in association with issues of standardization, it seems appropriate to also introduce a definition of the word, not least because some recent work in English spelling (Archer et al. 2015) has made explicit reference to terms like *normalization*. As a model or pattern, a norm is more or less codified, more or less prestigious, and it is an abstraction that emerges in a community, one which may have been formed by an authority for special purposes (Locher and Strässler 2008: 2). According to the *Oxford English Dictionary Online* (Simpson and Proffitt 2000–), a norm is "a value used as a reference standard for purposes of comparison," and, one may infer, *normalization* refers to the imposition of a norm as a reference standard. If the concepts of standard and norm are so closely associated, it is because a norm forms a natural basis for a standard: a linguistic norm can be selected and held up as a reference standard. However, when a linguistic norm is selected as a standard and used as a yardstick, it becomes a prestige norm and is associated with values of correctness, appropriateness and social status (see Bartsch 1985).

The definitions above fit naturally with the understanding of standardization as a set of norms which exist in incipient stages of development and then redevelop to become less likely to vary and easier to predict. In this chapter, the said understanding of standardization represents an inevitable assumption when talking about spelling development, but is not an inescapable requirement. In principle, being in possession of a standard written system with a clear set of rules to be followed is neither a necessary nor a sufficient condition for a language to exist, if we look upon language simply as the property of a speech community with shared norms (Labov 1972a: 27). However, if orthography is a core element in the ideological and symbolic production of societies and languages, there is one fundamental concept that runs through the history of English, which in turn makes this language particularly suited for discussing issues about spelling standardization. Standardization is inseparably bound up with the written language, as it is in this channel that uniformity of structure is most functional and obvious (Haugen 1966a: 929, Samuels 1972: 109, Poussa 1982: 81, Milroy 2000: 14, Schaefer 2006: 4, Lange 2012: 995). The process of standardization, therefore, revolves especially around the act of improving on existing means of written expression, making them more uniform and complete, as well as more logically consistent and predictable (Görlach 1990 [1988]: 14, Cheshire and Milroy 1993: 3). Traditionally, the process of standardization in English spelling has been described as a unified, unidirectional narrative of linguistic development. The unidirectional perspective sees the emergence and dominance of a growing, centralized standard of written English toward which all individual spellings, and the spelling system of English as a whole, gravitate (see Fisher 1996, especially pp. 36–83). The development of a growing standard spelling system in English was generally described as spreading irregularly over the course of two centuries (see, e.g., Scragg 1974: 67, Salmon 1999: 32, Nevalainen and Raumolin-Brunberg 2005: 42, Nevalainen 2012a: 151), and it is for this reason that this chapter focuses mainly on Early Modern English. General evolutionary principles (see, e.g., Hope 2000) also suggest that a complex trait like spelling, in the English language, may have evolved diachronically from simpler precursors.

The evolutionary linearity is imposed on history by a backward projection of present-day standard spelling on Early Modern English spelling, and it can be seen as a legitimate attempt to create a history for the standard language – to imagine a past for it and to determine a canon, in which normative forms are argued for and unorthodox forms rejected (Milroy 1994: 22–23). In a way, historicizing the language becomes a necessary condition for the concept of a standard to coexist with that of a norm, intended as an elevated set of rules to be followed. The most inevitable consequence of concentrating on a unique history of standardization for Early Modern English spelling is that a history of developments in individual graphemes or groups of graphemes, some of which may perhaps have been relatively autonomous from each other and apparently counterintuitive, is made to appear as unidimensional. Such a view of the history of standardization becomes, to use Roger Lass's words (1976: xi), "a single-minded march" toward regularity. In this sense, therefore, the concept of standardization in Early Modern English spelling is dependent on chronological dimensionality and rests on the point of view of the present-day spectator. It is especially within the remits of this point of view that one can talk about spelling standardization as a process of 'evolution' or 'forward-facing development'.

13.2 Synthesis of Competing Tendencies

In contrast to the linear theoretical model of standardization expressed above, a number of scholarly voices across generations have proposed a more complicated scenario, where standardization is the result of a synthesis of competing forms and tendencies. According to this view, standardization is seen as a nodal process which sees stages of development and redevelopment through adaptation and under the pressure of sociohistorical factors (Samuels

1972: 165–70, Görlach 1990 [1988]: 18–24, Wright 1994: 110–13). The advent of historical sociolinguistics has reinforced the idea above, not only uncovering and describing the existence of multiple competing sociolinguistic standards, but also developing a theoretical understanding of linguistic evolution as nonlinear and nonprescriptive (see, e.g., Bakhtin 1981, Bell 2007, Nevalainen and Raumolin-Brunberg 2012, Hernández-Campoy 2015, Nevalainen 2015). For historical sociolinguists, the standardization of English spelling would be the result of a convergence of multiple axes of linguistic change, each initially relatively autonomous from the other. The accumulation of multiple competing iterative processes would be in itself the essence of each axis in the process of historical development toward regularity and predictability. According to this framework, the standardization of English spelling would therefore be best described as a multiple, rather than a unitary process, one that more faithfully describes "the hybrid linguistic nature of Standard English" (Hope 2000: 49). The understanding of standardization as a convergence of multiple axes of linguistic change does not need to reject all internal irregularities as erroneous, but can accommodate them as "structured variation," markers of the process of linguistic selection between competing standards (Milroy 2000: 20–22). In other words, one can imagine the standardization of English spelling as the result of converging and diverging trajectories, a synergy of individual voices composing a polyphonic harmony in a chorus.

The development of structure in spelling, therefore, stems from the development of each individual spelling feature, which in turn comes out of a complex, dynamic and often unpredictable scenario. Among the linguistic elements which participated in defining English as we know it today, the development of spelling in particular is perhaps one of the most convoluted and unpredictable in the history of standardization. If any sensible generalization can be made at this point about spelling developments in English, it would be that spelling standardization as a whole is not something that we can usefully chart in a linear temporal continuum, to avoid oversimplifications and distortions of language history; instead, we can only represent aspects of spelling standardization, which can help us to glean insights into its continuous development. A more sophisticated way to understand the overall patterns of development in English would be to see orthographies within sections of the history of English as *Gleichzeitigkeit der Ungleichzeitigen* (see Burkhard 2002, Schlögl 2013) . This term translates to the 'simultaneity of the nonsimultaneous', and refers to the idea that any historical moment represents a section through the historical continuum, which reveals different time layers featuring phenomena of very different age and duration in continuous (re)development (Koselleck 1979: 132). It is perhaps due to the dynamic nature of the setting in which English develops that the spellings in the sixteenth and the seventeenth centuries in particular are in permanent development. In other words, the two requirements set for a standard language at the beginning of this chapter, maximum application and minimum variation (see Nevalainen and Tieken-Boon van Ostade 2006: 310), are only true for Early Modern English spelling if they are conceived as processes in the making.

The view of spelling standardization as a process that is never fully complete entails the idea that maximum application and minimum variation never reach a complete status, but increase in the degree of *focusing*, a term used by sociolinguists to refer to a high level of agreement in a language community as to what does and what does not constitute 'the language' at a given time (Trudgill 1986: 86). When interpreting patterns of convergence as indicators of standardization in spelling, therefore, standardization itself would be best intended as a matrix of focus rather than of fixity. In other words, individual historical spellers tended to a greater or lesser extent to conform to an idea of standard, but none of the individual texts surviving, or even a specific range of years within the sixteenth and the seventeenth centuries, can ever be said to demonstrate every characteristic of a standard. Thus, the developments toward new graphemic arrangements do not contribute to making a clear-cut set of fixed shibboleths. Instead, they give form to what the nineteenth-century scholar Alexander J. Ellis, who first described it, called a "sort of mean," a kind of fixed magnet of spelling forms toward which printed English tended (Smith 1996: 50). The sort of mean continues to be regionally and chronologically interfered with by the "pluricentric" nature of the English language, "one whose norms are focused in different local centres, capitals, centres of economy, publishing, education and political power" (Romaine 1998: 27). If we want to look upon spelling standardization in English from a large-scale point of view, the term *supralocalization* may come in particularly handy for addressing the conceptual difficulties that stem from a pluricentric language (see also Chapter 21, Chapter 25 and Chapter 30, this volume).

Supralocalization refers to the geographical diffusion of linguistic features beyond their region of origin, and, in this respect, it achieves the chief goal of standardization, to reduce the amount of permissible variation while increasing in focusing (Nevalainen and Tieken-Boon van Ostade 2006: 288). If supralocalization works well as a defining term to describe the spectrum of spelling developments from a large-scale perspective, however, it alone cannot capture the full essence of *spelling standardization*, which stems from all of the complex range of definitions and nuances expressed in the chapter so far as a whole. Spelling developments in Early Modern English in particular developed in a way that blurs many of the distinctions between *focusing*, *supralocalization* and *standardization* and were never a fixed point of reference. For this reason, it would be safer, I suggest, to describe the spelling system of the Early Modern English era (i.e. the period between the sixteenth and the seventeenth century) as a system in the process of *standardizing*. The theoretical challenges existing to date certainly reflect the complexity of the relation between standardization and spelling, but it is not just a theoretical problem. The challenges are also caused by our little knowledge about the complex dynamics behind spelling standardization in English. It is also for this reason that, I believe, more work on large-scale developments in English spelling is needed, especially in and around the Early Modern era. The following sections provide an overview of what we know to date about the dynamics in English spelling immediately prior to and during that era, drawing on some of the most relevant recent work in the field.

13.3 A Standardizing Variety of English

The process of standardization of English was a long and complex one, and saw some fundamental developments before the introduction of printing in England in 1476. In general, the origins of a standardized form of written English have been associated with four varieties of English, identified as Types I–IV, with characteristically focused spelling conventions (see Samuels 1969 [1963], Smith 1996: 70; see also Chapter 21, this volume), three of which were connected with the London area (Samuels 1969 [1963]: 404–18, Nevalainen 2012a: 133–34). Type I was the language of the Wycliffite manuscripts, some features of which appeared in vernacular medical writings from the Central Midlands in the fifteenth century (see Taavitsainen 2000, 2004b). Type II was the language of the documents from the Greater London area produced before 1370, and is "Essex in basis with accretions from Norfolk and Suffolk" (Samuels 1981: 49). Type III was the language of literary manuscripts, for example the earliest manuscripts of Geoffrey Chaucer's *Canterbury Tales*, Thomas Hoccleve's manuscripts and William Langland's *Piers Plowman*, as well as London guild account records. Type IV departed "from a combination of spoken London English and certain Central Midland elements" (Samuels 1969 [1963]: 413–14) to become the language of the Chancery, adopted for writing royal and government documents in 1430. Type IV appeared at least two generations after Type III and was a mixture of features from Type III, with elements from the Central Midlands (Samuels 1969 [1963]: 411–13, Benskin 2004: 2; compare, however, Nevalainen 2012a: 137).

Numerous scholars see the origin of a standardizing form of written English in the Chancery writings stemming from Type IV (Samuels 1969 [1963]: 411, Scragg 1974: 52, Richardson 1980: 728–29, 737, 740, Heikkonen 1996: 115–16, Nevalainen and Tieken-Boon van Ostade 2006: 274–75, Corrie 2012: 145–46, Nevalainen 2012a: 133, 136), and suggest that the 'Chancery standard' was derived from the variety selected by Henry V's Signet Office, then accepted as the Chancery norm. This presumably later developed as the supraregional standard for printers and the language community at large, possibly due to the authority of the Chancery and of the institutional endorsement (see Fisher 1977, 1996). Some of the conventions derived from the Chancery documents include the spellings of the words *not, but, such(e)*, <gh> as a velar sound in *light* and *knight*, <ig> in the word *reign*, and the preference for <d> (rather than <t>) in the past tense and past participle forms of weak verbs (Smith 1996: 68–69, Nevalainen and Tieken-Boon van Ostade 2006: 275–76). The written code adopted by the Chancery spread far and wide not only thanks to the circulation of documents, but also due to the frequent migrations of the clerks who had served their apprenticeships at the Chancery. While the above seems to be a widely shared agreement among most scholars, there are also contrasting voices that reject the claim that a single variety may have formed the basis for a standardized written form of English (see Hope 2000: 50, Benskin 2004: 1–40). Instead, they suggest that an inconveniently wide range of dialects contributed to the modern standard, and that the 'Chancery standard' features a great deal more variation than is generally admitted. More recently, a volume edited by Wright (2020b) has challenged the rather simplified development proposed by the orthodox origin explanations, and has pointed instead to a rather complex scenario where not only was English standardization geographically fragmented, but it was also shaped by nonlinear interactions between dialects, peoples and even foreign languages (e.g. Latin and French).

Regardless of the exact regional origins of the late medieval standardized varieties in England, it is quite clear that London was a linguistic pool from which a standard was emerging for the Early Modern English period (Rutkowska 2013a: 48). The English printing industry echoed the southern variety of English that had emerged by the late fifteenth century in the city, simply because it was there that the printing industry developed the most. Through wide-ranging trilingualism of the literate social ranks and extensive lexical borrowing, then, Latin and French spelling conventions also left their mark on the emerging standardized form of English that was being used in London. In systemic terms, the basic phonemic fit between English spelling and pronunciation, for example, was weakened by the adoption of new digraphs and grapheme/phoneme correspondences (Nevalainen 2012a: 132). Some other conventions that were adopted already from the Middle English period (especially from the 1200s onward) include <ou> corresponding to Middle English /uː/ and replacing the previous <u> in word spellings like *house*, <qu> for earlier <cw> in *queen*, and <o> for earlier <u> in *love*. In the fifteenth century, <ie> was taken over from French to represent Middle English /eː/ and, especially at the beginning, it appeared most frequently in words of French origin (Görlach 1991: 47). From the introduction of printing, London drew artisans and printing house staff from various parts of the country and from abroad, so that the London book business quickly became a melting pot of dialects and foreign languages (Howard-Hill 2006: 19). Contact influence inevitably played a role in shaping the emerging modern standard that was echoed by the introduction of printing, and increased the overall complexity of the variety of spellings used in print.

Among the more recent commentators, Salmon (1999), Nevalainen (2012a) and Rutkowska (2013a) showed evidence for interesting developments in the southern variety of English used in and around London. From the range of examples made available in their work, an increased level of focusing appears to have been in place already from the end of the sixteenth century, when attempts to systematize irregular features such as vowel length and, in some cases, vowel quality are apparent. Vowels could be doubled to mark length, and digraphs began to be used to indicate quality: for example, <ee> was used for /eː/, <oo> for /oː/ and <ea> for /ɛː/, as in *seen, soon* and *sea*. Word-final <e> could similarly indicate the length of the preceding vowel (*made, side, tune*), and consonant doubling a short vowel (*hill*). During the sixteenth century, effort went into keeping homophones apart, and spelling words like *all* and *awl* and *made* and *maid* differently. A third improvement was to regularize the orthography borrowed from medieval French by altering the spellings, so as to reflect their supposed Latin roots. Respellings such as *debt* (< Middle English *dette*; L *dēbitum*), *doubt* (< Middle English *doute(n)*; L *dubitāre*), and *victuals* (< Middle English *vitailes*; L *victuālia*), for example, would have represented preferable forms for those who knew Latin. Some of the most typical and widely known spelling changes that occurred over the seventeenth century, instead, are the distinction between vowels (<i> and <u>) and consonants (<j> and <v>), and the replacement of word-final <ie> with <y>.

Most recently, a couple of studies have expanded on the overview provided so far, providing interesting insights into spelling developments in English from a quantitative, large-scale point of view. Berg and Aronoff (2017), for example, conducted a diachronic investigation of spelling developments in four derivational suffixes, claiming that English spelling "gradually became more consistent over a period of several hundred years, starting before the advent of printers, orthoepists, or dictionary makers, presumably through the simple interaction of the members of the community of spellers, a sort of self-organizing social network" (2017: 37–38). While Berg and Aronoff's claims are interesting, there is another piece of research that has provided, in my view, more compelling details for the large-scale development of Early Modern English spelling. Basu's work (2016) goes beyond the specific case of suffixes, uses some more reliable corpus material, and makes less unorthodox claims about the process of standardization in English spelling.

13.4 Two Waves of Standardization

Basu's quantitative investigation was conducted using an early version of *Early English Books Online: Text Creation Partnership* (EEBO-TCP 2015–ongoing), and identified two major waves of spelling standardization in the Early Modern English era, one running over most of the sixteenth century and another one occurring in the seventeenth century. The work analyzed the cumulative transition periods of individual word tokens to find out whether there was a general time pattern to linguistic change, and showed all new word forms that gained wide acceptance between the two centuries. The results indicated some radical differences between the two waves of development within the first two centuries of English printing, intervaled by periods of relative lull in the rate of orthographic change (Figure 13.1). The first wave of standardization, which occurred around the mid-to-late sixteenth century, appeared to be larger than the second wave, and was correlated with the period where the process of printing matured in England. The rate of words becoming established as standard detected for the end of the sixteenth century was found to be not only higher, that is, featuring a greater number of words, but also broader than the seventeenth-century wave. This pattern was interpreted to indicate that the words which shifted in spelling before and around the mid-sixteenth century were not aberrations, but, according to Basu, part of a broad, expanding set of innovations. The second wave, which occurred around the time of the Civil War, on the other hand, was seen as fitting a traditional expectation of spelling standardization in English, because it appeared as well defined and easily identifiable. The relative broadness of the two frequency waves of standardization also showed that a degree of variation remained over the course of the Early Modern era. The norms that codified as standard resulted from supralocal developments which converged to become standard usages, and formed well-defined waves of development which tended toward standardization as a fluctuating development.

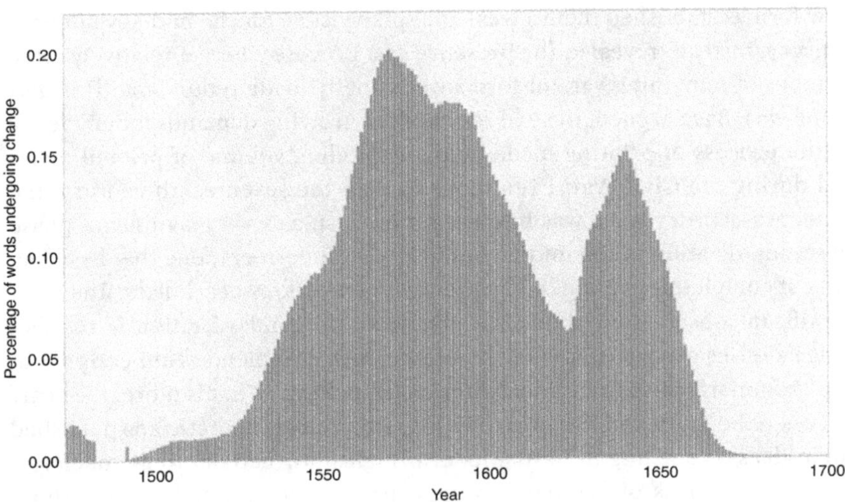

Figure 13.1 Percentage of orthographic forms per year coming into widespread use (from Basu 2016: 194)

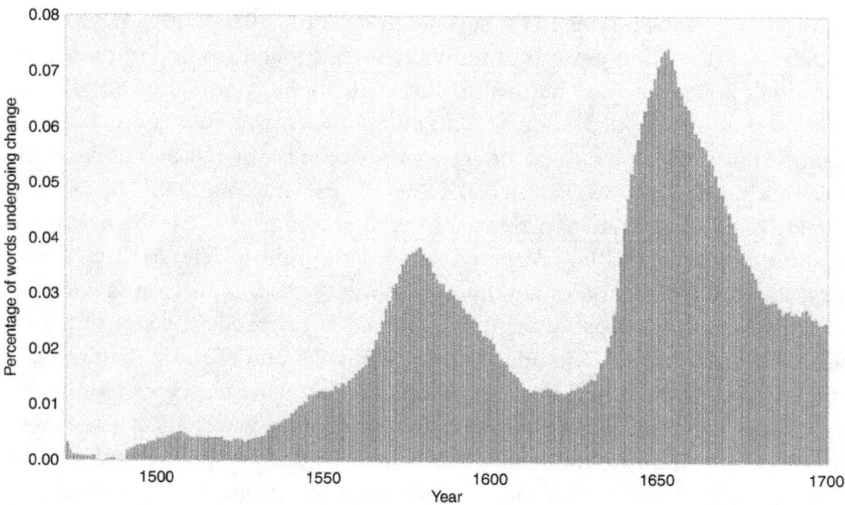

Figure 13.2 Percentage of orthographic forms per year undergoing a rapid decline in usage (from Basu 2016: 194)

A corresponding barplot, drawn as part of the exploratory work in the same study (Figure 13.2), visualized the number of words undergoing a downward transition in a given year – that is to say, it plotted the rates at which orthographic forms fell out of usage. A comparison of the two plots revealed interesting patterns of development, and showed that the rate of decline for these forms lagged slightly behind the rate of acceptance for new forms. Older spellings continued to occur in relatively low numbers, even after the new forms established themselves. The spike visible for the mid-seventeenth century, instead, revealed the presence of a process where a relatively large number of remaining variant forms were finally made redundant. This outcome was, Basu argued, the end result of the growing demands for efficiency in the process of printing made by the exploding volume of printed material during the Civil War. Even more so than the seventeenth century, the sixteenth-century wave was interpreted by Basu as a very significant phase of standardization in the middle of the Early Modern era, one that has been almost completely overlooked by previous generations of scholars. The most significant observation about the first wave of standardization is the fact that its onset predates most of the prescriptive comments from early modern grammarians on the standardization of spelling. What is more, the years between the 1570s and the 1620s, during which most theoreticians published their ideas on spelling in Early Modern English, turned out to be much less unstable in terms of orthography than previously assumed. Unlike those of Berg and Aronoff (2017), Basu's findings appear to be more in line with previous statements made on Early Modern English spelling as a whole. For

Howard-Hill (2006: 16), printing was the cradle of change and development toward standardization. Printers manipulated spelling, and were driven by typographic pressures to serve their own business, responding to the changes which affected the printing industry between the sixteenth and the seventeenth centuries. According to Smith, the introduction of printing in particular was a key "external event" that accelerated the process of standardization and encouraged a debate around linguistic reform (Smith 2012: 174). For Rutkowska (2013a: 62, 167, 252), combined influences from two main sources, theoreticians on the one hand and printers on the other hand, were probably responsible for shaping Early Modern English spelling in a modern direction and for influencing its speed of development. According to Tyrkkö (2013: 151), it has been "commonplace" to attribute the gradual standardization of English spelling in the Early Modern English period to the impact of printing technology.

To return to the model of standardization introduced at the incipit of this chapter, the two waves of development uncovered by Basu alert us to some important qualities of Early Modern English spelling and its process of standardization. First of all, the sixteenth and the seventeenth centuries were already beyond the selection stage: by the end of the Early Modern era, a standardizing form of English had been largely selected and accepted (perhaps by those who used the 'Chancery standard'), but codification, unlike for other European languages (for French, see, e.g., Ayres-Bennett 1994: 53), was still in its infancy. The two centuries over which the Early Modern English era stretches, therefore, can be seen as a continuation of the time of elaboration (see Kloss 1967, 1978, Fishman 2008) which had begun in the Middle English period, and had departed from the London 'standard' (Lange 2012: 1001). While it is generally agreed that elaboration is primarily a lexical process (Milroy and Milroy 2012 [1985a]: 31), it also affected orthography, as spelling was developing to become more predictable and more functional. Despite their tendency to achieve predictability and functionality, however, variant forms are expected to continue to persist as idiosyncrasies. When taken together, both of the individual waves of spelling developments describe a process of standardization in continuous tension, regulated by forces of supralocalization. The process of standardization in Early Modern English, therefore, certainly does not fix all irregularities, but instead allows for some variation in the spelling of English even when one particular orthographic form rises to become, in practical terms, a 'standard'.

A second interesting finding that stems from the results summarized from Basu relates to the overall conceptual understanding of standardization in Early Modern English spelling. The process of orthographic change was phased and discrete, rather than uniform and gradual, and proceeded not from chaos to order, but from coherence to coherence, through reiterative and individual changes. Moreover, standardization was an ongoing, slow development, which never fully completed by the end of the seventeenth century. For this reason, as mentioned earlier on, diachronic spelling developments in Early Modern English, which tend to become a more focused set of norms, should be seen as elements of an *incipient* and *ongoing* process of standardization, rather than complete, stand-alone elements of a standard. In light of the quantitative overview given in recent research, a distinction between *regularization*, seen as a univocal and unidirectional development toward standardization, and *standardization*, seen more as an umbrella term for encompassing multiple stages of regularization, should be retained also in future large-scale work on diachronic spelling development. Without a doubt, the findings made available by Basu from recent, preliminary work on large-scale developments in Early Modern English spelling represent a useful and inspirational point of departure for future work in the field. At the same time, however, much as for Berg and Aronoff's study, there are elements from Basu's work that need to be taken with caution.

In particular, some statements more than others, not least the bold claims about the wholesale influence of the printing press on large-scale spelling developments, need to be corroborated with more substantial linguistic evidence than was made available in Basu's chapter-long work. Previous statements in Basu's study (2016: 183–84), for example, suggest that graphemes form the basic units for the process of standardization in Early Modern English, which means that a more extensive quantitative focus on graphemes is a desideratum in order to glean an understanding of the dynamics involved in the standardization of English spelling. Moreover, the influence of theoreticians, schoolmasters, authors and readers, as well as printers, on the development of English spelling remains, to date, a widely debated, unsettled topic (see Scragg 1974: 52–87, Salmon 1999: 32, Nevalainen and Tieken-Boon van Ostade 2006: 290, Percy 2012: 1008). For Rutkowska (2016: 187; see also Chapter 22, this volume), "the question of the extent to which theoreticians, on the one hand, and printers, on the other, have impacted on the regularization of Early Modern English spelling is likely to remain a chicken-and-egg problem for quite a long time." In my opinion, this is because systematic, large-scale studies are necessary to give more meaningful answers to big questions like the one posed above. Recent work that seeks to fill this gap in an informed way (see, e.g., Condorelli 2020b, 2021a, 2021b, 2022b) needs a compendium of knowledge about the elements mentioned above. To this end, the following section describes the role and relevance of theoreticians, schoolmasters, authors and readers in the Early Modern English era. Another chapter in the present *Handbook* (see Chapter 23, this volume) gives more insights into printing and printers in England.

13.5 A Multiparty Affair

Prescriptivism in the English language is a practice almost as old as the Early Modern English era itself. The first comments concerning the need for a spelling reform in English appeared around the middle of the sixteenth century, as a response to John Cheke's and Thomas Smith's interest in the pronunciation of ancient Greek (Scragg 1974: 59). While Cheke did not explicitly formulate any reform proposals, his translation of fragments of the Gospel of Saint Matthew was an implicit statement in this sense (Dobson 1957, I: 43, Salmon 1999: 20). The most remarkable examples of spellings used by Cheke include the doubling of vocalic spelling and the use of word-final <e> to indicate vowel length (both as separate features and combined). The occasional doubling of consonant graphemes to indicate shortness of the preceding vowel also constituted a relatively regular feature in Cheke's translation (e.g. *Godd*, see Dobson 1957, I: 44). One of the first explicit improvements proposed for English spelling, instead, was occasioned by Thomas Smith, in his Latin treatise published in 1568. Smith's thoughts were echoed in English by John Hart, who was among the most innovative and productive advocates of a new spelling system based on pronunciation. John Hart maintained that it would be "much more easie and readie [...] for the writer and printer" (1955 [1569], fol. 4) to spell English if his suggestions were followed. Hart pointed out that "we should not neede to vse aboue the two thirds or three quarters at most, of the letters which we are nowe constreyned to vse, and to saue the one third, or at least the one quarter, of the paper, ynke, and time which we now spend superfluously in writing and printing" (fol. 5).

Among those that followed Hart, Puttenham (1968 [1589]: 120–21) actively promulgated rules and patterns for spelling the English language and warned his audience against adopting the speech and spelling habits of lower-class, uneducated people and countrymen (Salmon 1999: 17). Even more so than Puttenham, Bullokar was bitterly critical of contemporary usage among the linguistic philosophers. For Bullokar, spelling conventions had become unpredictable because of the absence of rigorous norms which could maintain correct spelling forms. "For lack of true orthography," he said, "our writing in Inglish hath altered in euery age, yea since printing began" (Bullokar 1968 [1580b]: 2). Unlike his predecessors and some of his contemporaries, William Bullokar heralded a line of language theoreticians who were active between the mid-sixteenth century and the early seventeenth century and who were opposed to a radical change of the English spelling system. Bullokar's approach reflected the growing need for control over orthography to allow for intercommunication, in a way that would not override the limitations of technology, while also avoiding complete subversion of the inherited English spelling system.

The complexity of the inconsistencies and variations in the English spelling system encouraged even further attempts at spelling reform, which were fueled by a strong interest in the Classical languages, and appreciation of their structure, literature, as well as fixed orthography (Görlach 1991: 50). Admittedly, even the earliest linguistic theoreticians had acknowledged the power and tenacity of custom as relevant for influencing English spelling. Hart had described custom as "any peoples maner of doings," and had affirmed that he was writing for the "good perswasion of a common commoditie" to those not "obstinate in their custome" (Hart 1569: 3–4). It was Richard Mulcaster, however, who was most receptive to the power and importance of custom, with all its imperfections, as a basis for shaping English spelling: "The vse & custom of our cuntrie, hath alredie chosen a kinde of penning, wherein she hath set down hir relligion, hir lawes, hir priuat and publik dealings" (Mulcaster 1582: N1 v). Mulcaster tended to juxtapose "custom" and "reason" to argue that any prescriptive or reasoned philosophical argument on spelling had to take prevalent scribal and printing practices into account, although he did emphasize writing as the true measure of "custom" compared to the often error-strewn process of printing (see also Chapter 5, this volume, for more discussion on the differences in views between Hart and Mulcaster).

As well as a language theorist, Mulcaster was an experienced schoolmaster, with an interest in designing, codifying and promulgating a system of spelling rules for the use of teachers and, perhaps indirectly, even pupils (Scragg 1974: 62). As evidenced with Mulcaster's example, the relationship between theoreticians and schoolmasters at the end of the sixteenth century was probably a close one. From Mulcaster's time onward, spelling books, grammars and dictionaries became increasingly common in the Early Modern English world, to such an extent that, according to some scholars, their prescriptivist attitude also affected the work of printers. According to Brengelman (1980: 333–34), schoolmasters sought and followed recommendations from early theoreticians, and most of the spelling principles that we use nowadays were in fact the result of a collaboration between the two. A similar idea resonates in Salmon (1999: 32, 34), who maintains that schoolbooks, and especially Mulcaster's *Elementarie*, most likely affected printers, presumably through schooling. Examples of late sixteenth-century and early seventeenth-century schoolbooks which may also have been influential include those by Clement (1587), Coote (1596), Hume (1617), Evans (1621), Brooksbank (1651) and Hodges (1653). For Rutkowska (2013a: 164), instead, lexicographers' practice may have gradually had a role in crystallizing some spelling principles. Key titles for dictionaries and word lists include the work written by Huloet as early as 1552, later republished in a substantially expanded edition by Huloet and Higgins (1572). The earliest English dictionary was written by Cawdrey (1604), a title which was likely later taken as a reference point by Butler (1633), Hodges (1644, 1649, 1653) and Wharton (1654).

If prescriptivism was a growing force, the figure of the author occupied a seemingly restricted, but nonetheless still important place in the thriving culture of the Early Modern English era. During the sixteenth and the seventeenth centuries, the author gradually joined the printer as a player in the story of the printing world, and was perceived as an important component within a broader system that created and distributed writing (Wall 2000: 69). The emerging figure of the professional author in Early Modern English is inevitably bound not only with that of the printer, but also that of the reader. Even before the introduction of printing in England in 1476, writers imagined readers as possessing the authority to change the text, turn a page or move away from a text, and often established a discourse that emphasized these and other modes of readers' participation. Along with recognizing readers' capabilities, authors also acknowledged both the potential and the threat offered by this participation to support or undermine authors' own power. In other words, the attention paid to writerly authority is incomplete without attending to its complement, readerly authority. One cannot understand Early Modern English authors without also taking into account Early Modern English readers, their relations to each other and the meaningful roles played by each party – both through the ways in which authors anticipated readers' participation, and as readers effected it (Blatt 2018: 2).

In practical terms, readers presented the potential for productive partnership with authors through their participatory engagement with texts, even as they concurrently threatened to disrupt the printing schedule. Accordingly, authors in early modern England focused on how readers could help or hinder through participatory reading practices, in order to maintain and develop their own status and engage readers in their projects (Blatt 2018: 9–10). Authors were deeply interested in shaping the practice of readers' corrections, seeking to guide how and what readers responded to before readers ever set pen to parchment. In a way, authors explored what readers might become to them by anticipating readers' enthusiasm for textual participation, and viewed readers as possessing a growing power to contribute in sophisticated ways to the literary language (Blatt 2018: 13, 19). Readers could in turn support or disrupt authors' plans for their texts and, by extension, also those of printers. Additionally, readers could read in ways that supported beneficial interpretations of a text, or not read in a productive way at all, limiting the success of a book. Thus, readers were, in their actions and in their potential, figures whose status provoked the ongoing interest and concern of authors and printers. Both readers and authors in the Early Modern English era, then, were in turn subjected to what Milroy and Milroy (2012 [1985a]: vii) call "the complaint tradition," a culture of tension toward the maintenance of a standardized written language. The surge of prescriptive influences between the sixteenth and the seventeenth centuries was only a prelude to the massive legislation and prescription which occurred during the second half of the eighteenth century (Stein 1994: 5). What Blank (1996: 9) terms "prescriptivism" in the early modern era was "diagnostic in its methods and its aims" and hence, in terms of the framework provided by Haugen (1966a), it can be located before the codification phase. Complaints about English that emerged from the very onset of printing in England often focused on the inadequacy of the vernacular, and did not establish a model to follow. Nevertheless, they still put pressures and expectations on individual authors and readers respectively (see Dobson 1955: 27, Görlach 1999: 475, Brackmann 2012: 56–57, Beal 2016: 309), a matter which takes us back, in a circular way, to the influence of theoreticians and schoolmasters.

Clearly, the context where Early Modern English spelling standardized was one of synergy and contrast between "competing magnets of prestige" (Smith 1996: 65). On the one hand, these parties most likely worked in conjunction with natural, language-internal processes of competition and self-organization (see, e.g., Kroch 1994, Ehala 1996, Rocha 1998, de Boer 2011), and operated in synchrony toward shaping the hybrid features of a more focused variety of English (Hope 2000: 52). On the other hand, if taken individually, each of the external parties identified above acted as impulses or as limiting factors toward regularization and standardization. Each of the parties may in principle have hindered, weakened, slowed down or, on the contrary, reinforced, accelerated or even helped standardization, for reasons existing within the nature of orthography itself. Orthography is a practice which is bound up with other practices to do with literacy, which are themselves embedded in the social, economic, cultural and technological layers of the society where the spelling has grown. For Sebba, "any explanatory account of orthography-as-practice must be sociocultural in nature" (Sebba 2007: 14) and "the practices involving literacy in which a community engages are inevitably related to the type of orthography which will emerge as one of the technologies underpinning those practices" (Sebba 2007: 23–24). These statements somewhat echo those made by scholars like Nevalainen, who has claimed that the standardization of English spelling was in fact "a multi-party affair" among language theoreticians, schoolmasters, authors, readers and printers (Nevalainen 2012a: 156).

13.6 Conclusion

This chapter has introduced readers to the concept of spelling standardization, offering an overview about the *ways* in which spelling standardization occurred, the *agents* behind the modern-like developments in historical spelling, and the *chronology* of the process of development in historical English. The chapter has departed from the idea that historical spelling represents one of the most complex facets of linguistic standardization, and one where disagreements exist about its overall process of development. The contribution has moved on to discuss the idea that standardization in English spelling was, for some scholars, an intralinguistic, spontaneous process of self-organization, and for others a multiparty affair that involved authors, readers, the printing press and linguistic commentators of the time. It is hoped that the present chapter will provide future scholars with useful information for a more informed approach to exploring issues and questions that remain unresolved in English spelling, following, for example, the quantitative steps laid out in Condorelli (2022b). With the experimentation of new tools to approach and understand the study of orthography, some of the existing questions can now be explored in a much more systematic way than before, giving researchers confidence to provide more meaningful answers. While implementing and testing quantitative methods geared specifically for studying something as complex as historical spelling are anything but easy tasks, they undoubtedly offer intriguing and not infrequently surprising insights into patterns that we would not be able to see with the naked eye.

Part IV
Empirical Approaches

14

Studying Epigraphic Writing

Katherine McDonald and Emmanuel Dupraz

14.1 Introduction

In this chapter, we focus on epigraphic writing (i.e. writing on hard materials such as stone, metal and ceramics) in ancient Italy, from around 300 to 50 BC. This material presents a whole host of methodological problems for the study of orthography, but also a wealth of opportunities for gaining insight into the mechanics of these languages and their wider social context. First, the problems. There were multiple steps in the production of epigraphic texts on stone or bronze, and each step (payment, commissioning, drafting, tracing onto the support, incising, painting) might be completed by one or more different people. It becomes difficult, therefore, to know who was in control of the orthography in any individual case. In some cases, the person commissioning the inscription, whose name and personal details may be recorded in the inscription, might have come prepared with a draft, which was faithfully copied; in other cases, his or her instructions might have been much vaguer; in others, the tracing of the text might have been done inexpertly or inaccurately, or the stonecutter might have made changes at a late stage. In yet other cases, such as some curse tablets and types of graffiti, it may be possible to shrink this multistage process down to the actions of one individual, but we can never be certain: many curse tablets, for example, were likely written or drafted by professionals, who themselves carried handbooks of example curses copied from elsewhere to be adapted for their clients (Gager 1992: 4–5, Dickie 2001: 48–49, McDonald 2015: 136). We have to assess each inscription carefully in its own context, looking for any clues as to how it was put together.[1]

We would like to thank Nicholas Zair for reading and commenting on a draft of this chapter, in addition to the two anonymous reviewers.

[1] Some transcription conventions particular to the ancient languages of Italy are used in this chapter. Texts written in the Latin alphabet are transcribed in italics. Texts written in the Etruscan alphabet, or an alphabet

Then there are the practical problems of studying languages with limited data. Small corpora of only a few hundred or a few thousand words limit the number of instances of each spelling, making it harder to find patterns. Damage to stones over the centuries can obscure some of the spelling variation. Dating the texts is also a constant problem. Many texts in ancient languages can only be dated to within a century or two, limiting our recognition of change over time. As a result, this kind of ancient written evidence is sometimes labeled 'bad data', at least from the point of view of traditional sociolinguistics (Labov 1972a: 100). However, these issues can be overcome. There has been a wealth of work on the fragmentary ancient languages of the Iron Age Mediterranean in the last decade or so, including Clackson 2015 (an overview), Dupraz 2012 (on Oscan and Umbrian), McDonald 2015, 2017 (on Oscan), Zair 2016 (on Oscan), Mullen 2013 (on Gaul), Steele 2013b (on Cyprus), Estarán Tolosa 2016 (on the western Mediterranean, including Iberia), Adiego 2006 (on Carian) and Tribulato 2012 (on Sicily), and we have made considerable inroads into establishing a solid methodological basis for understanding these languages and their writing systems (McDonald 2017).

As we discuss below, there often were identifiable spelling norms within communities or regions; interpreting the significance of these spelling norms is the next challenge. Our knowledge of what the ancient Italian education system was like – for professional scribes and inscription writers, for the elite, and for the wider population who had some knowledge of writing – is very limited. As a result, any notion of orthographic 'rules' or 'norms' has to be treated carefully. We know, however, that teaching and learning did occur, and that this involved more than teaching the basics of the alphabet. Some of the orthographic conventions that we see probably came about as spelling 'rules' taught to learners from the earliest stages of their education. Much of this teaching was very informal, but a considerable proportion of it centered on professional training – for scribes, priests and priestesses, craftsmen, stonemasons and other kinds of workers who made use of writing (for an overview of education in Italy at this period, see McDonald 2019). The 'schools' or 'tutors' used by the elite were another way in which orthography was transmitted. Latin, in particular, underwent a process of 'standardization' in the second and first centuries BC (Clackson and Horrocks 2007), and it seems likely, from the remarkable consistency of its orthographic conventions and letter shapes, that Oscan, a neighboring and closely related language, was experiencing a similar crystallization of rules at a similar time.

This does not mean, however, that these rules were as systematic as they are for contemporary languages, nor as fixed and rigid. On the contrary, the

derived from it (e.g. the Oscan and Umbrian alphabets) are transcribed in **bold**. Texts written in the Greek alphabet are transcribed in Greek characters. The following abbreviations for corpora are used in this chapter: AE = *L'Année Épigraphique*; CIL = *Corpus Inscriptionum Latinarum*.

notion of centralized reforms accepted by a wide community in any ancient language, which has sometimes been mooted in twentieth-century scholarship, should probably be given up. We should assume that the orthographic norms attested in the written record of any language in ancient Italy reflect both collectively accepted norms (explicitly taught in some kind of teaching system) and individual variations, preferences and innovations, which may have either become shared by individuals other than their inventor or sunk quickly into oblivion.

It is also important to note that many studies of ancient orthography consider multilingualism closely. This is partly because the ancient world was so profoundly multilingual that many of the slaves, craftsmen and soldiers involved in the creation of inscriptions spoke and wrote in multiple languages, and indeed in multiple alphabets. But also, because our knowledge of fragmentary languages often draws on our more detailed knowledge of languages like Latin and Greek, our best way into the epigraphic evidence in lesser-known languages like Oscan, Umbrian or Venetic is often through the study of contact and exchange.

In sum, the baseline assumptions of academics have changed profoundly in the past twenty years. Writing which was previously deemed incompetent, error-prone or careless is now much more likely to be assumed to be meaningful in some way – whether the writer or copyist was aware of the significance or not. This change of viewpoint has allowed a much deeper understanding of variation and change in ancient orthography. Spellings that look like errors or incompetence may be unconscious borrowings from another language known by the writer, or a particular orthography may have been used deliberately to evoke a specific effect. Nonstandard spelling may be the result of a lack of knowledge, or an experimentation with the orthography, or may show us a snapshot of a wider change in progress. Once the writing system of a particular area became more established, there was still an ongoing process of adaptation and change, in reference to other nearby alphabets, the changing phonology of the language, conscious archaism (or even false archaism) referencing older forms, processes of top-down standardization and so on. Ancient orthography can often be best understood on the micro level of individual inscriptions, taking into account their context, location and linguistic landscape – in other words, we must follow the principle of "informational maximalism" (Janda and Joseph 2003: 37).

14.2 Republican and Early Imperial Latin Orthography: Grammarians and Epigraphy

The surviving evidence of Latin epigraphy spans a millennium; the unique depth and breadth of the Latin corpus means that we have the opportunity to see orthographic fashions come and go. The most famous of these, perhaps, is that of the 'Claudian' letters – new characters invented and promoted by the somewhat scholarly emperor Claudius (ruled AD 41–54), which did not appear to outlive his reign (Suetonius *Life of Claudius* 41.3). More tenacious were the apex (a small stroke or 'accent' above long vowels, apart from <i>) and the i-longa (a taller version of <i>), which can be seen as early as the second century BC, most commonly in official and more expensive inscriptions. A nice example of the apex and i-longa in action is the inscription of in the College of the Augustales in Herculaneum (AE 1979 169; see Figure 14.1); however, they were never used consistently (Gordon 1983: 14, Clackson and Horrocks 2007: 95). We also have literary texts which provide a commentary on Latin spelling rules – advocating for some, and rejecting others. The epigraphic material provides a helpful warning against taking the literary texts too much at face value, as the 'rules' that writers espoused did not always match writing practices on the ground.

One example is the use of double graphemes to represent long vowels, such as <aa> for /aː/, also known as *geminatio vocalium*. This spelling convention is documented in the epigraphic record of Latin between about 140 and 50 BC, mostly in initial syllables, resulting in spellings such as *Maarcus*, *seedes* and *iuus* (Salomies 2015: 172). The earliest example may be *aaram* (CIL I^2 2238, 135/4 BC, Delos). Double <aa> is both the earliest and the most frequently attested

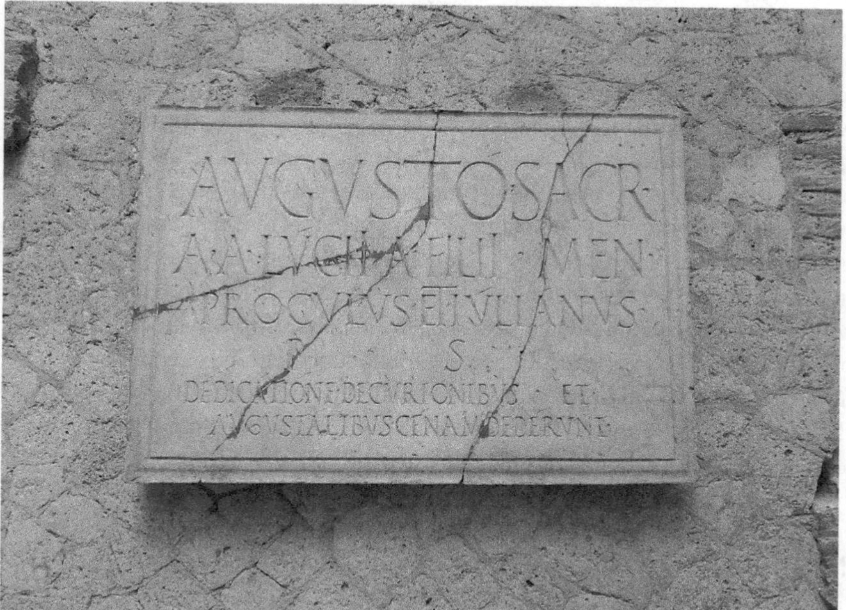

Figure 14.1 Dedication to Augustus, Herculaneum, first century AD
The use of the apex and i-longa is visible multiple times (e.g. the <u> and second <i> of Lucii in the second line).
(AE 1979, 169. Photo: K. McDonald)

double vowel spelling, with <uu> appearing around 117 BC and <ee> not until around 100 BC (Vine 1993: 269). The spelling <oo> is rare, and <ii> particularly rare, though not unknown (Chahoud 2019: 65), probably because of possible confusion with the cursive letter <e>, which was written as two vertical lines (Vine 1993: 272). The double vowel convention probably did not originate in Latin inscriptions, but in Oscan, a closely related language spoken in central and southern Italy, whose speakers (and writers) had been in sustained contact with Latin since the Roman expansion into Italy in the late fourth and early third century BC (Lejeune 1975: 240–42, Vine 1993: 267–86). Double vowels are attested in Oscan much earlier than in Latin, possibly as early as the third century BC (depending on the date of Pallanum 1/Fr 2, which was written some time from c. 300 BC onward; there are many examples from 200 BC onward).[2]

In Oscan, vowel length is only distinguished for stressed vowels, and the word stress falls on the initial syllable (see Meiser 1986: 135–51 for comments on both Umbrian and Oscan); as a result, the writing of long vowels as double is almost always confined to initial syllables. The spelling <aa> is by far the most common double vowel grapheme (about 55 percent of the attested examples). This can be ascribed to the phonology of Oscan vowels: the phonemes /ɛː/ and /ɔː/ do exist, but they are relatively infrequent, due to a proto-historic vowel shift (Meiser 1986: 39–54). As a result, the vowel /aː/ represents by far the most frequent open long vowel in the language. In Latin, in contrast, vowel length is relevant in all word positions; the word stress also does not necessarily fall on the first syllable of polysyllabic forms, because it falls on the penultimate or antepenultimate syllable. Furthermore, /aː/ was not particularly frequent compared to the other long vowels. However, the extant examples of double vowel graphemes used to represent long vowels in Latin inscriptions show exactly the same tendencies as in Oscan: double vowel graphemes are attested mainly in word-initial syllables (or in monosyllabic words), and double <aa> represents more or less half of all the documented examples. To give a few examples:

- Oscan **aasas** ('altars', nominative plural, ImIt Teruentum 34/ST Sa 1, line B 1, Agnone);
- Latin *aara* ('altar', nominative singular, CIL I² 1439, Bouillae);
- Oscan **Staattieís** ('Statius', masculine name, genitive singular, ImIt Abella 3/ST Cm 3, Abella);
- Latin *Staatius* ('Statius', masculine name, nominative singular, CIL I² 1845, Amiternum).

As can be seen from these examples, many words and names are common to both languages (as is understandable in two closely related languages

[2] Oscan inscriptions are numbered according to Crawford's *Imagines Italicae* and Rix's *Sabellische Texte* (Crawford 2011, Rix 2002).

spoken in neighboring areas, and sometimes spoken within the same communities). The shared names in particular, Vine has suggested, may have been the motivation for the cross-over of this orthographic convention (Vine 1993: 279–80, Chahoud 2019: 66). It seems reasonable to suppose that the double spelling of long vowels might have been introduced into Latin by Oscan/Latin bilinguals who were literate in both languages.[3] The new orthographic rule that some writers of Latin seem to have acquired can be expressed as follows: '(optionally) transcribe any long vowel in word-initial syllables and in stressed monosyllabic forms as a double vowel, especially if the vowel is an /aː/'. If we accept this explanation of the origin of this orthographic convention, some writers of Latin ended up following a convention that was (partly) based on the phonology of a non-Latin language. However, the rule also seems to have been subject to reinterpretations within Latin itself. The practice of writing long vowels with a digraph is mentioned by various Roman grammarians, with arguments both for and against the practice. The poet Lucius Accius (c. 170–c. 86 BC) seems to have been in favor, according to Terentius Scaurus:

> Accius wanted the syllables which are long by nature to be written with gemination of the vowel, whereas, otherwise, the fact that a vowel is long or short can be expressed by the addition or the suppression of an apex.
>
> (Dangel 1995, fr. XXI)

The poet Gaius Lucilius (c. 180–c. 102–101 BC), who is characterized as an "assertive voice delivering views on an unprecedented variety of themes" (Chahoud 2019: 46), and who had a special interest in orthography, seems to have rejected this rule, for the following reason:

> First, AA is a long, and A a short syllable: however, we will do the same for both, and, just as we speak, we shall write *pacem* [peace], *placide* [calmly], *Ianum* [Janus], *aridum* [dry], *acetum* [vinegar], as the Greeks do with Ἆρες Ἄρες [two allomorphs of the god-name Ares in the vocative, the first one with long /aː/, the second one with short /a/].
>
> (Lucilius fr. 9, 5, as quoted in Charpin 1991)

Lucilius advocated the use of what he considers a phonetic rule: just "as [the Romans] speak," they should write <a> in all cases. This means that Lucilius does not regard the suprasegmental opposition between short and long vowels as a truly phonetic one. And furthermore, Lucilius reminds his readers that the ancient Greek orthography also uses the same grapheme, alpha, both for short /a/ and for /a(ː)/, even though they have different letters for

[3] It also seems that the practice of writing double vowel graphemes was imported into the orthography of Faliscan, a variety closely related to Latin, under the influence of Latin, and possibly even extended beyond what was normal in Latin to include, for example, the doubling of <oo> (Adams 2007: 102–4, Chahoud 2019: 65).

some vowel sounds, for example, /e(:)/ and /o(:)/. His ancient Greek example (Ἄρες Ἄρες, Homer *Iliad* 5.31) is one also used by his younger ancient Greek contemporary, Dionysius Thrax, which suggests a common stock of examples on which they both drew, and shows how closely Lucilius was aligning himself with ancient Greek rather than 'local' or 'nonurban' orthographic norms (Vine 1993: 286, Chahoud 2019: 61, 65). Interestingly enough, however, it seems that Lucilius was only concerned with the transcription of the vowel /a(:)/ in the first syllable of word forms (Vine 1993: 279–80). As examples, he quotes *pācem, plăcidē, Iānum, āridum, ăcētum*, all of which contain the initial vowel /a/ or /a:/ in a stressed (in most cases) or in an unstressed syllable (*ăcētum*, in which the stressed vowel is /e:/). As we have shown, the doubling of /a:/ in initial syllables was the most common kind of vowel doubling in epigraphy, and this was perhaps partly what Lucilius had in mind.

Were either Accius or Lucilius aware of Oscan spelling conventions, including the double spelling <aa> for /a:/? Lucilius probably knew some Oscan (Charpin 1978: 11, Adams 2003: 120–22); Accius, on the other hand, was born in Pisaurum, an Umbrian-speaking area. Perhaps Lucilius's appeal to Greek models implicitly drew a contrast with some Romans' habit of sharing spelling rules with their Samnite neighbors – which had a very different social and cultural meaning. Of the two systems for marking long vowels, it was the apex which survived longer – Quintilian (c. AD 35–c. AD 100) referred to the double vowels as an obsolete practice (*Institutio oratoria* 1.4.10, also 1.7.14). It is worth remembering that authors' comments on orthographic rules are drawing a contrast between themselves and (a) other 'experts' and (b) the spellings being used among their contemporaries. For example, Quintilian, writing in the first century AD, advocated for a very sparing use of the letter <k>:

> For I think that in fact K should not be used in any words except those which can also be signified by the letter on its own [e.g. K can be used as an abbreviation for Kalendae, the first day of the month]. I mention this because some people believe that K is necessary whenever it is followed by the letter A, even though the letter C exists, which has the same quality in front of every vowel.
> (Quintilian *Institutio oratoria* 1.7.10)

Here, Quintilian explicitly limits the instances where <k> is correct, but he allows that there are other opinions on this matter. To a modern learner of Latin, the letter <k> is limited to a very small number of words – *Kalends, Karthago* and a few others. And Quintilian is right that, for the most part, writers of Latin of his time did not always use <k> before <a> (although this had been the orthographic convention a few hundred years before him). But we can see that what was 'incorrect' to Quintilian was not 'nonstandard' in the literate community more widely. For example, *karissimus/-a* and related words are extremely common words on tombstones, and this spelling is almost as common as *carissimus*.[4] The spelling with <k> may have been preferred by some writers and not others, as can be seen in the Vindolanda tablets, where letters to and from some of the generals and their wives show this spelling (Adams 1995: 119). The 'standard' orthography espoused by Quintilian was not the only possible spelling used even by profession and educated writers. These slight mismatches between the literary testimonia and the epigraphic evidence reminds us that neither 'education' nor 'literacy' were monolithic. A great deal of our evidence for education hinges on the accounts of male authors from a certain class and time period, writing for a particular audience; there were many literate people outside this social class who had their own understanding of what the 'rules' were and, of course, these rules changed considerably over time.

14.3 Oscan Orthography: Regional Communities of Practice

We have already touched on the possible influence of Oscan orthography on Latin orthography. How much do we know about orthographic norms in Oscan itself? Oscan is an unusual example of a fragmentary language in some respects. Firstly, it is written in (at least) three alphabets (Tikkanen 2020). The best-attested are the 'Oscan' or 'National' or 'Central' alphabet, which used the Etruscan alphabet as its direct model, the Greek alphabet (used particularly in Lucania and Bruttium) and the Latin alphabet (used particularly in the areas nearest Rome and in later inscriptions).[5] All of these alphabets were adapted to a greater or lesser extent to write Oscan: for example, Oscan in the Greek alphabet uses a special character for /f/, often in the shape of an <s>. The adaptation of the Greek alphabet to writing Oscan also required the creation of norms for how to write vowels and certain consonant clusters. We explore both of these examples below.

Secondly, Oscan is attested across a particularly wide range of different document types and, as a result, we have evidence of the spellings used by a range of people with different purposes in mind. Surviving inscriptions include legal texts, religious texts, inscriptions commemorating building work, dedications, curse tablets, graffiti, coins and artists' signatures. Thirdly, it is often considered to show an unusually high level of orthographic 'standardization' (Zair 2016: 124–25, Tikkanen 2020). This is not to say that there is no spelling variation – particularly in the texts written in the Greek and Latin alphabets. Several recent studies, including Zair (2016) and McDonald

[4] As a rough-and-ready estimate, the Epigrafik-Datenbank Clauss-Slaby shows 3,618 inscriptions containing *cariss** and 2,429 containing *kariss**.

[5] A small number of inscriptions use the Etruscan alphabet; a few early inscriptions are written in the so-called Nocera alphabet.

(2015), both discussed below, have looked at Oscan orthography and tried to make sense of some of this variation – although some spelling 'rules' have been proposed, the evidence is sparse and needs to be used carefully. All the same, the evidence leads us in some interesting directions, and suggests that even in communities with a great deal of spelling variation, there was probably some sense that 'rules' existed.

Zair (2016: 26–95) has explored the vowel orthography of Oscan in the Greek alphabet. The spelling of vowels presented a problem in all of Oscan's alphabets, because none of the alphabets had a catalogue of signs which mapped directly onto the number of vowels in the language. In the Oscan alphabet, diacritic marks were created c. 300 BC to mitigate this issue. In the Greek alphabet, however, the problem remained: how could a six-vowel system – /i(:)/, /e(:)/, /ɛ(:)/, /a(:)/, /o(:)/, /u(:)/, plus diphthongs – be written using the nine Greek vowel graphemes – <ι>, <ει>, <ε>, <η>, <α>, <ο>, <ω>, <ου>, <υ>?[6] This topic had previously been explored by Lejeune (1970), but considerable new evidence was uncovered in the second half of the twentieth century which invited a new evaluation of the issue. As described by Lejeune, there were two major stages in how vowels were written in Oscan in the Greek alphabet.[7] Lejeune believed in orthographic norms created in centralized scribal schools, the most important of which was centered on the sanctuary of Rossano di Vaglio (Lejeune 1970: 276). This understanding of the education system accounts for the possibility of a widespread and relatively quick spelling reform (as set out in Table 14.1).

Table 14.1 *Lejeune's analysis of vowel orthography in Oscan in the Greek alphabet*

	Stage 1 (up to 300 BC)	Stage 2 (after to 300 BC)	
/i/	ι	ι	
/e/	ε	ει	
/ɛ/	ε	ε	
/ɛi/	ει	ηι	
/a/	α	α	
/a/ in word-final position	ο	ο	
		Nonfinal syllables	Final syllables
/o/	ο	ο	ο, ου, ω
/o/ next to a labial	ο	ω	
/u/	υ	ου	ου, ο, ω
/u/ > /ju/ > /y/	υ	ιυ, υ	
/ou/	ου	ωϝ, ωυ	

[6] In Greek of this period, <ει> and <ου> were digraphs for long vowels, and not diphthongs. The signs <ι>, <α> and <υ> could represent long or short vowels in Greek.

[7] This system has often been used to date inscriptions, but cannot do so reliably.

However, Zair's analysis based on the current evidence has shown that, at the very least, a large minority of the extant inscriptions do not follow the system outlined by Lejeune (Zair 2016: 44). Rather than accepting that these exceptions are the products of other, minor scribal schools, or no scribal schools at all (which is how Lejeune explains spelling variation), Zair puts forward a different proposition. There was, in fact, a great deal more variation in vowel spelling than has previously been supposed, both across the whole time period when these inscriptions were being written, and within individual inscriptions. There was no single 'reform', but a collection of spellings from which writers could choose, most of which were in use from the fourth to the first century BC (as shown in Table 14.2).

This scrutiny of the vowel orthography is not done simply for its own sake – Zair shows in his analysis how a better understanding of the vowel orthography can help us produce better data for understanding Oscan etymology and morphology (Zair 2016: 80–83). It also gives us some insight into the education system, and the kinds of rules that people were (or were not) taught. They were not taught, for example, that spelling variation was to be avoided on principle, apart from perhaps as a matter for individual preference (Zair 2016: 91). However, there are hints at orthographic conventions which were taken up by many writers, such as the use of -ηι for the /εi/ diphthong. Forty-five of 48 instances of the spelling -ηι- occur in either the dative singular -ηι or the genitive singular –ηις,[8] so that it seems that there was a convention of sorts around how to write these particular noun endings. It is very likely that this was influenced by the same spelling found in dative endings in Greek (Zair 2016: 95).

Another recent study is McDonald's work on the writing of consonant clusters in Oscan in the Greek alphabet, in particular on /ps/, written either as <ψ> or <πς>, and /ks/, written either as <ξ> or <κς> (McDonald 2015: 82–93). The Greek letter *psi* is the most common way to spell the cluster

Table 14.2 *Zair's analysis of vowel orthography in Oscan in the Greek alphabet*

	Spelling 1	Spelling 2	Spelling 3
/i/	ι		
/e/	ι	ε	ει
/ε/	ε		
/εi/	ει (perhaps not in use in the first century BC)	ηι	
/a/	α		
/o/	ο	ω	
/u/	ου	ο	υ (only /y/ < *-u- after dental)

[8] The dative case roughly corresponds in meaning to the English prepositions 'to' and 'for', and is mostly commonly used in Oscan inscriptions to mark the indirect object; the genitive case roughly corresponds to English 'of', and is found in Oscan to mark possession or filiation ('son or daughter of').

/ps/, but it is not used consistently. Most notably, all our examples of *psi* are found in names, whether personal names or divine names (e.g. νοψιν, a male name in the accusative,[9] Laos 2/Lu 46, Laos), while our examples of <πϲ> are found in other kinds of words (e.g. (ω)πϲανω 'building (gerundive)', Potentia 1/Lu 5, Rossano di Vaglio). *Xi* follows the same pattern, but is even rarer. On its own, this might not tell us much – there are only a handful of examples of these spellings, and many Oscan inscriptions contain names exclusively, so we do not have enough other kinds of words to make a fair comparison. However, there is a regional pattern in the data. There is a split between names and other words everywhere except Messina, in Sicily, where we have the only nonname instance of a *xi* (μεδδειξ 'magistrate', nominative plural, Messana 4/Me 1) and the only name written with <κϲ> (μαμαρεκϲ, Messana 6, Me 4). Historically, the idea of a difference in orthographic norms between the Oscan speakers of Messina and other speakers using the Greek alphabet is plausible, because the Mamertines who occupied Messina were (supposedly) Oscan-speaking mercenaries hired in Campania, where the Oscan alphabet was used (McDonald 2015: 90–92). Perhaps they had the Oscan alphabet – which has no *psi* or *xi* – partly in mind. The pattern identified here may be due to chance, but it may also be the result of a small community of writers whose orthographic norms came from a different source to others writing in the same alphabet.

There are some mysteries among the apparent orthographic rules of Oscan. For example, although double consonants can be written either double or single in Oscan, in loanwords from Latin and Greek containing /-st-/, the /s/ is almost always written double (Zair 2016: 163–64). Examples include **kvaísstur** < Latin *quaestor*, **passtata** < Greek παστάς 'porch', **perisstul[leís]** < Greek περίστυλον 'colonnade'. Native words containing /st/, however, are written <st>. This may reflect some perceived difference in the quality of the Greek and Latin cluster compared to the sound of the cluster in Oscan. But, strikingly, the doubling of the <s> is not found when the same borrowed words are written in the Greek alphabet – so, for example, we have *quaestor* as κϝαιϲτορ. Zair suggests that perhaps writers in Lucania and Bruttium (using the Greek alphabet) were in close enough contact with the Oscan alphabet to be aware of some orthographic rules (e.g. 'double letters to write geminate consonants are noncompulsory'), but not close enough contact to be aware of more detailed exceptions to the rules, (e.g. 'more-or-less compulsory double writing of <s> for /sst/ in loanwords'; Zair 2016: 164). This example suggests not just that there were regional orthographic conventions, but that we might be able to reconstruct something of how the rules spread from place to place, being adapted, changed and simplified as they went.

[9] The accusative is the case used to mark the direct object of a verb, among other purposes. This example is from a list of names in the accusative, perhaps because a cursing phrase like 'I bind [X, Y, Z]' is implied.

14.4 Umbrian Orthography: Rules in the Iguvine Tables

Let us now discuss orthography in another language of fragmentary attestation: Umbrian, another Italic language closely related to Latin, written in and around Umbria from around the seventh century BC to the first century AD. It is mainly documented in an exceptional document known as the Iguvine Tables, which merits a detailed exploration. The Iguvine Tables are seven tablets made of bronze, on which are engraved the descriptions of six complex state rituals, together with four general regulations of the Atiedian Brotherhood which was in charge of these rituals, in the city-state of Gubbio (*Iguuium*). These texts were engraved at various times from the end of the third century to the beginning of the first century BC. It must be emphasized that they only represent the last stage of a written tradition which had arisen as early as the last decades of the fourth century BC, as well as a lengthy oral tradition (Maggiani and Nardo 2014). Most of the engraved texts contain older sections taken from some earlier version that had been written on a perishable support such as wood or waxed tablets (Rix 1985: 27–34, Dupraz 2011). As a result, the Iguvine Tables document the writing habitus of a restricted community of learned priests, who would have drafted the text to be inscribed. They tell us something about the orthographic norms used by a small number of individuals (elite priests and the craftspeople – who may have been enslaved, freed or freeborn – whom they hired to engrave their inscriptions) in one small city during a time span of about two centuries. We know little about the education of these people, but it probably mirrored the systems of learning to write found elsewhere in Italy: the professional training of both priests and stonecutters created and reproduced local spelling conventions. Our knowledge of Umbrian is so heavily based on this single series of documents that it is very difficult for us to speak of 'Umbrian' writing habits more broadly; however, the Iguvine Tables represent a uniquely long text in an Italic language other than Latin (four times longer than the next longest text, the Oscan Tabula Bantina), and they provide a rich resource for thinking about orthographic norms in a single community (Figure 14.2).

The Iguvine priests used two different writing systems: an Etruscan-based alphabet, usually known as the 'Umbrian' alphabet, and the Latin alphabet. The Umbrian alphabet used in the Tables can be further divided into two variants, in which the inventory of signs is the same although the shapes of some of the letters are different. The alphabets includes two letters unique to Umbrian which we usually transcribe <ř> and <ç>. The Latin alphabet is used on the last two and a half tablets, which were probably written last, around the first century BC. This change in the alphabet should not be explained as a form of decay or a 'forgetting' of the Umbrian alphabet over time; it is more likely to be a process of fitting Umbrian traditions into a changing political and social landscape, in competition first with other Umbrian city-states, and then with

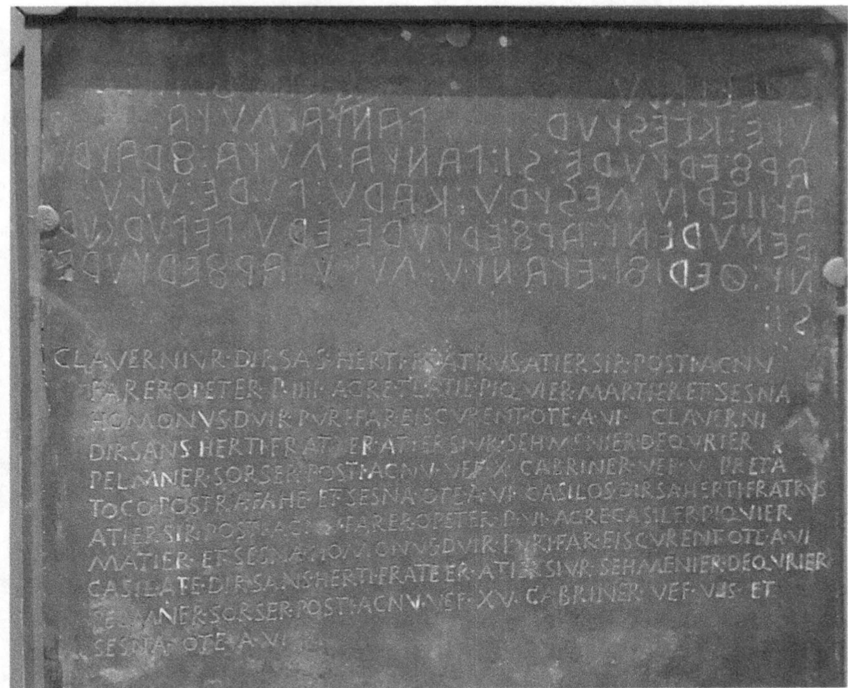

Figure 14.2 Table 5 of the Iguvine Tables, showing the end of the older text (in the Umbrian alphabet) followed by the beginning of the newer text (in the Latin alphabet)
(image: K. McDonald)

Rome (see McDonald and Zair 2017 for similar considerations for the Tabula Bantina). The orthography of the Iguvine Tables respects some general spelling conventions throughout; but these conventions left much room for individual freedom and creative innovation, and there is considerable internal variation in the document in how some phonemes are represented. Meiser, for instance, was able to establish the overall correspondences between phonemes and graphemes. The situation for the front vowels is as shown (Meiser 1986: 27–28, Dupraz 2016) in Table 14.3. The Umbrian language had three

Table 14.3 *Front vowels in Umbrian (simplified presentation)*

Phonemes	Graphemes (Umbrian alphabet)	Graphemes (Latin alphabet)
/iː/	<i>, <ih>	<i>, <ihi>
/i/	<i>	<i>
/eː/	<e>, <i>, <eh>	<e>, <i>, <ei>, <eh>, <ehe>
/e/	<e>, <i>	<e>, <i>, <ei>
/ɛ/	<e>	<e>
/ɛː/	<e>, <eh>	<e>, <ee>, <ehe>

front vowels (i.e. vowels produced with the high point of the tongue close to the front of the mouth).

Vowel length was distinctive only in stressed syllables (as in Oscan, but unlike Latin), and the stress lay on the initial syllable of the word. Specific strategies were optionally available for representing long vowels, and these are only documented in stressed syllables. The main one consisted of the use of the grapheme <h> as a marker of length, often combined, in the texts in the Latin alphabet, with the repetition of the vowel, so that for example /iː/ was written <ihi> (e.g. **persnihmu** 'he should pray', IV 11, 23, 25, alongside **persnimu**, IV 8, 10 and *persnihimu* VIb 17). The transcription of the mid-close vowel /e(ː)/ clearly raised a difficulty: neither the Etruscan alphabet, from which the Umbrian alphabet was adapted, nor the Latin alphabet had three symbols for front vowels. This problem was usually solved by using (arbitrarily) either the grapheme <e> or <i>, combined (in the Latin alphabet) with the marker of length <h> when relevant; however, a digraph <ei> also arose as a specific marker for this mid-close vowel.

This is the usual explanation of the orthography of front vowels in Umbrian, and it is quite correct overall, but it fails to account for the existence of some specific spelling conventions if we turn from the overall level of the whole corpus to analyze some subsets of words. The analysis of the orthographic rules of the Iguvine Tables, started more than one century ago by von Planta, is not yet complete (von Planta 1892). As we shall see, there is considerable methodological value in looking closely at individual forms and lexemes when using this kind of epigraphic evidence. To begin with, there seem to be orthographic rules relating to various morphological forms. The descriptions of rituals are mainly written in a specific mood called *the imperative II*, often known in Latin grammars as the 'future imperative', which means something like 'X should do' or 'X shall do'. The Tables contain hundreds of examples of this morphological form. The imperative II of the verbs of the *-ē-conjugation is almost always transcribed with an <e> in the texts written in the Umbrian alphabets, and with an <i> in the Latin alphabet (von Planta 1892: 1, 95), regardless of the other possibilities offered by the Umbrian orthography as a whole for /e/. See for instance the following examples:

habetutu 'they shall have' (I b 15, Umbrian alphabet);
kařetu 'you shall call' (I b 33, Umbrian alphabet), but *carsitu* (e.g. in VII a 43, Latin alphabet);
habetu 'you shall have' (e.g. in II b 23, 2×, Umbrian alphabet);
uřetu 'you shall lighten' (e.g. in III 12, Umbrian alphabet);
sersitu 'he shall be sitting' (VI b 41, Latin alphabet).

It seems clear that there was a collectively shared norm as to the orthography of the verbal suffix *-ē- in the imperative II, and the writers of the Iguvine

Tables are remarkably consistent in its application. Many questions remain open, of course (for instance, was this rule explicitly taught when learning to write?), but the existence of the convention is clear. A slightly different problem is that of the present active participles of the *-ē-conjugation. In these participles, the verbal suffix is always written with <e>, in both alphabets:

kutef 'being silent' (e.g. in I a 6, Umbrian alphabet);
zeřef 'sitting' (e.g. in I a 25, Umbrian alphabet);
serse 'sitting' (e.g. in VI b 41, 3×, Latin alphabet).

This raises a problem, which is quite often encountered when discussing the orthography of ancient languages, especially in languages of fragmentary attestation: is the spelling with <e> a purely orthographic rule? Or should it be ascribed to a specific phonetic property of the vowel in the suffix? There are reasons to believe that in the specific context of the present active participles, a prehistoric conditioned treatment known as Osthoff's law[10] shortened the etymologically long *-ē- to *-e-, which, following a vowel shift, became /ɛ/. This /ɛ/ vowel is always transcribed as <e> in Umbrian (Untermann 2000, see: **kutef**, Fortson and Weiss 2019: 639). On the other hand, as we have seen, <e> is also one of the usual notations for /e/ (< unstressed *-ē- after the vocalic shift), alongside <i> and <ei>.[11] So the quality of the vowel in this ending is somewhat in question.

The fact that in the texts written in the Latin alphabet the imperative II has always <i> (e.g. *sersitu* in VI b 41), whereas the present active participle has always <e> (e.g. *serse*, the participle of the same lexeme) seems to imply that a phonetic difference was felt between the two vowel qualities. It is to be assumed, therefore, that the scribes using the Umbrian alphabet did not want to devise a contrastive orthography (since they used <e> both for the imperative II and for the present active participle), and that this was a new spelling convention created by later priests who used the Latin alphabet.

[10] Osthoff's law: shortening of originally long vowels before sonorants in closed syllables, in this case, before the participial suffix *-*nt*-.

[11] The validity and dating of Osthoff's law in Italic are controversial. Therefore, at least two quite different interpretations of the spelling with in all these participial forms deserve consideration: (1) either the systematic use of reflects the fact that, synchronically, these participial forms contain the phoneme /ɛ/, which must be transcribed with <e> in Umbrian; this analysis presupposes that Osthoff's shortening did take place at some period in the prehistory of Umbrian (*-ē + nt- > *-e + nt- > /ɛ/); or (2) the systematic use of <e> is the effect of a specific orthographic norm which governs the transcription of the verbal suffix *-ē- in the participial forms, that is, it is the effect of an orthographic rule at a morphological level. In that case, the scribes have decided, for some reason, to generalize the use of the grapheme <e> and to avoid the variants <i> and <ei>, when transcribing the phoneme /e/ in the present active participles of the *-ē-conjugation. Should this hypothesis be correct, there would be no need to accept the validity of Osthoff's law in Umbrian (unstressed *-ē- + -nt- yields /e/ without Osthoff's shortening; this phoneme is always written with <e> in this particular morphological category, although other spellings are available). A third theoretical possibility is that Osthoff's law took place after the Umbrian vowel shift, resulting in a short /e/ in the participle before the shortening of the noninitial vowels, but this would probably be indistinguishable in the spelling (personal communication from Nicholas Zair).

In Umbrian, spelling conventions also existed at the lexical level – that is, there were spellings which stayed consistent across different attestations of the same word. It is probably significant, for instance, that the lexeme *frite* 'trust', which is unfortunately only attested in texts written in the Latin alphabet, is always transcribed with an <i> in the first syllable, although it contains a stressed *-ē- > /eː/, which may in principle appear as <e>, <i> or <ei>, or even as <eh> or <ehe>. This noun is attested in two different texts (the long version of the description of the *piaculum* ritual, VI a 1–VI b 47, 4×, and the long version of the *lustratio* ritual, VI b 48–VII a 54, 4×). Therefore, its uniform spelling is probably not to be interpreted as the choice of a single priest or scribe, but as a wider spelling convention.

The apparent variation in spelling when examining the corpus as a whole is often the effect of the existence of multiple smaller-scale norms, variously followed by different individuals. One example of this is the orthography of the demonstrative stem *eks- attested in the long version of the *lustratio* ritual.

Umbrian has a proximal demonstrative stem *eks- > /ɛss-/, which is almost always written as <es->. It seems that the vowel /ɛ/ was phonetically raised to /e/ before several consonant clusters, among which *-ks- > /ss/, when these were followed by a front vowel; this raising probably took place in some of the case forms of *eks-, but not in all (Meiser 1986: 110, Dupraz 2012: 84). However, the raising is not, in general, taken into account in the orthography of this demonstrative. The choice not to transcribe the phonetic opposition between stem vowels with and without raising should be interpreted as a lexical orthographic norm. On the one hand, the raising is almost never transcribed as such in the inflectional forms of this demonstrative (though it is not clear how all these forms were pronounced). On the other hand, however, it is always transcribed in the adverbs derived from the demonstrative stem, even in those in which the following vowel is not a front vowel (e.g. **isunt** 'in that same way', in which <i> represents /e/ (Dupraz 2012: 78–81, 84). This means that in this family of words a lexical orthographic rule has developed which does not reflect the original phonetic properties of the words in question.

There are only two exceptions to this lexical rule. The long version of the *lustratio* contains six examples of the dative-ablative plural of the stem *eks-.[12] In that case form, the stem is followed by the front vowel /e/ (ending /-er/ < *-oys or similar). Four of the six forms show the expected orthography *esir* (VII a 10, VII a 18, VII a 26, VII a 32); the last two, however, have *isir* (VII a 21, VII a 34). The four regular forms appear in two parallel long texts of prayer (VII a 9–VII a 20; VII a 25–VII a 34): the same prayer formula is quoted both in VII a 10 and in VII a 26; another formula is attested both in VII a 18 and in

12 The dative is the case roughly corresponding in meaning to the English prepositions 'to' and 'for'; the ablative is the case roughly corresponding in meaning to the English prepositions 'by', 'with' and 'from', among other uses. The dative and ablative are identical in form in the plural.

VII a 32. The context of the two irregular forms is significant: they appear in two short prayers following respectively the first and the second long prayer (VII a 21–VII a 23; VII a 34–VII a 36); in both these short prayers the form *isir* appears in the very same formula. It is unlikely to be a coincidence that the spelling <is> for the demonstrative stem *eks- appears only in these two parallel complementary prayers and nowhere else in the Iguvine Tables. We may speculate, for example, that the short complementary prayers were added by a different scribe who did not know or did not accept the convention that all forms of the demonstrative *eks-, regardless of their (original) pronunciation, were written with <es>. These kinds of micro-level examples help us to build up the complex history of how the prayers were copied and recopied, before making it into the version we see today.

In many cases, of course, the variation in orthographic practices happens not within a single text, but between different texts drafted and copied by different individuals – and so, we find some examples where a particular orthography is used consistently within one section of the Tables but contrasts with the orthography of another section. It is probably significant, for instance, that the ending of the first singular present active indicative of the *-ā-conjugation, which is attested both in the long version of the *piaculum* and in the long version of the *lustratio*, is written with <-au> in the *piaculum* (15×) and with <-auu> in the *lustratio* (8×). This ending may have been pronounced /a^{w}u/ with an intervocalic glide. The scribe in charge of the engraving of the long version of the *lustratio* seems to have tried to transcribe the glide, in contrast to his colleague; unfortunately this ending is not attested in the other sections of the text.

Finally, language contact must always be taken into account when investigating the orthographic norms in a corpus like that of the Iguvine Tables. To return to an orthographic convention we have already discussed: the double spelling of long vowels is attested in Umbrian as well as in Latin and Oscan as a specific marker of length, but only in seven word forms (Dupraz 2016: 18–21):

frateer ('brothers', nominative plural masculine, V b 16);
eest ('he will go', future indicative third singular, VI a 2);
ooserclom- ('watching tower (?)', accusative singular neuter, VI a 12);
meersta ('correct, righteous', accusative singular feminine, VI a 17);
eesona ('divine', accusative plural feminine, VI a 18);
eetu ('thou shalt go/he shall go', imperative II, VI b 54);
feetu ('he shall do', imperative II, VII a 41).

These forms appear in three of the four texts written in the Latin alphabet: the general regulation V b 8–V b 18, the long version of the *piaculum*, and the long version of the *lustratio*. These four texts date from the end of the second century and the beginning of the first century BC. It has been suggested that the Umbrian double vowel graphemes are an effect of language contact, probably with Latin, which at that period was beginning to become the prestige language in the whole peninsula (Prosdocimi 1984: 154–60). This argument is disputable. The extant documentation, however scanty, does not present the same pattern as in Latin (and in Oscan). Of the seven forms showing double vowels, six contain the digraph <ee>, and the last one has <oo>. The word *frateer* has its double vowel in a noninitial syllable. This is not what would be expected if the writers had taken on the Latin pattern for double vowels, which shows an overall predominance of <aa> in initial syllables. The phoneme /aː/ is fairly common in Umbrian, among others in word-initial syllables, and it is never written with <aa>.

While it may safely be assumed that the principle of doubling vowel graphemes did arise in contact with Latin (and perhaps also with Oscan), it seems that double vowels were used in Umbrian in a particular context. In fact, this spelling functions as a variant of a local orthographic convention unconnected to Latin and Oscan double vowels: the digraph |ee| is an allograph of the digraph <ei>, which is used in the later Iguvine Tables to transcribe the phonemes /e/ and /eː/. Both the digraph <ei> and the much rarer double vowel graphemes are mainly attested in forms in which the vowel (whether etymologically short or long) was originally followed by a consonant at the coda of the syllable, but where this consonant has undergone lenition and has been lost or weakened from a stop to a semivowel. This lost consonant may still have been pronounced as a semivowel yod, at least in the more formal registers.[13]

Therefore, even in languages of fragmentary attestation, the written tradition of which is often considered the worst possible 'bad data', language contact should not be regarded as the entire explanation for all orthographic changes, since orthography always presupposes an effort, however unconscious, to transcribe the specific properties of the language being used. In the present case, several of the Iguvine priests seem to have devised a new orthographic norm, perhaps taking the cue from their knowledge of a rule attested in contemporary Latin and Oscan, but adapting it carefully to the needs of their own language.

14.5 Venetic Orthography and Punctuation: Becoming Roman

To finish, we would like to briefly highlight punctuation as a part of orthography, and to emphasize the cultural meaning which can sometimes be tied up with orthography. In some languages, punctuation conventions are just

[13] For example, *feetu* is a variant of *feitu* and *fetu* < **feχtu*. The double and the digraph <ee> in such forms represent *-e- + spirant, where the spirant has been weakened, perhaps lost by some speakers but realized as a semivowel by others. The digraph also arose in other contexts such as the secondary lengthening in *meersta*, *frateer*. A similar orthographic rule may lie behind the exceptional spelling *ooserclom*, since here <oo> transcribes the vowel *o- + a weakened consonant. See Dupraz (2016: 9).

as important as spelling conventions, and can take on considerable significance for the writers. A key example is Venetic, a language of northeastern Italy attested from around the sixth to the first century BC; it is probably related to the other Italic languages such as Latin, Oscan and Umbrian, but may form a separate branch of the Italic language family. The most notable feature of the Venetic orthographic system is not its spelling but its punctuation. In the Venetic system of punctuation, any syllable which consists of consonant + vowel is left unmarked. However, any syllables which end in a consonant, diphthongs, or syllables which consist only of a vowel, are marked by placing dots or short lines around the letter which causes the syllable not to conform to the CV structure. For example: **.e.go vhu.k.s.siia.i. vo.l.tiio.m.mnina.i.** (Es 2, funerary inscription on stone, 475–350 BC, Pellegrini and Prosdocimi 1967: 54–56). This system was borrowed from an Etruscan punctuation system around the fifth century and then maintained until the first century BC, far outliving its use in Etruscan (Prosdocimi 1983: 79–84, Wachter 1986: 111–12, Bonfante and Bonfante 2002: 56). One of the most interesting phases in Venetic epigraphy is the period around the first century BC in which the Latin alphabet starts to be used, but the Venetic punctuation is still maintained in a few inscriptions (not always in accordance with the original rules). So, for example, an older urn reads, in the Venetic alphabet:

va.n.te.i. vho.u.go.n.tio.i. .e.go

'For Vants Fougontios I (am)'

Es 79, Este (Pellegrini and Prosdocimi 1967: 197)

But one of the more recent examples, which uses the Latin alphabet, reads:

frema. .i.uantina. .ktulistoi uesces

'Frema Iuantina for Ktulistos (as his) foster-child'

Es 104, Este (Pellegrini and Prosdocimi 1967: 222)

There is some recognition, even after the change to the Latin alphabet, that there 'should' be punctuation, and that sometimes it should be word-internal, but the clusters and diphthongs have not been marked as they would have been under the earlier rules. The initial <i-> has been marked, so there is perhaps some remaining understanding that initial vowels needed punctuation. Were there new orthographic rules in play that we have not yet understood? Or, as seems more likely, was the visual appearance of the orthography the main thing that was important to these writers? It is relevant that we see this orthographic archaism mainly on the inscriptions on funerary urns, which were buried in family groups of multiple generations. Each time a new family member was cremated and buried, the grave would be opened and the older urns would be visible once again. This perhaps influenced the orthography names on the new urns – the writers wanted their orthography to fit with the visual language which tied the family urns together.

14.6 Conclusion

We selected the case studies of ancient Italian epigraphy in this chapter to highlight just a few of the methodological issues that arise when studying ancient orthography, and some of the recent approaches taken by scholars to understand the orthography used by writers of this languages. As we have seen, although we are dealing with languages without a written 'standard language' (or, perhaps, languages in the very earliest stages of developing such a standard), we can still speak of spelling conventions and orthographic norms. These norms arose within communities or groups of writers, but were flexible and mutable – they were also subject to faster change over time than in a truly 'standardized' written language. Nevertheless, it seems likely that writers of many of these languages could have articulated some of the 'rules' they had been taught, if asked to do so, in greater or lesser detail.

When we investigate Latin orthography, we have both literary accounts and epigraphic evidence to guide us. These are frequently complementary, as literary authors are typically setting their own opinions up in contrast to the spellings used by the wider literate community. In more fragmentary languages, contact with Latin or Greek can be a way into the evidence, but frequently we have to take the texts on their own merits. As we have seen from the Umbrian examples in particular, sometimes the key is to work at levels other than the level of the entire corpus – we need to go text by text, lexeme by lexeme, or verb form by verb form, to uncover the orthographic conventions behind the apparently endless variation. Oscan, with its three alphabets, gives us a particularly striking case study of regionalism in orthographic practices across one language. And in both our Oscan and Venetic case studies, we have seen how there can be an awareness of orthographic 'rules', which may even have cultural meaning attached to them, without these rules being executed identically by all writers. Overall, like many other scholars working today, we advocate for an approach which prioritizes both textual detail and social context. In this way, we believe that it is possible to overcome the methodological issues of epigraphic texts to yield new information about ancient orthography.

15

Materiality of Writing

Giedrius Subačius

15.1 Introduction

Historically, orthography has always been dependent on the materiality (physicality) of writing tools and surfaces. In the development of orthographies, the perception of *durability* and *ephemerality* has been a significant factor as well: in certain cases, hopes for permanence as opposed to temporality encouraged orthographic differences in written (printed) texts. In ancient Rome, for example, capital letters carved in stone were more durable than the minuscules used on wax tablets. After the invention of movable type printing in fifteenth-century Europe, manuscripts became more ephemeral than printed texts. For instance, newspapers printed in Lithuania at the end of the nineteenth century were considered more perishable than printed books. The *materiality* of the printing milieu was one of the main reasons for the symmetry of the majuscules and minuscules in orthographies based on Latin script and for the absence of most of the abbreviations that are characteristic of medieval manuscripts. Constrained by the space available within printers' type cases, the number of typefaces would have been limited, which may have impacted the development of certain orthographies and may have constrained the abundance of diacritic marks. The *direct* materiality of a sheet of paper also may have influenced the presence of hyphens and abbreviations, and in certain cases, the choice of graphemes.

This chapter focuses on the *materiality* of orthography as approached from the perspective of such research fields as paleography, codicology and orthography. *Materiality* as a *physical* condition or reason for spelling transformations and variation is considered as either restrictive or encouraging physical reality for an applied orthography. The chapter then discusses the way the imaginary *durability* or *ephemerality* of the composed text might influence the orthographic approach (minuscules vs. majuscules, double parallel orthographies, and manuscripts vs. prints). *Symmetricity* of capital and non-capital graphemes in Latin script is approached as a result of the materiality of printers' work conditions. The chapter also discusses how manuscript orthographies might have been shaped after the imagined collections of types present in local printing shops, and how specificity of the writing material might have impacted certain orthographic peculiarities.

This chapter deals primarily with the European orthographic tradition and, within it, with some features of Lithuanian orthography, as history of Lithuanian orthography is my major area of expertise.

15.2 Paleography

15.2.1 Scope

In Europe, paleography was introduced in the seventeenth century by Jean Mabillon, who sought to identify the date at which a manuscript was created from the handwriting used to create it. Mabillon worked with the Latin manuscripts, and Latin remains very much a focus for paleographic research. Today, however, any old manuscript (e.g. Armenian, Egyptian, Chinese) falls within the scope of paleography. Paleographers read old manuscripts. Perception of orthographic nuances was always the key to deciphering ancient texts. By the middle of the twentieth century, codicology had branched out of paleography, developing into a separate science of manuscript books (codices). In a sense, paleography remained a 'bare' philological science, devoid of additional manuscript information, which was taken over by codicology. Orthography remains one of the foci of paleography, while codicology aims at other aspects of manuscript origination. Still, codicology may be aided by the orthography, especially in dating manuscripts and supplying more accurate judgments about the locations in which manuscripts might have been created. Orthography is not an object or a tool of codicology, but codicologists may exploit the results of orthographic research.

Paleography and codicology are often paired, and their proximity may be seen in books and in book chapters of the edited volume titled *Problemy paleografii i kodikologii v SSSR* (Li͡ublinskai͡a 1974), *The Makings of the Medieval Hebrew Book: Studies in Palaeography and Codicology* (Beit-Arie 1993), 'Paleography and codicology' (Mathisen 2008), 'Paleography and codicology: Bibliothèque Nationale de France, Arabe 328a' (Powers 2009), 'Palaeography, codicology and language' (Rambaran-Olm 2014) and, of course, the *Cambridge Studies in Palaeography and Codicology* series. The older of the two terms is *paleography* (from Greek παλαιός, 'old', and γράφειν 'to write'). The Merriam-Webster dictionary gives it a second meaning of "an ancient or antiquated manner of writing," which dates from

1749. Today, paleography is defined as a science whose focus is "the study of ancient or antiquated writings and inscriptions: the deciphering and interpretation of historical writing systems and manuscripts." *Encyclopaedia Britannica* defines it simply as the "study of ancient and medieval handwriting." Two salient attributes emerge from these definitions: age (old, ancient, medieval) and type of human activity (writing or handwriting). In short, paleography, the original meaning of which was old writing, today refers to the study of old writing.

The publication in 1681 of *De re diplomatica* (in Latin) by Mabillon, a French Benedictine monk (Mabillon 1681b, Boyle 1984: 12–13, Aris 1995: 417, Mathisen 2008: 140), is considered to mark the beginning of Latin paleography. Mabillon's purpose was to "[establish] the age of Latin manuscripts based on their handwriting and other internal considerations" (Mathisen 2008: 141). Reading, understanding and conveying the meaning of old texts are the main goals of paleography. As Carroll (1976: 39) put it, "Paleography is the science – and one might very well say the art – of deciphering texts." Paleographers also engage in the preparation of old texts for publication for modern readers; as Koster (2009: 258) noted, "a tradition of critical scrutiny and editing [...] has been one of the hallmarks of our discipline." Modern paleography considers many aspects of this work: form of writing, orthography, languages and dialects. Paleography began as the analysis of Latin texts, and it is sometimes claimed that "paleography is [currently] regarded as relating to Greek and Latin scripts with their derivatives, thus, as a rule, excluding Egyptian, Hebrew, and Middle and Far Eastern scripts" (*Encyclopaedia Britannica*). In practice, however, paleographers work with other scripts as well as Latin, and surely the analysis of any old manuscript may be termed *paleographic*. Consider, for instance, texts written by paleographers about Armenian, Egyptian, Aramaic and Chinese scripts: 'Album of Armenian paleography' (Clackson 2003, Russell 2006), 'Egyptian paleography' (Breasted 1910), 'Ancient Egyptian epigraphy and paleography' (Silverman 1979), 'A calligraphic approach to Aramaic paleography' (Daniels 1984), 'Wu Dacheng's paleography and artifact studies' (Brown 2011). Modern paleography deals with *any* ancient or medieval writing.

Paleographers, among other things, research scripts. Although the same script can be adopted for writing in various languages – Latin, Greek, Cyrillic and Arabic scripts, for example, are used for writing in many different languages – orthography usually characterizes writings of one language. In phases of prestandard orthographies, we may analyze the orthographies of a particular region (e.g. Wycliffite or Egyptian), of a particular time period, of a particular person or even of a particular phase within the creative biography of a single individual, for example Ion Heliade Rădulescu in Romanian (Close 1974) or Simonas Daukantas in Lithuanian (Subačius 2020).

15.2.2 Orthography in the Context of Paleography

Certainly, orthography is very important for paleography. Not all aspects of writing that matter to paleographers are objects of orthographic study, however. Features such as the introduction of letter extensions (in today's terminology, *descenders* and *ascenders*) for certain minuscules such as *b*, *d*, *g*, *h*, *p*, *q* and *ſ* in some early scripts – for instance, in New Roman Cursive, which had been in use since the third century BC (Marcos 2017: 16) – and in many other medieval minuscules is an object of paleography. This modification involves only the visuality of letter surfaces; the relationship of the letter to sounds, syllables and words as well as to other letters in the alphabet is unchanged. In other words, the system of graphemic signs (graphemes) remains intact. This is not the case with the minuscules *i* and *j*, however. Initially, there was only one letter *i*, and the shape of *j* was merely its elongated variant in certain strong positions, marked longer with a descender for easier reading. By the late medieval and early modern period, it had developed into two different graphemes, one signifying a vowel, and the other a consonant. Because the inventory of letters had been transformed, this development became an object not only of paleography but of historical orthography as well. The border into orthography was crossed because the graphic system expanded.

Before various rapid ways of writing were developed, a single alphabetic set of letters was sufficient, and many of the oldest writing systems did not employ majuscules and minuscules. The development of cursive and minuscule ways of writing was of great importance both for paleography and historical orthography. Writing more quickly generally led to modification of the shape of letters. In this way, the separate rounded letters carved in stone in ancient times became somewhat smaller, linked shapes on papyrus, wax tablets, parchment and paper. The more important texts continued to be rendered in capital letters, however, as if minuscules had less significance because they could be produced more quickly (see the use of capital letters for book titles and chapters and the use of minuscules in the body of texts today). As *systemic* modifications of scripts, cursives and minuscules were significant additions. Individual orthographies inherited this duality of majuscules and minuscules and it became an important characteristic of many of them. Not only were the shapes restyled, but the very system of graphemes changed. Today, many alphabets include both capitals and minuscules, or *uppercase* and *lowercase letters* as they are commonly known in English, designations derived from the typesetting case containing the capital letters which, in a traditional printer's shop, was situated above the tray containing their minuscule counterparts. Knowledge of orthographic rules helps paleographers to make sense of concrete signs and decipher old texts. Orthographic development, on the other hand, is an object of investigation on its own: historical orthography constitutes a separate scholarly discipline.

Orthography is a system of graphemes (as opposed to the letter shapes, known as glyphs) and other graphic signs (e.g. obligatory or optional diacritics), consisting of their relation within a word, of their connectivity into digraphs, trigraphs and so on. It is a system of ideas that rule our recognition and choice of graphemes, expressed through the shapes of particular letters (see also Baker 1997: 93 and Sebba 2007: 10). Imagine language as an invisible being with an audible voice and think of writing as a visible garment worn by that being. In this sense, language and writing are like Mr. Griffin in the notorious novel by Wells (1897), *The Invisible Man*: unseen yet dressed up and speaking. Visuality is present only in the garment – we cannot see language *per se*. Now imagine the orthography as the pattern used to construct that garment. That pattern represents the underlying principle of what we ultimately visualize as concrete signs (letters and so on). In prestandard periods, however, the inventory of graphemes, other graphic signs and their guiding rules were often unstable and characterized by an abundance of variation. Both the number of graphemes and the regulations governing them could fluctuate: consider, for example, the variety of letters with diacritics in Early Modern Latin, French, Polish and Lithuanian orthographies (Strockis 2007, Šinkūnas 2010, Baddeley 2012, Bunčić 2012). Paleographic research is bound in time by the appearance of printed texts. The study of printed texts is allotted to historians of printing.

15.3 Codicology

15.3.1 Scope

Codicology (from Latin *codex* 'notebook, book' and Greek λόγος 'word') is a much younger term than paleography. According to Merriam-Webster, which defines it as "the study of manuscripts as cultural artefacts for historical purposes," codicology dates back only to 1953 in the English language. The term codicology was not coined in English, however. The French term *codicologie* appeared first. The first to use this term systematically was Alphonse Dain in his 1949 book *Les manuscrits* (Dain 1949, Gruijs 1972: 92). There was an earlier attempt by Charles Samaran in 1934–35 to term the new science *codigraphie* to distinguish it from *bibliographie*, but it did not catch on (Gruijs 1972: 94). According to Delaissé, "the term *codicologie* or *codicology* usually signifies 'a wider knowledge of the mediaeval book'" (Delaissé, after Gruijs 1972: 101).[1] Also,

> codicology *(codicologie, Handschriftenkunde,* manuscript study) is concerned with such matters as inscriptions, format, number of lines to a page,

[1] Judging by the editor's note, the work by L. M. J. Delaissé *Archaelogy and History of the Medieval Book, Problems and Method* that was planned to appear in print in 1972/73, probably was never printed after Delaissé's death in January 1972: "It now seems unlikely that this book will ever be published" (Gruijs 1972: 91).

> dimensions of the text on the page, size and type of paper, watermarks, binding, clamps, foliation, type of ink, damp and grease stains, pin-prickings, arrangement of gatherings, decoration, and so on. All of these help to provide information about the origin and history of the codex, and about the society in which it was produced.
>
> (Ostrowski 1977: 264)

Codicology is used in a narrow and in a broad sense. According to Albert Gruijs, "[c]odicology – in the strictest sense – *is* archaeology. For, like the archaeologist, the codicologist examines the codex first and foremost as an object from the past" (Gruijs 1972: 90). Moreover, "codicology comprises the investigation of all physical aspects of codices, together with the indispensable interpretation of the results which such a synthesis has to provide for subsequent historical research" (Gruijs 1972: 102). In the broadest sense of the term, by contrast, codicology "virtually coincides with the modern conception of manuscript studies as a multidimensional approach to the codex as object-in-itself, and as cultural phenomenon" (Gruijs 1972: 102).

> An example of codicology in the wider sense [...] seems to me to be the book by Jean Destrez, *La pecia dans les manuscrits universitaires du XIIIe et du XIVe siécle* [...] In this work the author is in fact dealing with a social institution: the organisation and techniques employed in reduplicating university texts rapidly by lending separate quires, or *pecia*, to student copyists so that a whole book could be copied in the time it took one student to copy one quire.
>
> (Gruijs 1972: 103)

Gruijs also elaborates on what he considers to be codicology in a strict sense:

> a. a highly detailed description of the physical aspects of the object [...]; b. a synthesis based on this description which outlines the material evolution of the codex; [...] c. confrontation of this evolution with the actual contents of the item in question [...]. The whole gives a picture of the static and dynamic structure of the manuscript.
>
> (Gruijs 1972: 104)

Gruijs considers "everything not comprised by these principles to belong to *codicology in the wider sense*" (Gruijs 1972: 104). In Ostrowski's words, "[o]ne can distinguish between codicology in the broad sense, that is, the study of a manuscript in its social and historical context, and codicology in the narrow sense, that is, merely a description of the manuscript" (Ostrowski 1977: 264). Thus, in the narrower sense of the term, codicology is focused on the physical manuscript *per se*; more broadly, it is focused on all possible background cultural and environmental specificities in which that manuscript was created and preserved. Codicology deals with "physical and paratextual features" (Smith 2014: 37). The *materiality* of an object is important for *codicology* in its narrower sense. As van Beek put it, traditionally "we are supposed to know that matter doesn't matter" (van Beek 1996: 15). However, his own approach to the materiality of codicological things is different:

> It is ultimately a gut feeling that leads me to accept that material culture significantly contributes to our construction and perception of the world and that presumably this must have to do with the most superficial aspect (appearance) of objects: the materiality, tangibility of things. That is to say that material objects contribute something special that is different from the textual attributes of cultural meaning.
>
> (van Beek 1996: 10)

Historically, paleography encompassed aspects that today are considered codicology. Features that, for earlier paleographers, were nonessential, often neglected or studied superficially after receiving only casual attention, for codicologists became the major research object: the materiality of an object itself came to the forefront. Codicology branched out of paleography, thereby shrinking the object of paleography. In earlier works by paleographers, as well as the reading and analysis of old texts, details were provided in the preface or footnotes about the writing materials used, the conditions in which manuscripts were compiled, facts about their previous and current owners, particulars of historical circumstance of manuscript assembly and the institutions involved in the preservation of manuscripts. Since the mid-twentieth century, however, all these details have been an object of codicology, in both the narrow and the broad sense.

Generally, codicology is a pre–mid-twentieth century kind of paleography except for the study of texts. Codicology is what remains of early paleography after its object constriction to mere scripting, writing, reading and orthography. As Smith put it, paleography is the "philological counterpart" of codicology (Smith 2014: 35). Gruijs (1972: 90) has compared codicology to archaeology, describing "old books" as "archaeological 'finds'" which must be "subjected to different types of interpretation: material, historical, ethnological and artistic" (Lieftinck 1958–59, after Gruijs 1972: 89–90). Codicology, which is "sometimes called in English 'the archeology of the codex'", in Russian is called "archeografija" (Ostrowski 1977); in the former Soviet Union, the term codicology (*kodikologija*) did not appear in the title of a book until 1974 (Ostrowski 1977: 264). The term codicology "is increasingly being adopted to distinguish the study of old writing (paleography) from the study of the codex or manuscript in which the writing is found" (Ostrowski 1977: 264). At the same time, the science of codicology itself has been growing in importance: "over the past decades, interest has shifted from the contents of manuscripts to the 'complex network of historical circumstances and processes' [...] that must come together to produce these objects" (Echard 2013: 298; the embedded quotation comes from Pearsall 2011: xvi).

15.3.2 Orthography in the Context of Codicology

Both paleographers and codicologists analyze very old (ancient, medieval) writings and their physicality in a cultural milieu. While paleographers work with orthography as well as other features of writing (scripting), codicologists are more detached from orthography. Still, consideration of the dating and localization of a codex is an essential part of codicological research, and orthographic representation of that codex may help draw more precise conclusions. For instance, the Greek *Codex Alexandrinus* was believed to exhibit Egyptian Greek forms, but after quantitative analysis of certain orthographic patterns, Smith was able to assert that its "orthographic variations have very little in common with the variants found in Egyptian Koine" (Smith 2014: 243). Thus, he was able to disprove the Egyptian provenance of *Alexandrinus* via the orthographic research.

An analogy might be drawn with the so-called Qumran Hebrew Orthography, found in the Dead Sea Scrolls. Tov (1986) had claimed there was a separate 'Qumran orthography' which was characterized by the full rather than the short orthography (Tov 1986). However, after examining the orthography of other scrolls discovered around the same time, Kim challenged the stability of that orthography: "The Qumran sectarian works show a wide spectrum in their orthography, which refuses to be described uniformly. This clearly shows that the orthography of the Qumran literature was unstable" (Kim 2004: 81). For this reason, "the orthography can no longer tell where the text came from" (Kim 2004: 81). Orthographic features once again were used to shed light on the proposed origin of the manuscript. Here, we deal, however, with the scrolls rather than codices. It is not that orthography is a direct object of codicology; rather, orthographic research can contribute to codicological knowledge, helping to improve our understanding of the origin, time and location of the manuscript compilation. Without orthographic input, a codicologist may miss important points in the history of a codex.

Let us briefly take stock. Orthography helps paleographers to understand texts. It may help codicologists to characterize the provenance of a codex. Orthographic patterns and variations that allow the original date and locality of a codex to be established more precisely might be the line at which orthography meets codicology: orthographic data allow codicological inferences to be drawn about time and place.

15.4 Orthography and Materiality

In contrast to linguistic, ideological and social reasons for orthographic change, such as political intentions, regional traditions and dialectal variation, marking group belonging, materiality might be considered a physical condition or reason for spelling transformations and variation. Materiality is important for orthography when the choice of graphemes, other graphic elements and the rules thereof depend on neither phonetic nor cultural (social, political) dimensions and principles, but either on restrictions or encouragement of certain physical realities. The physical writing environment might become a factor not only for the style of a letter shape, but also for its orthographic adaptation.

Miller has argued that "a key question is to determine when, where and for whom the material attributes of things matter. Materiality like nature is mainly a potential presence. The solidity of the branch comes to matter mainly when you hit your head on it" (Miller 1996: 27). So, to expand on the metaphor, on what occasions might orthography hit its head on the solidity of a branch? What kind of influence might the tangible materiality of writing and printing exert on orthography? What impact might papyrus, parchment, paper, scroll, book, clay or wax tablet, pen or stylus, movable type, typewriter and computer monitor have on such an ideal aspect of writing as orthography – on its sets of rules, norms, combinations of graphemes, morphemes, punctuation, abbreviation and so on? How might the surface and space of a clay or wax tablet, or of a sheet of parchment or paper, affect orthographic particularities? It is common knowledge that the cuneiform writing system was devised for a stick or reed to be pressed into a wet clay (tablet, roll), but other writing tools were more appropriate for papyrus, parchment and paper, whose surface better accommodated the strokes of quill, pen or brush. In ancient Greece and Rome, a chisel was used to carve words in stone in majuscule (capitalization), but the wax tablet and stylus prompted the development of different shapes, what we call minuscule letters today. After the invention of movable print type, of course, text production changed dramatically; individual letter strokes in manuscripts were replaced by ready-made mirrored letter-blocks, known as types, set one by one on a composing stick, dipped in ink and pressed on paper.

Even some luxuriously prepared manuscript volumes have had a very unsettled orthography, containing signs of aesthetic play with variants, as in the case of Simonas Daukantas's *History of the Lithuanian Lowlands* (1831–34). In this book, the message of the solidity of Lithuania's past conveyed through the striking *material* shape of the volume was prioritized over the orthographic needs of a few potential readers. Individual attempts to develop orthographies have been characterized as much by an almost unrestrained imagination, a kind of challenge to the printing houses (e.g. Daukantas), as by the constraints imposed by available printers (e.g. Martynas Mažvydas, 1510–63, and Jurgis Ambrozijus Pabrėža, 1771–1849).

15.4.1 Durability and Ephemerality

The materiality of texts also means that they can be mutilated or destroyed. Despite the assertion by Roman emperor Caius Titus that *verba volant scripta manent*, as van Peer has argued, "[o]wing to their very materiality, written texts are prone to erosion and damage"; in fact, the written language is so vulnerable to material destruction that it "needs the creation and operation of special institutions in order to be preserved" (van Peer 1997: 35). Van Peer speaks about signs that are mutilated or erased for magical or political and economic reasons – any material destruction of texts or their parts. He considers that even editing one's own text and proofreading it is a form of mutilation. Although typically described as a cleaning process (as in "[t]his allowed us to do a more thorough job of editing and cleaning of typographical errors," Bernard 1980: 134), even typographical correction involves the alteration – and therefore the mutilation – of a former text. The concept of mutilation draws our attention to the importance of any text that may be produced, even those that are labeled flawed. Mutilation presupposes the significance of the text in its premutilated form, and of any chain of alterations made to the text before it reaches us in its so-called final form. In short, it presupposes that all surviving texts are worthy of study.

In practice, however, people often 'measure' texts according to their chances for survival: an 'erroneous' text is likely to be destroyed more readily than its 'corrected' counterpart. In earlier centuries, printers tended to destroy manuscripts once the book versions of them had been printed. Proofs were not preserved; it is rare to find a sheet with marked proofs from the sixteenth century (see the Newberry Library text with the 1570 proofs at Novickas 2004: 32). Even today we tend to perceive texts as either less or more worthy of preservation. Imagine a continuum of texts lined up according to their presumed intended perishability; at one end, the most preservable and durable writings would be placed, and at the other, the most ephemeral, those almost unworthy of a place under the sun. The dichotomy would be of what I call durability versus ephemerality. Manuscripts in general are recognized as more easily lost or destroyed than printed material. Consider Crain's analysis of the nineteenth-century children's books *Jack and the Bean-stalk* (1848) and *The Harper Establishment* (Abbott 1855), which describes how storybooks are made. Crain noted that

> [H]ere manuscripts are represented as an ephemeral and disposable stage of book production. Manuscripts, in their scruffy, fragile uniqueness, appear not as, for example, auratic signs of authorship but as "obscure and seemingly useless" rolls. Jack's story and *The Harper Establishment* promote and valorize both the "thingness" [...] of the codex, its seemingly durable materiality, and the collaborative labor (and laborers) invested in it.
>
> (Crain 2013: 159)

The codex in this context is a printed book as opposed to a manuscript roll. Books are regarded as durable, whereas manuscripts are ephemeral and disposable. This dichotomy may be discernible in other spheres as well.

Historically, as previously noted, minuscules were developed primarily to enhance the speed of writing, and the texts composed in them may have been perceived as prone to greater perishability than those written in majuscules – because minuscules were written on more perishable surfaces (i.e. wax tablets) and in less formal contexts. For example,

> [I]n the fifth century, during the lifetime of Sr. Mesrop Mashtots, who invented an alphabetic, fully phonetic script for Armenian, and certainly soon after him, there existed both the rounded and square forms of *erkat'agir* [majuscule]. These were suitable for more or less formal purposes with different media (stone, parchment, papyrus), and there was a nascent *bolorgir* [minuscule and other cursive book hands] as well, without any "transitional" stage.
>
> (Russell 2006: 278, Stone et al. 2002)

Similarly, an Egyptian rapid cursive known as "the book-hand" became "the hand used for religious books, while the rapid cursive [was] employed only for business and other secular affairs" (Breasted 1910: 136). Both minuscule letters and rapid cursive would appear to be associated with the more disposable, perishable end of the survivability continuum. Production of codices in late medieval England can be tentatively allocated into two other categories according to the level of commercialization: "an amount of porosity between 'non-commercial' and 'commercial' is an important way of considering the degree of necessary co-existence of the two paradigms" (Pouzet 2011: 238), "and indeed between professional and nonprofessional" (Echard 2013: 300) paradigms. This distinction of 'noncommercial' and nonprofessional manuscripts could suggest an awareness of their comparatively high perishability. Commercial and professional correlate with durability, whereas noncommercial and nonprofessional are associated with the more ephemeral nature of such texts.

Accordingly, how a scribe (or society) perceives the durability and ephemerality of a text may depend on the material used (i.e. on materiality) and the purpose of the text (e.g. sacred or quotidian). The ultimate goal of a text may be discerned from the effort that the scribe put into its production. The commerciality and professionalism of a text also depend on the extent to which it is widely distributed and on the scribe's ability to achieve and maintain a high standard of work. Thus, commerciality determines distribution, professionalism reflects ability, and durability indicates the degree to which a manuscript is intended to survive. That intention (i.e. the long- or short-term survival of the manuscript) is the primary concern of the scribe, followed by production (professional or otherwise), and then distribution (commercial or otherwise). Greater effort was put into the preparation and completion of texts that were meant to survive for longer, which generally were more accurate, tidier and better organized. In other words, the more durable the text, the stricter the orthographic norms. Texts intended to be preserved in perpetuity were expected to have a better kind of orthography. Carelessness can be a sign of greater ephemerality of writing, while meticulousness may signal the expectation of longer survival (Subačius 2021: 35, 38–39, 196, 539, 595, 625). The perceived materiality of a text, its chances for survival and its anticipated place in future society may have significantly influenced orthographic choices.

15.4.2 Printing

Manuscripts produced in the centuries that followed Antiquity and the Middle Ages fall outside the scope of either paleography or codicology. The print era nevertheless holds great interest for historians of orthography, as orthographic systems continued to develop. Not only do orthographies in manuscripts and prints sometimes differ, but some languages go through centuries of evolution before developing strong orthographic standards. Consider the *early dialect selection* standard languages in Europe, such as Danish, Dutch, English, French, German, Hungarian, Polish, Spanish and Swedish, all of which chose the dialectal norm as basis for their standard during the early modern period, and especially during the Renaissance (Subačius 2002). The basis for standard orthographies were laid then, but it took several hundred years until uniform orthographic standards were developed, most often during the eighteenth and nineteenth centuries. As for the *late dialect selection* standard languages such as Albanian, Croatian, Estonian, Finnish, Latvian, Lithuanian, Slovak, Slovenian and Ukrainian, the orthographic variation must have been even greater, as their orthographies typically were not standardized until the end of the nineteenth or the beginning of the twentieth century. Indeed, some European orthographies such as Galician, Macedonian, Rusyn, Valencian, Võru and Yiddish were evolving even after that, in the late twentieth century up to the present day. Some variation is still present even in highly standardized orthographies, such as German (*daß* and *dass*), English (*minuscule* and *miniscule*) and Portuguese (*carácter* and *caráter*) (Marquilhas 2015: 284).

The changing materiality of text production during the print era was also a stimulus for certain orthographic modifications. Initially, as is commonly known, printers aimed to follow closely the traditions associated with manuscript production, but with the passing of time they became emboldened to introduce a variety of changes. Most contemporary readers simply do not notice standardized orthography, in which graphemes appear to be wearing uniforms. One can predict the letters that will appear within words and is never surprised. In short, standard orthography is, most of the time, for most people, uninteresting, even boring. However, if its uniformity is disturbed even slightly, one notices the difference at once. For those who wish to read at speed, a disturbed orthography is an unwelcome distraction. We read more quickly and absorb the information the text contains more efficiently when the orthography is unmarked. We do not want to be distracted by orthographic discrepancies that do not comply with our expectations and hinder our progress through the text. Over many years of training, we develop the skills required to read machine-made (printed) texts quickly, and orthographic uniformity guarantees our proficiency and contributes greatly to our ability to compete with the many other skilled readers in our present-day society. The uniformity of standard orthography is an asset that enables thoughts and ideas to be shared and exchanged much more quickly than before.

When we read historical texts, however, we often encounter prestandard orthographies characterized by diversity and variation. In the early phases of orthographic development during the print era, the need for uniformity was first recognized not by readers but by the typesetters in the printing houses (see Voeste 2012: 176). It was they who introduced 'order' into orthography, and readers reaped the fruits of their labor. As in today's consumer society, a producer creates a product which in turn sparks demand for it. During the period of orthographic diversity, the introduction of a more uniform orthography carried the promise of greater efficiency and profitability for printers and typesetters of books and newspapers. As the upper and lower cases containing the type sets grew more standardized, typesetters became more skilled and were able to set words and entire texts more quickly. As the speed of production increased, the more profit the printer earned (see Voeste 2012: 174–76). The greater the profit, the more printers were able to invest in their businesses, enabling them to produce more texts – and the more texts to which readers are exposed, the more their reading skills improve. Thus, consumers benefited from the standardization of orthography achieved through printing.

Materiality had very different implications for printers than it had for manuscript writers. That difference could, in some cases, influence orthography, as printers altered orthography to ensure optimal speed of production. As they began to produce their own texts, printers found that majuscules and minuscules were often used in manuscripts. They adopted both. Today, the alphabets of many languages feature this dual system of letters; consider, for example, the Greek, Latin and Cyrillic scripts and the many alphabets based on them. Although some scripts or alphabets such as Arabic, Georgian, Hebrew, Hindi and Sanskrit are unicameral, meaning they have only one set of letters, we have inherited this duplicity from the manuscripts. Minuscule letters could be written more quickly with a quill than their majuscule equivalents. For a typesetter, however, the time required to set text in majuscules or minuscules was comparable. Had printing been introduced in early Antiquity, we can speculate that the printers would have created only one set of alphabetic letters (unicameral), since working with only one case of letters in front of them rather than with two would have enhanced the speed of production. But the tradition of two alphabetic sets was well rooted in manuscripts, so it was only natural that printers from the fifteenth century on would adopt it.

In a manuscript, one might write any sign with no loss of time or effort. Graphemic representation had no limits other than those set by the imagination, and any combination, diacritic mark, abbreviation and so on was possible. By contrast, a typesetter is constrained by the limited inventory of type in his cases – and the larger the inventory, the more intricate the process of setting. The two alphabetic sets of letters in manuscripts, based on Latin script, were not symmetric, and their asymmetricity was embraced by the early printers. Over time, however, printers made them symmetric. Consider the disappearance of the long graph *ſ* in orthographies based on Latin script. Until the end of the eighteenth century, texts in various languages contained two lowercase letters *ſ* and *s* and only one uppercase *S* for a single phoneme /s/ (*ſ* was used in the word-initial and median positions, *s* in the word-final position). At the end of the eighteenth century, printers in various European countries stopped including the asymmetrical long *ſ* in the font sets they were fashioning (Subačius 2004c: 239–43). With the long letter *ſ* missing from the sets of new fonts, printers were unable to employ it even if they wanted to. In his old age, the American politician, scientist and former printer Benjamin Franklin deplored the loss of the long *ſ*. Were it not for the printers, Latin-based alphabets might still have asymmetric features like the one that persists in the Greek alphabet, in which the capital sigma *Σ* has two corresponding lower case sigmas *σ* and *ς*.

Consider another asymmetry, of the letters *V* and *v*, *u*; *I* and *i*, *j* that in early modern times was almost omnipresent in Latin script-based alphabets. Printers modified these orthographic particularities by filling 'the gaps' in the upper case through adding symmetrical capitals *U* and *J*. Thus, the materiality of the printers' milieu encouraged them to make upper and lower cases more symmetrical, to help typesetters synchronize their skills for both typesetting cases. Consequently, the physicality of the printers' environment influenced the Latin script and the orthographies based on it. In sum, for orthographies based on Latin script, the 'order' achieved by the standardization and symmetry in the two sets was primarily developed through the efforts of printers.

Newly developing orthographies were often limited to the inventories of those printers who were ready to print texts, but only in other, earlier orthographies of other languages. Consider the case of Jan Weinreich, a sixteenth-century East Prussian printer who used to print Latin, German and Polish texts in Karaliaučius (Regiomons, Królewiec, Königsberg; today Kaliningrad). The author of the first printed book in Lithuanian, Martynas Mažvydas, took his text to Weinreich's shop to be published in 1547. There it was printed with two Polish letters *ą* and *ę* containing the diacritic mark *ogonek* ˛ to signify nasality. Polish orthography marked nasality only by these two letters, whereas Lithuanians used to pronounce four nasal phonemes. In the manuscripts of that period, other Lithuanian authors used to mark the nasality of these four letters (*i* and *u* in addition to *a* and *e*) with dots under the letters (Gelumbeckaitė 2008).

For a long time, the inventories available to printers determined that only the graphemes corresponding to nasals, that is <ą> and <ę>, were marked, and the diacritic dot under the letter that was present in manuscripts was never printed. The printers were ready to use the letters they had in Polish type sets, but any request for a new grapheme would have been a pain in the neck. Not only was it expensive to cut punches, make matrixes and cast the type in lead, but printers also had to think about where these new letters would be placed within their type cases, and changing the location of type undermined their skills and their ability to work efficiently. Today, Lithuanian orthography includes four nasal graphemes <ą>, <ę>, <į>, <ų>, indicating that the shape of the ogonek was chosen by the early printers and not by the Lithuanian authors, who initially preferred to use dots under the letters; the <į>, <ų> diacritics were modeled after <ą>, <ę> subsequently. The materiality of the printing environment (i.e. the inventories of printers) was a decisive factor in the choice of certain Lithuanian graphemes. One might label this a Polish orthographic influence, which was ensured by the printers' inventories.

15.4.3 Double Orthography: Prints and Manuscripts

As the printing process advanced, an important duplicity was recognized in divergent orthographies. Regarding eighteenth-century English orthography, Noel Osselton wrote:

> Lord Chesterfield speaks (in *The World*, 1754) of "two very different orthographies, the *pedantic*, and the *polite*" which were current at the time and it seems to me that the history of English spelling in that period must take account of this double standard which both existed and was recognized to exist. Dr. Johnson's letters are full of spellings he would never have countenanced in his Dictionary.
>
> (Osselton 1963: 274)

Orthographic duplicity developed as printed texts diverged from manuscript writing traditions. The difference between the two also stemmed from the formal and informal ways of using orthography in printed texts as opposed to manuscripts. According to Tieken-Boon van Ostade, there were "two spelling systems currently in use, a public spelling system and a private one" (Tieken-Boon van Ostade 1998: 457). Moreover,

> [t]he existence of a dual spelling system was recognized as such in the early eighteenth century, as the following quotation from *The Spectator* (1711)

shows: [...] "he told us [...] that he never liked Pedantry in Spelling, and that *he spelt like a Gentleman and not like a Scholar*."

(Tieken-Boon van Ostade 1998: 464)

Of course, pedantic and scholarly spellings were those used by the printers in contemporary terms. On the continuum from durability to ephemerality, the pedantic and scholarly way of spelling and those termed polite and gentlemanly would have been located at opposite ends, with the former being considered more durable than the latter. Different material reality of printers modified not only the ways the texts were produced and distributed, but also the orthography itself. As Rutkowska has noted in her review of *Orthographies in Early Modern Europe* (Baddeley and Voeste 2012b), a similar duplicity of orthography has been identified in many other European languages:

> The evidence for the significance of printing and printers in the process of standardisation can be seen in that printed books reached a relatively high level of spelling regularisation much earlier than handwritten documents which preserved idiosyncrasies for decades or even centuries longer. In fact, in several languages, two separate systems have been identified, one in printed books and the other in manuscripts, for example in English (Nevalainen, pp. 141–46), Polish (Bunčić, pp. 224–25), and Czech (Berger, pp. 264–65).
>
> (Rutkowska 2015b: 299–300)

Double orthographies may have existed within the scope of prints themselves. Around the turn of the twentieth century (c. 1899–1904), a double orthography was developing in the printed materials produced by the Lithuanian diaspora in America. The texts identified as worthy of longevity were printed in books, and those that were presumed to have a shorter life expectancy were found in newspapers. Book orthography included the 'new' graphemes <č> and <š> for the /tʃ/ and /ʃ/ phonemes, while newspaper orthography included the 'old' digraphs <cz> and <sz> for the same phonemes. It was not uncommon to find both in use in the same newspaper. Often on the same page, some columns would be printed in the older newspaper orthography and others in book orthography. The latter, which were wider and ended with the phrase 'to be continued', served to preserve the serialized texts in standing type form until the entire text was completed. These were then reprinted as a separate volume; book orthography was used in these columns in anticipation of their eventual transfer to book form (Subačius 2004b).

Comparable orthographic duplicity was used in Lithuanian newspapers of East Prussia (1890–93). One orthography was used in those newspapers that were aimed at more educated readers, which were considered more durable, and another in those which were aimed at the less educated, such as newspapers about farming, and therefore were more perishable (Venckienė 2004). In both cases, one Lithuanian orthography was coherently employed in some texts and another in others, as if both those orthographies were already partly standardized and the standards observed. Duplicity of orthography in printing was dependent less on the materiality of the production means than on the presumed survivability of the matter.

Prior to standardization, creative individuals may have been inventing new orthographies, perhaps with the intention of competing with tradition, or perhaps not. Consider the Lithuanian author Jurgis Ambrozijus Pabrėža, who compiled multiple manuscript volumes and never printed a line of them. His orthography of doubled vocalics <aa>, <ee>, <oo>, <ii> and <yy> stands out as the only attempt to introduce the doubled vocalics in the entire history of Lithuanian writing (Subačius 2011b: 448). Pabrėža's orthography, however, was designed to contain only those letters present in Polish orthography, because the printing types were adjusted to print Polish texts. Thus, knowledge of the material content of printing houses influenced Pabrėža's unique orthographic system.

An equally creative person was Simonas Daukantas, whose orthography, especially in his manuscripts, was probably the most diverse in the known history of written Lithuanian. In his voluminous manuscript *History of the Lithuanian Lowlands* (1831–34), for instance, Daukantas employed at least seven different digraphs <ei>, <ęi>, <yi>, <ij>, <ie>, <iei> and <iey> to render a single diphthong /əi/ of his Lowland Lithuanian dialect, even though he could have picked up a single uniform digraph had he followed a generalizing phonetic rule. The impressive size of the manuscript (553 leaves = 1,106 pages in folio) itself conveyed the message that the history of Lithuania was weighty and equipped with the Lithuanian language, that it had a concrete, material shape, and that it was solid and undeniable. The desire to impress readers of both Polish and Lithuanian with the sheer visuality, the sheer materiality of the volume was more important to Daukantas than generalizing orthographic rules. On the contrary, the emphasis on the materiality of the volume enabled Daukantas to take a relaxed approach to orthography. For instance, in approximately one half of his manuscript Daukantas experimented with the aesthetics of spelling variants: the long initial graphemes <l>, <t> and <p> with the ascenders and descenders correlated with the long variants of the digraphs <yi> and <ij>, <y> and <j> with the descenders (Subačius 2020; regarding aesthetic variation in orthography, see Voeste 2007b: 303). The striking materiality of the manuscript both encouraged and enabled the laxity of the newly developed individual orthography. Because orthography was less important than the materiality of the work, it became a playground for aesthetic individualism.

15.4.4 Text

The materiality of the laid-out text, as it stretches on a specific material surface (e.g. a page of paper), can also have an impact on orthographic decisions and variation. Traditional 'on-page' textual materiality, or *direct* materiality, may influence usage of abbreviations. The goal of saving precious writing material facilitated the development of a wide range of abbreviations in the manuscript culture of Latin and other languages in the Middle Ages. The most famous study of Latin and Italian abbreviations was completed more than a century ago by Cappelli (1912). Using textual abbreviations and ligatures conserved the expensive parchment used for handwritten texts and saved time for the scribe producing the text. Due to the scarcity of writing material, the scribe was expected to 'save' text, that is, to use fewer graphemes to render the same amount of text. The more expensive the writing material, the more abbreviations one was encouraged to apply.

Initially printers had imitated the traditional practices of scribes and used the abbreviations developed for manuscripts. This changed as printing became more developed. Paper was much more available during the print era, and setting entire words in print made the text much more legible and accessible. Printing changed the attitude of public toward abbreviations and led most of them to be abandoned. The dependence of orthography on the materiality of the page was evidenced by the practice of interrupting words at the end of a line and completing them on the next line. In earlier centuries, before the modern hyphen <-> became widely accepted, various approaches had been utilized, from a slash </>, to a double hyphen <=> to no sign at all. Then and now, the deployment of this mark depends on the position of the word at the end of the line, that is, on the direct materiality of the page. Position at the end of the line alone controls the rule, not any other orthographic principle. One more kind of direct materiality influenced the development of orthographic features: the different graphemes chosen in different positions on a page. For instance, in most places in his manuscripts, Pabrėža used to write the diagraph <sz> for the phoneme /ʃ/, but sometimes at the end of the line, and only in the final word of a line, he marked the 'old' ligature <ß> instead. Thus, the end-of-the-line position influenced graphemic variation. In such cases, the wider the sheet of paper used, the fewer <ß> ligatures would appear (Subačius 1996: 18–19).

15.5 Conclusion

The materiality of texts leaves them open to mutilation, destruction or preservation. People 'measure' texts according to their chances for survival. An 'erroneous' text (e.g. an earlier draft) is likely to be destroyed more rapidly than its 'corrected' counterpart. In certain cases, the development of changes in orthography may have been influenced by an awareness of worthiness for preservation and by the prediction of the length of their material life (durability or ephemerality of texts). Historically, minuscules were developed primarily to enhance writing speed, and texts composed in them may have been perceived as more perishable than those written in majuscules. Manuscripts are generally recognized as more perishable than printed texts. Texts intended for lengthy preservation were expected to have a more prestigious orthography. Simultaneous double orthographies developed in various societies, one being more prestigious than another.

Typesetters were the first to recognize the need for orthographic uniformity. In manuscripts, the two alphabetic styles of capital and noncapital letters, which were based on Latin script, were asymmetric, but over time printers made them symmetric by abandoning the 'redundant' long <ſ> and introducing uppercase <U> and <J>. Printing changed the attitude of the public toward abbreviations and led most of them to be abandoned. The hyphen at the end of a line is dependent on the word position at the end of the line, on the direct materiality of the page and not on any other orthographic principle. Sometimes different graphemes were positioned at the end of a line. Paleography involves using historical orthographies; codicology may be served by them. The dependence of historical orthography upon the 'direct' materiality of texts and upon the material aspects of text production is a comparatively new and developing field of research.

16

Data Collection and Interpretation

Anja Voeste

16.1 Introduction

This chapter is intended to offer assistance with the earliest stages of an empirical investigation, while you are contemplating how to design a study. For this reason, the underlying premises and assumptions of analysis, which are usually taken for granted, are stated here explicitly and hopefully clarified to some extent. For a project already in the planning phase, this chapter helps you to evaluate the advantages and disadvantages of a given method. Moreover, it helps you to understand which theoretical decisions are already inevitably made when choosing an empirical method. If you are aware of a method's theoretical prerequisites, you may be able to give your study a sounder theoretical basis and discuss its theoretical foundations more convincingly. A key issue, addressed at different points in the chapter, is that data collection and interpretation are always intertwined. Data collection is predetermined and controlled by prior findings or by your research objectives. Conversely, the modes of description applied during data collection lead to a preference for a specific set of interpretations. While many scholars rely on data that have been collected and described by others (e.g. when using historical corpora), analytical reasoning should be applied, hypotheses formulated and sound interpretations reached. Even large corpora and effective analysis tools will not spare us from this task. In the comic science fiction *The Hitchhiker's Guide to the Galaxy* (Adams 1979), '42' is the noninterpretable answer to the ultimate question of life, given by a supercomputer after several million years of computing time. It is still the case that '42' is not a good answer if this number is not interpreted in its historical context.

In the following, I briefly discuss two typical forms of historical spelling studies, namely the tracking of a specific spelling feature, that is, its emergence, spread or decline, and the observation of a spelling variable, that is, the alternation between different spelling variants. Both cases allow for comparative variable analysis, as tracking specific spelling features also works according to the pattern of 1:0 (occurrence vs. nonoccurrence; 1 = occurrence, 0 = nonoccurrence). Three possible methods are available for comparative variable analysis, which are presented in more detail in Section 16.2. These methods are the comparison of variants in a single text (TRAVA), the comparison of two or more texts (TERVA) and, as a subvariant of this second method, the comparison of different copies of the same text (CTVA). The advantages and disadvantages of each method can be taken into account if you are aware of each method's dangers and pitfalls. A targeted use of these methods or a use of two or more of them in combination may help you to strengthen your interpretation and/or to find alternative explanatory hypotheses.

16.2 Data Collection

The first step in any investigation involves basic decisions about which research questions to pursue and which analytical tools to use for the empirical investigation. In these times of 'computational revolution' and the widespread use of statistical methods, it is possible to draw on larger corpora of electronic data. This allows the researcher to rely on broader data as a foundation for their work and thus hopefully glean more significant and representative results. Even with the increasingly widespread use of computational technology, a key question remains: How good really is the material that we have in our hands for analysis? As is often pointed out, Labov (1994: 11) claimed that historical linguistics can be described as "the art of making the best use of bad data." Even if this seems to be true at first glance, especially from the point of view of 'big data', it may still be argued that the statement is misleading. Data are always incomplete, never perfect: historical data can never fully reflect the complexity of the linguistic reality in which we are actually interested. Even large corpora do not entirely mirror reality or guarantee objective knowledge. They are still highly filtered, codified and potentially distorted datasets (see also the demand for more representative corpora in Elspaß 2012a). The availability of more data does not necessarily mean that patterns would be less messy, more transparent or easier to interpret for the researcher.

On the contrary, the availability of more data may entice us into assuming the primacy of correlations over causal explanations (Mazzocchi 2015: 1252). However, correlations only inform us *that* something is happening; they cannot give us the crucial answer of *why* it is happening. In fact, we now know that with more datasets, the possibility of false or so-called spurious correlations increases: Calude and Longo (2017) confirmed that the bigger the database which one mines for correlations, the higher the chance of finding recurrent (spurious) regularities, which of course should not be interpreted as evidence of causation. Therefore, it should be borne in mind that the same epistemological difficulties as those inherent to the more narrow-scale, traditional methods remain when using 'big data' and applying statistical methods. The 'computational turn' has thus not resulted in electronic tools taking over the task of analytical reasoning. We still need to formulate hypotheses based on nondeductive inference rules (e.g. by induction or analogy) and test them for plausibility (Cellucci 2013, section 4).

Moreover, we still have to deduce creatively from the available data and include in our deductions even implausible inferences that might elude computer-based logic. The problem is easily demonstrated by the example of language contact where the texts under study are more or less influenced by a contact language. This is especially true for so-called invisible languages, a concept that was introduced by Havinga and Langer (2015: 1–34). The term refers to linguistic features or even entire varieties that were marginalized or systematically excluded from the written language at a certain point in time (e.g. Low German, South Jutish, North Frisian). Invisible languages may be stigmatized substrate languages or regional varieties which only become perceptible when interfering with the textual records of the elite language. That makes it even more important to rely on our experience and our interpretative strength to detect, for example, subtle contact phenomena in the records.

Hypotheses play a role even at the beginning of data collection. Data collection itself is controlled by hypotheses and prior findings. Pragmatic considerations must also be weighed, asking, for example, how much time is available, what the costs are, and what expertise is needed. In order to answer these questions and obtain relevant data, we first need to identify the research questions. In the field of historical orthography, identifying a research question typically involves two possible approaches: focusing on the usage (emergence, spread or decline) of a particular spelling feature or on the variable occurrence of different spellings. When starting with existing corpora or easily accessible sources, it makes sense, from a practical point of view, to investigate questions that are predetermined by the corpus or the given material. Therefore, it is more than likely that the corpora or the sources will affect our choice of questions. Alternatively, one could put together a corpus or modify the datasets of an existing corpus in order to address a previously defined research question. In either case, however, the data to be collected or used will not be an amorphous amount of data put together without any criteria, but rather they will always be a targeted and sensible selection of historical material carefully selected and compiled for researchers as a whole, or a specific research project.

For the first approach, if the usage (emergence, spread or decline) of a particular spelling feature is to be addressed, a number of additional parameters must be decided, for example, which time periods, which text types or which writing materials are to be included. This is where the first hypotheses and, of course, the researcher's expertise come into play: the selection is already determined by the consideration of which texts or which linguistic or external factors may be particularly relevant for one's investigation. Let us look at some simple examples. One could investigate the use of graphemes, graphs, glyphs or other characters, for example homoform digraphs (e.g. *aa* and *tt*), heteroform digraphs (e.g. *ae* and *th*), diacritics (e.g. *í* and *ñ*), ligature glyphs (e.g. *æ* and *fi*), allographs and contextual variants (e.g. |ſ| and |ς|), abbreviations (e.g. ꝰ and ꝫ), punctuation marks (e.g. ¿ and ⸗) or typographical spaces of different widths (*em-quad*, *en-quad*). At first glance, these examples may seem like superficial questions of form, but they nevertheless entail many potential problems that influence the researcher's hypotheses and, therefore, their data collection and methods. Homoform digraphs may indicate distinctive syllabic features (New High German *Ratte* /ʁaṭə/ 'rat' vs. *Rate* /ʁaː.tə/ 'rate'; dots indicating different syllable boundaries) and they may be subject to combinatorial restrictions (Early New High German **raatt* 'council'). Allographs and contextual variants may involve questions of capitalization and word separation, and so morphological, syntactic and semantic factors must be taken into account.

The investigation of graphotactic combinations of graphemes quickly leads to questions of specification and to those of possible minimum or maximum word constraints. Depending on the context, graphemes may be underspecified and overspecified. In German, <v> is underspecified because it may be pronounced as [f] or [v]. On the other hand, <g> may be overspecified in cases of final devoicing. Although <g> is to be pronounced voiceless at the end of the syllable, the logographic spelling specifies more than it usually does. It indicates paradigmatic congruency with word forms in which no final devoicing occurs (*Tag* according to *Tages*, *Tage*). Minimum or maximum word constraints describe the possible allowed length of word forms, that is, the minimal or maximal size of lexical words. In Polish, these constraints allow either minimum words like the preposition *w* 'in' or maximum words like the noun *konstantynopolitańczykowianeczka* 'young girl of Constantinople'.

Furthermore, the influence of external factors is to be expected. Abbreviations, for instance, may have been used predominantly by professional writers, or homoform digraphs might have been an important aid for a target group of unskilled readers. If we want to take a closer look into one of these issues, we will also have to collect or select data that shed light on any internal and external factors involved or use corpora for which the influence of these factors has already been proven. On the basis of prior findings, preliminary hypotheses and initial samples of our data, the researcher can then decide in favor of either a qualitative or a quantitative survey, and select a synchronic longitudinal study of individuals, a cross-sectional study (a 'snapshot' of a specific historical moment) or a comparative diachronic analysis of several points in time (time-series analysis). The researcher will probably want to choose a text type in which the spelling feature occurs frequently and a writing material that might be particularly interesting for their research question. Examples may include uncommon writing surfaces such as stone, wood or metal (epitaphs, house inscriptions, jewelry) (Balbach 2014, Schmid 1989) or the relationship of text and image on paintings or coins. One who considers undertaking a comparative analysis in a cross-sectional study may want to compare different writing materials, for example parchment and paper, scrolls and codices, block books and incunabula, or luxury editions and ordinary reading copies. Scrolls were more difficult to handle during the process of writing than codices, so scribes could not as easily move back and forth between paragraphs; therefore, spellings in scrolls may be less consistent. Block books contain lettering that has been carved out of woodblocks; they differ fundamentally in terms of production from printing with movable type. Can we expect differences in spelling or in punctuation between the two types? Luxury editions can physically weigh so much that no one would want to pick them up or hold them while reading, in contrast to ordinary reading copies. Did the scribes of those prestigious, luxury copies therefore put more effort or less effort into writing uniformly?

Now for the second approach to studying historical material – that of addressing a spelling variable. If occurrences of different spellings are to be investigated, the variables in question must first be properly defined. It may be helpful to remember that variables do not only consist of simple variants according to the pattern of *king* vs. *kyng* or Early New High German ***nahme*** vs. *na_me* 'name'.[1] Variables may also include sequenced elements, such as A + B vs. B + A (Early New High German ***raht/rath*** 'council'). Variants of these two types (so-called simple and complex paradigmatic variants) may even co-occur and make up variants that are multipart (so-called syntagmatic variants): ***bo_ke*** and ***book_*** or ***queen***, ***que_n***, ***cween***, ***cwe_n*** (see Wolfram 1991: 23–24, 2006: 334, Auer and Voeste 2012: 253–55 for corresponding grammatical variants). It must also be considered that variants may contain word boundaries. This is obvious in compound spellings (*hitchhiker/hitch-hiker/hitch hiker*) or in 'long-distance' assimilations such as Old High German ***mag ih*** vs. ***meg ih*** (*i*-mutation), but could also play a role in other cases, for example *wyth hys mount/with hys mount* (analogous to *satysfye/satisfye*).

The next step is to choose a method or to combine different methods in order to analyze the variables in question (as also discussed in Voeste 2020). *Intratextual variable analysis* (TRAVA) involves the investigation of the frequency and range of variants in a single text copy with the objective of comparing specific contexts and explaining particular usages of the variants. Since the external variables remain constant for a single text copy, this method is particularly useful for the detection of potential internal factors that trigger

[1] The underscore indicates that an element does not occur.

the choice of a spelling variant, such as lexical category, intervocalic position or syllabic characteristics. It is also helpful for detecting hypercorrect forms[2] or unintentional interferences[3] stemming from the local substrate variety or the native tongue of a scribe or typesetter. The *intertextual analytical method* (TERVA) aims to compare the results of two or more intratextual investigations, for example with respect to different external determinants such as time and place. This approach may also be used to identify diachronic or diatopic differences in order to exclude them from a study of other external constraints such as the influence of scribal 'schools' or language contact. The third method, namely *cross-textual variable analysis* (CTVA), is a subtype of the intertextual analytical method. It compares the variants of different versions of the same text. This method is also based on comparing alterations from one version to the other in order to detect a pattern of deliberate changes. As a precondition of its use, this approach requires successive textual records, such as a handwritten template and printed edition or different copies of the same text. Ideally, the three methods can be combined in order to uncover the impact of language-internal and external influencing factors on spelling, including diachronic, diatopic, text-type-specific or media-dependent aspects (concerning the writing material). In what follows, I present the advantages and disadvantages of the three methods in more detail. My examples stem from the early history of printing, as this is the working area that I am most familiar with as a researcher.

16.2.1 Intratextual Variable Analysis (TRAVA)

TRAVA is the most suitable method for determining possible internal factors that trigger the choice of a variant, such as syllable boundaries (Early New High German *menner* 'men' but *man* 'man'),[4] adjacent sonorous segments (Turkish *düğün* 'marriage') or assimilations (Hungarian *egyben* 'in one piece', *hatban* 'in six pieces'), and questions of word shape (so-called *graphematic weight*)[5] (Late Middle English 'Chancery standard' *theyre* 'their') or lexical category (German function words *in*/**inn*, *dir*/**dier* 'to you'). This intratextual approach by no means excludes language-external factors. Aspects such as regional origin, level of education and experience, or individual preferences (idiosyncrasies) of the scribes or typesetters involved may have led to the deliberate or unintentional use of certain variants. But if we deal with variability in one and the same text copy, diachronic, diatopic or text-type-specific explanatory factors are less likely.

[2] Hypercorrections are overapplications of perceived rules and may stem from the request or wish to use prestigious variants, for example Spanish *<bacalado> 'cod' instead of <bacalao> (following <pescado> 'fish').

[3] An example for an unintentional interference would be *<pescao> 'fish' (following dialectal [pes'kao]).

[4] Early New High German (ENHG) is the period 1350 to 1650.

[5] A word like <beet> is graphematically heavier than <bet>, see Evertz (2018: 125).

TRAVA has the advantage of allowing for detailed insights into a single text copy. This provides the opportunity to identify even factors that are not immediately apparent. It is advisable to use TRAVA as a preliminary study before starting a larger investigation in an intertextual variable analysis. Potential decisive factors identified in a single text can then be further investigated in a larger corpus. TRAVA is by no means simpler than other methods. Especially when looking at a low number of tokens, it is difficult to rely on percentages only. Consider the following example. Figure 16.1 shows the text of a pamphlet of about 1500 (ISTC ih00134500),[6] a Christian song about Mary's sufferings, in which I have highlighted the uppercase and lowercase letters of the *nomina sacra*: *Maria* (13), *maria* (7), *ihefus* (2), *Jhefus* (1), *Johannes* (2), *Jofeph* (2), *fymeon* (2), and *annas* (1). In total, 18 of the 30 tokens (i.e. 60 percent) are capitalized. If we were to conduct a time-series analysis, we would certainly observe that the percentages increase rapidly during the sixteenth century until all *nomina sacra* are capitalized (the topic is discussed thoroughly

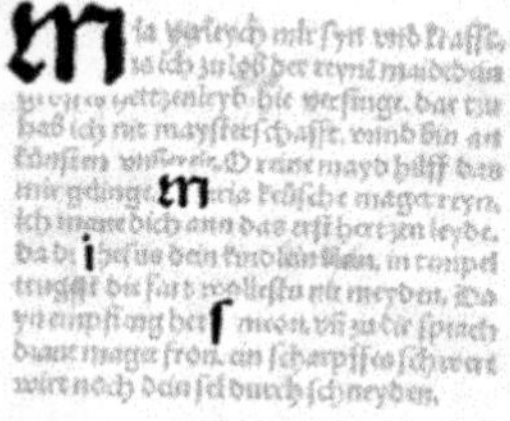

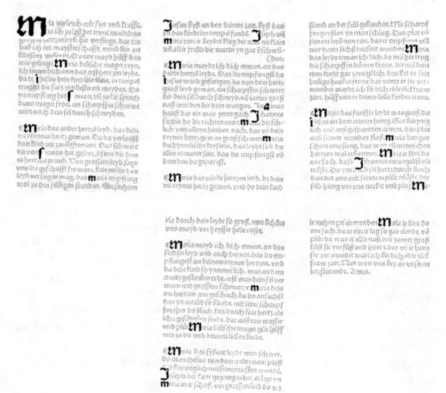

Figure 16.1 *Die sieben Herzensleiden Unserer Lieben Frau*, 5 pages, with highlighted uppercase and lowercase letters of *nomina sacra*
(ISTC ih00134500)

[6] ISTC (*International Short Title Catalogue*) is a database of fifteenth-century European prints.

in Bergmann and Nerius 2006). In the case of TRAVA, however, one cannot simply argue for a change in progress; one must also address the question of why variable spellings occur at all at a given point in time. Was the author or typesetter not aware that his spellings were inconsistent, or was his use of upper and lower case indeed intentional?

As preliminary work for such hypotheses and interpretations, the data must be carefully checked and described. If we take a closer look at the incunable, we can see that the name *Maria* is repeatedly placed at the beginning of a paragraph (opening the verse), namely as the initial word or after an alinea,[7] so that the use of upper case may have served as a structuring element. Furthermore, in 11 out of 13 instances, names as vocative expressions are written in upper case. Names also tend to be written in upper case when following a full stop (9 of 13 instances) or when they are the first word at the top of the page. Eventually, even exceptions can be explained. Sometimes the space in the line seems not to have been sufficient to use a capital letter (see Figure 16.2). All these considerations are of course only hypotheses based on the one incunable selected. They would, however, be a good starting point for a more detailed survey. If one wanted to plan a larger study on this basis, one would include the position (i.e. initial, after pilcrow, after full stop, at the top of the page) as well as the case (i.e. nominative) or the usage in a vocative expression and consider questions of line spacing (i.e. justification), and then one could determine which of the hypotheses would work in a large-scale approach.

16.2.2 Intertextual Variable Analysis (TERVA)

TERVA is a method that involves at least two different texts to investigate the influence of a particular variable, usually the influence of an external one such as time or place of text production. The comparison should be conducted in such a way that only one variable, the so-called independent variable, is examined as a possible causal determinant. TERVA is difficult to perform because it is usually based on the precondition of *ceteris paribus* ('all other things being equal'). If we want to find out whether the independent variable influences the dependent variables (the so-called regressands), it must be verified that no potentially confounding variables interfere. Consequently, all other variables have to remain the same. However, the main problem that has to be

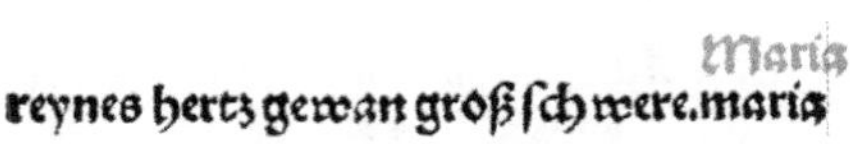

Maria
reynes hertz gewan groß sch were.maria

Figure 16.2 Maria in lower case (vocative after full stop)
(ISTC ih00134500, p. 4, line 15)

[7] An alinea or pilcrow sign is a paragraph mark (¶) indicating a new train of thought or the beginning of a paragraph, respectively.

addressed is the extent to which the *ceteris paribus* condition is fulfilled or can be fulfilled at all. Usually, historical studies do not strictly follow the criterion of *ceteris paribus*; for example, texts stemming from the same region or from the same decade or the same quarter of a century are often considered to be 'the same'. On the other hand, the *ceteris paribus* condition can be interpreted very strictly so that, for example, two London texts may only be regarded as 'the same' if they were produced in the same year, in the same printing shop or chancery, or even by the same typesetter or scribe. Sometimes, even if we focus on one and the same individual, challenges are never lacking. Bowie (2015) has shown that speakers behave a lot like sinusoidal curves, oscillating back and forth between variants during their lifetime. This has also been proven for spelling, morphology and syntax. A corpus analysis of Thomas Mann's works (Grimm 1991) has shown, for example, that his linguistic features are sometimes more consistent with his brother Heinrich's than with his own. Before engaging with a TERVA type of study, therefore, one should carefully consider when the *ceteris paribus* condition is sufficiently met and when it is not, in order to conduct a reliable study that produces meaningful results.

In the following example, I compare three theological treatises printed in Hanover in 1669/70.[8] The publication was motivated by the conversion of John Frederick, duke of the Welf dynasty in the northern territory of Brunswick-Calenberg, to the Roman Catholic Church. The increasing presence of the Catholic faith in Hanover, an exclusively Protestant *residence*,[9] led to a theological dispute, initiated by the chief court chaplain and general superintendent Justus Gesenius. Using the pseudonym Timotheus Friedlieb, Gesenius started the dispute by publishing a treatise entitled *Warum wilt du nicht Römisch=Catholisch werden/wie deine Vorfahren waren?* ('Why don't you want to be Roman Catholic like your ancestors were?'). The question was soon answered on behalf of the Duke by the Jesuit Gaspar Sevenstern and the Capuchin priest Christoph Kirchweg (Köcher 1895: 57). The analytical material that I present here meets the *ceteris paribus* condition sufficiently. My approach is based on three texts of the same type, printed within a few months in the same city. Despite these similarities, the treatises show striking differences. Both Sevenstern and Kirchweg chose Upper German variants, which were not typical of the northern territory of Brunswick-Calenberg and the city of Hanover (Ahlzweig and Pieske 2009). Compared to Gesenius, this is particularly evident in the use of the apocope (Habermann 1997, 2012: 75–78).[10] While Gesenius chose the variant with word-final *-e* (*Ende* 'end', *Worte*

[8] I am grateful to Claus Ahlzweig for bringing this controversy to my attention. The publications examined here are part of his written legacy.

[9] A residence or *Residenzstadt* is a city where the sovereign ruler resided.

[10] Apocope is the loss of a word-final vowel schwa (ə).

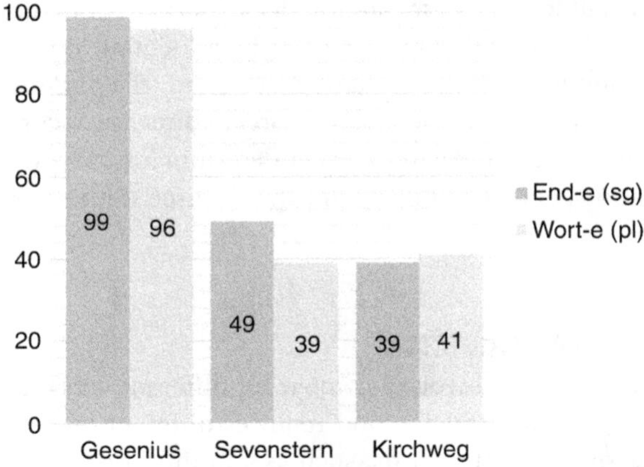

Figure 16.3 Percentages of final e in singular and plural

'words') in almost all instances, his opponents preferred apocopes in the singular and plural. Figure 16.3 shows the distribution of variants with final *-e* in percentage values. The percentages are based on at least 100 tokens in the singular and 50 in the plural per text (tokens in the dative singular case were excluded). Looking at these results, one question comes to mind immediately: How to explain the contrast between Gesenius's text (96–99 percent apocope) and Sevenstern's/Kirchweg's texts (39–49 percent apocope)? The crucial difference between the treatises is the conflicting theological position of the three opponents: Gesenius was a Lutheran, while Sevenstern and Kirchweg were both Roman Catholics. Therefore, a use of Upper German variants such as *Cron-⊘* 'crown' instead of *Crone* or *Zeugnus* 'testimony' instead of *Zeugnis* by Sevenstern and Kirchweg suggests that these southern variants functioned as Catholic shibboleth forms even in the North (for East Upper German, see Rössler 2005). The comparison shows that at the close of the seventeenth century, after the Counter-Reformation had come to an end with the Peace of Westphalia (1648), denominational differences still influenced the choice of variants.

Although the analysis of an isolated determinant based on the *ceteris paribus* condition is useful and convincing, it is not always the best choice. Consider that a causal relationship between a spelling variable and an external or internal constraint may be difficult to isolate since linguistic variables can be affected for more than one reason (for an introduction, see Walker 2010, 2014). In addition, various factors may affect each other or trigger the choice of a variant so that it would not be advisable to isolate a single causal determinant. Therefore, especially when looking into larger corpora, historical linguists work on the assumption of *mutatis mutandis* ('with the necessary modifications'), allowing other possible determinants to change as well. In a time-series analysis, for example, multiple factors (such as text type, dialect or social rank of the author) are correlated with each other while the aim is still to determine which one of them is particularly influential. While the *ceteris paribus* assumption is helpful for isolating causation, the *mutatis mutandis* concept suggests a multivariate analysis in order to measure correlations between a spelling variable and several other determinants, usually computed with the correlation coefficient *r* using the open-source software *R* (Gries 2013).

16.2.3 Cross-textual Variable Analysis (CTVA)

CTVA is a subtype of TERVA and it involves comparing different versions of the same text. As a precondition, this method requires different copies, reprints, editions or successive textual records, such as a draft, a first complete manuscript and a fair or final copy. CTVA adheres even more strongly to the principle of *ceteris paribus* because it retains the author and the text not just as similar but as identical factors. CTVA is particularly suitable if one wants to investigate changes that appear to have been made intentionally (and perhaps even systematically) from one version of a text to the next, possibly inserted by the scribe, the editor, the proofreader or the compositor. Those types of variation may indicate a sound change or characteristic regional or local features, and, even more interestingly, they may warrant a revaluation of spelling variants. Revaluations or reanalyses typically occur in folk etymologies or in so-called eggcorns (*eggcorn* is a misinterpretation of *acorn*). In spelling, they are most evident in capitalization or in word segmentation, when syllable or morpheme boundaries are explicitly clarified. Revaluations can be used as evidence for the grammatical editing of spelling variants.

In the following sample study, I compare three editions (A, B_1 and B_2) of a poem by Hans Witzstat, later used as a hymn text, *Der geiſtlich buchſsbaum. Von dem ſtreyt des fleyſchs wider den geyſt*, 'The sacred boxwood. On the conflict between flesh and spirit'. The title is probably an allusion to a popular song about a dispute between a boxwood and a willow. All three editions were printed in Nuremberg, first in 1526 (A) by Jobst Gutknecht and then reprinted, probably in 1528 (B_1 and B_2), by Kunigunde Hergot, who continued her husband's work after he was executed for political reasons in 1527. The *ceteris paribus* condition is strictly met for the texts mentioned above. Two copies even stem from the same printing shop. The editions consist of only seven pages in octavo. Nevertheless, there is a whole range of differences in terms of spelling. Texts A and B_1 differ in 148 instances, A and B_2 differ in 178 instances, while B_1 and B_2 differ in 72 instances only (see the examples below).

Particularly apparent are the frequently occurring differences in the graphic representation of the diphthong /aɪ/ or /ɛɪ/, which is written <ey> or <ei>, once also <ai> (in A, typical of Middle High German (MHG) /ɛɪ/ in Upper German dialects). Apart from the <ai> spelling of MHG /ɛɪ/, there is no historically justifiable pattern. MHG /ɛɪ/ and /iː/ appear both as <ei> and <ey>: examples include *reyn* 'clean'/*allein* 'alone' (MHG *reine, alein*) and *weyl* 'while'/*feindt* 'foe' (MHG *wîle, vî(e)nt*). There is, however, an interesting level of consistency among the texts: due to positional constraints, <i> never occurs at the end of a word (e.g. bey 'by, near', *drey* 'three', *frey* 'free'). At a first glance, the alternation between <ei> and <ey> seems to represent free variation, because the same types are realized as variants (*dein* ~ *deyn* 'your', *fleiſch* ~ *fleyſch* 'flesh', *ſtreit* ~ *ſtreyt* 'dispute'). However, the typesetters of each of the three texts proceeded according to different principles. Text A from Jobst Gutknecht's workshop shows a clear tendency to avoid <ei> in front of letters whose stems have ascenders, probably because the i-dot comes too close to the ascender (Figure 16.4). But while he opted for <ey> instead of <ei> here, he otherwise still used spellings with simple <i> in front of ascenders (*nit* 'not', *iſt* 'is', *will* 'want(s)' and so on). A comparison of the three editions shows that only compositor B_1 followed this practice to a large extent or at least abode closely by the template of typesetter A (Figure 16.5). He also adhered to this template in other cases, while typesetter B_2 did not follow their footsteps (a hypothesis which can also be confirmed by spellings such as *abendt, verporgen, ſtätig*). However, we cannot conclude from this congruence that typesetter B_1's avoidance of the sequence <ei> + ascender was a conscious decision. The typesetter of text B_2 probably did not comprehend this

Figure 16.4 Undesired combination of i-dot and ascender

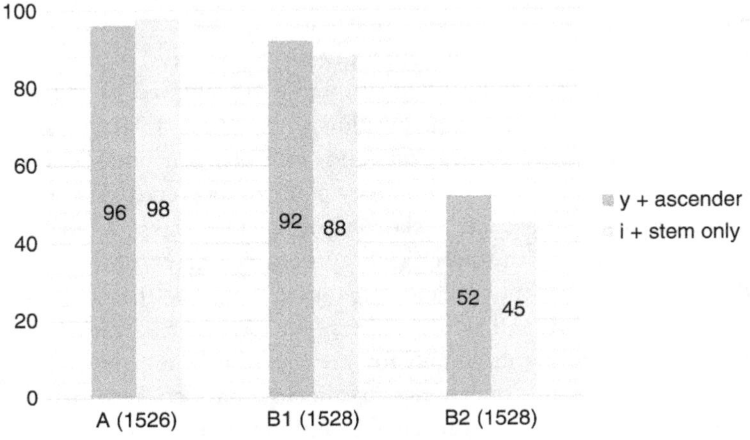

Figure 16.5 Percentages of <y> and <i> in relation to following ascenders/nonascenders (Σ 92)

aesthetic restriction, or if he was aware of it, he did not continue the practice. His deviations from the template (presumably A or B_1) rather speak in favor of free variation in text B_2.

The analysis reveals a different typesetting behavior, that is, a different action with respect to the variable, in each text copy. One of the typesetters (A) followed the aesthetic-typographical restriction to not use <ei> followed by letters with ascenders. The typesetter of the first reprint (B_1) adopted this special feature, just as he closely adhered to the template in typesetting and spelling. The third typesetter (B_2), on the other hand, used a completely different approach: in his copy, <ei> and <ey> alternate independently of subsequent letters with ascenders. A comparison via CTVA affords one the ability to detect such differences in the behavior of the craftsmen involved. Clearly, this method is of great value for developing a satisfactory historical interpretation, especially since such subtle differences fade away when large amounts of data are analyzed in historical corpora.

16.3 Data Interpretation

After having reviewed and analyzed the data, one usually has to arrive at relevant conclusions. However, this does not happen on neutral ground, because data interpretation and the previous data collection cannot be truly separated. As the examples above have shown from different angles, the annotation or the close inspection and description of data during the collection phase is a prerequisite for further hypotheses and interpretations. In turn, data collection is aided or even decisively influenced by focusing on the phenomena we consider relevant. Judgments about relevance may be based on specific research objectives, as our scholarly expertise or even our own interests and taste filter our view of the data and influence their description. Abbott (2004: 245) points out the problem of tunnel vision, in which researchers tend to see the same puzzles and answer the same questions over and over again. For political, individual or moral reasons, they may be tempted to address well-intended but repetitive research questions by, for example, focusing on particular social groups (women, workers, religious 'outsiders'). This focused research may miss the fact that many patterns are repeated within different social groups. Against this backdrop, we need to interpret our historical data and the behavior of scribes and typesetters with an open mind. We should always expect unknown determinants to influence the choice of variants, including determinants which we may not have considered previously. Unexpected determinants might, for instance, be connected to frequency effects, so that an ongoing change first occurs in function words but affects content words only with a time lag (see Phillips 2006: 181–96, Bybee 2007: 5–18). Or there might be questions of orthographic form and design to consider. Written characters and words may be extended, abbreviated, modernized or historicized because of the given space, format or material (Shute 2017). Shorter forms may have served to make better use of the limited space, or historical spellings may have been chosen to support the retrospective construction of tradition and thus to ensure social prestige (Voeste 2010: 2–7). Therefore, it is especially important to study the original writing surface and spacing (in large or small format, in single or multiple columns, with even or uneven lines) and not to rely solely on decontextualized spelling variants collected in electronic corpora.

16.4 Conclusion

If forming hypotheses depends so much on the method of data collection, what does this imply for the three methods presented? In principle, TRAVA takes all variants of a text into account in their full scope, although the variants are generally narrowed down to certain subsets (such as the use of uppercase letters). The potential set of hypotheses is initially unlimited; all language-internal and language-external variables can be considered as explanatory factors. Therefore, the advantage of TRAVA is its special usefulness for forming hypotheses. If you work thoroughly with this method, and if you study the variants in detail, you may come up with innovative hypotheses for variable correlations. TERVA, on the other hand, is a much more stringent method that is controlled by theoretical presumptions, since it is based on a defined testing arrangement and aims to test a predetermined explanation. The independent and dependent variables in question are previously specified and are then brought together for testing. Therefore, as a description technique, TERVA can be seen as a more focused method. In terms of research logic, everything that has been said about TERVA applies even more to CTVA. In this third and last method, the problem of *ceteris paribus* is reduced, though not wholly eliminated. The comparative investigation of temporally and spatially distant versions of one and the same text inevitably draws the researcher's attention to different material modes and to the text's various sociocultural contexts.

All three methods have their specific advantages and disadvantages, and none of them possesses an inherent superiority over the others. One can even attempt to combine all three methods and apply them consecutively to achieve the best possible outcome. But no matter which of the methods you choose or how you combine them, historical orthography remains a field for those who are thrilled by complex puzzles and bored by simple solutions.

17

Philological Approaches

Annina Seiler and Christine Wallis

17.1 Introduction

As a mode of study, philology has a long history, yet the way the term has been used, and the attitude of scholars to both the study of orthography and the meaning of orthographic variation, has changed substantially over time. This chapter outlines the origins and history of philology, from its roots in the Classical period to the present day, and discusses how far philological approaches pertain to the study of historical orthography. Philology's focus on material, historical and manuscript contexts makes it an especially fruitful way of interrogating historical texts, and philological methods have long been viewed as a particularly apt way of dealing with (among other features) the wide orthographic variation naturally present in medieval works. To illustrate the concerns and approaches of present-day philologists to the study of historical orthography, the chapter presents two case studies. The first focuses on scribal practices in Old English and provides an example of a manuscript-centered analysis of orthography. The second focuses on the scripting of Old English and Old High German and illustrates how historical orthographies can be analyzed by mapping spelling onto an etymological sound reference system.[1]

The term philology ultimately derives from Greek φιλολογία 'love of reasoning, love of learning and literature', which is a derivative of the compound adjective φιλόλογος 'fond of words'. It enters the modern European languages via Latin *philologia* in the later Middle Ages; compare French *philologie*, Spanish *filología*, Italian, Portuguese, Polish *filologia*, Czech *filologie*, Russian *филоло́гия*. The English and German words (*philology*, *Philologie*)

[1] Scripting describes the process by which a language is put into writing. For a discussion of the concept see Schaefer (2012: 1278, 1280) and the literature cited there.

are coined on the basis of the French form.[2] Philology involves a wide range of practices that are generally linked to the study of texts and languages. Initially tied to the task of editing works from Classical Antiquity (fifth century BC–fifth century AD), philology has split into separate branches, including Classical philology, comparative philology (or historical linguistics), manuscript studies, *Altertumskunde*, as well as literary criticism.[3] As a result of the differentiation of philology, the notion as to what philological approaches entail has changed considerably and also differs from discipline to discipline. Nevertheless, all philological practices are characterized by an orientation toward the material sources in which the languages and literatures of the past are attested.

Not only the notion of what philological approaches entail but also their appreciation has changed. Jacob Grimm (1785–1863) placed a very high value on philology when he famously claimed that "none among the sciences is prouder, more noble, more pugnacious than philology and more implacable against mistakes."[4] On the other hand, in the first half of the twentieth century, *Buchstabenphilologie* (i.e. philology of letters) came to be used as a derogatory term assigned to research that was held to rely too strongly on the written word. In the past decades, philology has undergone a rehabilitation, particularly in the context of historical sociolinguistics and pragmatics with a strong focus on the manuscript evidence. The different uses of philology have impacted philological approaches to orthography. Whether orthography was considered worthy of study has waxed and waned with the fortunes of philology itself.

17.2 Philology in Classical Antiquity and the Middle Ages

In Classical Antiquity (eighth century BC-fifth century AD) and the Middle Ages (fifth–fifteenth century), philology included all branches of learning, as illustrated by Martianus Capella's fifth century allegorical encyclopaedia *De nuptiis Philologiae et Mercurii* (ed. Willis 1983). This work gives an account of the seven maidens which Philology, a personification of learning, receives as a wedding gift from her husband Mercury. The maidens embody the seven liberal arts: grammar, dialectic, rhetoric (the *trivium* of medieval education); geometry, arithmetic, astronomy and music (the *quadrivium*).[5] The study of

[2] See the *Oxford English Dictionary Online* (Simpson and Proffitt 2000–), *Französisches etymologisches Wörterbuch* (von Wartburg 1928–2003), *Deutsches Wörterbuch* (Grimm and Grimm 1854–1961), s.vv.

[3] On the differentiation of philology into separate fields see, for example, Harpham (2009), Wolf and Blauth-Henke (2011), Turner (2014).

[4] German original: "keine unter allen wissenschaften ist hochmütiger, vornehmer, streitsüchtiger als die philologie und gegen fehler unbarmherziger" (Grimm 1864: I, 235). All translations are by the authors unless otherwise stated.

[5] On the *trivium* and *quadrivium* see, for example, Kintzinger 2016a, 2016b.

orthography lies at the very foundation of this curriculum as it represents the initial step of the *Ars grammatica*, the first discipline of the *trivium*. Classical and medieval discussions of orthography center on the concept of the *littera*, which combines *nomen* 'name', *figura* 'shape' and *vox* 'voice' (or *potestas* 'might', i.e. the sound value of a letter).[6] Thus, *littera* refers not only to the character as a visual unit of a writing system, but also to the sound a character represents, as well as to the name by which it is identified. Consequently, medieval discussions of orthography focus not only on the correct spelling of Latin words but also on their pronunciation. Regional differences of Latin are addressed by Abbo of Fleury in the tenth century: in his *Quaestiones grammaticales* (ed. Guerreau-Jalabert 1982), he criticizes the way his students at Ramsay Abbey apparently pronounced words like *civis*, using the spelling <qui> to represent what must have been the sound /k/.[7]

Medieval accounts of orthography do not normally focus on the vernacular languages. One notable exception is the twelfth-century *First Grammatical Treatise* (ed. and trans. Benediktsson 1972), which devises an orthographic system for Old Icelandic in which each speech sound is represented by a single character (Huth 2003: 444–57). While the First Grammarian's use of minimal pairs to establish differences between sounds is highly innovative and reminiscent of twentieth-century linguistic methodology, his terminology is firmly grounded in medieval grammatical theory; a *stafr*, for example, like its Latin counterpart *littera*, combines shape, sound and name (Benediktsson 1972: 44–45). Sharing the fate of many orthographic reforms, few of the First Grammarian's suggestions were incorporated into Old Icelandic spelling practice.

17.3 Orthography, Renaissance Philology and Beyond

In the Renaissance (fifteenth and sixteenth centuries), philology evolved as the set of methods necessary to edit Classical Greek and Latin texts.[8] The antiquarian interest of scholars in the sixteenth and seventeenth century also extended to the vernacular languages, which resulted in the establishment of 'modern' philology. Textual criticism necessitated the collation of different

[6] As, for example, stated by the fourth century AD Roman grammarian Donatus (*Ars grammatica*, I.2. 'De littera'; edited by Keil and Mommsen 2009 [1864]: 368, line 14). The tripartite differentiation goes back to Stoic language theory; the Greek equivalents (as attested by Diogenes of Babylon in the second century BC) for the different aspects of γράμμα are στοιχεῖον, χαρακτήρ and ὄνομα (see Vogt-Spira 1991: 301–2, 308). For an in-depth account, see Vogt-Spira (1991); see also Desbordes (1990: 123–25).

[7] Ironically, Abbo imposes a pronunciation resulting from Romance assibilation of /k/ > /ts/ and criticizes what must have been the Classical sound value. For a detailed discussion of Abbo's *Quaestiones*, see Roger Wright (2011).

[8] On the philological endeavors of the Renaissance, see Zanobini (2016).

manuscripts and, thus, resulted in fine-grained analyses of orthographic differences and their implications (see Zanobini 2016: 5). The method culminated in the nineteenth century in Lachmann's scientific approach to the reconstruction of the archetype of a text – still one of the tenets of Classical and medieval philology.[9]

On a theoretical level, Renaissance scholars started to rethink the Classical concept of *littera*. Julius Caesar Scaliger (1484–1558), was among the first to criticize the *Ars grammatica* and to argue that *littera* referred only to the written letter (Vogt-Spira 1991: 311–13). Scaliger adduced spurious etymological 'evidence' to support his view: he explained that *litera* – to be spelled with a single <t> – derives from *lineaturae*, that is, the lines drawn on the page. Vogt-Spira suggests a connection between this new conceptualization of writing and the practice of silent reading, which certainly became the norm with the spread of printed books, though it must have started some centuries earlier (Vogt-Spira 1991: 313–14).[10] Printing, in any case, did engender a wider debate on orthography, which manifested itself in suggestions for orthographic reforms for the modern languages across sixteenth- and seventeenth-century Western Europe (Neis 2011: 174). The aim of such propositions was to bring the spelling in line with contemporary pronunciation, as for example, by Louis Meigret (1500–58) for French, John Hart (d. 1574) for English and Gonzalo de Correas (1571–1631) for Spanish (Neis 2011, Salmon 1999: 15–21, Lucas 2000). Reform attempts were often informed by philological work on medieval texts. Some of the characters proposed by Sir Thomas Smith (1513–77) for English, for instance, were adopted from Anglo-Saxon scripts, for example <ð> and <þ> for the voiced and voiceless dental fricatives, respectively, or <ꝼ> for /v/ and <ʒ> for /ʤ/ (Lucas 2000: 6).

The use of these characters was closely linked to type design.[11] Such spelling reforms were generally unsuccessful (Liuzza 1996: 25); however, their influence is still visible in the International Phonetic Alphabet.[12] During the eighteenth-century boom in the publication of pronouncing dictionaries, elocutionists employed a variety of methods for conveying their preferred pronunciation, such as italic and Gothic fonts (Johnston 1764), accents and macrons (Jones 1798), numeric (Kenrick 1773) and alphanumeric notation (Walker 1791, Sheridan 1780), or devising their own systems (Spence 1775) to reconcile spelling and pronunciation.[13] However, spelling reform itself was not a concern of the eighteenth-century orthoepists.

9 For a detailed discussion of Lachmann's method, see Trovato (2014).

10 On the origins of silent reading, see Saenger (1997); for silent reading in the seventeenth and eighteenth centuries, see Jajdelska (2007).

11 On the print types for Anglo-Saxon texts, see Lucas (1999, cited in Lucas 2000: 6).

12 On orthography and phonetics in the sixteenth and seventeenth centuries, see MacMahon (2013: 112–14).

13 On eighteenth-century pronouncing dictionaries and the relationship between their notation and contemporary phonology, see Beal et al. (2020) and references therein.

17.4 Orthography and Comparative Philology

Philology took a new turn in the late eighteenth century with the identification of Sanskrit as an Indo-European language by Sir William Jones in 1786. This discovery resulted in a focus on the relationship and history of the Indo-European languages (Sonderegger 2000a: 417, 2000b: 443), as in the work undertaken by the Danish philologist Rasmus Rask (1787–1832) and the Germans Franz Bopp (1791–1867), and Jacob (1785–1863) and Wilhelm Grimm (1786–1859). Jacob Grimm discussed orthography in a lecture addressed to the Prussian Academy of Sciences in 1847. His starting point was contemporary German orthography, which he considered to be 'barbaric' in contrast with earlier spelling:

> More than 800 years ago, in St. Gall during the time of Notker, German orthography was in a better state, and great care was applied to the exact designation of our sounds; good things can still be said about the writings of the twelfth and thirteenth century; only since the fourteenth century has it started to deteriorate.
>
> (Grimm 1864: I, 349)

Grimm specifically criticized words in which the spelling deviates from the spoken language, for example, 'superfluous' letters in compounds like *Schifffahrt*,[14] etymological or hypercorrect spellings, as well as the different ways of representing vowel length (Grimm 1864: I, 330, 349–50). Interestingly, Grimm also took issue with features of written language that have no counterpart in the spoken language, such as hyphens or apostrophes, as well as word-initial capitals. His remarks illustrate that, in his view, an ideal writing system is closely aligned with the spoken language and has a one-to-one relationship between letters/graphs and sounds. This attitude is coupled with the belief that earlier orthographies represented this ideal state.[15] Grimm has been accused by later scholars of not being able to distinguish between letters and sounds (see Haas 1990: 10–13). While he may not have been an astute phonetician, part of this criticism arises from Grimm's *Deutsche Grammatik* (1822), whose Book 1 is entitled *Von den buchstaben*. Yet, Grimm's use of *buchstabe* stands in the Classical *littera* tradition: he clearly separated *zeichen* ('sign') and *laut* ('sound'), and he was very aware of the fact that the sounds of historical stages of languages can only partially be recovered from writing. Fowkes goes one step further in his defense of Grimm and argues "that his use of the term *Buchstabe* was tantamount to 'phoneme'" (Fowkes 1964: 60).[16] On

[14] Recent debates on German orthography still focus on the same issues; the prescribed spelling for *Schiff(f)ahrt*, to use one example, changed from two to three <f> in the *Rechtschreibreform* in 1996.

[15] For a critical discussion of this notion, see Stanley (1988).

[16] Fowkes also draws attention to Grimm's use of minimal pairs and speculates that he may have known the *First Grammatical Treatise* (Fowkes 1964: 61).

the other hand, as Haas (1990: 13) reminds us, as a philologist Grimm primarily dealt with letters and not with sounds.

The neogrammarians (*Junggrammatiker*) in the second half of the nineteenth century took the natural sciences, primarily anatomy and biology, as a model for their linguistic work.[17] On the one hand, this resulted in the application of empirical methods to the study of articulatory phonetics, or 'sound physiology'. On the other hand, based on the wide-reaching impact of Charles Darwin's *On the Origin of Species* (1859), it led to the adoption of the tree model for historical linguistics and resulted in the reconstruction of Proto-Indo-European. Orthography is largely ignored in comparative philology, even though an understanding of the letter–sound correlations of the earliest attested stages of languages is a prerequisite for any reconstruction. The attitude of historical linguistics toward writing is reflected in the handbooks on the earlier stages of languages; they traditionally start with a section on spelling and pronunciation before they move on to a more detailed discussion of the phonology and morphology (and rarely the syntax). However, in-depth discussions of the writing system itself are usually absent.[18] Only a few nineteenth-century studies focus specifically on orthography: there are, for example, Friedrich Wilkens's *Zum hochalemannischen Konsonantismus der althochdeutschen Zeit* (1891) and Friedrich Kauffmann's 'Über althochdeutsche Orthographie' (1892), both on Old High German spelling, or Karl D. Bülbring's 'Was lässt sich aus dem gebrauch der buchstaben *k* und *c* im Matthäus-Evangelium des Rushworth-Manuscripts folgern?' (1899) on Old English orthography.

A theoretical discussion of writing is provided by Hermann Paul (1846–1921) in *Prinzipien der Sprachgeschichte* (Paul 2009 [1880]). In his chapter 13, 'Language and writing' (*Sprache und schrift*), Paul stresses the fact that any linguistic information from the past is only accessible through "the medium of writing" (*das medium der schrift*, Paul 2009 [1880]: 245). However, he holds that it is impossible to fully reconvert writing into speech – even in the case of writing systems that are close to spoken language. To illustrate the relationship of spoken and written language, Paul uses two similes: first, spoken language and writing are as a line is to a number (Paul 2009 [1880]: 246), since speech sounds blend into each other whereas writing is discontinuous. Second, they are as a painting to a rough sketch, meaning that writing can never express all the nuances of speech, and only someone who is familiar

[17] On the Neogrammarians, see Putschke (1998), Burridge (2013: 157–65).

[18] See, for example, the grammars of the early Germanic languages, such as Wilhelm Braune's *Gotische Grammatik* (Braune 1880), his *Althochdeutsche Grammatik* (Braune 1886) or Eduard Sievers's *Angelsächsische Grammatik* (Sievers 1882). Haas (1990: 13) points out that the *Althochdeutsche Grammatik* only distinguishes letters and sounds from its thirteenth edition (Braune and Eggers 1975), and only in the fifteenth edition (Braune and Reiffenstein 2004) do we get a separate section on 'Schreibsysteme und Paläographie' (13–18, §§7–8), though some details were already included in §8 'Schriftsysteme' of the thirteenth and fourteenth editions.

with the language will be able to recover details such as quantity or stress (Paul 2009 [1880]: 249–50).

17.5 Saussure and the Structuralists

Starting with Ferdinand de Saussure's (1857–1913) ground-breaking publications, philology, referring to a diachronic analysis of language, came to be contrasted with synchronic linguistics. Saussure explicitly criticized philology for "attaching itself too slavishly to the written language and forgetting the living language" (Saussure 1995 [1916]: 14). In his view, the only function of writing was to represent spoken language; for those who study writing rather than language Saussure used a comparison similar to the one presented by Hermann Paul: "It is as if one believed that, in order to know someone, one should look at his photo rather than at his face" (Saussure 1995 [1916]: 45). Therefore, he argued, the sole object of linguistics is spoken language. The only reason for studying writing is that linguists need to understand its "functionality, defects and perils" (44) in order to recover language from written sources.

This view dominated the structuralists' approach to language, which culminated in Leonard Bloomfield's famous statement in his introduction to *Language* that, "[w]riting is not language, but merely a way of recording language by means of visible marks" (Bloomfield 1973 [1933]: 21). While Bloomfield considered writing an impediment, whose study is only needed in order to "get [...] information about the speech of past times" (Bloomfield 1973: 20–21), he nevertheless devoted one chapter to "Written records" (Bloomfield 1973: 297–313), in which he discussed the properties and history of different writing systems. Bloomfield also used a simile to illustrate the relationship of writing to language: "writing is [...] merely an external device, like the use of the phonography, which happens to preserve for our observation some features of the speech of past times" (Bloomfield 1973: 299). The generally negative attitude toward writing meant that, as Venezky (1970: 10) put it, "orthography was relegated to the backporch of the new linguistic science."

In the Prague linguistic circle, Josef Vachek (1909–96) began to rethink the structuralist stance on writing, identifying written language as a separate norm alongside spoken language. Vachek saw the two norms as independent but co-ordinated representations of a universal linguistic norm, or *langue*. Yet, he accorded independent status only to established writing systems and considered the earliest attempts at writing by a linguistic community as "a mere transposition of the spoken norm" (Vachek 1939: 102) or as "a kind of quasi-transcription" (Vachek 1945–49: 91) and, thus, as a secondary system of representation. Vachek's work heralded the development of grapholinguistics as a separate linguistic discipline. This field has been dominated by a debate on the relationship between writing and spoken language and the consequent methodological question whether to use an autonomistic or a relational approach for graphemic analysis. Proponents of an autonomistic approach call for an analysis of written language without making recourse to the spoken language.[19]

17.6 Philology in the Twentieth Century

Philological approaches to orthography in the twentieth century have largely eschewed autonomistic methods. Instead, they are characterized by a careful assessment of spelling evidence in combination with other philological methods. Particular significance has been attached to the letter–sound correlations of the Latin alphabet in different regions and time periods. An early study urging a reconsideration of the evidence of orthographic variation was Daunt's (1939) examination of the Old English spellings which were traditionally viewed as representing short diphthongs arising from a number of sound changes.[20] Under one such change (breaking), monophthongs which were followed by /r/ or /l/ plus another consonant (or by /h/ on its own) became diphthongs, for example *weorpan, eald, feohtan*. Daunt reinterpreted the digraphs <ea> and <eo>, not as evidence of short diphthongs, but as allophones of the short vowels /æ/ and /e/, the second vowel indicating the velar quality of the following consonant. According to Daunt, this was due to Irish influence on Old English orthography, where vowel graphs are used as diacritics to distinguish velarized and palatalized consonants.[21]

Important work on Old High German orthography and phonology was undertaken by Penzl. His numerous publications provided new impulses, in particular, by making explicit some of the methodological issues at stake (e.g. Penzl 1950, 1959, 1971, 1982, 1987).[22] For example, Penzl (1971: 305) proposes a method for establishing the phonological systems of early Germanic languages, which combines an "internal graphemic analysis" with a "diagraphic comparison." The first takes into consideration the "choice and distribution of graphemes" within a single text, while the latter entails an analysis of the spelling attested in earlier or later periods as well as in different dialects. Penzl illustrates the application of this method with an example from the St. Gall *Paternoster & Creed* (c. 790). This text uses <o>, <oo> in words like *losi, prooth, sonen, erstoont*. Comparing this material with the same words in

[19] For a summary and discussion of the different positions, see Glaser (1988); see also Chapter 5 (on relational and autonomistic approaches) and Chapter 6 (on grapholinguistics), this volume.

[20] For example, palatal diphthongization (Campbell 1959: 64–71), breaking (54–60), and back mutation (85–93).

[21] See Stockwell and Barritt (1951, 1955), and White (2000) for a further development of this argument. For a different opinion, see Kuhn and Quirk (1953, 1955); for a phonemic interpretation of Old English spelling, generally, see Kuhn (1961, 1970).

[22] For a selected bibliography of Penzl, see Rauch and Carr (1979: 11–18).

Notker's works (eleventh century), it becomes clear that for Notker there is a graphic contrast between <ô> (*lôse, brôt*) and <uô> (*[be]suônet, irstuônt*). Early St. Gall charter material (before 762) shows that Notker's <ô> corresponds to <au> or later <ao> (e.g. *Autmarus, Gaozberto*); this is not the case for Notker's <uô>, which corresponds to <o> in the charters. This evidence makes it clear that in the *Paternoster & Creed* "the two *o oo* must have been different, even if lack of symbols led to their graphic merger in the writing system of [St.] G[all] Pat[ernoster]'s scribe" (Penzl 1971: 306). Penzl's method also takes other types of evidence into consideration, which include comparative data from the wider language family, meter and rhyme, loanwords, typological aspects, as well as metalinguistic comments. On a theoretical level, Penzl (1971: 307) identified the "phonemic fit of the orthography" as "a major consideration" of any analysis of written texts. He questioned the structuralist assumption of biuniqueness (i.e. a one-to-one relation of graphemes and phonemes), which resulted either in misconceptions of the phonology represented by early orthographies or in a rejection of writing as an object worthy of study. In Penzl's work, by contrast, a careful consideration of the "complex orthographic solutions" (Penzl 1971: 307) leads to a deeper understanding of writing systems and their evolution.

In another work arguing for a more nuanced relationship between orthography and sound values, Clark (1992a) worked at the intersection of history and onomastics. She carefully considered the spellings of personal and place names in the *Domesday Book*, which routinely render /θ/ and /ð/ as <t> or <d>, for example. Clark disputed the traditional view that these unetymological spellings represented the effects of French speakers' pronunciation on insular names, and concluded that the Domesday scribes were "not consciously representing current pronunciations used either by scribes or by informants" (Clark 1992a: 320); rather, they were deliberately rendering insular names according to Latin (or, when that failed, French) orthographic norms, in the context of what was a Latin-language administrative text. Similar considerations involving detailed discussions of the pronunciation of medieval Latin, letter–sound correlations and vernacular phonology resulted, for example, in Harvey's (2011) reassessment of the origins of Celtic orthography (and publications cited there), or Dietz's (2006) analysis of digraphs in the transition from Old to Middle English. These studies demonstrate philology's continuing applicability to a number of related disciplines.

17.7 'New Philology' and Pragmaphilology

In the second half of the twentieth century, a renewed emphasis on the value of the manuscript sources of medieval texts lay at the heart of 'New Philology'. This approach arose from concerns among literary scholars that medieval studies – long seen as a bastion of the philological method – had become marginalized and widely perceived as irrelevant in the face of newer methodologies and advances, particularly in literary criticism. In a special volume of *Speculum*, Nichols (1990) describes New Philology in terms of a renewal, with a strong desire among its adherents to return to its origins in manuscript culture. This entailed a concentration on the materiality of the text (see Chapter 15, this volume), in contrast with earlier focuses on text stemmata and the reconstruction of an idealized, 'original' text as envisaged by its author. The new approach presented itself as a fundamental shift; whereas earlier efforts had had the effect of narrowing the variation (orthographic, morphological or lexical) naturally present in multiple-witness texts in an attempt to retrieve the author's 'original' text, New Philologists emphasized the importance of variety inherent in the different manuscripts.[23] Variety in the manuscript and linguistic variation were seen as fundamental aspects of the condition of medieval texts:

> If we accept the multiple forms in which our artifacts have been transmitted, we may recognize that medieval culture did not simply live with diversity, it cultivated it. The 'new' philology of the last decade or more reminds us that, as medievalists, we need to embrace the consequences of that diversity, not simply live with it, but to situate it squarely within our methodology.
>
> (Nichols 1990: 8–9)

New Philology's emphasis on the original manuscript text aligned literary studies more closely with some of the more language-oriented approaches to studying manuscript texts, although some questioned whether New Philology offered anything that was not already being done.[24]

More recent work has again returned to the question of manuscript transmission and how this can be elucidated by the evidence offered by orthographic variation.[25] Scholars in historical linguistics have also sought a return to the manuscript text; such a plea was at the heart of Lass's (2004) essay which, in focusing on the processes of textual selection in corpus-building, makes a strong case for the inclusion only of texts as they occur in their manuscript

[23] For an overview of New Philology and critical responses to the movement, see Yager (2010).

[24] See Baisch (2018) for German reactions to Nichols (1990). Breier's (1910) study of *The Owl and the Nightingale* established that the C and J manuscripts had been copied from an exemplar which had been written by two scribes, each using his own dialect. His work showing that the C scribe was a *literatim* copier who preserved the original spellings, in contrast with the J scribe's translating behavior, pre-dates some of the methods and concerns of later work in the area.

[25] See Lapidge (2000) for an attempt to provide further dating evidence for the archetype of *Beowulf* by deducing the likely paleographic forms underlying spelling variations and scribal errors in the poem's only existing manuscript. Neidorf (2013) analyzes errors rendering proper names in *Beowulf*, and discusses the implications this has for the scribes' understanding of their exemplar, and thus of the likely date of the original poem. Fulk (2010, 2012) analyzes non–West-Saxon spellings that occur throughout a body of anonymous Old English homiletic texts, concluding that they provide evidence for a more widespread Mercian literary production than previously assumed, the majority of which has not survived.

form. He advocates the faithful recording of features such as spelling, capitalization and punctuation, and rejects edited texts which normalize or modernize; building a corpus from edited texts runs the risk of incorporating the distortions of editorial choices into the evidence we are able to gain from corpus inquiry. Smith (1996: 14) also emphasizes the necessity of bringing together philological and linguistic approaches when studying Old or Middle English, as advocated in historical pragmatics and historical sociolinguistics. He points out that as our earliest records of the language are mediated to us through writing, an understanding of writing systems is essential if we are to undertake effective historical language research (Smith 1996: 56).[26]

The emergence of pragmaphilology as a discipline also reflects the increasing preoccupation of scholars with the written text in its context. In a seminal publication heralding the arrival of the new discipline, Jacobs and Jucker (1995: 11–12) state that "adequate (i.e. pragmatic) analysis of historical texts must study these texts in their entirety including sociohistorical context, their production process and – crucially – a faithful account not only of the syntactic/lexical level but also the physical and orthographic level." Among the more recent studies in the field are those which combine small details (e.g. punctuation or paleography) with morphosyntactic features and wider concerns such as the social contexts of a text's production, in order to produce a more nuanced and rounded picture of the text and its communicative function.[27] At heart, pragmaphilology, in common with New Philology and other recent fields in linguistics such as historical sociolinguistics, maintains a focus on original texts. As Taavitsainen and Fitzmaurice (2007: 18) note, "a prerequisite for the conduct of historical pragmatics is the acceptance of written texts as legitimate data." The increasing availability of high-quality facsimiles and online scans of manuscripts has been fundamental in enabling a more manuscript-centered approach which is able to account for factors such as paleographical data alongside areas which fall more traditionally under the domain of linguistics. Baisch (2018: 183) notes that the increasing availability of digital editions "has begun to open up new possibilities which reflect central preoccupations of the New Philology."

17.8 A Linguistic Atlas of Late Mediaeval English

While not always a mainstream approach, the philological focus on manuscript text and context repeatedly surfaces as a primary concern among scholars working on medieval language and literature. This holistic

[26] See also Labov (1994: 11) on the "bad data problem."

[27] See for example, Williams (2014), who includes orthographic variation as part of a range of features in a pragmaphilological study of the letters of the sixteenth-century Thynne sisters; Evans (2013) considers spelling evidence alongside morphosyntactic features in her historical sociolinguistic study of Elizabeth I's letters.

approach is exemplified by the substantial body of work undertaken in compiling *A Linguistic Atlas of Late Mediaeval English* (LALME, McIntosh et al. 1986a) and its subsequent counterpart, *A Linguistic Atlas of Early Middle English* (LAEME, Laing 2013–). The seeds of LALME were sown by McIntosh in an article in which he advocated the study of Middle English orthography in its own right, and not just as a way to devise or understand the correspondence between written and spoken Middle English (McIntosh 1956). His confidence in the value of the evidence of written language in its own right was not widely shared at the time, and put him at odds with the structuralist stance: "there is beyond doubt at present a fairly prevalent feeling that the approach to spoken manifestations of language is in some fundamental sense a more rewarding – not to say reputable – pursuit than that to written texts" (McIntosh 1956: 37). This approach was informed by McIntosh's earlier work as a dialectologist in present-day Scots, and his observations that orthographic patterns were apparent in surviving Middle English manuscripts which enabled him to make geographical or dialectal correspondences.

McIntosh's methodology was novel in that it treated each manuscript witness as a linguistic informant, the equivalent of a living speaker in a dialect survey. From each witness he collected counts of a wide range of variants akin to a dialect questionnaire to construct profiles for each scribe (McIntosh 1974: 602–3). These included 'S-features' (reflective of spoken language differences, such as *hem/þem*), 'W-features' (orthographic features, reflective of written language and which have no bearing on the pronunciation of a word, such as *sche/she*) and 'G-features' (paleographical features such as the shape of a particular graph). Throughout, McIntosh emphasizes the value of working across disciplines to view the problem in the round, because "it is sometimes the case that that a scribe fails to impose his own S-features on texts but does impose upon them various *scribal* characteristics of his own" (McIntosh 1974: 603). That is to say, paleographical variants are used alongside evidence from spellings which encode spoken variation, as well as those spellings which do not. This complementary evidence is used as part of the 'fit technique' to place writers geographically.[28]

This build-up of small details culled directly from the manuscripts themselves enabled LALME researchers to categorize scribal behavior into

[28] The 'fit technique' is a method used by McIntosh, adapted from modern dialectology, whereby "unlocalizable texts are assigned a geographical position by triangulation on the basis of features shared with texts of known provenance" (Fulk 2016: 100); texts whose provenance could be ascertained on external grounds were plotted on a map, and these points used to provide comparative data in order to position texts of unknown origin. Notably, McIntosh was able to successfully employ the technique due to his inclusion of features reflective of both written and spoken variation: "we must seek to detect significant variations within the written-language system as such, and not just those variations which seem to reflect differences within the spoken-language system" (McIntosh 1974: 602).

different types; for example, a scribe may choose to copy his exemplar text *literatim*, reproducing a near-identical text, or he may 'translate' the exemplar into his own linguistic norms, substituting his favored spellings for those he finds in his exemplar. Or he may choose to do something in between, perhaps beginning as a more *literatim* scribe before moving to translating behavior as he becomes more familiar with the exemplar's forms. Benskin and Laing (1981) also described the behavior of a *Mischsprache* scribe: one who produces both forms from the exemplar and those from his own preferred usage, but who, importantly, maintains this behavior throughout his copy. Altogether, this methodology not only tells us about the way the scribe of the surviving manuscript went about his task, but it can also allow us to build, through the collection of relict forms, an idea of the nature of the underlying exemplar. As Laing (1988: 83) notes, "dialectal analysis often provides the means to do far more than place a scribe on the map." More recent research has focused on what can be discovered about the writing systems employed by different scribes; careful and painstaking analysis has revealed the use by some writers of "litteral substitution sets" (where one sound is represented by several *litterae*), and by others of "potestatic substitution sets" (where one symbol represents several sounds; see Laing and Lass 2009: 1).[29] Laing (1999) details, for example, how changes in the written forms of <þ>, <p> and <y> during the Middle English period led to the interchangeable use of these graphs by some scribes to map a range of pronunciations including /ð/, /θ/, /w/ and /j/. Laing and Lass (2009) see scribal variation as overlapping function and formal equivalence, as systematic, and not a result of 'mental failure' or 'scribal error'.[30] This emphasis on the value of the input of the scribe (as a 'native speaker'), rather than trying to correct something that is perceived as an inferior version of the author's original, links the LALME/LAEME project's attitude to historical texts with that of new philologists, historical sociolinguists and pragmaphilologists: "[i]t is recognised that a 'corrupt' text may reflect the activity of a contemporary editor, critic, or adaptor rather than that of a merely careless copyist" (Laing 1988: 83).

[29] Laing, following Benskin (1997: 1) deliberately employs the medieval doctrine of *littera*, referring to the concepts *figura* (the letter-symbol), *nomen* (the letter-name) and *potestates* (the sound-value): "When one wishes to 'get inside the head' of a medieval copyist, reference to graphemes and allographs seems neither appropriate nor useful" (Laing 1999: 255). See also Section 17.2 above.

[30] "We use the terms 'confusion' and 'confused' without pejorative intent. We do not mean to imply any necessary mental failure on the part of the scribe(s). The terms refer to a formal equivalence and/or an overlap in function, which is normally systematic. They rarely denote intellectual confusion, or even inadvertence. Formal equivalence and functional overlap may sometimes lead to genuine intellectual confusions; but in our experience they are unusual. 'Confusions' are more often than not systematically explicable in terms of the writing praxis of the exemplar and/or of the copyist. Simple scribal error, whose existence in individual cases we of course do not deny, is comparatively uncommon" (Laing and Lass 2009: 3).

17.9 Case Study: Two Scribes of the Tanner Bede

The methods outlined by the compilers of LALME/LAEME are not only of use for the study of Middle English but can also be applied to Old English material, although the language situation is rather different; in general later writers of Old English appear to have used a focused variety (i.e. late West Saxon), whereas Middle English was "*par excellence*, the dialectal phase of English" (Strang 1970: 224), when writing routinely reflected local usage.[31] The important thing to bear in mind is that many surviving Old English texts are copies, rather than autograph writings, meaning that what we see on the page is not the result (as in our second case study below) of a considered scripting choice, but the outcome of the copying behavior of the latest scribe. Thus, in line with McIntosh's observations, we may detect orthographic features as well as morphosyntactic ones, which may have been transmitted from the exemplar text, or else translated into the scribe's own preferred usage. The difference between looking at late Old English and Middle English is that Old English literacy was probably far less widespread socially, being more or less restricted to the ecclesiastical elite. In addition, the destruction of Northumbrian and Mercian monasteries and their libraries during the Viking attacks of the ninth and tenth centuries means that a substantial part of our data for Old English comes from eleventh-century Wessex and the dialect written there (Fulk and Cain 2013: 21–22).

This case study examines the performance of two scribes from Oxford, Bodleian Library Tanner 10 (T), a late tenth-century copy of the Old English translation of Bede's *Historia ecclesiastica*, and is based on the methodology developed in Wallis (2013) and adapted from that of the LALME project. An examination of T alongside the other *Bede* manuscripts reveals that the original translation, which no longer exists, was written in a Mercian dialect, and the text was progressively West-Saxonized as a succession of scribes recopied it during the late tenth and eleventh centuries (Miller 1890, Wallis 2013). In total five scribes contributed to T, and the two under examination are referred to as T2 and T4.[32] A questionnaire was used to collect the variant spellings, from which five features are examined.[33] These are all conservative features

[31] Smith (1996: 66) defines a focused variety as "a centripetal norm to which speakers tend, rather than a fixed collection of prescribed rules from which any deviation at all is forbidden."

[32] T2 writes sections of text between ff. 103r–117v (Miller 1890: 352–90), and provides a total of 1,540 graphic units across four short stints which alternate with those by T1, before the copying task is taken over by T4 part way through f. 117v. T4's contribution falls into two stints, the first of which is considered here, and which consists of 3,561 graphic units between ff. 117v–126r. Scribal stints are measured in graphic units rather than in words, as spacing and word division can be rather irregular in the manuscript and words are frequently split over lines.

[33] A questionnaire with a greater number of features will allow a more nuanced picture, and may well include morphological and paleographical, as well as orthographic variants (McIntosh 1974: 610–11). For the sake of brevity only a limited number of features are considered here.

indicative of *Bede*'s original Mercian dialect: *ah* is a form of *ac* ('but') commonly found in Anglian dialects, rather than West Saxon (Hogg 1992a: 275), while *ec* is a spelling of *eac* ('also') which shows Anglian smoothing (Campbell 1959: 95). Spellings retaining <oe> represent the rounding of *ē*, found in non–West-Saxon dialects (Campbell 1959: 76–78, 133), while double vowel combinations, for example *tiid* for *tid* ('time'), are found in older texts representing long vowels (Campbell 1959: 13). *Cuom-* and *cwom-* represent early spellings of *com-* the past tense of *cuman* ('to come'), before the loss of *-w-* (Ringe and Taylor 2014: 339). These features are summarized in Table 17.1.

These features appear sporadically as relicts in other *Bede* manuscripts, as well as in T. It is important not only to ascertain the form(s) of each feature present, but also where each instance occurs, by folio. In that way we can detect whether a scribe's behavior is consistent throughout his stint, or whether it changes as he writes. Two main trends are noticeable about T2's performance. Firstly, he has a strong tendency to use the more conservative spellings; for example, he only ever uses *ah*, and never *ac*, while he transmits six <oe> spellings, including *roeðnis* 'storminess', *woedelnisse* 'poverty' and *woen* 'hope'. Another relict feature transmitted throughout his stint is the use of double vowels, rendering both proper and common nouns; his 23 examples include *tiidum* 'time', *cwoom* 'came' and the personal name *eedgils*. Finally, T2 only uses older spellings of the past tense of the verb *cuman*; while he vacillates between the older <u> for *w* and the newer *wynn*, it is notable that he never writes *com* (see our second case study on variation between <u> and *wynn* in Old English).[34] One place where T2 may introduce a form of his own is on a single occasion right at the beginning of his stint, where he writes *eac* (f. 103r). However, following this he always writes *ec* (three times), apparently following his exemplar. It would appear then that T2's copying behavior falls toward the *literatim* end of the spectrum; there is little evidence on the basis of the features discussed here to suggest that he brings many of his own preferred spellings to his copy, and he maintains conservative spellings throughout.

When T2 reached the end of his stint, the copying task was taken up by T4, whose approach over the next 18 folios is rather different. T4 begins by

Table 17.1 *Spelling variation in T2 and T4*

Relict feature	Newer variant
ah	ac
ec	eac
oe	e
double vowels: aa, ee, ii, oo, uu	a, e, i, o, u
cuom-, cwom-	com-

[34] By contrast, a study of the manuscript's main scribe (T1) shows that in his copy of Book 3 of the *Bede* he never writes *cuom*; however, he does write *cwom* (57× in Book 3), and occasionally *com* (5×).

reproducing a number of forms from his exemplar, and on the first two folios (f. 117v–118r) we find *ah, ec, cuom, cwom,* and *forðfoered* 'to depart, die' with an <oe> spelling. It is quite clear that as he continues, T4 gradually abandons these inherited spellings for ones which reflect his own training and preferences. What is notable, however, is that he does not change all these spellings at the same point in his copy; while *ec* is soon changed to *eac* on f. 118r, *com* makes its appearance a little later, on f. 119r. Rather later still is the change from *ah* to *ac* (f. 121v), suggesting that these changes happen perhaps at a lexical level, rather than at a systematic, orthographic level; previous exposure to a spelling does not seem to be a factor, as *ec* is written only once before the spelling is changed, while *ah* appears four times before it is replaced. It is rather more difficult to say whether the lack of <oe> forms in the later folios represents a conscious change by T4, or whether it was simply the case that no such forms existed in this part of the exemplar.

A different pattern is shown, however, by the four double vowel spellings, which appear, rather sporadically, throughout T4's stint in words such as *aa* 'always' and *riim* 'reckoning'. Although the contributions of both scribes are short, it appears that T2 is rather more likely to transmit a double vowel spelling than T4 (23 times in 1,540 graphic units, against T4's four times in 3,651 graphic units). It is possible that fewer double vowel spellings occurred in T4's section of the text than in T2's, although the fact that such spellings are also transmitted by scribes T1 and T5 suggests that this is unlikely. That double vowels occur in each scribe's stint, though to differing degrees, might suggest that they were not felt by the scribes to be too incongruous a spelling, or that they were part of the T scribes' passive repertoire (Benskin and Laing 1981: 58–59). T4, then, acts as a translator scribe, albeit one who starts out more *literatim*, before 'writing in' to his own preferred norms and style. Of course, without the original exemplar, we cannot be entirely sure to what extent either scribe made alterations in their text, and it should be stressed that this is not an exhaustive survey. Nevertheless, comparison of T2 and T4 with each other, and with other scribes of the *Bede* manuscripts, allows us to build a picture of the sorts of features we would expect to have been in the archetype, and which therefore may well have occurred in T's exemplar. Building up a scribal profile, which aims to analyze both the features used as well as their distribution, enables us to map the internal consistency of each scribe, in addition to their differences from one another.

17.10 Quantification in Philological Approaches to Orthography

Beyond the research on early English encouraged by the LALME/LAEME project, a number of philological approaches to orthography from the early decades of the twenty-first century have addressed written language by mapping spelling onto a linguistic reference system. This method was initially developed by Mihm and Elmentaler in the context of a project entitled *Niederrheinische Sprachgeschichte* at the University of Duisburg, which focused on administrative writing in Duisburg from the fourteenth to the seventeenth century (as described in Elmentaler 2003: 49–51). While rejecting an autonomistic analysis of written language as impractical, Elmentaler takes great pains to avoid circular reasoning. This is achieved by analyzing graphs (*Graphien*) according to their correspondence to *Lautpositionen* ('sound positions'), which are units defined by sound etymology and context. Elmentaler's research also relies on the strict separation of scribes and exact quantification (Elmentaler 2003: 60–63). Graphs and sound positions are correlated, which makes it possible to establish the grapheme systems of individual scribes and to assess the overlap in the representation of different sound positions. On a wider level, Elmentaler's research confirms that early written languages are fully functional, that the letter–sound correlations of Latin are persistent, and that change in written language is often discontinuous (Elmentaler 2003: 51–53).

Subsequent studies have applied Mihm and Elmentaler's approach to other types of material: Larsen (2001, 2004) has adopted it for a study on Middle Dutch statutes of the Flemish town of Ghent, Kawasaki (2004) for a graphemic analysis of the Old Saxon *Heliand*, and Seiler (2014) in the context of research on the earliest Old English, Old High German and Old Saxon sources. These studies address different research questions and, consequently, adapt the relational method to suit their own purpose: Larsen aims at establishing the entire grapheme systems represented in the material from Ghent; Kawasaki systematically compares the spellings for the dental letters *þ*, *d*, *đ* and *t* across the five extant manuscripts of *Heliand*; and Seiler investigates, on the one hand, how a number of consonant phonemes are represented and, on the other hand, how 'superfluous' graphemes like <k>, <q>, <x> and <z> are employed. These differences aside, the studies share a cautious stance when it comes to attributing exact sound values to the orthographic features under investigation and they all aim to elucidate the workings of nonstandardized writing systems.

17.11 Case Study: The Scripting of /w/ in Old English and Old High German

This second case study focuses on the spellings for one sound, the continuant of Proto-Germanic */w/ in Old English and Old High German. This sound was phonologically stable, yet it is represented in various ways since Latin had no corresponding sound and, therefore, the alphabet provided no suitable character.[35] The case study provides insights into the scripting of Old English and Old High German; the details presented here are based on a comparative analysis of early orthography (Seiler 2014), which relies on quantitative data to identify the factors determining graphemic choices. The methodology is adapted from Elmentaler (2003; see above), mapping spellings onto an etymological reference system. The results show that while, overall, the spellings for Old English and Old High German /w/ are variable, there are clear-cut diatopic and diachronic patterns. Furthermore, different orthographic solutions tend to be used for specific sound positions. Once these factors are taken into consideration, Old English and Old High German orthographies turn out to be surprisingly consistent.

When scribes in England and in Frankia started to write their vernacular languages with the Latin alphabet, three typologically distinct spellings for the representation of /w/ were available to them. The first option was to use single <u>, though this graph stood for labiodental /v/ in Latin; the second spelling consisted of the digraph <uu>, and a third option was to adopt the character <ƿ>, named *wynn* 'joy', from the runic script (ᚹ). All three spellings (as well as some others) are attested in Old English and Old High German sources, yet their patterns of distribution are very different. *Wynn* is the standard spelling in Old English from the ninth century onward and remained in use well beyond the end of the Anglo-Saxon period.[36] Early Old English sources, going back to the late seventh and eighth century, generally use <u> or <uu> instead, though rare instances of *wynn* occur. Single <u> dominates in the eighth-century versions of Cædmon's Hymn transmitted as part of Bede's *Ecclesiastical History* (see the extract from the Moore manuscript under (1) below) and is found in names attested in the earliest Anglo-Saxon charters. Even in texts that use <ƿ> or <uu> elsewhere, <u> is often retained as a spelling for /w/ in the consonant clusters /kw/, /hw/, /sw/ and so on, as for example in the Alfredian translation of the *Pastoral Care*, which normally employs <ƿ> but uses <cu>, <su> and so on for these clusters (2).[37] These spellings are clearly modeled on Latin words, like *suavis* 'sweet', which contain a bilabial semivowel (Stotz 1996: 142). Double <uu> occurs only occasionally, mostly in early Mercian sources as exemplified by examples from the Épinal Glossary (3). However, the digraph spelling continues to be used in Old English names in Anglo-Latin texts as in the *Vita St. Æthelwoldi*

[35] Old English and Old High German /w/ must have been a bilabial approximant [w]; Latin <u>, when used as a consonant, represented a labiovelar fricative [v] probably by the first century AD (Stotz 1996: 142 §108.2, 150–51 §113.1). See the difference between early (i.e. pre-650) borrowings from Latin into Old English, like *wine*, *wall* and later ones, such as *verse*, *vulture* (examples from Durkin 2014: 102–9).

[36] On early Old English spelling, see Scragg (1974: 1–14), and Blomfield (1935). The disappearance of *wynn* in the course of the Middle English period has not been investigated in detail, though Laing (1999) discusses its confusion with <þ> and <y> in later Middle English (see Section 17.8 above).

[37] See also the use of <cu> in the Tanner *Bede* in our first case study.

(4) (Lapidge and Winterbottom 1991: clxxxviii). Again, there is a restriction: <uu> is rarely used before the vowel /u/ (e.g. ***uulfgar*** and not *****uuulfgar***). The following text samples illustrate the range of spellings found in different Anglo-Saxon sources:

(1) *Nu scylun hergan hefaenricaes* ***uard****, metudæs maecti end his modgidanc,* ***uerc uuldurfadur****, sue he* ***uundra*** *gihuaes, eci dryctin, or astelidæ* (Cædmon's Hymn from the Moore manuscript, Cambridge University Library, MS Kk. 5.16, c. 737, ed. Dobbie 1942: 105; emphasis added here and throughout);

(2) *Ne cuæð he ðæt forðyðe he ænegum men ðæs* ***pyscte*** *oððe* ***pilnode****, ac he* ***pitgode*** ***sua sua*** *hit* ***gepeorðan*** *sceolde* (Old English *Pastoral Care*, Bodleian Library, Hatton MS 20, late ninth century, ed. Sweet 1871: I, 29.10);

(3) [232] *ca[ta]ractis*: ***uuaeterthruch*** 'water-pipe', [1026] *telum:* ***uueb*** 'web', [1040] *taberna:* ***uuinaern*** 'tavern', [1045] *talpa:* ***uuandaeuuiorpae*** 'mole', [1062] *uitelli:* ***suehoras*** 'fathers-in-law', [1088] *uirecta:* ***quicae*** 'green place' (Épinal Glossary, c. 700, ed. Pheifer 1974);

(4) *Est enim ciuitas quaedam modica, commerciis abunde referta, quae solito* ***uuealinga*** *ford appellatur, in qua uir strenuus quidam morabatur, cui nomen erat Ælfhelmus, qui casu lumen amittens oculorum cecitatem multis perpessus est annis. Huic in somnis tempore gallicinii sanctus AÐELVVOLDUS antistes adstitit eumque ut maturius* ***uuintoniam*** *pergeret et ad eius tumbam gratia recipiendi uisus accederet ammonuit* [...] (*Vita St. Æthelwoldi*, ed. Lapidge and Winterbottom 1991: 42).[38]

In Old High German, the digraph <uu> is already the regular spelling for *w* in the earliest sources in the eighth century. Its use is doubtless modeled on West Frankish spelling practice, where <uu> is attested in personal names on coins and charters from the late sixth century onward (e.g. *UUaldemarus, UUandeberctus*, see Wells 1972: 118–19, 144, 157, Felder 2003: 700). From Merovingian Frankia the digraph presumably also spread to Anglo-Saxon England (Seiler 2015: 119–20). Eventually, <uu> or <vv> were combined into a single character with touching or overlapping strokes, resulting in the establishment of a new letter <w>.[39] The runic character *wynn*, on the other hand, is restricted to a small number of texts and is rarely used consistently (Braune and Heidermanns 2018: 24). The presence of *wynn* in Old High German is generally attributed to Anglo-Saxon influence. One text in which it is found is in the *Hildebrandslied*, an alliterative heroic poem (5). The mixture of <uu> and <p> spellings suggests that *wynn* occurred in the exemplar from which

[38] The text printed above follows the spelling of Cotton MS Caligula A VIII (1st quarter of the 12th c.), f. 127v (available online at http://www.bl.uk/manuscripts/Viewer.aspx?ref=cotton_ms_caligula_a_viii_f127v [accessed 17 June 2023]).

[39] According to Bischoff (1990: 122), the composite form appears in the eleventh century, though "[i]t is almost attained in the tenth [...]." Sporadic attestations, however, already occur in Merovingian sources (Seiler 2014: 114).

the extant version was copied but was not normally used by the two scribes (see Lühr 1982: 32–34). The *Hildebrandslied* was copied in Fulda, one of the centers of the Anglo-Saxon mission on the Continent, which explains the presence of insular influence in the scriptorium.

The restrictions on <uu> found in Old English also apply to Old High German orthography: in consonant clusters and before the vowel /u/ many scribes prefer single <u> as a spelling for /w/ (5, 6, 7). One exception to this rule is Otfrid of Weissenburg, who explicitly speaks out in favor of 'triple-u' for the sequence /wu-/ in one of the prefaces to his *Evangelienbuch*: "Sometimes, as I believe, three *u* are necessary for the sound; the first two as consonants, as it seems to me, but the third keeping its vocalic sound" (ed. Magoun 1943: 880). Otfrid also insisted on this spelling being used in the *Evangelienbuch* (see Seiler 2010: 92–95, 99). For the representation of the cluster /kw/, many Old High German sources resort to <qu> or similar spellings, as in the Old High German translation of Tatian's *Diatessaron* (6). This spelling is clearly modeled on the large number of Latin words containing a labiovelar (*quia*, *quod* and so on). Incidentally, the same spelling occurs in some Old English sources (e.g. *quicae* in (3) above).

Overall, Old High German orthography is highly idiosyncratic and more prone to intricate digraph and trigraph spellings than Old English. The scribe of part Ka of the *Abrogans* glossary, for example, uses <ouu> to represent Proto-Germanic */w/ in clusters with /s/ or /z/, single <u> in other clusters and double <uu> elsewhere (7). It is possible that the trigraph owes its composition to the insertion of a parasitic vowel after the sibilant (Braune and Heidermanns 2018: 103); however, many intricate spelling rules are graphic in nature and unconnected to the sound level. The following examples illustrate the range of Old High German spellings for /w/:

(5) *[...] gurtun sih iro s**u**ert ana, helidos, ubar [h]ringa. do sie to dero hiltiu ritun. hiltibraht gimahalta, heribrantes sunu – her **uu**as heroro man, ferahes frotoro –; her fragen gistuont fohem **uu**ortum, [h]**ṕ**er sin fater **ṕ**ari* [...] (*Hildebrandslied* 5b–9, c. 830, ed. Lühr 1982, I, 2);[40]

(6) *Inti q**u**ad Zacharias zi themo engile: **uu**anan **uu**eiz ih thaz? ih bim alt, inti mīn q**u**ena fram ist gigangan in ira tagun* (Old High German *Tatian*, c. 830; ed. by Braune and Ebbinghaus 1994: 47);

(7) [12.19] *ambiguus*: *undar zo**uu**aim* 'going two ways', [12.20] *dubius*: *zo**uu**iual* 'doubt', [28.20] *natare*: *so**uu**imman* 'to swim', [29.02] *natabat*: *so**uu**am* 'swam'; [13.11] *ambitus: cadh**u**ing* 'region', [23.06] *ego inquid: ih qh**u**ad* 'I said', [30.16] *adfligit: th**u**ingit* 'he throws down'; [10.21] *almum: **uu**ih* 'holy', [25.16] *crescit: **uu**ahsit* 'it grows' (*Abrogans*, Cod. Sang. 911, c. 790, ed. Bischoff et al. 1977).

[40] In the extract printed here, <ṕ > is substituted for <w> used in Lühr's edition. For a facsimile see, for example, Lühr (1982, II, 799–800).

A comparison of the spellings for /w/ in Old English and Old High German suggests that similar factors were at work. Orthographic solutions are influenced by two opposing principles: firstly, a desire for an unambiguous representation of vernacular sounds and, secondly, the rules of Latin grammar. This leads to compromises such as single <u> in clusters and before the vowel /u/, while <uu> is used elsewhere. The dominance of Latin spelling practice and orthographic rules results in similarities between individual writing systems but also across the traditions of the West Germanic languages. Such similarities are owing to a shared background rather than to direct influence from one spelling system to another. Individual scribes define their own, sometimes intricate spelling rules, though Old English spelling coalesces toward a relatively uniform representation of the vernacular in the course of the Anglo-Saxon period. Old High German orthography, on the other hand, remains more fragmented. Finally, scribal choices are also affected by the text genre. In nonstandardized writing systems, spellings often carry associations beyond the sounds that they represent. The runic character *ƿ*, for example, is clearly a 'vernacular' graph. Single <u> but also the digraph <uu>, on the other hand, stand for (Merovingian) Latinity and are thus more suitable for the representation of vernacular elements in Latin texts.[41] On a more general level, this case study shows how core philological methods can be updated to reach a more sophisticated understanding of the writing systems of the past. This entails, on the one hand, a more nuanced assessment of the correlations of spellings and sounds and, on the other, investigating writing systems as culturally transmitted phenomena that contain features going beyond sound representation. By shifting attention squarely onto written language, the term *Buchstabenphilologie* may thus be reclaimed as the study of writing in its own right.

17.12 Conclusion

The popularity of philology has waxed and waned among scholars of historical texts. However, it has never been entirely eclipsed by other methods. It has frequently been noted that 'philology' is difficult to define (e.g. Nichols 1990: 2, Fulk 2016: 95), encompassing a wide range of methods and involving competence in a number of disciplines.[42] Nevertheless, it is because it is a fundamental part of textual scholarship that philology remains a relevant and valid approach to the study of historical texts on a variety of levels. While the concerns of philologists may have moved away from the tasks of textual editing and the recovery of the original authorial text, the methodology and expertise

[41] For more details on this last aspect, see Seiler (2021: 126, 146–48).

[42] See, for instance, the wide range of methods and topics covered in Neidorf et al. (2016).

developed by philologists now find their use in "mediating between the demands of linguistic methodology and the limitations that beset the records of prior states of the language available for linguistic analysis" (Fulk 2016: 96). It is precisely this mediating role which is most valuable; philology is easily absorbed by and combined with newer theoretical linguistic approaches, providing scholars with a deeper understanding of the "extralinguistic contexts of linguistic data" (Fulk 2016: 95). Thus, a range of scholarship has developed that combines philological sensitivities with the theoretical underpinning of, for example, variationist linguistics in historical sociolinguistics, or politeness theory in historical pragmatics. It is arguably in these fields, where philological methods are able to take advantage of advances in digital humanities such as corpus linguistics or digital editing, that we see the most fruitful combinations of many of the strands laid down by twentieth-century work (e.g. New Philology, pragmaphilology, LALME), much of which involves the study of historical orthographies, alongside several other features. Finally, there is an emphasis in these newer fields on finding new texts to study, often from the kinds of writers who have been overlooked by traditional scholarship, such as documents from lower-class writers in 'language history from below' (Elspaß 2012b). This means that the supply of historical documents is by no means exhausted, and there remains much work for philologists to do using such combined methods, both on existing documents and on those yet to be discovered.

18

Exploring Orthographic Distribution

Javier Calle-Martín and Juan Lorente-Sánchez

18.1 Introduction

"I'll call for pen and ink, and write my mind." This sentence from Shakespeare (*1 H6*, V, 3, 66, see Burns 2000) is a neat way to introduce our readers to the content and scope of this chapter. These are the Earl of Suffolk's words for when, in love with Margaret, he doubts whether or not to free her, and appeals for a pen and ink to let his intentions flow on a piece of paper. The present chapter examines the relationship between 'pen and paper' in the composition of early English manuscripts and printed books, on the basis of the hypothesis that some common practice on the matter was shared by scribes and printers alike. Old manuscripts and printed books are taken as the source of evidence to discuss the concept of *spacing* and *distribution*. The term *distribution* is not simply taken as the mere arrangement of the sentences and paragraphs on the page, but it is rather conceived in its widest sense referring to the writers' decisions both in the preparation of the writing surface and in the writing process itself.

This chapter discusses the arrangement of the external aspects of the text together with the distribution of internal features associated with spacing in Late Middle English (1350–1500) and Early Modern English (1500–1700). The focus is on the English language and Early Modern English in particular as the period when the standards on spacing were on the rise. In the following, we describe the rationale behind the composition of early English handwritten documents, reconsidering aspects such as the preparation of the writing

The present chapter has been funded by the Ministry of Economy and Competitiveness (grant number FFI2017-88060-P). This grant is hereby gratefully acknowledged. We are grateful to Dr. Jesús Romero-Barranco (University of Granada) for his valuable help and feedback on the previous drafts of this paper. We also wish to thank the three anonymous reviewers and the editors, whose thoughtful comments have substantially improved the final version of this chapter.

surface, the dimensions of the folio, margin conventions, frame and line ruling, the use of columns (and its association with the formality of the text) and line justification. Next, we explain the main notions of the concept of spacing, describing different types of line-final word division and its specific variants, and providing a general overview of existing research in the literature. Finally, two case studies are offered where we discuss the emergence of spacing in the Middle Ages and its development throughout the Early Modern English period, paying attention to both handwritten and printed sources. These studies are carried out by considering divisions both in the middle and at the end of a line. Divisions in the middle of a line, on the one hand, are described in light of the evidence of nominal and adjectival compounds, reflexives, adverbs and words which, although independent lexemes, are irregularly found together in the period. Line-final word division, in turn, considers the typology of boundaries, whether morphological, phonological or anomalous. We argue that it is from narrow case studies like these that we can effectively contribute to knowing more about our general understanding of orthographic distribution.

18.2 Formatting and Layout

The preparation of the writing surface was a time-consuming process according to which animal skin (sheepskin was more frequently used in Britain than goatskin) was turned into parchment as a result of the cleaning and the subsequent dehairing of the material. In itself, creating parchment was an arduous and lengthy process which made the resulting material a valuable product, a luxurious item which could only be afforded by the elite of the time. Parchment, and writing materials in general, had limited availability and was therefore an expensive item at the time. Consequently, careful planning of its use was crucial in order to make the most of this writing surface (Clemens and Graham 2007: 15–17).

In this context, columns were a recurrent practice among medieval and, to a lesser extent, Early Modern English scribes, although "in the fifteenth century a renewed preference among some for layouts with long lines is detectable, probably under Italian Humanistic influence" (Derolez 2003: 37). Even though there is not a one-to-one correspondence between the disposition of columns and the formality of the text, the use of columns is more strongly associated with particular registers and genres, especially those considered to have a higher level of formality. As far as genre is concerned, the use of columns is especially frequent in high-esteemed literary compositions, poetry in particular, often highly decorated and colored specimens. This is the case of MS Hunter 7, containing a decorated version of John Gower's *Confessio Amantis*; MS Hunter 197, housing a copy of Geoffrey Chaucer's *The Canterbury Tales*; or MS Hunter 5, a precious version of John Lydgate's *Fall of Princes* (Cross 2004).

As far as register is concerned, the presence of columns is also more widely connected with texts with a higher level of formality, and medical writing may be the best testimony to this scribal preference. Theoretical and surgical treatises were considered the most academic registers and belonged to the learned tradition, being mostly translations of learned Latin medicine with an academic origin designed for physicians of the highest class and (barber) surgeons. Remedies, in turn, portray the language used by lay people, as they were collections of recipes that families stored for their use at home. While the latter are seldom rendered in two columns for the purposes of private use, some theoretical/surgical treatises are often found with columns depending on the circulation and value of the item at hand. MS Hunter 95, for instance, is a beautiful two-column composition housing a Late Middle English version of the *Book of Operation*. From the beginning of the sixteenth century, however, the use of columns decreased among Early Modern English scribes.

The dimensions of the margins are in most cases a matter of convention in early English manuscript composition insofar as the foot margin is usually twice as wide as that at the top, and the side margins are greater than the top and less than the foot (Johnston 1945: 72). By doing this, medieval scribes ensured that "the height of the written space equalled the width of the page" (de Hamel 1992: 21). Regardless of its dimension, in a regular quire, consisting of eight leaves, the upper and lower margins measure approximately 20 mm and 35–40 mm, respectively, while the left and right margins amount to c. 15–20 mm and 15–35 mm. This can be taken as a milestone both in Late Middle English texts, as in MS Hunter 497 (Calle-Martín and Miranda-García 2012: 26), MS Wellcome 542 (Calle-Martín and Castaño-Gil 2013: 29) or MS Hunter 328 (Calle-Martín 2020: 15); and Early Modern English specimens, as in MS Wellcome 3009 (Criado-Peña 2018: 16) or MS Rylands 1310 (Calle-Martín 2020: 16). Figure 18.1 shows the average dimension of a manuscript

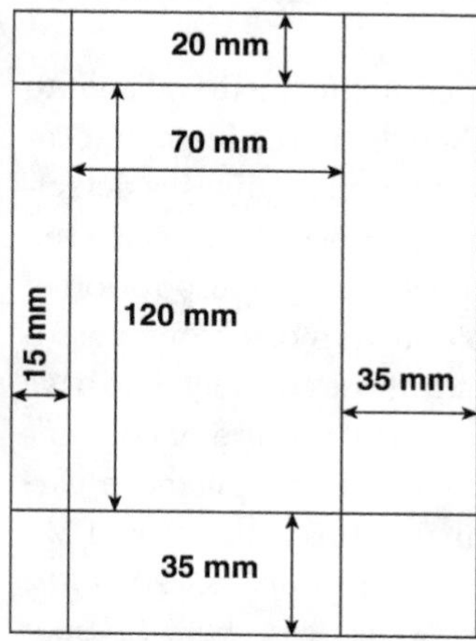

Figure 18.1 Margins and writing space in MS Hunter 497

folio with the approximate size of the margins and the actual writing space as found in the fifteenth-century English translation of Macer Floridus's *De viribus herbarum* (Glasgow University Library, MS Hunter 497).

Ruling techniques changed over time, however. Drypoints were used until the eleventh century, a method which consisted in pressing into the page with a sharp instrument, where only one side of the page needed to be ruled. Leadpoint, in turn, was in vogue until the thirteenth century and it was distinguished by its grey or reddish-brown color and, contrary to drypoint rule, it required the ruling of both sides of the page. Finally, ink began to be in use from the fourteenth century, often with the same color as the running text, even though this practice became less and less fashionable from the fifteenth century and, since then, only frame ruling remained (Derolez 2003: 55, Clemens and Graham 2007: 16–17). Even though frame ruling was a consistent practice in early English manuscripts, line ruling was more often associated with valuable copies to ensure that the text had a visually appealing layout (Calle-Martín 2020: 17). The number of lines of a handwritten composition depended on the size of the volume.

The history of English handwriting in the period 1400–1600 is characterized by the replacement of the Anglicana hand by the Secretary script, the latter more cursive and considerably smaller in size (Roberts 2005: 4, Calle-Martín 2011b: 35–54). The progressive spread of the Secretary hand had a crucial impact on the design of the manuscript page leaving more room for running text. Both from the fifteenth century, the scribe of MS Hunter 497 is consistent as to the use of a hybrid Anglicana hand, while MS Hunter 328 is rendered with a more cursive hand, allowing for more running words per page.

Line justification is also a matter of scribal choice in handwritten documents, depending in most cases on the value of the copy at hand. Even though there is a general commitment to make the most of the writing space, it is a fact that valuable copies are particularly respectful to the inner and outer margins, and line-fillers are frequent devices to avoid a blank line after the closing of a paragraph. Less valuable copies are more concerned with the importance of the writing space and, as a consequence, show a frequent use of margins for the running text – to the detriment of word division – together with a wider use of abbreviations. Printed texts, on the other hand, are obviously more prone to line justification, while at the same time avoided the use of line-fillers for visual purposes.

In addition to the size and spacing conventions of the written material, formatting was obviously the only means to provide the written text with some kind of organization. Decorative material was often employed to indicate major textual divisions in the text. The *litterae notabiliores* stand out as visual indicators of the beginning of a sentence, becoming "the primary way in which the reader was guided through the text" (Smith 2020b: 212). The cost of doing such hand-rubrication was then enormous and the use of underlining and/or colored ink, red in particular, were also frequent practices to indicate textual divisions within the text, thus guiding the eye of the reader to the important parts of the text. A hierarchy of scripts was also a common device for macro-structural purposes, both in handwritten and printed documents, where "square capitals [were used] for main headings, uncials for lower level headings and initial words, and Caroline minuscule for the main text" (Smith 1994: 36–38; Baron 2001: 22). MS Hunter 135, housing a sixteenth-century English version of *De chirurgia libri IV* (ff. 34r–73v), displays this kind of typographical arrangement of the text where section titles are reproduced with an italic script while the running text is rendered with a fairly legible Tudor Secretary hand.

Punctuation also played a decisive role in the organization of the text, understood as a means to divide the text into pages, lines and paragraphs. It was considered pragmatically and, besides pages and lines, the paragraph was taken as the earliest unit of punctuation, often unaccompanied by any internal mark of punctuation until the seventh century (Lennard 1995: 65–68). Written punctuation started thenceforth and by the eleventh century there was a set of symbols which, with overlapping uses, were devised for the expression of particular needs. The Middle Ages then stand out as a crucial period in the development of the system of punctuation in the sense that it consisted of overlapping repertoires of marks associated with a particular scriptorium or geographic area until the eleventh century, and of "a general repertoire with a wide European distribution" from the twelfth to the fourteenth century (Lennard 1995: 66). In light of this, apart from the paragraph itself, different punctuation marks appeared to create the *mise-en-page*, thus making the text more readable. The list includes, for instance, the *paragraphus* § and the *paraph* ¶ along with other symbols such as the *virgule* /, the *double virgule* // and the *perioslash* ./, each of these adopting various forms (.//, //., etc.). The paragraphus was mostly found as an indicator of divisions in a text. The paraph carried the pragmatic function of "a macro structural marker to indicate particular relationships within the paragraph as well as the major sections and subsections within the text" (Calle-Martín and Miranda-García 2005: 33). The virgule, and its variant forms, were recurrent symbols with section titles while at the same time also committed to the separation of sense units which are semantically and syntactically independent. The period, in turn, also served to circumscribe some key terms of a text, apart from other kinds of sentential, clausal and phrasal relationships.

18.3 Spacing: Word Division

The term *word division* is used to denote the threefold rendering of some words in historical compositions, which may appear either joined, hyphenated or separated, although the latter overwhelmingly predominated (Tannenbaum

1930: 146). In itself, word division is relevant to orthography in view of its connection with punctuation. The phenomenon dates back to the sixth century, when Irish and Anglo-Saxon scribes contributed decisively to the development of the system of *distinctiones*. These scribes were in need of visual marks in order to understand Latinate texts, most of them written in *scriptura continua*, and turned to the practice of word separation, with spaces and periods used therein (Clemens and Graham 2007: 83–84, Calle-Martín 2011a: 18). The phenomenon, however, has been traditionally shunned in most sources and the only references to it in the literature are limited to mentioning the lack of an orthographic standard until the first half of the sixteenth century (Denholm-Young 1954: 70, Petti 1977: 31).

Line-final word division is defined as the breaking of a word at the end of a line and, unlike divisions in other positions, the rules determining it differ according to phonological and morphological factors. The issue is also ignored in traditional handbooks on paleography, where its omission is assumed to be the rule rather than the exception. The only references to the topic reveal that there is no consensus, neither at a phonological nor at a morphological level, governing line-final word division among English penmen. The splitting of words at the end of lines is considered arbitrary in handwriting and the only precept "seems to have been that not less than two completing letters could be carried over to the second line" (Hector 1958; see also Denholm-Young 1954: 70, Petti 1977: 31). The modern tenets have discredited the traditional approaches proposing the existence of conventional patterns. The topic is open to interpretation, however. In Old English (OE), Hladký (1985a: 73) states that the main word division principle is basically morphological, including suffixed, prefixed and compound words. Lutz, in turn, affirms that the division of polysyllabic words reflects their phonological organization into syllables, thus assuming that line-final word division is based on the syllabification of OE (Lutz 1986: 193; see also Burchfield 1994: 182). There is not a univocal attitude in the period in view of the distinctive practices of scribes and, as such, the evidence found in these modern approaches cannot be generalized to represent the whole period.

To cope with this limitation, the last decade has witnessed a number of statistical analyses (Calle-Martín 2009, 2011a) addressing the phenomenon in terms of the particular choices of scribes to provide empirical data that may be eventually compared with other texts. From a methodological viewpoint, the rationale used for these investigations stems from Hladký's (1985a, 1985b) approach to the study of word division in some historical texts, proposing a classification of the topic in terms of the ultimate force of splitting, that is, morphology and phonology. The former recurs to the traditional word-formation principles of prefixation, suffixation and composition, as in *vn-curable*, *sauour-ing* and *som-what*, respectively. The latter divides words in terms of their actual pronunciation where the following types of phonological rules stand out: (i) the CV-CV rule, that is, the division after an open syllable, as in *sy-newes*; (ii) the C-C rule, the division between two consonants, as in *mer-curye*; (iii) the V-V rule, the division between two conjoining vowels, as in *api-um*; (iv) the ST rule, either the separation or the preservation of the cluster *-st*, as in *sub-stance* or *was-tyng*; (v) the CL rule, the keeping together of a consonant and a liquid on condition that both belong to the same syllable, as in *par-brakynge*; and (vi) the CT rule, the division between the pair *-ct*, as in *elec-tuaryes*. These statistical analyses have also added a third group (Calle-Martín 2009: 38, 2011a: 18) so as to account for those anomalous divisions which fall apart from this twofold classification, as in *ointme-nt*.

18.4 Case Studies

The present section explores the emergence of spacing in the Middle Ages and its development throughout the Early Modern English period, paying attention to both handwritten and printed sources. Spacing is examined here by considering divisions both in the middle and at the end of a line (see Subsections 18.4.1 and 18.4.2, respectively). Two case studies are used for explanatory purposes here to show that the methodology proposed for researching orthographic distribution works, and the focus on word division specifically is then offered as an example. The data used as source of evidence come from the two components of *The Málaga Corpus of Early English Scientific Prose*, both *The Málaga Corpus of Late Middle English Scientific Prose* (for the period 1350–1500) (Miranda-García et al. 2014) and *The Málaga Corpus of Early Modern English Scientific Prose* (for the period 1500–1700) (Calle-Martín et al. 2016). These corpora contain material from the three branches of early English scientific writing: specialized treatises, surgical treatises and recipe collections (Voigts 1984, Taavitsainen and Tyrkkö 2010). These two components of the Málaga corpus contain transcribed material using semi-diplomatic conventions to render an accurate reproduction of the original handwriting. In this fashion, the spelling, lineation, paragraphing, word division and punctuation have been exactly reproduced as by the scribal hand, while abbreviations have been systematically expanded in italics. The corpus has been automatically annotated with CLAWS7 (Constituent Likelihood Word-tagging System), developed by the UCREL team at the University of Lancaster (Garside 1987, Garside and Smith 1997),[1] whose tagset incorporates more than 160

[1] Based upon present-day English, it does not include the large amount of spelling variants and the archaic/obsolete words of early English. The spelling variation naturally poses a problem when automatically POS-tagging the text, where the accuracy of CLAWS decreases. To solve this shortcoming, a normalization process with the tool VARD was necessary before the actual CLAWS annotation, which yields two corpus files, the normalized corpus and the POS-tagged corpus (Baron and Rayson 2008: 5).

tags together with particular labels for the different marks of punctuation (Romero-Barranco 2020).[2]

The printed material comes from the *Early English Books Online* corpus, which contains a total of 755 million words from 25,368 texts from the period 1470–1700. Even though it includes material from a wide range of fields, such as literature, philosophy, history, religion, science and politics, among others, the present case study exclusively relies on the scientific component of the corpus so that all the data belong to the same typology of texts. The *EEBO* corpus has been supplemented with a small collection of texts on pharmacy, botany, alchemy and medicine from the sixteenth and seventeenth centuries that we have manually compiled following the *Málaga Corpus* editorial model (Brunschwig 1528, Dodoens 1578, Ruscelli 1595 and Hartman 1696). The size and format of *EEBO* allows for the examination of particular spelling features from a chronological perspective, word division included, both in the middle and at the end of a line.

The compilation of data has been a straightforward process. As far as the *Málaga Corpus* is concerned, the corpus contains a semi-diplomatic transcription of the original manuscript text. A simple search was required to obtain the instances of word division in the middle of the line as the modernized version of the corpus allows the generation of all the allomorphs of a given lexeme. Line-final breaks, in turn, were automatically generated by searching for the hyphen - and the double hyphen =, which are the punctuation symbols used to mark these breakings in handwritten texts. As far as printed texts are concerned, the instances of division in the middle of a line were generated automatically through the Sketch Engine interface,[3] and, in this case, different searches were needed to comply with the orthographic variation of Early Modern English. Next, line-final word division instances were automatically generated by means of the hyphen, which is also found to mark these breakings in printed texts. On quantitative grounds, divisions in the middle of a line have been represented with percentages (%) while the distribution of line-final word splits has been analyzed with normalized frequencies (n.f.).

18.4.1 Word Division

Compounds are taken to be the lexemes consisting of two independent lexemes (Bauer 2003: 40). Word division is here described according to the evidence provided by nominal or adjectival compounds (i.e. *headache*, *toothache*,

[2] See http://hunter.uma.es and http://modernmss.uma.es for the Late Middle English and the Early Modern English components of the corpus, respectively.

[3] Sketch Engine is a software tool which processes texts for the identification of words, phrases or particular linguistic constructions presenting the results in the form of word sketches, concordances or word lists. See www.sketchengine.eu for more detailed information about the tool and its potential for linguistic research.

aquavitae, rosemary, lukewarm and so on), compound adverbs (i.e. *therewith, within, inward* and so on), reflexive pronouns (i.e. *myself, himself, themselves* and so on) and other forms unequivocally rendered as two different lexemes in present-day English, but together for some time in the history of English (i.e. *shall be* and *as much*, among others). Figure 18.2 shows the distribution of nominal and adjectival compounds in the period 1350–1700, where the joined version of words is observed to proliferate over time. While there is a major preference for the separation of both members of the compound (72.2 percent) in the fifteenth century, the sixteenth century stands out as a transitional period marking the progressive decline of the separated form (58.8 percent) together with the rise of the joined form (38.2 percent). The seventeenth century shows the eventual standardization of the joined spelling with a rate of 66.2 percent, contrasting with the sporadic occurrence of both the hyphenated (17.7 percent) and the split forms (16.1 percent) in handwritten texts. Figure 18.3, in turn, presents the same state of affairs in printed documents inasmuch as split forms significantly predominate over joined forms in the sixteenth century (with rates of 71.1 percent and 28.1 percent, respectively). In the seventeenth century, however, there is a significant rise of joined forms (51.9 percent), which eventually outnumbered the occurrence of split forms (40.8 percent). Still, figures are surprisingly high if compared with their occurrence in handwritten documents.

The standardization of these compounds is not in all cases systematic as the adoption of the joined form seems to behave differently across the different compounds. There is, on the one hand, a group of compounds like *aquavitae, rosemary* and *quicksilver*, among others, which are systematically represented

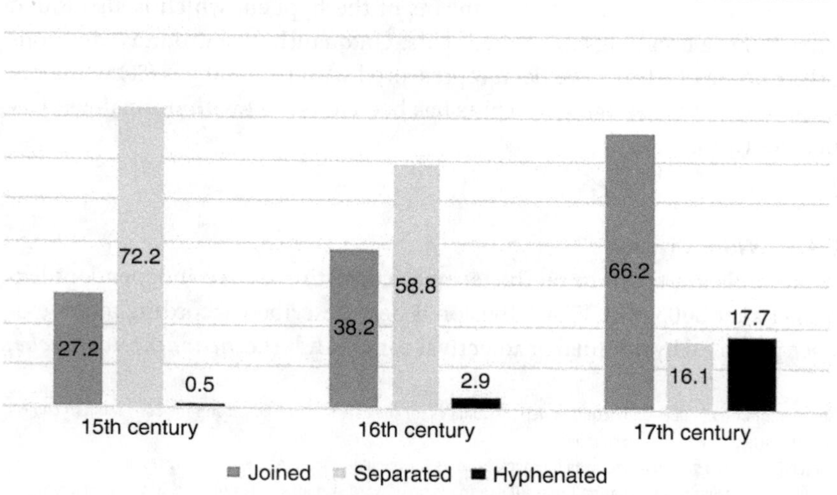

Figure 18.2 Nominal and adjectival compounds in handwritten texts (%)

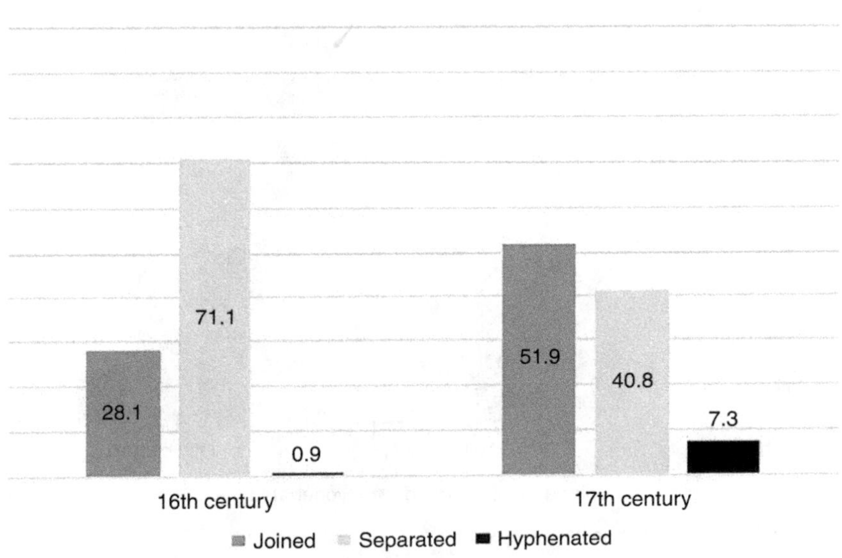

Figure 18.3 Nominal and adjectival compounds in printed texts (%)

in its full form at the beginning of the seventeenth century, with a minute occurrence of the separated and the hyphenated forms. There is, on the other hand, another set of compounds which are more reluctant to the adoption of the joined form and more bound to appear with the hyphen well into the seventeenth century. The list includes the *-ache* compounds (i.e. *headache, toothache*) together with other combinations such as *lukewarm*.

Figures 18.4 and 18.5 show the threefold representation of reflexives in handwritten and printed documents, respectively. As far as handwriting is concerned, a similar trend of development is observed with the final standardization of the full form of the reflexive at the beginning of the seventeenth century. There is an outstanding preference for the split form of the reflexive throughout the fifteenth and sixteenth centuries with rates of 76.9 percent and 67.9 percent, respectively, followed by the joined form (23.1 percent and 30.3 percent), while the use of the hyphenated form is sporadic. In the seventeenth century, the results again show the rise of the joined form (46.1 percent), which outnumbers the split (39.1 percent) and the hyphenated spellings (14.7 percent), although the split form of these reflexives is still considerably high in these texts. Printers, on the other hand, present a different attitude toward reflexives insofar as the split form is significantly preferred both in the sixteenth (94.1 percent) and the seventeenth centuries (68.7 percent). Even though there is a significant rise of the full version of reflexives in the seventeenth century (31.2 percent), the split form shows a wider distribution in printed documents.

There is also room for morphological variation in the distribution of reflexives depending on the person of the verb, with three clear diachronic

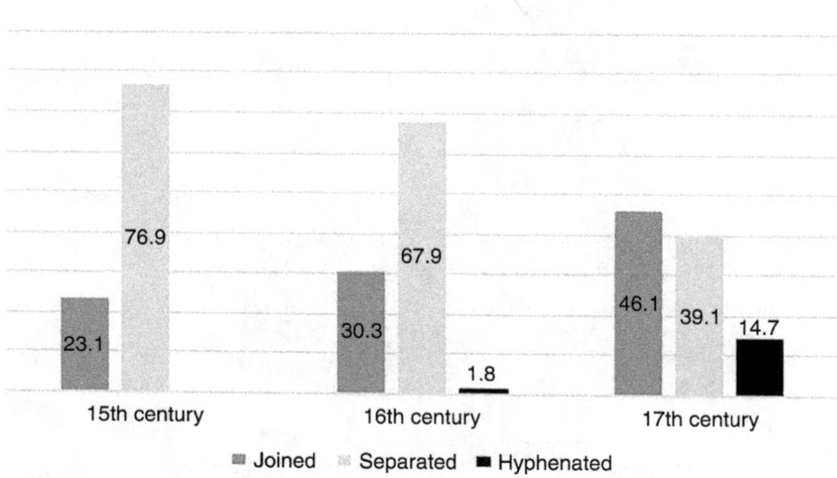

Figure 18.4 Reflexive forms in handwritten texts (%)

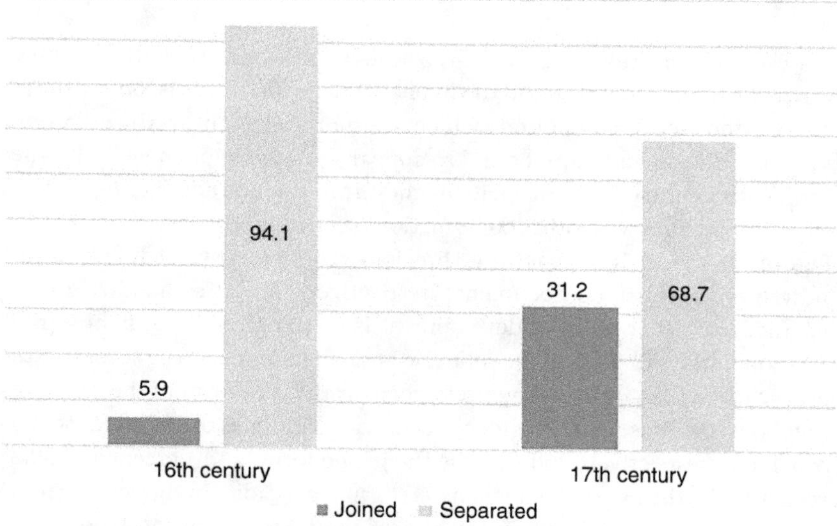

Figure 18.5 Reflexive forms in printed texts (%)

tendencies. First and second person pronouns are systematically separated in Late Middle (1350–1500) and Early Modern English (1500–1700) (i.e. *my self, your self, our selves, your selves*) both in handwritten and printed texts, with just occasional occurrences of the hyphenated and the joined spellings (i.e. *my-self, myself*). Third person plural pronouns, in turn, present another trend. Even though the split spelling is clearly the choice in the fifteenth-century (i.e. *them selves*), the full form begins to slightly outnumber the others in the sixteenth century, becoming the standard spelling at the turn of the following century (i.e. *themselves*). Third person singular pronouns would lie somewhere in between the previous tendencies with the preference for the split form throughout the fifteenth and sixteenth centuries and the rise of the joined form in the seventeenth century. The two spellings, *himself* and *him self*, are then found to have a balanced distribution throughout that century.

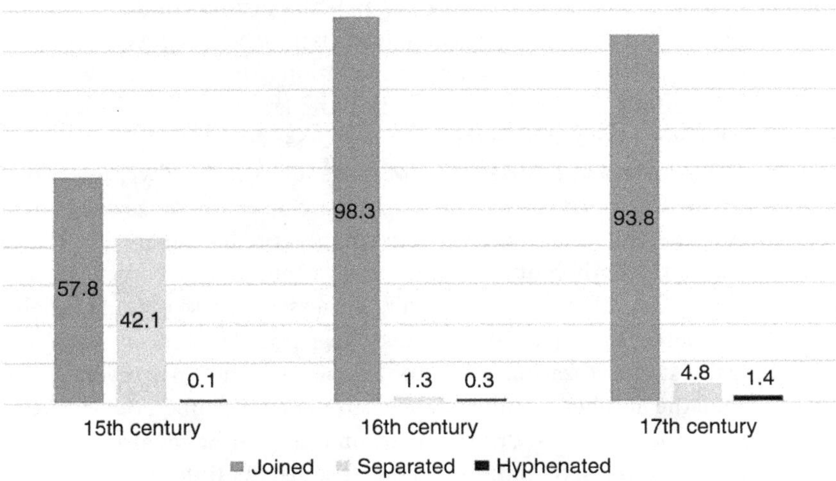

Figure 18.6 Other adverbs and prepositions in handwritten texts (%)

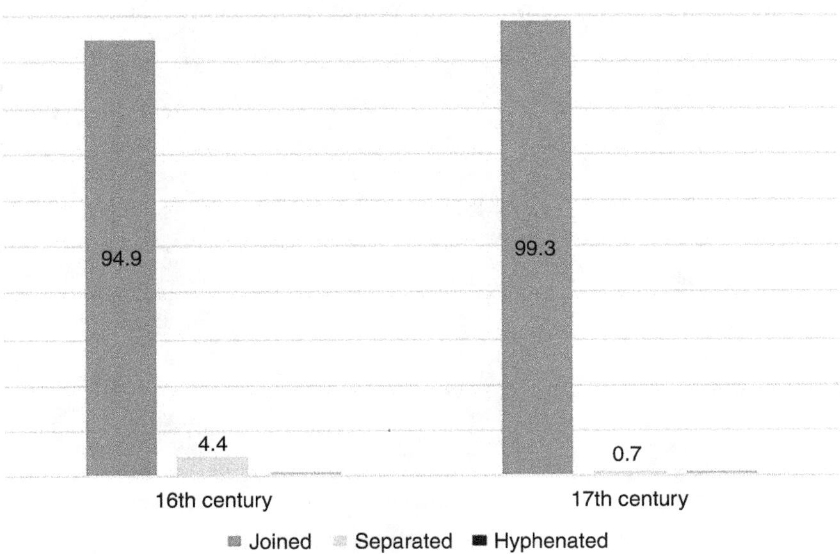

Figure 18.7 Other adverbs and prepositions in printed texts (%)

Figures 18.6 and 18.7 present the development of the spellings of the adverbs *afterward*, *inward*, *outward*, *therewith* and *within* together with the preposition *without* in handwritten and printed texts. These items are found to be somewhat more advanced in the standardization process with the adoption of a systematic form already in the sixteenth century. Adverbs are usually represented either joined or separated in the fifteenth century, with rates of 57.8 percent and 42.1 percent, respectively. One century later, however, the split form declines, leaving these words with an unequivocal spelling. The full form becomes general practice among penmen and printers in the sixteenth and seventeenth centuries. A different tendency is observed for lexemes which appear together without any apparent justification. This is particularly the case of combinations like *asmuch* and *shalbe*, the latter "found capriciously till the seventeenth century" (Denholm-Young 1954: 70).

Figure 18.8 presents the distribution of these items in handwritten texts. As shown, they developed irregularly with drastic ups and downs over time. Interestingly enough, there is a widespread practice of separating these lexemes among fifteenth-century scribes with a rate of 99.1 percent of the instances. The sixteenth century, however, witnesses the rise of joined spelling with 89.1 percent and just 10.7 percent of separated instances. As in the previous cases, standardization seems to take place in the early seventeenth century, when the number of split instances surpasses the joined version with 85.9 percent of the examples. Printed texts, on the other hand, already present split spelling in the sixteenth century with a distribution of 81.8 percent and 18.2 percent of split and joined instances, respectively (Figure 18.9). The printers' decision to avoid the joined form of these lexemes is already a consensus in the seventeenth century, with a rate of 98.2 percent of the instances.

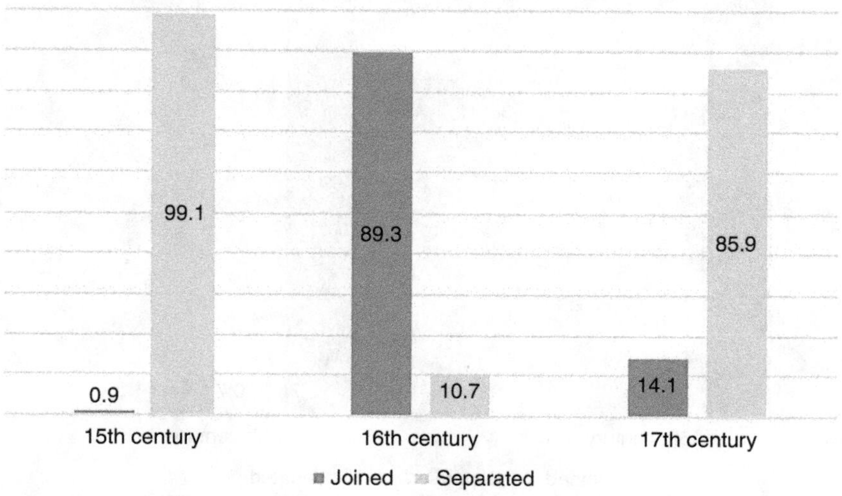

Figure 18.8 Development of *shalbe* and *asmuch* in handwritten texts (%)

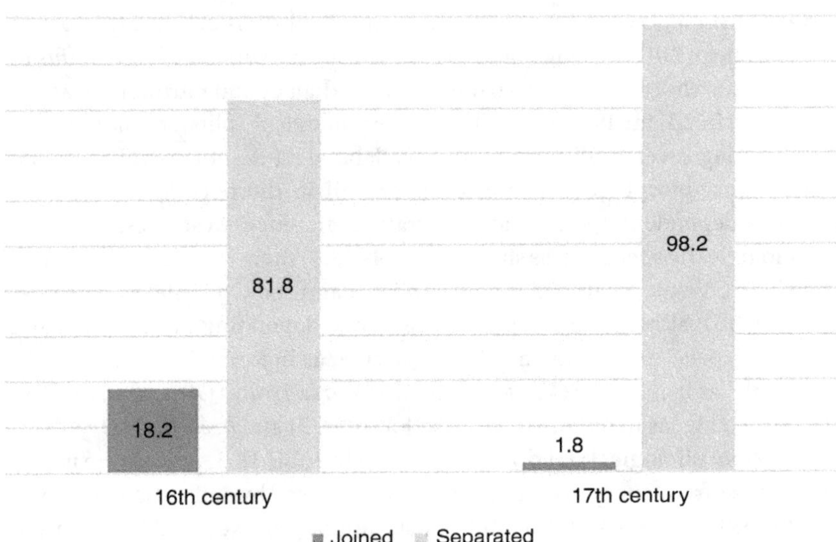

Figure 18.9 Development of *shalbe* and *asmuch* in printed texts (%)

18.4.2 Line-final Word Division

An empirical analysis of line-final word division in early English prose must necessarily stem from a statistical overview of the phenomenon in OE, the period marking off the beginning of this practice to validate the existence of a regular set of patterns among Anglo-Saxon scribes. The quantitative analysis of line-final word division comes to refute the argument of Hladký (1985a: 73) that the major principle determining divisions at the end of the lines in OE is fundamentally morphological. As shown in Table 18.1, phonological divisions are found to outnumber morphological breaks. The former amount to 86.97 occurrences, the latter to 70.11 occurrences. Anomalous boundaries are sporadic with just 7.22 instances.

A previous study on line-final breaks in OE sheds light on the erratic distribution of the phenomenon among Anglo-Saxon writers, more bound to make the most of the writing surface at the margin. Interestingly enough, phonological splits exceed morphological ones in MS Corpus Christi College 140, containing the Anglo-Saxon version of the *Gospel According to St. Matthew* (*Mt* for short), and MS Vitelius A.xv (*Vit* for short), housing the *Beowulf* manuscript and three prose tracts dated c. 1000 (Rypins 1998). There is, in turn, a

Table 18.1 *Type of division in OE (n.f.)*

Phonological	86.97
Morphological	70.11
Anomalous	7.22
Total	164.31

substantial preference for morphological line-final divisions in MS Corpus Christi College 201, housing a mid-eleventh-century version of *Apollonius of Tyre* (*AoT* for short), despite sharing the same dialect and chronology as *Mt* (Calle-Martín 2011a: 19–20). Although morphological splits are more widespread among several OE writers, the available data do not corroborate the principle that morphological breakings prevail in the period, as these are ultimately dependent upon the idiosyncratic preferences of scribes.

Phonologically speaking, as shown in Table 18.2, there is a major preference for the CV-CV rule, as in *cire-niscan* (*AoT*, li); and the C-C rule, as in *nih-tes* (*Vit*, 103r, 16), although other possibilities arise depending on the word and the factual space at the margin: (i) the V-V rule, as in *farise-isce* (*Mt*, xiv); (ii) the ST rule, as in *fæs-tenu* (*Vit*, fol. 112v, 17) or *arce-strates* (*AoT*, xxii, li);[4] and (iii) the CL rule, as in *wun-driende* (*Vit*, fol. 106v, 9) and *hreo-fla* (*Mt*, vii).

From a morphological standpoint, as shown in Table 18.3, prefixation is usually the most frequent type of division in OE, followed by suffixation and composition. While in *Vit* and *AoT* prefixes outnumber suffixes, in *Mt* suffixation slightly surpasses prefixation. Anomalous boundaries, in turn, are irregularly distributed in the OE period. In the majority of cases, this irregular separation is the result of limited space at the margin of the folios. The scribe was, to some extent, forced to break the word elsewhere, always on condition that there are at least two letters on the following line, as in *hlafo-rd* (*Mt*, xxvi). In other cases, the distortion might be explained in terms of an erroneous interpretation of the inflection by the scribe, as in *heof-enum* (*Mt*, vi).

Table 18.2 *Phonological boundaries in OE (n.f.)*

	Vit	*Mt*	*AoT*
CV-CV rule	59.8	51.6	1.5
C-C rule	50.5	42.7	6.1
V-V rule	0.9	1.9	–
ST rule	–	1.9	0.3
CL rule	0.9	–	–

(from Calle-Martín 2011a: 21)

Table 18.3 *Morphological boundaries in OE (n.f.)*

	Vit	*Mt*	*AoT*
Prefixation	47.7	24.3	22.9
Suffixation	41.1	33.7	4.5
Composition	10.2	8.4	3.1

(from Calle-Martín 2011a: 21)

[4] This rule is erratic in OE as there is no evidence of a consistent practice (Calle-Martín 2011a: 22; see also Hladký 1985a: 74).

As illustrated in Table 18.4, there is a growing importance of phonological boundaries in fifteenth-century handwritten documents coinciding with the gradual decline of morphological divisions, with just 15.02 occurrences – a negligible figure if compared with the total of anomalous divisions (Calle-Martín 2011a: 23, see also Hladký 1985a: 74–75, Hladký 1987: 137, Calle-Martín 2009: 40). Still, there are texts where line-final word division is subjected to an array of random rules by which some words are prone to be broken almost elsewhere (Calle-Martín 2011a; see also Calle-Martín 2009: 40). This is, for instance, the case of MS Peterhouse College 118 (P118 for short), which presents a significant number of anomalous splits.

From a phonological viewpoint, the CV-CV rule predominates, followed by the C-C rule (see Table 18.5). There are cases, however, where a consonant letter is spuriously added after the break, perhaps in the attempt to preserve the C-C rule rather than providing an irregular split. In MS Hunter 328 and MS Sloane 340 (H328 and S340 for short), for instance, the scribes prefer the writing of *vrin-nal* (S340, fol. 49v, 10) and *strang-gurie* (H328, fol. 26v, 23) to avoid the breaking of a syllable at the end of the line, even when other breaks would have also been possible, such as the CV-CV rule in *vri-nal* or *strangu-rie*. In addition to this, in contrast with OE, there is a growing specialization among fifteenth-century scribes in view of the slight increase in the use of V-V splits, always on condition that both vowels are pronounced, as in *ve-ynes* (S340, fol. 42v, 3);[5] the more frequent use of the ST rule, as in *dyges-tyon* (S340, fol. 40v, 24); and the appearance of the CT rule, as in *lac-tea* (H328, fol. 11r, 25).

Table 18.4 *Type of division in ME (n.f.)*

Phonological	151.88
Morphological	15.02
Anomalous	8.59
Total	175.49

Table 18.5 *Phonological boundaries in ME (n.f.)*

	E2622	*H328*	*S340*	*P118*	*H497*
CV-CV rule	56.08	36.52	104.82	87.81	127.12
C-C rule	25.67	10.80	57.24	29.27	103.47
V-V rule	2.70	1.86	8.27	9.06	6.39
ST rule	–	0.37	5.51	–	0.52
CT rule	–	0.37	–	–	0.27

(from Calle-Martín 2011a: 25, 2009: 41–45)

[5] In texts like MS Hunter 497 (H497), for instance, the rule substantially diffuses in the specialized terminology, usually of Latinate origin, as a clue for an appropriate reading, as in *siri-us*, *uari-ole* or *opi-um* (Calle-Martín 2009: 44).

From a morphological standpoint, Table 18.6 presents the distribution of morphological boundaries among fifteenth-century scribes where suffixation is observed to outnumber prefixation in most cases. This distribution is consistent, except for MS Egerton 2622 (E2622 for short) on account of its preference for prefixes, as in *for-sohte* (fol. 136v, 6), *up-warde* (fol. 155v, 8) or *y-do* (fol. 148r, 10).

Table 18.7 presents the distribution of line-final breaks among sixteenth and seventeenth-century penmen, where phonological boundaries are negligible in comparison with its frequency in previous centuries. As shown, there is a higher tendency for line-final division in printed texts than in handwritten texts (74.21 vs. 36.78 occurrences). Morphological division, in turn, is sporadic in both types of texts. Notwithstanding these general tendencies, there is also room for variation across some pieces insofar as anomalous boundaries are found to supersede the morphological in two early sixteenth-century compositions, MS Ryland 1310 (R1310 for short) and the *Booke of Dystyllacyon of Waters* (*Dyst* for short; Brunschwig 1528), in particular.

As far as phonological divisions are concerned, Tables 18.8 and 18.9 show that the CV-CV and the C-C rules are, as expected, the most widespread boundaries both in handwriting and printing, with all the other rules lagging

Table 18.6 *Morphological boundaries in ME (n.f.)*

	E2622	*H328*	*S340*	*P118*	*H497*
Prefixation	3.37	1.11	8.96	6.75	5.56
Suffixation	1.35	6.70	15.86	6.75	8.90
Composition	1.35	1.49	0.68	–	4.45

(from Calle-Martín 2011a: 25, 2009: 46–47)

Table 18.7 *Type of division in EModE (n.f.)*

	Handwriting	Printing
Phonological	36.78	74.21
Morphological	11.71	9.52
Anomalous	6.70	5.66
Total	55.19	89.39

Table 18.8 *Phonological boundaries in EModE handwritten texts (n.f.)*

	R1310	*H135*	*H95*	*FER7*	*W6812*
CV-CV rule	27.53	15.22	16.07	4.96	32.56
C-C rule	21.81	10.55	4.38	5.52	25.97
V-V rule	1.03	1.22	0	0.82	2.32
ST rule	5.71	1.96	0	0	2.32
CT rule	0.51	0.24	0	0.27	0.77
CL rule	2.07	1.96	5.84	0.55	2.71

Table 18.9 *Phonological boundaries in EModE printed texts (n.f.)*

	Dyst	*AoP*	*NH*	*FPh*
CV-CV rule	51.37	49.87	63.44	58.99
C-C rule	38.20	34.91	55.05	57.79
V-V rule	1.50	3.11	0	4.55
ST rule	4.32	0.62	2.33	2.87
CT rule	0.56	0	0	1.43
CL rule	3.38	4.98	10.73	9.35

well behind. There are, however, exceptions to this rule in some texts. For instance, the C-C rule outnumbers the CV-CV rule in MS Ferguson 7 (FER7 for short), housing an early-seventeenth-century handwritten extract of *The Secrets of Alexis of Piemont* and *A Niewe Herbal or Historie of Plants* (*AoP* and *NH* for short, respectively; Ruscelli 1595, Dodoens 1578); this is interpreted as an erratic practice of the scribe given the preference for the CV-CV rule in the printed versions of the same text. Apart from the preference for CV-CV, both handwritten and printed sources show a higher level of specialization in view of the constrained distribution of the V-V rule, on the one hand, and the ST rule, on the other, as in *indige-stion* (R1310 fol. 3r, 34), *ipo-stasis* (R1310 fol. 11v, 22), *Ma-sterwort* (*FPh*, p. 26) and so on. Likewise, there is a rebirth of the CL rule in the period, becoming more recurrent in printed compositions, *NH* and *FPh*, in particular (Dodoens 1578; Hartman 1696). In handwriting, MS Hunter 95 (H95 for short) stands out on account of its relative high frequency, as in *Com-frey* (fol. 1v, 55) and *con-tractum* (fol. 10r, 3).

Finally, morphological divisions are more erratic with the absence of a standard practice across penmen and printers. Tables 18.10 and 18.11 present the distribution of morphological boundaries in handwritten and printed documents. While in MS Wellcome 6812 (W6812 for short) suffixation sharply outnumbers composition, in H135 composition surpasses suffixation.

Table 18.10 *Morphological boundaries in EModE handwritten texts (n.f.)*

	R1310	*H135*	*H95*	*FER7*	*W6812*
Prefixation	1.03	0.98	2.92	0.55	0.77
Suffixation	4.15	3.92	4.38	2.20	15.50
Composition	4.15	7.61	1.46	2.76	5.42

Table 18.11 *Morphological boundaries in EModE printed texts (n.f.)*

	Dyst	*AoP*	*NH*	*FPh*
Prefixation	0.37	1.24	0	1.91
Suffixation	1.31	4.98	3.73	12.94
Composition	2.63	6.85	8.39	6.71

Prefixation, except for H95, becomes almost nonexistent in handwritten texts. In printed documents, however, composition is more widely disseminated, followed by suffixation and prefixation, the latter negligible across all the texts – with the only exception of *FPh*, where suffixation is preferred.

18.5 Some Follow-up Thoughts

Since the analysis section has been quite intense and data-driven, let us pause for a minute and take stock of what the whole purpose of the present contribution has been so far, before moving on to giving some follow-up thoughts. The core section of the chapter has been concerned with the emergence of spacing in the Middle Ages and its development in the Early Modern English period. After a brief description of the writing material and the arrangement of the text on the writing surface, the chapter has focused in greater detail on the concept of spacing applied to words broken in the middle and at the end of a line, as these are the two environments where both scribes and printers were bound to make choices as to the separation of a word. To this purpose, two case studies were offered, paying attention to the phenomenon both in handwritten and printed sources. As far as handwritten material is concerned, the data were drawn from the two components of *The Málaga Corpus of Early English Scientific Prose*, both *The Málaga Corpus of Late Middle English Scientific Prose* (for the period 1350–1500) and *The Málaga Corpus of Early Modern English Scientific Prose* (for the period 1500–1700). As for the printed material, the analyses have relied on the scientific component of the corpus of *Early English Books Online* together with other sixteenth- and seventeenth-century scientific texts, providing us with fresh data to evaluate the printers' attitude toward word division at the time.

Word division in the middle of the line has been explored in light of the evidence provided by nominal/adjectival compounds, compound adverbs, reflexives and words, which, although rendered unequivocally as two independent lexemes in present-day English, are irregularly found together in the history of English. The orthographic standardization of these words initiated in the sixteenth century and, after a period of competition between the joined and split forms, it was not until the seventeenth century that the solid version of these forms seems to be adopted. Notwithstanding this, reflexives present an unexpected development in the sense that the joined form is the rule in seventeenth-century handwritten documents, while the split form is still the dominant practice in printed texts. The shape of independent lexemes such as *shall be* and *as much*, however, was deemed to be the result of the scribes' and printers' choice insofar as they were mainly separated in the fifteenth century but overwhelmingly joined in the sixteenth century. Line-final word division was discussed in terms of the typology of breaking, whether morphological, phonological or anomalous. While the phenomenon is erratic in Old English to make the most of the writing surface, a more standard practice was observed among medieval and Early Modern English penmen. There is an increasing importance of phonological divisions in the period 1500–1700, with an outstanding preference for the CV-CV and the C-C rules, followed by the V-V rule. Morphological breaks, in turn, become sporadic, suffixation preferred over prefixation and composition. This rationale also seems to be the dominant pattern for breaking words at the end of a line in the early printed texts, where both the CV-CV and the C-C rules are systematically adopted by the printers.

With that said, what can our readers take from our case studies and from our chapter as a whole? We believe that they are a testimony of how little one can lay out from a scientific, linguistic point of view about orthographic distribution as a whole. Through research, however, one can glean more about the practical aspects of conducting empirical work on something as little explored as word separation, as a way to hopefully reach some encouraging generalization on at least one area of orthographic distribution. The study of word separation in historical documents is at times painstaking for the analyst in view of the number of irregular breaks which are scattered throughout the text with no other explanation than making the most of such an expensive writing surface as parchment or paper. In the absence of a standard pattern among scribes and printers, one of the methodological problems with studying word separation across time lies in the selection of data, which may, to some extent, bias the validity of the results. The different attitudes toward word division are commonplace in the historical analysis of the phenomenon and some of the texts under scrutiny have raised this same point. In spite of this shortcoming, the study of the phenomenon in handwritten texts also sheds light on some of the scribal attitudes toward word division in the medieval period, where both regular and irregular practices are found depending on the hand involved. The Renaissance, and the printing press in particular, marked off the beginning of a new era in which both scribes and printers were increasingly committed to the use of a more standard practice in the middle of the line – with a wider preference of solid forms toward the seventeenth century – and at the end of the line – with the increasing adoption of phonological divisions throughout the early modern period, the CV-CV and the C-C rules in particular.

Even though word division in the middle of the line was practically standardized toward the end of the seventeenth century, line-final word division still awaits the labor of other scholars to provide a more convincing picture of the phenomenon after the arrival of printing. This chapter has mostly shown one side of the coin, and there is still a long way ahead to gather some more evidence about it in other periods, genres or text types. The seventeenth century was crucial in the development of word division as a result of the printers' decisive contribution. The study of the phenomenon from the community-of-practice perspective would then open new doors to assess the role of the different printing houses in the dissemination of the sixteenth- and seventeenth-century practices on word division. Tyrkkö (2020: 70) argues that "printers formed a tight-knit professional community where new innovations, or deviations from current standards, were immediately noticed" and this community "is a valuable one to take when it comes to Early Modern printing and thus to spelling standardisation" (Tyrkkö 2013).

To wrap up, then, where can future research depart from in order to understand more orthographic distribution and its relation with word division? We believe that a diachronic study is a desideratum to reconsider the actual contribution of seventeenth-century printers, the role of eighteenth- and nineteenth-century prescriptive grammars and the eventual configuration of the phenomenon as it now stands in present-day English, worldwide varieties included. Genre and text-type variation would also be a revealing line of research in the light of the evidence provided by, for instance, magazine and newspaper material, which could have surely pioneered the standardization process in comparison with the timid contribution of text types such as fiction or science, among others.

18.6 Conclusion

The present chapter has provided an overview of issues relating to orthographic distribution and has then discussed the emergence of spacing in early English writing, considering the attitudes of both scribes and printers toward word division in the middle and at the end of the line. The two case studies have cast light on the existence of some level of orthographic variation throughout the fifteenth and the sixteenth centuries, when the phenomenon was mostly found to rely on the individual preferences of scribes. The seventeenth century, in turn, brought some fresh air to the issue with the progressive adoption of solid forms in the middle of the line and phonological divisions at the end of the line. This trend, however, is incipient at the turn of the seventeenth century, being still a very early date to propose some sort of orthographic standardization in the writing of these words. The case studies have, we hope, illuminated our knowledge about word division in early English and have provided a methodological framework for the study of word division across time. The topic surely awaits the future insight of other scholars to elucidate the moment and the forces which contributed to the eventual standardization of line-final word division in English. It is from relatively narrow areas of empirical work that, we believe, useful generalizations about such a big topic as orthographic organization can hopefully be drawn in the future.

19

Comparative and Sociopragmatic Methods

Marija Lazar

19.1 Introduction

From the outset of philological inquiries into texts on historical stages, the interest in text materiality (discussed in Chapter 15, this volume), has paved the way for the development of paleography, historical phonology and text criticism. In each of these fields, the graphic signs themselves as well as their systems have constantly played a subordinate role. It is only recently that the examination of *writing systems* themselves as well as *orthography* and *punctuation* have become truly independent research areas, whose consolidation continues, given that research on them remains dispersed in case studies across various disciplines. According to Coulmas (2013: 17–18), a *writing system* can, in this context, be understood as a set of graphic signs (*scripts*) in order to decode a language into its written form; *orthography* means a set of scripts, including a set of rules, that regulates its usage.[1]

The first attempts at systematizing script types were presented in *paleography* (e.g. Karskiĭ 1901, Zhukovskai͡a 1955; see also Chapter 15, this volume), an integrative part of historical science, which was to introduce a divide between historical science and philology. If we examine how language histories have been written over time, an endeavor that started simultaneously with paleography, the history of writing systems was by and large excluded from them on account of the fact that, on the one hand, the history of writing systems did not fit into the structuralist concept of language and, on the other,

[1] In historical linguistic studies, the distinction between writing systems and orthography is not always clearly drawn or, respectively, cannot be drawn, for the studies themselves are concerned with exploring a set of scripts used in a text or a group of texts and with finding regularities within them. The sole exceptions are those studies dealing with orthography reforms that clearly restrict the area of use of both terms.

it was already part of another discipline. However, it must be borne in mind that, as a practice, paleography was more interested in the shape of scripts; their inventory has been described with regard to this perspective, which Zalizni͡ak refers to, for example, as *calligraphy* in a broader sense (Zalizni͡ak 2002a [1979]: 560–61).

Subsequently, the divide in *text criticism* between historical science and philology deepened, while a separate editorial canon for the needs of historical science and for philology was developed, even though the very same texts were often to become objects of interest to both disciplines. Ultimately, this was to result in contradictory solutions in text materiality interpretation and representation, particularly regarding text normalization and modernization in historical editions, as well as its literal (diplomatic) reproduction in philological editions, which restricted their interoperability between both disciplines (Piotrowski 2012: 19, Sahle 2013: 107–10, 143–67, 225–53). The editor's vision, as conveyor of ultimate decisions about the shape of the edited text, often led to editorial encroachments for clarity's sake, notably concerning orthography. This procedure deviates from the original text and impedes an appropriate graphematic analysis (Černá-Willi 2012: E5–E7).

The philological editions were mostly used in linguistic *phonological research in diachrony*; the scripts, on the other hand, were interpreted as graphic representations of phonemes; this was the reason behind the faithful representation of the spelling used in source texts. However, authors of some studies distanced themselves from the prevailing paleographical praxis; instead, they described the set of graphemes and their corresponding functions as used in the language system under scrutiny. The phonological and graphemic reconstruction of linguistic proto-stages was based on structuralist oppositions: phoneme ~ allophone; grapheme ~ allograph (Lisowski 2001, Marti 2014, Stadnik-Holzer 2014). Research topics such as *capitalization, punctuation* and *text structure*, however, were not included in the scope of linguistic research over a longer period, for the modernization praxis in historical editions rendered them invisible, while philological editions frequently followed the same principle in order to ensure ease of reading. Ultimately, it was paleography that completed their description (e.g. Karskiĭ 1901: 232–57). From the 1990s on, linguistic interest in these research areas has burgeoned; the potential for its development has still not been realized, however.

Alongside a functional description, the description of users' concept of writing systems and their attitudes toward them had already been outlined in the late 1970s (Zalizni͡ak 2002 [1979]). The *user-based turn* was motivated both by the subjectivity of usage *in* and *of* writing systems and strove for a description of the system used; the latter obviously deviated from the prescribed one (Zalizni͡ak 2002a [1979]: 566–67). Ultimately, such considerations were to open up a vast field of sociolinguistic and sociopragmatic research into the usage of writing systems (see Section 19.3). Besides those descriptive studies that furnish an overview of writing systems in particular sources and – more broadly – languages, a comparative paradigm was deployed in more advanced studies. On the one hand, this approach provides a positivist exploration into similarities and divergences in graphic representation within single texts or between several texts. On the other, it can serve as an access to sociolinguistic and sociopragmatic variables in order to explain orthographic consistency or variation, as well as, paired with an appropriate digital mark-up, calculate and measure the regularity in variation. The starting point for this development can be observed in text criticism, whereby a holistic method was used for studying texts that involve both an in-depth investigation and a thorough reconstruction of the extralinguistic context.

In this chapter, comparative and sociopragmatic methods are illustrated based on material from Slavic languages written in early modern times, when their writing systems had already been developed to a great extent, thus corresponding, albeit sometimes with delayed timing, to the common European trend. Traditionally, Slavic studies have shown considerable interest in writing, orthography, and variation in and of the writing systems. And yet, as with other philologies, this research has not been completed within a specific sociolinguistic or sociopragmatic paradigm, even though it inevitably touches upon important concepts within it. This chapter equally serves as the summary of trends therein and is structured as follows.[2]

First, the most important directions in *comparative* studies on Slavic writing systems and orthographies are presented. Second, the theoretical preliminaries in *sociopragmatics* and the deployment of this framework for research on writing systems are discussed, for sociopragmatic concepts have largely been developed without taking writing systems into consideration. Then, *pragmaphilology* is presented as a promising direction emerging recently within Slavic studies, and it serves as an example of the shift from the initial paleographic interest in linguistic material to studying variation *in* and *of* several writing systems. To conclude, the chapter summarizes the criticism of both methods, evaluates their impact on future development within the discipline, and maps out prospective directions in how to best adopt those methods.

[2] Some exceptions that represent consolidated results and demonstrate a growing interest in the field of scripts, writing systems and orthography are the following recently published volumes: Čornejová et al. (2010), on Czech orthography from the tenth until the twentieth century; Baddeley and Voeste (2012b) as well as Condorelli (2020c), with case studies on orthographies from early modern times; Berger et al. (2009/2014), with chapters devoted to orthography und scripts in a comprehensive handbook on Slavic languages; Tomelleri and Kempgen (2015), on contact phenomena between Slavic writing systems; Bunčić et al. (2016), on biscriptality in a typological perspective with several case studies on Slavic languages; Kempgen and Tomelleri (2019), on sociopragmatics of Slavic writing systems.

19.2 Comparative Method: Exploring Variation

Given the relative scarcity of historical sources, the comparative method has been predominantly adopted for carrying out small-scale studies with a high zoom-in effect. These have resulted in detailed explorations and presuppose the existence of a certain number of comparable studies in order to provide sufficient evidence for verified generalizations (for further considerations, consult Section 19.5). The comparative method is deployed on selected sources and is used to explore the variation, either within a single text or between several copies of a text, in order to access an individual, a small-scale (e.g. communities of practice) or an institutionally driven (e.g. chanceries, printing houses) alternation between them (see Auer and Hinskens 2005: 336).[3]

This approach requires using serial, impactful texts, such as manuscript copies or book reprints. In research on writing systems and orthographies, the comparative method has, to date, been applied to various versions of the Bible (for Bibles printed in Czech see Fidlerová et al. 2010), or ecclesiastic literature such as Joannes de Caulibus's *Meditationes vitae Christi* (for translations printed in Polish such as Baltazar Opiec's *Żywot Pana Jezu Kristu*, see Lisowski 2001, Bunčić 2012). The advantage of focusing on such texts is their widespread circulation and their apparent, frequency-induced influence on the establishment of orthographic norms across society – either officially established or socially agreed upon. Both factors underpin the significance of serial sources for language and cultural history.

The vast majority of serial texts in the vernacular languages were originally *translations* (mainly from Latin) in the Middle Ages and in early modern times. However, this key factor was not always taken into consideration in previous philological scholarship; this led to isolated analyses of target texts without recourse to the source texts. Meanwhile, in *translation studies*, the use of comparisons between the source text and the target text, as well as between different translations of one and the same text, became an acknowledged analytical method. Similarly, here, the interest in the target text's quality of translation and in the source text's cultural transfer led to the focus on the mechanisms of cultural accommodation between those cultures that were in contact. Moreover, research on these mechanisms not only encompassed the motivation behind the translation, but also aesthetic and ideological programs that explain the interpretative deviations between the source and the target text, as well as between translations by different authors.

The impact of the linguistic shape of the source text on the target text (linguistic interference), particularly in translations from medieval and early modern times, became obvious as one consequence of cultural translation from the learned into the vernacular languages; this led to the unification of

[3] A comparable discussion is provided in Chapter 16, this volume.

the linguistic/philological research methods with those employed in translation studies (see Zemenová 2011, Lazar 2018, Maier and Shamin 2018). This interdisciplinary research has primarily concentrated on lexical and morphosyntactic interferences; the exploration of writing systems and orthographies was subsequently narrowed down to observing orthographic 'mistakes' that were interpreted as hasty or inattentive writing executed by someone lacking experience therewith. Notwithstanding the existence of such writing irregularities, the prospective studies on orthographic interferences in medieval and early modern times translations should provide fresh insights into the development of and interrelationships between European writing systems, where micro- and macro-linguistic variation remain to be explored.

For the *microlinguistic variation*, a careful and systemic examination of impactful orthographic practices by literate individuals could exemplify the orthographic practices of those social groups over whom they wielded influence, particularly in the situation of learning a language. This approach often reveals consistent writing principles as used by an expert writer.[4] This was the case in the 1607 Russian-German phrasebook and dictionary compiled by Tönnies Fonne, subsequently examined by Hendriks (2014: 81–138).[5] Fonne's phrasebook was compiled following the tradition of phrasebooks for German-speaking merchants trading in Eastern Europe, where East Slavic vernacular languages, including Russian, were spoken. These phrasebooks were used for language learning; thanks to them the essential speaking, writing, reading and cultural competency were developed and they are considered to have had considerable outreach.

The *macrolinguistic variation* in writing systems and orthography can be productively explored by examining serial texts from different regions. In this case, not only common features but also regionally induced divergence between the related writing systems can be explored. This approach is exemplified in translations of German municipal law into Czech and the Old Slovak language, which was used in East Central European towns during the fifteenth century.[6] In these closely related varieties, the onset of orthographic change from a simplified and digraphic orthography toward the use of diacritic orthography has been documented after the Hussite Wars (approximately 1419–34).[7] The shift toward diacritic orthography – under the premise

[4] In all likelihood, language itself as subject matter for such a kind of writing led to orthographic uniformity.

[5] The phrasebook is one of the earliest examples of consequent Latin transliteration of Russian words and sentences.

[6] The status of Old Slovak remains a disputed issue in research literature (see Lifanov 2001).

[7] The 'default' Latin alphabet did not suffice for encoding specific Slavic sounds (fricatives, palatalized consonants, long vowels). Hence, their graphic marking inventory was continuously expanded and was to become more and more consistent and unambiguous. For Czech and Old Slovak, three options were subsequently used: (1) the simplified orthography (usage of ambiguous writing signs), for example <ʒ> ~ <z> for both /z/ and /ʐ/; (2) the digraphic orthography, for example <sz> : /ʂ/; (3) the diacritic orthography, for

of the simultaneous usage of other orthographies – was motivated by two extralinguistic factors:

(1) Writing in Slavic varieties/translation into Slavic varieties and the appropriate use of spelling was part of the Hussite ideological program and, hence, translating activities and usage of diacritic orthography was a sign of affiliation to this movement.
(2) In times of uncertainty, the towns adhered to the symbolic re-establishment and legitimation of the German law in Slavic translations; these were compiled using the new and more progressive orthography.

The study discovered the use of diacritic orthography in the Old Slovak translation together with a simplified and digraphic orthography, while the Czech translation demonstrates, with some exceptions, the exclusive use of simplified and digraphic orthography. This divergence emerged on account of the comparative chronology of translations of the German law in two separate regions: in Bohemia, Czech translations were already coming out from the beginning of the fifteenth century (pre-Hussite period), while the Old Slovak translations in Upper Hungary date back to the mid-fifteenth century (post-Hussite period). The later onset of the Slavic written tradition in Upper Hungary was to facilitate implementing the diacritic orthography, while in Bohemia the established translation and orthography tradition hindered the breakthrough of the innovative, progressive orthography (Lazar 2016: 193–96). As the exemplified study shows, several variation types – in this case, diachronic and diatopic variation – may be explored at once.[8] Further exploration into orthographic principles applied to other languages or varieties will help to cluster the European writing systems according to common orthographic principles that cross linguistic boundaries and to explore systemic similarities and differences between them.

The comparative method is also frequently deployed in order to explore and compare writing systems found in *written* and *printed texts on various media or surfaces* (see Franklin 2019: 1–2, Rozhdestvenskai͡a 1992, Schaeken 2019).[9] In particular, the interplay of manifold text materiality with writing systems was primarily explored in the earlier stages of language development when the interdisciplinary collaboration of linguistics with archaeology and historical auxiliary sciences, such as sphragistics, numismatics, or epigraphy dealing with texts written on seals, coins, church walls and so

example <á> : /aː/. In the mid-fifteenth century all three options were already used and differently evaluated in different sources. In contemporary Czech and Slovak, the diacritic orthography won recognition; however, these writing systems contain some relics of the simplified and digraphic orthography.

[8] For an overview of orthographic variation types, see Rutkowska and Rössler (2012: 217–19).

[9] Franklin criticizes the focus of traditional scholarship on the written or printed word (usually, on parchment or on paper), for this excludes multiple other spaces and surfaces where the written word may be depicted (Franklin 2019: 1–18).

on, occurs (see Section 19.4). In later language stages, such collaboration is usually less intensive for the substantial growth of text stored on traditional media (manuscripts or prints). In particular, those sources written during the transition from the Middle Ages to early modern times have attracted interest among researchers across linguistic specializations, for the medial shift from manuscript to print was to constitute a seminal event in the history of European writing systems and orthographies. Such scholarship involved the study of similarities and discrepancies between writing systems on media and the motivation analysis for diverging graphemic choices (Lisowski 2001, Fidlerová et al. 2010, Bunčić 2012). However, the constantly growing interest in the role of written language in shaping urban space, as evidenced from the abovementioned studies on the beginnings of written languages, has revived synthetic approaches to writing systems and orthographies presented in urban spaces. Diachronic studies on *linguistic landscapes* (see Pavlenko 2010, Pavlenko and Mullen 2015) involve interdisciplinary approaches and multimodal corpora; the complete medial and material range of written texts, including pictures of billboards, information tables, shop names, street names, commemorative plaques, graffiti and so on, have been taken into consideration.

19.3 Theoretical Preliminaries in Sociopragmatics

The sociopragmatic paradigm in historical linguistics dates back to the mid-1990s and is usually divided into two branches: diachronic pragmatics and pragmaphilology (Taavitsainen and Fitzmaurice 2007: 13–15). As the discipline's name suggests, it unites two subdisciplines, pragmatics and sociolinguistics,[10] whose boundaries are elastic. Compared with historical linguistics studies, whose aim is to describe the earlier language stages, as well as to explain the causes behind linguistic change and genetic interrelations in languages, sociopragmatics also involves the historical conditions for text production, transmission and reception so as to be able to explain language change and reconstruct the meanings that texts conveyed within those settings (Taavitsainen 2012: 1464). Notwithstanding historical distance, this perspective ensures an appropriate interpretation of historical texts. This assertion is equally true for historical studies on writing systems and orthographies, for their development and change depend on sociolinguistic and sociopragmatic variables (Baddeley and Voeste 2012a: 11).

[10] Historical sociolinguistics came about ten years earlier, in the early 1980s (Nevalainen 2015: 243–44, Zalizni͡ak 2002a [1979]).

[11] Conceptual orality (also known as 'informality') is defined as a spoken utterance transposed in written form (Koch and Österreicher 1994: 587, 2008: 199–202).

The development of historical sociopragmatics has been facilitated by placing *conceptually oral* texts in the spotlight (Koch and Österreicher 1994: 587, 2008: 199–203),[11] that is, plays, dialogues, courtroom recordings, textbooks, phrase books, as well as ego-documents (letters, diaries, postcards, notes and so on),[12] writings that often draw upon an 'invisible' language history 'from below' (Elspaß 2007: 2–3, Taavitsainen and Fitzmaurice 2007: 18–21, Taavitsainen 2012: 1466–67, Havinga and Langer 2015: 2–5).[13] A significant characteristic of those texts is their heterogeneity on multiple levels of the language system; one needs to be aware, however, of constraints put in place by the genre-related encoding practices (for more details, see Taavitsainen and Fitzmaurice 2007: 18). Developing appropriate concepts mostly depends on available sources; this results in the abovementioned production of unique case studies that often provide an insufficient basis for generalizations. An exception exists for the English language, as the available corpora cover its entire history and have a relatively high level of representativeness compared to those compiled so far for other languages (Nevalainen 2012b: 1442). Hence, the following presentation of both branches, and the appropriate research frameworks used therein, is based on representative case studies that demonstrate their practical applications, advantages and perspectives.

19.4 Pragmaphilology Meets Diachronic Pragmatics

Differences between the philological and the historical sociopragmatic approach can be traced in the history of research on the Novgorodian birchbark letters – short texts of utilitarian character found in Northern Russian Novgorod by archaeologists, starting in 1951 until the present day. Dating back to between the eleventh and fourteenth centuries, these texts were written on birchbark strips in an East Slavic variety called the Old Novgorodian dialect. Initially, their linguistic interpretation was a supportive activity for historians who had been seeking to read the birchbark letters segmented into words and sentences whose difficult and incomprehensible contents were in need of explanation. In parallel to this work process, the significance of these texts has been acknowledged for the history of Slavic languages, and the first structuralist descriptions of the birchbark letters, which also include

[12] Also referred to as a 'throw-away literacy' designating the practice of discarding Novgorodian birchbark letters (Franklin 2002: 183–84, Schaeken 2019: 36–37).

[13] The concept of a language history 'from below' is juxtaposed with the concept of a language history 'from above', that is, language history written based on authoritative, codified and normalized textual sources, stemming from representatives of the upper class. Sources depicting language usage by lower social classes or in informal situations are often absent in the canon of language histories and are called 'invisible language histories'. These gaps have been consequently closed in publications that appeared in the Historical Sociolinguistics Network (HiSoN), notably in the *Journal of Historical Sociolinguistics*.

descriptions of paleography and phonology, have been published (Borkovskiĭ 1955). The writing system used in the birchbark letters differs from the writing system used on parchment; in earlier research it was even evaluated as a writing system that availed of fewer characters and was ascribed to society's less educated strata (Avanesov 1955, 80–81; compare criticism in Zalizni͡ak 1986: 93, 104, 217).

This particular writing system as well as its orthography have been described in great detail, notably by Zalizni͡ak (1986, 2002b). He demonstrated how both the birchbark letter's writing system and orthography followed a given set of rules, and, moreover, that discrepancies in the writing system and orthography used on parchment were not random in nature (Zalizni͡ak 1986: 96–97). In line with this recognition, observations on line-final word division showing orthographic conventions and text arrangement demonstrate a shift from the line-final open syllable, until c. 1350, to the possibility of dividing a word, thus also ending a line with a closed syllable, post-1350 (Schaeken 1995: particularly pages 101–2).[14] In Novgorodian society, a dichotomy existed between a *bookish* and an *everyday* writing system, as did, to a lesser extent, a dichotomy between two orthographic systems. As is shown below, these two orthographies used to have a social function. In structural terms, Zalizni͡ak (2002b: 594–95) speaks of a *default* and a *non-distinguished* writing system. Within the default writing system, the scripts <*ъ*> /ø/ – <*o*> /o/ and <*ь*> /ʲø/ – <*e*> /e/ were distinguished, while within the non-distinguished writing system they were interchangeable; moreover, intermediate writing systems with shared features of the default and non-distinguished system existed. In particular, within the non-distinguished system, the interchangeability of the scripts might have a more or less systemic character (Zalizni͡ak 1986: 100–5).

The use of the appropriate writing system depended not only on the author's referential perspective on the particular situation but also on the corresponding sustainability of a piece of writing (i.e. the time span a piece of writing was meant to serve). As Franklin (2002: 40) observes, "[s]cribes of parchment manuscripts kept half an eye on eternity; senders of birchbark letters would hardly have counted on the prying persistence of future archeologists." Following Koch's and Österreicher's distance and proximity communication model (Koch and Österreicher 1994: 588, 2008: 201), two referential perspectives are suggested: an *immediacy* and a *distance* perspective. Both perspectives are distinguished by the clusters of features distributed among them, as shown in Table 19.1.

However, the immediacy and distance perspectives were not impenetrable; this might explain idiosyncrasies within the material clusters (Schaeken 2011b: 354–8, Schaeken 2019: 49–53). Epigraphic inscriptions on church

[14] Line-final word division is further discussed in Chapter 18, this volume.

Table 19.1 *Clusters of features in Novgorodian writings with different authors' referential perspectives*

Features	Immediacy perspective	Distance perspective
Writing material[a]	Birchbark, church walls, everyday items, etc.	Parchment, ritual liturgical items
Writing system	Everyday (non-distinguished)	Bookish (default)
Orthography	Everyday	Bookish
Formulaic/formulation conventions	An everyday set	A bookish set
Conveyance practice	Conceptually oral	Conceptually written

[a] On the use of different items and surfaces for writing, see Rozhdestvenskaîa 1992: 152–55, Schaeken 2019: 44–47, Franklin 2019: 1–18.

walls serve as a good example for this phenomenon: they demonstrate the interchangeability whenever it came to choosing between everyday and bookish orthography. This decision primarily depended on the functionality the writer aspired to. It would be simplistic to state that the writing material impacted upon the choice of orthography (see Bunčić 2016: 137). Yet, birchbark as a material and everyday orthography definitely exhibit a regular co-occurrence (see Schaeken 2019: 49–50).[15] Hence, functionality (sustainability) was decisive whenever opting either for an everyday or for a bookish orthography. As the research summary on birchbark letters shows, the text materiality description within paleography paved the way for the description of *writing materiality* (writing system and orthography) from the perspective of historical linguistics. The example of the birchbark letters demonstrates that the *explanation* for using diorthographia in Novgorod was only feasible when reconstructing the sociopragmatic context of its use. Without taking the sociopragmatic perspective into account, the birchbark letters were merely interpreted as unlearned writings. The contextualization of their usage – as a strategy in a situation that required an immediacy or a distance perspective – led to the depiction of a competent and conscious user, who could readily switch between two writing systems.

Indeed, the further *pragmaphilological* research on birchbark letters confirmed the existence of such a type of competent writer. Over the last two decades the writing and delivery of the birchbark letters has been reconstructed in terms of its participants' communicative roles: this included the role of the messenger who delivered the letter, read aloud the message for the addressee, and later returned to the original sender with an answer (Gippius 2004, Gippius and Schaeken 2011, Schaeken 2019: 141–85). Subsequently, the

[15] Bunčić calls the dichotomy of two Novgorodian writing systems *medial diorthographia* (Bunčić 2016: 129–39); this suggests that the choice of a writing system depends on the choice of written material. By contrast, a more plausible explanation seems to be the author's referential perspective that includes the choice of writing system and written material as constitutive features.

structure of letters was disclosed as a polyphony of references concerning the author herself/himself, the messenger, the addressee and further individuals participating in the communicative situation. These findings resulted in the contents across a range of birchbark letters being reinterpreted and showed the necessity of sociopragmatic analysis for an adequate historical interpretation of these sources. Switching between the default writing system and a 'corrected' non-distinguished writing system marked a different referential perspective in several birchbark letters and served therefore for text structuring (Schaeken 2011b: 354–58).[16] The description of birchbark letters as conceptually oral texts "with limited interference of specific genre conventions" (Schaeken 2011a: 10) that unite several referential perspectives showed the motivation behind the usage of several writing systems.

19.5 Criticism, Impact and Perspectives

The issues facing historical orthography are akin to most issues that those working in historical linguistics are likely to encounter. They encompass the general sparsity of linguistic resources, their restricted availability and their selectiveness. While each of these factors has inhibited digital research in historical orthography on account of the unbalanced corpora, the automatic recognition of manuscripts and prints has already reached a high standard. This development, in turn, has facilitated text acquisition at least. Consequently, the scope for research in historical orthography within a digital environment is equally limited to accessible corpora. The range of languages involved, however, has grown and thus boosted the diversity of languages considered for research purposes.

The shift toward digitization in the humanities has led to expanding the range of research methods from hermeneutic to computer-based ones, and has ultimately promoted more comprehensive research into writing systems from the perspective of big data. These new methods have been underpinning the necessity of unambiguously and consistently encoding the characters in digital representations of analogue texts in order to ensure their retrieval through digital applications (Piotrowski 2012: 11). However, the most common praxis in text criticism and corpus linguistics involves modernizing orthography for the sake of a standardized retrieval (see the DIAKORP within the *Czech National Corpus*, CNC). Recently, however, this trend has changed; the interest in spelling and orthography in linguistics has

[16] As discussed in Zalizni͡ak (1986: 100–5), the Novgorodian writers used intermediate writing systems between the standard and the non-distinguished one. The Novgorodian birchbark letter no. 907, for instance, illustrates the usage of such a system: the nominative singular masculine ending <e> in the non-distinguished system was replaced by the standard ending <ъ> while other linguistic features were retained from the non-distinguished system.

burgeoned and the TEI-encoding initiative has offered a practicable way for tagging spelling irregularities as well as a systemic analysis of them. A multilayer representation of contents in a digital environment, being a powerful instrument, apparently resolves those prevailing discrepancies; this includes but is not restricted to interlinking transcripts and facsimiles. The multilayer representation of contents enables validation of the transcriber's solutions (when compared with the facsimile), or for the indication of possible variable solutions as proposed by a transcriber in the case of uncertainty (Vertan 2018: 55). Notwithstanding all the advantages that this powerful instrument can offer, a substantial amount of study both on writing systems and orthography is still carried out manually.

Similarly, as already highlighted in Section 19.1, historians are not interested in orthographic variation, but instead in content, and sometimes in text structure. In his comprehensive legal analysis, for example, Mikuła (2018: 24) points out the importance variation plays in text structure, for it might convey key changes in legal norms or in their interpretation. Yet, Mikuła also comments on the omission of language variation on other levels of his analysis. Jamborová (2010) clearly showed, however, that orthographic variation might be distinctive for lexical meaning and text interpretation, juxtaposing *město* (in the sense of *civitas*) and *miesto* (in the sense of *locus*) in the Czech legal codices of the fifteenth century. Curiously enough, the restricted orthographic variation, or lack thereof, might equally be an indicator for formalization as contrasted with the variable and informal context: such was the case of the n-gram *geden czlowiek* 'one man/somebody' in Middle Czech legal sources (Lazar forthcoming).

In order to verify already existing outcomes, the scope of genres to be examined needs to be broadened (Fidlerová et al. 2010: 303), not only focusing on serial texts, but also exploring longer time spans. This will enable a deeper look into the editorial praxis of printing houses and their respective programs to unify orthography on the eve of standardization of European languages. Legal texts constitute one such area to explore; they were usually updated and compiled several times according to evolving circumstances in their usage and, as the previous research shows, constitute a fruitful and promising field for research in historical orthography. In particular, specialized platforms that collect sources on selected topics and integrate research tools such as automatic comparison of text versions provide a promising environment for large-scale research (see the research area *Sources from Laws of the Past*, IURA for Polish legal texts). A longitudinal exploration into orthographic decisions made in a mixed community of practice, including translators and publishers, is feasible with materials from early newspapers that frequently contained news reports that had been translated. Some preliminary analyses in this direction, based upon articles from Russian newspapers in the first decades of the eighteenth century, has been completed by Maier and Shamin

(2018). Such large-scale studies afford a solid foundation for generalizations and subsequent typologies of orthographic changes as bundles of intra- and extra-linguistic factors across language boundaries or language families (see Baddeley and Voeste 2012b: 11, Condorelli 2020c).

Contact linguistics is the area where the contact and impact of several orthographic systems on each other needs to be more intensively explored in future. Orthographic systems came into contact primarily as a result of exchanges between and amidst professional networks, the acquisition of several writing systems or typesets, foreign language learning, as well as during the translation process itself. Some research on these topics has been presented in Section 19.2 (see also Chapter 11, this volume), but it still needs to cross the threshold of studies *sui generis*. In order to do so, a shift is called for: from a comparative approach, which undoubtedly was adopted on account of the peculiarities of the materials involved, toward a sociolinguistic approach in order to explain the comparison outcomes.

To sum up, recent developments in digital humanities have opened up new avenues for research in the diachronic examination into writing systems and orthographies, which for some time had been impeded by editorial practices. As a result of this shift, interdisciplinary approaches on the same material have been consolidated and synergy effects between the disciplines involved have emerged. Apart from the identification of the appropriate type of orthographic variation (see Rutkowska and Rössler 2012: 217–19), this synthetic view has enabled a broader and more diversified scope for explaining variation in writing systems and orthographies. This is precisely the direction that needs to be followed in future research.

19.6 Conclusion

The present chapter has drawn upon the comparative and sociopragmatic methods in historical orthography research. Having defined writings systems and orthography, including the potential overlap between these terms, I have described orthography as a supportive discipline on the fringes of other disciplines, such as paleography, historical phonology and text criticism. I have also explained the growing interest in studying writing systems and orthographies as independent disciplines. Section 19.2 has presented the adoption of the comparative method in Slavic studies and principal directions therein, for example, a proliferation of small-scale studies on individual and group variation, exploration of consecutive versions of biblical and ecclesiastical literature, microlinguistic and macrolinguistic approaches to variation as well as investigating and contrasting texts written on different types of medium and surface. Section 19.3 has summarized theoretical preliminaries in historical sociopragmatics, primarily based upon research on

English historical orthography, pointing to such aspects of sociopragmatic context as historical conditions for text production, transmission, reception, and the reconstruction of meanings conveyed by texts in the relevant context, with the focus on conceptually oral texts. In section 19.4, I have offered an overview of the most important concepts in Slavic studies (mostly involving Russian, Czech and Polish material). These have been roughly divided into pragmaphilology and diachronic pragmatics, with the differences and synergies between these approaches exemplified. In Section 19.5, the methods proposed have been critically appraised and their applicability for prospective research demonstrated.

20

Reconstructing a Prehistoric Writing System

Ester Salgarella

20.1 Introduction

How can we reconstruct the orthography of a writing system that is no longer used? How can we test our assumptions and reach definite conclusions? This chapter investigates the topic of orthographic reconstruction of a historical writing system by taking as case study the Linear B (LB) syllabary of Bronze Age Greece, used to render the oldest Greek dialect attested in written form, Mycenaean Greek. Reconstructing the orthography of a historical writing system poses challenges of both a structural and a linguistic nature. In the case of LB, the task is complicated by the paucity of evidence, its state of preservation (fragmentary texts) as well as its nature (economic records). The evidence we are left with are syllabic sequences such as *a-to-ro-qo, i-qo, po-me*: this is how the words 'man', 'horse', 'shepherd' were spelled in Mycenaean Greek. No doubt there is a considerable gap to gauge to connect these spellings to their alphabetic Greek counterparts ἄνθρωπος /ant^hro:pos/ 'man', ἵππος /hippos/ 'horse', ποιμήν /poime:n/ 'shepherd'. How did we arrive at such reconstructions? Understanding and systematically reconstructing the orthographic conventions devised to write this early form of Greek with a syllabic system was the first step toward establishing a methodology for reading and interpreting LB texts. Reconstructing orthographic conventions helped us make sense of the grapholinguistic units: knowing the way in which specific phonological and morphological features were encoded as recurrent patterns allowed us to 'reconstruct' the linguistic reality behind the writing system and to study the language in its diachronic development.

In the case of LB, orthographic reconstruction was a backward process, as based on (and borne out by) comparison with later evidence from alphabetic Greek. The methods used to reconstruct historical orthographies may be multiple, inasmuch as contextual. A global, overarching method may prove ill-suited to accounting for the peculiarities of the many contextual realities. Although some general 'universals' (e.g. phonotactics) may help to reconstruct historical orthographies, the *raison d'être* of each orthography remains context-based, as intertwining both writing and linguistic systems. For, as Faber (1991: 620) holds, "any linguistic interpretation of an orthography is based on an understanding of its creation and use." This contribution aims to prove useful to those interested in seeing how reconstructing the orthography of a historical writing system no longer in use gives us a finer appreciation of the language encoded, to be studied in its diachronic development. In this respect, the Greek language is unique in having a continuous written record from the Late Bronze Age (c. 1400–1200 BC) until today, although over time it was rendered with typologically different writing systems: first written with the LB syllabic system, adapted from the earlier Minoan Linear A syllabary, before the adoption of the alphabetic system, adapted from the Phoenician alphabet, in the Iron Age.

20.2 Writing in Bronze Age Greece: Linear B in Context

A number of writing systems were in use in Bronze Age Greece, having had as their cradle the island of Crete, situated in the middle of the Aegean Sea at a crossroads between Europe, Egypt and the ancient Near East. From a typological perspective, all these writing systems are syllabaries, meaning that each graphic sign represents a syllable (e.g. /pa/, /e/; see Tables 20.1–20.3) and is a phonological unit in the script. These syllabaries were also complemented with a set of logographic (or ideographic) signs, depicting real-world referents and standing for words/concepts, not individual syllables (e.g. a sign depicting a tripod cooking pot and standing for the world 'tripod'; a sign depicting a pig flanked by the syllabogram /si/ standing for the concept 'fattened pig', see Meissner 2019). Crete first saw the rise of Cretan Hieroglyphic and the Linear A script (LA): the former is understood to be a North/East Cretan phenomenon (with major find-spots at Knossos, Mallia and Petras) in use in the period c. 1900–1700 BC; the latter, with its original nucleus probably to be sought in central Crete (Phaistos), shows a much wider geographical distribution (across Crete, on the Aegean islands, some finds also in Asia Minor) as well as time span, c. 1800–1450 BC. Both scripts are still undeciphered and are understood to encode the indigenous language(s) of Bronze Age Crete (on LA see Schoep 2002, Davis 2014, Salgarella 2020, 2021; on Cretan Hieroglyphic see Olivier and Godart 1996, Ferrara 2015, Decorte 2017, 2018).

The role played by LA, and the civilization responsible for creating and making use of such writing – the so-called 'Minoans' in the literature – cannot be overestimated, so much so that over time LA was taken as a template (mother-script) for the creation of another two writing systems: LB, used on Crete and Mainland Greece in the period c. 1400–1190 BC; and

Table 20.1 *The LB 'basic' syllabary*

	/a/	/e/	/i/	/o/	/u/
Vowel	*a* /a/	*e* /e/	*i* /i/	*o* /o/	*u* /u/
d- /d/	*da* /da/	*de* /de/	*di* /di/	*do* /do/	*du* /du/
j- /j/	*ja* /ja/	*je* /je/		*jo* /jo/	
k- /k, g, kʰ/	*ka* /ka, ga, kʰa/	*ke* /ke, ge, kʰe/	*ki* /ki, gi, kʰi/	*ko* /ko, go, kʰo/	*ku* /ku, gu, kʰu/
m- /m/	*ma* /ma/	*me* /me/	*mi* /mi/	*mo* /mo/	*mu* /mu/
n- /n/	*na* /na/	*ne* /ne/	*ni* /ni/	*no* /no/	*nu* /nu/
p- /p, b, pʰ/	*pa* /pa, ba, pʰa/	*pe* /pe, be, pʰe/	*pi* /pi, bi, pʰi/	*po* /po, bo, pʰo/	*pu* /pu, bu, pʰu/
q- /kʷ, gʷ, kʷʰ/	*qa* /kʷa, gʷa, kʷʰa/	*qe* /kʷe, gʷe, kʷʰe/	*qi* /kʷi, gʷi, kʷʰi/	*qo* /kʷo, gʷo, kʷʰo/	

Table 20.1 *Continued*

r- /r, l/	*ra* /ra, la/	*re* /re, le/	*ri* /ri, li/	*ro* /ro, lo/	*ru* /ru, lu/
s- /s/	*sa* /sa/	*se* /se/	*si* /si/	*so* /so/	*su* /su/
t- /t, t^h/	*ta* /ta, t^ha/	*te* /te, t^he/	*ti* /ti, t^hi/	*to* /to, t^ho/	*tu* /tu, t^hu/
w- /w/	*wa* /wa/	*we* /we/	*wi* /wi/	*wo* /wo/	
z /z/	*za* /za/	*ze* /ze/		*zo* /zo/	

Darker shading for LB signs that have both the same shape and the same/approximate phonetic value in LA; lighter shading for signs that have only got the same shape (but not phonetic value) in LA; no shading for signs that are new LB introductions.
(drawings by the author based on actual attestations)

Cypro-Minoan, developed on Cyprus and used in the period c. 1600–1050 (on LB see Ventris and Chadwick 1973, Palmer 1963, Hooker 1980, Bernabé and Luján 2006, Duhoux and Morpurgo-Davies 2008, 2011, 2014, Melena 2014c, Del Freo and Perna 2019; on Cypriot scripts see Steele 2013a, 2013b, 2019). Both daughter-scripts render different languages from the template: LB was successfully deciphered in 1952 and proven to write an archaic form of Greek, while Cypro-Minoan is still undeciphered. In this chapter, the focus is on LB, since, being the only system currently deciphered and of which we thus have a better appreciation, it gives us the most insights into its diachronic development (starting from the process of adaptation from LA) and the reconstruction of the orthographic conventions used to write Greek by means of such system back in the Bronze Age.

As last remark, it needs stressing that the context of use of LB is restricted, as limited to the bookkeeping of bureaucratic transactions by palatial administrations: our evidence consists in inscribed clay tablets (and some vessels) which have been burnt and thus preserved to us as a result of a number of firing episodes which took place at the end of the Bronze Age. Therefore, due to the economic nature of the evidence, LB texts show a highly formulaic structure.

20.3 The Ancestry of the Syllabary

The first time Greek speakers set out to write down their language they made use of syllabic signs, since LB was molded and adapted from the LA writing system already in use on Crete. Scholars have long been working on reconstructing the process and circumstances of adaptation and script transmission from one system onto the other. Upon discovery of the first inscribed documents at the start of the twentieth century, British archaeologist Arthur Evans, who was then excavating the palatial center of Knossos on Crete (report on the first excavations in Evans 1901), coined and used the unifying label 'Minoan linear scripts' to refer to such writing, further subdivided into scripts of 'Class A' and 'Class B' (with a chronological connotation). Since very early on, in fact, it was apparent that a good number of signs were shared between the two systems as appearing in both (hence listed with the prefix 'AB' in the systematized sign list), implying that upon adaptation these signs had been directly borrowed from the template. Some of these shared signs are likely to have retained both the same shape and the same (or approximately comparable) phonetic value and are therefore standardly referred to as 'homomorphic and homophonic' signs; some other signs, instead, show a comparable sign form (homomorphic), but their correspondence in terms of phonetic value cannot be uncontroversially proved (lastly Steele and Meissner 2017). For this reason, and thanks to the decipherment of LB as Greek (see Section 20.4) allowing for the phonetic interpretation of syllabic signs, it is possible to at least read with an approximation LA texts. On top of this core of AB 'shared' signs, some 12 signs were also created *ex novo* in LB (see Section 20.8).

From a typological perspective, a syllabary is often deemed not to be the perfect fit for rendering Greek in writing: the syllabic structure of the LB system, which only encodes open syllables (i.e. those ending in a vowel), does not allow for the straightforward notation of final consonants (i.e. consonants in the coda of a syllable) and consonantal clusters, at times resulting in ambiguity as to the correct reading and interpretation of words (see Section 20.5).[1] This is the reason why, in mainstream scholarship, LB is often seen as an

[1] In this respect, an interesting comparison could be drawn with the closely related Cypriot syllabic system of the first millennium BC, which, although retaining the open-syllable structure to write Greek, developed quite different orthographic conventions (e.g. more extensive writing of final consonants /s/ and /n/, and of consonantal clusters). For Cypriot writing see especially Steele 2013a.

'unsuitable' system for writing Greek. However, it has to be acknowledged that in the Late Bronze Age the (logo-)syllabic system was the best (if not the only) 'game in town' in the Aegean area. Given the derivation of LB from LA, it is a reasonable assumption that the form of the syllabary may well reflect the characteristics of another language (Minoan), for which it was created, and not Greek. It may not be too far-fetched, in fact, to suppose that in the context of adaptation the first Mycenaean Greek writers may well have retained not only the script in its purely graphic form (i.e. its sign repertory), but also the orthographic conventions which were bound to it in the template system. This, in fact, would have been the most effortless solution for individuals who had to learn the writing technology *ex novo*, as well as how to notate their own – different – language in writing.

In this respect, the possibility may be entertained that the first writers of LB might have been bilinguals, mastering both Mycenaean Greek and Minoan (lastly Salgarella, 2020: 377), given the rather systematic regularity of spellings and the observance of orthographic conventions since the very early stage of LB writing documented to us. This could explain, at least in part, why the system was not adapted to reflect more accurately and explicitly the phonological repertory of the Greek language (e.g. voicing and aspiration, see Sections 20.5, 20.6). What is remarkable is that, all in all, the extant LB texts present a notable orthographic uniformity, across both time (some 200 years) and space (Crete and Mainland Greece). However, this is not to say that the system was completely standardized, as modifications, additions and local as well as chronological writing preferences can be observed nevertheless (see Section 20.8; on the possible existence of 'local scripts' within LB, see Melena 2014c: 84, Del Freo and Perna 2019: 137–38).

20.4 Reconstructing Orthographic Conventions

At this point we may well wonder how we arrived at reconstructing the orthographic conventions used to write Mycenaean Greek with the LB writing system. Regrettably, we do not have any contemporary records or accounts of writing conventions, and it was down to modern philologists to reconstruct the conventions that, it is believed, scribes followed when reducing the spoken language to syllabic writing. The reconstruction of orthographic conventions can be seen as a step-by-step process, which stretches from predecipherment to postdecipherment. In short, we could say that the method followed for the reconstruction was threefold. The first step involved looking for general recurrent patterns, and this was done before the decipherment by scholars working on the then still called 'Minoan scripts', that is, both LA and LB. To start with, Evans was already able to identify the presence of gender distinction (masculine/feminine) inferable from the juxtaposition of self-evident logograms depicting a man or a woman to words showing different endings (among which, for example, the signs later to be read as *jo*, masculine ending, and *ja*, feminine ending; Evans 1909: 35–36). On this wave, the American scholar Kober demonstrated the existence of not just two, but three grammatical cases, and showed proof for inflection by collecting sets of words containing sequences of the same signs but ending with different terminations: the so-called 'Kober's triplets' (Kober 1946, 1948; for a description of the LB decipherment process see Chadwick 1967, Pope 2008, Judson 2017b).

As a second step, building on Kober's results and on a further search for systematic patterns, Ventris carried out a methodical analysis of sign frequency and position in 20 'work notes' he circulated to scholars (Ventris and Sacconi 1988). By using a combinatory method, he arrived at establishing relative links between signs, resulting in a 'grid' in which each row included signs likely to share the same consonant, and each column signs likely to share the same vowel (although at this stage phonetic values had yet to be suggested). Variation in spelling also played a role in the construction of the 'grid': if two words differed by one sign only, by implication the two variant signs had to have something in common (either the same consonant or the same vowel). One such example is the word later to be transcribed as *a-re-pa-zo-o*, which also comes in the alternative spelling *a-re-po-zo-o*: although Ventris could not read it yet, he was able to list the two variant signs (*pa* and *po*) in the same row as arguably sharing the same consonant. The 'grid' was then tested against the texts.

At this point, Ventris made an educated guess by looking for the place name Amnisos (the harbor of Knossos) on the tablets, as he thought that place names were likely to have been recorded and the 'grid' already offered suggestions to read some signs as *a*, *n* + vowel, consonant + *i*. Fortunately, one of Kober's triplets showed exactly the desired pattern: *a-*i-n*-***, easily to be restored as *a-mi-ni-so*. By filling in the gaps with the new values and updating the 'grid' accordingly, Ventris started to allocate phonetic values to signs and, by consequence, tentatively to work out the readings of further words. The result of this work was what he called an 'experimental vocabulary' (Ventris and Sacconi 1988: 337–48): a list of LB words for which plausible Greek counterparts could be suggested, enabling him to demonstrate that the language encoded in LB showed enough features and vocabulary to be Greek. Ventris's decipherment was endorsed by classicist Chadwick, who, by testing Ventris's 'grid' further, was able to read another number of Greek words not included in the 'experimental vocabulary'. The collaboration between the two resulted in firmly establishing the phonetic values of the core LB syllabary. The third and final step to reconstruct orthographic conventions involved comparing the LB spellings with words known in alphabetic Greek on the one side, and their etymology in reconstructed Proto-Indo-European on the other. This allowed for a better and more nuanced appreciation of the readings, as well as the historical development of the Greek language.

As we can see, reconstructing orthographic conventions goes hand in hand with (and is a result of) the unfolding of the decipherment process: since the first stages of Ventris's analysis, it was reckoned that the words appearing on the LB documents, which started to sound quite like Greek, did show 'an unlikely set of spelling conventions' (Chadwick 1967: 67). Underneath this syllabic vest, the lexemes of Greek started to show themselves: the more words were given a Greek interpretation and read accordingly, the more the spelling conventions received confirmation. As Ventris himself announced on the BBC on July 1, 1952,

> I have come to the conclusion that the Knossos and Pylos tablets must, after all, be written in Greek – a difficult and archaic Greek, seeing that it is 500 years older than Homer and written in a rather abbreviated form, but Greek nevertheless. Once I made this assumption, most of the peculiarities of the language and spelling which had puzzled me seemed to find a logical explanation.
>
> (quoted in Chadwick 1967: 68, full transcript in Ventris and Sacconi 1988)

By the end of the decipherment process, it was only a matter of systematizing in a coherent way such conventions: these had first been put forward as the 'assumed rules of Mycenaean orthography' by Ventris and Chadwick in their after-decipherment technical article 'Evidence for Greek dialect in the Mycenaean archives' (1953) and firmly established later on in the pivotal publication *Documents in Mycenaean Greek* (1956, followed by a second edition in 1973). However, the uneasiness Chadwick and Ventris felt at reconstructing such 'rules' cannot be concealed and is on occasion expressed throughout their work:

> these rules had been forced upon us as the result of identifying the Mycenaean words as Greek; they were in many respect unexpected and unwelcome; [...] although they were empirically determined, they do form a coherent pattern
>
> (Chadwick 1967: 74)

and

> the inadequacy of the script led to considerable uncertainty about the exact form of many words, which could only be given intelligible shape by the assumption of certain rules of orthography. [...] These conventions are based on the general assumption that the pronunciation behind the spelling is a normal – though archaic – form of East Greek, such as had already been inferred for the period by philologists.
>
> (Ventris and Chadwick 1973: 67)

In the years that followed, scholars attempted to account for these complex (and at times rather puzzling) orthographic conventions in detail (see, e.g., Vilborg 1960, Palmer 1963, Doria 1965, Hooker 1980; in more recent reference volumes see Bartoněk 2003: 106–12, Risch and Hajnal 2006: 45–55), and developed approaches aimed at understanding the *raison d'être* of such spelling strategies, with a focus on the systematic principles behind the spelling of consonantal clusters (for which see Section 20.6). In this respect, two main currents of thought have been followed (summary in Woodard 1997: 19–132, Bernabé and Luján 2006: 45–52): one encompasses syllable-dependent approaches, hinging on the premise that orthographic conventions are dependent upon syllabic structure (Householder 1964, Beekes 1971, Ruijgh 1985: 105–26, Sampson 1985: 65–70, Morpurgo-Davies 1987: 91–104); the other, by contrast, encompasses non-syllable-dependent approaches, based on the idea that such spelling representations are sensitive to a set of hierarchical relations (e.g. sonority hierarchy), and not dependent upon syllabic structure (Tronskiĭ 1962, Viredaz 1983, Justeson 1988, Woodard 1994, 1997: 62–78, 112–32).[2] To this latter group belongs the theory of the 'hierarchy of orthographic strength' elaborated by Woodard (1994, 1997: 62–78, 112–32), which stands out for not only giving an accurate account of the principles behind the spellings, but also managing to predict spelling outcomes (more on this in Section 20.6).

In conclusion, LB writing conventions had first been established right after the decipherment and were refined over time by way of comparing LB spellings with the phonology of reconstructed Proto-Indo-European on the one side, and that of the later (first millennium) alphabetic Greek dialects on the other. The very regularity of these orthographic 'rules' (although with some exceptions, discussed in Section 20.7) implies that these conventions did exist. It remains to be demonstrated whether such conventions were created in the process of script-adaptation to write Greek in the LB syllabic system, or were continued, to some extent, from the previous system (LA) which, however, rendered a different language. In this chapter, the focus rests on the LB syllabary only (not the whole logo-syllabic set) to suit the theme of the present *Handbook*. In what follows an outline is given of the main orthographic conventions ('rules') that scholars have reconstructed for the orthography of the LB writing system. However, it has to be borne in mind that the LB sign repertory extends beyond its syllabic component (accounting for phonetic units) by also encompassing a set of logograms (i.e. picture-signs standing for real-word referents and commodities), a number of monograms (i.e. signs made up with all the individual signs, strongly interwoven, of the word they stand for), ligatures (i.e. combinations of logogram plus syllabogram) and measure signs (for exhaustive descriptions of the LB script and documents see works listed in Section 20.2).

[2] Consani's approach (Consani 2003, 2016) could also be taken as non-syllable-dependent. However, he states that the writing of onsets and omission of codas of syllables and words would privilege the lexical access and semantic identification of lexemes. On this view, LB orthographic conventions were "a precise choice operated by the LB users and cannot be considered dependent on the nature of the writing system" (Consani 2016: 96).

20.5 Writing Greek in Syllables

With respect to syllabic structure, LB signs represent open syllables of the type (C)V (consonant + vowel, e.g. /da/, or vowel alone, e.g. /a/). There are, however, some exceptions of signs with a CCV structure (consonant + consonant + vowel), where the second consonant is either a labialized sound (/w/, e.g. *dwo*) or a palatalized sound (/j/, e.g. *rja*) (see Section 20.7). The open syllable structure represents a structural constraint for writing Greek which has to be borne in mind since, as is explained below, those responsible for 'standardizing' the writing (orthographic) conventions upon adaptation of the LB script had to find ways of getting around the open syllable structure in order to account for consonants appearing in the coda of a syllable (a common feature in Greek, as an inflectional Indo-European language) as well as word-initial and word-internal consonantal clusters.

After the decipherment, scholars were able to arrange signs based on their phonetic value into 13 series (Table 20.1, horizontal rows): 12 consonantal series interlocking five vocalic sounds (/a/, /e/, /i/, /o/, /u/; Table 20.1, vertical columns). The entire syllabary, with a total of 87 signs, was subdivided into 'basic' and 'additional' syllabary. The former comprises some 59 signs and represents the fundamental nucleus of the script, with the basic set of sounds necessary to write down any Greek word (although not unambiguously). The latter comprises some 14 signs which are either 'doublets' (this is the case when one single sign is used to replace the sequence of two signs already present in the basic syllabary, e.g. *au* to replace *a-u*), or 'complex' signs representing consonantal clusters (discussed in Section 20.7). On top of these, there are some 14 still undeciphered signs (discussed in Section 20.9). In what follows, the main characteristics of the basic syllabary are outlined (in-depth descriptions in Melena 2014c: 26–53, Bernabé and Luján 2006: 19–21, 23–26, Del Freo and Perna 2019: 132–33).

The 12 consonantal series of the basic syllabary consist of stops (/d/, /k/, /p/, /t/), nasals (/m/, /n/), liquids (/l/, /r/), sibilant (/s/), labial approximant (/w/), palatal approximant (/j/), labio-velar (/k^w/)[3] and a *z*-series of still debated phonetic interpretation.[4] There is one vocalic series, with each grapheme standing for either a long or a short vowel. It can be noticed at first glance that the system, as it is, suffers from underrepresentation of phonemes

[3] Labiovelars are velar stops coarticulated with a labial sounds (e.g. /k^w/, /g^w/, /k^{wh}/), which Mycenaean Greek inherited from Indo-European and rendered by means of the *q*-series. Mycenaean is unique among the Greek dialects in still preserving these sounds in writing, as they had already been lost by the time of alphabetic Greek (with the only exception of the Arcadian and Cypriot dialects; see Woodard 1997: 181).

[4] The *z*-series may represent affricates (/t^s/, /d^z/), evolved into different sounds variably rendered (e.g. -σσ/ττ-, -ζ-, -δδ-) in the Greek dialects of the first millennium (Melena 2014c: 52–53). It has also recently been suggested that the *z*-series could represent the outcome of the depalatalization (or full palatalization) of former palatalized stops (Melena 2014c: 15, 46–53).

(from a present-day perspective). As to vowels, vowel length is not marked (e.g. the sign transliterated as 'o' may represent either /o/ or /oː/, likewise the sign transliterated as 'e' could be either /e/ or /eː/), nor is the presence of possible initial aspiration (the script has no series for the aspirate /h/, except for sign a_2 rendering /ha/). As for consonants, voice and aspiration are not marked in the series rendering stops, nor are these marked in the labiovelar series, and there is one single series for the rendition of liquids (/l/, /r/), which is conventionally transcribed as *r*-series (e.g. the syllabogram for *ra* is read as either /ra/ or /la/). Moreover, LB neither makes use of diacritics to mark the presence of accents or aspiration, nor has it a way of marking geminated (i.e. double) consonants (e.g. *mi-to-we-sa* /miltowessa/ *μιλτοϝεσσα 'painted red').

This 'minimum marking' is a crucial shortcoming of the system, not allowing for a straightforward phonetic and phonemic reading of Mycenaean Greek words. Hence, an adequate understanding of the contextual occurrences of words is often necessary for their correct interpretation and reconstruction. This shortcoming affects stops to a great extent, as the lack of differentiation between voiceless, voiced and aspirated stops results in having the graphemes of the *p*-series representing the phonemes /p/, /b/, /pʰ/, and the graphemes of the *k*-series representing the phonemes /k/, /g/, /kʰ/. Dental stops are the only exception, as in this case, in addition to the *d*-series (voiced /d/), the system has a dedicated *t*-series for marking voiceless /t/, and plausibly also aspirated /tʰ/.

These characteristics, alongside the LB orthographic conventions (Section 20.6) result in some 'obscuring' of the exact phonological reality of the word concealed behind the spelling. In fact, in certain contexts, the LB script may create ambiguity: for example, the spelling *pa-te* could be interpreted as either /pateːr/ (alphabetic Greek πατήρ) 'father' or /pantes/ 'all' (alphabetic Greek πάντες), and only a contextual analysis can give us the most suitable reconstruction. This brings us to the next section, illustrating the orthographic conventions as reconstructed.

20.6 Spelling 'Rules'

Once confronted with the technology of writing, those responsible for adapting the writing system to the needs of the Greek language established, and, to an extent, likely inherited, a number of writing conventions, also known in the scholarship as 'spelling rules' (most recent descriptions in Bernabé and Luján 2006: 31–52, Melena 2014c: 89–123, Del Freo and Perna 2019: 140–46). It has been mentioned earlier that the main feature of the LB syllabary is its open syllable structure (syllables of the (C)V or C(C)V type), and that this is a hindrance for the accurate rendering of Greek phonological and morphological features alike. This is particularly true when it comes to writing down closed syllables (CVC type: e.g. consonants at word-end as case markers) and consonantal clusters (CCV type), which are abundant in the Greek language (e.g. ἄνθρωπος /antʰroːpos/ 'man'). This was a critical issue that had to be dealt with; to overcome it, Mycenaean Greek writers ('scribes' in the literature) adopted mainly two procedures. Let us illustrate these with some examples.

The first solution, most economical and easy, was to simply omit the 'extra' consonant in the coda of a syllable: this always applies to consonants at word-end, and in case the consonant in the coda is one of the following: /l/, /r/ (liquid), /m/, /n/ (nasal), /s/ (sibilant). By reason of omission of a sound, this spelling is also called 'partial spelling' (Woodard 1997: 11). Thus, how would a word like χαλκός /kʰalkos/ 'bronze' be spelled out? Here the syllabification is *kʰal-kos*, showing a sequence of two closed syllables (CVC–CVC). Based on the rule outlined above, word-final /s/ is dropped, and /l/ in the word-internal cluster is dropped likewise because of its phonetic nature (liquid): hence, the resulting spelling is *ka-ko*. But what if the word-internal consonant is none of the above? In this case, the second procedure followed (a slightly more creative one) consisted in spelling out both consonants of the cluster, giving rise to two syllables sharing the same vocalic sound. This is the so-called 'empty vowel' (alternatively, 'dummy vowel'), as this vowel was not supposed to be pronounced (as not present in the phonological word). One such example is the graphic rendering of the word χρυσός /kʰrusos/ 'gold', whose syllabification is *kʰru-sos* (CCV–CVC), showing a consonantal cluster (/kʰr/) at word-start. With the aid of an 'empty vowel', added right after the first consonant of the cluster, the resulting spelling is *ku-ru-so* (with word-final /s/ regularly omitted).

Another such example is the spelling of the renowned site of Knossos on Crete: the place name is rendered as Κνωσσός /knoːssos/ in alphabetic Greek (and has remained the same until today), showing a word-initial consonantal cluster. In LB the term is written with an 'empty vowel', resulting in the spelling *ko-no-so*. The procedure employing the 'empty vowel' is used, rather systematically, for both word-initial and word-internal consonantal clusters starting with a stop (stop + stop; stop + /l/, /r/, /m/, /n/, sometimes also stop + /s/), and with the clusters /mn/ (e.g. Ἀμνισός /amnisos/ 'Amnisos' = *A-mi-ni-so*) and /sm/ (see below). This alternative spelling strategy is also called 'plenary spelling', given that in this case all consonants are clearly spelled (Woodard 1997: 11). At this point, some observations are in order on the spelling of /s/ in clusters, as its treatment is not systematic. We have already seen that word-final /s/ is always omitted. In word-initial and word-internal position, /s/ is normally omitted when starting a consonantal cluster comprising a stop (e.g. σπέρμον /spermon/ 'seed/grain' = *pe-mo*; φάσγανα /pʰasgana/ 'sword' = *pa-ka-na*; Ϝάστυ /wastu/ 'city' = *wa-tu*); however, /s/ is usually spelled out when the second consonant of the cluster is either /m/ (smV) or /w/ (swV) (e.g.

δοσμός /dosmos/ 'contribution' = *do-so-mo*). As a final remark, in addition to biconsonantal clusters, we can also find a few instances of triconsonantal clusters: in this context the 'empty vowel' rule applies and all three consonants are spelled out with the aid of the 'empty vowel' (e.g. the man's name *a-re-ku-tu-ru-wo* /Alektruōn/).

In sum, the two strategies used to spell consonantal clusters are either partial spelling (omission of a sound) or plenary spelling (full rendition of both consonants). It would appear that these two strategies are not accidental but compliant with the sonority hierarchy of consonantal sounds. Woodard (1994, 1997) has demonstrated that these spellings respect what he calls the 'hierarchy of orthographic strength' (Section 20.3). This theory is based on the assumption that orthographic strength progressively decreases from stops to liquids, following the sequence stop > fricative > nasal > glide > liquid. Thereby, Woodard (1997: 65) comes to the conclusion that "within a word, any two successive consonants will be represented with plenary spelling if, and only if, the orthographic strength of the first is greater or equal to that of the second; otherwise, partial spelling will be used." This non-syllable-dependent approach gives an accurate and elegant explanation of the systematic procedures used to write consonantal clusters and is therefore worth bearing in mind for any further analysis of syllabic spelling.

The next set of spelling rules concerns the treatment of vocalic sounds. As mentioned earlier, vowel length is not marked, neither is initial aspiration. The script, in fact, does not have a sign series for aspirated vowels, the only exception being sign a_2 (an LB innovation) standing for /ha/, which is attested in word-initial, word-internal (at compound boundary) and word-final position (see Melena 2014c: 73–78, Pierini 2014). The possibility may be entertained that some of the still undeciphered signs (Section 20.8) could potentially represent aspirated vocalic sounds, although no such cases have so far been clearly identified. Notwithstanding, there seem to have been ways of signaling the presence of intervocalic aspiration (although not explicitly marked): one of the methods used was the intentional omission of the so-called 'graphic glides'. Graphic glides is the name conventionally given to transitional sounds /j/ and /w/ following a syllable ending in /i/ and /u/, respectively, and preceding a following vocalic sound, in order to ease the phonetic transition between the two next-by vowels. The phonetic nature of glides is still problematic and it is unclear whether these are simply transitional sounds or actual subphonemic features (see Meissner 2008, Melena 2014c: 23). For this reason, their name for now remains 'graphic' glides. Let us see the above rule at work: the adjective *ko-no-si-jo* /knoːssios/ 'of Knossos' shows the glide /j/ placed between the vocalic sounds /i/ and /o/, likewise the noun *ta-ra-nu-we* /tʰraːnues/ 'footstools' (compare alphabetic Greek θρῆνοι/θρόνοι) shows the glide /w/ coming after /u/ and before /e/.

The use of glides is reasonably consistent (with a few contextual exceptions: see Melena 2014c: 116–17, 120–22, Del Freo and Perna 2019: 142) and their absence generally points to the presence of intervocalic aspiration: e.g. the noun *a-ni-o-ko* /hannihok^{h}os/ 'reins holder/charioteer', and the personal name *wa-tu-o-ko* / wastuhok^{h}os/.[5] Omission of glides in contexts where these would be expected is one way of marking intervocalic aspiration; another way of marking it, in environments that would not have featured a glide anyway, is through the presence of the hiatus: the hiatus, expressed by writing two consecutive vocalic sounds, blocks vowel contraction, pointing to the presence of intervocalic /h/. We can see this phenomenon in instances such as the neuter plural ending *-wo-a* /woha/ of the perfect participle, which may also show the most accurate alternative spelling *-wo-a*$_2$ (e.g. *te-tu-ko-wo-a* alongside *te-tu-ko-wo-a*$_2$ /tetuk^{h}woha/ 'completely built'); the dative-locative plural case-endings *-a-i* (a-stems) and *-o-i* (o-stems) representing /ahi/ and /ohi/ respectively (e.g. *e-qe-ta-i* /hek^{w}etahi/ 'to the Followers').

Let us now move on to another case of sequences of vocalic sounds – diphthongs. Mycenaean Greek has /i/ diphthongs and /u/ diphthongs, but there are no separate and complete sign series for the notation of diphthongs in the script. Therefore, a set of conventions had to be devised for their rendering. With respect to /i/ diphthongs, conventionally the second element, /i/, is not spelled out (with very few exceptions).[6] Examples include *po-me* /poimeːn/ 'shepherd' (alphabetic Greek ποιμήν), *ko-wa* /korwai/ 'girls' (alphabetic Greek κόρ(F)αι, nominative plural). By contrast, in /u/ diphthongs the second element, /u/, is always explicitly notated: for example *e-u-me-de* / eumeːdeːs/ 'Eumedes' (alphabetic Greek Εὐμήδης), *na-u-do-mo* /naudomoi/ 'ship builders'. It has to be pointed out that LB does have three signs that represent diphthongs: *a*$_3$ /ai/, *a*$_4$ /au/ and *ra*$_3$ /rai, lai/. These all belong to the 'additional syllabary', which is discussed in the next section.

20.7 Breaking the 'Rules'

The 'additional syllabary' (Table 20.2) consists of 14 signs which do not form complete series (in-depth discussion in Bernabé and Luján 2006: 26–30, Melena 2014c: 53–82, Del Freo and Perna 2019: 133–34). These are conventionally subdivided into 'doublets' and 'complex syllabograms'. The former group comprises signs whose phonetic value is understood to be somewhat similar to that of signs belonging to the basic syllabary (hence 'doublets').

[5] Both nouns are compounds with *-o-ko* /hok^{h}os/ 'holder' (<*seg^{h}-; compare alphabetic Greek ἔχω 'to have'). The first member of *a-ni-o-ko* is related to *a-ni-ja* /hanniai/ 'reins' (compare alphabetic Greek ἡνίαι), while the first member of *wa-tu-o-ko* is wa-tu /wastu/ 'city'.

[6] These are mostly limited to Knossos, for example *pa-i-to* /p^{h}aistos/ Φαιστός 'Phaistos'.

Table 20.2 *The LB 'additional syllabary'*

	a-series			*labialized group*			*yodized group*			*aspirated stop*
	aspiration	i-diphthong	u-diphthong	/Cwa/	/Cwe/	/Cwo/	/Cja/	/Cje/	/Cjo/	
a	 a_2 /ha/	 a_3 /ai/	 a_4 /au/							
d-					 dwe /dwe/	 dwo /dwo/				
n-				 nwa /nwa/						
p-								 pte </p^je/?		 pu_2 /p^hu, b^hu/
r-		 ra_3 /rai, lai/					 ra_2 /rja, lja/		 ro_2 /rjo, rjo/	
t-					 twe /twe/	 two /two/	 ta_2 /tja/			

Shading for signs that have only got the same shape (but not phonetic value) in LA; no shading for signs that are new LB introductions.
(drawings by the author based on actual attestations)

Classified as such are a_2 /ha/, a_3 /ai/, a_4 /au/, pu_2 /pʰu/, /b⁽ʰ⁾u/, ra_2 /rja, lja/ (giving /rra, lla/) and ro_2 /rjo, ljo/ (giving /rro, llo/),[7] ra_3 /rai, lai/, ta_2 /sta?/.[8] Of these, four are LB innovations (a_2, a_3, ro_2, ra_3), while four others (*au*, pu_2, ra_2, ta_2) have graphic antecedents in LA (shaded in Table 20.2). The latter group comprises signs of the CCV type, where the second consonant is either /w/ (labialized) or /j/ (yodized). To this group belong *dwe* and *dwo*, *twe* and *two*, *pte* (from *pʲe*?), *nwa*. Except for the latter (*nwa*), which has a graphic antecedent in LA, these signs are all new introductions in LB (for a discussion of additional syllabary signs and their role in reconstructing the LA to LB script-adaptation process see Judson 2017a).

It is worth noting that additional syllabary signs are used for the rendition of specific phonological traits, for example aspiration, gemination, and notation of diphthongs and of labialized and yodized clusters (CwV, CjV). The use of additional syllabary signs, however, is not systematic, and it seems to have been up to each individual writer to decide whether or not to make use of these signs instead of combinations of signs already available in the basic syllabary. Thanks to such spelling alternations it was thus possible to work out the phonetic value of most additional syllabary signs, which have been established through the joint effort of a number of scholars (*in primis* Meriggi 1955, Palmer 1955, Petruševski and Ilievski 1958, Ephron 1961, Lejeune 1962, Chadwick 1968). By way of example, the syllabogram ra_2 alternates with the digraph *-ri-ja* to represent the suffix /tria/ (compare alphabetic Greek -τρια) of feminine agent nouns (e.g. *a-ke-ti-ra*$_2$ and *a-ke-ti-ri-ja* /aske:triai/ 'weavers'), meaning that ra_2 was likely to represent the cluster /rja/. Using one sign instead of a sequence of two would have been a more economical choice for tablet writers.

There are other similar examples of variant spellings of the same word, with and without an additional syllabary sign: for example *pe-ru-si-nwa* alongside *pe-ru-si-nu-wa* (/perusinwa/ 'last year's', alphabetic Greek περυσινός), *pte-re-wa* alongside *pe-te-re-wa* (/ptelewa/ 'made of elm wood', alphabetic Greek πτελέα 'elm tree'), *o-da-twe-ta* alongside *o-da-tu-we-ta* and *te-mi-dwe-ta* alongside *te-mi-de-we-ta* (terms used to describe chariot wheels), *pa-we-a*$_2$ alongside *pa-we-a* (/pʰarweha/ 'clothes', compare Homeric φάρε(h)α), *pe-ra*$_3$*-ko-ra-i-ja* alongside *pe-ra-a-ko-ra-i-jo* (the 'Further Province' in Pylos). Interestingly, in some instances spelling variation is also witnessed within the graphic repertory of one single scribe (e.g. scribe H 32 at Pylos). It was possible, therefore, for scribes to 'break the rules' and make use of alternative spellings, as long as these did not compromise the understanding of the underlying phonological word.

[7] Yodized consonantal clusters are understood to have undergone a process of palatalization resulting in palatalized geminates.

[8] A question mark is placed after the phonetic reading of a sign if its phonetic value is doubtful (and still debated).

20.8 Scribal 'Creativity': Inconsistencies or Scribal Choices?

Overall, some 12 new signs were introduced in LB by the scribes, in both the basic and the additional syllabary (see Melena 2014c: 84–88). The basic syllabary was expanded with the addition of seven *o*-series signs (*do, jo, mo, no, qo, so, wo*)[9] and one *e*-series sign (*pe*). The additional syllabary was expanded with four 'doublets' (three signs of the *a*-series a_2 /ha/, a_3 /ai/, ra_3 /rai, lai/ and one of the *o*-series ro_2 /rjo, ljo/, arguably giving /rro/, /llo/) and all the new 'complex' syllabograms (except *nwa*). The fact that LB introduced most *o*-series signs has made some scholars argue that the template system, LA, and by implication the Minoan language, was a three-vowel system (/a/, /i/, /u/) (Palaima and Sikkenga 1999; objections in Davis 2014: 240–2, Melena 2014c: 86, Meissner and Steele 2017). The absence of *pe* in LA, which at least graphically has got a number of *e*-series signs also continued into LB, remains puzzling and yet to be convincingly explained.

As to the innovations in the additional syllabary, most of these signs were either introduced more clearly to express specific features or used in specific contexts. I have already mentioned that a_2 /ha/ is the only sign clearly marking aspiration and, given its most occurrences in either word-initial or word-internal position starting the second element of a compound, it has been suggested that a_2 may have originated as a demarcative sign used mainly at word-start or as a marker for a compound boundary (Melena 2014c: 74). Another sign created to suit a specific context is ra_3 /rai, lai/, as it was used at word-end to mark the nominative plural of feminine nouns. Moreover, ra_3 appears to be a Pylian creation: it is widely used at Pylos in such morphological contexts by a number of scribes (H 1, 2, 4, 21, 31), but is never attested elsewhere. However, this is not the only sign to have originated at Pylos (or at least to be limited to this site). In fact, also the complex syllabogram *two* is so far a one-off attestation used by Pylian scribe H 43 to write the man's name *o-two-we-o* (genitive singular). On the other hand, its counterpart *twe* is only attested at Knossos (and more widely employed), but never elsewhere. Whether this pattern of attestations is fortuitous and due to the partial state of preservation of the extant evidence or genuinely meaningful is a matter that remains to be ascertained.

What is interesting, however, is that the other two complex signs newly introduced in LB, namely *dwo* and *dwe*, show a comparable formation: these are labialized CCV signs belonging to the *o*-series and *e*-series. Moreover, we can be reasonably sure that *dwo* was a creation within LB. In fact, the shape of *dwo* is made of two mirroring *wo* signs, in other words 'a pair of *wo*'s'. It

[9] Some *o*-series signs have been tentatively argued to have a graphic antecedent in LA (Melena 2014c: 85; for *wo* Salgarella, 2020: 157, 171, 246). However, the issue of whether *o*-series signs were inherited from LA or newly invented in LB is still controversial.

has been argued (Risch 1957: 32) that its graphic form is itself an indication that *dwo* was created on the basis of the Greek language, since the Greek word for the numeral 'two' is δύο /duo/, sounding like 'duo *wo*' and therefore 'dwo'. In turn, *dwe* may well have originated from *dwo* by analogy. All in all, we may see here at play an underlying tendency to create pairs in an attempt at systematizing the new introductions. Moreover, it can be noted that a great number of new signs belong to the vocalic series most innovated in the basic syllabary (i.e. the newly expanded *e-*/*o*-series), and some of these signs seem to have been created on the basis of the analogic principle. This is likely to have been the case for ro_2 /rjo, ljo/ giving /rro, llo/, a sign arguably created by analogy with inherited ra_2 /rja, lja/, given that we do not have any examples of alternative spelling ro_2/*-ri-jo* (while we have the alternation ra_2/*-ri-ja*). Hence, the possibility may be entertained that the same principle also operated for the creation of the newly introduced sign a_3, representing the diphthong /ai/, by analogy with the inherited sign a_4, noting its /u/ diphthong counterpart /au/. A final note is worth adding in relation to *pte*, as this sign appears to stand out for not being part of any series, hence being somewhat isolated in the structure of the syllabary. It has been suggested (see lastly Melena 2014c: 69–70) that its phonetic value /pte/ developed from an original /pje/, where the palatalized labial never underwent full palatalization, but was replaced with the cluster /pt/ instead. Interestingly, and strangely enough given the assigned value, this sign is a LB innovation, not present in LA (or at least not found yet if it did exist), and is only used for the spelling of a limited number of words mainly at Knossos, Pylos and sporadically Tiryns.

By presenting and discussing the signs which were newly introduced in LB, this section has laid stress on the 'creativity' of the writers involved in the process of adapting the script to the Greek language. It has been shown that some creations were added to better account for Greek phonological features (e.g. aspiration); some others instead appear to be more restricted in both context of use and attestations (e.g. ra_3). All in all, such examples are worthy of the title of 'scribal creativity'.

20.9 Filling the Gaps and the Undeciphered Signs

Looking back at Tables 20.1 and 20.2, some irregularities catch the eye: Why are there still empty slots in the syllabic series? Some of these empty slots are to be expected for phonetic reasons and can therefore be taken as 'structural gaps'. this is most likely the case for the slots showing the phonetic sequences /(C)wu/ (including *qu* = /kʷu/), and maybe also for the sequence /ji/ (although Melena 2014a: 83, suggests a value /ji/ or /zi/ for the undeciphered sign **63*; for a possible, although still speculative, reconstruction of the general structure of the LB syllabary see: Melena 2014c: 88–89, Del Freo and Perna 2019: 138–40). Other empty slots, instead, may simply reflect our still partial understanding of the LB syllabary in its full form and stand a chance of being filled with some of the undeciphered signs. By way of example, the values /ju/, /zi/, /zu/ are not implausible and would fill in some of the partially complete series, making it reasonable as well as justifiable to look for their presence among the undeciphered signs.

In fact, although more than half a century has now gone by since the decipherment of LB, some 14 syllabograms (Table 20.3) are still enigmatic and remain untransliterated, hence called 'undeciphered', and conventionally referred to by their classification number preceded by an asterisk (see summary in Del Freo and Perna 2019: 134–35, with specific references; Judson 2020). Also in this case, some of these signs have been inherited and continued from LA (Table 20.3, shaded slots), while some others are only attested in LB. Most of the undeciphered signs are rarely used and usually occur to spell names of arguable non-Greek origin (e.g. a female name spelled **18-to-no* at Knossos). Moreover, a good number of these do not show a widespread geographical distribution, as their attestations (and therefore use) are limited to certain sites: for instance, signs **18*, **47* and **49* are only attested at Knossos; sign **63* only at Pylos and Thebes; signs **64*, **83*, **86* only at Knossos and Pylos.

Thanks to alternative spellings with signs of the basic syllabary as well as contextual analyses, some very speculative phonetic values have been advanced for a number of undeciphered signs. These have been put forward mainly by Melena (2014c: 88–89) and are given in Table 20.3 (with further references to specific discussions). For the time being, all these tentative values must be taken with due caution, as most values are not officially endorsed by the Mycenological Colloquia,[10] and the hypotheses that await confirmation need to be tested with further studies. In fact, as Judson's (2020) thorough analysis of the undeciphered signs points out, at present we are at an impasse, as there is no way to prove uncontrovertibly any of the values attributable to these signs, with a very few exceptions. The only sign whose phonetic value can be more securely determined is **65* (Melena 2014a: 75–79, 81–83), which is likely to be read as /ju/ because of some compelling spelling alternations (e.g. a place name variably spelled *ri-*65-no*, *ri-u-no*, *ri-jo-no*) and a possible etymological connection of the LB word *i-*65* (nominative), alternating with *i-je-we* (dative), with the Greek word for 'son' (/^{h}ius/ > υἱός). In case this reading is unanimously accepted, sign **65* is likely soon to be moved to the basic syllabary to fill the slot *ju* /ju/.

[10] The Mycenological Colloquium is an international conference taking place every five years, where scholars in the field of Mycenaean and Aegean studies discuss debated issues and agree on the final decisions to take to move the field forward.

Table 20.3 *The LB 'undeciphered' syllabograms*

Sign	Speculative value
 *18	/sto/? (Melena 1985: 483)
 *19	*ru*$_2$? (Melena, in preparation)
 *22	*pi*$_2$ /^{m}bi, p^{h}i/? (Melena 1987)
 *34/35	*a*$_5$ /^{h}ai/? (Melena 2014b)
 *47	*i*$_2$? (Melena, in preparation)
*49	-
 *56	*pa*$_2$ /^{m}ba, p^{h}a/? (Melena 1987)
*63	*zi*? (Melena 2014a)
 *64	/swi/ ? (Chadwick 1968) or /twi/? (Melena, in preparation)
 *65	*ju* /ju/ (Melena 2014a)
 *79	*wo*$_2$ /wjo/? (Melena 1978)
 *82	/swa/ or /twa/? (Melena 1983: 262–7)
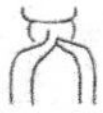 *83	/nwe/ or /ste/? (Melena 1985, in preparation)
 *86	/dwa/? (Melena 1983)

Shading for signs that have only got the same shape (but not phonetic value) in LA; no shading for signs that are new LB introductions.
(drawings by the author based on actual attestations)

20.10 Beyond Signs: Tablet Layout

In addition to orthographic conventions, the documents inscribed in LB are characterized by a peculiar set of 'layouts' (i.e. modalities of disposing textual information on the writing surface), which can be taken as some sort of *mise-en-page*. The purpose of this strategy appears to have been to enhance and ease legibility of the record as a whole for easier and quicker access to key information (e.g. place names, commodities listed, personnel involved) at first glance. As such, textual structure itself can be taken as carrier of information, as each item occupies a dedicated space. There are examples of 'capitalization', where the first word of the record is written in bigger characters and stands out from the remaining text (usually for its importance). One such example is given in Figure 20.1, where a man's name (*a-re-ke-se-u* /Alekseus/) is written in 'capitals', followed by the indication of a place name (*pa-i-to* 'Phaistos') in smaller characters on the second line, and the items (flock of sheep) recorded by means of logograms followed by numerals positioned at the far right end. This disposition arrangement places emphasis on the name of the individual (in this case a shepherd), in charge of the flock of sheep and its location, as well as pointing out the overall size of the flock (100 sheep): an easy and effective method.

Change in character size is a strategy used to separate words, but not the only one. Two other methods were devised by the 'scribes' for marking word division: leaving a space between two consecutive words (as we do), or using a word divider in the shape of a short, straight vertical line (represented by a comma in transliterations, as in Figure 20.1; on word division see Duhoux 1999: 227–36, Melena 2014c: 123–28, Del Freo and Perna 2019: 146–47, Meissner forthcoming). The latter method appears to have had an edge over the former, as it is the most frequently used (especially at Pylos), albeit not systematically. The word divider is a new introduction in LB, not present in LA. In some cases, we may even talk of scribal hypercorrection, as word dividers are sometime placed (unnecessarily) between a word and a logogram, between logograms, or even between logograms and their related numerical entry. There are, however, some exceptions to the use of either method: this is the case for formulae

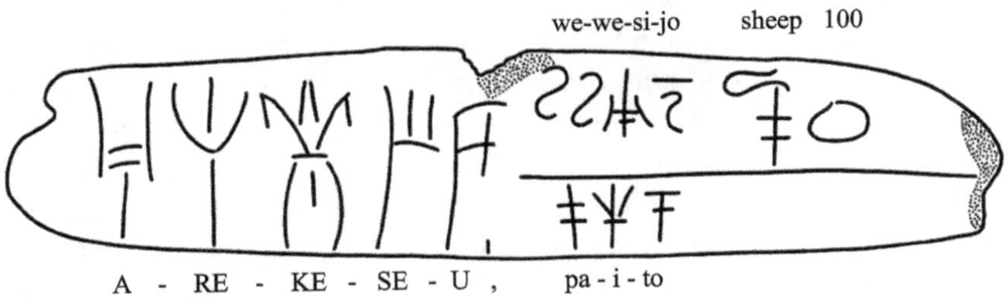

Figure 20.1 LB tablet from Knossos (KN Da 1156)
(drawing by the author after CoMIK, Chadwick et al. 1986–1998, vol. 2: 43)

(nominal compounds) and clitic particles. Some words are in fact simply juxtaposed, without graphic separation: for example *a-ne-mo-i-je-re-ja* 'priestess' (*i-je-re-ja* /hi^{j}erei^{j}a/, alphabetic Greek ἱερεία) 'of the winds' (*a-ne-mo* /anemo:n/, alphabetic Greek ἀνέμων, genitive plural), *pa-si-te-o-i* 'to all' (*pa-si* /pansi/, alphabetic Greek πα(ν)σί) 'the Gods' (*te-o-i* /t^{h}ehoihi/, alphabetic Greek θέοισι, dative plural). As for clitics, these are usually attached to word-start or word-end: *o-u-di-do-si* /ou didonsi/ 'they do not give', with proclitic *o-u-* /ou/ 'not' (alphabetic Greek οὐ) preceeding the verb; *e-ke-qe* /ek^{h}ei k^{w}e/ '(s/he) has', with enclitic *-qe* /k^{w}e/ (alphabetic Greek τε) following the verb (on Mycenaean particles see Salgarella 2018, 2019a, 2019b). As a last remark, in LB there are no cases of *scriptio continua* (also known as *scriptura continua*; see Chapter 18, this volume), nor are words ever split across lines (which, instead, happens quite often in LA). Moreover, writing lines may at times be ruled to ease directionality of writing; this is also a new feature introduced in LB (only a few LA texts show ruling, which is never consistent throughout the document). In conclusion, LB documents show neater writing on the tablet surface and appear to have improved on the *mise-en-page* for quicker information retrieval, resulting in an overall systematization of the writing practice as a whole.

20.11 Conclusion

This chapter has discussed the methods scholars used over the past decades to reconstruct the orthography of a writing system previously unknown and no longer in use, and the challenges they faced to reach as accurate an understanding as possible of both the writing system itself (Linear B) and the underlying language (Mycenaean Greek). It has been shown that the reconstruction of LB orthographic conventions was context-based, as well as context-driven. The historical and linguistic backdrop, within which the adaptation of an already existing writing system, LA, to render a different language, Greek, took place, played a major role in the reconstruction, which is still ongoing (e.g. 'undeciphered' signs). It has been shown that the reconstruction was a complex process, involving steps stretching from predecipherment (identification of recurrent patterns) to postdecipherment (systematic analysis of such patterns to work out orthographic conventions by comparing LB spellings with Proto-Indo-European and alphabetic Greek). This enabled scholars to draw up the 'rules' that governed the system and, by assessing deviations, to evaluate the extent to which these were adhered to. In fact, orthographic variation is also observable within the time span of LB itself (variant spellings, site-restricted signs). This chapter has illustrated how an initially unknown orthographic system was reconstructed, and how that reconstruction contributed to a more subtle appreciation of the diachronic development of Greek, here seen in its 'Bronze Age snapshot'.

Part V

Explanatory Discussions

21

Scribes and Scribal Practices

Peter J. Grund

21.1 Introduction

Anyone who has worked with manuscript texts in English (or many other languages for that matter) from especially the pre-print era is familiar with the wide variation in orthography (including spelling, capitalization, punctuation and other similar features) found in such texts. Variation is often evident even among versions of the same text. This is highlighted in the various orthographic conventions found in the opening phrase in copies of the late fifteenth-century English alchemical tract *Mirror of Lights* (Grund 2014: 591), cited in (1)–(8). The phrase differs slightly (or considerably) in the copies, but overall, it can be paraphrased as 'in seeking out the truth of this craft that people call alchemy'.

(1) *In the sechynge of the soothnesse of this craft that men callyn Alkemye/* (Cambridge, Trinity College, MS R. 14. 37, f. 115r)
(2) *In sekyng oute of the sothenesse of this craft þ^t men callys alkemye* (Cambridge, Trinity College, MS R. 14. 45, f. 67r)
(3) *In sekyng ouȝte of þe sothenes of this crafte þ^t men callen Alkemye* (Cambridge, University Library, MS Kk. 6. 30, f. 1r)
(4) *In schechyng owt þe soþenes of þis craft þ^t me clepud alkonomyȝe* (London, British Library, MS Sloane 513, f. 155r)
(5) *In seking owte the sowthnes of this crafte, that men do calle alkamye,* (Cambridge, Trinity College, MS O. 2. 33, 11)
(6) *In sechyng owte of the sothenes of the crafte that men callith Alkȳmȳe* (London, British Library, MS Harley 3542, f. 1r)

I am grateful to Matti Peikola, two anonymous reviewers, and the editors for comments on an earlier version of this chapter. Naturally, any errors are entirely my own.

(7) *In shewinge oute of yᵉ Southnes of philosophy* (London, British Library, MS Sloane 3580A, f. 193v)
(8) *In the seekinge of the sowthenesse, of this crafte that men call Vnxqymio* (London, British Library, MS Sloane 316, f. 18r)

In this short extract (which is not even a full clause), 'this' is found in two spellings (*this* and *þis*), 'out' in four spellings (*oute, owt, owte* and *ouȝte*) and 'soothness' (or 'truth') in as many as seven different spellings: *soothnesse, sothenesse, sothenes, soþenes, sowthnes, Southnes* and *sowthenesse.* Capitalization is applied differently, as can be seen in the spelling of 'alchemy' and 'soothness', and some manuscripts employ abbreviations while others do not (e.g. *þ*ᵗ for *þat*). This variation in copies of one and the same text may of course have multiple origins, but, crucially, the orthographic patterns reflect choices – conscious or unconscious – made by different *scribes* in responding to the text they are copying and in rendering a new text. Since much of our information about orthography before the advent of the printing press derives from scribal output, our knowledge about early English orthography is dependent on our knowledge about scribes, their identities, practices and motivations.

This chapter reviews what we know about scribal practices of orthography, how their orthographies have been studied and interpreted, and where avenues of future research lie. Section 21.2 is devoted to some fundamental aspects of studying scribes, showing the multidisciplinary interest in scribes and providing a broad backdrop for thinking about scribal variation in orthography. It covers issues such as the term and concept of a scribe, the contexts in which scribes worked, and how the role of the scribe has changed over time. Section 21.3 then focuses on research on scribal orthographies within three broad contexts: (1) studies focusing on phonology and phonetics, but using scribal orthography as the source of information; (2) research that concentrates on the intersection of phonology/phonetics and orthography; and (3) studies that are focused on orthography as an exclusively or primarily written phenomenon. Section 21.4 addresses the issue of orthographic standardization specifically, as scribes have been seen as central in this process, and touches on the various frameworks and approaches adopted for the study and interpretation of spelling regularization and standardization. Before a brief conclusion (Section 21.6), an outlook section (Section 21.5) points to some of the avenues open for new discoveries in the future.

Much has been written on scribes and their linguistic practices in various geographical, linguistic and temporal contexts (e.g. Wagner, Beinhoff and Outhwaite 2013). While we see interesting cross-linguistic and cross-cultural trends in scribal practices, this chapter cannot do justice to the complexities that arise in considering scribal work across a variety of geolinguistic contexts. The approach in this chapter is to keep the geolinguistic factor constant, focusing on scribes working with English. Some of the mechanics that have been outlined in studies of English are more widely applicable. But different cultures and time periods do open up questions that can only be convincingly answered by closely considering the specifics of the scribes, their status and practices in time periods and locations in which they were active.

21.2 Scribes: Terms, Definitions and Contexts

Scribes play a major role in the production and dissemination of text in historical periods, and, up until the era of printed texts starting in the late fifteenth century, much of our textual and hence linguistic evidence for English is extant in scribal copies rather than authorial holographs. Exactly how the role of scribes in text production should be understood and evaluated has been vigorously debated. In research on Old English (c. AD 500–1100), for example, scholars of poetry have variously emphasized scribes as corrupting an authorial text, as consciously participating in the construction of the text, or something in between (e.g. Doane 1994, Fulk 2003, Neidorf 2017).[1] Recent research in Middle English suggests that the distinction between scribe and author is not clear-cut, and that the relationship should more accurately be conceptualized as a continuum (e.g. Fisher 2012).

Irrespective of how to understand their contributions, the impact and hence significance of scribes is undeniable, and scribes have not surprisingly been studied and discussed – even praised and castigated – in scholarship in many overlapping areas, including text criticism, editing, paleography and book history, and historical linguistics. With such cross-disciplinary attention to scribes, studying their practices in orthography from a historical linguistic perspective by necessity involves drawing on the insights from allied fields. There is, for example, obvious overlap between linguistic approaches and paleography and book history. Spellings can be influenced by choices of scripts and handwriting, as in the well-known variation of <u> and <v>, representing both consonants and vowels, in the Middle English (c. 1100–1500) and Early Modern English (c. 1500–1750) periods (see, e.g., Grund et al. 2021). Manuscript space and scribes' professional goals may also impact the choice of alternative spellings: Scragg (1974: 52) suggests that "scriveners [could charge] by the inch and [add] to their income with superfluous letters." Similarly, punctuation is studied in complementary ways by scholars of historical orthography and paleographers, and there are obvious opportunities for cross-fertilization (e.g. Parkes 1993 [1992], Calle-Martín and Miranda-García 2008).

[1] I owe this point to one of the reviewers of the chapter.

The exact definition of *scribe* and the label used vary across studies and time periods considered. Scribes are often associated with a level of professionalism where copying is seen as conducted as part of a profession or calling (Beal 2008: s.v. *scribe*). The context and purpose of such copying of course change over time, as copying shifts from mainly monastic scriptoria to more commercial, guild-governed enterprises; hence scribes of the early Middle Ages were considerably different than their later counterparts (e.g. Scragg 1974: 34). However, *scribe* is not always equated with a professional category, and the term has been applied more generally to any person making a copy of a text (e.g. Beal 1998: 3, 2008: s.v. *scribe*, Wagner, Outhwaite and Beinhoff 2013: 3–4). A number of other labels with varying degrees of denotative and connotative overlap also occur in the literature: *copyist, clerk, scrivener, amanuensis, secretary, recorder* and *notary*. A term such as *copyist* is perhaps largely synonymous with *scribe*. *Clerk* and *scrivener*, on the other hand, often designate professionals with writing duties other than or in addition to copying texts, including the drafting of legal documents, but the terms are sometimes used more generally to mean 'copyist' or 'scribe' as well (e.g. Scragg 1974: 35–36, 64, 67).

The multiple terms not only underscore the complexity of interlinked writing contexts and activities, but they also signal a variety of developments in writing-related professions and the contexts of writing over time. In the Old English period and well into the post-Conquest Middle English period (after 1066), the copying of texts in English (as well as in Latin and later French) was primarily the domain of monasteries and churches, where monks, nuns and other ecclesiastics would undertake copying as part of their religious duties or possibly on commission (Gameson 2011). Much of the text production appears to have taken place in *scriptoria*, that is, rooms or workplaces devoted to the copying of text in ecclesiastical establishments, but copying was also undertaken in other locations, such as at the royal court or in less organized circumstances (Gameson 2011: 102–6). While we have some knowledge of individual scribes, we mostly lack information allowing us to connect texts with named individuals with known social background in the Old English period.

In the late medieval period (fourteenth and fifteenth centuries), text production shifted from primarily ecclesiastical contexts to more secular and commercial locations, and a number of professional delineations developed. From at least the late fourteenth century, a guild of 'textwriters' (which seems to have covered a number of allied book production professionals) existed in London. This guild later split into the Writers of the Court Letter or Scriveners Guild, whose members "could draft legally binding documents" (Mooney 2008: 185; see also Chapter 23, this volume), and what was eventually called the Stationers' Guild, which was concerned with text production and the book market more generally (Mooney 2008: 187; see also Chapter 23, this volume). Documentation in relation to the guilds and their members has revealed a complex picture of the 'scribal industry': scribes worked as part of commercial enterprises in close conjunction with other book artisans, but likely not within large organized scriptoria, and freelancing seems to have occurred outside the purview of the guilds (see Christianson 1989a, 1989b; Mooney 2008). Recent paleographical projects, including *Late Medieval English Scribes* by Mooney and associates, have also made it possible to connect a number of mainly literary manuscripts to particular scribes. The most notable discovery in this context is probably the identification of the London scribe Adam Pinkhurst and the attribution of well-known Chaucer manuscripts to him, although the attributions and identification continue to be debated (e.g. Mooney 2006, Warner 2015). Naturally, the London scene cannot be extended uncritically to other geographical locations, but, as discussed in Section 21.4, scribal work in London has been claimed to be especially important for our understanding of patterns and regularization in spelling in fifteenth-century England.

The advent of the printing press in the late fifteenth century has traditionally been seen as the end of the era of scribal copying (see, e.g., Schulz 1943: 382, Scragg 1974: 67). However, research over the past twenty years has proven such assumptions false or at least shown them to be oversimplified. On the more professional side, scribal 'publication' (commercial and otherwise) and copying of a wide range of literary texts, scientific writings and other genres continued for another two hundred years or so in England, and we know the identity of numerous scribes who undertook such work (e.g. Love 1993, Marotti 1995, Beal 1998, McKitterick 2003). Some professional contexts also relied heavily on scribal work, where printing could not replace the need for scribes, such as the legal system (where scribes are still active to some degree today). In the legal domain, there is an obvious overlap between *scribe* and *scrivener* (in the technical sense of someone who records legal documents), but legal scribes often undertook not only drafting but also copying of legal documents (e.g. Grund 2007, Hiltunen and Peikola 2007, Grund 2011). If *scribe* is taken in the more general sense of 'anyone who copies text', scribes are of course ubiquitous throughout historical periods and still present, but more in a role that can be taken on than in a clearly designated profession.

Scribal orthography must thus be understood against the backdrop of a number of historical, social and cultural factors and developments. Some scribes were professional; others were not. Some worked as part of close-knit communities; others were part of looser networks or on their own. And the types of texts they copied and for whom varied a great deal. All of these contexts and factors have a potential impact on orthographic patterns.

21.3 Scribal Practices of Orthography

As I have already suggested, it is a truism (though one that is not always explicitly acknowledged) that talking about the history of English orthography for certain periods is largely talking about the *scribal* history of English orthography. For Old English, the evidence is predominantly scribal (as far as we can tell).[2] The evidence for Middle English is more complex,[3] and we do see an increasing number of holograph manuscripts of, for example, letters at the end of the period (Bergs 2005). Before increasing regularization in especially spelling and the rise of 'standards' in the fifteenth century and beyond (see Section 21.4), scribes clearly treated the orthographic patterns of the text they copied in a variety of ways, and the resulting text may reflect a scribe's language entirely, partly or not at all. Which of these categories applies to any one copy of a text is not easily recoverable, and we often seem to be dealing with fractured, inconsistent and almost lawless orthographic use. This leaves us with a record that has been used, treated, conceptualized and theorized in a number of different ways in scholarship on orthography.

While the focus in this chapter is on orthographic patterns, it is important to recognize that such patterns are often studied for purposes other than exploring the history of orthography. Most notably, they are used as a window into the pronunciation of the past and phonetic/phonological developments over time. As such, variation in spelling is taken to signal variation in pronunciation, although the degree of transparency and direct linkage between spelling and pronunciation is usually problematized (see, e.g., Hogg 1992b: 68, Lass 1992: 27).[4] Perhaps in keeping with the book's general aim of catering to students, Horobin (2013a) focuses his chapter about Chaucerian spelling and pronunciation on how spelling reflects contemporaneous pronunciation (although comments are also given on spelling irrespective of possible phonological connections). Toon (1983), on the other hand, traces spelling variation as a reflection of phonological developments across the Old English period. Although they both acknowledge the scribal underpinnings of their evidence, the scribe is not used as an explanatory factor for the perceived patterns, which is a common feature of work focused on spelling as a phonological source of evidence.

[2] It is unclear to what extent runic inscriptions of Old English should be considered scribal or authorial, although they probably represent a mix (see Page 1999: 115–16).

[3] The twelfth-century *Ormulum*, for example, represents an early glimpse at authorial experimentation in orthography (Anderson and Britton 1999).

[4] Interestingly, both Hogg's and Lass's chapters in *The Cambridge History of the English Language* (vols. 1 and 2, respectively) are labeled 'Phonology and morphology'. Orthography (mainly spelling) does receive a separate, though, brief treatment in the chapters. Volume 3, on the other hand, has a chapter dedicated to 'Orthography and punctuation' (Salmon 1999).

While this type of phonological/phonetic study of orthography usually has little to say about the orthography *per se*, other strands of research explicitly take on the connection of the two, which usually means studying the details of both linguistic systems, with a possible emphasis on one or the other. Focused research on scribal copying behavior has revealed a complex picture of how scribes negotiate the intersection of pronunciation and spelling. Early interpretations of the seemingly erratic spelling habits of scribes in the early Middle English period (1100–1300) postulated that the patterns were due to Anglo-Norman scribes' insufficient familiarity with English conventions in orthography and pronunciation. This idea was firmly debunked by Clark in 1992, but she shows the longevity of this conception of scribal variation (Clark 1992b: 117–18). Building on Clark's (1992b) discussion, Laing (1999) suggests that early Middle English scribes tried to 'reinvent' English spelling after copying mostly in Latin and French. As they did so, their systems allowed for complex, yet systematic variations: a letter form (or *figura*) could represent various underlying pronunciations (or *potestates*), or various *figurae* could represent the same *potestas*, for one and the same scribe or for different scribes. For example, representing initial /j/, one scribe in Laing's (1999) study uses exclusively <y>, another <y> and <þ>, and yet another <þ> and <ȝ> (Laing 1999: 258). Following up on Laing's (1999) suggestions, Laing and Lass (2003, 2009) further emphasize the point that "[w]riting systems could be prodigal yet still systematic" in early Middle English (Laing and Lass 2003: 258). They provide additional formalization of this idea in the concepts of *litteral substitution sets* and *potestatic substitution sets* (ideas also partly touched on in Laing 1999). The former concept refers to the letter forms that can be used for a particular phonetic realization (such as <t> or <tt> for Old English /ht/), while the latter includes the orthographic reflection of a range of *potestates* (e.g. <ȝ> for /h/, /x/, /j/, /w/ and /ɣ/) (Laing and Lass 2009: 2). This approach makes it possible to evaluate and understand spelling conventions as an integral part of the scribes' systematic, yet variable negotiation of writing and pronunciation, and not as aberrant, emendable scribal corruptions.

Much recent scholarship has focused on orthography (especially spelling) in its own right, without possible connections with underlying representation of phonology/phonetics. At the forefront of this research are the *Linguistic Atlas of Late Mediaeval English* (McIntosh et al. 1986a), including its online version eLALME (McIntosh et al. 2013), *A Linguistic Atlas of Early Middle English 1150 to 1325* (Laing 2013–) and *A Linguistic Atlas of Older Scots, Phase 1, 1380 to 1500* (Williamson 2013), as well as associated studies by the compilers before and after the completion of the atlas projects (some of which have already been cited above). There had been long-standing interest in and attempts at systematic study of scribal variation in orthography, especially spelling, in late Middle English before the launch of the atlas projects (McIntosh et al. 1986b: 3–4). However, the methods, techniques and scope of LALME (and the subsequent atlases following its principles) brought the charting and understanding of scribal variation to an unparalleled level. Among many innovations in LALME, the compilers focus on the orthography (or written language more generally) as valid in itself, rather than primarily as a means for recapturing the spoken language of the past (McIntosh et al. 1986b: 5–6). This means that data were collected that have no obvious connection to pronunciation, such as the spelling of the ending *-ly* used to form adverbs, as *-le, -lee, -ley, -li, -lie, -lye* and *-ly* (McIntosh et al. 1986b: 455–56). The compilers collected information on over two hundred features, many orthographic, some lexical and morphological, from thousands of texts from mainly the period 1350–1450, allowing an extensive view of patterns in the period. Regionally localizable texts were used as 'anchor' texts for their atlas, showing where certain orthographic conventions were current. Additional data were supplied using the so-called 'fit technique', where, briefly put, non-localized manuscripts and texts could be placed on a map as their patterns matched or 'fit' with those of anchor texts (McIntosh et al. 1986b: 10).

Although the method and charting have their drawbacks (as the compilers acknowledge), this approach has had a tremendous impact on Middle English scholarship of all stripes, and not least on work on orthography. From this research, we can clearly see that medieval spelling is not haphazard, but systematic, with clear regional patterning. We can see the regional distribution of individual spellings of particular lexemes, such as for 'such' in its numerous variants (McIntosh et al. 1986b: 321–23), but also the linguistic profiles of scribes and manuscripts (McIntosh et al. 1986c). What regionalism tells us is not always clear, however. The compilers of LALME note that "the *Atlas* tells us, in essence, *where the scribe of a manuscript learned to write*; the question of where he actually worked and produced the manuscript is a matter of extrapolation and assumption" (McIntosh et al. 1986a: 23, italics original).

Developing the LALME method and surveying extant manuscripts that could be mined for information forced the compilers to chart and theorize the kinds of behaviors that scribes exhibit as they copy texts. The scribes' approach has a direct bearing on the orthographic record that they left behind and hence influences how we understand scribal systems of orthography. The most detailed and formalized classification of scribal approaches is that of Benskin and Laing (1981), drawing on McIntosh (1963: 8–9; see also McIntosh et al. 1986b: 12–23). Based on hypothetical scenarios as well as actual manuscript evidence, Benskin and Laing (1981) suggest a number of possible ways of evaluating the resulting manuscript evidence, dealing primarily with orthography, but to some extent morphology, lexis and syntax. At one end of the continuum is a *literatim* copyist that faithfully renders the original without any modification, while at the other end is the translating scribe, who fully 'translates' (if necessary) the text's language into the scribe's own language (see also Laing 1999, 2000). The most common strategy is not surprisingly somewhere in between, resulting in a so-called *Mischsprache*, a mixed language. The degrees of such *Mischsprachen* can vary a great deal, influenced by such factors as place in the text, type of text, medium (verse vs. prose) and other factors.

Some manuscripts show simply some insular *relict* forms inherited from the original in an otherwise meticulously translated text (Benskin and Laing 1981: 58), while others reveal complex patterns of adoption and adaptation. Benskin and Laing (1981: 58–59) propose that, in the mixing of linguistic features, the scribes' orthography may be conditioned by their active and passive repertoire of usage. The former includes the scribes' 'spontaneous usage' outside the copying context; the latter being a part of the scribes' knowledge of language and perhaps used in the community, even if not by the scribes themselves. How exactly a scribe negotiates these two repertoires is not always readily obvious but can only be surmised and hypothesized through close study of the textual evidence. Even more complexity is added to this picture when we consider that some *Mischsprachen* are not scribally produced but a result of textual production (so-called *pseudo-Mischsprachen*), where the textual history of the copied manuscript may obscure scribal patterns. For example, a scribe may copy *literatim* a text written by two scribes who have varying orthographies. The resulting text gives the impression that the copying scribe has a *Mischsprache* system, while it simply reflects two "inherited" spelling conventions (Benskin and Laing 1981: 63).

So how does awareness of different types of scribes help us study scribal systems of orthography? Clearly, it is crucial to know what kind of scribe or scribal behavior we are dealing with to know whether the scribe has a possible 'prodigal' (wide-ranging but systematic) spelling system (as suggested by Laing and Lass 2003 and 2009, reviewed above) or whether the spelling reflects a mixture of systems. The extent to which a particular type of manuscript is used for evidence in a study of orthography naturally depends on the specific research questions. After all, even a mixed usage is evidence of contemporaneous spelling (although diachronic layering is of course possible). However, these results underscore that scribal copying behaviors complicate use of a text as a straightforward linguistic 'informant' for orthographic use.

21.4 Orthographic Regularization, Supralocalization and Standardization

Present-day orthography commands a great deal of regularity, and there is a clear standard, perhaps more so than for other levels of linguistic structure in the written language. That does not mean that there is no variation: there are regional/varietal differences (such as between American and British English spelling and punctuation), as well as generic patterns (e.g. academic writing and text-messaging). The tension between variation and regularization or standardization has been present throughout the history of English, though in various shapes and guises, and the contributions of scribes to these patterns have varied over time. With the advent of the printing press, the regularization and standardization of English orthography entered a new stage, although the process was certainly gradual, negotiated and by no means straightforward (Scragg 1974: 64–87, Salmon 1999: 15–21).[5] We know little about whether and, if so, exactly how scribes contributed to processes of regularization and standardization in the print era. Differences in orthography between print and handwritten text are evident throughout the early modern and into at least the late modern periods (e.g. Osselton 1998 [1984], Salmon 1999, Fairman 2006: especially pages 75–80). However, for scribal texts specifically rather than handwritten sources in general, few studies appear to exist. Although primarily concerned with lexico-grammar rather than orthography, Nevalainen (2013) shows that Henry VIII's 'secretaries', who wrote letters in his name, were more conservative than the king in some features, but less so in others. On the orthographic side, the secretaries preferred the eventually standard form *you*, while Henry VIII used *yow*, in Nevalainen's (2013: 109) material.

In witness depositions spanning the early modern period, the scribes, who drafted as well as copied testimony, adhered to varying orthographic conventions – in terms of spelling, capitalization, punctuation and use of abbreviations (Grund 2011). It remains to be explored whether these scribes conformed to or developed patterns that can be attributed to community or professional standards. We do see increasing regularization and adherence to the developing standard of spelling over time, but the scribes do not appear to behave differently in this regard from writers in general (Grund 2011: 158–63). In the legal documents surviving from the witch trials in Salem, Massachusetts, in 1692–93 (Rosenthal et al. 2009), a different pattern emerges. The scribal context in Salem is complex. More than 200 writers of diverse backgrounds and professions were involved in recording some 1,000 documents; *scribe* must here therefore be seen as on a continuum of professionalism. As they recorded and copied texts, they seem to have been variously influenced by their own pronunciation (and possibly that of others), printed text and the developing standard (Grund et al. 2009: 72–77). The dynamics of these patterns have yet to be explored in detail.

Where we do see the clear and significant impact of scribes and scribal practices in regularization and standardization processes is in the Middle Ages, though in varying, complex ways across the period. Of course, this is not surprising, since most of the data at hand are scribal, as we have established before. However, these processes are intimately connected to who the

[5] For a discussion of standardization and regularization, see Chapter 13, this volume.

scribes were, where they worked and what they were trying to accomplish. Most of the research interested in processes of standardization has focused on the late medieval period (fourteenth and fifteenth centuries) when we see several supralocal varieties develop; that is, linguistic patterns appear that are no longer geographically coherent nor localizable (although distinctly regional writing also continued, as we shall see below in the discussion of Stenroos 2013; see also Chapter 13, Chapter 25 and Chapter 30, this volume). That does not mean that we do not see regularization and possible standardization (depending on how we define this process and the subsequent 'standard'; see below) before this date. At the end of the Old English period (the late tenth and early eleventh centuries), West Saxon, originally a southern regional dialect, was diffused across different regions and used in a variety of texts and genres. Gneuss (1972) hypothesized that this supralocal, 'standardized' variety was a conscious product, likely stemming from the monastery of Winchester, whose influence prompted other ecclesiastical centers, such as Canterbury and York, to adopt it, and we see it employed in a range of texts, such as the *Anglo-Saxon Chronicle* and translations of Bede's *Historia ecclesiastica*, as well as poetic works (Hogg 1992b: 78, Horobin 2013b: 66–67). However, unlike modern standard spelling, Late West Saxon was not entirely regular across writers and locations, and there may have been other prestigious varieties, such as Mercian (Horobin 2013b: 66–67). We see forms of spelling evidencing copying or translation from other dialects, which may indicate that non–Late West Saxon spellings and forms were part of the scribes' passive (if not active) repertoire, in Benskin and Laing's (1981) terminology (see Section 21.3). But misinterpretations also seem to be evident, as scribes negotiated unfamiliar spellings, especially if the original text and dialect were diachronically removed from the scribe (Neidorf 2017: 46). With the Norman Conquest, this 'standard' disappears and is not the foundation of our present-day standard spelling conventions.

The early Middle English period also witnessed systematicity in spelling, as evident in the charting of LAEME (Laing 2013–) (and the studies discussed in Section 21.3), although there is much more variability than in later periods: there are not the kinds of supralocal, standard(izing) patterns evident in late Old English nor late Middle English. Tolkien (1929) famously pointed to the regularity in spelling (and other features) between two early Middle English manuscripts from the southwest Midlands copied by different scribes (Cambridge, Corpus Christi College, MS 402, containing *Ancrene Wisse*, advice to anchoresses, and Bodleian Library, MS Bodley 34, which includes a number of spiritual texts, such as *Sawles Warde*). Tolkien (1929: 111) concluded that the patterns were indicative of a literary standard, which he labeled the *AB language*. While some scholars follow Tolkien's (1929) claim of a literary standard (see the sources listed by Benskin and Laing 1981: 98), the idea of a standard and some of Tolkien's (1929) other assumptions have been questioned and criticized, not least because of the lack of evidence of wider use of the AB language (e.g. Horobin 2013b: 99). Nonetheless, the existence of these manuscripts shows a concern for regularity and convention, perhaps stemming from a particular scriptorium or community.

More widespread and systematic regularization, supralocalization and standardization is evidenced in the late fourteenth and fifteenth centuries. Based on the collection of data from spelling (but also vocabulary and morphology) for LALME, Samuels suggested in the seminal 1963 article 'Some applications of Middle English dialectology' that four types of language occur in late medieval manuscripts "that are less obviously dialectal, and can thus cast light on the probable sources of the written standard English that appears in the fifteenth century" (Samuels 1963: 84; see also Horobin 2011: 73–74). He also refers to these varieties as "incipient standards" (Samuels 1963: 89).

Type I: 'Central Midland Standard', found especially in texts associated with the religious community of the Lollards, based on dialects in Northamptonshire, Huntingdonshire and Bedfordshire

Type II: English of the greater London area as evidenced in, for example, the Auchinleck manuscript (National Library of Scotland, Advocates' MS 19. 2. 1), with influences from East Anglian features

Type III: the London English of especially Geoffrey Chaucer, but also Thomas Hoccleve and other sources, influenced by Central Midlands features

Type IV: 'Chancery standard', as evidenced in documents disseminated by the London-based government and administration, influenced by Central Midlands and Northern and North Midlands features

These types should not be seen as straightforwardly linked in the sense that one gave way to the other or necessarily influenced the other, and, as indicated in the list and emphasized below, the different varieties likely had varying affinities to professional and religious communities and to different types of text production.[6] Samuels's (1963) basic framework continues to be influential, but his fairly brief outline – the article is 14 pages, with a third of the article taken up by graphs and tables – has been criticized, questioned, modified, nuanced and added to in numerous subsequent studies. Taavitsainen (2000, 2004), for example, shows the presence of Samuels's (1963) Type I, Central Midland Standard (as well as East Midlands features), in a range of medical and scientific texts, pointing to the broader applicability of this variety among scribes copying scientific works.[7] Scribes of scientific writing even seem to have retained this variety or features of it into the fifteenth and sixteenth

[6] The understanding of the term and concept of a 'standard' differs considerably in studies of early spelling developments, and often the concept remains undefined. For an early discussion of this issue in relation to Samuels's (1963) study, see Sandved (1981). See also Stenroos (2013) below.

[7] Samuels (1963: 85) had already noted, but not explored, some of these connections (see Taavitsainen 2004: 214).

centuries in the face of the growing prominence and influence of the putative 'Chancery standard'. Whether these patterns point to a centralized location with a particular 'house style' of orthography (and other features) remains unknown, but Taavitsainen (2004: 236) argues that the variation in some of the manuscripts is so limited that "they must have been produced under some kind of control."

In his discussion of Chaucer's language, Horobin (2003), on the other hand, is primarily concerned with Types II–IV, and especially Type III, which is characteristic of Chaucer manuscripts. Importantly, he demonstrates that these types are by no means inflexible standards, but allow for variation (unlike the present-day spelling standard). Though it suggests a great deal of uniformity in spelling, Horobin's comparison of a limited set of core words ('not', 'they', 'though', 'such', etc.) reveals variation (as in *þai, hij* for Type II for 'they', and *theyre, þeir* for Type IV for 'their') and overlap (as in *swich* for Types II and III for 'such'). Several additional convergences among these varieties appear to be evident in manuscripts that adhere primarily to one or the other type, emphasizing the complexity of the formation and negotiation of different writing standards (see also Benskin 2004: 3–4). It is also clear that Chaucer scribes retained Type III features even after Type IV (the 'Chancery standard') allegedly became more prevalent, perhaps because these features were seen as especially Chaucerian by the small community of scribes copying these manuscripts (Horobin 2003: 34). Like the scribes of the scientific texts discussed by Taavitsainen (2000, 2004), then, the Chaucer scribes did not immediately and uniformly adopt a 'Chancery standard', which underscores the negotiation and gradual adoption of such a variety.

As the putative ancestor of the modern standard, the 'Chancery standard' (Type IV) has not surprisingly garnered the most critical attention. Even so (or perhaps because of the attention), the identity, status, origin and development of this variety continue to be fiercely debated. In a series of articles from the 1970s to the 1990s (collected in Fisher 1996), Fisher builds on Samuels's (1963) brief comments on the 'Chancery standard'. Fisher argues for English, and Chancery English in particular, as consciously promoted by the Lancastrian monarchs in the fifteenth century through the Chancery, "the central agency for the administration both of justice and of national affairs" (Fisher 1996: 42). Indeed, he suggests that "[t]he essential characteristics of Modern written English were determined by the practice of the clerks in Chancery and communicated throughout England by professional scribes writing in Chancery script and under the influence of Chancery idiom" (Fisher 1996: 64). This strongly formalized view of the 'Chancery standard' (as well as some of its concomitant assumptions) has been questioned, especially by Benskin (e.g. Benskin 1992, 2004; see also Wright 2020a and 2020b discussed below). Among other issues, Benskin (1992: 79) points to 'Chancery English' as a misnomer for several reasons. The primary language of Chancery was

Latin, and when the scribes employed English, it appears to have been mainly when copying documents originating elsewhere, such as the Signet or Privy Seal Offices. The patterns are thus much broader than would be indicated by the term 'Chancery'. The dissemination and adoption of such a variety was also likely much less "linear and unidirectional" (to borrow descriptions from Wright 2000: 6, in her general characterization of standardization processes) than Fisher's (1996) narrative seems to suggest. A number of 'colorless' varieties appear to have developed in regions outside London before and concomitant with a 'Chancery standard', where strongly regional variation is reduced (though not completely deleted). These "incipient regional standards" (Benskin 1992: 84) may have paved the way for the subsequent adoption of a 'Chancery standard' (Benskin 1992: 82).

Concerns have been raised about how to understand and conceptualize *standard*, *incipient standard* and *standardization* in this context. Stenroos (2013) questions whether the term and concept of *standard* is appropriate for the fifteenth century, especially when understood to include notions of ideology and conformity. Instead, she favors the notion of *supralocalization* (adopted from Nevalainen and Raumolin-Brunberg 2003: 13), that is, the diffusion or adoption of features across regions (irrespective of whether they become part of a subsequent standard).[8] This point is reinforced through two case studies, one indicating that scribes translated texts originally written in a supralocal London English into a regionally marked West Midlands dialect apparently for a local market, which involved "unusual orthographic features which may point to a shared scribal tradition" (Stenroos 2013: 175). This underscores, again, that putative standards (or supralocal varieties) did not eliminate other varieties, which scribes used for particular purposes to reach specific audiences.

A different, though related, challenge to the current understanding of orthographic variation and standardization in late medieval England comes from Moore (2019). She argues that the lens of *communities of practice* (CoPs) helps us drill down into the details of scribal behavior that explanatory factors such as regionalism and migration cannot help us do. The CoP framework, which has been widely used in the social sciences and sociolinguistics, postulates communities characterized by members with a joint enterprise, mutual engagement and a shared repertoire of language, behaviors and so on (see also Kopaczyk and Jucker 2013 and Chapter 23, this volume). Viewing scribal work through this lens involves considering how the scribes negotiated and developed their language as part of fairly close-knit communities for whom language was one of their unifying characteristics. The regularized use and many 'incipient standards' that developed in late medieval England would thus be the result of such CoP negotiations, as scribes working together

[8] For more discussion about supralocalization, see Chapter 30, this volume.

within scriptoria or in less organized contexts developed in-house styles of spelling to carry out their joint enterprise.[9] In other words, the CoP concept gives us a concrete way of exploring what happened on the ground, in the scribes' workplaces and professional relationships.

The most fundamental criticism of earlier standardization accounts and of the concept of a 'Chancery standard' in particular is found in Wright (2020a, and in her earlier work cited therein). Based on the contributions in the edited volume in which her introductory piece occurs (Wright 2020b), Wright argues forcefully and convincingly that traditional narratives about the origins and later processes of standardization should be substantially revised or even rejected, and that 'Chancery standard' as a concept should be abandoned as lacking evidential and theoretical grounding (as already hinted in the earlier discussions above). Like earlier accounts, Wright (2020a) and the contributors to Wright (2020b) are not only concerned with spelling patterns (or orthography more broadly) but also words, grammatical forms and other linguistic features, and not only with scribal patterns but with writers of all kinds. It is clear that, as we consider more types of evidence from a broader range of sources, a different, less unilinear narrative emerges, which impacts how we think about scribal orthographies and their role in standardization. Among other things, Wright (2020a: 12–13) stresses the decentralized character of standardization processes, pointing to "[s]upralocal centres all over England, not specifically East or Central Midlands, not specifically London" (Wright 2020a: 12). Factors such as the pragmatics of the usage, different genres of writing, community dynamics (as in Moore 2019) and the multilingual context of language use in fourteenth- and fifteenth-century England are all highlighted as crucial aspects to consider in charting standardization processes. Emphasizing the openness and fluidity of the notion, but at the same time acknowledging the scholarly need for a crystallization of the new conceptualization, Wright (2020a: 13) offers the following formulation of the standardization of English:

> Over the fourteenth century, living standards rose, enabling a new class of people to find their voice. Monolingual English, shaped by its Anglo-Norman antecedent, was the written record of the trading classes.

21.5 Beyond Spelling

Much of my earlier discussion has focused on one aspect of orthography: spelling. This is to some extent natural and by necessity: most of the studies of orthography pertain to scribal patterns of spelling, while scribal punctuation,

[9] The connection of this framing to later standardization processes, such as the more widespread adoption of a 'Chancery standard', is less clear; most of Moore's (2019: 129) discussion focuses on "incipient standardization."

abbreviation, capitalization, word division and similar features have not been studied systematically and to the same extent. Investigation into the latter aspects of orthography has no doubt been hampered by modern editors often modernizing or normalizing such 'accidentals' in their editions (as in the case of most volumes of the *Early English Text Society*, which publishes the bulk of editions of Middle English and to some extent Old English works). That does not mean that aspects such as abbreviations and word division are unstudied, but they are usually approached on the basis of individual texts or manuscripts (e.g. Parkes 1997, Calle-Martín 2004). Despite such focused work, we lack a more general sense of how various scribes worked with and developed orthographic systems in this respect. A great deal of information can be gleaned from manuals of paleography and work on book history (e.g. Tannenbaum 1930, Parkes 1993 [1992]). At the same time, the broader representativeness of the descriptions is often unclear, as are the connections to scribes in particular. Furthermore, some of this work is not necessarily focused on English, which obscures particularly English patterns. However, this multilingual focus reminds us that many of the scribes wrote in several languages and were thus exposed to, generally familiar with, and hence likely to adopt cross-linguistic uses, if the scribes ever made a clear-cut distinction. Indeed, while much work on English orthography (and spelling in particular) is undertaken in isolation from other languages, the interaction of such languages and the multilingual context in which many scribes worked (especially in the Middle Ages) should not be forgotten, as research by Wright and others highlights (e.g. Wright 1996, 2020a, 2020b).

Recent work has pointed to new avenues and methods for the study of scribal orthography, especially features beyond spelling. Corpus linguistic and statistical approaches may hold great promise in this regard. Adopting such approaches, Honkapohja (2017, 2019) demonstrates that, rather than being haphazard and accidental, scribes' use of abbreviations are clearly influenced by factors such as language, types of text and type of word abbreviated. A desideratum is obviously more corpora and text databases that reliably reflect the use of the manuscripts and hence scribal usage in order to facilitate this kind of systematic approach. We are also starting to see more emphasis on the interaction of orthography with other types of textual features. Carroll et al. (2013) indicate how orthography overlaps with or is implicated in broader patterns of scribal practices. Such practices include rubrication, use of colors, line division, overall layout and so on, in addition to the use of punctuation marks (such as paraphs '⁋') and capitalization. These features perform various interlinked pragmatic, textual and interpersonal functions in manuscripts, and can be manipulated for different audiences or purposes (see also Varila et al. 2017 and contributions therein).

Finally, despite already receiving considerable attention, the question of orthographic regularization and standardization continues to be widely debated. As indicated by the sources cited in Section 21.4, it remains unclear how to understand various stages of regularization and whether and, if so, how to apply the concepts of standard and standardization to them (see also Smith 1996: 70). Moore's (2019) CoP perspective seems to offer a new way of thinking about the negotiation and selection of orthographic variants leading to regularized and possibly standardized use, and future applications of this framework to specific cases hold great promise. And the avenues opened up by Wright (2020a, 2020b) will no doubt encourage a new generation of research that takes a closer look at new features and genres to chart the dynamics of the 'living standards' of the fourteenth and fifteenth centuries and beyond.

21.6 Conclusion

This chapter has overviewed key concepts and major trends in scholarship on scribal practices connected to orthography (primarily in the sense of spelling). It has highlighted the crucial interdisciplinary nature of studying linguistic aspects of orthography, as social history and materiality (e.g. aspects of handwriting and manuscript production) play crucial roles in variation and change in orthographic systems. We have seen how spelling is studied from a variety of interrelated perspectives (as a means to get to phonological/phonetic variation and change as well as a linguistic domain with its own set of dynamics, irrespective of possible pronunciation connections). Scribal patterns of orthography are also implicated in larger trends of regularization, supralocalization and standardization of the English language. The scholarly narrative of these processes has shifted considerably over time, as new approaches, foci and materials have emerged.

Although much of our narrative about early English orthography is dependent on scribal evidence, we know frustratingly little about the identity, training and working conditions of these scribes. This is information that would help us understand some of the social and pragmatic motivations of their orthographic choices. At the same time, an increasing number of detailed accounts of scribal practices are providing us with new and more richly contextualized accounts (e.g. contributions in Wright 2020b). We may still never be able to access key sociolinguistic information for individual scribes, but we are getting a better sense of their milieu, their roles and engagement within local communities, and their participation in and contribution to broader trends involving all kinds of writers especially from the fourteenth century onward.

22

Orthographic Norms and Authorities

Carol Percy

22.1 Introduction

This chapter contextualizes conflicts over orthographies relating to the formation of late modern nations from the end of the eighteenth through the nineteenth centuries. A common language was one example of the imagined cultural distinctiveness that often inspired or justified the building of what has been called a *nation-state*, "an independent political state formed from a people who share a common national identity (historically, culturally, or ethnically)" (Hobsbawm 1992: 11–12, 21–22, 37, "nation-state, n." in the *Oxford English Dictionary Online*, Simpson and Proffitt 2000–). Yet a common language is rarely the defining characteristic of a state. National boundaries commonly contain a linguistically heterogeneous populace. State formation can be seen as a process in which such linguistic differences are erased. Orthographic conflicts inevitably arise as a common language is cultivated and imposed.

Historically, language policies and politics sometimes interacted in tandem (Hobsbawm 1992: 10, 21, Wright 2012). In early modern Europe, a 1539 Ordinance decreed French to be the sole administrative language of the kingdom of France, as its political unification continued (Rickard 1989: 81, 83); in 1714, Castilian Spanish was declared the language of Spain, after its borders had been established in the previous century with Portugal and with France (García 2011: 670). In the nineteenth century, citizens might be imaginatively unified while reading historical texts (Anderson 2006), or managed through

I am grateful for the patient assistance of our co-editors and for the resources of the University of Toronto Library, especially for librarians Graham Bradshaw, Graeme Slaght and Benjamin Walsh, and for the pandemic curbside service and Hathi Trust subscription. I have learned a great deal from Fatemeh Khavaninzadeh and Samantha Pong, my two RAs funded by the University of Toronto Work-Study program. Thanks also to David Clandfield, Juan Camilo Conde-Silvestre, Ana Deumert, Stefan Dollinger, Andrew Hope, Nils Langer, John Percy, Yannick Portebois, Keren Rice, Matthew Risling, Gijsbert Rutten, Jeremy Smith and Jessica Warner.

mass schooling and the printing press in a national language. I interpret consequent conflicts over orthographic norms through both linguistic and social perspectives (e.g. Sebba 2009). First, different orthographies can facilitate different practices of literacy (e.g. Seifart 2008: 287). Second, the choice of script, of character, of symbol–sound correspondences and/or of word spellings can express multiple group and individual identities. Finally, once any orthographic norms exist, change is inevitably resisted by most literate adults who have learned them: according to Fishman (1977: xvi), "the greater and grander the tradition of literacy, literature, and liturgy in an orthographic community, the less likely that even minor systematic orthographic change will be freely accepted and the less likely that any orthographic change will be considered minor."

I begin this chapter by categorizing some of the orthographic traditions inherited by nation-states: (re)forming national orthographies might involve replacing traditional orthographies associated with authoritative religious or literary or administrative vernacular texts. I sketch some typical tensions between more etymological and more phonemic orthographies, tensions often reflecting their typical origins and functions.

In the chapter's core, I use a structure that highlights such 'agents' or 'engines' of change, both internal (e.g. educators) and external (e.g. transnational academies) to states (see further Ó Ciosáin 2004: 6–8). The production of orthographic 'authority' has been linked with typical 'discourse fields', for instance pedagogical and political (Sebba 2009: 41). I relate such norm-forming discourses to agents' aims, finding orthographic correlates to group identities. The authorities surveyed in this chapter are illustrated with reference to several nineteenth-century national languages that 'unified' traditionally or historically multilingual regions or that became independent from empires. Examples include French, Norwegian and Russian, as well as transnational varieties of Dutch, English, German and Spanish.

This thematically organized chapter also draws on and consolidates what I hope will be useful resources for scholars investigating other periods, languages and regions. Some early modern foundations are laid for communities (Burke 2004: 89–110), Academy dictionaries (Considine 2014) and orthographies (Baddeley and Voeste 2012b), while a range of influential case studies are edited by Fishman (1977) and by Jaffe et al. (2012), and abstracted by Sebba (2007). Baker surveys numerous 'Problems and solutions' in 'Developing ways of writing vernaculars' (Baker 1997), while SIL International (2022) on its page about 'Orthography' provides links to subpages with bibliographies that are both topical and regional. And two chapters available in Spolsky's handbook of language policy (Spolsky 2012), namely those written by Coulmas and Guerrini, and Edwards, respectively, intersect historical and theoretical features of 'Writing reform' and 'Language management agencies' worldwide.

22.1.1 Conflicting Orthographic Norms: Focus on Functions

Traditional orthographic practices might reflect dialect variation within what would only later become nation-states, and/or perhaps the influences of foreign languages, whether Latin or vernacular. Dialects acquired supraregional status for a variety of reasons – more political in the case of Parisian French and Castilian Spanish; more literary in the case of Tuscan (Burke 2004: 97–8). For these Romance vernaculars, etymologically Latinate orthographies were sometimes inevitably developed by bilingual mediators. In Renaissance Venice, for example, from 1494 the printer Aldus Manutius affirmed the status of Tuscan vernacular literature – which he printed with the care and occasionally with some spelling conventions of Classical Latin, such as the etymological <h>, <t> rather than <c> in words like *giustitia*, and the use of <u> as both consonant and vowel (Burke 2004: 106–7, Michel 2012: 70–73). In premodern Scandinavia, German and Latin had sometimes served as languages of administration and of learning (Kristiansen 2003: 69–70, 80, Pettersson 2019: 139). Thus in Denmark, contemporary readers of the first (1524) translation in Scandinavia of the Christian New Testament complained about orthographic instability and the influence of both Latin and German (Pettersson 2019: 135), the latter likely reflecting at least the perceived influence of Martin Luther.

In Protestant Europe, a number of Bible translations mixed regional writing traditions: translators sought to accommodate and reach many people. Before standardization, writing traditions of "particular communities of practice" were generally "transmitted through the activities" of those groups (Smith 2020a: 25). Luther claimed to use 'general German', the East Upper (southern) German of the Habsburg chancery, while also drawing on another, pre-existing model, the East Central German of the Saxon chancery (Mattheier 2003: 216–17, Burke 2004: 101–2). The 1529 Danish translation of the New Testament was addressed to an audience of "alle Danske, Suenske oc Norske" "perhaps [...] to expand the possible market of the translation" (Berg 2016: 45); the translator Christiern Pedersen is also said to have removed unnecessary letters and reduced variability (Kristiansen 2003: 75–76). In newly independent Sweden, King Gustav's 1541 Bible drew on the western dialects of the translation committee members as well as written traditions from a southern religious center (Teleman 2003: 408–9); it simultaneously minimized "Danish traces" (Berg 2016: 46). Likewise, the 1637 *Statenbijbel* of the Dutch Republic blended northern and southern writing traditions to capitalize on the 1581 secession of northern provinces from Catholic Spain (Willemyns 2003: 100).

In the Low Countries and Geneva, Protestant printers perpetuated the phonemic spellings of French that sixteenth-century poets as well as Protestants had proposed; after the St. Bartholomew's Day Massacre of 1572, printers among other French Protestants had gone abroad (Baddeley 2012: 107–15).

According to Rickard, it was the influence of their imported foreign publications of French that provoked the intervention of the Académie Française in the seventeenth century (Rickard 1989: 107). Modern French orthography is more etymological, while Italian and especially Spanish principles are more phonemic, as the Spanish spelling of *ortografía* attests: in contrast, French *orthographe* uses <th> for /t/ and <ph> for /f/ (Llamas-Pombo 2012: 15). Among some remaining etymological spellings in Spanish are (as in French) silent <h> in words like *hoy* 'day' and the digraph <qu> in *que* (Llamas-Pombo 2012: 51), with ongoing debate about "learned consonant groups" (Tacke 2020: 570–71).

Standardized orthographies are useful for teaching (Stebbins 2001: 185), at least in Western settings. But standardization intensifies the power of orthographic elements to mark boundaries, difference and belonging (Sebba 2009: 39–41). For Gal (2018: 224), standardization is "a semiotic process operating through axes of differentiation." Language standards evoke universality, anonymity, progress and rationality, and oppose particularity, authenticity, tradition and emotion. Yet groups and individuals can have multiple relational identities, especially in 'minority' and/or postcolonial contexts. Efforts to reform existing orthographies might be resisted for various reasons.

The relative advantages and disadvantages of more etymological and more phonemic orthographies have been particularly considered by codifiers of unwritten and endangered languages (e.g. Smalley 1959, Baker 1997, Seifart 2008). More etymological (or "morphographic" or "deep") orthographies can more easily represent multiple dialects of a single language (Seifart 2008: 287), as well as reflecting relationships between otherwise differently pronounced words such as French *enfant* /ãfã/ and *enfanter* /ãfãte/ or English *reduce* and *reduction*; such orthographies are particularly useful for languages like English with many such "morphophonological changes" (Seifart 2008: 279). Deep orthographies are also cognitively easier for advanced readers to process (Seifart 2008: 282). In contrast, more phonemic or "shallow" orthographies are easier for beginning readers and for beginning writers, and for nonnative or nonfluent speakers (Seifart 2008: 283, 287). Yet proposals for new orthographies may be resisted by educated individuals with investments in traditional orthographies. Additional factors must be considered when developing orthographies for unwritten languages. In a still-influential article on developing writing systems for the latter, the missionary William Smalley ranks conflicts among criteria: "acceptance" by "the learner" and "society" precedes "maximum representation of speech," "ease of learning," "reproduction" and "transfer" to the dominant language (1959: 52–53). In a lengthy essay on 'Developing ways of writing vernaculars', Baker surveys numerous 'Problems and solutions in a historical perspective' (1997: 93).

Would-be orthographic innovators must remember that various elements of spelling have identity functions for individuals and groups, representing social as well as linguistic concepts at many levels (Sebba 2009: 39–41). Particular scripts can be linked with religions, often for political reasons (see further Coulmas 2003: 201–3, Spolsky 2009b, Pharo 2015). The Roman alphabet became initially associated with Christianity, for instance, along with the Latin it originally encoded (Coulmas 2003: 201). Canonical texts often symbolize a tradition, even when their orthographies have changed. For instance, the idea of Martin Luther's influence on Standard German remains powerful, although his texts have not directly influenced "actual language behaviour" since the seventeenth century (Mattheier 2003: 221) and his own later orthography was likely influenced greatly by his printers, for instance with respect to "increased (but not complete) capitalization" (Young and Gloning 2004: 215). And citations from literary authors like Miguel de Cervantes were so central to the first dictionary published by the Real Academia Española (RAE) (1726–39) that it would subsequently become known as the *Diccionario de autoridades* 'authorities' (Considine 2014: 115), although the spelling of *Don Quixote* would change from an <x> to a <j> with the eighth edition of the *Ortografía* (RAE 1815). Finally, characters, diacritics and spellings can also acquire group-specific meanings. In Spain, for instance, the 1815 *Ortografía* also banished from the Spanish alphabet the <k> found in some loanwords, though this elimination was only temporary (Tacke 2020: 572). And within and beyond Spain, "various subcultural groups" substitute <k> for Standard Spanish <c> or <qu> (Sebba 2007: 129); indeed, in other "places colonized by 'Latin' languages (and peoples associated with them) [...] a kind of orthographic nationalism and decolonization has been brought to us by the letter 'k'" (Thomas 2007: 964). In this chapter, I use the term 'orthographies' for the conventional correspondence of symbol (<c> or <k>) to sound (/k/) in a particular language, restricting the term 'spelling' to particular words (Dutch *cultuur* or Afrikaans *kultuur*).

22.1.2 Establishing Authorities: Theory and Practice

This section introduces representative human and institutional authorities who endeavored to form or reform orthographic norms in modern times. Once established, norms are difficult to dislodge. In the past, as Fishman famously observed, reformers had to contend with the "gatekeepers of written tradition, the poets, priests, principals and professors, with the institutions and symbols that they create and serve" (Fishman 1977: xvi; see also Geerts et al. 1977: 206). More recently, the public have increased in prominence and influence in linguistic debates. Gal and Woolard (2014 [2001a]: 7) "unpack" and "extend" the concept of the public: essential to their argument is the complex coexistence of an "authority of anonymity in the public sphere" with "an authority of authenticity" from "voices competing for recognition as the embodiment of a particular community." Context is crucial: the 'same' kinds of agents might promote different literacies. Unlike Fishman's poet-gatekeepers, for instance, some early modern poets resisted existing systems: in pro-Reformation Lyon, for instance, poets as well as printers hoped that more phonemic spelling would facilitate reading (Baddeley 2012: 113). And educators look forward as well as backward. Some promoted more phonemic spelling in the service of literacy instruction rather than defend the traditional spelling whose mastery is the source of their status: in seventeenth-century England, the schoolmaster Charles Butler rejected the Latin positional distribution of <u>/<v> and <i>/<j> and recommended that the graphs distinguish vowels (<i> and <u>) and consonants (<j> and <v>, Rutkowska 2016: 171; see also Condorelli 2021a: 811).

Even with digital resources, influence and authority are difficult to quantify. Butler's list of homophones was much plagiarized by later codifiers (Salmon 1999: 14). Yet the relationship between textbooks and texts has remained what Rutkowska acknowledges is a "chicken-and-egg" problem: texts before Butler used <i> and <u> as vowels, and if he did exert additional influence on later printers it was "not" "sudden" (Rutkowska 2016: 187; see also Chapter 13, this volume). In their big-data corpus study of the spelling of specific suffixes, Berg and Aronoff conclude with confidence that "[t]hroughout this entire period, there is no evidence of an external authority having any influence" (Berg and Aronoff 2017: 62). More recently, in his thorough survey of <i> and <u> Condorelli has recently concluded that their "large-scale standardisation developments [...] were not so much animated by intellectual debates on the English language, but rather they were dependent on professional and historical dynamics that affected the printing industry" (Condorelli 2021a: 800).

Can linguistic authority derive from either tradition (e.g. etymological orthography) and/or reason (e.g. phonemic orthography)? Some studies of language policy have used Weber's theories of political authority to explain how individual decisions have social impact (e.g. Cooper 1989: 173–75). In 'Politiks als Beruf' (1919), Weber conceptualized authority as tripartite: arising from traditional "custom," individual "charisma" and/or bureaucratic "legality" (Weber 2004 [1919]: 34) – with the latter authority ideally dominant in modern industrialized societies (Sica 2012). Writing specifically about "the basis for orthography selection," Eira (1998: 172) characterized it as "fundamentally a question of the location of authority, which is in turn a function of the prevailing discourses." While Eira identifies six discourses, Sebba (2007: 139–54) transforms these in his own work: Eira's "scientific, political, religious, technological, historical, and pedagogical" become "modernisation, globalisation and technology," "belonging, unity and separation," "cultural heritage: creation myths, history, permanence and decline," "economic," "pedagogical" and "prescription and optionality: the discourse of conformity." Edwards argues that any "language management agencies" must be seen as "points on continua of activity and attitude, and not as independent bodies whose workings can be understood in isolation" (Edwards 2012: 419).

Authority is difficult to theorize in part because "[l]anguage planning [...] encompass[es] virtually all aspects of the social life of language" (Edwards 2012: 432). Analyses of orthographic conflicts inevitably embed specific arguments and outcomes in their cultural contexts. In a widely cited study of 'Successes and failures in Dutch spelling reform', Geerts et al. (1977: 201–6) identify some of the arguments as group-specific – emotional and objective, anti-reform and pro-, general and *Belgian* (my emphasis). Arguments about orthographies "are really debates about the values held by opposing groups in society" and thus "at the deepest level, studies of identity" (Edwards 2012: 436). One essential question for every contest is "Why [...] now?" (Edwards 2012: 428). While this chapter is structured to find cross-cultural similarities among different kinds of agents and agencies, its content also and especially stresses the inevitable importance of context.

22.2 Creating Citizens of Nation-states

22.2.1 Overview

This section surveys typical conflicts over orthographic norms that follow the emergence of nation-states. The codification of norms often accompanies the consolidation of heterogeneous territories, as with the unification of Germany in 1871. In other cases, dissociations from different and/or multilingual empires generated efforts to align the new political boundary with a distinctive national language: representative countries include Chile (1810) and Norway (1814). Yet newly self-governing countries were usually multilingual, especially colonial regimes.

Corresponding orthographic conflicts reflect these political trends, although every political entity has a unique linguistic ecology. Pronunciation continued to diverge from traditional spellings, as in the past. Newly independent nations often considered spellings that differed from the mother country. Postcolonial Hispanic orthographies, for instance, have gone through divergence and reunification, while languages such as Flemish in Belgium have also secured status through transnational standards. Many nations consolidated standards through the nineteenth century to improve mass literacy – a particular challenge in multilingual countries. Such standardization is frequently controversial. Despite support from elementary educators, simplified spellings were often resisted by intellectuals and mocked in the press. Simplified spelling succeeded mostly in countries with low literacy rates and/or authoritarian governments such as the Union of Soviet Socialist Republics or the People's Republic of China (Coulmas and Guerini 2012: 450–52).

22.2.2 Individuals

Schoolmaster and lexicographer Noah Webster exerted some influence on American spelling after the American War of Independence (1775–83), though the process was slower and less radical than generally believed. He suggested drastic reforms in an appendix to his *Grammatical Institute* (1783–85) and more moderate ones in his *Compendious Dictionary of the English Language* (1806). These include more phonemic spellings of words such as *theatre* and omitting the superfluous <u> from words such as *honour*, which he saw as a vestige of the Norman oppression of England and by extension the British oppression of America (Webster 1806: viii–ix). Webster's self-positioning relative to Samuel Johnson shows the potential authority of lexicographers. Yet despite Webster's reforms being mocked in the press (Martin 2019: 33–34, 48, 112–20), many spellings that were codified in his magisterial *American Dictionary of the English Language* (1828) were eventually accepted but implemented at different rates (Venezky 2001: 345, Cummings 2016: 278–81, Mair 2019: 340–43) and likely in part through the influence of subsequent lexicographers (Martin 2019: 192–93) and newspapers (Anson 1990: 47).

The individuals who exerted the most immediate authority in establishing norms were those channeling the interests of the state. In the wake of the French Revolution, a Dutch popular movement overthrew the ruler of the confederated provinces and promoted national unity and democracy. Matthijs Siegenbeek, the first professor of the Dutch language at Leiden University (from 1797 to 1847) codified orthographic norms in 1804. Siegenbeek's treatise reflected his government's desire to nationalize education policy and was commissioned and "recommended for educational and governmental use" by the newly appointed Minister of National Education in the Batavian Republic (Geerts et al. 1977: 184). State support and his status as school inspector ensured his system's influence at that time, although his etymological distinction of the pronunciation of certain long vowels departed from earlier textbooks (Rutten et al. 2020: 266–77). Flemish populations increasingly contested Siegenbeek's spellings when they were imposed after the unification of the northern and southern provinces in 1814, and in 1830 when Belgium became independent (Geerts et al. 1977: 184–85).

After Denmark ceded Norway to Sweden (1814), contrasting linguistic and literary discourses would eventually result in two conflicting standards in Norway (see also Chapter 24), now known as Bokmål (literally 'book language', based on the old Danish system) and Nynorsk ('New Norwegian', with a newly created spelling system). Beginning in 1845, the headmaster Knud Knudsen promoted a minimally localized version of written Danish which was recognized in 1862 by an official orthographic reform that resulted in 'Dano-Norwegian', which was virtually identical with written Danish. From the 1850s, Ivar Aasen promoted a composite of the rural western dialects he had codified in a *Grammar* (1848) and *Dictionary* (1850). He encouraged the use of what he called Landsmaal 'rural country language' by writing a play, *Ervingen* (1855), and songs (1863). Aasen's Landsmaal standard and Knudsen's Dano-Norwegian both gained official status as a compromise solution in 1885, the year after the King's cabinet was dismissed by Parliament, and were mandated in schools by 1892, the same year in which Elias Blix's 1869 Landsmaal hymnal (Blix 1869) was authorized for churches. Other dialects, such as the urban working class, were unsuccessfully proposed as a single 'Samnorsk', literally 'levelled Norwegian', alternative to the conflicting authorities of educated cosmopolitans and illiterate peasants (Jahr 2014: 35–67, 81–89).

In the nineteenth century, such developments were seen not only in northern climes but also in southern spheres. Chile's bid for political independence, declared in 1810 and finally recognized by Spain in 1844, had inspired Venezuelan expatriate Andrés Bello to help found a Chilean university in 1842 as one stage toward planning a national public education system. This nation-building vision included a simplified orthography that would "embody, in writing, American liberation from Spain" and American pronunciation by eliminating <z> and replacing it with <s> (Villa 2015: 237), proposed by Argentinian exile Domingo Faustino Sarmiento, but which, repeating a familiar pattern, was opposed by Spanish sympathizers and conservative intellectuals (Villa 2015: 235–39). Bello had co-authored a somewhat more moderate proposal in the 1820s while in London advocating for his own newly independent homeland: this proposal was first published in 1823 (Bello and García del Río 1826 [1823]). Reflecting what Villa (2015: 239) describes as the "political and symbolic power in the education system and intellectual circles" of Bello's, elements of Bello and García del Río's more moderate orthography were recommended by the university to the government: these included eliminating silent <h> and <u> in words like *hilo* 'thread' and *queso* 'cheese' (Villa 2015: 233, 238). Bello's spelling accounted for most of the orthographic reforms introduced not only to newly independent Chile from 1844 but also to some other Spanish American nations – very fleetingly. The year 1844 also saw the Royal Decrees mandating "the exclusive use" of the RAE's orthographic rules in Spain (Villa 2013: 96). Academies and central states both had a vested interest in creating and enforcing universal standards. Indeed, through the nineteenth century the Academy spelling was progressively readopted through Latin America; Chile was the final country to comply, in 1927 (Llamas-Pombo 2012: 18).

22.2.3 Academies and Congresses

Many nation-states attempted to strengthen central authority through primary and public education, drawing on the resources of governments and academies. At least in theory, language was to be both instrument and symbol of national centralization and, with it, linguistic assimilation of minorities: "French was essential to the concept of France, even though in 1789 50% of Frenchmen did not speak it at all, only 12–13% spoke it 'correctly' – and indeed outside a central region [...] In northern and southern France virtually nobody talked French" (Hobsbawm 1992: 60, Weber 1976: 67–69). It is widely believed that the sixth edition of the *Dictionnaire de l'*Académie française (1835) set the orthographic standard, with an 1832 Decree making its norms official through public education and state examinations for public servants (Rickard 1989: 121). The 1832 Decree has been challenged as a 'myth', invented in the 1970s to resist reform and entrench authority (reported by Hemming 1993: 76–77, Sebba 2007: 146). The Academy's sixth dictionary registered and entrenched some changes reflecting pronunciation: in words like *français*, the <ai> spelling replaced <oi> when it represented /ɛ/. Other changes reflected the tendency in French to represent etymology and analogy: the plural noun *enfans* became *enfants* to correspond to the singular *enfant* and to the verb *enfanter*. And the dictionary's past authority is suggested by its popularity with pirating lexicographers: Nadeau and Barlow report four unauthorized abridgments in 1836 and 1837 alone (Nadeau and Barlow 2006: 178, 182).

The expansion of state education could cause conflicts between the state and its educators – and others. In the 1840s, the RAE rejected educators' calls for a simplified, phonemic orthography (Villa 2013: 95). Queen Isabella II endorsed the Academy's authority in 1844 when she signed a mandate for the use of RAE norms in elementary schools (Villa 2013: 96). Villa (2013: 93–98, 102–5) reports that the orthographic conflict reflected a larger one about teacher training and school administration. In Chile, at the same time, Sarmiento's promotion of simplified spelling was politically as well as pedagogically motivated (Villa 2015: 239). During this period, committees and conferences regularly convened to adjudicate orthographic norms. After unification in 1871, Germany made standardization a priority across numerous areas including education (Johnson 2005: 19). An 1876 conference involving educators, printers and linguists, and attended by representatives from Austria as well as the German states, reached a broad consensus to resolve variation among historical, regional and foreign orthographic conventions, though according to Johnson issues like capitalization were too controversial (Johnson 2005: 21). Among recommendations reached were the replacement of <th> by <t> in words like *Theil* → *Teil* 'part' and <c> by <k> or <z> in foreign words like *Classe* → *Klasse* and *Medicin* → *Medizin* (Johnson 2005: 21). Despite the linguistic authority of the delegates, their modest compromise between history and pronunciation was ultimately criticized by many journalists and thus also abandoned by the chancellor, Bismarck (Johnson 2005: 22); German provinces (*Länder*) "continued to issue their own orthographic dictionaries" (Dollinger 2019b: 19). As usual in such cases, objections were not only linguistic but political: journalists doubted the state's authority and demanded more public consultation.

A second conference was held in 1901, three years after Bismarck's death, and (reflecting its ultimately political impetus) involving fewer academics but still including some schoolteachers and a few representatives of the book trade among more regional politicians (Johnson 2005: 22–26). Standardizing a national language had implications elsewhere on its dialect continuum – that is to say, in other nations or regions. Indeed, from the late eighteenth century, Austria's distinctive written Imperial Standard had already begun to "invisibilize," to disappear from the written domain "even though it continued to be used and passed on to future generations in speech" (Havinga 2018: 1) when Empress Maria Theresa (1717–80, reigned 1740–80) appointed professors of German at diplomatic academies and universities and, with the aid of educational advisor Johann Ignaz von Felbiger (1724–88), introduced compulsory education in 1774 based on the East Central German norm (Havinga 2018, Dollinger 2019b: 17–18). The institutions of empire gave authority and influence to a woman and to a postmaster's son, the Empress and von Felbiger (Havinga 2018: 73). Until 1866, the nations that are currently Austria and Germany had shared a history as well as a language as territories in the Holy Roman Empire (dissolved in 1806) and subsequently the German Confederation (1815–66). But with the political split of the German-speaking areas into three political unities – the German Empire (unified under Prussia from 1871), Austria (as of 1919 as a republic) and Switzerland (as the consensual federation par excellence) – the German language situation became potentially complex.

For a lower-status language like Flemish in Belgium, the authority of transnational associations eventually proved tempting. After the newly independent kingdom of Belgium seceded from the United Kingdom of the Netherlands (1830), the Siegenbeek spelling of Dutch seemed particularly northern and Protestant (Geerts et al. 1977: 185–86). The difficulty of achieving consensus on a successor spelling model is evident from the rejection of all the competition entries by a government-appointed committee. The appeal of traditional spelling is demonstrated by the similarity to the Siegenbeek spelling of the committee's own counterproposal (1839), which got royal assent in 1844. Indeed, at an 1849 Congress at the University of Ghent, delegates from north and south laid out plans for a Dutch dictionary and orthography, the *Woordenboek der Nederlandsche Taal* (De Vries and Te Winkel 1864–2001). Continuing until 1912, the congresses provided contact and support from the Netherlands if the status of Dutch relative to French in Belgium was in danger of decreasing (Geerts et al. 1977: 185–86, Willemyns 2003: 102–7).

22.2.4 Lexicographers

State support greatly increased lexicographers' authority in codifying spelling norms. Linguists De Vries and Te Winkel began to compose the *Woordenboek der Nederlandsche Taal* (1864–2001) supported by two governments. Written in the tradition of the Grimms' historical dictionary of German, the dictionary itself was not completed before 1998 (with supplements in 2001) and after about 150 years; the spelling of its title ([...] *Nederlandsche Taal*) thus reflects past rather than contemporary conventions (Haß 2019: 479). Te Winkel had codified an orthography for the project in 1863, *De grondbeginselen der Nederlandsche spelling: ontwerp der spelling voor het aanstaande Nederlandsch Woordenboek*, and a royal decree established it in Belgium shortly thereafter (Geerts et al. 1977: 186, Willemyns 2003: 107). De Vries and Te Winkel by and large followed Siegenbeek, but there were a few noticeable differences: Siegenbeek's *magt* 'power' and *zaaijen* 'sow' became *macht* and *zaaien* respectively in De Vries and Te Winkel (van der Wal and Van Bree 2008: 318). In the Netherlands, the authority of the Siegenbeek spelling and authors' general fondness for their individual spellings delayed the acceptance of what would become known as the De Vries and Te Winkel spelling (1866), and conservatism slowed its eventual dissemination after its use for the King's speech in 1883. Geerts et al. (1977: 189–90) attribute its eventual acceptance not to royalty but educators. Of course, codifiers could also be opposed to the state. Around the 1880–81 war for independence, discussions of orthography in South Africa reflected resistance to (the) British as well as internal debates about the relationship between Dutch and Afrikaans: one domain of contention was religious (Willemyns 2013: 222). The *Genootskap van Regte Afrikaners* (est. 1875) promoted the use of written Afrikaans "in public domains hitherto reserved for English or Dutch" (Roberge 2003: 26) and in their *Eerste beginsels* 'First principles' of Afrikaans (1876) spelling that reflected Afrikaaner pronunciation: "Ons skryf ni *sch*, mar *sk*. Een Afrikaander seg nie *sch*ool, mar *sk*ool; nie *sch*apen, mar *sk*ape" [We write not *sch* but *sk*. An Afrikaner says not *sch*ool but *sk*ool; not *sch*apen but *sk*ape] (Du Toit 1876: 10, quoted by Roberge 2003: 27).

Some educators became influential lexicographers as vernacular norms were increasingly taught in state schools. The French schoolteacher Pierre Larousse published what Nadeau and Barlow (2006: 177) deem "the first full method for teaching French grammar and spelling ever published," the *Lexicologie des écoles primaires* (1850); his *Nouveau dictionnaire de la langue française* (1856) heralded the "virtual monopoly in schools" of smaller dictionaries published from the Larousse publishing house (Nadeau and Barlow 2006: 177). In Germany, teachers from different regions published their own orthographies, which exacerbated the lack of standardization. Duden savvily based his 1880 dictionary, *Vollständiges Orthographisches Wörterbuch der deutschen Sprache von Duden Konrad: Nach den neuen preußischen und bayerischen Regeln*, on the set of guidelines from the first Orthographic Conference from 1876, which were heavily influenced by the 'Prussian School Orthography' (Königliches Ministerium der geistlichen, Unterrichts- und Medizinal-Angelegenheiten

1880), "a specific set of guidelines for schools in Prussia" commissioned by the Prussian Minister for Education and Culture and introduced in 1880 (Johnson 2005: 22). Several German states and Austria continued to issue their own spellers, however. The press complained about the imposed guidelines, but by the Orthographic Conference in 1901, Duden's dictionary had become a *de facto* authority even in Switzerland and Austria. However, there were limits on this influence: until 1911, the German Kaiser Wilhelm II (along with anyone directly corresponding with him) was exempt from the 1902 spelling reform, which included "the shift from <th> to <t> in most words perceived to be of German origin" (Johnson 2005: 24–25; see also Mattheier 2003: 228–29, Johnson 2005: 22–26, Dollinger 2019b: 19–20) – so <th> remains in words like *Orthografie* [ɔrtograˈfiː]. And according to Dollinger (2019b: 19), "[a]fter the second conference, orthographic differences remained largely in the integration of loanwords, where the southern German states continued, against their political affiliation, to follow Austria's lead of integrating loanwords to a much lesser degree than in Prussia." By 1926, Austrian opposition was voiced by as prominent a man as Ludwig Wittgenstein in form of a school dictionary highlighting Austrian variants, the *Wörterbuch für Volks- und Bürgerschulen* (Dollinger 2019b: 19). By 1951, the *Österreichisches Wörterbuch* superseded Duden in Austria as the officially sanctioned dictionary for schools and government, much to the chagrin of German lexicographers and the press alike, which continues to this day (Dollinger 2019b: 39).

Establishing norms for transnational languages also challenged codifiers of Spanish: language remained as a legacy in its liberated colonies in America. In 1870, the Real Academia Española sought to strengthen central authority by supporting 'subsidiary' academies in Spanish America. In Mexico, related newspaper debates included the patriotism associated with its pre-existing academy and the status and spelling of local and especially Indigenous words. For instance, the local spelling of *México* (from Nahuatl) departed from the RAE's recommended *Méjico*. A first fruit of international collaboration was the twelfth edition of the Academy dictionary, the *Diccionario de la lengua castellana por la* Real Academia Española (1884), which according to Cifuentes (2013: 177) included about half the suggestions by the Mexican subsidiary (there spelled the Spanish way as *Academia Mejicana*, see Real Academia Española 1884: xiv). Provincialisms were slow to pervade normative texts, but pan-Hispanism appealed to educated elites in recently liberated nations. It appealed to tradition and unified the southern nations against the hegemonic English of the United States (Cifuentes 2013: 180).

22.2.5 Educators

Competing visions of education often reflect broader conflicts among teachers, politicians and other stakeholders. In late nineteenth-century France, contention over spelling recapitulated political divisions in the Third Republic. By 1889, these surfaced when philologists, teacher unions and secularists signed petitions to the Académie française supporting orthographic reform (Catach 1999 [1985]: 239). In 1891, the Ministry of Public Instruction joined the fray with a circular introducing the concept of *tolérances* for certain kinds of errors in classroom *dictées* and state examinations. In 1893, a retired senior educational administrator and distinguished *Académicien*, Octave Gréard, presented a *Note* to the Academy's Dictionary Committee recommending revisions in favor of spelling consistency (Arrivé 1994: 69). Examples included related words with different forms (e.g. *bonhomme* and *bonhomie*), loanwords, suffixes in *-ent/-ant*, and replacing *-x* with *-s* in noun plurals (e.g. *genoux*) (summarized by Catach 1999 [1985]: 243). The Dictionary Committee approved publication of Gréard's *Note* after protracted discussion and by a slim majority of one in the summer, when most members were absent (Catach 1999 [1985]: 243). The reaction came as the conservative *Figaro* launched an editorial campaign against the *Note*. Literary authors took sides (Catach 1999 [1985]: 240), and the full-strength Academy distanced itself from the *Note*, explaining that agreeing to its publication did not mean agreeing with its content (Arrivé 1994: 70). After further petitions, the state took a series of actions that staked out its own responsibility for spelling. In 1895–96, the Minister of Public Instruction struck a special committee which reported in 1900. A new Minister issued a decree enumerating orthographic *tolerances* and directing examiners not to penalize certain variants (Arrivé 1994: 71–72). The Academy opposed the confusion that *tolérances* would cause, but then issued a report suggesting some regularizations of spelling that might be considered, including some from the Gréard *Note*: removing plurals in *-oux*, regularizing related words (e.g. *charriot* for *chariot* by analogy with *charrette*) and suffixes in *-ciel/-tiel* (Catach 1999 [1985]: 247). Nevertheless, the existence of two authorities (Ministry and Academy) exempted both from ultimate responsibility: these proposals were not included in the next Academy dictionary, and the state's directives were never implemented (Catach 1999 [1985]: 248). This impasse reminds us of how political divisions in democratic states often inflect debates over language usage. In *belle époque* France, spelling reform took on the same weight in the national consciousness as secularized public education and the separation of Church and State (Catach 1999 [1985]: 241).

In other countries, associations of educators advocated spelling reform against the state. We have seen that a teachers' association lost the battle with the state in 1840s Spain, over orthography and more general educational issues (Villa 2013: 96–98). The United States uses only a few of the 11 and 12 simplified spellings recommended by the American Philological Association (1876) and The National Education Association (1898) – *catalog* and *program* (Yule and Yasuko 2016: 420). In the Netherlands, the teacher Kollewijn argued that pronunciation rather than etymology made spelling easier to learn. His proposal was taken seriously enough that in 1908 it was prohibited by the Dutch government (Geerts et al. 1977: 190–92). In South Africa, with lower literacy rates and less connection to tradition, a similar system would be supported by teachers, journalists and the Zuid-Afrikaansche Taalbond (South African Language Association), founded in 1890; codification of a simplified Dutch was delayed by the desire to get backing from the Netherlands, and by the Anglo-Boer War (Deumert 1999: 95–96, Steyn 2017: 234). The codification of Afrikaans helped to confirm its differentiation from Dutch. Afrikaans had been introduced as a medium of primary education in 1914 and by 1919 was supported by "the major Afrikaner teachers' organizations [...] as an instructional medium at all levels" (Roberge 2003: 31). The first edition of the South African Akademie's (est. 1909) Afrikaans orthography, *Afrikaanse woordelys en spelreëls* (1917), drew on Kollewijn's proposals (Willemyns 2013: 226): in the 1921 edition, the letter <k> for /k/ replaces <c> except for allowable variation in the words *christelik/kristelik*, *christen/kristen*, and *Christus/Kristus* (Bosman et al. 1921: x, 24, 81–82). Afrikaans "effectively superseded Dutch" when it became an official language in 1925 (Roberge 2003: 31) – and in 1933 when an Afrikaans biblical translation displaced the Statenbijbel in the Dutch Reformed churches, "the last bastion of Dutch in South Africa that Afrikaans had to conquer" (Willemyns 2013: 225).

The implementation of simplified spelling in Russia shows the insufficient influence of educators when compared to the more powerful agents of the state. Redundant symbols in the Russian alphabet were among the preoccupations of the Pedagogical Society of Russian language teachers in Moscow in the early twentieth century: the <ъ> sign "written at the end of every word ending in a hard consonant (except palatals [...])" was usually superfluous, and the three pairs of letters <ѣ> and <е>, <ѳ> and <ф>, and <и> and <i> duplicated each other phonetically, with very rare occasions to make grammatical or lexical distinctions (Comrie et al. 1996: 285). In 1903, their proposals for reform were rejected by the Russian Ministry of Education and debated in the press after some consideration by the Academy of Sciences (Comrie et al. 1996: 285). In 1912, further work by an Academy subcommission had little impact. It was only in early 1917 that a congress of secondary schoolteachers lobbied the Academy just before the monarchy fell. Although the Provisional Government's Ministry of Education was attacked by the press for accepting the Academy's suggestions in May 1917, the Bolshevik government implemented the reforms in all state and government institutions and schools in December 1917 shortly after it had taken power in October. Its success has been attributed to its ideological and practical function in combating illiteracy (Comrie et al. 1996: 286–95). The state also had the power to impose its reforms, confiscating the types for the old characters used by opposition printers, for <ъ>, <ѣ>, <ѳ>, <v> and <i> (Comrie et al. 1996: 295). More short-lived were the Roman scripts used by the Soviets to codify minority Turkic languages (Collin 2011: 52) and as many as 14 languages in Siberia, to facilitate mass literacy and education and industrialization (Grenoble and Bulatova 2018: 119, 122). In temporarily rejecting Cyrillic scripts, Collin argues that the Bolsheviks sought not only to "build general literacy" and "break the link with the Islamic Middle East" but also to appropriate the international association of the Roman alphabet for their hoped-for worldwide revolution (Collin 2011: 52). In restoring the Cyrillic scripts in the mid-1930s, Stalin might have been once again deterring connections with Turkey; in 1928, the adoption of the Roman script for Turkish reflected Atatürk's desire for links with Europe (Coulmas 2013: 114–15). Both the imposition of the Roman script in the early 1930s, and the subsequent Russifying restoration of the Cyrillic script in 1937 demonstrate Soviet politics and power as well as practical efforts to develop mass literacy (Grenoble and Bulatova 2018: 120–22).

22.2.6 The Press and Public Opinion

The press often undermined these centralizing tendencies in democratic contexts, whether by taking a stand or simply reporting dissent. In Germany, the press questioned imperial authority to reform spelling and criticized the compromise at the 1876 congress (Johnson 2005: 21–22). In France, the *Figaro* supported some academicians in mocking proposals for reform by a fellow academician and then by a minister: the minister's list of *tolérances* was modified and subsequently ignored. The importance of orthography to journalists is clear from their invited participation in commissions and congresses – in Germany and Russia, for instance – and in their role in the codification processes, for example Henry Louis Mencken in twentieth-century USA. Venezky's 2001 survey of American spelling draws extensively from the fourth edition of Mencken's *The American Language* (Mencken 1936).

The authority of the press and of public opinion is demonstrated by the eventual failure of simplified spelling in nineteenth-century Britain (Hoffman 2017) and in twentieth-century America (Zimmerman 2010). In the later nineteenth century, educators and industrialists supported simplified spelling in the interests of efficiency. In 1903, the industrialist Andrew Carnegie gave early support to a campaign for simplified spelling: he hoped that as many as 20 influential literary authors "would promise to adopt 12 condensed forms: program (instead of *programme*), tho, altho, thoro, thorofare, thru, thruout, catalog, prolog, decalog, demagog, and pedagog" (Zimmerman 2010: 370). In 1906, *the New York Times* reported supportively on the new Simplified Spelling Board and its list of "300 pruned words" (*New York Times*, April 1, 1906: 7, Zimmerman 2010: 371), and President Roosevelt in an August 1906 letter reproduced in the Board's *Simplified Spelling* printed *For the Use of Government Departments* ordered the White House printer to adopt simplified spellings ranging from *abridgment* to *wrapt* in "all Government

Simplified Spelling. 15

18. Words spelled with **s** or **z** (in the root). Rule: Choose **z**. Ex.: *Apprize, assize, comprize, raze, surprize, teazel.*

19. Words spelled with **s-** or **sc-**. Rule: Omit **c**. Ex.: *Simitar, sithe.*

20. Words spelled with or without silent **-ue**. Rule: Omit **-ue**. Ex.: *Catalog, decalog, demagog, pedagog, prolog.*

THREE HUNDRED WORDS.

Choose the simpler spelling, that at the left.

abridgment	abridgement
accouter	accoutre
accurst	accursed
acknowledgment	acknowledgement
addrest	addressed
adz	adze
affixt	affixed
altho	although
anapest	anapaest, anapæst
anemia	anaemia, anæmia
anesthesia	anaesthesia, anæsthesia
anesthetic	anaesthetic, anæsthetic
antipyrin	antipyrine
antitoxin	antitoxine
apothem	apothegm, apophthegm
apprize	apprise
arbor	arbour
archeology	archaeology, archæology
ardor	ardour
armor	armour
artizan	artisan
assize	assise
ax	axe
bans	banns
bark	barque

7401—06——3

Figure 22.1 A page from *Simplified Spelling. For the Use of Government Departments* (Simplified Spelling Board 1906: 15)

publications of the Executive Departments" (Simplified Spelling Board 1906: 5–6, 15, 23). The beginning of the list is reproduced as Figure 22.1 (Simplified Spelling Board 1906: 15). But journalists and cartoonists can of course also mock new developments: Roosevelt rescinded the order after four months of ridicule and satire (Zimmerman 2010: 372).

Although place names have been more successfully regulated by its Board on Geographic Names, founded in 1890 (Venezky 2001: 348), US public opinion sometimes forced the Board to reverse its decisions, for instance restoring the spelling of 'Pittsburgh' in 1911 after an earlier reform that included dropping "silent letters" such as "the final 'h' in the termination 'burgh'" (United States Board on Geographic Names 1892: 6, Venezky 2001: 349). The official renaming of a place can be particularly tricky in countries with coexisting orthographies such as Norway: after 1814, when the Danish orthographies of place names were Norwegianized, the dialect-derived Nynorsk orthography was felt to be less Danish than Bokmål (Jahr 2014: 107–8). Nineteenth-century Norwegianization included not only discarding Danish influence but also assimilating the minority Sámi and Kven populations (Pedersen 2016: 215). More recent debates (and not only in Norway) concern the representation of Indigenous place names: the Kven and Sámi place names that were replaced with Norwegian names are only slowly being restored, some on public signs provoking defacement and public debate "in the local newspapers and online" (Pedersen 2016: 224).

Newspapers' use of orthographic norms can publicize and differentiate attitudes and practices. In its brief career from 1858 through 1862, the *Canadian Phonetic Pioneer: A Monthly Journal Devoted to the Spread of the Writing, Printing, and Spelling Reform* briefly mediated the ultimately unsuccessful efforts at spelling reform by William Orr (Murray and Portebois 2016: 67). The *Chicago Tribune* not only supported spelling reform from 1880 but introduced reformed spellings in 1934: the "80 reformed spellings" included "<harken>, <tarif>, <jaz> and <burocrat>" (Yule and Yasuko 2016: 420); its publisher Colonel Robert R. McCormick "viewed state authority as inherently malign and menacing" and his *Tribune* "frequently denounced 'burocrats'" (Bates 2019: 428).

In Norway, periodicals have participated in the debates over Nynorsk vs. Bokmål by whether and how they use those standards: fewer use the "minority standard" Nynorsk (Jahr 2014: 167; Pedersen 2016: 219), while "the main conservative newspaper in Norway," *Aftenposten*, has "very conservative Bokmål [that] acts as an alternative style pattern to those promulgated by the state language planning authorities" (Millar 2005: 96). In postcolonial countries, nativized varieties of English can be subordinated through local newspapers' use of international standards. Conversely, a newspaper might lend increased authority to a Caribbean creole. In 1990s Jamaica, the academic Carolyn Cooper used biweekly newspaper columns to promote a combination of

Creole and phonemic spelling. Its simultaneous 'translation' by the more traditional literary dialect conventions epitomizes a typical conflict in the spelling of minority languages, between modern linguist "mediators" and more familiar "user-developers" (Devonish 2003: 55–56, Sebba 2016: 352–54).

22.3 Consequences for Other Languages

All of these efforts to standardize national languages demonstrate that linguistic uniformity is not characteristic of nation-states. Moreover, standardizing the orthography of a national language will have impacts on other languages, beyond and within the nation's borders. Beyond national borders, any standardization of orthography in the process of nation- and empire-building had implications for the norms of transnational languages, such as Austrian German, Flemish and Afrikaans among other postcolonial varieties of European languages (Sebba 2007: 81–101, 116–18). Within the nation, official national languages bring powerful and ongoing consequences for 'minority' languages and their speakers (Gal 2018: 225, Lane et al. 2018). Galician, for instance, is spoken in Spain and related to Spanish but more closely related to Portuguese: as its status in Spain rises, debates about its orthography intensify (O'Rourke 2018: 87). Finally, imposing European languages in settler nations has irrevocably endangered or eliminated many Indigenous languages and cultures (Goddard 1996: 3). Codifying Indigenous languages historically assimilated their speakers to national settler cultures and often to orthographic conventions of national languages (see, e.g., Biava 1990, Errington 2008: 154, 158, Spolsky 2009a, de Reuse 2019).

Devising and standardizing Indigenous orthographies more generally presents serious ethical as well as methodological challenges, even as part of language revitalization (see, e.g., Barros 1995, Jones and Mooney 2017). Written norms reflecting pronunciation and/or resembling those of the national language might be easier and preferable for learners (see, e.g., Hinton 2014), but fixing norms imposes colonial processes on what had been a predominantly oral tradition and reduces linguistic diversity and social equity (Stebbins 2001: 167, 188, Frawley et al. 2002: 9, Rice and Saxon 2002: 143). Consulting community members as authorities has produced diverse solutions (e.g. Hinton 2014: 142). In 1976, for instance, while a "unified orthography" for "the circumpolar Inuit community" (Burnaby 2013: 193) was accepted by many Inuit communities (and settler religious organizations), it was rejected by others – for instance by Nunavut elders who associated their original missionary system with the "words of God," and by the Labrador Inuit who associated the standard with the Northwest Territories (Patrick et al. 2018: 143). The common writing system for Inuktut more recently agreed upon uses elements from all the regional writing systems and does not displace these traditions– this process is seen not as 'standardization' but as 'unification' (Patrick et al. 2018: 148). In other cases, some communities rejected "written forms of their languages" (Burnaby 2013: 188). Perhaps new technologies like 'Talking Dictionaries' might begin to revitalize oral languages in an organic manner – recording individual usage and preserving linguistic diversity without an intermediate stage of writing or standardization (Lüpke 2011: 321, Harrison et al. 2019: 34).

In his monograph on *Creating Canadian English*, Dollinger considers how attempting to standardize the spelling of Indigenous proper names was "enacting colonial routines and expectations on another culture" with a "predominantly oral" tradition, "with spelling questions playing no role whatsoever" (Dollinger 2019a: 6). According to the recently published *Elements of Indigenous Style: A Guide for Writing by and about Indigenous Peoples*, the "preference" of Indigenous individuals explains such orthographic variation in proper names as *Sto:Loh* and *Stô:Lō* (Younging 2018: 21). The compiler advises any "editor or publisher trying to do the right thing in terms of accuracy, consistency, and showing respect on the page" to either "ask the Indigenous Peoples at the centre of a work for the spelling of their names" or to use some of the "current and useful compilations" of "names and spellings compiled by others in consultation with Indigenous Peoples" (Younging 2018: 72). Such recent attention to Indigenous style in Canada marks a more general awareness of the plight and rights of Indigenous peoples internationally.

22.4 Conclusion

This chapter has demonstrated that debates within nation-states about orthographic variations expose changing and conflicting cultural allegiances and pedagogical needs; successes and failures mark intersections as well as boundaries of influence and power. Among potential authorities, representative conflicts include tensions between traditional and simplified spellings for mass state education. European vernaculars inherited diverse writing practices from different discourse communities, including government chanceries, printing houses, religious translations and national language academies. Educators' engagement with the state reminds us that pedagogy is often a matter of politics. Successful reforms sometimes reflect intersections of low literacy and/or authoritarian states, though not always (Fishman 1977: xvii). Existing traditions can be difficult to displace, especially in democracies. Journalists can support or undermine proposed norms, whether using or reporting them. Many debates that raged in the nineteenth century have continued into modern times. And with the rise of social media, individuals can not only internalize but also influence and drive discourses of group identity: after 2015, French speakers on Twitter objecting to the belated implementation of the 1990 French orthography reform created a discourse of "the *ideal French speaker*" by characterizing those rectified spellings as ones that "the *lazy* or *stupid* French speaker cannot or chooses not to embrace" (Drackley 2019: 295, 308). Different variations on these themes would appear in stories about orthographic conflicts over national standards for Greek (Mackridge 2009), Italian (Migliorini and Griffith 1966: 372–75, Richardson 2001) or Portuguese (Marquilhas 2015), for instance; culturally specific trends emerge from comparative studies, for example of Romance languages more generally (Pountain 2016, Lebsanft and Tacke 2020). And different stakeholders have faced distinct linguistic challenges where languages have transnational religious or political associations (like Classical Arabic) or are roughly logographic (like Chinese) (Coulmas 2013: 54, 111). Every debate has its own context and considerations.

23

Networks of Practice across English and Dutch Corpora

Marco Condorelli and Chris De Wulf

23.1 Introduction

Over the last few decades, the use of corpora has become the standard, most widespread method of analyzing and explaining the diachronic development of standardization and variation in orthography. Corpora have reduced the time required for finding evidence of linguistic phenomena from past centuries and have exercised a significant influence in bringing theoretical and use-based analyses closer together (Rissanen 2012: 197). Corpora have also encouraged a more systematic typology of discourse communities, some features of which are a broadly agreed set of public goals expressed by a category of texts, and articulated by the operations of community members (see Swales 1990: 24–27, Diller 2001: 20). Within the remits of European orthographies, the relationships between different language communities and patterns of orthographic standardization have recently received more detailed attention from a more synergic perspective (see, e.g., Baddeley and Voeste 2012b, Condorelli 2022a, 2020c).[1] The present chapter attempts to move a small step forward in much the same direction, offering an overview of the historical and professional links underlying the formation of what we call *networks of practice*. Since the idea of a network of practice is, to our knowledge, entirely new, we do not presumptuously claim to give in this chapter a fully articulated, detailed definition, but rather we humbly put forward an initial concept which we hope future scholars can pick up on and develop further, if they find it as useful on a practical level as we think it is on a theoretical plane. With the term networks of practice, we refer to nonprototypical communities

Many thanks to Hanna Rutkowska and Gijsbert Rutten for giving very helpful suggestions on this chapter at its various stages of development.

[1] For parallels in the history of the book, see Rospocher et al. (2019).

of practice (CoPs) in English and Dutch book production and distribution, as well as between the worlds of manuscript and print. While links also exist between France and England, or between the Low Countries, the German lands and France, the case of English and Dutch is perhaps one of the most straightforward from a linguistic point of view. English and Dutch are of course linguistically closely related, being both derived from Germanic roots, a factor which increases the feasibility of comparative discussions between the two. Furthermore, English and Dutch have some close ties strictly related to orthography, caused by mutual interaction.

The Dutch influence on English in the process of composition, for example, led to the introduction into the English spelling system of some alien spelling conventions, most notably the Dutch custom of using <gh> for /g/ in words like *ghost* and *ghest* 'guest'; or the use of <oe> in *goed* 'good', which appears from time to time in some of William Caxton's printed editions (Salmon 1999: 24, Horobin 2013b: 127). The consonant spelling <gh> for a velar fricative sound in Middle Dutch was in turn most likely derived from French (Van Reenen and Huijs 2000: 162). Both English and Dutch were influenced by French to different degrees and at different periods of time, a process which further increases comparability between the two languages. With regard to English, <ou> was introduced by French scribes to represent /uː/, a spelling which survives in words like *through*, *wound* and French loanwords like *group* and *soup* (Scragg 1974: 48). Another interesting example is that of the French spelling <ie>, which survives in English and French loanwords like *brief*, *piece* and *relief*. This digraph was so widely used in Anglo-Norman that it became established in Parisian French words (e.g. in *chief*) and even in many native words in /eː/, later /iː/, for example *fiend* and *thief* (Scragg 1974: 49). With regard to Dutch, the Picardian French spelling <ou> for /oː/, later /uː/, was adopted in Flemish medieval spelling (e.g. in *bouc*, 'book'), but became obsolete in favor of the more popular spelling <oe> (e.g. in modern Dutch *boek*). For the /øː/ sound, the Picardian French spelling <eu> successfully replaced the local medieval Dutch alternatives <o>, <ue> and <oe> from the fourteenth century onward, for example in modern Dutch *keuze* and *neus*, 'choice' and 'nose' (De Wulf 2019: 163).

As a departing principle underlying our historical and professional overview between England and the Low Countries, we use the commonly shared assumption that the availability of different types of corpus resources inevitably leads researchers working in historical orthography to explore diverging empirical goals and to use different methodological frameworks. In what follows, however, we focus on the idea that networks of practice represent a key bridge across material which inevitably stimulates divergent research interests in the field. In our overview, we bring attention to some fundamental similarities with reference to early book production and local organization, and how communities involved in the production of the early modern texts operated forming links even between individuals or groups working on manuscripts and printed material. Furthermore, we aim to show examples of how the respective histories of book industry in England and the Low Countries are interrelated. Communities of book producers in English and Dutch, we suggest, were not self-standing entities within the remits of the two languages respectively, but engaged in more or less loose professional and social interactions which are still relevant in discourses about communicative communities. Due to the very early stage in which our proposed idea is found, we do not provide, in this chapter, specific examples of relations between networks of practice and the development of orthographic features, nor do we engage in a discussion of potential individual networks of practice behind specific text collections. With our contribution, instead, we aim to provide essential background information for future researchers to explore the intricate correlation between professional organization, culture and society, in the complex framework of early modern Europe.

23.2 Early Modern English and Early Modern Dutch Corpora

At the incipit of an insightful chapter about the social life behind early modern book production, Sherman (2011: 164) asserts that studying old texts often feels somewhat like walking through a deserted town. The pages surviving to the present day preserve the words of long-gone scriveners and printers, giving us insights into the social, intellectual and linguistic worlds that they represented. The texts themselves remain inanimate, even more so the further they travel from the individuals, as well as the actions and the contexts that first gave them life. This state is of course a condition of our growing distance from the past, one that we cannot escape or ignore, but that we can study and attempt to reconstruct. Because of the potential dangers of anachronism, the perils of discussing patterns of comparability and differences across corpora are certainly not few; boundaries across texts are sometimes difficult to pinpoint, and so are their overlaps. Problems of demarcation also arise by examining the supposed motives of scriveners and printers for producing a particular set of works. The corpora available for research in orthography, however, are generally each characterized by texts that respond to general conventions which readers expect and to which authors strive to conform. The characteristics of each category of text become perhaps increasingly obvious toward the end of the seventeenth century, as the differences are then often based on internal linguistic features resulting from a process of codification (see Taavitsainen 2001: 140). Needless to say, the differences are noticeable not only within each language, but even more so when comparing collections of material between English and Dutch.

For the English language, early modern orthographies of the southern variety of printed English largely developed in and around London, and are mostly represented in *Early English Books Online*. The selection of texts in this collection aims to be as representative as possible of the Early Modern English printed material surviving to date, and encompasses a diversified range of genres and text types, mostly books but also shorter documents and notes. Alongside generalist collections like the *Early English Books Online*, other corpora provide more modest collections of texts compiled following more specialized rationales, for example *An Electronic Text Edition of Depositions* (Kytö et al. 2011), the *Corpus of English Dialogues* (Culpeper and Kytö 2006), the *Early Modern English Medical Texts* (Taavitsainen et al. 2010), the *Lampeter Corpus* (Schmied et al. 1994), the *Newsbooks Corpus* (McEnery and Hardie 2007) and the *Shakespeare's First Folio*. These corpora contain facsimile and/or transcribed versions of printed material which ranges from legal documents, all the way through to collections of treatises and textbooks, recipe collections and compendia of medicine, as well as periodical publications like essays, pamphlets and newsbooks. All of the transcriptions from these texts present historically reliable spelling, with rare exceptions. For example, a subset of texts in the *Corpus of English Dialogues* contains normalized spelling (see Kytö and Walker 2006: 28) and should therefore be excluded by any researchers attempting to glean insights into orthographic patterns using transcriptions from this corpus.[2]

In addition to the corpora mentioned above, the *Corpus of Early English Correspondence* (Nevalainen et al. 1998) contains 'secondhand' handwritten texts from a wide range of writers, from literary authors to royals and even lower-class writers. The term *secondhand* refers here to the fact that the compilers included handwritten texts inherited from old printed editions. Even though the original editors claim that they left orthography untouched, this is sometimes not true in a number of cases, because some of the material underwent a degree of silent editing on orthography. Editing obviously curtails the reliability of a corpus for the purposes of studying orthography, but recent work has shown that, with all due caution, the *Corpus of Early English Correspondence* can become useful for some aspects of orthographic inquiry (see, e.g., Kaislaniemi et al. 2017, Sairio et al. 2018). Whatever corpora one might be more interested in for researching standardization in English

[2] While the collections above are useful for research in historical spelling, other corpora, like the *Innsbruck Letter Corpus* (Markus 1999) and the *Helsinki Corpus* (Rissanen et al. 1991), containing handwritten and printed texts, are not so relevant for the same purposes (see also Evans 2012 as well as Berg and Aronoff 2017 for contrasting views about this corpus). In the *Innsbruck Letter Corpus*, spellings were not compared against the original manuscripts in order to determine their faithfulness to the originals. For the *Helsinki Corpus*, on the other hand, the compilers compromised on the use of possibly edited versions of original texts where no other edition existed and on the categories of publication dates established in the corpus (1500–70, 1570–1640, 1640–1710 and 1500–1710).

orthography, the material available in and across each of them varies not only according to genre, but also communicative function, audience and even price in the original market (see Diller 2001). Most of the texts included in the available corpora also share particular processes of producing, distributing and consuming, and it is the combination of all or some of these variables that situates some of the texts in each corpus within more or less specific contrasting categories (see Fairclough 1992b: 126).

Much like for the English language, the early modern era has grown to become an important spot of interest for research in Dutch orthography (see Marynissen and Janssen 2014, Rutten et al. 2014). For the time being, however, the corpora available for researchers in Dutch offer a somewhat more patchy perspective into Early Modern Dutch orthography than is the case for English. In Dutch historical sociolinguistics, the seventeenth and eighteenth centuries have been of special interest for over a decade, particularly with respect to research into literacy, spelling and language policy (some references are available in Chapter 30, this volume). The most notable collection for research in Dutch orthography is the *Letters as Loot Corpus* (van der Wal et al. 2015, Rutten and van der Wal 2014, 2018). In Dutch, however, there is a gap for material published or written in the sixteenth century, because there are currently no collections of diplomatically transcribed texts made available for that period. *Bijbels digitaal,* a corpus of early modern Bible editions, which covers the years between 1477 and 1648, represents to date the only exception to the rule (Van der Sijs and Beelen 2008–12).

While the current gaps are unfortunate, high-quality medieval charter corpora such as the *Corpus Gysseling*, I (Gysseling and Pijnenburg 1977) and the *Corpus Van Reenen – Mulder* (Van Reenen and Mulder 1993) offer promising options for research into the thirteenth and fourteenth centuries, respectively.[3] Of course, we do not want to insinuate that medieval corpora can act as a replacement for missing material from the early modern era, but just that the current range of corpora available to Dutch researchers has created something of a less formal distinction between the fading end of the Middle Ages and the first half of the early modern era than is perhaps the case for English.[4] Having established this important caveat, the two charter corpora mentioned above span most of the Dutch-speaking area by design. *Letters as Loot* covers a large part of the Western Low Countries, as that was the main area from

[3] The charters are mostly private law contracts drawn up between local parties before local aldermen councils.

[4] A relatively large body of research exists for Middle English at the intersection between orthography and dialectology (among the existing contributions, Margaret Laing's publications are perhaps most relevant, see www.lel.ed.ac.uk/~esss09/). For Dutch, a multigenre *Historical Corpus of Dutch* currently being developed by Gijsbert Rutten, Wim Vandenbussche, Iris Van de Voorde, Marijke van der Wal and Rik Vosters at Vrije Universiteit Brussel and Leiden University promises to become a useful addition to the material available for the early modern era and beyond, as it will likely cover texts from the middle of the sixteenth, seventeenth, eighteenth and nineteenth centuries.

which the East India Company employees were recruited. An additional digital resource available for those interested in pursuing Dutch orthographic research in proximity to the early modern era is a compendium of 336 literary, handwritten texts (prose and lyric poetry) from the period 1250–1500, known as the *Corpus Middelnederlands* (1998). Much as for English, all of the Dutch corpora mentioned above contain diplomatic transcriptions of original texts, which means that the original orthographic variants within the texts have not been normalized to present-day Dutch. Some of the corpora have in part been compiled from later printed editions of manuscripts, as in the case of the *Corpus Van Reenen – Mulder*, but these have in turn been compared carefully against the original manuscripts and approved as reliable.

The slightly more irregular coverage of Dutch orthography for the early modern era stems from the practical limitations for the construction of new corpora, and the ones available to date are partially the result of a peculiar administrative setup that might not be present in larger language areas. The Dutch and the Flemish governments have transferred most of their language documentation and regulation responsibilities to the *Nederlandse Taalunie*. In addition to the academic institutions and the national funding organizations in Flanders and the Netherlands, the *Instituut voor de Nederlandse Taal*, a Taalunie dependency, is a binational institution mostly devoted to historical corpus-building and maintenance, lexicology and tool development, which mainly responds to the needs and interests of those who are affiliated to it.[5] The availability of much handwritten material has inevitably turned the focus of research in Dutch orthography to synchronic and diachronic aspects of social stratification and dialect variation (e.g. Rutten and van der Wal 2018, De Wulf 2019). As a consequence, the development of standardized orthography in Dutch is not the only, or perhaps even the main, focus of analysis in current research. A point of similarity with English research, on the other hand, may be found in the fact that almost every Dutch corpus, when taken in isolation, constitutes a relatively uniform entity when it comes to a range of textual characteristics. The corpora discussed here contain charters, epistolary material or literary manuscripts, a feature which in turn creates interesting fragmentations and contrasts within the remits of Dutch.

At this point, it will have become apparent even to the nonspecialist reader that the corpora available for research in Early Modern English and Early Modern Dutch orthographies present us with a very diversified and almost incompatible range of research material both within each language and, even more so, between the two languages. The material available for students of Early Modern English and Dutch orthography also clearly leads researchers

[5] There is fairly easy access to repositories of single-genre texts that for Middle Dutch and for seventeenth-century Dutch and beyond has impacted research in Dutch orthography, but on the flip side there is, as mentioned earlier in this chapter, a lack of corpora of a similar size for the fifteenth and sixteenth centuries.

to pursue different research goals and chronological portions of the early modern era, to a point that it is difficult to see any elements that can truly connect scholars of the two languages. In the following section, however, we argue that, despite the obvious differences arising from the corpora available to date, there is a macro-level historical and contextual thread connecting English and Dutch materials, one that runs through the concept of networks of practice. As we explain below, networks of practice represent a pivotal tool for finding the link between the two languages, as these were more broadly interlinked than perhaps previously discussed or assumed by students of orthography.

23.3 Communities and Networks of Practice

In recent work concerning historical orthography (Rogos 2013, Rutkowska 2013b, Sairio 2013, Tyrkkö 2013, Conde-Silvestre 2019, 2020), the concept of a CoP has been used to indicate individuals who produced communicative artifacts like books, whether they were handwritten or printed, and their relation with the process of language change. Our working definition of a CoP compares with the definition used in the recent publications above, which in turn mainly stems from Eckert and McConnell-Ginet (1992: 464). For these two co-authors, a CoP is defined both by its membership and by the practices in which the members engage. The term refers not just to a group of people who share a certain characteristic feature, but also to a group of people who interact and share ways of doing things. The concept of a CoP, however, goes back to even before Wenger's definition, because it is a relative of the concept of communicative communities, which were introduced as early as 1970 by Zabrocki (originally referred to as *kommunikative Gemeinschaften*). Zabrocki defined communicative communities as entities formed by at least two individuals who either feel the need or are forced to exchange information for any given reason (Zabrocki 1970: 3).

Over the last decade or so, the notions of communicative communities and CoPs have enjoyed ever-increasing interest and elaboration among scholars.[6] Today, the concept of a CoP denotes a team of people working together, sharing the same tools and following the same community procedures, but there is of course a lot of room for fuzziness even within and across these variables (see Tyrkkö 2013: 153). In any case, members of a CoP most likely share similar work conditions and are subject to similar technological limitations

[6] According to Rutkowska (2013b: 125), the various categories of communicative communities that have been at the center of scholarly attention so far are, in addition to communities of practice, "community of interest" (Henri and Pudelko 2003), "community of inquiry" (Garrison et al. 2000) and "community of action" (Cahier and Zacklad 2004).

(Rutkowska 2013b: 125). In a CoP, a group of individuals who collaborate and share experiences, procedures and tools are bound by the same regulations, and usually work in the same environment (Wenger 1998: 72–73). The people involved in the printing business, for example, often formed a tight-knit and intertwined social group with family ties and mutual commitments which were often reiterated across generations and where job roles were sometimes exchangeable (Adam 2010: 280). For Wenger (1998: 72–85), a CoP is identifiable according to three fundamental parameters: mutual engagement, joint enterprise and shared repertoire. As argued in recent work (Jucker and Kopaczyk 2013: 8), not all CoPs show all three parameters that are crucial for identifying a CoP to the same extent. In other words, CoPs are characterized to various degrees by their mutual engagement, and the geographical perspective taken to identify these communities is often rather narrow, and mainly limited to a national context.

With our contribution, we aim to encourage more work on the theory of the meso-level in sociolinguistics (see Nevalainen 2015: 248–49), by proposing a focus on an umbrella unit which includes the idea of a CoP, and that, for convenience, we call *networks of practice*. With this term, we intend a mid-level entity with a focus on specific individuals or identifiable groups, which is what makes the idea of a network of practice a potentially useful one. In contrast to networks of practice, discourse communities are more about the characteristics of a social interaction, in a more abstract way and at a higher generalization level than those of a network and a community of practice. In discourse communities, that is, one does not necessarily have to think about specific people from a local context. A CoP, on the other hand, is a more micro-level entity where ties among identifiable people are quite narrow; in fact, work relationships are so close in a CoP that the focus is often not so much on actual work connections but on negotiations among people (i.e. their agreed procedures, shared repertoire, common goals and actions, etc.).

By focusing on networks of practice, we would like to give more emphasis to CoPs where mutual engagement arises not necessarily by sharing the same workplace or guild, or even the same cultural, national and linguistic context, but simply through participation in a casual setup of work norms and collaborative relationships. These relationships, we believe, sit at the loosest end of the mutual-interaction spectrum which characterizes CoPs, largely because of the limitations imposed by cultural, linguistic and geographical distances. Networks of practice, as we envisage them, do not have a joint enterprise; that is to say, a common goal may be missing and there may not be any methods of controlling membership, genre ownership or foreseeable mechanisms of member intercommunication (see Jucker and Kopaczyk 2013: 4). However, there are still connections between people with a shared repertoire and mutual involvement, and it is these connections that make a network an entity in its own right. To give an example, it is true that printers generally formed

CoPs, especially when they worked closely on one and the same project and were located within the same printing workshop. Other printers, however, did not have common goals together, in the sense that they may have simply not shared workload with one another, but they were still linked by kinship and/or professional relationships. The question of whether membership of a network of practice is voluntary or not will have to remain unanswered at this point, as we believe that more empirical work in the future needs to build on these ideas in order to solidify and demonstrate their effectiveness. If membership is voluntary in CoPs, though, as it is, we can tentatively put forward the idea that it might not necessarily always be the same in networks of practice. Another question that one may raise at this point is whether there is an awareness of belonging to a network of practice like there is in a CoP, or whether there is some kind of explicit negotiation of meanings, practices and procedures among the networks of practice members like there is for a CoP. These, again, are all issues that need a shared set of agreements among scholars, but we can assume here, for the sake of theory and sheer discursiveness, that these qualities in networks of practice are frequently not there as they are for CoPs, or they may be fuzzier than in closer communities. Much like for CoPs more strictly, networks of practice can be distinguished from professional networks, that is, social networks of professionals,

> chiefly [by] method and focus. Network analysis typically deals with structural and content properties of the ties that constitute egocentric personal networks [... but] cannot address the issues of how and where linguistic variants are employed [...] to construct local social meanings. Rather, it is concerned with how informal social groups [...] support local norms or [...] facilitate linguistic change.
>
> (Milroy and Gordon 2003: 19)

Moreover, social networks (intended here as synonymous with networks of practice) are based on the existence of social ties between members, weak or strong as they may be. As Holmes and Meyerhoff (1999: 180) put it, "[a] social network requires quantity of interaction; a C[ommunity] of P[ractice] requires quality of interaction" and relies on mutual engagement. We can also assume that networks of practice require quality of interaction, though how much awareness there is of this quality of interaction among members (and how it contrasts with that of CoPs) is of course open for debate.

In the remaining part of this chapter, we give an overview of examples of historical and social contexts where networks of practice involved in handwritten and printed text production may have arisen. Handwriting and printing communities were connected to each other, at a time in history where the latter did not completely supplant the former, but rather specialized side by side in different areas within the book market. As members of a guild, professionals working on handwritten material formed a CoP in its own right, subject to the same legal regulations as printers, including privileges and duties (see Rogos 2013: 105–7). With regard to those working in printing, on the other hand, relatively large groups of workers doubtlessly interacted and shared goals, interests and techniques not only with those involved in handwriting, but also with individuals working in printing between the two countries (see Tyrkkö 2013: 153–54). Groups of printers in England and the Low Countries, we suggest, engaged in professional networks that created significant interactions and similarities between English and Dutch. It is in these overlapping historical similarities that networks of practice may be found. As briefly indicated above, networks of practice obviously may not respond to all requirements necessary to identify a prototypical CoP to the same degree, but are nevertheless still present and relevant – or rather they should be – for those who study orthography. For the case of English and Dutch, networks of practice are identifiable, we believe, on two essential levels: early production and local organization, on the one hand, and international networks, on the other hand.

The case of early production and local organization may be represented by the kinship situation mentioned earlier in this section, where colleagues may become related by family, friendship and other social ties unrelated to business. The case of international networks, instead, may well exemplify professional relationships of a looser type, where laborers are not necessarily bound by and committed to the same project on a daily basis, but happen to share some elements which eventually connect them, albeit more casually. Examples of these elements may be, for example, printing tools, like shared typefaces, or a temporary work connection where a laborer from one country contributes to the book production chain of another country. Since these are often conjectural situations where discussions may lead one to speculate, we refrain in the remaining part of this chapter from analyzing these situations any further, but we limit ourselves to acknowledging that relations may be found both on a personal (individual) level and on a group level. Taking this as a fixed point of departure, the following section offers background scenarios where it is likely that networks of practice might have formed, weaving a sociohistorical and professional context that should be useful, we hope, to those interested in exploring orthography as a product of networks of practice in future research endeavors.

All of the scenarios represented in the remaining part of this chapter are situations where references to texts, materials and people may be found by comparing and matching together in a complementary way the corpora available to date. Rather than providing a fragmented perspective of which corpus illustrates what historical and sociological context, we prefer to dip a toe in the water here by providing a more general overview of what all the inherited context available so far from these collections can do for us. Our hope is that this approach will nudge future researchers to begin exploring similarities and differences across the corpora discussed earlier in this chapter, and potentially to identify different networks of practice across them.

23.4 A Short Comparative Overview

23.4.1 Early Book Production and Local Organization

England and the Low Countries share a similar history of early book production, and communities involved in the production of handwritten and printed material coexisted and sometimes interacted with each other. From the end of the fifteenth century onward, the enterprise of various people involved in making, importing or selling printed books made London dominant in national book commerce. Migration to Paternoster Row or to streets and lanes nearby in London continued steadily throughout the fifteenth century; as many as 136 stationers and book artisans, at various times, established business premises and residence in the environs of St. Paul's Cathedral (Christianson 1999: 128–29). In the manuscript world, copyists, illuminators and bookbinders worked from their own shops or lodgings, supervised by a *stationarius* and linked by an intricate network of professional and private ties (Christianson 1989b: 207–8). Given the fact that the majority of book artisans in London operated from Paternoster Row, artisans working on the same manuscript could communicate with one another with relative ease (Christianson 1990: 29, Rogos 2013: 105). As nicely put by Rutkowska (2013b: 126), those working in a printing shop had not only a shared bag of information on how to produce a book, but also used many of the same tools, like movable type and woodcuts, which essentially were the result of an investment made by the master printer for the common good of all their workers. More frequently than not, those working in a printing shop borrowed tools from each other and sometimes even became in charge of a printing house if some of the key senior workers gave up their role due to illness, death or old age (Duff 1948 [1906]: 125, 132, 173). Between the end of the fifteenth century and the beginning of the sixteenth century, then, the jobs of booksellers and publishers, publishers and printers, or printers and compositors, overlapped to a large extent (Duff 1948 [1906]: 72, Pleij 1982: 21, de Hamel 1983: 29). It is due to the fuzzy nature of these roles that the word *stationer* was used in early print to refer to "anyone who made, bound, or sold books" (Raven 2007: 12, as referenced in Rutkowska 2013b: 126).

Overall, the book market in England was not a completely autonomous business over much of the fifteenth century, and it was only from the late seventeenth century that London, Oxford and Cambridge were on a par with Antwerp, Amsterdam, Paris and Frankfurt in the scholarly book market (Bland 2010: 214). In the Low Countries, the roles of those involved in early book production were as eclectic as those in England, and scriveners had been involved in literary work production as well as in local or regional administration for a long time before the introduction of printing. To give an example, thirteenth-century Dutch author Melis Stoke wrote, among other works, a rhymed chronicle of Holland, while also serving as a clerk for the city of Dordrecht and for the committal court of Holland (Rem 2003: 84). In the case of Stoke and his colleagues, spelling similarities and differences between the Holland administration, with clerks originating from different regions, and the local one in Dordrecht, bear witness to this interaction (Rem 2003: 269–71). Melis Stoke's activities as a literary author and clerk for different administrations bind him into overlapping networks, and also mean that his writing appears across Middle Dutch corpora of different genres. Much like London in England, cities like Bruges, Ghent, Lille, Antwerp and Brussels were heavily urbanized and acted as dominant cultural and economic hubs for a long time in the Low Countries (Stegeman 2014: 139–41). Initially, it looked as if the university town of Leuven, where Dirk Martens established the first printing office of the southern Low Countries in 1473, would become the epicenter of the book market in the area, but it was Antwerp that usurped that role rather quickly (Adam 2010: 275–78). The leading role of Antwerp in early printing becomes clear when one compares the number of original incunabula woodcuts that were used for the first time in this city with that of other printing centers in the Low Countries. Antwerp boasts 1,107 woodcut originals, the next city on the list, Delft, 640 (Kok 2013: xxi).[7] For most of the sixteenth century, Antwerp played a key role in combining the necessary funding, technology and culture for producing books, and enjoyed an independent economic status and cultural prosperity.

Both in England and in the Low Countries, the advent of printing did not make handwritten book production immediately obsolete. The manuscript industry stayed alive alongside the emerging printing industry well into the sixteenth century (Hellinga and Trapp 1999: 3, Pleij and Reynaert 2004: 3–7). In fact, the thriving manuscript production and its role in (performance-based) literary culture may have inhibited an early expansion of printing, for example in the southern Low Countries (Pleij 2010: 290). More importantly, printing and handwriting did not end up becoming competing technologies in the whole European scene until later in the early modern era. Both in production and in use, English and Dutch handwritten and printed materials also had some remarkable overlapping points within each of the two languages. Scriveners still engaged in jobs like producing copies of legal texts, literary works, letters and other documents of note, and were still regarded as an effective publication route (Woudhuysen 1996: 52–53). Most of the incunabula produced at the intersection between the age of manuscript and

[7] To a large extent, the large number of original woodcuts can be attributed to Gerard Leeu, who is responsible for about a quarter of the total number of (known) woodcuts in the Low Countries (Kok 2013: xxii).

that of print consciously imitated the layout and conventions of manuscripts; while every printed book was first a manuscript; even when a book had been printed, it might well be marked up and corrected for a later edition by hand. Readers might annotate or emend, making a book into a composite document and leave their traces, like the inky thumbprint of a pressman, in the margin. For many, the difference between print as a mechanized form of mass manuscript production and print as a technology with other aesthetic, technical and socioeconomic concerns was not self-evident, at least at the early stages of book production (Bland 2010: 83–84). It is easy to imagine how this type of close coexistence between manuscript and print may have fostered connections of the type that we assume in networks of practice.

The eventual fading of manuscript production, both in England and in the Low Countries, was not just a matter of a superior technology proving itself victorious. The gradual disappearance was also in part a societal change in which readership among commoners grew more consciously aware of the beauty of print, while the relevance of the monastic clergy, including their role as book manufacturers, declined (see Bell 1999: 254). From the late sixteenth century onward, England began to establish a more organized, competitive professional setup for printing; concurrently, the northern Low Countries became internationally renowned, continuing the previously southern tradition. With the grant of a Royal Charter to the Stationers' Company in 1557, English printers gained for the first time the legal power to take decisions about the trades over which it had jurisdiction, which essentially meant that the Company appropriated the craft of printing to itself (Gadd 1999: 37). The freedom granted by the Charter of Incorporation allowed the most powerful dozen patentees that controlled the printing trade in London to retain their decisional power even during much of the rigorously controlled Elizabethan era (1558–1603), until complaints raised by a number of minor printers about their licensing rights led to changes in the Company's administration policies. The sealing of the Star Chamber decree in 1586 created a more democratic share of publishing rights across more members of the Stationers' Company, and afforded more printers economic and administrative freedom in typography (Halasz 1997: 25).

Like members of the Stationers' Company, scriveners in England belonged to a guild that was originally known as the Writers of the Court Letter in the fifteenth century, and that was incorporated as the Company of Scriveners from 1617 (see Steer 1968; see also Chapter 21, this volume). Broadly speaking, the Stationers and the Scriveners had very similar structures, governance and responsibilities, and it is clear that the Charter for the Scriveners was based on that of the Stationers (Blayney 2003: 45–47). This situation may, once again, encourage one to think that there may have been some ties existing between the two, even if only because the formation of one guild may have inspired the other. Both companies had a Master, two Wardens and a Court of Assistants, as well as a Beadle and a Clerk. At the lower levels, a Stationer was first apprenticed, next freed as a yeoman, and then made a member of the livery. As a member of the livery, he had to serve as Junior and Senior Renter-Warden before rising to the Court of Assistants, from which the Master and Wardens were chosen (Blayney 2003: 41). In the Scriveners' Company, the junior ranks were referred to as Stewards and Younger Members (Blayney 2003: 49–53). Overall, we know very little about the organization of a scrivener's business, but it was likely that people involved in the manuscript business would sometimes migrate to working in print and vice versa, creating an amalgamation of language, knowledge and possibly even relationships across groups of workers. The Scriveners' Company would only include those scriveners that were involved in (re)producing legal matter, whereas the producers of literary manuscripts were part of the Stationers. Even the members of the Scriveners' Company, however, were known to take up other writing tasks when the demand for legal work was slow (Woudhuysen 1996: 60–64). Stationers and scriveners held close ties also when it came to circumventing some of the restrictions put in place by their companies' statutes, and they would exchange certain assignments and even apprentices, risking fines for doing so (Woudhuysen 1996: 58–59). Furthermore, stationers and booksellers would offer both printed and handwritten books for sale, which means their business relations had to include both printers and scriveners, and some scriveners had to live close to the book trade, for example in Lombard Street (Woudhuysen 1996: 48–50, 59). These relations inevitably created a fertile compendium of unspoken knowledge about book production as a whole, regardless of the types of technology used to produce the texts.

Unlike in England, Antwerp printers did not immediately start their own guild to protect their rights and their craft, nor did they join a stationers' guild. Organizations similar to those of English stationers or scriveners existed in the older, medieval cultural centers like Bruges, where craftsmen involved in manuscript production would gather together and were known as *librariërs*. Proof of such an official *Gild van Librariërs* exists from as early as 1457 (Schouteet 1964: 231). The guild would include illuminators, who would be the cause of friction between the librariërs' organization, on the one hand, and the painters' guild, on the other hand – the latter unsuccessfully trying to force the illuminators to join their guild throughout the first half of the fifteenth century (Schouteet 1964: 231–32). A powerful and separate librariërs' guild similar to the one in Bruges was absent in late fifteenth-century Antwerp, when printing arrived in the Low Countries. The printers' activities and their presumed usage of similar crafts and tools, however, caused friction with other professions, notably the Antwerp painters and illuminators, who, unlike those in Bruges, were joined under the guild of St. Luke (Adam 2010: 280). The authorities in the Low Countries also did not show much interest in sanctioning or reining in the printing industry. On the contrary, although the entourage of the late fifteenth-century Burgundian court and the local administration could use the possibilities of print whenever they saw fit for propaganda purposes, they did so to a much lesser extent than the kings of France, for example, as the Burgundian policy of peace meant there was little reason to meddle with the press (Speakman Sutch 2010: 254–55).

The absence of a specific professional guild for Dutch printers at the dawn of their industry may partially be owed to the independent, eclectic role of those who worked in the early printing houses. Since the end of the fifteenth century, the economic powerhouse that was Antwerp attracted insightful entrepreneurs like Gherard Leeu (Gouda, Holland) to set up a printing shop (Pleij 2010: 190). Leeu was involved in all stages of book production (acquirement, translation, redaction, publishing, wood-blocking, printing, binding and sale), a business method shared by contemporaries William Caxton and Thomas van der Noot (Pleij 1982: 21). Eventually, however, Antwerp printers were pressured by painters to join the St. Luke's guild, and were consequently never part of an organization of the type of the *Gild van Librariërs* in Bruges that could defend their own, separate interests (Adam 2010: 280). This association with other artists did not necessarily damage them, however. During the first half of the sixteenth century, Antwerp had become a huge production center for paintings, tapestries, books and all sorts of luxury items for the rest of the world: "Art had become a commodity and was marketed year-round by professional art dealers who handled large orders to be shipped abroad" (Vermeylen 2002: 4).

In one way or another, however, scriveners and printers in the Low Countries coexisted in similar and overlapping organizations, much like their English counterparts. Printing was seen as an extension of the activities of booksellers, binders and publishers, as, for example in Bruges, they were always assumed to join or already be part of the *Gild van Librariërs*, also known as the Guild of St. John the Evangelist (Schouteet 1964: 234, Geirnaert 1994: 121).[8] By joining the same guild, professional interactions between scriveners and printers were inevitable, because the two would often play complementary job roles. For example, it is likely that scriveners would have played an active part in the printing process by providing a matrix copy for texts that were to be printed (e.g. Baddeley 2012: 101), which means that even orthographic practices between scriveners and printers in Bruges may show immediately comparable features. Printers and scriveners would also occasionally be the same people: Colard Mansion, who worked with William Caxton in Bruges, and his contemporary Johannes Brito were successful scriveners and

[8] An early mentioning of the term appears in the sixteenth century dictionary Tresoor der Duytsscher talen: "Librarier; een boeckschriuere, boeckprintere, druckere oft vercoopere" (Van den Werve 1553: 101). The term encompasses book writers, book printers and booksellers. The difference between *boeckprintere* and *druckere* is unclear; the former are probably to be interpreted as woodblock makers and the latter as movable type printers (Dewitte 1996: 335).

translators before they entered the printing business (Geirnaert 1994: 120). Membership of the same guild meant that scriveners and printers would socialize and worship together, and, in the case of the *librariërs* in Bruges, even co-own liturgical objects that they could take along to different chapels (Dewitte 1996: 335). Printers and scriveners were, in other words, very much part of each other's lives and social circles.

23.4.2 International Networks

As well as sharing broadly comparable, sometimes interlinked histories of early production and local organizations, relevant individuals or identifiable groups in England and the Low Countries were also connected by international networks, predominantly related to the printing industry.[9] In the Low Countries, religious freedom was an important factor which encouraged a number of Englishmen, Frenchmen and other Protestant immigrants into exile in the Low Countries. The international nature of the community of printers in places like Antwerp becomes apparent by evidence of some of the surviving woodcuts and types. The catalogue of Dutch incunabula woodcuts in Kok (2013), for example, shows recurring and resembling woodcuts with different printers, implying collaborative networks of printers in different cities and in editions meant for non-Dutch markets (Kok 2013: xxvi). The recurrence of recognizable typographical material outside the Low Countries might be due partly to collaborations and partly to the fact that Antwerp printers such as Leeu also published English and other foreign-language translations of popular books, in which the woodcuts were reused (Driver 2014: 392). One of the most famous printers in the Low Countries was French-born Christophe Plantin, who set up his industrial printing office in Antwerp in 1555 with dozens of employees. The printer produced books in a plethora of languages meant to be exported all over the Low Countries and abroad, and, for this reason, inevitably influenced international printers, not least those in England (Voet 1969: 32).[10] Aside from purely language-based connections, there were also cultural reasons why the Low Countries were in close contact with England over the early modern period. In particular, English Protestant literature was produced quite regularly in the Low Countries, and Antwerp printer Martin de Keyser, for example, another Frenchman by birth, was

[9] Although manuscript production continued, it is likely that the distribution of handwritten books remained on a smaller scale than that of print, more local and relying on personal contact and short-distance networks (Tenger and Trolander 2010: 1039).

[10] For example, in the late sixteenth century, a modernized French orthography, adopted by French printers in favor of Reformation, was taken along with the Reformists who fled to the Low Countries due to the Counter-Reformation. There, the modernized French orthography survived and thrived in the books printed in French by Plantin and re-emerged as a model for later modern French spelling reforms in the seventeenth century (Baddeley 2012: 101).

especially keen to print works written by William Tyndale, among others (Lavinsky 2014: 196). Conversely, the works of Leeu, Colard Mansion, who collaborated with Caxton, Arend de Keyser, Jacob Bellaert, Richard Pafraet and Johan Veldener also exerted international influence in the printing industry, including the English one (e.g. Driver 2014: 393).

In general, most academics and professionals in England could avail themselves of more books printed abroad than books produced in the British Isles. Their expectations were set by those printed products whose standards were not matched by the books produced in Britain until well into the seventeenth century. Among the centers where high standards were achieved in the production of books for the university-educated, Leuven dominates, and English scholars were treated with respect in the city. Thomas More's *Utopia*, for example, was first published at Leuven by Dirk Martens, and a copy of it in the survey was given to Corpus Christi College, Oxford, by John Claymond (Lane Ford 1999: 192). For England, however, the reasons why strong international networks were in place were not so much cultural or intellectual, but more practical in nature. William Caxton, who was responsible for setting up the printing press in England in 1476, likely spent much of his time traveling back and forth between London and the Low Countries in the 1440s, before moving to Bruges to set up a cloth trade business. Caxton aimed to improve the quality of English cultural life by translating into his mother tongue works embodying the lively and more widespread literary ambience that he had come to know in Flanders. During his many years of residence in the Low Countries, Caxton had observed how a culture initially confined to the Burgundian court and its entourage had taken hold in a much wider social circle of civil servants, merchants and other citizens, within a flourishing urban context. Through his translations into English of works that had become popular in the social milieu with which he had become familiar, Caxton blended a foreign culture with the continuing preoccupations of the English (Hellinga and Trapp 1999: 3). In this context, there may be room for conjectures about some of the business relations entertained by Caxton abroad and how influential or indeed lasting they were when he migrated to England.

Aside from the specific case of William Caxton, then, there were larger-scale practical reasons behind the internationalized profile of printing, which related to the setup of English printing industry as a whole. Especially from the first half of the sixteenth century, English book production was almost entirely dependent on materials, techniques and skills brought in from overseas. Procuring suitable type was a priority for every printer, and there is much evidence that, for printers in England in the early modern era, it was usually obtained from abroad through well-established relations with punch-cutters and type-founders in France, Germany and the Low Countries, and, where necessary, foreign type was adapted for printing the English language (Hellinga 1991: 68, 1999: 71). Whether these types of relations entailed close interactions, however, remains unclear; in fact, it is likely that connections were not as strong and bonding as they would be in a CoP. A relatively large number of the books which circulated in the British market especially in the sixteenth century were also often imported from abroad: between the 1510s and the 1540s, Leuven and Antwerp made their presence felt particularly strongly in the affairs related to book trade, while Paris continued to act as a supply center to the British market until the 1540s–50s (Lane Ford 1999: 186–87, 193). The close international ties between England and the Low Countries were also fostered by the foreign presence in the English printing workforce and remained sustainable due to the fact that early printing involved the reiterative production of many of the same old book titles (Raymond 2011: 62).

The ever more frequent repetition of identical chapters and verses, owed to a constant republication of old classics, Bibles and early vernacular works during this time of history, would have encouraged the amplification and reinforcement of some of the 'standard' typographical norms that had been forged from the introduction of print, which in turn were relics of manuscript features (Hellinga 1999: 91). Between the end of the fifteenth century and the beginning of the sixteenth century, printers went to great lengths to use a large number of separate typographical units that represented scribal ligatures, contractions and variant forms for the same graphemes. This setup guaranteed continuous purchases of elaborated typographical materials from abroad and the need for expert composing hands often unavailable domestically (Hellinga 1999: 70). The accession of Edward VI (reigned 1547–53) to the throne of England heralded a period of unprecedented turbulence in the reiterative structure of publishing in London, but this seems not to have shaken at all the stability of the professional networks between England and the Low Countries. For a brief interval under Protector Somerset (Edward Seymour), the government allowed unheard-of liberty to Protestant authors, printers and booksellers (King 1999: 174).

The temporary cessation of censorship in 1547 and 1548 gave printers such a renewed enthusiasm for book production that they went on to produce material at a higher rate than at any point since Caxton's establishment of the first English printing press in 1476 (Bell and Barnard 1992: 51). During this time, almanacs and ballads gained popularity together with previously banned Protestant titles, and many of the books produced in London became the product of labor of repatriated Protestant printers who had gone into exile in the Low Countries and elsewhere abroad under Henry VIII (Capp 1979: 20, King 1999: 166, Barnard 2002: 13). These movements inevitably enriched the relationships that had been forged decades earlier, and contributed to mixing together workmen of England and the Low Countries, and perhaps creating some relatively loose bonds between the two countries. The reimposition of restraints under the Duke of Northumberland in 1549, and the subsequent ascension of Queen Mary I to the throne of England (reigned 1553–58), caused somewhat of a contraction in the overall production of books (Took 1977: 245, Loach 1986: 137, Bell and Barnard 1992: 52, King 1999: 170–71). Despite the reinstitution of traditional control measures on printing, the Marian government was generally no more successful than its predecessors at controlling the book trade, and relations between England and the Low Countries continued even after the officialization of the Stationers' Company in 1557 (King 1999: 175). While it is difficult to establish the exact time when the print-related relationship between England and the Low Countries ceased to exist as it had been for much of the sixteenth century, future research could nevertheless seek to provide answers to this question. In the meantime, the examples given here can be taken as sufficiently instructive for a concluding thought about how meaningful networks of practice in England and the Low Countries would have been throughout much of the early modern era.

If we want to fully understand the relationship between the material available for researchers of Early Modern English and Dutch orthography, we cannot disregard the wider networks of those who engaged in international professional interactions for the production of most of the material surviving to date. It is by means of relatively complex surroundings overseeing the existence of tight-knit CoPs that the material available between English and Dutch, with its inevitable imperfections and limits, can become virtually complementary. The respective histories of English and Dutch have some fundamental similarities also with reference to early book production and local organization, and operated forming links which extended beyond geographical, professional or cultural confines. When studying Early Modern English and Dutch orthography, either in isolation or comparatively, future researchers also need to be aware of another truth underlying every individual attempt to investigate manuscripts and printed books produced in early modern Europe: the Renaissance did not *invent* books, but only *printed* books. In many ways, the characteristics of those who produced books and the fact that there was a market for them at all are properly seen more as the realization of collaborative trends that had been developing since the thirteenth century than as a radical departure from them (Andersen and Sauer 2002: 7).

As a result of the close connection between the manuscript and the printed book worlds in the early modern era, a fundamental methodological axiom becomes apparent. Anyone seeking to embark on an empirical exploration of networks of practice using orthography as a primary source of evidence will have a wide range of starting-point elements at their disposal for analysis, which could be taken as immediate consequences of interactions at the level of networks of practice. For manuscripts, pertinent matters include calligraphic style, the use of *litterae* and abbreviations, and the occurrence of recognizable scriveners across different text genres (literary texts and administration at local as well as regional levels, as was the case with Melis Stoke). For printed books, relevant typographical and textual features include woodcuts, title page and signature styles, typefaces and individual types, abbreviations, page layout and size, and even the nature and origin of particular typographical errors. Some of these elements can be analyzed with more confidence than others using the corpora that we have presented in our chapter, drawing on facsimiles or transcriptions depending on the object of analysis and the size of the data surveyed. Overall, however, the material available to date for researches of Early Modern English and Dutch represents a sufficient basis to embark on investigations which follow the lines of inquiry suggested here.

23.5 Conclusion

The present chapter has provided an overview of some of the most important historical, cultural and professional contexts behind the formation of networks of practice, which overcame the boundaries of manuscript and print, and the physical confines between England and the Low Countries. The focus on networks of practice should of course never end up blurring some of the many CoPs that reside behind each given collection of texts, and within each language. Instead, it should encourage researchers to explore solutions to their questions about orthography that may also lie at the intersection between well-defined CoPs and narrow geographical boundaries. With our discussion, we hope to have been useful to future researchers of orthography in a twofold way. First, we have provided a short overview of the material available today for research in historical orthography with specific interest in the early modern era. Second, we have presented a broad contextualization for research in Early Modern English and Dutch orthography, from an angle that leans toward historical sociolinguistics. As modern-day historical linguists, in our efforts to decipher and describe the development of orthography, we cannot be mere late spectators of the production of earlier books, nor can we interpret orthography solely as the product of well-defined, unique categories, genres or even languages. Instead, we need to tailor our empirical interests to embrace orthography, text and society in harmony and in the awareness of a much broader, nuanced and often rather difficult-to-grasp context. With the experimentation of new ways to approach and understand the study of orthography, some of these perspectives can now be explored empirically for the first time in history and can be investigated in a more dynamic way. It is hoped that the present contribution will give researchers a thought-provoking starting point to explore more seriously and more intensively some of the possible context-driven similarities in historical writing on different media, and across European orthographies, and discuss what these might tell us about networks of practice.

24

Literacy and the Singular History of Norwegian

Agnete Nesse

24.1 Introduction

This chapter provides an overview of changes in the written varieties of Norway from a diachronic perspective. Emphasis is laid on the period after 1500, although also the first centuries of literacy are touched upon. Many language histories focus on the emergence of one standardized variety, and the most investigated features are those that can be seen as early examples of what came to be the modern standard (Rutten and van der Wahl 2014: 3). The history of writing in Norway offers a perspective that can shed light on the importance of external history such as migration, politics and ideologies for deciding which linguistic features survive the test of time in a linguistic community, and which disappear. For example, the immigration of German merchants led to changes in the vocabulary, the union with Denmark led to morphological simplification, and ideology led to the emergence of two written standards. Emphasis is placed on the following questions relating to Norway. What language was used and when? How did reading and writing skills develop in the population? What did people read? How was the spelling regulated, and how did input from reading in combination with regulations imparted through the schools influence the output? Orthography, in the broad sense that also includes the spelling of morphological features, has at times had strong political connotations. This is often referred to as *målstrid* 'language struggle', especially in the early twentieth century. Most literature on the issue addressed in this chapter is written in Norwegian. However, Haugen's *Language Conflict and Language Planning* (Haugen 1966a) gives a broad overview of the standardization process from the end of the nineteenth century until 1960. His book also discusses how politics and language planning were intertwined with one another during this period. Jahr deals with some of the same questions in his book *Language Planning as a Sociolinguistic Experiment* (Jahr 2014).

Norwegian is a North Germanic language used exclusively in Norway. There have historically been Norwegian speakers in the Americas, mostly in the United States, but also in Canada and South America (Haugen 1953); however, their number has been declining for a long time now (Johannessen and Salmons 2012, Kinn 2020). The estimated population of Norway in 2022, when this chapter was written, was approximately 5.4 million. The majority have Norwegian as their first language, but not all. Immigration from other parts of the world since the 1970s is one reason for this. In addition, there has, as long as records have been kept in Norway, been a minority in the northern part of the country that speak the Finno-Ugrian language Sámi. Finnish has also been spoken in many areas in the north since the eighteenth century. Neither Sámi nor Finnish is discussed further in this chapter but, in short, the period up until the mid-nineteenth century was characterized by multilingualism, where a significant portion of the northern population spoke Sámi, Finnish and Norwegian (Johansen 2013, Bull et al. 2018). However, as a result of the romantic-nationalist movement of the nineteenth century, which emphasized the slogan *one nation, one language*, there was a campaign to make all inhabitants of Norway speak the same language. The Sámi- and Finnish-speaking people were strongly encouraged, and in some cases forced, to give up their languages, and after a hundred years the use of these minority languages had diminished. The ideological turn around in the middle of the twentieth century led to very slow but persistent attempts to secure the minority languages, and today revitalization is vivid (Johansen 2013, Mæhlum 2019).

24.2 Orthography and Alphabets

One might claim that the shape of the letters is of minor importance for the study of orthography, since words are spelled the same no matter what kind of letters are used. However, several facts lead one to treat letters as core empirical elements in historical orthography. Knowing the function and use of each and every letter of an alphabet is vital for literacy, and being able to form signs that bear a meaning has in itself been looked upon as an important skill. Interesting is also the fact that language-internal factors, such as the introduction or disappearance of individual phonemes, has led to development of new letters in different alphabets when they were introduced to new languages (Mørck 2018: 309).

The orthographic history of Norwegian goes back to the first runic inscriptions in the first centuries AD (Spurkland 2005, Schulte 2015). The runic alphabet (usually called *fuþark* from the first six runes; see also Chapter 12, this volume) was used for more than a thousand years; the youngest inscriptions found are from the middle of the fifteenth century (Mørck 2018: 310).

During the thousand years of runic representation of Norwegian, the language structure went through vast changes, and the runic alphabet also changed after being influenced by the Latin alphabet, which was introduced in Norway together with the Christian faith during the late tenth and early eleventh centuries. Interestingly, the runic alphabet also had a graphic influence on the Latin alphabet used in Norway. The rune ᚦ representing /θ/ was included in the Latin alphabet. This consonant was also part of English, and it was by contact with English that the rune in question was accepted into the Latin alphabet that was used in Norway. By 1500 the corresponding letters had not been used any more, partly because the letter combinations *th* and *dh* were used instead of the single letters *þ* and *ð*, and partly because the sounds they represented were disappearing from spoken Norwegian. However, the letter combinations *dh* and *th* were used even if the consonants they represented merged with *d* and *t* (Mørck 2018: 309).

The Black Death, which reached Norway in AD 1349, also led to great changes in orthography. A common explanation for this is that most of those who were literate were clerics; they saw to the sick – and were infected by the plague. Therefore, a greater portion of literates, compared to illiterates, died. After the plague, there were fewer people who were able to instruct new writers in the old norm, and young people then had to find their own way in writing. Most likely, this led to the written language becoming a better representation of spoken Norwegian, including its geographic variation. In the historiography of the Norwegian language, the period between the plague and the Reformation of the Church, that is 1350–1536, is called Middle Norwegian (*mellomnorsk*). During this period, the language changed from Old Norse to Early Modern Norwegian. Most importantly, a number of grammatical distinctions were lost. In nouns, the four cases, nominative, accusative, dative and genitive, merged into one form. The verb inflection changed dramatically, too. Naturally, in such a large and sparsely inhabited country, these processes did not happen at the same time all over; there are still dialects with remnants of case and number endings on verbs (Berg et al. 2018: 225–28). The morphological changes coincided with changes in word order, which became more strictly regulated. In addition to phonological, morphological and syntactic changes, the vocabulary changed dramatically, as loads of Low German words and word-forming elements were introduced into all the Scandinavian varieties (Christensen 2012: 123–26, Mørck 2018: 330). The speed at which these changes became visible in the writing of people varies according to genre, geography and the rank of the writer (Mørck 1999: 276–81).

During the Middle Norwegian period, the three Scandinavian languages influenced one another more than they did during previous centuries, due to political contact. Indeed, Denmark, Sweden and Norway were united in changing alliances during this period, and if the so-called Kalmar Union (1389–1521), which united all three countries, had lasted, a common, Scandinavian written language might have emerged. However, this did not happen. Sweden ended up as an independent country with a written language of its own, while Norway became a part of Denmark, and gradually the Norwegians started writing Danish. This did not result from forcible intervention but from adopting what must have been perceived as a more prestigious and modern variety at the time. All these changes are in sum the reason why the sixteenth century is seen as the beginning of Modern Norwegian (Nesse and Torp 2018). It is thus at this point I begin my overview of reading, writing and orthography.

First, some words of caution. Whereas syntactic features can be easily identified as just that, the distinctions separating morphological, phonological and orthographic features are not always equally straightforward. Some graphic variables – such as the use of capital letters, the use of the letters *æ*, *ø* and *å*, or the use of diacritics – are easily defined. Drawing the line between phonological and orthographic changes is not always easy, however, and even morphology can sometimes be seen as orthography; in the Norwegian tradition it often is. In fact, to write about Norwegian orthography without including morphological variation and morphological changes is difficult. An example from modern Norwegian may be helpful here: the Bokmål standard has the suffix *-er* in the present tense of verbs like *hopper* 'jump(s)', *dømmer* 'judge(s)' and *leser* 'read(s)';[1] the Nynorsk standard has *hoppar*, *dømmer* and *skriv*, respectively, since the three verbs belong to different verb classes.[2] For accustomed writers of Bokmål trying to write Nynorsk, this can be a challenge. For those who do not have this division of suffixes in their dialects, and are not familiar with the concept of different verb classes, the variation between the endings may be conceived as mere orthographic coincidences. Since the verb class with the suffix *-ar* is the largest, a common mistake is to write *hoppar*, *dømmar* and *skrivar* using this most frequent ending, which fails to recognize the morphological aspect. This does not mean that linguists should not see this as morphology, but rather that the inclusion of such phenomena may deserve its place in the present chapter.

24.3 What Is Norwegian, and What Should We Call the Language?

For Norwegians this is a perfectly sound question. For non-Norwegians, however, it may seem like an unnecessary question to ask. But the concept of 'Norwegian', which first appeared in the written sources of the fifteenth century (see Sandøy 2018: 161), has been used in very different ways since

[1] Bokmål is a written standard based on the Danish-Norwegian koiné spoken by the urban upper classes from the eighteenth century on.

[2] Nynorsk is a written standard based on nineteenth-century rural dialects and Old Norse.

then. Present-day Norwegian consists of many dialects and two official written standards, both developed during the latter half of the nineteenth century as Ausbau languages (Kloss 1967, Trudgill 1997: 151–54). For both standards, dissimilarity to Danish was a major motivation for their creation. Bokmål 'book language' is based on an oral koiné based on both Danish and Norwegian that evolved in the educated classes from the late eighteenth century onward.[3] Today, approximately 90 percent of the population prefer to use this standard in writing. Nynorsk 'New Norwegian' is based on an oral koiné between several rural, mostly West Norwegian dialects and Old Norse. Today, approximately 10 percent of the population prefer to use this standard in writing. Both written Danish, Bokmål and Nynorsk (and Swedish) are to a large extent mutually intelligible (Haugen 1966b, Torp 2004), and the orthographic differences have played a major role in defining the two Norwegian varieties as different from Danish.

When working with the written language used in Norway during the Danish-Norwegian union, a difficulty has been the labeling of the written code used in Norway. Should the term *Norwegian* be used, because of the dialect features that can be found in the writings of Norwegians? Or should it be called *Danish*, since the norm center was at all times during this period the capital city Copenhagen? Some have applied double names like *Dansk-norsk* 'Dano-Norwegian' or *Norsk-dansk* 'Norwegian-Danish', but today the most common terminology is to call the dialects 'Norwegian' and the written code 'Danish'. An interesting point is that when the union between the two countries ended and Norway had its constitution in 1814, the fathers of the constitution stated that the language of the country should be *Norsk* 'Norwegian'; by this they meant the Danish they were used to. This may seem strange, but the reason is that Norway in 1814 had entered into a new union, this time with Sweden, and the important point for the writers of the Constitution was that the Swedish language should not be forced upon the Norwegians. Rather, the Norwegians should be allowed to use the written code that they were used to, the Danish one. Danish linguists protested fiercely against the naming of Danish as Norwegian, and the solution was that in schools, grammars and so on the written language was labeled *Modersmaalet* 'the mother tongue', which came to mean 'Danish with Norwegian interference' (Hoel 2018: 434–35).

During the first half of the twentieth century, language choice and language naming were tied to Norwegian politics. The conservatives were in favor of the Dano-Norwegian koiné, and the liberals were in favor of the rural koiné. Both sides wanted their variety to become the sole national language.

[3] *Bokmål* has been the official name since 1929. Before 1929 the two standards were called first *Rigsmaal* and *Landsmaal*, later *Riksmål* and *Landsmål*. In this chapter, the names *Bokmål* and *Nynorsk* are also used when discussing spelling from before 1929.

In 1929 the terms *Bokmål* and *Nynorsk* were introduced instead of the old terms *Rigsmaal* and *Landsmaal*. The new terms were controversial but are still in use (Haugen 1966a, Jahr 2014, Rambø 2018: 573–74). The emerging Labor party tried to stay out of the language conflict, claiming that economic matters were more important than spelling. Later, they became proponents of a uniform Norwegian that included features from both standards. The attempt to unite Bokmål and Nynorsk in a common standard was official Norwegian policy until 2002, when Parliament decided that the existence of two official written standards was to be actively promoted (Vikør 2018: 674).

24.4 Literacy in Norway

The ability to read and write, and a certain familiarity with the concept 'text' is often referred to as *literacy*. We use terms such as *illiterate societies* or we discuss 'the emergence of literacy in a certain country'. Obviously, knowing about orthographic patterns in the language one wants to read and/or write is an important part of this. But how developed must one person's ability to read or write be for us to call her or him 'literate'? It is commonly recognized that it was not until around 1900 that Norway became a truly literate society, in the sense that it could be expected that most people of a certain age were able to read and write (Hoel 2018: 452–53). An exception was to a certain degree the Sámi population in the north. Here the strategy of sending Sámi children to boarding schools where the Sámi language was banned failed in its aim to teach them to become fluent in reading and writing Norwegian (Rambø 2018: 552–53).

If we go back in history, the extent and the social distribution of literacy is less clear. Literacy in the early runic period seems, to judge by the inscriptions we can see today, not to have been a common skill (see Schulte 2015). Many inscriptions have the name of the rune master as part of the inscription, which may mean that carving runes was considered more of an art than an activity for everyone to take part in. From the Middle Ages, however, there seems to have been a more widespread distribution of this runic craftmanship, while at the same time a number of people learned to read and write the Latin alphabet (Haugen 2018: 201–2). The texts written in the two alphabets seem to differ systematically from one another. This divide may be due to several reasons. One may be the fact that the artifacts used to write Latin were expensive; pen, ink and parchment had to be specially made for the purpose. To write or carve runes, all you needed was a piece of wood and a knife. Wood was everywhere to be found, since it was used for heating, building houses, furniture, tools and so on. Norway was a country with great forests and few people, and wood was exported to other countries. Unlike many other places, in Norway a piece of wood was affordable writing material (Bagge and Mykland 1987: 126–30).

In addition to this, a knife was every person's most important tool, always carried in the belt. In Bergen, more than a thousand runic inscriptions from the Middle Ages have been found. Some seem to be writing exercises, when a stick simply contains the runic alphabet. Other inscriptions fall into the categories of religion or magic, or function as business letters (Liestøl 1963: 12–15, Hagland 2011). The majority, however, are simply short messages or labels on goods, the latter often with the name of the owner and the verb *á* 'owns' (Liestøl 1963: 6).

There are indications that runic writing in the Middle Ages was somewhat more orthophonic than texts with Latin letters. One such inscription from Bergen reads, in transcribed form, *gya: sæhir: atþu: kakhæim*, in normalized Old Norse *Gyða segir at þú gakk heim* 'Gyda (fem. name) tells you "go home"' (Liestøl 1963: 21). In the name *gya/Gyða* as well as in the verb *sæhir/segir* (present tense, third person singular), developments well known from other sources and newer dialect history can be seen. The *ð* was either changed to *d* or lost, and in this case we see that it had possibly been lost, since the runic inscription simply has *gya*. The *g* in *sæhir/segir* was most likely pronounced as a fricative /ɣ/; thus the spelling with *h* may have been a more accurate pronunciation of this word (Schulte 2011: 179). However, there are also features in this inscription that speak against the idea of orthophonic script, for instance the spelling *kak* for Old Norse *gakk* 'go!' (imperative). The runic alphabet went through different phases, and during one of them, voiced and unvoiced variants of the same phoneme were spelled with the same rune, so each of the pairs /g/ ~ /k/, /d/ ~ /t/, /b/ ~ /p/ shared one letter. Later, the voiced variants were marked by a diacritic, which could easily get lost since they were only dots. A wooden stick that has been lying in the ground for 700 years or more might easily have lost a small part where such a dot had been carved, so we cannot know for sure if the writer wrote *kak* or *gak*. Nevertheless, even if the runic inscriptions from medieval Bergen show that a number of common people seem to have been able to write and read runes, this does not mean that this is representative of the whole population. Traders have often been at the forefront of literacy. One of the great benefits of the Hanseatic League was its apt inclusion of writing in its business dealings. In medieval Bergen, most people were directly or indirectly connected to trade; this means that a larger portion of the population was literate compared to other places (Nesse 2017: 168–69).

The modern Norwegian period is to a considerable extent defined by the reformation of the Church. One might think that the Reformation led to increased literacy, due to Luther's emphasis on the closeness of each person to the religious texts. However, as far as existing research shows, it is not until the eighteenth century that the effect of the Reformation on the level of literacy becomes visible (Fet 1995, Bull 2015). The general growth in literacy is connected to the introduction of compulsory confirmation in

1736, which led to the establishment of public schools in 1739 (Haukland 2014: 541, Hagland et al. 2018: 48, Nesse and Torp 2018: 385). Earlier, the introduction of literacy had been a private matter; thus teaching children to read, and sometimes to write, was left to the family. Now there was an increased effort to secure all children's reading abilities regardless of the family's approach to literacy. Whereas today we look at this as a step forward for society, many people at the time were against it. Sending children to school made organizing the life of the family more difficult. The children were needed as working hands, and practicing reading and writing was best done during those periods of the year when there was less to do on the farm. Furthermore, the farmers had to board the new teachers as well as provide the school facilities, yet another expense that was hard for some to meet (Haukland 2014: 542). The reason for establishing the new schools was to ensure that all people were able to read so that they could read religious texts (Hagland et al. 2018: 48).

Writing was not made compulsory in public schools until 1827 (Fet 2005: 30), and competence in reading without competence in writing was quite common. This means that even if some of those who signed the constitution in 1814 signed "with pen in place"[4] (Vannebo 1984: 8), it is possible that they could read. Both Haukland (2014) and Vannebo (1984) show that there were social differences in literacy as well as differences between urban and rural communities. There seem to have been geographic differences too. This was probably a result of the fact that private initiatives came to play a major part in promoting literacy in certain areas (Kildal 1948, Haukland 2014). These initiators were people with resources who built collections of books and who encouraged less fortunate people to borrow books and take part in literacy. From 1777 and for some decades afterward, prizes were established for those who built such book collections (Kildal 1948). But these prizes were not money to help develop literacy; instead the collectors received books or even silver cups (Kildal 1948: 2).

Clerics were important actors in the development of literacy (Haukland 2014). As a part of the Lutheran confirmation, they checked that young people had read the important texts and both understood and remembered them. The pastors were often part of the school board in the parish, which decided what the children were to learn and read. However, during the period from the middle of the eighteenth and to the beginning of the nineteenth century, many pastors were inspired by Enlightenment ideas to the extent that they acquired the nickname *potetprester* 'potato pastors', because they were conceived to be more eager to teach the farmers to grow potatoes than to preach the Word (Nesse and Torp 2018: 386–90). Others, who

[4] Norwegian: *Med påholden pen*. Literally, it means that someone else holds the pen and writes for you. In practice, those who could not write set an *x* by their name.

argued that the Church should concentrate on souls and not farming techniques, were provoked by this eagerness to help the members of their congregation improve their livelihood. Independent groups started to conduct church services outside the premises of the state Church, either in private homes or even outside the churches after the ordinary service (Haukland 2014: 545). The largest of these movements was initiated by Hans Nielsen Hauge (1771–1824), and his followers were called *Haugianere* or *lesere* 'readers' (Haukland 2014).

One of Hauge's achievements was to encourage not only the reading of holy texts, but also writing. Letter-writing was used to spread the ideas of the group. Hauge himself wrote more than a thousand letters (Haukland 2014: 539) and 200,000 copies of his books were printed. Hauge had not, however, enjoyed higher education, and did not master the elaborate prose style of his better educated clerical adversaries. Haukland, who has studied his letters, states that "Hauge's uneducated language bothered him. He did not write in oral style on purpose, but because of his lack of normal education" (Haukland 2014: 552). As I understand Haukland, this seems to have had more to do with insufficient knowledge of contemporary stylistic patterns and syntax than insufficient mastery of orthographic rules. Overall, Norwegian literacy clearly was a gradual ability. The people of the High Middle Ages (1050–1350) who wrote their name on a stick with the verb 'own' in the present tense added to it (see Figure 24.1) may or may not have been able to write other, more elaborate texts. Such a label, for example *Arni á* 'Arne owns', is not far from a trademark. Also, handicraftsmen in the eighteenth century who were

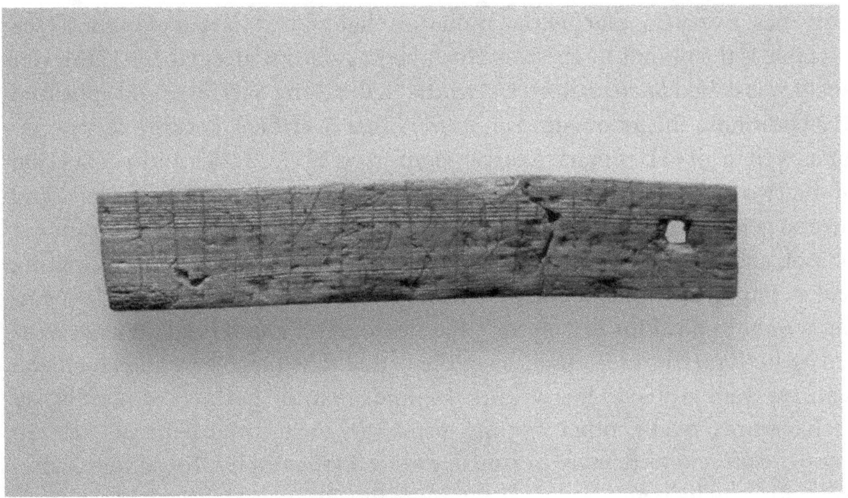

Figure 24.1 Runic stick from Bergen, the Middle Ages
(photo: Svein Skare, Bergen University Museum. License Attribution-ShareAlike, CC BY-SA)
These were fastened to goods in order to label the goods with the owner's name.

able to write a short receipt may or may not have been able to write a letter to a family member. Moreover, one should recognize that the ability to write was not only considered a communicative skill. Well into the beginning of the twentieth century, writing was also seen as handicraft in its own right, and the ability to form letters in a beautiful way was highly regarded in some groups (Gundersen 2005: 129).

24.5 What Did People Read?

In order to understand why the orthography developed the way it did, it is important to investigate what people read, since it is reasonable to assume that reading contributes to writing when it comes to both text style and orthographic details. For example, it is likely that reading influences the spelling of less frequent words, since more frequent words like personal pronouns or 'and', 'be' and so on are stored in the memory as more or less fixed entities. One methodological challenge when looking into reading habits as a way to learn more about orthography is that many texts that were once popular have not been preserved (Fet 2005: 21). There could be several explanations for this. Fet mentions low-quality paper, the sharing of texts, and the simple fact that they were not regarded as worth saving for the next generation. This means that there may be influential literature that cannot be investigated. Examples of such books may be the so-called folk books, tales, songs and other so-called low genres.

There are, on the other hand, popular books that have been kept through the centuries; a very popular genre within the religious texts is that of psalms. One example is the psalms by the poet Dorothe Engelbretsdatter (1634–1716). Her debut was called *Siælens Sang-Offer* [The Soul's Song Sacrifice] and appeared in 24 editions. The follow-up, *Taare offer* [Tear Sacrifice], became very popular as well in all of Denmark-Norway (Pettersen 1957: 11–12), and a collection of the two was published in 1699. Psalms were usually learned by heart, and several generations of children must have recited Engelbretsdatter's psalms at school, and with so many books sold we must assume that her way of writing had an important influence on people. Engelbretsdatter wrote in a style seemingly quite typical for her period. The monograph about her language written by Pettersen in 1957 emphasizes the extent to which Norwegian dialectal features were visible in her writing. He finds that the psalms did not display such features, but her other writings, especially the favored genre of letters in rhyme (*rimbrev*) were more personal, even in orthography. Those were, however, not read by many, and were therefore less influential. Engelbretsdatter's most famous psalm begins as follows in her original, seventeenth-century Danish-Norwegian orthography:

DAgen viger og gaar bort,
Lufften bliffver tyck og sort,
Solen har alt Dalet plat,
Det gaar ad den mørcke Nat.

[The day fades and goes away,
The air becomes thick and black,
The sun has already gone down,
We go toward the dark night.]

This psalm has been sung ever since it was written, but the spelling has been altered through the centuries. In the modern spelling from 1985 (Norsk salmebok 1985) it provides a good illustration of the way older texts have been modernized in lexicon, morphology and orthography. It is not only psalms that have been altered in this way; novels, plays and other texts published in new editions are modernized to a greater or lesser degree.

Dagen viker og går bort,
Himmelen blir tung og sort,
Solen har oss alt forlatt,
Nær oss er den mørke natt.

[The day fades and goes away,
The sky becomes heavy and black,
The sun has already left us,
Near us is the dark night.]

One characteristic feature in the spelling of Engelbretsdatter and other writers of her period is the use of capital letters. This had not yet reached the pattern we find later in the eighteenth century, when all nouns were marked by capital letters. In 1877, capitalization was (in principle) restricted to personal names and sentence-initial elements (Popp 1977), but the general use of capital letters in all nouns lingered on for decades. In Engelbretsdatter's time, capitalization could be a way to place emphasis on certain words, but in some instances it seems that aesthetic considerations – or simply old habit – governed its use.

Another feature is the consistent use of double *f*, often followed by a *v* or a *u*. The word *bliffver* 'becomes' was most likely pronounced /bli: ver/, which means that the sequence *ffv* or *ffu* represented the single consonant /v/. When looking at the writing of the time, it is clear that the letter *f*, both in handwriting and in print, is similar to other letters, such as *h* (in handwriting) and the 'long' *s*. This seems to be a reasonable explanation for the use of *ff* or *ffv* instead of just *f*, since one wanted to avoid misinterpretation of the words. The letter combination *ck*, which we find in *tyck* 'thick' and *mørcke* 'dark', is also worth mentioning. In present-day Norwegian, *tyck* appears as *tykk* and *mørcke* as *mørke*. In both words, the vowel is short, but present-day Norwegian shortens the geminated consonant in consonant clusters. This rule did not apply at the time when Engelbretsdatter was doing her writing. Back then, the combination *ck* simply signaled that the preceding vowel was short. Last, but not least, the period allowed for different realizations of the letter that Engelbretsdatter writes as *ø*. This marks a central, mid-high rounded vowel, which has been part of the alphabet for as long as Scandinavian languages have been written with Latin letters. Its graphic shape has been either *ø* or *ö* (both long and short), or as the ligature *œ*, used in Old Norse to mark the long vowel. Today, Danish and Norwegian use *ø*, while Swedish, like German, uses *ö*; in handwriting, different variants may occur.

Other ways to learn about people's reading habits – in addition to looking at books like Dorothe Engelbretsdatter's psalm collections – is to study lists of books that people owned. A unique work based on sources from several parts of rural Norway was conducted by Fet (1995, 2003). He went through 16,287 probated estates from the eighteenth century, recording all books mentioned in these estates. Fet's work provides interesting information about what kind of books people, mostly farmers, owned in rural Norway. One important fact is that a larger number of farmers owned books than had previously been assumed. Fet's findings also showed that even if religious texts such as psalms, devotional books and didactic books dominate in the estates, other kinds of texts show that reading was more varied than had been previously assumed.

In 1777, it was decided that all learned schools (*latinskolene*) in Denmark-Norway should use one and the same book for reading instruction. This was not a religious book, but a book about famous people who had served their country in spectacular ways. The book was specially designed for use in schools and its author was Ove Malling (1748–1829). The title was *Store og gode Handlinger af Danske, Norske og Holstenere* [Great and Good Deeds by Danes, Norwegians and Holsteinians] (Jacobsen 2010: 68–70). Since the children who read this book would later enter higher positions in society, it must have been influential as a guide for correct spelling. The book has therefore been considered the starting point for a unified spelling in the Danish-Norwegian state. For the majority of the population, who did not attend these schools, the reader on Christianity by the Danish bishop Erik Pontoppidan may have been equally important as a pattern for writing. This book was first published in 1737 and was used in Norway until the beginning of the twentieth century. During the eighteenth century, it appeared in more than 40 editions, and in some years more than 10,000 copies were printed (Horstbøll 2005: 59).

During the nineteenth century, Norwegians and Danes largely read the same books, and even if some grammar books had different titles, the content was usually identical in both countries. The Norwegian grammarian Maurits Hansen (1794–1842) changed the title of his grammar book for school children from edition to edition: *Forsøg til en Grammatik i Modersmaalet* (1822),

Grammatik i det norske og danske Sprog (1828) and finally *Norsk Grammatik* (1833). In the edition from 1828, he wrote in his preface that he hoped each reader would use the title that pleased him the best (Hoel 2018: 435). Not only the reading habits but even the literary market were one and the same in Denmark and Norway, long after the dissolution of the political union between the two countries. However, Nynorsk texts were not so easy for Danes to comprehend; therefore the common literary market was first and foremost for books written in Bokmål, which were by far the more common; and Bokmål was also the preferred variety for both Henrik Ibsen (1828–1906) and Bjørnstjerne Bjørnson (1832–1910). Bjørnson did have an interest in Nynorsk in his younger days, and some of his short stories were translated into Nynorsk (Hubacek 1996: 42–48). Later he realized the economic advantages of keeping the common Danish-Norwegian literary market alive and became a fierce advocate of Bokmål. In order to manage this balance between a common book market and growing changes in the written language in Norway, he provided word explanations for the Danish readers. His 1898 edition of the very popular tale of *Synnøve Solbakken* (Bjørnson 1898) had footnotes with word explanations on almost every page. Norwegian words like *Sau* 'sheep', *braane* 'to melt – about snow' and *sint* 'angry' were translated with the equivalent Danish words *Faar*, *smelte* and *vred*. How Norwegian readers reacted to this has not been investigated. Most likely, for some it contributed to strengthening their positive attitude toward linguistic separation from Danish.

There were several important writers who chose Nynorsk, in spite of the economic disadvantages. Nynorsk texts became rather popular, and not just in those areas where the dialects showed the greatest similarity to Nynorsk. An important literary genre where Nynorsk was frequently used was drama written for amateurs in the different youth associations (*ungdomslag*) across the country. Ivar Aasen, the creator of Nynorsk wrote a play entitled *Ervingen* (Aasen 1855) in addition to numerous poems. Walton (1987: 190) sees Aasen's linguistic, literary and political work as intertwined: "Whilst Aasen's linguistic work is the basis for his belletristic writing, this in turn casts light onto the counter-hegemonic aspirations which are the basis for the linguistic project." Another important author of plays was Hulda Garborg (1862–1934). She was the driving force in establishing the first professional Nynorsk theater in 1912, but before that, her plays had been performed by both amateur and professional actors (Skre 2011: 228). Most of her plays were written in Nynorsk, but in her preface to the comedy *Rationelt Fjøsstell* [Rational Dairy Management] (Garborg 1896), she writes (in Bokmål) that even if the plays are written in Nynorsk, she wishes that those who perform her plays should use their own dialect. This example shows us that already in the 1890s the amateur actors, who often were farmers and servants in the countryside, were expected to read both Nynorsk and Bokmål, as well as to be able to adjust a written standard to their own dialect. All in all, this is quite a sophisticated linguistic task.

During the twentieth century, most Norwegians were brought up learning to read, and to some extent write, both Nynorsk and Bokmål. In 1944 as many as 34 percent of new pupils were to have Nynorsk as their language of instruction (Rambø 2018: 596), but since then the number has declined gradually. In the academic year 2021–2022, 11.6 percent of the youngest pupils and 6 percent of the pupils in secondary schools had Nynorsk as their language of instruction. The language of instruction is chosen by the parents for the youngest pupils, and by the pupils themselves for the older ones (The Norwegian Directorate for Education and Training 2023). The majority of Norwegians during the twentieth and twenty-first centuries have had some experience in reading their mother tongue in more than one version, both Nynorsk and Bokmål. Furthermore, since there are many alternate forms of both Nynorsk and Bokmål, most Norwegians have read the same words in many forms. The following are a couple of examples: 'the bridge' can in Bokmål be spelled as *broen*, *broa*, *bruen* or *brua*; in Nynorsk, the verb 'to wish' can be spelled *ynska*, *ynske*, *ynskja*, *ynskje*, *ønska*, *ønske*, *ønskja*, *ønskje*. Fortunately, not all words have so many variants, but the examples illustrate the challenges Norwegians face when writing. The knowledge that most words have more than one possible variant can lead to uncertainty as to which spelling is correct. However, the ideology behind this is that the written norm should be inclusive – we should all find our own forms in at least one of the two standards. This writer prefers *broen* when she writes Bokmål, and *ønske* when she writes Nynorsk.

24.6 Ideas behind the Spelling Reforms

As discussed in Chapter 29, this volume, orthography is not separate from politics. Norway is a good case study for anyone who wants to investigate how certain suffixes can gain symbolic power in a society. This is not the place to deal in depth with the ideological basis of the spelling reforms (Haugen 1966a and Jahr 2014 discuss this issue in their books, both written in English). Nevertheless, roughly speaking, one can say that there have been three main ideologies, partly succeeding one another, but partly also competing with one another. One can be labeled *national honor*, the second *leveling of social class differences* and the third *actual use*. Since school is the one place where orthography is actually a theme, children's needs and pedagogical considerations have also played a part in the debate.

Both Norwegian standards were developed in the same cultural climate of nationalism and the ideas of Johann Gottfried Herder (1744–1803) that a nation could only truly express itself if it possessed a tongue of its own (Jahr 2014: 44). This national tongue should also be the written standard of the people of the nation. Both Nynorsk and Bokmål were seen as Norwegian by their creators and users, and both were indeed Norwegian – in the sense that they were both primarily used in Norway. Still, in the struggle for being most characteristically Norwegian, the urban elite was doomed to fail, since Bokmål was a mixed language, close to Danish. Scholars like Didrik Arup Seip (1884–1963) tried to demonstrate that the koiné derived from the Dano-Norwegian spoken by the urban elites was indeed not a koiné but purely Norwegian (Jahr et al. 2016: 48); nevertheless, things seemed to go the wrong way for Bokmål. The end of the Swedish-Norwegian union, which lasted from 1814 until 1905, had great symbolic impact as well. The Danish prince Carl (1872–1957) was invited to become Norway's king, and in doing so he changed both his own and his son Alexander's names, taking the old Norse kings names *Haakon* and *Olav*, respectively (Bomann-Larsen 2004: 456).

However, class struggles of the 1920s and 1930s made national ideology less important (Kjeldstadli 1994). The ideology of the communist leaders was to a great extent international, and other matters were more important than language. A much-used quote from leading men in the Labor party is that it does not really matter how we spell the expression 'the pot', what matters is that we have food to put into it (Sandøy 1975: 58). The expression 'the pot' was chosen deliberately, since within Bokmål there was a debate if *gryta* or *gryten* was the better form (Jahr 1994: 67–86, Rambø 2018: 580–81). In 1938, this was settled in a new reform that tried to combine the two standards, making *gryta* the main form in both Bokmål and Nynorsk. Conveniently, this was also the form that was used in the dialects of the populous lower classes in the urban areas of the southeast. These constituted an important group of voters for the Labor party, which gained much power during the 1930s (Jahr 1994: 67–86, Rambø 2018: 580–81).

The Second World War (in Norway 1940–45) led in some ways to the return of *national* as an important virtue, but the language question ended up being quite irrelevant. During the war the line between a good and a bad Norwegian only had to do with how one conducted oneself toward the German occupation, not how you wrote (Rambø 2018: 602). In the postwar period, the language conflict was not first and foremost between the advocates of Bokmål and Nynorsk, but between those in favor of amalgamation of the two standards, on the one hand, and more traditionally oriented people who wanted two different written standards, on the other. Parents organized protests against assimilated spelling, and they 'corrected' their children's schoolbooks with a pen; for example, *gryta* would be changed to *gryten* and *brua* to *broen* (Vikør 2018: 618–19). Eventually, toward the end of the twentieth century, the authorities gave up little by little the attempt to achieve one uniform norm for written Norwegian. The spelling reforms for Bokmål in 2005 and Nynorsk in 2012 were based on actual use in published books, newspapers and so on (Vikør 2018: 673–85). Neither national honor nor leveling of social class was used as an argument in the new spellings; rather use, authenticity and tradition were important ideological arguments.

24.7 The Actual Writing

When discussing the orthographic patterns or practices among those members of the population who had some or advanced writing skills, it is important to note that both printing and standardization came late to Norway. The first printing press was set up around 1643 (Hagland et al. 2018: 44), and the first Norwegian book store opened in 1771 (Haukland 2014: 541). Although books were sent to Copenhagen for publishing, the tradition of copying books by hand remained well into the eighteenth century (Hagland et al. 2018: 44–45). One book that was not published until a critical edition emerged in 1858 was *Bergens Fundas* (Nicolaysen 1858, Sørlie 1957, Nesse 2021), the first history book to be written about the city of Bergen. A total of 22 handwritten manuscripts have been saved of this book, about half of them in the Dano-Norwegian orthography of the time, the other half being translations into German.[5] The spelling varies, not only from one manuscript to another but also throughout the text of individual manuscripts. When the author writes about the distant past, he is influenced by the language of the Old Norse sources; when he writes about contemporary events, the linguistic anachronisms are fewer (Sørlie 1957: 16). An example from *Bergens Fundas* can serve as an illustration of sixteenth-century orthography:

> Anno MCDLXXvj Branndt Bryggenn Aldt sammens aff, Oc siiden denn tiidt haffuer de hinnde saa Ordentligen opbygdt, som hun nu er Funderrit. Thj tillforne da haffuer denn Platz verrit bygdt, liigesom Stranden nu er.
>
> [Anno 1476 the Pier burned, all of it, and afterward have they built it up again for real, the way it is founded now. For earlier that place has been built like the Beach is now. (from Sørlie 1957: 59)]

Bryggen 'the pier' and *Stranden* 'the Beach' denote places in Bergen, facing one another across the bay. The use of capital letters is not ruled by word class in this spelling system. In addition to the place names *Bryggen* and *Stranden*, *Platz* 'place' is the only noun in the extract. In *Bergens Fundas* there is a general tendency for nouns to be capitalized, but there are many exceptions. In the conjunction *Thj* 'though' we see the use of *j* to mark the vowel *i* /iː/. This was common both in writing words and numbers – 'three' was very often written *iij*, with *j* at the end. Gemination of letters is common in this text. In words like *Branndt* 'fire' and *sammens* 'together' the gemination of the consonant letters *n* and *m* marks that the vowel is short. On the other hand, it is uncertain whether the verb form *verrit* 'been' was pronounced with a long or short vowel. Words with the syllable structure VC in Old Norse, like *vera* 'to be', developed differently in different dialects, and both in the eastern part of

[5] German translations are not considered here. One of them is published in Nesse (2002).

Norway as well as in the city dialect of Bergen VCC has been common (East Norwegian commonly /væra/). Other West Norwegian dialects had VVC, as in /ve:ra/. In the early twentieth century, the pronunciation in the Bergen dialect was either /vuʁe/ or /væʁt/; from before that time we have no direct information about the pronunciation. The gemination of vowels, as in *siiden* 'after' and *tiidt* 'time', marks that the vowel is long. The exception to this system is the use of geminated *ff* or even *ffu* to write the consonant /v/ after a long vowel. This may be due, as mentioned in Section 24.5, to graphic considerations, since the handwritten *f* could be hard to distinguish from both *h* and the so-called long *s*.

Moving onward to the seventeenth century, we have a possibility to trace changes in writing habits through several generations of one family who stayed in the same city and belonged to the same social class (Nesse 2012, 2013: 94–105). The Meltzer family was, like many other merchant families in Bergen at the time, both German and Norwegian. The first Meltzer in Bergen, Clamer Meltzer (1656–1730) was an immigrant who wrote only German, but his wife, Anna Hammeken (1692–1774), who was born in Bergen as the daughter of a German merchant married to a Norwegian wife, wrote Dano-Norwegian. The only text we have from Anna Hammeken's hand is a short life description,[6] where she writes about important dates in her life from when she was born and until she had buried two husbands and several children. Her style possesses a certain literary quality and is very fluent. She has more dialectal features in her writing than her descendants, which shows that standardization had not come very far in Norway at the time, and that she, like most girls, may have received less formal education than boys of her social class. Spellings like *gott* 'good' and *ver* 'every' show deletion of consonants that were at the time mute in the spoken language, but retained in writing as *godt* and *hver*. There is no sign of German influence apart from certain graphic elements; for instance, Anna uses the letter *ß* quite frequently. A change from the spelling in *Bergens Fundas* is that she marks long vowels by the insertion of an *e* rather than by gemination: *goede* 'good, plural', *døede* 'died'. Short vowels are, like earlier, marked by gemination of the next consonant, as in *komme* 'come', or by *ck*, as in *fick* 'received'.

From Anna Hammeken's grandson Clamer Meltzer (1745–1815) we have a number of texts in an account book.[7] Texts of this genre provide interesting information about abbreviation practices, like the writing of *Hund*ʳ for *hundrede* 'hundred'. Dialect features used by Clamer Meltzer include *dager* 'days' and *Spruten* 'the fire hose' where *Dage* and *Sprøjten* would be the more correct forms. The morphological distinction in Danish where some masculine nouns (like *dag*) have the ending *-e* and some the ending *-er* did not

[6] The Norwegian Digital Archive

[7] Bergen, University Library, MS 613.

coincide with the Norwegian dialects, where some dialects have an *-r* in all masculine nouns and others a vowel (usually *-a* or *-e*). The Bergen dialect has *-r* in the plural of all nouns apart from monosyllabic neuters. So *dager* can be perceived as a dialectal form. The form *Spruten* seems to be a dialectal compromise between the Low German *Sprutte* and the Dano-Norwegian definite singular *Sprøjten*. Such forms were rather common in the bilingual society that Bergen was at the time. Furthermore, Clamer Meltzer uses capital letters much at random and has the same gemination practice that was common earlier, marking both long and short vowels. He uses *ck* instead of geminated *k*.

The next generation marks a change in many ways. From Clamer Meltzer's son, Fredrik Meltzer (1779–1855), we have letters and diaries, all to be found in the University library of Bergen. He was an active writer of a diary when he traveled, both in Norway and abroad, and he wrote numerous letters. Fredrik Meltzer was also one of those present when the Norwegian constitution was formed in 1814, and he owes his fame more to this than his occupation as merchant. His writing practice is less varied than the earlier members of the family, and standardization efforts can be easily traced. Even in his least formal texts, consisting of summaries of the first 20 years of his 13 children's lives written on uneven sheets of paper, his writing bears the mark of standardization based on the language of Copenhagen. This must mean that writing the same word in the same way every time he wrote must have become automatic. In addition to decreasing variation, there are other interesting changes. Fredrik Meltzer uses the letter *æ* much more frequently than his ancestors, as in words like *giæntagen* 'repeated', *Lærerne* 'the teachers' and *Knæerne* 'the knees'. Anna Hammeken writes *lerre* 'learn', which is derived from the same root as *Lærerne*. Both the change from *e* to *æ* and the change from geminated to simple consonant can be seen as typical results of the standardization process. It is unlikely that this new use of *æ* had anything to do with the Bergen dialect or with the pronunciation of Danish in Copenhagen. It was in essence a writing convention, and during the nineteenth century, the use of *æ* vs. *e* was the subject of much debate, both in Denmark and in Norway (Jacobsen 2010: 99, 480–82, Popp 1977).

Fredrik Meltzer's children were skilled writers. One of them, Harald (1814–62), became an author. Here, I use examples from letters written by Fredrik's daughter Lydia Meltzer (1821–1863).[8] The letters written to her brother Oscar (1822–1904) show a combination of oral and literary style. Like her father, she uses capital letters in all nouns; she also uses capital letters in second person pronouns, that is, *Du* 'you singular subject', *Dig* 'you, singular objec.' and *Dine* 'you, singular possessive', whereas her ancestor Anna Hammeken used capital letters in the first person pronoun *Jeg* 'I'. This is an interesting change; Anna's usage can be compared with present-day English, whereas Lydia's

8 Bergen, University Library, MS 936.B.2.

practice corresponds to present-day German (until the spelling reform of 1998/2005). Present-day Norwegian has clear restrictions on the use of capital letters, confining their use to the beginning of main clauses and proper names. In Lydia's letters, short vowels are marked by gemination of the following consonant, as in *sidde* 'sit'. As far as the letters *x* and *q* are concerned, which had a stable position in writing for centuries, Lydia Meltzer uses them in the traditional fashion, writing *strax* 'soon' with *x* representing /ks/, and *qvikke* 'quick, plural' with *q* for /kv/. During the latter half of the nineteenth century, a slow process started to remove the letters *c*, *q*, *w*, *x* and *z* from as many words as possible. These were replaced either by groups of consonants (*q* to *kv*, *x* to *ks* and *z* to *t* or *ts*), or by another letter (*c* was replaced by *k* and *w* was replaced by *v*).

The writings of the Meltzer family demonstrate a gradual change from an orthography allowing for considerable variation, including the use of dialect features, toward a more uniform standard variety. From Lydia's writing and onward, variation becomes more common again, but this time variation is not a reflection of the absence of a standard as in earlier centuries, but rather of uncertainty as to what the standard(s) should be. The changes can be followed along two dimensions: first, the establishing of two competing official standards, both of which were, from 1892, allowed as a language of instruction in schools; and, second, changes within the two standards, and the struggle to merge them. A merger was wanted by the authorities, but not in a random way allowing writers to be free to use spellings from either of the two standards as they felt inclined. The merger should be orchestrated by the authorities and was to be achieved in accordance with rules and regulations passed by Parliament (Rambø 2018: 582–87).

An example, written by a South Norwegian farmer in a protocol in the 1960s,[9] can serve as illustration (Nesse 2013: 144). He wrote Bokmål, but mixed both older forms and forms from Nynorsk into his writing. For instance, he wrote that *Regnskapen blei oplest og godkjent* 'The account was read aloud and approved'. The first word, *Regnskapen*, is declined as a masculine noun, which is correct in Nynorsk *rekneskapen*, but in Bokmål it is supposed to be *regnskapet*, of neuter gender. Whether this form is a dialectal form or a Nynorsk/Bokmål hybrid is hard to establish; both may in fact be the case. The auxiliary verb *blei* 'was' is a compromise form, allowed both in Nynorsk and in Bokmål. The main verb *oplest* 'read' shows pre-1938 Bokmål orthography; it was then changed to *opplest* in Bokmål and *opplesen* in Nynorsk, both with a geminated *p*. His form may serve as an example of how long it takes to implement changes in orthography. If we choose to see this farmer's writing from a strictly Norwegian diachronic perspective, there are no mistakes in this sentence, but the writer has mixed both

[9] The Norwegian Digital Archive.

Nynorsk and Bokmål, and newer and older forms. Even if our farmer wrote correct Norwegian in the broad sense, his way of writing would not be tolerated in schools. All schoolbooks were scrutinized in order to ensure that they followed the regulations that appeared every 20 years. The schools, and the books used in the schools, were meant to represent the future linguistic situation of the country; hence compromise forms allowed in both standards were favored or even required (Vikør 2018: 617–21). In order to present a picture of the changes that occurred in Norwegian orthography and writing during the twentieth century, up until 2005 (the year of the last Bokmål reform) and 2012 (the year of the last Nynorsk reform), two examples from the literature are given along with a translation into present orthography:[10]

Pre-1907 Bokmål

Men naar Efteraarsstormene kom, naar Lindetrærne i Kontorets Haver blev ribbet, mens Bladene føg langs Øvregaden og hobede sig op i Haug ved Hammeckens Trappe, naar Regnet piskede og skyllede ned som bedst, da kunde det hænde, at Hammecken blev lidt taus iblandt.

(Wiberg 1907: 5)

Bokmål 2020

Men når høststormene kom, når lindetrærne i Kontorets hager ble ribbet, mens bladene føk langs Øvregaten og hopet seg opp i haug ved Hammeckens trapp, når regnet pisket og skylte ned som best, da kunne det hende, at Hammecken ble litt taus i blant.

[But when the autumn storms came, when the linden trees in the gardens of the Kontor were ribbed, when the leaves blew along the Upper Street and gathered in a heap by the stairs to Hammecken's house, when the rain whipped and poured down at its worst, then it happened that Hammecken became silent from time to time.]

There is just one lexical change, that of *Efteraarsstormene* > *høststormene*. *Efteraar* was the Danish word, *høst* the Norwegian one. Most words have had their spelling changed: of the 43 words in the paragraph, only 20 are not changed, and these are mostly short words like the preposition *i* 'in', the conjunction *og* 'and', and the adverbs *da* 'then' and *ned* 'down'.

Nynorsk 1892

Mennerne i fatigstyre visste, at mannen i Kroken kasta burt so mykje for seg med drykk og sumling, og solengje det varde, var dei svert knipne med aa hjelpa han. Ei tunna korn elder tvo fek han um aare, men ikkje meir.

(Løland 1892: 10)

[10] Both translations (into Modern Norwegian and into English) are mine.

Nynorsk 2020
Mennene i fattigstyret visste, at mannen i Kroken kasta bort so mykje for seg med drykk og somling, og so lengje det varte, var dei svært knipne med å hjelpa han. Ei tønne korn eller to fekk han om året, men ikkje meir.

[The men of the local poverty board knew that the man in Kroken wasted so much for himself with drink and laziness, and as long as that lasted, they were very stingy in their help to him. He received a barrel or two of grain each year, but nothing more.]

In the Nynorsk example, none of the lexical items has changed, and the changes in spelling are not as revolutionary as those in Bokmål. Of the 43 words in the original paragraph, 30 remain unchanged.

24.8 Conclusion

This brief overview of the reading, writing and general literacy capacities of Norwegians from the early modern period onward shows that at most times throughout the history of Norwegian, the language has had several norms at the same time. Only during a comparatively short period at the end of the eighteenth and beginning of the nineteenth century did Norway experience a situation with one standardized, more or less unquestioned norm. However, the variation that existed before and after this period can be explained in various ways. Variation in spelling before standardization does not seem to have been salient for writers: skilled writers varied their way of writing a given word, even on the same page. After about 1850, on the other hand, variation became important for a different reason compared to the situation before 1750.

The creation of two separate Norwegian written standards was initiated as part of a nation-building process influenced by an ideology assuming the language to be the defining element, or 'soul', of a nation. Since there were different views on where Norway's 'soul' were to be located, in the cities or in the countryside, two standards came into being. In addition, within each standard there was a question of which speaker's variety one should model the written standard on. In the cities, was it the speech of the upper classes, as is most often the case with standard languages, or the speech of the lower classes? In the countryside, should one choose the rural dialects of the western, eastern or middle part of the country (the northern dialects were never seriously considered)? The result left Norwegians in 2022 with one language, several dialects and two written standards.

25

Authorship and Gender

Mel Evans

25.1 Introduction

Quite often, when we read a text, we wish to know more about its creator. To answer questions about the source of the language on a page, the researcher may explore the text's themes and content, or its paratextual material. They may also consider the linguistic forms of the text itself – and this includes the spelling. Investigating the relationship between spelling and a text's author is not an uncomplicated process. The notion of 'authorship' is itself a complex concept, encompassing the person or persons who developed the content of the text, which may or may not be distinct from those who produced the written form of the text being analyzed (see Love 2002). However, accounting for these aspects, the exploration of spelling in order to understand more about the creator of a text, or to look at how the biography of individuals or different social groups (e.g. women) correlates with particular spelling practices, can be a rewarding and insightful area of research. This chapter seeks to provide an overview of the main areas that a researcher should consider when starting to investigate the relationship between an author, their social background and their spelling. There are no rules proffered, as such, but rather some suggested guidelines of good practice (and some related cautionary tales) to help to ensure the research is original, robust and insightful.

The chapter is divided into three sections relating to the ways in which historical spelling – focusing on English examples – can be investigated from the perspective of authorship and authorial background, with a particular consideration of gender.[1] The first part considers the textual evidence of spelling in

[1] English orthography is well documented, with digital resources complementing traditional philological approaches to spelling variation. It is also the language variety best known to the present author. For this chapter, 'authorship' refers to the manual creator or producer of a written text – what Goffman (1981) would

English, and the social configuration of literacies which entails that histories of early English spelling are histories of elite men's spelling. The discussion considers how specialist literacies prior to c. 1500 shape our understanding of historical spelling and what claims we can robustly make based on such evidence. The second section looks at the relationship between authorship and spelling, and discusses what steps are needed if one seeks to use spelling for authorship attribution in printed and handwritten media. Finally, the chapter examines women's spelling in English, highlighting the potent ideologies operating with regard to gender, and suggests how metalinguistic evidence can be used as a means of critical evaluation. The chapter concludes with suggestions for possible directions for future research that may help to rectify some of the empirical gaps in our knowledge of spelling in historical varieties of English (and hopefully other languages as well) that relate to authorship and gender. An investigation into the relationship between the spelling used in a text or a range of texts, and the social background and identity of its author(s) may have a range of objectives. Such a study may seek to investigate the social and sociolinguistic dimensions of spelling for particular historical periods, genres and languages; to evaluate the significance of orthographic practices for the potential performative and pragmatic meanings for a writer's particular communicative objectives; or to serve as a diagnostic for authorship attribution, differentiating one potential writer from another. However, the investigation of spelling for all such purposes relies on the ability to identify the provenance of a text's spelling system: after all, in many cases (present day as well as historical), the named author of a text may not be the source of its spelling (see Kniffka 2007).

As Chapter 24, this volume, illustrates, practices of historical orthography are closely bound up with *literacy* skills. This connection has implications for any sociolinguistic reading of spelling in a text and the appraisal of its (possible) author. The degree of an individual's familiarity with written communication, both as reader and as writer, has been shown to shape spelling choices, whether that writer is using a standardized spelling system or is working in an 'a-standard' environment (a term that seeks to avoid any sense of predestination for varieties, such as English, that would later develop a standard; see Tagg and Evans 2020), such as English informal (handwritten) texts prior to the nineteenth century (see Section 25.4), or present-day Swiss German (e.g. Oppliger 2016). The inequalities surrounding access to education in historical societies are bound up with prevalent social hierarchical structures. Patriarchal and class-based systems have long had an impact on men and women's access to education, and on their opportunities to develop skills in

call the animator; 'authorial background' encapsulates the connection between linguistic forms (here, spelling) and a writer's social background and experiences. 'Gender' refers to the social construction of femininities and masculinities, including their association with male and female sex roles.

reading and writing. For instance, in sixteenth-century England, it is thought that around 20 percent of men could sign their name, and this falls to approximately 5 percent of women (Wheale 1999: 43). Moreover, the capacity to sign disguises a wider range of literacies, in which only some individuals could comfortably set about writing fluently and spontaneously. Consequently, any study of the social profile of the author (intended as the writer) of a text and its spelling properties necessarily must consider the impact of the social stratification of literacy, such as from the perspective of gender and of class.

In present-day writing, particularly on social media and in computer-mediated communication, standard and nonstandard spellings carry social meaning, with gender in particular emerging as a significant attribute in linguistic identity work. For example, Varnhagen et al. (2010) discuss gendered practices of nonstandard English spelling in instant messaging, Squires (2012) looks at punctuation practices in relation to affect and gender, and other research has investigated the intersectionality of gender, ethnicity and authenticity in computer-mediated interactions (Hinrichs 2012, Choi 2017). These present-day investigations illustrate how spelling, and more specifically spelling *variation*, has the capacity to acquire social meanings within certain contexts. Tracking back and exploring past spelling practices can be undertaken not only to enrich understanding of the process of standardization, or to reconstruct historical phonology, but to help us understand both the significance of spelling for the signaling of authorial identity of written documents, and also, I argue, the extent to which historical spellings systems had social meanings for their writers and readers, beyond the direct representation of language in written form. To illustrate how previous researchers have explored the connections between authorship and spelling, the chapter examines historical English evidence. The discussion begins with the earlier periods of evidence, before turning, in Sections 25.3 and 25.4, to early and late modern periods (roughly 1500–1900). For reasons of space, this chapter concentrates particularly on spelling, as opposed to the broader category of orthography (e.g. capitalization, punctuation), although in practice many studies consider all aspects equally. It aims to provide points of reference and raise pertinent questions relevant to those wishing to undertake their own spelling research linked to authorship and gender.

It is important to acknowledge that any exploration of spelling – particularly one interested in the identity of its creators – requires a careful, reflective approach. Spelling in standard writing systems is highly sensitive to linguistic ideologies, and perceptions of spelling practice often draw on a (subconscious) evaluation of that text in comparison with the institutional (regular, predictable, familiar) standard; a standard that is instilled via education typically from a very young age. Spelling-based linguistic ideologies are perpetuated in private and public discourse, as demonstrated in Richardson (2018), who discusses the example of a letter by British Prime Minister Gordon Brown, sent in 2009, which was attacked in the media for its nonstandard spelling. It is important to recognize that the value judgments are social, and not intrinsic to the spelling itself. At the same time, the meaning of spelling variation in a standardized system relies on the points of contrast; what Sebba (2012) calls the 'zone of social meaning'. However, it should be noted that some writing communities do not have a standardized system; what can be described as an 'a-standard' spelling environment. When examining spelling practice in a-standard contexts, a researcher needs to consider that the ideological frames of reference are not the same as for standard contexts, and this has implications both for how writers may use spelling variation as a pragmatic device, and how analysts should interpret spelling practice. Sönmez (2000) has forcefully argued that the reported (perceived) discrepancy between men and women's spelling in Early Modern English reflects present-day (standard language) bias toward particular types of spelling practice, and that such differences would not have been as relevant to early modern readers. This particular point is taken up and examined further in the final section of the chapter when looking at the metalanguage surrounding women's spelling in Early and Late Modern English.

25.2 Authors and Spelling: Archives and Evidence

When thinking about the social dimensions of historical English spelling, and in particular the authorship of the extant texts, the lacunae in historical archives becomes swiftly apparent. Scholarship that presents itself as being about 'historical spelling' is primarily an exploration of the history of men's spelling; a history that reflects the sociolinguistic and literacy practices of past societies. The historical trajectory of writing literacies (and therefore spelling) in English is one of slow, broadening participation, diffusing across different social groups – with women perhaps one of the last to benefit (see Shammas 2019). To begin an investigation of historical spelling, interested in the possible relationship between spelling practice and the social profile of an author, a researcher needs first to be aware of the materials that are available, and their affordances and limitations for the specific methods and lines of inquiry required for spelling research. In English historical orthography, research has tended to follow a private/public divide, and often a manuscript/print dichotomy as well (for an overview, see Condorelli 2020a). This reflects the nature of the extant evidence. For the pre-print era (before c. 1475), manuscripts are the primary site for written language. At this time, clerical activities fell within a largely male domain, originating as they did within the monasteries, although literacy within nunneries is also well attested (Blanton et al. 2013). The subject matter and functions (religious, administrative) of many early texts reflect this professional sphere of language use.

Studies of Old English (c. 500–1100) have examined spelling in order to better understand the provenance of manuscripts, due to the fact that, as discussed in Chapter 13, this volume, English spelling had regional 'standards' during the period. Thus, Davidson (1890) and McClumpha (1890) debate the spelling conventions used by different scribes in the Beowulf manuscript, and the extent to which shifts in preference indicate a transference from Northumbrian to West Saxon dialect. Other Old English surveys use spelling evidence to provide insights into the phonological properties of the language, such as tracking final-vowel loss (Minkova 1991) and to determine syllable structures (Minkova 2015b) in the earliest recorded texts. Minkova (2015b) notes that "lay literacy was practically non-existent [...]. The only linguistic instruction available to the scribes was Latin orthography" (Minkova 2015b: 151), and this training shapes the available evidence, with properties like word breaks following classical conventions. However, the narrow frame of extant Old English literature means that, beyond regional factors, our understanding of the scribes of the manuscripts themselves is relatively limited in scope.

In Middle English (c. 1100–1500), literacy began slowly to expand into the lay community, entailing a greater range of texts for analysis and consequently a greater diversity in writers and spelling practices. Writing remained a primarily male domain, and one that would be restricted to the upper social ranks for centuries to come. It was also socially stratified, in that the elite may not have received the education sufficient for writing, or that they perceived this activity as a manual task, unsuited to their status; authorship was not the same as the scribe's 'menial' role in copying and writing (Bergs 2005: 116; see also Fisher 2012). Hence, abbesses, as high-ranking individuals, likely delegated scribal responsibilities to professional male subordinates (Barratt 2010: 261), and similar practices are attested in the emergence of secretariats and scribes among families, as seen in the scribal activities of the Paston letters (Bergs 2005: 79–80). Middle English spelling is perhaps best known from the perspective of its regional varieties. *A Linguistic Atlas of Late Mediaeval English* (LALME, McIntosh et al. 1986a), first developed in the 1980s, demonstrates the dialectal properties of written texts (particularly literary manuscripts) prior to 1430, as well as documenting the gradual supralocalization of many of these varieties toward the 'Chancery standard', "the official language of the London administrators and the direct ancestor of modern Standard English" (McIntosh et al. 2013: section 5).

LALME is a valuable resource for those researching medieval spelling and its regional distribution, with the distribution of spelling variants plotted onto a dialect map. Because of the localization of Middle English spelling, it is possible for other texts to be profiled using the spelling variants in order to estimate its possible regional provenance, allowing for factors such as idiosyncratic scribal preference (particularly in the fifteenth century), the influence of the source text, bi-dialectal scribes and sociolinguistic variation (McIntosh et al. 2013, section 3.1.2). The nature of historical literacies entails that LALME continues to represent the spellings of predominantly male scribes. The makeup of the archives starts to change from the fifteenth century, as domains of literacy start to expand beyond the clerical and administrative to include vernacular, personal and private writing. This shift has implications for the kinds of analysis that can be done when researching the relationship between spelling and authorship. Correspondence is perhaps the genre that provides the greatest breadth (social, regional, topical), found in collections such as the Paston letters, the Cely letters and the Stonor correspondence.

While the scribe and named author may still not be the same, those employed as amanuenses were from more diverse backgrounds, such as servants within the author's household (Barratt 2010: 261, Wiggins 2016: 196). Nevertheless, English spelling typically continues to be *men's* spelling in these early collections of correspondence. Bergs's (2013) study of the Paston letters observes that there are "virtually no writings by female *scribes* left since there was an extremely high degree of illiteracy among female speakers before about 1600. Nevertheless, we do have texts by female *authors*" (Bergs 2013: 241). However, Bergs suggests that the extant female-authored texts still reflect their scribes' spelling conventions, even if other linguistic features, such as morphosyntactic variables, show properties more plausibly aligned with the named female author. Hernández-Campoy (2016b: 130) tests Bergs's hypothesis in the Paston letters, and finds that the chronological distribution of the <th> digraph vs. runic thorn is "chaotic and inconsistent" in the letters of the female Pastons, which he interprets as a consequence of different scribes. While there is a risk of the argument becoming circular (i.e. the letters are scribal therefore their spelling is inconsistent; inconsistency in spelling is evidence of scribal status), the study suggests that spelling variants pattern differently to morphosyntactic variants, and that the spelling variation is similar to the male Pastons (and the posited scribes). Thus, in manuscript records for Middle English, the spelling evidence reflects the gendered distribution of literacy: the general lacuna of women's spellings is, in a sense, what women's spelling looked like, an absence on the page.

Any investigation of late Middle English spelling should therefore treat evidence carefully, with consideration of the likely scribal and authorial contexts, and should aim to be explicit as to who, precisely, is represented in the spelling evidence under investigation. Some studies do acknowledge the gendered distribution of their orthographic evidence. Thus, Conde-Silvestre and Hernández-Campoy (2004) consciously focus on male spelling practices in late medieval correspondence in order to trace the permeation of the 'Chancery standard' from official administration documents to private writings, such as letters. They assert that "the absence of female 'informants' [...] is wholly conscious" because of high illiteracy rates and the resultant reliance on a scribe: "[e]ven if autograph letters by women had existed in the corpus, their role in the expansion of a typical change 'from above', like the diffusion of prestigious spellings connected to the Chancery standard, would have been minimal" (Conde-Silvestre and Hernández-Campoy 2004: 140). From their male-written corpus, they are able to identify the permeation of Chancery spelling, which is most prevalent among professional (e.g. legal) scribes, as might be expected, with the male writers of the lower gentry showing the least uptake of these particular forms. Other studies, such as Kaislaniemi et al. (2017) look at chronological spelling developments in correspondence in a general (i.e. nongendered) way but acknowledge that the kinds of spelling represented are shaped by the social profile of the writers that contribute to the linguistic data for any given period, with male writers tending to dominate the records, and women writers largely constrained to the highest social ranks.

For researchers interested in the potential gendered correlations of spelling practices, suitable material only really becomes available in the early modern period (1500–1700) as part of the wider shift in increasing literacies and the expansion of writing to less formal and officious domains. Although recent scholarship suggests that women acted as authors much earlier than this (women in religious houses being plausible candidates; see Watt 2013, 2019), the earliest examples of women's holograph English texts (i.e. texts written in the hand of their named author, rather than by a scribe) are primarily found in correspondence collections. Letters, such as those by royals including Margaret Tudor, sister to Henry VIII, date from the very early sixteenth century (so, slightly earlier than Bergs 2013 proposes), and provide the first kinds of equivalent written evidence from which to compare and explore spelling practices of men and of women – that is, in which genre and communicative context are similar.

Of course, the women with the educational training, and for whom holograph letters were pragmatically appropriate, are a small group, comprising mercantile, noble and royal women. Sabine Johnson (fl. 1545–51), for example, was the wife of London merchant John Johnson. Her extant correspondence provides valuable evidence of women's mercantile language that has yet to be properly examined for spelling, although her letters indicate her propensity for linguistic innovations (Nevalainen 1996: 81–82). Letters for royalty (e.g. Anne Boleyn, Katherine Parr) and nobility (e.g. Bess of Hardwick) are more numerous. While caution is required when assuming that a holograph letter is representative of the language of its named author, rather than that of a third party (see examples discussed in Wiggins 2016), there is nevertheless a close connection between the marks extant on the page and the spelling practices of the named author; and this connection increases in strength throughout the sixteenth and seventeenth centuries. As Williams (2014) observes, spelling is part of what might be considered an epistolary voice; a linguistic-material act of communication that represents a named author's identity. In the early modern period, therefore, we can compare the practices of men and women on a fairly robust like-for-like basis. The period offers a context in which spelling may have started to accrue some kinds of indexical significance, perhaps at a very localized level (research relevant to these points is considered further in Section 25.4). There is thus scope to design comparative projects that consider spelling in relation to the author and/or scribe's social rank, education and gender, as well as (although to a less extent than earlier periods) for its regional properties.

The early modern period also offers a wealth of evidence from other media, reflecting the expansion of printed material in the period (see Gillespie and Powell 2014). Printed texts provide large-scale evidence of historical spelling. However, early modern print production processes entail that the connection between text and named author is problematic. Studies of English spelling have observed that printed texts show a fairly swift homogenization in the spelling forms used, with regularization generally dated to the seventeenth century (Salmon 1999: 32). There have been, and continue to be, extensive debates over the factors informing this process: the extent to which it was a conscious process, whether it was informed by economic considerations and/or shaped by prescriptive forces (see Brengelman 1980, Howard-Hill 2006, Berg and Aronoff 2017, 2018). Shute (2017) tests the long-standing assertion that Caxton (who introduced the printing press to England) encouraged his compositors to alter the spelling of a word to fulfill the justification requirements of the printed page (e.g. Reid 1974). Shute's quantitative analysis finds no strong evidence to support the hypothesis of this practice being performed among early printing houses: spelling variation between compositors shows an equal distribution of short and longer spellings, as well as those with no impact on overall word length, and "no patterning as to *where* the spelling changes occurred on the page" (Shute 2017: 274). Shute proposes that other strategies, such as enjambement (words split across lines), abbreviation and space manipulation (orthography in its fuller sense, rather than spelling) were the main strategies used. Adjusting spaces is straightforward, whereas spelling modification requires far more complex (and therefore less temporally economic) adjustments. Spelling variation in print should be associated with compositor preference and/or "natural variation in spelling at that time" (Shute 2017: 281).

Compositors were, like their scribal predecessors, typically men with specialist training, and "the spelling norms that were transmitted through the print medium were therefore largely shaped by men" (Nevalainen 2012a: 159: 8). By the eighteenth century, authors such as Robert and Sarah Fielding expected their manuscripts to be regularized as part of the print process (Tieken-Boon van Ostade 1998: 458). That said, women were not excluded from the printing industry: Jocelin's *The Mothers Legacie* (first edition 1624) shows how women could be involved in all parts of a printed book's production: author, publisher, printer (Werner 2014). Joan Orwin printed Edmund Coote's *The English Schoole-maister* (1596), a work targeted at women (Nevalainen 2012a: 154–55). There is potential, therefore, to explore the possible practices between different printers, and to see how the gender of their printing master informs, if at all, the spelling systems in use.[2]

More recent periods of history provide greater diversity in spelling evidence across the social spectrum. Looking at the eighteenth, nineteenth and twentieth centuries, we find a range of genres and media that can inform our understanding of the relationship between spelling and the author (writer) in English. This includes the telegram, in which the technology's economic requirements influenced the spelling practices of its trained engineers, and potentially the much larger reading public (O'Brien 1904: 467). Telegrams were a technology open to the masses, and their significance for perceptions of spelling norms warrants further investigation. Another roughly contemporaneous technology is the postcard: a form that offers insights into "the everyday writing of all people," including those for whom other written modes, such as letter-writing, were not accessible (Gillen and Hall 2010: 170). Postcards were more public texts than contemporaneous correspondence, although some writers developed ciphers to conceal their messages (Gillen and Hall 2010: 172). As the preceding discussion has shown, an author's literacy and writing experience informs their communicative practice, including their spelling choices, and this is captured in genres like postcards, providing evidence of language use 'from below'. Thus, late modern materials can help to address the elite bias of earlier historical evidence; other potential text types suitable for investigation include pauper letters (e.g. Fairman 2015) and migrant correspondence (e.g. Moreton 2016).

25.3 Spelling, Authorship and Attribution

Despite the challenges of provenance, spelling has repeatedly been used as a diagnostic feature for authorship attribution in English. This section provides an overview and evaluation of these studies, and highlights points of conceptual and methodological caution for a researcher hoping to use spelling to identify the author of a text. This discussion should be seen as part of a wider conversation surrounding orthographic markers of authorship, such as paleography (see Chapter 15, this volume).

Authorship attribution is an expanding field with present-day and historical applications. It relies heavily on quantitative and computational methods, using descriptive and monitored statistical approaches to look for trends

[2] Bunčić (2012: 245) reports that the first owner of a Kraków print shop was a woman, who wished that "not only men but also women or girls learn to read texts in their own language, especially those that add to their advantage and also their delight."

across linguistic features in a set of texts (for a survey see Stamatatos 2009). The approach relies on the principle that all language users have a set of linguistic preferences that are sufficiently distinct from anyone else; therefore, if a text can be profiled using the same techniques, it can be evaluated as being 'like' or 'unlike' a set of texts known to be by a given author.

The principles underpinning the use of spelling to identify the author of a given text are relatively straightforward. In present-day English, in a standardized context of use, individual writers may have their own spelling idiosyncrasies that differentiate their writing from their contemporaries. These idiosyncrasies might be considered, by some, as 'errors' or 'mistakes', reflective of low literacy levels, but may also be connected to register and medium (compare digital media). In cases of disputed authorship, the analyst looks for marked spelling errors (i.e. unusual nonstandard spellings) and for evidence of regionality, such as UK and US spelling variants (Olsson 2012: 145). Spelling, as a means of attributing authorship, has played a role in legal cases, such as the investigation into the murder of Ashleigh Hall in 2009, in which respellings characteristic of Ashleigh's text messages, versus those of the man convicted of her murder, contributed to the case for the prosecution (Olsson 2018: 125–33). The rise of social media offers new interactive spaces in which standard spelling is not necessarily expected, due to factors such as economy, register and the identity-work potential of nonstandard spellings, and therefore offers scope for useful diagnostic evidence for authorship attribution analyses in combination with other linguistic features (e.g. Iqbal et al. 2008, Sousa-Silva et al. 2011, Peng et al. 2016).

That said, spelling is not the most robust evidence for authorship even in present-day materials produced within a standardized system: writers are inconsistent in their misspellings, and the relevant text sample may not necessarily contain the relevant words for analysis (Juola 2006: 120). An investigation of the speeches of Ronald Reagan, for example, hypothesized that Canadian versus American spellings (e.g. *theatre* and *theater*) might be diagnostically useful in differentiating Reagan from other candidates, except that the American president "spelled such words both ways" (Airoldi et al. 2007: 504), was generally inconsistent, and that spelling was often changed, anyway, in the process of typing up the drafts. Standard, and perhaps a-standard, spelling can be understood on a sociolinguistic scale of attention, spanning "informal" to "very strongly accurate formal orthographic writing" (Kniffka 2007: 182). In present-day texts our modern tools, such as spell checkers, neutralize idiosyncratic spellings, and are exploited by those seeking to mask authorship features. Some digital texts, such as programming code, contain few contexts in which spelling can plausibly vary, for example comments within the code, but not the code itself (Burrows 2010). Spelling is therefore indirect evidence of a text's authorship (Kniffka 2007: 169), and forensic and attribution work commonly includes spelling as part of a much larger set of linguistic evidence. Some attribution investigations in fact regularize variant spellings in order to isolate lexical and syntactic information, as spelling can often contribute more 'noise' to an attribution analysis than meaningful evidence (see, e.g., Evans and Hogarth 2020).

Indeed, research into automated spelling standardization can itself yield information about spelling variation (for a valuable critique on the methodological application of concepts such as 'regularization' and 'normalization', see Condorelli 2020b). Tagg et al. (2012) look at the thresholds of standardness in a corpus of English text-messaging, and Pilz et al. (2007) explore variant identification in English and German historical texts. Trials using automated spelling normalization derived from statistical machine translation (natural language processing) methods have assessed the impact of language-external factors for different historical texts. Schneider et al. (2017), using *A Representative Corpus of Historical English Registers* (ARCHER, Biber and Finegan 1990–2013), developed probabilistic normalization based on a small training sample of early and late modern English. They found that the training set was most accurate when using texts from a restricted (century-long) temporal period, and then applied to texts of the same period – reflecting the diachronic changes in English spelling systems. Conversely, studies (Hämäläinen et al. 2018, 2019) using the *Corpus of Early English Correspondence* (CEEC, Nevalainen et al. 1993–98) found that temporal data, as well as social metadata, had little impact on regularization accuracy, perhaps because the variation within the letters corpus was too fine-grained to capture using probabilistic rule-based approaches like neural linguistic programming.

Regardless of methodological and disciplinary approach, the challenge for researchers is to recognize what insights the available evidence may yield, and to complement any claims about an author's spelling with other relevant linguistic and nonlinguistic evidence. The situation for texts and authorship produced in a-standard environments involves greater variation across texts and genres. Research into early and late modern periods of English suggests that individual writers had repertoires of preferred forms (Sairio et al. 2018: 92). This is most acute in the early modern period, during the shift from regional varieties to a supralocalized standard spelling system (see Nevalainen 2012a: 141; see also Chapter 13, Chapter 21 and Chapter 30, this volume). Some scribal practices are innovations, such as the Peterborough Chronicle scribe who uses the digraph <th> for thorn, anticipating its widespread adoption by centuries (Bergs 2013: 252–56). Similarly, spelling practices of the Beryn scribe and his scriptorium can connect other manuscripts with this center of production (Mosser and Mooney 2014: 46–50).[3] Such examples offer insights

[3] The Beryn scribe contributed to many significant works in Middle English, copying versions of *Brut* and Chaucer's *Parliament of Fowls*, as well as the sole extant version of *Tale of Beryn* (Alnwick Castle, Duke of Northumberland MS 455). The interaction of the Beryn scribe's hand with other scribes in some of the manuscripts has led to the hypothesis that the scribe oversaw a scriptorium for the production of literary, vernacular works (Mosser and Mooney 2014: 49).

into the capacity for individual scribal practice, alongside community-level norms, to be appraised. However, unlike the forensic linguistic cases outlined above, the focus of these studies is profiling the spelling system of a text, rather than its connection to a specific author.

An interpretation of spelling and authorship that accounts for the provenance of the text in question appears the most advisable approach. While variation may be greater in historical texts, the obscure processes of text production increase the potential for unidentified interference. Nevertheless, scholars have used spelling as evidence in verification tests of authorship, drawn from both printed evidence and manuscripts. Typically, analysis concentrates on the prevalence of marked spellings: forms which typify a particular writer's practice, and appear in the questionable text. Markedness in an a-standard spelling system encompasses forms that might be deemed archaic, those which deviate from conventional graph combinations, or which are, based on the extant reference material, quantitatively rare. Kniffka (2007: 186), writing about present-day texts, cautions against the use of "direct one-to-one matching of individual items and/or features of writing systems to one particular writer/typist," because there is not presently a suitable empirical baseline of normative practices. Given the greater variability and instability in the historical corpus, diagnostic techniques and interpretations in historical authorship attribution based on spelling warrant similar notes of caution.

If a researcher wishes to investigate authorship of a text or texts using spelling evidence, then many of the potential insights, and pitfalls, can be observed among the existing scholarship on William Shakespeare (1564–1616), which represents something of a cautionary tale. Shakespeare's canon continues to be interrogated for authorship (see, e.g., Vickers 2018), with spelling evidence used for attribution purposes. However, the evidence relies almost exclusively on printed materials, with the associated complexities and uncertainties of the production process on the linguistic evidence. Jackson (2008), for instance, acknowledges the "potential effects of scribes and compositors on early modern printed texts," but argues that there remain "a sprinkling of the idiosyncratic spellings" (Jackson 2008: 286) that typify authorial holographs. Jackson uses marked spellings to argue for Shakespeare's authorship of the sonnet 'A Lover's Complaint' (Shakespeare 1640), based on a search of spelling forms in the *Literature Online* (LION) database. The use of a baseline point of reference here is important; as he acknowledges, any spelling evidence put forward in support of authorship needs to be "gathered in a systematic manner that facilitates its evaluation"; that is, to ascertain how rare or marked the identified spellings actually are. Jackson (2008: 289) identifies other printed works containing so-called unusual spellings in the questioned sonnet. In support of his argument, many of these are exclusively Shakespearean texts: for example, *greeuance* appears in *Othello* (Shakespeare 1622a) and *Romeo and Juliet* (Shakespeare 1622b); *parradise* occurs twice in

Love's Labour's Lost (Shakespeare 1598). Collectively, Jackson summarizes the plays with "three or more rare spelling links to *LC*," listing five plays by Shakespeare and one (*The Second Maiden's Tragedy*, extant only in manuscript: London, British Library, Lansdowne MS 807) by Middleton (Begor Lancashire 1978), with other plays and authors grouped by the replication of two rare spellings and one rare spelling: a patterning that, Jackson suggests, makes "Shakespeare's predominance [...] glaringly obvious" (Jackson 2008: 295). However, despite the recourse to the database, it is not possible to confirm that the Shakespearian prominence is genuinely an "obvious" marker of authorship. Jackson does not conduct an equivalent test for other authors using the same database, for example, to establish if other spellings are similarly distinctive; nor is there a consideration of whether Shakespeare's known texts show the same profiling tendency based on unusual spellings. As Kniffka (2007: 210–13) cautions, we need a greater understanding, via an empirical baseline, of spelling norms, interpreted according to social and genre properties, to fully appreciate the potential significance of individual spelling variation, and its validity as evidence of authorship.

Other studies have looked at compositor 'authorship'. McKenzie's (1969) classic comparison of bibliographic analysis with historical records of the printing house is another important cautionary tale: bibliography suggested two compositors, whereas the actual records for the printing house reveal at least six. Rizvi (2016) is highly critical of efforts to identify early modern compositors from spelling. He suggests that even statistically significant differences in spellings within a text are not necessarily indicative of authorship, because correlation is not causation, and early modern spelling is so chaotic that statistical testing for significance is inappropriate. Dahl (2016: 170) offers a similar warning, particularly in treatments of spelling variation in mediated print contexts, noting the "textual scholar's narrative adaptability"; that is, confirmation bias shapes the feature selection and interpretation (e.g. of a spelling's markedness) in a way that suits the researcher's preferred hypothesis.

As these examples show, we simply do not know enough yet about the ways in which compositors appropriated or changed the spellings of their source manuscripts to make robust assertions about authorship/writership relations. However, the availability of digitized texts (through LION, EEBO-TCP and other repositories) means that we can now start to collect evidence pertinent to questions about authorship, such as establishing the markedness of a particular spelling form (EEBO N-gram Browser is an excellent resource). In more formal public texts, spelling variation is aligned with different standardized systems (e.g. British and American spellings), with private texts providing richer opportunities to associate spelling forms with idiolectal practices into the present day. DiMeo (2011) uses spelling characteristics alongside paleographical and internal evidence to establish that the hand in the seventeenth-century Boyle Family Receipt Book (Wellcome Library MS 1340)[4] is not the hand of Lady Ranelagh, but instead that of Margaret, Countess of Orrery (DiMeo 2011: 269–70).

Studies of spelling and authorship may also engage with the ideologies around spelling variation and their significance for authorial identity, for instance in the spelling of proper names. In Early Modern English, the practices of literate, high-profile or high-status individuals complicate the potential meanings attached to stability, or variation, in the spelling of one's name. For instance, playwright Ben Jonson (1572–1637) purportedly changed the spelling of his surname, losing the conventional <h> to differentiate himself from others publishing under that name (Wildenthal 2018: 2). The historical record shows that Shakespeare, quite famously, has six extant signature spellings, including *Shaksper* and *Shakspeare*, used on his will (The National Archives, PROB 1/4A), but not the present-day conventional spelling *Shakespeare*. For proponents of the non-Stratfordian interpretation (those that believe Shakespeare was a businessman and actor from Stratford, but not the author of the plays associated with that name), this is of great significance. As Wildenthal (2018: 4) observes, records associated with Shakespeare "the Stratfordian" show extensive variation in the spellings of his name, whereas printed records denoting the author are far more consistent. Yet the greater regularity of print spelling in the period complicates the robustness of this interpretation (see Whalen 2015).

Work on other sixteenth-century individuals suggests a range of practices: monarchs spell their names uniformly, with the spelling closely bound up with handwriting. Consistency is likely a security measure, although Elizabeth I's (1533–1603) calligraphic display seems also to have indexed her learning (for a discussion of Tudor royal signatures, see Evans 2020: 57–60). For noble writers, the evidence is more mixed. Edward Seymour (c. 1500–52), Duke of Somerset and Lord Protector during the first half of the reign of Edward VI, maintains consistent spelling and handwriting throughout his career, excepting for the upgrades in his titles. Other writers show greater variation – and this may partly arise from differences in status and/or educational training. Elizabeth Bacon (1541–1621), despite being a fairly consistent speller overall, shows extensive variation in writing her name in her correspondence, for example *Elizabeth*, *Elezabeth*, *Elisabeth* and *Elyzabeth* (Evans and Tagg 2020: 214–15). Bess of Hardwick (c. 1527–1608) shows similar variation in her personal name and title; her married name *Cavendish* is rendered at least four ways, although this stabilizes later in life, which could reflect a connection between onomastic uniformity and social status (Wiggins 2016: 139–40). There is the potential for more empirical work to be done on signatures and spelling to ascertain common practice and any potential associated

[4] London, Wellcome Library, Wellcome MS 1340. "The Boyle Family Receipt Book." Boyle Family Collection of 712 Medical receipts, with some cookery receipts, compiled in a book by members of the Boyle family, c. 1675–1710.

ideologies, which may have ramifications for the arguments concerning a certain early modern dramatist.

The studies surveyed here suggest that the lack of baseline evidence impedes authorship attribution work using only, or primarily, spelling. For instance, Merriam (2011: 242; see also Merriam 2006) suggests that it is unlikely that the presumed author of *John a Kemp*, Anthony Munday (1560–1633), completely switched spelling forms between compiling plays, preferring to interpret the scenario as one of scribal influence in the composition of *Sir Thomas More*. However, Merriam's interpretation is largely supposition: we do not actually know the extent to which a writer's spelling system might typically evolve or change during their lifespan. Some research, such as Evans (2013), Evans and Tagg (2020) and Sairio (2009, 2018), has demonstrated distinctive developments in the spelling systems of some early modern writers; but more research is needed if we are to understand the properties and proclivities of spelling in private writing in the history of English.

However, the researcher faces challenges in accessing the kinds of large-scale material needed to construct the envisaged empirical baseline. Handwritten texts and informal texts are not so readily accessed in a digital format that enables quantitative analyses, as is the case with contemporaneous print. The ERRATAS project has sought to establish whether early (e.g. Victorian) print editions of historical manuscripts are suitable for orthographic investigations. Early printed texts are the source materials for various linguistic corpora, including the CEEC (Nevalainen et al. 1993–98), and these already digitized and marked-up texts would be ideal for investigating private spelling *if* they were found to be suitably reliable.[5] ERRATAS looks at the extent to which editors silently regularized and/or modernized their source texts and found that some orthographic properties such as <u> ~ <v> and word divisions (e.g. *to morrow* > *tomorrow*) have been silently modernized in the majority of editions, rendering these features unsuitable for inquiry (Sairio et al. 2018: 80, 87). However, other spelling features were unaffected by editorial interference, and could therefore be identified using temporally appropriate analysis. To establish the spelling reliability in editions of seventeenth-century correspondence, the authors suggest that it is possible to simply look for a preponderance of 'old' rather than 'new' spellings, because the standard was not yet established in private writing. For the eighteenth century, however, a nonstandard/standard dichotomy was becoming established, entailing that the absence of nonstandard forms does not necessarily mean that an edition has been modernized (Sairio et al. 2018: 89), and analysis must privilege particular forms that cluster together within an editor's textual principles.

In sum, the work on spelling and authorship attribution demonstrates the opportunities for further investigation and innovation; arguably, we have

[5] For work using CEEC (cautiously), see Kaislaniemi et al. (2017) and Evans (2013).

relevant methods, but we still need to establish some kind of norm for comparison and interpretation. Hopefully, the developments in digital humanities (e.g. handwriting recognition software) and digitization projects will enable this baseline to be ascertained for different varieties of English and for other languages, therefore allowing authorship attribution statements to be made about individual spelling preferences and exceptionality with a reference to a robust comparative dataset.

25.4 Gendered Spelling: Stereotypes and Empirical Evidence

The chapter so far has offered a summary of research exploring the relationship between spelling practices and authorship, in order to highlight the opportunities and challenges of this area of research through the lens of historical varieties of English. This survey has highlighted the importance of ideologies around spelling (and literacy) which not only affect the material themselves (i.e. in terms of the social groups represented by historical evidence) but potentially, too, a researcher's interpretations of the spelling data. In this final section, I explore more closely how spelling research can identify and address the linguistic ideologies that prevail in relation to spelling variation and change. The discussion focuses on the gendering of spelling in historical periods of English, considering different truisms about women's spelling, and the extent to which they are verified by empirical evidence. As noted in Section 25.2, until the early modern period spelling was primarily men's spelling. The limitations of literacy and education opportunities entailed that women rarely learned to read, never mind wield a pen. From the late fifteenth century, this begins to change, although we do not find gender parity in basic vernacular literacy until the early 1900s, when early education was made compulsory for boys and girls (Arnot and Phipps 2003: 2). Thus, between 1500 and 1900, the differing opportunities in education potentially manifest in different practices in spelling, and, at least, there appears to be widespread belief that this should be the case.

Discussions of historical literacy suggest there is a gendered discrepancy in spelling that arises from stratified access to education and writing experience; but this discrepancy is not always treated objectively, showing the influence of standardized ideologies. Fritz (2010: 246–47) offers an important reminder that spelling practice intersects with broader social structures. In the nineteenth century, Australian women had more educational opportunities than their British or American counterparts, meaning that the emerging Australian English Standard does not align with one gender more than the other. For British English, however, there is a general narrative that women's spelling is typically "naive" (Sönmez 2000: 410) or "less 'careful'" than that of male contemporaries (Wyld 1956: 133). Sönmez (2000) argues persuasively that the critical appraisal of women's spelling (in particular, that of seventeenth-century women) reflects a bias of the critics, shaped by anachronistic values of standardized spellings toward a-standard evidence. Comparing the writings of William Cavendish, Duke of Newcastle (1593–1676) and Lady Brilliana Harley (1598–1643), she proposes that spelling variation is characteristic of both authors, but that the differences in the kinds of variation determine the salience for a present-day reader. Harley's lesser education inclines her to use "phonetically obscure spellings" linked to stress patterns, forms not aligned with derivational morphology (e.g. affixes) and syllabic word breaks (e.g. *a fraide*). The same features are evident in the spelling system of Newcastle to a far lesser extent (Sönmez 2000: 420–22). Sönmez proposes that the salience of women's spelling is, in part, a product of modern perceptual bias, which backgrounds variants that are aligned with present-day phonetic principles, but foregrounds those "which are neither orthodox nor phonetic" (Sönmez 2000: 429).

Appraisals of women's spelling of this kind can be divided into two groups: firstly, assertions contemporaneous with the spelling system being evaluated, such as claims made by the authors and educators publishing spelling books in the sixteenth to nineteenth centuries; and secondly, the evaluations and assessments made by editors and scholars working on materials from earlier periods than their own. These sources of appraisal of spelling rely on metalanguage – comments made about spelling – which can be as useful for an exploration into the social background of authors and their spelling practices as the evidence of spelling itself (e.g. Rutten and Vosters 2010). Metalinguistic comments require a qualitative approach, but can be extracted using digital resources and search techniques. For Early Modern English, the EEBO-TCP database offers one resource for identifying metalinguistic commentary relevant to spelling. The commentaries commonly occur in publications with an interest in educating and instructing their readers, including the spelling books published over the course of the sixteenth and seventeenth centuries, and more general works on pedagogy. Many publications, it should be pointed out, do not refer to women as their envisaged audience at all. In *An A, B, C for Children* (1570: A1 r), the preface asserts that "by this Booke, a man that hath good capacitie, and can no letter in the Book, may learne to read in the ſpace of ſixe weekes [...]. Alſo you may learne therby to write Engliſh truely and to knowe the true Ortographie of the Engliſhe tung." John Brinsley's *Ludus literarius* (1612) similarly foregrounds the text's capacity to improve the learning of young boys. Other publications, however, single out ladies and gentlewomen as a demographic who would benefit from greater guidance in spelling, and literacy more generally. Thus, John Chalmers 1687 publication is fully entitled: *English Orthography, Containing The Art of Writing Right And Spelling Well: With Directions for Reading English and Writing Letters to Persons of all Qualities. Very necessary for young Persons both Men and Women, especially those who have not learned the Grammar.* In the introduction he advises that "[t]he *onely* way for *Ladies*, and *ſuch* who have not had *Grammar-erudition*, is to obſerve *carefully* these following *Dire[ct]ions*" (Chalmers 1687: 15). Other, well-known educational treatises and guides, including Richard Mulcaster's *Positions vvherin those primitiue circumstances* (1581), Edmund Coote's *The English Schoole-master* (1596), Cawdrey's *Table Alphabeticall* (1604) and Thomas Blount's *The Academie of Eloquence* (1654), among others, all single out ladies or gentlewomen as potential beneficiaries of their publications.

The greater attention toward women readers correlates with broader changes in educational opportunities for men and women, in which literacy became more accessible. At the same time, women were denied training in skills, such as Classical languages, and instead encouraged to prioritize domestic abilities. In 1698, Ainsworth offered a scathing assessment of the impact of women on a (male) child's learning, which illustrates the bifurcation of male and female spheres of learning:

> If they do take care to send 'em to *School*, perhaps 'tis to ſome *Woman* who never knew any thing of *Orthography*, tho' ſhe may make a ſhift to read her *Prayers*, or Murder a *Gazette*, confounding one Period with another, which ſhe muſt needs do, having ne-ver been acquainted with the *Rules of Pointing* [punctuation]. Hence it comes to paſs, that *Vulgar People*, who only have learn'd to *Read* and *Write* at this rate, commit ſuch horrible blunders in *Spelling*, and making no *Points*, are at the hazard of having no one, that writes *true*, to underſtand what they mean.
>
> (Ainsworth 1698: 7)

Ainsworth's publication, which is a general education guide, points specifically to women's limited capacity with written language. The criticism extends those of Sir Thomas Elyot in the previous century, in his *Boke named the Gouernour*, which advised parents not to leave their children with a (female) nurse whose accent may have a detrimental impact on the pronunciation of their charges (Elyot 1531: 19 v). In the final decades of the seventeenth century, attention appears to have shifted from speech to writing. By the eighteenth century, similar pedagogic publications made scathing criticisms of the curriculum offered to women, in contrast to that of men, recognizing the impediment this presents for their literacy skills, of which spelling was an important part. While a woman might be offered schooling in spelling, this is considered one of the "auxiliary accomplishments" that, when in competition with more frivolous activities like dancing, were easily forgotten, according to the author of *The History of Women* (Alexander 1779: 37–38). In *The Accomplish'd Housewife: or, the Gentlewoman's Companion* (1745: 7), the book's female readership is singled out for poor spelling: "This Ignorance, indeed, being almoſt univerſal in the Sex, ought not to refle[ct] a Diſhonour on it, or be imputed to them for a Crime"; yet, at the same time, the weaknesses in spelling require urgent correction. The anonymous editors helpfully suggest that the housewife should read "every Day to your husband or ſome Friend" (1745: 388) and collect examples of good spelling from their personal libraries. Good spelling, they suggest, is one of the "perpetual Comforts" (1745: 388) that a good wife can offer her husband.

The increasing salience of women's spelling was presumably a consequence of the standardization of English spelling more generally, which began to permeate private as well as printed modes of writing. The decreasing variance of English orthography, and the broadening reach of literacy, entailed that deviations from the emergent norm would be foregrounded, and therefore available for comment and evaluation. Spelling, as the example of the conduct manual suggests, became associated with 'good' femininity. Goodman (2002) has described a similar association between gender roles and spelling in France in the same period. Views of women's speech and writing shifted from being the more 'natural' rendering of the French language in the sixteenth century, to becoming unlearned, corrupt and simplistic, in need of correction and improvement, by the eighteenth century. Such attitudes illustrate the increasing social capital of writing and literacy, and the capacity for one's spelling to index not only learning, but indirect properties such as social rank, and feminine and masculine attributes (Goodman 2002: 222–23).

The criticisms of women's spelling extend to more recent periods as well. Using the Google Books digital search tool to explore the Camden Society editions (old and new series) and Early English Text Society (original series), my investigations suggest that it is generally the case that spelling is not commonly remarked upon by editors, except to point out variant forms of personal names and placenames. However, in the instances in which an editor does draw attention to the spelling, women's writing receives a more critical account. Thus, spelling variation is accounted for in a matter-of-fact way when it relates to the writing activities of male scribes: a rendering of 'vassy' (*vecci*) in the *Plumpton Correspondence* is explained as a logical byproduct of a scribe working from dictation: "the scribe having to trust solely to his ear for catching rightly the sound of the name as pronounced to him, the subscription of the personage himself to the document being simply a cross mark" (Stapleton 1839: x). The evaluation of male-authored spelling uses limited descriptive terms: George Villiers (1628–87) the Duke of Buckingham's letter is transcribed in full "to show that some of the peculiarities of the uncouth orthography of the Rawdon MS [now London, British Library, Add. MS 34206] were in use by contemporaries of the highest rank and literary distinction" (Davies 1863: 124–25). "Uncouth" is the preferred epithet for the spelling found in the correspondence of Colonel John Birch (1615–91) (Webb 1873: 53).

In the editions that refer to women's spelling, however, more space is given to describing and evaluating their orthography. Elizabeth I's spelling, in her translation of Boethius, is introduced as having been "untrammelled by any rules whatever. The same word is seen on one page spelt in two or three different ways" (Pemberton 1899: 25), a description that, on the face of it, does not suggest the queen's practice was in fact much different to the private manuscript spellings of her (male) contemporaries. Of her epistolary spelling, Bruce (1849: xxii) asserts that it is "often very strange," albeit comprehensible. There is a romantic tinge to the accounts: Bruce notes that there are

> personal peculiarities, which although minute are not altogether without interest. When Elizabeth writes 'swarve', 'desarve' [...] and 'vacabond'; or James [VI/I] 'aither', 'yow', 'airt' and 'uillaine' or Charles I 'Agust,' pronounced 'āgust' we can scarcely doubt that we are informed of the very way in which those words ordinarily fell from the royal lips.
>
> (Bruce 1849: xxii)

Similarly, noblewoman Lady Brilliana Harley's spelling is considered "varied and irregular," despite her "bold and legible hand" (Lewis 1854: xiv). The editor of the Hatton correspondence provides a full-throated critique of women's spelling in the seventeenth century: "Nothing can be greater than the difference between their diction and their spelling, and the fearful atrocities committed in the latter respect prove what a painful operation letter-writing must have been to the greater number of women of that time" (Maunde 1878: iv). Maunde sees these failings as a consequence of the educational system of the period, rather than an essentialist failing of the women themselves, and notes that in aspects such as content and self-expression, women's letters are often of more interest than men's (Maunde 1878: v). Yet the view of such "atrocities" is one shaped by the subsequent standardized spelling system, in which uniformity was the measure of excellence. Recent uproars over nonstandard spellings in digital media testify to the long-standing entrenched association between quality and uniformity in English spelling (see Thurlow 2006).

One productive, developing area of research has started to consider the characteristics of historical women's spelling, looking at the ways in which their practices compare with their male/educated contemporaries, and whether spelling variation carried any social meanings relevant to the textual construction of their identity. In the early modern period, Evans and Tagg (2020) examine the spelling of four women letter-writers of the sixteenth century (Elizabeth I, Bess of Hardwick, Elizabeth Bacon and Joan Thynne). The study examines the consistency of spelling in their correspondence, calculated quantitatively (i.e. their spelling systems as a whole), as well as looking at particular forms with potential psychosocial salience (e.g. personal names or placenames). The analysis compares each woman's spelling practices, interpreted in light of their educational training, and also looks for any significant developments in their spelling across the lifespan. What is notable is that, perhaps contrary to the impression given by early modern publications and subsequent editorials, all four women use one or two variant forms for the majority of words. The subset with more than three variants spellings is small, and tends to comprise words which combine common, conventional graph substitutions (e.g. word-medial <u> ~ <v>, word-medial and word-final <i> ~ <e> ~ <y>). Interauthor comparison suggests that educational training correlates with a writer's spelling consistency. Elizabeth I is the most consistent speller, presumably reflecting her Humanist education. Joan Thynne (1558–1612), whose training was more limited, although sufficient to enable her to use letter-writing to run her household, shows greater variation. The results offer an important counterpoint to the generic truisms about historical women's spellings (see Sönmez 2000). Elizabeth I's spellings are very consistent, and demonstrative of her experience in writing; that they are 'strange' simply reflects her preference for forms that do not later become the standard spelling (e.g. 'which' as *wich*; Scragg 1974: 69 makes a similar observation of the queen's consistency, although without quantitative evidence). Of course, in the sixteenth century there was no standard, and it is erroneous to interpret any writer's spellings solely on such comparative terms, regardless of their gender.

For later periods of English, studies suggest that, for some women at least, the inconsistency of their spelling was of no apparent consequence. The epistolary spelling of Elizabeth Montagu (1718–1800) of the Bluestocking Network shows an increase in inconsistency over the course of her life – despite her education and status as a published, literary author. Variant spellings include contractions for past tense verbs and part participles, respellings for economy (e.g. *shd* for 'should'), and *-ck* for now-standard *-c* e.g. *dramatick* (Sairio 2018: 640–42). While Montagu was not "the primary target audience" (Sairio 2018: 637) for the grammars and spelling books of the period, her modest shift toward normative spellings in her private writings suggests that she valued the nonstandard variants for her private writing, perhaps because of the informality and potential intimacy they signaled, as well as her capacity to write letters in such an informal style, as an established woman in society (Sairio 2018: 644, 648). Sairio notes that preferences for past-tense forms are highly idiolectal, rather than gendered, although other sociolinguistic factors, such as age, are relevant to the uptake of the emergent standard forms; for example, younger writers use the incipient standard *-ed* spelling more than the older generation (Sairio 2018: 646). Curiously, however, Montagu's epistolary spelling shows a possible sensitivity to the gender of her recipient, with "more informal and speechlike" (Sairio 2018: 650) spellings used when writing to women. This may in fact reflect concerns around social distance, with Montagu constructing a more formal (perhaps modeled on the emerging standard) epistolary 'voice' when writing to male superiors (Sairio 2018: 650). Montagu's practices demonstrate the capacity for some writers to harness variants for their social meaning in a nascent standard system. More work is needed to establish the extent to which identity and interpersonal work was undertaken using spelling variation. It is telling, perhaps, that studies of individual or small-network spelling practices thus far tend to have women at their center. This is a logical corrective to the longer (i.e. premodern) narrative of English men's spelling. Yet there is need for much greater work on writers across the social spectrum, and a clearer sense of what constitutes the unmarked kind of variance and inconsistency for individuals' spelling systems in the Early and Late Modern English periods. Such studies can be undertaken on a small scale, compared to other kinds of spelling investigation, and offer a useful starting point for those wishing to explore the relationship between an author, their social experiences (such as gendered opportunities and expectations) and their spelling.

25.5 Conclusion

This chapter has surveyed three areas relevant to authorship and gender in (English) historical orthography. The discussion has considered how the kinds of material available for investigation, and the implications of literacy norms, shape the questions that can be asked and investigated. It has assessed the potential value of spelling in authorship attribution work in print and manuscript evidence, and evaluated the common truisms, their empirical validity and the relevant social contexts relating to women's spelling in the history of English. The survey is, necessarily, selective, and the English language offers only one part of the wider research narrative (see Condorelli 2020a). Yet English is a useful illustrator of spelling, authorship and gender, offering relatively copious quantities of evidence for multiple historical periods which show very acutely the impact of technology and linguistic mode upon spelling practices. It is also the case that, rightly or wrongly, English spelling largely dominates research into historical authorship attribution and historical corpus investigations interested in orthographic variation.

The chapter highlights the many areas for potential future research. If we are to understand the connections between an author's spelling and their social background, like gender, genre or time period, then a broader baseline is required. Individual writers, such as Shakespeare, Elizabeth I or Elizabeth Montagu, are a logical starting point: these writers have (semi-)defined corpora of work, much of which is digitized, and the interest in spelling typically arises from larger questions about these individuals' literacy, social status and textual 'performance'. However, advances in digital humanities and computational linguistics mean we can widen the orthographic investigative net. This chapter has argued for the importance of robust evidence, systematic analysis and an awareness of linguistic ideologies that shape both data and interpretations. Despite these challenges for the researcher, there is much to investigate.

26

Sociolinguistic Variables in English Orthography

Juan Manuel Hernández-Campoy

26.1 Introduction

One of the main foundational tenets in sociolinguistics is the conception of the speaker's sociolinguistic behavior as inextricably based on social meaning, where language constitutes a social practice (see Trudgill 1983, Le Page and Tabouret-Keller 1985). Given the strong relationship between language and society, language is viewed not solely as a means of communicating information or establishing and maintaining social relationships, but also as a very important instrument for conveying social information about the speaker's identificational, attitudinal and ideological profile (Pride 1971, Trudgill 1983). Language transmits social meaning through sociolinguistic variation and through the choices speakers make, because language acts *are* always acts of identity (Le Page and Tabouret-Keller 1985: 14). Registers, genres and text types constitute amalgams of conventional discourse categorizations where style plays a pivotal role through variation cross-sectionally for the transmission of social and linguistic meaning (see Hernández-Campoy 2016a). In the following pages of this chapter, the social significance of orthography and its adequate status as a level of language description at which sociolinguistic variables can be identified are claimed. The indexical potential of orthographic variation and its instrumentalization in (historical) sociolinguistics are explored at the levels of style, register, dialect, genre and other text-type-specific conventions through relevant research already carried out in the area. This examination of orthographic variables as sociolinguistic variables sheds light on the potential effect of orthographic variation for the construction and transmission of social meaning not just linguistically and conceptually, but mostly and crucially, at sociolinguistic and pragmatic levels. According to Coulmas (2003: 233–34), given that language is both a mental and a social fact, biscriptality and mere spelling variation are not perceived by their users as value-neutral, but rather with a wide scope of symbolic instrumentalization and interpretation (see also Chapter 8, this volume).[1] Given their role as rule-governed graphic representation of language, orthographic choices in their social context also reflect the subtleties of social meaning: "the signs carry not only linguistic meaning, but also a social meaning at the same time" (Sebba 2007: 7). The licensed or unlicensed deviation from spelling standard conventions, therefore, makes orthography represent the intersection point for language as a formal object and also as a social and cultural phenomenon.

Given that pronunciation and orthography represent the core of the relationship between spoken and written language, its manifestation on language production has been subject to social indexicalization. According to Bullough (1991: 1–38), the Carolingian reform of Latin in the early eighth century AD, for example, aiming at an *ad litteras* pronunciation was a deliberate attempt to establish and standardize written Latin as the unified model of the language throughout the empire, given the proliferation of local varieties in the wake of Roman expansion (see also Coulmas 2003: 227–29). Spelling pronunciation became a concept and a linguistic reality, and also a reflection of the existence of geolinguistic and sociolinguistic variation. This process simultaneously fostered not only the intended convergence and homogeneity but also divergence, since those Romance languages diverging from their Latin source also experienced a development into internally heterogeneous separate entities as they became written languages: "the *ad litteras* reform did not spawn the family of Romance languages, but it served as a catalyst for the process of language divergence" (Coulmas 2003: 227). These processes were found in Latin and its Romance languages such as the dialect of Castilian Spanish for Spanish, or Tuscany for Italian, Île-de-France for French, as well as in the Germanic and Slavonic language families in other areas of Europe (see Condorelli 2020c), or the Indo-Aryan, Dravidian, Tibeto-Burmese and Austro-Asiatic distinct language families in the Indian subcontinent, and so on (see Wurm 1994, Daswani 2001).

There are languages, such as Spanish, German, Czech or Russian, where the relationship between spoken (pronunciation) and written (orthography) language is clear and predictable, so that a grapheme corresponds to a phoneme, as the prototypical case of biuniqueness: the uniqueness of pronunciation of a grapheme and the uniqueness of spelling of phoneme, or the sound-to-symbol/symbol-to-sound simplicity (see Luelsdorff 1987: ix, Sgall 1987: 4, Upward and Davidson 2011: ix; see also Chapter 2, Chapter 4, Chapter 5, Chapter 8 and Chapter 17, this volume). In fact, Katz and Frost (1992a: 1) underline the dependence of writing and reading on spoken language and

[1] Biscriptality is the use of two different scripts, writing systems or orthographies for the same language; see Bunčić et al. (2016), Elti di Rodeano (2019), Ambrosiani (2020). Alternatively, see Grivelet (2001) and Coulmas (2003) for digraphia. See also Chapter 8, this volume.

view this as a putative relationship between language and reading that follows the principle of an isomorphic relation between letter and phoneme: "writing systems are designed primarily to represent spoken language," where each orthography reflects a unique relationship to its own language's structural characteristics (see also Mattingly 1992). However, there are many other languages and dialects where biscriptality is not – or has not been – uncommon, having two or more scripts, writing systems or orthographies for the same language (see Zima 1974, Luelsdorff 1987, Frost and Katz 1992, Carney 1994, Grivelet 2001, Coulmas 2003, Sebba 2007, Baddeley and Voeste 2012b, Bunčić et al. 2016, Condorelli 2020c). Examples include Swiss vs. German varieties, Chinese vs. Taiwanese and Hindi vs. Urdu, or, to bring the matter closer to home for many, the diorthographic difference between British vs. American English – as in *theatre* ~ *theater*, *centre* ~ *center* or *defence* ~ *defense*. In these cases, according to Coulmas (2003: 233–34), digraphia may act as an identificational symbol, becoming the nexus between writing and language identity through choice. Geographical variation (*you-youse* in English) and historical variation (*shew* < *show*, *phantasy* > *fantasy* in English) may also be reflected through spelling (see Scragg 1974, Sebba 2007, Upward and Davidson 2011). In fact, as Sebba (2007: 11) points out, the relationship between phonology and orthography and dialect has traditionally allowed language history to trace phonological change through spelling (see Scragg 1974).

Sometimes some digraphia situations are the result of writing reform projects, which lead to transitional periods of variation of the old and new systems used side by side, as in the case of the Runic alphabet in English. During the Old English period (450–1100), the Celts and the Anglo-Saxons used a Germanic alphabet of runes (see Chapter 12 and Chapter 24, this volume). But the early Christian missionaries introduced the Roman alphabet when they brought Christianity, literacy and European culture during the early seventh century AD (Upward and Davidson 2011, Crystal 2012). As Millward and Hayes (2012: 84) point out, "Christianization is an important landmark in the history of the English language because it brought England and English-speakers into the only living intellectual community of Europe, that of the Latin Church. England immediately adopted the Latin alphabet, and English was soon being written down extensively." Initially, the one-to-one correspondence between letter and sound was maintained (see Figure 26.1).[2]

The adoption of continental practices at the expense of autochthonous ones was rapid except for a few letters that did not have an equivalent in Latin and thus prevailed until the end of the Middle Ages: 'thorn' <þ> (>*th*) and 'wynn' <p> (> *uu* ~ *w*). Other variants were introduced by Irish monks, such as 'eth' <Ð> ~ <ð>, 'ash' <Æ> ~ <æ> or 'ethel' <Œ> ~ <œ> (see Scragg 1974: 6–11, Hogg 1992b: 73–81, Upward and Davidson 2011: 3). The replacement of the

[2] Source: https://wiki.ultimacodex.com/wiki/Runic_alphabet.

Figure 26.1 Germanic alphabet of runes

runic <þ> with the Roman digraph <th>, as in *þing* > *thing*, *broþer* > *brother* and *comeþ* > *cometh*, was therefore a contact-induced change in the English spelling of the late Middle English period (between 1300 and 1500), and the thorn was a relic grapheme still resisting continental orthographic influence. This process was observed by Conde-Silvestre and Hernández-Campoy (2013) and Hernández-Campoy, Conde-Silvestre and García-Vidal (2019) in different generations of the Paston family. The scrutiny of these forms in the *Paston Letters* showed a positive monotonic pattern that proceeded gradually, cumulatively and consecutively from generation to generation from 1425 to 1503. The *Paston Letters* constitute a collection of 422 authored documents (246,353 words) written during the most part of the fifteenth century by different generations of this minor gentry Norfolk family, about whom there is extensive personal biographical information (see Davis 1971). Different studies on this biscriptual variation between the autochthonous runic letter <þ> and the Roman digraph <th> in this Paston family are presented along this chapter to illustrate different types of instrumentalization of its indexical nature.

26.2 Orthographic Variation and Sociolinguistic Variables

One of the main achievements in sociolinguistics was the empirical demonstration that linguistic variation in interpersonal communication is not normally free at all, but rather constrained by social and/or contextual factors (see Labov 1966, 1972a, or Trudgill 1974). For this reason, the exploration of orthographic variation across style, register, genre and any text type from a sociolinguistic perspective becomes inherently inevitable. The *linguistic variable* appeared as its main construct and is conceived as a linguistic unit with two or more variants involved in covariation with extralinguistic variables (see Trudgill 1974: 80),[3] allowing a distinction between interspeaker (social) and intraspeaker (stylistic) variation: "[t]he social dimension

[3] In variationist sociolinguistics, linguistic variables are represented between parentheses or keywords in capitals, for example variable (ing) or variable ING, respectively (see Chambers 1995: 17, or Meyerhoff 2006: 8).

denotes differences between the speech of different speakers, and the stylistic denotes differences within the speech of a single speaker" (Bell 1984: 145).

Linguistic variables occur at all levels of linguistic analysis, depending on the nature of the linguistic feature under observation. Obviously, current sociolinguistic theory has mostly been based on spoken language, using both phonological and grammatical variables, such as the rhotic or nonrhotic realization of postvocalic /r/ in New York City (Labov 1966, 1972a) or the omission of the copula *be* in *She nice* (rather than *She is nice*) in Afro-American Vernacular English (Wolfram 1969), among many others. This practice, however, constitutes a challenge in historical sociolinguistics due to the nature of its linguistic materials available as archival sources. But, fortunately, the treatment and reliability of orthographic variables as (socio)linguistic variables has already been tested at both micro and macro levels of historical sociolinguistic research, evidencing patterns of language variation and change (see Hernández-Campoy and Conde-Silvestre 1999, Taavitsainen 2000, 2004, Rutkowska 2003, 2005, Stenroos 2004, 2006, Bergs 2005, Sairio 2009, Rutkowska and Rössler 2012, Conde-Silvestre and Hernández-Campoy 2013, Schiegg 2016, 2018, or Hernández-Campoy and García-Vidal 2018a, 2018b, among others).

As Rutkowska and Rössler (2012: 213) point out, structural variability "exists not only at the generally recognized levels of phonology, morphology, and syntax, but also at the level of orthography"; and its evolution has to be understood as part of the interplay between intra- and extralinguistic processes and pressures. Thus, an orthographic variable can be seen as "a feature of an orthographic system of a given language, related to the phonological, morphological, or lexical levels of that language system, and realized by different variants under specific extra-linguistic circumstances" (Rutkowska and Rössler 2012: 219). The extralinguistic factors conditioning the use of different spelling forms in those cases of variability are usually production, geographical location, sociodemographics (sex, age, rank), social networks, text type (and genre), style, register and medium (handwritten vs. printed). In fact, in a period, like the late Middle Ages, when written correspondence was one of the most frequent modes of communication and when a well-established and fixed standard variety was lacking, orthographic variation must have been a source of social meaning (see Baddeley and Voeste 2012b, Voeste 2018a).

Therefore, as the following sections show in different ways, and following Rutkowska and Rössler (2012: 217–19), the nature of sociolinguistic variation in orthography may perfectly be functionally constrained by diachronic, diatopic, diaphasic, diastratic, diasituative and aesthetic variants as a reflection of external factors, such as style, register, genre and specific text-type conventions.

26.2.1 Style and Register

Style-shifting currently appears overlapping with or disguised under the form of accents, dialects, registers or genres, largely resembling a functionally rule-governed code-switching process. Some terminological clarification is thus needed. In this sense, Coseriu (1970: 32) proposed a typology of linguistic variation with four dimensions: diaphasic, diastratic, diatopic and diachronic. Diaphasic variation refers to intraspeaker variation according to the communicative setting, yielding different styles or registers. Diastratic variation is interspeaker variation according to the sociodemographic and/or biological characteristics of the speaker in different social groups, giving way to sociolects. The diatopic dimension is associated with geographical variation in the form of geolects or dialects. Finally, diachronic variation refers to the different historical stages within the evolution of a language. Both *style* and *register* have been indistinctly used as diaphasic variation to refer to particular ways of language use in particular sociosituational contexts. Hallidayan linguistics uses the term 'register' for all types of sociosituational varieties (including technical/occupational ones), assuming 'styles' as an aesthetic option with no functional value in the communicative process (see Halliday 1975, 1978, Gregory and Carroll 1978, Crystal and Davy 1969, Biber and Finegan 1994, Biber 1995, 2006 or Biber and Conrad 2009). Contrarily, Labovian sociolinguistics uses the term 'style' to refer to sociosituational varieties, restricting 'registers' to technical or occupational ones (see Labov 1966, 1972a, Trudgill 1974, Coupland 1980, 2007, Bell 1984 or Ferguson 1994). All speakers, therefore, use different styles in also different situations depending on the context of situation (topic, addressee and the medium), but not all speakers have the same proficiency in registers or verbal repertoire:

Style (formality)	Register (occupation)
tired vs. *fatigued*	*word* vs. *lexical item*
bust vs. *break*	*collar-bone* vs. *clavicle*

Halliday (1978) conceived language as a systemic resource for meaning – rather than merely a system of signs – where every single linguistic act involves choice from a describable set of options at any level for its communicative purposes. The sets of meaning resources are selected and used by individuals in particular social contexts that facilitate disambiguation, with *field* (subject matter or topic), *tenor* (roles of the participants in an interaction) and *mode* (channel of communication) as variables in *registers* – rather than styles. Since then, different typological classifications of styles (registers, or functional styles) have been proposed without consensus (see Hernández-Campoy 2016a: 24–28). In Fowler's (1986: 192) view, different 'fields' produce different kinds of language, especially at the lexical level. According to Crystal (1980: 292), 'tenor' might stand as a roughly equivalent term for 'style', and 'mode' refers to the symbolic organization of the communicative situation (written, spoken and so on) and even the genre of the text. Halliday's theory inspired the communicative-function model accounting for style-shifting, known as Register Axiom, developed by Douglas Biber and Edward Finegan in sociolinguistics (see Biber 1995, Biber and Finegan 1994, Biber and Conrad 2009).

Following Biber and Conrad's (2009) framework for analyzing register variation, Yáñez-Bouza (2015) and Rutten and Krogull (2022) have found different situational characteristics, such as participants, channel, setting, communicative purpose and topic in different types of historical ego-documents. The question is whether there are differences at the level of spelling. In medieval England, the Chancery Office was the administrative writing office, responsible for the production of official documents, together with the Exchequer, the Privy Seal Office and the Signet Office from c. 1430 onward: "The Inns of Chancery and Inns of Court were active in training their staff, other clerks, and common lawyers to master the form and content of these documents in Latin and French, and, it is assumed, also in English" (see Nevalainen 2012a: 134). Despite its institutional stance – initially beginning as part of the royal household – the 'Chancery English standard'[4] texts also showed multiple spelling conventions practiced, betraying the geographical origin of clerks, as the variation found in *such* (including *sich, sych, seche, swich* and *sweche*) (Nevalainen 2003: 133). However, according to Nevalainen and Tieken-Boon van Ostade (2006: 276), the regularization of the digraph <gh> for the fricative [x] ~ [ç] instead of <ʒ> in *light* or *plough*, the use of the dental suffix <d> instead of <t> for the past tense and past participle of weak verbs, or the use of capital <I> for the first person singular subject pronoun, as well as other spelling practices, were led by the Chancery.

Evans (2020) has recently studied the use of verbal and visual features in the language of royal texts of Tudor England to construct and project the image of royal power and authority – in addition to other resources such as rituals and ceremonies, body images (coins, portraiture, woodcuts), physical and geographical properties (clothing, jewelry, architecture), etc. Metapragmatics is also crucial in this iconography of the power and authority of the royal persona projected through verbal and visual features. In this sense, Evans's (2020: 12–13) notion of the royal social voice is understood within Biber and Finegan's (1994) conception of *register* and *style*, Agha's (2005, 2011) *enregisterment*,[5] and their connections with *genres*. The study of royal language and

[4] 'Chancery standard' was suggested by Samuels (1989 [1963]: 71) to refer to that variety of English used in the governmental offices in fifteenth-century England and which was assumed to be the direct ancestor of modern Standard English. According to Fisher (1977) and Richardson (1980), the 'Chancery standard' practices were based on King Henry V's (1413–22) personal writing office (the Signet Office). More recently, Benskin (2004) has questioned the role of the Chancery Offices in standardization by claiming the importance of Latin as the majority language of administration and the insignificant use of English (and with a great deal of geographical variation) by the body of clerks at the Signet Office.

[5] Enregisterment is defined by (Agha 2003: 231–32) as "the processes through which a linguistic repertoire becomes differentiable within a language as a socially recognized register of forms."

its metacommunicative strategies for enregisterment is thus relevant because they reflect a particular addresser's stance and the addressee's interpretation in their interaction, considering linguistic and nonlinguistic conventions in terms of production and consumption. Similarly, in a different study, Tagg and Evans (2020) also work on the social meanings of orthographic standardization by comparing spelling variation in sixteenth-century correspondence and in twenty-first-century text messages and the ideological ground conditioning in their respective practices. Despite the four-century temporal gap, their transhistorical pragmatic approach shows that both periods share similar motivations in spelling practices, such as identity construction/projection and the dynamics of social interaction, and so does a gender-based approach carried out (see Evans and Tagg 2020). Raumolin-Brunberg and Terttu Nevalainen (1990) investigated spelling variation in official and private texts written between 1500 and the mid-1550s using the *Helsinki Corpus of English Texts* (Rissanen et al. 1991) as linguistic archival source. They found less degree of spelling variation in official documents than in private ones, reflecting both the specific characteristics of the registers (and genres) and the professional, educational and regional extraction. Their results also allowed these authors to conclude that public writings were linguistically more focused than private ones even in the sixteenth century.

Register variation in Labovian sociolinguistics, according to Ferguson (1994: 20), is a communication situation that recurs regularly in a society (in terms of participants, setting, communicative functions and so on) with developed identifying markers of language structure differentiated from other communication situations. Style enjoys a central position in sociolinguistic variation, where *stylistic* variation constitutes a main component together with *linguistic* and *social* variation (Rickford and Eckert 2001: 1). Sociolinguistic studies, as Bell (1984: 145) pointed out, are not only concerned with social variation between individuals of different social ranks (interspeaker variation) but also with stylistic variation within the speech of a single informant (intraspeaker variation). Historical sociolinguistics has recently started focusing on styles to move further in our understanding of the speaker's sociolinguistic behavior in the social interaction of speech communities from the past. As Coulmas (2003: 241) states, "[t]he range of linguistic varieties in literate society includes registers, styles and dialects that are closer to or further divorced from the written standard, the literacy rate being one of the factors that determine the specific arrangement of functionally distributed varieties characteristic of a given society." Figures of speech (*figurae verborum*) and figures of thought (*figurae sententiarum*) have traditionally been assumed to constitute the rhetorical devices that enhance speaking or writing as stylistic elements of display since the ancient Graeco-Roman cultures. More recently, style-shifting has been demonstrated to cause its own effects in the transmission of social meaning and positioning (see Hernández-Campoy 2016a). Style-shifting is materialized through different linguistic resources and mechanisms present in language varieties which are available to speakers as "a clustering of linguistic resources, and an association of that clustering with social meaning" (Eckert 2001: 123).

The *Paston Letters*, for example, illustrate the way some fifteenth-century letter-writers exploited the indexical nature of the orthographic variable (th) as a mechanism to mark formality and politeness, accommodating to the social rank of letter addressees through stylistic choice. As seen above, in a context of a strong continental magnetism, the Roman-based form <th> was a socially and stylistically conscious external choice in England, a Labovian change 'from above', that became overtly popular during the fifteenth century, acquiring overt prestige and entering the linguistic norm (see Benskin 1982, Stenroos 2004, 2006). Given the socially meaningful nature of this orthographic variable, the choice and use of its variants seems to have participated in medieval speaker's both inter- and intraspeaker variation, pivoting for both social and stylistic dimensions. As observed by Hernández-Campoy and García-Vidal (2018b: 399), in this family, John I's sociolinguistic behavior in social interaction demonstrates that the principles of *graded style-shifting* and *range of variability* characterizing Labov's (1966) and Bell's (1984) models of stylistic variation also governed intraspeaker variation in English medieval society: that is, no single speaker is monostylistic, though the range of the individual's verbal repertoire is always conditioned by external factors such as situational context and social background (see Hernández-Campoy 2016a: 83–85). John I's letters reveal that he has a linguistic repertoire (range of variability), as well as accommodative competence and awareness of sociolinguistic conventions on the indexical nature of variable (th): the innovative variant <th> is more extended in those groups of the social rank that enjoy overt prestige, a fact which enables John Paston I to vary and adapt his style according to the addressee: 100 percent when addressing royalty, 97 percent with nobility, 82 percent with his wife, 74 percent with other minor gentry interlocutors and 73 percent with legal professionals. Together with audience-based style-shifting processes through the use of the orthographic innovation <th>, in Hernández-Campoy and García-Vidal's (2018b: 404) study, there is also register-based variation. Upward adjustments occur when addressing royalty (100 percent) and nobility (97 percent), which were the most overtly prestigious groups. But it is also somehow high with legal professionals (73 percent), considering this is an inferior rank, and very close to the group of equals (minor gentry: 74 percent). In fact, individual comparisons between groups also suggest the existence of significant variation between them at $p < 0.01$, except between legal professionals (398/545: 73 percent) and minor gentry (594/801: 74 percent), where $p > 0.05$. This is probably because of the technicality of the official language of law, business and administration, as well as, more crucially, due to the distant nature of those trained interlocutors (see also Palander-Collin et al. 2009: 12).

26.2.2 Style and Dialect

Dialects, accents, styles and registers of speech have traditionally been conceived in association with social categories and different situations of language use and user (see Trudgill 1983: 100–22): variation according to use (style or register) and variation according to user (sociolect, geolect, etc.). As a result, if styles bring up situationally defined varieties and registers to occupational ones (when not equated to styles), dialects and accents, on the other hand, constitute varieties associated with different groups of speakers. In fact, accent and dialect have usually been related to the 'speaker', style to the 'situation' and register to the 'topic', 'subject' or 'activity' (Trudgill 2006: 119–21). Though both are closely connected, if style is a variety defined according to *use*, dialect constitutes a variety defined according to the *user*. The concept of 'dialect' and its nature has always been controversial in sociolinguistic traditions (see Ammon 2004, Britain 2004), with the concepts of 'geolect' initially or 'patois' later to refer to a 'regional dialect' or any nonstandard varieties. But the terms 'sociolect', 'social dialect', 'urban dialect' or 'class dialect' emerged during the 1960s as an urbanized equivalent to the regional dialect, denoting variation associated with social class stratification.

During the process of language standardization at the end of medieval times in Europe, the need of a national standard variety also affected orthography. In England, during the 1100s, after the Norman Conquest, the spelling system changed under the influence of Latin and Norman French. The coexistence of three orthographic systems (Latin, French and English) was a source of confusion and linguistic instability. As a result, widespread regional variation and general instability due to the multiplicity of spelling conventions in English texts complicated the emergent English orthographic norms (Blake 1992: 10–11). A sense of a standard orthography did not start until the fifteenth century, taking about two centuries to complete (Smith 2012: 134, Rutkowska and Rössler 2012: 222). For example, under the influence of Latin, in addition to the fixation of <th> instead of <þ> and <ð>, other non-Latin letters such as 'ash' <æ>, 'wynn' <ƿ> and 'yogh' <ȝ>, also extensively used in Old and Early Middle English, were gradually replaced by Roman-based equivalents: <a> instead of <æ> (*thæt* > *that*), <uu> and <w> instead of <ƿ> (*ƿeg* > *weg*) and <gh> and <y> for <ȝ> (*plouȝ* > *plough*, *ȝou* > *you*). Due to French influence, the digraph <ou> came to be used for the Middle English long vowel /uː/ (*hūs*>*house*), and <o> in the context of minims (<m>, <n>, <v>) or other letters with down strokes (<l>, <ch>), as in *cume* > *come*, *Lundon* > *London*, *luve* > *love* or *wulf* > *wolf*, began to be used for the short vowel /u/ to facilitate manuscript legibility. The di-/trigraphs <sh>, <sch> and even <ss> in the north replaced <sc> (*sceal* > *shal* ~ *schal* ~ *ssal* ~ *xall* > *shall*), and <ch> was used instead of <c> for /ʧ/ (*cild* > *child*). The digraph <qu> replaced <cw> in words such as *cwen* > *queen*. Long vowels came to be spelt with double letters to mark vowel length, as in <ee> for /eː/ (*geese*) and <oo> for /oː/ (*doom*), while double consonants were used to mark a preceding short vowel (*cuþþe* 'kindred'). In addition to the regular <s> spelling (*see*), <c> started to be used for /s/ before <e, i> (corresponding to front vowels) both in loan words (*cellar*) and also in native words (*mice*). New spelling conventions were introduced and <j> and <v> came to be used as allographs of <i> and <u> respectively, showing instability (*lyfe* ~ *life*: 'life'; *ier* ~ *yeer*: 'year'; *vre* ~ *ure*: 'our'; *driuen* ~ *driven*: 'driven') in word-medial position till the second half of the sixteenth century (see Scragg 1974: 38–51, Nevalainen 2012a: 132–33, Rutkowska 2013a: 117–40, 2016, Condorelli 2021a, 2021b, 2022b; see also Chapter 13, this volume).

As seen in Subsection 26.2.1, dialectal coloring and other variability options became suppressed but affected different text types in different ways, mostly starting with official government documents, such as the 'Chancery standard' in England (see Fisher 1977 and Benskin 2004). The subsequent extension of orthographic standard conventions to other types of texts and genres was in high correlation with sociodemographic factors, such social rank, mobility, gender or education, and/or geographical origin. Hernández-Campoy and Conde-Silvestre (1999, 2005), for example, examined the diffusion of incipient standard orthographic practices in late fifteenth-century private correspondence of some members of the geographically different families of Paston (Norfolk), Cely (London) and Stonor (Oxfordshire) in England: <sh> (vs. <sch>, <ssh>, <ss> and <x>) as in *shall*, <wh> (vs. <qw>, <qu>) as in *which*, and <u> (vs. <e>, <o>, <y>, <uy>, <wy> or <ui>) as in *such*. This interdialectal perspective compares the treatment of the three orthographic variables in the letters written by the three families included in the diachronic part of the *Helsinki Corpus of English Texts* (Rissanen et al. 1991).

The scores for these variables in the three families revealed that the Pastons from Norfolk exhibit lower frequencies of usage of the incipient standard spelling practices (30 percent), as opposed to the 63 percent of the Celys and the 89 percent of the Stonors. This is possibly connected with the linguistic similarity of their respective local varieties to the new norm (the South-Western in the case of the Stonors, and the South-Eastern in the case of the Celys). In fact, according to these authors, both varieties had an important linguistic influence on the configuration of the London dialect in the fourteenth century, while East Anglian features, the local variety of the Pastons in Norfolk, started to pour into the London dialect later in the Middle English period. Additionally, the correlation between graphemic innovations through particular diagnostic lexical items selected and age, gender, status, social networks and styles allowed Hernández-Campoy and Conde-Silvestre (1999, 2005) to conclude that social rank and weak ties within medieval loose-knit networks also played a crucial role in the diffusion in time of incipient standard spellings. Sociodemographically speaking, the most mobile members of the upper gentry and also of urban nongentry (merchants) appeared as more "prominent in the use of the spellings that would become standard practices" (Hernández-Campoy and Conde-Silvestre 2005: 126). And stylistically, the "increase in the use of early standard variants in the course of time is parallel to their extension from formal to informal documents" (Hernández-Campoy and Conde-Silvestre 2005: 126).

Osselton (1984) studied the development of two standard spelling practices in the seventeenth and eighteenth centuries by comparing printed public writings of literary authors (such as Johnson, Gray, Addison, Defoe and Dryden) as a result of the expansion of the printing press and handwritten private letters. He paid attention to noun capitalization, the derivational suffix *-al*, the orthographic realizations of the inflectional ending *-ed* in past tense and past participles of weak verbs, and lexical abbreviations. His results indicated the presence of a more fixed orthography in public writings and, contrarily, a wider range of variation in handwritten private correspondence which is based on inherent genre and even stylistic categorizations highly conditioned by the medium (handwritten/printed). Although he asserted that "epistolary spelling is a graphic system which leads its own linguistic life" (1984: 125), he also found "a time-lag of between 50 and 100 years between epistolary and printers' spelling" (1984: 132) in the move toward orthographic uniformity. Similarly, the existence of two standards of spelling and the greater amount of spelling variation in eighteenth-century private letters than in printed texts was also confirmed by Tieken-Boon van Ostade (1998, 2006a) with her comparison between the spelling practices in letters by Sarah Fielding, Robert Lowth, Laurence Sterne and James Boswell, and those of contemporary printers.

But the role of printers in the regularization of English spelling in this context of highly inconsistent and chaotic practices in Early Modern English seems to have contributed to the fixation of a standardized orthography, as Rutkowska (2013a, 2020a: 41–42) and Condorelli (2021a, 2022b) have been able to show. In her study investigating over 30 orthographic variables in 13 editions of the *Kalender of Shepherdes* (published between 1506 and 1656), Rutkowska (2013a) found a decrease in variation and the subsequent increase in the consistency of spelling patterns from the first to the last edition of this incunable almanac, evidencing the impact of publishing houses. Later, with her quantitative analysis of third person singular present tense inflectional endings of verbs (*-eth*, *-ethe*, *-yth*, *-ythe*, *-ith*, *-ithe*, *-th* and *-the*) in six editions of *The Book of Good Maners* (1487–1526), printed by William Caxton, Richard Pynson and Wynkyn de Worde, Rutkowska (2020a: 41–42) also suggests an overt influence of printing houses in the mid-sixteenth century before the codification stage took place with the subsequent availability of grammars and spelling books. In fact, given Caxton's awareness of the difficulties for communication of the absence of a common variety because of his activity as a printer, he advocated that "books had to be printed in a dialect and use conventional spelling that could be understood by all" (Brinton and Arnovick 2011: 312), as he expressed in the Preface to his translation of *Eneydos* (1490).

Similarly, Condorelli (2021a, 2022b) recently explored the positional spelling redistribution, fixation and standardization of word-initial <v> ~ <u> (*vntil ~ until, vnfaithful ~ unfaithful*) and <i> ~ <j> (*iudge ~ judge, iolly ~ jolly*) between 1500 and 1700 across a range of printed English texts from a sampled version of the database *Early English Books Online*. The regularization of <u> and <j> for initial position and <v> and <i> for elsewhere goes together with redistribution of <u> ~ <i> to represent vowels and <v> ~ <j> to represent consonants. According to his results, these diachronic developments seem to have occurred between the 1620s and 1640s in close connection with pragmatic factors that affected the Early Modern English printing industry. A similar situation also affected the fixation of <i> in word-initial position to the detriment of <y> (*yf ~ if, lyttle ~ little*) as well as the regularization of <y> in word-final position at the expense of <i> (*my ~ mi, by ~ bi*) in Early Modern English, neutralizing these traditional random graphemic alternations (see Condorelli 2021a).

Kaislaniemi et al. (2017) observed variation for the word-medial vowel digraph <ie ~ ei> (*friend ~ freind, believe ~ beleive* or *receive ~ recieve*) in order to study orthography and the codification of spelling norms in England from the fifteenth to the eighteenth centuries. The vowel digraph <ie> ~ <ei> exhibited a clear progression across the 400-year dataset covered for one variant (*friend, believe, receive*) to become dominant from the mid-1550s onward after a period of variability in strong competition, at least in the process of standardization of this epistolary spelling. If social, register, audience and/or context-based idiolectal variation dominated the fifteenth and sixteenth centuries, with no uniform patterns of spelling practices, then generational change started to make the number of variants decrease in the seventeenth century, moving away from the array of medieval regional norms and its multiplicity of spelling conventions and leading to the emergent standard spelling form (fixed) in the eighteenth century (Kaislaniemi et al. 2017: 204).

If, as Nevalainen (2003: 138) stated, the codification of English spelling was completed in print by 1650 approximately, in holographic writing the fixation of conventions occurred much later, which allowed Osselton's (1963) distinction between public spelling – that of print houses – and private spelling (handmade writing). The subsequent minimal variation in the contemporary spelling of worldwide English is the global success of spelling standardization and the codification of orthography through continuous institutional support (Nevalainen and Tieken-Boon van Ostade 2006: 310). Sociodemographically, from the point of view of the gender of letter-writers, although men tended to be leading the standardization process for these variables, sex-based differences had entirely leveled out at the end of the eighteenth century. In terms of social groups, if upper ranks used to lead the change until the beginning of 1700, after the 1720s it was the middle and lower ranks (professionals and merchants) that became ahead of standard conventions. Geographically, London was in the vanguard of the standardization process in every period, with northerners and the Home Counties behind (see Kaislaniemi et al. 2017: 207–8).

As Rössler (2000) stated, orthography and specific spellings may often also be used for some especially creative stylistic purposes agentively. With the application of Silverstein's (2003) notion of 'indexical meaning' to language production varieties, registers and styles are recently being seen as "cultural models of action that link diverse behavioral signs to enactable effects, including images of persona, interpersonal relationship, and type of conduct" (Agha 2006: 145). As shown in Hernández-Campoy and García-Vidal (2018a), Sir John Paston II appears as a member of the Paston family who instrumentalized the indexical nature of the spelling forms <þ> and <th> following a proactive agency in choice and use to pursue a particular goal. During the civil war (1455–87), the Duke of Norfolk seized Caister Castle in 1469, at that time held by the Pastons, and took the rents of the manor until approximately 1476. In a letter addressed to King Edward IV in 1475, John Paston II asked him to intervene and help his family to get the Caister manor back. Regarding this variable, John II was characterized as a user of the incipient standard spelling mostly (78 percent) in his letters, and also exhibiting a graded style-shifting with different audience-based verbal attunements: 100 percent with nobility, 79 percent with clergy, 91 percent with other minor gentry interlocutors or 89 percent when addressing legal professionals. However, unexpectedly, he was just 33 percent standard when addressing the king. According to Hernández-Campoy and García-Vidal (2018a: 21–23), his sociolinguistic behavior when addressing King Edward IV – violating expectations for rank and audienceship – is based on the socioconstructionist Speaker Design Theory.[6] This deliberate and proactive underuse of the protostandard form by Sir John Paston II with the royalty group by exceeding the use of the nonstandard variant <þ> may be understood as a conscious and deliberate case of *hypervernacularization* to pursue a communicative effect and some kind of stylistic coloring; that is, the use of nonstandard forms correctly though inappropriately according to sociodemographic and/or stylistic parameters, and whose counterpart would be hyperstandardization – also known as hypercorrection (see Cutillas-Espinosa et al. 2010: 34). The unexpected use of a vernacular form (the old runic spelling <þ>) with downward rather than

[6] The Speaker Design Theory is a recent multidimensional as well as multifaceted socioconstructionist approach to stylistic variation in sociolinguistics that emphasizes the socially constructive potential of style-shifting for the creation and projection of social meaning in interpersonal discourse. In this way, speakers make personal and strategic stylistic choices deliberately in order to hint at a precise social categorization and transmit a particular social positioning in society (see Coupland 2007: 82–176, Hernández-Campoy 2016a: 146–84).

upward accommodation indicates that John II was not shifting his epistolary language production in reaction to formality and audienceship. Rather, he used an obsolete dialectal spelling feature to project the defenselessness of his humble family against the power and strength of the Duke of Norfolk, in pursuit of what became a successful petition.

26.2.3 Style and Genre

Genre variation in sociolinguistics is conceived as conventionalized message-forms, so that a genre appears as a message type that recurs regularly in a community – in terms of semantic content, participants, occasions of use and so on. This kind of message-form has its own developed identifying internal structure differentiated from other message types in the repertoire of the community (Ferguson 1994: 21): for example, the legal form of a power-of-attorney document, a notarial deed, the psalm-form of religious poetry, primary school riddles and so on, in addition to traditionally literary epic, lyric, drama and subsequent subgenres (see Devitt 2004, but also Biber 1995). When establishing the difference between register, genre and style, Biber and Conrad (2009: 16) view them as different approaches to the same text, rather than as different kinds of texts or different varieties. The three perspectives are based on (i) the texts considered for analysis, (ii) the linguistic characteristics considered for the analysis, (iii) the distribution of those linguistic characteristics and (iv) the interpretation of linguistic differences.

The development and diversification of digitalized archival data sources is allowing scholars to deal with intraspeaker variation at the level of ego-documents, genre categorizations and other text types, as well as specific aspects of formulaic epistolary language such as formality levels, literacy and linguistic repertoire, politeness strategies, address formulae and so on (see Rutkowska 2003, Tieken-Boon van Ostade 2006a, Dossena and Fitzmaurice 2006, Sairio 2009, 2017, Pahta et al. 2010, Dossena and Del Lungo Camiciotti 2012, Auer 2015). Among others, Hogg (2006: 395–416) claimed that the incorporation of variables such as style, register and text type into the analysis of linguistic variation in texts belonging to early periods such as Old English could provide valuable sociolinguistic insights into those historical stages. Similarly, as suggested by Laing and Lass (2006: 419–20), the study of scribal documents with the collaborative expertise of textual scholars, paleographers and codicologists contributes importantly to the analysis of sociolinguistic and geolinguistic variation in the Middle Ages. This collaborative exploration provides us with both social and linguistic information on the complex relations between the scribes' native varieties and their transcribing of foreign languages, as well as with the text genres, the provenance of exemplars and the different modes of copying, the order to which a given scribe belonged (such as Franciscan or Benedictine), the kind of script he used and the particular scriptorium where he wrote (see Dumville 1993, Blake and Thaisen 2004, Traxel 2004, Thaisen 2005, 2017).[7]

Ego-documents, such as letters, diaries, travel accounts, court records, memoranda, wills, indentures and recipes, have been demonstrated to be adequate materials for sociolinguistic analysis and the exploration of their role as genres is also becoming a source for research (see Nevala and Palander-Collin 2005, Tieken-Boon van Ostade 2006a, Palander-Collin 2010, Elspaß 2012b, Voeste 2018a). Some authors have also confirmed the relevance of these documents to reconstruct the sociolinguistic contexts of language variation and change in the past (see Dossena and Fitzmaurice 2006, Nevalainen and Tanskanen 2007, Dossena and Tieken-Boon van Ostade 2008, Dossena and Del Lungo Camiciotti 2012, van der Wal and Rutten 2013, Rutten and van der Wal 2014, Auer et al. 2015, Amador-Moreno 2019, Brown 2019). Among some of the most recent contributions, Kaislaniemi et al. (2017) demonstrate the usefulness of archival sources such as the *Corpus of Early English Correspondence* (CEEC; Nevalainen et al. 1993–98) to study orthography and the codification of spelling norms in England from the fifteenth to the eighteenth century.

In a kind of historical patholinguistic research, Schiegg (2018) explored the use of standard spelling practices in German by mentally ill patients in a corpus of letters written in a psychiatric hospital from 1891 to 1905,[8] focusing on (i) the appearance of the spelling <c> in combination with <h>, as in *ich* 'I' (standard) versus *ih* (nonstandard), and (ii) the use of indicators of vowel quantity, such as *bitte* 'you're welcome' (standard) versus *bite* (nonstandard), or the nonstandard grapheme <f> instead of the <v> (e.g. *fon* ~ *von* 'from; of'), <ai> instead of <ei> (e.g. *waib* ~ *weib* 'wife'), <d> instead of <t> (e.g. *dete* ~ *täte* 'would do'), etc. As Hernández-Campoy and García-Vidal (2018b) found, one of Schiegg's informants (Martin B.) exhibits an audience-based sociolinguistic behavior, with higher frequencies in the use of a standard orthography in formal letters – addressed to the local mayor and his brother-in-law (81.2 percent and 87.4 percent) – and, conversely, lower frequencies

[7] Sometimes the choice of the variants for an orthographic variable might not have been so much conditioned by factors related to sociodemography, context, register or genre. When dealing with handwritten materials from the past, paleographical aspects may often come into consideration, given that both topic and corpus data ultimately rest on manuscript evidence (see Vázquez and Marqués-Aguado 2012). Scribes were prone to mistakenly repeat letters within a given word or even word or phrases (dittographies), or the omission of letters, syllables, words or phrases where similar words or syllables are involved (haplography), as well as to calculations of writing space and the graphic environment where the letter and possible abbreviations were supposed to stand (see Osselton 1963, 1984, Taavitsainen 2000, 2004, Tieken-Boon van Ostade 2006b, Thaisen 2017, Honkapohja 2017, Claridge and Kytö 2020, Honkapohja and Liira 2020).

[8] The source of linguistic materials was the southern German psychiatric hospital of Kaufbeuren, which kept its thousands of old patient files dating back to 1849. In these files, a diverse array of text types are available: "medical records, certificates, doctors' notes, telegrams, letters from public authorities and different institutional documents, as well as documents by the patients themselves, many of which are letters to (and from) their families, to doctors, and to other authorities" (Schiegg 2018: 117; see also Schiegg 2015: 75).

in informal ones, such as those addressed to his aunt (67.8 percent) or his wife (22.4 percent). Informant Martin B. had enough range of variation and accommodative competence to be able to consciously shift from different styles and choose between different variants, practicing upward and downward accommodation despite his limited education. Even more interestingly, Schiegg (2018) also found a regular pattern, which is the impact of age and health condition on correctness and standardness; that is, the more the mental health of patients in the psychiatric hospital deteriorated, the more uncareful their handwriting was and the less willingness (or faculty) they had to use the standard variety (see also Schiegg 2015).

As Markus (2006) found, the use of abbreviations was a gender and register/genre-based practice, with female writers using fewer than male ones, and being more usual in business letters. Similarly, as revealed by Tieken-Boon van Ostade's (2006b) research, the level of formality also constituted a factor conditioning the use of abbreviations and contractions in private letters, especially in informal letters, drafts and short notes.

26.3 Conclusion

Historical sociolinguistics has recently highlighted the indexical potential of orthography as a level at which sociolinguistic variables can be identified, especially through the exploration of style, register, genre and text types in written materials from the past. The relevance of orthographic variables is exceptional to reconstruct the sociolinguistic contexts of language variation and change in past communities and also to shed light on the resources and driving forces for sociolinguistic variability and diaphasic choice by individuals in past societies. The incorporation of textual variables such as style, register, genre and text type into the analysis of linguistic variation in documents belonging to past periods provides valuable sociolinguistic insights into those historical stages. The role of new genres and text types is also being highlighted as linguistic sources worth studying for both inter- and intra-speaker variation, especially to study orthography and the codification of spelling norms in a given language, such as English. The extralinguistic factors conditioning the use of different spelling forms in cases of variability are usually based on production, geographical location, sociodemographics (sex, age, rank), social networks, text type (and genre), style, register and medium (handwritten vs. printed). In earlier periods of a given language – when private correspondence was the most frequent means of written communication and without the existence of a well-established and fixed standard variety – orthographic variation was an overt source of social meaning and its research avenues should be extended.

27

Sociolinguistic Implications of Orthographic Variation in French

Sandrine Tailleur

27.1 Introduction

This chapter is intended to give empirical evidence to support the idea that, within the field of historical sociolinguistics, variation in spelling is now considered a type of linguistic variable (Rutkowska and Rössler 2012).[1] This idea in itself is an innovation, one that needs further support, given the fact that, for early variationists, oral language is usually the exclusive object of study. For Labov (1994: 18), for instance, to observe language change in progress is to study quantitatively extensive oral corpora of spontaneous speech, "using the present to explain the past." The history of languages' orthographies shows that they are systems resulting of conscious top-down processes – a literate social elite creates the system and imposes its views on users of the language. It is therefore difficult to reconcile such consciously created entities to theories of language change, which is by definition unconscious (unlike variation, which can be more or less conscious). Moreover, language change is most often studied through communities, using extensive corpora, whether historical or modern, not at the individual level – see for instance Kroch (2001) or, for a discussion about the role of individuals in language change (sound level), Tamminga (2019) and MacKenzie (2019). This chapter is of particular interest to any researcher working in historical variationist sociolinguistics,[2] since it provides a discussion about types of data and individual variation.

This article received the financial support from *Fonds de recherche du Québec – Société et culture* (grant #2019-NP-252988 *La variation linguistique chez l'individu*). I would like to thank the editors of this volume and the anonymous reviewers for their insight. I am also very grateful to France Martineau, from the University of Ottawa, and to Ailís Cournane, from New York University, for their precious comments and advice on this chapter.

[1] See also Chapter 5 and Chapter 26, this volume.

[2] The variationist approach in sociolinguistics considers that "language requires an understanding of variable as well as categorical processes, and that the variation witnessed at all levels of language is not random" (Bayley 2013: 117).

We know that contextualizing data within a specific theoretical framework or a specific historical period is crucial to ensure that the analyses presented in our studies are valid. A lot is to be taken into consideration when it comes to types of data, especially historically, and this chapter offers evidence to help a historical sociolinguist navigate through it and make the right methodological decisions. Many studies of historical orthographies (e.g. Catach 2001) have looked at the prescriptive literature (mainly dictionaries) and metalinguistic comments on the formation of a writing system. This is important to understand the processes of standardization that happened in all European languages at various stages (see also Vandenbussche 2002, Nevalainen 2012a). However, fewer studies (see, e.g., Chapter 26 and Chapter 30, this volume) have actually considered spelling practices as examples of variable usage of language, to the same extent that a variable usage of morphological or phonological variants might inform us about the internal grammar of the speaker. Throughout this chapter, I ask the following questions: Can a variable usage of spelling features by a writer be used in the same way as other types of linguistic variables? And can we use orthographic usages to know more about language variation and change?

The aim of this chapter is to review studies of French orthography that have focused on the spelling practices of 'regular' users of the language (in crucial opposition to writers from the literate elite – norm makers). By discussing conclusions put forward by these studies, I shed light on what they can tell us about processes of language change as exemplified by spelling variation. Note that these studies do not include orthographic variation that is *allowed* by the standard system (such as geographic variation, to which I come back below), but look instead at how actual users of the written language deviate from standard forms (or, when applicable, how they react when confronted with fluctuating standards). This chapter situates French orthographic variables within the broader language evolution context. What are spelling variations telling us about the writer's attitudes toward the norm (written or spoken), toward the written form, and toward his or her linguistic community as a whole? How does spelling variation compare to other types of language variation? For instance, morphosyntactic variation is widely recognized as being part of the actual language system of the writer, while spelling is not, since it is a phenomenon exclusively associated with the written medium. It is therefore very useful to compare morphosyntactic and spelling variations within the same speakers, whenever the studies allow it, in order to better understand how to treat orthographic variation.

We know that morphosyntactic variation can be used to identify vernacular or regional features in writing, but only when the imperfect mastery of the written medium can safely be ruled out as a cause for variation (see Martineau 2013 for a discussion). For spelling variation, it is different: some spelling variants are loaded with social and political meanings – one could think of the spelling differences between British and American English, and the in-between that is represented by the Canadian English spelling (which uses *colour* (British), not *color* but *analyze* (American), not *analyse*). In these cases, the choice of one variant over another forces the writer to take a stand for one or the other national culture, when he or she is aware of the differences, which is of course not always the case for unskilled writers (I come back to this fact in the review of studies presented in Section 27.3). In French, such clear spelling choices are not available to writers coming from France, Belgium, Canada or others; the spelling norm is very much centralized in France. Therefore, spelling variation cannot, in most cases, be linked to regional or geographical variation. We are therefore left with register variation (relative distance to the norm or norms) and diachronic variation. Both aspects are addressed in this chapter. This chapter concentrates almost exclusively on the French language, and the studies that I review all address either regional French from France or different varieties of French in Canada (based on important work by Martineau and Dionne 2008, Martineau and Tailleur 2011, Martineau 2014, Martineau and Remysen 2019). The transplantation of French from France to Canada during the eighteenth and nineteenth centuries is at the center of at least one of the studies presented in this chapter.

The outline of this chapter is as follows. In Section 27.2, I give an overview of the theoretical assumptions needed to consider orthography within a language variation and change approach, since specificities concerning the study of oral and written languages need to be clarified. Section 27.3 addresses the concept of 'orthographic variable' and clarifies how it is used in studies about historical French. It presents a detailed review of studies, most within the variationist framework (see for instance Chambers 1995), by researchers who chose to examine orthographic variations. The studies are all about eighteenth- and nineteenth-century French, and the focus in this section is to emphasize the link between, on the one hand, spelling variation, and on the other, morphosyntactic variation within the social contexts of each specific act of writing. The norm is addressed each time, but only as a way to contextualize variation. Finally, I conclude this chapter with a discussion about what the studies teach us and about the importance of mixing individual and community-level approaches when considering a historical text. I show, through a careful presentation of selected historical sociolinguistic studies, that writers' variable choices of orthography can inform us about broader mechanisms of language variation and change, but always alongside other types of variation or linguistic information. It is emphasized that the influence of the writer, within the process of writing, seems to remain the most important factor to take into consideration in studies of orthographic variation.

27.2 Language Change and Written Language: A Few Theoretical Assumptions

Language change is a broad concept, but one that is unanimously accepted within all fields of linguistics: languages continuously change. Although it is sometimes possible to slow down change in progress through external interventions (normative ones, for instance, as discussed in Chapter 22, this volume), it is absolutely impossible to stop it (see Trudgill 2001 for a sociolinguistic approach to language change). Additionally, language change is hard to grasp; synchronically we can observe variation, but we cannot observe language change. Labov (1994: 25) speaks of "synchronic study of linguistic change in progress," and he proposes that we observe change both in variation across time (real time), and in variation across generations (apparent time). Labov (1994: 26) proposed that, in order "[t]o extract evidence for change in progress, we must separate the variation due to change from the variation due to social factors like sex, social class, social networks, and ethnicity, and from the variation due to internal factors like sentence stress, segmental environment, word order and phrase structure." This is what the studies chosen for this chapter attempt to demonstrate, but using written data and, among their variables, orthographic ones. In this section, I assume that what Labov proposed for oral data could be transposed to historical writing, given the appropriate types of written data that have been used in studies focused on historical variation and change.

In the last few years, advances in historical sociolinguistics, among other domains, have overcome the binary nature of the difference between vernacular and standard languages (see Hernández-Campoy and Conde-Silvestre 2012). An approach in terms of a register continuum is now preferred, and historical sociolinguists always carefully describe the type of data under study so that it can be situated on the continuum (see Watts 2015: 5–6). Oral and written languages may also be considered to fall on a continuum with respect to each other – of course, when language is written down (by hand, on a typewriter, a press or a computer), it is no longer oral, so this aspect is binary. However, researchers, and historical sociolinguists in particular, have described types of nonstandard written data that are often closer to vernacular language than to the standard one. Such nonstandard data can contain features of oral language, like traces of pronunciation in the spelling (for a detailed discussion on different types of such data, see, among others, Elspaß 2012b and Martineau 2013). Although I do not posit that we can find truly oral language in historical written sources, I argue that with the right type of written data, we can consider written data the same way that sociolinguists working on modern data consider oral data: as a manifestation of the writer-speaker's linguistic system. The diversity of data emphasizes the fact that language is heterogeneous regardless of mode, especially when we address it in terms of the individual speaker-writer (e.g. Auer 2007).

For it to be the 'right' kind of data, it needs to have a certain level of spontaneity, which can be found for instance in personal correspondence (e.g. Elspaß 2012b). Of course, correspondence produced by semiliterate people (described by Branca-Rosoff and Schneider 1994, see Subsection 27.3.1) might share more characteristics with oral speech than texts written by highly skilled writers. But even these texts written by people who spent more time mastering the written medium (through more years of schooling, for instance), when private, can still contain a certain level of spontaneity (see the work of Martineau 2014, Martineau and Remysen 2019, described below). These facts, which are well accepted within the field of historical sociolinguistics (as attested by the references cited), give us a motive to investigate the role of orthography in the processes of language variation and change, despite its purely written nature. If we accept that certain types of written data can be studied within a variation and change type of framework, then it is necessary to have a finer understanding of elements that are specific to the medium itself, such as orthography.[3] The review of the data presented in this chapter contributes to this understanding.

I argue here that recent works in historical sociolinguistics within a variationist approach have been using orthographic variation as a tool to better understand language change. Crucially, I do not assume that orthographic variation can lead directly to language change. We know that, in theory, it could lead to changes in normative rules; if this were to happen, it would be an example of a change 'from below' in spelling. However, we know that historically, this type of change is very rarely attested. Thus, in practice, despite the hybrid types of written data that are now used in historical sociolinguistics, I believe that we do not have evidence that there is a direct link between orthography and language change – rather, we usually see that writing reflects changes. This is therefore why one needs to investigate what role, if any, orthographic variables can play in studies of language variation and change.

27.3 Orthographic Variables

Most studies in historical sociolinguistics that have looked at orthography in a systematic way have used it to measure the level of literacy of writers. It is often, more than a way to study variation, an indication of an imperfect

[3] Other examples of elements specific to the medium of writing could be the context surrounding the acquisition of writing (schooling, literacy rates within the family, the community and so on), formulaic language (typical of correspondence) and so on.

mastery of the written register (e.g. Martineau 2013). Branca-Rosoff and Schneider (1994: 41) say that studying orthography "allows us to measure the efficiency of learning [i.e. education] and contributes to culturally situate writers" (my translation). This has slightly different consequences according to the period in question; from one century to the next, spelling variation did not have the same social connotation. Whereas it was people from higher social classes who wrote during the seventeenth and eighteenth centuries, since they were generally the only ones with means of entry into education, writing became much more accessible during the nineteenth century. It is during that time that 'literate societies' developed in industrialized countries, in which, for the first time in history, a majority of citizens were able to read and write (e.g. Verrette 2002, Vandenbussche 2007a). The studies reviewed in the next section of this chapter present both orthographic and morphosyntactic variation, one from the eighteenth century, and the others from the nineteenth century. The reason for this asymmetry is twofold: (1) I found more studies about French that included at least one orthographic variable available for the nineteenth century; (2) with the democratization of education during the nineteenth century in both France and Canada, it is easier to find writings produced during this period by a wider array of writers, coming not only from higher social classes but also from working classes. I could more easily, focusing on the nineteenth century, distinguish the social classes of the writers by looking at their orthographic usages. In addition, the democratization of education forced the better educated social classes to mark a distance between themselves and the lower ones by showing off their mastery of the subtle art of spelling conventions.

For the purposes of the present discussion, a choice was made to stay away from what is presented as 'pronunciation' variation. We know that one of the main ways to have access to clues with regard to historical pronunciation is via spelling (see, e.g., Lodge 2010 for a discussion), but I chose to only present the results of studies which consider orthographic variants as such, and not as examples of possible evidence for oral language in writing. Since the investigation into historical pronunciation is an already well-attested use of historical orthographic variation, I wanted to explore things further and bring to light different approaches. Therefore, all studies presented here use a type of written data that is "heterogeneous yet written, non-standard yet polished" (Branca-Rosoff and Schneider 1994: 29, my translation), which is not the same as oral; the link between oral and written is everything but binary or symmetrical, as discussed in the previous section. In some cases, I present orthographic variables that are part of the writer's 'culture', encompassing his or her relationship with the act of writing itself; in other cases, I present what Branca-Rosoff and Schneider (1994: 41) call "diachronic variants," which are variants that represent changes in progress, and where multiple norms could be coexisting during the same period. These two types of orthographic variables, when combined with other types of variables and with nonlinguistic information contextualizing the act of writing, can inform us about language variation and change, and this is what I explore further in this section.

27.3.1 The Eighteenth Century

In France, the *Dictionnaire de l'Académie* was one of the main carriers of the French written norm. There were four editions of the *Dictionnaire de l'Académie* published during the eighteenth century alone (in 1718, 1740, 1762 and 1798). There had been one during the seventeenth century (the first edition in 1694), two during the nineteenth century (sixth and seventh editions in 1835 and 1878) and the eighth edition in the 1930s. The Academy is still working on its ninth edition (1992–). The study presented in this section uses a corpus dating from around the French Revolution (1789 and after), so it is important to briefly provide an overview of the main normative references available at the time.[4] During the second half of the eighteenth century, it was the fourth and fifth editions of the *Dictionnaire* that were published (1762 and 1798). Linguists specializing in the history of orthography agree that the third edition (1740) mainly, but also the fourth (1762), were the ones that introduced the majority of changes in the French writing system; Catach (2001: 232) mentions that approximately 48 percent of changes that are listed between the eight editions of the *Dictionnaires de l'Académie* were introduced in 1740. These two are, therefore, the editions that led to the modern spelling system.

Branca-Rosoff and Schneider (1994) thus use this very bustling historical period as a backdrop to study the diffusion of norms in written language. They looked at spelling variation in revolutionary correspondence. With the publication of these dictionaries, among other contemporary linguistic normative innovations, there existed in France more than one norm to follow. In addition, even the concept of 'norm' (or what is included in it and, most crucially, excluded from it) was not yet very well defined or understood at the time (Branca-Rosoff and Schneider 1994: 45). The extensive work led by these two linguists was among the first looking at the writing of semiliterate people (*peu-lettrés*), and using spelling variations as a means to study phenomena that are not exclusively linked to contemporary pronunciations (although they do address this kind of variation; see Branca-Rosoff and Schneider 1994: 50–53). It is remarkable to see that in 1994, these authors were already talking about the possible link between language change in progress and spelling

[4] Only the *Dictionnaires de l'Académie* are mentioned here for space reasons, but there was obviously a multitude of grammars, spelling manuals and other norm-making (or norm-diffusing) documents published during the same period. It is also important to note that although considered a definite reference, dictionaries were almost always late adopters of changes that were already happening in literary and scientific publications of the time (Catach 2001: 222).

variation: “For each writer, different variables have different significance. [...] Sociolinguists usually interpret these oscillations between concurring systems (the mix of ‘old’ and ‘new’ forms) as evidence for changes in progress” (Branca-Rosoff and Schneider 1994: 45, my translation).

Branca-Rosoff and Schneider (1994) focused on variants that were eventually integrated into the norm (just like Martineau 2014, Martineau and Remysen 2019; see next section). They identified the change in many normative documents of the time (the year in which the dictionary or grammar incorporated it) and were then able to contextualize the variation in terms of distance to the norm for each usage, and each writer. Since their corpus is from the southern part of France, around the city of Marseilles, where people were mostly speaking Occitan, one of their research questions was to see whether they could identify regional features (that could be attributed to an Occitan influence) in French texts. French was the language of administration and power, so knowledge of it varied greatly from person to person, depending mainly on access to education (Branca-Rosoff and Schneider 1994: 26). Branca-Rosoff and Schneider study two orthographic variables: the so-called ‘graphic word’ (i.e. word divisions) and the use of three different diacritics, including *accents aigus* (*é*), *accents graves* (*è*, *à*, *ù*) and *accents circonflexes* (*î* and *ê*). The first variable is directly linked to the level of mastery of the written medium, whereas the second one is more linked to the fluctuating norm of the time.

In general, even if all writers from their corpus could be considered semiliterate, there are very few cases of *agglutination*, where boundaries between each word, marked by a graphic space, are not respected (Branca-Rosoff and Schneider 1994: 42). It is the writers from the most isolated places in the corpus that exhibit the highest numbers of these types of ‘mistakes’, which also correlates for these writers with a higher number of lexical spelling mistakes. They show that the number of lexical spelling mistakes varies greatly from writer to writer (out of 100 words, from as few as 3 mistakes to more than 28) (Branca-Rosoff and Schneider 1994: 44). Most importantly, they also show, through studying the use of accents, that overall norms took a long time to reach southern France writers’ usages, even when printers had already adopted it (Branca-Rosoff and Schneider 1994: 46–50). More precisely, a few writers were late to adopt the *accent aigu* in the final position (even though it was generalized in print), and most writers were very late adopters of accents *graves* and *circonflexes*. But, once again, they show that some writers’ orthographic behaviors are different from those of others, and it is difficult to come up with a unique generalization.

Branca-Rosoff and Schneider (1994) also studied morphological and syntactic variables within the same documents. They did not directly and explicitly compare orthographic to other types of variables (these analyses are part of different chapters), but I am taking this step here to try to demonstrate the possible links between different levels of variation in writing. In terms of morphological and syntactic variation, (nonstandard) variants in this study are divided according to the following three types: those associated with southern France varieties (regionalisms); those associated with "permanent tendencies in French" (i.e. variations due to vernacular language influence, Branca-Rosoff and Schneider 1994: 64); and those associated with changes that are said to have been caused (or exacerbated) by the Revolution (Branca-Rosoff and Schneider 1994: 66). The authors do not offer a variationist study of each variant encountered, so I cannot say anything about a possible pattern, or whether a specific writer uses more or fewer of these three types of variants, since the systematic work underlying the research was not presented. However, Branca-Rosoff and Schneider mention that all texts under study contain nonstandard morphological and syntactic variants. Foreseeably, in texts where they found spelling variants that do not correspond to the accepted norm, they also found nonstandard morphological and syntactic variants, associated with regional varieties and, more generally, with vernacular varieties (they mention the localities from which the texts are written, so this is how I make comparisons between morphosyntactic and orthographic variations). It is unfortunately not possible to know if each text contains all these variants at once, since we do not have access to the original data.

Another interesting element that is worth mentioning are the conclusions that the authors reach after both chapters (see Branca-Rosoff and Schneider 1994: 45 about orthography and 1994: 73 about morphological and syntactic variation), which could be summarized in this way: linguistic behaviors (orthographic, morphological or syntactic) vary according to the individual writer, and even within a single writer's usages. The authors reach these conclusions and insist on the heterogeneity of their corpus even without having conducted a systematic analysis (i.e. a study of variable patterns) of each writer.

27.3.2 The Nineteenth Century

In French, the turn of the nineteenth century following the French Revolution marks a pivotal period for orthographic norms (also a consequence of the fact that the eighteenth century had seen a surge in normative pressures and standardization). Moreover, as mentioned before, the nineteenth century saw the rates of literacy increase exponentially; for instance, in the province of Quebec (a mainly French-speaking Canadian province), literacy increased steadily throughout the century, with an important peak between 1850 and 1900, to reach a rate of approximately 75 percent of literate people by 1900 (Verrette 2002: 92).[5] The present section offers a summary of three studies that address variable spelling (among other written practices) in nineteenth-century French Canada.

[5] Note that this rate is based on the period's definition of *literate*, which meant roughly being able to sign one's name.

27.3.2.1 Canada vs. France: High-class Writers

Martineau and Remysen (2019) (based on Martineau 2014) studied the writings of higher-class Canadian French speakers to see how the changes affecting the norm in France after the Revolution were followed in North America. Through studying the usages of different generations of writers, they show the transition from older (*Ancien Régime*, i.e. pre-dating the French Revolution) variants to new ones. They chose three orthographic variables for which the norm changed in France during the eighteenth and nineteenth centuries (see below for details). Just like for Branca-Rosoff and Schneider's (1994) study described in the previous section, they picked their variables for two main reasons: (i) the norm, for each variant, was fluctuating (so variation was expected); (ii) given the orthographic nature of the variables, their rate of use is very high in writing (more so than, for example, morphosyntactic variables). In addition, since Martineau and Remysen (2019) worked with a corpus produced by highly literate people, they also expect that some if not all these variables might have social connotations, to which some if not all writers might be sensitive. The difference between the spelling variables discussed here and variables that are (morpho)syntactic in nature such as the variable use of negation (with or without the *ne* in French, see Table 27.3) is the fact that spelling variation, in order to be meaningful in a language change context, needs to be linked to a changing norm. However, the authors did not limit their study to the link between the use of each variant and the norm; they also linked each writer's usage of variables with different external factors. They mainly focused on two: the writer's generation (linked to the year of birth – see Table 27.1) and the individual's social trajectory (see Table 27.2).

Martineau and Remysen (2019) studied three orthographic variables used by six writers from France and Canada over two generations (divided between writers born before 1760 – before the Revolution – and writers born before 1795 – just around the Revolution). Variable 1 was the sound [ɛ] spelled as *es, oi* or *ai*, where the *es, oi* are conservative and the *ai* is innovative; variable 2 was the spelling of the modern *-ère* as *-ere*, *-ére* (conservative) or *-ère* (innovative); and variable 3 was the plural of the present participle as *-ans/-ens* (conservative) or *-ants/-ents* (innovative) (Martineau and Remysen 2019: 283, 286, 291).

They found that practices varied greatly according to individual writers: they could not posit usage generalizations per generation, nor per place of birth (France vs. Canada). In Table 27.1, I provide a summary of the writers' behaviors according to their generation, where grey cells represent majority usages, and where "!" means categorical (i.e. 100 percent) use.[6]

[6] I took the numbers from tables 1 through 9 of Martineau and Remysen (2019: 283–92) and only kept the following information: which variant was the majority one (to get the big picture for each external factor), and the generation and the place of birth for each writer. Note that Martineau and Remysen give all the details on each writer, as well as the exact number of occurrences.

Table 27.1 *Conservative (CONS) vs. innovative (INNOV) use of orthographic variables according to writer and generation*

		Variable 1		Variable 2		Variable 3	
Gen		CONS	INNOV	CONS	INNOV	CONS	INNOV
1	Writer A	!		!			
	Writer B						
	Writer C						!
2	Writer D		!				
	Writer E						
	Writer F						

In a situation where a perfect shift can be observed (i.e. change reaching near completion), we would expect all writers from the first generation to use the conservative variant in the majority of contexts, and writers from the second generation to use the innovative variants most of the time. Martineau and Remysen (2019) show that this is not the case, at least not perfectly; it depends not only on the writer, but also on the variable. Writer A of the first generation is categorically conservative when it comes to the use of the first two variables, but he uses mostly the innovative variant for the third variable (the *t* in the plural of present participles). Writer F from the second generation is the only writer of the six to be consistent throughout all three variables: he is conservative across the board (which is surprising for a second-generation writer). The others all vary – sometimes conservative, sometimes innovative – depending on the variable. No variable shows a perfect pattern in which all first-generation writers would use the conservative one in the majority of contexts, and the second generation would do the opposite. We can also notice that variable 2, the spelling of the modern *-ère*, varies less than the others: only one writer out of the six uses the innovative variant most of the time. Martineau and Remysen chose three variables that were changing at the time (as attested by the high level of variation for each), but not at the same rate – we see that variable 2 was slower to change than the others, based on these six writers' practices.

In recent studies on language change, the focus has been put on "leaders of change" (Denis 2011: 61): Which members of the speech community are the ones leading changes? The data from Martineau and Remysen (2019) allow them to address this question directly. If they had looked at only one variable, they might have concluded that writer D was the leader of change in this community (he uses the innovative variant most of the times for variables 1 and 2); however, this is not the case for variable 3, where it is writer E that seems to be leading the change. The individual differences are striking – this is in line with what Waters and Tagliamonte (2017) show, using modern oral data: high use of a specific innovative variant does not predict high use of another innovative variant from another variable.

I now explore the second research question that Martineau and Remysen (2019) addressed: Are changes happening at the same time in Canada and in France? In other words, is the distance between France and Canada stopping the change from happening in the latter community? To answer these questions, they looked at three French writers and three Canadian writers. Table 27.2 summarizes the findings divided by place of birth (Tables 27.1 and 27.2 are based on the same data, but with different groupings of writers; grey cells represent majority usages and "!" means categorical use).

Table 27.2 *Conservative (CONS) vs. innovative (INNOV) use of orthographic variables according to writer and place of birth*

			Variable 1		Variable 2		Variable 3	
Birthplace		Gen	CONS	INNOV	CONS	INNOV	CONS	INNOV
Canada	Writer A	1	!		!			
	Writer D	2		!				
	Writer E	2						
France	Writer B	1						
	Writer C	1						!
	Writer F	2						

Usages are as 'messy' as in the previous table: specific practices do not align with the place of birth. The only variable for which it is the case is variable 2, where writers from France all use the conservative variant in a majority of (not all) contexts (but the opposite is not true for Canadian writers for the same variable). Martineau and Remysen (2019) show that French writers are slightly more conservative, since only two writers use only two of the innovative variants in a majority of contexts (compared to all three Canadian writers on four occasions). The authors explain their results, comparing the networks of each of these writers to determine if we can see why writers D and E, for instance, despite being both Canadian from the second generation, behave in completely opposite ways when it comes to orthographic practices. They show that open networks (Milroy and Milroy 1992 use the term *weak network ties*, and *loose-knit networks*) can lead to a more innovative use of certain variables, but not all variables have the same social connotation. In addition, they show that, based on their corpus, writers do not change their spelling usage throughout their lifetime (Martineau and Remysen 2019: 294, see also Martineau 2014 for a similar conclusion). The contribution made by Martineau and Remysen's article to knowledge on orthographic practices is crucial, since they show empirically that it is as important to consider the individual writer's social trajectory as it is to understand the macro norms of the time. They state that "the back and forth between micro- and macro-linguistic analyses allows nuanced pictures of communities which are defined by much more than just territorial borders" (Martineau and Remysen 2019: 293, my translation). And, again, they show how usages vary not only from one writer to the next, according to their social trajectory (social network open or loose-knit vs. closed or close-knit), but even within the texts of the same writer, usage can fluctuate between conservative and innovative variants, depending on how specific variables are socially connotated, namely as associated with a supraregional norm or not.

27.3.2.2 Acadian French Corpus: Lower-class Writers

The corpus under study in Martineau and Remysen (2019) described above is composed of personal correspondence, but it is written by people with a high level of literacy. Usages extracted from this corpus can thus be compared to a certain norm, since it is plausible that these people had direct access to a norm, most likely through schooling. However, when the writers are unskilled (*peu-lettrés*), as was the case for the ones studied by Branca-Rosoff and Schneider (1994) for the eighteenth century, it is not as evident that a norm was readily accessible to them (even if they had to have a certain level of familiarity with it, as is required for any act of writing, mastered or not). It is also the case in the corpus that Martineau and Tailleur (2011) studied to compare the written usages of different members of a single family during the nineteenth century.[7] The language under study is Acadian French, which is a Canadian variety spoken in the Maritimes region (the Atlantic side) of the country.[8] What makes the corpus under study especially interesting is the fact that it is composed of letters by writers who are considered unskilled in the act of writing itself, and who are also speakers of a regional variant of French which is typically only used orally (akin to the situation described by Branca-Rosoff and Schneider in eighteenth-century southern France).

Therefore, in this study by Martineau and Tailleur (2011), the focus is not so much on comparison between the orthographic usage and a norm (although the norm is always presented as a reference for the period), but rather to situate spelling variants with respect to the high level of vernacularity in the corpus as well as regional traces in the written language. This is exemplified

[7] The corpus in this study and the corpus studied in Martineau (2014) and Martineau and Remysen (2019) are from Martineau's (2005–) major collection of corpora: *Corpus de français familier ancien.*

[8] Acadian French is one of the varieties of French spoken in Canada (and in parts of the United States). It is widely accepted that dialectal boundaries exist between Acadian French in the East and Laurentian French, from Quebec all the way to the westernmost provinces, where French speakers represent a small minority of the population. Different varieties exist all over the country, but they are usually divided according to their origins, Laurentian or Acadian (see Mougeon and Beniak 1989 for detailed descriptions of these varieties).

through variable uses of three morphosyntactic features. Spelling 'mistakes' are presented as evidence for the imperfect mastery of the written language – for instance, they show that out of the 19 writers represented in the corpus, only 4 show more than 50 percent mastery of number agreement spelling. The spelling 'mistakes' (in this case only concerning grammatical agreement) are then put alongside morphosyntactic variants deemed vernacular, to show a more complete portrait of the writer's usages. Table 27.3 shows such a comparison for one of the most prolific writers of the corpus, Wallace Landry, born in 1884.

Table 27.3 *Frequency of vernacular features/spelling errors in Wallace Landry's letters*

Use of *je vas* (vs. *je vais*)	Deletion of *ne*	Spelling number agreement
85.7% (18/21)	85.2% (52/61)	22.9% (33/144)

(from Martineau and Tailleur 2011: 160)

This table shows that the writer named Wallace has a very high rate of use of vernacular features (the first two columns), and a fairly low number of correct spelling agreement. This is what we would expect from a nonexpert writer, for whom the line between oral and written languages is blurry, and where rules specific to the act of writing are not all mastered. Martineau and Tailleur (2011: 159) also consider regional features, in addition to the more 'mainstream' vernacular features (i.e. general to Canadian French as a whole, which the authors consider more 'neutral') presented in Table 27.3. They found that Wallace indeed uses features that come from the (spoken) Acadian dialect. He uses the *-ont* ending where more standard French would use *-ent* (*ils disont* instead of *ils disent* 'they say'); he uses the *avoir* (have) auxiliary with pronominal verbs (i.e. verbs with reflexive pronouns) instead of *to be* (*je **m'ai** préparé* instead of *je **me suis** préparé* 'I prepared myself'); and he uses, albeit rarely, the pronoun *je* in the first person plural contexts (*je marchons* instead of *nous marchons* 'we walk') (Martineau and Tailleur 2011: 162–69).

Another writer, named Norine Landry, also shows a low percentage of correct number agreement spelling (18 percent – 4 out of 22 examples), but does not use as many vernacular features as Wallace does. The authors hypothesize that the sensitivity that the writers seem to have is not toward a written norm, which would likely be visible through spelling, but more toward normative pressures put on their dialectal features (Martineau and Tailleur 2011: 170). It gives great evidence for the sensitivity of the average speaker-writer to subtle differences found between the various ways one can use language. This study shows that certain spelling variations can be associated with a vernacular way of using the written language, but this does not carry to regional features that are specific to the Acadian oral variety. The authors' treatment of spelling variations (in this case grammatical spelling, as opposed to the less systematic lexical spelling) is a tool to show writers' distance to very specific normative pressures.

27.3.2.3 Lower-class Writers: The Case of Nineteenth-century Montreal

In a similar way, the next study shows how mastery of the orthographic conventions (norms) can be a "way to social advancement" (*outil de promotion sociale*, Martineau and Dionne 2008: 232). Martineau and Dionne's (2008) study of unskilled writers from Montreal during the second half of the nineteenth century shows very clearly how three members of the same family have very different masteries of orthographic rules. The careful study of orthographic plural agreement even allowed the authors to determine that one of the members of the family, the father, was not actually writing his own letters. They identified, through clues in the texts and calligraphy, three different writers for the letters all signed by the father. This study is mentioned only briefly since spelling is not studied in comparison to other types of variation. Rather, it is used as a way to show how, even within one family, each writer can have his or her own way to use orthographic rules, some faithful to the norm, some very idiosyncratic. Either way, the authors show that, in working-class Montreal from the second half of the nineteenth century, mastering orthographic norms is one of the ways displayed by writers to gain prestige and rise socially. This is a slightly different conclusion from the ones reached by the other studies, which brings a diversity of evidence to the point being made in this chapter.

27.4 Orthographic Variation and the Linguistic Variable

The few studies that were reviewed in this chapter had in common that they considered spelling variations as a type of linguistic variable, and treated them in a systematic way, akin to what is most often done with morphosyntactic (or phonetic, in oral corpora) features. The results presented show that orthographic variation (with respect to a certain norm) cannot be unified in terms of its treatment; for variation to become linguistic evidence of a phenomenon, it needs to be very well contextualized. It seems that orthography, just like the writing system as a whole, is only one of the tools that a speaker of a language uses to express themselves. For some speakers, it is a way toward a form of empowerment through the written medium, whereas for others it is an obstacle to self-expression. Without much surprise, it seems that it is the nineteenth century that gave a specific meaning to each 'kind' of orthography, since the written norm became a visible entity, albeit not accessible for all.[9]

One of the key elements to retain from this review is that spelling variation can successfully be used as a linguistic variable, as was argued by Rutkowska and Rössler (2012: 229). I have shown that spelling behaviors are influenced by one main external factor: the individual writer.[10] Whereas communities can be studied as linguistic entities with the help of large corpora, the relationship that one writer entertains toward written conventions and orthographies is his or her own. It is always influenced by education (i.e. schooling), networks and other external factors, but it cannot be correlated directly to a specific use of another linguistic variant; in other words, a certain 'orthographic behavior' could not predict (or be correlated to) a certain morphosyntactic usage, or vice versa.

To consider exclusively written phenomena within a definition of a linguistic variable in the study of language variation is crucial, and I argue that it is completely compatible with the complexity of the object of study in historical sociolinguistics: there is "writing with respect to orality, and writing with respect to writing" (Martineau 2017: 212). Indeed, on the one hand, we study writing to study the 'language' of past speakers and communities, to know more about language change and evolution within a single language, or in a diachronic way, to better understand today's language facts and variations. On the other hand, we also study writing in a more microscale way, to understand the relationship, throughout time, that the speaker-writer entertained with the act of writing itself, as a means and as a goal. This perspective also allows us to study in detail the link between norm and usage, especially in

[9] Note that this conclusion is also linked to the fact that studies like the ones we described for the nineteenth century do not really exist for earlier centuries. I chose to talk about Branca-Rosoff and Schneider (1994) for the eighteenth century since it is such an important study, despite not adopting the variationist framework employed in the others.

[10] The original definition of a linguistic variable by Labov (1972a: 8) is as follows: "First, we want an item that is frequent, which occurs so often in the course of undirected natural conversation that its behavior can be charted from unstructured contexts and brief interviews. Secondly, it should be structural: the more the item is integrated into a larger system of functioning units, the greater will be the intrinsic linguistic interest of our study. Third, the distribution of the feature should be highly stratified: that is, our preliminary explorations should suggest an asymmetric distribution over a wide range of age levels or other ordered strata of society." This chapter shows that the first two aspects of the definition are definitely compatible with orthography. As for the third one, an anonymous reviewer pointed out that the heavy influence of the individual writer seems to weaken the claim and asked if orthography could thus really be considered a linguistic variable within the field of variationist sociolinguistics. It is a very valid and important point, whose scope is not limited to orthographic variables: When the individual speaker/writer comes up as the most influential factor of variation, what do we make of it in terms of community variation, and eventually, change? The studies presented in this chapter definitely prove that leaders of change are difficult to identify, and that the individual speaker/writer cannot be ignored. However, I do not believe that it weakens the claim that orthography could be a variable, since Labov, who worked at a larger community scale, never considered the type of data involved here, as argued in Section 27.2. I thank the anonymous reviewer for such a pertinent comment, which points to interesting possibilities for further work.

terms of spelling. The common denominator of the studies reviewed in this chapter is as follows: the meaning behind variations in orthography is very much writer-specific. To each speaker-writer his or her own relationship with orthography. This often corresponds to his or her relationship to the act of writing, more generally. For some writers, direct links could be made with usages of other levels of language, but for others, orthographic variation was only a way to assess his or her relationship to the written medium. I therefore believe that once a linguist is able to establish the social, political, historical and geographical context of a specific act of writing, and especially the state of the norm(s) of the time, the parallels that are thereby created with different morphosyntactic variables within a written piece actually teach us about language variation, and eventually about change in progress.

The studies reviewed also show that there is an urgent need to look at writers individually to understand language change. The multiple variables considered in each of the studies, including mainly orthographic ones, demonstrate that individual factors play such an important role in language usage and attitudes that we cannot afford to ignore them. Studies of language communities should be done alongside studies of individuals to be able to benefit from both the large amount of data that comes with community studies, and the information about the detailed dynamics between a writer/speaker and his or her environment (Martineau 2021).

27.5 Conclusion

The link between language variation and change, and orthography, when not concerned with spelling pronunciation, regional variations or standardization processes, is not obvious. Despite this, considering spelling behaviors within studies of writers in a historical context is to have access to one extra piece of information about the writer's relationship to language itself, in all its forms. With the help of example case studies, I have shown that for writers with a limited education, there is usually co-occurrence of nonstandard spelling variants and vernacular (sometimes regional) morphological and syntactic nonstandard variants (Branca-Rosoff and Schneider 1994, Martineau and Tailleur 2011). For highly educated writers, there is co-occurrence of conservative variants with closed networks and innovative spelling variants with open networks (Martineau 2014, Martineau and Remysen 2019). Although these conclusions are expected in a community-level approach, each study clearly shows that when given more attention to individual writers, these co-occurrences become less generalized. The individual speaker-writer has his or her own relationship to (the act of) writing; Martineau and Dionne (2008) showed how for a working-class Montreal family at the end of the nineteenth century, mastery of the spelling system (and lack thereof) had social significance in a context where individuals tried to improve their own social conditions. While the search for 'leaders of language change' is still ongoing (see for instance Denis 2011, for a take on specific individuals as innovators within a community, or Nevalainen and Raumolin-Brunberg 2003, for the role of women as leaders of change), written language is the only data we can use to give historical depth to this search. We therefore need to consider any factor influencing the speaker/writer's use of language, but also his or her linguistic behavior. Orthographic variation is yet another instrument in the historical sociolinguist's toolbox; its study brings us closer to the much-needed complete picture leading to a better understanding of language change.

28

Orthography and Language Contact

Israel Sanz-Sánchez

28.1 Introduction

The emergence of orthographic standards is almost universally preceded by a phase of variation in spelling options, whether among different writing systems or among spelling alternatives from the same writing system (e.g. the alternation between <x> and <j> or <g> in eighteenth-century Spanish, between <ize> and <ise> in verbs from Greek -ίζειν historically in English, and *ſ* and *s* in several Western European languages). While this process can be seen at work in monolingual societies, the historical and ideological dynamics of this process are particularly apparent in situations of language contact. In these situations, spelling options come to symbolize specific ethnolinguistic affiliations and linguistic ideologies, and become a tool in the formulation of new group identities (see Jaffe 1999, 2000b, Coulmas 2013, 2014, Sebba 2015, Bunčić et al. 2016, among others). Consequently, several questions become paramount when researching the dynamics of orthographic development and standardization in settings of pervasive language contact. How are spelling conventions negotiated in these situations, and how are they shaped by the broader sociolinguistic and cultural context of language contact? What role do various sociocultural agents and their interests play in this process? How does the emergence of specific orthographic norms reflect the larger patterns of cultural conflict and adaptation typical of language contact settings?

This chapter illustrates several cross-cultural and cross-linguistic themes common to the development of orthographic norms in language contact situations, by exploring the interface between the sociolinguistics of contact and the emergence of spelling trends. It also provides a case study of the development of orthographic norms in one such situation of intense cultural and linguistic contact, namely the adaptation of alphabetic script to the writing of Nahuatl in central Mexico during the Spanish colonial period (1521–1810).

This example can be used as a test case for the complex interface among sociolinguistic, cultural and ideological factors involved in the emergence of orthographic norms and standards in other situations of language contact. To accomplish these goals, this chapter first provides a review of the literature on the interface between orthography and language contact in a variety of historical contexts, and outlines a general framework for the application of a historical sociolinguistic lens (Auer et al. 2015) to the study of historical orthographies as an *ecological* process (see, for instance, Barton 1994, 1995, Mufwene 2001, 2018, Lüpke 2011). Second, this sociohistorical, ecological framework is applied to study of the introduction of alphabetic writing to central Mexico and its adaptation to Nahuatl.

A common observation in the literature on orthography and language contact is that, within the larger context of negotiation of sociolinguistic and cultural norms typical of contact societies, spelling norms become a tool for various groups to claim cultural agency (see Coulmas 2014, Jaffe 1999, 2000b, Sebba 2015). From this perspective, the emergence of spelling traditions in contact situations can be considered an *ecological* process (see Barton 1994, 1995, Lüpke 2011) and is a central part of the local sociolinguistic dynamics of contact (see Sebba 2007, 2009, 2015, Coulmas 2013; see also Section 28.2 below). An ecologically informed approach to historical orthographies "examines the social and mental embeddedness of human activities in a way that allows change. Instead of studying the separate skills which underlie reading and writing, it involves a shift to studying *literacy*, a set of social practices associated with particular symbol systems and their related technologies" (Barton 1994: 32). In an ecological approach, the development of spelling is not seen merely as the conception of a technology for language notation that is detached from the social and cultural context of writing and language use. Much on the contrary, spelling is both a function of this context and one of its elements: for instance, specific orthographies and spellings can become iconically associated with groups of people and their assumed values (see Jaffe 1999, 2000b, Johnson 2005, Sebba 2015) and can thus play an important role in sociopolitical conflict (see Villa and Vosters 2015a).

An adjective often connected to ecological approaches to various forms of systemic change is *evolutionary*. Barton (1994, 1995) opposes the ecological study of historical spellings as an evolutionary phenomenon on the argument that specific writing systems do not exhibit qualitative properties on a universal scale. But *evolution* need not be teleological: instead, it can also be taken as *adaptive*, as seen in applications of biological theory to language transmission, contact and change (see Croft 2000, Mufwene 2001, 2018) and in sociopragmatic approaches to language use and language variation (see Ellis and Larsen-Freeman 2009). From this perspective, languages are seen as *complex adaptive systems*: population-wide patterns (akin to language or dialect norms) emerge as individuals engage in the selection of linguistic features, and these selections are directly shaped by the characteristics of the environment in which individuals communicate with each other. These approaches explicitly reject the teleological understanding of evolution, which "should not be interpreted as progress [but as] adaptations to a changing ecology" (Mufwene 2001: 147). Similarly, although aspects of spelling may be carefully planned to fit specific purposes, there is no such thing as a demonstrable historical progression toward 'better' orthographies, and even in contexts of heightened awareness about spelling choices, orthographic alternatives may survive to fit specific (and often competing) communicative or ideological goals (see Sebba 2009).

28.2 Previous Approaches to Language Contact and Historical Orthography

In situations of pervasive sociolinguistic contact, as commonly acknowledged by historical sociolinguists (see Tuten 2003, Trudgill 2004), linguistic and cultural norms are oftentimes thoroughly renegotiated. Orthographic norms are usually a part of this renegotiation. As a matter of fact, language contact situations are a prime context for the introduction of new writing systems (or new spelling variants) to a community: "only rarely in the history of literacy has a language community developed its own indigenous writing system independently of other systems already in existence. Much more commonly, writing – and with it, an orthographic system – is introduced through contact with another culture" (Sebba 2007: 59).

Insofar as cultural contact is often accompanied by language contact, the introduction of these new writing systems is directly affected by the context of language contact and learning: "[i]t is by means of this process of adapting to the demands of a new language that most of the significant developments in writing systems have taken place" (Barton 1994: 121). However, while "the nature of bilingualism in the language community is one important factor in the emergence of orthographies for new written traditions," other factors also play a key role, including "the types of literacy practices which the orthography supports or is intended to support, and the prevailing language ideologies concerning those practices and the language varieties involved in them" (Sebba 2007: 60).

Historically, such settings have included new borders, invasions, waves of heavy cultural foreign influence and colonial situations. In the latter, the introduction of new writing systems may be intended by the dominant class as a tool of acculturation and subordination of indigenous groups, leading to the disruption of the local cultural and linguistic practices (Coulmas 2013: 8). The initial agents in the introduction of writing are often members of a learned group operating in close association with the interests of the ruling class (Barros 1995, Sebba 2007: 79). At the same time, the indexical potential of writing practices and spelling systems is always susceptible to reformulation (see Sebba 2007, 2015, Villa and Vosters 2015a), which will then allow the members of subordinate groups to claim agency and use spelling as a tool for ideological affirmation and cultural resistance.

Despite the ideological nature of these processes, the study of orthographic change as an ideologically motivated process has not always been a key concern among scholars of historical orthography in contexts of language contact. Instead, research on the emergence of orthographic norms (or more generally, spelling) in language contact settings initially focused exclusively on linguistic aspects. For instance, spellings of Old French loanwords in medieval documentation in Middle High German (c. 1100–1500), or medieval Castilian Spanish loanwords in Andalusian Arabic (c. 1100–1492) have been used to reconstruct the phonological inventories of the languages in contact (see Joos 1952, Pocklington 1986). While these studies approached spelling primarily as a representation of contact language features, other studies have explored the potential role of orthographic norms in shaping the linguistic behavior of language users in contact situations. This approach follows the rationale articulated by Coulmas (2014: 2): "[w]riting systems, rather than being neutral devices for recording speech and making it visible, are constitutive of certain linguistic varieties that by virtue of being written acquire a standard or canonical status. Therefore, influences of language on writing and of writing on language have to be reckoned with." One example concerns the possibility of *spelling pronunciations*, where the spelling of a foreign item is interpreted through the lens of the donor language phonology. Although this is usually only the case for specific items in a language, spelling-based pronunciations may occasionally have more far-reaching systemic consequences: for instance, in nineteenth-century Finnish, old /ð/, spelled <d>, came to be articulated as /d/ because of the prestige of Swedish, where <d> was pronounced as a plosive (Campbell 1991: 317). The new plosive articulation eventually became part of the standard language.

Following the blooming of sociolinguistics from the 1970s onward, studies of language contact came to grapple with the role of social factors in the emergence of patterns of language use. Studies of written systems and orthography followed suit and began to pay more attention to the *sociolinguistics of writing* (see Sebba 2007, 2009, 2015, Jaffe et al. 2012, Blommaert 2013, Coulmas 2013, 2014). From this perspective, orthographic practices are a part of the sociolinguistics of the community, and they operate both as a cultural product for the expression of identities via symbolic meanings and as a tool for political struggle. Settings of pervasive language contact, which oftentimes are also characterized by ethnolinguistic hybridity and sensitivity on the part of language users to the symbolic value of cultural and linguistic practices, allow for the complex interaction of social factors in the formulation of innovative orthographies. In addition, the recent expansion of digital communication technologies has provided a new conduit for written language contact effects, especially in contexts where ideological resistance to standard sociopolitical discourses is expressed. Themistocleous (2010) offers a review of *online orthographies* in noncontact and contact environments. A major trend appears to be the romanization of languages that used to be written in scripts other than the Latin one (including varieties of Arabic, Greek, several Slavic languages and Chinese), a move initially motivated by the limitations of computers to represent systems other than the Latin script. Technological advances, such as the development of the Unicode Standard (see Chapter 3, this volume), have made many scripts other than Latin available, which gives hope regarding a revitalization of traditional scripts in these languages.[1]

A leitmotiv of the literature on language contact and orthography is the frequent conscious manipulation of spelling options by individuals and institutions to enact symbolic connections relevant to the contact setting. For instance, in a review of literature on orthography and language contact, Guerini (2019) emphasizes the importance of the ideological backdrop of contact in determining the symbolic value that specific options acquire (whether the choice of scripts or orthographic norms, or the use of specific graphemes). Guerini (2019: 77–80) speaks of "language contact in the written mode," emphasizing the degree to which written norms may be studied as an area of language contact in their own right. In her review, she identifies four areas where this type of approach may be applied productively: the study of the iconic nature of individual graphemes, the orthographic treatment of loanwords, the orthographic choices in contexts of digital communication and the practice of *typographical mimicking*. In this practice, a specific visual element of a writing system or script becomes a stereotype of a culture or language and is imitated in a different script to evoke that cultural association (see also Coulmas 2014: 16–19 for a discussion of relevant examples).

In very general terms, the relationship between language contact in the written mode and language contact as a sociolinguistic process can apply to two separate types of settings: (a) situations where language contact is not sociolinguistically widespread, and (b) contexts of pervasive societal bi- or multilingualism. In the first case, contact is primarily between writing systems, scripts or orthographies, although language contact can also play a role in these situations as a vehicle for the introduction of scriptal or orthographic innovations among specific social groups, as noted by Sebba (2007). A common outcome in this case is the differentiated use of more than one written

[1] According to the Unicode Consortium, "Unicode has encoded scripts for all of the world's languages [...]. Unicode also includes many historic scripts used to write long-dead languages, as well as lesser-used regional scripts that may be used as a second (or even third) way to write a particular language" (Unicode Consortium 2019) and continues to develop updates to allow for the use of these encoded scripts in all possible platforms (including cell phones).

systemic option, distributed according to linguistic or social variables (for instance, ethnic group or the variety of the language being written). Bunčić et al. (2016) have coined the term *biscriptality* to refer to this situation (see also Chapter 8, this volume), and have elaborated a typology of attested biscriptal strategies that subsumes various forms of spelling or orthographic alternation for the writing of the same language (e.g. *digraphia*, based on the use of two spelling systems, or *diorthographia*, with two orthographies in the same spelling system for the same language). Biscriptal environments include well-known cases, such as the historical competition between Latin and Cyrillic alphabets in Serbo-Croatian, as well as other less commonly discussed examples, such the use of scripts in ancient Egypt or postcolonial Africa. This typology allows for diachronic and cross-linguistic comparisons among contact settings. In many of these cases, the emergence of biscriptal protocols must be sought precisely in historical situations of language contact. For instance, Iyengar (2021) describes the complex dynamics of spelling in Sindhi, which has historically exhibited an option between Perso-Arabic and Devanāgarī. This study demonstrates that multilingualism by groups of Sindhi speakers in languages like Urdu, Farsi, Arabic, Hindi and Sanskrit has been one of several important sociolinguistic catalysts driving this spelling choice between Perso-Arabic and Devanāgarī.

Many of the characteristics of biscriptal (or multiscriptal) contexts can also be seen in situations where language contact in the written mode has occurred amidst intense societal multilingualism. An example includes the various scripts for Tuareg (Tifinagh, Arabic and Latin), which have alternated for centuries amidst contact among Tuareg, Arabic and French (see Savage 2008). Sometimes, it is the very situation of language contact that spurs the creation of a new scriptal or orthographic system to note the specific phonological characteristics of one of the languages, or as an instrument to protect the ethnolinguistic integrity of one of the groups in contact. Such was the case of Canadian Aboriginal Syllabics, which was developed in the mid-1800s by European missionaries to note a variety of Indigeneous languages in Canada (Nichols 1996: 599–606). To this day, identity-motivated debates persist within Canadian Indigeneous communities about the use of specific orthographies (see, e.g., for Inuit languages, Patrick et al. 2018). Settings of national or ethnic affirmation, which frequently fall at different points along the spectrum of societal bilingualism, constitute particularly interesting cases to study the interaction among sociolinguistics, identity politics and spelling norms. One such case is North Macedonia, studied by Kramer (2015), who analyzes the complex interactions between the ideological debates around the place of Macedonian ethnicity in the southern Balkans and the choice of specific scripts (Cyrillic vs. Latin) and specific orthographies (Serbian, Bulgarian or local variants of the Cyrillic script). Diorthographic settings often illustrate similar tensions, especially in the case of minority languages, where orthographic choices are symbolically connected to dependence or autonomy from majority languages. Examples include the orthographic debates in Corsican vs. French (see Jaffe 1999) and in Galician vs. Portuguese and Spanish (see Álvarez-Cáccamo and Herrero Valeiro 1996). These cases underscore the operation of writing systems as tools for literate language users to navigate contact settings.

From a methodological and heuristic perspective, the multiple factors that impact the development and choice of written systems in language contact situations complicate the study of contact historical orthographies. Specific challenges include the scarcity of data, questions about the representativeness of the extant data and the impossibility of accessing the ideological and sociolinguistic underpinnings of contact among writing systems, spellings and orthographies in real time (see Coulmas 2014, Sebba 2009). These same obstacles also hinder research on language variation, contact and change in historical situations. Consequently, the application of theoretical and methodological approaches that have proven effective in *historical sociolinguistics* (see Romaine 1982, Auer et al. 2015) offers a potentially productive approach to tackle these hurdles also in the study of historical orthographies (see Rutkowska and Rössler 2012). Within this area, recent applications range from variationist analyses of corpora of private correspondence (e.g. letters by Elizabeth I, Evans 2012; see also Chapter 25, this volume) to diachronic studies of the emergence of spelling norms in historical situations of language or dialect contact (e.g. the orthography of Scots, Bann and Corbett 2015) and sociopolitical approaches to orthography in the construction of national historical narratives (e.g. the various European cases described in Villa and Vosters 2015a). While the bulk of the sociohistorical studies of orthography in language contact situations have tended to focus on western languages, other geographical and cultural settings are starting to be studied from this same historical sociolinguistic approach (e.g. Bondarev et al. 2019).

Within the larger area of historical sociolinguistics, as advanced in Section 28.1, ecological approaches to language contact and change stress the degree to which individual agents select elements from the features available to them to form individual repertoires, with communal norms emerging from these choices (see Mufwene 2001, 2018, Clancy Clements 2009). If, as often proposed in studies of language contact in the written mode, orthography is one of the sites of language contact, it follows that orthographic practices are part of the ecology of contact and should be expected to be sensitive to many of the same triggers as those operating on spoken (or signed) languages. Explicitly applying this framework to endangered languages, Lüpke (2011) speaks of an *ecology of writing*, and underscores the way in which different types of writers and readers can actively use orthographic options as resources, rather than as competing options, as usually assumed in historical sociolinguistic approaches to orthography (e.g. Nelde 1997). A particularly revealing area for the study of the interface between language contact and new orthographic norms is provided by *loanwords*, which can become symbolic of the source culture. Consequently, the spelling of loanwords can be subject to specific forms of manipulation (see Klöter 2010), as shown by the differentiated writing strategies of loanwords in Japanese (use of *katakana*), Greek (Latin script for loans from other European languages, primarily English) or English (diacritics in French loanwords), to name but a few cases (on this point, see Section 28.7).

In the remainder of this chapter, the possibilities of a sociohistorical and ecological framework to study the complexities of orthographic negotiation in language contact contexts are exemplified with a case study hitherto unexplored from a historical sociolinguistic perspective: the development of alphabetic written Nahuatl during the Spanish colonial period, with a focus on the phonological class of sibilants. Although logically rooted in the local circumstances of language contact in colonial Mesoamerica, this case study is of interest to the analysis of orthographic norm development and standardization in other ecologies, particularly in colonial settings: it exemplifies the social dynamics of importation of a metropolitan spelling norm in a situation of language contact, eventually leading to the development of local practices among the indigenous population. All these ingredients are typical of the emergence of orthographic norms in other language contact contexts (see Sebba 2007, 2015).

28.3 Contact Ecologies and the Ecology of Writing in Colonial Mexico

The arrival of Europeans to Mesoamerica in the early 1500s not only altered the local demographic and sociolinguistic landscapes – it also triggered radical changes in the traditional Mesoamerican technologies of writing and their social embedding (see Cifuentes 1998, Lockhart 1991, 1992, Olko 2015, Reyes Equiguas 2016). The most important innovation in this area was the introduction of alphabetic writing. In this section, I briefly describe the development of alphabetic writing among Nahuatl speakers in central Mexico as a process of ecological adaptation to a new environment of cultural and sociolinguistic contact, as outlined in Section 28.2.

Before the arrival of the Europeans, several nonalphabetic writing systems were in use in Mesoamerica. Because virtually no pre-conquest sample of writing from central Mexico has survived,[2] our knowledge of early Nahua writing is based mostly on the earliest post-conquest codices, assumed to be closest to pre-conquest styles, as well as on descriptions of Nahua writing in

[2] The few pre-conquest codices that have been preserved originate in other areas of present-day Mexico. They include some Mixtec and Mayan codices.

Spanish sources. Following Lockhart (1992: 327–31), three complementary modes of writing can be identified in pre-conquest Nahua writing: (a) a pictographic mode, which directly depicted the concept that is being represented; (b) a logographic mode, in which specific signified referents were represented by means of conventionalized ideograms; and (c) phonetic transcription, in which conventionalized glyphs/ideograms were used as representations of the initial syllables of the original glyph. This last mode was the closest to a phonologically based system of writing, but it did not operate independently from the pictographic symbols that justified the phonological interpretation of each sign (see Whittaker 2009).

Writing in post-conquest Mexico exhibits continuities with pre-conquest written modes. For instance, Europeans' use of paper was analogous to the use of bark paper (*amatl*) in pre-conquest Mesoamerica (sometimes deer skin was also used, not unlike the European use of parchment), as was the use of ink (*tlilli*). Mesoamerican 'books' (*amoxtli*) were typically long folded sheets rather than collections of bound folios, but each sheet often provided a unit of spatial organization, just like the folios or pages in a book (Lockhart 1992: 326–27).[3] In other respects, the introduction of alphabetic writing did represent a clear departure from pre-conquest writing, but the phonetic mode appears to have provided Nahuas a partial conceptual analogue to the phonetic base of European alphabets. Thus, for several decades, we see an expanded use of phonetically based glyphs in some Nahuatl texts, which may be a direct response to the introduction of alphabetic writing. For instance, the Spanish female name *Clara* was represented with a compound glyph consisting of the glyph for *house* (Nahuatl root *cal-*) and the glyph for *water* (root *a-*), rendering *cal-a*, a phonetic approximation to *Clara* (Lockhart 1992: 333–34; see Whittaker 2009 for more examples of incorporation of phonetic glyphs in early colonial alphabetic texts). In addition, a trend toward the elimination of pictorial elements in Nahua writing is clear, and by the mid-1600s, they became exceptional (Lockhart 1992: 353). As a matter of fact, the bulk of post-conquest writing in Nahuatl is entirely alphabetic. The persistence of at least some forms of pictorial representation in combination with alphabetic writing can be considered a part of the *internal ecology* (see Mufwene 2001, 2018) of alphabetic writing in colonial central Mexico.

Besides these internal interactions among different writing systems, changes in the *external ecology* of writing in colonial central Mexico involved the emergence of new agents and new uses (see below). Initially, the development of alphabetic norms for Nahuatl was the product of direct intervention by Spanish Franciscan friars, who worked in close collaboration with members of the Nahua nobility (see Olko 2015). This early stage of alphabetic

[3] It is no surprise, therefore, that the meanings of these three Nahuatl terms were simply extended to refer to their new European counterparts.

writing in Nahuatl can be linked to specific institutions (e.g. the Franciscan school of Santa Cruz de Tlatelolco, founded in 1536 on the outskirts of Mexico-Tenochtitlan for the education of indigenous clergy). In these institutions, several generations of Nahua students were exposed to alphabetic writing in Latin, Spanish and Nahuatl (see Cifuentes 1998, Reyes Equiguas 2016). However, the indigenous municipalities (*altepetl*) progressively became the new centers of production of writing in Nahuatl – here, Nahuatl-dominant (or usually monolingual) scribes learned to write alphabetically, sometimes from local Spanish clergy, but more often from other literate Nahuas (Lockhart 1991: 105, Olko 2015). Far from the norms for written Nahuatl initially devised and used by European clergy, conditions were right for the implementation of alternative orthographic strategies. Just as writers became more diverse, the applications of alphabetic writing also expanded, going from just catechetical or historical texts initially to encompass also administrative (e.g. wills, land deeds, municipal records) and private uses by the end of the colonial period (see Lockhart 1992, Olko 2015).

Despite these changes, the external ecology of writing in colonial Nahuatl also exhibits continuities throughout this whole period. One such continuity concerns the relationship between alphabetic writing and language learning. From the beginning, the implementation of alphabetic spelling and the development of orthographic norms for Nahuatl took place against the larger background of mutual language acquisition: Europeans undertook the adaptation of Latin script to Nahuatl as a tool in their learning of the language, but the Nahuas that were instrumental in that process also participated as they learned Latin and Spanish (Cifuentes 1998, Parodi 2006). Later on, the spread of alphabetic writing away from urban centers took place amid a parallel increase in societal bilingualism in Spanish and Nahuatl among the indigenous population of central Mexico (Lockhart 1991, 1992, Olko 2015). Therefore, as observed in other situations of language contact (see Section 28.2), a close sociolinguistic relationship emerged between the development of bilingual repertoires and the development of alphabetic writing skills among the indigenous scribes. Overall, as explained below, the selection of specific spelling options in this environment of linguistic and cultural brokerage can be expected to reflect a broad array of ecological interactions. In turn, these triggers played a critical role in the emergence of orthographic norms in Nahuatl, a point to which I now turn.

28.4 The Emergence of Orthographic Norms in Colonial Nahuatl

The development of an alphabetic orthography for Nahuatl can be traced back to the first Franciscan-led circles in the years following the Spanish conquest (1520s–1530s) (Canger 1997, Karttunen 1985: 41, Lockhart

1992: 330).[4] Although at the time of contact with the Europeans Nahuatl was dialectally varied (Olko and Sullivan 2013), the target of the first alphabetic norms was the high register of the language used in the central valley of Mexico (i.e. what has generally come to be known as 'Classical Nahuatl', e.g. Launey 2011), as codified in colonial *artes* (i.e. grammars of Nahuatl). In the earliest extant one, Andrés de Olmos offers the first explicit articulation of an alphabetic Nahuatl orthography:

> Orthography, spelling and pronunciation [*manera de escribir y pronunciar*, literally, 'the manner of writing and pronouncing'] are usually taken from the writings of wise men and old authors whenever they are available. But in this language, since they had no writing, this guide is missing, and so we need to guess [*andar adeuinando*].
>
> (Olmos 1875 [1547]: 196, my translation)

While Olmos was likely not the first to devise an orthography for Nahuatl,[5] many elements of his orthographic thinking became a common staple in subsequent *artes*. Such elements include the following: a listing of the phonemes (presented as *letras* 'letters', see below) that Nahuatl is said to lack (which include < b>, <d>, <g>, <r>, <s>, <v>); the noting of conspicuous gaps between spelling and pronunciation created by allophonic variation (as when the grammars refer to the pronunciation of letter <k> as <g> in certain contexts, in reality the alternation between [k] and [g] as allophones of /k/); and warnings about the limits of the Latin alphabet to note specific characteristics of Nahuatl phonology, such as the phonemes /tɬ/ and /ts/, the contrastive differences in vowel length, and the so-called *saltillo* ('little jump', i.e. the glottal stop). In such cases, most grammars either resorted to whatever was perceived to be the closest equivalence afforded by Latin script or ignored these features as targets of written representation (for instance, Carochi's 1645 and Aldama y Guevara's 1754 grammars are the only ones to systematically represent vowel length and the glottal stop).

Although this orthographic development process is often presented merely as an adaptation of the Latin script to Nahuatl (e.g. Cifuentes 1998), it was specifically its Castilian Spanish version that was used (see Lockhart 1992: 335–36, Smith-Stark 2005, Olko and Sullivan 2013). The fact that the friars were relying on the spelling of Spanish can be seen in the use of the digraphs

[4] The activity by colonial Catholic clergy in Mesoamerica to describe, codify and alphabetize indigenous languages is part of a much larger enterprise to transplant and impose European colonial ideological hierarchies to non-European societies (see Errington 2001, Rabasa 1993). In the context of Spanish colonialism, the Latin and Greek grammatical tradition and its adaptation to the description of European languages (most notably, Antonio de Nebrija's 1492 *Gramática de la lengua castellana*) were the models used in the grammatical description and alphabetical development of indigenous languages (see Cifuentes 1998, Guzmán Betancourt 2001, Smith-Stark 2005).

[5] We know that there were at least two earlier Nahuatl *artes* that have not been preserved (Canger 1997: 59).

<tl> and <tz>, absent in Latin script but justified as spellings for /tɬ/ and /ts/ based on the pronunciation of Spanish, as well as in the justification of deviations from what would be the expected pronunciation for Spanish sequences, such as <ll>. For instance, in Antonio del Rincón's 1595 grammar, the association between graphemes and phonemes in Spanish is explicitly assumed as the starting point for the alphabetization of Nahuatl, as exemplified in the following quote: "they [= Nahuatl speakers] do not use [...] the two <ll> as in the Spanish way, for instance they do not say *villa* ['town'] as in Spanish [i.e. not as a lateral palatal /ʎ/], but as in Latin, pronouncing each <l> separately" (1885 [1595]: 62, my translation).

These first attempts at the alphabetization of Nahuatl took place in close linguistic and cultural contact among Spanish and Nahuatl speakers, and were directly shaped by the European friars' orthographic choices described in the preceding paragraph. Overall, the spelling choices in the earliest texts in Nahuatl written by Nahuas reflect a high degree of proximity to these early orthographic norms (Lockhart 1992: 335–36). As alphabetic writing progressively spread to other areas beyond the core cities of the central valley of Mexico (see Section 28.3), several innovations departing from the system devised by the Spanish friars and their indigenous students were introduced. The most important of these departures in these regional colonial Nahuatl texts was the focus on the phonological form of language rather than on the spelling of specific words (Lockhart 1992: 338–39, Olko and Sullivan 2013: 190–91). More specifically, each letter was meant as a representation of sound in a given context, regardless of the role of that sound in the morphological structure of the word or whether it had a different pronunciation in a different context. For instance, these regional colonial Nahuatl texts exhibit considerable variation in the use of <n> in syllabic codas, which seems to be due to the combined function of the morphophonological rules of Nahuatl, stylistic factors and hypercorrection, and even less predictable individual variation (see *intrusive nasality*, Karttunen and Lockhart 1976: 11–12). These variable innovations progressively gave way to specific spelling traditions in each *altepetl* (Lockhart 1992: 342–43).

From the beginning, the adaptation of Spanish loanwords by Nahua scribes stood out as a prime area for orthographic experimentation, as typically attested for loanwords in other language contact settings (see Section 28.2). To spell these loanwords, Nahua scribes often applied substitutions for Spanish sounds that Nahuatl lacked. For instance, Nahuatl does not have voiced plosives, so <p> was frequently used for Spanish <b> and <v> (*capilto*, see Spanish *cabildo* 'town council'), and <t> for <d> (*totor*, see Spanish *doctor* 'doctor'). Hypercorrections also abound (*brigo*, see Spanish *pregón* 'public decree'; *desurello*, see Spanish *tesorero* 'treasurer'). Variation in loanword spelling among scribes from the same region and period spans the whole colonial period, and appears to be the product of various sociolinguistic and cultural triggers (see

Lockhart 1992, Olko and Sullivan 2013, Olko 2015). These triggers can be seen at work most clearly in the spelling for loanwords containing sounds that exhibited pervasive variation in colonial Spanish. In the following sections, I focus on one such case: the spelling for sibilant sounds.

28.5 Case Study: The Orthography of Sibilants in Colonial Nahuatl

In order to interpret the spelling for sibilants in Spanish loanwords in Nahuatl, we must consider the phonology of sibilants in colonial Spanish and in Nahuatl, as well as their orthographic interpretation in alphabetic Nahuatl spelling. Because of space limitations, this review is necessarily brief – the reader is invited to refer to the literature referenced in this section for more details. Medieval Castilian Spanish (c. 1200–1500) appears to have had as many as six contrastive fricative sibilant segments. These contrasts were based on a three-way place of articulation distinction and a voicing contrast, as shown in Table 28.1.

During the late medieval period (c. 1350–1500), this system underwent complex changes geographically and socially (Cano Aguilar 2004, Penny 2004). In some dialects, the loss of the voicing distinction yielded a three-way contrast: /s̪/ – /s̺/ – /ʃ/. In other areas, the loss of voicing was combined with the loss of the distinction between dentoalveolars and apicoalveolars, a phenomenon that has come to be known as *seseo* and that resulted in a two-way contrast between /s/ and /ʃ/. The first form of merger is commonly attested in central and northern Castile, while *seseo* is more commonly attested in southern varieties, including Andalusian. By the mid-1500s, the system in Table 28.1 appears to have represented a socially infrequent but still prestigious option. In addition to sociolinguistic variation within Castilian Spanish, bilingualism with other Iberian languages (Basque, Portuguese, Catalan) and with the languages of African slaves and other L2 speakers provided additional opportunities for diversification and merger (see Plans 2004). By contrast, all dialects of Nahuatl featured a single contrast between a front, dental or dentoalveolar fricative sibilant /s/ and a back, palatal or palatoalveolar fricative sibilant /ʃ/ (Launey 2011: 4; see Karttunen and Lockhart 1976: 5 for the possibility of allophonic variation in the articulation of /ʃ/), just like *seseo* dialects in colonial Spanish.

Table 28.1 *Medieval central Castilian system of sibilant fricatives*

Dentoalveolar		Apicoalveolar		Palatoalveolar	
[–voice]	[+voice]	[–voice]	[+voice]	[–voice]	[+voice]
/s̪/	/z̪/	/s̺/	/z̺/	/ʃ/	/ʒ/

When interpreting the spelling of Spanish loanwords in Nahuatl, it is important to keep in mind that the L1 Spanish input presented to Nahuatl speakers was sociolinguistically unsystematic: once in the colonies, demographic mixture and dialect and language contact blurred the sociolinguistic correlates of Spanish dialects operative in Spain. Crucially enough, therefore, the L1 Spanish input that L2 learners had access to was highly variable, especially in the first decades, and it featured segments not present in Nahuatl that were challenging in terms of acquisition (most notably the apicoalveolar sibilant still in vogue in northern and central Castilian varieties; see Smith-Stark 2005: 28–29, Sanz-Sánchez 2019: 223–25). In addition, two facts of colonial Spanish American dialectology are highly relevant to the interpretation of Nahuatl spellings: (a) over time, *seseo* spread among L1 Spanish speakers in the colonies, and it seems to have been characteristic of colony-born Spaniards by the early 1600s (see Frago Gracia 1999, Sanz-Sánchez 2019), and (b) palatoalveolar /ʃ/ was backed to velar /x/ (often articulated as [h]) in most dialects of European and American Spanish over the course of the seventeenth century (see Cano Aguilar 2004).

In addition to spoken Spanish, exposure to elements of written Latin and Spanish must have also shaped the orthographic repertoires of Nahua scribes. In the case of Spanish, the roots of a more or less stable orthography can be traced back to the court of Alfonso X 'the Wise', king of Castile and León (1252–84), whose royal chancery promoted a spelling system that targeted the six-way sibilant repertoire presented in Table 28.1. This system is presented in (1):

(1) a Dentoalveolars
<c> (|c| and |ç|) = /ts/ (> late medieval /s̻/) <z> = /dz/ (> late medieval /z̻/)
b Apicoalveolars
<s> (word-initial), <ss> (intervocalic) = /s̺/ <s> (intervocalic) = /z̺/
c Palatoalveolars
<x> = /ʃ/ <j> and <g> = /ʒ/

Although this norm continued to offer a prestigious spelling model as late as the 1600s, scrupulous adherence to it in early colonial texts is infrequent (Sanz-Sánchez 2019). Spanish friar-grammarians used this orthographic tradition to arrive at a consensus on how to note the two sibilant phonemes of Nahuatl. An analysis of the 13 published colonial Nahuatl *artes* reveals some clear orthographic tendencies since the earliest grammars.[6] The spelling

[6] The grammatical treatises reviewed here include the following (in chronological order): Olmos (1875 [1547]), Molina (1571), del Rincón (1885 [1595]), Galdo Guzmán (1890 [1642]), Carochi (1645), Vetancurt (1673), Vázquez Gastelu (1689), Guerra (1692), Pérez (1713), de Tapia Zenteno (1753), Aldama y Guevara (1754), Cortés y Zedeño (1765), Sandoval (1965 [1810]).

choice for /ʃ/ is always <x>. For /s/, there is some diachronic variation. The early grammars select <c> in onset position (with |c| before <e, i> and |ç| before <a> and <o>), and <z> for all syllabic coda positions. Over time, spelling becomes more unstable: <c> is sometimes replaced by <z> in word-initial and intervocalic position, but there are also examples of <z> used across the board for any /s/ (e.g. Guerra 1692). Sample spellings are shown in (2):

(2a)	Early grammars			
	tlaçotla	*cihuatl*	*eztli*	*nicochiz*
	/tɬasoˀtɬa/	/ˈsiwa: tɬ/	/ˈestɬi/	/niˈkoʧis/
	'to love'	'woman'	'blood'	'I will sleep'

(2b)	Later grammars			
	tlaçotla ~ tlazotla	*cihuatl ~ zihuatl*	*eztli*	*nicochiz*

With only a few exceptions (e.g. Aldama y Guevara 1754), the *artes* make no reference to allophonic variation in the pronunciation of neither /s/ nor /ʃ/. Alternation in spellings is thus exclusively orthographically motivated. These conventions appear to be a function of both the spelling norms for Castilian Spanish in vogue at the beginning of the colonial period as well as changes in the pronunciation of Spanish in Mexico. The early grammarians seem to have still been familiar enough with the pronunciation and spelling of the old Castilian norm to equate Nahuatl /s/ (a front sibilant) with Castilian dentoalveolar /s̪/ rather than with the slightly retracted apicoalveolar /s̺/, and consequently selected <c> (as either |ç| or |c|) and <z> as the graphemes for that sound (see example (1) above). Confirmation for this hypothesis can be found in the recurrent comment in all colonial grammars that Nahuatl does not have <s>, which can be easily understood if we assume that <s> in their mind stood for the apicoalveolar Castilian sibilant (see Table 28.1). The distribution of <c> (as either |ç| or |c|) and <z> depending on syllable position and following vowel in onset is also an adaptation of the old Castilian orthographic system, as shown in example (1). Note that voicing was not contrastive in coda position, so that even in medieval Castilian texts <z> can be frequently found for coda dentoalveolars, regardless of voicing. As *seseo* spread socially in spoken colonial Mexican Spanish (see Section 28.5), later grammarians were forced to negotiate their knowledge of the phonetic value of Nahuatl sibilants and their representation in the earlier orthographic norms with their awareness about the new phonetic value of Spanish graphemes. By 1673, Vetancurt writes that if *cihuatl ~ zihuatl* 'woman' "was written with s. instead of z. it would have the same pronunciation" (f. 1 r, my translation). Most of these authors justify sticking with the use of <z> instead of <s> based on the existence of an established written norm.

While clear spelling continuities can be identified between medieval Spanish orthographies and the new norms preconized by Nahuatl grammars, the influence of these norms among Nahua scribes was uneven. Adherence to these norms appears to have been most consistent among scribes in close communication with Spanish clergy during the initial phase of alphabetization (1530s–70s, see Section 28.3 above). As time went by and alphabetic writing broke loose from these original circles, alternative sibilant spellings emerged. These orthographic innovations "tend to correspond to linguistically plausible phenomena" (Lockhart 1991: 122–23). For instance, a 1750 land grant from the town of Calimaya in the area of Toluca, southwest of Mexico City, uses <s> for all cases of /s/ regardless of phonetic context (*sacatitla* 'next to the grassland', *ysihuahuatzin* 'his honorable wife', *quixitinis* 'will/may harm it'; compare classical spelling *zacatitla, icihua(hua) tzin, quixitiniz*) (Archivo General de la Nación, Tierras 2541, expediente 11, f. 3, transcribed in Lockhart 1991: 108–9). This phenomenon is rooted in the sociolinguistic ecology of Nahuatl literacy in the late colonial period (1650–1810): as language shift to Spanish advanced among the indigenous communities of central Mexico, most writing in Nahuatl came to be practiced by bilingual Nahuatl-dominant scribes of a lower social rank with little to no familiarity with the orthographic norms proposed in grammatical treatises (Lockhart 1991: 133–34, Olko 2015). However, other orthographic uses were much more stable. For instance, in the same land grant, <tz> and <x> are consistently used for /ts/ and /ʃ/, as prescribed since the earliest *artes*.

While language shift does appear to account for some of the orthographic developments in these Nahuatl texts, it is likely that other triggers also operated in the context of widespread social and cultural change typical of colonial central Mexico. The spelling of sibilants in Spanish loanwords offers a prime example of these multiple ecological effects.

28.6 Sibilants in Nahuatl Documents: Spanish Loanwords

The corpus used in the present study relies on the collection of colonial Nahuatl texts used in Karttunen and Lockhart (1976), one of the foundational studies in twentieth-century Nahuatl philology, which presents a survey of a corpus of alphabetic texts ranging from the 1540s to the 1790s (for the sources used by the authors to compile their corpus, see Karttunen and Lockart 1976: 126). The Spanish loanwords in this collection are listed in a lengthy appendix (Karttunen and Lockhart 1976: 52–90), constituting the corpus for this chapter. Following a rigorous philological approach, the authors are careful enough to note the words "as [they] appear in the Nahuatl text" (Karttunen and Lockhart 1976: 52), which allows us to use the data in this appendix as evidence for orthographic variation and adaptation in these texts. Of these word tokens 476 (representing 350 lexical types) feature sibilant sounds in the Spanish source lexical item. Since words can contain more than one sibilant, the total number of sibilant spelling tokens (506) is higher than that of word tokens. Overall, the loanwords in this list illustrate the semantic trends of lexical borrowing from Spanish into Nahuatl throughout the colonial period, with lexical borrowings concentrating in specific fields like artifacts, types of people, and religious and biological concepts. Since alphabetized Nahuatl was, at least initially, an adaptation of Castilian Spanish spelling, the loanwords are classified here according to their adherence or deviation from attested orthographic practices for Spanish sibilants (see Section 28.5). Four types of spellings are represented in the corpus, as shown in (3–6):

(3) Etymological spellings, reflecting the medieval Castilian norm (see Section 28.5): Nahuatl *hordenaças* 'decrees' (1547) < medieval Castilian Spanish *ordenanças*;[7]
(4) Spellings suggesting devoicing: *coçina* 'kitchen' (1549) < *cozina*;
(5) Spellings suggesting merger between dentoalveolars and apicoalveolars (i.e. *seseo*): *hasucar* 'sugar' (1683) < *azucar*;
(6) Spellings suggesting merger across the 'back' sibilant categories, that is, apicoalveolars and palatoalveolars: *pexo* 'type of currency unit' (1635) < *peso*.[8]

After these sibilant spellings were classified, they were plotted chronologically into four periods of approximately 50 years each. The last period is somewhat longer to accommodate the fact that the corpus only includes six texts written after 1750, and the low density of data for this period would have skewed the overall chronological distribution if considered separately. Figure 28.1 shows the distribution of each type of spelling, in percentages.

As can be seen, the data reveal several clear trends. First, most spellings are etymological in every period. Examples (7–9) illustrate this type of spelling:

(7) *mesa* 'table' (1549) < *mesa*;
(8) *cevara* 'barley' (1610) < *cebada*;
(9) *panrenjan* 'couple' (1736) < *pareja*.

Although these etymological spellings are very frequent, their proportion drops as the colonial period proceeds. This drop is largely compensated by the rise in the proportion of spellings suggesting *seseo*, which make up over one fourth of all examples in the later documents. Examples include (10–12):

(10) *çiera* 'saw' (1597) < *sierra*;
(11) *ycalson* 'underskirt, gaiters' (1611) < *calçon*;
(12) *obligasio* 'obligation' (1716) < *obligacion*.

[7] Throughout the remainder of this study, attested Nahuatl forms and year of attestation are given first, followed by medieval Castilian Spanish etyma.

[8] A very small number of words with sibilants in the Spanish source presented no sibilant in the Nahuatl loanword, or highly idiosyncratic spellings not found in other texts – such spellings were not included in the analysis.

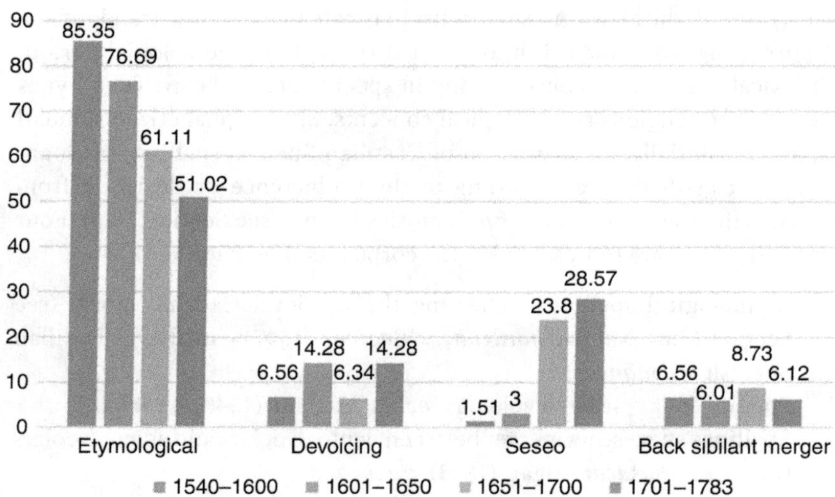

Figure 28.1 Distribution of sibilant spellings in the loanwords in Nahuatl manuscripts (N=506) (from Karttunen and Lockhart 1976)

Other spelling trends are represented in a minority of cases, but they persist throughout the colonial period in slightly varying proportions. These include spellings suggesting devoicing, as in examples (13–14), and spellings suggesting merger of apicoalveolars and palatoalveolars, as in examples (15–16):

(13) *posision* 'possession' (1550) < *possession*;
(14) *mestiço* 'mestizo' (1607–1629) < *mestizo*;
(15) *sovon* 'doublet, jerkin' (1575) < *jubon*;
(16) *xonbla* 'shadow, shade' (1610) < *sombre*.

In addition, specific lexical items exhibit different behaviors. On the one hand, sibilant spellings in some words maintain their etymological form throughout the colonial period, as shown by the reflexes for Spanish *español* 'Spaniard, Spanish' (17) and for *juez* 'judge' (18):

(17) *español* (1547), *espanol* (1550–60), *españolesme* (1570), *espannor* (1617);
(18) *jueztito* (1548), *juezti* (1553), *juezhuia* (1607–29), *jueztica* (1609).

By contrast, most items exhibit pervasive variation, particularly in words that reoccur throughout the corpus, as can be seen in adaptations of *camisa* 'shirt' in (19) and *solar* 'lot of clear land' in (20):

(19) *camissatli* (1549), *camixachiuhqui* (1550–60), *camisatli* (1555, 1606);
(20) *solar* (1549), *jular* (1550–60), *xollal* (1682), *xotlal* (1734).

Overall, the distribution of spellings for sibilant segments in Spanish loanwords in the corpus of colonial Nahuatl texts shows frequent variation, but also several clear diachronic trends pointing to the emergence of diachronic norms. In the next section, these trends are interpreted as a function of the adaptation of written practices to various historical ecological triggers specific to this context of cultural and linguistic contact.

28.7 The Ecology of Sibilant Spellings and the Emergence of Orthographic Norms

Previous approaches to the incorporation of Spanish loanwords in Nahuatl texts have used these spellings as evidence of L2 articulatory patterns among Nahuatl speakers (Karttunen and Lockhart 1976, Karttunen 1985, Lockhart 1991, 1992, Hidalgo 2001). While nonnative language learning is clearly an important factor, other sociolinguistic and cultural triggers can be seen at work. Following Lockhart (1991, 1992), colonial Nahuatl texts feature two strategies for the spelling of Spanish loans: an 'orthographic' approach, whereby scribes adhere to Spanish spelling norms, and a 'phonetic' approach, with loanwords reflecting characteristics of nonnative pronunciation of Spanish lexical items. In the corpus, the spellings in the etymological class are the clearest examples of the orthographic trend. As stated above (see Section 28.5), this etymological norm had little support in actual spoken practice already in the sixteenth century. Therefore, adherence to this norm in the corpus must be interpreted as a function of the influence of prestige models of written Spanish (Karttunen and Lockhart 1976: 113). In this respect, the diachronic evolution of the frequency of these spellings is significant, since it mirrors the progressive spread of alphabetic practices away from the urban centers of central Mexico to rural areas (see Sections 28.3 and 28.4): as alphabetic writing in Nahuatl spilled away from direct contact with learned models of literacy in both Spanish and Nahuatl, Nahua scribes appear to have been less motivated to abide by the canonical spelling of sibilants typical of metropolitan norms. But the persistence of etymological spellings also bespeaks the strength of the social networks in which Nahua scribes transmitted and learned alphabetic practices: even as Nahua scribes lost direct touch with written norms of the first stage of Nahuatl alphabetization, they continued to largely produce loanwords that respected traditional Spanish orthography, as shown by the data analyzed in Section 28.6.

On the other hand, the L2-based phonetic trend identified by Lockhart can be seen most clearly in the other types of spellings that occur at lower frequency in the corpus. The clearest example of phonetic influence of Nahuatl is in the spellings suggesting merger among apicoalveolar and palatoalveolar sibilants. Spellings suggestive of this type of merger are attested in L1 Spanish dialects on both sides of the Atlantic (Cano Aguilar 2004: 842) as a low-frequency feature until about the mid-1600s. By contrast, in my corpus, this alternation occurs across a variety of lexical items, including many for which these variants are seemingly unattested in Castilian Spanish (e.g. *casa* 'box' (1548); *xilla* 'chair' (1549); *quixitol* 'inquisitor' (1576); *xinola* '(Spanish) lady' (c. 1700), see Spanish *caja, silla, inquisidor, señora*). Rather than a preservation of articulatory modes imported by L1 Spanish speakers, these spellings appear to reflect the adaptation of the Spanish apicoalveolar sibilant by L1 Nahuatl speakers, who perceived this sibilant as more retracted than their /s/ and equated it with Nahuatl palatal /ʃ/ (Sanz-Sánchez 2019: 223–25). Note, too, that the proportion of these spellings, although low, is fairly consistent throughout the whole period, even though in L1 Spanish, palatal /ʃ/ became velar /x/ by the late 1600s (Sánchez Méndez 2003: 246–47). The spread of bilingualism in Spanish among Nahua communities and the increase in L1 Spanish speakers in indigenous communities would lead us to expect that <x>, <g> and <j> spellings for Spanish /s/ items, and <s> or <ss> for Spanish /ʃ/ items would have become disfavored, since Nahuas now had evidence that previous /ʃ/ items no longer exhibited a sibilant in Mexican Spanish. Not only does the persistence of these spellings show that these forms had been fully incorporated into the lexicon of Nahuatl – it also demonstrates that they had become entrenched in Nahuatl orthographies (Karttunen and Lockhart 1976: 7–8, Lockhart 1992: 315).

While much of the data appears to be have been driven by the dichotomy between adherence to Spanish orthographic norms and L2 Nahuatl pronunciation invoked by Lockhart, spelling variation in specific texts calls into question this simple dichotomy as the sole explanatory factor. Spellings suggesting *devoiced* articulations are a good example. The maintenance of spelling distinctions related to voicing can be rightly assumed to have been challenging for Nahuatl-dominant speakers since the beginning, given the lack of voicing contrasts in Nahuatl obstruents (Launey 2011: 4). But devoicing is, as seen above (Section 28.5), a well-established trend in L1 Spanish as well. In addition, since the loss of voicing in L1 forms of Spanish, alternation in the spellings within each of the medieval phonological classes (<c> and <z>, and <s> and <ss>) is widespread in colonial texts authored by native Spanish speakers (Cano Aguilar 2004: 834–37, Sanz-Sánchez 2019). Exposure to such forms can be expected to also have motivated these spelling choices in texts written by Nahuas.

Another diachronic fact that resists explanation simply in terms of adherence to Spanish canonical orthography or L2 phonology is the increase in the spellings suggesting *seseo*. As explained above (Section 28.5), this phenomenon became categorical in local forms of Mexican Spanish since at least around 1600. Therefore, these spellings reflect a trend, already noted elsewhere (Karttunen and Lockhart 1976), for changes in the pronunciation of sibilants in L1 forms of Spanish to be reflected in Nahuatl texts. At the same time, these spellings contradict analyses that have identified a general trend for Spanish loanwords to be presented in a more 'standard' way as time went by (e.g. Lockhart 1992: 316). While this may be the case with spellings noting other phonological categories present in Spanish but absent in Nahuatl, such as the voicing difference in stops (see Section 28.4), sibilants do not conform to this general diachronic pattern.

This apparent contradiction, however, can be comfortably accommodated by an ecological adaptive framework (see Section 28.1), where orthographic practices reflect concurrent and often conflicting triggers. In particular, these Nahuatl spellings may be interpreted as reflecting two parallel ecological catalysts: on the one hand, the increase in bilingualism in Spanish in Nahua communities, which logically must have triggered a parallel increase in familiarity with colloquial forms of spoken Spanish; and, on the other hand, a rise in the frequency of interaction with written forms of Spanish, which in many areas of central Mexico increasingly included evidence of *seseo* in writing. Orthographic *seseo* is widespread in eighteenth-century texts in Spanish authored by Nahuas (Lockhart 1991: 111–12), as well as in the written production of L1 Spanish speakers from the same period (see Frago Gracia 1999). Such spellings, therefore, are more a transparent representation of the types of written and spoken Spanish that late colonial Nahuas came into contact with than they are of 'standard' orthography in Spanish, which could only be highly influential in the case of the writing of individuals in close contact with learned circles.

The data on *seseo* spellings also shed light on the ways in which Nahua speakers may have conceived of the use of the spelling of loanwords as a tool to negotiate linguistic and cultural contact. As mentioned above (see Section 28.5), as time went by, both L1 Spanish and Nahuatl came to share the same front sibilant /s/, the only difference being in the back sibilant (with /ʃ/ becoming /x/ in Spanish but not in Nahuatl; see Section 28.5). Therefore, an orthographically and phonologically straightforward solution would have been to spell all cases of /s/ with the same grapheme, for example <s>, regardless of the language of origin of the lexical item in question. As a matter of fact, this is exactly what we find in many Nahuatl texts in the late colonial period (Lockhart 1991: 106–9; see also Section 28.5). In these texts, the orthographic alternation between <c> (as either |ç| or |c|), and <z> for Nahuatl /s/ preconized by most *artes* and typical of early post-conquest alphabetic Nahuatl texts has been eliminated in favor of <s>. This choice without doubt stems from the identification of <s>, already the highest-frequency spelling for Spanish /s/, as the most appropriate for the same sound in Nahuatl. Since <s> was not one of the orthographic options preconized by the early grammars nor by the orthographic norms in early Nahuatl alphabetic writing (see Section 28.5), this change represents a clear example of the diachronic ecological interaction between orthographies in both languages.

However, the same is not true for Spanish loanwords. While *seseo* spellings do become more common, etymological spellings according to the medieval norm remain the most common sibilant spelling category even in the last decades covered by the corpus. The 1750 land grant (see Section 28.5) exemplifies this different orthographic treatment for Spanish loanwords: while virtually all cases of Nahuatl /s/ are spelled with <s>, Spanish /s/ is given a much more variable treatment than its Nahuatl counterpart: for instance, noncanonical *petision* 'petition' and *pedaso* 'piece' contrast with canonical *juez* 'judge' or *oficiales* 'officials'. How can one explain this apparent contradiction? One possibility is that continued exposure to alternation of sibilant spellings in Spanish, which was far from standardized even in the eighteenth century in many forms of writing, triggered a similar alternation in Spanish loanwords used in Nahuatl texts. However, it is also possible that this alternation may reflect the persistence of internal traditions for the spelling of Spanish loanwords developed from the earliest period of development of alphabetic writing in Nahuatl. From this perspective, Nahua writers may have been aware of the potential of spellings like <c> and <z> to indexically symbolize linguistic origin and cultural difference between 'Nahuas' and 'Spaniards' (i.e. a case of *attribution*, Sebba 2015). This type of effect has been described by Lüpke (2011: 331) as a consequence of the ecology of contact in communities under cultural pressure, where writers and readers may be especially sensitive to the iconic value of orthography. While tantalizing, this hypothesis would benefit from a more detailed quantitative comparison between sibilants in written Nahuatl items and in Spanish loans than can be attempted here. Future research will have to confirm whether (and how) the patterns of variation in these loanwords differ from the observed evolution in orthographic norms for Nahuatl texts in specific groups of texts, by period, text type or area of provenance, and if Nahua scribes used these differential orthographic strategies to visually signal a difference between Nahuatl and Spanish.

All in all, the diachronic evolution of sibilant spellings in these data can be summarized as a progressive process of detachment from initial norms modeled on medieval Castilian Spanish orthography and a gradual development of more autonomous spelling protocols. Although late colonial Nahuatl sibilants as spelled by Nahua scribes were not standardized, indications of homogeneous norms (e.g. spelling of all /s/ as <s>) were starting to emerge. Spanish loanwords, with their iconic potential in a situation of language contact, appear to have operated as orthographic islands by partially resisting some of the trends applied to Nahuatl lexicon. Overall, the spelling of Nahuatl exhibits a parallel behavior to the historical development of orthographic norms in other language contact situations, where "the orthography of one language initially modelled on the norms of another may de-standardise and take on new normative principles" (Bondarev 2019: 19). As is often the case in normative processes, complete homogenization was not reached: with the end of the colonial period, the dissolution of the indigenous municipalities radically altered the ecology of writing in Nahuatl, and written Nahuatl all but disappeared (see Karttunen 1985). A variety of present-day orthographies exist, but the debate on how Nahuatl should be spelled is far from settled (see Pharao Hansen 2016).

28.8 Conclusion

This chapter has shown that the complex sociolinguistics of language contact can be a major contributor to the patterns of variation and change in historical orthographies. The literature in this area demonstrates that situations of language contact are often the site for the emergence of new orthographic norms. By taking linguistic variation and contact as the default in any community, historical sociolinguistic approaches to historical orthographies are particularly well positioned to account for these multiple environmental effects. In addition, ecological models that see population-wide norms as emerging from individuals' adaptive choices can be applied productively to account for similarities and differences at various social scales of analysis, from individual writers to regional, national and international norms.

As an illustration, the sociohistorical ecological adaptive framework presented at the beginning of this chapter has been applied to the emergence of alphabetic orthographies in colonial Nahuatl. The analysis strongly suggests that the spelling protocols used by colonial Nahua scribes were highly sensitive to a variety of environmental motivations. These motivations include the influence from historical writing and orthographic traditions, various degrees of proficiency in Spanish and Nahuatl, membership in specific social networks, and possibly ideologies about language use, writing and ethnolinguistic affiliation. More importantly, this case offers a transparent illustration of the applicability of a multicausational, ecological approach to the study of orthographic variation and norm creation in other high-contact sociolinguistic settings.

29

Discourse and Sociopolitical Issues

Laura Villa Galán

29.1 Introduction

This chapter deals with the study of orthography from a sociopolitical historical perspective. This innovative approach to the study of spelling will be of interest for those concerned with how *language* and *power* are intertwined. Historical orthographic studies have traditionally paid more attention to linguistic issues, that is, the development of the formal characteristics of a specific writing system over time. Sociopolitical studies of orthography focus instead on nonlinguistic issues, that is, the motivations for and implications of adopting or reforming a specific writing system in a particular moment in time. A key underlying assumption for this approach is that language (including practices, norms and ideas about language) is socially and politically charged. This is so because language never exists in the abstract but rather it is always used, managed and thought of in concrete historical contexts and in specific interactions among people who hold different positions in the social structure and different amounts of power to dictate the norms of communication.

Linguistic hierarchies and commonsense ideas about language are, in fact, powerful mechanisms to justify *social inequality* in class societies because they validate *social difference* through language: they legitimize that people perceived as better spoken are more prestigious in our society than those who are seen as linguistically deficient. This is so because notions such as language correctness, appropriateness or prestige are understood as the consequence of natural processes (see Woolard and Schieffelin 1994, Irvine and Gal 2000, Flores and Rosa 2015). Consequently, it is assumed that everyone has the same access to prestigious ways of speaking and that everyone is judged equally when they speak, neither of which assumptions holds, as a vast number of studies in critical sociolinguistics and linguistic anthropology have definitively proven.[1] Similarly, research that assumes a sociopolitical historical perspective seeks to show that language is not a mere arbitrary system of communication that undisputedly develops over time. Instead, it is a sociohistorical construct, and therefore "in any attempt to understand how and why some views of language gradually emerge as dominant, while others are suppressed and marginalised, we need to attend to the historical processes that inform the dynamics of social power as these obtain in particular times and places" (Johnson 2005: 5–6). Consequently, far from being natural phenomena, linguistic hierarchies and commonsense ideas about language (for instance, the existence of a national standard orthography and our unquestioned acceptance of the need for such spelling norms) are indeed the result of historical struggles.

In this chapter, I offer, first, a literature review that provides the reader with examples of research questions, methodological approaches and theoretical perspectives in the area of sociopolitical studies of orthography. Then, I present a case study, the officialization of a particular orthographic system in Spain in 1844. This event is especially pertinent to understanding how power struggles lie behind specific orthographic debates and how nonlinguistic factors play a significant role in the development of spelling norms. In addition, this case study seeks to serve as an example of the kind of critical questions with which researchers interested in the discursive and political nature of language approach their corpus. The goal of these critical questions is to better understand how language (including practices, norms and beliefs) changes in history as part of historical processes that materialize in specific sociopolitical events which involve specific actors with specific sociopolitical interests. More generally, these critical questions seek to understand how language and power intertwine.

The scholarly works discussed in the following pages represent a wide range of research interests, theoretical conceptualizations and analytical procedures that converge in a common concern for the social nature of language and linguistic instruments, that is, grammars, dictionaries, and, of course, orthographies. Researchers that take such a perspective conceive orthography as a cultural artifact and as social practice. This implies that issues such as the selection of a script, the codification of a writing system or the establishment of spelling norms are no longer approached as ideologically neutral scientific endeavors but are rather understood as historically situated political

[1] In recent years, for instance, raciolinguistics (an area of study within those disciplines) has helped us to better understand the biased way in which society judges appropriateness in relation to who is the speaker rather than what is said or how. Scholars have found that racialized subjects are overwhelmingly marked as linguistically deficient not based on the objective materiality of their linguistic practices but due to their subordinated position in the social structure. Likewise, scholars working with the concept of raciolinguistic ideologies have explained that linguistic discrimination and racism are intertwined systemic problems that have their roots in colonial history and that continue to perpetuate the subjugation of racialized communities today (see Flores and Rosa 2015, Rosa and Flores 2017).

activities. From this point of view, orthographies are studied, for instance, as powerful instruments of inclusion and exclusion in relation to the construction and enactment of social identities. They are also examined as gatekeeping devices that exacerbate and naturalize social inequalities by preventing certain groups and individuals from accessing capital resources for upward mobility in society. Moreover, they are analyzed as ideological mechanisms that reinforce (or challenge) a given political entity, most commonly the capitalist nation-state. In short, orthographies are practical and symbolic tools strategically used to impose, maintain or resist particular social identities or politico-economic orders (see Jaffe 1999, 2000a, Sebba 2007, 2009, Jaffe et al. 2012). However, the sociopolitical effects of orthographic choices are not necessarily conscious and, in fact, the ideological nature of orthography is unnoticed and uncontested by most people.

Linguistic anthropology and critical sociolinguistics (the two fields more readily concerned with discursive and sociopolitical issues) are disciplines committed to studying language as a nonneutral code, as a form of social organization and as a system of differentiation (see Duranti 2011). It is through language that power relations are constructed, and that social difference is maintained. Thus, it is only by looking at language in context and language in action, by analyzing situated practices and everyday interactions (i.e. by studying discourse) that we will be able to understand how power operates and how inequality is perpetuated (see Fairclough 1992a, Jaworski and Coupland 1999). Due to their interest in matters of power, control and inequality, linguistic anthropologists and sociolinguists pay particular attention to the production, reproduction and sociopolitical effects of *language ideologies* (see Schieffelin et al. 1998, Kroskrity 2000). Defined as the "mediating link between social forms and forms of talk" (Woolard and Schieffelin 1994: 55) or as "representations, whether explicit or implicit, that construe the intersection of language and human beings in a social world" (Woolard 1998: 3), the study of language ideologies allows us to better comprehend "the tie of cultural conceptions to social power" (Woolard 1998: 10). Three features shared by all language ideologies expose this tie:

> first, their *contextuality*, that is, their embedding in a cultural, political, and/or social order; second, their *naturalizing function*, that is, their normalizing effect on a particular extralinguistic order; and third, their *institutionality*, that is, their production and reproduction in institutionally organized practices that support specific forms of power and authority.
>
> (del Valle 2007: 21)

One subfield of inquiry within sociolinguistics in which the concept of language ideology has been particularly revealing (and one that is of special interest to the study of orthography) is that of *language planning*. First defined by Einar Haugen as "the activity of preparing a normative orthography, grammar, and dictionary for the guidance of writers and speakers in a non-homogeneous speech community" (Haugen 1961: 68), language planning was at the time seen as a technical activity that should result in the top-down implementation for the nation as a whole of a *standard language* with "two mutually supporting aspects, on the one hand a generally accepted orthography, and on the other a prestige dialect imitated by the socially ambitious" (Haugen 1961: 134). This technical approach to *standardization* became particularly influential in a variety of sociolinguistic contexts between the 1950s and the 1970s. In a context of decolonization, Western-trained linguists embarked on various language planning activities in Africa, Asia and South America (Ricento 2006: 12–15). They participated, for instance, in numerous efforts to 'reduce to writing' previously oral languages, and applied sociolinguistic knowledge in the implementation processes in order to achieve the acceptance of those new writing systems by the speech communities. As Fishman put it,

> [t]he creation of writing systems is itself necessarily an outgrowth of culture contact, if not of political and economic domination from outside. Thus, the creation of a writing system is singularly unlikely to be viewed dispassionately and its propagation and acceptance by indigenous networks are necessarily viewed as having implications for group loyalty and group identity.
> (Fishman 1977: xiv–xv)

Since the late 1970s to the 1990s, researchers started to question "some of the assumptions that informed the early work in LP," inspired by a more critical approach to language planning that led them to explore its role in the "reproduction of social and economic inequality" (Ricento 2006: 13). The goal of the field and the task of the linguists shifted from intervening in real decision-making situations to analyzing the consequences of such interventions, including the disenfranchisement brought about by the development of standard languages, the power struggles beneath the manifestation of *normativity* and *prescriptivism*, and the political processes behind the rise of *linguistic authorities* (see Milroy and Milroy 1985a, Joseph 1987, Crowley 1989, Cameron 1995, Gal and Woolard 2001b). Scholars have increasingly underlined that the motivations for standardization are "various social, political and commercial needs" and that "absolute standardization of a spoken language is never achieved" (Milroy and Milroy 1985a: 19). Accordingly, they have proposed "to speak more abstractly of standardization as an *ideology*, and a standard language as an idea in the mind rather than a reality – a set of abstract norms to which actual usage may conform to a greater or lesser extent" (Milroy and Milroy 1985a: 19).

Following that critical approach to the study of language planning, this chapter discusses both the usage of nonstandard orthographies and the standardization of orthography (including the creation of new writing systems and the reform of languages with a long written tradition) as activities both charged with sociopolitical meaning and carrying sociopolitical consequences. As mentioned above, Section 29.2 offers an overview of recent literature concerned with sociocultural considerations in relation to the study of orthography. Particular attention is given to studies that take on a historical perspective, either to enrich the analysis of contemporary orthographic issues or to explore the conditions under which a particular written system was selected and codified in the past, usually in the context of nation-building or (de)colonialization processes. Section 29.3 applies the theoretical and methodological tools presented in the two previous sections to a particular case study: the officialization of the Spanish orthography in mid-nineteenth-century Spain. Finally, Section 29.4 offers some concluding remarks.

29.2 The Sociolinguistics of Orthography

While orthographies are usually presented by linguists (and understood by the general public) as conventional systems, highly codified and standardized for the functional purpose of communication in writing, sociolinguistics has long showed that culture, politics and identity lie behind many aspects of orthographic design, implementation and usage (see Sebba 2007, 2009). Given the intricate relationship between orthography and the sociopolitical world, scholars have suggested understanding orthography not as a neutral technology but as social practice (see Sebba 2007; see also Jaffe et al. 2012). It is because orthography involves *variation* (both regarding script selection and spelling options) that orthographic practices can be used "to iconize difference at a wide range of linguistic levels *and* levels of social organization" (Sebba 2012: 7). As Jaffe, a visionary pioneer in the field, put it, "[o]rthographic choices and their interpretation are read as metalinguistic, socially conditioned phenomena which shed light on people's attitudes towards both specific language varieties and social identities and on the relationship between linguistic form and the social world in general" (Jaffe 2000b: 499). Building on the basic sociolinguistic principle that variation involves social meaning, in the last few decades sociolinguists and linguistic anthropologists have produced a systematic body of work that explores the connections between orthographic variation and social inequality, showing "how scriptural practices both index and constitute social hierarchies, identities and relationships and how in some cases, they become the focus for public debates around language ideologies" (Sebba 2012: 10).

In his monograph on the subject of spelling and society – a remarkable effort to systematize theoretical and methodological approaches to the sociolinguistics of orthography – Sebba (2007) wonders what the purpose of spelling might be. He explains, from a sociocultural standpoint, that

> we spell because orthography is part of the elaboration of our culture; because there is a natural tendency for all human activities which involve choice to take on social meaning; because literacy itself is embedded in and important to our culture and social actions, and orthography is essentially bound up with literacy.
>
> (Sebba 2007: 160)

It is social motivations and not just practical reasons, he claims, that drive "the compulsion to have a standardized, almost invariant system of orthography, with all the regulatory apparatus that that entails" (Sebba 2007: 159–60). Sebba's book explores five general areas in which the compulsion to orthographic standardization materializes: orthography as a source of identity formation, creation of writing systems, orthographic standardization in postcolonial situations, orthographic standardization of vernaculars, and orthographic reform. Drawing on Sebba's work, this review of the literature follows the same organization.

As mentioned above, a departing point of the social study of orthography is to understand it as social practice. The potential of orthographic variation to acquire extralinguistic significance leads us to explore how orthographic practices intertwine with issues of social identity and social representation. The nation-state context (the development of national identities through orthographic differentiation, whether in discourse or in practice) has been a privileged site of study in the field. Studies that take this approach include Ahmad (2012) on the alignment of Urdu and Hindi with Muslim and Hindu respectively as the outcome of a language ideological debate in late nineteenth-century India, and Vosters et al. (2012) on the discursive exploitation of orthographic features as markers of Southerners in the Low Countries (1750–1830), a discursive differentiation that does not correspond, however, with actual orthographic practices.

An interesting body of research in this area of investigation is the study of the social meaning of nonstandard orthographic practices (see Jaffe 2000a). Nonstandard spelling can be mobilized in order to construct alternative social groups as well as to index belonging to them. Examples of the sociopolitical significance of nonstandard orthographies are the social and symbolic value of spelling transgressions in German punk fanzines (Androutsopoulus 2000) or the politically laden use in Basque subculture of Basque orthographic conventions that differ from Spanish orthographic conventions when spelling Spanish words (Urla 1995). Often, the identities in question are unconventional or subversive because of the potential of nonstandard orthographies to "expose and thus call into question dominant language ideologies and the social hierarchies in which they are embedded" (Jaffe 2000b: 511). Conversely, "non-standard ideologies also always dramatize power and status differentials between language varieties and their speakers" (Jaffe 2000b: 498) because of “the powerful symbolic coupling of standard orthographies with linguistic and social authority” (Jaffe 2000b: 511). Thus, besides being a source of disruption of the hierarchical social order, nonstandard orthographies can inversely be interpreted as illegitimate deviations from the norm whose utilization – willingly or not – promotes the stigmatization of the groups associated with those nonstandard orthographic practices. In this sense, Jaffe (2012) and Preston (2000) offer insightful analyses of the use of nonstandard orthographies in scholars’ transcribing practices.

Another fruitful area to examine the sociopolitical nature of orthography and its history is the emergence of new writing systems. Unseth (2008), for instance, presents a collection of works on the sociolinguistics of script selection. Sebba (2007: 58–72) emphasizes that the introduction of writing in formerly oral languages (a process that responded to various political, economic and religious interests) was usually carried out by literate bilinguals who applied orthographic conventions from one language to another. Often the substituting language was that of the colonial ruler. In recent times, however, linguists “have been successful in creating a market for their services” (Sebba 2007: 73) as they have increasingly taken the role of language experts in orthographic development. Sebba questions the absolute need for linguistic expertise in this matter, and situates the rise of linguists as language planners at the crossroads between the professionalization of linguistics and the politicization of the spread of literacy (which has nowadays been declared a priority by many national and supranational organizations, such as UNESCO). An important early work on the emergence of writing systems, one that also promotes a critical reflection concerning the consequences of reducing oral languages to writing, is Mühlhäusler’s (1990) study on language and ideology regarding the introduction of literacy in the Pacific. Mühlhäusler discusses the negative repercussions of the emergence of writing during colonial times in the islands of Melanesia, Micronesia and Polynesia, among them the loss of linguistic heterogeneity and the shift from traditional modes to colonial ideas, ways of life and religion. He concludes that

> vernacular literacy is neither a ‘tame pursuit’ nor a neutral medium for recording pre-existing knowledge and experiences, but rather an agent of linguistic, religious and social change. It is best seen as a transitional phenomenon in all but a few large languages: on the one hand it prepares speakers for transition to reading skills in a non-local (typically metropolitan) language [...] [O]n the other hand literacy accelerates the transition from traditional to modern (westernized) societies. Past advocates of vernacular literacy in the Pacific have tended to overestimate the benefits and underestimate the dyseconomies of the process.
>
> (Mühlhäusler 1990: 203)

The introduction of writing systems and the subsequent standardization of the new orthographies are not only carried out during colonial periods, but are also emblematic processes of postcolonial politics. Sebba (2006), for instance, studies the script changes undergone by Tartar during the Soviet era (1922–91) and after the dissolution of the Soviet Union. Thomas (2007) analyzes the anticolonial and revolutionary symbolism of letter *k* and orthographic reform in the Philippines in the late nineteenth century. Similarly, Wyrod (2008) examines the success of the N'ko alphabet after French colonialization in West Africa. Now, if in general "orthographic choice is really about 'imagining' the past and the future of a community" (Schieffelin and Doucet 1994: 176), in postcolonial situations the sociopolitical tensions are particularly salient because in these contexts orthographic debates are also "deeply tied to issues of representation at both the national and international levels" (Schieffelin and Doucet 1994: 187). This holds true for the debates over the orthography of Haitian Creole studied by these authors. Since the mid-1920s onward, pro-phonemicists proposing a systematic orthography independent from French have confronted pro-etymologists advocating to maintain Kreyòl's orthography closely tied to the colonial language as well as intermediaries supporting a phonology-based orthographic system that also respects French conventions. Schieffelin and Doucet's influential article is an excellent example of how a discursive and sociopolitical analytical approach can enrich our understanding of the historical developments and debates over orthography in relation to the weight of particular social forces. As they put it,

> [o]rthographic debates when situated within the broader framework of language ideology – the cultural beliefs that underlie the language practices, choices, and attitudes of a people – can be seen as articulating historically grounded tensions between groups that do not hold equal shares in the social and political system. Often, these inequalities developed during colonial encounters and were maintained after the original colonists were no longer present.
>
> (Schieffelin and Doucet 1994: 187)

The previous quote can certainly be applied to many contexts of standardization of vernacular languages as well. In linguistic anthropology the concept of the vernacular usually refers to minority languages geographically located in a broader nation-state within which they may be recognized – or erased – at different levels. Orthographic standardization of minority languages may take a variety of forms (from sporadic, localized endeavors to planned, comprehensive actions) and involve diverse actors with their different shares of power (from state or regional governmental agencies to local language activists). Studied from a sociopolitical perspective, the actions and discourses that shape orthographic standards reveal explicit or implicit confrontations of political stances, economic projects and language ideologies. Examples of sociopolitical studies concerned with the orthography of minority languages are Álvarez Cáccamo and Herrero Valeiro (1996) (whose work focuses on the struggle over Galician identity vis-à-vis Portuguese and Spanish embedded in competing orthographic options), Guerini (2018) (with an analysis of the symbolic value of orthographic choices in public signage in Bergamasco, an unstandardized and unrecognized language in Italy) and Schwartz (2018) (whose study examines the pedagogical and cultural significance of orthography in Chiwere, a Native American language without fluent speakers that has been revitalized on the basis of written texts).

In the area of studies of minority languages and orthographic standardization, reference to Jaffe's (1996, 1999) work on Corsican is due. Her analysis of the symbolic meaning of the 1988 Corsican spelling contest is embedded in a broader examination of Corsican language activism that began in the 1970s coupled with regionalist political movements. Built on the intertwined examination of language practices, language ideologies and language political economy, Jaffe's study of Corsican orthography explores "the 'historically specific' and 'culturally shaped' nature of the form that resistance [to French language dominance] takes" (Jaffe 1996: 817). She concludes that orthographic standardization (and, more broadly, language planning in Corsica) is grounded on "a dominant ideology of linguistic value" that activates "a series of culturally conditioned responses to domination/authority which act as obstacles to the program of linguistic revitalization that planners wish to promote, and create new forms of linguistic insecurity and alienation" (Jaffe 1999: 246).

The last area of research that Sebba (2007: 132–56) identifies as a rich site for the study of spelling and society is the reform of the orthography of languages with an established written tradition. In this area of research, Baddeley and Voeste (2012b) gather studies on the development of national orthographies in early modern Europe, while Villa and Vosters (2015b) offer a collection of papers on orthographic conflicts over Dutch, German, Lithuanian, Macedonian, Portuguese and Spanish. Similarly, Bermel (2007) analyzes the history of Czech orthographic reforms, Johnson (2005) studies past and present language ideological debates over German, Portebois (2003) examines the politicization of spelling reform in nineteenth-century France, and Rothstein (1977) focuses on the 1930s debates over Polish orthographic reform. These studies show that orthographic reform is an activity particularly prone to generate confrontation and that "even slight modifications of an existing orthography can lead to an enormous outcry" (Sebba 2007: 154). This is so because orthographic features and orthographic systems become iconic embodiments of both the language itself and the country that it represents (of their present image and of their past glories). Moreover, the potential for orthographic reforms to spark public disputes derives from the fact that a multitude of interests are at stake: from the pedagogical aspirations of educators to the economic interests of publishers; from the political goals of governmental agencies to the material and symbolic interests of various social groups and organizations.

Indeed, the conceptualization of these controversies over orthography as "contexts under which language becomes an important theme for public debate as well as an important object for politicization" (Blommaert 1999: 427) has led a great number of studies in historical orthography (particularly, although not exclusively, in relation to orthographic reforms) to rely on Blommaert's crucial concept of *language ideological debate* (see, e.g., Johnson 2005, Bermel 2007, Ennis 2008, Ahmad 2012, Villa 2012, 2013, 2017, Villa and Vosters 2015b). Despite language being the center of public discussions, language ideological debates are not merely linguistic controversies. They are understood as emerging from broader sociopolitical processes and, therefore, both the debates themselves and their outcomes are seen as embedded in particular relationships of power, social hierarchies and forms of discrimination (Blommaert 1999: 3–4). Of crucial importance is Blommaert's discussion of the problem of historical research. Concerned with the analysis of texts instead of with the study of discourse, historical linguistics has privileged synchronic studies and focused on "language-related ideational phenomena [...] often seen as ideas which people just happen to have" (Blommaert 1999: 6). This analytical preference, Blommaert explains, has produced "an abstraction of the historical process in which the genesis of such ideational phenomena is contained, sometimes amounting, in fact, to a dehistorization of the phenomena" (Blommaert 1999: 6). Blommaert proposes, instead, to practice historical materialism, that is, to focus on

> the real historical actors, their interests, their alliances, their practices, and where they come from, in relation to the discourses they produce – where discourse is in itself seen as a crucial symbolic resource onto which people project their interest, around which they can construct alliances, on and through which they exercise power.
>
> (Blommaert 1999: 7)

This idea of historical research is the foundation that supports the case study presented in the next section, which examines the public debate that surrounded the officialization in 1844 of the spelling norms defended by the Royal Spanish Academy (RAE for its Spanish name, Real Academia Española). In the first part of Section 29.3, I offer a critical overview of the mainstream narrative of the history of the orthography of Spanish. Then, I analyze the debate between an association of elementary schoolteachers and prominent political and cultural figures in the 1840s in Madrid (Spain), explaining it in relation to a broader political debate over the centralization of the education system. Finally, I succinctly refer to the connections between the orthographic controversy in Spain and another language ideological debate over orthography that took place in Chile, also in the 1840s.

29.3 Orthography in History: The Case of the Spanish Language

In the last few decades, Spanish linguistic historiography has been producing a great amount of work on the orthographic ideas of both salient authors in the history of the Spanish language, such as Antonio de Nebrija, Gonzalo Correas or Andrés Bello, and other less prominent figures outside scholarly fields. Connected in a chronological manner, such orthographic milestones have formed a well-established narrative of the development of the Spanish orthography since the language became independent from Latin to the present day (see Rosenblat 1951, Marcos Marín 1979, Esteve Serrano 1982, Martínez Marín 1992, Martínez Alcalde 1999, 2010, Battaner Moro 2009, Berta 2017; for an analysis from a discursive and political perspective, see Godoy 2015). Today, this narrative of the history of the Spanish orthography has transcended academic and scholarly circles to become institutionalized through its incorporation into the orthographic books published by the RAE, whose popularity and selling success is well known (see RAE 1999, REA and Asociación de Academias de la Lengua Española [ASALE] 2010).

Briefly, this mainstream historical account begins with the standardizing efforts made by Alfonso X (1221–84), who is represented as the earliest codifier of the spelling of the Castilian vernacular. After that initial moment of the standardization process, the historical account continues to present a period of orthographic irregularity until the introduction of printing and the emergence of Spain's first great orthographer, Antonio de Nebrija (1444?–1522). Then, the sixteenth and seventeenth centuries appear as times of great instability, characterized by the existence of numerous orthographic treatises, ranging from the most conservative proposals to the most radical simplifications. This orthographic variability – the historical account concludes – ended with the creation of the RAE in 1713 and the imposition of its spelling norms in the nineteenth century (RAE and ASALE 2010: 30–33). In the dominant narrative, the officialization of the RAE's orthography is explained as the response to a radical, capricious simplification of the orthography intended by a group of teachers in Madrid. The queen – the historical account claims – had to intervene in order to stop this meddling of the teachers in the language and did so by imposing the RAE's orthography by royal decree in 1844 (RAE 1999: v–vi). This move would eventually result in the acceptance of this orthographic norm across the Spanish-speaking world.

By overemphasizing particular historical figures, even when contradicting informed research on the matter – see, for instance, Tuten and Tejedo-Herrero's clarification regarding the role of Alfonso X in the selection of Castilian and the codification of its orthography (Tuten and Tejedo-Herrero 2015) – this historical account creates a grand narrative that naturalizes the oversimplification of orthographic issues instead of accepting the complexity of each historical context and each orthographic outcome. In order to fill in the gaps of a history actually made of disconnected dots, the dominant narrative relies on two unifying threads. The first one is the presentation of the continuous conflict between two orthographic principles – phoneticism and etymologism – as the inner force that triggered the development of the Spanish orthography over time (see Martínez Alcalde 1999, 2010). Correspondence between phonemes and graphemes is taken to be the natural tendency of the Spanish language. Therefore, gradual simplification was the teleological principle that guided the changes toward that orthographic ideal. The second unifying thread is the significance of the creation of the RAE in 1713, to the extent that it is portrayed as a historical necessity. Represented as a milestone in the history of the Spanish language as a whole, the establishment of the institution is also considered to mark a 'before' and 'after' in the history of its orthography. So much so that the period before the RAE is commonly referred to as a chaotic or conflictive orthographic time, while the officialization of the institution's spelling norms in 1844 is presented as the highlight of the Spanish orthography (see Esteve Serrano 1982, RAE 1999, Martínez Alcalde 2010, RAE and ASALE 2019).

It is this particular moment in history – the officialization of the RAE's spelling norms in 1844 – that I revisit in the remainder of this section drawing on my previous work (Villa 2012, 2013, 2015, 2017). However, before delving into the case study itself, it seems useful to make a few comments concerning the two unifying threads of the dominant history of the Spanish language that I have presented in the previous paragraph. Regarding the first one, it may seem evident by now that from a sociopolitical, materialist perspective the opposition of *a priori* abstract categories necessarily results in an ahistorical analysis. Evidently, the clash between phoneticism and etymologism does not account for the heterogeneity of the actual proposals made by specific actors in concrete moments of the history of the Spanish language. In fact, this heterogeneity suggests that it would be better to conceive of the opposition between phoneticism and etymologism as a continuum of dynamic orthographic tendencies (that may vary even within one single author's work) than as a polarized, fixed dichotomy. In addition, and even more significantly, orthographic arguments can only acquire full (historical) meaning when they are contextualized due to the fact that in any given linguistic debate it is not orthographic principles that confront one another, but rather individuals and groups of individuals with their particular social positions, their political interests, their alliances and so on.

In relation to the second unifying thread – the representation of the RAE as a historical necessity, as the culmination of the Spanish orthography – I see this as the natural outcome of the teleological character of the historical account itself. However, this depiction of the institution involves several analytical problems. First, it is inaccurate to represent the creation of the RAE as a pivotal moment in the history of the Spanish orthography since, at the time of its foundation, the institution was not interested in the standardization of the orthography, given that its first spelling norms were subsidiary to the compiling of the dictionary (Martínez Alcalde 2010). Second, it is misleading to depict the RAE as a unitary, homogeneous, stable actor instead of as a collective of individuals who hold different political and linguistic ideas at various times – and even at the same time (see del Valle and Villa 2012). And finally, it is mystifying – and mythicizing – to take for granted the authority of the institution as a natural gift when, as I hope to show in the subsequent analysis, the attainment of this authoritative position resulted, in fact, from political actions and power alliances that took place in specific times and places with their particular social hierarchies and political dynamics (Villa 2013).

I move now to present the circumstances that surrounded the officialization of the Spanish orthography in mid-nineteenth-century Spain (for a more extensive treatment of the arguments in the rest of this section, I refer the reader to Villa 2012, 2013, 2015, 2017). At the beginning of the 1840s a group of teachers associated in the Literary and Scientific Academy of Elementary Education designed a simplified orthographic system and started to implement it in their schools.[2] Their phonology-based orthography consisted of 24 letters with the simplification of pairs of letters for the same sound, the substitution of digraphs with single letters and the elimination of silent letters (see Figure 29.1). As part of their implementation strategies, the teachers contacted the RAE in April 1843, urging the institution to endorse the reformed orthography. Quite the opposite, the RAE refused to support the teachers' simplification, arguing that

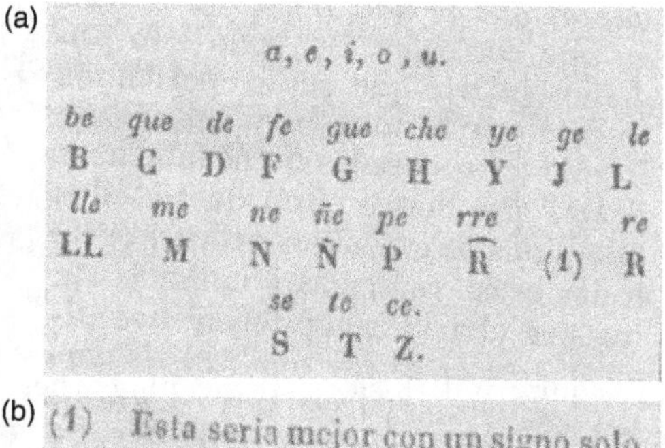
(a)

a, e, i, o, u.

be *que* *de* *fe* *gue* *che* *ye* *ge* *le*
B C D F G H Y J L
lle *me* *ne* *ñe* *pe* *rre* *re*
LL M N Ñ P R̂ (1) R
se *te* *ce.*
S T Z.

(b) (1) Esta seria mejor con un signo solo.

Figure 29.1 Reformed alphabet implemented by Madrid teachers in the 1840s (El Educador 1842: 4)

[2] In Spanish, Academia Literaria y Científica de Instrucción Primaria Elemental y Superior or, following the reformed orthography, Academia Literaria i Zientífica de Instruczion Primaria Elemental i Superior. This nongovernmental organization was established in 1840 on the basis of its predecessor (Academia de Profesores de Primera Educación). The Literary and Scientific Academy held monthly public meetings to discuss different matters regarding appropriate contents and teaching methodologies for elementary school children. It also organized teacher training workshops. Because of their loud and public opposition to the government, this institution was banned by royal order in 1853 (see Gil de Zárate 1855, Molero Pintado 1994, Villa 2013, 2017).

the innovations, as expressed in the response letter to the teachers, "*would result in serious inconveniences and no advantages.*" One year after this episode, the recently formed Council for Public Instruction (an organism created to oversee the public education system, which counted several members of the RAE among its representatives) asked Queen Isabella II (1830–1904) to intervene in the orthographic dispute. Agreeing with the petition, the queen signed a royal decree on April 25, 1844 that mandated the exclusive use of the RAE's orthography in Spain's schools, threatening to revoke the teaching licenses of those who disobeyed (Colección de leyes 1844: 629–30).

The officialization of the RAE's spelling norms intensified the language ideological debate over Spanish orthography. The teachers took actions to contest the imposition by moving the debate to the public sphere. For instance, they organized a public meeting in October 1844 to openly defend both their reformed orthography and their legitimacy to rule on linguistic issues related to education. Regarding the defense of their proposal, the teachers relied on a pedagogical argument to support their innovations because they trusted that the simplified orthography would facilitate the learning of reading and writing. Even more important than supporting their orthographic proposal, however, was the need for the teachers to defend their right to intervene in linguistic matters. The royal decree had legitimized the position of the RAE by representing it – in a legal document, no less – as a "respectable corporation that can measure the advantages and disadvantages of each variation and establish the way to carry out those that are truly useful" (Colección de leyes 1844: 630). Conversely, the teachers strategically relied on their experience teaching elementary school children in order not only to present themselves as a legitimate actor in the language debate, but also to discredit their political opponents:

> Is it likely that the government knows, understands and sees this situation? No sir, because it does not practice this profession. And what about the Council for Public Instruction? They do not either, for the same reason. And the Academy of the Spanish Language? They do not either, unless some of its members have practice teaching.
>
> (Academia Literaria y Científica de Instrucción Primaria 1844: 21)

This language ideological debate, beyond a struggle over authority in language, was a struggle over the control of education. In the central decades of the nineteenth century, Spain's politicians undertook an extensive nation-building project that intended to move the country (a formal imperial power that had lost the majority of its territories in the first third of the century) from absolutism and feudalism to a constitutional monarchy and an incipient capitalist system (see Suárez Cortina 2006, La Parra López et al. 2012, Pérez Ledesma and Saz 2014). The centralization of the administration (an important pillar of this nation-building process) was felt with particular intensity in the area of education since the public school system started to be conceived at that time as a powerful state mechanism to shape and control the citizenry (see Escolano Benito 2000, Ramírez Aisa 2003, Puelles Benítez 2010). As a result, independent groups, such as the Literary and Scientific Academy of Elementary Education, were losing decision-making power and influence over the educational market. This broader sociopolitical and economic context helps us to better understand the teachers' investment in a potentially controversial orthographic reform as well as the intensity with which they publicly opposed the officialization of the RAE's spelling norms. Needless to say, this controversy was not the only one – nor even the most intense one – in which the teachers were involved against the government. Indeed, their main warhorse had been the opposition to the normal schools whose establishment, starting in 1839, came to jeopardize the teacher's control over a significant niche of the educational market: teacher training (Gil de Zárate 1855, Molero Pintado 1994, Villa 2012, 2013). Their livelihood was at stake, and so the teachers displayed a number of strategies to resist the centralization of education ranging from open confrontation (through public meetings, publications and newspaper articles) to sabotage of governmental institutions, and even alignment with political opposition to the government coming from revolutionary groups.

While the teachers strategically utilized public confrontation and radical alliances to mobilize social forces against the government, the latter used state power (legal mechanisms, for instance) to blunt the teachers' resistance to the centralization of education. In order to fully understand the role of the orthographic debate in this context, it is important to point out that several members of the RAE were also politicians that held positions of responsibility in the government, many of them in the area of education (Zamora Vicente 1999). To name just the two most prominent figures, Francisco Martínez de la Rosa (1787–1862), the institution's director, was Secretary of State between 1844 and 1846 and, more crucially, Antonio Gil de Zárate (1793–1861) became General Director of Public Instruction at the end of 1843. The Council for Public Instruction (the agency that requested the queen's intervention in the orthographic debate) operated under the umbrella of the organism directed by Gil de Zárate. Given the close personal ties between the central administration and the RAE, the officialization of the Spanish orthography emerges as another battlefield in which the struggle over the control of education was fought.

In addition, the public debate became an excellent opportunity to reinforce the alliance between the RAE and the government. It also strengthened the image of the institution in the eyes of the country as Spain's linguistic authority, as an organization endorsed by the crown and the government, although independent from them. That alliance, as well as the consequent uplifting of the RAE and the consolidation of the standard language as a symbol of the nation, acquires full meaning when we go beyond the national context and look at the political dynamics in the international arena. As mentioned above, Spain had lost most of its colonial territory in Latin America between 1810 and 1825. However, the American process of independence was a political enterprise still very present in Spain's political and economic life in 1844 (Van Aken 1959, Cortada 1994). These circumstances urge us to mention, if only briefly, another language ideological debate over orthography that took place in Chile in parallel to the controversy between the RAE and the teachers in Madrid (Villa 2015).

The Chilean debate started in October 1843 when Domingo Faustino Sarmiento (1811–88), a well-known writer and intellectual exiled from Argentina, proposed a radical simplification of the orthography based on the American pronunciation, seeking to symbolically embody in the language the country's political emancipation (see Contreras 1993, Arnoux 2008, Ennis 2008). The public confrontation that ensued from his proposal ended with the imposition of a less radical simplification of the orthography, the one proposed by prominent grammarian, writer and politician Andrés Bello (1781–1865). This officialization of the Chilean orthography was ratified on April 25, 1844, coinciding with the imposition of the RAE's spelling norms in Spain. Similar to the Spanish language ideological debate, the Chilean controversy over orthography touches on several sociopolitical issues of local, national and international scope. First, the positioning of intellectuals in the public and cultural arena (this was not, far from it, the only heated debate involving Sarmiento that flooded the Chilean press). Second, the emergence of a national education system under the umbrella of the University of Chile, whose rector was Andrés Bello, at the time when Sarmiento was Director of the Normal School. Third, the sociocultural relationship between Chile and Spain; in fact, Sarmiento's proposition to mark America's emancipation in the spelling system and his contempt for Spain's literary scene and the RAE were the center of the public debate sparked by his simplification proposal.

I bring up the Chilean controversy over orthography for two reasons. On the one hand, this episode attests to the value of placing politics at the center of the study of language. Indeed, the Chilean orthographic conflict highlights the need to examine the individual actors participating in a given language debate – their alliances and interests – in order to fully understand the development of specific linguistic features and ideas about language in a particular moment and time. On the other hand, the material and symbolic connections between the orthographic conflicts in Chile and Spain draw attention to the significance of the new postcolonial order as a key historical development to construe this particular moment in the history of the Spanish orthography (Villa 2015). The need for Spain to reposition itself vis-à-vis the American republics (and vice versa) in a postcolonial era is crucial for an in-depth analysis of these language ideological debates. It is that underlying political process which gives full meaning, for instance, to the coincidence of the date on which the officialization of the orthography in both countries took place. April 25, 1844, was not only the day that the spelling norms defended by Bello and the

RAE were officially sanctioned, but also – and more importantly – the day that Queen Isabella II signed in Madrid the treaty of peace and friendship between Chile and Spain. That legal document officially reinstated, for the first time after Chile's independence, political and commercial relationships between the two countries (Tratado de paz 1846).

In sum, my analysis of the officialization of the RAE's orthography in this section has attended to the particular sociopolitical circumstances of the mid-nineteenth century instead of explaining it as the natural development of the historical confrontation between orthographic forces. I have concluded that the events that surrounded the officialization of the RAE's spelling norms in 1844 were shaped by a complex intersection of national and international political interests and alliances. These include Spain's efforts to centralize education as part of an intense nation-building project which was, in turn, linked to broader political changes brought about by the fall of the Spanish empire and the death of Spain's last absolutist monarch. They also include the repercussions of those large-scale policies at a local level (for instance, changes in the labor practices of elementary schoolteachers in Madrid) as well as at an institutional and symbolic level (e.g. the position of key members of the RAE in the government, which resulted in the consolidation of the institution as the linguistic authority of the nation).

Following a historical materialist approach, I have contextualized the orthographic proposals made by all language brokers in relation to their social positions and political agendas. In so doing, I hope to have enriched our understanding of this specific moment of particular salience of the Spanish orthography in history. Above all, I hope to have shown its political complexity by unveiling the agency of both the teachers and the members of the RAE and their strategic moves to impose their spelling norms as a means to consolidate their position in specific national and international spaces. In addition, I hope that my analysis contributes to exposing how the decontextualized mainstream grand narrative of the history of the Spanish orthography reproduces the standard language ideology by erasing the struggles beneath its imposition and by naturalizing a depoliticized image of the linguistic authorities that, in fact, as we have seen, struggled to impose it. Needless to say, this was not an isolated episode but one of many instances in the history of the RAE that show the efforts made by its members to position the institution as a linguistic authority in the Spanish-speaking world, that is, as a cultural institution of reference in different domestic and global political spaces.[3]

[3] See Fries (1989), del Valle and Gabriel-Stheeman (2002) and Senz and Alberte (2011). See also Medina (2013) for an exploration of the political environment of unrest in which the RAE was established and recognized. See Garrido Vílchez (2012) and Villa (2013) for analyses of the significance of the 1857 Ley Moyano, which imposed the RAE's grammatical and orthographic norms and textbooks in Spain's education system. See del Valle (2010, 2011, 2013) for studies of the RAE's agenda in different moments of its history from the second half of the nineteenth century onward.

29.4 Conclusion

This chapter has presented the main theoretical and methodological trends in the study of orthography from a discursive and sociopolitical perspective. Scholars working with this approach take a deliberate stance to discuss issues of dominance and power, access and distribution of resources, emergence and circulation of language ideologies, as well as perpetuation of social inequality. From a discursive and sociopolitical perspective, an orthography is no longer understood as an undisputed technical device but rather seen as the result of historical struggles between social actors with different political agendas and different amounts of power to influence the outcomes of the debates. Consequently, orthographies are studied as social practice due to the potential for orthographic proposals, choices and features to acquire social meaning.

After offering a general overview of the theories, methods and literature in the field, I presented a case study of the Spanish language: the language ideological debate surrounding the officialization of the RAE's orthography in 1844. I explained this milestone in the history of the language as resulting from a complex intersection of local, national and international political conditions. My research explicitly questions the dominant narrative of the history of the Spanish orthography regarding its aseptic account of this specific episode, in particular, and the dehistoricized image of the language that it promotes, in general. I hope to have shown that orthographies carry their history in their materiality; that they embody all the past actions that contributed to their current configuration, even when the historical struggles that shaped them are imperceptible or silenced in the present. It is the researcher's task to shed light on the dark spots of the history of the orthography by examining how in each specific context of analysis orthographic changes, debates and ideas were bonded to concrete power relationships, social orders and language ideologies.

30

Transmission and Diffusion

Gijsbert Rutten, Iris Van de Voorde and Rik Vosters

30.1 Introduction

Theories of language change often focus on the various ways in which innovations spread from one language user to another. Following Labov (2007), *transmission* and *diffusion* are two crucial concepts in this context. On the one hand, transmission is used for changes in language passed down and incrementally amplified from one generation to the next, where innovations move in a similar direction across generations. Diffusion, on the other hand, is used to signal changes across communities, with innovations spreading, for instance, from one dialect group or one part of a language area to another, and involving imperfect adult language learning. Since their introduction, both concepts have gained wide currency in sociolinguistics, but the implications and relevance of this twofold distinction for orthographic change have not been assessed in great detail.

Exploring the relevance of the transmission versus diffusion dichotomy is exactly what we set out to do in this *Handbook* chapter. Departing from the classic definitions of transmission and diffusion by Labov in Section 30.2, we evaluate their applicability to diachronic orthography, comparing them to other, related concepts, to a large extent based on the work of Milroy (2007). We then move on to discuss examples of transmission (Section 30.3) and diffusion (Section 30.4). In Section 30.5, we shift our attention to another layer of orthographic variation and change, above the notion of the community that underpins transmission and diffusion, namely the layer of multiple standards in situations of pluricentricity. We then move to a broader reflection comparing diachronic perspectives on spelling variation and change to other instances of language change, while discussing the issue of transmission versus diffusion within the larger framework of standardization and the development of linguistic norms within and across speech communities over time (Section 30.6). Section 30.7 concludes.

In line with our own research expertise, we adopt a historical sociolinguistic approach to the topic outlined above, delving into several examples of regionally or socially motivated language change. As such, we do not only look at the peculiarities of spelling as a learned behavior, but also explore the link between orthographic change, diffusion and supralocalization, which offers clear implications for the study of standardization as a historical process. We argue against a 'tunnel view' of the standardization process, where regional writing traditions lead to one clear and exclusive national standard. Instead, we focus on how such regional standards actually give rise to a more multilayered sociolinguistic landscape, as is the case for many pluricentric languages. To evaluate the different theoretical concepts discussed in this chapter, we draw on different case studies from our own research on Dutch language history, but also from case studies in German and English historical sociolinguistics. By taking this cross-linguistic perspective, we explore to which extent issues related to the diffusion and transmission of orthographic change are similar across languages, pointing to interesting avenues for comparative historical sociolinguistic work and applications to other languages and language families.

30.2 Transmission, Diffusion and Writing Traditions

The two main models of language change discussed by Labov (2007) are transmission and diffusion, which differ in a number of ways. The most important difference is the type of language learning implied in the model. Transmission involves native-language acquisition by children, ensuring continuity across generations. Children are seen as capable of replicating faithfully the language of their parents' generation so that the phonological system – Labov's theory primarily deals with sound change – of each new generation copies that of the previous generation. This does not exclude change, quite the contrary in fact, but where change occurs it is usually in the same direction across the generations, for example, by generalizing an innovation to more phonetic contexts than before. Labov (2007: 246) calls this process *incrementation*. Transmission and incrementation thus lead to internal change, that is to say, change from within the system of the language, also termed change 'from below': properties of the system are transmitted to new generations who may increment these to new contexts. This first model of language change ties in with the tree model used in historical linguistics (Schleicher 1853), which also works on the combined assumptions of intergenerational transmission and increasing difference to other languages as a result of internal change. It may be clear that this model is primarily and perhaps only applicable to relatively stable and homogenous speech communities.

Social changes and occurrences such as famine, war and migration may render communities less stable and less homogenous, and may foster contact between speech communities. In such contact situations, language change occurs through the diffusion of forms from one community to the other. Since this involves the importation of forms from other language systems, language change occurs 'from above'. In the prototypical case, this involves adult learning, which is often imperfect. This means that specific sounds, for example, may be borrowed, but the intricate phonological system ruling these sounds in the donor language will remain obscure to the adult learners, as such intricacies are generally only learnable by children. In other words, only some properties diffuse. This kind of diffusion across communities, as opposed to transmission within communities, ties in with the wave model in traditional historical linguistics (Schmidt 1872).

Labov's approach has given rise to much research on innovation and change, largely on synchronic data, and it has subsequently been criticized and refined, for example by Cheshire et al. (2011), Stanford and Kenny (2013), Tagliamonte and Denis (2014). Cheshire et al. (2011: 156) consider it to be a useful toolkit for the study of language change, and this is also the perspective that we take. We ask whether transmission and diffusion, though primarily based on sound change in the present, are useful concepts in the study of diachronic orthography. One could argue that this is a curious question, as orthography – and more generally writing – is a much more conscious act than speaking, and moreover not part of natural language acquisition but exclusively learnt through instruction (Coulmas 2013: 98). From this observation, it would follow that the distinction between internal changes 'from below' and changes 'from above' does not hold: all orthography being 'from above', diffusion would be the only concept needed. The orthographic systems of European languages are furthermore not bound specifically to their respective communities. On the contrary, many communities have adopted the Latin script and Latin-based phoneme–grapheme correspondences, after which the writing system was adapted in order to represent sounds not part of the Latin phoneme inventory (Coulmas 2002). In this sense, orthography can be seen as one colossal contact phenomenon, as a technique imported through diffusion from another language. We argue, however, that orthographic change can often be modeled in much the same way as 'normal' language change: it frequently follows an S-curve, for example, and is subject to a range of internal and external factors (see Sections 30.4 and 30.5). As we discuss, orthographic practices are also not only the result of explicit instruction, but can equally be picked up during reading in a less conscious manner (see Subsection 30.3.1). It does therefore not seem justified to treat orthography differently from other language levels *a priori*. In addition, we argue in Section 30.3 that instances of transmission can also be found in the history of orthography.

Even if we treat orthography as a regular language phenomenon akin to phonology and morphosyntax, Labov's approach comes with one serious drawback. The distinction between transmission and diffusion is based on the ability to define concrete and separable language communities, that is communities of language users with shared sets of norms. Transmission and incrementation take place within such communities, whereas diffusion is a contact phenomenon transcending the limits of communities. The two processes can be distinguished particularly in comparative analyses of well-defined and fairly homogenous communities with different migration and settlement histories (Tagliamonte and Denis 2014). But communities themselves can be multilingual, bringing in language contact as an intrinsic property (see Cheshire et al. 2011). More generally, contact should be treated as a normal phenomenon in language histories affecting any community, if only because early and late modern population growth in northwestern Europe can often only be explained by in-migration, as until recently death rates outnumbered birth rates, particularly in urban areas (Milroy 2007: 150). At the same time, delineating language communities can be challenging in the case of historical periods for which sufficient contextual information is lacking. Labov (2007: 348) also acknowledges that his concept of the community may be strongly influenced by the present-day North American communities that he has worked on, and he points out that European dialectology usually focuses on the diffusion of variants in historical dialect areas, from one region to the other, less so on transmission through incrementation.

Milroy (2007) introduces a distinction similar to Labov's (2007) transmission and diffusion, while placing contact at the heart of the matter. Diffusion can be compared to *supralocal* changes, which are available 'off the shelf': they seem to travel easily from community to community, over large territories, and are picked up by speakers across the language area, or even across the globe (see also Cheshire et al. 2011). This also means that direct contact between speakers is not necessary. The sociolinguistic profile of such changes is still under-researched (Milroy 2007: 162), but obvious present-day examples are popular expressions such as *be like* (see Tagliamonte and Denis 2014). Transmission occurs within *local*, close-knit networks and communities, where intense, direct and ongoing contact enables speakers to replicate the fine-grained constraints that regulate the variable system. Milroy and Milroy (1985b: 363) have emphasized the importance of language *maintenance* in such local, high-contact settings. Local changes occur when the network structure changes, or through contact with other networks and communities via peripheral network members with relatively loose ties.

Labov (2007) focuses on the difference between children's and adults' ability to learn linguistic rules. Milroy's (2007) view also has implications for acquisition, but it is not a central theme, since maintenance within networks affects both children and adults. The Milrovian contact-centered view does not assign different models of language change to different age groups. Interestingly, Stanford and Kenny (2013) argue that density of interaction is in fact sufficient for a computational model of Labov's (2007) results, and can explain the outcomes of transmission and diffusion without taking into account possible language acquisition differences between children and adults. Another reason to not accept the difference between children and adults lies in the inherent reversibility of orthography: anyone can take the time to learn the phonetic and/or phonological intricacies underlying a specific spelling system, and usually language users can return to their writings in order to amend the spelling. There is no critical threshold for the acquisition of orthographic rules, as other factors can, of course, also play a role in the acquisition of orthography.

For the present chapter, we depart from the notion of *writing traditions*, particularly from regionally bound orthographic practices emerging in the course of the medieval period and undergoing changes throughout medieval and postmedieval times. In European settings, among the most pervasive and significant changes are without any doubt *supralocalization* and subsequent *standardization* (Nevalainen and Tieken-Boon van Ostade 2006, Rutten 2016b), understood as the increase of the geographical span of certain variants at the expense of other variants, moving toward a more focused variety (Le Page and Tabouret-Keller 1985).[1] In line with the European research tradition, we take *diffusion* to be the main source of orthographic change, defining it in general terms as the spread of innovations through the language area as a result of contact (and not restricting it to adult learning effects across communities). We avoid *transmission* in the traditional sense as much as possible as it depends on the debatable notion of homogenous communities, although we also claim that it may be a useful concept in specific sociohistorical contexts: these include explicit instruction in schools, for example, in which orthographic norms are consciously transmitted to the next generation, but also in close-knit networks of adults. We prefer to call this phenomenon 'transmission' instead of 'maintenance', as it often involves educational settings, and also because new orthographic norms may be introduced and transmitted before any kind of maintenance is logically possible.

30.3 Transmission

30.3.1 Transmission through Instruction

As we already discussed, in general, orthography represents explicitly learnt behavior. Although there are language users who largely acquire reading and

[1] See also Chapter 13, this volume, for a discussion on standardization and supralocalization. The latter is also discussed in Chapter 21, Chapter 25 and, although briefly, Chapter 4, this volume.

writing skills independently through self-teaching, the acquisition of reading and writing usually involves explicit instruction by someone who is already experienced. The key issue here is the transmission of conventions, without which continuity in the written tradition would not exist. Like today, transmission of orthographic conventions was institutionalized in medieval and postmedieval European history, with monasteries and schools providing the typical contexts where children, adolescents and adults learnt to spell (Boekholt and De Booy 1987: 1–9). In addition, home teaching resulted in reading and writing skills among a larger part of the population, including women, although it should be noted that many places also offered schools for girls (Boekholt and De Booy 1987: 30).

Apart from the observable continuity in writing traditions, another piece of indirect evidence of transmission comes from the extensive metalinguistic traditions found all over Europe. The Dutch, German, English, French, Italian, Spanish and Portuguese grammatical traditions begin in the sixteenth century, or just a bit earlier, and orthography is a prominent topic therein (Carvalhão Buescu 2000 for Portuguese, Dibbets 2000 for Dutch, Esparza Torres 2000 for Spanish, Kristol 2000 for French, Marazzini 2000 for Italian, Rössing-Hagar 2000 for German and Verrac 2000 for English). The sources testify to the practice of orthographic transmission, but the general problem with analyzing transmission in this way is similar to the problem connected to the institutional and family settings mentioned above: we can assume metalinguistic texts played a role in the transmission of orthographic conventions, as we can assume children and adults learnt to read and write through instruction by parents and peers, but in general we lack detailed information about the exact ways in which conventions were transmitted to new languages users. For example, we do often not know whether extant metalinguistic texts were actually used in the historical classroom, and if so, which texts exactly, and to what extent and how the teacher made use of them (Vandenbussche 2007b: 29). With respect to the normative grammatical tradition of the early and late modern period (approximately sixteenth to nineteenth centuries), research is in fact quite skeptical of direct influence on patterns of language use (see Rutten et al. 2014, and Anderwald 2016 and the references therein).

The observable continuity in orthographic conventions in itself provides evidence of transmission, but the conclusion, for example, that <f> and <v> have been used for labiodental fricatives throughout history, does not generate much insight into how this convention was transmitted. Nonetheless, discontinuity or divergence from common norms can indirectly reveal teaching practices. The variable use of <h> in Middle English sources, including both deletion of expected <h> and prothesis of <h> in vocalic onsets, strongly suggests that speakers who lacked the phoneme /h/ had been taught to write <h> or had seen it written in words where they would normally not pronounce /h/. Milroy (1992a: 199) lists many thirteenth-century examples from East

Anglia including forms of the verb 'to have' such as *adde*, *adden*, *aue*, and also *ate* for *hate*, *is* for *his*, *om* for *home* and many more, as well as the addition of 'unhistorical' *h* in words such as *ham* for *am*, *his* for *is* and *hure* for *our*. This kind of discontinuity, resulting from a conflict between pronunciation and orthographic conventions, can itself be quite continuous: Hundt (2015: 97), for example, discusses words such as *as* for *has*, *ealth* for *health*, and also *ham* for *am* and *hare* for *are* in English private letters from 1846.

Similar instances of *h*-dropping and *h*-prothesis can be found in Middle Dutch texts, in particular from the southwest of the language area such as Flanders, and these writing practices also appear to have been continued into the early modern period. Rutten and van der Wal (2014: 24–25) report on a range of variable features found in seventeenth-century private letters from the Zeeland region in the southwest of the present-day Netherlands. Apart from prevocalic deletion of <h> as in *andt* for *handt* meaning 'hand' and prevocalic prothesis as in *hacht* for *acht* meaning 'eight', they mention two additional and related effects of teaching an orthographic system with <h> to language users who lack /h/ in the spoken language. One of the historical Dutch pronunciations of the letter <h> is [haː], rendered [aː] by speakers lacking /h/. The letter <a> is, however, also rendered [aː]. This means that for *h*-less language users, the alphabet provides two graphemes with the same phonetic value, which led seventeenth-century letter-writers from Zeeland to substitute <a> for <h> as in *aebben* instead of *hebben* 'have', as well as use <h> for <a> as in *hpril* for *april* 'April'.

These English and Dutch examples demonstrate divergences from what was presumably transmitted, and they thus provide indirect evidence of teaching practices. There are, however, also historical sociolinguistic situations where explicit transmission can be better reconstructed, together with its effects on patterns of language use. What is needed is (1) evidence of actual teaching practices, and (2) a well-defined, real or imagined language community. To measure the effect of explicit transmission, we also need (3) a balanced corpus of original sources. Requirement 1 is without doubt the hardest to meet. Archival sources fulfilling requirements 1 and 2 are discussed, for example, by Van der Feest Viðarsson (2017), who analyzes Icelandic student essays from the nineteenth century. These are produced within a well-defined educational community setting, and corrected by the teachers, providing evidence of corrective attitudes and practices.

An excellent opportunity to study transmission through instruction is provided by the new Dutch language policy developed around 1800 in the context of nation-state building, which resulted in official rules for the spelling and grammar of Dutch, published in 1804 and 1805 (Rutten 2019). At a time when the nationalist ideology started to supersede older, regional identities and was politicized into a nation-building project in the first decades of the nineteenth century, the new language policy was connected to the simultaneous reorganization of the field of education, which led to a national system of school inspection (Schoemaker and Rutten 2019). The extensive archives of the school inspection show a profound awareness of the language policy among teachers and school inspectors alike, and provide evidence that, already in the first decade of the nineteenth century, many schoolteachers made an effort to transmit the newly devised prescriptions to their pupils. Schoemaker and Rutten (2019) and Rutten et al. (2020) show that schoolbooks almost immediately shifted to the new orthographic norms, again suggesting a high awareness of these new norms. The explosion of new schoolbooks and of revised editions of old books also implies general exposure to the new orthography. Furthermore, corpus studies of private letters, diaries and regional newspapers from before and after the new policy show a great influence of the new orthography on the writing practices of individual language users, even in private writings (Krogull 2018). We can assume language users adhered to new orthographic norms both to show erudition and to signal loyalty to the nation-building endeavor. For a range or spelling variables, an almost complete shift from older conventions to the new prescriptions can be found. The fact that newspapers quickly shift again implies that exposure to written language often implied exposure to the new rules (Krogull 2018).

The Dutch case of the decades around 1800 shows that the transmission of orthographic norms can be fruitfully studied if archival sources are available providing evidence of norm transmission as well as norm acceptance in language use (requirements 1 and 3 mentioned above). The ideological background is the official effort to create, through the educational system, a homogenous community constituted by the inhabitants of the Dutch nation-state (requirement 2).

30.3.2 Transmission within Networks and Communities

As explained in the previous subsection, we do not limit transmission to child language acquisition. We should rather investigate whether certain adult contact situations outside the educational settings discussed in Subsection 30.3.1 may count as instances of transmission. Close-knit networks and communities constitute possible sociohistorical contexts in which orthographic practices are transmitted from one language user to the other, either as instances of orthographic maintenance or as examples of orthographic change (requirement 2). In the absence of explicit instruction, requirement 1 cannot be met, which shifts the burden of proof to empirical sources demonstrating norm enforcement (requirement 3). Nevalainen and Raumolin-Brunberg (2016: 220–21) discuss language variation and change as found in English letters related to the sixteenth-century Johnson merchant family network. They show how the language use of some individuals within this network seems to pattern similarly with respect to six morphosyntactic changes in progress (e.g. use of single negation); they do not discuss spelling. Interestingly, the similarities appear to follow the social pattern of master–apprentice bonds. The sociolinguistic profile of the London-based merchant, John Johnson, is closely matched by his apprentice based in Calais, Henry Southwick. Likewise, Johnson's relative Anthony Cave has a profile similar to that of his apprentices Richard Johnson and Ambrose Saunders. Nevalainen and Raumolin-Brunberg (2016: 221) argue that this shows that generational transmission not only takes places from parents to children, but also from masters to apprentices.

Studies that focus on spelling transmission include Sairio (2009) and Conde-Silvestre (2019). Sairio (2009: 226–92) seeks evidence of network-based orthographic similarities in the eighteenth-century Bluestocking network around Elizabeth Montagu. An important conclusion is that correlations between network strength and spelling choices are not strong, and that other factors such as social position, gender and the type of relationship between writer and addressee are more important. Conde-Silvestre (2019) analyzes the fifteenth-century Stonor letters, a collection of English letters centered on Sir Thomas Stonor II. Conde-Silvestre (2019) argues that the letter-writers constituted a community of practice (CoP) (Eckert 2000) as they were all engaged in the same endeavor of maintaining the feudal system known as *enfeoffment*. He compares the spelling in these letters to a related collection of letters, also part of the Stonor collection, though not produced by people participating in the same system of *enfeoffment*. For a number of spelling variables, Conde-Silvestre (2019) shows that the language of the CoP is more focused, and thus less variable, clearly suggesting orthographic norm enforcement.

Metalinguistic networks and communities constitute another context in which orthographic convergence may occur. It is traditionally claimed that medieval scribes and early modern printers advanced spelling convergence (see also Voeste 2007a). Rogos (2013), Rutkowska (2013b) and Tyrkkö (2013) demonstrate that this convergence can be interpreted as a function of the scribes and printers being part of communities of practice. Tyrkkö (2013) analyzes 124 English books published by 88 different printers between 1500 and 1700, and shows a remarkable decline of spelling variation. Rogos (2013) focuses on fifteenth-century scribes copying one of Chaucer's *Canterbury Tales* and the "centrifugal tendencies" (Rogos 2013: 118) characterizing consonant spelling and abbreviations. Rutkowska (2013b) makes similar claims for sixteenth-century printers based in London. She also argues that in order to account for focusing, also diachronically, we need to consider that early printers operated within communities of practice at three different levels: at the most local level, people collaborated within printing houses; in addition, different printers were active at the same time, part of the same guild, and often had their offices in the same street or neighborhood; finally, within these communities, particular ways of presenting texts were also transmitted to younger generations.

A fruitful way to study metalinguistic transmission is by focusing on variants that were nonexistent or very low-frequency at the time when they were prescribed in metalinguistic publications. McLelland (2014: 266) shows that the German seventeenth-century grammarian Schottelius advocated *kk*-spellings in words such as *wekken* 'to wake' (compare present-day German *wecken*). For about one generation, quite a few elitist language commentators and literary authors followed this practice, but by the final decades of the seventeenth century, *kk* had already disappeared again from spellings like the example above. Flemish grammarians of the eighteenth century represent a similar case (Vosters et al. 2012, Vosters and Rutten 2015). They prescribed a complex system of diacritics to distinguish etymologically different *e*- and *o*-sounds. Here, too, the spelling was taken over primarily by other language commentators and a limited number of printers. Such cases are indicative of transmission processes within professional communities.

30.4 Diffusion

So far, we have singled out certain sociohistorical contexts that may be analyzed from the perspective of transmission. In this section, we focus on the more general process of diffusion, in particular on three main types, that is diffusion across regions, across social groups, and across genres and contexts. We limit ourselves, in the context of this chapter, to a few illustrative examples. Since language is seen as a variable social system in our historical sociolinguistic approach, a main concern for diachronic orthography is to gain access to sizable corpora of historical sources, as equally as possible distributed across social variables such as region, social rank and gender. In addition, it is important to compare similar genres and/or registers, produced in similar contexts and with similar purposes, as it is well-known that different spelling systems have historically been used for different genres and/or registers: Salmon (1999) discusses differences between print and manuscript spelling in the history of English, and Rutkowska and Rössler (2012: 225–26) refer to the so-called 'double spelling standard' in eighteenth-century English, when authors, grammarians included, used different orthographies in their private letters and printed texts.

30.4.1 Regional Diffusion

Studying regional diffusion requires substantial sources from various regions, preferably from similar genres, and where possible from different times. Relative proportions of variants at one moment in time can of course, in line with the apparent time construct, indicate an ongoing change, but one advantage of historical sociolinguistics is that it is possible to study language change in real time. Focusing on printed sources, Rössler (2005) analyzes regional diffusion in a corpus of texts originating from Bavaria, in southern Germany, and Austria. The corpus comprises various genres, organized into two major types: religious texts and secular texts. The sources date back to the sixteenth, seventeenth and eighteenth centuries, when religious conflicts and, in connection with these, religious texts were significant, and when orthographic supralocalization occurred along with metalinguistic reflection, while regional writing traditions remained important. The sources are localizable based on the places where they were printed; the cities taken into account are Vienna, Graz, Klagenfurt, Salzburg, Linz, Innsbruck, Munich and Passau. Rössler explains that many more historical actors were involved in text production than just the author: books were usually printed in offices with multiple typesetters and proofreaders so that the number of people responsible for the language of the final product exceeded the number of authors. Rössler even argues that typesetters and proofreaders influenced the spelling and morphology of a text more strongly than the author, at least until the individual author gained significance as a cultural figure from the middle of the eighteenth century onward. The text samples in the corpus are 4,000 to 5,000 words on average, per genre, per three-decade period and per city, resulting in a corpus of 437,279 words.

The principled setup of the corpus allows Rössler to perform detailed analyses of the gradual reduction of variation characteristic of the period. This reduction takes place at various levels: the number of competing variants decreases, but also the number of competing regional writing traditions. The latter development, in particular, signals supralocalization. Crucial in the analysis of such diachronically diverse writing traditions is the empirical baseline evidence against which the orthographic changes are measured. This can only be a reliable historical phonological reference system (see Elmentaler 2003: 97). On the basis of such a system, Rössler helpfully distinguishes between various levels of analysis. The lowest level is that of the concrete *variants* found in textual sources. Texts are often not homogeneous, displaying several variants for one phoneme. The individual variants of a text taken together constitute its *writing variety* (*Schreibvarietät*). The aggregate of multiple localizable writing varieties taken together constitute the *writing variety of an area* (*Schreibvarietät eines Raums*), which we can also call *regional writing traditions*. Regional diffusion in this case means that a variant or the variants used in a given text are considered to be part of a different regional writing tradition than the text itself.

While regional diffusion in orthography may be seen as a phenomenon characteristic of medieval and early modern times, pre-dating the advent of standardization impulses, various studies of historical Dutch have shown that particularly manuscript sources from more recent times may also show intriguing patterns of regional diffusion, often in direct connection with standardization and/or language planning. Vosters et al. (2012) and Vosters and Rutten (2015) show how Flemish administrative sources from the early nineteenth century display an orthographic shift within only six years, namely between 1823 and 1829. These years represent the beginning and the end of the Dutchification policy during the United Kingdom of the Netherlands (1814–30). The oldest sources have an average of about 42 percent of spelling variants usually considered typically southern, that is, Flemish. By 1829, after just six years, these variants have decreased to a mere 24 percent in usage, while the typically northern, that is, Dutch forms have diffused further among southern writers.

Regional diffusion often implies the introduction of graphemes and/or grapheme–phoneme correspondences exogenous to the region to which the variants are diffusing. The result is a further widening of the gap between the spoken and the written language. Rutten and van der Wal (2014: 19–74) demonstrate this on the basis of an analysis of the interplay of phonology and orthography in the *Letters as Loot Corpus*, comprising seventeenth- and eighteenth-century Dutch private letters. One example concerns the representation of etymologically different *e*-sounds, where one area, namely Zeeland, maintains the historical difference between so-called sharplong *e*, deriving from Germanic diphthongs, and the so-called softlong *e*, which are the product of vowel lengthening, while another region, that is, Holland, has a merger. Various regional writing traditions coexisted in the seventeenth and eighteenth centuries: a southern tradition incorporating the etymological difference in the spelling, and various northern traditions indicating the merger by adopting morphemic or syllabic spelling principles (see Rutten and Vosters 2013). The southern writing tradition was backed up by metalinguistic discourse and became officially standardized in 1804 (see Subsection 30.3.1). In the meantime, however, many letter-writers from Zeeland had shifted to the merging spelling systems characteristic of Holland. The example shows that the regional diffusion of orthographic practices can lead writers to disregard phonological differences that they maintain in their spoken language even if presumably prestigious metalanguage promoted an orthography in line with their speech.

30.4.2 Social Diffusion

Older manuscripts, such as medieval administrative texts, are often localizable and thus enable research on regional diffusion. Social diffusion is a more difficult topic when it comes to the availability of representative sources. It is not only essential to identify the actual or main author of a text, in the case of multiple authorship; it is also necessary to identify the author in terms of relevant social characteristics such as position or rank within a network, community or in society at large, level of education, degree of participation in the written culture, gender, age or generation, religious beliefs and so on. This requires ardent sociohistorical research and, admittedly, some sheer luck. A diversity of social characteristics in the sources, imperative for a comparison across social variables, can be reached by focusing on texts 'from below', that is on genres that were widely produced and used by large portions of historical populations, also from more humble social backgrounds, such as letters and diaries (Elspaß et al. 2007, van der Wal and Rutten 2013). More easily available sources, such as literary texts, are often bound to specific social groups, for example well-educated men. However, texts 'from below' were more often reused or thrown away, and their authors have left fewer traces in the archives, which impedes research on their social characteristics (Elspaß 2012b: 159).

Rössler (2005), discussed above, circumvents the issue of authorship by focusing on the place of printing. This enables him to analyze the influence of religion on orthographic choices. A major change in his materials is the gradual disappearance of Upper German spellings in his corpus of Upper German texts, signaling the ongoing supralocalization in German orthography. This change is, however, halted or temporarily reversed in the seventeenth century during the intense Catholic Counter-Reformation. In this specific sociohistorical context, a regional writing tradition with Upper German elements came to index locally supported Catholicism. Later in the century, this effect disappeared, and supralocalization advanced.

When there is enough information about authors and their social profile, meaningful analyses of the interplay of social variables and orthographic practices can be undertaken at the level of individual language users. Elspaß (2005) presents research on a corpus of 648 German private letters amounting to about 375,000 words. Most letters are so-called emigrant letters sent from and to North America in the nineteenth century following the migration waves. Elspaß could determine the educational background of quite a few writers in the corpus, adopting a two-way distinction between those with solely primary and those with primary and secondary education. For a number of orthographic variables, Elspaß is able to show that this social difference marks a considerable divide in spelling. Spelling variants such as *wier, mier* and *dier* for *wir, mir, dir,* for instance, almost never occur in the writings of scribes with a higher than elementary education, while they do occur to varying degrees (between 7 and 17 percent of all variants) in the writings of less educated scribes (Elspaß 2005: 439).

An even more fine-grained social division is part of the aforementioned *Letters as Loot Corpus* (Rutten and van der Wal 2014). This corpus is socially stratified in terms of gender and social rank. In addition to considerable numbers of letters written by women, it also comprises letters associated with four different social layers in contemporary Dutch society. Rutten and van der Wal distinguish between the lower, lower-middle, upper-middle and upper ranks, largely based on education and occupation, and ranging from hardly educated sailors and their wives in the lower ranks to established captains and their wives in the upper ranks. In this corpus, punctuation is a relatively marginal phenomenon in two respects. More letters lack than contain punctuation, and if punctuation is used, it is often inconsistently and not throughout the entire letter (Rutten and van der Wal 2014: 268). On the basis of the social stratification of the corpus, it can be shown that punctuation in private manuscript sources rises in this period as a social change 'from above'. Only 27 percent of the seventeenth-century letters have some kind of punctuation, which increases to 42 percent in the eighteenth century. Crucially, upper and upper-middle ranked men are the leaders of this change with c. 60–70 percent of letters with punctuation already in the seventeenth century. They are closely followed by upper-ranked women, whose use increases from 14 percent in the seventeenth to over 60 percent in the eighteenth century. Among the lower and lower-middle ranks, punctuation is still infrequent in the eighteenth century. Rutten and van der Wal (2014: 269) interpret these social constraints of rank and gender as symptoms of the same social variable, namely writing experience, taken as the degree to which individuals participate in the written culture.

30.4.3 Diffusion across Genre and Context

When studying regional and social diffusion based on the regional and social characteristics of text producers, such as printers and writers, it is important to keep in mind that genre can be a crucially intervening factor. The genre will normally not vary in the case of diachronic comparisons, while synchronically, comparisons across genres are indeed quite informative. Classifications of genres, text types and also situational contexts will often depend on the specific sociohistorical situation from which the sources emerge. Stenroos (2004) presents a detailed analysis of the spread of the spelling <th> in Middle English based on fourteenth- and fifteenth-century data taken from *A Linguistic Atlas of Late Mediaeval English* (LALME, McIntosh et al. 1986a). The spelling <th> was and still is used for dental fricatives, both voiced and unvoiced, in initial, medial and final position (e.g. *think, either, both*). In the period under investigation, it competed with the older letter thorn, <þ>, and the more recent innovation <y>. Stenroos (2004) distinguishes various systems used in northern and southern areas, some with graphemic mergers, others which maintain differences between the graphemes. One factor influencing the choice of grapheme is voice: <th> occurs first in voiceless positions, only later in voiced ones. The overall picture, thus, is one of regional diversity and graphemic as well as phonetic conditions. But Stenroos (2004) also shows that genre is a major factor. Grouping the various texts in LALME into two major genres, that is, documents and literary texts, it turns out that southern documents are very progressive with almost 100 percent instances of <th> by the middle of the fifteenth century, when the use thereof is still fairly marginal in literary texts. In northern areas, <th> is well advanced in voiceless positions, both in documents and literary texts. It is a minority form, however, in voiced contexts. Stenroos then argues that the spread in the north and the south, though different in terms of pace, and of graphemic and phonetic conditioning, was crucially associated with genre. In particular, the use of <th> diffused from legal texts from the London/Westminster area to legal texts elsewhere as a function of the centralized legal education system in Westminster.

Genre-related variation persists in the early and late modern period, even in administrative sources at a time when standardization gains high significance. The aforementioned corpus of Flemish administrative sources from the early nineteenth century comprises two variational dimensions related to genre and context (Vosters 2011, Vosters et al. 2012). The first relates to genre or text type in a conventional way: the three main types in the corpus are police reports, interrogation reports and indictments, where indictments clearly constitute the most formal type. The proportion of typically southern/Flemish spellings is c. 30 percent in the police and interrogation reports, but drops below 20 percent in the indictments. The second dimension concerns the institutional level at which the texts are produced, and so is more related to context than to genre *per se*. The results are similar in that locally and regionally produced sources display c. 30 percent typically southern/Flemish spellings, which drops below 20 percent in supraregional sources (Vosters 2011: 319–20).

30.5 Diffusion and Pluricentricity

30.5.1 Introduction

Above (Section 30.4), we have discussed examples of diffusion at different levels and different stages: we evidenced how emerging regional writing traditions spread geographically in the process which we labeled supralocalization, which then provided impulses for processes of standardization at an even larger level. However, adopting a more macro-level perspective, we can also observe how processes of supralocalization and ensuing standardization, in combination with the emergence of regional and (proto)national borders, may lead to a new situation: multiple centers may emerge from which norms are diffused, thus giving rise to distinct yet related national or regional language norms. Such is the case for pluricentric languages, which are "used in more than one country as national or regional official language" and where this situation "has resulted in differences in the standard variety" (Ammon et al. 2016: xxxix). We believe that taking a pluricentric perspective on language history can help to combat the so-called "tunnel vision version" of language history (Watts and Trudgill 2002: 1; see also Watts 2011: 585): a highly teleological view presenting "language history as the inexorable march towards a uniform standard" (Elspaß 2007: 4). Such a teleological view generally implies a focus on regional variation in the medieval period, which gives way to an exclusive focus on standardization and a unified standard language as the clear and exclusive outcome of this process from early modern times onward. Historical sociolinguistic research (see Rutten 2016b) has advocated a shift away from this tunnel view of standardization, in favor of a more nuanced and multilayered perspective, in which we give prominence to ongoing variability in written language use. In fact, in many cases, we argue, one can observe how regional writing traditions, instead of leading to a sole and exclusive national standard, in fact evolve into a pluricentric landscape. This is the case for the standardization history of Dutch, which we discuss in more detail as our primary case study by focusing on diffusion and historical pluricentricity across the centuries.

30.5.2 A Case Study: The Diffusion of Long a

Our case study concerns the orthographic representation of long *a* in closed syllables. For this variable, the traditional practice, originating from Middle Dutch (approximately twelfth to sixteenth centuries) spelling praxis, was to indicate lengthening by adding an <e> (rarely <i>) to the original vowel <a>, resulting in spellings such as *maend* 'month' and *daer* 'there'. From the seventeenth century onward, however, this older writing practice was increasingly being replaced by the doubling of the original vowel as the incoming form, largely irrespective of the pronunciation of the long *a*. This resulted in <aa> rather than <ae> spelling, for example *maand* 'month' or *daar* 'there'.[2] As such, we focus on how the incoming orthographic variant <aa> was diffused across the language area instead of older <ae>.

To investigate this orthographic change, we used a preliminary test version of the multigenre *Historical Corpus of Dutch*, which was developed at Vrije Universiteit Brussel and Leiden University. This corpus includes texts from the middle of the sixteenth, seventeenth, eighteenth and nineteenth centuries, and the preliminary version we used comprises a component of pamphlets and a component of so-called ego-documents. Pamphlets are printed texts, mostly commentaries or polemics about current affairs, political or religious topics, as well as some public ordinances and similar documents.

[2] Some other spelling variants also existed (e.g. <a> spellings), but they hardly played any role from the early modern period onward. For this reason, we limit our attention to the two main variants, <ae> and <aa>.

Ego-documents, on the other hand, were not meant to be published: they are more personal, handwritten texts, such as diaries, travelogues and personal chronicles of local events or family history, often primarily produced for the authors and their family members (see Elspaß 2012b). The corpus was built with the aim of studying pluricentricity in Dutch language history, and as such it includes material from both the central area (Holland) and a more peripheral region (Zeeland) in the north of the language area (i.e. the later Kingdom of the Netherlands), as well as material from the center (Brabant) and the periphery (Vlaanderen) in the south of the language area (i.e. the Dutch-speaking territories of what would be later called the Kingdom of Belgium). While the northern province of Holland became the center of standardization from the seventeenth century onward, Brabant remained a central and influential region in the south.

The diachrony of the ongoing change from <ae> to <aa>, as shown in Figure 30.1, tells us that the incoming form first appears in the mid-seventeenth century, gains significant ground by the mid-eighteenth century, and clearly becomes dominant by the mid-nineteenth century. Overall, of all tokens (n=4,745), the incoming variant accounts for 35.3 percent in the ego-document subcorpus (n=827), whereas it accounts for 37.4 percent in the pamphlet subcorpus (n=898): as such, the pamphlets are slightly quicker in adopting the new form, but this difference is really small. More generally, however, the incremental change from <ae> to <aa>, which visually appears

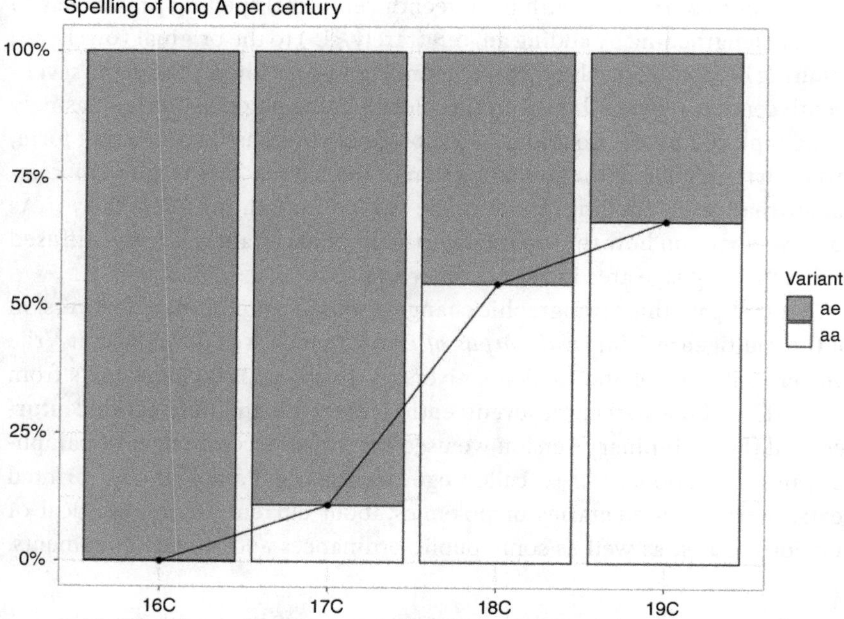

Figure 30.1 The incremental change of <ae> to <aa> across centuries

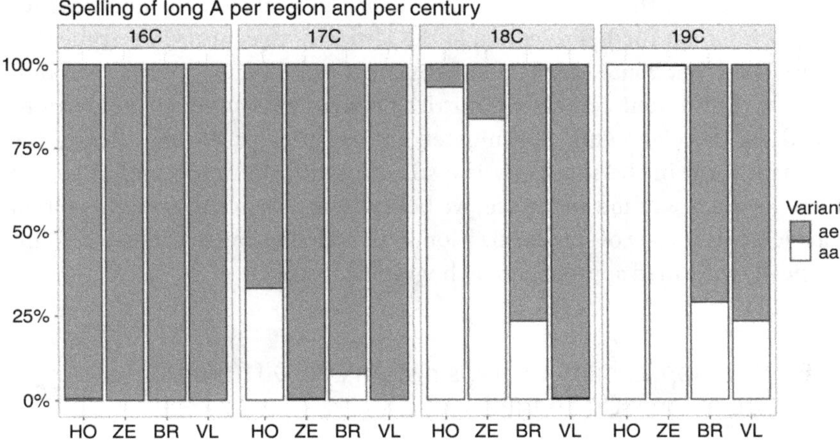

Figure 30.2 The change from <ae> to <aa> across regions and centuries

as the first stages to a traditional S-curve, seems to suggest that spread could be taking place across generations.

However, splitting up the data per region, as in Figure 30.2, we see how the rise of <aa> rather seems to be due to geographical diffusion, originating from the northern center of Holland, and spreading across regions from there. In the mid-seventeenth century, Holland clearly leads the change, but by the mid-eighteenth century, the innovation has been diffused from Holland across the north, to the more peripheral region of Zeeland. At the same time, it seems to have also spread to the south of the language area, gaining ground in the more central region of Brabant. It is not until the nineteenth century, however, that it has finally spread to the more peripheral region of the south, Flanders, at a time when the change was already completed in both the center and the periphery of the north. As such, we can see a shift in the pluricentric landscape of the Dutch-speaking Low Countries, which changes from a constellation where Holland is the normative center where this innovation arises in the seventeenth century and from where it subsequently spreads, to more of a strict division between the north and the south of the language area from the eighteenth century onward, where we can also observe Brabant as an additional normative center for the southern territories. The eighteenth and nineteenth centuries show fairly distinct and thus presumably separate dynamics in the north and the south, precisely at the time when the political and sociocultural border between both areas started to develop and grow in importance.

These results illustrate how the spread of the incoming orthographic <aa> variant is a case of diffusion across regions, while also offering significant diachronic depth so that we can link the findings to the ongoing standardization process. However, rather than limiting ourselves to a description of how <aa>

won out by establishing itself in the dominant region of Holland, and was thus taken as input for further selection in the seventeenth century, we argue that this variable contributed to the development of a pluricentric normative landscape, with different centers (in north and south) from which innovations spread: in the eighteenth and nineteenth centuries, <ae> was clearly the dominant form in the south. By investigating diffusion processes at such a macro level across time and space, we believe it is possible to avoid the pitfall of a teleological view of standardization, thus contributing to a more sociolinguistically informed approach to orthographic history.

30.6 The Applicability of Transmission and Diffusion in Diachronic Orthography

We have discussed the concepts of transmission and diffusion, departing from their definitions in the original Labovian sense, with a focus on the type of language learning or acquisition involved, as well as in the Milrovian sense, which emphasizes the type of contact among speakers, either between or within communities. We have also discussed particularities of orthographic change, mainly centered around the observation that spelling is by definition a learned behavior. As such, we have argued that diffusion can be seen as the main source of orthographic change, which can typically be described as change 'from above' in the Labovian sense. In fact, we have observed that changes often spread across geographically defined communities in a process which can also be labeled supralocalization: regionally bound orthographic practices in the late medieval period thus often develop into supraregional writing traditions in postmedieval times. Needless to say, such supraregionalization processes can provide fertile ground for later standardization efforts, although they often also lead to pluricentric linguistic landscapes, where various normative centers coexist at a national and/or at a regional level.

Another topic addressed in the chapter has been the possibility of transmission in orthographic terms, as many changes in spelling practices actually seem to follow normal S-curve patterns with relatively incremental increases in usage. From this perspective, we can foreground the fact that orthography is also often picked up in a less conscious manner, for instance through reading – in that sense, orthography is not so different from other levels of the language. Therefore, we have argued, transmission can also be a useful concept in particular historical settings, for instance where we can link continuity in orthographic conventions to instruction and teaching practices, or in cases of close-knit networks and dense community structures, where changes are transmitted from one user to the next. The distinction between transmission and diffusion, however, can only be deemed useful if both concepts provide us with different models and different predictions concerning patterns of change. We wonder, in other words, what we can gain by adopting the concept of transmission, and whether we cannot merely limit ourselves to diffusion as the main driver of orthographic changes. The view we have taken in this chapter is that the Labovian distinction in terms of learnability, based on the opposition of child versus adult language acquisition or learning, is harder to apply in historical settings, as cases of transmission, according to this perspective, demand fairly extensive investigations of the exact mechanisms underlying transmission. We deem the Milrovian distinction between local and supralocal changes to be more useful, which can be linked to transmission and diffusion respectively by foregrounding the scale of the contact situation.

Building on the contact and community-based perspective of Milroy (2007), we have also observed that diffusion-type changes in cases of spelling seem to follow more gradual, incremental patterns of change over the centuries, in line with the traditional S-curve model. This was, among other examples, the case for the spread of the innovative <aa> spellings in Dutch, as discussed in the final case study: <aa> forms gradually appear and spread across time and place between the seventeenth and the nineteenth centuries. At the same time, however, cases of transmission of spelling norms do allow for more abrupt and possibly also deliberate changes, as we have discussed in the case of the Dutch spelling and educational policy, which caused significant changes in orthographic practices in a relatively short period of time (Krogull 2018). In addition, note that we have treated both concepts mostly as independent concepts, and we have not focused much on the interaction between transmission and diffusion. In reality, of course, both types of changes co-occur and indeed interact. In Section 30.4.1, for instance, we discussed the regional diffusion of orthographic practices indicating a long *e* merger from Holland to Zeeland, but in fact, this change 'from below' was later reversed to a significant extent by a change 'from above'. This process occurred when the officialized Siegenbeek norms (see Section 30.3.1) reintroduced the distinction between both etymologically distinct *e* sounds, and such norms were transmitted within the community through education (Rutten et al. 2020). Such and similar instances, where transmission overrules diffusion, open up promising avenues for future research, but fall outside of the scope of the present contribution.

30.7 Conclusion

Taking the observations and analyses in this chapter together, we argue that orthographic changes resemble changes in other levels of the language in the sense that they all allow for changes of both the local, transmission type, and the supralocal, diffusion type. They also differ, however, in the sense that orthographic changes seem to be more incremental in cases of diffusion, and possibly more abrupt in cases of transmission – which is exactly the opposite from what you would expect for other domains of language. Taking a diachronic perspective on spelling variation and change, we observe gradual geographical, social and other types of diffusion as fairly typical. Overall, a highly frequent and therefore important pattern of change seems to be that of a transition from local or regionally circumscribed writing traditions to the supralocal level by means of (geographical) diffusion, often followed by standardization on the one hand, but also leading to situations of pluricentricity on the other hand.

31

Analogy and Extension

Yishai Neuman

31.1 Introduction

In this chapter, I focus on the relationship between analogy, extension and orthography. *Analogy* is an automatic cognitive process by which what is known is projected on what is thought as similar just to provide a similar result, that is *extension*, as when an infant conflates dogs and cats, thinking they are all dogs in virtue of limited past experience. Further experience and cognitive development may allow refraining from erroneous analogy, as when infants begin distinguishing cats from dogs, whereas cognitive stagnation in some adults or in entire social groups prevents them from distinguishing realities which others distinguish well. Extension through perceptual analogy in conventional semiotic systems ends up changing the system and thus involves no error, but rather an evolution of human perception. Semiotic systems evolve through analogy-induced extension in general, and particular subdomains of semiotics (understood as the study of signs; see, e.g., Chandler 2017: 2), like language and graphemics, may serve as good examples. Analogy between graphemic systems in contact may produce intergraphemic extension, and analogy between different categories of a single graphemic system may produce intragraphemic extension. Since writing systems relate to language in various ways, including to components of phonemic and morphemic systems but not solely thereto, analogy involving graphemics often produces intersemiotic extension either from language to graphemics, or vice versa. What seems like perfect correlation between graphemics and components of language in synchronic analysis may quite often result from historical analogy and extension between them; the study of this historical evolution falls within the diachronic analysis of language–writing relations.

Let us start with a short historical background. The beginning of writing was not language-oriented, but visually iconic, pictographic or object-associated (see Chapter 2, this volume, for more discussion on the origins of writing). Engraved forms on stone and clay were at first pure pictograms, like today's emojis (e.g. 🚗). They alluded to concrete objects without relating to the writers' languages, whether *car, voiture, Auto,* מכונית /mexonit/ or سيارة /sajja:ra/. This means that pictographic and consequently more abstract ideographic writing could in principle be understood across languages. Indeed, as early as the fourth millennium BC, the Sumerian ideogram ▽ 'woman' needed no translation. When writing consists of pictograms only, it is generally cross-cultural and incidentally cross-linguistic. In a pictogram-only writing system, every pictogram indicates the same basic object in practically all languages, except for specific cultural differences. For people who employ a pictographic writing system, then, each pictogram indicates first an object universally, and incidentally, in their particular language, it also corresponds to a phonemic sequence, to a single spoken word. This means that for various languages whose speakers were using a pictographic writing system there could hypothetically be drawn a visual-articulatory list of correspondences between pictograms and phonemic words. Such a list would be intuitive for all speakers since spontaneous metalinguistic awareness of children and naïve people attains its limits at the word-object level and does make the difference between 'things' and 'words', a reality corroborated by polysemous terms for the two notions in ancient languages such as Hebrew and Aramaic.

Few of the languages, however, whose speakers were using a pictographic writing system, happened to be *typologically monosyllabic,* that is, languages whose set of basic lexical or grammatical morphemes is largely monosyllabic. In those languages, many pictograms corresponded to a syllable-word, and object-oriented metalinguistic awareness was incidentally also syllable-oriented, since "syllabic segmentation can be based on simple auditory perception" (Bentin 1992: 197), even if only for a slim minority of relatively sophisticated or less naïve speakers. Creative writers among the speakers of those entirely (e.g. Chinese) or relatively (e.g. Sumerian) *typologically monosyllabic* languages could play with puns by assigning the secondary syllable–pictogram correspondence a primary role. Analogy from a one-type word-pictogram logo- or morphographic sign and extension toward other occurrences of that morpheme syllable elsewhere in the lexicon could trigger the emergence of syllable-based writing. Thus, analogy from pictographic nonlinguistic writing in largely typologically monosyllabic languages laid the premise for extension of the primary pictogram-object writing to syllable-oriented language-associated writing, as pointed out by Coulmas (1999: 481): "Like ancient Chinese, Sumerian words were largely monosyllabic with many homonyms. It is thought that extensive homonymy made early Sumerian pictographic scribes recognize the possibility of rebus-based writing which led to phonetization." This accounts for the formation processes which brought about the emergence of three initially syllabic writing systems: Sumerian, Chinese and Mayan (Daniels 1992: 93–95).

The fact that language-oriented writing emerged only in these three monosyllabic languages is not fortuitous: only in these languages was the pictogram-to-syllable analogy possible, and then followed the extension of the primary relation to a general morphemic syllabic writing. Languages whose monosyllabic lexicon – not necessarily the entire lexicon – covered all of the phonotactically possible syllables thus served as a point of departure for analogy from that part of the lexicon and for extension on adding sound to meaning relations in writing (Daniels 1992: 93–95). There is a good chance that other pictographic communication systems prevailed among speakers of languages whose core lexicon was not mainly monosyllabic, where consequently no such analogy was possible, nor any extension thereof. As a result, those local nonlinguistic writings never became language-associated and at some point disappeared as the outcome of a cultural natural selection. The cognitive process of analogy is thus responsible for the very introduction of linguistic features into writing. Further extension of the primary syllable–pictogram correspondence created the anachronistic illusion that writing has always been language-oriented and is thus responsible for the language bias in practically all modern linguistic general accounts of writing. Ferdinand de Saussure's (1983: 24 [1916: 45]) twofold claim with respect to the relations maintained between language and writing is a good example for the language bias in accounting for written communication: "[a] language and its written form constitute two separate systems of signs. The sole reason for the existence of the latter is to represent the former."

Saussure's *first* claim is clairvoyantly descriptive: language and writing are two separate semiotic systems. This truism could not be stated more simply or more accurately. It should have naturally led, however, to the study of language and writing as semiotic systems in contact. Nevertheless, owing to Saussure's powerful taboo on the question, this evident truism had not led to such studies for very long. Instead, the *second* claim, completely unfounded, has marked twentieth-century linguistics so strongly that the overwhelming majority of scholars who treat writing–language relations seem to compete with each other on which of them best echoes Saussure's 'sole-reason' axiom, like Bloomfield (1927: 433): "Now, writing, of course, is merely a record of speech"; or Hall (1950: 31): "As a matter of fact, writing is essentially a way of representing speech." Until recently only a few free thinkers dared to consider language and writing outside of Saussure's assumed scope of dominant–dominated or deriving–derived relations. Further evolution of language–writing relations brought about ongoing systemic convergence to phonemic writing due to cognitive analogy and extension of existing correspondences. Moving from syllabic to phonemic writing by the acrophonic principle occurred in parallel from Sumerian-Akkadian to the Ugaritic alphabet and from

(Sumerian-inspired, see Daniels 1992: 95) Egyptian to Canaanite, thence to the Phoenician consonantal alphabet, from which emerged the Hebrew-Aramaic alphabet with partial notation of vowels and in parallel the Greek alphabet with full vowel notation. The very evolution of graphic communication from pictures to language-oriented writing is, at its inception, the fruit of analogy between some pictures and their monosyllabic morphemes, and the extension of these relations to other parts of language.

31.2 Language and Writing Reciprocal Analogy and Extension

Once writing has been aligned on language, even if only slightly, systemic gaps between components of writing and aspects of language have constantly been candidates for analogical reasoning and thence to extension of existing principles of correspondence. Let us assume the logically first creative pun which allowed 'spelling' the name *Carmen* by a rebus based on the sequence of two pictograms like 🚗👥 which was the beginning of aligning writing on language. Then, similarly to the increase in the force of gravity as the distance between two bodies decreases, the attraction between writing and language grew stronger as the systemic overlap between them increased. It ended up in what might have seemed a perfect match from the beginning. On its way to such 'perfection', however, a series of analogy-based extensions operated.

Unlike mainstream linguistic thought, language–writing convergence goes both ways. This is true particularly but not solely when it comes to the relationship between graphemics and phonemics. Graphemics has undoubtedly evolved analogically to the phonological structure of corresponding languages. Both orthography and popular spelling often follow phonemics in extending existing phonographemic correspondences, though in different paces (Neuman 2021). The opposite direction of analogy-based extension of graphophonemic correspondences has also been operating, and much more so than phonocentric linguists might be inclined to consider. For example, the historic adaptations of French graphemics are to some degree inspired by the phonological evolution of the language (Catach 2001), but on the other hand, when graphemics resisted phonology and remained structurally remote, mainly for cultural reasons, phonology often ended up adapting to orthography, since "[t]he semi-literate adjust their pronunciation to spelling by uttering the silent letters as actual consonants only to show that they are educated and can spell correctly" (Buben 1935: 15).

Analogy-based extension of graphemic and phonemic relations operates in both directions: from phonemics to graphemics and from graphemics to phonemics. The following sections thus present various case studies of both categories. Whereas in times of relatively low literacy graphemics tends to adapt to the phonological structure, as literacy grows, we witness a strong tendency in the opposite direction. Indeed, the establishment of a chosen 'correct' spelling as an authoritative convention is responsible for the alignment of the phonological system on orthography.

31.3 Graphophonemic Analogy: From Correspondences to Operators

One of the salient features in human behavior is the cognitive process of *analogy*, whereby one's familiar area of experience serves as a model for dealing with what is less familiar. In linguistics, analogy is responsible for morphological leveling of what is less frequent with what is more frequent; for example, the past tense of the verb *help* was once *holp* (compare the German cognate perfect *geholfen*) but under the pressure of the significantly more frequent *-ed* system shifted to *helped* alongside other "strong verbs that became weak" (Baugh and Cable 2002: 163–64). Analogy can operate on the relations between language and writing, in particular between phonology and spelling. For example, since the phonemic sequence /aɪC/ corresponds more frequently to <iCe> than to <ighC> (the C representing any consonant or consonant grapheme), popular texts, unbound by rules of orthography, may display novel spellings such as *nite* instead of traditional *night* (Sebba 2007: 125), whereby the new spelling *nite* is analogous to the graphophonemic correspondence between /taɪd/ and *tide*. Just as analogy may modify the spelling of words, it may operate the other way around, that is, from spelling to phonology. All the more, given the cognitive primacy of visual over auditory stimuli, and in light of the higher social prestige and authority of the written at the expense of the oral, analogous formations in spelling based on pronunciation are less likely to appear among literate adults or to resist social and educational pressure in young spellers than analogous pronunciations based on orthography.

The parallel examination of the phonemic sequence and of the graphemic sequence in Modern English (from 1500 on) has revealed a set of graphophonemic (from graphemes to phonemes) and phonographemic (from phonemes to graphemes) correspondences (Deschamps 1992, 1994, Carney 1994). Based on these graphemic analyses, it becomes clear that a given phonemic sequence may correspond to several graphemic sequences, but at a certain hierarchy of frequency, as in /aɪC/ corresponding to <iCe> more often than to <ight> (Carney 1994: 151–54). Similarly, a given graphemic sequence may correspond to several phonemic sequences, but, there too, displaying a certain hierarchy of frequency, as in <ea>, which corresponds much more often to /iː/ (e.g. *plead, weak, veal*) than to /ɛ/ (e.g. *head, deaf, death, breath*). This means that each grapheme or graphemic sequence has one primary phonemic correspondent, and a few possible secondary phonemic correspondents in decreasing frequency. A full account of the graphemics of a given orthography may thus provide a list of all graphophonemic correspondences with the primary graphophonemic correspondent for each one. In turn, the primary graphophonemic correspondent becomes the default phonemic value for a transformation rule which I have termed *graphophonemic operator* (Neuman 2013: 135–36). This is the pivotal moment when quantity translates into quality. Indeed, when assigning phonemes to graphemes analogically to frequent graphophonemic correspondences, literate speakers extend the range of the existing default phonemic value by activating frequency-motivated graphophonemic operators. One such operator, <t> → /t/, resulted in the insertion of /t/ in what became the oft-cited /ˈɒfən/ ~ /ˈɒftən/ variation.

From a sociolinguistic point of view, once society becomes literate, its members may indeed be able to read, but are not always familiar with the oral tradition associated with the unfamiliar vocabulary of the newly acquired written language (Neuman 2009: 311–13). This situation is fertile ground for phonological modifications which would not occur via the sole phonemic filter between the source and the target language or dialect, but rather through analogical graphophonemic assignment according to operators of the target language applied to vocabulary originating from elsewhere. This is how many French-originated English words came to exhibit consonants which had not been part of the phonemic makeup of those words at the time of lexical transfer. In his *History of English Spelling*, Scragg (1974) elaborates on the lexical impact of the "French invasion" (pp. 38–51) and on the ensuing reshaping of that impact during the "Renaissance and re-formation" (pp. 52–63); he illustrates this process by the following example: "from the Latin participle *perfectum* French derived an adjective which passed into English as *parfit*, also spelt in the sixteenth century as *parfit*. [...] *parfit* was respelt *perfect*" (Scragg 1974: 54). The impact of this respelling is the insertion of /k/, still absent from French *parfait* /paʁfɛ/. In effect, such conditions may allow for a phonemic zero to be replaced by a phoneme if the graphemic counterpart is a grapheme liable to be interpreted by the semi-educated, who ignore the oral transmission, as the default phonemic counterpart of the grapheme at hand (Koeppel 1901). This process also happened systematically in many loanwords as well as autochthonous words around the globe (Neuman 2009: 309–705). In what follows I present a selection of case studies of graphophonemic analogy and extension.

31.3.1 Anglo-Norman, Modern French and Germanic <t> → English /t/

The default correspondence of English <t> is /t/. In the Anglo-Norman lexical component of Middle and Early Modern English, between the second half of the twelfth century and the first half of the seventeenth century, as well as in later lexical borrowing from French, words like *format*, whose graphemic <t> corresponded to no consonant, kept this graphophonemic discrepancy as long as they remained rare in vernacular usage. This category of words has not resisted the process described above, and the phoneme /t/ is the most frequently introduced phoneme in Anglo-Norman vocabulary. Indeed, the comparison of phonological variations between the 1917 and the 1937 editions of Daniel Jones's *Dictionary of English Pronunciation* is very illustrative of this process as it allows us to observe change in the course of happening. Thus, *format* is transcribed as [ˈfɔːma] in 1917 but [ˈfɔːmæt] in 1937, with the former pronunciation in brackets (Horn and Lehnert 1954: 1212). Importantly, Jones the phonetician uses square brackets for [ˈfɔːma] and [ˈfɔːmæt], but it should be maintained that the variation is not phonetic, but phonemic. Indeed, the gradual change from the former /ˈfɔːma/ to the newer /ˈfɔːmæt/ results from the graphophonemic operator <t> → /t/, and not from some occasional weakness of /t/. Apart from the *format* case, all references on spelling pronunciation point to the most famous example of the operator <t> → /t/. Thus, Scragg (1974: 41) says that "/t/ is frequently heard now in *often, Christmas, postman.*" Coye elaborates further:

> Speaker confidence in a pronunciation can fluctuate in the everyday realm too, as seen in the remarkable change in *often*. This word has been pronounced without /t/ for centuries, but as literacy increased and awareness of the written *t* grew, people everywhere apparently began to think it ought to be pronounced.
>
> (Coye 1998: 183–84)

Kökeritz (1964: 139) mentions the emergence of /t/ in *often* and *pestle*; the example *often* is mentioned under 'spelling pronunciation' also by Wilson (1993), Chalker and Weiner (1998) and McArthur (1998). The absence of *often* from Koeppel's (1901) extensive account is indicative of how late the /t/ emerged in this word.

31.3.2 Anglo-Norman <h> → English /h/

The gradual loss of the British English pharyngeal voiceless fricative from late eighteenth century on may find an authentic echo in the title of an 1866 manual by Charles W. Smith: *Mind your H's and take care of your R's: exercises for acquiring the use & correcting the abuse of the letter H, with observations* [...]. The instruction of spelling and the educated orthoepy based thereon have resulted in the reintroduction of the phoneme /h/ in many words which had lost it. Thus, according to Henry Sweet,

> [i]nitial (h), which was preserved through First and Second Modern English, began to be dropped at the end for the last century, but has now been restored in Standard English by the combined influence of the spelling and of the speakers of Scotch and Irish English [...] It has been almost completely lost in the dialects of England.
>
> (Sweet 1892: 280)

From a sociolinguistic point of view, had the Scots and the Irish been the only /h/-carriers in nineteenth-century England (*albaphobia* and *hibernophobia*, respectively), this phoneme might have been stigmatized as 'foreign' or 'low-class' and would have been rejected even more. The graphemic salience of <h>, however, prompted the operation of the graphophonemic operator <h> → /h/ among the educated, thus inversing the rapport of prestige between *h*-full and *h*-less speakers. Whereas in native English vocabulary the operator <h> → /h/ can be said to have restored the /h/ in places in which it had been lost, its introduction into French words, which had neither <h> nor /h/ upon arrival from Early Middle English (1100–1300) on, constitutes the rise of a new phoneme within the phonemic sequence completely *ex scripto* ('from writing'), both in synchronic and in diachronic analyses. Koeppel (1901: 4–6) enumerates some English words of French origin, all of which had neither /h/ nor <h> in Middle English (1100–1500), but with gradually introduced <h> spellings from Modern English on, and this respelling of French words was followed by the gradual introduction of /h/ into their English phonemic makeup, all of which display an initial /h/ today: ME *abit* vs. ModE *habit*, ME *Ebrewe* (still attested in the fifteenth century) vs. ModE *Hebrew*, ME *oste* vs. ModE *host*, ME *umble* vs. ModE *humble*. In other initial <h> French-originated words, the English /h/ is a graphophonemic extension based on analogy with the existing vocabulary, for example *horrible*, *heritage*. Hesitations between <a> and <an> before *historical* demonstrate clearly the original /h/-less phonological makeup of the word.

Conversely to the spelling pronunciation's bad reputation as isolated and inconsistent, the analogical emergence of an initial /h/ in these words is rather systematic. Except for the words *heir*, *honour*, *hour* and *honest*, which survived the wholesale process of spelling pronunciation, to which one should add American English *herb*, all *h*-less French words which were gradually respelled with a historic <h> ended up acquiring the additional phoneme /h/ through the graphophonemic operator <h> → /h/ (Scragg 1974: 41). To realize how gradual the emergence of /h/ was and how relatively recent the currently prevailing situation is, consider the entry *humour* in the 1901 edition of the *New English Dictionary on Historical Principles* (Murray et al. 1888–1928, later known as the *Oxford English Dictionary*, Murray et al. 1933): "The pronunciation of the initial *h* is only of recent date, and many still omit it" (Murray et al. 1901: 452). A similar case is found in present-day German, whereby the final-syllable grapheme <h>, whose duty is vowel length marking, ends up producing an analogical /h/. For example, against singular *Kuh* /kuː/ 'cow' the plural *Kühe* alternates between the morphophonologically expected /kyɛ/ and the graphophonemically analogical /kyhɛ/ (Lindqvist 1997: 200). Finally, two interesting cases of spelling-analogy <h> → /h/ extension appear in the English gentilic terms *Hebrew* and *Hungary*/*Hungarian*. Both display an initial /h/ unlike any other language (German has /h/ in *Hebräisch* but none in *Ungarn*/*Ungarisch*). One may only speculate what possible oral tradition or scribal practice of those gentilic terms possibly underlies their initial seemingly ghost /h/.

31.3.3 Interdental Phonemization of Hellenized Spelling: <th> → English /θ/

The composite grapheme <th> replaced the grapheme <t> in present-day English words which were thought at some point to descend from Greek words displaying <θ>. Consequently, the graphophonemic operator <th> → /θ/ gradually remodeled the phonemic makeup of these words in English, thus replacing their Middle English or Early Modern English (1100–1700) /t/ by Modern English (from 1500 on) /θ/. Among those words are *theater, theme, throne, Catholic, anthem, amethyst, apothecary, arthritic, authentic, lethargy, panther*. Some of them have been mistakenly thought to stem from Greek words with <θ>. Scragg (1974: 57) mentions the unetymological <h> in *author* and *anthem* (Middle English *auctor, antem*) and Levitt (1978: 46) adds the name *Arthur*, whose /t/, still extent in the shorter name *Art*, was remodeled into /θ/, too. It thus becomes clear that etymological authenticity is not a criterion for the success or failure of the operator <th> → /θ/ or for spelling pronunciation in general. For a while, those words displayed /t/~/θ/ variation until the variant better corresponding to spelling won and the variation became history (Koeppel 1901: 21–22). It would be wrong to consider, however, that the /t/~/θ/ variation is merely historic. Kerek (1976: 326) estimates that while the operator <th> → /θ/ has successfully prompted the emergence of the phoneme /θ/ at the expense of /t/ in some words, it "is currently exerting pressure in others (*thyme, asthma, clothes, isthmus, Waltham, Thames, height*, and so on, in the latter case via visual metathesis) leaving only a small residue still apparently untouched (*Thomas, Thomson*)."

The diachronic impact of the /t/→/θ/ conversion on the English phonological system is twofold. In some cases it prompts the conditioned phonemic split /t/ → /θ/ ~ /t/; and in other cases, it dissolves homophones and prompts the emergence of minimal pairs such as *thyme* vs. *time, theme* vs. *team*. Both types of impact have led to an increase in the overall functional load of /θ/ and in the overall number of distinctions. Dissolving homophones through regular analogical spelling pronunciation is what Levitt (1968: 28) considers as a therapeutic device to cure "phonetic erosion" in French. Kerek's consideration of visual metathesis in the colloquial form /haɪθ/ is not necessarily exact since this noun correlates to the adjective /haɪ/ within the paradigmatic relations /haɪ/-/haɪθ/, so the colloquial noun may stem from be morphological analogy to other terms designating dimensions (e.g. /diːp/-/depθ/).

The suffix /θ/ also designates English ordinals (e.g. *seventh*); Levitt relates the story of some ordinals as follows:

> English numerals ending in a fricative originally had ordinals ending in t – *fift, sixt, twelft*. In the seventeenth century, by analogy with other ordinal numbers which ended in *th*, an *h* was added, and *th* was subsequently pronounced [θ], according to spelling.
>
> (Levitt 1978: 46–47)

As we have seen, the operator <th> → /θ/ in English is not limited to true or false Greek etymology, and it generally follows intentional respelling by language authorities. There are, however, some 'accidents' too. It so happens that when <t> and <h> are adjacent on both sides of a morpheme boundary, the phonemic sequence /t/ or /th/ (depending on whether or not the <h> is initially silent) is liable to be replaced by /θ/. Similarly, the initially *ham*-ending names of the Massachusetts towns of *Waltham* and *Wrentham*, like *Wenham* and *Framingham* still are, ended up displaying /θəm/.

31.3.4 Latinization of Early Modern English: Latin <c> → English /k/

The sequence /kt/ is one of the Latin consonantal (obstruent) clusters to have been simplified in Old French (the eighth to fourteenth centuries) into /t/. Old French words with /t/ which had originated in Latin /kt/ passed into Middle English orally, thus displaying /t/ both in the source and in the target languages. Later Latinization of Early Modern English spelling of Latinate vocabulary involved the respelling of French <t> to English <ct>. With the advent of learning, the work of orthoepists and finally later universal literacy, English words with /t/ vs. <ct> phonographemic incongruity ended up aligning the phonemic sequence on the graphemic sequence. This accounts for the emergence of /k/ in terms that had lost it in Old French several centuries earlier. For example, Old French *parfait* ~ *parfit* entered Middle English as *parfet* ~ *parfit* and was later respelled to the savant orthography *perfect*, which is based on Latin *perfectum*. In the sixteenth century there is evidence for only /k/-less pronunciation, but in the eighteenth century orthoepists are already divided on the question whether the <c> should be pronounced. Since then, the /kt/ pronunciation has gradually attained stability, and nowadays the graphemic and phonemic sequences match perfectly (Koeppel 1901: 9–10).

In addition to *parfet* → *perfect*, the graphophonemic operator <c> → /k/ has affected also *verdit* → *verdict* and *suget* → *subget* → *subject*, with quite similar evolution from Old French and Middle English /k/ to Latin and present-day English /kt/. Interestingly, the savant drift has not spared Modern French (from 1700 on) either, where alongside *parfait* /parfɛ/ stemming from the oral uninterrupted transmission there is a new Latin savant derivative *perfection*

/pɛrfɛksjõ/, with both its vowel /e/ (instead of the phonemically evolved /a/) and the obstruent group /kt/. The same applies for present-day French *sujet* /syʒɛ/ and *subjectif* /sybʒektif/. For present-day French *verdict* /verdikt/, however, there is apparently no popular phonemically evolved counterpart, probably because the term belongs to a professional legal jargon which is learned by definition. A contrastive analysis of these three terms and their nominal derivatives in present-day English and in present-day French, like /perfekt/-/perfekʃən/ vs. /parfɛ/-/pɛrfɛksjõ/, shows that the difference between the partial spelling Latinization in French and the wholesale Latinization in English and the ensuing spelling pronunciations in both are responsible for higher paradigmatic coherence at the morphemic level in English than in French.

31.3.5 Latin <us> → Hungarian /uʃ/

Let us consider the phonemic makeup of the Latin masculine nominative suffix *-us* in two Central European languages: Austrian German and Hungarian (Neuman 2009: 499–501). The orthoepic rules of nonvernacular Latin in German were such that Latin <s> was orthoepically performed as German /s/ in word-final position, for example the frequent greeting *Servus* 'hello' (compare 'at your *service*') in colloquial Austrian German (still today), and thence the lexical transfer in spoken Hungarian *Szervusz* /sɛrvus/. There is a total of 52 /us/ terms (spelled <usz>) in Hungarian: *plusz, mínusz, kókusz* (Papp 1994: 445); all are lexical transfers from Latin terms which were first vernacularized in colloquial German. Later, however, from the mid-nineteenth century on, the study of Latin gained currency in Hungary, and Hungarian scholars began importing Latin terms directly into Hungarian without the mediation of spoken German. Under the new circumstances, Latin spelling was maintained in the target culture, but since Hungarian <s> corresponds to /ʃ/, the more recent <us>-ending terms came to exhibit the new graphophonemic form /uʃ/: *glóbus, nótárius, típus* 'type', *ciklus* 'cycle' and so on. The original Latin suffix in Hungarian now oscillates between a closed set of German-mediated older terms displaying /us/ and an open set of terms adapted directly from *written* Latin, by definition, and whose number based on Papp's (1994) inverse dictionary amounts to 662. With respect to phonological adaptation, graphophonemic analogy based on conventional Hungarian orthography is responsible for the emergence of the new suffix /uʃ/ in spoken Hungarian completely *ex scripto*. One must note that the terms in /uʃ/ are by no means restricted to written or even educated spoken Hungarian, for example *március* /maːrcjuʃ/ 'March', *május* /maːjuʃ/ 'May'. Transfer from Latin to Hungarian has thus been put into a graphemically administered grid and, rather than following natural sound rules, has started to follow one particular analogical rule of graphophonemic assignment: <us> → /uʃ/.

31.3.6 Reversing Sonorant Vocalization in English: <l> → /l/

The vocalization of lateral /l/ is well attested in world languages (Johnson and Britain 2007). The consonant /l/ may soften into a glide, either /j/ like in French *conseil* (/kõsɛj/ from Latin *consili*) 'counsel, advice', or /w/ like in Dutch *zawt* /zawt/ 'salt'. Languages displaying the gliding of /l/ are as different and remote as Polish and Aramaic. In some cases, when the output glide follows a vowel, the descending diphthong may contract into a (long) vowel, from which emerge V~/l/ paradigmatic alternant pairs such as *maudire* /modiːr/ 'to curse' and *malediction* /malediksiõ/ 'a curse' in French. When instances of /l/-originated glides evolve into vowels, one may safely speak of /l/-vocalization (Recasens 2012). The process of /l/-vocalization has not spared English. The most renowned cases are *walk* and *talk*, where spelling testifies to an authentic historic /l/ (Wright 1924: 28). Thanks to their extremely high frequency in daily speech, their phonemic evolution is protected from analogical spelling-based restructuring, at least in English, since French anglicism *talkie-walkie* 'walkie-talkie' displays two extant /l/ consonants (Tournier 1998: 549). In lower frequency vocabulary, however, the oral transmission might be too weak to prevent an orthographic <l> from inducing a phonemic /l/.

The gradual operation of <l> → /l/ is observable in several English words. Horn and Lehnert (1954: 1212) note that the word *salve* has evolved from /sɑːv/ to /sælv/ as shown by two consecutive editions of Daniel Jones's *Pronunciation Dictionary*, the former still in the 1917 edition, the latter in 1937. Also, *scalp* changes from /skåːp/ in the seventeenth century to /skælp/ nowadays. With respect to *almost*, the form /åmust/ prevailing in the seventeenth century while the pronunciation with /l/ is marginal and considered barbaric; at the turn of the twentieth century, it is the residual pronunciation without /l/ which is looked at as vulgar. Similarly, French *hallebarde* became *halbarde* in English, whence its sixteenth-century vocalization to *hauberde*, but an etymologizing spelling *halberd* ended up reintroducing the /l/. These examples illustrate the role of schooling not only in introducing sounds that are synchronically new to the oral transmission but also in labeling the linguistic effects of this introduction as prestigious. The correlation between school, spelling pronunciation and prestige in language use is reaffirmed (Koeppel 1901: 10). Besides these historic examples, there are more contemporary cases, in which the process can be caught in action. This is notably what happens when one's own astonishment at a word displaying spelling pronunciation is matched with the interlocutors' astonishment for opposite reasons, as Fred Householder's statement tells us:

> About eight years ago I heard a radio announcer pronounce the trade-name Palmolive with a distinctly audible [l] before the [m]. At the time I took it to be merely an isolated instance, the sort of thing to be expected from radio

> announcers. But when I mentioned it one day in class to illustrate extreme spelling-pronunciations, I was surprised to discover that most of my students also pronounced [l] in the words of this series – and were amazed and shocked at my suggestion that this was not normal.
>
> (Householder 1948: 155)

This mutually shocking experience encouraged Householder to conduct a study on different words of the category. His findings were that while literary words, lacking a stable oral transmission, generally obeyed spelling pronunciation, words that are more frequent in speech would maintain a back vowel, corroborating the historic /l/-vocalization, but at the same time, at least in the younger generation, also displayed /l/. And since the study has "not yet found a single person under the age of 30 who does not pronounce [l] in most or all of these words" (Householder 1948: 156), this means that the process studied by Householder affected the generation born in the 1920s and later. Nowadays, only a century later, the process must be complete, so that even without variation we may safely consider those /l/ instances as resulting from spelling pronunciation. The possibility of capturing the process in the happening, as Householder does, allows a better understanding of the impact of the spelling component of graphemics on phonology also in cases which have been studied only when the process had been completed.

Catching a process in action is also possible in cases of traditional vs. general contexts. Such is the synchronic introduction of word-final obstruents through spelling-based analogy and extension to phonology in French following the mandatory instruction of universal literacy within the establishment of modern State schools (The Jules Ferry Laws, France 1881–82). French linguist Michel Masson (1938–) relates (by personal communication): "I remember that my grand-father (born in 1870) used a big, heavy, cylinder stump on which he put logs to chop them and called it *un bloc* but he pronounced that /blo/; however, in other contexts, he used the word with the common pronunciation /blok/." The English graphophonemic operator <l> → /l/ also affects loanwords, as Kökeritz (1959: 222) shows for the Gallicism *cul-de-sac*: "In American English the spelling-pronunciation is complete, /ˈkʌldəˈsæk/."

31.3.7 Old English Toponymy Exhibiting /ʧ/: <c> → Modern English /k/ ~ /s/

Between the eighth and the twelfth centuries, Old English (eighth to twelfth centuries) spelling evolved from primarily variable local or personal spelling through harmonization to a system much closer to what is considered conventional orthography. The diacritic function of <h> may serve as a good example (Scragg 1974: 46–47). Present-day English <h> can function as a diacritic letter to distinguish minimal graphemic pairs vis-à-vis the corresponding phonemic inventory, for example, <th> from <t> as in *thin* vs. *tin*, <sh> from <s> as in *ship* vs. *sip*, and <ch> from <c> as in *char* vs. *car*. But in spite of the functional unity which the diacritic <h> shows nowadays, these composite graphemes do not follow similar historical evolution. Dietz (2006) shows that the linguistic history of the corresponding phonemes, on the one hand, and the history of their graphemic counterparts, on the other hand, are two well-distinct histories. The composite grapheme <ch> was adopted in Old English texts from the scholarly Latin of the British Isles in the tenth century. At that time, it corresponded in English phonemics to either /k/ or /x/, and only occasionally to /ʧ/, the latter being neither regular nor stable (Dietz 2006: 22–23, 29–35). Then, with the Norman invasion in 1066, the more recent correspondence of <ch> to /ʧ/ is massively represented in Anglo-Norman, when French /ʧ/ had not yet been simplified to /ʃ/. This correspondence was on its way to becoming stabilized in the beginning of the twelfth century and would become the sole productive correspondence to /ʧ/ by the fifteenth century (Scragg 1974: 44–45, Dietz 2006: 331–33). Regularity and stability of the correspondence <ch> → /ʧ/ arrive later, indeed owing to Anglo-Norman influence. This graphophonemic evolution results in, from that moment on, <c> without <h> corresponding generally to /k/ except before front vowels, where it corresponded to /s/. Consequently, by analogy to the more stable correspondence, the atypical maintaining of <c>: /ʧ/ in the archaic spelling of several places names in England diverted their pronunciation by graphophonemic extension from /k/ to /s/.

According to Dietz (2006: 11), place names in England such as *Cerne Abbas* and *Cirencester* display the fricative /s/ instead of the etymologically expected affricate /ʧ/. It is generally accepted that this particularity represents a substitution which results from a phonological transformation in Anglo-Norman. As he shows, however, relatively recently edited sources suggest that the /s/ in these names stem from medieval spelling pronunciation. The history of this category of toponyms begins at the unstable graphemics of Old English but then displays conditioned graphemic or phonemic splits by analogy either to graphemics or to phonemics. Thus, either <c> was adapted analogically to phonemics and was replaced by <ch>, as in *Manchester*, which maintains the oral tradition; or <c> was maintained in archaic spellings and /ʧ/ was replaced graphophonemically either by /s/, as in *Cerne Abbas* and *Cirencester*, or by /k/, as in *Lancaster*. Analogy between phonemics and graphemics in this category has led to both types of extension, either from the local linguistic tradition to official orthography or from archaic spelling to a new phonological makeup of these place names.

31.3.8 Peripheral Diphthong Conveying Systemic Foreignness: <oi> → English /ɔɪ/

In an instructive study on peripheral phonemes in the English phonological system, Vachek (1964: 78–84) devotes a chapter to the synchronic foreignness of the diphthong /ɔɪ/ in present-day English. The scholar, whose notation is kept loyal to the source for the sake of systematicity, sketches the vowel system of English as presented in Figure 31.1 (adapted from Vachek 1964: 78):

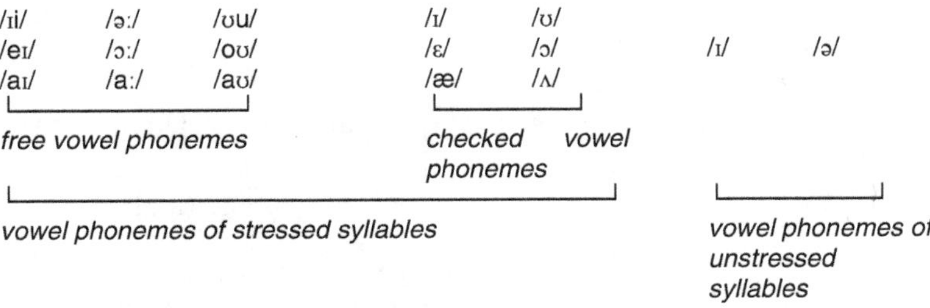

Figure 31.1 The English vowel system
(adapted from Vachek 1964: 78)

Following his explanation (Vachek 1964: 81) that English front diphthongs consisting of [ɪ], namely /ɪi/, /eɪ/ and /aɪ/, are systematically paralleled by a series of back diphthongs ending in /ʊ/, namely /ʊu/, /oʊ/ and /aʊ/, Vachek points out that the heterogeneous (consisting of back and front components) diphthong /ɔɪ/ is not paralleled by the expected */ɛʊ/. Moreover, this diphthong occurs only in loanwords the overwhelming majority of which stem from French.

From a diachronic point of view, elaborates Vachek, Middle English diphthongs /ui/ (as in *joint* and *point*) and /ɪi/ were neutralized to /əi/ and later, at the Great Vowel Shift (GVS) (Lass 1999: 72–84), became /aɪ/. This is how seventeenth- and still even eighteenth-century sources display evidence for rhyming pairs such as *refines* and *joins*. In effect, after the neutralization of both diphthongs into /əi/ and the latter's transformation into /aɪ/, one would expect that such pairs keep rhyming forever, whatever their graphemic makeup. But things evolved otherwise. Whereas the diphthongs /əi/ > /aɪ/ stemming from the homogenous diphthong /ɪi/ had evolved into /aɪ/ and remained so, those of the diphthongs /əi/ > /aɪ/ which had stemmed from the heterogeneous diphthong /ui/ remained /aɪ/ in some British Southern dialects (and therefore also stigmatized as low) but became /ɔɪ/ in Standard English, however without any apparent phonological motivation. Simply put, one has to explain why some /əi/ diphthongs evolved to /aɪ/ and remained this way while other such diphthongs evolved further to /ɔɪ/.

Vachek (1993: 82) is of the opinion that, since the phonological data alone cannot account for the phonemic bifurcation at hand, resorting to spelling is unavoidable. In effect, the graphemic sequence is the only component capable of explaining the phonemic shape of words such as *choice* /ʧɔɪs/, in which the diphthong /ɔɪ/ does not stem from a historic /ui/, but rather from /oi/. This is also how this class of words is explained by two other scholars:

> I look upon these *oi*-forms as originally inverted spellings of eNE /əɪ/, showing the leveling of the reflexes of ME *i* and *iu*, which in the case of *foist(y)* has given rise to a spelling-pronunciation /ɔɪ/.
>
> (Kökeritz 1959: 224)

> The first member of *ui* was usually written *o*; thus, poison for *puison*. In modern times this written form gave rise to a spelling-pronunciation that has prevailed in standard speech.
>
> (Malone 1959: 262)

Nevertheless, Vachek (1964: 82) wonders, the evolution of words such as *come*, *done* and *love*, pronounced in Middle English as /kum, dun, luv/, in the early seventeenth century as /kəm, dən, ləv/ and in present-day English as /kʌm, dʌn, lʌv/, exhibits no trace of influence of the grapheme <o>. What then, he continues, allows us to suppose any graphophonemic influence of <o> in *point* if the same <o> does not exercise a similar influence on *love*? In the absence of an additional factor, one might object to the hypothesis of a spelling-induced pronunciation and claim it is not strong enough. To this objection he responds:

> In attempting to answer this question one should realize that the impact of the written norm of language upon its spoken counterpart is only a specific instance of a more general phenomenon, viz. of the influence of external factors of the development of the system of language. The interventions of such external factors are, of course, qualitatively different from the internal changes taking place within the structure of the spoken norm. As, however, these internal changes often appear to be motivated by the structural needs and wants of the system of language, a hypothesis may emerge to the effect that also the intervention of the written norm may be somehow connected with the structural situation obtaining the system. In other words, one should ask whether the penetration of the spelling pronunciation in words like *joint*, *point* may not have been motivated be the structural needs and wants of the corresponding spoken norm.
>
> (Vachek 1964: 83)

This is an illustration of the twofold functions of graphophonemic realization of loanwords. In many cases it serves as a means of *integration* and *appropriation*, such as the French /s/ in the German-language toponym *Strasbourg* which displays /ʃ/ (also vowel-wise respelled from *Straßburg*). In the category at hand we are witnessing the contrary: the graphophonemic operator <oi>

→ /ɔɪ/ serves as a means of *alienation*, a way to keep these French words apart from the English inherited vocabulary. Words identified as foreign are thus kept in phonemic 'quarantine' through graphophonemic realization, which echoes other practices of foreign words' structural 'quarantine' (Masson 1986, Schwarzwald 1998). This is being realized by analogy with graphophonemic correspondences of words already felt as foreign, and whose feature [+foreign] is phonemically manifest since they have not had time to adapt to the phonological system of the target language. What this means is that given the phonological foreignness of the diphthong /ɔɪ/ in originally French words such as *choice* and *joy*, /ɔɪ/, resulting from graphophonemic analogy with words displaying [ɔɪ] ↔ <oi> / <oy>, perceived as foreign (French), was assigned to words such as *point* and *joint*. These words were, until then, integrated with /aɪ/ in English but not in the system of graphophonemic correspondences of its writing system.

The ultimate conclusion of this question is that French-originated English words that display the graphophonemic correspondence /ɔɪ/ ↔ <oi> ~ <oy> would exhibit no /ɔɪ/ in the absence of the graphemic sequence <oi> or <oy>. This conclusion, however obvious, does not conform with Chomsky and Halle's (1968: 191–92) consideration of each present-day English diphthong as presumably resulting from Middle English long vowels according to their Vowel Shift Rule (VSR), that is, "diphthongization, vowel shift, and various rounding and backness adjustments," as summarized by Jaeger's (1984: 15) critique of Chomsky and Halle's method. In this case, then, Chomsky and Halle take the liberty of inventing a historic long vowel which would be the 'logical' source of /ɔj/, although we pertinently know that these words did not follow the evolution of the core stratum of the English lexicon; rather, it appeared late in French-originated words whose phonemic makeup was shaped based on their spelling. Vachek's (1964) analysis was already accessible to scholars in 1968, but Chomsky and Halle preferred not only to ignore it in this case, but more generally to tailor the data to fit their preconceived theory, whatever its historical or cognitive validity.

Finally, later in the history of English and without immediate rapport with the evolution of British English, two North American French-spelt toponyms exhibit an analogous phenomenon: given the eighteenth- to nineteenth-century French <oi> ↔ [wɛ]/[wa] correspondence, the Native American place name [ilinwe] was spelt by French settlers as *Illinois* and the city of *Detroit* owes its name to the French common noun *détroit* /detrwa/ 'strait'. Both place names initially followed French phonographemic rules [wɛ] → <oi>; however, they ended up displaying the graphophonemic diphthong /ɔɪ/ in English and consequently in other languages except French, where *Illinois* maintains the original pronunciation /ilinwa/ while *Detroit* has been remodeled on the American English pronunciation for the sake of differentiation from the homonymic common noun. In the absence of the homonymy constraints, foreign words with <oi> may adopt the analogical pronunciation /wa/ in present-day French, for example English *gasoil* → mid-twentieth-century French /gazwal/, nowadays largely outdated and replaced by *gazole* (Neuman 2009: 793–94).

31.3.9 Derivational Productivity of Vowel Alternations

As is known to people who have learned to read and write English, English spelling is difficult to master. Its makeup is notoriously inconsistent in corresponding to sounds. One may cite, in this respect, George Bernard Shaw's humorous *ghoti* spelling for *fish*: <gh> for /f/ as in *enough*, <o> for /ɪ/ as in *women* and <ti> for /ʃ/ as in *nation* (Stubbs 1980: front cover; see also Chapter 9, this volume, about the origin of this spelling). Generations of educators, centuries-old respelling societies and numerous self-nominated language reformers deemed English spelling inconsistent with sound and therefore unsuitable for the sound system of the English language. Then, totally unexpectedly, in a completely surprising sequence of events, come Chomsky and Halle and, departing from the original scope of the science of language, declare English spelling to be "a near optimal system for the lexical representation of English words" (Chomsky and Halle 1968: 49–50).

There are numerous references in the *Sound Pattern of English* (Chomsky and Halle 1968) which state that the abstract morphophonemic representations are similar in form to orthographic forms. The similarity between spelling and what Chomsky and Halle choose to postulate as their underlying representations is indeed striking, and this apparent coincidence has been noticed and analyzed much in detail (Giegerich 1999: 151–60). But an unbiased observation cannot rule out orthography as the source for Chomsky and Halle's VSR. What is even more striking is that, in their analysis, the authors recapitulate the historic GVS into a synchronically operative VSR. In turn, Chomsky and Halle would like the VSR to suit, to a large extent, the shifting sounds corresponding to stable letters in the spelling, for example both the diphthong in /tʃaɪld/ *child* and the vowel in /tʃɪldrən/ *children* correspond to one and only <i> in the orthography. Educational application of Chomsky and Halle's (1968) VSR appears with only a little delay. In full compliance with Chomsky and Halle (1968), Carol Chomsky (1970), an education scholar in literacy acquisition at Harvard (and spouse of Noam Chomsky), argues that Chomsky and Halle's assertion regarding English spelling as "a near optimal system" means that English spelling is not a problem for the acquisition of literacy in spite of its apparent letter–sound notorious inconsistencies:

> In *The Sound Pattern of English* Chomsky and Halle demonstrate a variety of ways in which the relation of conventional English orthography to the sound structure of the language is much closer than is ordinarily assumed. Simply

> stated, the conventional spelling of words corresponds more closely to an underlying abstract level of representation within the sound system of the language, than it does to the surface phonetic form that the words assume in the spoken language. [...] When viewed in its correspondence to this underlying form, English spelling does not appear as arbitrary or irregular as purely phonetic criteria might indicate.
>
> (Chomsky 1970: 288)

For the Chomskys, teaching how to read English and doing phonology go hand in hand. One cannot refute Carol Chomsky's observation that ascribing different sounds to a single (vowel-)letter using some relatively regular graphophonemic correspondences turns out to be beneficial for the didactics of literacy: knowing that the letter which corresponds to /aɪ/ also regularly corresponds to /ɪ/ and that when two words have somewhat similar meanings they may display coherent spelling does by all accounts make it easier to learn how to read and write in English. This indeed works. But is Noam Chomsky's parallel VSR also tenable? Are there, in synchronic analysis, underlying abstract vowel units which surface 'in the spoken language' as different vowels or diphthongs just as they are assumed to have evolved in the historic GVS? In other terms, can one rightfully recapitulate the assumed diachronic evolution into synchronic cognitive linguistic processes? Does the GVS keep operating whenever speakers of English (presumably process the underlying form /ma:ke/ and finally) utter /meɪk/? The synchronic validity of Chomsky and Halle's VSR in present-day English has been challenged in a number of studies from the 1970s on. Here is a short synopsis of a few critiques:

> Whether English speakers have actually internalized such a rule as the VSR as C&H [Chomsky and Halle] claim is questionable, especially since contrary evidence has been collected by some investigators.
>
> (Steinberg and Krohn 1975: 235)

> However, Chomsky and Halle intended for these rules to represent psychologically real synchronic, rather than diachronic processes (Jaeger 1984: 15). This rule has its origin in the orthographic system of English.
>
> (Jaeger 1984: 33)

> In their highly influential study of what they called the 'sound pattern' of English, for example, Chomsky and Halle (1968) proposed an analysis that essentially duplicated the historical changes of the Great Vowel Shift to be part of the phonological competence of contemporary speakers and characterized one of the rules involved to be 'without doubt the pivotal process of Modern English phonology'.
>
> (Derwing 1992: 194)

There is a lexical criterion which must be taken into account, too. Many of the tense vowels and diphthongs emanating from the historic GVS go back to the Germanic word stock. Those words either display no alternation, like /maɪnd/ *mind*, /neɪm/ *name* and /stəʊn/ *stone*, or display lexically set flectional alternations of strong nouns and verbs within the core vocabulary of Old English, for example /tʃaɪld/ *child* vs. /tʃɪldrən/ *children*. In other cases, while displaying lexically set vowel alternation, words may be spelt according to the vowel at hand, like Germanic strong inflection, for instance tense inflection *sleep* vs. *slept*, adjective-noun inflection *wide* vs. *width*, as well as some Latinate vocabulary, such as *pronounce* vs. *pronunciation*; but in the absence of supportive spelling, VSR has been shown essentially unproductive (Smith and Baker 1976). In other terms, outside strong noun and verb inflections, VSR is either supported by spelling or it does not exist. Indeed, upon examination of the existence of underlying forms which the VSR may transform into surface forms, production of diphthongs turns out to be conditioned essentially by spelling:

> No strong evidence has been found for underlying forms; Orthographic devices such as double consonants and *es* appear to influence performance through their effect on perceived morphemic structure, not on more abstract forms.
>
> (Smith and Baker 1976: 284)

If one considers stable diphthongs such as in /maɪnd/ *mind*, /neɪm/ *name* and /stəʊn/ *stone*, as well as a limited number of lexically set flectional alternations such as *child* vs. *children* and *sleep* vs. *slept*, mostly in strong plurals and verbs, on the one hand, and derivational alternations, such as /laɪn/ *line* vs. /lɪnɪər/ *linear*, on the other hand, an etymological pattern comes to light: vowels and diphthongs alternate productively mainly in lexical derivatives of Latinate vocabulary. In effect, strong inflections like *child* ~ *children* in nouns and *write* ~ *written* in verbs represent closed lexical sets, and the vowel alternations which they may display are not productive in later derivation, for example *childish* with a diphthong like in *child*. They were created by the historic GVS in the passage from Middle English to Modern English, and since spelling remained unchanged, graphemes began corresponding to variations as different as diphthongs, as in /tʃaɪld/, and lax vowels, as in /tʃɪldrən/. In general, outside the strong inflecting lexicon, all of which is etymologically Germanic, words which underwent the GVS display the resulting vowel with no alternation, be they Germanic like *high* or not, mostly Middle English everyday French loanwords, for example *tower* /ˈtaʊər/ (compare French *tour* /tuːr/). Both Germanic vocabulary and French loanwords from the Middle English period are closed lexical sets and display no vowel alternation in lexical derivation. This may plead for the following analysis: the historic GVS has indeed left its mark on English phonology, but this phonological shift is not active in present-day English.

A large number of later lexical loans, however, do display vowel alternations in derivations (e.g. *divine* ~ *divinity*). Those words, however, are all *learned words*: they come from books and their phonological makeup thus results from spelling pronunciation. Indeed, for the Latinate vocabulary, rather than underlying Old English long vowels becoming diphthongs and tense vowels in the vernacular, there are graphemic vowels which sophisticated users perform using graphophonemic operators analogically to existing vocabulary. Some of these newly created words, with no phonological history in English, end up displaying alternations between lax vowels and diphthongs or tense vowels. Therefore, the phonological makeup of these words was created through graphophonemic assignment and this feature of the Latinate vocabulary in present-day English continues to operate whenever language users meet a written English word for which they dispose of no or little oral tradition. The phonology of this stratum of the English lexicon can thus be explained in terms of relative chronology, and this set of facts and analyses should be taken into account when considering the variation it displays compared to the core Germanic vocabulary, which *did* evolve through the GVS. Giegerich (1992), explains the alternation between the schwa and the diphthong in the last syllable of *Anderson* and the adjectival derivation *Andersonian* as literate derivation, whereby the letter <o> is assigned a diphthong. To account for this situation, Giegerich (1992: 413) formulates a spelling pronunciation rule for phonological relationships in derivation when phonological rules are irrelevant.

In a later work, Giegerich (1999: 131–66) devotes a chapter to showing this point. His disciple, Montgomery, studies similar questions in two other publications (Montgomery 2001, 2005). Both Giegerich and Montgomery convincingly integrate spelling pronunciation into their accounts of literacy-dependent processes in present-day English. In effect, the GVS has left its mark on the old strata of English vocabulary in the form of stable diphthongs and tense vowels, with little alternation, mostly in core Germanic morphologically strong lexica. Stated simply, from a purely phonological point of view, Chomsky and Halle's attempt to convert the GVS into a modern VSR is scientifically untenable. Several languages with a long writing tradition display cases in which phonologically obsolete processes seem to continue to operate while their operation is really maintained graphophonemically (Neuman 2009: 673–700). Like in other cases of orthography-dependent operation of phonologically obsolete processes, a modern reflex of the historic GVS operates through graphophonemic operators. The continued operation of the historic GVS therefore enjoys an artificially maintained productivity.

This is to say that when Carol Chomsky (1970) pleads for the teaching of English literacy using spelling consistency corresponding to phonological variation while believing she is taking on the relationship between underlying forms and surface forms, what she is really doing is teaching literacy instructors and students the history of the spelling pronunciation rules in the way schoolmasters used them to willfully *shape* the school pronunciation of Latinate words in Early Modern English. This also means that when Chomsky and Halle (1968) claim that English spelling miraculously matches the supposed underlying representation which they put forward, all they are really saying is that given the spelling-based *genesis* of the phonological makeup of the Latinate lexicon in English, its phonological behavior matches its spelling, on which they have chosen to construe their VSR. From the point of view of general linguistic theory, putting forward a description of written language instead of that of language itself is what Harris (1981) designates by the term *scriptism*, namely "the tendency to analyse spoken language as if it were written language *avant la lettre*" (Harris 2003: 233). Since most Latinate English terms had not entered English when the GVS ceased its operation, even the historical component of Chomsky and Halle's analysis is more anachronistic than really diachronic. And their synchronic analysis thus conflates natural phonology with graphophonemics, which makes their reasoning an obvious case of scriptism.

It is now clear that the analogy going from vernacular Middle English phonographemic relations to graphophonemic extension in later book-to-speech oralized Latinate learned vocabulary has been institutionalized in present-day English. Later application of the very same analogy, however, is now a sign of poor acquaintance with the oral tradition of English, and may be associated with poor education. Indeed, as long as British and later American diplomats and foreign ministers were the only English speakers concerned with Middle Eastern countries, the lax vowel /ɪ/ of *Iraq*, ingrained in the oral tradition which is based on the initial monophthong in Arabic, was safe from analogical pronunciation. But once US troops invaded Iraq, in 2003, the country became the concern of many speakers unfamiliar with the place name. Consequently, in Michael Moore's documentary film *Fahrenheit 9/11* (Moore 2004), the interviewed journalists and diplomats maintain the orally transmitted form /ɪræk/ while several soldiers' parents and a US president introduce the analogical novelty /aɪræk/.

31.3.10 Postvocalic /r/ in American English Becomes Analogical to <r>

In his ground-breaking study 'The social stratification of (r) in NYC department stores', leading sociolinguist Labov (1972a: 64) studies the social correlation of (r-0) and (r-1) pronunciations, namely postvocalic *r*-less and *r*-ful pronunciations. He goes on to explain that "[b]efore World War II, the New York City schools were dominated by an Anglophile tradition which taught that (r-1) was a provincial feature [...] and that the correct pronunciation of orthographic *r* in *car* was (r-0), [kɑ·] [...]." To support his explanation, he cites (note 10) a 1940 text by the New York City Department of Education (Raubicheck et al. 1940) designed for New York City schools. In the chapter 'Problems of phonetics' (pp. 287–374), there is a section on 'The sounds of English' (pp. 297–349) and a subsection on 'The consonants' (pp. 325–49), in which the authors lose sight of the ongoing /l/ insertion in words like *calm* (see Subsection 31.3.6 in this chapter) and discuss what they conceive as the problematic pronunciation of /r/:

> There are many people who feel that an effort should be made to make the pronunciation conform to the spelling, and for some strange reason, they are particularly concerned with *r*. We all pronounce *calm, psalm, almond, know, eight, night,* and there without worrying [...] Yet people who would not dream of saying kni: or psai'kɒlədʒi insist on attempting to sound the *r* in words like pɑ:k or fɑðə just because an *r* marks the spot where our ancestors used a trill [...].
>
> (Raubicheck et al. 1940: 336)

First of all, before moving forward with understanding the relevant implications of Labov's own findings, it is important to point out that both of the above texts – namely (1) his (1972a) explanation about the pre-WWII (r-0) correct pronunciation of orthographic *r* as in *car* [kɑ:] and (2) the expressive manifest of the NYC department of education (1940) presumably attributing similar status to the <gh> of *night* and to the <r> of *car* – are really telling us that teaching English spelling to a population of (r-0) speakers requires an effort to keep this (r-0) feature from changing to (r-1). Was this 1940-reported effort of any use? Labov, when conducting his (1972a) study some 30 years later, finds out that this effort was completely fruitless. His results concerning the sociolinguistic relations of /r/ pronunciation in NYC show a tendency to depart from the Anglophile prestige *r*-less pronunciation in postvocalic position and move toward an *r*-ful pronunciation. In Labov's analysis of the facts, he maintains that the pace of change is stratified according to social class. Upon closer look, however, shifting from *r*-less old prestige to *r*-ful new prestige is in closest correlation with higher education. His choice of words makes precisely this point, though only implicitly:

> The process of linguistic socialization is slower for lower-middle-class groups who do not go to college than for upper-middle-class speakers who begin adjusting to the new norm in the upper class tracks of the academic high schools.
>
> (Labov 1972a: 65)

What Labov is really saying is that the better educated lead the move from *r*-less to *r*-ful and that the less educated follow their steps with a certain delay. This means that a certain component in education promotes the articulation of /r/ when there is <r>. In other terms, this is a story of the gradual success of the spelling-analogical graphophonemic operator <r> → /r/ pending the level of literacy. College attendees are more literate than "groups who do not go to college," as Labov puts it. Then, the prestige of literacy, including the component of spelling, is such that college kids identify the new prestige form with that which is implied by spelling and go on unconsciously leading the move from the previous spelling-independent old prestige *r*-less form to the spelling-dependent new prestige *r*-ful form. The shift which Labov portrays is thus a case of wholesale spelling pronunciation, that is, orthography-based analogy and extension to the phonological structure. Interestingly, throughout his study, Labov (1972a: 65) utters the sequences "orthographic *r*" and "make the pronunciation conform to the spelling" only when relating others' positions. No mention of writing-related terms, however, is made in his own analysis. For reasons pertaining to the twentieth-century linguistic taboo over writing, Labov keeps his silence when it comes to the spelling factor, which is nonetheless an indispensable component in the analysis of his own findings. This is a perfect illustration of a case in which the orthographic elephant in the sociophonological room goes unnoticed.

31.3.11 Nasal Consonants Preceded by Nasal Vowels in French

For the sake of convenience of the majority of the readership of this *Handbook*, the phenomenon of graphophonemic analogical formation has thus far in this chapter been illustrated mainly for English. Other languages nevertheless display it no less than English, as I have shown extensively (Neuman 2009). In what follows, I shall give a taste of the phenomenon at hand in some of these languages. For lack of space, the remainder of the illustration includes only single examples from French, Hebrew, Arabic and Yiddish.

The historical phonology of French teaches that an oral vowel in front of a nasal consonant becomes nasalized by regressive assimilation. This applied to the vowels of Old French between the eleventh and the fourteenth century. Then, by phonetic dissimilation, if the nasal consonant was at syllable-final position, it became mute; otherwise, it persisted and the nasal vowel became denasalized. Dissimilation in Middle French thus prevented any sequence of a nasal vowel and a nasal consonant. Complementary distribution between VC̃ (oral V, nasal C) and Ṽ (nasal V) was conditioned by whether the next component was a vowel or not, for example /ɛ̃vizibl/ *invisible* and /inodibl/ *inaudible*, also /sõ/ *son* 'sound' and /sonor/ *sonore* (Carton 1974: 185, Catach 1984: 45, Klausenburger 1978: 23, 1984: 63, Bourciez 1958: 33–34, Fouché 1959: 356–64, Zink 1999: 81–85, Joly 1995: 165–81).

In the case of the French morpheme *en*, however, phonological inconsistency emerges. This morpheme is either the preposition *en* /ã/ as in *en retard* 'late' or the verbal prefix as in *endormir* 'put to sleep'. Then, before a vowel the preposition displays the hybrid sequence of a nasal vowel followed by a nasal consonant /ãn/ except in the frozen composition /dor**en**avã/ *dorénavant* 'from now on', in which this morpheme displays the expected alternation. The hybrid phonemic sequence /ãn/ appears wherever the component <en> occurs as a separate graphemic word, for example /ãnavã/ *en avant* 'forward', both of whose morphemes happen to be contained also in *dorénavant.* The sequence /ãn/ in /ãnavã/, then, results from the expected prevocalic /n/, which initially leads to /**en**/ as in *dorénavant*, but at the same time the preceding oral vowel /**e**n/ becomes nasalized /ãn/, not as a result of some new phonological transformation, but as an analogical extension from the lexical graphemic word <en>, whose unmarked alternant is /ã/. In other terms, the phonologically expected /en/ and the graphemically induced /ã/ have summed up to /ãn/ whenever the preposition *en* precedes a vowel. Farther extension of the process may be observed in verbs such as /ãnivre/ *enivrer* 'intoxicate', whose prefix *en* has been identified by orthoepists as the same component as the preposition. At this point they started an entire campaign meant to uproot the popular realization /enivre/, however expected according to the one nasal segment (consonant of vowel) per syllable constraint. The graphemic word <en> is thus the nucleus of the analogy from /ã/ to the prevocalic hybrid extension /ãn/ as in /ãnavã/ *en avant* 'forward', and the sole remnant of the expected phonemic sequence, which managed to escape the analogy due to its graphemic 'spaceless refuge' within the graphemic word, is /dor**en**avã/ *dorénavant* 'from now on'. This example demonstrates the analogical impact of graphemic word boundary (space) on otherwise phonemically conditioned alternating morphemes in deflecting these morphemes from their expected path to alignment on graphemic consistency (Neuman 2009: 346–55).

31.3.12 The Zero Grapheme in Hebrew, Arabic and Yiddish: <ø> → /a/

Whereas all consonants in Hebrew and Arabic, as well as in the Hebrew lexical component within Yiddish, correspond to material graphemes, some vowels may correspond to the zero grapheme <ø>, though constrained differently in the three languages. It so happens that in both Hebrew and Arabic the most frequent graphophonemic correspondence of the zero grapheme is the vowel /a/, and less so in the Hebrew component of Yiddish (Neuman 2013: 143–44). The quantitatively following correspondences are /e/ and /i/, and others follow in a descending scale of frequency. In lexical items whose oral transmission has for some reason been weakened, or never existed, or does not exist in synchronic analysis, or has been relativized by spelling for various sociolinguistic reasons, vowels other than /a/, and which correspond to the zero grapheme, become /a/, based on analogy from the most frequent graphophonemic correspondence. Thus, the /a/ insertion in the Yiddish "direct Hebrew verb formation" of the *CaCC+en* type, that is, Hebrew consonantal root + Germanic verbal suffix (Weinreich 1965: 28), also results from the high frequency of <ø> → /a/, as implicitly put forward by Masson (1976: 168); this is so especially in light of the graphemic rather than phonemic reality of the Hebrew root, at least during the nonvernacular period of Hebrew (Neuman 2009: 646). A very similar use of the abstract 'root morpheme + noun' may be traced in the present-day Hebrew compound R-M-Z 'hint' + /'or/ 'light' →/ramzor/ 'traffic lights' (Neuman 2009: 613, 2013: 143). The analogical graphophonemic operator <ø> → /a/ also reshapes existing forms in Hebrew and Arabic: ספרות *SFRWT*, meaning 'literature' /sifrut/ exhibits the uneducated by-form /safrut/, تذكرة *TĐKRH*, meaning 'message, note' /taðkira/ → /taðkara/, "[m]ostly pronounced *taðkara*," according to Wehr (1976: 310), alongside similar cases in Arabic (Neuman 2009: 507–8). Also, 'nectarine' entered Hebrew as /naktarína/ due to the <ø> grapheme in נקטרינה *NQṬRYNH* and in spite of existing though rare /nektar/; the composite term רכבל *RKBL* /rakével/, meaning 'aerial tramway' is mostly known and used as /raxbal/ based on analogical graphophonemic realization; the term /pesími/ 'pessimistic' has a widespread by-form /pasími/. Finally, the Franciscan institution *Terra Santa* in Jerusalem has been generally known as /tara santa/ for local speakers of Hebrew and for speakers of Arabic not only in Jerusalem but also around other sites held by the Franciscans throughout the Middle East – in both languages for the same reason (Neuman 2009: 609–16).

31.4 Conclusion

As long as spelling is spontaneously or institutionally adapted to linguistic components such as phonology and morphology, analogical formation can be said to be working in the direction going from morphophonemics to graphemics. Prestabilized spelling variation is thus subject to analogical modifications based on speech variation. These dynamics are what allows historical linguists to reconstruct the development of language, especially morphophonemics, based on observations and analyses of spelling variation. The institutionalization of spelling, however, bodes the emergence of *orthography*, that is, 'correct' spelling. Once spelling is liable to be correct or incorrect, knowing how to spell correctly becomes a status symbol, and thence new phonemic makeups emerge, which now compete with existing phonemic makeups that do not qualify as a perfect match of the orthography. The competition between linguistic forms which draw from the oral tradition and spelling-based pronunciations usually results in the victory of the latter. Rather than a marginal phenomenon, this type of analogy from spelling to phonology is quite the rule in literate societies. The above account offers a selection of case studies, mostly drawn from the English-illustrated part of a much larger multilingual collection of systematic analogical transformations between languages and their writing systems (Neuman 2009).

What the readership of the present *Handbook* may wish to take from this chapter on analogy and extension concerns both the linguistic impact on writing and the graphemic impact on language. The linguistic impact on writing has gradually adapted spelling to various aspects of language, especially morphophonemics. And the impact of writing on language becomes significant particularly at the point where spelling is institutionalized on its way to becoming orthography. Whereas spontaneous spelling is relatively fluid and thus tends to adapt to the development of language to a large degree, orthography as a social institution is intentionally stable and permanent; it is inherently 'correct' or 'incorrect', and thus mastering it is associated with social prestige. In view of the prestige that comes with the command of orthography, this semiotic artifact may become a factor in the development of the morphophonemic system. Thus, rather than representational relations between writing and language, it is safer to assert that spelling is usually analogous to morphophonemics whereas morphophonemics may in many cases be analogous to orthography. From a general semiotic perspective, analogical reasoning is responsible, on the one hand, for the spelling extension of morphophonemics, and, on the other hand, for the morphophonemic extension of orthography.

Bibliography

Aasen, Ivar 1848. *Det norske Folkesprogs Grammatik*. Kristiania: Werner
1850. *Ordbog over det norske Folkesprog*. Kristiania: Trykt hos C .C. Werner
1855. *Ervingen. Sangspil i een Akt*. Kristiania: Det norske Theaters Forlag
1863. *Symra: tvo Tylfter med nya Visor*. Kristiania: Malling

Abercrombie, David 1949. 'What is a "letter"?' *Lingua* 2: 54–63

Abbott, Andrew 2004. *Methods of Discovery. Heuristics for the Social Sciences*. New York/London: Norton

Abbott, Jacob 1855. *The Harper Establishment, or, How the Story Books Are Made*. New York: Harper's

Abecele lėtuviškaj-rusiška, del naŭdos lemėntorišku mokslinijčiu͡ [...] 1865. Warsaw: Spaŭstuvee Kommissiios Apšvėtimo Publično

Academia Literaria y Científica de Instrucción Primaria 1844. *Sesión Publica celebrada el día 3 de octubre de 1844, en el salón del instituto español. Por la Academia de profesores de primera educación, para demostrar las ventajas que ofrece la reforma de ortografía adoptada y publicada por la misma Academia. Dedicada a los profesores y amantes de la educación*. Madrid: Imprenta de Dª. Francisca Estevan

Académie française 1694. *Le dictionnaire de l'Académie française*. Paris: Coignard
1718. *Le dictionnaire de l'Académie française*. Paris: Coignard (2nd ed.)
1740. *Le dictionnaire de l'Académie française*. Paris: Coignard (3rd ed.)
1762. *Le dictionnaire de l'Académie française*. Paris: Brunet (4th ed.)
1798. *Le dictionnaire de l'Académie française*. Paris: Smits (5th ed.)
1835. *Le dictionnaire de l'Académie française*. Paris: Firmin-Didot (6th ed.)
1878. *Le dictionnaire de l'Académie française*. Paris: Firmin-Didot (7th ed.)
1932–35. *Le dictionnaire de l'Académie française*. Paris: Hachette (8th ed.)
1992–. *Le dictionnaire de l'Académie française*. Paris: Imprimerie Nationale (9th ed.)

Adam, Isabell 2013. 'Graph', in Martin Neef, Said Sahel and Rüdiger Weingarten (eds.), *Schriftlinguistik/Grapholinguistics* (Wörterbücher zur Sprach- und Kommunikationswissenschaft/Dictionaries of Linguistics and Communication Science 5). Berlin/Boston: De Gruyter, www.degruyter.com/view/db/wsk

2014. 'Allograph', in Martin Neef, Said Sahel and Rüdiger Weingarten (eds.), *Schriftlinguistik/Grapholinguistics* (Wörterbücher zur Sprach- und Kommunikationswissenschaft/Dictionaries of Linguistics and Communication Science 5). Berlin/Boston: De Gruyter, www.degruyter.com/view/db/wsk

Adam, Renaud 2010. 'Imprimeurs en Brabant et en Flandre au temps de Philippe le Beau', in Hanno Wijsman (ed.), *Books in Transition at the Time of Philip the Fair. Manuscripts and Printed Books in the Late Fifteenth and Early Sixteenth Century Low Countries*. Turnhout: Brepols Publishers n.v., pp. 273–85

Adams, Douglas 1979. *The Hitchhiker's Guide to the Galaxy*. London: Pan Books

Adams, James N. 1995. 'The language of the Vindolanda writing tablets: an interim report', *Journal of Roman Studies* 85: 86–134

2003. *Bilingualism and the Latin Language*. Cambridge: Cambridge University Press

2007. *The Regional Diversification of Latin, 200 BC–AD 600*. Cambridge: Cambridge University Press

Adamska-Sałaciak, Arleta 1996. *Language Change in the Works of Kruszewski, Baudouin de Courtenay and Rozwadowski*. Poznań: Motivex

Adiego, Ignacio J. 2006. *The Carian Language*. Leiden: Brill

Agata, Mari 2011. 'Improvements, corrections, and changes in the *Gutenberg Bible*', in Jacob Thaisen and Hanna Rutkowska (eds.), *Scribes, Printers, and the Accidentals of Their Texts*. Frankfurt am Main: Peter Lang, pp. 135–55

Agha, Asif 2003. 'The social life of cultural value', *Language and Communication* 23: 231–73

2005. 'Voice, footing, enregisterment', *Journal of Linguistic Anthropology* 15 (1): 38–59

2006. *Language and Social Relations*. Cambridge/New York: Cambridge University Press

2011. 'Commodity registers', *Journal of Linguistic Anthropology* 21 (1): 22–53

Ahlzweig, Claus and Pieske, Knut 2009. Protestantisch-katholische Kontroversen in Hannover im 17. Jahrhundert. Oral presentation at the annual meeting of the Arbeitskreis für historische Stadtsprachenforschung, Augsburg, October 6, 2009

Ahmad, Rizwan 2012. 'Hindi is perfect, Urdu is messy: the discourse of delegitimation of Urdu in India', in Alexandra M. Jaffe, Jannis K.

Androutsopoulos, Mark Sebba and Sally A. Johnson (eds.), *Orthography as Social Action: Scripts, Spelling, Identity and Power* (Language and Social Processes 3). Boston/Berlin: De Gruyter, pp. 104–33

Ainsworth, Robert 1698. *The Most Natural and Easie Way of Institution Containing Proposals for Making a Domestic Education Less Chargeable to Parents and More Easie and Beneficial to Children: By Which Method, Youth May Not Only Make a Very Considerable Progress in Languages, but Also in Arts and Sciences, in Two Years.* London: Printed for Christopher Hussey

Airoldi, Edoardo M., Fienberg, Stephen E. and Skinner, Kiron K. 2007. 'Whose ideas? Whose words? Authorship of Ronald Reagan's radio addresses', *PS: Political Science & Politics* 40 (3): 501–6, https://doi.org/10.1017/S1049096507070874

Aitchison, Jean 2013. *Language Change. Progress or Decay?* Cambridge: Cambridge University Press (4th ed.)

Akiner, Shirin 2009. *Religious Language of a Belarusian Tatar Kitab: A Cultural Monument of Islam in Europe. With a Latin-Script Transliteration of the British Library Tatar Belarusian Kitab (OR 13020) on CD-ROM.* Wiesbaden: Harrassowitz Verlag

2017. 'Cultural hybridity in the religious literature of the Tatars of North-Eastern Europe', *Slavonic and East European Review* 95 (3): 401–28

Aldama y Guevara, José A. 1754. *Arte de la lengua mexicana.* Mexico City: Biblioteca Mexicana

Alexander, William 1779. *The History of Women, from the Earliest Antiquity, to the Present Time; Giving Some Account of Almost Every Interesting Particular Concerning That Sex, among All Nations, Ancient and Modern.* Dublin: Printed by J. A. Husband

Allen, Julie D., Anderson, Deborah, Becker, Joe, Cook, Richard, Davis, Mark, Edberg, Peter, Everson, Michael, Freytag, Asmus, Jenkins, John H., McGowan, Rick, Moore, Lisa, Muller, Eric, Phillips, Addison, Suignard, Michel and Whistler, Ken (eds.) 2012. *The Unicode Standard. Version 6.2 – Core Specification.* Mountain View: Unicode Consortium, https://unicode.org/versions/Unicode6.2.0/

Almeida Cabrejas, Belén 2014. 'Scriptores con bajo y medio nivel socioeducacional en documentos del siglo XIX del Archivo Municipal de Alcalá de Henares: acercamiento a sus usos gráficos', in Rocío Díaz Moreno and Belén Almeida Cabrejas (eds.), *Estudios sobre la historia de los usos gráficos en español.* Lugo: Axac, pp. 167–210

Alnwick Castle, Duke of Northumberland MS 455

Althaus, Hans Peter 1980 [1973]. 'Graphetik', in Hans Peter Althaus, Helmut Henne and Herbert E. Wiegand (eds.), *Lexikon der germanistischen Linguistik*, Tübingen: Niemeyer, pp. 105–18 [138–42], https://doi.org/10.1515/9783110960846.138

Altmann, Gabriel 2008. 'Towards a theory of script', in Gabriel Altmann and Fengxiang Fan (eds.), *Analyses of Script: Properties of Characters and Writing Systems*. Berlin/New York: De Gruyter, pp. 149–64

Álvarez Cáccamo, Celso and Herrero Valeiro, Mario 1996. 'O continuum da escrita na Galiza: entre o espanhol e o português', *Agália: Revista da Associaçom Galega da Língua* 46: 143–56

Amador-Moreno, Carolina 2019. *Orality in Written Texts: Using Historical Corpora to Investigate Irish English 1700–1900*. London: Routledge

Ambrosiani, Per 2019. 'Slavic alphabets and languages in publications by the *Propaganda Fide* during the 17th and 18th centuries', in Sebastian Kempgen and Vittorio Tomelleri (eds.), *Slavic Alphabets and Identities*. Bamberg: University of Bamberg Press, pp. 1–27

2020. 'Graphematic features in Glagolitic and Cyrillic orthographies: a contribution to the typological model of biscriptality', in Marco Condorelli (ed.), *Advances in Historical Orthography, c. 1500–1800*. Cambridge: Cambridge University Press, pp. 46–66

Amirova, Tamara A. 1977. *K istorii i teorii grafemiki*. Moscow: Nauka

1985. *Funk͡tsional'na͡ia vzaimosv͡iaz' pis'mennogo i zvukovogo ͡iazyka*. Moscow: Nauka

Ammon, Ulrich 2004. 'Standard variety', in Urlich Ammon, Norbert Dittmar, Klaus J. Mattheier and Peter J. Trudgill (eds.), *Sociolinguistics: An International Handbook of the Science of Language and Society*, vol. 1. Berlin: De Gruyter, 273–83

Ammon, Ulrich, Bickel, Hans and Lenz, Alexandra N. 2016. *Variantenwörterbuch des Deutschen. Die Standardsprache in Österreich, der Schweiz, Deutschland, Liechtenstein, Luxemburg, Ostbelgien und Südtirol sowie Rumänien, Namibia und Mennonitensiedlungen*. Berlin: De Gruyter

Amsler, Mark 2012. *Affective Literacies. Writing and Multilingualism in Late Middle Ages* (Late Medieval and Early Modern Studies). Turnhout: Brepols Publishers

2016. 'Multimodality and medieval multimodalities'. Paper presented at the Medieval/Digital Multimodalities seminar for the New Chaucer Society, The New Chaucer Society Twentieth International Congress, July 2016, Queen Mary University of London

An A,B,C for children Here is an A,B,C, deuised with sillables, with the Pater noster, the Creed & the ten Commaundments in English [...]. 1570. London: Abraham Veale, dwelling in Paules Churchyard at the signe of the Lamb (EEBO, ProQuest)

Ananiewa, Natalia 2013. 'Teksty Polaków pisane grażdanką w syberyjskiej wsi Wierszyna', *Acta Baltico-Slavica* 37: 287–98

Andersen, Jennifer L. and Sauer, Elizabeth 2002. 'Current trends in the history of reading', in Jennifer L. Andersen and Elizabeth Sauer (eds.), *Books and Readers in Early Modern England: Material Studies*. Philadelphia: University of Pennsylvania Press, pp. 1–20

Anderson, Benedict 2006. *Imagined Communities: Reflections on the Origin and Spread of Nationalism*. London/New York: Verso (revised ed.)

Anderson, John and Britton, Derek 1999. 'The orthography and phonology of the *Ormulum*', *English Language and Linguistics* 3 (2): 299–334

Anderwald, Lieselotte 2016. *Language between Description and Prescription. Verbs and Verb Categories in Nineteenth-Century Grammars of English*. Oxford: Oxford University Press

Androutsopoulos, Jannis 2000. 'Non-standard spelling in media texts: the case of German fanzines', in Alexandra M. Jaffe (ed.), *Non-Standard Orthography*, special issue of *Journal of Sociolinguistics* 4 (4): 514–33

Angermeyer, Philipp S. 2005. 'Spelling bilingualism: script choice in Russian American classified ads and signage', *Language in Society* 34 (4): 493–531

2011. 'Bilingualism meets digraphia: script alternation and script hybridity in Russian-American writing and beyond', in Mark Sebba, Shahrzad Mahootian and Carla Jonsson (eds.), *Language Mixing and Code-Switching in Writing: Approaches to Mixed-Language Written Discourse*. New York/London: Routledge, pp. 255–72

Anis, Jacques 1983. 'Pour une graphématique autonome', *Langue française* 53: *Le signifiant graphique* (ed. by Jacques Anis): 31–44

2017 [1988]. *L'écriture: théories et descriptions*. Brussels: De Boeck Université

Anis, Jacques, Chiss, Jean-Louis and Puech, Christian 1988. *L'écriture. Théories et descriptions*. Brussels: De Boeck Université

Anson, Chris M. 1990. '*Errours* and *endeavors*: a case study in American orthography', *International Journal of Lexicography* 3 (1): 35–63

Antonovich, Anton K. 1968. *Belorusskie teksty, pisannye arabskim pis'mom i ikh grafiko-orfograficheskai͡a sistema*. Vilnius: Vil'ni͡usskiĭ gosudarstvennyĭ universitet im. V. Kapsukasa

Arabyan, Marc 1994. *Le paragraphe narratif. Étude typographique et linguistique de la ponctuation textuelle dans les récits classiques et modernes*. Paris: L'Harmattan

2018. 'Histoire et emplois de l'alinéa ouvrant en diachronie (XIIIe–XVIIe siècles)', *Signata. Annales des sémiotiques* 9: 427–58

Archer, Dawn, Kytö, Merja, Baron, Alistair and Rayson, Paul 2015. 'Guidelines for normalising Early Modern English corpora: decisions and justifications', *ICAME Journal* 39: 7–42

Archivo General de la Nación, Tierras 2541, expediente 11. Land grant in Calimaya

Aris, Rutherford 1995. 'Complementary viewpoints: some thoughts on binocular vision in mathematical modeling and Latin paleography', *New Literary History* 26 (2): 395–417

Aristotle 1963. *Categories and De Interpretatione* (trans. and ed. by John L. Ackrill). Oxford: Clarendon Press

Arnot, Madeleine and Phipps, Alison 2003. 'Paper Commissioned for the EFA Global Monitoring Report 2003/4, the Leap to Equality. Gender and Education in the United Kingdom'. *Education for All Global Monitoring Report* 2003/4

Arnoux, Elvira N. 2008. *Los discursos sobre la nación y el lenguaje en la formación del Estado (Chile 1842–1862).* Buenos Aires: Santiago Arcos

Aronoff, Mark. 1989. 'The orthographic system of an early English printer: Wynkyn de Worde', *Folia Linguistics Historica* 8 (1–2): 65–97

1992. 'Segmentalism in linguistics: the alphabetic basis of phonological theory', in Pamela Downing, Susan D. Lima and Michael Noonan (eds.), *The Linguistics of Literacy.* Amsterdam: John Benjamins, pp. 71–82

Arrivé, Michel 1994. 'Un débat sans mémoire: la querelle de l'orthographe (1893–1991)', *Langages* 114: 69–83

Auer, Anita 2015. 'Stylistic variation', in Anita Auer, Daniel Schreier and Richard J. Watts (eds.), *Letter Writing and Language Change.* Cambridge: Cambridge University Press, pp. 133–55

Auer, Anita, Peersman, Catharina, Pickl, Simon, Rutten, Gijsbert and Vosters, Rik 2015. 'Historical sociolinguistics: the field and its future', *Journal of Historical Sociolinguistics* 1 (1): 1–12

Auer, Anita, Schreier, Daniel and Watts, Richard J. (eds.) 2015. *Letter Writing and Language Change.* Cambridge: Cambridge University Press

Auer, Anita and Voeste, Anja 2012. 'Grammatical variables', in Juan Manuel Hernández-Campoy and Juan Camilo Conde-Silvestre (eds.), *The Handbook of Historical Sociolinguistics.* Chichester: Wiley-Blackwell, pp. 253–70

Auer, Peter (ed.) 2007. *Style and Social Identities: Alternative Approaches to Linguistic Heterogeneity.* Berlin/New York: De Gruyter

Auer, Peter and Hinskens, Frans 2005. 'The role of interpersonal accommodation in a theory of language change', in Peter Auer, Frans Hinskens and Paul Kerswill (eds.), *Dialect Change: Convergence and Divergence in European Languages,* Cambridge/New York: Cambridge University Press, pp. 335–57

Augst, Gerhard 1986. 'Descriptively and explanatorily adequate models of orthography', in Gerhard Augst (ed.), *New Trends in Graphemics and Orthography.* Berlin: De Gruyter, pp. 25–42

Avanesov, Ruben I. 1955. 'Fonetika', in Viktor I. Borkovskiĭ (ed.), *Paleograficheskiĭ i lingvisticheskiĭ analiz novgorodskikh beresti͡anykh gramot.* Moscow: Izdatel'stvo Akademii Nauk SSSR, pp. 79–102

Ayres-Bennett, Wendy 1994. 'Elaboration and codification: standardization and attitudes towards the French language in the sixteenth and seventeenth centuries', in Mair M. Parry, Winifred V. Davis and Rosalind A.

M. Temple (eds.), *The Changing Voices of Europe. Social and Political Changes and Their Linguistic Repercussions*. Temple: University of Wales Press, pp. 53-73

Backhouse, Anthony E. 1984. 'Aspects of the graphological structure of Japanese', *Visible Language* 18 (3): 219–28

Baddeley, Susan 2012. 'French orthography in the 16th century', in Susan Baddeley and Anja Voeste (eds.), *Orthographies in Early Modern Europe*. Berlin/Boston: De Gruyter, pp. 97–125

Baddeley, Susan and Biedermann-Pasques, Liselotte 2004. 'Histoire des systèmes graphiques du français à travers des manuscrits et des incunables (IXe–XVe siècle). Segmentation graphique et faits de langue', *Revue de linguistique romane*, 269–70: 181–201

Baddeley, Susan and Voeste, Anja 2012a. 'Introduction. Orthographies in Early Modern Europe: a comparative view', in Susan Baddeley and Anja Voeste (eds.), *Orthographies in Early Modern Europe*. Berlin/Boston: De Gruyter, pp. 1–13

(eds.) 2012b. *Orthographies in Early Modern Europe*. Berlin/Boston: De Gruyter

Bagge, Sverre and Mykland, Knut 1987. *Norge i dansketiden*. Oslo: Cappelen

Bagley, Robert W. 2004. 'Anyang writing and the origin of the Chinese writing system', in Stephen D. Houston (ed.), *The First Writing: Script Invention as History and Process*. Cambridge: Cambridge University Press, pp. 190–249

Baines, John 2004. 'The earliest Egyptian writing: development, context, purpose', in Stephen D. Houston (ed.), *The First Writing: Script Invention as History and Process*. Cambridge: Cambridge University Press, pp. 150–89

Baisch, Martin 2018. 'Transmission and materiality: philology, old and new, in German medieval studies', *Digital Philology* 6 (2): 177–95

Baker, Philip 1997. 'Developing ways of writing vernaculars: problems and solutions in a historical perspective', in Andrée Tabouret-Keller, Robert B. Le Page, Penelope Gardner-Chloros and Gabrielle Varro (eds.), *Vernacular Literacy: A Re-Evaluation*. Oxford: Clarendon, pp. 93–141

Bakhtin, Mikhail M. 1975. *Voprosy literatury i ėstetiki: Issledovanii͡a raznykh let*. Moscow: Khudozhestvennai͡a literatura

1981. *The Dialogic Imagination* (ed. by Michael Holquist; trans. by Caryl Emerson and Michael Holquist). Austin: University of Texas Press

Balbach, Anna-Maria 2014. *Sprache und Konfession. Frühneuzeitliche Inschriften des Totengedächtnisses in Bayerisch-Schwaben*. Würzburg: Ergon

Balestra, Miriam, Appelt, Annalen and Neef, Martin 2014. 'Systematische Beschränkungen für Schreibungen im grammatischen Wortschatz des Deutschen: der Konsonant [f]', *Zeitschrift für Sprachwissenschaft* 33 (2): 129–63, https://doi.org10.1515/zfs-2014-0006

Bann, Jennifer and Corbett, John 2015. *Spelling Scots. The Orthography of Literary Scots, 1700–2000*. Edinburgh: Edinburgh University Press

Barnard, John 2002. 'Introduction', in John Barnard and Donald F. McKenzie (eds.), *The Cambridge History of the Book in Britain*, vol. 4: *1557-1695*. Cambridge: Cambridge University Press, pp. 1–25

Barnes, Michael P. 2012. *Runes: A Handbook*. Woodbridge: Boydell

Baron, Alistair and Rayson, Paul 2008. 'VARD 2: a tool for dealing with spelling variation in historical corpora', in *Proceedings of the Postgraduate Conference in Corpus Linguistics*. Birmingham: Aston University

Baron, Naomi S. 2001. 'Commas and canaries: the role of punctuation in speech and writing', *Language Sciences* 23: 15–67

Barratt, Alexandra 2010. *Women's Writing in Middle English: An Annotated Anthology*. Old Tappan: Taylor and Francis

Barros, Maria C. 1995. 'The missionary presence in literacy campaigns in the indigenous languages of Latin America (1939–1952)', *International Journal of Educational Development* 15 (3): 277–87

Barteld, Fabian, Hartmann, Stefan and Szczepaniak, Renata 2016. 'The usage and spread of sentence-internal capitalization in Early New High German: a multifactorial approach', *Folia Linguistica* 50 (2): 385–412

Barton, David 1994. *Literacy: An Introduction to the Ecology of Written Language*. London: Blackwell

1995. 'Some problems with an evolutionary view of written language', in Stanisław Puppel (ed.), *The Biology of Language*. Amsterdam: John Benjamins, pp. 19–31

Bartoněk, Antonín 2003. *Handbuch des Mykenischen Griechisch*. Heidelberg: Winter

Bartsch, Renate 1985. 'The influence of language standardisation on linguistic norms', *Studia Linguistica* 39: 23–50

Bassetti, Benedetta 2012. 'Bilingualism and writing systems', in Tej K. Bhatia and William C. Ritchie (eds.), *The Handbook of Bilingualism and Multilingualism*. Hoboken: John Wiley and Sons, pp. 649–70 (2nd ed.)

Basso, Keith H. 1974. 'The ethnography of writing', in Richard Bauman and Joel Sherzer (eds.), *Explorations in the Ethnography of Speaking*. Cambridge: Cambridge University Press, pp. 425–32

Basu, Anupam 2016. 'Ill shapen sounds, and false orthography: a computational approach to early English orthographic variation', in Laura Estill, Michael Ullyot and Diane Jackaki (eds.), *New Technologies in Medieval and Renaissance Studies*. Tempe: Arizona Center for Medieval and Renaissance Studies/Iter, pp. 167–200

Bates, Stephen 2019. 'Prejudice and the press critics: Colonel Robert McCormick's assault on the Hutchins commission', *American Journalism* 36 (4): 420–46

Battaner Moro, Elena 2009. 'La investigación sobre ortografía, fonética y fonología en la tradición lingüística española', in Teresa Bastardín Candón and Manuel Rivas Zancarrón (eds.), *Estudios de historiografía lingüística*. Cádiz: Universidad de Cádiz, pp. 27–43

Bauer, Laurie 2003. *Introducing Linguistic Morphology*. Washington, DC: Georgetown University Press (2nd ed.)

Baugh, Albert C. 1957. *A History of the English Language*. New York: Appleton-Century-Crofts

Baugh, Albert C. and Cable, Thomas 1993. *A History of the English Language*. Upper Saddle River: Prentice Hall (4th ed.)

2002. *A History of the English Language*, Upper Saddle River: Prentice Hall (5th ed.)

Baxter, William H. and Sagart, Laurent 2014. *Old Chinese: A New Reconstruction*. Oxford: Oxford University Press

Bayley, Robert 2013. 'Variationist sociolinguistics', in Robert Bayley, Richard Cameron and Ceil Lucas (eds.), *The Oxford Handbook of Sociolinguistics*. Oxford: Oxford University Press, https://doi.org/10.1093/oxfordhb/9780199744084.013.0001

Bazell, Charles E. 1981 [1956]. 'The grapheme', in Piotr Ruszkiewicz (ed.), *Graphophonemics: A Book of Readings*. Katowice: Uniwersytet Śląski, pp. 66–70 (reprint from *Litera* 3: 43–46)

Beal, Joan C. 2016. 'Standardisation', in Merja Kytö and Päivi Pahta (eds.), *The Cambridge Handbook of English Historical Linguistics*. Cambridge: Cambridge University Press, pp. 301–17

Beal, Joan C., Sen, Ranjan, Yáñez-Bouza, Nuria and Wallis, Christine (eds.) 2020. *Studies in Late Modern English Historical Phonology Using the Eighteenth-Century English Phonology Database (ECEP)*, special issue of *English Language and Linguistics* 22 (3). Cambridge: Cambridge University Press

Beal, Peter 1998. *In Praise of Scribes: Manuscripts and Their Makers in Seventeenth-Century England*. Oxford: Clarendon Press

2008. *A Dictionary of English Manuscript Terminology, 1450–2000*. Oxford: Oxford University Press

Beekes, Robert 1971. 'The writing of consonant groups in Mycenaean', *Mnemosyne* 24: 338–39

Begor Lancashire, Anne (ed.) 1978. *Thomas Middleton. The Second Maiden's Tragedy*. Edited from British Library Lansdowne MS 807. Manchester: Manchester University Press

Behaghel, Otto 1911. *Geschichte de deutschen Sprache. Dritte vollständig umgearbeitete Auflage*. Strasbourg: Verlag von Karl J. Trübner

Beit-Arie, Malachi 1993. *The Makings of the Medieval Hebrew Book: Studies in Palaeography and Codicology*. Jerusalem: Magnes Press

Bell, Allan 1984. 'Language style as audience design', *Language in Society* 13: 145–204

2007. 'Style and the linguistic repertoire', in Carmen Llamas, Louise Mullany and Peter Stockwell (eds.), *The Routledge Companion to Sociolinguistics*. London: Routledge, pp. 95–100

Bell, David N. 1999. 'Monastic libraries: 1400–1557', in Lotte Hellinga and Joseph B. Trapp (eds.), *The Cambridge History of the Book in Britain*, vol. 3: *1400–1557*. Cambridge: Cambridge University Press, pp. 229–54

Bell, Maureen and Barnard, John 1992. 'Provisional count of STC titles 1475–1640', *Publishing History* 31: 49–55

Bello, Andrés and García del Río, Juan 1823. 'Indicaciones sobre la conveniencia de simplificar i uniformar la ortografía en América', in *La Biblioteca Americana, o, Miscelánea de Literatura, Artes i Ciencias: Por Una Sociedad de Americanos* 1: 50–62. London: en la imprenta de don G. Marchant

1826 [1823]. *Indicaciones sobre la conveniencia de simplificar i uniformar la ortografía en América*. Caracas: Imprenta de Domingo Navas Spínola

Benediktsson, Hreinn 1972. *The First Grammatical Treatise: Introduction, Text, Notes, Translation, Vocabulary, Facsimiles* (University of Iceland Publications in Linguistics 1). Reykjavík: Institute of Nordic Linguistics

Benskin, Michael 1982. 'The letters <þ> and <y> in later Middle English, and some related matters', *Journal of the Society of Archivists* 7: 13–30

1992. 'Some new perspectives on the origins of standard written English', in Jan A. van Leuvensteijn and Jan B. Berns (eds.), *Dialect and Standard Language in the English, Dutch, German and Norwegian Language Areas: 17 Studies in English or German*. Amsterdam: Netherlands Academy of Arts and Science, pp. 71–105

1997. 'Texts from a township in late medieval Ireland', *Collegium Medievale* 10: 91–173

2004. 'Chancery Standard', in Christian J. Kay, Carole Hough and Irene Wotherspoon (eds.), *New Perspectives on English Historical Linguistics*, vol. 2: *Lexis and Transmission*. Amsterdam/Philadelphia: John Benjamins, pp. 1–40

Benskin, Michael and Laing, Margaret 1981. 'Translations and *Mischsprachen* in Middle English manuscripts', in Michael Benskin and Michael L. Samuels (eds.), *So Meny People Longages and Tonges: Philological Essays in Scots and Mediaeval English Presented to Angus McIntosh*. Edinburgh: Middle English Dialect Project, pp. 55–106

Bentin, Shlomo 1992. 'Phonological awareness, reading, and reading acquisition: a survey and appraisal of current knowledge', in Ram Frost and Leonard Katz (eds.), *Orthography, Phonology, Morphology, and Meaning*. London/Amsterdam: North-Holland, pp. 193–210

Berg, Ivar 2016. 'The making of the Scandinavian languages', in Gijsbert Rutten and Kristine Horner (eds.), *Metalinguistic Perspectives on Germanic Languages: European Case Studies*. Oxford: Peter Lang, pp. 35–55

Berg, Ivar, Bugge, Edit, Sandøy, Helge and Røyneland, Unn 2018. 'Geografisk og sosial variasjon', in Brit Mæhlum (ed.), *Praksis*, vol. 2 of Helge Sandøy and Agnete Nesse (eds.), *Norsk språkhistorie*. Oslo: Novus, pp. 163–256

Berg, Kristian 2014. 'Morphological spellings in English', in Kristian Berg, Franzizka Buchmann and Nanna Fuhrhop (eds.), *The Architecture of Writing Systems*, special issue of *Written Language and Literacy* 17 (2). Amsterdam/Philadelphia: John Benjamins, pp. 282–307

2016. 'Graphemic analysis and the spoken language bias', *Frontiers in Psychology* 7: 388, https://doi.org/10.3389/fpsyg.2016.00388

2019. *Die Graphematik der Morpheme im Deutschen und Englischen*. Berlin/Boston: De Gruyter, https://doi.org/10.1515/9783110604856

Berg, Kristian and Aronoff, Mark 2017. 'Self-organisation in the spelling of English suffixes: the emergence of culture out of anarchy', *Language* 93 (1): 37–64, https://doi.org/10.1353/lan.2017.0000

2018. 'Further evidence for self-organization in English spelling', *Language* 94 (1): e48–e53, https://doi.org/10.1353/lan.2018.0013

Berg, Kristian and Evertz, Martin 2018. 'Graphematik – die Beziehung zwischen Sprache und Schrift', in Stefanie Dipper, Ralf Klabunde and Wiltrud Mihatsch (eds.), *Linguistik: Eine Einführung (nicht nur) für Germanisten, Romanisten und Anglisten*. Berlin/Heidelberg: Springer, pp. 187–95

Berg, Kristian, Primus, Beatrice and Wagner, Lutz 2016. 'Buchstabenmerkmal, Buchstabe, Graphem', in Beatrice Primus and Ulrike Domahs (eds.), *Laut – Gebärde – Buchstabe*. Berlin/New York: De Gruyter, pp. 337–55

Bergen, University Library, MS 613

Bergen, University Library, MS 936.B.2

Berger, Tilman 2012. 'Religion and diacritics: the case of Czech orthography', in Susan Baddeley and Anja Voeste (eds.), *Orthographies in Early Modern Europe*. Berlin/Boston: De Gruyter, pp. 255–68

Berger, Tilman, Gutschmidt, Karl, Kempgen, Sebastian and Kosta, Peter (eds.) 2009/2014. *Die slavischen Sprachen. Ein internationales Handbuch zu ihrer Struktur, ihrer Geschichte und ihrer Erforschung, Bd. 1–2/The Slavic Languages: An International Handbook of Their Structure, Their History and Their Investigation*, 2 vols. Berlin/Munich/Boston: De Gruyter

Bergeron, Réjean and Ornato, Ezio 1990. 'La lisibilité dans les manuscrits et les imprimés à la fin du Moyen Âge: préliminaires d'une recherche', *Scrittura e Civiltà* 14: 151–98

Bergmann, Rolf 1999. 'Zur Herausbildung der deutschen Substantivgroßschreibung: Ergebnisse des Bamberg-Rostocker Projekts', in Walter Hoffmann (ed.), *Das Frühneuhochdeutsche als sprachgeschichtliche Epoche*. Frankfurt am Main/New York: Peter Lang, pp. 59–79

Bergmann, Rolf and Nerius, Dieter 1998. *Die Entwicklung der Großschreibung im Deutschen von 1500 bis 1710*. Heidelberg: Winter

2006. *Die Entwicklung der Großschreibung im Deutschen von 1500 bis 1700*. Heidelberg: Winter (4th ed.)

Bergs, Alexander 2005. *Social Networks and Historical Sociolinguistics: Studies in Morphosyntactic Variation in the Paston Letters (1421–1503)*. Berlin: De Gruyter

2013. 'Writing, reading, language change – a sociohistorical perspective on scribes, readers, and networks in medieval Britain', in Esther-Miriam Wagner, Ben Outhwaite and Bettina Beinhoff (eds.), *Scribes as Agents of Language Change*. Berlin: De Gruyter, pp. 241–60

Berkenbusch, Eckhard 1997. *Übungsbuch der chinesischen Schriftzeichen für praktisches Chinesisch*, vol. 1. Beijing: Kommerzieller Verlag

Berlanda, Elena 2006. 'New perspectives on digraphia: a framework for the sociolinguistics of writing systems'. Major research paper, York University, Toronto

Bermel, Neil 2007. *Linguistic Authority, Language Ideology, and Metaphor: The Czech Orthography War*. Berlin: De Gruyter

Bernabé, Alberto and Luján, Eugenio R. 2006. *Introducción al Griego Micénico: Gramática, selección de textos y glosario*. Zaragoza: Prensas Universitarias de Zaragoza

Bernard, H. Russell 1980. 'Orthography for whom?', *International Journal of American Linguistics* 46 (2): 133–36

Berrendonner, Alain and Reichler-Béguelin, Marie-José 1989. 'Décalages: les niveaux de l'analyse linguistique', *Langue française* 81: 99–125

Berta, Tibor 2017. 'La norma ortográfica en el contexto de la historia de la lengua española. La utopía de la ortografía fonémica', *Acta Hispanica* 22: 15–23

Biava, Christina 1990. 'Native American languages and literacy: issues of orthography choice and bilingual education', *Kansas Working Papers in Linguistics* 15 (2): 45–59

Biber, Douglas 1995. *Dimensions of Register Variation: A Cross-Linguistic Comparison*. Cambridge: Cambridge University Press

2006. *University Language: A Corpus-Based Study of Spoken and Written Registers*. Amsterdam/Philadelphia: John Benjamins

Biber, Douglas and Conrad, Susan 2009. *Register, Genre and Style*. Cambridge: Cambridge University Press

Biber, Douglas and Finegan, Edward (eds.) 1990–2013. *A Representative Corpus of Historical English Registers* (ARCHER). Originally compiled under the supervision of Douglas Biber and Edward Finegan at Northern Arizona University and University of Southern California; modified and expanded by subsequent members of a consortium of universities. Current member universities are Bamberg, Freiburg, Heidelberg, Helsinki, Lancaster, Leicester, Manchester, Michigan, Northern Arizona, Santiago de Compostela, Southern California, Trier, Uppsala and Zurich, www.projects.alc.manchester.ac.uk/archer/

(eds.) 1994. *Sociolinguistic Perspectives on Register*. Oxford: Oxford University Press

Bilet͡s′ka, Olena 2015. 'Stanovlenni͡a hrafichnoï linhvistyky i͡ak kompleksnoï nauky: analitychnyĭ ohli͡ad', *Naukovyĭ visnyk Khersons'koho derzhavnoho universytetu, ser. Linhvistyka* 19: 18–28, http://ekhsuir.kspu.edu/handle/123456789/1648

Birk, Elisabeth 2013. 'Graphem', in Martin Neef, Said Sahel and Rüdiger Weingarten (eds.), *Schriftlinguistik/Grapholinguistics* (Wörterbücher zur Sprach- und Kommunikationswissenschaft/Dictionaries of Linguistics and Communication Science 5). Berlin/Boston: De Gruyter, www.degruyter.com/view/db/wsk

Bischoff, Bernhard 1990 [1979]. *Latin Palaeography: Antiquity and the Middle Ages* (trans. by Dáibhí Ó Cróinín and David Ganz). Cambridge: Cambridge University Press

Bischoff, Bernhard, Duft, Johannes and Sonderegger, Stefan (eds.) 1977. *Das älteste deutsche Buch: Die Abrogans-Handschrift der Stiftsbibliothek St. Gallen*. St. Gallen: Zollikofer

Bjørnson, Bjørnstjerne 1898. *Synnøve Solbakken*. Copenhagen: Gyldendal

Blake, Norman F. 1965. 'English versions of *Reynard the Fox* in the fifteenth and sixteenth centuries', *Studies in Philology* 62 (1): 63–77

1992. 'Introduction', in Norman F. Blake (ed.), *The Cambridge History of the English Language*, vol. 2: *1066–1476*. Cambridge: Cambridge University Press, pp. 1–22

Blake, Norman F. and Thaisen, Jacob 2004. 'Spelling's significance for textual studies', *Nordic Journal of English Studies* 3 (1): 93–107

Bland, Mark 2010. *A Guide to Early Printed Books and Manuscripts*. London: Wiley-Blackwell

Blank, Paula 1996. *Broken English: Dialects and the Politics of Language in Renaissance Writings*. London: Routledge

Blanton, Virginia, O'Mara, Veronica and Stoop, Patricia (eds.) 2013. *Nuns' Literacies in Medieval Europe: The Hull Dialogue*. Turnhout: Brepols Publishers

Blatt, Heather 2018. *Participatory Reading in Late-Medieval England*. Manchester: Manchester University Press

Blayney, Peter W. M. 2003. *The Stationers' Company before the Charter, 1403–1557*. London: Worshipful Company of Stationers

Bliss, Charles K. 1965. *Semantography (Blisssymbolics): A Logical Writing for an Illogical World*. Sydney: Semantography (Blissymbolics) Publications (2nd ed.)

Blix, Elias 1869. *Nokre Salma, gamle og nye*. Christiania: Forlagt av det Norske Samlaget

Blomfield, Joan E. 1935. 'The origins of Old English orthography, with special reference to the representation of the spirants and w'. B. Litt. thesis, Oxford University, UK

Blommaert, Jan 2013. 'Writing as a sociolinguistic object', *Journal of Sociolinguistics* 17: 440–59

(ed.) 1999. *Language Ideological Debates*. Berlin: De Gruyter

Bloomfield, Leonard 1927. 'Literate and illiterate speech', *American Speech* 2: 432–39

1933. *Language*. New York: Holt, Rinehart and Winston

1935 [1933]. *Language*. London: George Allen and Unwin

1973 [1933]. *Language*. London: George Allen and Unwin (a British, revised ed., 11th reprint)

Blount, Thomas 1654. *The academie of eloquence containing a compleat English* [...]. London: T. N. for Humphrey Moseley (EEBO, ProQuest)

Boduėn de Kurtenė, Ivan 1912. *Ob otnoshenii russkogo pis'ma k russkomu i͡azyku*. Saint Petersburg: Redakt͡sii͡a zhurnala 'Obnovlenie shkoly', http://books.e-heritage.ru/book/10075813

Boekholt, Petrus Th. F. M. and De Booy, Engelina P. 1987. *Geschiedenis van de school in Nederland vanaf de middeleeuwen tot aan de huidige tijd*. Assen/Maastricht: Van Gorcum

Boesch, Bruno 1946. *Untersuchungen zur alemannischen Urkundensprache des 13. Jahrhunderts. Laut- und Formenlehre*. Bern: Francke

1968. 'Die deutsche Urkundensprache. Probleme ihrer Erforschung im deutschen Südwesten', *Rheinische Vierteljahrsblätter* 32: 1–28

Bolinger, Dwight 1946. 'Visual morphemes', *Language* 22: 333–40

Bomann-Larsen, Tor 2004. *Folket. Haakon & Maud II*. Oslo: Cappelen

Bondarev, Dmitry 2019. 'Introduction: orthographic polyphony in Arabic script', in Dmitry Bondarev, Alessandro Godi and Lameen Souag (eds.), *Creating Standards: Interactions with Arabic Script in 12 Manuscript Cultures*. Berlin: De Gruyter, pp. 1–37

Bondarev, Dmitry, Godi, Alessandro and Souag, Lameen (eds.) 2019. *Creating Standards: Interactions with Arabic Script in 12 Manuscript Cultures*. Berlin: De Gruyter

Bonfante, Giuliano and Bonfante, Larissa 2002. *The Etruscan Language: An Introduction*. Manchester/New York: Manchester University Press (revised ed.)

Borkovskiĭ, Viktor I. (ed.) 1955. *Paleograficheskiĭ i lingvisticheskiĭ analiz novgorodskikh berestîanykh gramot*. Moscow: Izdatel'stvo Akademii Nauk SSSR

Borleffs, Elisabeth, Maassen, Ben A. M., Lyytinen, Heikki and Zwarts, Frans 2017. 'Measuring orthographic transparency and morphological-syllabic complexity in alphabetic orthographies: a narrative review', *Reading and Writing* 30: 1617–38

Bosman, D. B., Le Roux, T. H., Malherbe, D. F. and Smith, Johannes J. 1921. *Afrikaanse Woordelys en Spelreëls*. Bloemfontein: Die Nasionale Pers

Bottéro, Françoise 2004. 'Writing on shell and bone in Shang China', in Stephen D. Houston (ed.), *The First Writing: Script Invention as History and Process*. Cambridge: Cambridge University Press, pp. 250–61

Bourciez, Édouard 1958. *Précis historique de phonétique française*. Paris: Klincksieck (9th ed.)

Bowie, David 2015. 'Phonological variation in real time: patterns of adult linguistic stability and change', in Annette Gerstenberg and Anja Voeste (eds.), *Language Development: The Lifespan Perspective*. Amsterdam: John Benjamins, pp. 39–58

Boyle, Leonard E. 1984. *Medieval Latin Palaeography: A Bibliographic Introduction*. Toronto: University of Toronto Press

Brackmann, Rebecca 2012. *The Elizabethan Invention of Anglo-Saxon England*. Cambridge: D. S. Brewer, pp. 55–83

Bradley, Henry 1919 [1913]. *On the Relations between Spoken and Written Language, with Special Reference to English*. Oxford: Clarendon Press (reprint)

Brajerski, Tadeusz 1990. *Język staro-cerkiewno-słowiański*. Lublin: Wydawnictwo Katolickiego Uniwersytetu Lubelskiego (7th ed.)

Branca-Rosoff, Sonia and Schneider, Nathalie 1994. *L'écriture des citoyens. Une analyse linguistique de l'écriture des peu-lettrés pendant la période révolutionnaire*. Paris: Klincksieck

Brandt, Carmen 2016. 'Hindi–Urdu', in Daniel Bunčić, Sandra L. Lippert and Achim Rabus (eds.), *Biscriptality: A Sociolinguistic Typology*. Heidelberg: Winter, pp. 149–58

Braune, Wilhelm 1880. *Gotische Grammatik: mit einigen Lesestücken und Wortverzeichnis. Sammlung kurzer Grammatiken germanischer Dialekte 1*. Halle: Niemeyer

1886. *Althochdeutsche Grammatik* (Sammlung kurzer Grammatiken germanischer Dialekte 5). Halle: Niemeyer

Braune, Wilhelm and Ebbinghaus, Ernst A. 1994. *Althochdeutsches Lesebuch*. Tübingen: Niemeyer (17th ed.)

Braune, Wilhelm and Eggers, Hans 1975. *Althochdeutsche Grammatik*. Tübingen: Niemeyer (13th ed.)

Braune, Wilhelm and Heidermanns, Frank 2018. *Althochdeutsche Grammatik I: Laut- und Formenlehre*. Berlin: De Gruyter (16th ed.)

Braune, Wilhelm and Reiffenstein, Ingo 2004. *Althochdeutsche Grammatik*. Tübingen: Niemeyer (15th ed.)

Breasted, James H. 1910. 'Egyptian paleography', review of *Hieratische Palaeographie. Die Aegyptische Buchschrift in Ihrer Entwicklungvon der Fünften Dynastie bis zur Römischen Kaiserzeit* by Georg Moeller, *American Journal of Semitic Languages and Literatures* 26 (2): 133–36

Bredel, Ursula 2005. 'Zur Geschichte der Interpunktionskonventionen des Deutschen - dargestellt an der Kodifizierung des Punktes', *Zeitschrift für Germanistische Linguistik* 33: 179–211

2008. *Die Interpunktion des Deutschen. Ein kompositionelles System zur Online-Steuerung des Lesens*. Tübingen: Niemeyer

2009. 'Das Interpunktionssystem des Deutschen', in Angelika Linke and Helmuth Feilke (eds.), *Oberfläche und Performanz. Untersuchungen zur Sprache als dynamischer Gestalt*. Tübingen: Niemeyer, pp. 117–35

Brehmer, Bernhard and Golubović, Biljana (eds.) 2010. *Serbische und kroatische Schriftlinguistik. Geschichte, Perspektiven und aktuelle Problem* (Studien zur Slavistik 25). Hamburg: Verlag Dr. Kovač

Breier, Willi 1910. *'Eule und Nachtigall': eine Untersuchung der Überlieferung und der Sprache, der örtlichen und der zeitlichen Entstehung des me. Gedichts*. Halle: Niemeyer

Brekle, Herbert E. 1995. 'Neues über Groß- und Kleinbuchstaben. Theoretische Begründung der Entwicklung der römischen Majuskelformen zur Minuskelschrift', *Linguistische Berichte* 155: 3–22

Brengelman, Frederick H. 1980. 'Orthoepists, printers and the rationalization of English spelling', *Journal of English and Germanic Philology* 79: 332–54

Bright, William 1999. 'A matter of typology: alphasyllabaries and abugidas', *Written Language and Literacy* 2 (1): 45–55

Brinsley, John 1612. *Ludus literarius: or, the grammar schoole shewing how to proceede from the first entrance into learning, to the highest perfection required in the grammar schools* [...]. London: [Humphrey Lownes] for Thomas Man (EEBO, ProQuest)

Brinton, Laurel J. and Arnovick, Leslie K. 2006/2011. *The English Language. A Linguistic History*. Ontario: Oxford University Press (2nd ed.)

Britain, David 2004. 'Dialect and accent', in Urlich Ammon, Norbert Dittmar, Klaus J. Mattheier and Peter J. Trudgill (eds.), *Sociolinguistics: An International Handbook of the Science of Language and Society*, vol. 1. Berlin: De Gruyter, 267–73

Brooks, Greg 2015. *Dictionary of the British English Spelling System*. Cambridge: Open Book Publishers, www.openbookpublishers.com/product/325

Brooksbank, Joseph 1651. *An English Monosyllabary* [...]. London: Printed for Edward Brewster

Brown, Goold 1859 [1850]. *The Grammar of English Grammars*. New York: Samuel S. and William Wood (4th ed.)

Brown, Joshua 2019. *Historical Heritage Language Ego-Documents: From Home, from Away, and from Below*, special issue of *Journal of Historical Sociolinguistics* 5 (2). Berlin: De Gruyter

Brown, Keith and Miller, Jim 2013. *The Cambridge Dictionary of Linguistics*. New York: Cambridge University Press

Brown, Michelle P. 1990. *A Guide to Western Historical Scripts from Antiquity to 1600*. London: The British Library

Brown, Shana J. 2011. *Pastimes: From Art and Antiquarianism to Modern Chinese Historiography*. Honolulu: University of Hawai'i Press

Bruce, John (ed.) 1849. *Letters of Queen Elizabeth and King James VI of Scotland*. London: Camden Society

Brunschwig, Hieronymus 1528. *The Vertuose Boke of Distyllacyon of Waters of all Maner of Herbes: with the Fygures of Styllatoryes*. London: Laurens Andrewe

Brzezina, Maria 1997. 'Propozycje zastosowania grażdanki do języka polskiego z drugiej połowy XIX wieku', in Anna Bolek, Adam Fałowski and Bożena Zinkiewicz-Tomanek (eds.), *Słowianie Wschodni. Między językiem a kulturą. Księga jubileuszowa dedykowana Profesorowi Wiesławowi Witkowskiemu w siedemdziesiątą rocznicę urodzin*. Kraków: Wydawnictwo Grell i córka s.c., pp. 161–67

Buben, Vladimir 1935. *Influence de l'orthographe sur la prononciation du français moderne*, Bratislava: University Komenského

Buck, Carl D. 1928. *A Grammar of Oscan and Umbrian: With a Collection of Inscriptions and a Glossary*. Boston: Ginn (2nd ed.)

Buckley, Eugene 2018. 'Core syllables vs. moraic writing', in Merijn Beeksma and Martin Neef (eds.), *Understanding Writing Systems*, special issue of *Written Language and Literacy* 21 (1). Amsterdam/Philadelphia: John Benjamins, pp. 26–51

Bülbring, Karl D. 1899. 'Was lässt sich aus dem Gebrauch der Buchstaben *k* und *c* im Matthäus-Evangelium des Rushworth-Manuscripts folgern?', *Anglia Beiblatt* 9 (10): 289–300

Bull, Ida 2015. 'Leseopplæring og lesebehov i norske byer før 1750', *Heimen* 52: 265–78

Bull, Tove (ed.) 2018. *Ideologi*, vol. 3 of Helge Sandøy and Agnete Nesse (eds.), *Norsk språkhistorie*. Oslo: Novus

Bull, Tove, Karlsen, Espen, Raanes, Eli and Theil, Rolf 2018. 'Andre språk i Noreg', in Brit Mæhlum (ed.) *Praksis*, vol 2 of Helge Sandøy and Agnete Nesse (eds.), *Norsk språkhistorie*. Oslo: Novus, pp. 417–532

Bullokar, William 1580a. *Bullokars Booke at large, for the Amendment of Orthographie for English speech: wherein, a most perfect supplie is made, for the wantes and double sounde of letters in the olde Orthographie.* London: Henry Denham

1968 [1580b]. *The Amendment of Orthographie for English Speech.* Amsterdam: Theatrum Orbis Terrarum (reprint)

Bullough, Donald A. 1991. *Carolingian Renewal: Sources and Heritage.* Manchester: Manchester University Press

Bunčić, Daniel 2012. 'The standardization of Polish orthography in the 16th century', in Susan Baddeley and Anja Voeste (eds.), *Orthographies in Early Modern Europe*. Berlin/Boston: De Gruyter, pp. 219–54

2016. 'Diorthographia', in Daniel Bunčić, Sandra L. Lippert and Achim Rabus (eds.), *Biscriptality: A Sociolinguistic Typology.* Heidelberg: Winter, pp. 129–48

forthcoming. 'Graphematik', in Daniel Bunčić, Hagen Pitsch and Barbara Sonnenhauser (eds.), *Einführung in die Linguistik der slavischen Sprachen*

Bunčić, Daniel, Lippert, Sandra L. and Rabus, Achim (eds.) 2016. *Biscriptality: A Sociolinguistic Typology.* Heidelberg: Winter

Burchfield, Robert 1994. 'Line-end hyphens in the *Ormulum* manuscript (MS Junius I)', in Malcolm Godden, Douglas Gray and Terry Hoad (eds.), *From Anglo-Saxon to Early Middle English.* Oxford: Clarendon Press, pp. 182–87

Burke, Peter 2004. *Languages and Communities in Early Modern Europe.* Cambridge: Cambridge University Press

Burkhard, Conrad 2002. 'Zur Ungleichzeitigkeit in der Weltgesellschaft. Erkenntnistheoretische Kommentare zur Kriegsursachenforschung, Arbeitspapier 1/2002'. Universität Hamburg – IPW, Forschungsstelle Kriege, Rüstung und Entwicklung, www.wiso.uni-hamburg.de/fachbereich-sowi/professuren/jakobeit/forschung/akuf/archiv/arbeitspapiere/weltgesellschaft-conrad-2002.pdf

Burnaby, Barbara 2013. 'How have Aboriginal North Americans responded to writing systems in their own languages?', in Katy Arnett and Callie Mady (eds.), *Minority Populations in Canadian Second Language Education.* Bristol/Buffalo/Toronto: Multilingual Matters, 184–98

Burns, Edward (ed.) 2000. *King Henry VI Part 1, by William Shakespeare.* London: The Arden Shakespeare

Burridge, Kate 2013. 'Nineteenth-century study of sound change from Rask to Saussure', in Keith Allan (ed.), *The Oxford Handbook of the History of Linguistics.* Oxford: Oxford University Press, pp. 141–65

Burrows, Steven D. 2010. 'Source code authorship attribution'. Doctoral dissertation, RMIT University, Melbourne, Australia

Butler, Charles 1633. *The English Grammar* [...]. Oxford: William Turner

Bybee, Joan L. 2007. *Frequency of Use and the Organization of Language.* Oxford: Oxford University Press

Bynack, Vincent P. 1984. 'Noah Webster and the idea of a national culture: the pathologies of epistemology', *Journal of the History of Ideas* 45: 99–114

Cahier, Jean-Pierre and Zacklad, Manuel 2004. 'Socio-semantic web applications: towards a methodology based on the theory of the communities of action', in *Proceedings of International Conference on the Design of Cooperative Systems*, French Riviera, May 11–14

Cahill, Michael 2018. 'Orthography design and implementation for endangered languages', in Kenneth L. Rehg and Lyle Campbell (eds.), *The Oxford Handbook of Endangered Languages*. Oxford: Oxford University Press, pp. 326–46

Cahill, Michael and Rice, Keren (eds.) 2014. *Developing Orthographies for Unwritten Languages*. Dallas: SIL International

Calle-Martín, Javier 2004. 'Punctuation practice in a 15th-century arithmetical treatise (Ms. Bodley 790)', *Neuphilologische Mitteilungen* 105 (4): 407–22

2009. 'Line-final word division in late Middle English *Fachprosa*', in Javier Díaz Vera and Rosario Caballero (eds.), *Textual Healing: Studies in Medieval English Medical, Scientific and Technical Texts*. Frankfurt am Main: Peter Lang, pp. 35–53

2011a. 'Line-final word division in early English handwriting', in Jacob Thaisen and Hanna Rutkowska (eds.), *Scribes, Printers, and the Accidentals of Their Texts*. Frankfurt am Main: Peter Lang, pp. 15–29

2011b. 'Through the looking glass: the palaeography of Benvenutus Grassus' English vernacular tradition', in Antonio Miranda-García and Santiago González (eds.), *Benvenutus Grassus' On the Well-proven Art of the Eye (Practica Oculorum and De Probatissima Arte Oculorum), as Found in MSS Hunter 503 and 513)*. Frankfurt am Main: Peter Lang, pp. 35–54

(ed.) 2020 *John Arderon's* De judiciis urinarum. *A Middle English Commentary on Giles of Corbeil's* Carmen de urinis *in Glasgow University Library, MS Hunter 328 and Manchester University Library, MS Rylands Eng. 1310*. Liverpool: Liverpool University Press

Calle-Martín, Javier and Castaño-Gil, Miguel Á. (eds.) 2013. *A Late Middle English Remedybook (MS Wellcome 542, ff. 1r–20v). A Scholarly Edition*. Frankfurt am Main: Peter Lang

Calle-Martín, Javier and Miranda-García, Antonio 2005. 'Editing Middle English punctuation: the case of MS Egerton 2622 (ff. 136–165)', *International Journal of English Studies* 5 (2): 27–44

2008. 'The punctuation system of Elizabethan legal documents: the case of G.U.L. MS Hunter 3 (S.1.3)', *The Review of English Studies* 59 (240): 356–78

(eds.) 2012. *The Middle English Version of* De viribus herbarum (*GUL MS Hunter 497, ff. 1r–92r*). *Edition and Philological Study*. Frankfurt am Main: Peter Lang

Calle-Martín, Javier, Moreno-Olalla, David, Esteban-Segura, Laura, Marqués-Aguado, Teresa, Romero-Barranco, Jesús, Thaisen, Jacob and

Rutkowska, Hanna 2016–. *The Málaga Corpus of Early Modern English Scientific Prose* (MCEMESP). Málaga: University of Málaga, https://modernmss.uma.es

Calude, Cristian S. and Longo, Giuseppe 2017. 'The deluge of spurious correlations in big data', *Foundations of Science* 22 (3): 595–612

Cambridge, Corpus Christi College, MS 402

Cambridge, Peterhouse College, MS 118 (ff. 29v–35r)

Cambridge, Trinity College, MS O. 2. 33

Cambridge, Trinity College, MS R. 14. 37

Cambridge, Trinity College, MS R. 14. 45

Cambridge, University Library, Corpus Christi College MS 140 (ff. 2r–45v)

Cambridge, University Library, Corpus Christi College MS 201 (ff. 131r–145r)

Cambridge, University Library, MS Kk. 5.16

Cambridge, University Library, MS Kk. 6.30

Cambridge, University Library, MS Mm. 5.37

Camden Old Series (1838–1872), The Camden Society, www.cambridge.org/core/journals/royal-historical-society-camden-fifth-series/past-title/camden-old-series/information/D31C6EA940BA40A21E1A8A3621AA0F2F

Camden New Series (1872–1901). The Camden Society, www.cambridge.org/core/journals/royal-historical-society-camden-fifth-series/past-title/camden-new-series/information/9666A1DDBEA0833FDC6777B01BF5EFAB

Cameron, Deborah 1995. *Verbal Hygiene*. London/New York: Routledge

Campbell, Alistair 1959. *Old English Grammar*. Oxford: Oxford University Press

Campbell, Lyle 1991. *Historical Linguistics: An Introduction*. Cambridge, MA: The MIT Press

Camps, Jean-Baptiste 2016. '*La Chanson d'Otinel*: édition complète du corpus manuscrit et prolégomènes à l'édition critique'. Doctoral dissertation, Université Paris-Sorbonne (Paris IV), France, https://doi.org/10.5281/zenodo.1116735

Canger, Una 1997. 'El *arte* de Horacio Carochi', in Klaus Zimmermann (ed.), *La descripción de las lenguas amerindias en la época colonial*. Madrid/Frankfurt am Main: Iberoamericana/Vervuert, pp. 59–74

Cano Aguilar, Rafael 2004. 'Cambios en la fonología del español durante los siglos XVI y XVII', in Cano Aguilar, Rafael (ed.), *Historia de la lengua española*. Barcelona: Ariel, pp. 593–612

Capp, Bernard 1979. *English Almanacs 1500–1800: Astrology and the Popular Press*. London: Faber and Faber

Cappelli, Adriano 1899. *Lexicon Abbreviaturarum Dizionario di Abbreviature Latine ed Italiane*. Milan: Ulrico Hoepli

1912. *Dizionario di Abbreviature Latine ed Italiani*. Milan: Ulrico Hoepli

Carney, Edward 1994. *A Survey of English Spelling.* London: Routledge

Caro Reina, Javier and Akar, Işık 2021. 'The development of the apostrophe with proper names in Turkish', *Zeitschrift für Sprachwissenschaft* 40 (3): 371–400, https://doi.org/10.1515/zfs-2021-2036

Caro Reina, Javier and Engel, Eric 2020. 'Worttrennung am Zeilenende in frühneuzeitlichen Hexenverhörprotokollen', in Renata Szczepaniak, Lisa Dücker and Stefan Hartmann (eds.), *Hexenverhörprotokolle als sprachhistorisches Korpus: Fallstudien zur Erschließung der frühneuzeitlichen Schriftsprache.* Berlin: De Gruyter, pp. 49–80

Carochi, Horacio 1645. *Compendio del arte de la lengua mexicana.* Mexico City: Biblioteca Mexicana

Carroll, Carleton W. 1976. 'Medieval romance paleography: a brief introduction', in Christopher Kleinhenz (ed.), *Medieval Manuscripts and Textual Criticism.* Chapel Hill: University of North Carolina Press, pp. 39–82

Carroll, Ruth, Peikola, Matti, Salmi, Hanna, Varila, Mari-Liisa, Skaffari, Janne and Hiltunen, Risto 2013. 'Pragmatics on the page: visual text in late medieval English books', *European Journal of English Studies* 17 (1): 54–71

Carton, Fernand 1974. *Introduction à la phonétique du français.* Paris/Brussels/Montreal: Bordas

Carvalhão Buescu, Maria L. 2000. 'Les premières descriptions grammaticales du portugais', in Sylvain Auroux, Ernst F. K. Koerner, Hans-Josef Niederehe and Kees Versteegh (eds.), *History of the Language Sciences/Geschichte der Sprachwissenschaften/Histoire des sciences du langage.* Berlin/Boston: De Gruyter, pp. 756–64

Catach, Nina 1968. *L'orthographe française à l'époque de la Renaissance.* Geneva: Droz

1980. 'La ponctuation', *Langue Française* 45: Nina Catach (ed.), *La ponctuation*: 16–27

1984. *La phonétisation automatique du français: les ambiguïtés de la langue écrite.* Paris: Éditions du CNRS

1986. 'The grapheme: its position and its degree of autonomy with respect to the system of the language', in Gerhard Augst (ed.), *New Trends in Graphemics and Orthography.* Berlin: De Gruyter, pp. 1–10

(ed.) 1990 [1988]. *Pour une théorie de la langue écrite. Actes de la Table Ronde internationale C.N.R.S.–H.E.S.O. Paris, 23–24 octobre 1986.* Paris: Éditions du CNRS

1995 [1980]. *L'orthographe française. Traité théorique et pratique avec des travaux d'application et leurs corrigés.* Paris: Nathan

1999 [1985]. 'La bataille de l'orthographe aux alentours de 1900', in Gérald Antoine and Robert Martin (eds.), *Histoire de la langue française, 1880–1914*. Paris: Éditions du CNRS, pp. 237–51

2001. *Histoire de l'orthographe française*. Paris: Honoré Champion Éditeur

Cavallo, Guglielmo and Maehler, Herwig 1987. *Greek Bookhands of the Early Byzantine Period, AD 300–800*. London: University of London, Institute of Classical Studies

Cawdrey, Robert 1604. *A table alphabeticall conteyning and teaching the true writing, and vnderstanding of hard vsuall English wordes, borrowed from the Hebrew, Greeke, Latine, or French* [...]. London: [I. Roberts] for Edmund Weauer (EEBO, ProQuest)

CBN POLONA online library, https://polona.pl

Cellucci, Carlo 2013. *Rethinking Logic. Logic in Relation to Mathematics, Evolution, and Method*. Dordrecht: Springer

Černá-Willi, Rahel 2012. *Polnisches Deutsch – Deutsches Polnisch. Edition und Analyse einer Sammlung von Paralleltexten des 18. Jahrhunderts aus Teschen/Oberschlesien*. Bern/Berlin/Frankfurt am Main: Peter Lang

Cerquiglini, Bernard 2004. *La genèse de l'orthographe française (XIIe–XVIIe siècle)*. Paris: Champion

Chadwick, John 1967. *The Decipherment of Linear B*. Cambridge: Cambridge University Press

1968. 'The group sw in Mycenaean', *Minos* 9: 62–65

1990. 'Linear B and related scripts', in James T. Hooker (ed.), *Reading the Past: Ancient Writing from Cuneiform to the Alphabet*. New York: Barnes and Noble, pp. 136–95

Chadwick, John, Godart, Louis, Killen, John T., Olivier, Jean-Pierre, Sacconi, Anna, Sakellarakis, Ioannis A. 1986–98. *Corpus of Mycenaean Inscriptions from Knossos* (CoMIK), vols. 1–4. Cambridge/Rome: Cambridge University Press/Edizioni dell'Ateneo

Chahoud, Anna 2019. 'Lucilius on Latin spelling, grammar, and usage', in Barnaby Taylor and Giuseppe Pezzini (eds.), *Language and Nature in the Classical Roman World*. Cambridge: Cambridge University Press, pp. 46–78

Chalker, Sylvia and Weiner, Edmund 1998. 'Spelling pronunciation', *The Oxford Dictionary of English Grammar*. Oxford: Oxford University Press

Chalmers, John 1687. *English Orthography. Or The Art of Writing and Spelling True English in Three Parts* [...]. London: Printed for Joseph Hindmarsh at the Golden Ball (EEBO, ProQuest)

Chambers, Jack K. 1995. *Sociolinguistic Theory: Linguistic Variation and Its Social Significance*. Oxford: Blackwell

Chambers, Jack K. and Trudgill, Peter J. 1998. *Dialectology*. Cambridge: Cambridge University Press (2nd ed.)

Chandler, Daniel 2017 [2002]. *Semiotics: The Basics*. Abingdon/New York: Routledge (3rd ed.)

Chang, Li-Yun, Chen, Yen-Chi and Perfetti, Charles A. 2018. 'GraphCom: a multidimensional measure of graphic complexity applied to 131 written languages', *Behavior Research Methods* 50 (1): 427–49

Charpin, François 1978. *Lucilius, Satires, Tome I. Livres I–VIII. Texte établi, traduit et annoté*. Paris: Les Belles Lettres

1991. *Lucilius, Satires, Tome III. Livres XXIX, XXX et Fragments Divers. Texte établi et traduit*. Paris: Les Belles Lettres

Chassant, Alphonse A. L. 1846. *Dictionnaire des Abréviations Latines et Francaises Usitées Dans les Inscriptions Lapidaires et Métalliques, les Manuscrits et les Chartes du Moyen Ăge*. Évreux: Cornemillot

Cheshire, Jenny, Kerswill, Paul, Fox, Susan and Torgersen, Eivind 2011. 'Contact, the feature pool and the speech community: the emergence of Multicultural London English', *Journal of Sociolinguistics* 15: 151–96

Cheshire, Jenny and Milroy, James 1993. 'Syntactic variation in non-standard dialects: background issues', in James Milroy and Lesley Milroy (eds.), *Real English: The Grammar of English Dialects in the British Isles*. London: Longman, pp. 3–33

Cheung, Yat-Shing 1992. 'The form and meaning of digraphia: the case of Chinese', in Kingsley Bolton and Helen Kwok (eds.), *Sociolinguistics Today: International Perspectives*. London: Routledge, pp. 210–15

Chiss, Jean-Louis and Puech, Christian 1983. 'La linguistique et la question de l'écriture: enjeux et débats autour de Saussure et des problématiques structurales', *Langue française* 59: 5–24

Choi, Lee Jin 2017. 'Performing "authentic" bilingualism: authenticity, novel respelling forms, and language ideology in South Korea', *Multilingua* 36 (2): 125–46, https://doi.org/10.1515/multi-2015-0091

Chomsky, Carol 1970. 'Reading, writing, and phonology', *Harvard Educational Review* 40: 287–309

Chomsky, Noam and Halle, Morris 1968. *The Sound Pattern of English*. New York: Harper and Row

Chrisomalis, Stephen 2009. 'The origins and co-evolution of literacy and numeracy', in David R. Olson and Nancy Torrance (eds.), *The Cambridge Handbook of Literacy*. Cambridge: Cambridge University Press, pp. 59–74

Christensen, Birgit 2012. 'A survey of Low German loanwords in Danish in the medieval period and the transition from Low German to High German as the written language in tønder in the 17th century', in Lennart Elmevik and Ernst H. Jahr (eds.), *Contact between Low German and Scandinavian in the Late Middle Ages. 25 Years of Research*. Uppsala: Kungl. Gustav Adolfs Akademien för svensk folkkultur, pp. 123–36

Christianson, C. Paul 1989a. 'Evidence for the study of London's late medieval manuscript-book trade', in Jeremy Griffiths and Derek Pearsall (eds.), *Book Production and Publishing in Britain 1375–1475*. Cambridge: Cambridge University Press, pp. 87–108

1989b. 'A community of book artisans in Chaucer's London', *Viator* 20: 207–18

1990. *A Directory of London Stationers and Book Artisans, 1300–1500*. New York: The Bibliographical Society of America

1999. 'The rise of London's book trade', in Lotte Hellinga and Joseph B. Trapp (eds.), *The Cambridge History of the Book in Britain*, vol. 3: *1400–1557*. Cambridge: Cambridge University Press, pp. 128–47

Cifuentes, Bárbara 1998. *Letras sobre voces: multilingüismo a través de la historia*. Mexico City: CIESAS and INI

2013. 'The politics of lexicography in the Mexican Academy in the late nineteenth century', in José del Valle (ed.), *A Political History of Spanish*. Cambridge: Cambridge University Press, pp. 167–81

Clackson, James 2003. Review of *Album of Armenian Paleography* by Michael E. Stone, Dickran Kouymjian and Henning Lehmann, *Bulletin of the School of Oriental and African Studies* 66 (2): 270–71

2015. *Language and Society in the Greek and Roman Worlds*. Cambridge: Cambridge University Press

Clackson, James and Horrocks, Geoffrey 2007. *The Blackwell History of the Latin Language*. Malden/Oxford: Wiley-Blackwell

Clancy Clements, Joseph 2009. *The Linguistic Legacy of Spanish and Portuguese: Colonial Expansion and Language Change*. Cambridge: Cambridge University Press

Claridge, Claudia and Kytö, Merja (eds.) 2020. *Punctuation in Context: Past and Present Perspectives*. Berlin: Peter Lang

CLARIN ERIC infrastructure 2021. Historical corpora, www.clarin.eu/resource-families/historical-corpora

Clark, Cecily 1992a. 'Domesday Book – a great red-herring: thoughts on some late-eleventh-century orthographies', in Carola Hicks (ed.), *England in the Eleventh Century: Proceedings of the 1990 Harlaxton Symposium*. Stamford: Paul Watkins, pp. 317–31

1992b. 'The myth of "the Anglo-Norman scribe"', in Matti Rissanen, Ossi Ihalainen, Terttu Nevalainen and Irma Taavitsainen (eds.), *History of Englishes: New Methods and Interpretations in Historical Linguistics*. Berlin: De Gruyter, pp. 117–29

Clemens, Raymond and Graham, Timothy 2007. *Introduction to Manuscript Studies*. Ithaca/London: Cornell University Press

Clement, Francis 1587. *The Petie Schole with an English Orthographie* [...] London: Thomas Vautrollier

Cleminson, Ralph 2015. 'Slavonic palaeography', in Alessandro Bausi, Pier Giorgio Borbone, Françoise Briquel-Chatonnet, Paola Buzi, Jost Gippert, Caroline Macé, Marilena Maniaci, Zisis Melissakis, Laura E.

Parodi and Witold Witakowski (eds.), *Comparative Oriental Manuscript Studies: An Introduction*. Hamburg: COMSt, pp. 310–15

Close, Elizabeth 1974. *The Development of Rumanian*. Oxford: Oxford University Press

Coe, Michael D. 1992. *Breaking the Maya Code*. New York: Thames and Hudson

Cohen, Marcel 1956. *Pismo. Zarys dziejów* (trans. by Irena Pomian). Warsaw: Państwowe Wydawnictwo Naukowe [Cohen, Marcel 1953. *L'écriture*. Paris: Éditions Sociales]

Coleccion de las leyes, decretos y declaraciones de las Cortes, y de los reales decretos, ordenes, resoluciones y reglamentos generales expedidos por los respectivos ministerios. Desde 1º de Enero hasta fin de Junio de 1844 1844, vol. XXXII. Madrid: Imprenta Nacional

Collin, Richard O. 2011. 'Revolutionary scripts: the politics of writing systems', in Michael A. Morris (ed.), *Culture and Language: Multidisciplinary Case Studies*. Frankfurt am Main: Peter Lang, pp. 29–67

Coltheart, Max 1984. 'Writing systems and reading disorders', in Leslie Henderson (ed.), *Orthographies and Reading*. London: Lawrence Erlbaum Associates, pp. 67–79

Comrie, Bernard, Stone, Gerald and Polinsky, Maria 1996. *The Russian Language in the Twentieth Century*. Oxford/New York: Clarendon Press (2nd ed.)

Conde-Silvestre, Juan Camilo 2012. 'The role of social networks and mobility in diachronic sociolinguistics', in Juan Manuel Hernández-Campoy and Juan Camilo Conde-Silvestre (eds.), *The Handbook of Historical Sociolinguistics*. Chichester: Wiley-Blackwell, pp. 332–52

Conde-Silvestre, Juan Camilo 2019. 'Spelling focusing and proto-standardisation in a fifteenth-century English community of practice', *Studia Neophilologica* 91: 11–30

2020. 'Communities of practice, proto-standardisation and spelling focusing in the Stonor letters', in Laura Wright (ed.), *The Multilingual Origins of Standard English*. Berlin/Boston: De Gruyter Mouton, pp. 443–66

Conde-Silvestre, Juan Camilo and Hernández-Campoy, Juan Manuel 2004. 'A sociolinguistic approach to the diffusion of Chancery written practices in late fifteenth century private correspondence', *Neuphilologische Mitteilungen* 105 (2): 133–52

2013. 'Tracing the generational progress of language change in fifteenth century English: the digraph <th> in the *Paston Letters*', *Neuphilologische Mitteilungen* 114 (3): 279–99

Condorelli, Marco 2019. 'Irregularity of the <ie> spellings in West-Saxon: the problem of pronouns', *SELIM* 24 (1): 29–52

2020a. 'From the early modern era to an international research area', in Marco Condorelli (ed.), *Advances in Historical Orthography, c. 1500–1800*. Cambridge: Cambridge University Press, pp. 1–15

2020b. 'Towards a relativity of spelling change', in Marco Condorelli (ed.), *Advances in Historical Orthography, c. 1500–1800*. Cambridge: Cambridge University Press, pp. 219–37

(ed.) 2020c. *Advances in Historical Orthography, c. 1500–1800*. Cambridge: Cambridge University Press

2021a. 'Positional spelling redistribution: word-initial <u>/<v> and <i>/<j> in Early Modern English (1500–1700)', *English Language and Linguistics*, 24 (2): 799–823

2021b. 'The standardisation of *i* and *y* in Early Modern English (1500–1700)', *English Studies* 102 (1): 101–23

2022a. *Introducing Historical Orthography*. Cambridge: Cambridge University Press

2022b. *Standardising English Spelling: The Role of Printing in Sixteenth and Seventeenth-Century Graphemic Developments*. Cambridge: Cambridge University Press

Condorelli, Marco and Voeste, Anja 2020. 'Synergic dialogue in historical orthography. national philologies, comparability and questions for the future', in Marco Condorelli (ed.), *Advances in Historical Orthography, c. 1500–1800*. Cambridge: Cambridge University Press, pp. 238–49

Consani, Carlo 2003. *Sillabe e sillabari fra competenza fonologica e pratica scrittoria*. Alessandria: Edizioni dell'Orso

2016. 'In search of the "perfect fit" between speech and writing: the case of the Linear B writing', in Paola Cotticelli-Kurras and Alfredo Rizza (eds.), *Variation within and among Writing Systems. Concepts and Methods in the Analysis of Ancient Written Documents*. Wiesbaden: Reichert Verlag, pp. 89–104

Considine, John 2014. *Academy Dictionaries 1600–1800*. Cambridge: Cambridge University Press

(ed.) 2019. *The Cambridge World History of Lexicography*. Cambridge: Cambridge University Press

Contreras, Lidia 1993. *Historia de las ideas ortográficas en Chile*. Santiago: Editorial Universitaria

Cook, Vivian and Bassetti, Benedetta 2005. 'An introduction to researching second language writing systems', in Vivian Cook and Benedetta Bassetti (eds.), *Second Language Writing Systems*. Bristol: Multilingual Matters, pp. 1–67

Cook, Vivian and Ryan, Des (eds.) 2016. *The Routledge Handbook of the English Writing System*. London/New York: Routledge

Cooper, Jerrold S. 1996. 'Sumerian and Akkadian', in Peter T. Daniels and William Bright (eds.), *The World's Writing Systems*. New York: Oxford University Press, pp. 37–57

2004. 'Babylonian beginnings: the origin of the cuneiform writing system in comparative perspective', in Stephen D. Houston (ed.), *The First*

Writing: Script Invention as History and Process. Cambridge: Cambridge University Press, pp. 71–99

Cooper, Robert L. 1989. *Language Planning and Social Change*. Cambridge/ New York: Cambridge University Press

Coote, Edmund 1596. [*The English Schoole-maister teaching all his scholers, the order of distinct reading, and true writing our English tongue*]. London: Widow Orwin, for Ralph Jackson, and Robert Dextar (EEBO, ProQuest)

Čornejová, Michaela, Rychnovská, Lucie and Zemanová, Jana (eds.) 2010. *Dějiny českého pravopisu (do r. 1902). Sborník příspěvků z mezinárodní konference Dějiny českého pravopisu (do r. 1902). 23.–25. září 2010, Brno, Česká Republika. History of Czech Orthography (up to 1902). Proceedings of the International Conference History of Czech Orthography (up to 1902). 23.–25. September 2010, Brno, Czech Republic*. Brno: Host, Masarykova univerzita

Corpus Inscriptionum Latinarum (CIL) 1862–. Berlin

Corpus Middelnederlands (Version 1.0) [Dataset] 1998. Available at the Dutch Language Institute, http://hdl.handle.net/10032/tm-a2-j6

Corrie, Marilyn 2012. 'Middle English – dialects and diversity', in Lynda Mugglestone (ed.), *The Oxford History of English*. Oxford: Oxford University Press, pp. 106–46 (updated ed.)

Cortada, James W. (ed.) 1994. *Spain in the Nineteenth-Century World. Essays on Spanish Diplomacy, 1789–1898*. Westport: Greenwood Press

Cortés y Zedeño, Gerónimo 1765. *Arte, vocabulario, y confessionario en el idioma mexicano, como se usa en el obispado de Guadalaxara*. Puebla: Colegio Real de San Ignacio

Coseriu, Eugen 1970. *Einfürhrung in die Strukturelle Betrachtung des Wortschatzes*. Tübingen: Tübinger Beiträge zur Linguistik

Cottereau, Emilie 2005. 'La copie et les copistes français de manuscrits aux XIVe et XVe siècles: étude sociologique et codicologique'. Doctoral dissertation, Université Paris Panthéon-Sorbonne, France

Coulmas, Florian 1989. *The Writing Systems of the World*. Oxford: Blackwell

1991. *The Writing Systems of the World*. Oxford: Blackwell (reprint)

1992. 'Writing systems', in William Bright (ed.), *International Encyclopedia of Linguistics*, vol. 4. New York/Oxford: Oxford University Press, pp. 253–57

1996a. *The Blackwell Encyclopedia of Writing Systems*. Cambridge, MA: Blackwell

1996b. 'Typology of writing systems', in Hartmut Günther and Otto Ludwig (eds.), *Schrift und Schriftlichkeit/Writing and Its Use. Ein interdisziplinäres Handbuch internationaler Forschung/An Interdisciplinary Handbook of International Research*, vol. 1. Berlin/New York: De Gruyter, pp. 1380–87

1999. *The Blackwell Encyclopedia of Writing Systems*, Chichester: John Wiley and Sons (paperback ed.)

2000. *The Writing Systems of the World*. Oxford/Cambridge, MA: Blackwell (2nd ed., reprint)

2002. *Writing Systems: An Introduction to Their Linguistic Analysis*. Cambridge: Cambridge University Press, https://doi.org/10.1017/CBO9781139164597

2003. *Writing Systems: An Introduction to Their Linguistic Analysis*. Cambridge/New York: Cambridge University Press (2nd ed.)

2012. *Writing Systems: An Introduction to Their Linguistic Analysis*. Cambridge: Cambridge University Press (online ed.)

2013. *Writing and Society: An Introduction*. Cambridge: Cambridge University Press

2014. 'Writing systems and language contact in the Euro- and Sinocentric worlds', *Applied Linguistics Review* 5: 1–21

Coulmas, Florian and Guerini, Federica 2012. 'Literacy and writing reform', in Bernard Spolsky (ed.), *The Cambridge Handbook of Language Policy*. Cambridge: Cambridge University Press, pp. 437–60

Coupland, Nikolas 1980. 'Style-shifting in a Cardiff work setting', *Language in Society* 9: 1–12

2007. *Style: Language Variation, and Identity*. Cambridge: Cambridge University Press

Coye, Dale F. 1998. 'Orthoepic piracy: spelling pronunciations and Standard English', *American Speech* 73 (2): 178–96

Crain, Patricia 2013. 'Reading childishly? A codicology of the modern self', in N. Katherine Hayles and Jessica Pressman (eds.), *Comparative Textual Media: Transforming the Humanities in the Postprint Era*. Minneapolis: University of Minnesota Press, pp. 155–82

Crawford, Michael H. 2011. *Imagines Italicae*. London: Institute of Classical Studies, School of Advanced Study, University of London

Criado-Peña, Miriam (ed.) 2018. *The Early Modern English Version of Elizabeth Jacob's* Physicall and Chyrurgical Receipts. Cambridge: Cambridge Scholars

Croft, William 2000. *Explaining Language Change: An Evolutionary Approach*. New York: Longman

Cross, Rowin 2004. *A Handlist of Manuscripts Containing English in the Hunterian Collection Glasgow University Library*. Glasgow: Glasgow University Library

Crossland, Ronald A. 1956. 'Graphic linguistics and its terminology', *Mechanical Translation* 3 (1): 8–11

Crowley, Tony 1989. *Standard English and the Politics of Language*. Urbana/Chicago: University of Illinois Press

Crystal, David 1985 [1980]. *A Dictionary of Linguistics and Phonetics*. Oxford: Basil Blackwell (2nd ed.)

2003. *The Cambridge Encyclopedia of the English Language*. Cambridge: Cambridge University Press (2nd ed.)

2012. *Spell It Out: The Singular Story of English Spelling*. London: Profile Books

Crystal, David and Davy, Derek 1969. *Investigating English Style*. London: Longman

Culpeper, Jonathan and Kytö, Merja (compilers) 2006. *A Corpus of English Dialogues: 1560–1760*, CD-ROM. Uppsala: Uppsala Universitet

Cummings, Darrell W. 2016. 'The evolution of British and American spelling', in Vivian Cook and Des Ryan (eds.), *The Routledge Handbook of the English Writing System*. London/New York: Routledge, pp. 275–93

Curran, Michael 1984. *The Antiphonary of Bangor and the Early Irish Monastic Liturgy*. Dublin: Irish Academic Press

Cushman, Ellen 2012. *The Cherokee Syllabary: Writing the People's Perseverance*. Norman: University of Oklahoma Press

Cutillas-Espinosa, Juan A., Hernández-Campoy, Juan Manuel and Schilling-Estes, N. 2010. 'Hyper-vernacularisation in a speaker design context: a case study', *Folia Linguistica* 44: 1–22

Czech National Corpus (CNC), https://korpus.cz

Czernecki, Józef 1902. *1 Jana Januszowskiego: Nowy Karakter Polski z r. 1594. 2 Stanisława Serafina Jagodyńskiego: Kalligraphia abo Cancellaria z r. 1695. Odbitka z "Praktyki szkolnej" dodatku do "Szkoły"*. Lviv: Nakładem Towarzystwa Pedagogicznego

Dąbrowska-Partyka, Maria 2000. 'Pismo jako znak tożsamości', in Maria Bobrownicka (ed.), *Język a tożsamość narodowa: Slavica*. Kraków: Towarzystwo Autorów i Wydawców Prac Naukowych "Universitas", pp. 169–82

Dahl, Marcus 2016. 'Authors of the mind', *Journal of Early Modern Studies* 5: 157–73

Dahlet, Véronique 2003. *Ponctuation et énonciation*. Guadeloupe: Ibis Rouge Éditions

Dain, Alphonse 1949. *Les manuscrits*. Paris: Les Belles Lettres

Daines, Simon 1640. *Orthoepia Anglicana: Or, The First Principal Part of the English Grammar: Teaching The Art of right speaking and pronouncing English, With certaine exact rules of Orthography, and rules of spelling* [...] London: Robert Young and Richard Badger for the Company of Stationers

Dale, Ian R.H. 1980. 'Digraphia', *International Journal of the Sociology of Language* 26: 5–13

Danecki, Janusz 1994. *Gramatyka Języka Arabskiego*. Warsaw: Wydawnictwo Akademickie Dialog

2011. 'Literature of the Polish Tatars', in Katarzyna Górak-Sosnowska (ed.), *Muslims in Poland and Eastern Europe: Widening the European*

Discourse on Islam. Warsaw: University of Warsaw Faculty of Oriental Studies, pp. 40–52

Danesi, Marcel 2017. *The Semiotics of Emoji: The Rise of Visual Language in the Age of the Internet*. London/New York: Bloomsbury Academic

Dangel, Jacqueline 1995. *Accius, Oeuvres (Fragments)*. Paris: Les Belles Lettres

Daniels, Peter T. 1984. 'A calligraphic approach to Aramaic paleography', *Journal of Near Eastern Studies* 43 (1): 55–68

1990. 'Fundamentals of grammatology', *Journal of the American Oriental Society* 110 (4): 727–31

1992. 'The syllabic origin of writing and the segmental origin of the alphabet', in Pamela Downing, Susan D. Lima and Michael Noonan (eds.), *The Linguistics of Literacy*. Amsterdam: John Benjamins, pp. 83–110

1996a. 'The study of writing systems', in Peter T. Daniels and William Bright (eds.), *The World's Writing Systems*. New York: Oxford University Press, pp. 3–17

1996b. 'The first civilizations', in Peter T. Daniels and William Bright (eds.), *The World's Writing Systems*. New York: Oxford University Press, pp. 21–32

1996c. 'The invention of writing', in Peter T. Daniels and William Bright (eds.), *The World's Writing Systems*. New York: Oxford University Press, pp. 579–86

2000. 'On writing syllables: three episodes of script transfer', *Studies in the Linguistic Sciences* 30 (1): 73–86

2001. 'Writing systems', in Mark Aronoff and Janie Rees-Miller (eds.), *The Handbook of Linguistics*. Oxford: Blackwell, pp. 43–80

2006. 'Three models of script transfer', *Word* 57 (3): 371–78

2009. 'Grammatology', in David R. Olson and Nancy Torrance (eds.), *The Cambridge Handbook of Literacy*. Cambridge: Cambridge University Press, pp. 25–45

2013. 'The history of writing as a history of linguistics', in Keith Allan (ed.), *The Oxford Handbook of the History of Linguistics*. Oxford: Oxford University Press, pp. 53–69

2017. 'Writing systems', in Mark Aronoff and Janie Rees-Miller (eds.), *The Handbook of Linguistics*. Hoboken: Wiley-Blackwell, pp. 75–94 (2nd ed.), https://doi.org/10.1002/9781119072256.ch5

2018. *An Exploration of Writing*. Sheffield/Bristol: Equinox

Daniels, Peter T. and Bright, William (eds.) 1996. *The World's Writing Systems*. New York: Oxford University Press

Daniels, Peter T. and Share, David L. 2018. 'Writing system variation and its consequences for reading and dyslexia', *Scientific Studies of Reading* 22 (1): 101–16

Das Bonner Frühneuhochdeutsch-Korpus, Korpora.org, https://korpora.zim.uni-duisburg-essen.de/FnhdC/

Daswani, Chander J. 2001. 'Issues of literacy development in the Indian context', in David R. Olson and Nancy Torrance (eds.), *The Making of Literate Societies*. Oxford: Blackwell, pp. 284–95

Daunt, Marjorie 1939. 'Old English sound-changes reconsidered in relation to scribal tradition and practice', *Transactions of the Philological Society* 38 (1): 108–37

Davidson, Chas 1890. 'Differences between the scribes of "Beowulf"', *Modern Language Notes* 5 (2): 43–45

Davies, Robert (ed.) 1863. *The Life of Marmaduke Rawden of York, or Marmaduke Rawdon the Second of That Name*. London: Camden Society

Davies, W. Vivian 1990. 'Egyptian hieroglyphs', in James T. Hooker (ed.), *Reading the Past: Ancient Writing from Cuneiform to the Alphabet*. New York: Barnes and Noble, pp. 74–135

Davis, Brent 2014. *Minoan Stone Vessels with Linear A Inscriptions*. Leuven: Peeters

Davis, Norman 1971. *Paston Letters and Papers of the Fifteenth Century*, 2 vols. Oxford: Clarendon

De Beaugrande, Robert 2006. 'Speech versus writing in the discourse of linguistics', *Miscelánea: A Journal of English and American Studies* 33: 31–45

De Boer, Bart 2011. 'Self-organization and language evolution', in Maggie Tallerman and Kathleen R. Gibson (eds.), *The Oxford Handbook of Language Evolution*. Oxford: Oxford University Press, pp. 612–20

Decorte, Roeland P.-J. E. 2017. 'Cretan "Hieroglyphic" and the nature of script', in Philippa M. Steele (ed.), *Understanding Relations between Scripts: The Aegean Writing Systems*. Oxford/Philadelphia: Oxbow Books, pp. 33–56

2018. 'The origins of Bronze Age Aegean writing: Linear A, Cretan Hieroglyphic and a new proposed pathway of script formation', in Silvia Ferrara and Miguel Valério (eds.), *Paths into Script Formation in the Ancient Mediterranean. Studi Micenei ed Egeo-Anatolici, Nuova Serie, Supplemento 1*, pp. 13–50

DeFrancis, John 1984a. *The Chinese Language: Fact and Fantasy*. Honolulu: University of Hawai'i Press

1984b. 'Digraphia', *Word* 35 (1): 59–66

1989. *Visible Speech: The Diverse Oneness of Writing Systems*. Honolulu: University of Hawai'i Press

2002. 'The ideographic myth', in Mary S. Erbaugh (ed.), *Difficult Characters: Interdisciplinary Studies of Chinese and Japanese Writing*. Columbus: National East Asian Language Resource Center, Ohio State University, pp. 1–20

DeFrancis, John and Unger, Marshall J. 1994. 'Rejoinder to Geoffrey Sampson, "Chinese script and the diversity of writing systems"', *Linguistics* 32: 549–54

De Hamel, Christopher F. R. 1983. 'Reflexions on the trade in books of hours at Ghent and Bruges', in Joseph B. Trapp (ed.), *Manuscripts in the Fifty Years after the Invention of Printing: Some Papers Read at a Colloquium at the Warburg Institute on 12–13 March 1982*. London: The Warburg Institute, University of London, pp. 29–33

1992. *Scribes and Illuminators*. London: British Museum Press

Del Freo, Maurizio and Perna, Massimo (eds.) 2019. *Manuale di epigrafia micenea. Introduzione allo studio dei testi in lineare B*, 2 vols. Padua: Libreria Universitaria.

Del Rincón, Antonio 1885 [1595]. *Arte mexicana*. Mexico City: Secretaría de Fomento

Del Valle, José 2007. 'Glotopolítica, ideología y discurso categorías para el estudio del estatus simbólico del español', in José del Valle (ed.), *La lengua, ¿patria común? Ideas e ideologías del español*. Madrid/Frankfurt am Main: Iberoamericana/Vervuert, pp. 13–29

2010. 'La lengua, los bicentenarios y la estrategia del acompañamiento', *Revista de crítica literaria latinoamericana* 36 (71): 127–48

2011. 'Panhispanismo e hispanofonía: breve historia de dos ideologías siamesas', *Sociolinguistic Studies* 5 (3): 465–84

2013. 'Linguistic emancipation and the academies of the Spanish language in the twentieth century: the 1951 turning point', in José del Valle (ed.), *A Political History of Spanish: The Making of a Language*. Cambridge: Cambridge University Press, pp. 229–47

Del Valle, José and Gabriel-Stheeman, Luis (eds.) 2002. *The Battle over Spanish between 1800 and 2000. Language Ideologies and Hispanic Intellectuals*. London/New York: Routledge

Del Valle, José and Villa, Laura 2012. 'La disputada autoridad de las academias: debate lingüístico-ideológico en torno a la Ortografía de 2010', *Revista Internacional de Lingüística Iberoamericana* 1 (19): 29–53

Demartini, Silvia 2011. 'Ortografia', in *Enciclopedia Italiana di Scienze, Lettere ed Arti*, www.treccani.it/enciclopedia/ortografia_(Enciclopedia-dell%27Italiano)

Den Heijer, Johannes, Schmidt, Andrea B. and Pataridze, Tamara (eds.) 2014. *Scripts beyond Borders. A Survey of Allographic Traditions in the Euro-Mediterranean World*. Leuven: Peeters

Denholm-Young, Noël 1954. *Handwriting in England and Wales*. Cardiff: University of Wales Press

Denis, Derek 2011. 'Innovators and innovation: tracking the innovators of and stuff in York English', *University of Pennsylvania Working Papers in Linguistics* 17 (2): 61–70

De Reuse, Willem 2019. 'Missionary and subsequent traditions in North America', in John Considine (ed.), *The Cambridge World History of Lexicography*. Cambridge: Cambridge University Press, pp. 597–613

Derolez, Albert 2003. *The Palaeography of Gothic Manuscript Books. From the Twelfth to the Early Sixteenth Century.* Cambridge: Cambridge University Press

Derrida, Jacques 1967. *De la grammatologie.* Paris: Les Éditions de Minuit

2016 [1967]. *Of Grammatology* (trans. by Gayatri Chakravorty Spivak). Baltimore: Johns Hopkins University Press

Derwing, Bruce L. 1992. 'Orthographic aspects of linguistic competence', in Pamela Downing, Susan D. Lima and Michael Noonan (eds.), *The Linguistics of Literacy.* Amsterdam/Philadelphia: John Benjamins, pp. 193–210

Desbordes, Françoise 1990. *Idées romaines sur l'écriture.* Lille: Presses Universitaires de Lille

1997. 'The notion of orthography: a Latin inheritance', in Clotilde Pontecorvo (ed.), *Writing Development: An Interdisciplinary View.* Amsterdam/Philadelphia: John Benjamins, pp. 117–28

Deschamps, Alain 1992. 'De l'anglais écrit à l'anglais oral: esquisse d'une graphématique', *Les langues modernes* 86 (3): 23–29

1994. *De l'écrit à l'oral et de l'oral à l'écrit: phonétique et orthographe de l'anglais.* Paris: Ophrys

De Tapia Zenteno, Carlos 1753. *Arte novissima de lengua mexicana.* Mexico City: Viuda de José Bernardo de Hogal

Deumert, Ana and Vandenbussche, Wim 2003. 'Standard languages: taxonomies and histories', in Ana Deumert and Wim Vandenbussche (eds.), *Germanic Standardizations: Past to Present.* Amsterdam/Philadelphia: John Benjamins, pp. 1–14

Deumert, Andrea 1999. 'Variation and standardisation: tthe case of Afrikaans (1880–1922)'. Doctoral dissertation, University of Cape Town, South Africa

Devine, Andrew M. and Stephens, Laurence D. 1994. *The Prosody of Greek Speech.* New York: Oxford University Press

Devitt, Amy 2004. *Writing Genres.* Carbondale: Southern Illinois University Press

Devonish, Hubert 2003. 'Caribbean creoles', in Ana Deumert and Wim Vandenbussche (eds.), *Germanic Standardizations: Past to Present.* Amsterdam/Philadelphia: John Benjamins, pp. 41–67

De Voogt, Alex 2012. 'Invention and borrowing in the development and dispersal of writing systems', in Alex de Voogt and Joachim Friedrich Quack (eds.), *The Idea of Writing: Writing across Borders.* Leiden: Brill

De Vries, Matthias and Te Winkel, Lambert A. 1866. *Woordenlijst voor de spelling der Nederlandsche Taal.* The Hague: Nijhoff

(principal eds.) 1864–2001. *Woordenboek Der Nederlandsche Taal*, 29 vols. plus supplements. The Hague: Nijhoff

Dewitte, Alfons 1996. 'Het Brugse St-Jans en St.-Lucasgilde der librariërs 1457, 1469', *Biekorf* 96: 334–40

De Wulf, Chris 2019. *Klankatlas van het veertiende-eeuwse Middelnederlands. Het dialectvocalisme in de spelling van lokale oorkonden.* Ghent: Koninklijke Academie voor Nederlandse Taal en Letteren

Dibbets, Geert R. W. 2000. 'Frühe grammatische Beschreibungen des Niederländischen (ca. 1550–ca. 1650)', in Sylvain Auroux, Ernst F. K. Koerner, Hans-Josef Niederehe and Kees Versteegh (eds.), *History of the Language Sciences/Geschichte der Sprachwissenschaften/Histoire des sciences du langage*. Berlin/Boston: De Gruyter, pp. 784–92

Dickie, Matthew W. 2001. *Magic and Magicians in the Greco-Roman World.* London: Routledge

Dickinson, Jennifer A. 2015. 'Introduction: language ideologies and writing systems', *Pragmatics* 25 (4): 507–16

Die syben hertzenleyt von vnnser lieben Frawen in dem gulden regenbogen Don. ~1500 [Nuremberg: Ambrosius Huber] (ISTC ih00134500)

Dietz, Klaus 2006. *Schreibung und Lautung im mittelalterlichen Englisch: Entwicklung und Funktion der englischen Schreibungen ch, gh, sh, th, wh und ihrer kontinentalen Entsprechungen* (Anglistische Forschungen 364). Heidelberg: Winter

Diller, Hans-Jürgen 2001. '*Genre* in linguistic and related discourses', in Hans-Jürgen Diller and Manfred Görlach (eds.), *Towards a History of English as a History of Genres.* Heidelberg: Winter, pp. 3–43

DiMeo, Michelle 2011. 'Lady Katherine Ranelagh or Lady Margaret Orrery? Reattributing Authorship of The Boyle Family Receipt Book', *Early Modern Women: An Interdisciplinary Journal* 6: 268–70

Di Renzo, Anthony 2000. 'His master's voice: Tiro and the rise of the Roman secretarial class', *Journal of Technical Writing and Communication* 30 (2): 155–68, https://doi.org/10.2190/B4YD-5FP7-1W8D-V3UC

Diringer, David 1943. 'The origins of the alphabet', *Antiquity* 17: 77–90

1948. *The Alphabet. A Key to the History of Mankind.* London/New York/Toronto/ Melbourne/Sydney/Cape Town: Hutchinson's Scientific and Technical Publications

1949. *The Alphabet: A Key to the History of Mankind.* New York: Philosophical Library (2nd ed.)

1962. *Writing.* London: Thames and Hudson

Doane, Alger N. 1994. 'The ethnography of scribal writing and Anglo-Saxon poetry: scribe as performer', *Oral Tradition* 9 (2): 420–39

Dobbie, Elliott van Kirk 1942. *The Anglo-Saxon Minor Poems* (The Anglo-Saxon Poetic Records 6). London: Routledge

Dobson, Eric J. 1955. 'Early Modern standard English', *Transactions of the Philological Society* 54 (1): 25–54

1957. *English Pronunciation 1500–1700*, 2 vols. Oxford: Clarendon Press

Dodoens, Rembert 1578. *A Niewe Herball, or, Historie of Plants: wherin is Contayned the Whole Discourse and Perfect Description of All Sortes of Herbes and Plantes.* London: Gerard Dewes

Dollinger, Stefan. 2019a. *Creating Canadian English: The Professor, the Mountaineer, and a National Variety of English*. Cambridge/New York: Cambridge University Press

2019b. *The Pluricentricity Debate: On Austrian German and Other Germanic Standard Varieties*. New York/London: Routledge

Doria, Mario 1965. *Avviamento allo studio del Miceneo: struttura, problemi e testi*. Rome: Edizioni dell'Ateneo

Dossena, Marina and Del Lungo Camiciotti, Gabriella (eds.) 2012. *Letter Writing in Late Modern Europe*. Amsterdam/Philadelphia: John Benjamins

Dossena, Marina and Fitzmaurice, Susan (eds.) 2006. *Business and Official Correspondence: Historical Investigations*. Bern: Peter Lang

Dossena, Marina and Tieken-Boon van Ostade, Ingrid (eds.) 2008. *Studies in Late Modern English Correspondence: Methodology and Data*. Bern: Peter Lang

Drackley, Patrick 2019. '"Je suis circonflexe": grassroots prescriptivism and orthographic reform', *Language Policy* 18 (2): 295–313

Driver, Martha W. 2014. 'Ina Kok: woodcuts in incunabula printed in the Low Countries', *Journal of the Early Book Society* 17: 392–94

Drozd, Andrzej 1994. 'Zastosowanie pisma arabskiego do zapisu tekstów polskich (zarys historyczny)', in Marek M. Dziekan (ed.), *Plenas Arabum domos*. Warsaw: Instytut Orientalistyczny, Uniwersytet Warszawski, pp. 75–93

1997. 'Wpływy chrześcijańskie na literaturę Tatarów w dawnej Rzeczypospolitej. Między antagonizmem a symbiozą', *Pamiętnik Literacki* 88 (3): 3–34

2000. 'Piśmiennictwo Tatarów polsko-litewskich (XVI–XX w.). Zarys problematyki', in Andrzej Drozd, Marek M. Dziekan and Tadeusz Majda (eds.), *Katalog zabytków tatarskich*, vol. 3: *Piśmiennictwo i muhiry Tatarów polsko-litewskich*. Warsaw: Res Publica Multiethnica, pp. 12–37

Dubrovskiĭ, Pëtr P. 1866 [1852]. *Obrazt͡sy pol'skogo i͡azyka v" proz͡ie i stikhakh" dli͡a russkikh"* [...]. Saint Petersburg: Tipografii͡a Imperatorskoĭ Akademīi Nauk"

Dücker, Lisa, Hartmann, Stefan and Szczepaniak, Renata 2020. 'The emergence of sentence-internal capitalization in Early New High German: towards a multifactorial quantitative account', in Marco Condorelli (ed.), *Advances in Historical Orthography, c. 1500–1800*. Cambridge: Cambridge University Press, pp. 67–89

Duden, Konrad 1880. *Vollständiges Orthographisches Wörterbuch der deutschen Sprache von Duden Konrad: Nach den neuen preußischen und bayerischen Regeln*. Leipzig: Bibliographisches Institut

Duff, Edward G. 1948 [1906]. *The Printers, Stationers and Bookbinders of Westminster and London from 1476 to 1535*. Cambridge: Cambridge University Press

Duhoux, Yves 1999. 'La séparation des mots en linéaire B', in Sigfrid Deger-Jalkotzy, Stefan Hiller and Oswald Panagl (eds.), *Floreant Studia Mycenaea. Akten sed X. Internationalen Mykenologischen Colloquiums in Salzburg vom 1.–5. Mai 1995. Band II.* Vienna: Verlag der Österreichischen Akademie der Wissenschaften, pp. 227–36

Duhoux, Yves and Morpurgo Davies, Anna (eds.) 2008. *A Companion to Linear B: Mycenaean Greek Texts and Their World*, vol. 1. Leuven: Peeters

2011. *A Companion to Linear B: Mycenaean Greek Texts and Their World*, vol. 2. Leuven: Peeters

2014. *A Companion to Linear B: Mycenaean Greek Texts and Their World*, vol. 3. Leuven/Walpole: Peeters

Dumville, David 1993. *English Caroline Script and Monastic History: Studies in Benedictinism AD 950–1030*. Woodbridge: The Boydell Press

Duncan, Henry 1857. 'An account of the remarkable monument in the shape of a cross inscribed with Roman and runic letters, preserved in the Garden of Ruthwell Manse, Dumfriesshire', *Archaeologia Scotica: Or, Transactions of the Society of Antiquaries of Scotland* 4: 313–26

Dupraz, Emmanuel 2011. 'Osservazioni sulla coesione testuale nei rituali umbri: il caso delle Tavole I e II a', *Alessandria* 5: 49–66

2012. *Sabellian Demonstratives: Forms and Functions*. Leiden: Brill

2016. 'Über den umbrischen Digraph -ei-/-ei-', *Historische Sprachforschung* 129: 13–38

Duranti, Alessandro 2011. 'Linguistic anthropology: the study of language as a non-neutral medium', in Rajend Mesthrie (ed.), *The Cambridge Handbook of Sociolinguistics*. Cambridge: Cambridge University Press, pp. 28–46

Durkin, Philip 2014. *Borrowed Words: A History of Loanwords in English*. Oxford: Oxford University Press

Dürscheid, Christa 2006. *Einführung in die Schriftlinguistik*. Göttingen: Vandenhoeck and Ruprecht (3rd ed.)

2016. *Einführung in die Schriftlinguistik*. Göttingen: Vandenhoeck and Ruprecht (5th ed.)

Dürscheid, Christa and Meletis, Dimitrios 2019. 'Emojis: a grapholinguistic approach', in Yannis Haralambous (ed.), *Graphemics in the 21st Century: Grafematik, Brest, June 13–15, 2018: Proceedings* (Grapholinguistics and Its Applications 1). Brest: Fluxus Editions, pp. 167–83

Du Toit, Stefanus J. 1876. *Eerste Beginsels van Die Afrikaanse Taal*. Cape Colony: Die Genootskap van Regte Afrikaners

Dziekan, Marek M. 1997. 'Chamaił Aleksandrowicza', *Rocznik Tatarów Polskich* 4: 27–35

2011. 'History and culture of Polish Tatars', in Katarzyna Górak-Sosnowska (ed.), *Muslims in Poland and Eastern Europe: Widening the European Discourse on Islam*. Warsaw: University of Warsaw Faculty of Oriental Studies, pp. 27–39

2015. 'Uwagi o językach i literaturach bośniackiej, serbskiej i chorwackiej pisanych alfabetem arabskim', in Marta Wida-Behiesse and Konrad Zasztowt (eds.), *Islam w Europie: Nowe kierunki badań. Księga ku czci Profesor Anny Parzymies*. Warsaw: Wydawnictwo Akademickie Dialog, pp. 201–14

Early English Text Society Original Series, https://users.ox.ac.uk/~eets/

Ebert, Robert P., Reichmann, Oskar, Solms, Hans-Joachim and Wegera, Klaus-Peter 1993. *Frühneuhochdeutsche Grammatik*. Tübingen: Niemeyer

Echard, Siân 2013. Review of *The Production of Books in England 1350–1500* (Cambridge Studies in Palaeography and Codicology 14) by Alexandra Gillespie and Daniel Wakelin (eds.), *Speculum* 88 (1): 298–300

Eckert, Penelope 2000. *Linguistic Variation as Social Practice*. Oxford: Blackwell

2001. 'Style and social meaning', in Penelope Eckert and John Rickford (eds.), *Style and Sociolinguistic Variation*. Cambridge: Cambridge University Press, pp. 119–26

Eckert, Penelope and McConnell-Ginet, Sally 1992. 'Think practically and look locally: language and gender as community-based practice', *Annual Review of Anthropology* 21: 461–90

Edgerton, William F. 1941. 'Ideograms in English writing', *Language* 17 (2): 148–50

Edwards, Anthony S. G. 2000. 'Representing the Middle English manuscript', in Derek Pearsall (ed.), *New Directions in Later Medieval Manuscript Studies*. Bury St. Edmunds: York Medieval Press, pp. 65–79

Edwards, John 2012. 'Language management agencies', in Bernard Spolsky (ed.), *The Cambridge Handbook of Language Policy*. Cambridge: Cambridge University Press, pp. 418–36

Early English Books Online (EEBO) 2017. Part of the SAMUELS project (ed. by Mark Davies), www.english-corpora.org/eebo/

Early English Books Online: Text Creation Partnership (EEBO-TCP) 2000–20, www.textcreationpartnership.org/

Ehala, Martin 1996. 'Self-organization and language change', *Diachronica* 13 (1): 1–28

Ehlich, Konrad 2007. *Sprache und sprachliches Handeln*. Berlin: De Gruyter

Eira, Christina 1998. 'Authority and discourse: towards a model for orthography selection', *Written Language and Literacy* 1 (2): 171–224

Eisenstein, Elizabeth L. 1979. *The Printing Press as an Agent of Change: Communications and Cultural Transformations in Early Modern Europe*. Cambridge: Cambridge University Press

1983. *Printing Revolution in Early Modern Europe*. Cambridge: Cambridge University Press

Eisenberg, Peter 1983. 'Orthografie und Schriftsystem', in Klaus B. Günther and Hartmut Günther (eds.), *Schrift, Schreiben, Schriftlichkeit: Arbeiten zur Struktur, Funktion und Entwicklung schriftlicher Sprache*. Tübingen: Niemeyer, pp. 41–68

1996. 'Zur Typologie der Alphabetschriften. Das Deutsche und die Reform seiner Orthographie', in Ewald Lang and Gisela Zifonun (eds.), *Deutsch – Typologisch*. Berlin/Boston: De Gruyter, pp. 615–31

2009. 'Phonem und Graphem', in Kathrin Kunkel-Razum and Franziska Münzberg (eds.), *Die Grammatik*, vol. 4. Mannheim/Vienna/Zurich: Dudenverlag, pp. 19–94

2013. *Grundriß der deutschen Grammatik*, vol. 1: *Das Wort*. Stuttgart: J. B. Metzler (4th ed.)

El Educador 1842, July 31, number 17, pp. 3–4

Elementarz dla dzieci wiejskich 1865. Saint Petersburg: Tipografii͡a Ivana Bochkareva

Elementarz dla dzieci wiejskich 1866. Warsaw: Drukarni͡a I͡Ana Kotti (2nd ed.)

Ellis, Nick and Larsen-Freeman, Diane (eds.) 2009. *Language as a Complex Adaptive System*. London: Blackwell

Elmentaler, Michael 2003. *Struktur und Wandel vormoderner Schreibsprachen*. Berlin/New York: De Gruyter

2011. 'Prinzipien und Motive des Schreibens in vormoderner Zeit', in Elvira Glaser, Annina Seiler and Michelle Waldispühl (eds.), *LautSchriftSprache. Beiträge zur vergleichenden historischen Graphematik*. Zurich: Chronos, pp. 17–30

2018. *Historische Graphematik des Deutschen. Eine Einführung*. Tübingen: Narr Francke Attempto Verlag

Elspaß, Stephan 2005. *Sprachgeschichte von unten. Untersuchungen zum geschriebenen Alltagsdeutsch im 19. Jahrhundert*. Tübingen: Niemeyer

2007. 'A twofold view "from below". New perspectives on language histories and language historiographies', in Stephan Elspaß, Nils Langer, Joachim Scharloth and Wim Vandenbussche (eds.), *Germanic Language Histories 'from Below' (1700–2000)* (Studia Linguistica Germanica 86). Berlin/Boston: De Gruyter, pp. 3–9

2012a. 'Wohin steuern Korpora die Historische Sprachwissenschaft? Überlegungen am Beispiel des "Neuhochdeutschen"', in Péter Maitz (ed.), *Historische Sprachwissenschaft*. Berlin: De Gruyter, pp. 201–25

2012b. 'The use of private letters and diaries in sociolinguistic investigation', in Juan Manuel Hernández-Campoy and Juan Camilo Conde-Silvestre (eds.), *The Handbook of Historical Sociolinguistics*. Chichester: Wiley-Blackwell, pp. 156–69

Elspaß, Stephan, Langer, Nils, Scharloth, Joachim and Vandenbussche, Wim (eds.) 2007. *Germanic Language Histories 'from Below' (1700–2000)* (Studia Linguistica Germanica 86). Berlin/Boston: De Gruyter

Elti di Rodeano, Sveva 2019. 'Digraphia: the story of a sociolinguistic term', in Yannis Haralambous (ed.), *Graphemics in the 21st Century: Grafematik,*

Brest, June 13–15, 2018: Proceedings (Grapholinguistics and Its Applications 1). Brest: Fluxus Editions, pp. 111–26

Elyot, Thomas 1531. *The Boke Named the Gouernour Deuised by Thomas Elyot Knight*. London: In edibus Tho. Bertheleti

Emiliano, António 2011. 'Issues in the typographic representation of medieval primary sources', in Yuji Kawaguchi, Makoto Minegishi and Wolfgang Viereck (eds.), *Corpus-Based Analysis and Diachronic Linguistics*. Amsterdam/Philadelphia: John Benjamins, pp. 153–73

Encyclopedia Britannica, www.britannica.com

Engelbretsdatter, Dorothe 1699. *Dorothe Engelbrets-Datters Aandelige Sang- og Taare-Offer*. Copenhagen: Bekostet af H. Kong. Højh. Bogtr. Joachim Schmedtgen, https://urn.nb.no/URN:NBN:no-nb_digibok_2019120928001

Ennis, Juan Antonio 2008. *Decir la lengua: debates ideológico-lingüísticos en Argentina desde 1837*. Frankfurt am Main: Peter Lang

Ephron, Henry D. 1961. 'Mycenaean Greek: a lesson in cryptanalysis', *Minos* 7: 63–100

Epigrafik-Datenbank Clauss-Slaby, www.manfredclauss.de/

ERRATAS (Orthography): Investigating the Orthographic Reliability of Historical Corpora 2016–19. Project members: Anni Sairio, Samuli Kaislaniemi, Anna Merikallio and Terttu Nevalainen. Funded by the Academy of Finland Digital Humanities Programme, https://blogs.helsinki.fi/stratas-project/subprojects/erratas/

Errington, J. Joseph 2001. 'Colonial linguistics', *Annual Review of Anthropology* 30: 19–39

2008. *Linguistics in a Colonial World: A Story of Language, Meaning, and Power*. Malden: Blackwell

Escolano Benito, Agustín 2000. *Tiempos y espacios para la escuela. Ensayos históricos*. Madrid: Biblioteca Nueva

Esparza Torres, Miguel A. 2000. 'Frühe grammatische Beschreibungen des Spanischen', in Sylvain Auroux, Ernst F. K. Koerner, Hans-Josef Niederehe and Kees Versteegh (eds.), *History of the Language Sciences/Geschichte der Sprachwissenschaften/Histoire des sciences du langage*. Berlin/Boston: De Gruyter, pp. 749–55

Estarán Tolosa, M. José 2016. *Epigrafía bilingüe del Occidente romano. El latín y las lenguas locales en las inscripciones bilingües y mixtas*. Zaragoza: Prensas Universitarias de Zaragoza

Esteve Serrano, Abraham 1982. *Estudios de teoría ortográfica del Español*. Murcia: Universidad de Murcia

Ethnologue, www.ethnologue.com

Evans, Arthur J. 1901. 'Knossos: summary report of the excavations in 1900: the palace', *The Annual of the British Schools at Athens* 6: 3–70

1909. *Scripta Minoa: The Written Documents of Minoan Crete, with Special Reference to the Archives of Knossos*. Oxford: Clarendon Press

Evans, John 1621. *The Palace of Profitable Pleasure* [...]. London: W. Stansby

Evans, Mel 2012. 'A sociolinguistics of early modern spelling? An account of Queen Elizabeth I's correspondence', in Jukka Tyrkkö, Matti Kilpiö, Terttu Nevalainen and Matti Rissanen (eds.), *Outposts of Historical Corpus Linguistics: From the Helsinki Corpus to a Proliferation of Resources* (Studies in Variation, Contacts and Change in English 10). Helsinki: VARIENG, https://varieng.helsinki.fi/series/volumes/10/evans/

2013. *The Language of Queen Elizabeth I: A Sociolinguistic Perspective on Royal Style and Identity*. Chichester: Wiley/Blackwell

2020. *Royal Voices: Language and Power in Tudor England*. Cambridge: Cambridge University Press

Evans, Mel and Hogarth, Alan 2020. 'Stylistic palimpsests: computational stylistic perspectives on precursory authorship in Aphra Behn's drama', *Digital Scholarship in the Humanities* 36 (1): 64–86, https://doi.org/10.1093/llc/fqz085

Evans, Mel and Tagg, Caroline 2020. 'Women's spelling in Early Modern English: perspectives from new media', in Marco Condorelli (ed.), *Advances in Historical Orthography, c. 1500–1700*. Cambridge: Cambridge University Press, pp. 191–218

Evertz, Martin 2016. 'Graphematischer Fuß und graphematisches Wort', in Beatrice Primus and Ulrike Domahs (eds.), *Laut – Gebärde – Buchstabe*. Berlin/New York: De Gruyter, pp. 377–97

2018. *Visual Prosody. The Graphematic Foot in English and German*. Berlin/Boston: De Gruyter

Evertz, Martin and Primus, Beatrice 2013. 'The graphematic foot in English and German', *Writing System Research* 5 (1): 1–23

Ewald, Petra 2004. 'Das morphematische Prinzip bei den Grammatikern des 18. Jahrhunderts', *Sprachwissenschaft* 29: 75–132

Faber, Alice 1991. 'Interpretation of orthographic forms', in Philip Baldi (ed.), *Linguistic Change and Reconstruction Methodology*. Berlin/New York: De Gruyter, pp. 619–37

1992. 'Phonemic segmentation as epiphenomenon', in Pamela Downing, Susan D. Lima and Michael Noonan (eds.), *The Linguistics of Literacy*. Amsterdam: John Benjamins, pp. 111–34

Fairclough, Norman 1992a. *Critical Discourse Analysis. The Critical Study of Language*. London: Longman

1992b. *Discourse and Social Change*. Cambridge: Polity Press

Fairman, Tony 2006. 'Words in English record office documents of the early 1800s', in Merja Kytö, Mats Rydén and Erik Smitterberg (eds.),

Nineteenth-Century English: Stability and Change. Cambridge: Cambridge University Press, pp. 56–88

2015. 'Language in print and handwriting', in Anita Auer, Daniel Schreier and Richard J. Watts (eds.), *Letter Writing and Language Change* (Studies in English Language). Cambridge: Cambridge University Press, pp. 53–71

Farmer, Steve, Sproat, Richard and Witzel, Michael 2004. 'The collapse of the Indus-script thesis: the myth of a literate Harappan civilization', *Electronic Journal of Vedic Studies* 11 (2): 9–57

Favriaud, Michel 2004. 'Quelques éléments d'une théorie de la ponctuation blanche – par la poésie contemporaine', *L'information grammaticale* 102 (1): 18–23

Fayol, Michel and Jaffré, Jean-Pierre 2016. 'L'orthographe: des systèmes aux usages', *Pratiques* 169–70: 1–15, https://journals.openedition.org/pratiques/2984

Fazzioli, Edoardo 1986. *Chinese Calligraphy. From Pictograph to Ideogram: The History of 214 Essential Chinese/Japanese Characters* (calligraphy by Rebecca Hon Ko). New York: Abbeville

Felder, Egon 2003. *Die Personennamen auf den merowingischen Münzen der Bibliothèque nationale de France*. Munich: Verlag der Bayerischen Akademie der Wissenschaften

Feldman, Laurie B. and Barac-Cikoja, Dragana 1996. 'Serbo-Croatian: a biscriptal language', in Peter T. Daniels and William Bright (eds.), *The World's Writing Systems*. New York: Oxford University Press, pp. 769–72

Ferguson, Charles 1994. 'Dialect, register, and genre: working assumptions about conventionalization', in Douglas Biber and Edward Finegan (eds.), *Sociolinguistic Perspectives on Register*. Oxford: Oxford University Press, pp. 15–30

Ferrara, Silvia 2015. 'The beginnings of writing on Crete: theory and context', *Annual of the British School at Athens* 110: 27–49

Fet, Jostein 1995. *Lesande bønder. Litterær kultur i norske allmugesamfunn*. Oslo: Universitetsforlaget

2003. *Skrivande bønder. Skriftkultur på Nord-Vestlandet 1600–1850*. Oslo: Samlaget

2005. 'Utfordringar og svar. Streiftog gjennom eit forskingsfelt', in Atle Døssland and Geir Hjorthol (eds.), *Lesande og skrivande bønder. Foredrag frå eit symposium*. Volda: Høgskulen i Volda, pp. 13–31

Fidlerová, Alena A., Dittmann, Robert and Vladimírová, Veronika S. 2010. 'Užívání velkých písmen v českých tištěných Biblích raného novověku', in Michaela Čornejová, Lucie Rychnovská and Jana Zemanová (eds.), *Dějiny českého pravopisu (do r. 1902). Sborník příspěvků z mezinárodní konference Dějiny českého pravopisu (do r. 1902). 23.–25. září 2010, Brno, Česká Republika. History of Czech Orthography (up to 1902). Proceedings of the International Conference History of Czech Orthography (up to 1902). 23.–25. September 2010, Brno, Czech Republic*. Brno: Host, Masarykova univerzita, pp. 285–308

Fischer, Steven R. 2001. *A History of Writing*. London: Reaktion Books

Fisher, John H. 1977. 'Chancery English and the emergence of standard written English', *Speculum* 50 (4): 870–99

1996. *The Emergence of Standard English*. Lexington: University of Kentucky Press

Fisher, Matthew 2012. *Scribal Authorship and the Writing of History in Medieval England*. Columbus: The Ohio State University Press

Fishman, Joshua A. 1977. 'Advances in the creation and revision of writing systems', in Joshua Fishman (ed.), *Advances in the Creation and Revision of Writing Systems*. The Hague: Mouton, pp. xi–xxviii

2008. 'Rethinking the Ausbau-Abstand dichotomy into a continuous and multivariate system', *International Journal of the Sociology of Language* 191: 17–26

Fleischer, Wolfgang 1966. *Strukturelle Untersuchungen zur Geschichte des Neuhochdeutschen*. Berlin: Akademie-Verlag

1969. 'Die Entwicklung des neuhochdeutschen Graphemsystems', in Erhard Agricola, Wolfgang Fleischer and Helmut Protze (eds.), *Kleine Enzyklopädie. Die deutsche Sprache*. Leipzig: Bibliographisches Institut, pp. 228–34

1970. *Untersuchungen zur Geschäftssprache des 16. Jahrhunderts in Dresden*. Berlin: Akademie-Verlag

Flores, Nelson and Rosa, Jonathan 2015. 'Undoing appropriateness: raciolinguistic ideologies and language diversity in education', *Harvard Educational Review* 85 (2): 149–71

Fortson IV, Benjamin W. 2020. 'An overlooked usage of apices an *I longae*? Notes on *CIL* VI 2080', *Zeitschrift für Papyrologie und Epigraphik* 214: 67–79

Fortson IV, Benjamin W. and Weiss, Michael 2019. 'Oscan Kúnsíf Deívúz and the Di Consentes', *Classical Philology* 114 (4): 637–45

Fouché, Pierre 1959. *Traité de prononciation française*. Paris: Klincksiek (2nd ed.)

Fowkes, Robert A. 1964. 'The linguistic modernity of Jakob Grimm', *Linguistics* 2 (8): 56–61

Fowler, Roger 1986. *Linguistic Criticism*. Oxford: Oxford University Press

Foxvog, Daniel A. 2014. *Introduction to Sumerian Grammar*. CreateSpace Independent Publishing Platform

Frago Gracia, Juan A. 1999. *Historia del español de América: Textos y contextos*. Madrid: Gredos

Francis, W. Nelson 1958. *The Structure of American English*. New York: The Ronald Press Company

Franklin, Simon 2002. *Writing, Society and Culture in Early Rus, c. 950–1300*. Cambridge: Cambridge University Press

2019. *The Russian Graphosphere, 1450–1850*. Cambridge: Cambridge University Press

Frawley, William, Hill, Kenneth C. and Munro, Pamela 2002. 'Making a dictionary: ten issues', in William Frawley, Kenneth C. Hill and Pamela Munro (eds.), *Making Dictionaries. Preserving Indigenous Languages of the Americas*. Berkeley: University of California Press, pp. 1–22

Friedlieb, Timotheus (i.e. Gesenius, Justus) 1669. *Erörterung der Frage: Warumb wilt du nicht Römisch=Catholisch werden/wie deine Vorfahren waren?* s.l. [Hanover] (VD17 3: 003742Z)

Fries, Dagmar 1989. *'Limpia, Fija y da Esplendor': La Real Academia Española ante el Uso de la Lengua*. Madrid: Sociedad General Española de Librería, S. A.

Fritz, Clemens W. A 2010. 'A short history of Australian spelling', *Australian Journal of Linguistics* 30 (2): 227–81, https://doi.org/10.1080/07268601003678635

Frost, Ram and Katz, Leonard (eds.) 1992. *Orthography, Phonology, Morphology, and Meaning*. London: North-Holland (Elsevier Science Publisher)

Frost, Ram, Katz, Leonard and Bentin, Shlomo 1987. 'Strategies for visual word recognition and orthographical depth: a multilingual comparison', *Journal of Experimental Psychology: Human Perception and Performance* 13 (1): 104–15

Fuhrhop, Nanna 2008. 'Das graphematische Wort (im Deutschen): Eine erste Annäherung', *Zeitschrift für Sprachwissenschaft* 27: 189–228

2018. 'Graphematik des Deutschen im europäischen Vergleich', in Angelika Wöllstein, Peter Gallmann, Mechthild Habermann and Manfred Krifka (eds.), *Grammatiktheorie und Empirie in der germanistischen Linguistik*. Berlin/Boston: De Gruyter, 587–615

Fuhrhop, Nanna and Buchmann, Franziska 2009. 'Die Längenhierarchie. Zum Bau der graphematischen Silbe', *Linguistische Berichte* 218: 127–55

2011. 'Buchstabenformen und ihre Relevanz für eine Schriftgrammatik. Erwiderung auf einige Thesen von Oliver Rezec', *Linguistische Berichte* 225: 77–88

2016. 'Graphematische Silbe', in Beatrice Primus and Ulrike Domahs (eds.), *Laut – Gebärde – Buchstabe*. Berlin/New York: De Gruyter, pp. 356–76

Fuhrhop, Nanna, Buchmann, Franziska and Berg, Kristian 2011. 'The length hierarchy and the graphematic syllable: evidence from German and English', *Written Language and Literacy* 14 (2): 275–92

Fuhrhop, Nanna and Peters, Jörg 2013. *Einführung in die Phonologie und Graphematik*. Stuttgart/Weimar: J. B. Metzler

Fulk, Robert D. 2003. 'On argumentation in Old English philology, with particular reference to the editing and dating of *Beowulf*', *Anglo-Saxon England* 32: 1–26

2010. 'Localising and dating Old English anonymous prose, and how its inherent problems relate to Anglo-Saxon legislation', in Stefan Jurasinski, Lisi Oliver and Andrew Rabin (eds.), *English Law before Magna Carta: Felix Liebermann and Die Gesetze der Angelsachsen*. Turnhout: Brepols, pp. 59–79

2012. 'Anglian features in Late-West-Saxon prose', in David Denison, Ricardo Bermudez-Otero, Chris McCully and Emma Moore (eds.), *Analysing Older English*. Cambridge: Cambridge University Press, pp. 63–74

2016. 'Philological methods', in Merja Kytö and Päivi Pahta (eds.), *The Cambridge Handbook of English Historical Linguistics*. Cambridge: Cambridge University Press, pp. 95–108

Fulk, Robert D. and Cain, Christopher M. 2013. *A History of Old English Literature*. Malden: Wiley-Blackwell (2nd ed.)

Gadd, Ian A. 1999 '"Being like a field": corporate identity in the Stationers' Company 1557–1684'. Doctoral dissertation, University of Oxford, UK

Gager, John G. 1992. *Curse Tablets and Binding Spells from the Ancient World*. New York: Oxford University Press

Gal, Susan 2018. 'Visions and revisions of minority languages: standardization and its dilemmas', in Pia Lane, James Costa and Haley De Korne (eds.), *Standardizing Minority Languages*. London/New York: Routledge, pp. 222–42

Gal, Susan and Woolard, Kathryn 2014 [2001a]. 'Constructing languages and publics: authority and representation', in Susan Gal and Kathryn Woolard (eds.), *Languages and Publics: The Making of Authority*, 1–12

(eds.) 2001b. *Language and Publics. The Making of Authority*. London/York: Routledge

Galdo Guzmán, Diego 1890 [1642]. *Arte mexicano*. Mexico City: Museo Nacional de México

Gallmann, Peter 1985. *Graphische Elemente der geschriebenen Sprache. Grundlagen für eine Reform der Orthographie* (Reihe Germanistische Linguistik 60). Tübingen: Niemeyer, https://doi.org/10.1515/9783111630380

1986. 'The graphic elements of German written language', in Gerhard Augst (ed.), *New Trends in Graphemics and Orthography*. Berlin/New York: De Gruyter, pp. 43–79

Gameson, Richard 2011. 'Anglo-Saxon scribes and scriptoria', in Richard Gameson (ed.), *The Cambridge History of the Book in Britain*, vol. 1: *c. 400–1100*. Cambridge: Cambridge University Press, pp. 94–120

Garborg, Hulda 1896. *"Rationelt Fjøsstell". En Komedie-Akt*. Kristiania: Feilberg and Landmark

García, Ofelia 2011. 'Planning Spanish: nationalizing, minoritizing and globalizing performances', in Manuel Díaz-Campos (ed.), *The Handbook of Hispanic Sociolinguistics*. Oxford: Wiley-Blackwell, pp. 665–85

Garrido Vílchez, Gema B. 2012. 'De la *Gramática* al *Epítome*: la Real Academia Española ante la enseñanza gramatical. El caso de 1857', *Revista argentina de historiografía lingüística* 4 (2): 101–15

Garrison, Randy, Anderson, Terry and Walter, Archer 2000. 'Critical inquiry in a text-based environment: computer conferencing in higher education', *The Internet and Higher Education* 2 (2–3): 87–105

Garside, Roger 1987. 'The CLAWS Word-tagging System', in Roger Garside, Geoffrey Leech and Geoffrey Sampson (eds.), *The Computational Analysis of English: A Corpus-Based Approach*. London: Longman, pp. 30–41

Garside, Roger and Smith, Nicholas 1997. 'A hybrid grammatical tagger: CLAWS4', in Roger Garside, Geoffrey Lech and Anthony McEnery (eds.), *Corpus Annotation: Linguistic Information from Computer Text Corpora*. London: Longman, pp. 102–21, https://ucrel.lancs.ac.uk/claws/

Gažáková, Zuzana 2014. 'Some remarks on aljamiado literature and the use of arebica in Bosnia and Herzegovina', in Johannes den Heijer, Andrea Schmidt and Tamara Pataridze (eds.), *Scripts beyond Borders. A Survey of Allographic Traditions in the Euro-Mediterranean World*. Leuven: Peeters, pp. 453–71

Geerts, Guido, van den Broek, Jef and Verdoodt, Albert. 1977. 'Successes and failures in Dutch spelling reform', in Joshua A. Fishman (ed.), *Advances in the Creation and Revision of Writing Systems*. The Hague/Paris: Mouton, pp. 179–245

Geirnaert, Noël 1994. 'Boeken in het middeleeuwse Brugge: een verhaal van eeuwen', *Vlaanderen* 43: 121–24

Gelb, Ignace J. 1952. *A Study of Writing*. Chicago: Chicago University Press

1963. *A Study of Writing*. Chicago: University of Chicago Press (2nd ed.)

1969. *A Study of Writing*. Chicago/London: University of Chicago Press (reprint)

Gelumbeckaitė, Jolanta (ed.) 2008. *Die litauische Wolfenbütteler Postille von 1573. Kritische kommentierte Edition der Handschrift 1: Kritische Edition und textkritischer Apparat* (Lithuanian Sermons of Wolfenbüttel of 1573. Critical Commented Edition and Critical Apparatus). Wiesbaden: Harrassowitz

Giegerich, Heinz J. 1992. 'The limits of phonological derivation: spelling pronunciations and schwa in English', *Linguistische Berichte* 142: 413–36

1999. 'Phonology and the literate speaker: orthography in Lexical Phonology', in Heinz Giegerich (ed.), *Lexical Strata in English: Morphological Causes, Phonological Effects*. Cambridge: Cambridge University Press, pp. 131–66

Gieysztor, Aleksander 2009. *Zarys dziejów pisma łacińskiego*. Warsaw: Wydawnictwo Naukowe PWN (2nd ed.)

Gil, Alexander 1619. *Logonomia Anglica. Qua Gentis Sermo Facilius Addiscitur*. London: John Beal

Gil de Zárate, Antonio 1855. *De la Instruccion pública en España*, 3 vols. Madrid: Imprenta del Colegio de Sordo-Mudos

Gillen, Julia and Hall, Nigel 2010. 'Edwardian postcards: illuminating ordinary writing', in Barton, David and Papen, Uta (eds.), *The Anthropology of Writing: Understanding Textually Mediated Worlds*. London/New York: Continuum, pp. 168–89

Gillespie, Vincent and Powell, Susan (eds.) 2014. *A Companion to the Early Printed Book in Britain, 1476–1558*. Cambridge: D. S. Brewer

Gillmann, Melitta 2018. 'Das Semikolon als Kohäsionsmittel. Eine Korpusstudie in der überregionalen Pressesprache', *Zeitschrift für germanistische Linguistik* 46 (1): 65–101

Gippert, Jost 2013. 'An outline of the history of Maldivian writing', in Shu-Fen Chen and Benjamin Slade (eds.), *Grammatica et Verba, Glamor and Verve: Studies in South Asian, Historical, and Indo-European Linguistics in Honor of Hans Henrich Hock on the Occasion of His Seventy-Fifth Birthday*. Ann Arbor: Beech Stave Press, pp. 81–98

Gippius, Alekseĭ A. 2004. 'K pragmatike i kommunikativnoĭ organizat͡sii berest͡ianykh gramot', in Valentin L. I͡Anin, Andreĭ A. Zalizni͡ak and Alekseĭ A. Gippius (eds.), *Novgorodskie gramoty na bereste (iz raskopok 1997–2000 gg.)*, vol. 11. Moscow: Russkie slovari, pp.183–232

Gippius, Alekseĭ A. and Schaeken, Jos 2011. 'On direct speech and referential perspective in Birchbark letters no. 5 from Tver' and no. 286 from Novgorod', *Russian Linguistics* 35: 13–32

Glaser, Elvira 1985. *Graphische Studien zum Schreibsprachenwandel vom 13. bis 16. Jahrhundert: Vergleich verschiedener Handschriften des Augsburger Stadtbuches*. Heidelberg: Winter

1988. 'Autonomie und phonologischer Bezug bei der Untersuchung älterer Schriftlichkeit', *Beiträge zur Geschichte der deutschen Sprache und Literatur* 110: 313–31

1998. 'Das Graphemsystem der Clara Hätzlerin im Kontext der Handschrift Heidelberg, Cpg. 677', in Peter Ernst and Franz Patocka (eds.), *Deutsche Sprache in Raum und Zeit. Festschrift für Peter Wiesinger zum 60. Geburtstag*. Vienna: Edition Praesens, pp. 479–94

Glasgow, University Library, Ferguson MS 7 (ff. 1r-20v, 23r–48v, 59r)

Glasgow, University Library, Hunter MS 5

Glasgow, University Library, Hunter MS 7

Glasgow, University Library, Hunter MS 95 (ff. 34r–239v)

Glasgow, University Library, Hunter MS 95 (ff. 1r–11v)

Glasgow, University Library, Hunter MS 135 (ff. 34r–121v)

Glasgow, University Library, Hunter MS 197

Glasgow, University Library, Hunter MS 328 (ff. 1r–68v)

Glasgow, University Library, Hunter MS 497 (ff. 1r–92r)

Glessgen, Martin-Dietrich 2012. 'Trajectoires et perspectives en scriptologie romane', *Medioevo Romanzo* 36 (1): 5–23

Glessgen, Martin-Dietrich, Kihaï, Dimitru and Videsott, Paul 2010. 'L'élaboration philologique et linguistique des *Plus anciens documents linguistiques de la France*, édition électronique', *Bibliothèque de l'École des Chartes* 158: 5–94

Glück, Helmut 2016. 'Schrifsystem', in Helmut Glück and Michael Rödel (eds.), *Metzler Lexikon Sprache*. Stuttgart: J.B. Metzler Verlag, pp. 597–98

Głuszkowski, Michał 2012. 'Dwa języki – jedna tożsamość. Wierszyna – polska wieś na Syberii', in Ewa Golachowska and Anna Zielińska (eds.), *Konstrukcje i destrukcje tożsamości*, vol. 2: *Tożsamość wobec wielojęzyczności*. Warsaw: Slawistyczny Ośrodek Wydawniczy, pp. 119–30

Gnanadesikan, Amalia E. 2009. *The Writing Revolution: Cuneiform to the Internet*. Malden: Wiley-Blackwell

2011. 'Syllables and syllabaries: what writing systems tell us about syllable structure', in Charles E. Cairns and Eric Raimy (eds.), *Handbook of the Syllable*. Leiden/Boston: Brill, pp. 397–414

2012. 'Maldivian Thaana, Japanese kana, and the representation of moras in writing', *Writing Systems Research* 4 (1): 91–102

2017. 'Towards a typology of phonemic scripts', *Writing Systems Research* 9 (1): 14–35

Gneuss, Helmut 1972. 'The origin of standard Old English and Æthelwold's school at Winchester', *Anglo-Saxon England* 1: 63–83

Goddard, Ives 1996. 'Introduction', in Ives Goddard (ed.), *Handbook of North American Indians*, vol. 17: *Languages*. Washington, DC: Smithsonian Institution, pp. 1–16

Godoy, Lucía F. 2015. 'La regulación ortográfica de la lengua castellana. Perspectiva Glotopolítica', *Exlibris* 4: 472–82

Goebl, Hans 1975. 'Qu'est-ce que la scriptologie?', *Medioevo romanzo* 2: 3–43 (reprinted in '*Le Rey est mort, vive le Roy*: nouveaux regards sur la scriptologie', *Travaux de linguistique et de littérature* 13 (1): 145–210)

1995. 'Französische Skriptaformen III. Normandie. Les scriptae françaises III. Normandie', *Lexikon der romanistischen Linguistik* 2 (2): 314–37

Goffman, Erving 1981. *Forms of Talk*. Philadelphia: University of Pennsylvania Press

Goodman, Dena 2002. 'L'ortografe des dames: gender and language in the old regime', *French Historical Studies* 25 (2): 191–223

Google Books, https://books.google.com/

Gordon, Arthur E. 1983. *Illustrated Introduction to Latin Epigraphy*. Berkeley: University of California Press

Görlach, Manfred 1990. 'The development of standard Englishes', in Manfred Görlach (ed.), *Studies in the History of the English Language*. Heidelberg: Winter, pp. 9–64 (English version of Manfred Görlach 1988. 'Sprachliche Standardisierungsprozesse im englischprachigen Bereich', in Ulrich Ammon, Klaus J. Mattheier and Peter H. Nelde (eds.), *Sociolinguistica. Internationales Jahrbuch für Europäische Soziolinguistik 2*. Tübingen: Niemeyer)

1991. *Introduction to Early Modern English*. Cambridge: Cambridge University Press (revised ed.)

1999. 'Regional and social variation', in Roger Lass (ed.), *The Cambridge History of the English Language*, vol. 3: *1476–1776*. Cambridge: Cambridge University Press, pp. 459–538

Gossen, Charles-Théodore 1967. *Französische Skriptastudien. Untersuchungen zu den nordfranzösischen Urkundensprachen des Mittelalters*, Vienna: Hermann Böhlaus

1979. 'Méditations scriptologiques', *Cahiers de Civilisation Médiévale* 87: 263–83

Goswami, Usha 2006. 'Orthography, phonology, and reading development: a cross-linguistic perspective', in R. Malatesha Joshi and P. G. Aaron (eds.), *Handbook of Orthography and Literacy*. Mahwah: Lawrence Erlbaum, pp. 463–80

Gregory, Michael and Carroll, Susanne 1978. *Language and Situation: Language Varieties and Their Social Contexts*. London: Routledge and Kegan Paul

Grenoble, Lenore A. and Bulatova, Nadezhda Ja. 2018. 'Language standardization in the aftermath of the Soviet language empire', in Pia Lane, James Costa and Haley De Korne (eds.), *Standardizing Minority Languages*. New York/London: Routledge, pp. 118–34

Gries, Stefan T. 2013. *Statistics for Linguistics with R: A Practical Introduction*. Berlin/Boston: De Gruyter (2nd ed., revised)

Grigor′eva, Tat′i͡ana M. 2004. *Tri veka russkoĭ orfografii (XVIII–XX vv.)*. Moscow: Ėlpis

Grigori͡an, Vartan R. 1980. *Istorii͡a armi͡anskikh koloniĭ Ukrainy i Pol'shi (Armi͡ane v Podol'e)*. Yerevan: Izdatel'stvo AN Armi͡anskoĭ SSR

Grigoryan, Vartan R. and Pisovich‘, Andrey 1964. *'Hayataṛ leheren vaveragrerě'*, *Banber Matenadarani* 7: 225–36

Grimm, Christian 1991. *Zum Mythos Individualstil. Mikrostilistische Untersuchungen zu Thomas Mann*. Würzburg: Königshausen and Neumann

Grimm, Jacob 1822. *Deutsche Grammatik*, vol. 1. Göttingen: In der Dieterischschen Buchhandlung (2nd ed.)

1864. 'Über das pedantische in der deutschen sprache: Vorgelesen in der öffentlichen sitzung der akademie der wissenschaften am 21 october 1847', in *Kleinere Schriften*, vol. 1. Berlin: Dümmler, pp. 328–55

Grimm, Jacob and Wilhelm Grimm 1854–1961. *Deutsches Wörterbuch*, 16 vols. Leipzig: Hirzel

Grivelet, Stéphane 2001. 'Digraphia in Mongolia', *International Journal of the Sociology of Language* 150: 75–93

Grot, I͡Akov K. 1885. *Russkoe pravopisanīe* [...]. Saint Petersburg: Tipografīi͡a Imperatorskoĭ Akademīi Nauk" (2nd ed.)

Gruaz, Claude 1990. *Du signe au sens. Pour une grammaire homologique des composants du mot* (Publications de l'Université de Rouen N° 158). Mont-Saint-Aignan: Publications de l'Université de Rouen

Gruijs, Albert 1972. 'Codicology or the archaeology of the book? A false dilemma', *Quærendo* 2 (2): 87–108

Grund, Peter J. 2007. 'From tongue to text: the transmission of the Salem witchcraft examination records', *American Speech* 82 (2): 119–50

2011. 'Scribes and scribal practices', in Merja Kytö, Peter J. Grund and Terry Walker (eds.), *Testifying to Language and Life in Early Modern England*. Amsterdam: John Benjamins, pp. 147–80

2014. 'The "forgotten" language of Middle English alchemy: exploring alchemical lexis in the *MED* and the *OED*', *Review of English Studies* 65 (271): 575–95

Grund, Peter J., Hiltunen, Risto, Kahlas-Tarkka, Leena, Kytö, Merja, Peikola, Matti and Rissanen, Matti 2009. 'Linguistic introduction', in Bernard Rosenthal, Gretchen A. Adams, Margo Burns, Peter J. Grund, Risto Hiltunen, Leena Kahlas-Tarkka, Merja Kytö, Matti Peikola, Benjamin C. Ray, Matti Rissanen, Marilynne K. Roach and Richard B. Trask (eds.), *Records of the Salem Witch-Hunt*. Cambridge: Cambridge University Press, pp. 64–90

Grund, Peter J., Peikola, Matti, Rastas, Johanna and Xin, Wen 2021. 'The <u> and <v> alternation in the history of English: spelling dynamics in the handwritten legal documents from the Salem witch trials (1692)', *American Speech* 96 (2): 127–60, https://doi.org/10.1215/00031283-8661851

Grüter, Majana 2007. *Die Entwicklung der englischen Groß- und Kleinschreibung in der frühen Neuzeit am Beispiel ausgewählter Texte*. Osnabrück: Universität Osnabrück, https://repositorium.ub.uni-osnabrueck.de/handle/urn:nbn:de:gbv:700-201001305204

2009. 'Optimalitätstheoretische Modellierung von Groß- und Kleinschreibung: eine Beispielanalyse englischer Texte um 1730', *Zeitschrift für Sprachwissenschaft* 28 (2): 203–30

Grzega, Joachim 2012. 'Lexical-semantic variables', in Juan Manuel Hernández-Campoy and Juan Camilo Conde-Silvestre (eds.), *The Handbook of Historical Sociolinguistics*. Chichester: Wiley-Blackwell, pp. 270–92

Guerini, Federica 2018. 'Orthography as an identity marker: the case of bilingual road signs in the province of Bergamo', in Kate Beeching, Chiara Ghezzi and Piera Molinelli (eds.), *Positioning the Self and Others: Linguistic Perspectives*. Amsterdam/Philadelphia: John Benjamins, pp. 263–83

2019. 'Orthography and graphemics', in Jeroen Darquennes, Joseph C. Salmons and Wim Vandenbussche (eds.), *Language Contact: An International Handbook*, vol. 1. Berlin: De Gruyter, pp. 76–88

Guerra, Juan 1692. *Arte de la lengua mexicana, segun la acostumbran a hablar los indios en todo el obispado de Guadalaxara, parte del de Guadiana y del de Mechoacan*. Mexico City: Viuda de Francisco Rodríguez Lupercio

Guerreau-Jalabert, Anita 1982. *Abbo Floriacensis: Quaestiones grammaticales*. Paris: Les Belles Lettres

Gundersen, Trygve R. 2005. 'Meningens håndarbeidere. Skrift, materialitet og kommunikasjon i Jostein Fets Skrivande bønder', in Atle Døssland and Geir Hjorthol (eds.), *Lesande og skrivande bønder. Foredrag frå eit symposium*. Volda: Høgskulen i Volda, pp. 123–44

Günther, Hartmut 1988. *Schriftliche Sprache. Strukturen geschriebener Wörter und ihre Verarbeitung beim Lesen* (Konzepte der Sprach- und Literatur- wissenschaft 40). Tübingen: Niemeyer, https://doi.org/10.1515/9783110935851

1990. 'Typographie, Orthographie, Graphetik. Überlegungen zu einem Buch von Otl Aicher', in Christian Stetter (ed.), *Zu einer Theorie der Orthographie. Interdisziplinäre Aspekte gegenwärtiger. Schrift- und Orthographieforschung* (Reihe Germanistische Linguistik 99). Tübingen: Niemeyer, pp. 90–104, https://doi.org/10.1515/9783111372280.90

Günther, Hartmut and Ludwig, Otto (eds.) 1994–96. *Schrift und Schriftlichkeit/Writing and Its Use. Ein interdisziplinäres Handbuch internationaler Forschung/An Interdisciplinary Handbook of International Research*, 2 vols. Berlin/New York: DeGruyter Mouton

Guzmán Betancourt, Ignacio 2001. 'La investigación lingüística en México durante el siglo XVII', *Dimensión Antropológica* 21: 33–70

Gysseling, Maurits and Pijnenburg, Willy (compilers) 1977. *Corpus van Middelnederlandse teksten (tot en met het jaar 1300) uitgegeven door M. Gysseling. M.m.v. en van woordindices voorzien door W. Pijnenburg. Reeks I: Ambtelijke bescheiden*. The Hague: M. Nijhoff

Haarmann, Harald 2006. 'Language planning: graphization and the development of writing systems', in Ulrich Ammon, Norbert Dittmar, Klaus J. Mattheier and Peter J. Trudgill (eds.), *Sociolinguistics: An International Handbook of the Science of Language and Society*, vol. 3. Berlin: De Gruyter, pp. 2402–20

Haas, Walter 1990. *Jacob Grimm und die deutschen Mundarten* (Zeitschrift für Dialektologie und Linguistik, Beihefte 65). Stuttgart: Steiner-Verlag Wiesbaden

Haas, William 1970. *Phono-Graphic Translation*. Manchester: Manchester University Press.

1976. 'Writing: the basic options', in William Haas (ed.), *Writing without Letters*. Manchester: Manchester University Press, pp. 131–208

1983. 'Determining the level of a script', in Florian Coulmas and Konrad Ehlich (eds.), *Writing in Focus*. Berlin: Mouton, pp. 15–29

Habermann, Mechthild 1997. 'Das sogenannte "Lutherische e". Zum Streit um einen armen Buchstaben', *Sprachwissenschaft* 22: 435–77

2012. 'Leichenpredigten des 17. Jahrhunderts im konfessionellen Kontext', in Jürgen Macha, Anna-Maria Balbach and Sarah Horstkamp (eds.), *Konfession und Sprache in der Frühen Neuzeit. Interdisziplinäre Perspektiven*. Münster: Waxmann, pp. 63–84

Hagland, Jan Ragnar 2011. 'Literacy and trade in late medieval Norway', *Journal of Northern Studies* 1: 29–37

Hagland, Jan Ragnar, Nesse, Agnete and Otnes, Hildegun. 2018. 'Skriftkunne og språkmedium', in Brit Mæhlum (ed.), *Praksis*, vol. 3 of Helge Sandøy and Agnete Nesse (eds.), *Norsk språkhistorie*. Oslo: Novus, pp. 29–118

Hagland, Jan Ragnar and Page, Ray 1998. 'Runica manuscripta and runic dating: the expansion of the younger fuþark', in Audun Dybdahl and Jan Ragnar Hagland (eds.), *Innskrifter og datering – Dating Inscriptions*. Trondheim: Tapir, pp. 55–71

Haile, Getatchew 1996. 'Ethiopic writing', in Peter T. Daniels and William Bright (eds.), *The World's Writing Systems*. New York: Oxford University Press, pp. 569–76

Halasz, Alexandra 1997. *The Marketplace of Print: Pamphlets and the Public Sphere in Early Modern England*. Cambridge: Cambridge University Press

Hall, Robert A., Jr. 1950. *Leave Your Language Alone*. Ithaca: Linguistica

1960. 'A theory of graphemics', *Acta Linguistica*, 8 (1): 13–20

1961. *Sound and Spelling in English*. Philadelphia: Chilton Books

Halliday, Michael A. K. 1975. *Learning How to Mean*. London: Edward Arnold

1978. *Language as Social Semiotic: The Interpretation of Language and Meaning*. London: Edward Arnold

1985. *An Introduction to Functional Grammar*. London: Edward Arnold

Haładewicz-Grzelak, Małgorzata 2014. 'Neogrammarian Ferdinand: a natural hermeneutics of *Mémoire sur le système primitif des voyelles dans les langues indo-européennes*, *Acta Neophilologica* 14 (1): 27–40

Hämäläinen, Mika, Säily, Tanja, Rueter, Jack, Tiedemann, Jörg and Mäkelä, Eetu 2018. 'Normalizing early English letters to present-day English spelling', in Beatrice Alex, Stefania Degaetano-Ortlieb, Anna Feldman, Anna Kazantseva, Nils Reiter and Stan Szpakowicz (eds.), *Proceedings of the Second Joint SIGHUM Workshop on Computational Linguistics for Cultural Heritage, Social Sciences, Humanities and Literature*

(LaTeCH-CLfL-2018). Stroudsburg: Association for Computational Linguistics, pp. 87–96

Hämäläinen, Mika, Säily, Tanja, Rueter, Jack, Tiedemann, Jörg and Mäkelä, Eetu 2019. 'Revisiting NMT for normalization of early English letters', in Beatrice Alex, Stefania Degaetano-Ortlieb, Anna Kazantseva, Nils Reiter and Stan Szpakowicz (eds.), *Proceedings of the Third Joint SIGHUM Workshop on Computational Linguistics for Cultural Heritage, Social Sciences, Humanities and Literature (LaTeCH-CLfL-2019*. Stroudsburg: Association for Computational Linguistics), pp. 71–75

Hammarström, Göran 1981 [1964]. 'Type and typeme, graph and grapheme', in Piotr Ruszkiewicz (ed.), *Graphophonemics: A Book of Readings*. Katowice: Uniwersytet Śląski, pp. 89–99

Hansen, Maurits 1822. *Forsøg til en Grammatik i Modersmaalet*. Christiania

1828. *Grammatik i det norske og danske Sprog*. Christiania

1833. *Norsk Grammatik*. Christiania

Haralambous, Yannis 2020. 'Grapholinguistics, TeX, and a June 2020 conference in Paris', *TUGboat* 41 (1): 12–19, https://tug.org/TUGboat/tb41-1/tb127haralambous-grapholinguistics.pdf

(ed.) 2019. *Graphemics in the 21st Century: Grafematik, Brest, June 13–15, 2018: Proceedings* (Grapholinguistics and Its Applications 1). Brest: Fluxus Editions, http://fluxus-editions.fr/gla1.php

(ed.) 2021. *Grapholinguistics in the 21st Century, Paris, June 17–19, 2020. Proceedings*(Grapholinguistics and Its Applications 4). Brest: Fluxus Editions, www.fluxus-editions.fr/grafematik2020-proceedingsI.pdf

Haralambous, Yannis and Dürst, Martin 2019. 'Unicode from a linguistic point of view', in Yannis Haralambous (ed.), *Graphemics in the 21st Century: Grafematik, Brest, June 13–15, 2018: Proceedings* (Grapholinguistics and Its Applications 1). Brest: Fluxus Editions, pp. 167–83, https://doi.org/10.36824/2018-graf-hara1

Haring, Ben 2015. '*Halaḥam* on an ostracon of the Early New Kingdom?', *Journal of Near Eastern Studies* 74: 189–96

Harpham, Geoffrey G. 2009. 'Roots, races, and the return to philology', *Representations* 106 (1): 35–62

Harrauer, Hermann 2010. *Handbuch der Griechischen Paläographie*. Stuttgart: Anton Hiersemann Verlag

Harris, Roy 1981. 'Scriptism', in Roy Harris (ed.), *The Language Makers*. Ithaca: Cornell University Press, pp. 6–16

1986. *The Origin of Writing*. London: Duckworth

1995. *Signs of Writing*. London/New York: Routledge

2003. *Rethinking Writing*. London/New York: Continuum

2009. 'Speech and writing', in David R. Olson and Nancy Torrance (eds.), *The Cambridge Handbook of Literacy*. Cambridge: Cambridge University Press, pp. 46–58

Harrison, K. David, Lillehaugen, Brook Danielle, Fahringer, Jeremy and Lopez, Felipe H. 2019. 'Zapotec language activism and talking dictionaries', in Iztok Kosem and Simon Krek (eds.), *Electronic Lexicography in the 21st Century (Elex 2019): Proceedings of the Elex 2019 Conference, 1–3 October, 2019, Sintra, Portugal*. Brno: Lexical Computing CZ s.r.o., pp. 31–50, https://elex.link/elex2019/proceedings-download/

Hart, John 1569. *An Orthographie, conteyning the due order and reason, howe to write or paint thimage of mannes voice, most like to the life or nature. Composed by I. H. Chester Heralt*. London: William Seres

1955 [1569]. *An Orthographie*, in Bror Danielsson (ed. and trans.), *John Hart's Works on English Orthography and Pronunciation* [1551. 1569. 1576], 2 vols. Stockholm: Almqvist and Wiksell, pp. 165–228

Hartman, George 1696. *The Family Physitian, or a Collection of Choice, Approv'd and Experience'd Remedies, for the Cure of Almost All Diseases Incident to Humane Bodies, whether Internal or External*. London: Richard Wellington

Harvey, Anthony 2011. 'Reading the genetic code of early medieval Celtic orthography', in Elvira Glaser, Annina Seiler and Michelle Waldispühl (eds.), *LautSchriftSprache: Beiträge zur vergleichenden historischen Graphematik*. Zurich: Chronos, pp. 155–66

Haß, Ulrike 2019. 'The Germanic languages other than English from c. 1700', in John Considine (ed.), *The Cambridge World History of Lexicography*. Cambridge: Cambridge University Press, pp. 460–83

Haugen, Einar 1950. *The First Grammatical Treatise: The Earliest Germanic Philology* (Language Monograph 25), *Language* 26 (4): 4–64

1953. *The Norwegian Language in America. A Study in Bilingual* Behavior I. Philadelphia: University of Pennsylvania Press

1961. 'Language planning in modern Norway', *Scandinavian Studies* 33 (2): 68–81

1966a. *Language Conflict and Language Planning: The Case of Modern Norwegian*, Cambridge, MA: Harvard University Press

1966b. '*Semicommunication*: the language gap in *Scandinavia*', *Sociological Inquiry* 36 (2): 280–97

1966c. 'Dialect, language, nation', *American Anthropologist* 68 (4): 922–35

1987. 'Language planning', in Ulrich Ammon, Norbert Dittmar, Klaus J. Mattheier and Peter J. Trudgill (eds.), *Sociolinguistics*, vol. 1. Berlin/New York: De Gruyter, pp. 626–37

Haugen, Odd E. (ed.) 2013. 'Dealing with glyphs and characters. Challenges in encoding medieval scripts', *Document numérique* 16 (3): 97–111

2018. 'Høgmellomalderen 1050–1350', in Agnete Nesse (ed.) *Tidslinjer*, vol. 4 of Helge Sandøy and Agnete Nesse (eds.), *Norsk språkhistorie*. Oslo: Novus, pp. 197–292

Haukland, Linda 2014. 'Hans Nielsen Hauge: a catalyst of literacy in Norway', *Scandinavian Journal of History* 39 (5): 539–59

Havelock, Eric 1999. 'The Greek legacy', in David Crowley and Paul Heyer (eds.), *Communication in History: Technology, Culture, Society.* New York: Longman, pp. 54–60 (3rd ed.)

Havinga, Anna D. 2018. *Invisibilising Austrian German: On the Effect of Linguistic Prescriptions and Educational Reforms on Writing Practices in 18th-Century Austria*, vol. 18. Berlin/Boston: De Gruyter

Havinga, Anna D. and Langer, Nils (eds.) 2015. *Invisible Languages in the Nineteenth Century.* Bern: Peter Lang

Healey, John F. 1990. 'The early alphabet', in James T. Hooker (ed.), *Reading the Past: Ancient Writing from Cuneiform to the Alphabet.* New York: Barnes and Noble, pp. 197–257

Hebda, Anna 2012. 'Phonological variables', in Juan Manuel Hernández-Campoy and Juan Camilo Conde-Silvestre (eds.), *The Handbook of Historical Sociolinguistics.* Chichester: Wiley-Blackwell, pp. 237–57

Hector, Leonard C. 1958. *The Handwriting of English Documents.* London: Edward Arnold

1966 [1958]. *The Handwriting of English Documents.* Ilkley: Scholar Press (2nd ed.)

Heikkonen, Kirsi 1996. 'Regional variation in standardization: a case study of Henry V's Signet Office', in Terttu Nevalainen and Helena Raumolin-Brunberg (eds.), *Sociolinguistics and Language History: Studies Based on the Corpus of Early English Correspondence.* Amsterdam: Rodopi, pp. 111–27

Heimann, David and Kay, Richard 1982. 'Preface', in Adriano Capellli, *The Elements of Abbreviation in Medieval Latin Paleography* (trans. by David Heimann and Richard Kay). Lawrence: University of Kansas Libraries, pp. i–iv

Hellinga, Lotte 1991. 'Importation of books printed on the Continent into England and Scotland before c. 1520', in: Sandra Hindman (ed.), *Printing the Written Word: The Social History of Books, circa 1450-1520.* Ithaca/London: Cornell University Press, pp. 205–24

1999. 'Printing', in Lotte Hellinga and Joseph B. Trapp (eds.), *The Cambridge History of the Book in Britain*, vol. 3: *1400–1557.* Cambridge: Cambridge University Press, pp. 65–108

2014. *Texts in Transit: Manuscript to Proof and Print in the Fifteenth Century.* Leiden: Brill

Hellinga, Lotte and Trapp, Joseph B. 1999. 'Introduction', in Lotte Hellinga and Joseph B. Trapp (eds.), *The Cambridge History of the Book in Britain*, vol. 3: *1400–1557.* Cambridge: Cambridge University Press, pp. 1–30

Hemming, T. D. 1993. 'Authority and orthography', in Rodney Sampson (ed.), *Authority and the French Language. Papers from a Conference at the University of Bristol.* Münster: Nodus Publikationen, pp. 75–85

Henderson, Leslie 1982. *Orthography and Word Recognition in Reading.* London: Academic Press

1985. 'On the use of the term "grapheme"', *Language and Cognitive Processes* 1 (2): 135–48

Hendriks, Pepijn 2014. *Innovation in Tradition. Tonnies Fonne's Russian-German Phrasebook (Pskov, 1607).* Amsterdam/New York: Rodopi

Henri, France and Pudelko, Béatrice 2003. 'Understanding and analysing activity and learning in virtual communities', *Journal of Computer Assisted Learning* 19: 474–87

Hernández-Campoy, Juan Manuel 2015. *Sociolinguistic Styles* (Language in Society). Malden: Wiley-Blackwell

2016a. *Sociolinguistic Styles.* Malden: Wiley-Blackwell

2016b. 'Authorship and gender in English historical sociolinguistic research: samples from the Paston Letters', in Cinzia Russi (ed.), *Current Trends in Historical Sociolinguistics.* Warsaw/Berlin: De Gruyter, pp. 108–42, https://doi.org/10.1515/9783110488401-009

Hernández-Campoy, Juan Manuel and Conde-Silvestre, Juan Camilo 1999. 'The social diffusion of linguistic innovations in 15th century England: Chancery spellings in private correspondence', *Cuadernos de Filología Inglesa* 8: 251–74

2005. 'Sociolinguistic and geolinguistic approaches to the historical diffusion of linguistic innovations: incipient standardisation in Late Middle English', *International Journal of English Studies* 5 (1): 101–34

(eds.) 2012. *The Handbook of Historical Sociolinguistics.* Chichester: Wiley-Blackwell

(eds.) 2014. *The Handbook of Historical Sociolinguistics.* Oxford: Wiley-Blackwell (paperback ed.)

Hernández-Campoy, Juan Manuel, Conde-Silvestre, Juan Camilo and García-Vidal, Tamara 2019. 'Tracing patterns of intra-speaker variation in early English correspondence: a change from above in the *Paston Letters*', *Studia Anglica Posnaniensia* 54 (1): 287–314

Hernández-Campoy, Juan Manuel and García-Vidal, Tamara 2018a. 'Persona management and identity projection in English medieval society: evidence from John Paston II', *Journal of Historical Sociolinguistics* 4 (1): 1–31

2018b. 'Style-shifting and accommodative competence in Late Middle English written correspondence: putting audience design to the test of time', *Folia Linguistica Historica* 39 (2): 383–420

Hernández-Campoy, Juan Manuel and Schilling, Natalie 2012. 'The application of the quantitative paradigm to historical sociolinguistics: problems with the generalizability principle', in Juan Manuel Hernández-Campoy and Juan Camilo Conde-Silvestre (eds.), *The Handbook of Historical Sociolinguistics.* Chichester: Wiley-Blackwell, pp. 63–79

Herrick, Earl M. 1975. Letters with alternative basic shapes. *Visible Language* 9 (2): 133–44

Hidalgo, Margarita 2001. 'Sociolinguistic stratification in New Spain', *International Journal of the Sociology of Language* 149: 55–78

Hill, Archibald A. 1967. 'The typology of writing systems', in William M. Austin (ed.), *Papers in Linguistics in Honor of Leon Dostert*. The Hague: Mouton, pp. 92–99

Hiltunen, Risto and Peikola, Matti 2007. 'Trial discourse and manuscript context: scribal profiles in the Salem witchcraft records', *Journal of Historical Pragmatics* 8 (1): 43–68

Hinrichs, Lars 2012. 'How to spell the vernacular: a multivariate study of Jamaican emails and blogs', in Alexandra M. Jaffe, Jannis K. Androutsopoulos, Mark Sebba and Sally A. Johnson (eds.), *Orthography as Social Action: Scripts, Spelling, Identity and Power* (Language and Social Processes 3). Boston/Berlin: De Gruyter, pp. 325–58

Hinton, Leanne 2014. 'Orthography wars', in Michael Cahill and Keren Rice (eds.), *Developing Orthographies for Unwritten Languages*. Dallas: SIL International Publications, pp. 139–68

Historical Sociolinguistics Network (HiSoN), https://hison.org/

Hjelmslev, Louis 1961. *Prolegomena to a Theory of Language*. Madison: The University of Wisconsin Press

Hladký, Josef 1985a. 'Notes on the history of word division in English', *Brno Studies in English* 16: 73–83

1985b. 'Word division in Caxton and Dryden', *Philologica Pragensia* 28: 135–41

1987. 'Word division and syllabification in English', *Brno Studies in English* 17: 123–30

Hobsbawm, Eric J. 1992. *Nations and Nationalism since 1780: Programme, Myth, Reality*. Cambridge/New York: Cambridge University Press (2nd ed.)

Hockett, Charles F. 1951. Review of *Nationalism and Language Reform in China* by John DeFrancis, *Language* 27 (3): 439–45, https://doi.org/10.2307/409788

1958. *A Course in Modern Linguistics*. New York: Macmillan

Hodges, Richard 1644. *A Special Help to Orthographie* [...]. London: Richard Cotes

1649. *The Plainest Directions for the True-Writing of English* [...]. London: William Dugard for Thomas Euster

1653. *Most Plain Directions for True-Writing* [...]. London: William Dugard

Hoel, Oddmund L. 2018. 'Unionstida med Sverige 1814–1905', in Agnete Nesse (ed.), *Tidslinjer*, vol. 4 of Helge Sandøy and Agnete Nesse (eds.), *Norsk språkhistorie*. Oslo: Novus, pp. 425–502

Hoffman, A. Robin 2017. 'The means and end(s) of spelling reform in the Victorian press', *Victorian Periodicals Review* 50 (4): 737–51

Hogg, Richard M. 1992a. *A Grammar of Old English*, vol. 1: *Phonology*. Chichester: Wiley-Blackwell

1992b. 'Phonology and morphology', in Richard M. Hogg (ed.), *The Cambridge History of the English Language*, vol. 1: *The Beginnings to 1066*. Cambridge: Cambridge University Press, pp. 67–167

2006. 'Old English dialectology', in Ans van Kemenade and Bettelou Los (eds.), *The Handbook of the History of English*. Oxford: Blackwell, pp. 395–416

Holmberg, Börje 1956. *James Douglas on English Pronunciation, c. 1740*. Lund: Gleerup

Holmes, Janet and Meyerhoff, Miriam 1999. 'The community of practice: theories and methodologies in language and gender research', *Language in Society* 28: 173–83

Holtus, Günter, Metzeltin, Michael and Schmitt, Christian (eds.) 1995. *Lexicon der Romanistischen Linguistik* (LRL), vol. 2, 2: *Die einzelnen romanischen Sprachen und Sprachgebiete vom Mittelalter bis zur Renaissance*. Tübingen: Niemeyer, *Französische Skriptaformen I–VII, Frankoprovenzalische Skriptae*, pp. 289–405; *Okzitanische Skriptaformen*, pp. 405–66; *Katalanische Skriptae*, pp. 486–512; *Aragonese und Navarresische Skriptae*, pp. 512–27; *Das Altkastilische in seinen Texten*, pp. 537–64

Honkapohja, Alpo 2013. 'Manuscript abbreviations in Latin and English: history, typologies and how to tackle them in encoding', in Anneli Meurman-Solin and Jukka Tyrkkö (eds.), *Principles and Practices for the Digital Editing and Annotation of Diachronic Data* (Studies in Variation, Contacts and Change in English 14). Helsinki: VARIENG, https://varieng.helsinki.fi/series/volumes/14/honkapohja/

2017. '"Latin in recipes?" A corpus approach to scribal abbreviations in 15th-century medical manuscripts', in Päivi Pahta, Janne Skaffari and Laura Wright (eds.), *Multilingual Practices in Language History: New Perspectives*. Berlin: De Gruyter, pp. 243–71

2019. 'Anchorites and abbreviations: a corpus study of abbreviations of romance and Germanic lexicon in the *Ancrene Wisse*', in Merja Stenroos, Martti Mäkinen, Kjetil V. Thengs and Oliver M. Traxel (eds.), *Current Explorations in Middle English*. Frankfurt am Main: Peter Lang, pp. 35–64

Honkapohja, Alpo and Liira, Aino 2020. 'Abbreviations and standardisation in the Polychronicon: Latin to English, and manuscript to print', in Laura Wright (ed.), *The Multilingual Origins of Standard English*. Berlin: De Gruyter, pp. 269–316

Hooker, James T. 1980. *Linear B: An Introduction*. Bristol: Bristol Classical Press

Hope, Jonathan 2000. 'Rats, bats, sparrows, and dogs: biology, linguistics, and the nature of standard English', in Laura Wright (ed.), *The Development of Standard English, 1300–1800: Theories, Descriptions, Conflicts* (Studies in English Language). Cambridge/New York: Cambridge University Press, pp. 49–56

Horley, Paul 2009. '*Rongorongo* script: carving techniques and scribal corrections', *Journal de la Société des Océanistes* 129: 249–61

Horn, Wilhelm and Lehnert, Martin 1954. *Laut und Leben: englische Lautgeschichte der neueren Zeit (1400–1950)*. Berlin: Deutscher Verlag der Wissenschaften

Horobin, Simon 2001. 'The language of the fifteenth-century printed editions of *The Canterbury Tales*', *Anglia* 119 (2): 249–58

2003. *The Language of the Chaucer Tradition*. Cambridge: D. S. Brewer

2011. 'Mapping the words', in Alexandra Gillespie and Daniel Wakelin (eds.), *The Production of Books in England 1350–1500*. Cambridge: Cambridge University Press, pp. 59–78

2013a. *Chaucer's Language*. Basingstoke: Palgrave Macmillan (2nd ed.)

2013b. *Does Spelling Matter?* Oxford: Oxford University Press

2016. 'The etymological inputs into English spelling', in Vivian Cook and Des Ryan (eds.), *The Routledge Handbook of the English Writing System*. London/New York: Routledge, pp. 113–24

Horsley, Greg H. R. and Waterhouse, Elisabeth R. 1984. 'The Greek *nomen sacrum* XP- in some Latin and Old English manuscripts', *Scriptorium* 38 (2): 211–30

Horstbøll, Henrik 2005. 'Bogmarkedet og læserevolutionen i Danmark-Norge i det lange 18. århundrede', in Arne Døssland and Geir Hjorthol (eds.), *Lesande og skrivande bønder. Foredrag frå eit symposium*. Volda: *Høgskulen* i Volda, pp. 55–73

Householder, Fred W. 1948. 'Balm, calm, palm', *American Speech* 23 (2): 155–56

1964. 'A morphophonemic question and a spelling rule', in Emmett L. Bennett (ed.), *Mycenaean Studies: Proceedings of the Third International Colloquium for Mycenaean Studies Held at 'Wingspread' 4–8 September 1961*. Madison: University of Wisconsin Press, pp. 71–76

1969. Review of *Language and Its Structure: Some Fundamental Linguistic Concepts* by Ronald W. Langacker, *Language* 45 (4): 886–97

Houston, Stephen D. 1994. 'Literacy among the pre-Columbian Maya: a comparative perspective', in Elizabeth Hill Boone and Walter D. Mignolo (eds.), *Writing without Words: Alternative Literacies in Mesoamerica and the Andes*. Durham: Duke University Press, pp. 27–49

2004. 'Writing in early Mesoamerica', in Stephen D. Houston (ed.), *The First Writing: Script Invention as History and Process*. Cambridge: Cambridge University Press, pp. 274–309

Howard-Hill, Trevor H. 2006. 'Early modern printers and the standardization of English spelling', *The Modern Language Review* 101 (1): 16–29

Hubacek, Svern-Erik 1996. 'Die Landsmaalbewegung in Bergen von den Anfängen bis sum Tode Henrik Krohns 1879', vol. 1. Doctoral dissertation, University of Vienna, Austria

Huloet, Richard 1552. *Abcedarium anglico latinum* [...]. London: William Riddel

Huloet, Richard and Higgins, John 1572. *Huloets Dictionarie* [...]. London: Thomas Marsh

Hume, Alexander 1617. *Of the Orthographie and Congruitie of the Britan Tongue* [...]. London: Tübner and Co.

1865 [1617]. *Of the Orthographie and Congruitie of the Britan Tongue: A Treates, noe shorter then necessarie for the Schooles*. London: Trübner, www.gutenberg.org/files/17000/17000-h/17000-h.htm

Hundt, Marianne 2015. 'Heterogeneity vs. homogeneity', in Anita Auer, Daniel Schreier and Richard J. Watts (eds.), *Letter Writing and Language Change*. Cambridge: Cambridge University Press, pp. 72–100

Huth, Dirk 2003. '"Jedes Volk schreibt seine Sprache mit seinen eigenen Buchstaben": Der altisländische Erste Grammatische Traktat und sein Entwurf eines orthographischen Standards', in Michèle Goyens and Werner Verbeke (eds.), *The Dawn of the Written Vernacular in Western Europe*. Leuven: Leuven University Press, pp. 441–61

International Short Title Catalogue (ISTC), https://data.cerl.org/istc/_search

Iqbal, Farkhund, Hadjidj, Rachid, Fung, Benjamin C. M. and Debbabi, Mourad 2008. 'A novel approach of mining write-prints for authorship attribution in e-mail forensics', *Digital Investigation* 5 (September): 42–51, https://doi.org/10.1016/j.diin.2008.05.001

Irvine, Judith and Gal, Susan 2000. 'Language ideologies and linguistic differentiation', in Paul V. Kroskrity (ed.), *Regimes of Language. Ideologies, Polities, and Identities*. Santa Fe: School of American Research Press, pp. 35–84

Irvine, Martin 2006. *The Making of Textual Culture: 'Grammatica' and Literary Theory 350–1100*. Cambridge: Cambridge University Press

Ivan Łuckievič's kitab (KL), MS from the eighteenth century; photocopy in Miškinienė, Galina, Namavičiūtė, Sigita, Pokrovskaja, Jekaterina and Durgut, Hüsein 2009. *Ivano Luckevičiaus kitabas: Lietuvos totorių kultūros paminklas*. Vilnius: Lietuvių kalbos institutas

Iverson, Gregory K. and Salmons, Joseph C. 2007. 'Domains and directionality in the evolution of German final fortition', *Phonology* 24: 121–45

Ivković, Dejan 2013. 'Pragmatics meets ideology: digraphia and non-standard orthographic practices in Serbian online news forums', *Journal of Language and Politics* 12 (2): 335–56

2015a. 'Jezički krajolik Srbije (prvi deo): percepcija prisustva ćirilice i latinice u javnoj sferi', *Antropologija* 15 (2): 87–110

2015b. 'Jezički krajolik Srbije (drugi deo): žanrovska digrafija i semiotizacija pisama', *Antropologija* 15 (3): 69–99

Iyengar, Arvind 2021. 'A diachronic analysis of Sindhi multiscriptality', *Journal of Historical Sociolinguistics* 7 (2): 207–41

Jack and the Bean-Stalk: A New Version, to which is added Little Jane and her Mother 1848. Boston: William J. Reynolds

Jackson, MacDonald P. 2008. 'The authorship of "A Lover's Complaint": a new approach to the problem', *Papers of the Bibliographical Society of America* 102 (3): 285–313

Jacobs, Andreas and Jucker, Andreas H. 1995. 'The historical perspective in pragmatics', in Andreas Jucker (ed.), *Historical Pragmatics: Pragmatic Developments in the History of English*. Amsterdam: John Benjamins, pp. 3–33

Jacobsen, Henrik G. 2010. *Ret og skrift. Officiel dansk retskrivning 1739–2005 Bind 1 Direktiver – Aktører – Normer.* Odense: Syddansk universitetsforlag

Jaeger, Jeri J. 1984. 'Assessing the psychological status of the Vowel Shift Rule', *Journal of Psycholinguistic Research* 13: 13–36

Jaffe, Alexandra M. 1996. 'The second annual Corsican spelling contest: orthography and ideology', *American Ethnologist* 23 (4): 816–35

1999. *Ideologies in Action: Language Politics on Corsica*. Berlin: De Gruyter

2000a. *Non-Standard Orthography*, special issue of *Journal of Sociolinguistics* 4 (4)

2000b. 'Introduction: non-standard orthography and non-standard speech', in Alexandra M. Jaffe (ed.), *Non-Standard Orthography*, special issue of *Journal of Sociolinguistics* 4 (4), pp. 497–513

2012. 'Transcription in practice: nonstandard orthography', in Alexandra M. Jaffe, Jannis K. Androutsopoulos, Mark Sebba and Sally A. Johnson (eds.), *Orthography as Social Action: Scripts, Spelling, Identity and Power* (Language and Social Processes 3). Boston/Berlin: De Gruyter, pp. 203–24

Jaffe, Alexandra M., Androutsopoulos, Jannis K., Sebba, Mark and Johnson, Sally A. (eds.) 2012. *Orthography as Social Action: Scripts, Spelling, Identity and Power* (Language and Social Processes 3). Boston/Berlin: De Gruyter

Jagić, Vatroslav 1913. *Entstehungsgeschichte der kirchenslavischen Sprache*. Berlin: Weidmannsche Buchhandlung (2nd ed.)

Jahr, Ernst H. 1994. *Utsyn over norsk språkhistorie etter 1814*. Oslo: Novus

2014. *Language Planning as a Sociolinguistic Experiment: The Case of Modern Norwegian*. Edinburgh: Edinburgh University Press

Jahr, Ernst H., Nedrelid, Gudlaug and Nielsen, Marit A. 2016. *Språkhistorieskriving og språkideologi*. Oslo: Novus

Jajdelska, Elspeth 2007. *Silent Reading and the Birth of the Narrator*. Toronto: University of Toronto Press

Jakobson, Roman 1960. 'Closing statement: linguistics and poetics', in Thomas Albert Sebeok (ed.), *Style in Language*. Cambridge, MA: The MIT Press, pp. 350–77

1962. *Selected Writings*. Berlin: Mouton

Jakubczyk, Marcin 2014a. 'Polszczyzna grażdańska w słowniku carycy Katarzyny II', *Poradnik Językowy* 2: 78–95

2014b. 'Słownik carycy Katarzyny Wielkiej w kontekście europejskich teorii językowych II połowy XVIII wieku i na tle tradycji leksykograficznej', *Poradnik Językowy* 9: 64–77

Jamborová, Martina 2010. 'Kvantita jako významový diferenciační činitel ve středověkém právnickém textu', in Michaela Čornejová, Lucie Rychnovská and Jana Zemanová (eds.), *Dějiny českého pravopisu (do r. 1902). Sborník příspěvků z mezinárodní konference Dějiny českého pravopisu (do r. 1902). 23.–25. září 2010, Brno, Česká Republika. History of Czech Orthography (up to 1902). Proceedings of the International Conference History of Czech Orthography (up to 1902). 23.–25. September 2010, Brno, Czech Republic*, Brno: Host/Masarykova univerzita, pp. 120–34

Janda, Richard D. and Joseph, Brian D. 2003. 'On language, change and language change – or, of history, linguistics and historical linguistics', in Brian D Joseph and Richard D. Janda (eds.), *The Handbook of Historical Linguistics*. Oxford: Blackwell, pp. 3–180

Januszowski, Jan 1594. *Nowy karakter polski* [...]. Kraków: Druk. Łazarzowa, Jan Januszowski

Jaworski, Adam and Coupland, Nikolas 1999. 'Part six. Power, ideology and control', in Adam Jaworski and Nikolas Coupland (eds.), *The Discourse Reader*. London/New York: Routledge, pp. 493–588

Jespersen, Otto 1909. *A Modern English Grammar on Historical Principles*, vol. 1: *Sounds and Spelling*. Heidelberg: Winter

Jocelin, Elizabeth 1624. *The mothers legacie, to her vnborne childe*. London: Iohn Hauiland, for William Barre (EEBO, ProQuest)

Johannessen, Janne B. and Salmons, Joseph C. 2012. 'Innledning', *Norsk i Amerika Norsk Lingvistisk tidsskrift* 30 (2): 139–48

Johansen, Åse M. 2013. 'Overcoming silence: language emancipation in a coastal Sámi-Norwegian community', *Sociolinguistic Studies* 7 (1–2): 57–77, https://doi.org/10.1558/sols.v7i1-2.57

Johnson, Janet H. 2010. 'Egyptian demotic script', in Christopher Woods, Emily Teeter and Geoff Emberling (eds.), *Visible Language: Inventions of Writing in the Ancient Middle East and Beyond*. Chicago: Oriental Institute, pp. 165–71

Johnson, Sally A. 2005. *Spelling Trouble? Language, Ideology and the Reform of German Orthography*. Clevedon/Buffalo/Toronto: Multilingual Matters

Johnson, Wyn and Britain, David 2007. 'L-vocalisation as a natural phenomenon: explorations in sociophonology', *Language Sciences* 29: 294–315

Johnston, Edward 1945. *Writing and Illuminating, and Lettering.* London: Pitman

Johnston, William 1764. *A pronouncing and spelling dictionary.* London: Printed for W. Johnston

Joly, Geneviève 1995. *Précis de phonétique historique du français.* Paris: Armand Colin

Jones, Daniel 1917. *An English Pronouncing Dictionary (on Strictly Phonetic Principles).* London/Toronto: J. M. Dent and Sons

1937. *An English Pronouncing Dictionary.* New York: E. P. Dutton and Company (4th ed., revised and enlarged)

Jones, Mari C. and Mooney, Damien 2017. 'Creating orthographies for endangered languages', in Mari C. Jones and Damien Mooney (eds.), *Creating Orthographies for Endangered Languages.* Cambridge: Cambridge University Press, pp. 1–35

Jones, Stephen 1798. *Sheridan improved: A general pronouncing and explanatory dictionary of the English language.* London (3rd ed.)

Joos, Martin 1952. 'The medieval sibilants', *Language* 28: 222–31

Joseph, John 1987. *Eloquence and Power: The Rise of Language Standards and Standard Languages.* New York: Basil Blackwell

Joshi, R. Malatesha and Aaron, P. G. (eds.) 2014. *Handbook of Orthography and Literacy.* London/New York: Routledge

Journal of Historical Sociolinguistics, www.degruyter.com/view/journals/jhsl/jhsl-overview.xml

Joyce, Terry 2002. 'The Japanese mental lexicon: the lexical retrieval and representation of two-kanji compound words from a morphological perspective'. Doctoral dissertation, University of Tsukuba, Japan

2011. 'The significance of the morphographic principle for the classification of writing systems', in Susanne R. Borgwaldt and Terry Joyce (eds.), *Typology of Writing Systems*, special issue of *Written Language and Literacy* 14 (1). Amsterdam/Philadelphia: John Benjamins, pp. 58–81

2016. 'Writing systems and scripts', in Andrea Rocci and Louis de Saussure (eds.), *Verbal Communication.* Berlin/Boston: De Gruyter, pp. 287–308

2019. 'The significance of the partial versus full writing dichotomy for the typology of writing systems'. Presentation at *Diversity of Writing Systems: Embracing Multiple Perspectives* (12th International Workshop on Written Language and Literacy), 26–28 March 2019, Faculty of Classics, Cambridge University, UK

Joyce, Terry and Borgwaldt, Susanne R. 2011. 'Typology of writing systems: special issue introduction', in Susanne R. Borgwaldt and Terry Joyce (eds.), *Typology of Writing Systems*, special issue of *Written Language and Literacy* 14 (1). Amsterdam/Philadelphia: John Benjamins, pp. 1–11, https://doi.org/10.1075/wll.14.1.01joy

Joyce, Terry, Hodoščєk, Bor and Nishina, Kikuko 2012. 'Orthographic representation and variation within the Japanese writing system: some corpus-based observations', in Terry Joyce and David Roberts (eds.), *Units of Language – Units of Writing*, special issue of *Written Language and Literacy* 15 (2). Amsterdam/Philadelphia: John Benjamins, pp. 254–78

Joyce, Terry and Masuda, Hisashi 2018. 'Introduction to the multi-script Japanese writing system and word processing', in Hye Pae (ed.), *Writing Systems, Reading Processes, and Cross-Linguistic Influences: Reflections from the Chinese, Japanese and Korean Languages*. Amsterdam/Philadelphia: John Benjamins, pp. 179–99

2019. 'On the notions of graphematic representation and orthography from the perspective of the Japanese writing system', in Terry Joyce and Robert Crellin (eds.), *Past, Present (... and Future?)*, special issue of *Written Language and Literacy* 22 (2). Amsterdam/Philadelphia: John Benjamins, pp. 248–80

Joyce, Terry and Meletis, Dimitrios 2021. 'Alternative criteria for writing system typology: cross-linguistic observations from the German and Japanese writing systems', *Zeitschrift für Sprachwissenschaft*, 40 (3), 257–77

Jucker, Andreas H. and Kopaczyk, Joanna 2013. 'Communities of practice as a locus of language change', in Joanna Kopaczyk and Andreas H. Jucker (eds.), *Communities of Practice in the History of English*. Amsterdam: John Benjamins, pp. 1–16

Jucker, Andreas H. and Taavitsainen, Irma 2012. 'Pragmatic variables', in Juan Manuel Hernández-Campoy and Juan Camilo Conde-Silvestre (eds.), *The Handbook of Historical Sociolinguistics*. Chichester: Wiley-Blackwell, pp. 293–306

Judson, Anna P. 2017a. 'Process of script adaptation and creation in Linear B: the evidence of the "extra" signs', in Philippa M. Steele (ed.), *Understanding Relations between Scripts: The Aegean Writing Systems*. Oxford/Philadelphia: Oxbow Books, pp. 111–26

2017b. 'The decipherment: people, process, challenges', in Anastasia Christophilopoulou, Yannis Galanakis and James Grime (eds.), *Codebreakers and Groundbreakers (Fitzwilliam Museum, Cambridge, 2017: Catalogue of Exhibition Held Oct 2017–Feb 2018)*. Cambridge: Charlesworth Press, pp. 15–29

2020. *The Undeciphered Signs of Linear B*. Cambridge: Cambridge University Press

Juola, Patrick 2006. 'Authorship attribution for electronic documents', in Martin S. Olivier and Sujeet Shenoi (eds.), *Advances in Digital Forensics II*. Boston: Springer, pp. 119–30, www.nowpublishers.com/article/Details/INR-005

Justeson, John S. 1976. 'Universals of language and universals of writing', in Alphonse Juilland (ed.), *Linguistic Studies Offered to Joseph Greenberg on the Occasion of His Sixtieth Birthday*. Saratoga: Anma Libri, pp. 57–94

1986. 'The origin of writing systems: preclassic Mesoamerica', *World Archaeology* 17 (3): 437–58

1988. Review of *Writing Systems: A Linguistic Introduction* by Geoffrey Sampson, *Language* 64: 423

2012. 'Early Mesoamerican writing systems', in Deborah L. Nichols and Christopher A. Pool (eds.), *The Oxford Handbook of Mesoamerican Archaeology*. Oxford: Oxford University Press, pp. 830–44

Justeson, John S. and Stephens, Laurence D. 1993. 'The evolution of syllabaries from alphabets: transmission, language contrast, and script typology', *Die Sprache* 35 (1): 2–46

Juška, Liudvikas 1901-09-08: *Petition letter to Bishop Mečislovas Paliulionis*. Lithuanian State Historical Archives: F. 1671, ap. 4, b. 179, 776–81

1901-09-15: *Petition letter to Bishop Mečislovas Paliulionis*. Lithuanian State Historical Archives: F. 1671, ap. 4, b. 179, 680-4

Kaislaniemi, Samuli, Evans, Mel, Juvonen, Teo and Sairio, Anni 2017. '"A graphic system which leads its own linguistic life?" Epistolary spelling in English, 1400–1800', in Tanja Säily, Arja Nurmi, Minna Palander-Collin and Anita Auer (eds.), *Exploring Future Paths for Historical Sociolinguistics* (Advances in Historical Sociolinguistics 7). Amsterdam: John Benjamins, pp. 187–213, https://doi.org/10.1075/ahs.7.08kai

Kao, Henry S. R., van Galen, Gerard P. and Hoosain, Rumjahn (eds.) 1986. *Graphonomics: Contemporary Research in Handwriting*. Amsterdam: North-Holland

Källström, Magnus 2018. 'Haraldær stenmæstari – Haraldus magister: a case study on the interaction between runes and Roman script', in Alessia Bauer, Elise Kleivane and Terje Spurkland (eds.), *Epigraphy in an Intermedial Context*. Dublin: Four Courts, pp. 59–74

Kämpfert, Manfred 1980. 'Motive der Substantivgroßschreibung. Beobachtungen an Drucken des 16. Jahrhunderts', *Zeitschrift für deutsche Philologie* 99: 72–98

Karlsson, Fred 1983. *Finnish Grammar* (trans. by Andrew Chesterman). Porvoo: Söderström

Karlsson, Stefán 2002. 'The development of Latin script II: in Iceland', in Oskar Bandle (ed.), *The Nordic Languages. An International Handbook of the History of the North Germanic Languages*. Berlin/New York: De Gruyter, pp. 832–40

Karskiĭ, Efim F. 1901. *Ocherki slavyanskoĭ kirillovskoĭ paleografii. Iz lekt͡sciĭ, chitannykh v Imperatorskom Varshavskom universitete*. Warsaw: Tipografii͡a Varshavskago Uchebnago Okruga

Karttunen, Frances 1985. *Nahuatl and Maya in Contact with Spanish*. Austin: Texas Linguistic Forum/University of Texas at Austin

Karttunen, Frances and Lockhart, James 1976. *Nahuatl in the Middle Years: Language Contact Phenomena in Texts of the Colonial Period*. Berkeley: University of California Press

Katz, Leonard and Feldman, Laurie B. 1983. 'Relation between pronunciation and recognition of printed words in deep and shallow orthographies', *Journal of Experimental Psychology: Learning, Memory, and Cognition* 9 (1): 157–66

Katz, Leonard and Frost, Ram 1992a. 'Orthography, phonology, morphology, and meaning: an overview', in Ram Frost and Leonard Katz (eds.), *Orthography, Phonology, Morphology, and Meaning*. London: North-Holland (Elsevier Science Publisher), pp. 1–8

1992b. 'The reading process is different for different orthographies: the orthographic depth hypothesis', in Ram Frost and Leonard Katz (eds.), *Orthography, Phonology, Morphology, and Meaning*. Amsterdam: Elsevier Science Publishers B.V., pp. 67–84

Kauffmann, Friedrich 1892. 'Über althochdeutsche Orthographie', *Germania* 37 (n.s. 25): 243–64

Kawasaki, Yasushi 2004. *Eine graphematische Untersuchung zu den Heliand-Handschriften*. Munich: Iudicium

Kaye, Alan S. 1996. 'Adaptations of Arabic', in Peter T. Daniels and William Bright (eds.), *The World's Writing Systems*. New York/Oxford: Oxford University Press, pp. 743–62

Keil, Heinrich and Theodor Mommsen (eds.) 2009 [1864]. *Grammatici Latini*, vol. 4: *Probi, Donati, Servii qui feruntur De arte grammatica libri, et Notarum laterculi*. Leipzig: Teubner (reprint by Cambridge: Cambridge University Press)

Kempgen, Sebastian and Tomelleri, Vittorio S. (eds.) 2019. *Slavic Alphabets and Identities*. Bamberg: University of Bamberg Press, https://fis.uni-bamberg.de/handle/uniba/45157

Kenrick, William 1773. *A New Dictionary of the English Language*. London: Printed for John and Francis Rivington, William Johnston, Thomas Longman, and Thomas Cadell

Kerek, Andrew 1976. 'The phonological relevance of spelling pronunciation', *Visible Language* 10 (4): 323–38

Keszler, Borbála 2003. 'A magyar írásjelhasználat és Európa', *Magyar Nyelvőr* 127: 24–36

2004. *Írásjeltan. Az írásjelhasználat szabályai, problémái és történet*. Budapest: National Textbook Publisher

Kettmann, Gerhard 1967. *Die kursächsische Kanzleisprache zwischen 1486 und 1546. Studien zum Aufbau und zur Entwicklung*. Berlin: Akademie-Verlag

Kildal, Arne 1948. *Boksamlinga åt Sivert Årflot 150 år*. Oslo: Samlaget

Kim, Dong-Hyuk 2004. 'Free orthography in a strict society: reconsidering Tov's "Qumran Orthography"', *Dead Sea Discoveries* 11 (1): 72–81

King, John H. 1999. 'The book-trade under Edward VI and Mary I', in Lotte Hellinga and Joseph B. Trapp (eds.), *The Cambridge History of the Book in Britain*, vol. 3: *1400–1557*. Cambridge: Cambridge University Press, pp. 164–75

Kinn, Kari 2020. 'Stability and attrition in American Norwegian nominals: a view from predicate nouns', *Journal of Comparative Germanic Linguistics* 23 (1): 3–38

Kintzinger, Martin 2016a. 'Trivium', in Gert Melville and Martial Staub (eds.), *Brill's Encyclopedia of the Middle Ages Online*, https://doi.org/10.1163/2213-2139_bema_SIM_033838

2016b. 'Quadrivium', in Gert Melville and Martial Staub (eds.), *Brill's Encyclopedia of the Middle Ages Online*, https://doi.org/10.1163/2213-2139_bema_SIM_033842

Kirchhoff, Frank 2017. *Von der Virgel zum Komma: die Entwicklung der Interpunktion im Deutschen* (Germanistische Bibliothek 61). Heidelberg: Universitätsverlag Winter

Kirchhoff, Frank and Primus, Beatrice 2016. 'Punctuation', in Vivian Cook and Des Ryan (eds.), *The Routledge Handbook of the English Writing System*. London/New York: Routledge, pp. 114–31

Kirchweg, Christoph 1670. *Res pro anima. Eine Seelen Sach/Welche um Rettung der irrigen Gewissen vorgenommen ist Uber die Frage: Wie lang wilst du noch Lutherisch bleiben?* Hanover: Schwendimann (VD17 1: 078180X)

Kjeldstadli, Knut 1994. *Et splittet samfunn 1905–35*, in Knut Helle, Knut Kjeldstadli, Even Lange and Sølvi Songer (eds.), *Aschehougs norgeshistorie*, vol. 10. Oslo: Aschehoug

Klausenburger, Jürgen 1978. 'French linking phenomena: a natural generative analysis', *Language* 54 (1): 21–40

1984. *French Liaison and Linguistic Theory*. Wiesbaden: F. Steiner

Klein, Jared, Joseph, Brian and Fritz, Matthias 2017. *Handbook of Comparative and Historical Indo-European Linguistics*. Berlin: De Gruyter

[Kleinas, Danielius 1653]. GRAMMATICA Litvanica Mandato & Autoritate SERENISSIMI ELECTORIS BRANDENBURGICI adornata, & præviâ Cenſurâ primùm in lucem edita à M. DANIELE Klein [...] REGIOMONTI, Typis & ſumptibus JOHANNIS REUSNERI, ANNO χριστογονίας cIↄ. Iↄc. LIII, http://seniejirastai.lki.lt/db.php?source=42

[1666]. Σὺν τῷ Θεῷ. Neu Littauſches / verbeſſert=und mit vielen neuen Liedern vermehretes Geſangbuch [...]. NAUJOS GIESMJU KNYGOS. [...] KARALAUCZUJE Iśſpaude ſawo iſſirádimais PRIDRIKIS REUSNERIS Metůſe M. DC. LXVI, http://seniejirastai.lki.lt/db.php?source=40

Klemensiewicz, Zenon, Lehr-Spławiński, Tadeusz and Urbańczyk, Stanisław 1955. *Gramatyka historyczna języka polskiego.* Warsaw: Państwowe Wydawnictwo Naukowe

Klinkenberg, Jean-Marie and Polis, Stéphane 2018. 'On scripturology', *Signata. Annals of Semiotics 9/Signatures. Sémiotique de l'écriture* 9: 57–102

Kloss, Heinz 1967. 'Abstand languages and Ausbau languages', *Anthropological Linguistics* 9 (7): 29–41

1978. *Die Entwicklung neuer Germanischer Kultursprachen seit 1800.* Düsseldorf: Schwann (revised ed.)

Klöter, Henning 2010. 'What is being borrowed? Language and script contact in Taiwan', in Alex de Voogt and Irving Finkel (eds.), *The Idea of Writing: Play and Complexity.* Leiden: Brill, pp. 93–115

Kniffka, Hannes 2007. *Working in Language and Law: A German Perspective.* Hampshire: Palgrave Macmillan, https://doi.org/10.1057/9780230590045

Kober, Alice E. 1946. 'Inflection in Linear Class B: I – Declension', *American Journal of Archaeology* 50: 268–76

1948. 'The Minoan scripts: facts and theory', *American Journal of Archaeology* 52: 82–103

Koch, Peter and Österreicher, Wulf 1994. 'Schriftlichkeit und Sprache', in Hartmut Günther and Otto Ludwig (eds.), *Schrift und Schriftlichkeit/Writing and Its Use. Ein interdisziplinäres Handbuch internationaler Forschung/An Interdisciplinary Handbook of International Research.* 1, vol. 1. Berlin/New York: De Gruyter, pp. 587–604

2008. 'Mündlichkeit und Schriftlichkeit von Texten', in Nina Janich (ed.), *Textlinguistik. 15 Einführungen*, Tübingen: Narr, pp. 199–215

Köcher, Adolf 1895. *Geschichte von Hannover und Braunschweig, 1648–1714*, vol. 2. Leipzig: Hirzel

Koeppel, Emil 1901. *Spelling-Pronunciations: Bemerkungen über den Einfluß des Schriftbildes auf den Laut im Englischen* (Quellen und Forschungen 89). Strasbourg: Karl J. Trübner

Kohrt, Manfred 1985. *Problemgeschichte des Graphembegriffs und des frühen Phonembegriffs.* Tübingen: Niemeyer

1986. 'The term 'grapheme' in the history and theory of linguistics', in Gerhard Augst (ed.), *New Trends in Graphemics and Orthography.* Berlin: De Gruyter, pp. 80–96, https://doi.org/10.1515/9783110867329.80

1987. *Theoretische Aspekte der deutschen Orthographie* (Reihe Germanistische Linguistik 70). Tübingen: Niemeyer

Kok, Ina 2013. *Woodcuts in Incunabula Printed in the Low Countries.* Houten: Hes and De Graaf

Kökeritz, Helge 1959. 'English place-name elements by A. H. Smith', *Speculum* 34: 135–40

1964. 'Spelling-pronunciation in American English', D. Abercrombie (ed.), *In Honor of Daniel Jones: Papers Contributed on the Occasion of His Eightieth Birthday 12 September 1961*, London: Longmans, pp. 137–45

Konopacki, Artur 2010. *Życie religijne Tatarów na Ziemiach Wielkiego Księstwa Litewskiego w XVI–XIX wieku*. Warsaw: Wydawnictwa Uniwersytetu Warszawskiego

2015. 'Autorzy, kompilatorzy, kopiści – rzecz o rękopisach Tatarów Wielkiego Księstwa Litewskiego', in Joanna Kulwicka-Kamińska and Czesław Łapicz (eds.), *Tefsir Tatarów Wielkiego Księstwa Litewskiego: Teoria i Praktyka Badawcza*. Toruń: Wydział Filologiczny UMK, pp. 271–86, www.tefsir.umk.pl/pliki/Tefsir_Tatarow_WKL.pdf

Königliches Ministerium der geistlichen, Unterrichts- und Medizinalangelegenheiten 1880. *Regeln und Wörterverzeichnis für die deutsche Rechtschreibung zum Gebrauch in den preußischen Schulen*. Berlin: Weidmannsche Buchhandlung

Kopaczyk, Joanna 2011. 'A V or not a V? Transcribing abbreviations in seventeen manuscripts of the "Man of Law's Tale" for a digital edition', in Jacob Thaisen and Hanna Rutkowska (eds.), *Scribes, Printers, and the Accidentals of Their Texts*. Frankfurt am Main: Peter Lang, pp. 91–106

Kopaczyk, Joanna and Jucker, Andreas H. (eds.) 2013. *Communities of Practice in the History of English*. Amsterdam: John Benjamins

Kopaczyk, Joanna, Molineaux, Benjamin, Karaiskos, Vasilios, Alcorn, Rhona, Los, Bettelou and Maguire, Warren 2018. 'Towards a grapho-phonologically parsed corpus of medieval Scots: database design and technical solutions', *Corpora* 13 (2): 255–69, https://doi.org/10.3366/cor.2018.0146

Korkiakangas, Timo 2018. 'Spelling variation in historical text corpora: the case of early medieval documentary Latin', *Digital Scholarship in the Humanities* 33 (3): 575–91

Korkiakangas, Timo and Lassila, Matti 2018. 'Visualizing linguistic variation in a network of Latin documents and scribes', *Journal of Data Mining and Digital Humanities* (Special Issue on Computer-Aided Processing of Intertextuality in Ancient Languages), 4472, https://jdmdh.episciences.org/4472

Kornicki, Peter F. 2018. *Languages, Scripts, and Chinese Texts in East Asia*. Oxford: Oxford University Press

Koselleck, Reinhart 1979. *Vergangene Zukunft. Zur Semantik geschichtlicher Zeiten*. Frankfurt am Main: Suhrkamp

Koster, Josephine A. 2009. 'Most excellent and curious hands: the future of paleography and related arts in early modern studies', *The Sixteenth Century Journal* 40 (1): 255–58

Kraków, Jagiellonian Library, MS 1961

Kramer, Christina 2015. 'Macedonian orthographic controversies', in Laura Villa and Rik Vosters (eds.), *The Historical Sociolinguistics of Spelling*, special issue of *Written Language and Literacy* 18 (2). Amsterdam/Philadelphia: John Benjamins, pp. 287–308

Kristiansen, Tore 2003. 'Danish', in Ana Deumert and Wim Vandenbussche (eds.), *Germanic Standardizations: Past to Present*. Amsterdam/Philadelphia: John Benjamins, pp. 69–91

Kristol, Andres M. 2000. 'Les premières descriptions grammaticales du français', in Sylvain Auroux, Ernst F. K. Koerner, Hans-Josef Niederehe and Kees Versteegh (eds.), *History of the Language Sciences/Geschichte der Sprachwissenschaften/Histoire des sciences du langage*. Berlin/Boston: De Gruyter, pp. 764–70

Kroch, Anthony S. 1994. 'Morphosyntactic variation', in Katherine Beals, Jeannette Denton, Robert Knippen, Lynette Melnar, Hisami Suzuki and Erica Zeinfeld (eds.), *Papers from the 30th Regional Meeting of the Chicago Linguistic Society*, vol. 2: *The Parasession on Variation in Linguistic Theory*. Chicago: Chicago Linguistic Society, pp. 180–201

2001. 'Syntactic change', in Mark Baltin and Chris Collins (eds.), *The Handbook of Contemporary Syntactic Theory*. Oxford/Cambridge, MA: Blackwell, pp. 698–729

Krogull, Andreas 2018. *Policy versus Practice. Language Variation and Change in Eighteenth- and Nineteenth-century Dutch* (dissertation, Leiden University, Leiden, the Netherlands). Utrecht: Netherlands Graduate School of Linguistics (LOT)

Kroskrity, Paul V. (ed.) 2000. *Regimes of Language. Ideologies, Polities, and Identities*. Santa Fe: School of American Research Press

Kuhn, Sherman M. 1961. 'The syllabic phonemes of Old English', *Language* 37: 522–38

1970. 'On the consonantal phonemes of Old English', in James L. Rosier (ed.), *Philological Essays: Studies in Old and Middle English Language and Literature in Honour of Herbert Dean Meritt*. The Hague: Mouton, pp. 16–49

Kuhn, Sherman M. and Quirk, Randolf 1953. 'Some recent interpretations of Old English digraph spellings', *Language* 29: 143–56

1955. 'The Old English digraphs: a reply', *Language* 31: 390–401

Küster, Marc W. 2019. 'Open and closed writing systems: some reflections', in Yannis Haralambous (ed.), *Graphemics in the 21st Century. Brest, June 13–15, 2018. Proceedings* (Grapholinguistics and Its Applications 1). Brest: Fluxus Editions, pp. 17–26, https://doi.org/10.36824/2018-graf-kues

Kytö, Merja, Grund, Peter J. and Walker, Terry (compilers) 2011. *An Electronic Text Edition of Depositions, 1560–1760*, CD-ROM, in Merja Kytö, Peter J. Grund and Terry Walker (eds.), *Testifying to Language and Life in Early Modern England*. Amsterdam: John Benjamins

Kytö, Merja, Grund, Peter J. and Walker, Terry 2011. *Testifying to Language and Life in Early Modern England: Including CD-ROM: An Electronic Text Edition of Depositions 1560–1760*. Philadelphia: John Benjamins

Kytö, Merja and Walker, Terry 2006. *Guide to A Corpus of English Dialogues 1560–1760* (Acta Universitatis Upsaliensis, Studia Anglistica Upsaliensia 130). Uppsala: Uppsala University

Labov, William 1972a. *Sociolinguistic Patterns*. Philadelphia: University of Pennsylvania Press

1972b. 'Some principles of linguistic methodology', *Language in Society* 1: 97–120

1994. *Principles of Linguistic Change*, vol. 1: *Internal Factors*. Oxford/ Cambridge, MA: Blackwell

2006 [1966]. *The Social Stratification of English in New York City*. Cambridge: Cambridge University Press (2nd ed.)

2007. 'Transmission and diffusion', *Language* 83: 344–87

Labs-Ehlert, Brigitte 1993. *Versalschreibung in Althochdeutschen Sprachdenkmälern: ein Beitrag über die Anfänge der Großschreibung im Deutschen unter Berücksichtigung der Schriftgeschichte*. Göppingen: Kümmerle

Laing, Margaret 1988. 'Dialectal analysis and linguistically composite texts in Middle English', *Speculum* 63: 83–100

1999. 'CONFUSION "WRS" CONFOUNDED: litteral substitution sets in early Middle English writing systems', *Neuphilologische Mitteilungen* 100 (3): 251–70

2000. 'The linguistic stratification of the Middle English texts in Oxford, Bodleian Library, MS Digby 86', *Neuphilologische Mitteilungen* 101 (4): 523–69

2004. 'Multidimensionality: time, space and stratigraphy in historical dialectology', in Marina Dossena and Roger Lass (eds.), *Methods and Data in Historical Dialectology*. Bern: Lang, pp. 49–96

2013–. *A Linguistic Atlas of Early Middle English 1150 to 1325* (LAEME), Version 3.2. Edinburgh: University of Edinburgh, www.lel.ed.ac.uk/ ihd/laeme2/laeme2.html

Laing, Margaret and Lass, Roger 2003. 'Tales of the 1001 nists: the phonological implications of litteral substitution sets in some thirteenth-century South-West Midland Texts', *English Language and Linguistics* 7 (2): 257–78

2006. 'Early Middle English dialectology: problems and prospects', in Ans van Kemenade and Bettelou Los (eds.), *The Handbook of the History of English*. Oxford: Blackwell, pp. 417–51

2009. 'Shape-shifting, sound-change and the genesis of prodigal writing systems', *English Language and Linguistics* 13 (1): 1–31

2014. 'On Middle English she, sho: a refurbished narrative', *Folia Linguistica Historica* 35 (1): 201–40

2019. 'Old and Middle English spellings for OE hw-, with special reference to the 'qu-' type: in celebration of LAEME, (e)LALME, LAOS and CoNE', in Rhona Alcorn, Joanna Kopaczyk, Bettelou Los and Benjamin Molineaux (eds.), *Historical Dialectology in the Digital Age*. Edinburgh: Edinburgh University Press, pp. 91–112

Lam, Joseph 2010. 'The invention and development of the alphabet', in Christopher Woods, Emily Teeter and Geoff Emberling (eds.), *Visible Language: Inventions of Writing in the Ancient Middle East and Beyond*. Chicago: Oriental Institute, pp. 189–95

Lamb, Sydney M. 1966. *Outline of Stratificational Grammar*. Washington, DC: Georgetown University Press

Lane, Pia, Costa, James and De Korne, Haley (eds.) 2018. *Standardizing Minority Languages: Competing Ideologies of Authority and Authenticity in the Global Periphery*. New York/London: Routledge, www.taylorfrancis.com/books/e/9781315647722

Lane Ford, Margaret 1999. 'Importation of printed books into England and Scotland', in Lotte Hellinga and Joseph B. Trapp (eds.), *The Cambridge History of the Book in Britain*, vol. 3: *1400–1557*. Cambridge: Cambridge University Press, pp. 179–201

Lange, Claudia 2012. 'Standardization: standards in the history of English', in Alexander Bergs and Laurel J. Brinton (eds.), *English Historical Linguistics: An International Handbook*, vol. 1. Berlin/Boston: De Gruyter, pp. 994–1006

L'Année Épigraphique (AE) 1889–. Paris

La Parra López, Emilio, Pérez Ledesma, Manuel, Luis, Jean-Philippe, Portillo Valdés, José M. , Fuentes, Juan Francisco, Romeo Mateo, María Cruz, Ramos Santana, Alberto and Romero Ferrer, Alberto 2012. *El nacimiento de la política en España (1808–1869)*. Madrid: Editorial Pablo Iglesias

Lapidge, Michael 2000. 'The Archetype of *Beowulf*', *Anglo-Saxon England* 29: 5–41

Lapidge, Michael and Winterbottom, Michael (eds.) 1991. *The Life of St. Aethelwold*. Oxford: Clarendon Press

Larousse, Pierre 1850. *Lexicologie des écoles primaires. Première année. Nature et rapport des mots*. Paris: L'auteur

1856. *Nouveau dictionnaire de la langue française* [...]. Paris: Larousse et Boyer

Larsen, Niels-Erik 2001. *Grafematische analyse van een Middelnederlandse tekst: het grafeemsysteem van de Vroegmiddelnederlandse Statuten van de Gentse Leprozerie uit 1236*. Amsterdam: Rozenberg Publishers

2004. 'Historical linguistics and graphemic analysis', *NOWELE* 44: 3–19

Lass, Roger 1976. *English Phonology and Phonological Theory.* Cambridge: Cambridge University Press

1992. 'Phonology and morphology', in Norman Blake (ed.), *The Cambridge History of the English Language*, vol. 2: *1066–1476*. Cambridge: Cambridge University Press, pp. 23–155

1997. *Historical Linguistics and Language Change.* Cambridge: Cambridge University Press

1999. 'Phonology and morphology', in Roger Lass (ed.), *The Cambridge History of the English Language*, vol. 3: *1476–1776*. Cambridge: Cambridge University Press, pp. 56–186

2004. 'Ut custodiant litteras: editions, corpora and witnesshood', in Marina Dossena and Roger Lass (eds.), *Methods and Data in English Historical Dialectology.* Bern: Peter Lang, pp. 21–48

2015. 'Interpreting alphabetic orthographies: Early Middle English spelling', in Patrick Honeybone and Joseph Salmons (eds.), *The Oxford Handbook of Historical Phonology.* Oxford: Oxford University Press, pp. 100–20

Lass, Roger and Laing, Margaret 2010. 'In celebration of early Middle English "h"', *Neuphilologische Mitteilungen* 111 (3): 345–54

Late Medieval English Scribes, www.medievalscribes.com/

Laufer, Roger 1972. *Introduction à la textologie. Vérification, établissement, édition des textes.* Paris: Larousse

Launey, Michel 2011. *An Introduction to Classical Nahuatl* (trans. and adapted by Christopher Mackay). Cambridge: Cambridge University Press

Lavinsky, David 2014. 'An early sixteenth-century Lutheran dialogue and its Wycliffite excerpt', *Journal of the Early Book Society for the Study of Manuscripts and Printing History* 17: 195–220

Lazar, Marija 2016. 'Transfer des Rechts und Transfer der Rechtssprache. Sächsisch-magdeburgisches Recht und seine Verbreitung im Ostmitteleuropa nach den Hussitenkriegen', in Holger Kuße and Hana Kosourová (eds.), *Persönlichkeiten in der tschechischen Sprach- und Kulturgeschichte. Beiträge zum 8. Bohemicum Dresdense: Tomáš Garrigue Masarik (1850–1937) 07. 11.2014und 9. Bohemicum Dresdense: Jan Hus (~1370–1415) – Erbe und Bedeutung 30. 10.2015* (Specimina Philologiae Slavicae. Bd. 191). Leipzig: Biblion Media, pp. 177–202

2018. 'Übersetzen, übertragen, deuten. Übersetzungspraktiken als Einflussfaktor für den Transfer des sächsisch-magdeburgischen Rechts in Ostmitteleuropa', in Gabriele Köster, Christina Link and Heiner Lück (eds.), *Kulturelle Vernetzung in Europa. Das Magdeburger Recht und seine Städte. Wissenschaftlicher Begleitband zur Ausstellung "Faszination Stadt".* Dresden: Sandstein Verlag, pp. 195–214

forthcoming. 'Rechtssprache als systemischer Erkenntnisgegenstand und Wege seiner digitalen Erforschung', in Wieland Carls (ed.),

IVS SAXONICO-MAIDEBVRGENSE IN ORIENTE. Das Sächsisch-magdeburgische Recht als kulturelles Bindeglied zwischen den Rechtsordnungen Ost- und Mitteleuropas. Bestandsaufnahme und Perspektiven der Forschung (IVS SAXONICO-MAIDEBVRGENSE IN ORIENTE 6). Berlin: De Gruyter

Lebsanft, Franz and Tacke, Felix 2020. 'Romance standardology: roots and traditions', in Franz Lebsanft and Felix Tacke (eds.), *Manual of Standardization in the Romance Languages*. Berlin/Boston: De Gruyter, pp. 3–59

Lehfeldt, Werner 2001. 'L'écriture arabe chez les Slaves', *Slavica occitania* 12: 267–82

Lehr-Spławiński, Tadeusz and Bartula, Czesław 1976. *Zarys gramatyki języka staro-cerkiewno-słowiańskiego na tle porównawczym*. Wrocław/Warsaw/Kraków/Gdańsk: Zakład Narodowy im. Ossolińskich (7th ed.)

Leith, Dick 1983. *A Social History of English*. London: Routledge and Kegan Paul

Lejeune, Michel 1962. 'Les signes TA_2 et TWO', *Revue de Philologie* 36: 217–24

1970. 'Phonologie osque et graphie grecque', *Revue des Études Anciennes* 72: 271–316

1975. 'Réflexions sur la phonologie du vocalisme osque', *Bulletin de la Société de Linguistique de Paris* 70 (1): 233–51

Lennard, John 1995. 'Punctuation: and – "Pragmatics"', in Andreas H. Jucker (ed.), *Historical Pragmatics: Pragmatic Developments in the History of English*. Amsterdam: John Benjamins, pp. 65–98

Le Page, Robert and Tabouret-Keller, Andrée 1985. *Acts of Identity: Creole-Based Approaches to Language and Ethnicity*. Cambridge: Cambridge University Press

Lepschy, Anna L. and Lepschy, Giulio 2008. 'Punteggiatura e linguaggio', in Bice Mortara Garavelli (ed.), *Storia della punteggiatura in Europa*. Rome/Bari: Laterza, pp. 3–24

Levenshtein, Vladimir I. 1966. 'Binary codes capable of correcting deletions, insertions, and reversals', *Soviet Physics Doklady* 10 (8): 707–10

Levitt, Jesse 1968. 'Spelling-pronunciation in Modern French: its origin and its functional significance', *Linguistics* 42: 19–28

1978. 'The influence of orthography on phonology: a comparative study (English, French, Spanish, Italian, German)', *Linguistics* 208: 43–67

Lewicka, Magdalena 2015. 'Kitabistics a new direction of the Islam studies in Poland (the literature of Polish-Lithuanian Tatars)', in Redzaudin Ghazali, Mohamad Rofian Ismail and Che Wan Shamsul Bahri C. W. Ahmad (eds.), *E-Proceeding of the 2nd International Conference on Arabic Studies & Islamic Civilization 2015*. Kuala Lumpur: World Conferences, pp. 290–303

2016. 'The literature of the Tatars of the Grand Duchy of Lithuania – characteristics of the Tatar writings and areas of research', *Journal of Language and Cultural Education* 4 (1): 1–16

Lewis, Thomas T. 1854. *Letters of the Lady Brilliana Harley, Wife of Sir Robert Harley, of Brampton Bryan, Knight of the Bath, with Introduction and Notes*. London: Camden Society

Liberman, Alvin M., Cooper, Franklin S., Shankweiler, Donald P. and Studdert-Kennedy, Michael 1967. 'Perception of the speech code', *Psychological Review* 74 (6): 431–61

Liberman, Isabelle Y., Shankweiler, Donald, Fischer, F. William and Carter, Bonnie 1974. 'Explicit syllable and phoneme segmentation in the young child', *Journal of Experimental Child Psychology* 18: 201–12

Liestøl, Aslak 1963. *Runer frå Bryggen*. Bergen: Bryggens Museum

Lifanov, Konstantin V. 2001. *Genezis slovackogo literaturnogo jazyka*. Munich: LINCOM Europa

Lindqvist, Christer 1997. 'Schriftinduzierter Sprachwandel: Synchrone und diachrone Auswirkungen im Deutschen', in Thomas Birkmann, Heinz Klingenberg, Damaris Nübling and Elke Ronneberger-Sibold (eds.), *Vergleichende germanische Philologie und Skandinavistik: Festschrift für Otmar Werner*. Tübingen: Niemeyer, pp. 193–212

Linguistic Typology 20 (3) 2016

Lisowski, Tomasz 2001. *Grafia druków polskich z 1521 i 1522 roku. Problemy wariatywności i normalizacji*. Poznań: Wydawnictwo Naukowe UAM

2020. 'A phonological-graphemic approach to the investigation of spelling functionality, with reference to Early Modern Polish', in Marco Condorelli (ed.), *Advances in Historical Orthography, c. 1500–1800*. Cambridge: Cambridge University Press, pp. 16–45

Literature Online (Proquest), https://proquest.libguides.com/lionpqp

Litovskīi͡a narodnyi͡a pi͡esni: s" perevodom" na russkīĭ i͡azyk". I. A. I͡Ushkevicha 1867. Saint Petersburg

Li͡ublinskai͡a, Aleksandra D. (ed.) 1974. *Problemy paleografii i kodikologii v SSSR*. Moscow: Nauka

Liuzza, Roy M. 1996. 'Orthography and historical linguistics', *Journal of English Linguistics* 24 (1): 25–44

Llamas-Pombo, Elena 2007. 'Réflexions méthodologiques pour l'étude de la ponctuation médiévale', in Alexei Lavrentiev (ed.), *Systèmes graphiques de manuscrits médiévaux et incunables français. Ponctuation, segmentation, graphies*. Chambéry: Université de Savoie, pp. 11–48

2009. 'Variación gráfica y secuenciación de la palabra en manuscritos medievales hispánicos', in Pedro M. Cátedra (ed.), *Los códices literarios de la Edad Media. Interpretación, historia, técnicas y catalogación*. San Millán de la Cogolla: Cilengua, pp. 225–57

2012. 'Variation and standardization in the history of Spanish spelling', in Susan Baddeley and Anja Voeste (eds.), *Orthographies in Early Modern Europe*. Berlin/Boston: De Gruyter, pp. 15–62

2019. 'Pour une étude de la ponctuation du *Halotti beszéd és könyörgés* dans un contexte européen', in Zsófia Ágnes Bartók and Balázs Horváth (eds.), *Írások a Pray-kódexről*. Budapest: Argumentum Kiadó, pp. 111–27

2020. 'Punctuation in sixteenth- and seventeenth-century French and Spanish: a model of diachronic and comparative graphematics', in Marco Condorelli (ed.), *Advances in Historical Orthography, c. 1500–1800*. Cambridge: Cambridge University Press, pp. 93–123

Loach, Jennifer 1986. 'The Marian establishment and the printing press', *English Historical Review* 101: 135–48

Locher, Miriam A. and Strässler, Jürg 2008. 'Introduction: standards and norms', in Miriam A. Locher and Jürg Strässler (eds.), *Standards and Norms in the English Language*. Berlin: De Gruyter, pp. 1–20

Lockhart, James 1991. *Nahuas and Spaniards: Postconquest Central Mexican History and Philology*. Stanford: Stanford University Press

1992. *The Nahuas after the Conquest: A Social and Cultural History of the Indians of Central Mexico, Sixteenth through Eighteenth Centuries*. Stanford: Stanford University Press

Lockwood, David G. 2001. 'Phoneme and grapheme: how parallel can they be?', *LACUS Forum* 27: 307–16

2009 [2001]. 'Phoneme and grapheme: how parallel can they be?' *LACUS Forum* 27: 307–16 (reprint)

Lodge, Anthony 2010. 'Les Lettres de Montmartre (1749) et l'histoire du français parlé', in Michael Abécassis (ed.), *Les voix des Français*, vol. 1. Bern: Peter Lang, pp. 11–29

Løland, Rasmus 1892. *Paa sjølvstyr*. Bergen: Mons Litlere

Lomagistro, Barbara 2004. 'Paleografska pitanja periodizacije i klasifikacije glagoljice', in Marija-Ana Dürrigl, Milan Mihaljević and Franjo Velčić (eds.), *Glagoljica i hrvatski glagolizam*. Zagreb/Krk: Staroslavenski institut – Krčka biskupija, pp. 453–83

2008. 'La scrittura cirillica minuscola: genesi ed evoluzione', in Alberto Alberti, Stefano Garzonio, Nicoletta Marcialis and Bianca Sulpasso (eds.), *Contributi italiani al 14. congresso internazionale degli Slavisti*. Florence: Firenze University Press, pp. 111–48

London, British Library, Add MS 34206

London, British Library, Cotton MS Caligula A VIII

London, British Library, Cotton MS Nero A X

London, British Library, Egerton MS 2622 (ff. 136r–165v)

London, British Library, Harley MS 3542

London, British Library, Lansdowne MS 807

London, British Library, Royal MS 18 D II

London, British Library, Sloane MS 316
London, British Library, Sloane MS 340 (ff. 39v–63v)
London, British Library, Sloane MS 513
London, British Library, Sloane MS 3580A
London, British Library, Vitelius MS A.xv (ff. 94r–131v)
London, Wellcome Library, Wellcome MS 542 (ff. 1r–20v)
London, Wellcome Library, Wellcome MS 1340
London, Wellcome Library, Wellcome MS 3009 (ff. 17r–90r)
London, Wellcome Library, Wellcome MS 6812 (ff. 1r–91v)

Lorenc, Anita 2018. 'Articulatory characteristics of Polish retoflex sibilants. Analysis using electromagnetic articulography', *Logopedia* 47 (2): 131–49

Love, Harold 1993. *Scribal Publication in Seventeenth-Century England*. Oxford: Clarendon Press

2002. *Attributing Authorship: An Introduction*. New York: Cambridge University Press

Lucas, Peter J. 1999. 'Parker, Lamparde and the provision of special sorts for printing Anglo-Saxon in the sixteenth century', *Journal of the Printing Historical Society* 28: 41–69

2000. 'Sixteenth-century English spelling reform and the printers in continental perspective: Sir Thomas Smith and John Hart', *Library: The Transactions of the Bibliographical Society* 1 (1): 3–21

Luelsdorff, Philip A. 1990. 'Principles of orthography', *Theoretical Linguistics* 16 (2-3): 165-214

(ed.) 1987. *Orthography and Phonology*. Amsterdam/Philadelphia: John Benjamins

Lühr, Rosemarie 1982. *Studien zur Sprache des Hildebrandliedes*, vol. 1: *Herkunft und Sprache*. Frankfurt am Main: Peter Lang

Lüpke, Friederike 2011. 'Orthography development', in Peter K. Austin and Julia Sallabank (eds.), *The Cambridge Handbook of Endangered Languages*. Cambridge: Cambridge University Press, 312–36

Luto-Kamińska, Anetta 2015. '*Alfurkan tatarski* Piotra Czyżewskiego – opis zabytku (grafia z elementami fonetyki)', *Studia z Filologii Polskiej i Słowiańskiej* 50: 18–47

Lutz, Angelika 1986. 'The syllabic basis of word division in Old English manuscripts', *English Studies* 67 (3): 193–210

Łapicz, Czesław 1986. *Kitab Tatarów Litewsko-Polskich: Paleografia. Grafia. Język*. Toruń: Uniwersytet Mikołaja Kopernika

2017. 'Kitabistyka: źródła, metodologia i badawcze', *Poznańskie Studia Polonistyczne. Seria Językoznawcza* 24 (2): 111–23

Łoś, Jan 1907. *Jakóba syna Parkoszowego traktat o ortografii polskiej*. Kraków: Nakładem Akademii Umiejętności

Maas, Utz 1985. '*Schrift – Schreiben – Rechtschreiben*', *Diskussion Deutsch* 16: 4–25

2007. 'Die Grammatikalisierung der satzinternen Großschreibung. Zur schriftkulturellen Dimension der Orthographieentwicklung', in Angelika Redder (ed.), *Diskurse und Texte. Festschrift für Konrad Ehlich*. Tübingen: Stauffenburg, pp. 385–99

Mabillon, Jean 1681a. *De Re Diplomatica. Libra VI*. Paris: Carol Robuster

1681b. *De Re Diplomatica*. Paris: Sumtibus Ludovici Billaine

MacKenzie, David N. 1971. *A Concise Pahlavi Dictionary*. London: Oxford University Press

MacKenzie, Laurel 2019. 'Perturbing the community grammar: individual differences and community-level constraints on sociolinguistic variation', *Glossa: A Journal of General Linguistics* 4 (1): 28, https://doi.org/10.5334/gjgl.622

Mackridge, Peter 2009. *Language and National Identity in Greece, 1766–1976*. Oxford: Oxford University Press

MacMahon, Michael K. C. 2013. 'Orthography and the early history of phonetics', in Keith Allan (ed.), *The Oxford Handbook of the History of Linguistics*. Oxford: Oxford University Press, pp. 105–21, https://doi.org/10.1093/oxfordhb/9780199585847.013.0006

Maddieson, Ian 2013. 'Consonant inventories', in Matthew S. Dryer and Martin Haspelmath (eds.), *The World Atlas of Language Structures Online*. Leipzig: Max Planck Institute for Evolutionary Anthropology, http://wals.info/chapter/1

Maggiani, Adriano and Nardo, Andrea 2014. 'Le Città umbre e la scrittura', in Orazio Paoletti (ed.), *Gli umbri in età preromana – atti del XXVII convegno di studi etruschi ed italici – Perugia – Gubbio – Urbino – 27–31 ottobre 2009*. Pisa/Rome: Fabrizio Serra, pp. 391–411

Magoun, Francis P. 1943. 'Otfrid's Ad Liutbertum', *Publications of the Modern Language Association of America* 58: 869–90

Maier, Ingrid and Shamin, Stepan M. 2018. 'Gathering information for the *Kuranty* and translation technique at the Collegium of Foreign Affairs in the 1720s', in *Science Journal of VolSU. History. Area Studies. International Relations* 23 (2): 71–88

Mair, Christian 2019. 'American English: no written standard before the twentieth century?', in Nuria Yáñez-Bouza, Emma Moore, Linda van Bergen and Willem B. Hollmann (eds.), *Categories, Constructions, and Change in English Syntax*. Cambridge: Cambridge University Press, pp. 336–65

Mair, Victor H. 1996. 'Modern Chinese writing', in Peter T. Daniels and William Bright (eds.), *The World's Writing Systems*. New York: Oxford University Press, pp. 200–8

Maisels, Charles K. 1993. *The Near East: Archaeology in the 'Cradle of Civilization'*. London/New York: Routledge

Makaruk, Larysa 2013. 'Hrafichna linhvistyka: stanovlenni͡a, suchasnyĭ stan ta perspektyvy rozvytku', *Inozemna filolohii͡a* 125: 16–21, http://

publications.lnu.edu.ua/collections/index.php/foreighnphilology/article/view/301

Malling, Ove 1777. *Store og gode Handlinger af Danske, Norske og Holstenere*. Copenhagen: Gyldendals Forlag

Malone, Kemp 1959. 'Diphthong and glide', in *Mélanges de linguistique et de philologie: Fernand Mossé in memoriam*. Paris: Didier, pp. 256–66

Manchester, John Rylands University Library, Rylands MS 1310 (ff. 1r–21r)

Marazzini, Claudio 2000. 'Early grammatical descriptions of Italian', in Sylvain Auroux, Ernst F. K. Koerner, Hans-Josef Niederehe and Kees Versteegh (eds.), *History of the Language Sciences/Geschichte der Sprachwissenschaften/Histoire des sciences du langage*. Berlin/Boston: De Gruyter, pp. 742–49

Marcos, Juan-José 2017. *Fonts for Paleography. User's Manual* (5th ed.), www.academia.edu/29815961/Short_manual_of_LATIN_PALEOGRAPHY_January_2017 and http://guindo.pntic.mec.es/jmag0042/LATIN_PALEOGRAPHY.pdf

Marcos Marín, Francisco 1979. *Reforma y modernización de la lengua española*. Madrid: Cátedra

Marcus, Joyce 2006. 'Mesoamerica: scripts', in Keith Brown (ed.), *Encyclopedia of Language and Linguistics*, vol. 8. Oxford: Elsevier, pp. 16–27 (2nd ed.)

Maretić, Tomo 1889. *Istorija hrvatskoga pravopisa latinskijem slovima*. Zagreb: Jugoslavenska akademija znanosti i umjetnosti

Marković, Ivan 2015. 'O grafemu i hrvatskoj abecedi', *Filologija* 65: 77–112

Markus, Manfred (compiler) 1999. *Innsbruck Computer-Archive of Machine-Readable English Texts* (ICAMET). *Innsbrucker Beitraege zur Kulturwissenschaft, Anglistische Reihe 7*. Innsbruck: Leopold-Franzens-Universitaet Innsbruck

Markus, Manfred 2006. 'Abbreviations in Early Modern English correspondence', in Marina Dossena and Susan Fitzmaurice (eds.), *Business and Official Correspondence: Historical Investigations*. Bern: Peter Lang, pp. 107–29

Marotti, Arthur F. 1995. *Manuscript, Print, and the English Renaissance Lyric*. Ithaca: Cornell University Press

Marquilhas, Rita 2015. 'The Portuguese language spelling accord', in Laura Villa and Rik Vosters (eds.), *The Historical Sociolinguistics of Spelling*, special issue of *Written Language and Literacy* 18 (2). Amsterdam/Philadelphia: John Benjamins, pp. 275–86

Marti, Roland 2012. 'On the creation of Croatian: the development of Croatian Latin orthography in the 16th century', in Susan Baddeley and Anja Voeste (eds.), *Orthographies in Early Modern Europe*. Berlin/Boston: De Gruyter, pp. 269–320

2014. 'Historische Graphematik des Slavischen: Glagolitische und kyrillische Schrift', in Sebastian Kempgen, Peter Kosta, Tilman Berger and

Karl Gutschmidt (eds.), *Die slavischen Sprachen/The Slavic Languages*, vol. 2. New York: De Gruyter, pp. 1497–513

Martin, Hans-Jürgen 1997–. '"Rechtschreibreform": Aktuell', in 'Rechtschreibung and "Rechtschreibreform"', www.schriftdeutsch.de/orthogra.htm

Martin, Peter 2019. *The Dictionary Wars: The American Fight over the English Language*. Princeton/Oxford: Princeton University Press

Martineau, France (ed.) 2005–. *Le corpus LFFA (Laboratoire de français familier ancien)*, https://diachronie.org/2016/08/01/corpus-lffa-francais-familier-ancien/

2013. 'Written documents: what they tell us about linguistic usage', in Marijke J. van der Wal and Gijsbert Rutten (eds.), *Touching the Past: Studies in the Historical Sociolinguistics of Ego-Documents*. Amsterdam/Philadelphia: John Benjamins, pp. 129–47

2014. 'L'Acadie et le Québec: convergences et divergences', *Minorités linguistiques et société/Linguistic Minorities and Society* 4: 16–41

2017. 'Entre les lignes: écrits de soldats peu-lettrés de la Grande Guerre' in Henry Tyne, Mireille Bilger, Paul Cappeau and Emmanuelle Guerin (eds.), *La variation en question(s). Hommages à Françoise Gadet*, Brussels: Peter Lang, pp. 211–35

2021. 'Parler entre les lignes', in Emilie Urbain and Laurence Arrighi (eds.), *Retour en Acadie: penser les langues et la sociolinguistique à partir des marges. Textes en hommage à Annette Boudreau*. Quebec City: Presses de l'Université Laval, pp. 63–86

Martineau, France and Dionne, Jennifer 2008. 'Morphologie du nombre dans les échanges épistolaires d'une famille ouvrière de Montréal au XIXe siècle' in Alain Desrochers, France Martineau and Yves Charles Morin (eds.), *Orthographe française: Évolution et pratique*. Ottawa: Les Éditions David, pp. 229–57

Martineau, France and Remysen, Wim 2019. 'Bouleversements sociaux et normes orthographiques: l'exemple du Régime anglais dans l'histoire du français québécois', in Andreas Dufter, Klaus Grübl and Thomas Scharinger (eds.), *Des parlers d'oïl à la francophonie: contact, variation et changement linguistique* (Beihefte zur Zeitschrift für romanische Philologie 440). Berlin: De Gruyter, pp. 271–98

Martineau, France and Tailleur, Sandrine 2011. 'Written vernacular: variation and change in 19th century Acadian French', in Tim Pooley and Dominique Lagorgette (eds.), *On Linguistic Change in French: Socio-Historical Approaches/Le changement linguistique en français: aspects socio-historiques*. Chambéry: Université de Savoie, Laboratoire Langages, Littératures, Sociétés, pp. 153–74

2014. 'Hybridity in French written documents from the nineteenth century', in Gijsbert Rutten, Rik Vosters and Wim Vandenbussche (eds.),

Norms and Usage in Language History, 1600–1900: A Sociolinguistic and Comparative Perspective. Amsterdam/Philadelphia: John Benjamins, pp. 223–48

Martínez Alcalde, María José (ed.) 1999. *Textos clásicos sobre la historia de la ortografía castellana*. Madrid: Mapfre-Fundación Histórica Tavera-Digibis Publicaciones Digitales

2010. *La fijación ortográfica del Español: norma y argumento historiográfico*. Bern: Peter Lang

Martínez Marín, Juan 1992. 'La ortografía española: perspectiva historiográfica', *Cauce* 14–15: 125–34

Marynissen, Ann and Janssen, Theo A. J. M. 2014. 'Vroegnieuwnederlands voor commercie en cultuur', in Freek Van de Velde, Hans Smessaert, Frank Van Eynde and Sara Verbrugge (eds.), *Patroon en argument. Een dubbelfeestbundel bij het emeritaat van William Van Belle en Joop Van der Horst*. Leuven: Universitaire Pers, pp. 500–12

Masson, Michel 1976. *Les mots nouveaux en hébreu moderne*. Paris: Publications orientalistes de France

1986. *Langue et idéologie: les mots étrangers en hébreu modern*. Paris: Éditions du CNRS

Masuda, Hisashi and Joyce, Terry 2018. 'Constituent-priming investigations of the morphological activation of Japanese compound words', in Hye Pae (ed.), *Writing Systems, Reading Processes, and Cross-Linguistic Influences: Reflections from the Chinese, Japanese and Korean Languages*. Amsterdam/Philadelphia: John Benjamins, pp. 221–44

Mathisen, Ralph W. 2008. 'Paleography and codicology', in Susan Ashbrook Harvey and David G. Hunter (eds.), *The Oxford Handbook of Early Christian Studies*. Oxford: Oxford University Press, pp. 140–66

Mattheier, Klaus J. 1990. 'Otfrid als Orthographiereformer? Überlegungen zu den Bemerkungen Otfrids von Weissenburg über den Gebrauch der Buchstaben <z> und <k> im Evangelienbuch', in Werner Besch (ed.), *Deutsche Sprachgeschichte: Grundlagen, Methoden, Perspektiven: Festschrift für Johannes Erben zum 65. Geburtstag*. Frankfurt am Main: Lang, pp. 67–83

2003. 'German', in Ana Deumert and Wim Vandenbussche (eds.), *Germanic Standardizations: Past to Present*. Amsterdam/Philadelphia: John Benjamins, pp. 211–44

Mattingly, Ignatius 1992. 'Linguistic awareness and orthographic form', in Ram Frost and Leonard Katz (eds.), *Orthography, Phonology, Morphology, and Meaning*. London: North-Holland (Elsevier Science Publisher), pp. 11–26

Maunde, Edward 1878. *Correspondence of the Family of Hatton, Being Chiefly Letters Addressed to Christopher, First Viscount Hatton, AD 1601–1704*, vol. 1 of 2. London: Camden Society

Maxwell, Kate 2016. 'Beyond sound, image, and text: the (more) hidden modes of the manuscript'. Paper presented at the Medieval/ Digital Multimodalities seminar for the New Chaucer Society, The New Chaucer Society Twentieth International Congress, July 2016, Queen Mary University of London

Mazzocchi, Fulvio 2015. 'Could Big Data be the end of theory in science? A few remarks on the epistemology of data-driven science', *EMBO Reports* 16 (10): 1250–55, https://doi.org/10.15252/embr.201541001

Mæhlum, Brit K. 2019. 'Southern Saami language and culture – between stigma and pride, tradition and modernity', in Håkon Hermanstrand, Asbjørn Kolberg, Trond Risto Nilssen and Leiv Sem (eds.), *The Indigenous Identity of the South Saami. Historical and Political Perspectives on a Minority within a Minority*. Springer Open, pp. 17–28, https://link.springer.com/book/10.1007/978-3-030-05029-0

McArthur, Tom 1998. 'Spelling pronunciation', *Concise Oxford Companion to the English Language*. Oxford: Oxford University Press

McClumpha, Charles F. 1890. 'Differences between the scribes of "Beowulf"', *Modern Language Notes* 5 (4): 193

McConchie, Roderick W. 2011. 'Compounds and code-switching: compositorial practice in William Turner's *Libellus de re Herbaria Novvs*, 1538', in Jacob Thaisen and Hanna Rutkowska (eds.), *Scribes, Printers, and the Accidentals of Their Texts*. Frankfurt am Main: Peter Lang, pp. 177–90

McDonald, Katherine 2015. *Oscan in Southern Italy and Sicily: Evaluating Language Contact in a Fragmentary Corpus*. Cambridge: Cambridge University Press

2017. 'Fragmentary ancient languages as "bad data"', *Sociolinguistica* 31: 31–48

2019. 'Education and literacy in ancient Italy: evidence from the Dedications to the Goddess Reitia', *Journal of Roman Studies* 109: 131–59

McDonald, Katherine and Zair, Nicholas 2017. 'Changing script in a threatened language: reactions to Romanisation at Bantia in the first century BC', in Mari C. Jones and Damien Mooney (eds.), *Orthography Development for Endangered Languages*. Cambridge: Cambridge University Press, pp. 291–304

McEnery, Tony and Hardie, Andrew (compilers) 2007. *The Lancaster Newsbooks Corpus*. Lancaster: University of Lancaster

McIntosh, Angus 1956. 'The analysis of written Middle English', *Transactions of the Philological Society* 55: 26–55

1961. '"Graphology" and meaning', *Archivum Linguisticum* 13: 107–20

1963. 'A new approach to Middle English dialectology', *English Studies* 44 (1): 1–11

1974. 'Towards an inventory of Middle English scribes', *Neuphilologische Mitteilungen* 75: 602–74

McIntosh, Angus, Samuels, Michael L. and Benskin, Michael, with the assistance of Margaret Laing and Keith Williamson 1986a. *A Linguistic Atlas of Late Mediaeval English* (LALME), 4 vols. Aberdeen: Aberdeen University Press

1986b. *A Linguistic Atlas of Late Mediaeval English*, vol. 1: *General Introduction, Index of Sources, Dot Maps*. Aberdeen: Aberdeen University Press

1986c. *A Linguistic Atlas of Late Mediaeval English*, vol. 3: *Linguistic Profiles*. Aberdeen: Aberdeen University Press

McIntosh, Angus, Samuels, Michael L. and Benskin, Michael, with the assistance of Margaret Laing and Keith Williamson, revised and supplemented by Benskin, Michael and Laing, Margaret, webscripts by Karaiskos, Vasilis and Williamson, Keith 2013. *An Electronic Version of A Linguistic Atlas of Late Mediaeval English* (eLALME), vol. 1, www.lel.ed.ac.uk/ihd/elalme/elalme.html

McKenzie, Donald F. 1969. 'Printers of the mind: some notes on bibliographical theories and printing-house practices', *Studies in Bibliography* 22: 1–75

McKitterick, David 2003. *Print, Manuscript, and the Search for Order, 1450–1830*. Cambridge: Cambridge University Press

McLaughlin, John C. 1963. *A Graphemic-Phonemic Study of a Middle English Manuscript*. The Hague: Mouton

McLelland, Nicola 2014. 'Language description, prescription and usage in seventeenth-century German', in Gijsbert Rutten, Rik Vosters and Wim Vandenbussche (eds.), *Norms and Usage in Language History, 1600–1700. A Sociolinguistic and Comparative Perspective*. Amsterdam/Philadelphia: Benjamins, pp. 251–75

Mechkovskai͡a, Nina B. 2017. 'Pervyĭ opyt sot͡siolingvisticheskoĭ tipologii dvugrafichnykh situat͡siĭ. O knige Danièli͡a Bunchicha i drugikh "Biscriptality: A Sociolinguistic Typology"' (Heidelberg, 2016)', *Slověne* 2017 (2): 721–39

Medina, Alberto 2013. 'The institutionalization of language in eighteen-century Spain', in José del Valle (ed.), *A Political History of Spanish: The Making of a Language*. Cambridge: Cambridge University Press, pp. 77–92

Meisenburg, Trudel 1990. 'Die großen Buchstaben und was sie bewirken können: Zur Geschichte der Majuskel im Französischen und Deutschen', in Wolfgang Raible (ed.), *Erscheinungsformen kultureller Prozesse. Jahrbuch 1988 des Sonderforschungsbereichs "Übergänge und Spannungsfelder zwischen Mündlichkeit und Schriftlichkeit"*. Tübingen: Narr, pp. 281–315

Meiser, Gerhard 1986. *Lautgeschichte der Umbrischen Sprache*. Innsbruck: Institut für Sprachwissenschaft der Universität Innsbruck

Meissburger, Gerhard 1965. 'Urkunde und Mundart', in Werner Besch, Wolfgang Kleiber, Friedrich Maurer, Gerhard Meissburger and Horst Singer (eds.), *Vorarbeiten und Studien zur Vertiefung der südwestdeutschen Sprachgeschichte*. Freiburg: Eberhard Albert Verlag, pp. 47–103

Meissner, Torsten 2008. 'Mycenaean spelling', in Anna Sacconi, Maurizio Del Freo, Louis Godart and Mario Negri (eds.), *Colloquium Romanum: atti del XII colloquio internazionale di micenologia, Roma, 20–25 febbraio 2006*, vol. 2. Pisa/Rome: Fabrizio Serra, pp. 507–19

2019. 'Griechisch σίαλος Mastschwein', *Glotta* 95: 190–200

forthcoming. 'Mycenaean word division', in John T. Killen and Anna Morpurgo Davies (eds.), *Documents in Mycenaean Greek*. Cambridge: Cambridge University Press (3rd ed.)

Meissner, Torsten and Steele, Philippa M. 2017. 'Linear A and Linear B: structural and contextual concerns', in Marie-Louise Nosch and Hedvig Landenius Enegren (eds.), *Aegean Scripts. Proceedings of the 14th International Colloquium on Mycenaean Studies, Copenhagen, 2–5 September 2015*, vol. 1. Rome: Edizioni dell'Ateneo, pp. 99–114

Melchert, H. Craig 1994. *Hittite Historical Phonology*. Amsterdam: Rodopi

Melena, José L. 1978. 'En torno a la identification del silabograma *79 del silabario micénico', in *Actas del V Congreso Espagñol de Estudios Clásicos*, pp. 751–57

1983. 'Notas de philologia micénica, III: El silabograma *86', *Emerita* 51: 255–67

1985. 'Notas de philologia micénica, IV: El silabograma *83', in *Serta Gratulatoria in Honorem Juan Régulo*. La Laguna: Universidad de La Laguna, pp. 473–86

1987. 'On untranslitterated syllabograms *56 and *22', in Petar Ilievski and Ljiljana Crepajac (eds.), *Tractata Mycenaea. Proceedings of the Eighth International Colloquium on Mycenaean Studies, Held in Ohrid (15–20 September 1985)*. Skopje: Macedonian Academy of Sciences and Arts, pp. 203–32

2014a. 'Filling gaps in the basic Mycenaean syllabary', in Alberto Bernabé and Eugenio R. Luján (eds.), *Donum Mycenologicum: Mycenaean Studies in Honour of Francisco Aura Jorro*. Leuven/Walpole: Peeters, pp. 75–85

2014b. 'Filling gaps in the Mycenaean Linear B additional syllabary: the case of syllabogram *34', in A. Martínez Fernández, B. Ortega Villaro, H. Velasco López, H. Zamora Salamanca (eds.), *AGALMA Homenaje a Manuel García Teijeiro*. Valladolid: Editorial Universidad de Valladolid, pp. 207–26

2014c. 'Mycenaean writing', in Yves Duhoux and Anna Morpurgo Davies (eds.), *A Companion to Linear B: Mycenaean Greek Texts and Their World*, vol. 3. Leuven/Walpole: Peeters, pp. 1–186

in preparation. 'On the structure of the Mycenaean Linear B syllabary. I. The untransliterated syllabograms. Preliminary report'

Meletis, Dimitrios 2015a. *Graphetik. Form und Materialität von Schrift.* Glückstadt: Verlag Werner Hülsbusch

2015b. 'Graphetik', in Martin Neef, Said Sahel and Rüdiger Weingarten (eds.), *Schriftlinguistik/Grapholinguistics* (Wörterbücher zur Sprach- und Kommunikationswissenschaft/Dictionaries of Linguistics and Communication Science 5). Berlin/Boston: De Gruyter, www.degruyter .com/view/db/wsk

2018. 'What is natural in writing? Prolegomena to a Natural Grapholinguistics', in Merijn Beeksma and Martin Neef (eds.), *Understanding Writing Systems*, special issue of *Written Language and Literacy* 21 (1). Amsterdam/Philadelphia: John Benjamins, pp. 52–88, https://doi.org/10.1075/wll.00010.mel

2019a. 'The grapheme as a universal basic unit of writing', *Writing Systems Research* 11 (1): 26–49

2019b. 'Naturalness in scripts and writing systems: outlining a Natural Grapholinguistics'. Doctoral dissertation, University of Graz, Austria

2020a. *The Nature of Writing. A Theory of Grapholinguistics* (Grapholinguistics and Its Applications 3). Brest: Fluxus Editions, www .fluxus-editions.fr/meletis-the-nature-of-writing-2020.pdf

2020b. 'Types of allography', *Open Linguistics* 6 (1): 249–66, https://doi .org/10.1515/opli-2020-0006

2022. 'Universality and diversity in writing systems', *LACUS Forum* 46 (1): 72–83

Meletis, Dimitrios and Christa Dürscheid 2022. *Writing Systems and Their Use. An Overview of Grapholinguistics.* Berlin/Boston: De Gruyter Mouton

Mencken, Henry L. 1936. *The American Language: An Inquiry into the Development of English in the United States.* New York: A. A. Knopf (4th ed.)

Meredith-Owens, Georg M. and Nadson, Alexander 1970. 'The Byelorussian Tartars and their writings', *Journal of Belarusian Studies* 2 (2): 141–76

Meriggi, Piero 1955. 'I testi micenei in trascrizione', *Athenaeum* 33: 64–92

Merriam, Thomas 2006. 'Orthographic changes in John A Kent and Hand M of More', *Notes and Queries* 53 (4): 475–78, https://doi.org/10.1093/ notesj/gjl161

2011. 'Moore the Merier', *Notes and Queries* 58 (2): 241–42, https://doi.org/ 10.1093/notesj/gjr056

Merriam-Webster.com. 2011, www.merriam-webster.com

Meyer, Wilhelm 1905. *Gesammelte Abhandlungen zur mittellateinischen Rythmik*, vol. 2. Berlin: Weidmannsche Buchhandlung

Meyerhoff, Miriam 2006. *Introducing Sociolinguistics.* London: Routledge

Michel, Andreas 2012. 'Italian orthography in Early Modern times', in Susan Baddeley and Anja Voeste (eds.), *Orthographies in Early Modern Europe*. Berlin/Boston: De Gruyter, pp. 63–96

Migliorini, Bruno and Griffith, T. Gwynfor (trans.) 1966. *The Italian Language* (The Great Languages). London: Faber

Mihm, Arend 2000. 'Zur Deutung der graphematischen Variation in historischen Texten', in Annelies Häcki Buhofer (ed.), *Vom Umgang mit sprachlicher Variation: Soziolinguistisk, Dialektologie, Methoden und Wissenschaftsgeschichte: Festschrift für Heinrich Löffler zum 60. Geburtstag*. Tübingen: Francke, pp. 367–90

2016. 'Zur Theorie der vormodernen Orthographien. Straßburger Schreibsysteme als Erkenntnisgrundlage', *Sprachwissenschaft* 41 (3–4): 271–309

2017. 'Sprachwandel in der frühen Neuzeit. Augsburg und Köln im Vergleich', in Markus Denkler, Stephan Elspaß, Dagmar Hüpper and Elvira Topalović (eds.), *Deutsch im 17. Jahrhundert*. Heidelberg: Winter, pp. 265–319

Miklas, Heinz, Gau, Melanie and Hürner, Dana 2016. 'Preliminary remarks on the Old Church Slavonic Psalterium Demetrii Sinaitici', in Alexander Kulik, Catherine M. MacRobert, Svetlina Nikolova, Moshe Taube and Cynthia M. Vakareliyska (eds.), *The Bible in Slavic Tradition*. Leiden/Boston: Brill, pp. 21–88

Mikšas, Jurgis, 1885-11-06: *Postcard to Martynas Jankus*. Vilnius University Library, Manuscript collection: F. 1 - D584

Mikuła, Maciej 2018. *Prawo miejskie Magdeburskie* (Ius Municipale Magdeburgense) *w Polsce XIV–pocz. XVI w. Studium o ewolucji adaptacji prawa*. Kraków: Wydawnictwo Uniwersytetu Jagiellońskiego

Milkamanowič's kitab (KM), MS from the eighteenth/nineteenth century (the photocopy of the document kept at the Nicolaus Copernicus University in Toruń)

Millar, Robert McColl 2005. *Language, Nation and Power: An Introduction*. Houndmills, Basingstoke/New York: Palgrave Macmillan

2012. *English Historical Sociolinguistics*. Edinburgh: Edinburgh University Press

Miller, Daniel 1996. 'Why it's safer to build on concrete than epistemology: a comment on "On Materiality" by Gosewijn van Beek', *Etnofoor* 9 (1): 25–27

Miller, Thomas (ed.) 1890. *Bede's Ecclesiastical History of the English People* (Early English Text Society, old series 95–6, 110–1). London: Oxford University Press

Millward, Celia M. and Hayes, Mary 2012 [1989]. *A Biography of the English Language*. Boston: Wadsworth (3rd ed.)

Milroy, James 1992a. *Linguistic Variation and Change*. Oxford/Cambridge: Blackwell

1992b. 'Middle English dialectology', in Norman Blake (ed.), *The Cambridge History of the English Language*, vol. 2: *1066–1476*. Cambridge: Cambridge University Press, pp. 156–206

1994. 'The notion of "standard language" and its applicability to the study of Early Modern English pronunciation', in Dieter Stein and Ingrid Tieken-Boon van Ostade (eds.), *Towards a Standard English 1600-1800*. Berlin/New York: De Gruyter, pp. 19-29

2000. 'Historical description and the ideology of the standard language', in Laura Wright (ed.), *The Development of Standard English, 1300–1800: Theories, Descriptions, Conflicts* (Studies in English Language). Cambridge/New York: Cambridge University Press, pp. 11–28

2001. 'Language ideologies and the consequences of standardization', *Journal of Sociolinguistics* 5 (4): 530–55

Milroy, James and Milroy, Lesley 1985a. *Authority in Language: Investigating Language Prescription and Standardisation*. London: Routledge and Kegan Paul

1985b. 'Linguistic change, social network and speaker innovation', *Journal of Linguistics* 21: 339–84

1999 [1985a]. *Authority in Language: Investigating Language Prescription and Standardisation*. London: Routledge (3rd ed.)

2012 [1985a]. *Authority in Language: Investigating Standard English*. London: Routledge (4th ed.)

Milroy, Lesley 2002. 'Social networks', in Jack K. Chambers, Peter J. Trudgill and Natalie Schilling-Estes (eds.), *The Handbook of Language Variation and Change*. Malden: Blackwell, pp. 549–72

2007. 'Off the shelf or under the counter? On the social dynamics of sound changes', in Christopher M. Cain and Geoffrey Russom (eds.), *Studies in the History of the English Language*, vol. 3: *Managing Chaos: Strategies for Identifying Change in English*. Berlin: De Gruyter, pp. 149–72

Milroy, Lesley and Gordon, Matthew 2003. *Sociolinguistics. Method and Interpretation*. Oxford: Blackwell

Milroy, Lesley and Milroy, James 1992. 'Social network analysis and social class: towards an integrated research model', *Language in Society* 21 (1): 1–26, www.jstor.org/stable/4168309

Miltenov, I͡Avor 2009–10. 'Kirilski rŭkopisi s glagolicheski vpisvanii͡a', *Wiener slavistisches Jahrbuch* 55: 191–219; 56: 83–98

2013. 'Glagolit͡sa v kirilski rŭkopisi kato tekstologicheski marker', *Krakowsko-Wileńskie Studia Slawistyczne* 8: 39–48

Minkova, Donka 1991. *The History of Final Vowels in English: The Sound of Muting*. Berlin/New York: De Gruyter

2015a. 'Establishing phonemic contrast in written sources', in Patrick Honeybone and Joseph Salmons (eds.), *The Oxford Handbook of Historical Phonology*. Oxford: Oxford University Press, pp. 72–85

2015b. 'Metrical resolution, spelling, and the reconstruction of Old English syllabification', in Michael Adams, Laurel J. Brinton and Robert D. Fulk (eds.), *Studies in the History of English Language VI: Evidence and Method in Histories of English*. Berlin: De Gruyter, pp. 137–60

Miranda-García, Antonio, Calle-Martín, Javier, Moreno-Olalla, David, González Fernández-Corugedo, Santiago and Caie, Graham D. 2014. *The Málaga Corpus of Late Middle English Scientific Prose* (MCLMESP). Málaga: University of Málaga, https://hunter.uma.es

Miškinienė, Galina 2001. *Seniausi Lietuvos totorių rankraščiai: Grafika. Transliteracija. Vertimas. Tekstų struktūra ir turinys*. Vilnius: Vilniaus Universitetas

2015. *'K istorii transliterat͡sii slavi͡anoi͡azychnykh arabografichnykh rukopiseĭ litovskikh tatar: na primere Vil'ni͡usskoĭ shkoly kitabistiki'*, in Joanna Kulwicka-Kamińska and Czesław Łapicz (eds.), *Tefsir Tatarów Wielkiego Księstwa Litewskiego: Teoria i praktyka badawcza. Toruń: Wydział Filologiczny UMK*, pp. 61–72, www.tefsir.umk.pl/pliki/Tefsir_Tatarow_WKL.pdf

Miškinienė, Galina, Namavičiūtė, Sigita, Pokrovskaja, Jekaterina and Durgut, Hüseyin 2009. *Ivano Luckevičiaus kitabas: Lietuvos totorių kultūros paminklas*. Vilnius: Lietuvių kalbos institutas

Molero Pintado, Antonio 1994. *Ciento cincuenta años de perfeccionamiento del magisterio en España. Desde las academias de profesores a la creación de los CEPs. 1840–1984*. Madrid: Universidad de Alcalá de Henares

Molina, Alonso de 1571. *Arte de la lengua mexicana y castellana*. Mexico City: Pedro Ocharte

Montfaucon, Bernard de 1708. *Palaeographia Graeca, sive, De Ortu et Progressu Literarum Graecarum*. Paris: L. Guerin

Montgomery, Scott 2001. 'The case for synchronic orthographic primacy: the effect of literacy on phonological processing'. Doctoral dissertation, University of Edinburgh, UK

2005. 'Lax vowels, orthography and /ə/: the need for orthographic primacy', *Linguistische Berichte* 201: 14–64

Mooney, Linne R. 2006. 'Chaucer's scribe', *Speculum* 81 (1): 97–138

2008. 'Locating scribal activity in late-medieval London', in Margaret Connolly and Linne R. Mooney (eds.), *Design and Distribution of Late Medieval Manuscripts in England*. York: York Medieval Press, pp. 183–204

Moore, Colette 2019. 'Communities of practice and incipient standardization in Middle English written culture', *English Studies* 100 (2): 117–32

Moore, Michael 2004. *Fahrenheit 9/11*. FLIC Distributors/Lionsgate Films

Morala Rodríguez, José R. 1998. 'Norma gráfica y variedades orales en el leonés medieval', in José M. Blecua, Juan Gutiérrez and Lidia Sala (eds.), *Estudios de grafemática en el dominio hispánico*. Salamanca: Universidad de Salamanca, pp. 169–88

2004. 'Norma y usos gráficos en la documentación leonesa', *Aemilianense* 1: 405–29

2015. 'Norma y variación en el romance de la documentación leonesa del siglo XIII', in Ramón Mariño Paz and Xavier Varela Barreiro (eds.), *Lingüística histórica e edición de textos galegos medievais, Verba,* Anexo 73. Universidade de Santiago de Compostela, Santiago, pp. 11–28

Mora-Marín, David F. 2003. 'The origin of Mayan syllabograms and orthographic conventions', *Written Language and Literacy* 6 (2): 193–238

Moran, Steven and Cysouw, Michael 2018. *The Unicode Cookbook for Linguists. Managing Writing Systems Using Orthography Profiles*. Berlin: Language Science Press

Mørck, Endre 1999. 'Sociolinguistic studies on the basis of medieval Norwegian charters', in Ernst H. Jahr (ed.), *Language Change. Advances in Historical Sociolinguistics*. Berlin/New York: De Gruyter, pp. 263–90

2018. 'Seinmellomalderen 1350–1536', in Agnete Nesse (ed.) *Tidslinjer*, vol. 4 of Helge Sandøy and Agnete Nesse (eds.), *Norsk språkhistorie*. Oslo: Novus, pp. 293–356

2019. 'The Reformation and the linguistic situation in Norway', *Nordlit* 43: 115–26, https://doi.org/10.7557/13.4903

Moreno-Olalla, David 2020. 'Spelling practices in late Middle English medical prose: a quantitative analysis', in Laura Wright (ed.), *The Multilingual Origins of Standard English*. Berlin/Boston: De Gruyter, pp. 141–63

Moreton, Emma 2016. '"I never could forget my darling mother": the language of recollection in a corpus of female Irish emigrant correspondence', *The History of the Family* 21 (3): 315–36, https://doi.org/10.1080/1081602X.2016.1155469

Morpurgo Davies, Anna 1987. 'Mycenaean and Greek syllabification', in Petar Ilievski and Ljiljana Crepajac (eds.), *Tractata Mycenaea. Proceedings of the Eighth International Colloquium on Mycenaean Studies, Held in Ohrid (15–20 September 1985)*. Skopje: Macedonian Academy of Sciences and Arts, pp. 91–103

Mortara Garavelli, Bice 2008. *Storia della punteggiatura in Europa*. Rome-Bari: Laterza

Moser, Hans 1977. *Die Kanzlei Kaiser Maximilians I. Graphematik eines Schreibusus. Teil I: Untersuchungen. Teil II: Texte*. Innsbruck: Institut für deutsche Philologie der Universität Innsbruck

Moser, Virgil 1929. *Frühneuhochdeutsche Grammatik. I. Band: Lautlehre. 1. Hälfte: Orthographie, Betonung, Stammsilbenvokale* (Germanische Bibliothek). Heidelberg: Winter

Mosser, Daniel W. and Mooney, Linne R. 2014. 'More manuscripts by the Beryn scribe and his cohort', *The Chaucer Review* 49 (1): 39–76

Mougeon, Raymond and Beniak, Édouard 1989. 'Présentation', in Édouard Beniak and Raymond Mougeon (eds.), *Le français canadien parlé hors Québec: aperçu sociolinguistique*. Quebec City: Presses de l'Université Laval, pp. 1–16

Moulin, Claudine 1990. *Der Majuskelgebrauch in Luthers Deutschen Briefen (1517–1546)*. Heidelberg: Winter

2004. 'Das morphematische Prinzip bei den Grammatikern des 16. und 17. Jahrhunderts', *Sprachwissenschaft* 29: 33–73

Mufwene, Salikoko 2001. *The Ecology of Language Evolution*. Cambridge: Cambridge University Press

2018. 'Language evolution from an ecological perspective', in Alwin Fill and Hermine Penz (eds.), *The Routledge Handbook of Ecolinguistics*. New York: Routledge, pp. 73–88

Mugdan, Joachim 1984. *Jan Baudouin de Courtenay (1845–1929): Leben und Werk*. Munich: Wilhelm Fink

Mühlhäusler, Peter 1990. '"Reducing" Pacific languages to writings', in John Joseph and Talbot Taylor (eds.), *Ideologies of Language*. London/New York: Routledge, pp. 189–205

Mulcaster, Richard 1581. *Positions vvherin those primitiue circumstances be examined, which are necessarie for the training vp of children, either for skill in their booke, or health in their bodie*. London: Thomas Vautrollier for Thomas Chare [Chard] (EEBO, ProQuest)

1582. *The First Part of the Elementarie vvhich Entreateth Chefelie of the right writing of our English tung*. London: Vautroullier (EEBO, ProQuest)

Mullen, Alex 2013. *Southern Gaul and the Mediterranean: Multilingualism and Multiple Identities in the Iron Age and Roman Periods*. Cambridge: Cambridge University Press.

Müller, Ernst E. 1953. *Die Basler Mundart im ausgehenden Mittelalter*. Bern: Francke

Müller, Rudolf W. 1964. *Rhetorische und syntaktische Interpunktion. Untersuchungen zur Pausenbezeichnung im antiken Latein*. Tübingen: Eberhard-Karls-Universität Tübingen.

Murray, Heather and Portebois, Yannick 2016. 'Steam writing in the urli daiz: William Orr, the Canadian phonetic pioneer, and the cause of phonographic reform', *Papers of The Bibliographical Society of Canada* 54 (1–2): 57–92, https://doi.org/10.33137/pbsc.v54i1-2.22657

Murray, James A. H., Bradley, Henry, Craigie, William A. and Onions, Charles T. 1888–1928. *A New English Dictionary on Historical Principles: Founded Mainly on the Materials Collected by The Philological Society*, 10 vols. Oxford: Oxford Clarendon Press

1901. *A New English Dictionary on Historical Principles: Founded Mainly on the Materials Collected by The Philological Society*, vol. 3. Oxford: Oxford Clarendon Press

1933. *The Oxford English Dictionary: Being a Corrected Re-Issue with an Introduction, Supplement and Bibliography, of A New English Dictionary on Historical Principles: Founded Mainly on the Materials Collected by the Philological Society*, 10 vols. Oxford: Oxford Clarendon Press

Murzynowski, Stanisław 1551. *Ortografia*. Królewiec: Aleksander Aujezdecki

Musakova, Elisaveta 2004. 'Kirilski rŭkopisi s glagolicheski vpisvanii͡a', in Marija-Ana Dürrigl, Milan Mihaljević and Franjo Velčić (eds.), *Glagoljica i hrvatski glagolizam*. Zagreb/Krk: Staroslavenski institut-Krčka biskupija, pp. 523–47

Nadeau, Jean-Benoît and Barlow, Julie 2006. *The Story of French*. New York: St. Martin's Press

National Library of Scotland, Advocates' MS 19. 2. 1

Naumann, Carl L. 1989. *Gesprochenes Deutsch und Orthographie. Linguistische und didaktische Studien zur Rolle der gesprochenen Sprache in System und Erwerb der Rechtschreibung*. Frankfurt am Main: Peter Lang

Naveh, Joseph 1982. *Early History of the Alphabet: An Introduction to West Semitic Epigraphy and Paleography*. Jerusalem: Magnes Press, Hebrew University

Nebrija, Antonio de 1492. *Gramática de la lengua castellana*. Salamanca: Juan de Porras, Biblioteca digital hispánica, bdh0000174208

Needham, Paul 1999. 'The custom rolls as documents for the printed book trade in England', in Lotte Hellinga and Joseph B. Trapp (eds.), *The Cambridge History of the Book in Britain*, vol. 3: *1400–1557*. Cambridge: Cambridge University Press, pp. 148–63.

Neef, Martin 2005. *Die Graphematik des Deutschen*. Tübingen/Berlin: Niemeyer/De Gruyter, https://doi.org/10.1515/9783110914856

2012. 'Graphematics as part of a modular theory of phonographic writing systems', *Writing Systems Research* 4 (2): 214–28, https://doi.org/10.1080/17586801.2012.706658

2013. 'Das Konzept des morphologischen Prinzips und seine Rolle in einer modularen Schriftsystemtheorie', in Martin Neef and Carmen Scherer (eds.), *Die Schnittstelle von Morphologie und geschriebener Sprache*. Berlin/Boston: De Gruyter, pp. 9–38

2015. 'Writing systems as modular objects: proposals for theory design in grapholinguistics', *Open Linguistics* 1: 708–21, https://doi.org/10.1515/opli-2015-0026

Neef, Martin and Balestra, Miriam 2011. 'Measuring graphematic transparency: German and Italian compared', in Susanne R. Borgwaldt and Terry Joyce (eds.), *Typology of Writing Systems*, special issue of

Written Language and Literacy 14 (1). Amsterdam/Philadelphia: John Benjamins, pp. 109–42

Neef, Martin, Neijt, Anneke and Sproat, Richard 2002. 'Introduction', in Martin Neef, Anneke Neijt and Richard Sproat (eds.), *The Relation of Writing to Spoken Language*. Tübingen: Niemeyer, pp. 1–7

Neef, Martin and Primus, Beatrice 2001. 'Stumme Zeugen der Autonomie – Eine Replik auf Ossner', *Linguistische Berichte* 187: 353–78

Neef, Martin, Sahel, Said and Weingarten, Rüdiger (eds.) 2012. 'Schriftlinguistik'/'Grapholinguistics', in *Wörterbücher zur Sprach- und Kommunikationswissenschaft/Dictionaries of Linguistics and Communication Science* 5. Berlin/Boston: De Gruyter, www.degruyter.com/view/db/wsk

Neidorf, Leonard 2013. 'Scribal errors of proper names in the *Beowulf* manuscript', *Anglo-Saxon England* 42: 249–69

2017. *The Transmission of* Beowulf*: Language, Culture, and Scribal Behavior*. Ithaca: Cornell University Press

Neidorf, Leonard, Pascual, Rafael J. and Shippey, Tom (eds.) 2016. *Old English Philology: Studies in Honour of R. D. Fulk*. Woodbridge: Boydell and Brewer

Neis, Cordula 2011. 'European conceptions of writing from the Renaissance to the eighteenth century', in Gerda Hassler (ed., with the assistance of Gesina Volkmann), *History of Linguistics 2008: Selected Papers from the 11th International Conference on the History of the Language Sciences (ICHOLS XI), Potsdam, 28 August–2 September 2008* (Studies in the History of the Language Sciences 115). Amsterdam: John Benjamins, pp. 169–86

Nelde, Peter 1997. 'Language conflict', in Florian Coulmas (ed.), *The Handbook of Sociolinguistics*. Oxford: Blackwell, pp. 285–300

Nemirovskiĭ, Evgeniĭ L. 2008. 'Sosushchestvovanie kirillovskogo t͡serkovnoslavi͡anskogo i grazhdanskogo shriftov v XVIII v.', in Aleksandr I͡U. Samarin (ed.), *Tri stoletii͡a russkogo grazhdanskogo shrifta (1708–2008)*. Moscow: Pashkov dom, pp. 156–59

Nerius, Dieter (ed.) 2007. *Deutsche Orthographie*. Hildesheim/Zurich/New York: Georg Olms Verlag

Nerius, Dieter and Augst, Gerhard (eds.) 1988. *Probleme der geschriebenen Sprache. Beiträge zur Schriftlinguistik auf dem XIV. internationalen Linguistenkongreß 1987 in Berlin* (Linguistische Studien, A, 173). Berlin: Akademiede Wissenschaften der DDR

Nesse, Agnete 2002. *Språkkontakt mellom norsk og tysk i hansatidens Bergen*. Oslo: Novus

2003. 'Written and spoken languages in Bergen in the Hansa era', in K. Braunmüller and G. Ferraresi (eds.), *Aspects of Multilingualism in European Language History*. Amsterdam/Philadelphia: John Benjamins, pp. 61–84

2011. '"Norskheter i språket hos..." – Et eksempel på minimalistisk språkhistorieskriving?', in Helge Sandøy and Ernst H. Jahr (eds.), *Norsk språkhistorie i eldre nynorsk tid (1525–1814)*. Oslo: Novus, pp. 32–47

2013. *Innføring i norsk språkhistorie*. Oslo: CappelenDamm

2017. 'Language choice in forming an identity: linguistic innovations by German traders in Bergen', in Esther-Miriam Wagner, Bettina Beinhoff and Ben Outhwaite (eds.), *Merchants of Innovation. The Languages of Traders*. Boston/Berlin: De Gruyter, pp. 158–78

2021. *Bergens Fundas. Til moderne norsk ved Agnete Nesse*. Bergen: Kapabel

Nesse, Agnete and Torp, Arne 2018. 'Dansketiden (1536–1814)', in Agnete Nesse (ed.), *Tidslinjer*, vol. 4 of Helge Sandøy and Agnete Nesse (eds.), *Norsk språkhistorie*. Oslo: Novus, pp. 357–424

Neuman, Yishai 2009. 'L'influence de l'écriture sur la langue'. Doctoral dissertation, Université Sorbonne Nouvelle, France

2013. 'Graphophonemic assignment', in Geoffrey Khan (ed.), *Encyclopedia of Hebrew Language and Linguistics*. Boston/Leiden: Brill, vol. 2: *G–O*, pp. 135–45

2021. 'Sociocultural motivation for spelling variation in Modern Hebrew', in Yannis Haralambous (ed.), *Grapholinguistics in the 21st Century, Paris, June 17–19, 2020. Proceedings* (Grapholinguistics and Its Applications 4). Brest: Fluxus Editions, pp. 489–99

Nevala, Minna and Palander-Collin, Minna 2005. 'Letters and letter writing: introduction', *European Journal of English Studies* 9 (1): 1–7

Nevalainen, Terttu 1996. 'Gender difference', in Terttu Nevalainen and Helena Raumolin-Brunberg (eds.), *Sociolinguistics and Language History: Studies Based on the Corpus of Early English Correspondence*. Amsterdam: Rodopi, pp. 77–92

2003. 'English', in Ana Deumert and Wim Vandenbussche (eds.), *Germanic Standardizations. Past to Present*. Amsterdam/Philadelphia: John Benjamins, pp. 127–56

2012a. 'Variable focusing in English spelling between 1400 and 1600', in Susan Baddeley and Anja Voeste (eds.), *Orthographies in Early Modern Europe*. Berlin/Boston: De Gruyter, pp. 127–65

2012b. 'New perspectives, theories and methods: historical sociolinguistics', in Alexander Bergs and Laurel J. Brinton (eds.), *English Historical Linguistics: An International Handbook*, vol. 2. Berlin/Boston: De Gruyter, pp. 1438–57

2013. 'Words of kings and counsellors: register variation and language change in early English courtly correspondence', in Esther-Miriam Wagner, Bettina Beinhoff and Ben Outhwaite (eds.), *Scribes as Agents of Language Change*. Berlin: De Gruyter, pp. 99–119

2014. 'Norms and usage in seventeenth-century English', in Gijsbert Rutten, Rik Vosters and Wim Vandenbussche (eds.), *Norms and Usage in Language History, 1600–1900: A Sociolinguistic and Comparative Perspective*. Amsterdam/Philadelphia: John Benjamins, pp. 103–28

2015. 'What are historical sociolinguistics?', *Journal of Historical Sociolinguistics* 1 (2): 243–69

Nevalainen, Terttu and Raumolin-Brunberg, Helena 2003. *Historical Sociolinguistics: Language Change in Tudor and Stuart England*. London: Pearson

2005. 'Sociolinguistics and the history of English: a survey', *International Journal of English Studies* 5 (1): 33–58

2012. 'Historical sociolinguistics: origins, motivations, and paradigms', in Juan Manuel Hernández-Campoy and Juan Camilo Conde-Silvestre (eds.), *The Handbook of Historical Sociolinguistics*. Chichester: Wiley-Blackwell, pp. 22–40

2016. *Historical Sociolinguistics: Language Change in Tudor and Stuart England*. London: Routledge (2nd ed.)

Nevalainen, Terttu, Raumolin-Brunberg, Helena, Keränen, Jukka, Nevala, Minna, Nurmi, Arja and Palander-Collin, Minna 1993–98. *Corpus of Early English Correspondence* (CEEC). Department of Modern Languages, University of Helsinki, www2.helsinki.fi/en/researchgroups/varieng/corpus-of-early-english-correspondence

Nevalainen, Terttu, Raumolin-Brunberg, Helena, Keränen, Jukka, Nevala, Minna, Nurmi, Arja, Palander-Collin, Minna, Taylor, Ann, Pintzuk, Susan and Warner, Anthony 2006. *Parsed Corpus of Early English Correspondence* (PCEEC), Oxford Text Archive, https://ota.bodleian.ox.ac.uk/repository/xmlui/handle/20.500.12024/2510

Nevalainen, Terttu and Tanskanen, Sanna-Kaisa (eds.) 2007. *Letter Writing*. Amsterdam/Philadelphia: John Benjamins

Nevalainen, Terttu and Tieken-Boon van Ostade, Ingrid 2006. 'Standardisation', in Richard Hogg and David Denison (eds.), *A History of the English Language*. Cambridge: Cambridge University Press, pp. 271–311

Nichols, John 1996. 'The Cree syllabary', in Peter T. Daniels and William Bright (eds.), *The World's Writing Systems*. New York: Oxford University Press, pp. 599–611

Nichols, Stephen 1990. 'Introduction: philology in a manuscript culture', *Speculum* 65 (1): 1–10

Nicolaysen, Nic 1858. *Norske Magasin*, vol. 1. Christiania: Johan Dahls forlagshandel

Nievergelt, Andreas 2009. *Althochdeutsch in Runenschrift. Geheimschriftliche volkssprachige Griffelglossen*. Stuttgart: Hirzel

Nordlund, Taru 2012. 'Standardization of Finnish orthography: from reformists to national awakeners', in Susan Baddeley and Anja Voeste (eds.), *Orthographies in Early Modern Europe*. Berlin/Boston: De Gruyter, pp. 351–72

Norsk salmebok 1985. Oslo: Verbum

Novgorodian Birchbark Letters, http://gramoty.ru

Novickas, Elizabeth 2004. 'The printer and the scholar: the making of Daniel Klein's *Grammatica Litvanica*', *Archivum Lithuanicum* 6: 17–42

Nowak, Jessica 2019. 'Zur Diachronie der satzinternen Großschreibung im Kontrast: Englisch – Niederländisch – Deutsch', *Jahrbuch für Germanistische Sprachgeschichte* 10 (1): 96–118

Nübling, Damaris, Dammel, Antje, Duke, Janet and Szczepaniak, Renata 2017. *Historische Sprachwissenschaft des Deutschen. Eine Einführung in die Prinzipien des Sprachwandels* (Narr Studienbücher). Tübingen: Narr (5th ed.)

Nunberg, Geoffrey 1990. *The Linguistics of Punctuation*. Stanford: CSLI

Nunberg, Geoffrey, Briscoe, Ted and Huddleston, Rodney D. 2002. 'Punctuation', in Rodney D. Huddleston and Geoffrey K. Pullum (eds.), *The Cambridge Grammar of the English Language*. Cambridge: Cambridge University Press, pp. 1723–78

O'Brien, Robert L. 1904. 'Machinery and English style', *Atlantic Monthly* 94: 464–72

Ó Ciosáin, Niall 2004. *Explaining Change in Cultural History* (Historical Studies 23). Dublin: University College Dublin Press, pp. 1–12

O'Connor, Michael P. 1983. 'Native speaker analysis, and the earliest stages of Northwest Semitic orthography', in Carol L. Myers and Michael P. O'Connor (eds.), *The Word of the Lord Shall Go Forth: Essays in Honor of David Noel Freedman in Celebration of His Sixtieth Birthday*. Winona Lake: Eisenbrauns, pp. 439–65

Oczkowa, Barbara 2004. 'Głagolityzm i neogłagolityzm w Chorwacji', *Biuletyn Polskiego Towarzystwa Językoznawczego* 60: 56–63

Okasha, Elisabeth 2018. 'Roman script and runes in Anglo-Saxon inscriptions: an intermedial usage?', in Alessia Bauer, Elise Kleivane and Terje Spurkland (eds.), *Epigraphy in an Intermedial Context*. Dublin: Four Courts, pp. 31–42

Oldireva Gustafsson, Larisa 2002. *Preterite and Past Participle Forms in English: 1680–1790*. Stockholm: Uppsala Universitet

Olivier, Jean-Pierre 1986. 'Cretan writing in the second millennium BC', *World Archaeology* 17 (3): 377–89

Olivier, Jean-Pierre and Godart, Louis (eds.) 1996. *Corpus Hieroglyphicarum Inscriptionum Cretae*. Paris: De Boccard

Olko, Justyna 2015. 'Alphabetic writing in the hands of the colonial Nahua nobility', *Contributions in New World Archaeology* 7: 177–98

Olko, Justyna and Sullivan, John 2013. 'Empire, colony and globalization: a brief history of the Nahuatl language', *Colloquia Humanistica* 2: 181–216

Olmos, Andrés de 1875. *Grammaire de la langue nahuatl ou mexicaine*. Paris: Imprimerie Nationale (originally written in 1547 as *Arte para aprender la lengua mexicana*)

Olsson, John 2012. *Wordcrime: Solving Crime through Forensic Linguistics.* London: Continuum

2018. *More Wordcrime: Solving Crime with Linguistics.* London/New York: Bloomsbury Academic

Ong, Walter J. 2005 [1982]. *Orality and Literacy: The Technologizing of the Word.* London/New York: Routledge Taylor and Francis Group

Open Language Archives Community (OLAC), olac.ldc.upenn.edu

Oppliger, Rahel 2016. 'Automatic authorship attribution based on character g-grams in Swiss German', in Stefanie Dipper, Friedrich Neubarth and Heike Zinsmeister (eds.), *Proceedings of the 13th Conference on Natural Language Processing (KONVENS 2016)*, 16. Bochum: Bochumer Linguistische Arbeitsberichte, pp. 177–85

O'Rourke, Bernadette 2017. 'Negotiating the standard in contemporary Galicia', in Pia Lane, James Costa and Haley De Korne (eds.), *Standardizing Minority Languages.* New York/London: Routledge, pp. 84–100

Osselton, Noel E. 1963. 'Formal and informal spelling in the 18th century: *errour, honor,* and related words', *English Studies: A Journal of English Language and Literature* 44 (4): 267–75

1984. 'Informal spelling in Early Modern English, 1500–1800', in Norman F. Blake and Charles Jones (eds.), *English Historical Linguistics: Studies in Development.* Sheffield: CECTAL, University of Sheffield, pp. 123–37

1985. 'Spelling-book rules and the capitalization of nouns in the seventeenth and eighteenth centuries', in Mary-Jo Arn and Hanneke Wirtjes (eds.), *Historical and Editorial Studies in Medieval and Early Modern English, for Johan Geritsen.* Groningen: Wolters-Noordhoff, pp. 49–61

1998 [1984]. 'Informal spelling systems in Early Modern English: 1500–1800', in Mats Rydén, Ingrid Tieken-Boon van Ostade and Merja Kytö (eds.) 1998. *A Reader in Early Modern English.* Frankfurt am Main: Peter Lang, pp. 33–45 (reprinted from Norman F. Blake and Charles Jones (eds.), *English Historical Linguistics. Studies in Development.* Sheffield: Department of English Language, University of Sheffield, pp. 123–37)

Ostrowski, Donald G. 1977. Review of *Problemy paleografii i kodikologii v SSSR. Jahrbücher für Geschichte Osteuropas, Neue Folge* 25 (2): 264–65

Oxford, Balliol College, MS 224a

Oxford, Bodleian Library, Bodley MS 34

Oxford, Bodleian Library, Hatton MS 20

Oxford, Bodleian Library, Tanner MS 10

Page, Raymond I. 1999. *An Introduction to English Runes.* Woodbridge: Boydell and Brewer (2nd ed.)

Pahta, Päivi, Nevala, Minna, Nurmi, Arja and Palander-Collin, Minna (eds.) 2010. *Social Roles and Language Practices in Late Modern English.* Amsterdam/Philadelphia: John Benjamins

Palaima, Thomas G. and Sikkenga, Elizabeth 1999. 'Linear A > Linear B', in Philip P. Betancourt, Vassos Karageorghis, Robert Laffineur and Wolf-Dietrich Niemeier (eds.), *Meletemata: Studies in Aegean Archaeology Presented to Malcolm H. Wiener as He Enters His 65th Year*, vol. 2. Liège/Austin: Histoire de l'art et archéologie de la Grèce antique, Université de Liège/Program in Aegean Scripts and Prehistory, University of Texas at Austin, pp. 599–608

Palander-Collin, Minna 2010. 'Correspondence', in Andreas H. Jucker and Irma Taavitsainen (eds.), *The Handbook of Historical Pragmatics*. Berlin/New York: De Gruyter, pp. 677–703

Palander-Collin, Minna, Nevala, Minna and Nurmi, Arja 2009. 'The language of daily life in the history of English: studying how macro meets micro', in Arja Nurmi, Minna Nevala and Minna Palander-Collin (eds.), *The Language of Daily Life in England (1400–1800)*. Amsterdam/Philadelphia: John Benjamins, pp. 1–23

Palionis, Jonas 1995. *Lietuvių rašomosios kalbos istorija*. Vilnius: Mokslo ir enciklopedijų leidykla

Pallas, Peter S. 1787, 1789. *Linguarum totius orbis vocabularia comparativa; augustissimae cura collecta* [...] *Linguas Europae et Asiae complexae*, 2 vols. Petrópolis: Typis Iohannis Caroli Schnoor

Palmer, Leonard R. 1955. 'Observations on the Linear B tablets from Mycenae', *Bulletin of the Institute of Classical Studies* 2: 36–45

1963. *The Interpretation of Mycenaean Greek Texts*. Oxford: The Clarendon Press

Palumbo, Alessandro 2020. *Skriftsystem i förändring. En grafematisk studie av de svenska medeltida runinskrifterna*. Uppsala: Institutionen för nordiska språk, Uppsala universitet

2022. 'How Latin is runic Latin? Thoughts on the influence of Latin writing on medieval runic orthography', in Edith Marold and Christiane Zimmermann (eds.), *Studien zur runischen Graphematik: Methodische Ansätze und digitale Umsetzung*. Uppsala: Institutionen för nordiska språk, Uppsala universitet, pp. 177–218

Papp, Ference 1994. *A Magyar Nyelv Szóvégmutató Szótára*. Budapest: Akadémiai Kiadó

Parkes, Malcolm B. 1987 'The contribution of insular scribes of the seventh and eighth centuries to the "grammar of legibility"', in Alfonso Maierù (ed.), *Grafia e interpunzione del latino nel medioevo (Seminario Internazionale, Roma, 27–29 septembre 1984)*. Rome: Edizioni dell'Ateneo, pp. 15–31

1992. *Pause and Effect. An Introduction to the History of Punctuation in the West*. Aldershot: Scholar Press

1993 [1992]. *Pause and Effect: An Introduction to the History of Punctuation in the West*. Berkeley: University of California Press

1997. 'Punctuation in copies of Nicholas Love's *Mirror of the Blessed Life of Jesus Christ*', in Shoichi Oguro, Richard Beadle and Michael G. Sargent (eds.), *Nicholas Love at Waseda*. Cambridge: D. S. Brewer, pp. 47–59

Parkosz, Jakub from Żórawice [Parcossii, Jacobus de Zoravice] c. 1470. *Pugna pro patria* (incunabulum), MS, in Marian Kucała (ed.) 1985, *Jakuba Parkosza traktat o ortografii polskiej*. Warsaw: Państwowe Wydawnictwo Naukowe, pp. 41–54

Parodi, Claudia 2006. 'The indianization of Spaniards in New Spain', in Margarita Hidalgo (ed.), *Mexican Languages at the Dawn of the Twenty-First Century*. Berlin: De Gruyter, pp. 29–52

Parpola, Asko 1994. *Deciphering the Indus Script*. Cambridge: Cambridge University Press

Patrick, Donna, Murasugi, Kumiko and Palluq-Cloutier, Jeela 2018. 'Standardization of Inuit languages in Canada', in Pia Lane, James Costa and Haley De Korne (eds.), *Standardizing Minority Languages: Competing Ideologies of Authority and Authenticity in the Global Periphery*. New York/London: Routledge, pp. 135–53

Paul, Hermann 1909. *Prinzipien der Sprachgeschichte*. Halle: Niemeyer (4th ed.)

2009 [1880]. *Prinzipien der Sprachgeschichte*. Halle: Niemeyer (reprinted by Cambridge University Press)

Paul, Hermann and Klein, Thomas 2007. *Mittelhochdeutsche Grammatik*. Tübingen: Niemeyer (25th ed.)

Pavlenko, Aneta 2010. 'Linguistic landscape of Kyiv, Ukraine: a diachronic study', in Elana Shohamy, Eliezer Ben-Rafael and Monica Barni (eds.), *Linguistic Landscape in the City*. Bristol: Multilingual Matters, pp. 133–50

Pavlenko, Aneta and Mullen, Alex 2015. 'Why diachronicity matters in the study of linguistic landscapes', *Linguistic Landscapes* 1 (1–2): 108–26

Pearsall, Derek 2011. 'Foreword', in Alexandra Gillespie and Daniel Wakelin (eds.), *The Production of Books in England 1350–1500* (Cambridge Studies in Palaeography and Codicology 14). Cambridge: Cambridge University Press, pp. xv–xvi

Pedersen, Aud-Kirsti 2016. 'Is the official use of names in Norway determined by the Place-Names Act or by attitudes?', in Guy Puzey and Laura Kostanski (eds.), *Names and Naming: People, Places, Perceptions and Power*. Bristol: Multilingual Matters, pp. 213–28

Peikola, Matti 2011. 'Copying space, length of entries, and textual transmission in Middle English tables of lessons', in Jacob Thaisen and Hanna Rutkowska (eds.), *Scribes, Printers, and the Accidentals of Their Texts*. Frankfurt am Main: Peter Lang, pp. 107–24

Pellat, Jean-Christophe 1988. 'Indépendance ou interaction de l'écrit et de l'oral? Recensement critique des définitions du graphème', in Nina

Catach (ed.), *Pour une théorie de la langue écrite*. Paris: Éditions du CNRS, pp. 133–46

Pellegrini, Giovanni B. and Prosdocimi, Aldo L. 1967. *La lingua venetica*. Padua: Instituto di glottologia dell'Università

Pemberton, Caroline 1899. *Boethius, De Consolatione Philosophiae, AD 1593, Plutarch, De Curiositate, Horace, De Arte Poetica (Part), AD 1598. Edited from the Unique MS, Partly in the Queen's Hand, in the Public Record Office, London* (Early English Text Society). London: Kegan Paul, Trench, Trübner and Co

Peng, Jian, Choo, Kim-Kwang Raymond and Ashman, Helen 2016. 'Bit-level n-gram based forensic authorship analysis on social media: identifying individuals from linguistic profiles', *Journal of Network and Computer Applications* 70 (July): 171–82, https://doi.org/10.1016/j.jnca.2016.04.001

Penny, Ralph 2004. 'Evolución lingüística en la Baja Edad Media: evoluciones en el plano fonético', in Cano Aguilar, Rafael (ed.), *Historia de la lengua española*. Barcelona: Ariel, pp. 593–612

Penzl, Herbert 1950. 'Orthography and phonemes in Wulfila's Gothic', *Journal of English and Germanic Philology* 49: 217–30

1957. 'The evidence for phonemic changes', in Ernst Pulgram (ed.), *Studies Presented to Joshua Whatmough on His Sixtieth Birthday*. The Hague: Mouton, pp. 193–208

1959. 'Konsonantenphoneme und Orthographie im althochdeutschen Isidor', *Mélanges de linguistique et de philologie Fernand Moddé in memoriam*. Paris: Didier, pp. 354–61

1971. 'Scribal practice, phonological change, and biuniqueness', *The German Quarterly* 44 (3): 305–10

1982. 'Zur Methodik der historischen Phonologie: Schreibung – Lautung und die Erforschung des Althochdeutschen', *Beiträge zur Geschichte der deutschen Sprache und Literatur* 104: 169–89

1987. 'Zur alphabetischen Orthographie als Gegenstand der Sprachwissenschaft', in Philip A. Luelsdorff (ed.), *Orthography and Phonology*. Amsterdam: John Benjamins, pp. 225–38

Percy, Carol 2012. 'Standardization: codifiers', in Alexander Bergs and Laurel J. Brinton (eds.), *English Historical Linguistics: An International Handbook*, vol. 1. Berlin/Boston: De Gruyter, pp. 1006–20

Pérez, Manuel 1713. *Arte de el idioma mexicano*. Mexico City: Francisco de Ribera Calderón

Pérez Ledesma, Manuel and Saz, Ismael (eds.) 2014. *Historia de las culturas políticas en España y América Latina*. Madrid/Zaragoza: Marcial Pons Historia/Prensas Universitarias de Zaragoza

Peters, Robert 2017. *Atlas spätmittelalterlicher Schreibsprachen des niederdeutschen Altlandes und angrenzender Gebiete (ASnA)*, 3 vols. Berlin/Boston: De Gruyter

Petruševski, Mihail D. and Ilievski, Petar H. 1958. 'The phonetic value of the Mycenaean syllabic sign *85', *Živa Antika* 8: 265–78

Pettersen, Egil 1957. *Norskhet i språket hos Dorothe Engelbretsdatter*. Bergen: Universitetsforlaget

Pettersson, Eva and Megyesi, Beáta 2018. 'The HistCorp collection of historical corpora and resources', in Eetu Mäkelä, Mikko Tolonen and Jouni Tuominen (eds.), *DHN 2018: Proceedings of the Digital Humanities in the Nordic Countries 3rd Conference*. Helsinki: University of Helsinki, pp. 306–20

Pettersson, Jonatan 2019. 'The Swedish Bible translations and the transition from Old Swedish to Early Modern Swedish', in Mikko Kauko, Miika Norro, Kirsi-Maria Nummila, Tanja Toropainen and Tuomo Fonsén (eds.), *Languages in the Lutheran Reformation: Textual Networks and the Spread of Ideas*. Amsterdam: Amsterdam University Press, pp. 129–48

Petti, Anthony G. 1977. *English Literary Hands from Chaucer to Dryden*. Cambridge, MA: Harvard University Press

Pharao Hansen, Marcus 2016. 'How to spell Nahuatl? Nawatl? Nauatl?', http://nahuatlstudies.blogspot.com/2016/07/how-to-spell-nahuatl-nawatl-nauatl.html

Pharo, Lars K. 2015. 'Authorities of scriptural technologies in America', in Vincent L. Wimbush (ed.), *Scripturalizing the Human: The Written as the Political*. New York/London: Routledge, 150–75

Pheifer, Joseph D. 1974. *Old English Glosses in the Épinal-Erfurt Glossary*. Oxford: Clarendon Press

Phillips, Betty S. 2006. *Word Frequency and Lexical Diffusion*. New York: Palgrave Macmillan

Pierini, Rachele 2014. 'Ricerche sul segno 25 del sillabario miceneo', in Alberto Bernabé and Eugenio R. Luján (eds.), *Donum Mycenologicum: Mycenaean Studies in Honour of Francisco Aura Jorro*. Leuven/Walpole: Peeters, pp. 105–37

Pilz, Thomas, Ernst-Gerlach, Andrea, Kempken, Sebastian, Rayson, Paul and Archer, Dawn 2007. 'The identification of spelling variants in English and German historical texts: manual or automatic?' *Literary and Linguistic Computing* 23 (1): 65–72, https://doi.org/10.1093/llc/fqm044

Piotrowski, Michael 2012. *Natural Language Processing for Historical Texts*. San Rafael: Morgan and Claypool

Pisowicz, Andrzej 2014 [2001]. *Gramatyka ormiańska (grabar – aszcharabar)*. Kraków: Księgarnia Akademicka

2000. 'Ormianie polscy. Problem świadomości narodowej a kwestia języka', in Maria Bobrownicka (ed.), *Język a tożsamość narodowa: Slavica*. Kraków: Towarzystwo Autorów i Wydawców Prac Naukowych "Universitas", pp. 135–42

Plans, Antonio S. 2004. 'Los lenguajes especiales y de las minorías en el Siglo de Oro', in Cano Aguilar, Rafael (ed.), *Historia de la lengua española*. Barcelona: Ariel, pp. 771–97

Pleij, Herman 1982. *De wereld volgens Thomas van der Noot, boekdrukker en uitgever te Brussel in het eerste kwart van de zestiende eeuw*. Muiderberg: Dirk Coutinho

2010. 'Printing as a long-term revolution', in Hanno Wijsman (ed.), *Books in Transition at the Time of Philip the Fair. Manuscripts and Printed Books in the Late Fifteenth and Early Sixteenth Century Low Countries*. Turnhout: Brepols Publishers, pp. 297–307

Pleij, Herman and Reynaert, Joris 2004. 'Inleiding. Boekproductie in de overgang van het geschreven naar het gedrukte boek', in Herman Pleij and Joris Reynaert (eds.), *Geschreven en gedrukt. Boekproductie van handschrift naar druk in de overgang van de Middeleeuwen naar de moderne tijd*. Ghent: Academia Press, pp. 1–18

Pocklington, Robert 1986. 'El sustrato arábigo-granadino en la formación de los dialectos orientales del andaluz', *Revista de Filología Española* 61: 75–100

Pope, Maurice 1999. *The Story of Decipherment: From Egyptian Hieroglyphs to Maya Script*. London: Thames and Hudson (revised ed.)

2008. 'The decipherment of Linear B', in Yves Duhoux and Anna Morpurgo Davies (eds.), *A Companion to Linear B: Mycenaean Greek Texts and Their World*, vol. 1. Leuven: Peeters, pp. 1–23

Popp, Daniel 1977. *Asbjørnsen's linguistic reform. I Orthography*. Oslo/Bergen/Tromsø: Universitetsforlaget

Portebois, Yannick 2003. 'La réforme de l'orthographe, une affaire d'état', *Histoire, Épistémologie, Langage* 25 (1): 71–85

Poser, William. J. 1992. 'The structural typology of phonological writing'. Oral presentation at the annual meeting of the Linguistic Society of America, Philadelphia, USA

Poussa, Patricia 1982. 'The evolution of early standard English', *Studia Anglica Posnaniensia* 14: 69–85

Pountain, Christopher J. 2016. 'Standardization', in Adam Ledgeway and Martin Maiden (eds.), *The Oxford Guide to the Romance Languages*. Oxford: Oxford University Press, pp. 634–43

Pouzet, Jean-Pascal 2011. 'Book production outside commercial contexts', in Alexandra Gillespie and Daniel Wakelin (eds.), *The Production of Books in England 1350–1500* (Cambridge Studies in Palaeography and Codicology 14). Cambridge: Cambridge University Press, pp. 212–38

Powell, Barry B. 2009. *Writing: Theory and History of the Technology of Civilization*. Chichester: Wiley-Blackwell

Powers, David S. 2009. 'Chapter 8: Paleography and codicology: Bibliothèque nationale de France, Arabe 328a', in *Muhammad Is Not the Father of Any of Your Men: The Making of the Last Prophet*. Philadelphia: University of Pennsylvania Press

Prakulevičius, Stanislovas, 1879-01-05: *Letter to Mykolas Godliauskis and His Family*. Vilnius University Library, Manuscript collection: F. 1 – E441.

Preston, Dennis 2000. 'Mowr and mowr bayud spellin': confessions of a sociolinguist', in Alexandra M. Jaffe (ed.), *Non-Standard Orthography*, special issue of *Journal of Sociolinguistics* 4 (4): 614–21

Pride, John 1971. *The Social Meaning of Language*. London: Oxford University Press

Primus, Beatrice 2003. 'Zum Silbenbegriff in der Schrift-, Laut- und Gebärdensprache - Versuch einer mediumübergreifenden Fundierung', *Zeitschrift für Sprachwissenschaft* 22 (1): 3–55

2004. 'A featural analysis of the modern Roman alphabet', in Martin Neef and Beatrice Primus (eds.), *From Letter to Sound: New Perspectives on Writing Systems*, special issue of *Written Language and Literacy* 7 (2). Amsterdam/Philadelphia: John Benjamins, pp. 235–74

2006. 'Buchstabenkomponenten und ihre Grammatik', in Ursula Bredel and Hartmut Günther (eds.), *Orthographietheorie und Rechtschreibunterricht*. Tübingen: Niemeyer, pp. 5–43

2007. 'The typological and historical variation of punctuation systems: comma constraints', in Guido Nottbusch and Eliane Segers (eds.), *Constraints on Spelling Changes*, special issue of *Written Language and Literacy* 10 (2). Amsterdam/Philadelphia: John Benjamins, pp. 103–28

2010. 'Strukturelle Grundlagen des deutschen Schriftsystems', in Ursula Bredel, Astrid Müller and Gabriele Hinney (eds.), *Schriftsystem und Schrifterwerb: linguistisch – didaktisch – empirisch*. Tübingen: Niemeyer, pp. 9–45

2011. 'Buchstabendekomposition – Replik auf Oliver Rezec', *Linguistische Berichte* 225: 63–76

Prosdocimi, Aldo L. 1983. 'Puntuazione sillabica e insegnamento della scrittura nel venetico e nelle fonti etrusche', *AION (Ling)* 5: 75–126

1984. *Le Tavole Iguvine*, vol. 1. Florence: Leo S. Olschki

Puchmír, Jaroslav 1851. *Pravopis rusko-český*. Prague: Bohumil Haase (2nd ed.)

Puelles Benítez, Manuel 2010. *Estado y educación en la España liberal, 1809–1857. Un sistema educativo nacional frustrado*. Barcelona: Pomares

Pulgram, Ernst 1951. 'Phoneme and grapheme: a parallel', *Word* 7: 15–20

Putschke, Wolfgang 1998. 'Die Arbeiten der Junggrammatiker und ihr Beitrag zur Sprachgeschichtsforschung', in Werner Besch, Anne Betten, Oskar Reichmann and Stefan Sonderegger (eds.), *Sprachgeschichte: Ein Handbuch zur Geschichte der deutschen Sprache und ihrer Erforschung* (Handbücher zur Sprach- und Kommunikationswissenschaft, 2.1). Berlin: De Gruyter, pp. 474–94 (2nd ed.)

Puttenham, George 1968 [1589]. *The Arte of English Poesie*. Menston: Scholar Press

Quintilian 1920. *Institution Oratoria* (with a translation by Harold E. Butler). Cambridge, MA: Harvard University Press

Rabasa, José 1993. 'Writing and evangelization in sixteenth-century Mexico', in Jerry Williams and Robert Lewis (eds.), *Early Images of the Americas: Transfer and Invention*. Tucson: University of Arizona Press, pp. 65–92

Rada Języka Polskiego przy Prezydium PAN (ed.) 2007. *Język polski*. Warsaw: Rada Języka Polskiego przy Prezydium PAN

Radziszewska, Iwona 2015. *'Przegląd autorskich systemów transliteracji i transkrypcji. Uwagi do zestawienia tabelarycznego'*, in Joanna Kulwicka-Kamińska and Czesław Łapicz (eds.), *Tefsir Tatarów Wielkiego Księstwa Litewskiego: Teoria i praktyka badawcza. Toruń: Wydział Filologiczny UMK*, pp. 173–94, www.tefsir.umk.pl/pliki/Tefsir_Tatarow_WKL.pdf

Rambaran-Olm, Mary R. 2014. 'Chapter 1: Palaeography, codicology and language', in *'John the Baptist's Prayer' or 'The Descent to Hell' from the Exeter Book: Text, Translation and Critical Study*. Rochester: Boydell and Brewer

Ramírez Aisa, Elías 2003. *Educación y control en los orígenes de la España liberal*. Madrid: UNED/Biblioteca Nueva

Raschellà, Fabrizio 1994. 'Rune e alfabeto latino nel trattato grammaticale di Óláfr Þórðarson', in Gísli Sigurðsson, Guðrún Kvaran and Sigurgeir Steingrímsson (eds.), *Sagnaþing helgað Jónasi Kristjánssyni sjötugum 10. apríl 1994*. Reykjavík: Hið íslenska bókmenntafélag, pp. 679–90

Raubicheck, Letitia E., Davis, Estelle H. and Carll, Lydia A. 1940. *Voice and Speech Problems*, New York: Prentice-Hall

Remacle, Louis 1948. *Le problème de l'ancien wallon*. Liège: Faculté de Philosophie et Lettres

Rambø, Gro-Renée 2018. 'Det selvstendige Norge 1905–1945', in Agnete Nesse (ed.), *Tidslinjer*, vol. 4 of Helge Sandøy and Agnete Nesse (eds.), *Norsk språkhistorie*. Oslo: Novus, pp. 503–602

Rastle, Kathleen 2019. 'EPS mid-career prize lecture 2017: writing systems, reading, and language', *Quarterly Journal of Experimental Psychology* 72 (4): 677–92

Rauch, Irmengard and Carr, Gerald F. (eds.) 1979. *Linguistic Method: Essays in Honor of Herbert Penzl* (Janua linguarum. Series maior 79). The Hague: Mouton

Raumolin-Brunberg, Helena and Nevalainen, Terttu 1990. 'Dialectal features in a corpus of Early Modern Standard English?', in Graham Caie, Kirsten Haastrup, Arnt Lykke Jakobsen, Jørgen Erik Nielsen, Jørgen Sevaldsen, Henrik Specht and Arne Zettersten (eds.), *Proceedings from the Fourth Nordic Conference for English* Studies, vol. 1. Copenhagen: Department of English, University of Copenhagen, pp. 119–131

Raven, James 2007. *The Business of Books: Booksellers and the English Book Trade 1450–1850*. New Haven: Yale University Press

Ravida, Fausto 2012. *Graphematisch-phonologische Analyse der Luxemburger Rechnungsbücher (1388–1500). Ein Beitrag zur historischen Stadtsprachenforschung*. Heidelberg: Winter

Raymond, Joad 2011. 'Development of the book trade', in Joad Raymond (ed.), *The Oxford History of Popular Print Culture*, vol. 1: *Cheap Print in Britain and in Ireland to 1660*. Oxford: Oxford University Press, pp. 59–75

Rayner, Keith and Pollatsek, Alexander 1989. *The Psychology of Reading*. Englewood Cliffs: Prentice Hall

Read, Charles 1983. 'Orthography', in Margaret Martlew (ed.), *The Psychology of Written Language: Developmental and Educational Perspectives*. New York: John Wiley and Sons, pp. 143–62

Read, Charles, Zhang Yun-Fei, Nie Hong-Yin and Ding Bao-Qing 1986. 'The ability to manipulate speech sounds depends on knowing alphabetic writing', *Cognition* 24: 31–44

Real Academia Española 1815. *Ortografía de la lengua castellana*. Madrid: Imprenta Real (8th ed.)

1884. *Diccionario de la lengua castellana por la Real Academia Española*. Madrid: Imprenta de Gregorio Hernando (12th ed.)

1999. *Ortografía de la lengua española*. Madrid: Espasa

Real Academia Española and Asociación de Academias de la Lengua Española 2010. *Ortografía de la lengua española*. Madrid: Espasa Calpe

Real Academia Española and Asociación de Academias de la Lengua Española 2019. *Gramática y ortografía básicas de la lengua española*. Madrid: Espasa Calpe

Recasens, Daniel 2012. 'A phonetic interpretation of the sound changes affecting dark /l/ in Romance', in Maria-Josep Solé and Daniel Recasens (eds.), *The Initiation of Sound Change: Perception, Production, and Social Factors*. Amsterdam/Philadelphia: John Benjamins, pp. 57–76

Reczek, Józef 1987. 'Językowa polonizacja Ormian', *Język Polski* 67 (1–2): 1–8

Reid, S. W. 1974. 'Justification and spelling in Jaggard's Compositor B', *Studies in Bibliography* 27: 91–111

Reiner, Erica 2000. 'The Sumerian and Akkadian linguistic tradition', in Sylvain Auroux, Ernst F. K. Koerner, Hans-Josef Niederehe and Kees Versteegh (eds.), *History of the Language Sciences/Geschichte der Sprachwissenschaften/Histoire des sciences du langage*. Berlin/Boston: De Gruyter, pp. 1–5.

Rem, Margit 2003. *De taal van de klerken uit de Hollandse grafelijke kanselarij (1300–1340). Naar een lokaliseringsprocedure voor het veertiende-eeuwse Middelnederlands*. Amsterdam: Stichting Neerlandistiek VU

Reyes Equiguas, Salvador 2016. 'El scriptorium del Colegio de la Santa Cruz de Tlatelolco a través de los códices Florentino y De la Cruz-Badiano', in Esther Hernández and Pilar Máynez (eds.), *El Colegio de Tlatelolco: Síntesis de Historias, Lenguas y Culturas*. Mexico City: Destiempos, pp. 26–38

Rezec, Oliver 2010. 'Der vermeintliche Zusammenhang zwischen Buchstabenformen und Lautwerten. Erwiderung auf einige Thesen von Beatrice Primus', *Linguistische Berichte* 223: 343–66

2011. 'Der vermeintliche Zusammenhang zwischen Buchstabenformen und Lautwerten. Zweite Erwiderung', *Linguistische Berichte* 225: 89–100

2013. 'Ein differenziertes Strukturmodell des deutschen Schriftsystems', *Linguistische Berichte* 234: 227–54

Rice, Keren and Saxon, Leslie 2002. 'Issues of standardization and community in Aboriginal language lexicography', in William Frawley, Kenneth C. Hill and Pamela Munro (eds.), *Making Dictionaries. Preserving Indigenous Languages of the Americas*. Berkeley: University of California Press, pp. 125–54

Ricento, Thomas 2006. 'Language policy: theory and planning. An introduction', in Thomas Ricento (ed.), *Language Policy: Theory and Planning*. Malden/Oxford: Blackwell, pp. 10–23

Richardson, Brian 2001. 'Questions of language', in Zygmunt G. Barański and Rebecca J. West (eds.), *The Cambridge Companion to Modern Italian Culture*. Cambridge/New York: Cambridge University Press, pp. 63–80

Richardson, Kay P. 2018. 'Spelling-gate: politics, propriety and power', *Journal of Language and Politics* 17 (6): 812–30, https://doi.org/10.1075/jlp.17072.ric

Richardson, Malcolm 1980. 'Henry V, the English Chancery and Chancery English', *Speculum* 55: 726–50

Rickard, Peter 1989. *A History of the French Language*. London: Unwin Hyman (2nd ed.)

Rickford, John and Eckert, Penelope 2001. 'Introduction', in Penelope Eckert and John Rickford (eds.), *Style and Sociolinguistic Variation*. Cambridge: Cambridge University Press, 1–18

Rimzhim, Anurag, Katz, Leonard and Fowler, Carol A. 2014. 'Brāhmī-derived orthographies are typologically Āksharik but functionally predominantly alphabetic', *Writing Systems Research* 6: 41–53

Rinas, Karsten 2017. *Theorie der Punkte und Striche. Die Geschichte der deutschen Interpunktionslehre*. Heidelberg: Winter

Ringe, Don and Taylor, Ann 2014. *The Development of Old English*. Oxford: Oxford University Press

Risch, Ernst 1957. 'Mykenisch wo-wo ko-to-no', *Minos* 5: 28–34

Risch, Ernst and Hajnal, Ivo 2006. *Grammatik des mykenischen Griechisch*, http://sprawi.at/de/content/mykenisches_griechisch

Rissanen, Matti 2012. 'Corpora and the study of the history of English', in Merja Kytö (ed.), *English Corpus Linguistics: Crossing Paths*. Amsterdam/ New York: Rodopi, pp. 197–220

Rissanen, Matti, Kytö, Merja, Kahlas-Tarkka, Leena, Kilpiö, Matti, Nevanlinna, Saara, Taavitsainen, Irma, Nevalainen, Terttu and Raumolin-Brunberg, Helena (compilers) 1991. *The Helsinki Corpus of English Texts*. Department of Modern Languages, University of Helsinki, https://varieng.helsinki.fi/series/volumes/14/rissanen_tyrkko/

Risse, Ursula 1980. *Untersuchungen zum Gebrauch der Majuskel in deutschsprachigen Bibeln des 16. Jahrhunderts: ein historischer Beitrag zur Diskussion um die Substantivgroßschreibung* (Studien zum Frühneuhochdeutschen 5). Heidelberg: Winter

Rix, Helmut 1985. 'Descrizioni di rituali in etrusco e in italico', in Adriana Quattordio (ed.), *L'etrusco e le lingue dell'Italia antica. Atti del Convegno della Società italiana di glottologia, Pisa, 8 e 9 dicembre 1984*. Pisa: Giardini, pp. 21–37

2002. *Sabellische Texte. Die Texte des Oskischen, Umbrischen und Südpikenischen*. Heidelberg: Winter

Rizvi, Pervez 2016. 'The use of spellings for compositor attribution in the First Folio', *The Papers of the Bibliographical Society of America* 110 (1): 1–53, https://doi.org/10.1086/685663

Roberge, Paul T. 2003. 'Afrikaans', in Ana Deumert and Wim Vandenbussche (eds.), *Germanic Standardizations: Past to Present*. Amsterdam/ Philadelphia: John Benjamins, pp. 15–40

Roberts, David 2011. 'A tone orthography typology', in Susanne R. Borgwaldt and Terry Joyce (eds.), *Typology of Writing Systems*, special issue of *Written Language and Literacy* 14 (1). Amsterdam/Philadelphia: John Benjamins, pp. 82–108

Roberts, Jane 2005. *Guide to Scripts Used in English Writings Up to 1500*. London: The British Library

Robertson, John S. 2004. 'The possibility and actuality of writing', in Stephen D. Houston (ed.), *The First Writing: Script Invention as History and Process*. Cambridge: Cambridge University Press, pp. 16–38

Robinson, Andrew 1995. *The Story of Writing: Alphabets, Hieroglyphs and Pictograms*. London: Thames and Hudson

2009. *Writing and Script: A Very Short Introduction*. Oxford: Oxford University Press

Rocha, Luis M. 1998. 'Selected self-organization and the semiotics of evolutionary systems', in Gertrudis van de Vijver, Stanley N. Salthe and Manuela Delpos (eds.), *Evolutionary Systems: Biological and Epistemological Perspectives on Selection and Self-Organization*. Dordrecht: Kluwer Academic Publishers, pp. 341–58

Rogers, Henry 2005. *Writing Systems: A Linguistic Approach*. Malden: Blackwell

Rogos, Justyna 2013. 'Crafting text language: spelling systems in manuscripts of the "Man of Law's Tale" as a means of constructing scribal community of practice', in Joanna Kopaczyk and Andreas H. Jucker (eds.), *Communities of Practice in the History of English*. Amsterdam/ Philadelphia: John Benjamins, pp. 105–21

Rogos-Hebda, Justyna 2016. 'The visual text: bibliographic codes as pragmatic markers on a manuscript page', *Studia Anglica Posnaniensia* 51 (3): 37–44

2020. 'Visual pragmatics of abbreviations and otiose strokes in John Lydgate's *Siege of Thebes*', *Journal of Historical Pragmatics* 21 (1): 1–27

2023. 'Multimodal contexts for visual code-switching: scribal practices in two manuscrips of Gower's *Confessio Amantis*', in Matylda Włodarczyk, Jukka Tyrkkö and Elżbieta Adamczyk (eds.), *Multilingualism from Manuscript to 3D: Intersections of Multimodalities from Medieval to Modern Times*. London: Routledge, pp. 19–34

Rollings, Andrew G. 2004. *The Spelling Patterns of English*. Munich: Lincom

Romaine, Suzanne 1982. *Socio-Historical Linguistics: Its Status and Methodology*. Cambridge: Cambridge University Press

1998. 'Introduction', in Suzanne Romaine (ed.), *The Cambridge History of the English Language*, vol. 4: *1776–1997*. Cambridge: Cambridge University Press, pp. 1–56

Romero-Barranco, Jesús 2020. 'Spelling normalisation and POS-tagging of historical corpora: the case of GUL, MS Hunter 135 (ff. 34r–121v)', in Miguel Fuster-Márquez, Carmen Gregori-Signes and José Santaemilia Ruiz (eds.), *Multiperspectives in Analysis and Corpus Design*. Granada: Comares, pp. 103–14

Rosa, Jonathan and Flores, Nelson 2017. 'Unsettling race and language: toward a raciolinguistic perspective', *Language in Society* 46: 621–47

Rosenblat, Ángel 1951. 'Las ideas ortográficas de Bello', in Ángel Rosenblat, *Obras completes*, vol. 5: *Estudios gramaticales*. Caracas: Ministerio de Educación, pp. ix–cxxxviii

Rosenthal, Bernard, Adams, Gretchen A., Burns, Margo, Grund, Peter J., Hiltunen, Risto, Kahlas-Tarkka, Leena, Kytö, Merja, Peikola, Matti, Ray, Benjamin C., Rissanen, Matti, Roach, Marilynne K. and Trask, Richard B. (eds.) 2009. *Records of the Salem Witch-Hunt*. Cambridge: Cambridge University Press

Rospocher, Massimo, Salman, Jeroen and Hannu, Salmi (eds.) 2019. *Crossing Borders, Crossing Cultures: Popular Print in Europe (1450–1900)*. Berlin/ Boston: De Gruyter

Rospond, Stanisław 1953. 'Problem genezy polskiego języka literackiego: uwagi polemiczne do artykułów T. Milewskiego oraz W. Taszyckiego', *Pamiętnik Literacki* 44 (2): 512–47

Rössing-Hagar, Monika 2000. 'Frühe grammatische Beschreibungen des Deutschen', in Sylvain Auroux, Ernst F. K. Koerner, Hans-Josef Niederehe and Kees Versteegh (eds.), *History of the Language Sciences/ Geschichte der Sprachwissenschaften/Histoire des sciences du langage*. Berlin/Boston: De Gruyter, pp. 777–84

Rössler, Paul 2000. 'Von der Virgel zum Slash. Zur Zeichensetzung zwischen Gutenberg und Internet', *Zeitschrift für Germanistik* 3: 508–20

2005. *Schreibvariation, Sprachregion, Konfession. Graphematik und Morphologie in österreichischen und bayerischen Drucken vom 16. bis ins 18. Jahrhundert*. Frankfurt am Main: Peter Lang

Rössler, Paul, Besl, Peter and Saller, Anna (eds.) 2021. *Vergleichende Interpunktion – Comparative Punctuation*. Berlin/New York: De Gruyter

Rothstein, Robert 1977. 'Spelling and society: the Polish orthographic controversy of the 1930s', in Benjamin Stolz (ed.), *Papers in Slavic Philology I*. Ann Arbor: University of Michigan, pp. 225–36

Rozhdestvenskaia͡, Tat'i͡ana V. 1992. *Drevnerusskie nadpisi na stenakh khramov: novye istochniki XI–XV vv*. Saint Petersburg: Izdatel'stvo Sankt-Peterburgskogo universiteta

Ruge, Nikolaus 2004. *Aufkommen und Durchsetzung morphembezogener Schreibungen im Deutschen 1500–1770*. Heidelberg: Winter

2013. 'Graphematik', in Martin Neef, Said Sahel and Rüdiger Weingarten (eds.), *Schriftlinguistik/ Grapholinguistics* (Wörterbücher zur Sprach- und Kommunikationswissenschaft/Dictionaries of Linguistics and Communication Science 5). Berlin/Boston: De Gruyter, www.degruyter .com/view/db/wsk

Ruijgh, Cornelius 1985. 'Problèmes de philologie mycénienne', *Minos* 19: 105–67

Rumble, Alexander R. 1994. 'Using Anglo-Saxon manuscripts', in Mary P. Richards (ed.), *Anglo-Saxon Paleography: Basic Readings*. New York: Garland Press, 3–24

Ruscelli, Girolamo 1595. *The Secrets of the Reuerend Maister Alexis of Piemont, Containing Excellent Remedies Against Diuerse Diseases, Wounds, and Other Accidents*. London: Peter Short

Russell, James R. 2006. Review of *Album of Armenian Paleography* by Michael E. Stone, Dickran Kouymjian and Henning Lehmann, *Speculum* 81 (1): 278–79

Russi, Cinzia (ed.) 2016. 'Introduction', in Cizia Russi (ed.), *Current Trends in Historical Sociolinguistics*. Berlin: De Gruyter, pp. 1–18

Russon, Allien R. 2016. 'Shorthand', *Encyclopedia Britannica Online*, www .britannica.com/topic/shorthand

Ruszkiewicz, Piotr 1972. 'Tytus Benni's views on English graphemics', *Acta Philologica* 5: 5–37

1976. *Modern Approaches to Graphophonemic Investigations in English.* Katowice: Uniwersytet Śląski

1978. 'Jan Baudouin de Courtenay's theory of the grapheme', *Acta Philologica* 7: 111–28

Rutkowska, Hanna 2003. *Graphemics and Morphosyntax in the* Cely Letters *(1472–88).* Frankfurt am Main: Peter Lang

2005. 'Selected orthographic features in English editions of the *Book of good maners (1487–1507)*', *SELIM* 12 (2003–2004): 127–42

2012. 'Linguistic levels: orthography', in Alexander Bergs and Laurel J. Brinton (eds.), *English Historical Linguistics. An International Handbook*, vol. 1. Berlin/Boston: De Gruyter, pp. 224–37

2013a. *Orthographic Systems in Thirteen Editions of the* Kalender of Shepherdes *(1506–1656).* Berlin: Peter Lang

2013b. 'Typographical and graphomorphemic features of five editions of the *Kalender of Shepherdes* as elements of the early printers' community of practice', in Joanna Kopaczyk and Andreas H. Jucker (eds.), *Communities of Practice in the History of English.* Amsterdam/Philadelphia: John Benjamins, pp. 123–49

2013c. 'Towards regularisation: morphological spelling in several editions of the *Kalender of Shepherdes*', *Studia Anglica Posnaniensia* 48 (1): 7–28

2015a. 'Late medieval dialectal and obsolescent spellings in the sixteenth-century editions of the *Kalender of Shepherdes*', in Juan Camilo Conde-Silvestre and Javier Calle-Martín (eds.), *Approaches to Middle English.* Frankfurt am Main: Peter Lang, pp. 129–47

2015b. Review of *Orthographies in Early Modern Europe* by Susan Baddeley and Anja Voeste (eds.), *Journal of Historical Sociolinguistics* 1 (2): 297–302

2016. 'Orthographic regularization in Early Modern English printed books: grapheme distribution and vowel length indication', in Cinzia Russi (ed.), *Current Trends in Historical Sociolinguistics.* Warsaw/Berlin: De Gruyter, pp. 165–93

2017. 'Orthography', in Alexander Bergs and Laurel Brinton (eds.), *The History of English*, vol. 1: *Historical Outlines from Sound to Text.* Berlin: De Gruyter, pp. 200–17

2020a. 'Morphological spelling: present-tense verb inflection in the early editions of *The Book of Good Maners*', *International Journal of English Studies* 20 (2): 31–45

2020b. 'Visual pragmatics of an early modern book: printers' paratextual choices in the editions of *The School of Vertue*, in Caroline Tagg and Mel Evans (eds.), *Message and Medium: English Language Practices across Old and New Media* (Topics in English Linguistics 105). Berlin: De Gruyter Mouton, pp. 199–231

Rutkowska, Hanna and Rössler, Paul 2012. 'Orthographic variables', in Juan Manuel Hernández-Campoy and Juan Camilo Conde-Silvestre (eds.), *The Handbook of Historical Sociolinguistics*. Chichester: Wiley-Blackwell, pp. 213–36

Rutten, Gijsbert 2016a. 'Historicizing diaglossia', *Journal of Sociolinguistics* 20 (1): 6–30

2016b. 'Diaglossia, individual variation and the limits of standardization: evidence from Dutch', in Cinzia Russi (ed.), *Current Trends in Historical Sociolinguistics*. Berlin: De Gruyter, pp. 194–218

2019. *Language Planning as Nation Building. Ideology, Policy and Implementation in the Netherlands, 1750–1850*. Amsterdam/Philadelphia: Benjamins

Rutten, Gijsbert and Krogull, Andreas 2022. 'The observee's paradox: theorizing linguistic differences between historical ego-documents', *Neuphilologische Mitteilungen* 122 (1–2): 284–318

Rutten, Gijsbert, Krogull, Andreas and Schoemaker, Bob 2020. 'Implementation and acceptance of national language policy: the case of Dutch (1750–1850)', *Language Policy* 19: 259–79

Rutten, Gijsbert and van der Wal, Marijke J. 2011. 'Local dialects, supralocal writing systems: the degree of orality of Dutch private letters from the seventeenth century', *Written Language and Literacy* 14 (2): 251–74

2014. *Letters as Loot: A Sociolinguistic Approach to Seventeenth- and Eighteenth-Century Dutch*. Amsterdam/Philadelphia: John Benjamin, https://doi.org/10.1075/ahs.2

2018. 'Dutch private letters from the seventeenth and eighteenth centuries: the linguistic experiences of the lower and middle ranks', in Joachim Steffen Harald Thun and Rainer Zaiser (eds.), *Classes populaires, scripturalité, et histoire de la langue. Un bilan interdisciplinaire*. Kiel: Westensee-Verlag, pp. 227–49

Rutten, Gijsbert and Vosters, Rik 2010. 'Chaos and standards: orthography in the southern Netherlands (1720–1830)', *Multilingua* 29 (3–4): 417–38, https://doi.org/10.1515/mult.2010.020

2013. 'Une tradition néerlandaise? Du bon usage aux Pays-Bas (1686–1830)', in Wendy Ayres-Bennett and Magali Seijido (eds.), *Bon usage et variation sociolinguistique. Perspectives diachroniques et traditions nationales*. Lyon: Éditions de l'École Normale Supérieure (ENS), pp. 233–43

Rutten, Gijsbert, Vosters, Rik and Vandenbussche, Wim (eds.) 2014. *Norms and Usage in Language History, 1600–1900: A Sociolinguistic and Comparative Perspective*. Amsterdam/Philadelphia: John Benjamins

Ruus, Hanne 2005. 'The development of Danish from the mid-16th century to 1800', in Oskar Bandle, Kurt Braunmüller, Ernst H. Jahr, Allan Karker, Hans-Peter Naumann and Ulf Teleman (eds.), *The Nordic Languages: An International Handbook of the History of the North Germanic Languages* (Handbücher zur Sprach- und Kommunikationswissenschaft 22.2). Berlin: De Gruyter, pp. 1282–91

Ryan, Des 2016. 'Linguists' descriptions of the English writing system', in Vivian Cook and Des Ryan (eds.), *The Routledge Handbook of the English Writing System*. London/New York: Routledge, pp. 41–64

2017. 'Principles of English spelling formation'. Doctoral dissertation, Trinity College Dublin, Ireland, www.academia.edu/36177552/Principles_of_English_spelling_formation_final_Ph.D._thesis_

Rypins, Stanley (ed.) 1998. *Three Old English Prose Texts in MS.* Cotton Vitellius A xv (Early English Text Society OS 161). London: Oxford University Press

Saenger, Paul 1997. *Space between Words: The Origins of Silent Reading* (Figurae: Reading Medieval Culture). Stanford: Stanford University Press

2000. *Space between Words. The Origins of Silent Reading.* Palo Alto: Stanford University Press (paperback ed.)

Sahle, Patrick 2013. *Digitale Editionsformen. Zum Umgang mit der Überlieferung unter den Bedingungen des Medienwandels.* 3 Bände. Norderstedt: Books on Demand

Sairio, Anni. 2009. *Language and Letters of the Bluestocking Network: Sociolinguistic Issues in Eighteenth-Century Epistolary English* (Mémoires de La Société Néophilologique de Helsinki 75). Helsinki: Société Néophilologique

2010. '"if You think me obstinate I can't help it": exploring the epistolary styles and social roles of Elizabeth Montagu and Sarah Scott', in Päivi Pahta, Minna Nevala, Arja Nurmi and Minna Palander-Collin (eds.), *Social Roles and Language Practices in Late Modern English*. Amsterdam: John Benjamins, pp. 87–109

2013. 'Elizabeth Montagu's Shakespeare essay (1769): the final draft and the first edition as evidence of two communities of practice', in Joanna Kopaczyk and Andreas H. Jucker (eds.), *Communities of Practice in the History of English*. Amsterdam: John Benjamins, pp. 177–97

2017. *Bluestocking Corpus: Letters of Elizabeth Montagu, 1730s–1780s*. Helsinki: University of Helsinki, http://bluestocking.ling.helsinki.fi/

2018. 'Weights and measures of eighteenth-century language: a sociolinguistic account of Montagu's correspondence', *Huntington Library Quarterly* 81 (4): 633–56, https://doi.org/10.1353/hlq.2018.0024

Sairio, Anni, Kaislaniemi, Samuli, Merikallio, Anna and Nevalainen, Terttu 2018. 'Charting orthographical reliability in a corpus of English historical letters', *ICAME Journal* 42 (1): 79–96, https://doi.org/10.1515/icame-2018-0005

Salgarella, Ester 2018. 'Some thoughts on Mycenaean o-u-qe', in Anna Margherita Jasink and Maria E. Alberti (eds.), *Akrothinia 2: Contributi di giovani ricercatori agli studi egei e ciprioti*. Florence: Firenze University Press, pp. 249–57

2019a. 'Non-connective behaviour of the particle -qe in the Linear B documents from Pylos', *Studi Micenei ed Egeo-Anatolici. Nuova Serie* 5: 71–84

2019b. 'Form and function of clausal particles in the Mycenaean documents from Pylos', *Journal of Greek Linguistics* 19: 196–214

2020. *Aegean Linear Script(s): Rethinking the Relationship between Linear A and Linear B*. Cambridge: Cambridge University Press

2021. 'Imagining Cretan scripts: the influence of visual motifs on the creation of script-signs in Bronze Age Crete', *Annual of the British School at Athens* 116: 63–94, https://doi.org/10.1017/S0068245421000034

Salmon, Vivian 1999. 'Orthography and punctuation', in Roger Lass (ed.), *The Cambridge History of the English Language*, vol. 3: *1476–1776*. Cambridge: Cambridge University Press, pp. 13–55

Salomies, Olli 2015. 'The Roman Republic', in Christer Bruun and Jonathan Edmondson (eds.), *The Oxford Handbook of Roman Epigraphy*. Oxford: Oxford University Press, pp. 153–77

Sampson, Geoffrey 1985. *Writing Systems: A Linguistic Introduction*. London: Hutchinson/Stanford: Stanford University Press

1994. 'Chinese script and the diversity of writing systems', *Linguistics* 32: 117–32

2015. *Writing Systems*. Sheffield: Equinox (2nd ed.)

2016a. 'Typology and the study of writing systems', *Linguistic Typology* 20 (3): 561–67

2016b. 'Writing systems: methods for recording language', in Keith Allan (ed.), *The Routledge Handbook of Linguistics*. London/New York: Routledge, pp. 47–61

2018a. 'The redundancy of self-organization as an explanation of English spelling', *Language* 94 (1): e43–e47

2018b. 'From phonemic spelling to distinctive spelling', in Merijn Beeksma and Martin Neef (eds.), *Understanding Writing Systems*, special issue of *Written Language and Literacy* 21 (1). Amsterdam/Philadelphia: John Benjamins, pp. 3–25

Samuels, Michael L. 1963. 'Some applications of Middle English dialectology', *English Studies* 44 (2): 81–94

1969 [1963]. 'Some applications of Middle English dialectology', in Roger Lass (ed.), *Approaches to English Historical Linguistics*. New York: Holt, Rinehart and Winston, pp. 404–18 (reprinted from *English Studies*, 44, pp. 81–94)

1972. *Linguistic Evolution, with Special Reference to English*. Cambridge: Cambridge University Press

1981. 'Spelling and dialect in the late and post-Middle English periods', in Michael Benskin and Michael L. Samuels (eds.), *So Meny People Longages and Tonges: Philological Essays in Scots and Mediaeval English Presented to Angus McIntosh*. Edinburgh: Middle English Dialect Project, pp. 43–54

1989 [1963]. 'Some applications of Middle English dialectology', in Angus McIntosh, Michael L. Samuels and Margaret Laing (eds.), *Middle English Dialectology: Essays on Some Principles and Problems*. Aberdeen: Aberdeen University Press, pp. 64–80

Sánchez Méndez, Juan 2003. *Historia de la lengua española en América*. Valencia: Tirant Lo Blanc

Sánchez-Prieto Borja, Pedro 2012. 'Para una historia de la escritura romance en León, Castilla y Aragón: algunas claves interpretativas', *Medioevo romanzo* 36: 24–61

Sandoval, Rafael 1965 [1810]. 'Arte de la lengua mexicana', *Estudios de cultura náhuatl* 5: 221–76

Sandøy, Helge 1975 *Språk og politikk*. Oslo: Det norske Samlaget

2018. 'Idéhistoria om norsk språk', in Tove Bull (ed.), *Ideologi*, vol. 3 of Helge Sandøy and Agnete Nesse (eds.), *Norsk språkhistorie I–IV*. Oslo: Novus, pp. 149–243

Sandøy, Helge and Nesse, Agnete (eds.) 2016–18. *Norsk språkhistorie*, 4 vols. Oslo: Novus

Sandved, Arthur O. 1981. 'Prolegomena to a renewed study of the rise of standard English', in Michael Benskin and Michael L. Samuels (eds.), *So Meny People Longages and Tonges: Philological Essays in Scots and Mediaeval English Presented to Angus McIntosh*. Edinburgh: Middle English Dialect Project, pp. 31–42

Sanz-Sánchez, Israel 2019. 'Documenting feature pools in language expansion situations: sibilants in Early Colonial Latin American Spanish', *Transactions of the Philological Society* 117: 199–233

Sapir, Edward 1921. *Language: An Introduction to the Study of Speech*. New York: Hartcourt, Brace and Company

Sartininkai parishioners, c. 1901. *Petition letter to Bishop Mečislovas Paliulionis*. Lithuanian State Historical Archives: F. 1671, ap. 4, b. 179, 806

Sass, Benjamin 2005. *The Alphabet at the Turn of the Millennium: The West Semitic Alphabet ca. 1150–850 BCE: The Antiquity of the Arabian, Greek, and Phrygian Alphabets* (Journal of the Institute of Archaeology of Tel Aviv University Occasional Publications, 4). Tel Aviv: Emery and Claire Yass Publications in Archaeology

Sassoon, Rosemary 2004 [1995]. *The Acquisition of a Second Writing System*. Bristol: Intellect Books

Saturno, William A., Stuart, David and Beltrán, Boris 2006. 'Early Maya writing at San Bartolo, Guatemala', *Science* 311 (5765): 1281–83

Saussure, Ferdinand 1983 [1916]. *Course in General Linguistics*. London: Duckworth

1993 [1916]. *Troisième cours de linguistique générale (1910–11) d'après les Cahiers d'Emile Constantin* (ed. by Eisuke Komatsu and Roy Harris). Oxford: Pergamon Press

1995 [1916]. *Cours de linguistique générale.* Publié par Charles Bailly et Albert Séchehaye avec la collaboration de Albert Riedlinger. Édition critique préparée par Tullio de Mauro. Postface de Louis-Jean Calvet. Paris: Éditions Payot and Rivages

2011 [1916]. *Course in General Linguistics* (trans. by Wade Baskin; ed. by Perry Meisel and Haun Saussy). New York: Columbia University Press

Savage, Andrew 2008. 'Writing Tuareg: the three script options', *International Journal of the Sociology of Language* 192: 5–13

Scancarelli, Janine 1996. 'Cherokee writing', in Peter T. Daniels and William Bright (eds.), *The World's Writing Systems.* New York: Oxford University Press, pp. 587–92

Schaefer, Ursula 2006. 'The beginnings of standardization: the communicative space in fourteenth-century England', in Ursula Schaefer (ed.), *The Beginnings of Standardization: Language and Culture in Fourteenth-Century England.* Frankfurt am Main: Peter Lang, pp. 3–24

2012. 'Interdisciplinarity and historiography: spoken and written English – orality and literacy', in Alexandre Bergs and Laurel Brinton (eds.), *English Historical Linguistics: An International Handbook*, vol. 2. Berlin/Boston: De Gruyter, pp. 1274–88, https://doi.org/10.1515/9783110251609.1274

Schaeken, Jos 1995. 'Line-final word division in Russian birchbark documents', *Russian Linguistics* 19 (1): 91–108

2011a. '"Don't shoot the messenger." A pragmaphilological approach to Birchbark Letter no. 497 from Novgorod', *Russian Linguistics* 35 (1): 1–11

2011b. 'Sociolinguistic variation in Novgorod birchbark documents: the case of no. 907 and other letters', *Russian Linguistics* 35 (3): 351–59

2019. *Voices on Birchbark: Everyday Communication in Medieval Russia.* Leiden: Brill

Scherer, Carmen 2013. 'Kalb's Leber und Dienstag's Schnitzeltag: Zur funktionalen Ausdifferenzierung des Apostrophs im Deutschen', *Zeitschrift für Sprachwissenschaft* 32 (1): 75–112

Schieffelin, Bambi and Doucet, Rachelle C. 1994. 'The "real" Haitian Creole: ideology, metalinguistics, and orthographic choice', *American Ethnologist* 21 (1): 176–200

Schieffelin, Bambi, Woolard, Kathryn and Kroskrity, Paul (eds.) 1998. *Language Ideologies: Practice and Theory.* New York/Oxford: Oxford University Press

Schiegg, Markus 2015. 'The invisible language of patients from psychiatric hospital', in Anna Havinga and Nils Langer (eds.), *Invisible Languages in the 19th Century.* Oxford: Peter Lang, 71–94

2016. 'Code-switching in lower-class writing: autobiographies by patients from Southern German psychiatric hospitals (1852–1931)', *Journal of Historical Sociolinguistics* 2 (1): 47–81

2018. 'Factors of intra-speaker variation in nineteenth-century lower-class writing', *Neuphilologische Mitteilungen* 119: 101–20

Schleicher, August 1853. 'Die ersten Spaltungen des Indogermanischen Urvolkes', *Allgemeine Monatsschrift für Wissenschaft und Literatur* 3, pp. 786–87

Schlieben-Lange, Brigitte 1994. 'Geschichte der Reflexion über Schrift and Schriftlichkeit', in Hartmut Günther and Otto Ludwig (eds.), *Schrift und Schriftlichkeit/Writing and Its Use. Ein interdisziplinäres Handbuch internationaler Forschung/An Interdisciplinary Handbook of International Research*, vol. 1. Berlin/New York: De Gruyter, 102–21

Schlögl, Rudolf 2013. *Alter Glaube und moderne Welt.* Frankfurt am Main: S. Fischer Verlag

Schmandt-Besserat, Denise 1986. 'The origins of writing: an archaeologist's perspective', *Written Communication* 3 (1): 31–45

Schmid, Hans U. 1989. *Die mittelalterlichen deutschen Inschriften in Regensburg.* Frankfurt am Main: Peter Lang

Schmidt, Johannes 1872. *Die werwandtschaftsverhältnisse de indogermanischen sprachen.* Weimar: Hermann Böhlau

Schmidt, Karsten 2018. *Phonographie und Morphographie im Deutschen. Grundzüge einer wortbasierten Graphematik.* Tübingen: Stauffenburg

Schmied, Josef, Claridge, Claudia and Siemund, Rainer (compilers) 1994. *The Lampeter Corpus of Early Modern English Tracts.* Chemnitz: Chemnitz University of Technology

Schneider, Edgar W. 2002. 'Investigating variation and change in written documents', in Jack K. Chambers, Peter J. Trudgill and Natalie Schilling-Estes (eds.), *The Handbook of Language Variation and Change.* Malden: Blackwell, pp. 67–96

Schneider, Gerold, Pettersson, Eva and Percillier, Michael 2017. 'Comparing rule-based and SMT-based spelling normalisation for English historical texts', in Gerlof Bouma and Yvonne Adesam (eds.), *Proceedings of the NoDaLiDa 2017 Workshop on Processing Historical Language.* Linköping: Linköping University Electronic Press, pp. 40–46

Schoemaker, Bob and Rutten, Gijsbert 2019. 'One nation, one spelling, one school: writing education and the nationalisation of orthography in the Netherlands (1750–1850)', *Paedagogica Historica* 55: 754–71

Schoep, Ilse 2002. *The Administration of Neopalatial Crete. A Critical Assessment of the Linear A Tablets and Their Role in the Administrative Process.* Salamanca: Ediciones Universidad de Salamanca

Scholfield, Phil 2016. 'Modernization and standardization since the seventeenth century', in Vivian Cook and Des Ryan (eds.), *The Routledge*

Handbook of the English Writing System. London/New York: Routledge, pp. 143–61

Schouteet, Albert 1964. 'Inventaris van het archief van het voormalige gilde van de Librariërs en van de vereniging van de schoolmeesters te Brugge', *Handelingen van het Genootschap voor geschiedenis* (formerly *Annales de la Société d'Emulation de Bruges*) 100: 228–69

Schubart, Wilhelm 1925. *Griechische Palaeographie*. Munich: C. H. Beck'sche Verlagsbuchhandlung

Schulte, Michael 2011. 'The rise of the younger fuþark: the invisible hand of change', *NOWELE. North-Western European Language Evolution* 60/61: 45–68

2015. 'Runology and historical sociolinguistics: on runic writing and its social history in the first millennium', *Journal of Historical Sociolinguistics* 1 (1): 87–110, https://doi.org/10.1515/jhsl-2015-0004

2020. 'On the history of the dotted runes and the connexion to the British Isles', *Beiträge zur Geschichte der deutschen Sprache und Literatur* 142 (1): 1–22

Schulz, Herbert C. 1943. 'The teaching of handwriting in Tudor and Stuart times', *Huntington Library Quarterly* 6 (4): 381–425

Schwartz, Saul 2018. 'Writing Chiwere: orthography, literacy, and language revitalization', *Language & Communication* 61: 75–87

Schwarzwald, Ora R. 1998. 'Word foreignness in Modern Hebrew', *Hebrew Studies* 39: 115–142

Scragg, Donald G. 1974. *A History of English Spelling* (Mont Follick Series 3). Manchester/New York: Manchester University Press/Barnes and Noble Books

Sébastianoff, François 1991. 'Graphèmes et phonogrammes', *La Linguistique* 27 (1): 15–28

Sebba, Mark 2006. 'Ideology and alphabets in the former USSR', *Language Problems and Language Planning* 30 (2): 99–125

2007. *Spelling and Society: The Culture and Politics of Orthography around the World*. Cambridge/New York: Cambridge University Press

2009. 'Sociolinguistic approaches to writing systems research', *Writing Systems Research* 1 (1): 35–49

2011. 'Researching and theorising multilingual texts', in Mark Sebba, Shahrzad Mahootian and Carla Jonsson (eds.), *Language Mixing and Code-Switching in Writing: Approaches to Mixed-Language Written Discourse*. New York/London: Routledge, pp. 1–26

2012. 'Orthography as social action: scripts, spelling, identity and power', in Alexandra M. Jaffe, Jannis K. Androutsopoulos, Mark Sebba and Sally A. Johnson (eds.), *Orthography as Social Action: Scripts, Spelling, Identity and Power* (Language and Social Processes 3). Boston/Berlin: De Gruyter, pp. 1–19

2015. 'Iconisation, attribution and branding in orthography', in Laura Villa and Rik Vosters (eds.), *The Historical Sociolinguistics of Spelling*, special issue of *Written Language and Literacy* 18 (2). Amsterdam/Philadelphia: John Benjamins, pp. 208–27

2016. 'The orthography of English-lexicon pidgins and creoles', in Vivian Cook and Des Ryan (eds.), *The Routledge Handbook of the English Writing System*. London/New York: Routledge, pp. 347–64

Seelbach, Ulrich 2016. 'Schreibsprachen in Kärnten: Vorstudie zu einer formularunterstützen Schreibsprachenbstimmung für mittelalterliche Handschriften', *Sprachwissenschaft* 41 (3–4): 311–33

Seifart, Frank 2008. 'Orthography development', in Jost Gippert, Nikolaus P. Himmelmann and Ulrike Mosel (eds.), *Essentials of Language Documentation*. Berlin/New York: De Gruyter, pp. 275–99

Seiler, Annina 2010. '*Latinis regulis barbara nomina stringi non possunt*, or: how to write the vernacular', in Pamela R. Robinson (ed.), *Teaching Writing, Learning to Write: Proceedings of the XVIth Colloquium of the Comité International de Paléographie Latine*. London: King's College London, Centre for Late Antique and Medieval Studies, pp. 91–101

2011. 'Litteras Superfluas – Zum Gebrauch "Überflüssiger" Buchstaben Im Althochdeutschen, Altsächsischen Und Altenglischen', in Elvira Glaser, Annina Seiler and Michelle Waldispühl (eds.), *Lautschriftsprache. Beiträge Zur Vergleichenden Historischen Graphematik*. Zurich: Chronos, pp. 167–83

2014. *The Scripting of the Germanic Languages: A Comparative Study of 'Spelling Difficulties' in Old English, Old High German and Old Saxon*. Zurich: Chronos

2015. 'Writing the Germanic languages: the early history of the digraphs <th>, <ch> and <uu>', in Aidan Conti, Orietta Da Rold and Philip Shaw (eds.), *Writing Europe, 500–1450: Texts and Contexts*. Cambridge: D. S. Brewer, pp. 101–21

2021. 'Germanic names, vernacular sounds, and Latin spellings in early Anglo-Saxon and Alemannic charters', in Robert Gallagher, Edward Roberts and Francesca Tinti (eds.), *The Languages of Early Medieval Charters: Latin, Germanic Vernaculars, and the Written Word* (Brill's Series on the Early Middle Ages 27). Leiden: Brill, pp. 117–53

Selvelli, Giustina 2015. 'Caratteri arabi per la lingua bosniaca', in Daniele Baglioni and Olga Tribulato (eds.), *Contatti di lingue – Contatti di scritture: Multilinguismo e multigrafismo dal Vicino Oriente Antico alla Cina contemporanea*. Venice: Edizioni Ca' Foscari – Digital Publishing, pp. 197–217

Senz, Silvia and Alberte, Montserrat (eds.) 2011. *El dardo en la Academia. Esencia y vigencia de las academias de la lengua española*, 2 vols. Barcelona: Melusina

Sevenstern, Gaspar 1669/70. *Gegengespräch Uber die Frage: Warum wilt du nicht Römisch Catholisch werden/wie dein [!] Vorfahren gewesen?* Hanover: Schwendimann (VD17 3: 301691S)

Sgall, Petr 1987. 'Towards a theory of phonemic orthography', in Philip A. Luelsdorff (ed.), *Orthography and Phonology*. Amsterdam/Philadelphia: John Benjamins, pp. 1–30

Shakespeare, William 1598. *A pleasant conceited comedie called, Loues labors lost* [...]. London: William White for Cutbert Burby (EEBO, ProQuest)

1622a. *The tragœdy of Othello, the Moore of Venice As it hath beene diuerse times acted at the Globe, and at the Black-Friers, by his Maiesties Seruants. Written by VVilliam Shakespeare* [...]. London: Nicholas Okes for Thomas Walkley (EEBO, ProQuest)

1622b. *The most excellent and lamentable tragedie, of Romeo and Iuliet* [...]. London: William Stansby for Iohn Smethwicke (EEBO, ProQuest)

1640. 'A Lover's Complaint', in *Poems: vvritten by Wil. Shake-speare. Gent.* London: Tho. Cotes (EEBO, ProQuest)

Shakespeare First Folio, Oxford Text Archive, https://ota.ox.ac.uk/desc/0119

Shammas, Carole 2019. 'Acquiring written communication skills as the vernacular standardizes: a case study of an English family's letters 1560–1700', *Huntington Library Quarterly* 82 (3): 429–82, https://doi.org/10.1353/hlq.2019.0022

Share, David L. 2014 'Alphabetism in reading science', *Frontiers in Psychology* 5 (752): 1–4

Share, David L. and Daniels, Peter T. 2016. 'Aksharas, alphasyllabaries, abugidas, alphabets and orthographic depth: reflections on Rimzhim, Katz and Fowler (2014)', *Writing Systems Research* 8 (1): 17–31

Shaughnessy, Edward L. 2010 'The beginnings of writing in China', in Christopher Woods, Emily Teeter and Geoff Emberling (eds.), *Visible Language: Inventions of Writing in the Ancient Middle East and Beyond*. Chicago: Oriental Institute, pp. 215–21

Sheridan, Thomas 1762. *A Course on Elocution: Together with Two Dissertations on Language; and Some Other Tracts Relative to those Subjects*. London: W. Strahan

1780. *A general dictionary of the English language*. London

Sherman, William H. 2011. 'The social life of books', in Joad Raymond (ed.), *The Oxford History of Popular Print Culture*, vol. 1: *Cheap Print in Britain and in Ireland to 1660*. Oxford: Oxford University Press, pp. 164–71

Shute, Rosie 2017. 'Pressed for space: the effects of justification and the printing process on fifteenth-century orthography', *English Studies* 98 (3): 262–82, https://doi.org/10.1080/0013838X.2017.1250197

Sica, Alan 2012. 'Max Weber'. Oxford Bibliographies Online in Sociology, www.oxfordbibliographies.com/view/document/obo-9780199756384/obo-9780199756384-0064.xml

Sievers, Eduard 1882. *Angelsächsische Grammatik* (Sammlung kurzer Grammatiken germanischer Dialekte 3). Halle: Niemeyer

SIL International 2022. 'Orthography', www.sil.org/orthography

Silverman, David P. 1979. Reviewed works: *Ancient Egyptian Epigraphy and Paleography: 'The Recording of Inscriptions and Scenes in Tombs and Temples,'* by Ricardo Caminos; *'Archeological Aspects of Epigraphy and Paleography,'* by Henry G. Fischer. *Journal of the American Research Center in Egypt* 16: 183–84

Silverstein, Michael 2003. 'Indexical order and the dialectics of sociolinguistic life', *Language and Communication* 23: 193–229

Simplified Spelling Board 1906. *Simplified Spelling. For the Use of Government Departments*. Washington, DC: Government Printing Office

Simpson, John A. and Proffitt, Michael (eds.) 2000–. *Oxford English Dictionary Online* (John A. Simpson ed. –2013, Michael Proffitt ed. 2013–). Oxford University Press, http://oed.com/

Šinkūnas, Mindaugas 2010. 'XVI–XVII amžiaus Mažosios Lietuvos raštų akcentografija'. Doctoral dissertation, Lietuvių kalbos institutas and Vytauto Didžiojo universitetas, Lithuania

2014. 'Mažosios Lietuvos raštų ortografijos reforma XVII amžiuje. I. Pučiamųjų priebalsių ir afrikatų žymėjimas', *Archivum Lithuanicum* 16: 9–58

2016. 'Kristus, Krystus, Christus, Chrystus ar Cristus? Vardo rašybos raida XVI–XIX amžiaus raštuose', *Archivum Lithuanicum* 18: 185–220

Skazka o rybak͡ie i rybk͡ie. Pasaka ape žuvinika ir žuvele 1902. Suwałki: Tipografi͡ia B. Brinmana

Sketch Engine, www.sketchengine.eu

Skre, Arnhild 2011. *Hulda Garborg. Nasjonal strateg*. Oslo: Samlaget

Smalley, William A. 1959. 'How shall I write this language?' *The Bible Translator* 10 (2): 49–69

Smalley, William A., Koua Vang, Chia and Yee Yang, Gnia 1990 *Mother of Writing: The Origin and Development of a Hmong Messianic Script*. Chicago: University of Chicago Press

Smilga, Kazimieras 1901. Book Ownership Inscription. Kaunas County Public Library, Collection of Old and Rare Prints

Smith, Andrew 2014. *A Study of the Gospels in Codex Alexandrinus: Codicology, Palaeography, and Scribal Hands*. Leiden: Brill

Smith, Charles W. 1866. *Mind your H's and take care of your R's: exercises for acquiring the use & correcting the abuse of the letter H, with observations and additional exercises on the letter R*. London: Lockwood

Smith, Daisy 2018. 'The predictability of {-S} abbreviation in Older Scots manuscripts according to stem-final littera', in Rhona Alcorn, Joanna Kopaczyk, Bettelou Los and Benjamin Molineaux (eds.), *Historical Dialectology in the Digital Age*. Edinburgh: Edinburgh University Press, pp. 187–211

Smith, Jeremy J. 1996. *An Historical Study of English: Function, Form and Change*. London/New York: Routledge

2008. 'Issues of linguistic categorisation in the evolution of written Middle English', in Graham D. Caie and Denis Renevey (eds.), *Medieval Texts in Context*. Abingdon: Routledge, pp. 211–24

2012. 'From Middle to Early Modern English', in Lynda Mugglestone (ed.), *The Oxford History of English*. Oxford: Oxford University Press, pp. 147–79 (updated ed.)

2020a. 'On scriptae: correlating spelling and script in Late Middle English', *Revista Canaria de Estudios Ingleses*, https://riull.ull.es/xmlui/handle/915/19292

2020b. 'The pragmatics of punctuation in Middle English documentary texts', in Merja Stenroos and Kjetil V. Thengs (eds.), *Records of Real People. Linguistic Variation in Middle English Local Documents* (Advances in Historical Sociolinguistics 11). Amsterdam: John Benjamins. 205–18

Smith, Margaret M. 1994. 'The design relationship between the manuscript and the incunable', in Robin Myers and Michael Harris (eds.), *A Millenium of the Book: Production, Design, and Illustration in Manuscript and Print, 900–1900*. Winchester: Oak Knoll Press, pp. 23–43

Smith, Philip T. and Baker, Robert G. 1976. 'The influence of English spelling patterns on pronunciation', *Journal of Verbal Learning and Verbal Behavior* 15: 267–85

Smith, Thomas 1568. *De recta & emendata linguae Anglicae scriptione, dialogus*. Paris: Robert Stephan

1963 [1568]. *De Recta et Emendata Linguæ Anglicanæ Scriptione Dialogus* (Stockholm Studies in English 56), in Bror Danielsson (ed. and trans.), *Sir Thomas Smith's Literary and Linguistic Works*, vol. 3. Stockholm: Almqvist and Wiksell

Smith-Stark, Thomas 2005. 'Phonological description in New Spain', in Otto Zwartjes and Cristina Altman (eds.), *Missionary Linguistics II/ Lingüística misionera II: Orthography and Phonology. Selected papers from the Second International Conference on Missionary Linguistics, São Paulo, 10–13 March 2004*. Amsterdam: John Benjamins, pp. 3–64

Sonderegger, Stefan 2000a. 'Ansätze zu einer deutschen Sprachgeschichtsschreibung bis zum Ende des 18. Jahrhunderts', in Werner Besch, Anne Betten, Oskar Reichmann and Stefan Sonderegger (eds.), *Sprachgeschichte: Ein Handbuch zur Geschichte der deutschen Sprache und ihrer Erforschung* (Handbücher zur Sprach- und Kommunikationswissenschaft 2.1). Berlin: De Gruyter, pp. 417–42

2000b. 'Sprachgeschichtsforschung in der ersten Hälfte des 19. Jahrhunderts', in Werner Besch, Anne Betten, Oskar Reichmann and Stefan Sonderegger (eds.), *Sprachgeschichte: Ein Handbuch zur Geschichte der deutschen Sprache und ihrer Erforschung* (Handbücher

zur Sprach- und Kommunikationswissenschaft 2.1). Berlin: De Gruyter, pp. 443–73

Sönmez, Margaret 1993. 'English spelling in the seventeenth century: a study of the nature of standardisation as seen in the MS and printed versions of the Duke of Newcastle's "A New Method..."'. Doctoral dissertation, University of Durham, UK

2000. 'Perceived and real differences between men's and women's spellings of the early to mid-seventeenth century', in Dieter Kastovsky and Arthur Mettinger (eds.), *The History of English in a Social Context: A Contribution to Historical Sociolinguistics* (Trends in Linguistics 129). Berlin/New York: De Gruyter, pp. 405–36

Sørlie, Mikjel 1957. *Bergens Fundas*. Bergen: J. D. Beyer

Sources from Laws of the Past (IURA), https://iura.uj.edu.pl/dlibra

Sousa-Silva, Rui, Laboreiro, Gustavo, Sarmento, Luís, Grant, Tim, Oliveira, Eugénio and Maia, Belinda 2011. ''twazn me!!! ;(' Automatic authorship analysis of micro-blogging messages', in Rafael Muñoz, Andrés Montoyo and Elisabeth Métais (eds.), *Natural Language Processing and Information Systems: 16th International Conference on Applications of Natural Language to Information Systems, NLDB 2011, Alicante, Spain, June 28–30, 2011, Proceedings* (Lecture Notes in Computer Science 6716). Berlin/New York: Springer, pp. 161–68

Speakman Sutch, Susie 2010. 'Politics and print at the time of Philip the Fair', in Hanno Wijsman (ed.), *Books in Transition at the Time of Philip the Fair. Manuscripts and Printed Books in the Late Fifteenth and Early Sixteenth Century Low Countries*. Turnhout: Brepols Publishers, pp. 231–55

Spence, Thomas 1775. *The grand repository of the English language*. Newcastle: T. Saint

Spitzmüller, Jürgen 2012. 'Floating ideologies: metamorphoses of graphic "Germanness"', in Alexandra M. Jaffe, Jannis K. Androutsopoulos, Mark Sebba and Sally A. Johnson (eds.), *Orthography as Social Action: Scripts, Spelling, Identity and Power* (Language and Social Processes 3). Boston/Berlin: De Gruyter, pp. 255–88

2015. 'Graphic variation and graphic ideologies: a metapragmatic approach', *Social Semiotics* 25 (2): 126–41

Spolsky, Bernard 2009a. 'Language management for endangered languages: the case of Navajo', in Peter K. Austin (ed.), *Language Documentation and Description*, vol. 6. London: SOAS, pp. 117–31

2009b. 'Religious language policy', in Bernard Spolsky (ed.), *Language Management*. Cambridge: Cambridge University Press, pp. 31–52

(ed.) 2012. *The Cambridge Handbook of Language Policy*. Cambridge/New York: Cambridge University Press

Sproat, Richard 2000. *A Computational Theory of Writing Systems*. Cambridge: Cambridge University Press

2010. *Language, Technology, and Society*. Oxford: Oxford University Press

Sproat, Richard and Gutkin, Alexander 2021. 'The taxonomy of writing systems: how to measure how logographic a system is', *Computational Linguistics*, 47 (3): 477–528

Spurkland, Terje 2005. *Norwegian Runes and Runic Inscriptions*. Woodbridge: Boydell Press

2017. 'The (dis-)ambiguation of the grapheme in the high medieval runic script', in Gaby Waxenberger, Hans Sauer and Kerstin Kazzazi (eds.), *Von den Hieroglyphen zur Internetsprache. Das Verhältnis von Schrift, Laut und Sprache*. Wiesbaden: Reichert, pp. 149–56

Squires, Lauren 2012. 'Whos punctuating what? Sociolinguistic variation in instant messaging', in Alexandra M. Jaffe, Jannis K. Androutsopoulos, Mark Sebba and Sally A. Johnson (eds.), *Orthography as Social Action: Scripts, Spelling, Identity and Power* (Language and Social Processes 3). Boston/Berlin: De Gruyter, pp. 288–324

Stachowski, Stanisław 2010. 'Polonizacja języka ormiańsko-kipczackiego', *LingVaria* 2 (10): 213–27

Stadnik-Holzer, Elena 2014. 'Diachrone Phonologie', in Karl Gutschmidt, Tilman Berger, Sebastian Kempgen and Peter Kosta (eds.), *Die slavischen Sprachen. Ein internationales Handbuch zu ihrer Struktur, ihrer Geschichte und ihrer Erforschung. Bd. 2./The Slavic Languages: An International Handbook of Their Structure, Their History and Their Investigation*, vol. 2. Berlin: De Gruyter, pp. 1525–64

Stamatatos, Efstathios 2009. 'A survey of modern authorship attribution methods', *Journal of the American Society for Information Science and Technology* 60 (3): 538–56

Stanford, James N. and Kenny, Laurence A. 2013. 'Revisiting transmission and diffusion: an agent-based model of vowel chain shifts across large communities', *Language Variation and Change* 25: 119–53

Stankevich, I͡An 1933. 'Belaruski͡ia musul'mane i belaruska͡ia litaratura arabskim pis'mom', *Hadavik Belaruskaha navukovaha Tavarystva* (Adbitka z Hadavika Belaruskaha Navukovaha Tavarystva Kn. I). Vilnius: Drukarni͡a I͡A. Levina)

Stanley, Eric G. 1988. 'Karl Luick's "Man schrieb wie man sprach" and English historical philology', in Dieter Kastovsky and Gero Bauer (eds.), *Luick Revisited: Papers read at the Luick-Symposium at Schloß Liechtenstein, 15.–18.9.1985* (Tübinger Beiträge zur Linguistik 288). Tübingen: Gunter Narr Verlag, pp. 311–34

Stapleton, Thomas 1839. *Plumpton Correspondence, a Series of Letters, Written in the Reigns of Edward IV, Richard III, Henry VII and Henry VIII, from Sir Edward Plumpton's Book of Letters*. London: Camden Society

Stauder, Andréas 2010. 'The earliest Egyptian writing', in Christopher Woods, Emily Teeter and Geoff Emberling (eds.), *Visible Language: Inventions*

of Writing in the Ancient Middle East and Beyond. Chicago: Oriental Institute, pp. 137–47

Stebbins, Tonya 2001. 'Emergent spelling patterns in Sm'algyax (Tsimshian, British Columbia)', *Written Language and Literacy* 4 (2): 163–94

Steele, Philippa M. 2013a. *Syllabic Writing on Cyprus and Its Context*. Cambridge: Cambridge University Press

2013b. *A Linguistic History of Ancient Cyprus: The Non-Greek Languages, and Their Relations with Greek, c. 1600–300 BC*. Cambridge: Cambridge University Press

2019. *Writing and Society in Ancient Cyprus*. Cambridge: Cambridge University Press

Steele, Philippa M. and Meissner, Torsten 2017. 'From Linear B to Linear A: the problem of the backward projection of sound values', in Philippa M. Steele (ed.), *Understanding Relations between Scripts: The Aegean Writing Systems*. Oxford/Philadelphia: Oxbow Books, pp. 93–110

Steer, Francis W. (ed.) 1968. *Scriveners' Company Common Paper 1357–1628: With a Continuation to 1678*. London: London Record Society

Stegeman, Jelle 2014. *Handbuch Niederländisch. Sprache und Sprachkultur von den Anfängen bis 1800*. Darmstadt: Wissenschaftliche Buchgesellschaft

Stein, Dieter 1994. 'Sorting out the variants: standardization and social factors in the English language 1600–1800', in Dieter Stein and Ingrid Tieken-Boon van Ostade (eds.), *Towards a Standard English 1600-1800*. Berlin/New York: De Gruyter, pp. 1–14

Steinberg, Danny D. and Krohn, Robert K. 1975. 'The psychological validity of Chomsky and Halle's Vowel Shift Rule', in John Odmark and J. Howard Shaw (eds.), *The Transformational–Generative Paradigm and Modern Linguistic Theory* (Current Issues in Linguistic Theory [CILT] 1). Amsterdam: John Benjamins, pp. 233–59

Stenroos, Merja 2004. 'Regional dialects and spelling conventions in late Middle English. Searches for (th) in LALME data', in Marina Dossena and Roger Lass (eds.), *Methods and Data in English Historical Dialectology*. Bern: Peter Lang, 257–85

2006. 'A Middle English mess of fricative spellings: reflections on thorn, yogh and their rivals', in Marcin Krygier and Liliana Sikorska (eds.), *To Make his Englissh Sweete upon his Tonge*. Frankfurt am Main: Peter Lang, pp. 9–35

2013. 'Identity and intelligibility in late Middle English scribal transmission: local dialect as an active choice in fifteenth-century texts', in Esther-Miriam Wagner, Bettina Beinhoff and Ben Outhwaite (eds.), *Scribes as Agents of Language Change*. Berlin: De Gruyter, pp. 159–81

2020a. 'The "vernacularisation" and "standardisation" of local administrative writing in late and post-medieval administrative writing', in Laura

Wright (ed.), *The Multilingual Origins of Standard English*, Berlin/ Boston: De Gruyter, pp. 39–85

2020b. 'Regional variation and supralocalization in late medieval English: comparing administrative and literary texts', in Merja Stenroos and Kjetil V. Thengs (eds.), *Records of Real People: Linguistic Variation in Middle English Local Documents* (Advances in Historical Sociolinguistics 11). Amsterdam: John Benjamins, pp. 95–128

Stęplewski, Artur 2018. *Semioza Pisma: Cyrylica i Łacinka w Serbskim i Chorwackim Dyskursie Narodowym na Tle Słowiańskim*. Poznań: Wydawnictwo Naukowe UAM

Stetson, Raymond H. 1937. 'The phoneme and the grapheme', in J. Wils, R. Meesters and W. Slijpen, *Mélanges de linguistique et de philologie offerts à Jacq. van Ginneken*. Paris: C. Klincksieck, pp. 353–56

Steyn, Jacob C. 2017. 'Die laaste projek van die "Hollandse taalbeweging in Suid-Afrika": Die Vereenvoudigde Hollandse Spelling', *Tydskrif Vir Geesteswetenskappe* 57 (2–1): 233–48

Stockwell, Robert P. and Barritt, C. Westbrook 1951. *Some Old English Graphemic-Phonemic Correspondences: æ, ea, and a* (Studies in Linguistics, Occasional Papers 4). Washington, DC: Georgetown University

1955. 'The Old English short digraphs: some considerations', *Language* 31: 372–89

Stone, Michaele, Kouymjian, Dickran and Lehmann, Henning 2002. *Album of Armenian Paleography*. Aarhus: Aarhus University Press

Stopka, Krzysztof 2000. *Ormianie w Polsce dawnej i dzisiejszej*. Kraków: Księgarnia Akademicka

Stotz, Peter 1996. *Handbuch zur lateinischen Sprache des Mittelalters*, vol. 3: *Lautlehre*. Munich: Beck

Strang, Barbara M. H. 1970. *A History of English*. London: Methuen

Strelcyn, Stefan 1952. 'Obecny stan badań nad pochodzeniem alfabetu fenickiego', *Przegląd Orientalistyczny* 4: 3–33

Strockis, Mindaugas 2007. 'Klasikinių kalbų kirčio žymėjimo įtaka lietuvių kirčio žymėjimui'. Doctoral dissertation, Vilniaus universitetas, Lithuania

Strycharska-Brzezina, Maria 2006. *Polskojęzyczne podręczniki dla klasy I szkoły elementarnej w Królestwie Polskim drukowane grażdanką. Wydanie warszawskie ze zbiorów Biblioteki Jagiellońskiej w Krakowie: Rozprawa filologiczno-historyczna i edycja*. Kraków: Polska Akademia Umiejętności

Stubbs, Michael 1980. *Language and Literacy: The Sociolinguistics of Reading and Writing*. Boston: Routledge and Kegan Paul

Suárez Cortina, Manuel (ed.) 2006. *La redención del pueblo. La cultura progresista en la España liberal*. Santander: Servicio de Publicaciones de la Universidad de Cantabria

Subačius, Giedrius 1996. 'Jurgio Ambraziejaus Pabrėžos žemaičių kalba', *Lietuvių Atgimimo istorijos studijos 8: Asmuo: tarp tautos ir valstybės.* Vilnius: Mokslo ir enciklopedijų leidykla, pp. 10–113

2002. 'Two types of standard language history in Europe', *Res Balticae* 8: 131–50

2004a. 'Lietuviška ir rusiška lietuviškų spaudinių kirilika 1864–1866 metais', in Darius Staliūnas (ed.), *Raidžių draudimo metai.* Vilnius: Lietuvos istorijos instituto leidykla, pp. 139–73

2004b. 'Double orthography in American Lithuanian newspapers at the turn of the twentieth century', in Philip Baldi and Pietro U. Dini (eds.), *Studies in Baltic and Indo-European Linguistics: In Honor of William R. Schmalstieg.* Amsterdam/Philadelphia: John Benjamins, pp. 189–201

2004c. 'Grafemos netektis Lietuvos ſpaudiniuose', *Archivum Lithuanicum* 6: 239–64

2005a. 'Development of the Cyrillic orthography for Lithuanian in 1864–1904', *Lituanus* 51 (2): 29–55

2005b. 'The choice of a symbolic codifying work in the history of standard European languages', in Jolanta Gelumbeckaitė and Jost Gippert (eds.), *Das Baltikum im sprachgeschichtlichen Kontext der europäischen Reformation.* Vilnius: Lietuvių kalbos instituto leidykla, pp. 124–33

2011a. *Lietuvių kalbos ekspertai Rusijos imperijos tarnyboje: Dmitrijus Kaširinas, Zacharijus Liackis, Andrius Poidėnas.* Vilnius: Lietuvių kalbos institutas

2011b. 'The forgotten model of a separate Standard Lowland Lithuanian: Jurgis Pabrėža (1771–1849)', in Joshua A. Fishman and Ofelia Garcia (eds.), *Language and Ethnic Identity 2: The Success-Failure Continuum in Language and Ethnic Identity Efforts.* Oxford: Oxford University Press, pp. 444–56

2012. 'The Influence of clandestine standard Lithuanian in the Latin alphabet on the official Lithuanian in Cyrillic letters (1864–1904)', in Konrad Maier (ed.), *Nation und Sprache in Nordosteuropa im 19. Jahrhundert.* Wiesbaden: Harrassowitz Verlag, pp. 231–40

2018. *Simono Daukanto Rygos ortografija (1827–1834).* Vilnius: Lietuvos istorijos institutas

2020. 'Orthographic variation and materiality of a manuscript: pre-standard Lithuanian spellings in Simonas Daukantas's *History of the Lithuanian Lowlands* (1831–1834)', in Marco Condorelli (ed.), *Advances in Historical Orthography, c. 1500–1800.* Cambridge: Cambridge University Press, pp. 124–40

2021. *Simono Daukanto Sankt Peterburgo Ortografija (1834–1846).* Vilnius: Lietuvos istorijos institutas

Swales, John 1990. *Genre Analysis: English in Academic and Research Settings.* Cambridge: Cambridge University Press

Sweet, Henry 1871. *King Alfred's West-Saxon Version of Gregory's Pastoral Care* (Early English Text Society, original series, 45, 50). London: Trübner

1888. *A History of English Sounds from the Earliest Period, with Full Word-Lists*. Oxford: Clarendon Press

1892. *A New English Grammar: Logical and Historical. Part I: Introduction, phonology, and accidence*. Oxford: Clarendon Press

Swiggers, Pierre 1996. 'Transmission of the Phoenician script to the West', in Peter T. Daniels and William Bright (eds.), *The World's Writing Systems*. New York/Oxford: Oxford University Press, pp. 261–70

Taavitsainen, Irma 2000. 'Scientific language and spelling standardisation 1375–1550', in Laura Wright (ed.), *The Development of Standard English 1300–1800: Theories, Descriptions, Conflicts*. Cambridge: Cambridge University Press, pp. 131–54

2001. 'Changing conventions of writing: the dynamics of genres, text types, and text traditions', *European Journal of English Studies* 5 (2): 139–50

2004. 'Scriptorial "house-styles" and discourse communities', in Irma Taavitsainen and Päivi Pahta (eds.), *Medical and Scientific Writing in Late Medieval English*. Cambridge: Cambridge University Press, pp. 209–40

2012. 'New perspectives, theories and methods. Historical pragmatics', in Alexander Bergs and Laurel J. Brinton (eds.), *English Historical Linguistics. An International Handbook*, vol. 2. Berlin/Boston: De Gruyter, pp. 1457–74

Taavitsainen, Irma and Fitzmaurice, Susan M. 2007. 'Historical pragmatics: what it is and how to do it', in Susan M. Fitzmaurice and Irma Taavitsainen (eds.), *Methods in Historical Pragmatics*. Berlin/New York: De Gruyter, pp. 11–36

Taavitsainen, Irma, Pahta, Päivi, Hiltunen, Turo, Mäkinen, Martti, Marttila, Ville, Ratia, Maura, Suhr, Carla and Tyrkkö, Jukka (compilers) 2010. *Early Modern English Medical Texts*, CD-ROM. Amsterdam: John Benjamins

Taavitsainen, Irma and Tyrkkö, Jukka 2010. 'The field of medical writing with fuzzy edges', in Irma Taavitsainen and Päivi Pahta (eds.), *Early Modern English Medical Texts. Corpus Description and Studies*. Amsterdam/Philadelphia: John Benjamins, pp. 57–61

Tacke, Felix 2020. 'Spanish', in Franz Lebsanft and Felix Tacke (eds.), *Manual of Standardization in the Romance Languages*. Berlin/New York: De Gruyter, pp. 559–79

Tagg, Caroline, Baron, Alistair and Rayson, Paul 2012. '"I didn't spel that wrong did i. Oops": analysis and normalisation of SMS spelling variation', *Lingvisticæ Investigationes* 35 (2): 367–88, https://doi.org/10.1075/li.35.2.12tag

Tagg, Caroline and Evans, Mel 2020. 'Spelling in context: a transhistorical pragmatic perspective on orthographic practices in English', in Caroline Tagg and Mel Evans (eds.), *Message and Medium: English Language Practices across Old and New Media* (Topics in English Linguistics 105). Berlin: De Gruyter, pp. 55–79

Tagliamonte, Sali A. and Denis, Derek 2014. 'Expanding the transmission/diffusion dichotomy: evidence from Canada', *Language* 90: 90–136

Taha, Haitham Y. 2016. 'Deep and shallow in Arabic orthography: new evidence from reading performance of elementary school native Arab readers', *Writing Systems Research* 8 (2): 133–42, https://doi.org/10.1080/17586801.2015.1114910

Tamminga, Meredith 2019. 'Interspeaker covariation in Philadelphia vowel changes', *Language Variation and Change* 31 (2): 119–33, https://doi.org/10.1017/S0954394519000139

Tamošiūnaitė, Aurelija 2010. 'Viena kalba – dvi abėcėlės: kirilika ir lotyniška abėcėle rašyti Petro Survilo laiškai', *Archivum Lithuanicum* 12: 157–82

2011. '*Ukiškasis kalendori͡us 1902 metams* ir *Pasaka ape žuvinika ir žuvele*: rengėjo problema', *Archivum Lithuanicum* 13: 85–112

2013. 'Ankstyvas lietuviškos kirilikos egodokumentuose liudytojas – Stanislovo Prakulevičiaus 1879 metų laiškas Godliauskių šeimai', *Archivum Lithuanicum* 15: 431–51

2015. 'Defining 'Lithuanian': orthographic debates at the end of the nineteenth century', in Laura Villa and Rik Vosters (eds.), *The Historical Sociolinguistics of Spelling*, special issue of *Written Language and Literacy* 18 (2). Amsterdam/Philadelphia: John Benjamins, pp. 309–26

Tannenbaum, Samuel A. 1930. *The Handwriting of the Renaissance*. New York: Columbia University Press

Tarėlka, Mikhail U. 2015. 'Adaptat͡syi͡a arabskaha pis'ma dli͡a peredachy slavi͡anskikh (belaruskikh i pol'skikh) tėkstaŭ', in Vittorio S. Tomelleri and Sebastian Kempgen (eds.), *Slavic Alphabets in Contact*. Bamberg: University of Bamberg Press, pp. 263–89

Tarėlka, Mikhail U. and Synkova, Irina A. 2006. 'Tėkst sufiĭskaha pakhodz͡hanni͡a z belaruska-tatarskaha khamaila', in S͡iarheĭ Vaz͡hnik and Ala Koz͡hynava (eds.), *Aktual'nyi͡a prablemy palanistyki*. Minsk: Prava i ėkanomika, pp. 29–54

2008. '»Ad trast͡sy ŭ nowym harshku z͡habu vysushyt͡s' i z vodkaĭ pit͡s'...«. Na skryz͡havanni kul'tur: znakharski tėkst z belaruskatatarskaha khamaila', in *Mezhdunarodnai͡a ėlektronnai͡a konferent͡sii͡a »Belorusskiĭ tekst: ot rukopisi k ėlektronnoĭ knige« (K Dni͡u belorusskoĭ pis'mennosti, senti͡abr'' 2008)*. [Minsk], www.belrus-seminar2008.narod.ru/Tarelka-Synkova.pdf

Taylor, Insup 1988. 'Psychology of literacy: east and west', in Derrick de Kerckhove and Charles J. Lumsden (eds.), *The Alphabet and the Brain: The Lateralization of Writing*. Berlin/Heidelberg: Springer, pp. 202–33

Taylor, Insup and Taylor, M. Martin 2014. *Writing and Literacy in Chinese, Korean, and Japanese.* Amsterdam/Philadelphia: Benjamins (revised ed.)

Taylor, Isaac 1883. *The Alphabet: An Account of the Origin and Development of Letters.* London: Kegan Paul, Trench

Teeuwen, Mariken 2014. 'Voices from the edge. Tironian notes in the margin', https://voicesfromtheedge.huygens.knaw.nl/?p=36

Tefsir from Francis Skaryna Belarusian Library and Museum in London (TL), MS from 1725, copyist Bohdan ibn Ševban Asanovič; photocopy in Georg M. Meredith-Owens and Alexander Nadson 1970, 'The Byelorussian Tartars and their writings', *The Journal of Belarusian Studies* 2 (2): 141–76 (p. 171)

Teleman, Ulf 2003. 'Swedish', in Ana Deumert and Wim Vandenbussche (eds.), *Germanic Standardizations: Past to Present.* Amsterdam/ Philadelphia: John Benjamins, pp. 405–29

Tenger, Zeynep and Trolander, Paul 2010 'From print versus manuscript to sociable authorship and mixed media: a review of trends in the scholarship of early modern publication', *Literature Compass* 7 (11): 1035–48

Ter Horst, Tom and Stam, Nike 2018. 'Visual diamorphs: the importance of language neutrality in code-switching from medieval Ireland', in Päivi Pahta, Janne Skaffari and Laura Wright (eds.), *Multilingual Practices in Language History: English and Beyond.* Berlin: De Gruyter, pp. 199–222

Te Winkel, Lambert A. 1863. *De grondbeginselen der Nederlandsche spelling: ontwerp der spelling voor het aanstaande Nederlandsch Woordenboek.* Leiden: Noothoven van Goor

Thackston, Wheeler M. 1993. *An Introduction to Persian.* Bethesda: Iranbooks (3rd ed.)

Thaisen, Jacob 2005. 'Orthography, codicology, and textual studies: the Cambridge University Library, Gg.4.27 *Canterbury Tales*', *Boletín Millares Carlo* 24–25: 379–94

2011. 'Adam Pinkhurst's short and long forms', in Jacob Thaisen and Hanna Rutkowska (eds.), *Scribes, Printers and the Accidentals of Their Texts.* Frankfurt am Main: Peter Lang, pp. 73–90

2017. 'Secretary letter-shapes in County Durham', *Folia Linguistica Historica* 51 (s38): 263–80

The Accomplish'd Housewife; or, the Gentlewoman's Companion 1745. London: For J. Newbery, at the Bible and Sun near the Chapter-House in St Paul's Church-yard

The Jules Ferry Laws, France 1881–82, http://dcalin.fr/textoff/loi_1882_vo.html

The Library of Congress, ALA-LC Romanization Tables, www.loc.gov/catdir/cpso/roman.html

Themistocleous, Christiana 2010. 'Online orthographies', in Rotimi Taiwo (ed.), *Handbook of Research on Discourse Behaviour and Digital Communication: Language Structures and Social Interaction*. Hershey: IGI Global, pp. 318–34

The National Archives, 'Prerogative Court of Canterbury: Wills of Selected Famous Persons' PROB 1/4A

The Norwegian Directorate for Education and Training 2023. 'Målformer in grunnskolen', www.udir.no/regelverkstolkninger/opplaring/Malform/malformer-i-grunnskolen12?depth=0&print=1

Thomas, Megan C. 2007. 'K is for de-kolonization: anti-colonial nationalism and orthographic reform', *Comparative Studies in Society and History* 49 (4): 938–67

Thompson, Edward M. 1893. *An Introduction to Greek and Latin Palaeography*. Oxford: Clarendon Press

Thurneysen, Rudolf 1946. *A Grammar of Old Irish* (trans. by D. A. Binchy and Osborn Bergin). Dublin: Dublin Institute for Advanced Studies

Thurlow, Crispin 2006. 'From statistical panic to moral panic: the metadiscursive construction and popular exaggeration of new media language in the print media', *Journal of Computer-Mediated Communication* 11 (3): 667–701, https://doi.org/10.1111/j.1083-6101.2006.00031.x

Tieken-Boon van Ostade, Ingrid 1998. 'Standardization of English spelling: the eighteenth-century printers' contribution', in Jacek Fisiak and Marcin Krygier (eds.), *Advances in English Historical Linguistics (1996)* (Trends in Linguistics 112). Berlin/New York: De Gruyter, pp. 457–70

2006a. 'Eighteenth-century English letters: in search of the vernacular', *Linguistica e Filologia* 21: 113–46

2006b. '"Disrespectful and too familiar"? Abbreviations as an index of politeness in 18th-century letters', in Christiane Dalton-Puffer, Dieter Kastovsky, Nikolaus Ritt and Herbert Schendl (eds.), *Syntax, Style and Grammatical Norms: English from 1500–2000* (Linguistic Insights 39). Frankfurt am Main: Peter Lang, pp. 229–47

2008. *Grammars, Grammarians and Grammar-Writing in Eighteenth-Century England*. Berlin/New York: De Gruyter

2010. *The Bishop's Grammar: Robert Lowth and the Rise of Prescriptivism*. Oxford: Oxford University Press

Tikkanen, Karin W. 2020. 'Lost – and found – in transmission: the creation of the Oscan alphabet', in James Clackson, Patrick James, Katherine McDonald, Livia Tagliapietra and Nicholas Zair (eds.), *Migration, Mobility and Language Contact in and around the Ancient Mediterranean*. Cambridge: Cambridge University Press, pp. 98–121

Tolkien, John R. R. 1929. 'Ancrene Wisse and Hali Meiðhad', *Essays and Studies by Members of the English Association* 14: 104–26

Tomelleri, Vittorio S. and Kempgen, Sebastian (eds.) 2015. *Slavic Alphabets in Contact*. Bamberg: University of Bamberg Press, https://fis.uni-bamberg.de/handle/uniba/21440

Took, Patricia 1977. 'Government and the printing trade, 1540–1560'. Doctoral dissertation, University of London, UK

Toon, Thomas E. 1983. *The Politics of Early Old English Sound Change*. New York: Academic Press

Torp, Arne 2004. 'Skandinavisk nabospråksforståelse – ideal eller virkelighet?', in *Språknytt* 3–4:45–48

Tournier, Jean 1998. *Les mots anglais du français*. Paris: Belin

Tov, Emanuel 1986. 'The orthography and language of the Hebrew scrolls found at Qumran and the origin of these scrolls', *Textus* 13: 31–57

Tranter, Nicolas 2013. 'Logography and layering: a functional cross-linguistic analysis', *Written Language and Literacy* 16 (1): 1–31

Tratado de paz y amistad, celebrado entre España y la República Chilena en 25 de abril de 1844. 1846. Madrid: Imprenta Nacional

Traube, Ludwig 1907. *Nomina Sacra. Versuch einer Geschichte der christlichen Kürzung*. Munich: C. H. Beck'sche Verlagsbuchhandlung

Traxel, Oliver M. 2004. *Language Change, Writing and Textual Interference in Post-Conquest Old English Manuscripts: The Evidence of Cambridge University Library, Ii. l. 33*. Frankfurt am Main: Peter Lang

Tribulato, Olga 2012. *Language and Linguistic Contact in Ancient Sicily*. Cambridge: Cambridge University Press

Trice Martin, Charles 1892. *The Record Interpreter: A Collection of Abbreviations, Latin Words and Names Used in English Historical Manuscripts and Records*. London: Reeves and Turner

Trigger, Bruce G. 2004. 'Writing systems: a case study in cultural evolution', in Stephen D. Houston (ed.), *The First Writing: Script Invention as History and Process*. Cambridge: Cambridge University Press, pp. 39–68

Tronskiĭ, Iosif M. 1962, 'Slogovai͡a struktura drevnegrecheskogo i͡azyka i grecheskoe slogovoe pis'mo', *Drevniĭ mir: akademiku Vasilii͡u Vasil'evichu Struve*. Moscow: Izdatel'stvo vostochnoĭ literatury, pp. 620–26

Trovato, Paolo 2014. *Everything You Always Wanted to Know about Lachmann's Method: A Non-Standard Handbook of Genealogical Textual Criticism in the Age of Post-Structuralism, Cladistics, and Copy-Text* (Storie e linguaggi 7). Limena: Libreriauniversitaria.it edizioni

Trudgill, Peter J. 1974. *The Social Differentiation of English in Norwich*. Cambridge: Cambridge University Press

1983. *Sociolinguistics: An Introduction to Language and Society*. Harmondsworth: Penguin Books

1986. *Dialects in Contact*. Oxford: Blackwell

1997. 'Norwegian as a normal language', in Unn Røyneland (ed.), *Language Contact and Language Conflict. Proceedings of The International Ivar Aasen Conference 14–16 November 1996*. Volda: Volda College, pp. 151–58

2001. *Sociolinguistic Variation and Change*. Edinburgh: Edinburgh University Press

2004. *New-Dialect Formation: The Inevitability of Colonial Englishes*. Edinburgh: Edinburgh University Press

2006. 'Standard and dialect vocabulary', in Keith Brown (ed.), *Encyclopedia of Language and Linguistics*. Oxford: Elsevier, 119–21 (2nd ed.)

Trunte, Nikolaos 2004. 'Das Šafařík-Triodion und das Ende der Digraphie', *Palaeoslavica* 12 (2): 306–17

Tryjarski, Edward 1960. 'Ze studiów nad rękopisami i dialektem kipczackim Ormian polskich', *Rocznik Orientalistyczny* 23 (2): 7–55

1976. 'A fragment of an unknown Armeno-Kipchak text from Polish collections', *Rocznik Orientalistyczny* 38: 291–302

Turner, James 2014. *Philology: The Forgotten Origins of the Modern Humanities*. Princeton: Princeton University Press

Tuten, Donald 2003. *Koinéization in Medieval Spanish*. Berlin: De Gruyter

Tuten, Donald and Tejedo-Herrero, Fernando 2015. 'The relationship between historical linguistics and sociolinguistics', in Manuel Díaz-Campos (ed.), *The Handbook of Hispanic Sociolinguistics*. Malden/Oxford: Wiley-Blackwell, pp. 283–302

Tyrkkö, Jukka 2013. 'Printing houses as communities of practice: orthography in early modern medical books', in Joanna Kopaczyk and Andreas H. Jucker (eds.), *Communities of Practice in the History of English*. Amsterdam: John Benjamins, pp. 151–75

2020. 'Early modern medicine in manuscript and print: a triangulation approach to analysing spelling standardisation', *International Journal of English Studies* 20 (2): 69–95

Ukiškasis kalendorius 1902 metams, turintėms 365 dėnas 1902. Suwałki: Tipografiia M. L. Sheĭnmana, byvshaia A. Marksona

Uldall, Hans J. 1944. 'Speech and writing', *Acta Linguistica* 4: 11–16

Unger, J. Marshall 2015. 'Interpreting diffuse orthographies and orthographic change', in Patrick Honeybone and Joseph Salmons (eds.), *The Oxford Handbook of Historical Phonology*. Oxford: Oxford University Press, pp. 86–99

Unger, J. Marshall and DeFrancis, John 1995. 'Logographic and semasiographic writing systems: a critique of Sampson's classification', in Insup Taylor and David R. Olson (eds.), *Scripts and Literacy: Reading and Learning to Read Alphabets, Syllabaries and Characters*. Dordrecht/Boston/London: Kluwer Academic Publishers, pp. 45–58

Unicode Consortium (ed.) 2019. *The Unicode Standard, Version 12.1.0.* Mountain View: Unicode Consortium, https://home.unicode.org

United States Board on Geographic Names 1892. *First Report of the United States Board on Geographic Names. 1890–1891.* Washington, DC: Government Printing Office

Unseth, Peter (ed.) 2008. *The Sociolinguistics of Script Choice*, special issue of *International Journal of the Sociology of Language* 192

Untermann, Jürgen 2000. *Wörterbuch des Oskisch-Umbrischen.* Heidelberg: Winter

Upward, Christopher and Davidson, George 2011. *The History of English Spelling.* Malden: Wiley-Blackwell

Urbańczyk, Stanisław 1986. 'Polszczyzna Ormian lwowskich', in Reinhold Olesch and Hans Rothe (eds.), *Festschrift für Herbert Bräuer zum 65. Geburtstag am 14. April 1986.* Cologne/Vienna: Böhlau, pp. 667–73

Urla, Jacqueline 1995. 'Outlaw language: creating alternative public spheres in Basque free radio', *Pragmatics* 5 (2): 245–61

Uspenskiĭ, Boris A. 2004. 'Nikolaĭ I i pol'skiĭ i͡azyk (I͡Azykovai͡a politika Rossiĭskoĭ imperii v otnoshenii T͡Sarstva Pol'skogo: voprosy grafiki i orfografii)', *Die Welt der Slaven* 49 (1): 1–38

Vachek, Josef 1939. 'Zum Problem der geschriebenen Sprache', *Travaux du Cercle Linguistique de Prague* 8: 94–104

1945–49. 'Some remarks on writing and phonetic transcription', *Acta Linguistica* 5: 86–93

1964. 'On peripheral phonemes of Modern English', *Brno Studies in English* 4: 7–109

1973. *Written Language.* The Hague: Mouton

1976 [1939]. 'Zum Problem der geschriebenen Sprache', in Josef Vachek (ed.), *Selected Writings in English and General Linguistics.* The Hague: Mouton, pp. 112–33 (reprinted from *Travaux du Cercle Linguistique de Prague* 8: 94–104)

1976 [1945–49]. 'Some remarks on writing and phonetic transcription', in Josef Vachek (ed.), *Selected Writings in English and General Linguistics.* The Hague: Mouton, pp. 127–33 (reprinted from *Acta Linguistica* 5: 86–93)

1976 [1972]. 'The present state of research in written language', in Josef Vachek (ed.), *Selected Writings in English and General Linguistics.* The Hague: Mouton, pp. 134–45 (reprinted from *Folia Linguistica* 6: 47–61)

1993. 'Present-day (w), its form and function in present-day English', *Brno Studies in English* 20: 11–15

Van Aken, Mark J. 1959. *Pan-Hispanism. Its Origin and Development to 1866.* Berkeley/Los Angeles: University of California Press

Van Beek, Gosewijn 1996. 'On materiality', *Etnofoor* 9 (1): 5–24

Van den Bosch, Antal, Content, Alain, Daelemans, Walter and De Gelder, Beatrice 1994. 'Measuring the complexity of writing systems', *Journal of Quantitative Linguistics* 1 (3): 178–88

Vandenbussche, Wim 2002. 'The standardization of Dutch orthography in lower, middle and upper class documents in 19th century Flanders', in Andrew Linn and Nicola McLelland (eds.), *Standardization. Studies from the Germanic Languages*. Amsterdam: Benjamins, pp. 27–42

2007a. '"Lower-class language" in 19th century Flanders', *Multilingua* 26: 277–88

2007b. 'Shared standardization factors in the history of sixteen Germanic languages', in Christian Fandrych and Reinier Salverda (eds.), *Standard, Variation und Sprachwandel in germanischen Sprachen*. Tübingen: Gunter Narr Verlag, pp. 25–36

Van den Werve, Jan II 1553. *Het tresoor der Duytsscher talen*. Brussels: Hans de Laet. Diplomatic transcription from Ghent University Library, accession number BHSL.RES.0535, www.dbnl.org/tekst/werv004scha01_01/

Van der Feest Viðarsson, Heimir 2017. 'The syntax of others: "un-Icelandic" verb placement in 19th- and early 20th-century Icelandic', in Ingrid Tieken-Boon van Ostade and Carol Percy (eds.), *Prescription and Tradition in Language: Establishing Standards across Time and Space*. Bristol: Multilingual Matters, pp. 152–67

Van der Kuijp, Leonard W. J. 1996. 'The Tibetan script and derivatives', in Peter T. Daniels and William Bright (eds.), *The World's Writing Systems*. New York: Oxford University Press, pp. 431–558

Van der Sijs, Nicoline and Beelen, Hans (compilers) 2008–12. *Bijbels Digitaal*. Nederlands Bijbelgenootschap, www.bijbelsdigitaal.nl/

Van der Wal, Marijke and Rutten, Gijsbert (eds.) 2013. *Touching the Past: Studies in the Historical Sociolinguistics of Ego-Documents*. Amsterdam/ Philadelphia: John Benjamins

Van der Wal, Marijke, Rutten, Gijsbert, Nobels, Judith and Simons, Tanja (compilers) 2015. *The Letters as Loot/ Brieven als Buit Corpus*. Compiled by Marijke van der Wal (Programme leader), Gijsbert Rutten, Judith Nobels and Tanja Simons, with the assistance of volunteers of the Leiden-based Wikiscripta Neerlandica transcription project, and lemmatised, tagged and provided with search facilities by the Institute for Dutch Lexicology (INL) (2nd release). Leiden University, https://brievenalsbuit.ivdnt.org/

Van der Wal, Marijke and Van Bree, Cor 2008. *Geschiedenis van Het Nederlands*. Utrecht: Spectrum

Vannebo, Kjell I. 1984. *En nasjon av skriveføre. Om utviklinga fram mot allmenn skriveferdighet på 1800-tallet*. Oslo: Novus

Van Peer, Willie 1997. 'Mutilated signs: notes toward a literary paleography', *Poetics Today* 18 (1): 33–57

Van Reenen, Pieter and Huijs, Nanette 2000. 'De harde en de zachte g, de spelling gh versus g voor voorklinker in het veertiende-eeuwse Middelnederlands', *Taal en Tongval* 52: 159–81

Van Reenen, Pieter and Mulder, Maaike (compilers) s.d. *Corpus Van Reenen – Mulder*, s.l. 1993. 'Een gegevensbank van 14de-eeuwse Middelnederlandse dialecten op computer', *Lexikos* 3: 259–79, www.diachronie.nl/corpora/crm14

Varila, Mari-Liisa, Salmi, Hanna, Mäkilähde, Aleksi, Skaffari, Janne and Peikola, Matti 2017. 'Disciplinary decoding: towards understanding the language of visual and material features', in Matti Peikola, Aleksi Mäkilähde, Hanna Salmi, Mari-Liisa Varila and Janne Skaffari (eds.), *Verbal and Visual Communication in Early English Text*. Turnhout: Brepols, pp. 1–20

Varnhagen, Connie K., McFall, Peggy G., Routledge, Lisa, Suminda-MacDonald, Heather and Kwong, Trudy E. 2010. 'Lol: new language and spelling in instant messaging', *Reading and Writing* 23 (6): 719–33

Vázquez, Nila and Marqués-Aguado, Teresa 2012. 'Editing the medieval manuscript in its social context', in Juan Manuel Hernández-Campoy and Juan Camilo Conde-Silvestre (eds.), *The Handbook of Historical Sociolinguistics*. Chichester: Wiley-Blackwell, pp. 123–39

Vázquez Gastelu, Antonio 1689. *Arte de lengua mexicana*. Puebla: Diego Fernández de León

Védénina, Ludmilla G. 1989. *Pertinence linguistique de la présentation typographique*. Paris: Peeters-Selaf

Venckienė, Jurgita 2004. 'Dvejopa XIX a. pabaigos lietuviškų laikraščių rašyba', in Darius Staliūnas (ed.), *Raidžių draudimo metai*. Vilnius: Lietuvos istorijos instituto leidykla, pp. 207–12

2006. 'Kirilika rašyti lietuviški XIX amžiaus pabaigos ir XX amžiaus pradžios rankraštiniai tekstai', *Archivum Lithuanicum* 8: 319–32

Venezky, Richard L. 1970. *The Structure of English Orthography* (Janua Linguarum, Series Minor 82). The Hague/Paris: Mouton

1999. *The American Way of Spelling*. New York/London: Guildford Press

2001. 'Spelling', in John Algeo (ed.), *The Cambridge History of the English Language*, vol. 6: *English in North America*. Cambridge: University Press, pp. 340–57

2004. 'In search of the perfect orthography', in Martin Neef and Beatrice Primus (eds.), *From Letter to Sound: New Perspectives on Writing Systems*, special issue of *Written Language and Literacy* 7 (2). Amsterdam/Philadelphia: John Benjamins, pp. 139–63

Ventris, Michael 1988. *Work Notes on Minoan Language Research and Other Unedited Papers* (ed. by Anna Sacconi). Rome: Edizioni dell'Ateneo

Ventris, Michael and Chadwick, John 1953. 'Evidence for Greek Dialect in the Mycenaean Archives', *Journal of Hellenic Studies* 73: 84–103

1956. *Documents in Mycenaean Greek*. Cambridge: Cambridge University Press

1973. *Documents in Mycenaean Greek*. Cambridge: Cambridge University Press (2nd ed.)

Ventris, Michael and Sacconi, Anna (eds.) 1988. *Work Notes on Minoan Language Research and Other Unedited Papers*. Rome: Edizioni dell'Ateneo

Vermeylen, Filip R. 2002 'Art and economics: the Antwerp art market of the sixteenth century'. Doctoral dissertation, Columbia University, USA

Verrac, Monique 2000. 'Les premières descriptions grammaticales de l'anglais', in Sylvain Auroux, Ernst F. K. Koerner, Hans-Josef Niederehe and Kees Versteegh (eds.), *History of the Language Sciences/Geschichte der Sprachwissenschaften/Histoire des sciences du langage*. Berlin/Boston: De Gruyter, pp. 771–77

Verrette, Michel 2002. *L'alphabétisation au Québec 1660–1900: en marche vers la modernité culturelle*. Sillery: Septentrion

Vertan, Cristina 2018. 'A framework for annotating and interpreting vagueness in historical documents', in Victor Baranov, Patricia Engel, Jürgen Fuchsbauer and Heinz Miklas (eds.), *El'Manuscript 2018. 7th International Conference on Textual Heritage and Information Technologies. Vienna and Krems, Austria, 14–18 September 2018*. Sofia: Sofia University Press St. Kliment Ochridski, p. 55

Vetancurt, Agustín de 1673. *Arte de lengua mexicana*. Mexico City: Francisco Rodríguez Lupercio

Vickers, Brian 2018. 'The "Dial Hand" epilogue: by Shakespeare, or Dekker?', *Authorship* 7 (2), https://doi.org/10.21825/aj.v7i2.9735

Videsott, Paul 2009. *Padania scrittologica: analisi scrittologiche e scrittometriche di testi in italiano settentrionale antico dalle origini al 1525*. Tübingen: Niemeyer

Vikør, Lars 2018. 'Det moderne Noreg (1945–2015)', in Agnete Nesse (ed.), *Tidslinjer*, vol. 4 of Helge Sandøy and Agnete Nesse (eds.), *Norsk språkhistorie*. Oslo: Novus, pp. 603–95

Vilborg, Ebbe 1960. *A Tentative Grammar of Mycenaean Greek*. Gothenburg: Almqvist and Wiksell

Villa, Laura 2012. '"Because when governments speak, they are not always right": national construction and orthographic conflicts in mid-nineteenth century Spain', in Nils Langer, Steffan Davies and Wim Vandenbussche (eds.), *Language and History, Linguistics and Historiography*. Bern: Peter Lang, pp. 209–27

2013. 'The officialization of Spanish in mid-nineteenth-century Spain: the Academy's authority', in José del Valle (ed.), *A Political History of Spanish*. Cambridge: Cambridge University Press, pp. 93–105

2015. 'Official orthographies, spelling debates and nation-building projects after the fall of the Spanish Empire', in Laura Villa and Rik Vosters (eds.), *The Historical Sociolinguistics of Spelling*, special issue of *Written Language and Literacy* 18 (2). Amsterdam/Philadelphia: John Benjamins, pp. 228–47

2017. 'Real orden del 25 de abril de 1844 que oficializó las normas ortográficas de la Real Academia Española', *Anuario de Glotopolítica* 1: 263–77

Villa, Laura and Vosters, Rik 2015a. 'Language ideological debates over orthography in European linguistic history', in Laura Villa and Rik Vosters (eds.), *The Historical Sociolinguistics of Spelling*, special issue of *Written Language and Literacy* 18 (2). Amsterdam/Philadelphia: John Benjamins, pp. 201–7

(eds.) 2015b. *The Historical Sociolinguistics of Spelling*, special issue of *Written Language and Literacy* 18 (2). Amsterdam/Philadelphia: John Benjamins

Vine, Brent 1993. *Studies in Archaic Latin Inscriptions*. Innsbruck: Institut für Sprachwissenschaft der Universität Innsbruck

Viredaz, Rémy 1983. 'La graphie des groupes de consonnes en mycénien et cypriote', *Minos* 18: 125–207

Vlasto, Alexis P. 1986. *A Linguistic History of Russia to the End of the Eighteenth Century*. Oxford: Clarendon Press

Voeste, Anja 2007a. 'Traveling through the Lexicon: "self-organized" spelling changes', in Guido Nottbusch and Eliane Segers (eds.), *Constraints on Spelling Changes*, special issue of *Written Language and Literacy* 10 (2). Amsterdam/Philadelphia: John Benjamins, pp. 89–102

2007b. 'Variability and professionalism as prerequisites of standardization', in Stephan Elspaß, Nils Langer, Joachim Scharloth and Wim Vandenbussche (eds.), *Germanic Language Histories 'from Below' (1700–2000)* (Studia Linguistica Germanica 86). Berlin/Boston: De Gruyter, pp. 295–307

2008. *Orthographie und Innovation: Die Segmentierung des Wortes im 16. Jahrhundert*. Hildesheim/Zurich/New York: Georg Olms Verlag

2010. 'Die Norm neben der Norm. Zum Zusammenhang von Graphienwahl und Überlieferungsform', in Fest-Platte für Gerd Fritz, www.festschrift-gerd-fritz.de/files/voeste_2010_norm-neben-der-norm.pdf

2012. 'The emergence of suprasegmental spellings in German', in Susan Baddeley and Anja Voeste (eds.), *Orthographies in Early Modern Europe*. Berlin/Boston: De Gruyter, pp. 167–91

2015. 'Proficiency and efficiency: why German spelling changed in early modern times', in Laura Villa and Rik Vosters (eds.), *The Historical Sociolinguistics of Spelling*, special issue of *Written Language and Literacy* 18 (2). Amsterdam/Philadelphia: John Benjamins, pp. 248–59

2016. *'A mensa et thoro*: on the tense relationship between literacy and the spoken word in early modern times', in Cinzia Russi (ed.), *Current Trends in Historical Sociolinguistics*. Berlin: De Gruyter, pp. 237–61

2018a. 'The self as a source: a peasant farmer's letters from prison (1848–1852)', *Journal of Historical Sociolinguistics* 4 (1): 97–118

2018b. 'Interpunktion und Textsegmentierung im frühen deutschsprachigen Prosaroman', *Beiträge zur Geschichte der deutschen Sprache und Literatur* 140: 1–22

2020. 'Investigating methods: intra-textual, inter-textual and cross-textual variable analyses', in Marco Condorelli (ed.), *Advances in Historical Orthography, c. 1500–1800*. Cambridge: Cambridge University Press, pp. 141–53

2021. 'Spelling variation and text alignment: an investigation of German *Mirabilia Romae* from the year 1500', *Zeitschrift für Sprachwissenschaft* 40 (3): 279–95, https://doi.org/10.1515/zfs-2021-2032

Voet, Leon 1969. *The Golden Compasses: A History and Evaluation of the Printing and Publishing Activities of the* Officina Plantiniana *at Antwerp. 1. Christophe Plantin and the Moretuses: Their Lives and Their World*. Amsterdam: Vangendt

Vogt-Spira, Gregor 1991. 'Vox und littera: Der Buchstabe zwischen Mündlichkeit und Schriftlichkeit in der grammatischen Tradition', *Poetica* 23 (3/4): 295–327

Voigts, Linda E. 1984. 'Medical prose', in Anthony S. G. Edwards (ed.), *Middle English Prose: A Critical Guide to Major Authors and Genres*. New Brunswick: Rutgers University Press, pp. 315–35

Von Lieven, Alexandra and Lippert, Sandra L. 2016. 'Egyptian (3000 BCE to ca. 400 CE)', in Daniel Bunčić, Sandra L. Lippert and Achim Rabus (eds.), *Biscriptality: A Sociolinguistic Typology*. Heidelberg: Winter, pp. 256–76

Von Planta, Robert 1892. *Grammatik der Oskisch-Umbrischen Dialekte*. Strasbourg: K. J. Trübner

Von Polenz, Peter 2020 [1978]. *Geschichte der deutschen Sprache*. Berlin/Boston: De Gruyter (11th ed.)

Von Raumer, Rudolf 2019 [1870]. *Geschichte der germanischen Philologie*. Munich: Oldenbourg Wissenschaftsverlag (reprint by De Gruyter)

Von Wartburg, Walther (ed.) 1928–2003. *Französisches etymologisches Wörterbuch: eine Darstellung des galloromanischen Sprachschatzes*, 25 vols. Bonn: Klopp

Vosters, Rik 2011. 'Taalgebruik, taalnormen en taalbeschouwing in Vlaanderen tijdens het Verenigd Koninkrijk der Nederlanden Een historisch-sociolinguïstische verkenning van vroeg-negentiende-eeuws Zuidelijk Nederlands'. Doctoral dissertation, Vrije Universiteit Brussel, Belgium

Vosters, Rik, Belsack, Els, Puttaert, Jill and Vandenbussche, Wim 2014. 'Norms and usage in nineteenth-century Southern Dutch', in Gijsbert Rutten, Rik Vosters and Wim Vandenbussche (eds.), *Norms and Usage in Language History, 1600–1900: A Sociolinguistic and Comparative Perspective*. Amsterdam/Philadelphia: John Benjamins, pp. 73–100

Vosters, Rik and Rutten, Gijsbert 2015. 'Three Southern shibboleths: spelling features as conflicting identity markers in the Low Countries', in Laura Villa and Rik Vosters (eds.), *The Historical Sociolinguistics of Spelling*, special issue of *Written Language and Literacy* 18 (2). Amsterdam/ Philadelphia: John Benjamins, pp. 260–74

Vosters, Rik, Rutten, Gijsbert and Vandenbussche, Wim 2012. 'The sociolinguistics of spelling: a corpus-based case study of orthographical variation in nineteenth-century Dutch in Flanders', in Ans van Kemenade and Nynke de Haas (eds.), *Historical Linguistics 2009. Selected Papers from the 19th International Conference on Historical Linguistics*. Amsterdam/ Philadelphia: Benjamins, pp. 253–73

Vosters, Rik, Rutten, Gijsbert, van der Wal, Marijke and Vandenbussche, Wim 2012. 'Spelling and identity in the Southern Netherlands (1750–1830)', in Alexandra M. Jaffe, Jannis K. Androutsopoulos, Mark Sebba and Sally A. Johnson (eds.), *Orthography as Social Action: Scripts, Spelling, Identity and Power* (Language and Social Processes 3). Boston/Berlin: De Gruyter, pp. 135–59

Waal, Willemijn 2012. 'Writing in Anatolia: the origins of the Anatolian hieroglyphs and the introduction of the cuneiform script', *Altorientalische Forschungen* 39 (2): 287–315

Wachter, Rudolf 1986. 'Die etruskische und venetische Silbenpunktierung', *Museum Helveticum* 43: 111–26

Wagner, Esther-Miriam, Beinhoff, Bettina and Outhwaite, Ben (eds.) 2013. *Scribes as Agents of Language Change*. Berlin: De Gruyter

Wagner, Esther-Miriam, Outhwaite, Ben and Beinhoff, Bettina 2013. 'Scribes and language change', in Esther-Miriam Wagner, Bettina Beinhoff and Ben Outhwaite (eds.), *Scribes as Agents of Language Change*. Berlin: De Gruyter, pp. 3–18

Wakelin, Daniel 2011. 'Writing the words', in Alexandra Gillespie and Daniel Wakelin (eds.), *The Production of Books in England 1350–1500* (Cambridge Studies in Palaeography and Codicology 14). Cambridge: Cambridge University Press, pp. 34–58

Walder, Adrienne 2020. 'Das versale Eszett. Ein neuer Buchstabe im deutschen Alphabet', *Zeitschrift für Germanistische Linguistik* 48 (2): 211–37

Waldispühl, Michelle 2018. "Deutsch" oder "nordgermanisch"? Sprachliche Bestimmung von Namen im Reichenauer Verbrüderungsbuch vor dem Hintergrund von Sprachkontakt und Mehrsprachigkeit', in Christoph

Hoffarth and Benjamin Scheller (eds.), *Ambiguität und die Ordnungen des Sozialen im Mittelalter*. Berlin: De Gruyter, pp. 129–50

2020a. 'Historische Rufnamen im Kontakt. Integration der altisländischen Pilgernamen auf der Reichenau in die mittelhochdeutsche Schreibsprache', in Luise Kempf, Damaris Nübling and Mirjam Schmuck (eds.), *Linguistik der Eigennamen*. Berlin: De Gruyter, pp. 17–37

2020b. 'Roman and runic in the Anglo-Saxon inscriptions at Monte Sant'Angelo: a sociolinguistic approach', *Futhark: International Journal of Runic Studies* 9–10 (2018–2019): 135–58

Walker, James A. 2010. *Variation in Linguistic Systems*. London/New York: Routledge

2014. 'Variation analysis', in Robert J. Podesva and Devyani Sharma (eds.), *Research Methods in Linguistics*. Cambridge: Cambridge University Press, pp. 440–59

Walker, John 1791. *A Critical Pronouncing Dictionary and Expositor of the English Language*. London

Wall, Wendy 2000. 'Authorship and the material conditions of writing', in Arthur F. Kinney (ed.), *The Cambridge Companion to English Literature, 1500–1600*. Cambridge: Cambridge University Press, pp. 64–89

Wallis, Christine 2013. 'The Old English Bede: transmission and textual history in Anglo-Saxon manuscripts'. Doctoral dissertation, University of Sheffield, UK, http://etheses.whiterose.ac.uk/id/eprint/5459

Wallis, John 1670. 'A Letter of Doctor John Wallis to Robert Boyle Esq. concerning the said Doctors Essay of Teaching a person Dumb and Deaf to speak, and to understand Language, together with the success thereof, made apparent to his Majesty, the Royal Society, and the University of Oxford', *Philosophical Transactions* 61: 1087–99

Walton, Stephen J. 1987. *Farewell the Spirit Craven. Ivar Aasen and National Romanticism*. Oslo: Det norske Samlaget

Warner, Lawrence 2015. 'Scribes, misattributed: Hoccleve and Pinkhurst', *Studies in the Age of Chaucer* 37: 55–100

Waters, Cathleen and Sali A. Tagliamonte 2017. 'Is one innovation enough? Leaders, covariation, and language change', *American Speech* 92 (1): 23–40

Watkins, Calvert 1976. 'Observations on the "Nestor's Cup" inscription', *Harvard Studies in Classical Philology* 80: 25–40

Watt, Diane 2013. 'The earliest women's writing? Anglo-Saxon literary cultures and communities', *Women's Writing* 20 (4): 537–54, https://doi.org/10.1080/09699082.2013.773761

2019. *Women, Writing and Religion in England and beyond, 650–1100* (Studies in Early Medieval History). New York: Bloomsbury Academic

Watt, Tessa 1991. *Cheap Print and Popular Piety, 1550–1640*. Cambridge: Cambridge University Press

Watt, William C. 1998. 'The old-fashioned way', *Semiotica* 122 (1–2): 99–138

Watts, Richard J. 2011. *Language Myths and the History of English*. Oxford: Oxford University Press

2015. 'Setting the scene: letters, standards and historical sociolinguistics', in Anita Auer, Daniel Schreier and Richard J. Watts (eds.), *Letter Writing and Language Change*, Cambridge: Cambridge University Press, pp. 1–13

Watts, Richard J. and Trudgill, Peter J. (eds.) 2002. *Alternative Histories of English*. Milton Park/New York: Routledge

Waxenberger, Gaby 2017. 'The development of the Old English fuþorc', in Gaby Waxenberger, Hans Sauer and Kerstin Kazzazi (eds.), *Von den Hieroglyphen zur Internetsprache. Das Verhältnis von Schrift, Laut und Sprache*. Wiesbaden: Reichert, pp. 209–47

Waxenberger, Gaby forthcoming. *A Phonology of Old English Runic Inscriptions with a Concise Edition and Analysis of the Graphemes*. Berlin/Boston: De Gruyter

Webb, Thomas W. (ed.) 1873. *Military Memoir of Colonel John Birch, Sometime Governor of Hereford in the Civil War between Charles I and the Parliament, Written by Roe, His Secretary*. London: Camden Society

Weber, Eugen 1976. *Peasants into Frenchmen: The Modernization of Rural France, 1870–1914*. Stanford: Stanford University Press

Weber, Max 2004 [1919]. 'Politik als Beruf', in David S. Owen and Tracy B. Strong (eds.), *The Vocation Lectures* (trans. Rodney Livingston). Indianapolis: Hackett, pp. 32–94

Weber, Walter R. 1958. *Das Aufkommen der Substantivgroßschreibung im Deutschen: ein historisch-kritischer Versuch*. Munich: Uni-Druck

Webster, Noah 1783–85. *A Grammatical Institute, of the English Language* [...]. Hartford: Parts 1 and 2: Hudson and Goodwin for the author, 1783, 1784; Part 3: Barlow and Babcock for the author, 1785

1806. *A Compendious Dictionary of the English Language* [...]. Hartford: Sidney

1828. *An American Dictionary of the English Language* [...], 2 vols. New York: S. Converse

Wehr, Hans 1976. *A Dictionary of Modern Written Arabic*. Edited by John Milton Cowan. Ithaca/New York: Spoken Language Services (3rd ed.)

Weingarten, Rüdiger 2011. 'Comparative graphematics', in Susanne R. Borgwaldt and Terry Joyce (eds.), *Typology of Writing Systems*, special issue of *Written Language and Literacy* 14 (1). Amsterdam/Philadelphia: John Benjamins, pp. 12–38

Weingarten, Rüdiger, Nottbusch, Guido and Will, Udo 2004. 'Morphemes, syllables and graphemes in written word production', in Thomas Pechmann and Christopher Habel (eds.), *Multidisciplinary Approaches to Language Production*. Berlin/New York: De Gruyter, pp. 1–28

Weinreich, Uriel 1965. *Ashkenazic Hebrew and the Hebrew Component in Yiddish*, Jerusalem: The Academy of the Hebrew Language

Wells, Christopher 1972. 'An orthographic approach to early Frankish personal names', *Transactions of the Philological Society* 71 (1): 101–64

Wells, Herbert G. 1897. *The Invisible Man*. New York/London: Harper and Brothers Publishers

Wenger, Étienne 1998. *Communities of Practice: Learning, Meaning, and Identity*. New York: Cambridge University Press

Werner, Sarah 2014. 'Finding women in the printing shop', *Collation. Folger*, https://collation.folger.edu/2014/10/finding-women-in-the-printing-shop

Wertheim, Suzanne 2012. 'Reclamation, revalorization, and re-tatarization via changing Tatar orthographies', in Alexandra M. Jaffe, Jannis K. Androutsopoulos, Mark Sebba and Sally A. Johnson (eds.), *Orthography as Social Action: Scripts, Spelling, Identity and Power*. Boston/Berlin: De Gruyter, pp. 65–101

Wexler, Paul 1988. 'Christian, Jewish and Muslim translations of the Bible and Koran in Byelorussia: 16th–19th centuries', *The Journal of Belarusian Studies* 6 (1): 12–19

Whalen, Richard F. 2015. 'Was "Shakspere" also a spelling of "Shakespeare"? Strat Stats fail to prove it', *Interdisciplinary Journal of Authorship Studies* 6: 33–50

Wharton, Jeremiah 1654. *The English-Grammar* [...]. London: William Du-Gard

Wheale, Nigel 1999. *Writing and Society: Literacy, Print, and Politics in Britain, 1590–1660*. London/New York: Routledge

White, David L. 2000. 'Irish influence and the interpretation of Old English spelling'. Doctoral dissertation, The University of Texas at Austin, USA

Whitney, William D. 1889. *A Sanskrit Grammar: Including Both the Classical Language, and the Older Dialects, of Veda and Brahmana*. Leipzig: Breitkopf and Härtel (2nd ed.)

Whittaker, Gordon 2009. 'The principles of Nahuatl writing', *Göttinger Beiträge zur Sprachwissenschaft* 16: 47–81

Wiberg, Christian K. 1907. *Jomfru Pegelau*. Kristiania: Aschehoug

Wiese, Richard 2004. 'How to optimize orthography', in Martin Neef and Beatrice Primus (eds.), *From Letter to Sound: New Perspectives on Writing Systems*, special issue of *Written Language and Literacy* 7 (2). Amsterdam/Philadelphia: John Benjamins, pp. 305–31

Wiggins, Alison 2016. *Bess of Hardwick's Letters: Language, Materiality, and Early Modern Epistolary Culture*. London: Routledge

Wildenthal, Bryan H. 2018. 'Reflections on spelling and the Shakespeare authorship question: "What's in (the spelling of) a name?"', *Thomas Jefferson School of Law Research Paper No. 3185805*, 1–4

Wilkens, Friedrich 1891. *Zum hochalemannischen Konsonantismus der althochdeutschen Zeit: Beiträge zur Lautlehre und Orthographie des ältesten Hochalemannischen, auf Grundlage der deutschen Eigennamen in den St. Galler Urkunden (bis zum Jahre 825)*. Leipzig: Gustav Fock

Willemyns, Roland 2003. 'Dutch', in Ana Deumert and Wim Vandenbussche (eds.), *Germanic Standardizations: Past to Present*. Amsterdam/ Philadelphia: John Benjamins, pp. 93–125

2013. *Dutch: Biography of a Language*. Oxford: Oxford University Press

Williams, Graham T. 2014. *Women's Epistolary Utterance: A Study of the Letters of Joan and Maria Thynne, 1575–1611* (Pragmatics and Beyond New Series 233). Amsterdam: John Benjamins

Williamson, Keith 2013–. *A Linguistic Atlas of Older Scots, Phase 1: 1380–1500*. Edinburgh: University of Edinburgh, www.lel.ed.ac.uk/ihd/ laos1/laos1.html

Willis, James (ed.) 1983. *Martianus Capella*. Bibliotheca scriptorum Graecorum et Romanorum Teubneriana. Leipzig: Teubner

Wilson, Kenneth G. 1993. 'Spelling pronunciations', in *The Columbia Guide to Standard American English*. New York: Columbia University Press

Wittgenstein, Ludwig 1926. *Wörterbuch für Volks- und Bürgerschulen*. Vienna: Hölder-Pichler-Tempsky AG

Witzstat, Hans 1526 (A). *Der geyſtlich Buchsbaum/ Von dem ſtreyte des fleyſches wider den geyſt*. Nuremberg: Jobst Gutknecht (VD16 W 4082)

1528 (B_1). *Der geiſtlich buchſzbaum. Von dem ſtreyt des fleyſchs wider den geyſt*. Nuremberg: Kunigunde Hergot (VD16 ZV 26909)

1528 (B_2). *Der geiſtlich buchſzbaum. Von dem ſtreyt des fleyſchs wider den geiſt*. Nuremberg: Kunigunde Hergot (VD16 W 4083)

Wolańska, Ewa 2019. *System grafematyczny współczesnej polszczyzny na tle innych systemów pisma*. Warsaw: Dom Wydawniczy Elipsa

Wolf, Johanna and Blauth-Henke, Christine 2011. 'Methode als Grenze? Zur Spaltung von Philologie und Sprachwissenschaft im 19. Jahrhundert', in Gerda Hassler (ed.), *History of Linguistics 2008. Selected Papers from the Eleventh International Conference on the History of the Language Sciences (ICHoLS XI), 28 August–2 September 2008, Potsdam*. Amsterdam: John Benjamins, pp. 49–68

Wolfram, Walt 1969. *A Sociolinguistic Description of Detroit Negro Speech*. Washington, DC: Center for Applied Linguistics

1991. 'The linguistic variable: fact and fantasy', *American Speech* 66 (1): 22–32

2006. 'Variation and language: overview', in Keith Brown (ed.), *Encyclopedia of Language and Linguistics*, vol. 13. Amsterdam/Boston: Elsevier, pp. 333–41 (2nd ed.)

Woodard, Roger D. 1994. 'On the interaction of Greek orthography and phonology: consonant clusters in the syllabic scripts', in William C. Watt (ed.), *Writing Systems and Cognition. Neuropsychology and Cognition*, vol 6. Dordrecht: Springer, pp. 311–34

1997. *Greek Writing from Knossos to Homer. A Linguistic Interpretation of the Origin of the Greek Alphabet and the Continuity of Ancient Greek Literacy*. Oxford: Oxford University Press

Woods, Christopher 2010a. 'Visible language: the earliest writing systems', in Christopher Woods, Emily Teeter and Geoff Emberling (eds.), *Visible Language: Inventions of Writing in the Ancient Middle East and Beyond*. Chicago: Oriental Institute, pp. 15–25

2010b. 'The earliest Mesopotamian writing', in Christopher Woods, Emily Teeter and Geoff Emberling (eds.), *Visible Language: Inventions of Writing in the Ancient Middle East and Beyond*. Chicago: Oriental Institute, pp. 33–50

Woolard, Kathryn 1998. 'Language ideology as a field of inquiry', in Bambi Schieffelin, Kathryn Woolard and Paul Kroskrity (eds.), *Language Ideologies: Practice and Theory*. New York/Oxford: Oxford University Press, pp. 3–50

Woolard, Kathryn and Schieffelin, Bambi 1994. 'Language ideology', *Annual Review of Anthropology* 23: 55–82

Woudhuysen, Henry R. 1996. *Sir Philip Sidney and the Circulation of Manuscripts, 1558–1640*. Oxford: Clarendon Press

Wrenn, Charles L. 1967 [1943]. 'The value of spelling as evidence', in Charles L. Wrenn (ed.), *Word and Symbol: Studies in English Language*. London: Longmans

Wright, Joseph 1924. *An Elementary Historical New English Grammar*. London: Oxford University Press

Wright, Laura 1994. 'On the writing of the history of Standard English', in Francisco Moreno Fernández, Miguel Fuster and Juan Jose Calvo (eds.), *English Historical Linguistics 1992* (Current Issues in Linguistic Theory 113). Amsterdam: John Benjamins, pp. 105–15

1996. *Sources of London English: Medieval Thames Vocabulary*. Oxford: Clarendon Press

2000. 'Introduction', in Laura Wright (ed.), *The Development of Standard English 1300–1800: Theories, Descriptions, Conflicts*. Cambridge: Cambridge University Press, pp. 1–8

2002. 'Code-intermediate phenomena in medieval mixed-language business texts', *Language Sciences* 24 (3–4): 471–89

2011. 'On variation in medieval mixed-language business writing', in Herbert Schendl and Laura Wright (eds.), *Code-Switching in Early English*. Berlin: De Gruyter, pp. 191–218

2020a. 'Introduction', in Laura Wright (ed.), *The Multilingual Origins of Standard English*. Berlin: De Gruyter, pp. 3–15 (ed.) 2020b. *The Multilingual Origins of Standard English*. Berlin: De Gruyter

Wright, Roger 2011. 'Abbo of Fleury in Ramsey (985–987)', in Elizabeth M. Tyler (ed.), *Conceptualizing Multilingualism in England, c.800–c.1250* (Studies in the Early Middle Ages 27). Turnhout: Brepols, pp. 105–20, https://doi.org/10.1484/M.SEM-EB.4.8006

Wright, Sue 2012. 'Language policy, the nation and nationalism', in Bernard Spolsky (ed.), *The Cambridge Handbook of Language Policy*. Cambridge: Cambridge University Press, pp. 59–78

Writing Systems Research, www.tandfonline.com/toc/pwsr20/current

Written Language and Literacy, https://benjamins.com/catalog/wll

Wurm, Stephen 1994. 'Graphisation and standardisation of languages', in Georges Lüdi (ed.), *Sprachstandardisierung*. Fribourg: Universitätsverlag, 255–72

Wyld, Henry C. 1956. *The Universal Dictionary of the English Language* [...]. London: Routledge/Kegan Paul (8th ed.)

Wyrod, Christopher 2008. 'A social orthography of identity: the N'ko literacy movement in West Africa', in Peter Unseth (ed.), *The Sociolinguistics of Script Choice*, special issue of *International Journal of the Sociology of Language* 192: 27–44

Yager, Susan 2010. 'New Philology', in Albrecht Classen (ed.), *Handbook of Medieval Studies: Terms, Methods, Trends*, vol. 2. Berlin: De Gruyter, pp. 999–1006

Yakubovich, Ilya 2010. 'Anatolian hieroglyphic writing', in Christopher Woods, Emily Teeter and Geoff Emberling (eds.), *Visible Language: Inventions of Writing in the Ancient Middle East and Beyond*. Chicago: Oriental Institute, pp. 203–7

Yáñez-Bouza, Nuria. 2015. '"Have you ever written a diary or a journal?" Diurnal prose and register variation', *Neuphilologische Mitteilungen* 116: 449–74

Yip, Po-Ching and Rimmington, Don 2016. *Chinese: A Comprehensive Grammar*. London/New York: Routledge (2nd ed.)

Young, Christopher and Gloning, Thomas 2004. *A History of the German Language through Texts*. London/New York: Routledge, https://doi.org/10.4324/9780203488072

Younging, Gregory 2018. *Elements of Indigenous Style: A Guide for Writing by and about Indigenous Peoples*. Edmonton: Brush Education

Yule, Valerie and Yasuko, Ishi 2016. 'Spelling reform', in Vivian Cook and Des Ryan (eds.), *The Routledge Handbook of the English Writing System*. London/New York: Routledge, pp. 413–27

Zabrocki, Ludwik 1970. 'Kommunikative Gemeinschaften und Sprachgemeinschaften', *Folia Linguistica* 4 (1–2): 2–23

Zair, Nicholas 2016. *Oscan in the Greek Alphabet*. Cambridge: Cambridge University Press

Zalizni͡ak, Andreĭ A. 1986. 'Novgorodskie berestyanye gramoty s lingvisticheskoĭ tochki zreniya', in Valentin L. I͡Anin and Andreĭ A. Zalizni͡ak (eds.), *Novgorodskie gramoty na bereste (iz raskopok 1977–1983 gg.)*, vol. 8. Moscow: Nauka, pp. 89–219

2000. 'Paleografii͡a beresti͡anykh gramot', in Valentin L. I͡Anin and Andreĭ A. Zalizni͡ak (eds.), *Novgorodskie gramoty na bereste (iz raskopok 1990–1996 gg.)*, vol. 10. Moscow: Russkie slovari, pp. 134–274

2002a [1979]. 'O poni͡atii grafemy', in Andreĭ A. Zalizni͡ak, *"Russkoe imennoe slovoizmenenie" s prilozheniem izbrannykh rabot po sovremennomu russkomu i͡azyku i obshchemu i͡azykoznanii͡u*. Moscow: I͡Azyki slavi͡anskoĭ kul'tury, pp. 559–76

2002b. 'Drevnerusskai͡a grafika so smesheniem *ъ-o* i *ь-e*', in Andreĭ A. Zalizni͡ak, *"Russkoe imennoe slovoizmenenie" s prilozheniem izbrannykh rabot po sovremennomu russkomu i͡azyku i obshchemu i͡azykoznanii͡u*, Moscow: I͡Azyki slavi͡anskoĭ kul'tury, pp. 577–612

2004. *Drevnenovgorodskiĭ dialekt*. Moscow: I͡Azyki slavi͡anskoĭ kul'tury (2nd ed.)

Zamora Vicente, Alonso 1999. *Historia de la Real Academia Española*. Madrid: Espasa

Zanobini, Michele 2016. 'Philology, Renaissance', in Marco Sgarbi (ed.), *Encyclopedia of Renaissance Philosophy*. Cham: Springer, pp. 1–9

Zemenová, Markéta 2011. 'Nástin překladatelských postupů a metod v období raného *novověku v kontaktu německo-českém/A Study on the Techniques and Methods in German-Czech Translations at the Time of the Renaissance and the Reformation*'. MA dissertation, Univerzita Karlova v Praze, Czech Republic

Zheltukhin, Alexander 1996. *Orthographic Codes and Code-Switching: A Study in 16th-Century Swedish Orthography*. Stockholm: Almqvist & Wiksell

2012. 'Variable norms in 16th-century Swedish orthography', in Susan Baddeley and Anja Voeste (eds.), *Orthographies in Early Modern Europe*. Berlin/Boston: De Gruyter, pp. 193–218

Zhukovskai͡a, Lidii͡a P. 1955. 'Paleografii͡a', in Viktor I. Borkovskiĭ (ed.), *Paleograficheskiĭ i lingvisticheskiĭ analiz novgorodskikh beresti͡anykh gramot*, Moscow: Izdatel'stvo Akademii Nauk SSSR, pp. 13–78

Ziegler, Johannes C. and Goswami, Usha 2005. 'Reading acquisition, developmental dyslexia, and skilled reading across languages: a psycholinguistic grain size theory', *Psychological Bulletin* 131: 3–29

Zifonun, Gisela, Hoffmann, Ludger and Strecker, Bruno 1997. *Grammatik der Deutschen Sprache*. Berlin: De Gruyter

Zimmer, Ben 2008. '"Ghoti" before Shaw', *Language Log*. Posted Apr. 23, https://languagelog.ldc.upenn.edu/nll/?p=81

Zimmerman, Jonathan 2010. 'Simplified spelling and the cult of efficiency in the 'Progressiv' era', *The Journal of the Gilded Age and Progressive Era* 9 (3): 365–94

Zink, Gaston 1999. *Phonétique historique du français*. Paris: Presses Universitaires de France

Znamenskaya, Tatiana A. 2004. *Stylistics of the English Language: Fundamentals of the Course*. Moscow: YPCC

Zima, Petr 1974. 'Digraphia: the case of Hausa', *Linguistics* 124: 57–69

Žagar, Mateo 2007. Grafolingvistika srednjovjekovnih tekstova. Zagreb: Matica hrvatska

2013. *Uvod u glagoljsku paleografiju I (X. i XI. stoljeće.)*. Zagreb: Institut za hrvatski jezik i jezikoslovlje

2020. 'Orthographic solutions at the onset of Early Modern Croatian: an application of the grapholinguistic method', in Marco Condorelli (ed.), *Advances in Historical Orthography, c. 1500–1800*. Cambridge: Cambridge University Press, pp. 176–90

Name Index

Aasen, Ivar, 443, 489
Abbott, Andrew, 336
Abbott, Jacob, 314
Abercrombie, David, 97, 106
Accius, Lucius, 290–91
Adam, Isabell, 126
Adam, Renaud, 464–71
Adams, Douglas, 324
Adams, James N., 291–92
Adelung, Johann C., 120
Agata, Mari, 7
Agha, Asif, 265, 526, 533
Ahlzweig, Claus, 332
Ahmad, Rizwan, 583, 587
Ainsworth, Robert, 515
Airoldi, Edoardo, 507
Akar, Işık, 70
Akiner, Shirin, 239–40
Aldama y Guevara, José A., 565
Alexander, William, 515
Alfonso X, King, 568, 588–89
Allen, Julie D., 64–67
Althaus, Hans P., 127
Altmann, Gabriel, 157–58
Álvarez Cáccamo, Celso, 561, 586
Amador-Moreno, Carolina, 535
Ambrosiani, Per, 16, 175, 180
Amirova, Tamara A., 5, 124, 130
Ammon, Ulrich, 529, 611
Amsler, Mark, 206
Ananiewa, Natalia, 235
Andersen, Jennifer L., 71–72, 475
Anderson, Benedict, 436
Anderwald, Lieselotte, 601
Androutsopoulus, Jannis, 583
Angermeyer, Philipp S., 178
Anis, Jacques, 121, 128–29, 168
Anson, Chris M., 443
Antonovich, Anton K., 240
Arabyan, Marc, 169
Archer, Dawn, 266
Aris, Rutherford, 307
Aristotle, 96–100
Arnot, Madeleine, 513
Arnoux, Elvira, 593
Arnovick, Leslie, 532
Aronoff, Mark, 8, 42, 115, 272–76, 441, 505
Arrivé, Michel, 449
Atatürk, Mustafa Kemal, 451
Auer, Anita, 114, 328, 534–35, 556, 561
Auer, Peter, 384, 541
Augst, Gerhard, 96, 102, 109, 123
Avanesov, Ruben I., 389
Ayres-Bennett, Wendy, 275

Backhouse, Anthony, 144
Bacon, Elizabeth, 511, 517
Baddeley, Susan, 5, 8, 75, 79, 83–92, 112, 171, 260, 264, 309, 387, 393, 437–39, 441, 471, 521–24, 586
Bagge, Sverre, 482
Bagley, Robert, 36
Baines, John, 35, 40
Baisch, Martin, 348
Baker, Philip, 439
Baker, Robert G., 636
Bakhtin, Mikhail M., 93, 268
Balbach, Anna-Maria, 328
Bann, Jennifer, 561
Barac-Cikoja, Dragana, 179
Barbarić, Vuk-Tadija, 15
Barlow, Julie, 444–48
Barnard, John,474
Barnes, Michael, 262
Barratt, Alexandra, 502–3
Barritt, C. Westbrook, 102, 105
Barros, Maria C., 454, 558
Barteld, Fabian, 71
Barton, David, 555–57
Bartoněk, Antonín, 403
Bartsch, Renate, 266
Bartula, Czesław, 227
Bassetti, Benedetta, 176, 179
Basso, Keith, 111
Basu, Anupam, 272–76

Bates, Stephen, 453
Battaner Moro, Elena, 588
Baudouin de Courtenay, Jan, 52, 100, 103, *see also* Boduėn de Kurtenė, Ivan
Baugh, Albert C., 621
Bazell, Charles E., 102, 107
Beal, Joan C., 280
Beal, Peter, 422–23
Bede, the Venerable, 351, 355, 429
Beekes, Robert, 403
Begor Lancashire, Anne, 510
Behaghel, Otto, 101
Beinhoff, Bettina, 420–22
Beit-Arie, Malachi, 306
Bell, Allan, 268, 523–28
Bell, David N., 469
Bell, Maureen, 474
Bellaert, Jacob,473
Bellen, Hans, 461
Bello, Andrés, 444, 588, 593
Benediktsson, Hreinn, 257, 340
Benskin, Michael, 270–71, 350, 353, 426–32, 528, 530
Bentin, Shlomo, 618
Berg, Ivar, 438
Berg, Kristian, 51–52, 54, 58–59, 63, 115, 272–76, 441, 479, 505
Berger, Tilman, 8, 90, 320
Bergmann, Rolf, 71, 257, 331
Bergs, Alexander, 424, 502–4, 508
Berkenbusch, Eckhard, 62
Berlanda, Elena, 175–77
Bermel, Neil, 586–87
Bernabé, Alberto, 398, 402–4, 405, 408
Bernard, H. Russell, 314
Berrendonner, Alain, 169
Berta, Tibor, 588
Biava, Christina, 454
Biber, Douglas, 525, 534
Biedermann-Pasques, Liselotte, 172
Birk, Elisabeth, 123
Bischoff, Bernhard, 208–12, 218, 357
Bismarck, Otto von, 445
Bjørnson, Bjørnstjerne, 489
Blake, Norman F., 8, 116, 529, 535
Bland, Mark,467
Blank, Paula, 280
Blanton, Virginia, 501
Blatt, Heather, 279
Blayney, Peter W. M., 469
Blix, Elias, 444
Blommaert, Jan, 558, 587
Bloomfield, Leonard, 7, 31, 101, 120, 150, 344, 619
Blount, Thomas, 515
Boduėn de Kurtenė, Ivan, 123, *see also* Baudouin de Courtenay, Jan
Boekholt, Petrus Th. F. M., 601
Boesch, Bruno, 255
Boleyn, Anne, 504
Bolinger, Dwight, 104
Bomann-Larsen, Tor, 491
Bondarev, Dmitry, 561, 576
Bonfante, Giuliano, 303
Bonfante, Larissa, 303
Bopp, Franz, 101, 342
Borgwaldt, Susanne R., 79, 142, 145, 152, 154
Borkovskiĭ, Viktor I., 389
Boswell, James, 531
Bottéro, Françoise, 36
Bourciez, Édouard, 640
Bowie, David, 332
Boyle, Leonard E., 307
Brackmann, Rebecca, 280
Bradley, Henry, 103
Brajerski, Tadeusz, 227
Branca-Rosoff, Sonia, 541–54
Brandt, Carmen, 178
Braune, Wilhelm, 356–57
Breasted, James H., 307, 315
Bredel, Ursula, 67–70
Brehmer, Bernhard, 124
Brengelman, Frederick H., 116, 201, 278, 505
Bright, William, 31, 41–44, 154
Brinsley, John, 514
Brinton, Laurel, 532
Britain, David, 529, 628
Brito, Johannes,471
Brooks, Greg, 165
Brooksbank, Joseph, 278
Brown, Goold, 100
Brown, Gordon, 500
Brown, Joshua, 535
Brown, Keith, 124–26
Brown, Michelle P., 212, 215
Brown, Shana, 307
Bruce, John, 517
Brunschwig, Hieronymus, 376
Buben, Vladimir, 620
Buchmann, Franziska, 55, 59, 60–63
Buckley, Eugene, 42
Bulatova, Nadezhda Ja., 450
Bülbring, Karl D., 343
Bull, Tove, 478, 483
Bullokar, William, 98, 277
Bullough, Donald, 521
Bunčić, Daniel, 5, 8, 71, 75, 83, 120, 126, 133, 135, 175–78, 309, 320, 384, 387, 555, 560
Burchfield, Robert, 365
Burke, Peter, 437–38
Burkhard, Conrad, 268
Burnaby, Barbara, 454
Burrows, Steven D., 507
Butler, Charles, 278, 441
Bybee, Joan L., 336
Bynack, Vincent P., 186

Cable, Thomas, 621
Cahill, Michael, 47
Cain, Christopher M., 351
Calle-Martín, Javier, 7, 20, 362–66, 376, 421
Calude, Cristian S., 325
Cameron, Deborah, 581
Campbell, Alistair, 352
Campbell, Lyle, 558
Camps, Jean-Baptiste, 221
Canger, Una, 564
Cano Aguilar, Rafael, 567–68, 573
Capp, Bernard, 474
Cappelli, Adriano, 206–9, 213–18, 322
Carl, Prince, 491

Carnegie, Andrew, 451
Carney, Edward, 76, 80–85, 110, 522, 621
Caro Reina, Javier, 70
Carochi, Horacio, 565
Carroll, Carleton W., 307
Carroll, Ruth, 434
Carroll, Susanne, 525–27
Carton, Fernand, 640
Carvalhão Buescu, Maria L., 601
Castaño-Gil, Miguel Á., 362
Catach, Nina, 109, 124, 165, 166–69, 449, 543, 620, 640
Caulibus, Johannes de, 384
Cave, Anthony, 604
Cavendish, William, 514
Cawdrey, Robert, 515
Caxton, William, 458, 471, 473–74, 505, 531
Cellucci, Carlo, 326
Černá-Willi, Rahel, 382
Cerquiglini, Bernard, 8
Cervantes, Miguel de, 440
Chadwick, John, 33, 398, 400–2, 410, 541
Chahoud, Anna, 288–91
Chalker, Sylvia, 623
Chalmers, John, 514
Chambers, Jack K., 113, 539
Chandler, Daniel, 617
Chang, Li-Yun, 158
Charles I, King, 517
Charpin, François, 290
Chassant, Alphonse A. L., 207, 213, 216
Chaucer, Geoffrey, 219, 270, 361, 423–24, 430–31, 604
Cheke, John, 277
Cheshire, Jenny, 267, 598–99
Cheung, Yat-Shing, 176
Choi, Lee Jin, 500
Chomsky, Carol, 107–8, 634–38
Chomsky, Noam, 107, 633–38
Chrisomalis, Stephen, 37
Christensen, Birgit, 479
Christianson, C. Paul, 423, 467
Cicero, 210
Cifuentes, Bárbara, 448, 562–66
Clackson, James, 286–88, 307
Clancy Clements, Joseph, 561
Clark, Cecily, 346, 425
Claymond, John,473
Clemens, Raymond, 208, 213, 216, 361–65
Clement, Francis, 97, 278
Cleminson, Ralph, 176
Close, Elizabeth, 307
Coe, Michael D., 35, 195
Cohen, Marcel, 226–27, 243
Collin, Richard O., 450
Coltheart, Max, 102
Comrie, Bernard, 181, 450
Conde-Silvestre, Juan Camilo, 7, 114, 463, 503, 522–24, 530–31, 540, 604
Condorelli, Marco, 5–10, 18, 22, 116, 170, 276, 281, 393, 441, 457, 501, 508, 519, 521–22, 530–32
Conrad, Susan, 525, 534
Considine, John, 437, 440
Contreras, Lidia, 593
Cook, Vivian, 176, 179
Cooper, Carolyn, 453
Cooper, Jerrold S., 35, 45
Cooper, Robert L., 441
Coote, Edmund, 278, 506, 515
Corbett, John, 561
Correas, Gonzalo, 588
Corrie, Marilyn, 270
Cortada, James W., 593
Coseriu, Eugen, 525
Cottereau, Emilie, 221
Coulmas, Florian, 31, 47, 50, 53, 56–67, 74–75, 78–86, 111, 129, 138–54, 234, 381, 437, 440, 442, 456, 520, 527, 555–59, 598, 618
Coupland, Nikolas, 525, 580
Court de Gébelin, Antoine, 235
Coye, Dale F., 623
Crain, Patricia, 314
Croft, William, 556
Cross, Rowin, 361
Crossland, Roland A., 106–7
Crowley, Tony, 581
Crystal, David, 3, 525–26
Cutillas-Espinosa, Juan, 533
Cyril, 227
Cysouw, Michael, 64
Czernecki, Józef, 232

Dahl, Marcus, 510
Dahlet, Véronique, 168
Dain, Alphonse, 309
Dale, Ian R. H., 175–77
Danecki, Janusz, 239
Danesi, Marcel, 151
Dangel, Jacqueline, 290
Daniels, Peter T., 30–36, 41–48, 56, 123–25, 138–42, 145–58, 307, 618–20
Darwin, Charles, 343
Daswani, Chander J., 521
Daukantas, Simonas, 87, 305–7, 321
Daunt, Marjorie, 345
Davidson, Chas, 502
Davidson, George, 521–24
Davies, Robert, 516
Davies, W. Vivian, 34
Davis, Brent, 396, 411
Davy, Derek, 525
De Booy, Engelina P., 601
De Hamel, Christopher F. R., 362–65
De Keyser, Arend,473
De Keyser, Martin,472
De Reuse, Willem, 454
De Voogt, Alex, 47
De Vries, Matthias, 446
De Wulf, Chris, 22, 462
Decorte, Roeland P.-J. E., 396
DeFrancis, John, 31, 35, 40, 43, 147, 150–51, 155–56, 176
Del Freo, Maurizio, 398, 400, 404, 405–10, 413, 415
Del Lungo Camiciotti, Gabriella, 534–35
Del Rincón, Antonio, 566
Del Valle, José, 580, 590
Demartini, Silvia, 192
Den Heijer, Johannes, 175
Denholm-Young, Noël, 365, 372
Denis, Derek, 548, 554, 598–99

Derolez, Albert, 208, 217–20, 361–65
Derrida, Jacques, 30, 123
Derwing, Bruce, 635
Desbordes, Françoise, 142–44
Deschamps, Alain, 621
Deumert, Ana, 265
Deumert, Andrea, 450
Devitt, Amy, 534
Devonish, Hubert, 454
Dewitte, Alfons,472
Di Renzo, Anthony, 210
Dibbets, Geert R. W., 601
Dickie, Matthew, 285
Dietz, Klaus, 346, 629–30
Diller, Hans-Jürgen, 457, 461
DiMeo, Michelle, 510
Diomedes, 97
Dionne, Jennifer, 551, 553
Diringer, David, 31, 41, 46, 146, 151, 154, 226–29
Doane, Alger, 421
Dobbie, Elliott van Kirk, 356
Dobson, Eric J., 277, 280
Dodoens, Rembert, 377
Dollinger, Stefan, 445, 448, 455
Donatus, 97–98
Doria, Mario, 402
Dossena, Marina, 534–35
Doucet, Rachelle C., 585
Douglas, James, 99
Drackley, Patrick, 456
Driver, Martha W., 472
Drozd, Andrzej, 240, 242
Du Toit, Stefanus J., 447
Dubrovskiĭ, Pëtr P., 236–38, 241
Dücker, Lisa, 71, 264
Duden, Konrad, 447–48
Duff, Edward G., 467
Duhoux, Yves, 398, 415
Dumville, David, 535
Dupraz, Emmanuel, 18, 286, 296, 300–2
Duranti, Alessandro, 580
Dürscheid, Christa, 52–53, 80, 118–30
Dürst, Martin, 129
Dziekan, Marek M., 240

Echard, Siân, 311, 315
Eckert, Penelope, 115, 463, 527, 604
Edgerton, William F., 104
Edward IV, King, 533
Edward Seymour, Protector Somerset, 474
Edward VI, King, 511
Edwards, Anthony S. G., 221
Edwards, John, 437, 441
Egbertus, 247
Ehala, Martin, 280
Ehlich, Konrad, 75
Eira, Christina, 441
Eisenberg, Peter, 54, 76
Eisenstein, Elizabeth, 70, 221
Elizabeth I, Queen, 511, 516–19, 561
Ellis, Alexander J., 269
Ellis, Nick, 556
Elmentaler, Michael, 51, 64, 90, 248, 251–52, 256, 258–60, 353–55, 606
Elspaß, Stephan, 325, 359, 388, 540, 607–12
Elyot, Thomas, 515
Emiliano, António, 75
Engel, Eric, 70
Engelbretsdatter, Dorothe, 486–88
Ennis, Juan Antonio, 587, 593
Ephron, Henry D., 410
Errington, J. Joseph, 454
Escolano Benito, Agustín, 592
Esparza Torres, Miguel A., 601
Estarán Tolosa, M. José, 286
Esteve Serrano, Abraham, 588–89
Evans, Arthur J., 399–401
Evans, John, 278
Evans, Mel, 7, 23, 115, 116, 499–501, 508, 511–12, 517, 526, 561
Evertz, Martin, 51, 54–56
Ewald, Petra, 257

Faber, Alice, 42, 154, 396
Fairclough, Norman, 461, 580
Fairman, Tony, 428, 506
Farmer, Steve, 36
Favriaud, Michel, 169
Fayol, Michel, 167
Felder, Egon, 356
Feldman, Laurie B., 83, 179
Ferguson, Charles, 525, 527, 534
Ferrara, Silvia, 396
Fet, Jostein, 483–88
Fidlerová, Alena A., 384, 387, 392
Fielding, Robert, 505
Fielding, Sarah, 505, 531
Finegan, Edward, 525
Fischer, Steven R., 66, 153
Fisher, John H., 267, 270, 431, 530
Fisher, Matthew, 421, 502
Fishman, Joshua A., 275, 437–40, 455, 581
Fitzmaurice, Susan, 348, 387, 388, 534–35
Flores, Nelson, 578
Fonne,Tönnies, 385
Fortson IV, Benjamin W., 16, 299
Fouché, Pierre, 640
Fowkes, Robert A., 342
Fowler, Roger, 525
Foxvog, Daniel A., 38
Frago Gracia, Juan A., 568, 575
Francis, W. Nelson, 101
Franklin, Benjamin, 318
Franklin, Simon, 176–81, 386, 389
Frawley, William, 454
Friedlieb, Timotheus, 332
Fritz, Clemens W. A., 513
Frost, Ram, 83, 143, 156, 521
Fuhrhop, Nanna, 50, 54–55, 57, 58–64, 130–35
Fulk, Robert D., 5, 351, 358, 421

Gadd, Ian A., 469
Gager, John G., 285
Gal, Susan, 439, 454, 578, 581
Gallmann, Peter, 71, 128–29
Gameson, Richard, 422
Garborg, Hulda, 489
García del Río, Juan, 444
García, Ofelia, 436
García-Vidal, Tamara, 524, 528, 533–35

Garside, Roger, 366
Gažáková, Zuzana, 180
Geerts, Guido, 440–50
Geirnaert, Noël, 471
Gelb, Ignace J., 31, 34–37, 46, 122, 140, 146–51, 155–56, 226
Gelumbeckaitė, Jolanta, 319
Gesenius, Justus. *see* Friedlieb, Timotheus
Giegerich, Heinz J., 634, 637
Gieysztor, Aleksander, 226
Gil de Zárate, Antonio, 592
Gil, Alexander, 97–98
Gilferding, Aleksander F., 236
Gillen, Julia, 506
Gillespie, Vincent, 505
Gillmann, Melitta, 70
Gippert, Jost, 190
Gippius, Alekseĭ A., 390
Glaser, Elvira, 254–56
Glessgen, Martin-Dietrich, 170
Gloning, Thomas, 440
Glück, Helmut, 76
Głuszkowski, Michał, 235
Gnanadesikan, Amalia E., 13, 31, 39, 41–44, 47, 78, 139–41, 149–54, 157
Gneuss, Helmut, 429
Godart, Louis, 396
Goddard, Ives, 454
Godoy, Lucía F., 588
Goebl, Hans, 170
Golubović, Biljana, 124
Goodman, Dena, 516
Gordon, Arthur E., 288
Gordon, Matthew,465
Görlach, Manfred, 266–68, 271, 278–80
Gossen, Charles-Théodore, 170
Gower, John, 219, 361
Górnicki, Łukasz, 231–32
Graham, Timothy, 208, 213, 216, 361–65
Gréard, Octave, 449
Gregory, Michael, 525–27
Grenoble, Lenore A., 450
Gries, Stefan T., 334
Griffith, T. Gwynfor, 456
Grigor′eva, Tat′i͡ana M., 83, 181
Grigori͡an (Grigoryan), Vartan R., 242
Grimm, Christian, 332
Grimm, Jacob, 99–101, 339, 342–43, 447
Grimm, Wilhelm, 342
Grivelet, Stéphane, 522
Gruijs, Albert, 309–11
Grund, Peter J., 7, 21, 115, 419, 421–23, 428
Grüter, Majana, 71
Grzega, Joachim, 114
Guerini, Federica, 442, 559, 586
Guerra, Juan, 569
Guerreau-Jalabert, Anita, 340
Guerrini, Federica, 437
Gundersen, Trygve R., 486
Günther, Hartmut, 122, 127–31
Gustav, King, 438
Gutkin, Alexander, 156

Haarmann, Harald, 138
Haas, Walter, 342
Haas, William, 80, 108, 110, 146, 151, 152
Habermann, Mechthild, 332
Hagland, Jan Ragnar, 262, 483–84, 492
Hajnal, Ivo, 403
Halasz, Alexandra, 469
Hall, Ashleigh, 507
Hall, Nigel, 506
Hall, Robert A., Jr., 31, 106–8, 619
Halliday, Michael A. K., 111, 525–26
Haładewicz-Grzelak, Małgorzata, 101
Hämäläinen, Mika, 508
Hammarström, Göran, 102
Hammeken, Anna, 493–95
Hansen, Maurits, 488
Haralambous, Yannis, 119, 125, 129, 164
Hardie, Andrew, 460
Hardwick, Bess of, 504, 511, 517
Harley, Brilliana, 514, 517
Harris, Roy, 29, 46, 75, 95, 112, 150
Harrison, K. David, 455
Hart, John, 98, 277–78, 341
Hartman, George, 377
Hartmann, Stefan, 14
Harvey, Anthony, 346
Haß, Ulrike, 447
Hätzlerin, Clara, 255
Haugen, Einar, 97, 113, 265–66, 477–82, 490, 580
Haugen, Odd E., 65, 482
Haukland, Linda, 483–85, 492
Havelock, Eric, 47
Havinga, Anna D., 326, 388, 446
Hayes, Mary, 522
Healey, John F., 43
Hebda, Anna, 114
Hector, Leonard C., 222, 365
Heikkonen, Kirsi, 270
Heimann, David, 206
Hellinga, Lotte, 9, 221, 468, 473–74
Hemming, T. D., 445
Henderson, Leslie, 52–53, 56–58, 102, 143, 149
Hendriks, Pepijn, 385
Henry V, King, 270
Henry VIII, King, 428, 504
Herder, Johann G., 490
Hernández-Campoy, Juan Manuel, 7, 23, 115, 268, 503–4, 520, 523–31, 533, 540
Herrero Valeiro, Mario, 561, 586
Herrick, Eral M., 60
Hidalgo, Margarita, 573
Higgins, John, 278
Hill, Archibald A., 145–46, 152–54
Hiltunen, Risto, 423
Hinrichs, Lars, 500
Hinskens, Frans, 384
Hinton, Leanne, 454
Hjelmslev, Louis, 108
Hladký, Josef, 365
Hobsbawm, Eric J., 436, 445
Hoccleve, Thomas, 270, 430
Hockett, Charles F., 30, 108, 140
Hodges, Richard, 278
Hoel, Oddmund L., 481–82, 489
Hoffman, A. Robin, 451
Hogarth, Alan, 508
Hogg, Richard M., 352, 424, 429, 534

Holmberg, Börje, 99
Holmes, Janet,465
Holtus, Günter, 170
Honkapohja, Alpo, 8, 212, 220–22, 434
Hooker, James T., 33, 191, 398, 402
Hope, Jonathan, 267–71, 280
Horley, Paul, 36
Horn, Wilhelm, 623, 628
Horobin, Simon, 8, 92, 424, 429–31, 458
Horrocks, Geoffrey, 286–88
Horsley, G. H. R., 211
Horstbøll, Henrik, 488
Householder, Fred W., 31, 403, 628
Houston, Stephen D., 30, 36, 47
Howard-Hill, Trevor H., 7, 271, 275, 505
Huijs, Nanette,458
Huloet, Richard, 278
Hume, Alexander, 98, 278
Hundt, Marianne, 602
Huth, Dirk, 257, 340

Ilievski, Petar H., 410
Ilsung, Sebastian, 255
Iqbal, Farkhund, 507
Irvine, Judith, 578
Irvine, Martin, 97
Isabella II, Queen, 445, 591, 594
Ivković, Dejan, 178
Iyengar, Arvind, 560

Jackson, MacD. P., 509
Jacobs, Andreas, 348
Jacobsen, Henrik G., 488, 494
Jaeger, Jeri J., 633, 635
Jaffe, Alexandra M., 94, 112–14, 437, 555–56, 558–61, 580–86
Jaffré, Jean-Pierre, 167
Jahr, Ernst H., 444, 453, 477, 482, 490
Jakobson, Roman, 108
Jakubczyk, Marcin, 235
Jamborová, Martina, 392
Janda, Richard D., 287
Janssen, Theo A. J. M., 461
Januszowski, Jan, 231–32
Jaworski, Adam, 580
Jocelin, Elizabeth, 505
Johannessen, Janne B., 478
Johansen, Åse M., 478
Johnson, John, 504, 604
Johnson, Richard, 604
Johnson, Sabine, 504
Johnson, Sally A., 445–48, 451, 556, 579, 586–87
Johnson, Samuel, 443
Johnson, Wyn, 628
Johnston, Edward, 362–65
Johnston, William, 341
Joly, Geneviève, 640
Jones, Daniel, 623, 628
Jones, Mari C., 454
Jones, Stephen, 341
Jones, William, 342
Joos, Martin, 558
Joseph, Brian D., 287
Joseph, John, 581
Joyce, Terry, 15, 59, 78–79, 139–45, 149–59
Jucker, Andreas H., 114, 115, 348, 432
Judson, Anna P., 401, 410, 413
Juola, Patrick, 507
Justeson, John S., 32, 36–38, 40, 46, 403

Kaislaniemi, Samuli, 116, 460, 504, 532–35
Källström, Magnus, 258
Kämpfert, Manfred, 71
Karadžić, Vuk, 120
Karlsson, Stefán, 257
Karskiĭ, Efim F., 381–82
Karttunen, Frances, 564–77
Katz, Leonard, 83, 143, 156, 521–22
Kauffmann, Friedrich, 343
Kawasaki, Yasushi, 354
Kay, Richard, 206
Keil, Heinrich, 97
Kenny, Laurence A., 598–600
Kenrick, William, 341
Kerek, Andrew, 625
Keszler, Borbála, 173
Kettmann, Gerhard, 255
Kildal, Arne, 484
Kim, Dong-Hyuk, 312
King, John H., 474–75
Kinn, Kari, 478
Kirchhoff, Frank, 68–70
Kirchweg, Christoph, 332
Kjeldstadli, Knut, 491
Klausenburger, Jürgen, 640
Klein, Jared, 163
Kleinas, Danielius, 84
Klinkenberg, Jean-Marie, 52–53, 58, 121–27, 133, 164–65
Kloss, Heinz, 275, 481
Klöter, Henning, 562
Kniffka, Hannes, 499, 507–10
Knudsen, Knud, 443
Kober, Alice E., 401
Koch, Peter, 388–89
Kochanowski, Jan, 231–33
Köcher, Adolf, 332
Koeppel, Emil, 623–26, 628
Kohrt, Manfred, 52, 56, 76, 102, 109
Kok, Ina, 468, 472
Kökeritz, Helge, 623, 629, 632
Kollewijn, Roeland A., 449
Konopacki, Artur, 240
Kopaczyk, Joanna, 8, 114–16, 432, 464
Korkiakangas, Timo, 264
Kornicki, Peter F., 66
Koselleck, Reinhart, 268
Koster, Josephine A., 307
Kramer, Christina, 560
Kristiansen, Tore, 438
Kristol, Andres M., 601
Kroch, Anthony, 280, 537
Krogull, Andreas, 603, 615
Krohn, Robert K., 635
Kroskrity, Paul V., 580
Küster, Marc W., 129
Kytö, Merja, 221, 460

La Parra López, Emilio, 591
Labov, William, 266, 523, 527, 537, 540, 596–600, 638–40
Labs-Ehlert, Brigitte, 70–71

Laing, Margaret, 8, 249, 348–50, 353, 425–30, 534
Lam, Joseph, 43
Landry, Norine, 550
Landry, Wallace, 550
Lane Ford, Margaret, 473–74
Lane, Pia, 454
Lange, Claudia, 266, 275
Langer, Nils, 326, 388
Lapidge, Michael, 355–56
Larousse, Pierre, 447
Larsen, Niels-Erik, 354
Larsen-Freeman, Diane, 556
Lass, Roger, 8, 245–47, 251, 267, 347, 350, 424–27, 534, 631
Lassila, Matti, 264
Laufer, Roger, 169
Launey, Michel, 565, 567, 574
Lavinsky, David, 473
Lazar, Marija, 20, 384–86, 392
Le Page, Robert, 520, 600
Lebsanft, Franz, 456
Leeu, Gherard,471
Lehfeldt, Werner, 180
Lehnert, Martin, 623, 628
Lehr-Spławiński, Tadeusz, 227
Leith, Dick, 265
Lejeune, Michel, 289, 293–94, 410
Lepschy, Anna L., 173
Lepschy, Giulio, 173
Levenshtein, Vladimir I., 264
Levitt, Jesse, 625
Lewis, Thomas T., 517
Liberman, Alvin, 31
Liberman, Isabelle, 42
Liira, Aino, 8, 220–22
Lindqvist, Christer, 624
Lippert, Sandra L., 176, 179
Lisowski, Tomasz, 8, 382, 384, 387
Li͡ublinskai͡a, Aleksandra D., 306
Liuzza, Roy M., 96, 102, 341
Llamas-Pombo, Elena, 7–8, 16, 89–90, 172–73, 439, 444
Loach, Jennifer, 475
Locher, Miriam, 266
Lockhart, James, 562–75
Lockwood, David G., 58, 131–34
Lodge, Anthony, 542
Løland, Rasmus, 496
Lomagistro, Barbara, 176, 180
Longo, Giuseppe, 325
Lorente-Sánchez, Juan, 20
Lotman, Yuri, 224
Love, Harold, 423, 498
Lowth, Robert, 531
Lucas, Peter J., 341
Lucilius, Gaius, 290–91
Ludwig, Otto, 122
Luelsdorff, Philip A., 76, 521
Lühr, Rosemarie, 356–57
Luján, Eugenio R., 398, 403, 405, 408
Lüpke, Friederike, 455, 561, 576
Luther, Martin, 438–40, 483
Luto-Kamińska, Anetta, 17
Lutz, Angelika, 365
Łapicz, Czesław, 240
Maas, Utz, 72, 96
Mabillon, Jean, 212, 305–7
Mackenzie, David N., 191
MacKenzie, Laurel, 537
Mackridge, Peter, 456
Maddieson, Ian, 45
Mæhlum, Brit K., 478
Maggiani, Adriano, 296
Maier, Ingrid, 385, 392
Mair, Christian, 443
Malling, Ove, 488
Malone, Kemp, 632
Mann, Thomas, 332
Mansion, Colard,471
Manutius, Aldus, 438
Marazzini, Claudio, 601
Marcos Marín, Francisco, 588
Marcos, Juan-José, 218, 308
Marcus, Joyce, 29
Maretić, Tomo, 120–21
Margaret, Countess of Orrery, 511
Maria Theresa, Empress, 446
Marković, Ivan, 125, 132
Markus, Manfred, 7–8, 536
Marotti, Arthur F., 423
Marquilhas, Rita, 316, 456
Martens, Dirk, 473
Martens, Thierry, 468
Marti, Roland, 90, 179, 382
Martin, Peter, 443
Martineau, France, 75
Martínez Alcalde, María José, 588–90
Martínez de la Rosa, Francisco, 592
Martínez Marín, Juan, 588
Mary I, Queen, 475
Marynissen, Ann, 461
Mashtots, Mesrop, 243
Masson, Michel, 629, 633, 642
Mathisen, Ralph W., 306
Mattheier, Klaus J., 250, 438, 440, 448
Mattingly, Ignatius, 522
Maunde, Edward, 517
Maxwell, Kate, 206
Mažvydas, Martynas, 318
Mazzocchi, Fulvio, 325
McArthur, Tom, 623
McClumpha, Charles F., 502
McConchie, Roderick W., 8
McConnell-Ginet, Sally, 463
McCormick, Robert R., 453
McDonald, Katherine, 18, 285–86, 294–97
McEnery, Tony, 460
McIntosh, Angus, 99, 105–8, 204, 425–26, 502–3, 609
McKenzie, Donald F., 510
McKitterick, David, 423
McLaughlin, John C., 104–7
McLelland, Nicola, 605
Mechkovskai͡a, Nina B., 175
Megyesi, Beáta, 264
Meisenburg, Trudel, 71
Meiser, Gerhard, 289, 297, 300
Meissburger, Gerhard, 255–56
Meissner, Torsten, 396–99, 407, 411, 415
Melchert, H. Craig, 194
Melena, José L., 398, 400, 404, 405–16

Meletis, Dimitrios, 5, 50–52, 57–58, 64, 75, 118–37, 138, 140–42, 159, 164–65, 167–68
Meltzer, Clamer, 493
Meltzer, Fredrik, 494
Meltzer, Harald, 494
Meltzer, Lydia, 494
Meltzer, Oscar, 494
Mencken, Henry L., 451
Meredith-Owens, Georg M., 240
Meriggi, Piero, 410
Merriam, Thomas, 512
Methodius, 227
Meyerhoff, Miriam, 465
Michel, Andreas, 8, 90, 438
Middleton, Thomas, 510
Migliorini, Bruno, 456
Mihm, Arend, 246–56, 353–54
Miklas, Heinz, 180
Mikucki, Stanisław J. K., 236
Mikuła, Maciej, 392
Millar, Robert McColl, 113–14, 453
Miller, Daniel, 313
Miller, Jim, 124–26
Miller, Thomas, 351
Millward, Celia M., 522
Milroy, James, 112–14, 265–68, 275, 279, 549, 581, 601
Milroy, Lesley, 25, 112–14, 265, 275, 279, 549, 581, 596, 599–600, 615
Miltenov, I͡Avor, 179–80
Minkova, Donka, 246, 502
Miranda-García, Antonio, 362, 366, 421
Miškinienė, Galina, 240
Molero Pintado, Antonio, 592
Mommsen, Theodor, 97
Montagu, Elizabeth, 518–19, 604
Montfaucon, Bernard de, 212
Montgomery, Scott, 637
Mooney, Damien, 454
Mooney, Linne R., 422, 508
Moore, Colette, 432–35
Moore, Michael, 638
Mora-Marín, David F., 38
Moran, Steven, 64
Mørck, Endre, 478–79
More, Thomas,473
Moreno Olalla, David, 7
Moreton, Emma, 506
Morpurgo-Davies, Anna, 398, 403
Mortara Garavelli, Bice, 173
Moser, Hans, 251, 255–56
Moser, Virgil, 259
Mosser, Daniel W., 508
Moulin, Claudine, 71, 257
Mufwene, Salikoko, 555–57, 561, 563
Mühlhäusler, Peter, 584
Mulcaster, Richard, 98–99, 278, 515
Mulder, Maaike,461
Mullen, Alex, 286, 387
Müller, Ernst E., 255
Müller, Rudolf W., 67
Munday, Anthony, 512
Murray, Heather, 453
Murray, James A. H., 624
Murzynowski, Stanisław, 232
Musakova, Elisaveta, 180
Mykland, Knut, 482

Nadeau, Jean-Benoît, 444–48
Nadson, Alexander, 240
Nardo, Andrea, 296
Naveh, Joseph, 43
Nebrija, Antonio de, 588
Needham, Paul, 222
Neef, Martin, 30–31, 52–53, 56, 76–77, 82–86, 118–24, 130–31, 135, 140, 142–45, 164
Neidorf, Leonard, 421, 429
Neis, Cordula, 341
Nelde, Peter, 561
Nemirovskiĭ, Evgeniĭ L., 181
Nerius, Dieter, 71, 76, 123, 257, 331
Nesse, Agnete, 23, 480, 483–85, 492–96
Neuman, Yishai, 26, 621–22, 627, 634, 637, 640–43
Nevalainen, Terttu, 8, 75, 117, 265–72, 276, 280, 388, 428, 432, 464, 504–9, 526, 530, 532, 535, 538, 554, 600, 603
Nichols, John, 560
Nichols, Stephen, 346–47, 358
Nievergelt, Andreas, 256
Nordlund, Taru, 90
Novickas, Elizabeth, 314
Nowak, Jessica, 71–72, 264, 475
Nübling, Damaris, 260
Nunberg, Geoffrey, 67–71

O'Brien, Robert L., 506
O'Connor, Michael P., 31
O'Rourke, Bernadette, 454
Oczkowa, Barbara, 230
Okasha, Elisabeth, 258
Oldireva Gustafsson, Larisa, 7
Olivier, Jean-Pierre, 36, 396
Olko, Justyna, 562–66, 570
Olmos, Andrés de, 564–65
Olsson, John, 507
Ong, Walter J., 224
Opiec, Baltazar, 384
Oppliger, Rahel, 499
Orr, William, 453
Orwin, Joan, 506
Osselton, Noel E., 71, 319, 428, 531, 532
Österreicher, Wulf, 388–89
Ostrowski, Donald G., 309–11
Outhwaite, Ben, 420–22
Ó Ciosáin, Niall, 437

Pabrėža, Jurgis A., 321
Pafraet, Richard, 473
Page, Ray, 262
Pahta, Päivi, 534
Palaima, Thomas G., 411
Palander-Collin, Minna, 528, 535
Palionis, Jonas, 77
Pallas, Peter S., 235
Palmer, Leonard R., 398, 402, 410
Palumbo, Alessandro, 252, 263
Papłoński, Jan, 236
Papp, Ference, 627
Parkes, Malcolm B., 172, 421, 434
Parkosz, Jakub, 230, 232

Parodi, Claudia, 564
Parpola, Asko, 36
Parr, Katherine, 504
Paston, John II, 533
Patrick, Donna, 454–55, 560
Paul, Hermann, 101, 343–44
Pavlenko, Aneta, 387
Pearsall, Derek, 311
Pedersen, Aud-Kirsti, 453
Pedersen, Christiern, 438
Peikola, Matti, 7, 423
Pellat, Jean-Christophe, 165
Pellegrini, Giovanni B., 303
Pemberton, Caroline, 517
Peng, Jian, 507
Penny, Ralph, 567
Penzl, Herbert, 102, 345–46
Percy, Carol, 22, 276
Pérez Ledesma, Manuel, 591
Perna, Massimo, 398, 400, 404, 405–10, 413, 415
Peter the Great, Tsar, 229
Peters, Jörg, 50, 57, 130–35
Peters, Robert, 263
Petruševski, Mihail D., 410
Pettersen, Egil, 486
Pettersson, Eva, 264
Pettersson, Jonatan, 438
Petti, Anthony G., 214–17, 364–65
Pharao Hansen, Marcus, 577
Pharo, Lars K., 440
Pheifer, Joseph D., 356
Phillips, Betty S., 336
Phipps, Alison, 513
Pierini, Rachele, 407
Pieske, Knut, 332
Pilz, Thomas,507
Pinkhurst, Adam, 423
Piotrowski, Michael, 382, 391
Pisowicz, Andrzej, 242–43
Plans, Antonio S., 567
Plantin, Christophe,472
Pleij, Herman, 467–71
Pocklington, Robert, 558
Polis, Stéphane, 52–53, 58, 121–27, 133, 164–65
Pollatsek, Alexander, 68
Pontoppidan, Erik, 488
Pope, Maurice, 35, 401
Popp, Daniel, 487, 494
Portebois, Yannick, 453, 586
Poser, William, 42
Pountain, Christopher, 456
Poussa, Patricia, 266
Pouzet, Jean-Pascal, 315
Powell, Barry B., 138, 149–51, 154
Powell, Susan, 505
Powers, David S., 306
Prakulevičius, Stanislovas, 80
Preston, Dennis, 584
Pride, John, 520
Primus, Beatrice, 51–56, 59–60, 68–69, 131–34
Priscian, 97
Proffitt, Michael, 3, 102, 266, 436
Prosdocimi, Aldo L., 301–3
Puchmír, Jaroslav, 236
Puelles Benítez, Manuel, 592
Pulgram, Ernst, 105–7
Puttenham, George, 277
Pynson, Richard, 531

Quintilian, 96–101, 183–84, 291–92

Rambaran-Olm, Mary R., 306
Rambø, Gro-Renée, 481–83, 490–91
Ramírez Aisa, Elías, 592
Ranelagh, Lady, 511
Raschellà, Fabrizio, 257
Rask, Rasmus, 101, 342
Rastle, Kathleen, 150
Raubicheck, Letitia E., 639
Raumolin-Brunberg, Helena, 267–68, 432, 527, 554, 603
Raven, James, 467
Ravida, Fausto, 251, 256
Raymond, Joad, 474
Rayner, Keith, 68
Read, Charles, 42, 145, 154
Reagan, Ronald, 507
Recasens, Daniel, 628
Reczek, Józef, 242
Reichler-Béguelin, Marie-José, 169
Reid, S. W., 505
Reiner, Erica, 31
Rem, Margit, 468
Remacle, Louis, 170
Remysen, Wim, 541, 544, 546–50, 553
Reyes Equiguas, Salvador, 562–64
Reynaert, Joris, 468
Rezec, Oliver, 58–60
Rice, Keren, 47, 454
Ricento, Thomas, 581
Richardson, Brian, 456
Richardson, Kay P., 500
Richardson, Malcolm, 270
Rickard, Peter, 436, 439, 445
Rickford, John, 527
Rimmington, Don, 67
Rimzhim, Anurag, 43
Rinas, Karsten, 70
Ringe, Don, 352
Risch, Ernst, 402, 412
Rissanen, Matti, 457, 527, 530
Risse, Ursula, 71
Rix, Helmut, 296
Rizvi, Pervez, 510
Roberge, Paul T., 446–50
Roberts, David, 84
Roberts, Jane, 363–65
Robertson, John S., 157
Robinson, Andrew, 138
Rogers, Henry, 31–33, 42, 53–57, 62, 79, 83–85, 103, 112, 139–56
Rogos-Hebda (Rogos), Justyna, 7–8, 17, 116, 208, 217, 604
Rollings, Andrew G., 110
Romaine, Suzanne, 111, 269, 561
Romero-Barranco, Jesús, 367
Roosevelt, Theodore, 451
Rosa, Jonathan, 578
Rosenblat, Ángel, 588
Rosenthal, Bernard, 115, 428

Rössing-Hagar, Monika, 601
Rössler, Paul, 3, 6–9, 76–77, 84, 113–14, 173, 333, 393, 528–33, 537, 552, 561, 605–8
Rothstein, Robert, 586
Rozhdestvenskaia, Tat'iana V., 386
Ruge, Nikolaus, 124, 259–60
Ruijgh, Cornelius, 403
Rumble, Alexander R., 218
Ruscelli, Girolamo, 377
Russell, James R., 307, 315
Russon, Allien R., 210
Ruszkiewicz, Piotr, 52, 95, 99–103
Rutkowska, Hanna, 3, 6–9, 15, 52, 64, 75–79, 84, 88, 113–16, 263, 271–78, 320, 393, 441, 463–64, 467, 528–35, 537, 552, 561, 604–5
Rutten, Gijsbert, 8, 25, 75, 91–92, 112, 443, 477, 514, 535, 600–11, 615
Ruus, Hanne, 71
Ryan, Des, 76, 80–85, 92
Rypins, Stanley, 373

Sacconi, Anna, 401–2
Saenger, Paul, 47, 172
Sahle, Patrick, 382
Sairio, Anni, 7, 114–16, 460, 508, 512, 518–19, 524, 534, 604
Salgarella, Ester, 21, 396, 400, 416
Salmon, Vivian, 112, 116, 267, 272, 276–78, 341, 428, 441, 458, 505, 605
Salmons, Joseph C., 478
Salomies, Olli, 288
Sampson, Geoffrey, 31, 35, 42–44, 88, 136, 141, 143, 147–48, 403
Samuels, Michael L., 266–71, 430–31
Sánchez Méndez, Juan, 574
Sánchez-Prieto Borja, Pedro, 170
Sandøy, Helge, 480, 491
Sanz-Sánchez, Israel, 24, 568, 573–74
Sapir, Edward, 6, 101
Sarmiento, Domingo Faustino, 444–45, 593
Sass, Benjamin, 44
Sassoon, Rosemary, 174
Saturno, William A., 36
Sauer, Elizabeth,475
Saunders, Ambrose, 604
Saussure, Ferdinand de, 7, 101–4, 113, 120, 344, 619
Savage, Andrew, 560
Saxon, Leslie, 454
Saz, Ismael, 591
Scancarelli, Janine, 41
Schaefer, Ursula, 266
Schaeken, Jos, 181, 386–91
Scherer, Carmen, 70
Schieffelin, Bambi, 578, 580, 585
Schiegg, Markus, 524, 535–36
Schleicher, August, 597
Schlieben-Lange, Brigitte, 96
Schlögl, Rudolf, 268
Schmid, Hans U., 328
Schmidt, Johannes, 598
Schmidt, Karsten, 55
Schmied, Josef, 460
Schneider, Gerold, 508
Schneider, Nathalie, 541–54
Schoemaker, Bob, 603
Schoep, Ilse, 396
Scholfield, Phil, 86, 92
Schouteet, Albert, 470
Schulte, Michael, 261–63, 478, 482–83
Schulz, Herbert C., 423
Schwartz, Saul, 586
Schwarzwald, Ora R., 633
Scragg, Donald G., 76, 84–88, 111, 267, 270, 276–78, 421–23, 428, 458, 518, 521–24, 623–25, 630
Sebba, Mark, 94, 112, 117, 143, 179, 196, 280, 436–42, 445, 454, 501, 555–62, 576, 580–87, 621
Seelbach, Ulrich, 263
Seifart, Frank, 436–39
Seiler, Annina, 20, 170, 264, 354–57
Seip, Didrik A., 491
Selvelli, Giustina, 180
Sevenstern, Gaspar, 332
Seymour, Edward, 511
Sgall, Petr, 95, 109, 521
Shakespeare, William, 360, 509–11, 519
Shamin, Stepan M., 385, 392
Shammas, Carole, 501
Share, David L., 46, 158
Shaughnessy, Edward L., 36
Shaw, George Bernard, 184, 634
Sheridan, Thomas, 99, 341
Sherman, William H., 459
Shute, Rosie, 7–9, 221, 337, 505
Sica, Alan, 441
Siegenbeek, Matthijs, 443, 446, 615
Sikkenga, Elizabeth, 411
Silverman, David P., 307
Silverstein, Michael, 533
Simpson, John A., 3, 102, 266, 436
Šinkūnas, Mindaugas, 84–86, 309
Skre, Arnhild, 489
Smalley, William A., 439
Smith, Andrew, 310–12
Smith, Charles W., 623
Smith, Jeremy J., 8, 101, 269–71, 275, 348, 435, 438
Smith, Nicholas, 366
Smith, Philip T., 636
Smith, Thomas, 97–98, 277, 341
Smith-Stark, Thomas, 565, 568
Sonderegger, Stefan, 342
Sönmez, Margaret, 7–8, 501, 513, 518
Sørlie, Mikjel, 492
Sousa-Silva, Rui, 507
Southwick, Henry, 604
Speakman Sutch, Susie, 471
Spence, Thomas, 341
Spitzmüller, Jürgen, 94, 176
Spolsky, Bernard, 437, 440, 454
Sproat, Richard, 31, 36, 40, 43, 138, 145–49, 155
Spurkland, Terje, 258, 262, 478
Squires, Lauren, 500
Stadnik-Holzer, Elena, 382
Stalin, Joseph, 451
Stam, Nike, 219
Stamatatos, Efstathios, 507
Stanford, James N., 598–600
Stankevich, IAn, 240
Stapleton, Thomas, 516
Stauder, Andréas, 35, 48

Stebbins, Tonya, 439, 454
Steele, Philippa M., 286, 396–99, 411
Steer, Francis W., 469
Stegeman, Jelle, 468
Stein, Dieter, 280
Steinberg, Danny D., 635
Stenroos, Merja, 6–8, 221, 429, 432, 524, 528, 609–10
Stephens, Laurence D., 46
Sterne, Laurence, 531
Stetson, Raymond H., 104
Stockwell, Robert P., 102, 105
Stoke, Melis, 468
Stone, Michaele, 315
Stonor, Thomas, 604
Stotz, Peter, 355
Strang, Barbara M. H., 351
Strässler, Jürg, 266
Strelcyn, Stefan, 226
Strockis, Mindaugas, 309
Stubbs, Michael, 110–11
Suárez Cortina, Manuel, 591
Subačius, Giedrius, 9, 19, 75, 81–88, 92–93, 172, 307, 316, 320–22
Sullivan, John, 564–66
Swales, John, 457
Sweet, Henry, 356, 623
Synkova, Irina A., 240
Szczepaniak, Renata, 14

Taavitsainen, Irma, 7, 114, 270, 348, 366, 387–88, 430–31, 459, 524
Tabouret-Keller, Andrée, 520, 600
Tacke, Felix, 439–40, 456
Tagg, Caroline, 8, 112, 116, 499–501, 511–12, 517, 527
Tagliamonte, Sali A., 548, 598–99
Taha, Haitham Y., 136
Tailleur, Sandrine, 24, 75, 539, 547, 549–50
Tamminga, Meredith, 537
Tamošiūnaitė, Aurelija, 14, 75, 80–83, 88, 92–93
Tannenbaum, Samuel A., 364, 434
Tanskanen, Sanna-Kaisa, 535
Tarėlka, Mikhail U., 240
Taylor, Ann, 352
Taylor, Insup, 45–47, 66–67, 153
Taylor, Isaac, 31, 46
Taylor, M. Martin, 45–47, 66–67
Te Winkel, Lambert A., 446
Teeuween, Mariken, 210
Tejedo-Herrero, Fernando, 588
Teleman, Ulf, 438
Ter Horst, Tom, 219
Thackston, Wheeler M., 196
Thaisen, Jacob, 7–9, 535
Themistocleous, Christiana, 559
Thomas, Megan C., 440, 585
Thompson, Edward M., 206, 211
Thurlow, Crispin, 517
Thurneysen, Rudolf, 193
Thynne, Joan, 517
Tieken-Boon van Ostade, Ingrid, 7–8, 75, 265–71, 276, 319, 505, 526, 531–36, 600
Tikkanen, Karin, 292
Tiro, Marcus Tulius, 210
Tolkien, John R. R., 429
Took, Patricia, 475
Toon, Thomas E., 424
Torp, Arne, 479–85
Tournier, Jean, 628
Tov, Emanuel, 312
Trapp, Joseph B., 468, 473
Traube, Ludwig, 206, 209, 215
Traxel, Oliver M., 535
Tribulato, Olga, 286
Trice Martin, Charles, 207, 217–18
Trigger, Bruce G., 46, 146, 155
Trudgill, Peter, 113, 269, 481, 520, 523–25, 529, 540, 557, 611
Trunte, Nikolaos, 180
Tryjarski, Edward, 242
Tudor, Margaret, 504
Tuten, Donald, 557, 588
Tyndale, William, 473
Tyrkkö, Jukka, 8, 116, 275, 366, 463–66, 604

Uldall, Hans J., 104–8
Unger, J. Marshall, 147, 155–56, 246
Unseth, Peter, 584
Untermann, Jürgen, 299
Upward, Christopher, 521–24
Urbańczyk, Stanisław, 242
Urla, Jacqueline, 583

Vachek, Josef, 104–11, 344, 631–34
Van Aken, Mark J., 593
Van Beek, Gosewijn, 311
Van de Voorde, Iris, 25
Van den Bosch, Antal, 143
Van der Feest Viðarsson, Heimir, 602
Van der Kuijp, Leonard W. J., 66
Van der Noot, Thomas, 471
Van der Sijs, Nicoline, 462
Van der Wal, Marijke, 75, 91–92, 461–62, 535, 602, 607–9
Van Peer, Willie, 313–14
Van Reenen, Pieter,458
Vandenbussche, Wim, 265, 538, 542, 601
Vannebo, Kjell I., 484
Varila, Mari-Liisa, 434
Varnhagen, Connie K., 500
Védénina, Ludmilla G., 169
Veldener, Johan, 473
Venckienė, Jurgita, 82, 320
Venezky, Richard L., 76–78, 85, 99–102, 110–12, 344, 443, 451–53
Ventris, Michael, 398, 401–2
Vermeylen, Filip R., 471
Verrac, Monique, 601
Verrette, Michel, 542, 545
Vertan, Cristina, 392
Vetancurt, Agustín de, 569
Vickers, Brian, 509
Videsott, Paul, 170
Vikør, Lars, 482, 491, 496
Vilborg, Ebbe, 402
Villa Galán (Villa), Laura, 8, 25, 94, 112, 444–45, 449, 556, 558, 561, 586–87, 589–94
Vine, Brent, 288–91
Viredaz, Rémy, 403

Vlasto, Alexis P., 93
Voeste, Anja, 5–8, 19, 75–76, 82, 85–93, 112–14, 171, 253, 259–60, 321, 328, 337, 387, 393, 437, 522, 535, 586, 604
Voet, Leon, 472
Vogt-Spira, Gregor, 341
Voigts, Linda E., 366
Von Felbiger, Johann Ignaz, 446
Von Lieven, Alexandra, 176, 179
Von Planta, Robert, 298
Von Raumer, Rudolf, 99
Von Weissenburg, Otfrid, 250
Vosters, Rik, 8, 25, 75, 94, 112, 514, 556, 558, 561, 583–87, 605, 606–10

Waal, Willemijn, 36
Wachter, Rudolf, 303
Wagner, Esther-Miriam, 420–22
Waldispühl, Michelle, 18, 254–56
Walker, James A., 333
Walker, John, 341
Walker, Terry, 460
Wall, Wendy, 279
Wallis, Christine, 20, 351
Wallis, John, 99
Walton, Stephen J., 489
Warner, Lawrence, 423
Waterhouse, E. R., 211
Waters, Cathleen, 548
Watkins, Calvert, 199
Watt, Diane, 504
Watt, William C., 121
Watts, Richard J., 540, 611
Waxenberger, Gaby, 258, 260–63
Webb, Thomas W., 516
Weber, Eugen, 445
Weber, Max, 441
Weber, Walter R., 70
Webster, Noah, 186, 443
Wehr, Hans, 642
Weiner, Edmund, 623
Weingarten, Rüdiger, 30–31, 78, 88, 136, 139–44, 163, 165
Weinreich, Jan, 318
Weinreich, Uriel, 642
Wells, Christopher, 356
Wells, Herbert G., 309
Wenger, Étienne,464
Werner, Sarah, 506
Wertheim, Suzanne, 176
Wexler, Paul, 240
Whalen, Richard F., 511
Wharton, Jeremiah, 278
Wheale, Nigel, 500
Whitney, William D., 198
Whittaker, Gordon, 29, 34, 562–63
Wiberg, Christian K., 496
Wiese, Richard, 77
Wiggins, Alison, 503–5, 511
Wildenthal, Bryan H., 511
Wilhelm II, Kaiser, 448
Wilkens, Friedrich, 343
Willemyns, Roland, 438, 446–50
Williams, Graham, 504
Williamson, Keith, 425
Willis, James, 339
Wilson, Kenneth G., 623
Winterbottom, Michael, 355–56
Wittgenstein, Ludwig, 448
Witzstat, Hans, 334
Wolfram, Walt, 328
Woodard, Roger D., 403, 406–7
Woods, Christopher, 31, 35
Woolard, Kathryn A., 440, 578–81
Woudhuysen, Henry R., 468
Wrenn, Charles L., 102, 104
Wright, Joseph, 628
Wright, Laura, 219, 222, 268, 431–35
Wright, Sue, 436
Wurm, Stephen, 521
Wyld, Henry C., 513
Wynkyn de Worde, 531
Wyrod, Christopher, 585

Yakubovich, Ilya, 36
Yasuko, Ishi, 449, 453
Yip, Po-Ching, 67
Young, Christopher,440
Younging, Gregory, 455
Yule, Valerie, 449, 453

Zabrocki, Ludwik, 463
Žagar, Mateo, 118, 120, 125–27, 137, 179
Zair, Nicholas, 286, 292–99
Zalizni͡ak, Andreĭ A., 181, 381–83, 388–89
Zamora Vicente, Alonso, 592
Zanobini, Michele, 341
Zemenová, Markéta, 385
Zheltukhin, Alexander, 8, 90
Zhukovskai͡a, Lidii͡a P., 381
Zima, Petr, 522
Zimmer, Ben, 183
Zimmerman, Jonathan, 451
Zink, Gaston, 640

Subject Index

abbreviations, 204–23
  Latin, 85, 89, 205–20, 322
  medieval Italian, 206
abjad, 43, 79, 141, 147–49, 191, 196, 226, 234
  Arabic, 79, 147, 239, 240
    adapted in Bosnian, *see* arebica
  Greek, 317
  Hebrew, 79, 147, 317
  Nabataean, 191
  Old Hebrew, 191
  Phoenician, *see* Phoenician
  Semitic, 191
abugida, 41, 43, 79, 147–49, 198
  Brāhmī, *see* Brāhmī (Brahmi)
  Devanāgarī, *see* Devanāgarī
  Ethiopic, *see* Ethiopic
acceptance by the community, 113, 581, 588, 603
acrophonic principle, 44, 619
acrophony, 38
AE, *see L'Année Épigraphique*
Afrikaans, 454
  words, 440
Akkadian, 35, 39, 619
akshara, 33, 41–46
Albanian, 316
aljamiado, 240
allographic spellings, 102, 197
allography, 56–58, 61, 64, 158, 167, 214, 232–33, 254, 258, 302, 327, 382, 530, 569
  as a synonym of biscriptality, 175
  in grapholinguistics, 129–34
  in the relational approach, 105–7
alphasyllabary, 41, 198
alphasyllabic writing system, *see* abugida
amanuensis, 422
analogy, 617–33, 638–43
Anglo-Boer War, 450
Anglo-Norman, 3, 433, 622–24, 630
  scribes, 425
Antiquity, 96, 205–10, 316, 317
  Classical, 338–40
  Graeco-Roman, 150
apostrophe, 68, 128, 342
Arabic, 135, 167, 241, 641
  alphabet, 224, *see also* abjad
  letters, 178
Aramaic, 44, 48, 628
  alphabet, 191
  script, 43, 307
archaeology, 386
ARCHER, *see Representative Corpus of Historical English Registers, A*
arebica/arabica, 178, 180
Armenian alphabet, 224
audiences, 114, 210, 217, 277, 292, 432, 434, 438, 514, 518, 528, 532–36
Ausbau languages, 481
Australian English Standard, 513
Austrian German, 454
authorship, 115, 314, 498–519, 608
  multiple, 607
autonomistic approach, 53, 63, 102–9, 129, 168, 345
Azeri, 234

Belarusian, 176, 229, 239–40
Bergamasco, 586
Bible prints, 72
Bible translators, 438
Bible, the, 240, 384
bicameral script, 227, 239, 243
biglyphism, 176, *see also* biscriptality
bigraphism, 176
Bijbels digitaal, 457
bilingualism, 179, 400, 438, 494, 557, 560, 564, 567, 584, *see also* trilingualism, multilingualism
  in German and Italian, 174
  in Oscan and Latin, 290
  in Spanish and Nahuatl, 573–75
biorthographism, 176–78, 181
biscriptality, 164, 175–82, 560, *see also* multiscriptality
Black Death, 479
Bluestocking Network, 518

book history, 421, 434
book industry, 459
book market, 465
book production and distribution, 458
bookbinders, 467
booksellers, 467, 470
bopomofo, 197
bosančica, 180
Bosnian, 178, 180
boustrophedonic writing, 226
Brāhmī (Brahmi), 45, 49, 189–90
Buddhism, 189
Bulgarian, 229, 560
Byzantine culture, 229

Cædmon's Hymn, 355
calligraphy, 382
capitalization, 64, 67, 69–73, 308, 313, 318, 323, 327, 348, 382, 434, 445, 480
  Dutch, 72
  English, 71
  French, 71
  German, 58, 71
  Latin, 65, 305
  Linear B, 415
  nomina sacra, 330
  Norwegian, 487, 492–95
  of nouns, 128
  patterns, 77
  scribal, 420
  sentence-initial, 128
  sentence-internal, 71, 257
  Spanish, 438
  word-initial, 342
Castilian Spanish, 436–38, 521, 558, 565–71, 576, 588
Catholic
  Church, 71, 212, 522
    Roman, 332
  Counter-Reformation, *see* Counter-Reformation
  shibboleth forms, 333
  Spain, 438
  Upper Sorbian, 178
CEEC, *see Corpus of Early English Correspondence*
Chancery standard, 270–71, 275, 329, 430–33, 502–4, 526, 530
change 'from above', 504, 528, 598, 609, 614–15
change 'from below', 257, 359, 388, 506, 541, 597–98, 615
character (definition), 65
Chinese, 34–41, 45–48, 135, 155–58, 167, 185–87, 522
  ancient, 619
  characters, 35, 48, 62, 152, 187, 197, 201
  dialects, 197
  Mandarin, 40, 196
  punctuation, *see* punctuation
  standard, 176
  writing system (script), 36, 40, 45, 57, 157, 167, 307
  written, 63, 185
Chiwere, 586
Christianity, 479
  Byzantine, 88
  Latin, 88–92, 261, 440, 488, 522
  Latin terms, 215
  nomina sacra, see nomina sacra
CIL, *see Corpus Inscriptionum Latinarum*
Civil War in England, 273–74
classifiers, 71, 128, 133
close-knit networks, *see* networks
CNC, *see* Czech National Corpus
codicology, 172, 208, 305–6, 309–12, 534
codification
  of a simplified Dutch, 450
  of Afrikaans, 450
  of Castilian, 588
  of form, 113, 265, 275, 280
  of graphemic rules, 50
  of Indigenous languages, 454
  of Nahuatl, 565
  of norms, 442, 446
  of spelling norms, 531–33, 535, 579
  of spelling rules, 278
  of Turkic languages, 450
  of unwritten languages, 439
  of writing systems, 582
  processes, 451
codified
  norms, 273, 443
  spelling system, 75
  spellings, 443
  standard, 113
codifiers, 441, 447, 588
  of Spanish, 448
CoMIK, *see Corpus of Mycenaean Inscriptions from Knossos*
communicative communities, 459
communities of practice (CoPs), 115–16, 380, 384, 392, 432, 438
comparative method, 384–87
comparative variable analysis, 325
  cross-textual (CTVA), 329, 334–36
  intertextual (TERVA), 329, 331–34
  intratextual (TRAVA), 328, 329–31
compositors, 334, 505, 509–11, *see also* typesetters
computer-mediated communication, 500
consonantal alphabet, *see* abjad
copyists, 287, 310, 350, 422, 426
corpora, 457
  Early Modern Dutch, 461
  Early Modern English, 267
  Middle Dutch, 354
Corpus Gysseling, 461
Corpus Inscriptionum Latinarum, 288–89
Corpus Middelnederlands, 462
Corpus of Early English Correspondence, 508, 512, 535
Corpus of English Dialogues, 460
Corpus of Mycenaean Inscriptions from Knossos, 415
Corpus Van Reenen – Mulder, 461
Corsican, 561, 586
Counter-Reformation, 333, 608
critical sociolinguistics, 578–80
Croatian, 180, 316, 336
  Glagolitic texts, 127
  orthography, 120
cultural accommodation, 384
cuneiform, 194, 313
  Hurrian, 48

Mesopotamian, *see* Sumerian
Sumerian, *see* Sumerian
Ugaritic, 48
Cypro-Minoan, 398
Cyrillic alphabet, 48, 61, 179, 227, 317, 560
adapted, 196, 229, 234–38
in Bosnian, *see* bosančica
in Lithuanian, 92
evolution, 229
graždanka, *see* Polish
Czech, 88–90, 236, 320, 385
legal codices, 392
orthographic reforms, 586
printed Bibles, 384
publications, 236
translation, 386
Czech National Corpus, 391

Danish, 71, 252, 479–81, 486–96
pronunciation, 494
readers, 489
words, 489, 496
written, 443, 481
Danish-Norwegian, 443, 486, 491, 493
literary market, 489
norm, 497
orthography, 492
state, 488
union, 481
Dano-Norwegian, *see* Danish-Norwegian
dash, 68, 168
dependency hypothesis, 126
Devanāgarī (Devanagari), 33, 79, 178, 188, 560
Dhivehi, 190
diacritic orthography, 385
diacritics, 33, 53, 65, 67, 84, 188–91, 195, 228–30, 233, 237–38, 241, 252, 257, 262, 293, 305, 309, 318–19, 327, 405, 440, 480, 483, 562, 605, 630
ogonek, 230–31, 237, 318
dialect
contact, 561
continuum, 446
selection, 316
dialectal
features, 87, 92
variation, 47, 525–27, 529–30
dialectology, 114
European, 599
Middle English, 430
Spanish American, 568
dialects
Acadian, 550
Armenian, 242
Chinese, 522
French, 537
German, 251–60, 334, 522
Greek, 395, 402
Lithuanian, 321
Middle English, 349, 351, 502
Nahuatl, 565
Norwegian, 443, 477–97
Old English, 351, 429, 502
Romance, 169
Slavic, 227, 388
Southern British, 631
Spanish, 521, 558, 568, 573
dictionary makers, 272
Dictionnaire de l'Académie, 543
diffusion, 596–600, 605–15
across communities, 598
across genre and context, 609–10
across regions, 432
across social groups, 501
of accepted variety, 113
of incipient standard, 530
of innovative spellings, 262
of linguistic features, 269
of norms, 543
of orthographic change, 597
of prestigious spellings, 504
of standard practices, 530
of West Saxon, 429
of writing systems, 138, 149
regional, 605–7
social, 607–9
digraph, 63, 81, 86–87, 97, 165–66, 228, 233, 237–38, 248, 251, 258, 271, 298, 302, 309, 320–23, 345–46, 355–58, 410, 503, 508, 565, 590
digraphia, 175, 560
digraphic orthography, 385
diorthographia, 560
discourse communities, 457
Dutch, 195, 437, 446–50, 457–76, 586, 597, 602–3, 628
book production, 458
government, 449
historical, 606
history of, 611
incunabula woodcuts, 468
influence on English, 458
language, 443
language policy, 602
nation-state, 603
orthography, 461
printers, 471
private letters, 91, 607, *see also* ego-documents
pronunciations, 602
society, 609
spelling, 615
spelling reform, 442
words, 440
writing system, 92
writing traditions, 438
Zeeland Dutch, 91
Dutchification policy, 607

early books production, 458
Early English Books Online, 116–17, 367, 378, 510
Text Creation Partnership, 272, 510, 514
Early Modern Alemannic, 253
Early Modern Dutch, 461
corpora, 468
Early Modern English, 267–69, 272–80, 360, 370, 421, 501, 511, 514, 622, 638
corpora, 468
orthographic variation, 367
period, 361, 366
scribes, 361
spelling, 626

Early Modern English Medical Texts, 460
Early Modern Latin, 309
Early Modern Norwegian, 479
Early New High German, 82, 85–91, 246–48, 257, 327
ecological
  adaptation, 557, 562
  framework, 556, 562, 575
  interactions, 564
  process, 556
  triggers, 573
ecology
  external, 563
  internal, 563
  linguistic, 442
  of contact, 576
  of Nahuatl literacy, 570
  of writing, 561, 576
  sociolinguistic, 570
editors, 174, 236, 334, 348, 350, 367, 382, 392, 434, 455, 512–18
EEBO, *see Early English Books Online*
EEBO-TCP, *see Early English Books Online, Text Creation Partnership*
ego-documents, 534–36
  Dutch, 611–13
  German, 608
  Lithuanian, 75, 83, 86
Egyptian, 147, 307, 312, 620
  Classical, 176
  hieroglyphs, *see* hieroglyphs
  rapid cursive, 315
elaboration of function, 113, 265, 275
eLALME, *see Linguistic Atlas of Late Mediaeval English, An Electronic Version of a*
Electronic Text Edition of Depositions, An, 460
English, 437
  alphabet, 59
  orthographic depth, 84
  spelling reform, 341
enregistrement, 526
epigraphy, 209, 386, *see also* inscriptions
Estonian, 316
Ethiopic, 79, 148
Etruscan alphabet, 298
  adapted, 296
    in Oscan, 292
etymological
  dictionaries, 248
  spelling, 88, 91, 107, 116, 171, 199–202, 338, 342, 441, 445, 571–76, 607, 628, 636
etymologism, 589
European languages, 72, 169, 174, 316, 338, 392
  orthographic debates, 112
  orthographic norms, 112
  orthographic traditions, 75
  orthographies, 75, 89, 316, 320
  spelling and vocabulary, 201
  vernaculars, 84, 90, 219
  writing systems, 77, 385, 386
European manuscript traditions, 86
extension, 617–25, 629–30, 638–43

Finnish, 147, 155, 316, 478, 558
  orthographic system, 112, 194
fit technique, 349
Flemish, 354, 442, 446, 454
  administrative sources, 607, 610
  government, 462
  grammarians, 605
  medieval spelling, 458
  populations, 443
  spellings, 610
focusing, 266, 269–70, 272
French, 71, 83, 134, 199, 202, 271, 339, 437, 628
  Acadian, 549
  diacritics, 309
  graphophonemic correspondences, 167
  influences in English and Dutch, 458
  manuscripts, 89
  orthographic depth, 84
  orthographic development, 89
  orthography, 439
  prestige of, 171
  pronunciation, 346
  spelling conventions, 271
  spelling reform, 341
  spelling system, 89, 166
  written, 79
French Academy, 439
French Revolution, 443, 543–46
futhark, *see* inscriptions, runic
futhorc, *see* inscriptions, runic

Galician, 454, 561
  identity, 586
  orthography, 316
gender, 115, 498–500, 503–6, 513–19, 527, 530–36, 604–9
  grammatical, 400, 495
generality, 266
genre, 114, 221, 249, 255, 358, 361, 379, 388–91, 423, 429, 433, 479, 486–89, 493, 499, 503–10, 520, 523–36, 605–12
Georgian script, 317
German, 53, 64, 82, 85, 88, 176, 199, 200, 245, 256, 260, 263, 437, 446, 488, 492, 535, 586, 624, 632
  alphabet, 59
  Austrian, 454, 627
  contemporary orthography, 342
  Empire, 446
  grapholinguists, 128
  historical texts, 508
  law, 386
  lexicographers, 448
  ligatures, 232
  linguistic tradition, 51
  literature on graphematics, 59
  occupation, 491
  orthographic systems, 256
  orthographies, 57
  premodern, 252, 257
  printed texts, 85
  provinces, 445
  researchers, 123
  scholars, 76
  script, 232
  scriptualization, 250
  spelling practices, 88

spelling principles, 259
spelling transgressions, 583
spelling variation, 253, 316
spoken, 627
Standard German orthography, 76, 440
universities, 137
writing system, 57, 128
Germanic
diphthongs, 607
languages, 71, 345
names, 250
roots, 458
sound values, 258
strong inflection, 636
vocabulary, 636
Germanic languages, 90
Glagolitic alphabet, 179–80, 227–28, 230
glyph, 51, 59, 64, 132, 176, 309, 327, 563
definition, 65
grammarians
Chilean, 593
eighteenth-century English, 605
Flemish, 605
German, 605
medieval, 97, 340
Norwegian, 488
of Sanskrit, 198
premodern, 274
Roman, 290
Spanish, 565, 568–69
grammatical traditions
in European languages, 601
grammatology, 30, 122, 126, 140
Grand Duchy of Lithuania, 239–40
graphematics, 30–31, 50, 57–59, 124–37, 144
grapheme
definitions, 52–56, 102–9, 128–35, 165–69
origin of the concept, 100, 123
graphemic space, 68
graphemics, 31, 50, 102, 105–6, 124–25, 620–22, 629–30
graphetics, 50, 62, 124–37
grapholinguistic
framework, 127
units, 395
grapholinguistics, 31, 118–37, 140, 164, 344
graphology, 30, 119, 140
graphonomy, 30
graphophonemic
analogy, 622, 627, 633
assignment, 637
correspondences, 167, 620–22, 633, 635, 641
diphthong, 633
evolution, 630
extension, 622–24, 638
influence, 632
isomorphy, *see* orthographic transparency
operator, 621–33, 637–40, 642
realization, 642
graphophonemics, 638
graphotactic
changes, 90
combinations, 327
constraints, 75–78, 85–88, 93
features of Russian, 93
rules, 76–77
spellings, 87
variation, 87
graphotactics, 86, 249
graždanka, *see* Polish
Great Vowel Shift, 631, 634–38
Greek, 88, 147, 287, 395–416, 456, 562
abbreviations, 85, 211
allography, 133
alphabet, 33, 46–49, 154, 199, 226–28, 317–18, 620
adapted in Oscan, 292–95
ancient orthography, 290
archaic, 398
Classical texts, 340
Codex Alexandrinus, 312
early manuscripts, 209
etymology, 143
graphemes, 58, 232
inscriptions, *see* inscriptions
nomina sacra, 211
prestige of, 201
shorthand, 210
spelling, 294
words, 146, 625

Haitian Creole, 585
Han'gŭl, 43, 147–49
handwriting, 140, 421, 511, 536
handwritten documents, 83, 115, 208, 221, 235, 307, 322, 360–80, 492, 512, 612, *see also* ego-documents
handwritten vs. printed texts, 87, 114, 132, 175, 218, 221, 320, 329, 360–80, 428, 487, 499, 531, 605
Hebrew, 211, 641
Hebrew-Aramaic alphabet, 620
Helsinki Corpus of English Texts, 527, 530
hieroglyphs, 33–40, 99
Anatolian, 36, 48
Cretan, 36, 44, 396
Egyptian, 33, 35, 39, 185
Maya, 35, 40, 185, 195
High German Consonant Shift, 250
Hindi, 33, 135, 178, 317, 522, 560, 583
Hispanic orthographies, 442
Historical Corpus of Dutch, 611
historical linguistics, 130, 325, 339, 343, 347, 387, 390–91, 421, 587, 597–98
historical orthography (definition), 5
historical pragmatics, 339, 348, 388
historical sociolinguistics, 7, 110–16, 170, 249, 263, 268, 339, 348, 499, 524, 527, 536, 537–44, 552–54, 557, 561–62, 577, 596–616
Hittite, 194, 200
holographs, 421, 424, 504–5, 509, 532
homography, 115, 116
Hungarian, 175, 329, 627
Hussite Wars, the, 385
hybridity, 225
hypercorrection, 329, 342, 415, 566
hyphen, 168, 305, 322, 323, 342, 367, 368–71

Iberian languages, 567
iconography, 29–30, 37–38
ideogram, 34–35, 44, 128, 216, 563, 618

ideograph, 35
ideographic
  forms, 100
  hieroglyphs, 35
  orthography, 104
  writing, 618
ideography, 151
Iguvine Tables, the, *see* inscriptions, Umbrian
illuminated initials, 221
illuminators, 467
incrementation, 597
incunabula, 328
  woodcuts, 468
indigenous
  communities, 570, 574
  groups, 557
  languages, 396, 560
  languages and cultures, 454
  municipalities, 564, 576
  names, 453
  networks, 581
  orthographies, 454
  peoples, 455
  population, 562, 564
  proper names, 455
  scribes, 564
  students, 566
  style, 455
  words, 448
  writing system, 557
Indo-European
  languages, 239, 342, 404
  linguistics, 163
inscriptions
  Chinese, 40
  Glagolitic, 230
  Greek, 47
  Greek and Latin, 198
  in ancient Italy, 285–304
  in Cyprus, 204
  in Mesoamerica, 36
  Latin, 187, 195, 209, 287–90
  on church walls, 389
  Oscan, 289, 292–95
  Polish grave, 235
  runic, 245, 252, 262, 478, 483–85
  runic and Latin, 258, 261
  Sumerian, 37
  Umbrian, 296–302
  Venetic funerary, 303
internal factors, 540
International Phonetic Alphabet, 4, 47, 196, 341
Inuit
  communities, 454
  languages, 560
Inuktut, 454
ISTC. *International Short Title Catalogue, The*, 147
Italian, 456, 521
  ancient education system, 286
  epigraphy, 304
  Humanistic influence, 361
  orthographic principles, 439
  phonology and spelling, 191–94
  spelling system, 89
IURA, *see Sources from Laws of the Past*

Japanese, 42, 48, 67, 79, 135, 141–45, 155–57, 201, 562, *see also* kana
  education, 197
  punctuation, *see* punctuation
  writing system, 141, 144, 167

Kalmar Union, 479
kana, 42, 48, 79, 147, 189, 190, 197, 201
  hiragana, 142
  katakana, 142, 562
kanji, 67, 79, 142, 157, 197, 201
Kipchak, 242
kitabistics, 240
koiné, 312, 481, 491
Korean, 135, 155, 167
  Han'gŭl, Hangul, hangŭl, *see* Han'gŭl
Kreyòl, 585

L'Année Épigraphique, 288
LAEME, *see Linguistic Atlas of Early Middle English 1150 to 1325, A*
LALME, *see Linguistic Atlas of Late Mediaeval English, A*
Lampeter Corpus, 460
Landsmaal, *see* Norwegian
language contact, 561
language families, 521
language ideologies, 112, 557, 580–87, 591–95
language policy, 461
Latin, 147, 271
  abbreviations, *see* abbreviations, Latin
  administrative writing, 264
  alphabet, 30, 180, 246, 263, 317, 345, 355, 440, 451, 479, 482, 522, 565
    adapted, 216, 228–34, 257, 258
      in Chinese, 197
      in Lithuanian, 92
      in Old Icelandic, 257
      in Oscan, 292
      in Polish, 224, 230
      in Romanian and Moldovan, 196
      in Scandinavian languages, 488
      in Umbrian, 296–302
      in Venetic, 303
    evolution, 187
    in German, 250
    modern, 59–63, 70
  Carolingian reform of, 521
  Classical texts, 340
  grammar, 358
  in Chancery, 432
  inflection, 627
  inscriptions, *see* inscriptions, Latin
  languages descended from, 163, 169, 521
  letters, 176, 178, 210, 237, 483, 488
  literacy, 205
  manuscripts, 206, 215, 306
  medicine, 362
  medieval, 346
  orthography, 292, 304, 358, 502, 627
  phonological system, 171
  phonology, 598
  prestige of, 201
  pronunciation, 566
  scholarly, 630

spelling conventions, 271
texts, 358
writing tradition, 89
Latinate
origin of words, 201
texts, 365
vocabulary, 626, 636–38
Latvian, 316
layout of
page, 361, 434
text, 363
Letters as Loot Corpus, 607
lexical
information, 508
level, 348
lexical spelling, 107
lexicographers, 443–48
Lexicon der Romanistischen Linguistik, 170
ligature, 84, 127, 228, 232, 241, 321–23, 327, 403, 488
linguistic anthropology, 578–80, 585
Linguistic Atlas of Early Middle English 1150 to 1325, A, 348–51, 353, 425, 429
Linguistic Atlas of Late Mediaeval English, A, 204, 348–54, 359, 425–27, 502–3, 609
Linguistic Atlas of Late Mediaeval English, An Electronic Version of a, 425
Linguistic Atlas of Older Scots, A, 425
linguistic hierarchies, 578
linguistic levels, 127
linguistic variants
typology, 525
LION, *see Literature Online*
literacy, 47, 83, 110–12, 115, 179, 197, 204–7, 260, 280, 292, 499–504, 513–19, 522, 534, 541, 556–57, 582–84, 623, 637
acquisition, 634
author's, 506
competence, 204
in Chinese, 45
in Europe, 173
in Norway, 477–78, 482–86, 497
instruction, 441
Latin, 252, 263
level, 83, 549, 640
low, 455, 507, 620
mass, 450
Nahuatl, 570, 573
Old English, 351
practices, 437, 501, 557
pre-print, 222
rates, 92, 442, 450, 527, 545
skills, 499
Spanish, 573
specialist, 499
universal, 626
literatim copying, 349–53, 426
Literature Online, 509–11
Lithuanian, 80–93, 307, 316, 318–23, 586
Cyrillic, 80
diacritics, 309
diaspora, 320
graphic inventory, 88
Latin Lithuanian spelling, 83
newspapers, 320
orthography, 319, 320
Polish influence, 319
script reform, 88
spelling system, 82
texts, 77, 81, 84, 86
writing system, 92
littera, the concept of, 97–101, 339–43, 425
litterae notabiliores, 169, 363
litterae singulares, 209
litteral substitution sets, 350, 425
litterati, 204, 208, 217
logogram, 32–35, 38–41, 45–47, 59, 66, 79, 167, 185, 196, 401, 403, 415, *see also* morphogram
logographic
signs, 396
writing (system), 32, 39, 41, 45, 47, 185, 197, 201, 563
logography, 40, 43, 46, 48, 146, 148, 152, 155, *see also* morphography
logosyllabary, 40
Low German, 263, 479, 494
scribes, 251
LRL, *see Lexicon der Romanistischen Linguistik*
Luxembourgish, 71
luxury
editions of books, 221, 328
manuscripts, 313

Macedonian, 586
ethnicity, 560
orthography, 229
maintenance
of correct spellings, 277
of etymological form, 572
of grapheme differences, 609
of language, 599
of Latin spelling, 627
of phonological differences, 607
of the standard, 265
of the standard variety, 113
of written standard, 279
orthographic, 603
within networks, 599
Málaga Corpus of Early English Scientific Prose, The, 366, 378
manuscript transmission, 347
manuscript versions, 419
manuscript vs. printed page, 205
Marathi, 33
materiality
of scripts, 124
of text, 313–22, 347, 381–82, 386, 390, 435
of writing, 128–29, 305, 310, 312, 390
Maya(n) writing, *see* hieroglyphs, Maya
medium
handwritten vs. printed, 114, 524
Mesopotamian cuneiform, *see* Sumerian cuneiform
metapragmatics, 526
Mexican Spanish, 574
Middle Ages, 70, 205–19, 230, 232, 246, 316, 322, 338, 339, 361, 366, 378, 387, 428, 482–85
dialect fragmentation, 169
education, 97
geolinguistic variation, 534
scribes, 422

Middle Czech, 392
Middle Dutch, 354, 602, 611
  corpora, 468
Middle English, 271–72, 275, 329, 347–51, 360–78, 421–27, 502–4, 530, 601, 609, 624–27, 632, 636
Middle French, 3
Middle High German, 199, 257, 334, 558
Middle Indic, 198
Middle Low German, 248
Middle Norwegian, 479
Middle Persian, 191
Minoan, 400, 411
Mischsprache copying, 350, 427
mise-en-page, 221, 415
Modern Roman Alphabet, 59
Moldovan, 178, 196
monosyllabic writing system, 618–19
mora, 42
moraic
  consonants, 42
  phonography, 148
morphogram, 32, 79, 167
morphograph, 59, 107
morphographic
  language, 89
  linguistic level, 142
  rules, 109
  sign, 618
  writing (system), 32, 59, 79, 149
morphographization, 92
morphography, 85, 90, 149, 153, 156–57
morphological spelling, 82–84, 89–92, 116, 257–60, 294
morphology, 60, 83, 91, 115, 121, 140, 156, 249, 332, 343, 365, 426, 480, 487, 524, 606
  derivational, 514
  inflectional, 196
  natural, 136
morphosyllabary, 158
movable type, 305, 313, 328
multilingualism, 255, 260–63, 287, 434, 436, 437, 442, 478, 559, 562, 599, *see also* bilingualism, trilingualism
multimodality, 205
multiscriptality, 256, 260, 262, 560, *see also* biscriptality
Muslim
  religious literature, 239
  speakers, 180
  Tatars, 239
Mycenaean Greek, 33, 44, 191, 395, 400, *see also* Greek
  diphthongs, 408
  orthography, 402
  words, 402, 405
  writers, 400, 406

Nabataean, 191
Nāgarī, *see* Devanāgarī
Nahuatl, 448, 555–57, 562–77
nationalist movement
  in Norway, 478
nation-state, 436–45, 454, 580, 583, 585, 602
natural grapholinguistics, 136
naturalness theory, 130, 136–37
neogrammarians, 101, 343
Nepali, 33
networks, 608
  close-knit, 599–600, 603, 614
  metalinguistic, 604
  strength, 604
networks of practice, 463
New High German, 258, 327
Newsbooks Corpus, 460
nomina sacra, 206–12, 330
nonstandard
  orthography, 178, 581, 583
  spelling, 112–14, 116, 287, 500, 501, 507, 512, 516–19, 533, 535, 553, 583
  variants, 545
  varieties, 529
  written data, 540
nonstandardized writing systems, 354, 358
norm (definition), 266
normalization, 266
Norman Conquest, 111, 429, 529
Norman French, 529
Norwegian, 437, 477–97
  Bokmål, 443, 480–82, 489–97
  constitution, 494
  Dano-Norwegian, 481
  Landsmaal, 444
  literacy, 485
  Nynorsk, 443, 480–82, 489–91, 495–97
  politics, 481
  spoken, 479
  standards, 490
  writing traditions, 252
  written norm, 491
  written standards, 497
Norwegianization of Danish, 453
Norwegians, 490
notae iuris, 210–11
notation, 29–30, 37, 556
  alphanumeric, 341
  astronomical, 35
  mathematical, 29
  musical, 29
  numerical, 37
  of consonants, 399
  of diphthongs, 408, 410
  of vowels, 42–43, 620, 631
  symbolic, 29
  technical, 65
notational system, 36, 231
numismatics, 209, 386
Nunavut, 454

Occitan, 544
Old Armenian, 243
Old Church Slavonic, 88, 177, 179–80, 227–29
Old English, 250, 257–62, 338, 343–45, 348, 351–58, 365, 373–75, 379, 421–25, 429, 502, 522, 534, 629–30, 636
Old French, 202
Old Hebrew, 191
Old High German, 250, 328, 338, 343, 345, 354–58
Old Norse, 254, 479–88
  normalized, 483

sources, 492
syllable structure, 492
Old Polish, 240
Old Saxon, 258, 354
Old Slovak, 385, 386
Old Swedish, 252
onomastics, 346
orthoepic norms/rules, 201, 627
orthoepists, 97, 115, 272, 341, 626, 641
orthoepy, 623
orthographic depth, 83, 84, 156, 259, *see also* orthographic transparency
orthographic reform, 440
orthographic transparency, 83, 259, 424, 522, *see also* orthographic depth
orthographic variants
typology, 113, 170
orthotypography, 174–75, *see also* typography
Oscan, 195, 286–304
etymology, 294
morphology, 294
Oxford English Dictionary, 624
Oxford English Dictionary Online, 3, 102, 266, 436

Pahlavi, 243
alphabet, 191
paleography, 106, 127, 172, 206–20, 305–11, 349, 365, 381–83, 389, 421, 434, 506, 510, 534
Parsed Corpus of Early English Correspondence, 117
PCEEC, *see Parsed Corpus of Early English Correspondence*
Persian alphabet, 229, 241
Perso-Arabic, 196, 560
philography, 31
Phoenician, *see also* abjad
alphabet, 191
writing system (script), 42–48, 147, 226, 396, 620
phonematics, 125
phoneticism, 589
phonetics, 100, 119, 126, 128, 168, 343, 420, 425, 639
phonogram, 32–35, 38–40, 47, 79, 166, 185
phonographemic correspondences, 620
phonographic writing (system), 79–80, 89, 143, 147, 171, 250
phonography, 38–49, 52, 64, 89–90, 100, 147–56, 166, 249–53, 344, 621
types, 148
phonology, 33, 38, 47, 54, 56, 64, 83, 91, 115, 119–21, 126, 131, 140, 170, 249, 287, 343, 346, 365, 381, 389, 420, 425, 522, 599, 607, 620–21, 629, 635–43
historical, 246, 500
levels of, 524
natural, 136
of Latin, 598
of Nahuatl, 565–77
of Oscan vowels, 289
of Proto-Indo-European, 403
of Spanish, 590
of the donor language, 558
Picardian French, 460
pictogram, 34, 185, 617–20
pictograph, 146
pictographic writing (system), 563, 617–18
pictography, 151–52
pīnyīn, 62, 67, 197
pluricentric languages, 597
pluricentricity, 165, 177, 180, 596, 610–16
Polish, 71, 88, 178, 224–44, 318–21, 628
alphabet, *see* Latin alphabet
Armenians, 243
consonants, 237
diacritics, 309
graphemes, 238
graždanka, 224, 229, 235–38
legal texts, 392
letters, 318
lexemes, 241
literature, 236
nasal vowels, 241
orthographic reform, 586
present-day, 231
texts, 243, 318, 321
type sets, 319
vowels, 238
writing, 230
Portuguese, 316, 456, 586
potestatic substitution sets, 350, 425
pragmaphilology, 346–48, 383, 387–91
pragmatic
domain, 172
functions, 208, 214, 217, 364
level, 128
principles, 71
pragmatics, 387, 433
Prakrit, 45
prescriptivism, 50, 70, 75, 112, 140, 143, 144, 200, 274, 277–80, 505, 538, 581, 603
prestige dialect, 581
print market, 208
printed editions of manuscripts, 462
printed texts, 71–72, 75, 83–85, 169, 305, 309, 319, 341, 360, 421, 505, 509
early, 216, 379
in Croatian, 180
in Dutch, 611
in English, 269, 532
in German, 259, 606
in Norwegian, 488
in Polish, 321
in Soviet Russia, 181
religious, 235
printers, 208, 221, 270, 272–81, 305, 314–23, 360, 369–72, 378, 438–41, 445, 450, 506, 531, 544, 604, 609
early modern, 115–17
printing
development, 230, 273
history of, 329
houses, 317, 321, 380, 455, 505, 510, 531, 532, 604
industry, 271, 275, 441, 505, 532
introduction of, 70, 111–12, 270, 279, 305, 420, 492, 588
practices, 278, 378
process, 471
shops, 306, 308, 332, 334
technological innovations, 171
proofreaders, 334, 606

Protestant
Bible translations, 438
city, 332
English literature, 472
German Bible prints, 72
printers, 438
spelling, 446
Upper Sorbian, 178
Protestants
French, 438
immigrants, 472
poets and printers, 441
Proto-German, 357
Proto-Indo-European, 343, 401–3, 416
Prussian Academy of Sciences, 342
publishers, 392, 453, 455, 506, 586
punctuation, 54, 64–70, 72, 164, 168–69, 210, 239, 327, 348, 364–67, 381, 382, 421, 434, 500, 609
Chinese, 67
Etruscan, 303
Finnish, 69
French, 67, 173, 174
German, 67, 69, 72
Hungarian, 69
Japanese, 67
Korean, 67
of Germanic languages, 173
of Romance languages, 173
Spanish, 67, 173, 174
Venetic, 303

Qumran Hebrew Orthography, 312
Quran, the, 240

raciolinguistics, 579
RAE, *see* Real Academia Española
Real Academia Española, 165, 440, 448, 587
Reformation, 112, 441, 479, 483
reforms
of orthographies, 89, 98, 102, 176–81, 186, 201, 257, 262, 275–78, 287, 293, 340–42, 439, 443–53, 490–91, 494–96, 521, 578, 583–92, 634
of scripts, 88, 92, 229
register, 114, 181, 362, 507, 520, 523–29, 532–36, 539–42, 605
formal, 302
high, 565
relational approach, 96, 100–2, 105–7, 252, 255, 260, 345, 354
Renaissance, 111–12, 231–32, 316, 340
Carolingian, 208
Representative Corpus of Historical English Registers, A, 508
rōmaji, 142
Roman script, *see* Latin alphabet
Romance
languages, 456
vernaculars, 438
romanization of languages, 559
Royal Academy of Spain, 440
runic
alphabet, 478
period in Norwegian, 482–86
script, 355–58
signs, 246
writing, 252–53, 257–63, 483
Russian, 83–93, 311, 385, 388, 437
alphabet, 229, 450
birchbark documents, 181
biscriptality, 177
manuscripts, 176
newspapers, 392
orthographic norms, 88
orthographic reforms, 181
orthography, 85, 176–78, 192
publications, 178
Romanticism, 236
script reform, 92
spelling practice, 86
words, 93, 235

Sámi (Sami), 478, 482
place names, 453
Sanskrit, 45–46, 147, 197–200, 317, 342, 560
Schriftlinguistik, 118, 123, 140
Scots, 561
scribal variation, 420
scribes, 66, 87, 89–90, 101, 115–16, 179–80, 191, 205–20, 246–64, 286, 299–301, 315, 322, 328–36, 346–58, 360–65, 372–80, 400, 410–11, 420–35, 502–9, 516, 534, 564–77, 604, 608, 618
scripta, -ae, 170
scriptology, 169
scriptoria, 207, 251–52, 357, 364, 433, 508, 535
scriptura continua, 365
scripturology, 121, 164, 169
scriveners, 421–23
S-curve, 598, 613, 614–15
Second World War, the, 491
selection of norm, 113
semantic
categories, 48, 249
content, 33, 534
convention, 239
determinatives, 34, 39, 40
distinctions, 69, 106
domain, 172
elements in *kanji*, 157
extension, 38
factors, 327
function, 254
indicators, 188
level, 128
principles, 71
trends, 571
values, 65
semantically informed writing systems, 147
semantics, 38, 90, 109
semasiographic writing (system), 147
semasiography, 151–52
semiotics, 617–20
Semitic
alphabet, 42–46, 59, 189, *see also* abjad
scripts, 65
Septuagint, 211
Serbian, 176, 178, 560
Serbo-Croatian, 84, 179, 560

Shakespeare's First Folio, 519
siglum, -a, 209–13
sign languages, 54, 150
SIL International, 437
simplified spelling, 442–45, 449–53, 455
Simplified Spelling Board, 451
Sindhi, 560
Slavic
  consonants, 241
  languages, 224, 230, 234, 238, 242
  vernaculars, 385
  vowels, 240
Slovak, 316
Slovenian, 316
social factors
  age, 518
  ethnicity, 540
  social class, 540, 542
social networks, 114–15, 524, 530, 536, 540, 549, 553, 573, 577
sociolinguistic variation, 502, 520–36, 567, 638
sociolinguistics, 387, 432, 527, 534, 558
  of contact, 555–77, 624, 641
  of literacy, 622
  of orthography, 582–87
  of writing, 558
  variationist, 114, 537, 561
sociopragmatics, 382–83, 387–91
Sources from Laws of the Past, 392
Spanish, 437, 564, 586, 589
  Castilian, *see* Castilian Spanish
  clergy, 564, 570
  colonial, 567
  colonial period, 555, 562
  conquest, 36
  empire, 594
  Franciscans, 563
  graphemes, 569
  history of orthography, 587
  loanwords in Nahuatl, 566, 570–77
  medieval orthographies, 569
  medieval period, 171
  orthographic norms, 574
  orthographic principles, 439
  orthographic rules, 583
  orthography, 165, 582, 588–94
  phonology and spelling, 191–93
  speakers, 566, 574
  spelling adaptation, 571
  spelling and pronunciation, 565
  spelling reform, 341
  spelling system, 89
  spoken, 575
  Standard, 440
Spanish America, 448
Spanish American nations, 444
spelling patterns
  for <i/j>, 441
  for <u/v>, 88, 441
spelling pronunciation, 553, 558, 623–40
sphragistics, 386
standardization, 438–39, 442, 445–48, 454–55, 495
  of spelling, 265–81
stationers, 422
Stationers' Company, 475
Stationers' Guild, 422
structural principles, 76
structuralism, 125, 133, 137, 346, 349, 381–82, 388–89
structuralists, 101, 106, 113, 119, 344–45
style, 353, 486, 493, 520, 523–36
  and dialect, 529–34
  and genre, 534–36
  and register, 525–28
  calligraphic, 475
  elaborate prose, 485
  formal, 201
  Indigenous, 455
  informal, 518
  of writing, 226, 253
  oral and literary, 494
  orthographic, 256, 431
    economical vs. prodigal, 251
  pre-conquest in Nahuatl, 562
Sumerian, 35–41, 618–20
  cuneiform, 32–40, 45, 48, 185–88
  ideogram, 618
  inscriptions, *see* inscriptions, Sumerian
  pictographic scribes, 618
  words, 618
  writing system, 187
supralocalization, 92, 269–70, 273, 428–35, 502, 508, 597, 600, 605–16
Swedish, 252, 481, 488
  prestige of, 558
  runic inscriptions, *see* inscriptions, runic
Swedish-Norwegian union, 491
Swiss German, 57, 499, 522
syllabary, 33, 41–46, 79, 146–48, 154, 185, 189–90, 200–1, 396, *see also* syllabogram
  ancestry of, 399
  Linear A, 396
  Linear B, 395–416
  Mesopotamian cuneiform, 33
syllabic writing system, 146, 147, *see also* syllabary
syllabogram, 33, 38–42, 47, 59, 196, 403, 408–13
syntactic
  contexts, 198
  domain, 172
  factors, 327
  features, 480
  information, 508
  level, 128, 348
  principles, 71
  variation, 545, 553
Syrian, 243

Tamil, 135, 167
Tatars, 176, 239–40
tetragraph, 166
text structure, 382
text type, 114, 247–49, 326–28, 379, 520, 523–24, 530, 534–36, 576, 609–10
Thai, 135, 167
Tironian note, 209–11
translation studies, 384
translations
  in early modern times, 384
  in the Middle Ages, 384
translator scribe (copying), 353

translators, 174, 392, 438
transmission, 596–605
  generational, 604
  metalinguistic, 605
  of conventions, 601
  of language, 556
  of linguistic meaning, 520
  of orthographic change, 597
  of script, 399
  of social meaning, 520, 527
  of texts, 387
  of writing systems, 138
  oral, 622, 629, 641
  through instruction, 602
  within communities, 598
trigraph, 165, 166, 228, 238, 250, 258, 309, 357
trilingualism, 271, *see also* bilingualism, multilingualism
Tuareg, 560
Turkic languages, 450
Turkish, 329, 451
  alphabet, 177, 180, 241
Turkmen, 234
Tuscan vernacular literature, 438
typefaces, 57
typesetters, 249, 254, 257, 259, 263, 317–18, 323, 328–37, 606, *see also* compositors
typography, 50, 64–67, 87, 122, 124, 129, 188, 327, 336, 559, *see also* orthotypography
  errors and correction, 314

Ukrainian, 316
Umbrian, 286–91, 296–304
unetymological spelling, 346, 625
Unicode Consortium, 35
Upper German, 259, 332, 608
  scribes, 254
Urdu, 178, 522, 560, 583
Uzbek, 234

variables, 336, 337, 520–36
  dependent, 331
  extralinguistic, 7, 114, 249, 328, 331, 523
  graphic, 480
  independent, 331
  linguistic, 538, 551
    definition, 114, 523
  morphological, 544
  morphosyntactic, 503, 550, 553
  orthographic, 114, 528, 535, 608
    definition, 114, 524
    in French, 457
  social, 560, 605, 608, 609
  sociolinguistic, 383, 520, 536
  sociopragmatic, 383, 387
  spelling, 94, 324, 328, 333, 602–4
  syntactic, 544
Venetic, 287, 302–4
Võru orthography, 316
vowel length indication, 116, 191, 195, 200, 272, 277, 289, 298, 342, 405, 407, 529, 565, 624
vowel notation, *see* notation of vowels

West Germanic, 248
  languages, 195, 358
West Norwegian dialects, 481, 493
women's spelling, 499, 513–19
word division, 55, 174, 186, 367–72, 415, 512
  in French, 174
  in Spanish, 174
  line-final, 360–80, 389
word spacing, 47

Yiddish, 641
  orthography, 316